P9-DUG-953
RARY

Masters: Book Arts

JULIE CHEN ■ CLAIRE VAN VLIET ■ BRIAN DETTMER
MARGARET COUCH COGSWELL ■ SHANNA LEINO ■
SUSAN KING ■ BARBARA TETENBAUM
■ HARRY REESE AND SANDRA LIDDELL REESE ■
SARAH BRYANT ■ SUSAN GOETHEL CAMPBELL
■ BONNIE STAHLECKER ■ KAREN KUNC
■ PETER MADDEN ■ WILBER SCHILLING ■ HEDI KYLE ■
INES VON KETELHODT AND PETER MALUTZKI
■ ADÈLE OUTTERIDGE ■ IAN BOYDEN ■

TIMOTHY ELY ■ JODY ALEXANDER ■ MACY CHADWICK ■ KEN BOTNICK ■ GENIE SHENK ■ JULIE LEONARD ■ ANDREA DEZSÖ ■ SARAH BODMAN ■ DANIEL ESSIG ■ KAREN HANMER ■ KEITH SMITH ■ BARBARA MAURIELLO ■ VERONIKA SCHÄPERS ■ DANIELA DEEG AND CYNTHIA LOLLIS ■ LYNNE AVADENKA ■ ROBIN PRICE ■ ELSI VASSDAL ELLIS ■ BÉATRICE CORON ■ PATI SCOBEY ■ DANIEL KELM ■ LAURA WAIT ■ JULIE FREMUTH ■

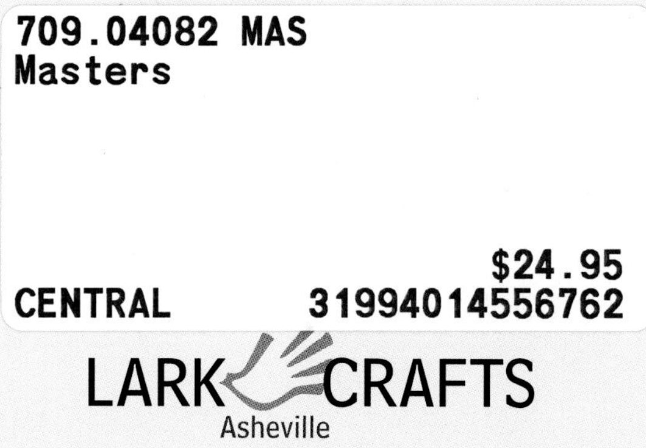

EDITORS:
Julie Hale
Beth Sweet

ART DIRECTOR:
Travis Medford

COVER DESIGNER:
Travis Medford

FRONT COVER, LEFT TO RIGHT:

Jody Alexander
The Odd Volumes of Ruby B. (Boxed Set), 2009

Shanna Leino
Looong Snakey, 2007

Margaret Couch Cogswell
Excessive Talking, 2007

BACK COVER:

Laura Wait
X, Letter of Danger, Sex, and the Unknown: Vol. VI, 2006

SPINE:

Macy Chadwick
The Topography of Home, 2009

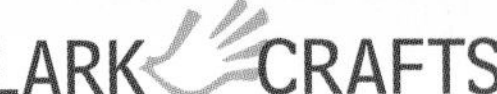
LARK CRAFTS
An Imprint of Sterling Publishing
387 Park Avenue South
New York, NY 10016

If you have questions or comments about this book, please visit: larkcrafts.com

Library of Congress Cataloging-in-Publication Data

Masters : book arts : major works by leading artists. -
p. cm.
Includes index.
ISBN 978-1-60059-497-7 (pb-pbk. with deluxe flaps : alk. paper)
1. Artists' books--Themes, motives. I. Hale, Julie. II. Title: Book arts.
N7433.3.M39 2011
709.04'082--dc22
2010025892

10 9 8 7 6 5 4 3 2

Published by Lark Crafts, an Imprint of
Sterling Publishing Co., Inc.
387 Park Avenue South, New York, NY 10016

Distributed in Canada by Sterling Publishing,
c/o Canadian Manda Group, 165 Dufferin Street
Toronto, Ontario, Canada M6K 3H6

Distributed in the United Kingdom by GMC Distribution Services,
Castle Place, 166 High Street, Lewes, East Sussex, England BN7 1XU

Distributed in Australia by Capricorn Link (Australia) Pty Ltd.,
P.O. Box 704, Windsor, NSW 2756 Australia

Manufactured in China

ISBN 13: 978-1-60059-497-7

For information about custom editions, special sales, and premium or corporate purchases, please contact Sterling Special Sales Department at 800-805-5489 or specialsales@sterlingpub.com.

Requests for information about desk and examination copies available to college and university professors must be submitted to academic@larkbooks.com. Our complete policy can be found at www.larkcrafts.com.

Contents

Introduction

I VIVIDLY REMEMBER THE MOMENT I first became aware of a book as more than simply words on paper in the form of a paperback romance or mystery novel. I was a junior in college when my mother gave me a trade edition of the Pennyroyal Press's *The Robber Bridegroom* by Eudora Welty. A longtime admirer of Ms. Welty, I lived in her neighborhood and always hoped to catch a glimpse of her at our local grocery store, the Jitney Jungle No. 14. I never saw her there, but that book, with its confluence of exquisite typography, wood engravings by Barry Moser, and Welty's narrative, activated in me a keen awareness and appreciation for the book arts that have never diminished.

The awakening of key senses—visual, tactile, aural—is a vital part of encountering the physicality of a well-designed book. The reader cannot fully experience the subtleties and richness of a book by viewing one page or several spreads; a book must be handled, read, and assimilated into the reader's reservoir of personal experiences to be truly appreciated. By triggering a reader's emotions, books can activate other levels of awareness. Many of the content-based works featured here do just that by relating a personal experience, a political statement, or a poem.

Book arts as an overarching term includes a variety of independent and highly specialized areas of expertise, including bookbinding, fine press books, artist's books, design binding, sculptural books, and box making. Yet the wonderful open-endedness of the medium—its inclusiveness and accessibility—made my role as curator challenging. I started with a list of 250 artists, from which I selected 43 individuals—truly a daunting task—and my goal was to present a broad cross-section of the form. The artists I chose use the book format in unique and personalized ways to convey their artistic messages.

Many of the pieces I selected display a departure from the traditional role of the book. I picked these works because I wanted to give equal value to the conceptual, visual, and sculptural areas of book arts. Regardless of its form, a great book is well paced, has rhythm, and conveys the message of the maker in its color, tone, and scale. As you'll see when you flip through these pages, the pieces here possess all of these qualities while succeeding as cohesive works.

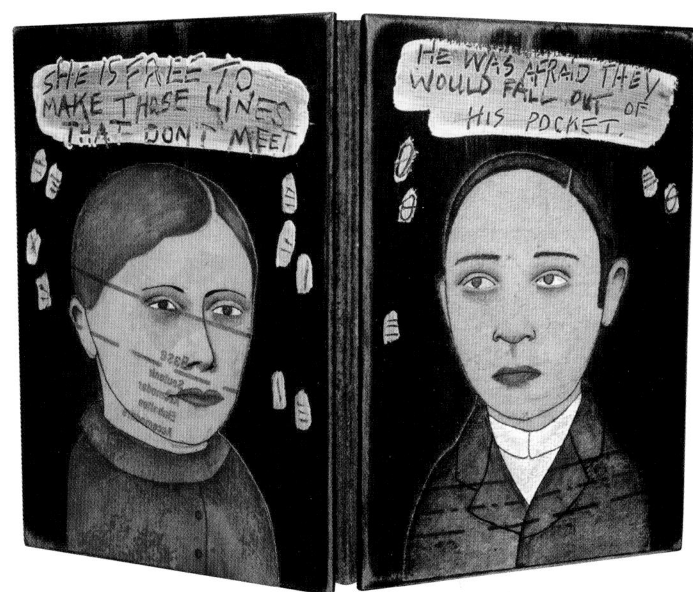

▲ **Julie Fremuth**
She Is Free | 2007

Many book artists appreciate having influence over the way readers move through their work. Julie Chen maximizes a book's capability to both conceal and reveal information in her exquisite pieces, which feature lace-like, cut pages. Macy Chadwick uses the atmospheric translucency of ink on paper to create physical layers of information. On the opposite end of the structural paradigm are books that can be viewed in their entirety at once. Artists accomplish this unique effect through a range of dramatically different design solutions. Adèle Outterridge employs striking, see-through plastic bindings that allow the viewer to take in the whole of a piece, while Laura Wait creates vibrant wall books that are extended and displayed in full when hung.

Each of the books in this volume starts with a story—even when words aren't physically present. Explaining content without using accompanying text is difficult to do, but it's accomplished with great confidence in numerous ways by the artists featured here. Jody Alexander and Barbara Mauriello create magnificent environments and artifacts for personalities, both real and imagined. Julie Fremuth's empathetic character portraits provide a foundation for understanding the universality of human situations.

For some artists, the book serves as a point of departure. Brian Dettmer uses sculptural applications in his work, turning vintage dictionaries and encyclopedias into topographical marvels, while Bonnie Stahlecker creates wall pieces that pay affectionate homage to the form of the book. Others use the book as a centerpiece for larger constructions. Daniel Essig gives it pride of place in his solemn, totemic pieces, and Margaret Couch Cogswell showcases it in her whimsical, vivid assemblages.

As a means of communicating thoughts, ideas, and emotions, the book is part of a long tradition. With intelligence and a taste for experimentation, these artists bear witness to its past while acting as advocates for the role it will play in the future. In forms as diverse and exciting as the art of storytelling itself, they offer work that's engaging and provocative, displaying a deep respect for the book and the position it holds as the center of their artistic practice. I'm honored to present their work to you.

—Eileen Wallace, Curator

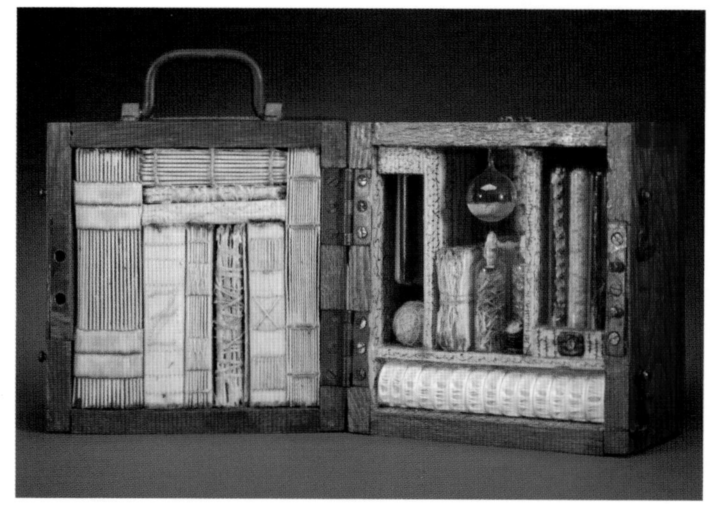

▲ **Jody Alexander**

If She Thought It Would Help, Zelda Would Use Her Antediluvian Curse Cache to Attain Her Revenge | 2004

Julie Chen

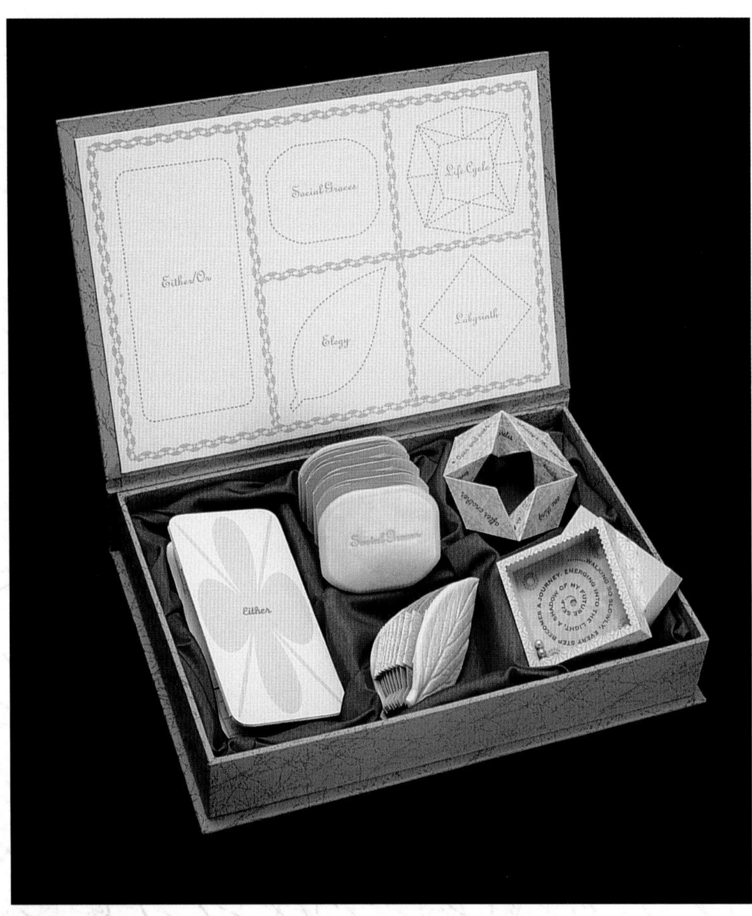

▲ **Bon-Bon Mots** | 1998

Box: 7 x 10 x 1¾ inches (17.8 x 25.4 x 4.4 cm)
Assorted papers and book cloth, binder's board, plastic sheeting, polymer clay; letterpress printed using photopolymer plates
Photo by Sibila Savage

OPERATING WITHIN a broad framework of what constitutes a book, Julie Chen is known for crafting intricate works featuring multi-layered text and non-traditional structures. Characterized by exquisite craftsmanship and masterful printing, Chen's work often demands active participation from readers. She uses games, sliding panels, and turning wheels to fully engage her audience and provide a meaningful experience. Her lyrical books demonstrate the broad technical and artistic potential of the book arts.

Chen's boundary-pushing art is rooted in the concept of the book as a time-based medium. Only by pausing and turning pages can the reader fully experience her whimsical, wonderful work. Chen lives in Berkeley, California, and publishes her limited-edition books under the Flying Fish Press imprint. Her work can be found in galleries worldwide, including the Museum of Modern Art in New York City and the Victoria and Albert Museum in London, England.

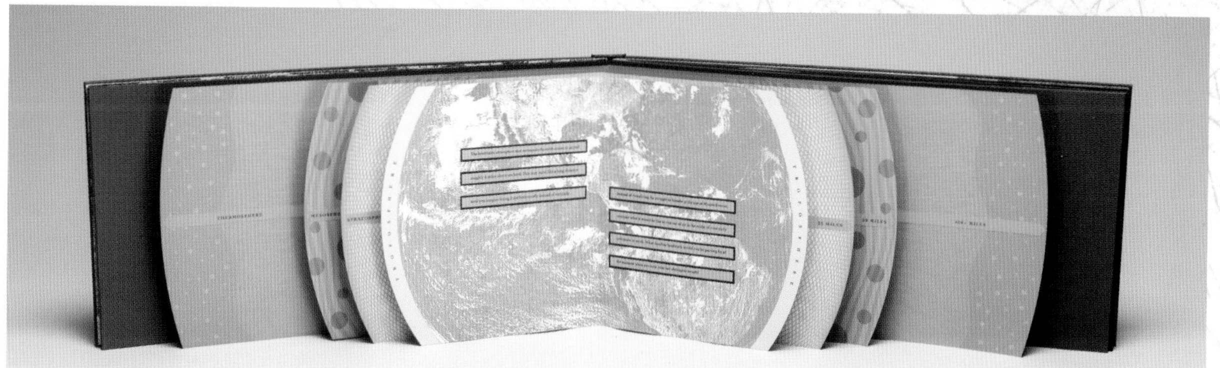

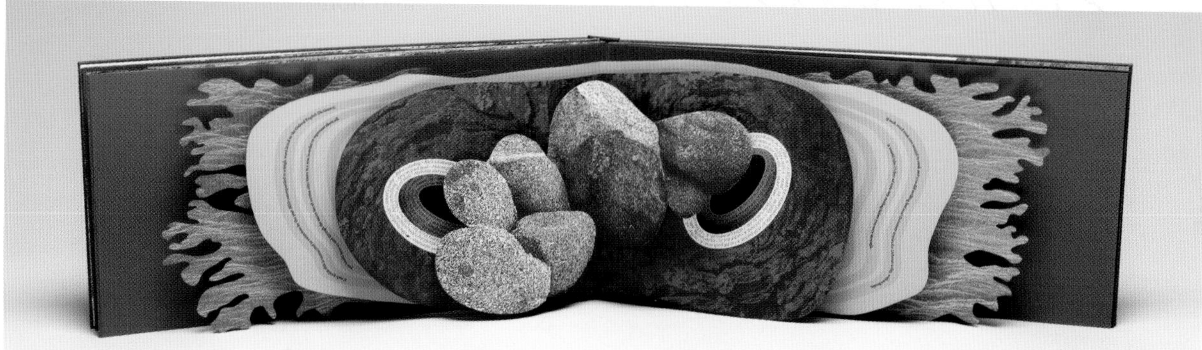

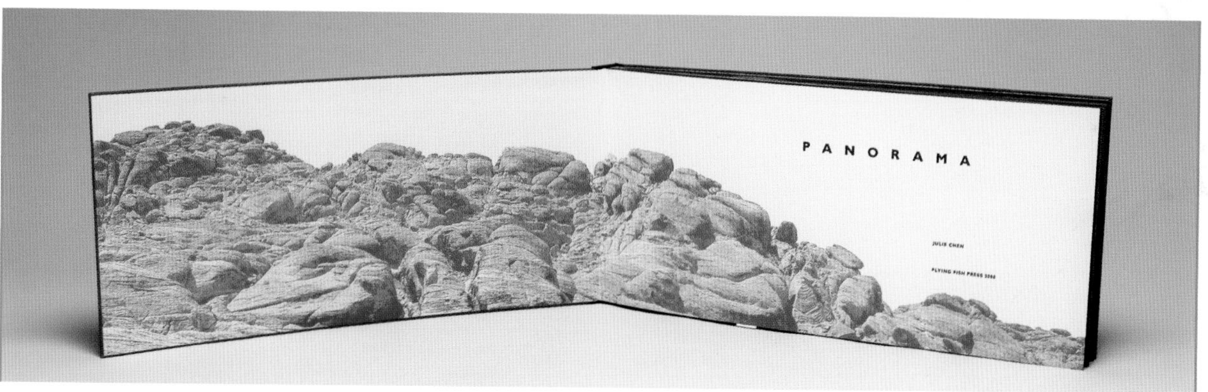

▲ **Panorama** | 2008

9½ x 20¼ x 1¼ inches (24.1 x 51.4 x 3.2 cm)
Assorted papers and book cloth, binder's board, magnets; letterpress printed using wood blocks and photopolymer plates

Photos by Sibila Savage

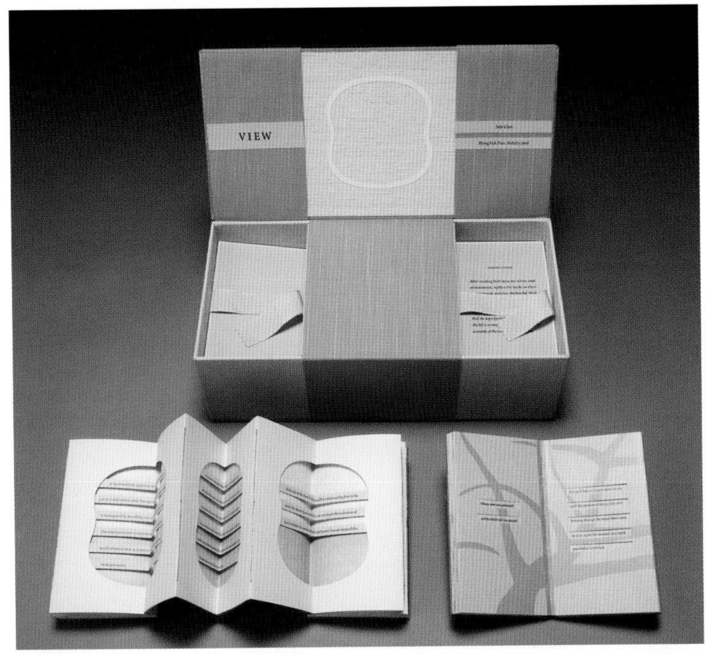

" I'm fascinated with the idea of giving order to personal experience through the use of mapping, charting, and numbering. These systems allow me to present personal content in my work in ways that can be easily understood and translated through the reader's own experience. "

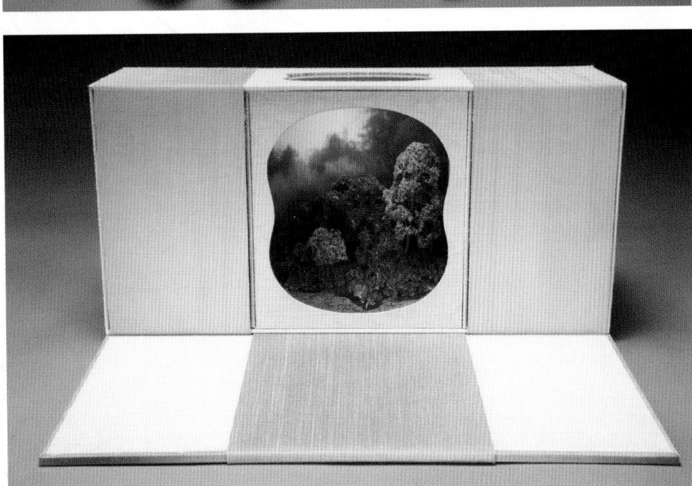

◀ **View** | 2007

Box: 6⅜ x 13⅝ x 4½ inches (16.2 x 34.6 x 11.4 cm)
Books when closed: 6 x 3⅝ x 1⅛ inches (15.2 x 9.2 x 2.9 cm)
Assorted papers and book cloth, binder's board, plastic sheeting, miniature landscape materials, resin, ribbon; letterpress printed using photopolymer plates and wood blocks
Photos by Sibila Savage

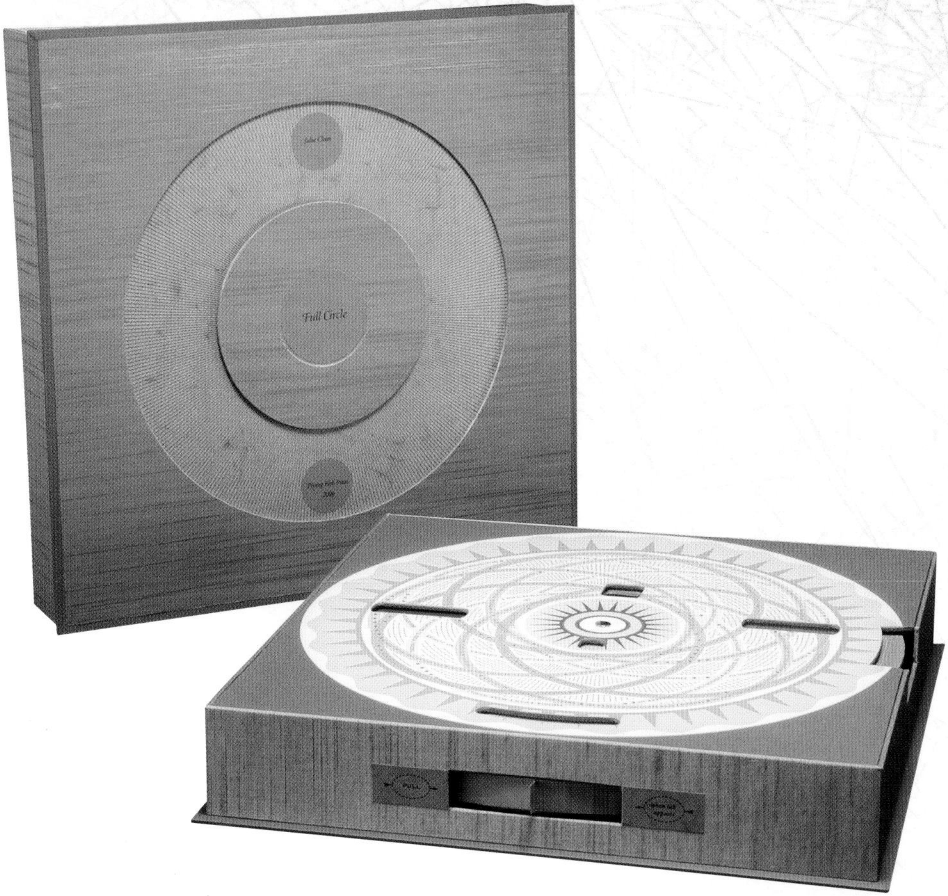

▲ **Full Circle** | 2006

15½ x 15½ x 3 inches (39.4 x 39.4 x 7.6 cm)
Assorted papers and book cloth, binder's board, plastic sheeting, found objects; letterpress printed using photopolymer plates

Photos by Sibila Savage

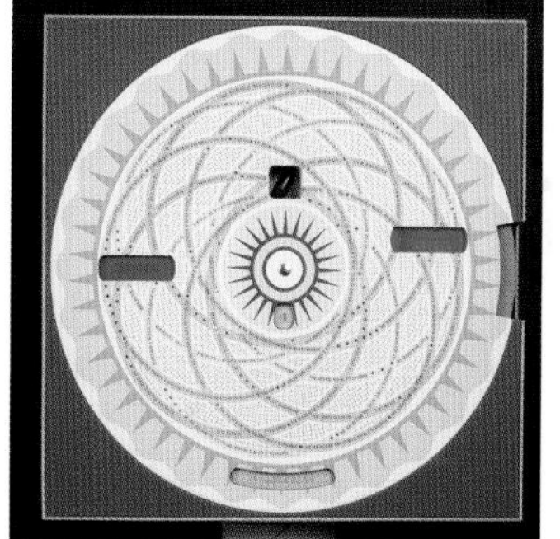

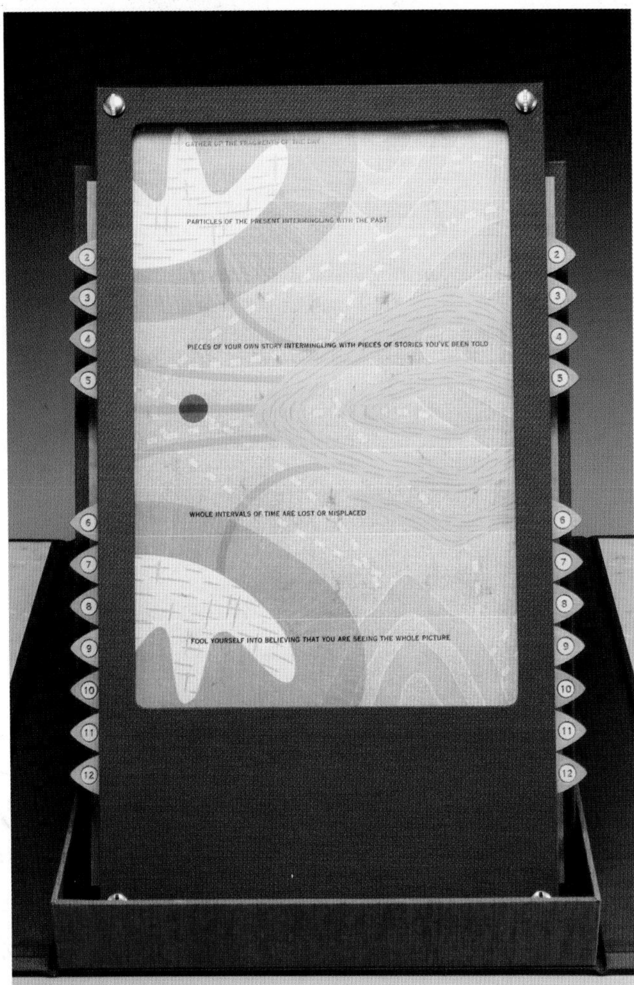

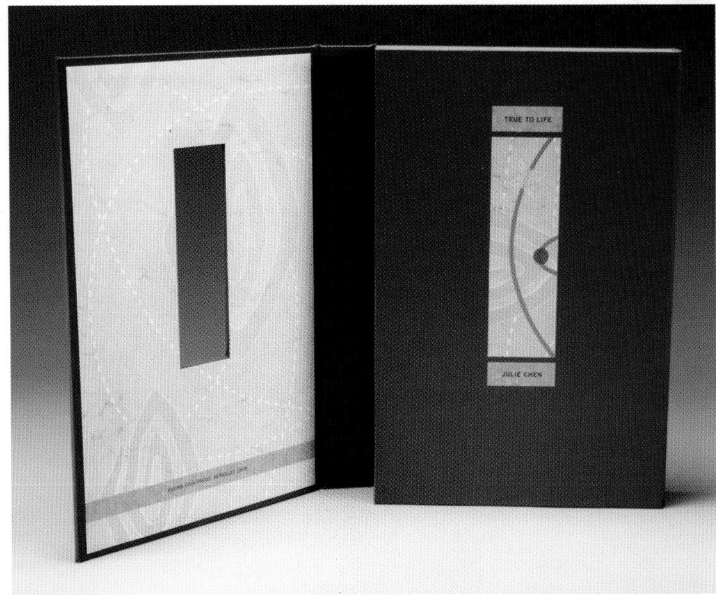

▲ **True to Life** | 2005

14¾ x 9½ x 1 inches (37.5 x 24.1 x 2.5 cm)
Assorted papers and book cloth, binder's board, plastic sheeting, wood; letterpress printed using photopolymer plates and wood blocks

Photos by Sibila Savage

" My personal definition of a book is very broad, with boundaries that are in constant flux. "

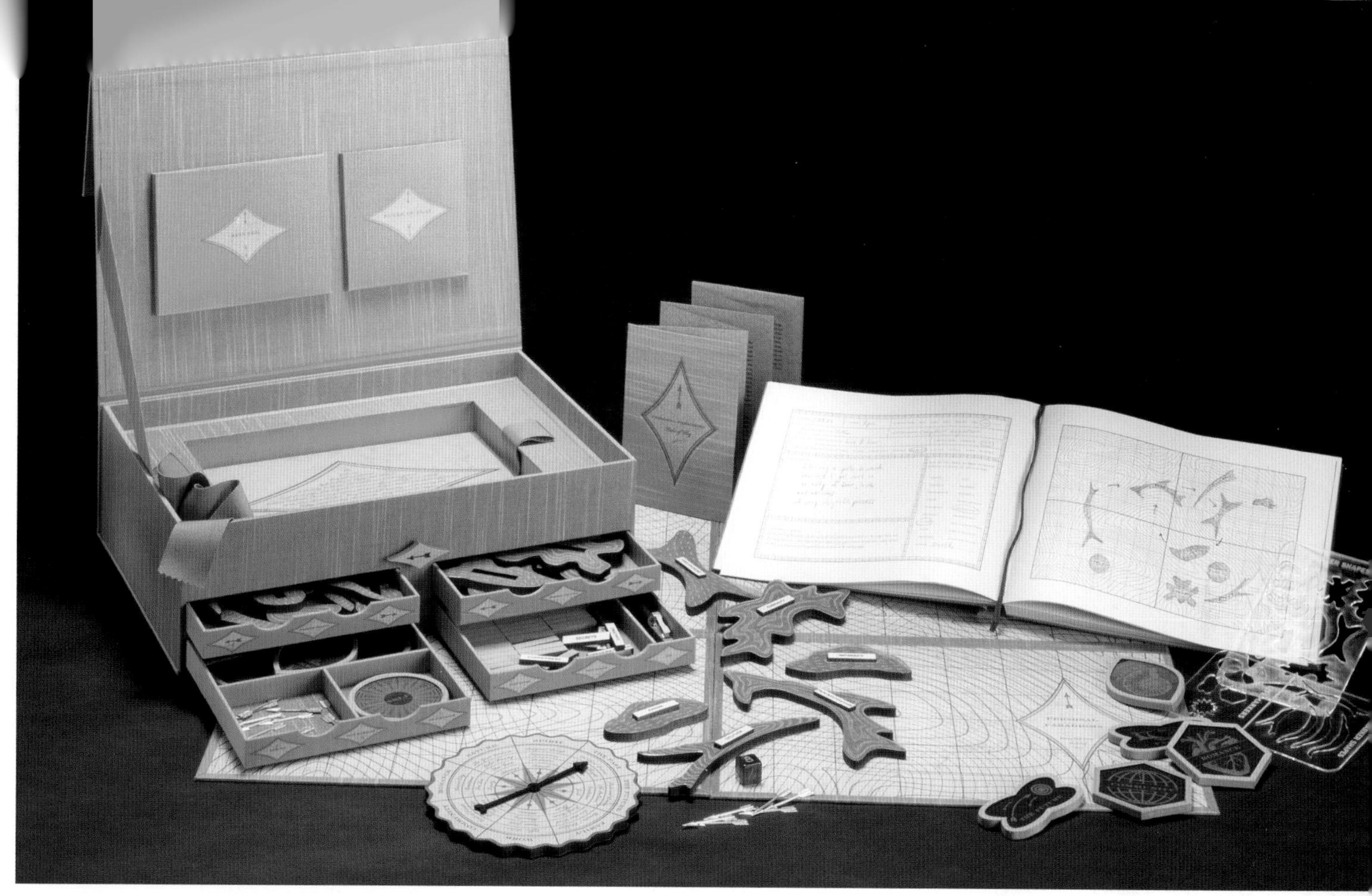

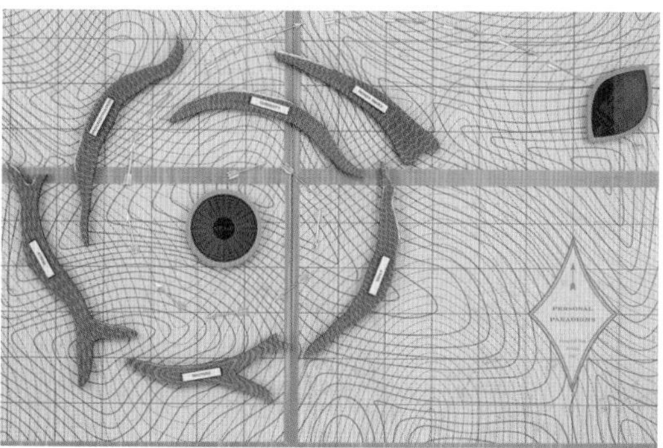

▲ **Personal Paradigms: A Game of Human Experience** | 2005

Box: 15½ x 11¼ x 4¾ inches (39.4 x 28.6 x 12.1 cm)
Game board: 21 x 30 inches (53.3 x 76.2 cm)
Assorted papers and book cloth, binder's board, plastic sheeting, wood, resin, colored pencils; letterpress printed using photopolymer plates, offset printed

Photos by Sibila Savage

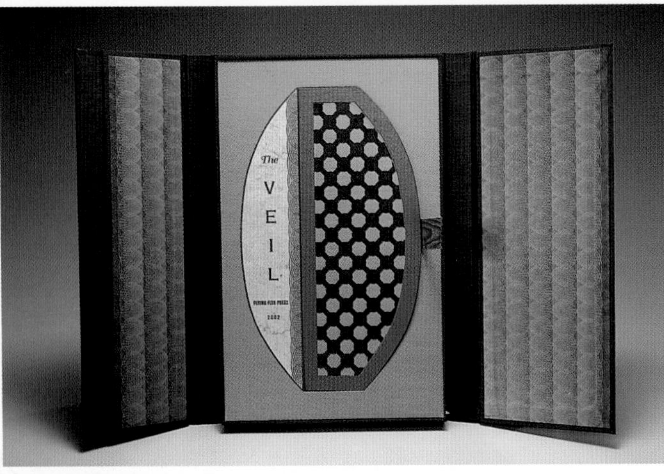

The Veil | 2005

10½ x 4½ inches (26.7 x 11.4 cm)
Assorted papers and book cloth, binder's board, magnets; letterpress printed using photopolymer plates
Photos by Sibila Savage

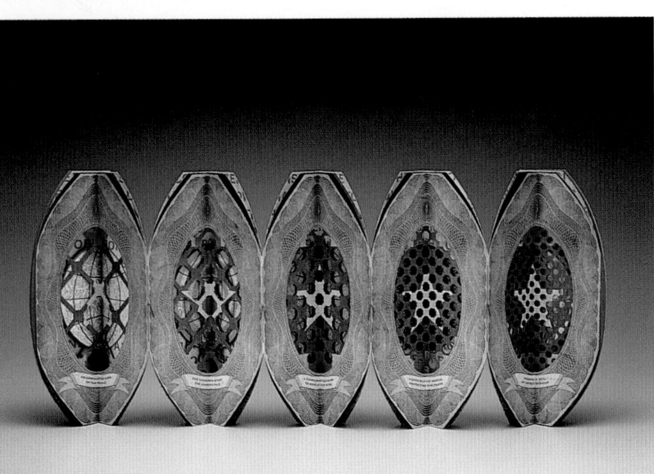

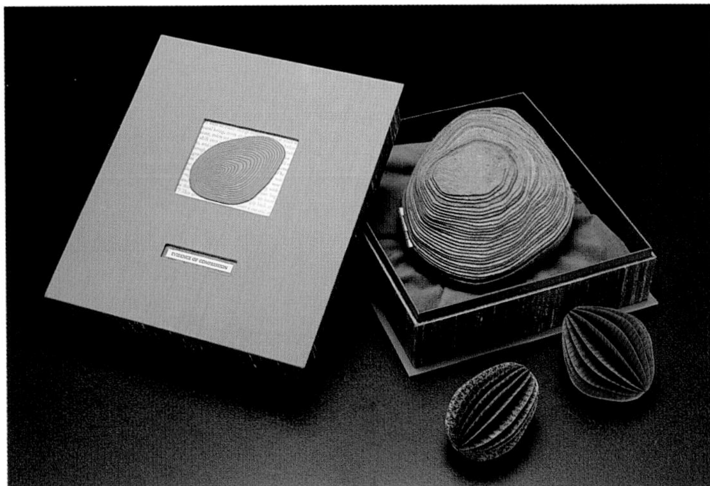

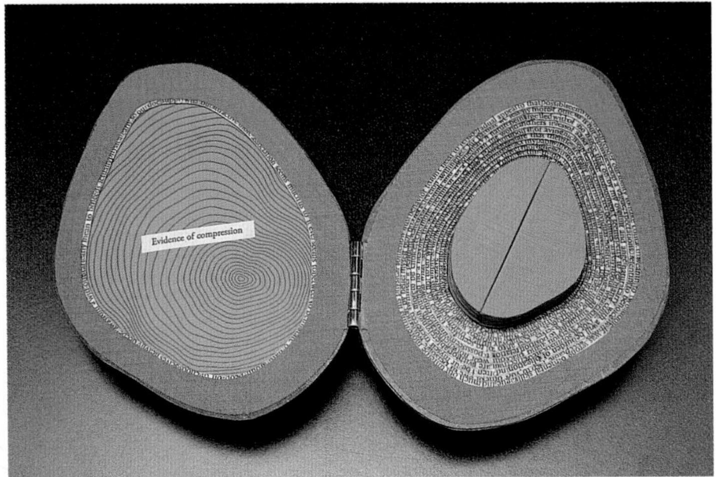

Evidence of Compression | 2001

Box: 9⅛ x 8 x 3½ inches (23.2 x 20.3 x 8.9 cm)
Outer book: 7 x 5¼ x 2¾ inches (17.8 x 13.3 x 7 cm)
Inner books: 3 x 1¼ x ⅝ inches (7.6 x 3.2 x 1.6 cm)
Assorted papers and book cloth, binder's board, magnets, brass hinge; letterpress printed using photopolymer plates
Photos by Sibila Savage

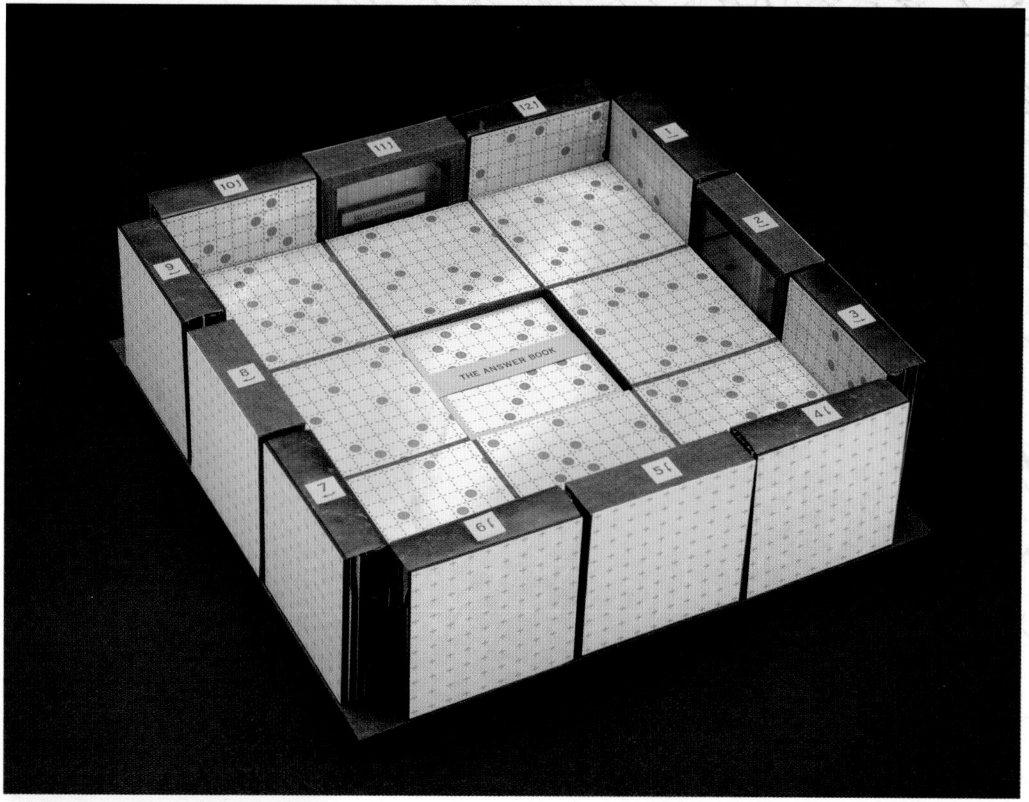

" I strive to present the reader with an object that challenges preconceived ideas of what a book is while providing a deeply engaging and meaningful experience of form and content. "

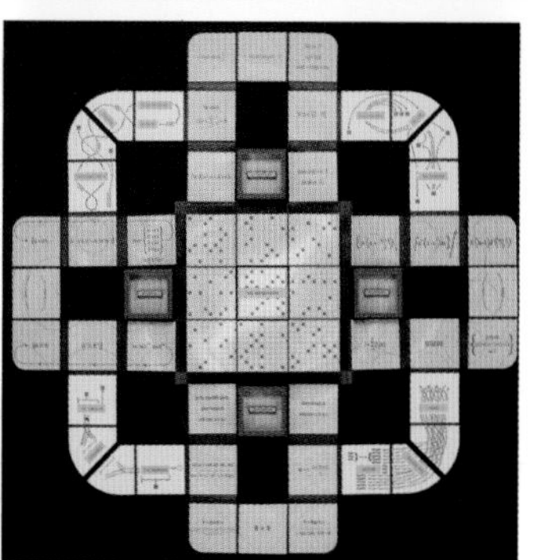

▲ **A Guide to Higher Learning** | 2009

11 x 11 x 3⅛ inches (27.9 x 27.9 x 7.9 cm)
Assorted papers and book cloth, museum board, magnets, plastic sheeting, wood; letterpress printed using photopolymer plates

Photos by Sibila Savage

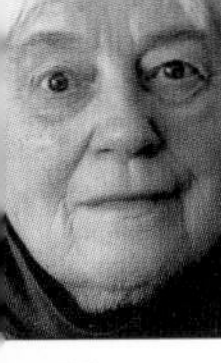

Claire Van Vliet

ACHIEVING A BEAUTIFUL BALANCE OF TEXT AND IMAGE while elegantly synthesizing elements such as ink, binding, and typography, Claire Van Vliet excels at every aspect of her art. The desire to publish books that fully integrate text, form, and visual elements motivated her to create unique non-adhesive book structures that enhance the reading experience. Allowing her books to take shape slowly, she considers each detail along with the reader's potential sensory reactions—how he or she will respond to the feel of the paper and the placement of text, and how typefaces will influence the reading experience.

Van Vliet founded the Janus Press in 1955 and has since published many notable writers, including Raymond Carver, Ted Hughes, and John le Carré. She credits the collaborative process with pushing her work in unexpected and fruitful directions. The vast range of her artistic vision is reflected in five decades of remarkable work. Van Vliet lives in Newark, Vermont. Her work is in institutions worldwide, including the National Gallery of Art in Washington, D.C.; the Victoria and Albert Museum in London, England; and the Library of Congress in Washington, D.C.

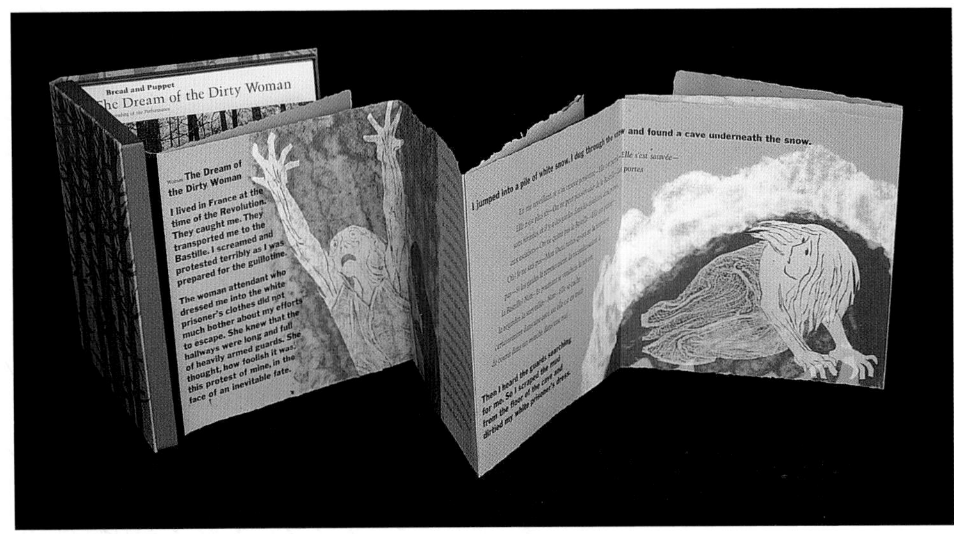

▲ **The Dream of the Dirty Woman: Bread and Puppet (Elka Schumann)** | 1980

12¼ x 11⅞ x 1 inches (31.1 x 30.2 x 2.5 cm)

Pulp-painted paper, relief prints, LP record, clamshell box with printed linen cover; letterpress printed, accordion binding

Photo by John Somers

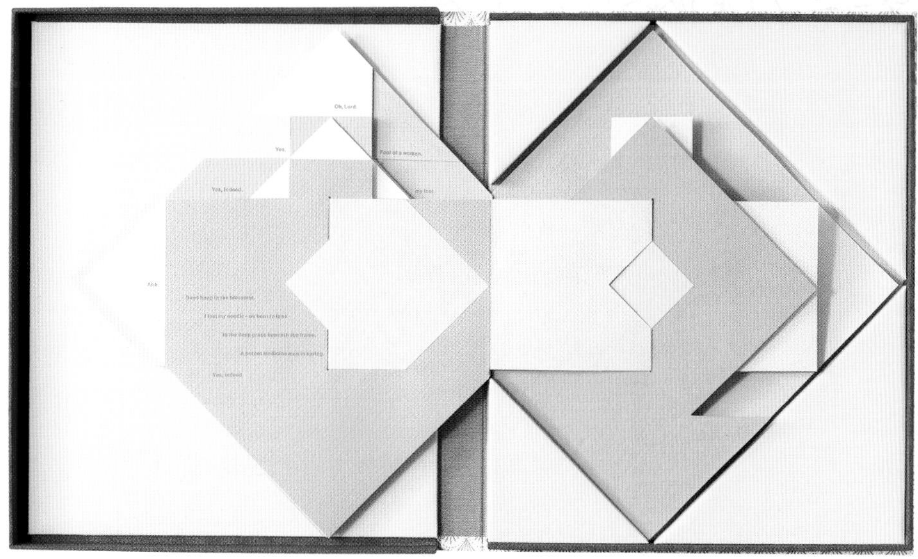

Aunt Sallie's Lament
by Margaret Kaufman | 1988

11¼ x 9¼ x 1 inches (28.6 x 23.5 x 2.5 cm)
Handmade papers, clamshell box covered in upholstery cloth; letterpress printed, concertina threaded binding

Photo by Melville McLean

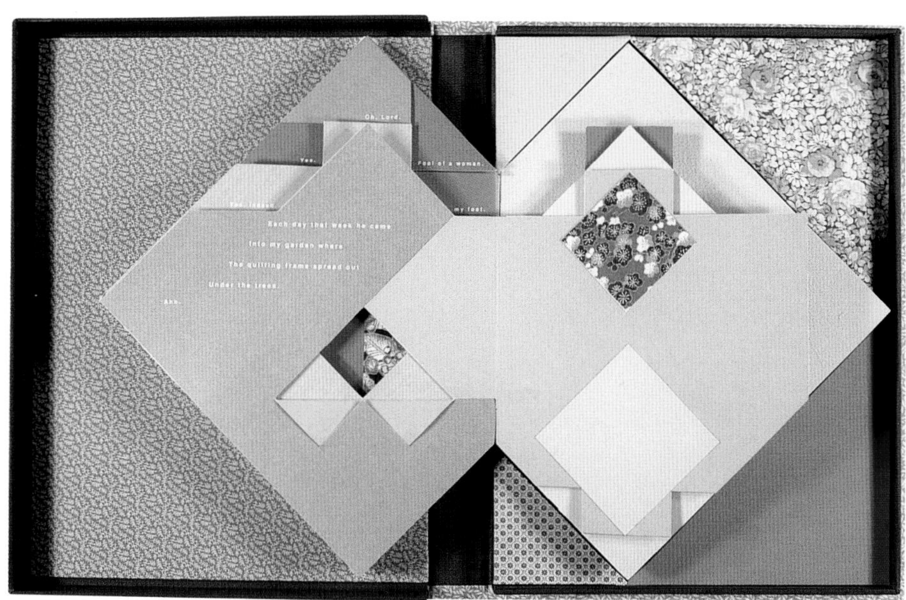

Aunt Sallie's Lament (Altered)
by Margaret Kaufman | 2004

8 x 8 x 1 inches (20.3 x 20.3 x 2.5 cm)
Permalin, handmade papers, chiyogami paper, clamshell box with various calico cloths and upholstery cloth; gocco, letterpress printed, inkjet printed

Photo by John Somers

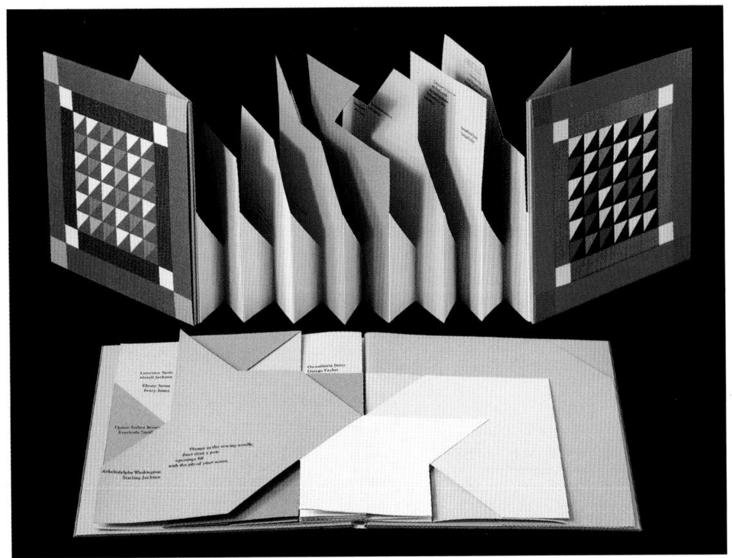

◀ **Designating Duet by Sandra McPherson** | 1989

Each: 7⅝ x 7⅝ x 1 inches (19.4 x 19.4 x 2.5 cm)
Various mold-made and handmade papers, abaca paper, clamshell box; letterpress printed, concertina threaded binding

Photo by Melville McLean

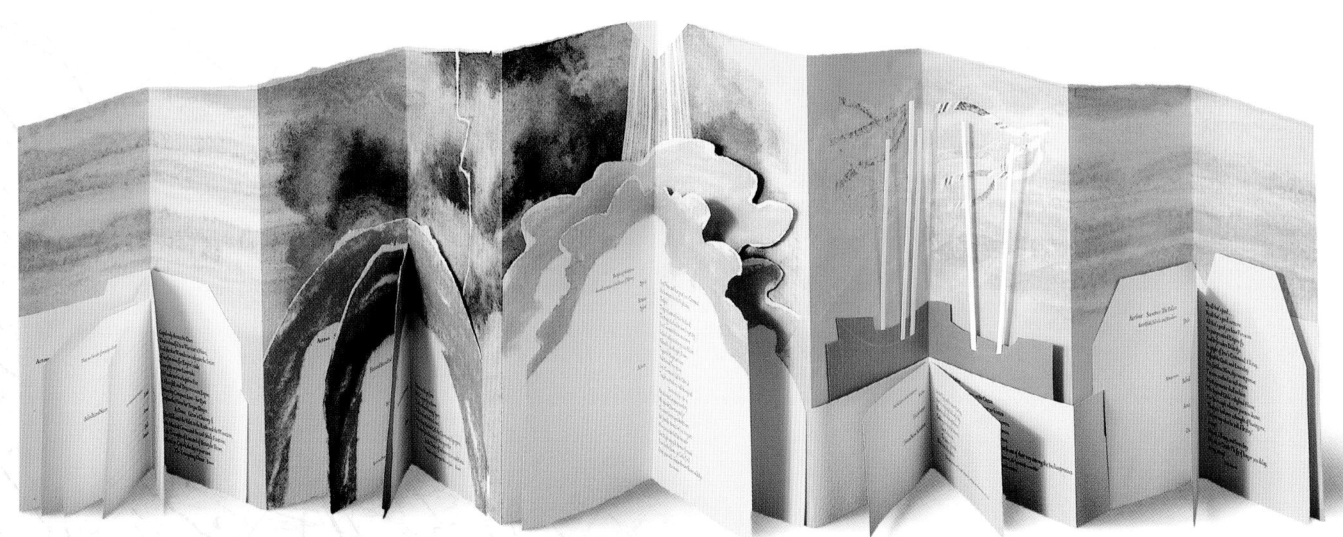

▲ **Dido and Aeneas by Henry Purcell and Nahum Tate** | 1989

14⅝ x 6½ x 1 inches (37.1 x 16.5 x 2.5 cm)
Pulp paint, handmade paper; letterpress, collage, pamphlets sewn into accordion binding

Photo by Melville McLean

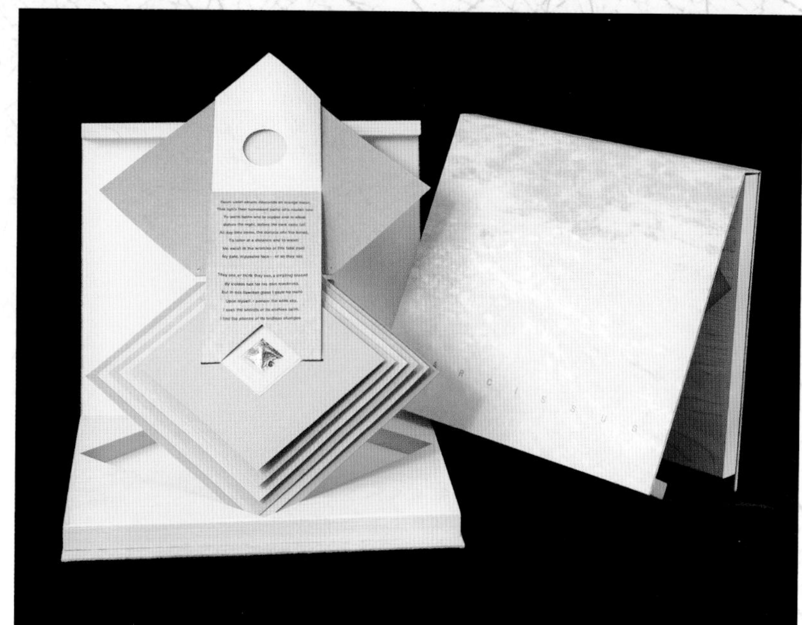

Narcissus by WR Johnson | 1990 ▶

9 x 11½ x 1 inches (22.9 x 29.2 x 2.5 cm)
Various handmade papers, abaca binding strip, clamshell box with slipcase; digital printed, letterpress printed
Photo by Melville McLean

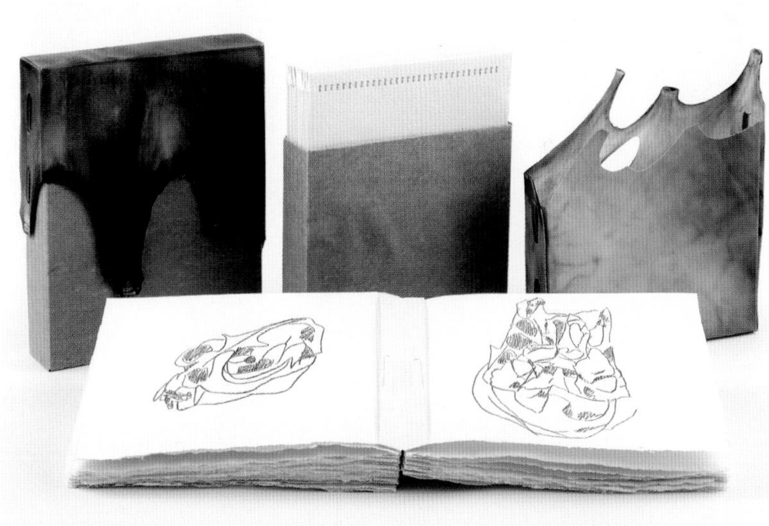

Bone Songs by Clifford Burke with drawings by Ruth Fine | 1992 ▶

10 x 8 x 1½ inches (25.4 x 20.3 x 3.8 cm)
Barcham Green RWS and Renaissance IV papers, abaca binding strips, double slipcase of paper and drum vellum; letterpress printed
Photo by Alan Jacubek

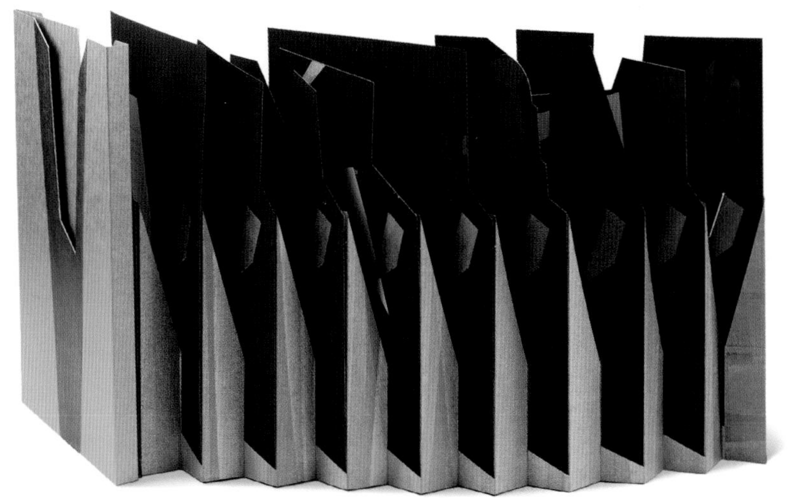

> " I love the fact that a single book can incorporate several forms. It can be held in the hand and paged in sequence, spread out sculpturally, and hung scroll-like. "

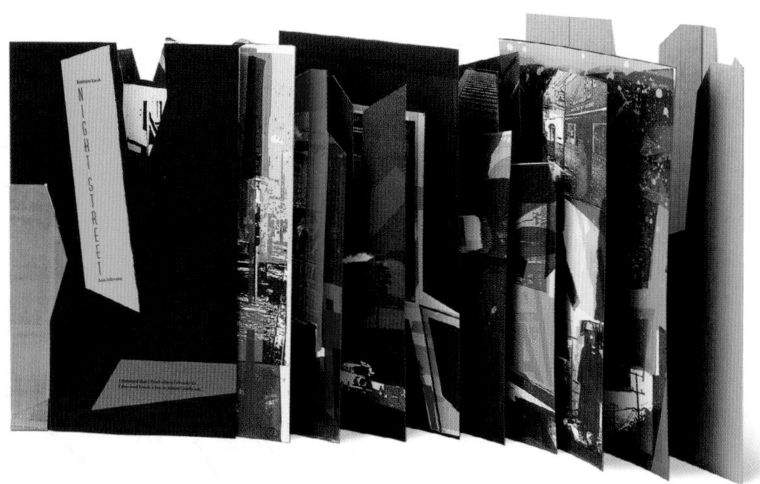

◀ **Night Street by Barbara Luck with images by Lois Johnson** | 1993

13½ x 8½ x 1 inches (34.3 x 21.6 x 2.5 cm)
Rives, Arches, and Miliani Ingres papers, Rowlux, abaca strips, double slipcase, elephant hide; letterpress printed, offset printed, concertina binding, silk-screened, collage

Photos by Melville McLean

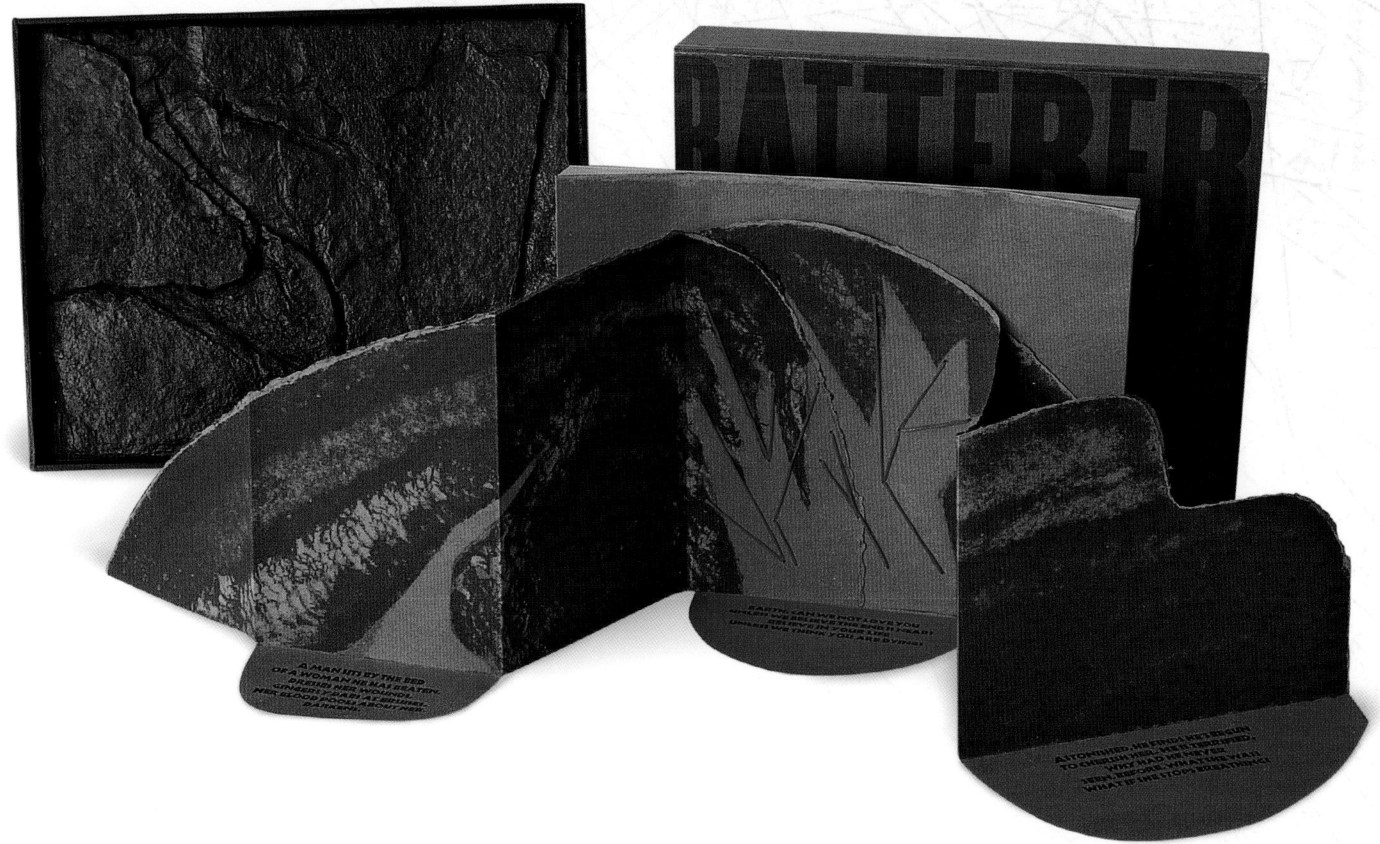

▲ **Batterers by Denise Levertov** | 1996

12 x 15 x 2 inches (30.5 x 38.1 x 5.1 cm)
Pulp-painted paper made at MacGregor-Vinzani, wood cradles, linen thread, wood frame, printed linen slipcase; letterpress printed
Photo by John Somers

" The reader of a book is open, curious, and unthreatened—and he wants what's inside the book. This makes the book an unusually receptive medium for a contemporary artist to work in. "

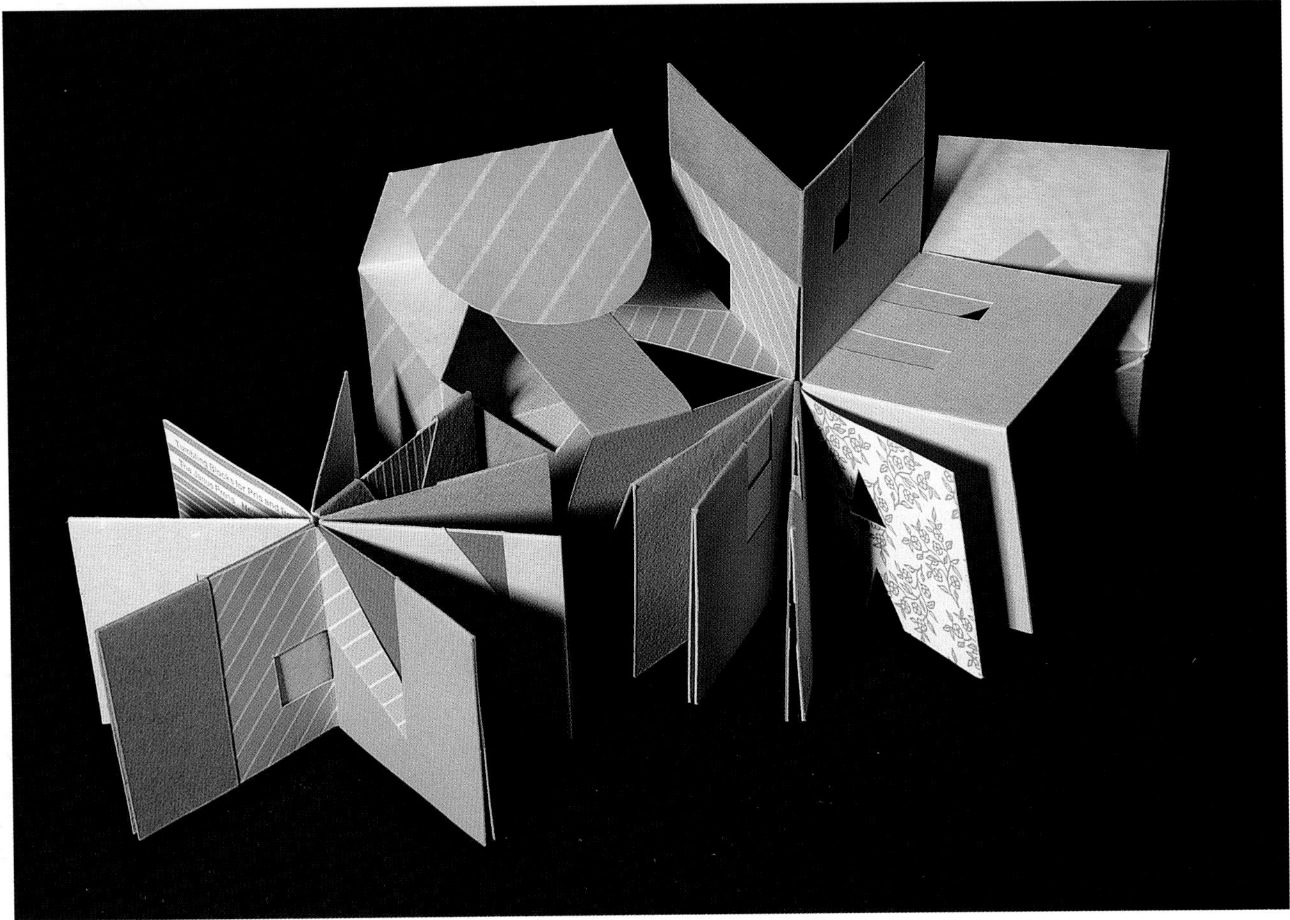

▲ **Tumbling Blocks** | 1996

2¼ x 2¼ x 2¼ inches (5.7 x 5.7 x 5.7 cm)
Various handmade papers, non-adhesive cube of MacGregor-Vinzani abaca; letterpress printed
Photo by John Somers

" All of the physical components of a book can act as facilitators to the essence of the text. They can engage the senses and widen the reader's comprehension of the text. "

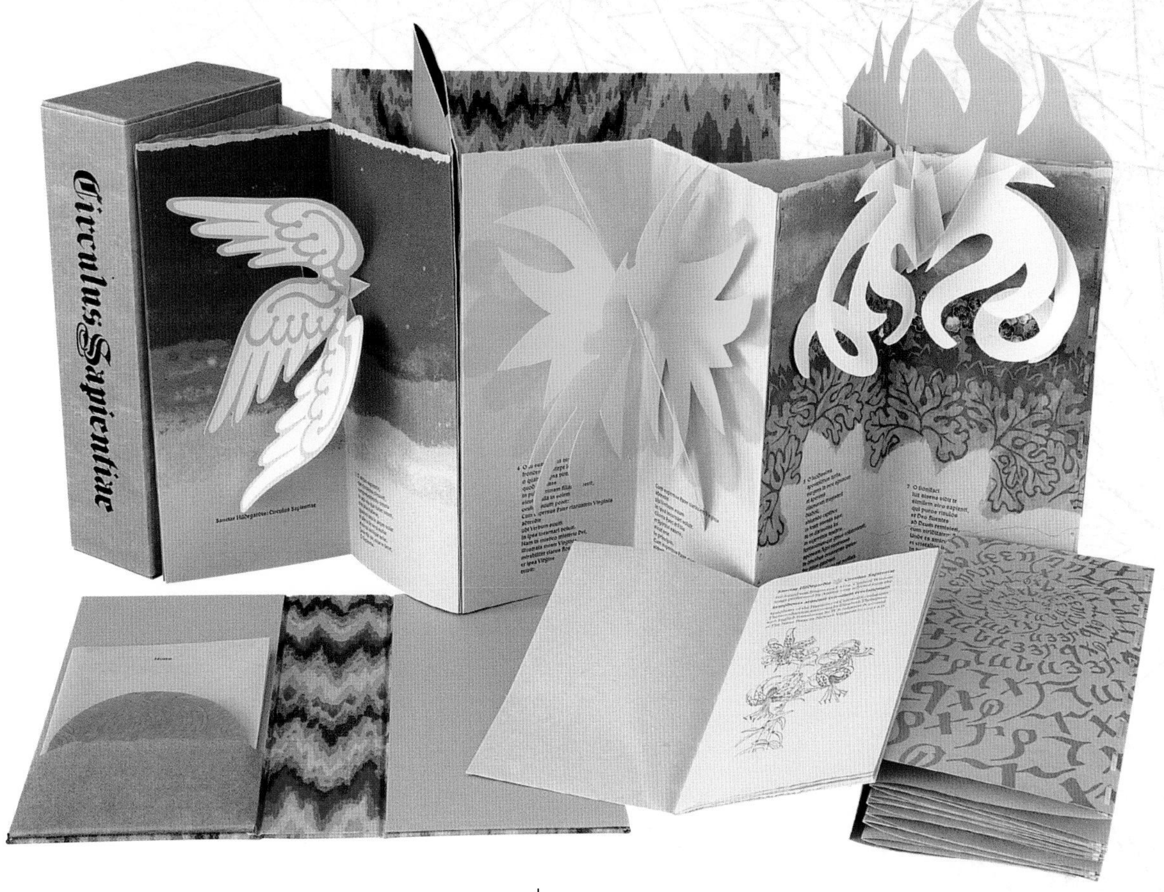

▲ **Circle of Wisdom by Hildegard of Bingen** | 2001

12 x 5½ x 2¼ inches (30.5 x 14 x 5.7 cm)

Pulp paint, handmade paper, chiyogami, paste paper, chemise, slipcase covered with Barcham Green Renaissance IV paper; stenciled, linocut, letterpress, collage, accordion binding

Photo by John Somers

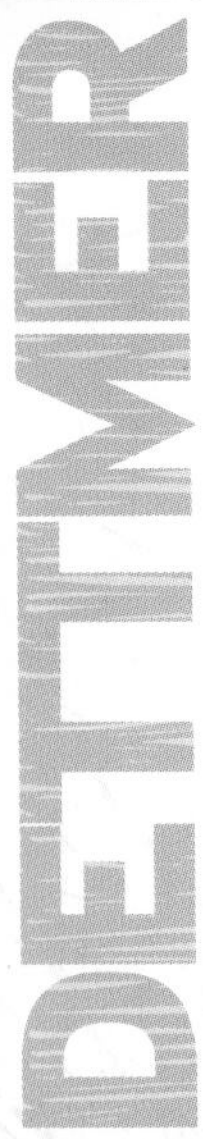

Brian Dettmer

TAKING AN ARCHAEOLOGICAL APPROACH TO the altered book, Brian Dettmer creates works that feature revealing compositions and intriguing visual relationships. Dettmer uses an exclusively reductive technique to create his breathtaking pieces, excavating existing books from cover to cover and transforming physical pages into intricate landscapes of text and image.

Dettmer begins work by sealing the edges of a book. He then cuts into the surface of the book and dissects through it from the front. Working with knives, tweezers, and surgical tools, he carves one page at a time and adds varnish to strengthen the structure. As he reveals the anatomy of a book, he exposes the new relationships and alternate histories that lie hidden within. Dettmer's magical work has been featured in the *Village Voice, The New York Times*, and *Harper's Magazine*. His books are in private and public collections around the world. He lives in Atlanta, Georgia.

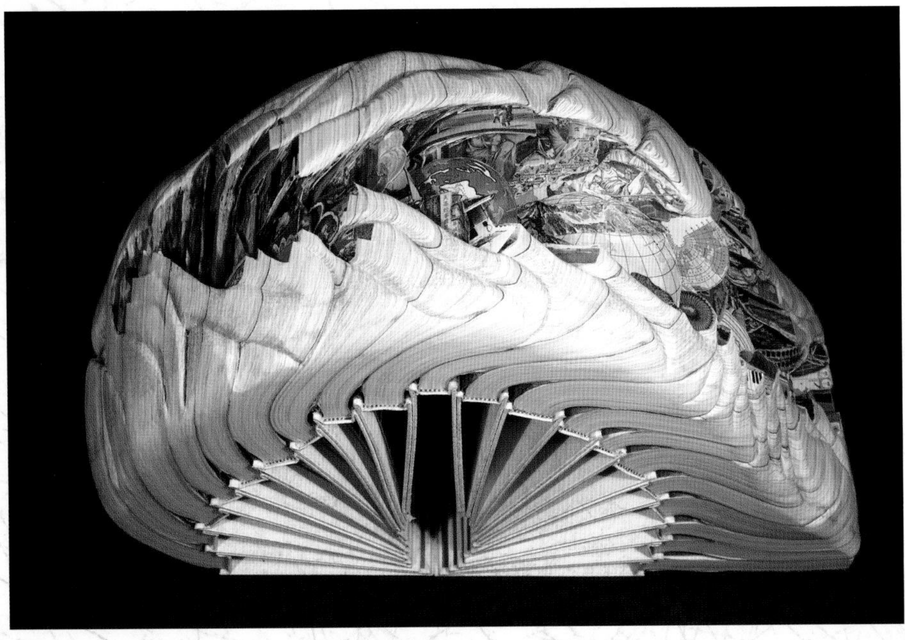

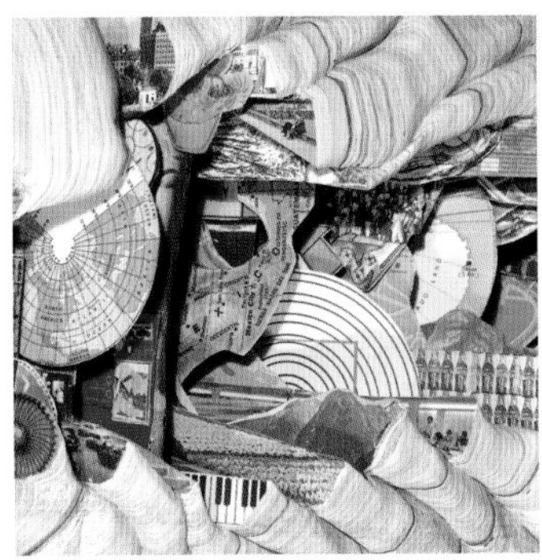

◀ **New Books of Knowledge** | 2009
16 x 26½ x 10 inches (40.6 x 67.3 x 25.4 cm)
Vintage encyclopedias; altered
Photos by artist

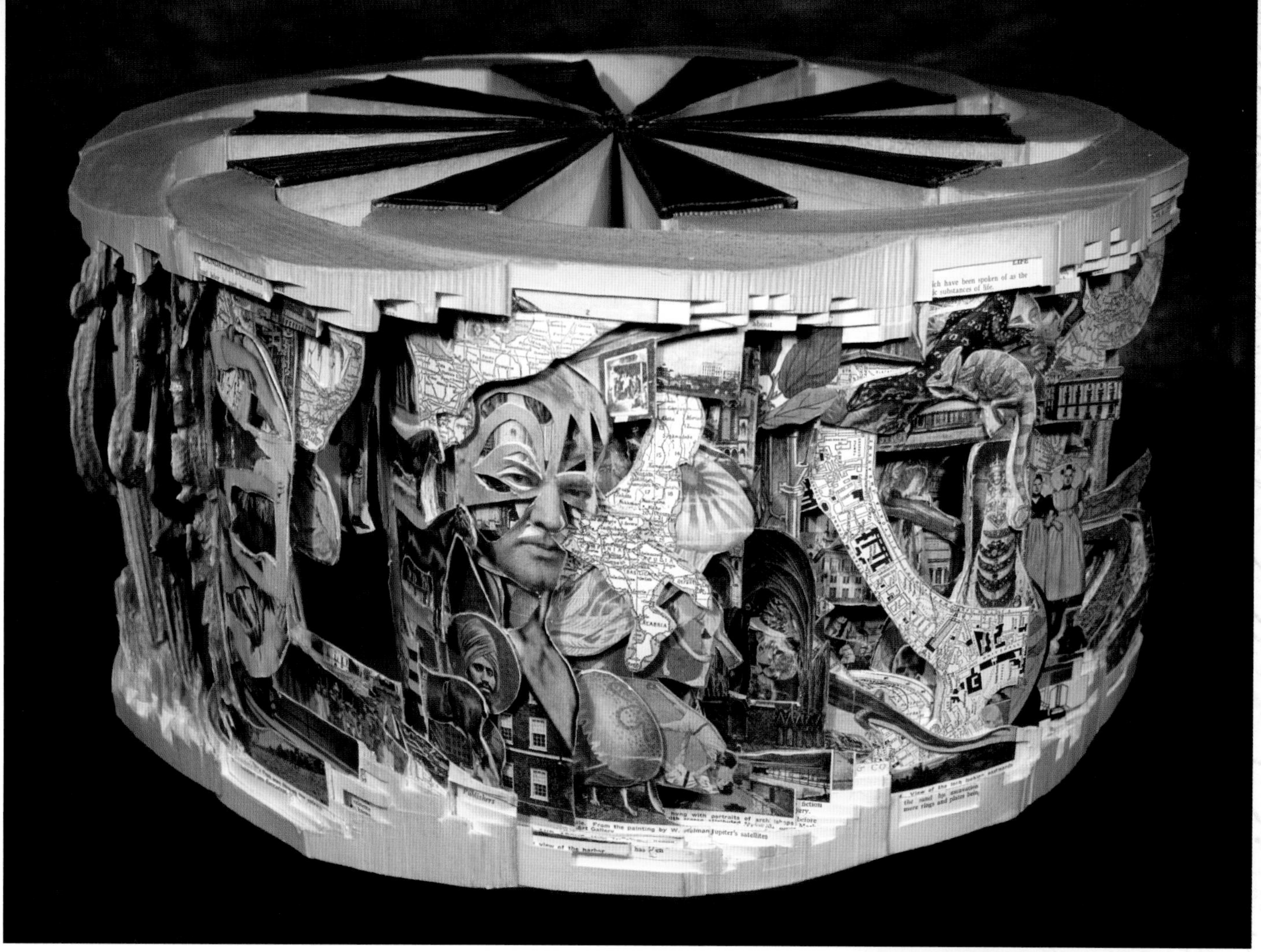

▲ **Doubleday** | 2009

10 x 19 x 19 inches (25.4 x 48.3 x 48.3 cm)
Vintage encyclopedias; altered
Photos by artist

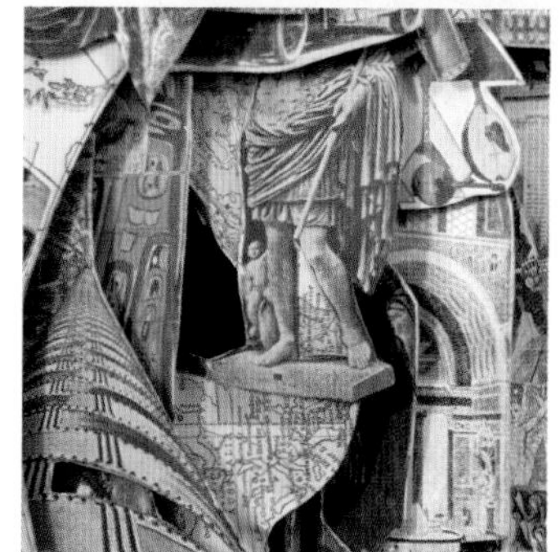

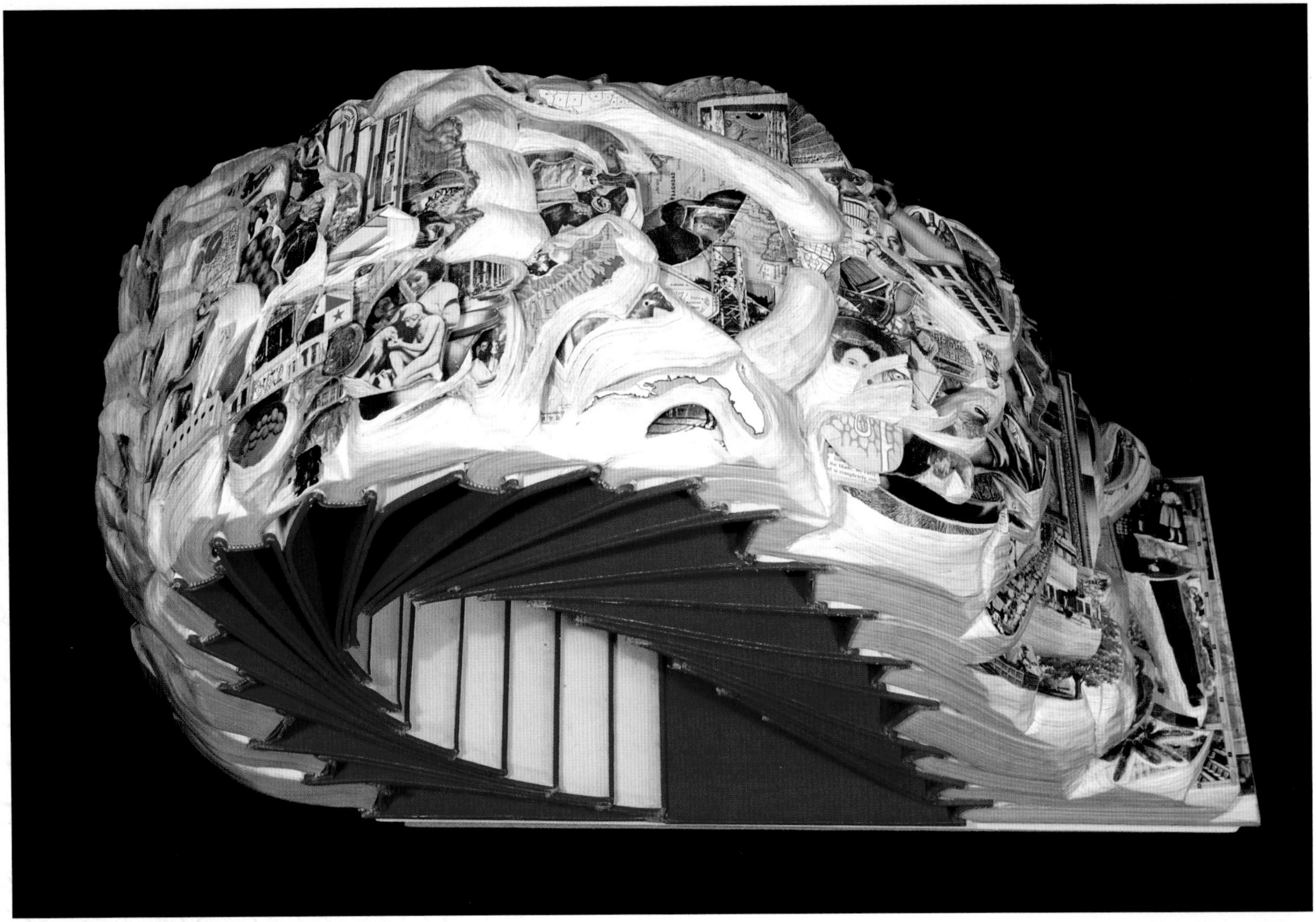

▲ **World Series** | 2009

16¼ x 26½ x 10¼ inches (41.3 x 67.3 x 26 cm)
Vintage encyclopedias; altered

Photos by artist

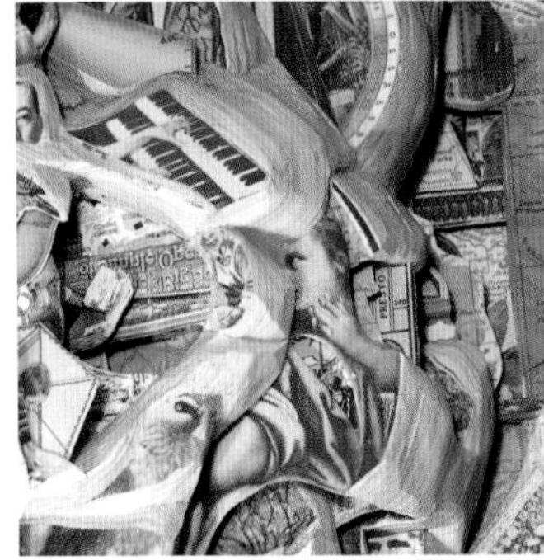

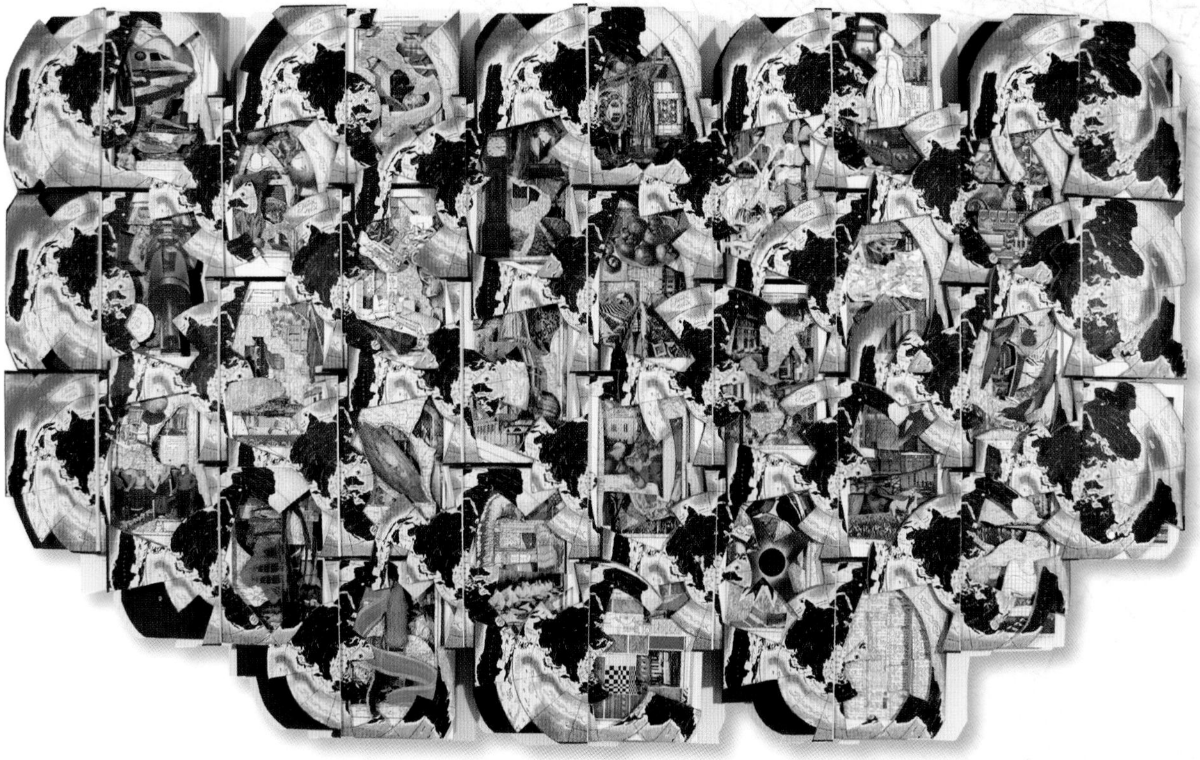

▲ **Americana** | 2009

40½ x 70½ x 2½ inches (102.9 x 179.1 x 6.4 cm)
Vintage encyclopedias; altered

Photos by artist

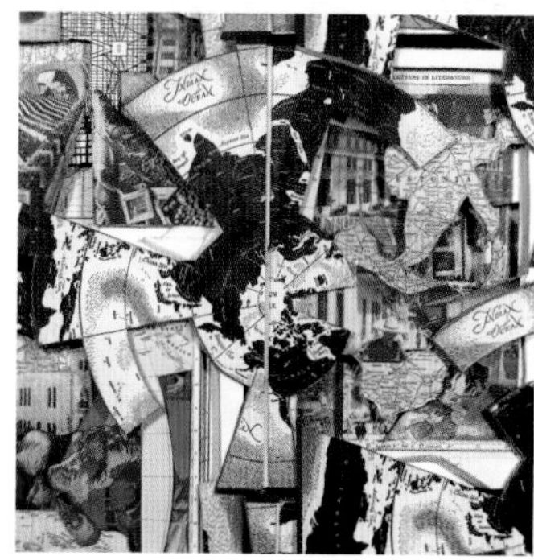

" Through concise alteration I edit objects such as books, maps, and tapes. I transform the roles of these media, re-contextualizing their content, so that new meanings emerge. "

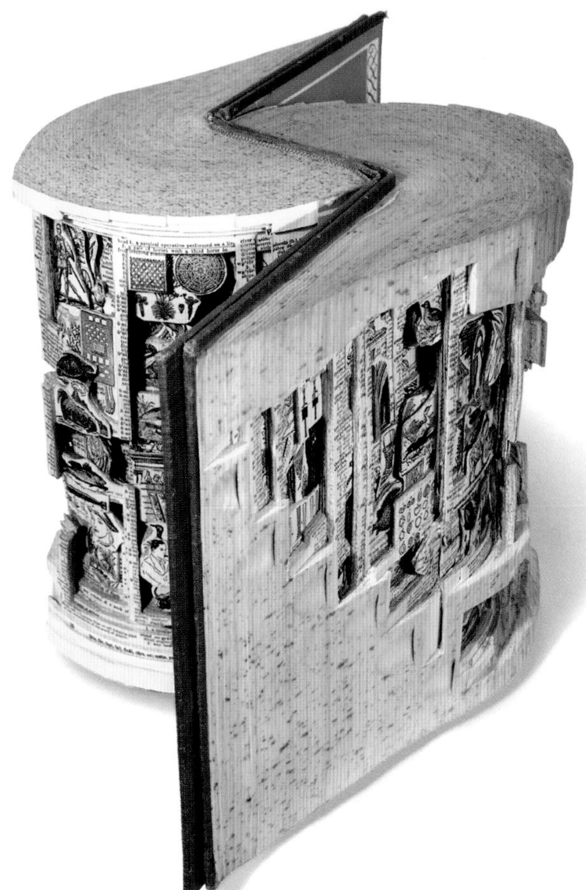

▲ **Webs New Inter Diction** | 2007

12 x 11½ x 5 inches (30.5 x 29.2 x 12.7 cm)
Dictionary; altered
Photo by artist

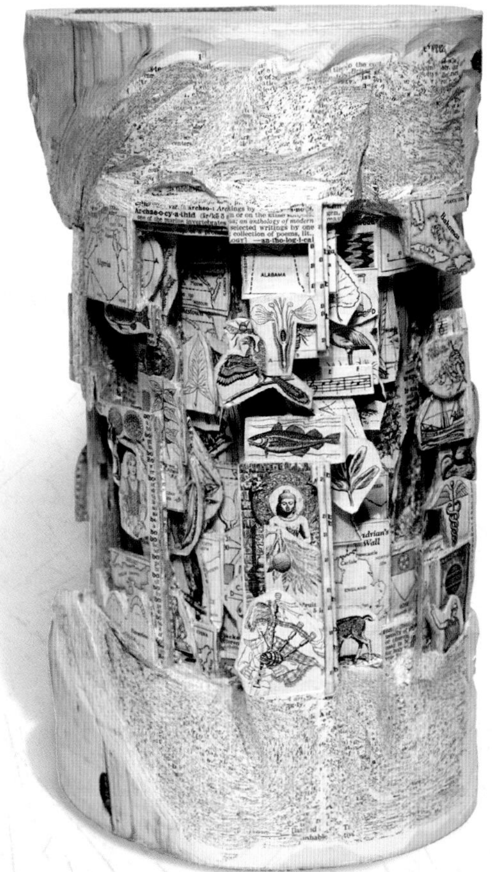

◀ **Column 1** | 2007

12 x 7 x 5½ inches (30.5 x 17.8 x 14 cm)
Book; altered
Photo by artist

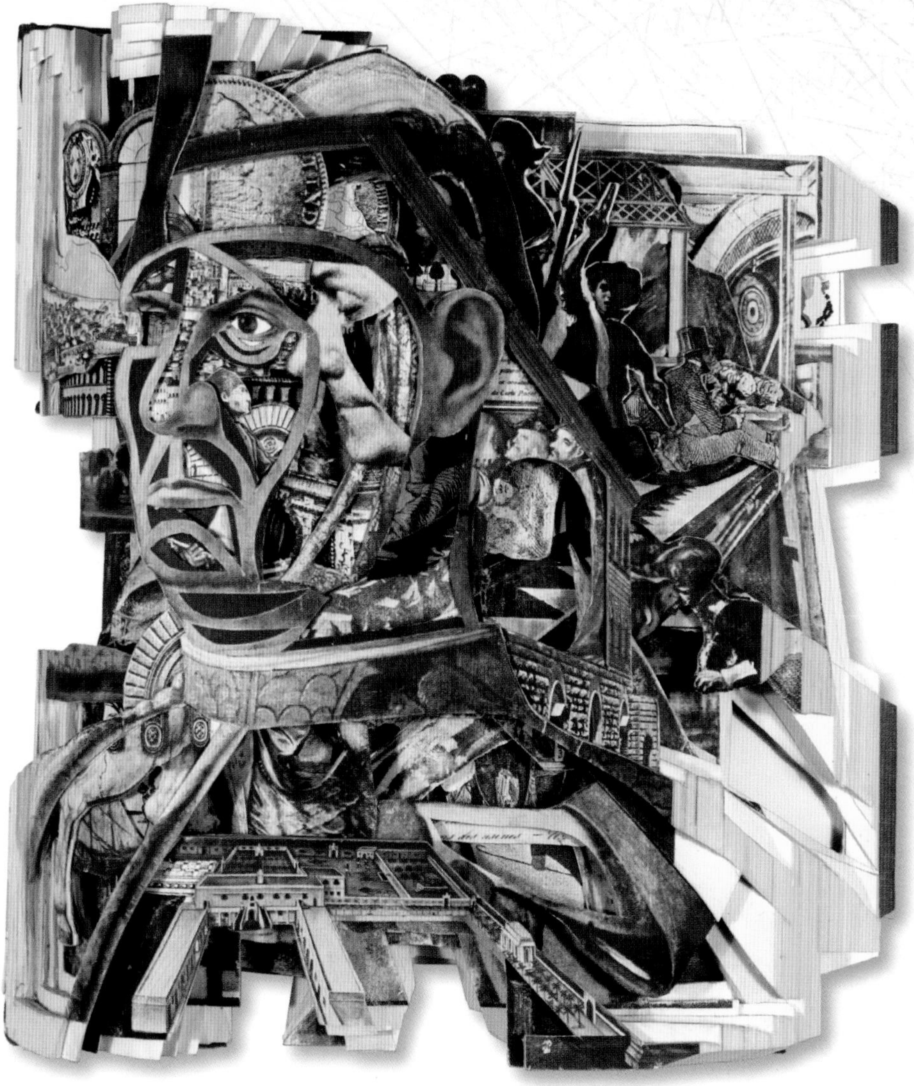

" As I work, I alter physical forms of information and shift preconceived functions. In this way, new and unexpected roles emerge in each book. "

▲ **A History of the Modern World** | 2009

10 x 9 x 2 inches (25.4 x 22.9 x 5.1 cm)
Book; altered
Photos by artist

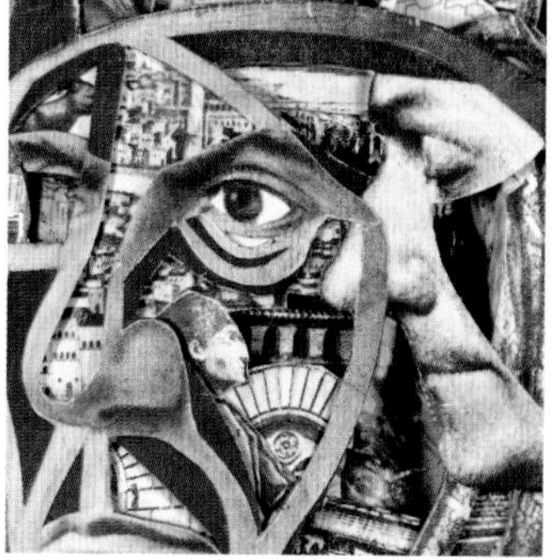

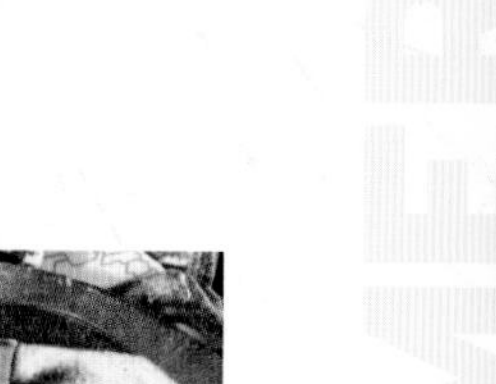

BRIAN DETTMER

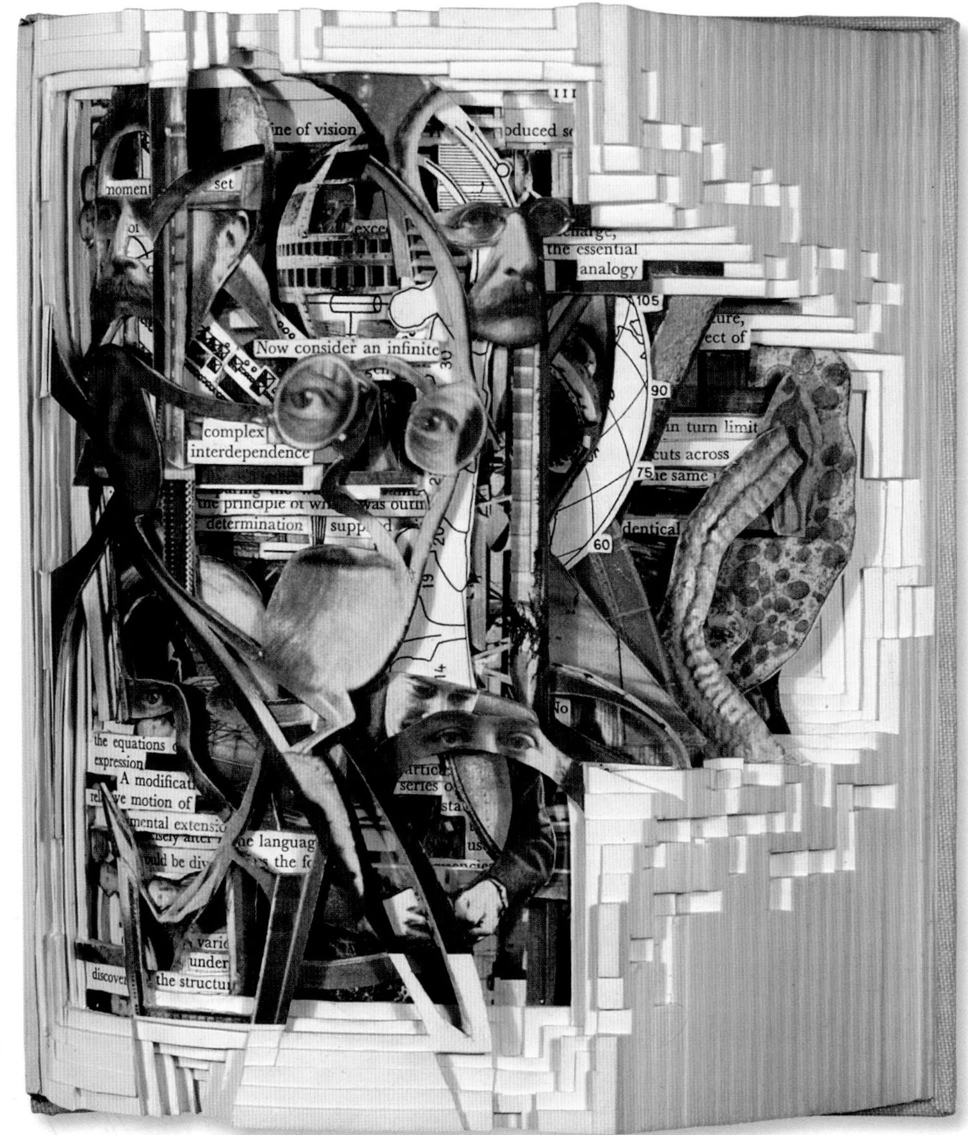

▲ Science in the Twentieth Century | 2009

9½ x 8⅜ x 2½ inches (24.1 x 21.3 x 6.4 cm)

Book; altered

Photo by artist

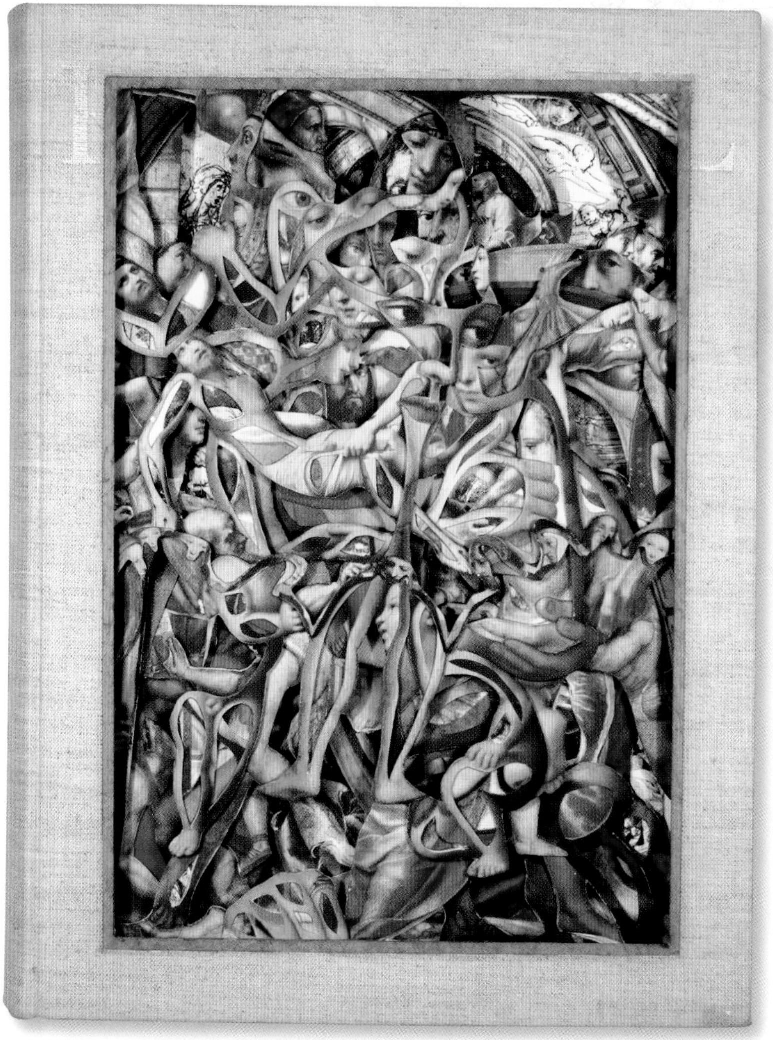

" My work is a collaboration—a communion with the existing material and its past creators. "

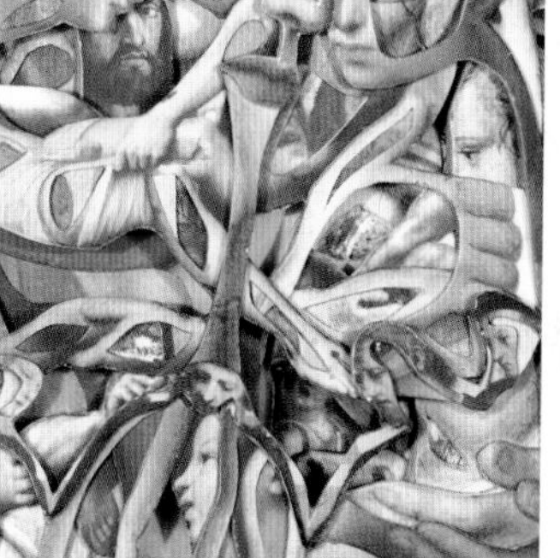

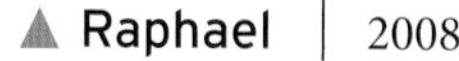

▲ Raphael | 2008

15 x 11½ x 2½ inches (38.1 x 29.2 x 6.4 cm)
Book; altered
Photos by artist

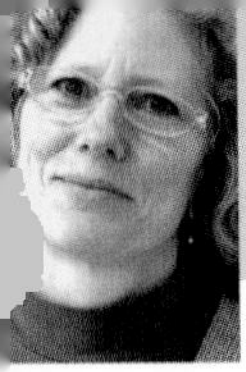

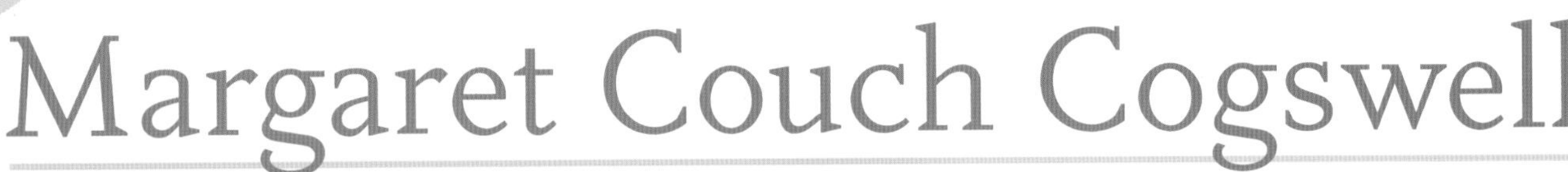

Margaret Couch Cogswell

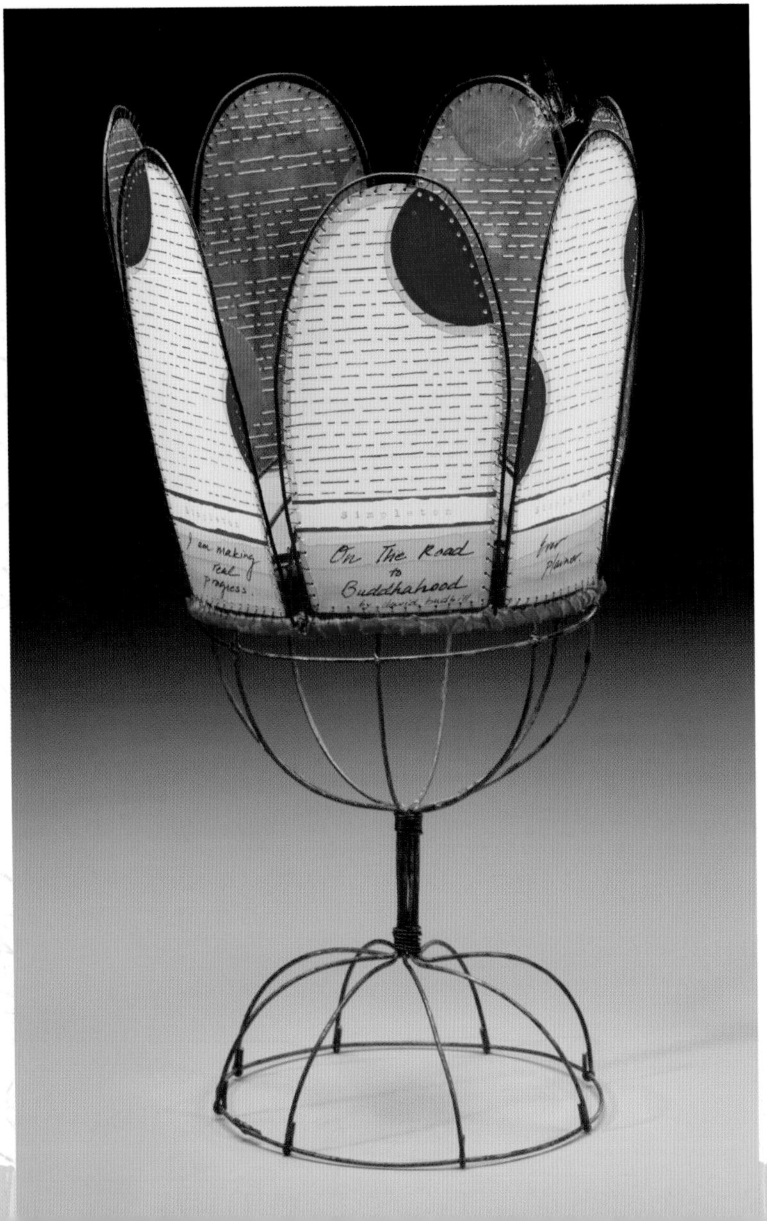

UNEXPECTED PAIRINGS of disparate objects form whimsical compositions in the work of Margaret Couch Cogswell. A storyteller at heart, Cogswell employs simple materials and a low-tech approach to inject a personal quality into her work. She uses humor to disarm the reader even as she delivers thought-provoking subject matter.

Cogswell's distinctive story crowns embody her thematic ideas, acting as metaphors for the anxieties, fears, and judgments that we hold about others and ourselves. Vivid color, stitching, and subtle handwriting combined with found and repurposed objects play a key role in supporting her aesthetic—a uniquely challenging combination of the rough and the refined.

Cogswell teaches and lectures regularly. She lives in Asheville, North Carolina.

◀ **Simpleton** | 2009

7½ x 8½ x 9½ inches (19.1 x 21.6 x 24.1 cm)
Wire, book pages, decorative paper, ink, thread, fabric, shellac, gesso; hand painted
Photo by Steve Mann

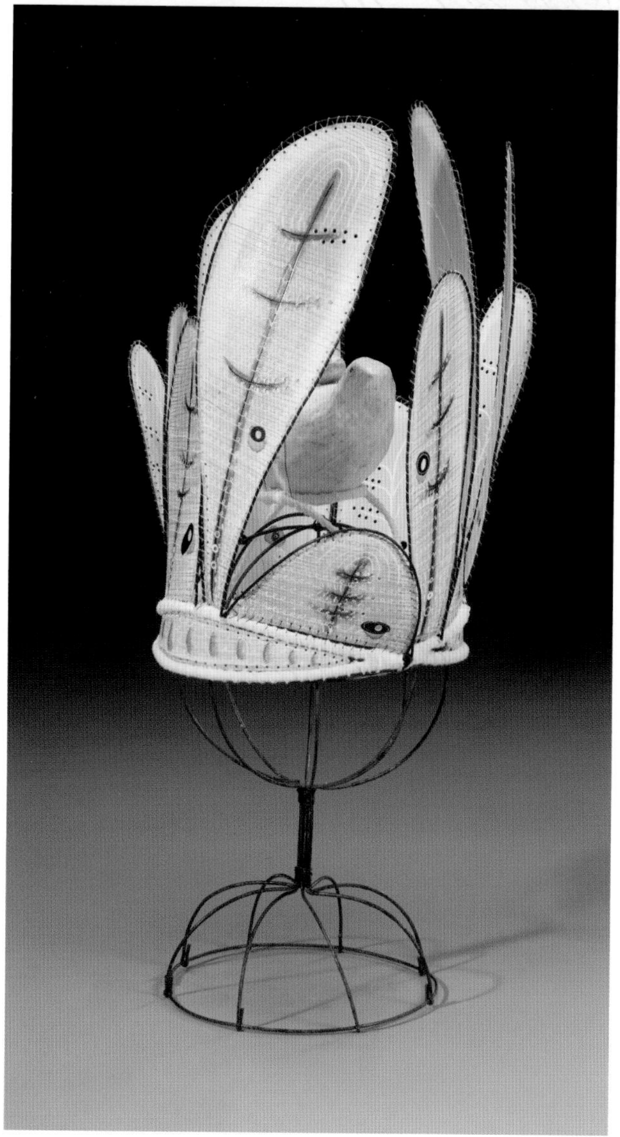

▲ **Birdbrain** | 2009

14 x 14 x 11 inches (35.6 x 35.6 x 27.9 cm)
Wire, book pages, papier-mâché, thread, fabric, graphite, gouache, ink, gesso; hand painted

Photo by Steve Mann

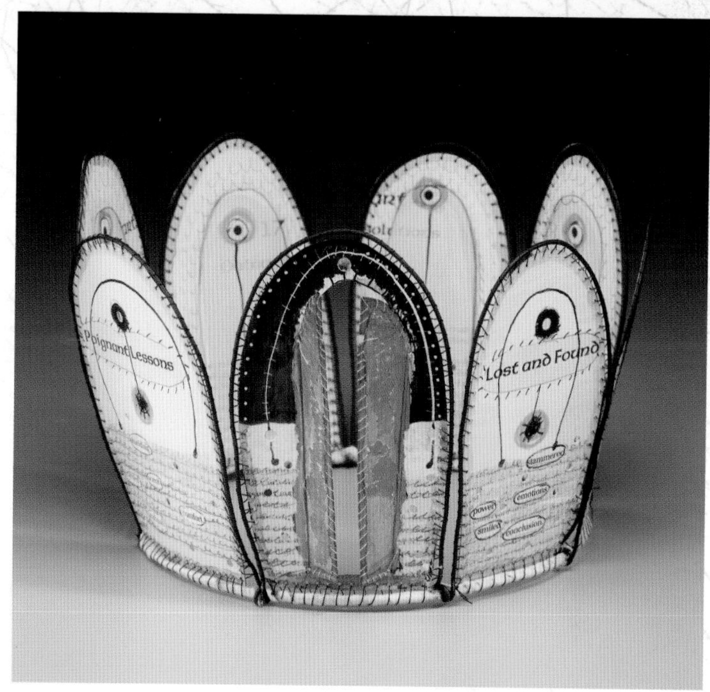

▲ **Doorway Crown** | 2007

7 x 9 x 9 inches (17.8 x 22.9 x 22.9 cm)
Wire, book pages, ink, gesso, gouache, thread, fabric, graphite, shellac; hand painted

Photo by Steve Mann

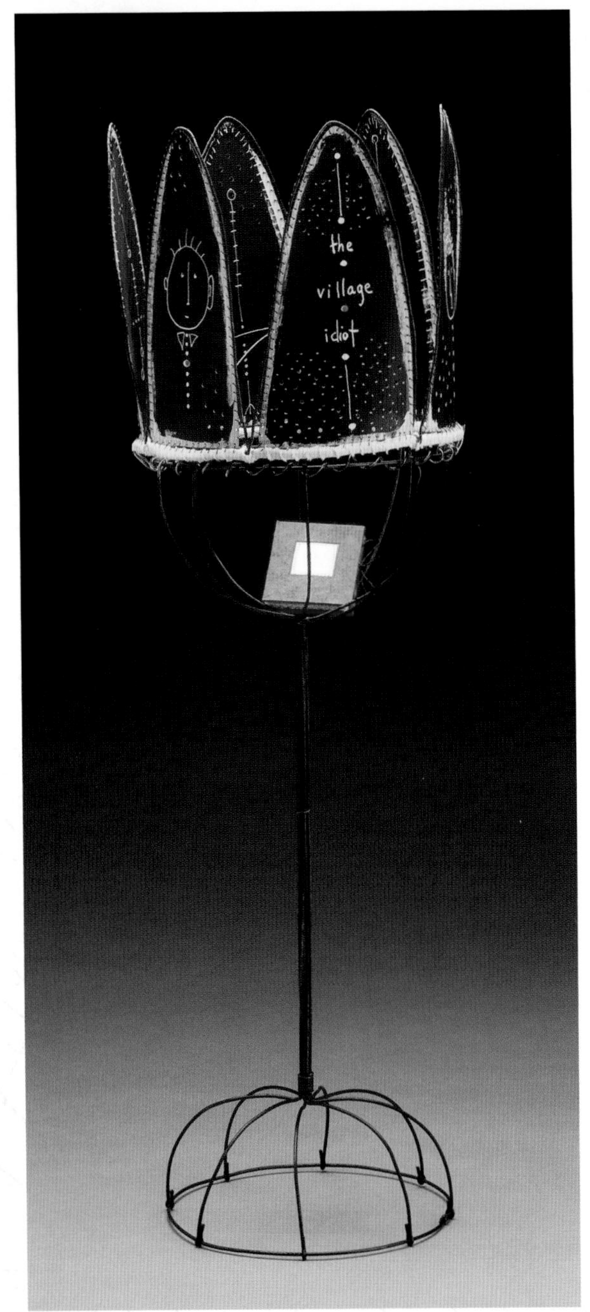

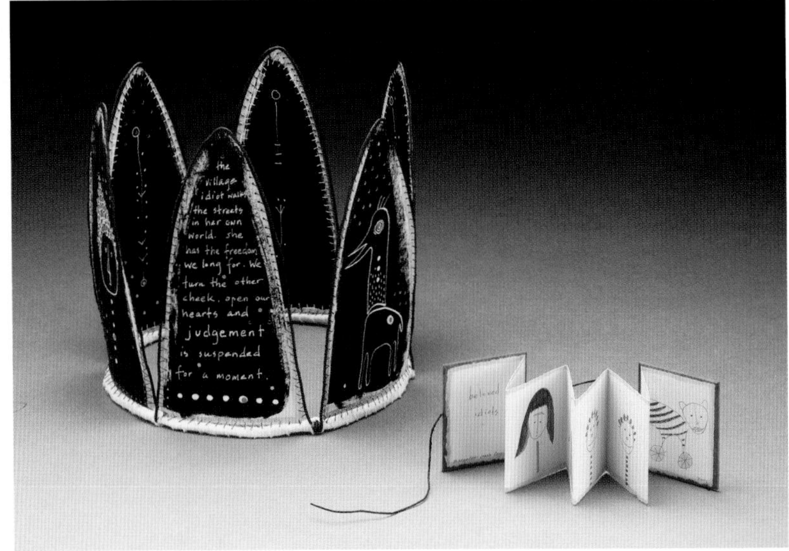

▲ **The Village Idiot** | 2008

Crown: 7 x 8 x 8 inches (17.8 x 20.3 x 20.3 cm)
Book: 2½ x 2 inches (6.4 x 5.1 cm)

Wire, book pages, gesso, ink, graphite, gouache, decorative paper, thread, fabric; hand painted, accordion-fold binding

Photos by Tom Mills

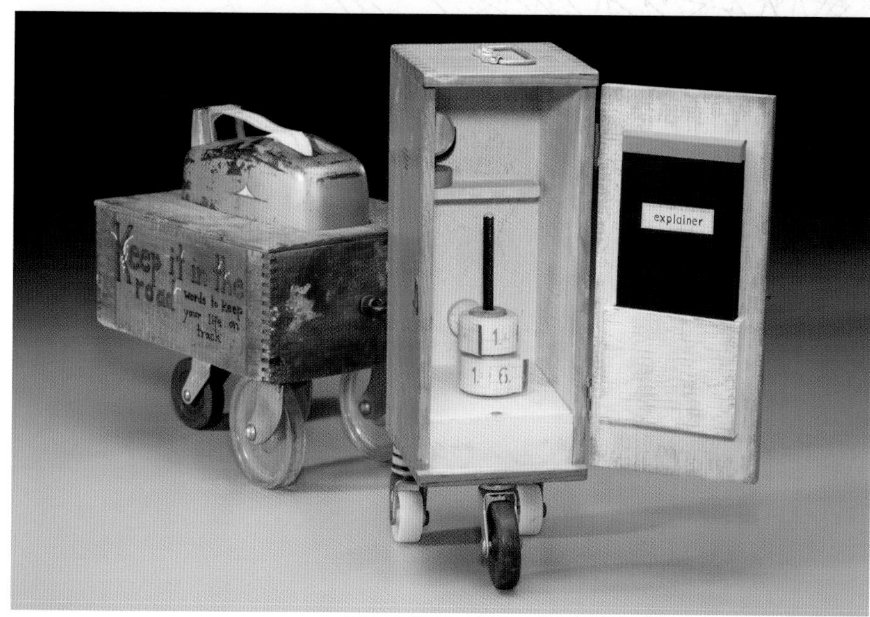

"I often employ comedy and a child-like sensibility in order to engage readers. I tend to conceal more sensitive or sophisticated content beneath the surface of a work."

▲ **Keep It in the Road** | 2009

9 x 22½ x 7½ inches (22.9 x 57.2 x 19.1 cm)
Found wooden boxes, wheels, tape dispenser, wooden dowels, hardware, tape, acrylic paint, found paper, ink; assembled, pamphlet-stitch binding

Photo by Steve Mann

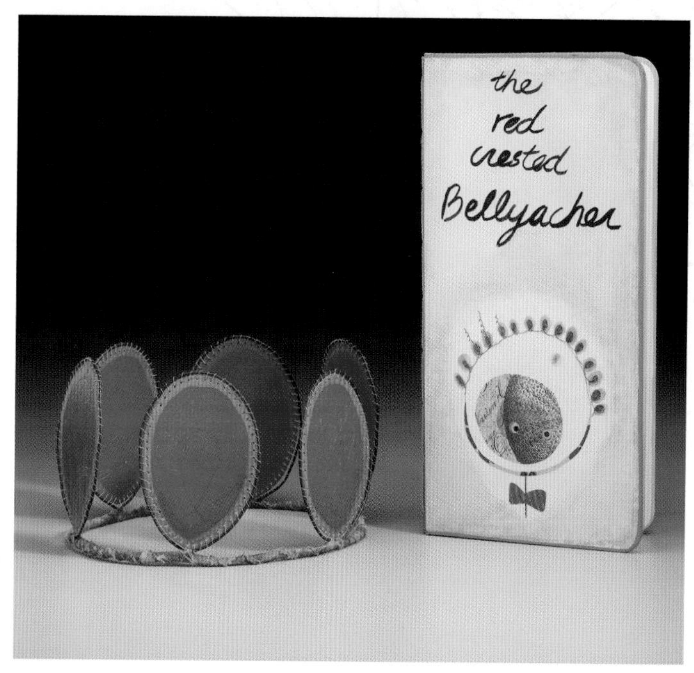

The Red-Crested Bellyacher | 2007 ▶

Crown: 4½ x 7 x 7 inches (11.4 x 17.8 x 17.8 cm)
Book: 11 x 5¾ inches (27.9 x 14.6 cm)

Wire, book pages, thread, fabric, acrylic paint, graphite, shellac, decorative paper, ink, gouache; hand painted, assembled, pamphlet-stitch binding

Photo by Steve Mann

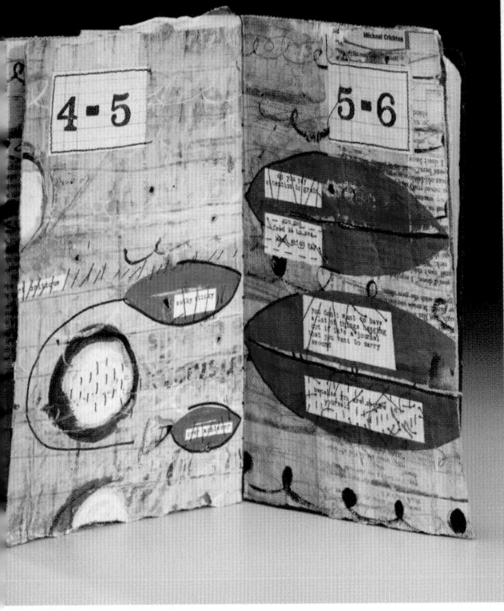

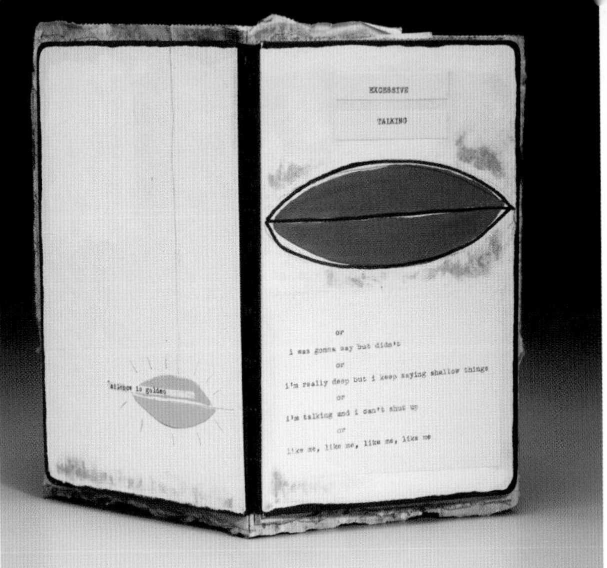

◀ **Excessive Talking** | 2007

10 x 6 inches (25.4 x 15.2 cm)
Paper bag, book pages, found paper, gesso, shellac, acrylic paint, gouache, ink, spray paint, graphite, thread; assembled, pamphlet-stitch binding

Photos by Steve Mann

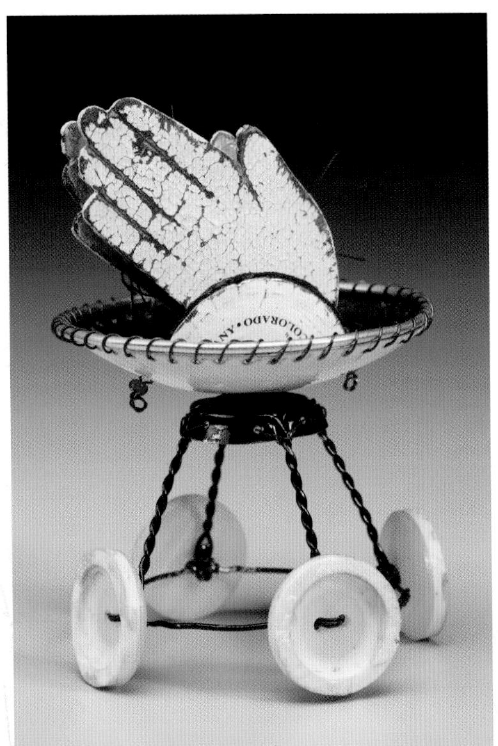

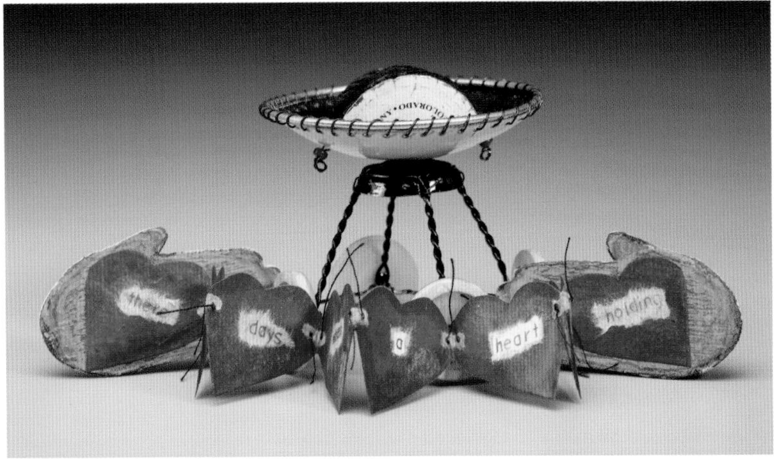

▲ **There Are Days . . .** | 2007

4 x 2¾ x 2¾ inches (10.2 x 7 x 7 cm)
Champagne cage, buttons, wire, tin can lid, bottle cap, leather, book board, milk paint, thread, beads, spray paint, decorative paper; accordion fold, assembled

Photos by Steve Mann

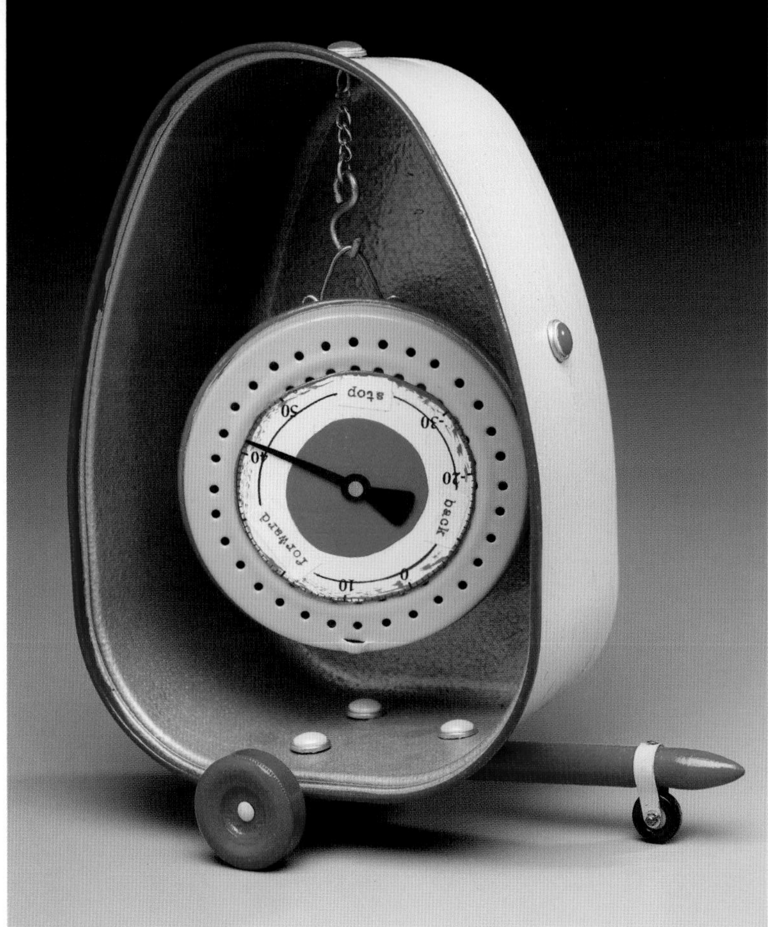

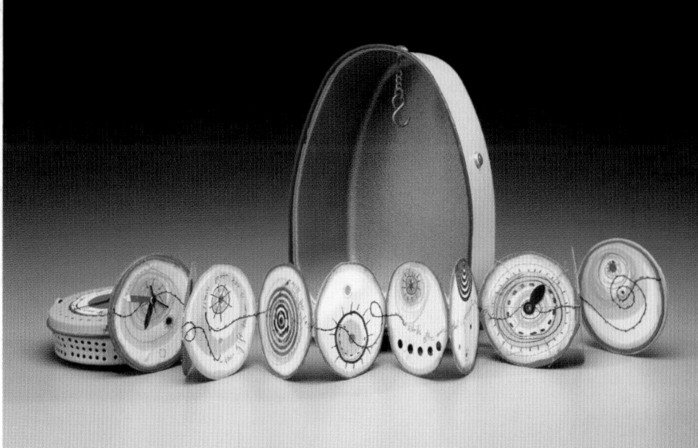

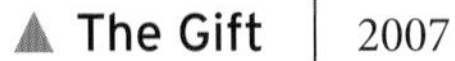 **The Gift** | 2007

Can: 8½ x 7 x 3½ inches (21.6 x 17.8 x 8.9 cm)
Book: 3½ x 3½ inches (8.9 x 8.9 cm)

Ham can, wood, tea strainer, wooden wheels, found objects, Rives BFK paper, graphite, thread, ink; assembled, accordion-fold binding

Photos by Steve Mann

" The hand of the maker is always apparent and visible in my books. This conveys my interest in and appreciation of the rough, unpolished moments in our existence. "

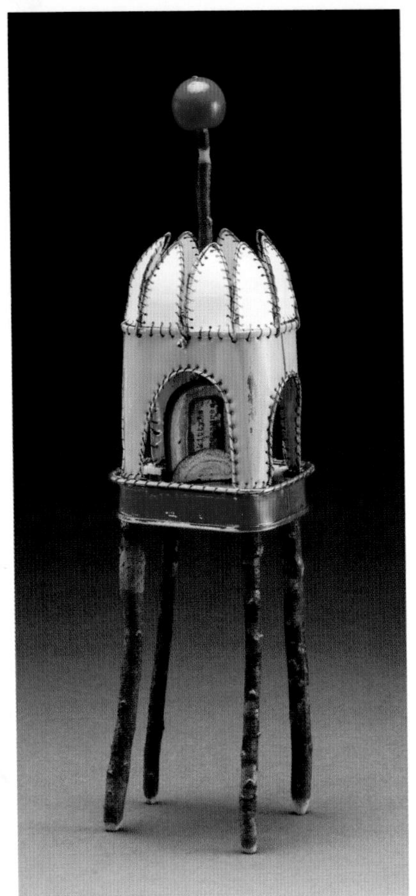

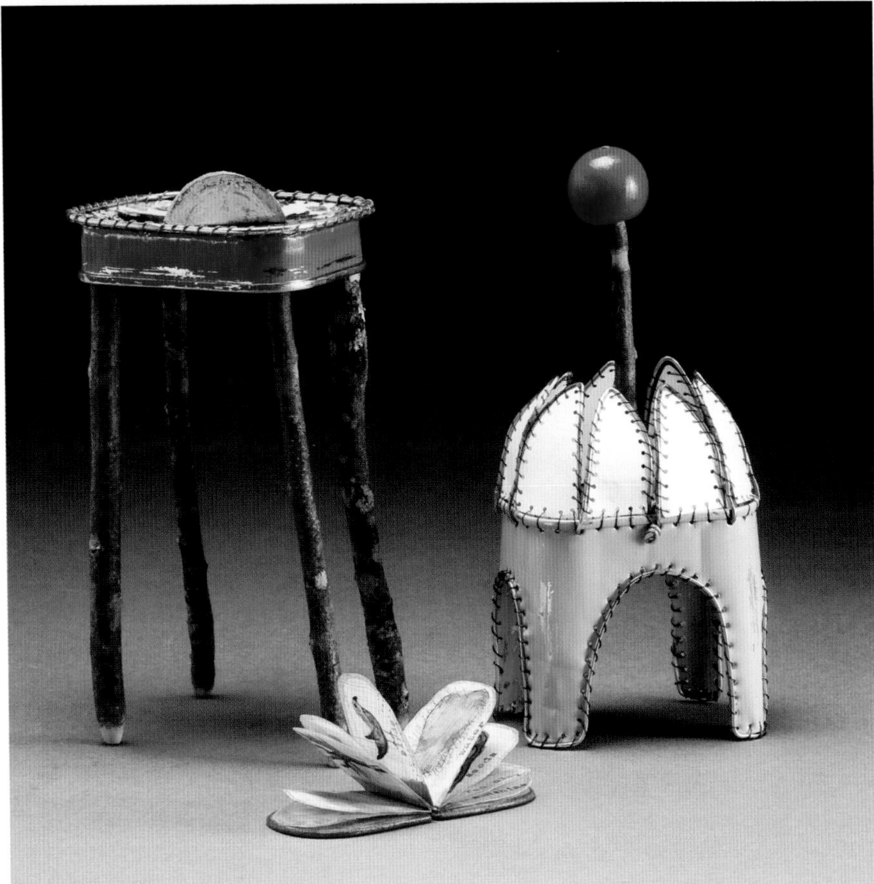

▲ Kitty's Treasures | 2008

Structure: 11 x 4½ x 3 inches (27.9 x 11.4 x 7.6 cm)
Book: 1¾ x 1¼ inches (4.4 x 3.2 cm)

Cans, spray paint, Tyvek, wood, bottle cap, wire, papyrus, gouache, graphite, ink; pamphlet-stitch binding

Photos by Tom Mills

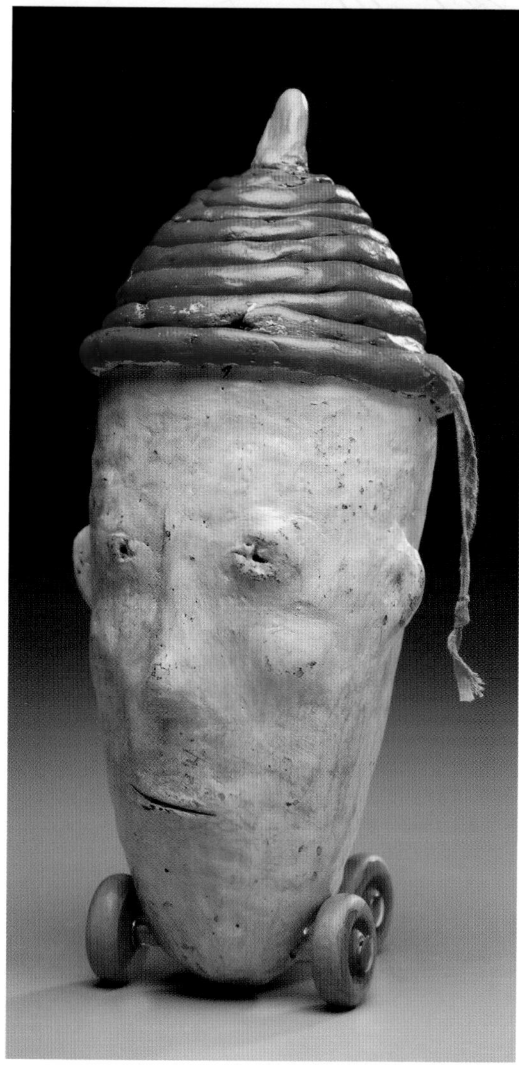

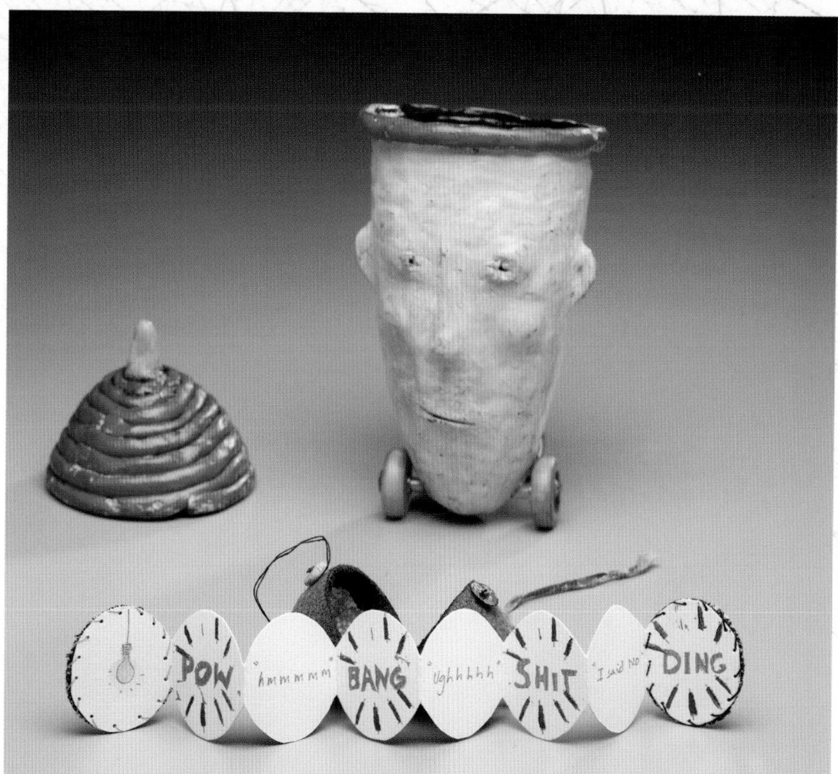

▲ **What's Going On in There?** | 2007

12½ x 5½ x 7 inches (31.8 x 14 x 17.8 cm)
Clay, wooden wheels, fabric, button, plastic kiwi, acrylic paint, ink, graphite, thread, gouache; assembled, hand stamped, accordion-fold binding

Photos by Steve Mann

" I work in books because of the interactive quality they offer. I want viewers to have a sensory experience through handling, wearing, and playing with my books. "

LEINO

Shanna Leino

WORKING PRIMARILY ON A DIMINUTIVE SCALE, Shanna Leino crafts striking, meticulously designed books from bone, metal, and paper. Leino references traditional bookbinding methods in her work, bringing the past into the present with finesse, creativity, and technical expertise. Stitches are integral to her structures. She often uses colorful silk thread to form intricate end bands—colorful patterns that serve as the finishing touches for her pieces.

Leino's books are the results of a long, slow process that reflects her deep respect for the traditions and materials of her craft. Planing wood, carving bone, and paring leather are typical procedures that she employs to give each work a distinctly handcrafted feel. Leino lives in Harrisville, New Hampshire, where she manufactures a line of tools for bookbinders and craftspeople. She teaches workshops regularly throughout the United States.

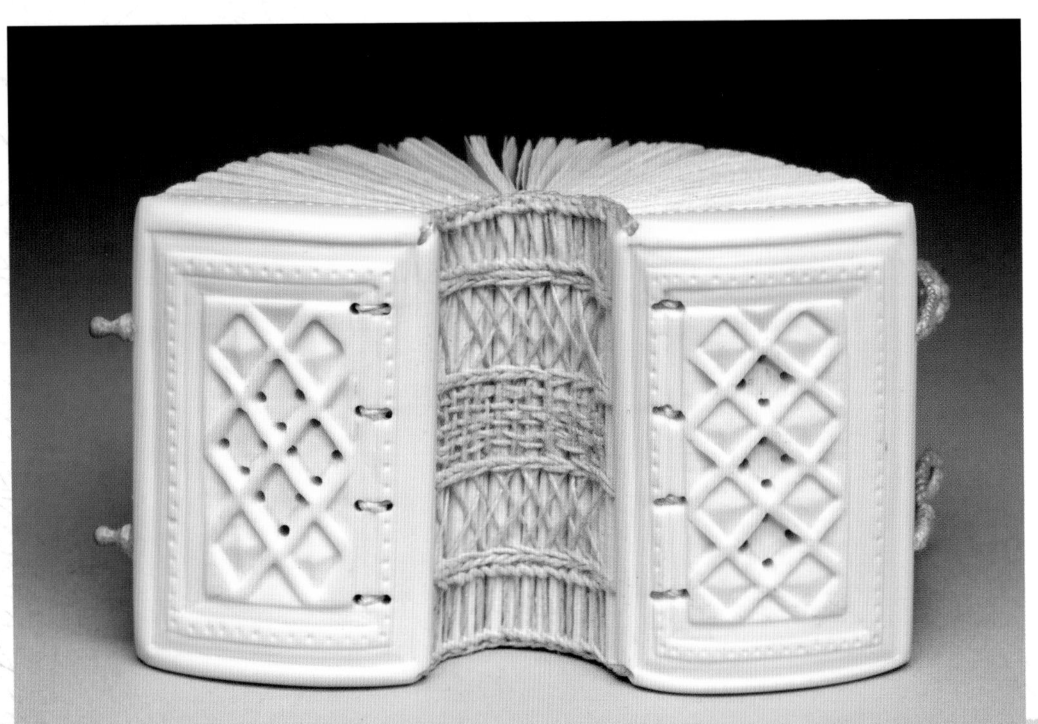

Carved Knot Book | 2008

1½ x 1 x 1 inches
(3.8 x 2.5 x 2.5 cm)
Elk bone, handmade flax paper, serviceberry wood, linen thread

Photo by Walker Montgomery

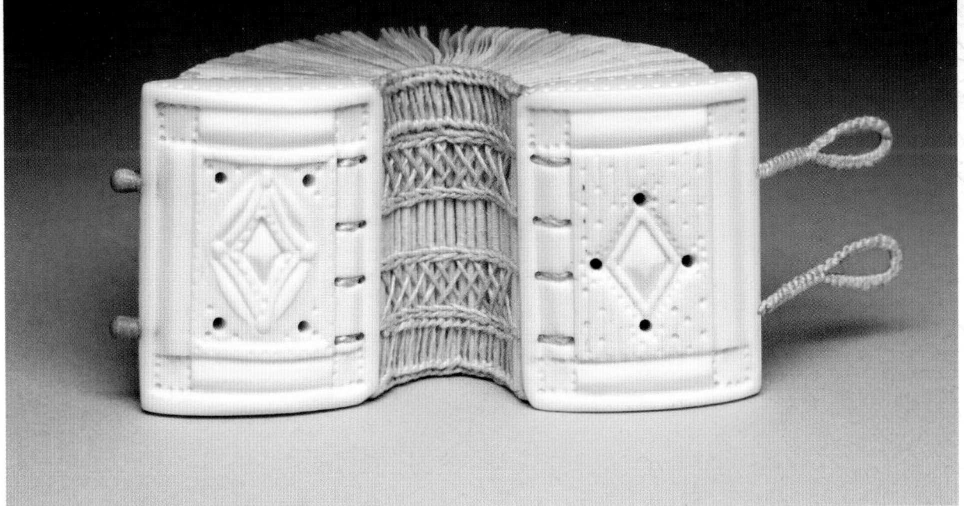

▲ **Tiny Elk-Bone Book** | 2008

1 x ¾ x ¾ inches (2.5 x 1.9 x 1.9 cm)
Elk bone, handmade flax paper, serviceberry wood, linen thread

Photo by Walker Montgomery

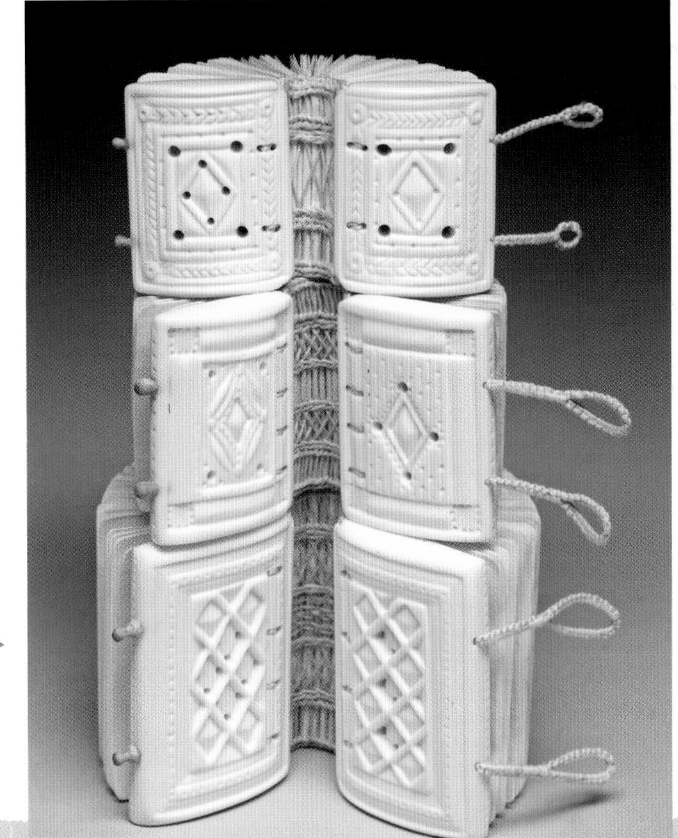

Carved Elk-Bone Books, Group of 3 | 2008 ▶

Tallest: 1½ inches (3.8 cm)
Elk bone, handmade flax paper, serviceberry wood, linen thread

Photo by Walker Montgomery

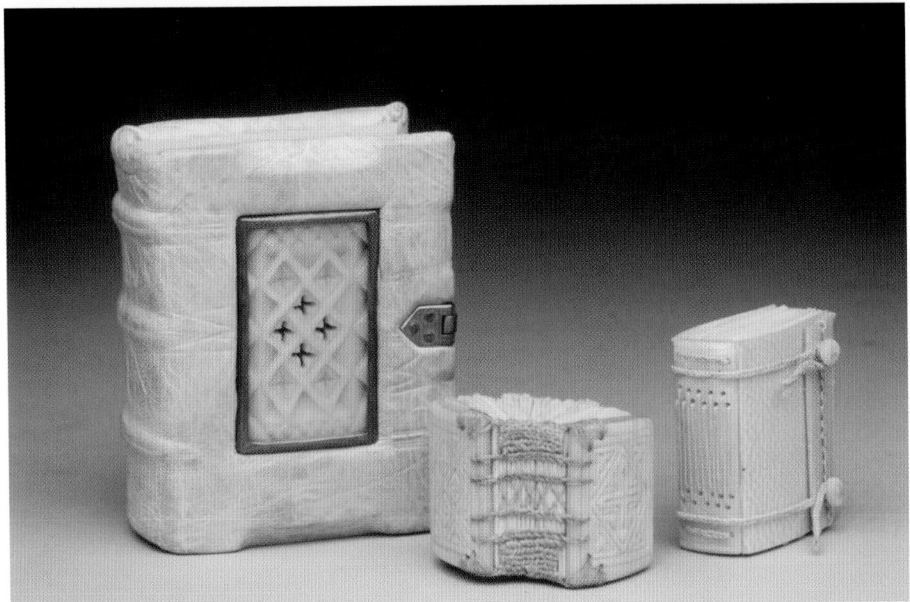

▲ **Group of Books, Featuring Elk Bone** | 2001

Various dimensions
Elk bone, handmade paper, vellum, brass, alum taw, mica, oak, linen thread; hand carved
Photo by Walker Montgomery

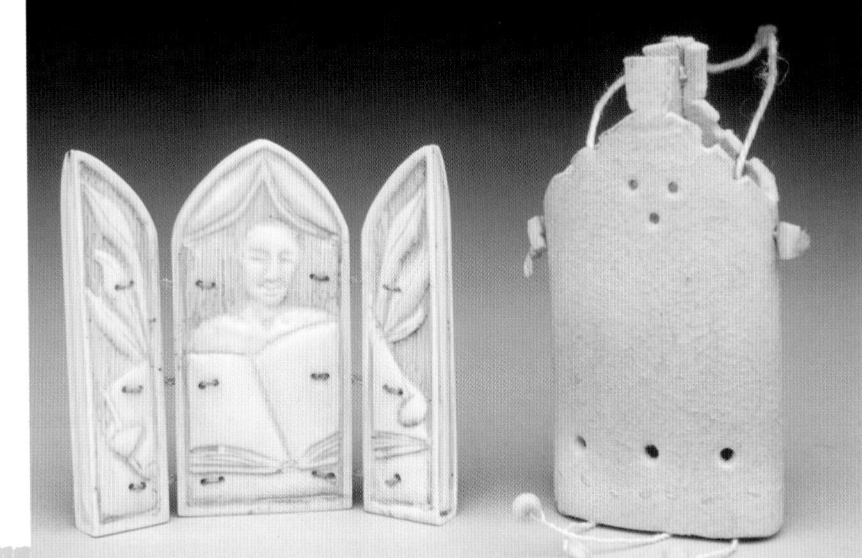

Carved Ivory Triptych | 2002 ▶

2¼ x 1⅛ x ½ inches
(5.7 x 2.9 x 1.3 cm)
Ivory, linen thread, suede
Photo by Walker Montgomery

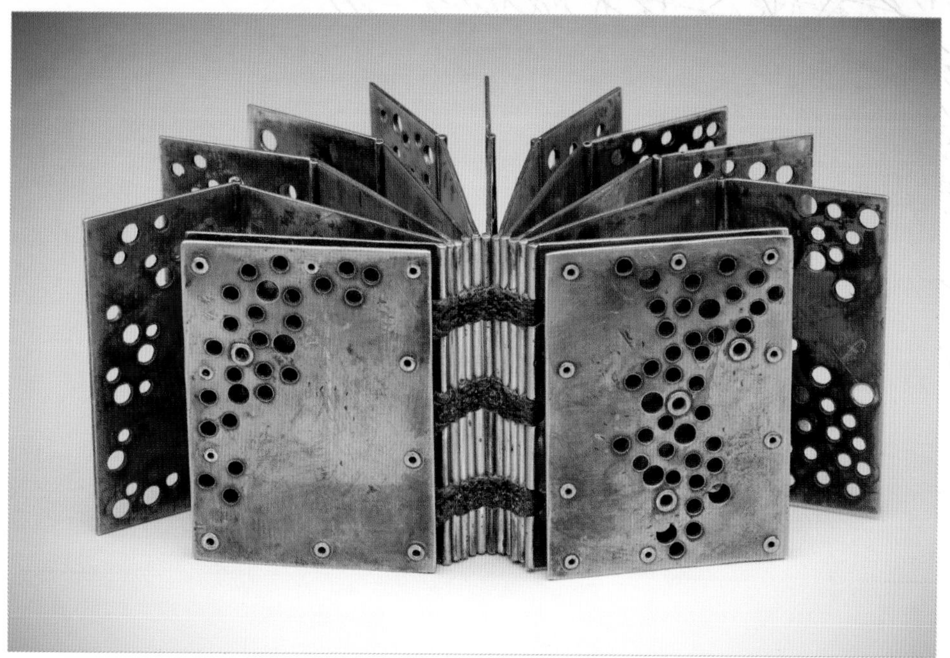

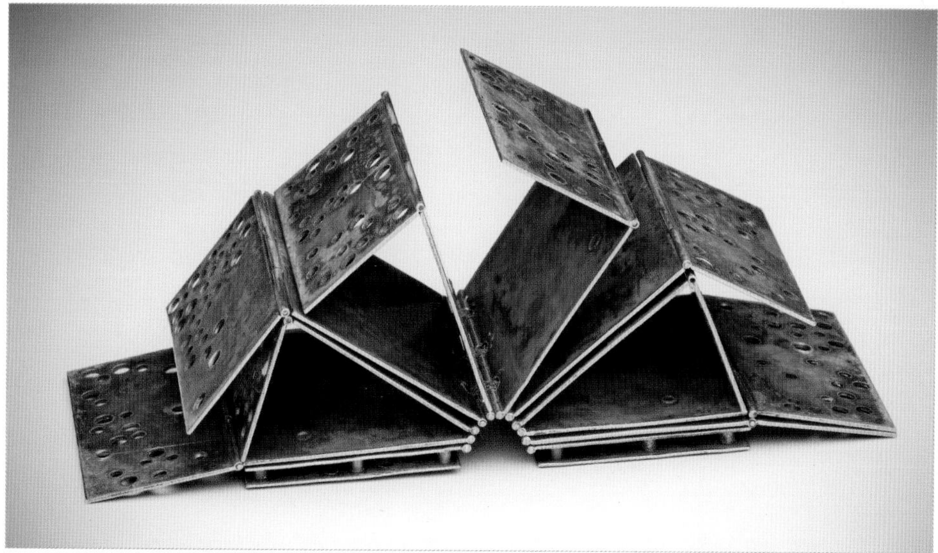

" I've kept a journal all my life and was frequently disappointed as a child by the machine-made books I used. They would inevitably fall apart before I was done filling them. Making a sturdy journal that would survive the tough love of regular use was my first book-making challenge. "

◀ **For the Love of . . .** | 2008
2 x 2½ x 1 inches (5.1 x 6.4 x 2.5 cm)
Brass, linen thread
Photos by Walker Montgomery

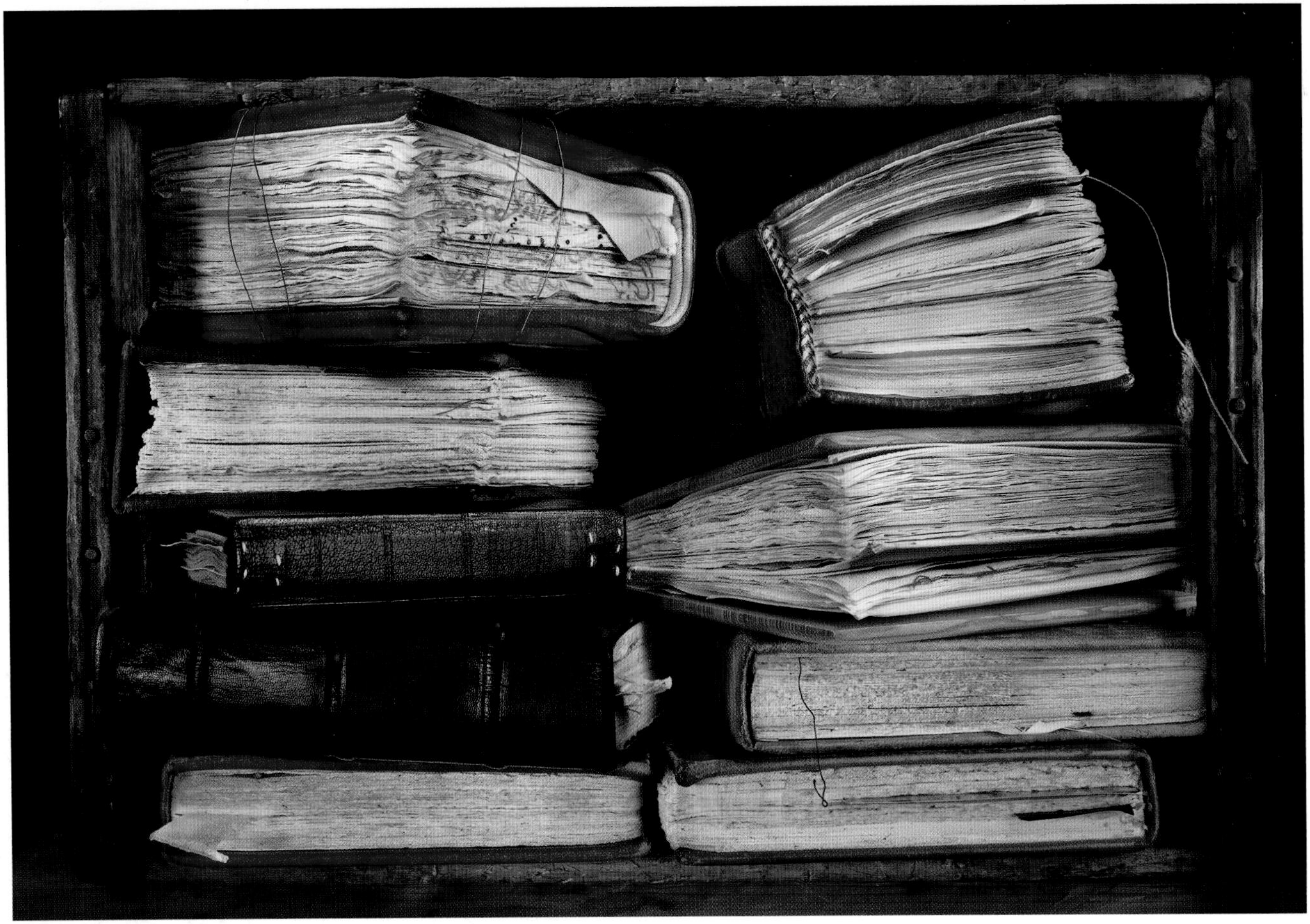

▲ Journals

Various dimensions
Various woods, paper, silk, linen and cotton thread, vellum, leather, binder's board, aluminum cans
Photo by Nancy Belluscio

> " The feeling of a treasure found, of something lost being rediscovered—this is the quality I chase in my work. "

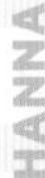

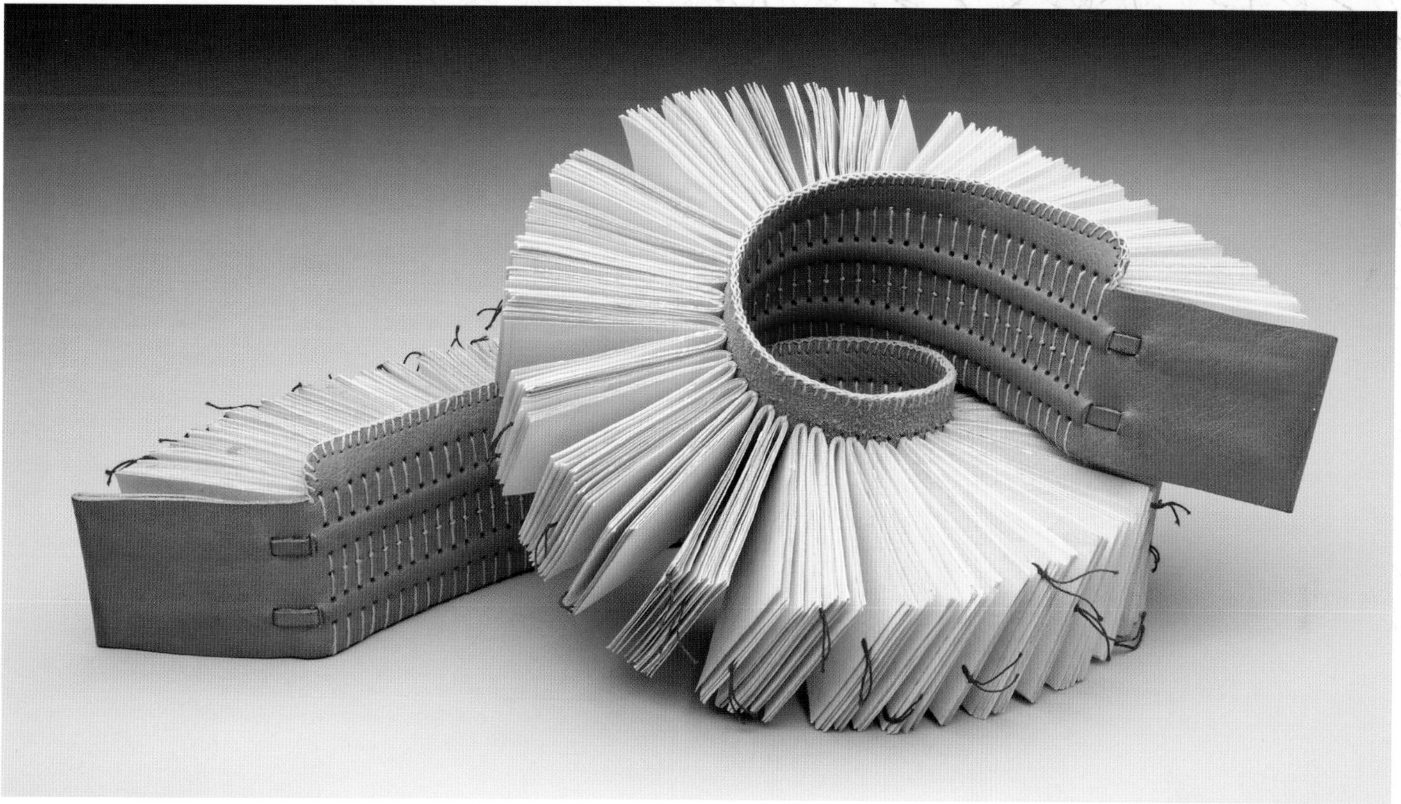

▲ **Looong Snakey** | 2007

2 x 14 x 3 inches (5.1 x 35.6 x 7.6 cm)

Leather, paper, linen and silk thread

Photos by Walker Montgomery

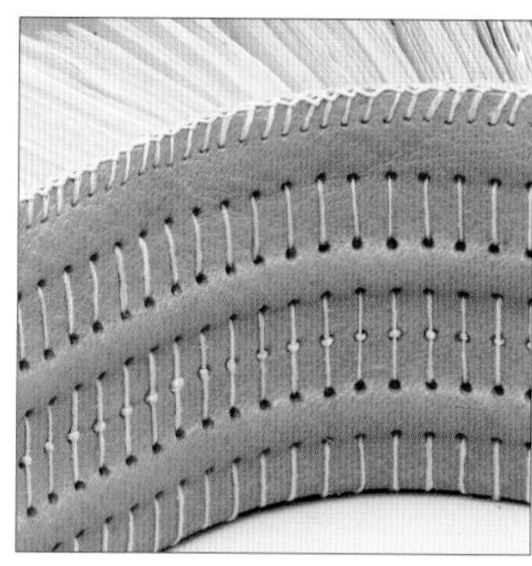

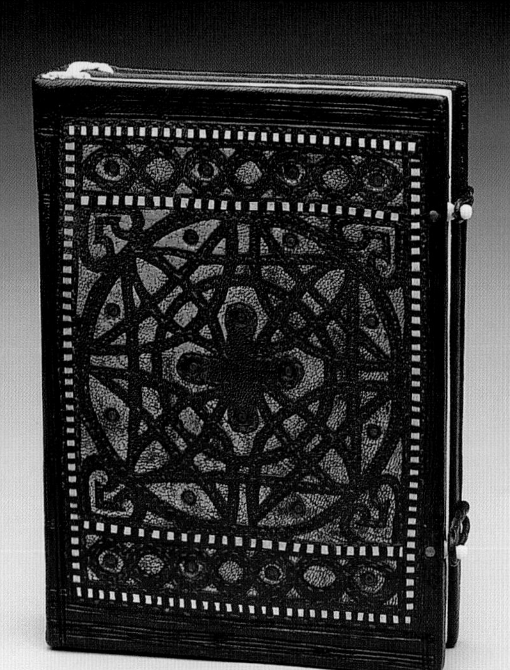

◀ **Appliquéd Coptic Binding Model** | 2000

5½ x 4 x 1¼ inches (14 x 10.2 x 3.2 cm)
Laminated paper, handmade cotton paper, leather, elk bone, vellum, linen and silk thread, brass

Photo by Walker Montgomery

" Small is my preferred scale. Quite often my books end up being bite sized. I like it when a piece will fit into the coin pocket of my jeans. "

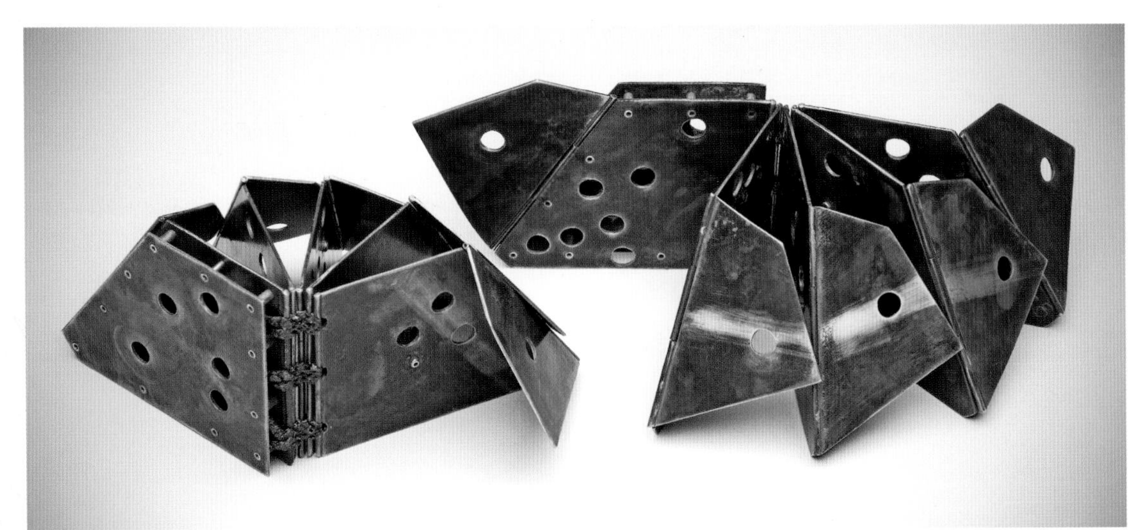

Splits | 2008 ▶

Each: 2 x 3 x 1 inches
(5.1 x 7.6 x 2.5 cm)
Brass, linen thread

Photo by Walker Montgomery

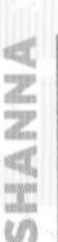

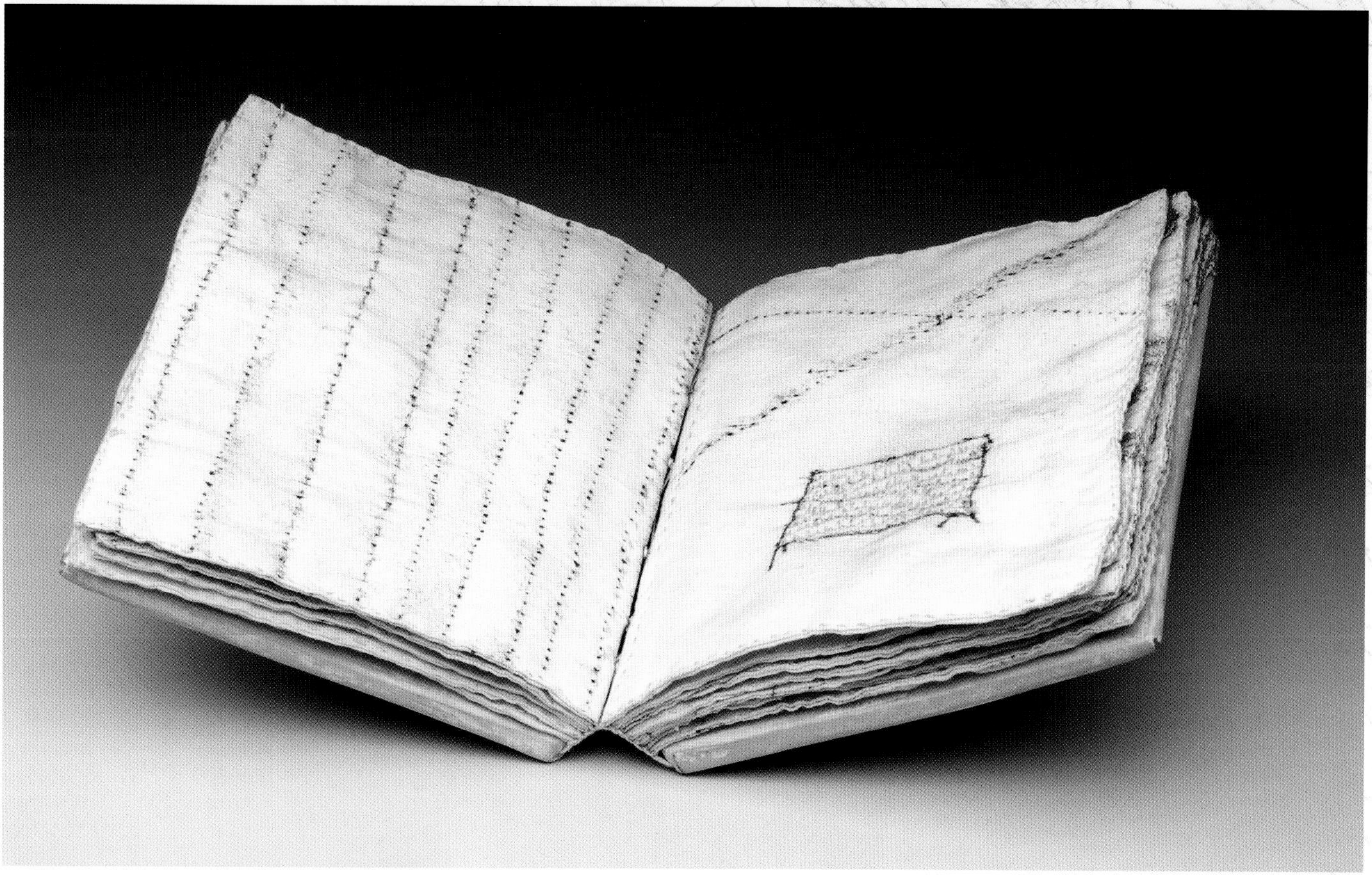

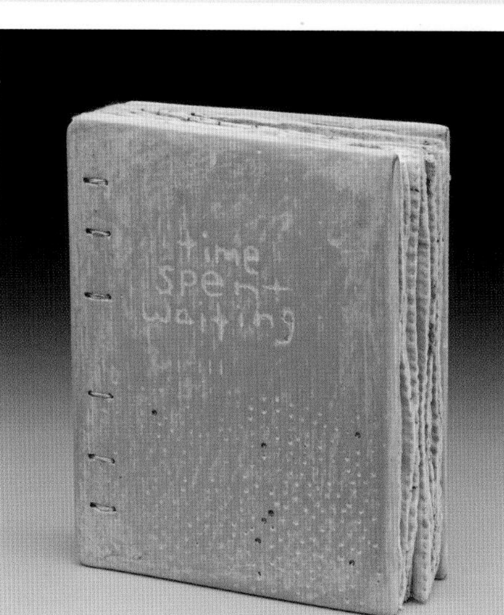

▲ **Time Spent Waiting III** | 2007

5 x 4 x 1 inches (12.7 x 10.2 x 2.5 cm)
Wood, milk paint, monoprinted silk cloth, linen thread
Photos by Walker Montgomery

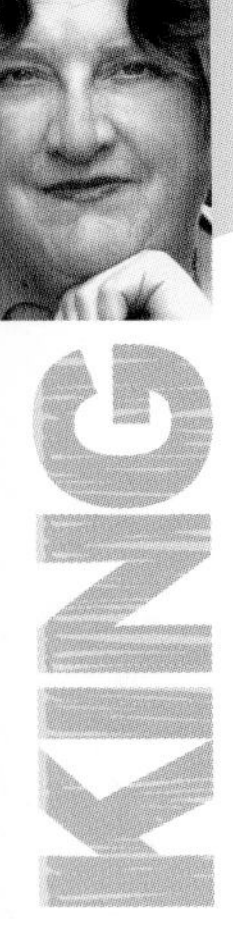

Susan King

IN EVOCATIVE AND MOVING BOOKS THAT BLEND the personal and the universal, Susan King demonstrates her special gift for making emotional connections with readers. Her poignant work investigates a variety of issues, including mortality, feminism, and family. King always allows content to dictate form, producing eloquent books that maximize structural opportunities in order to communicate ideas. By sharing her personal experiences, she cultivates an awareness in others of the validity of their own stories.

As she applies her vision in new ways to the book-making process, King richly explores connections between form and content. She uses the tactile qualities of her medium to their fullest. King's work can be found in institutions around the world, including the Library of Congress in Washington, D.C.; the Victoria and Albert Museum in London, England; and the Musée National d'Art Moderne–Centre Georges Pompidou in Paris, France. She lives in Mount Vernon, Kentucky.

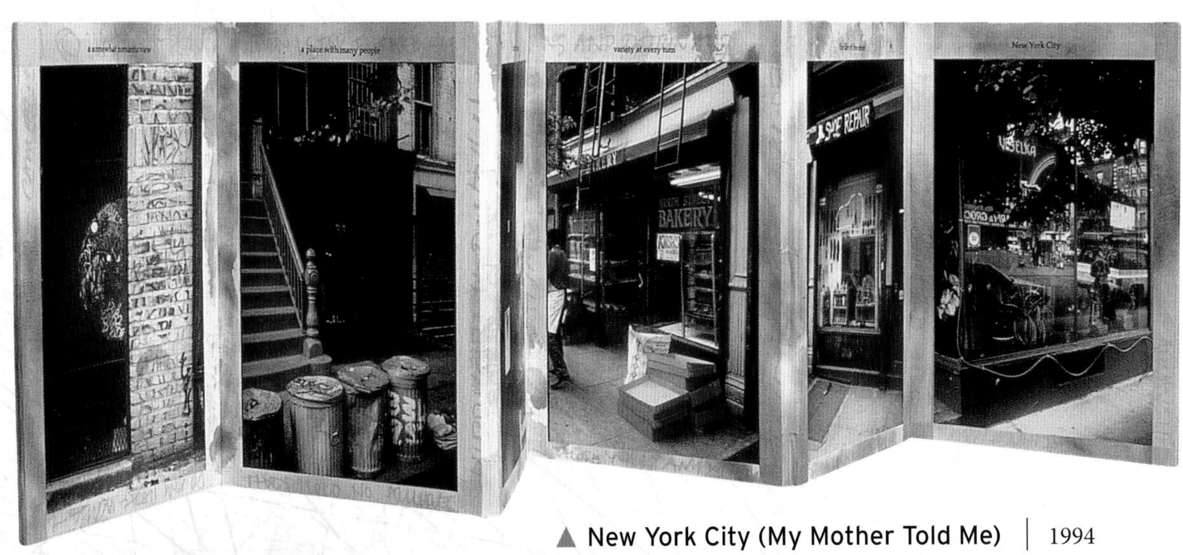

▲ **New York City (My Mother Told Me)** | 1994

11½ x 48 inches (29.2 x 121.9 cm)

Japanese paper, gouache, oil pastels; double-hinged screen binding, laser printed

Photo by John Kiffe

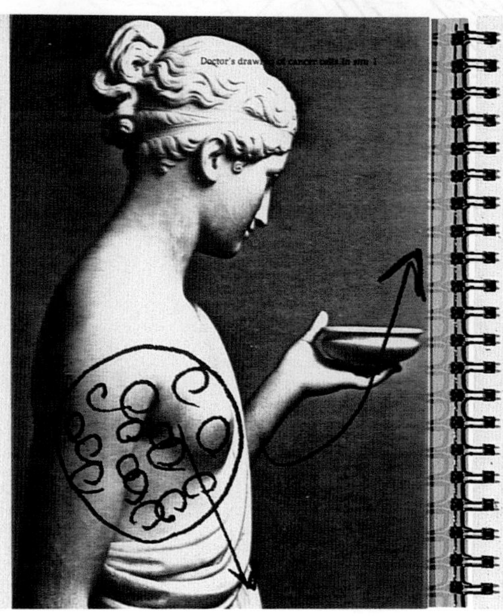

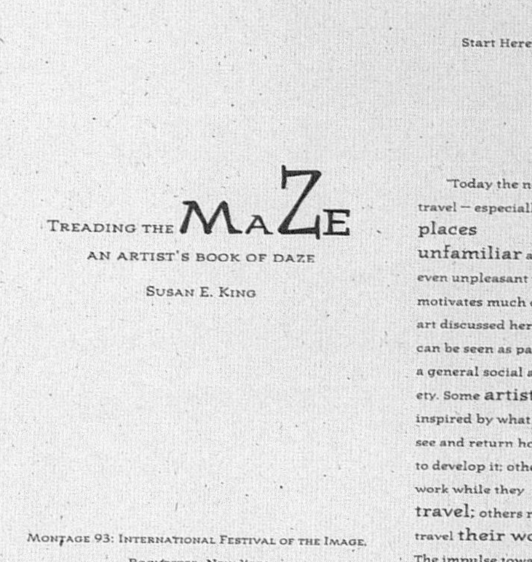

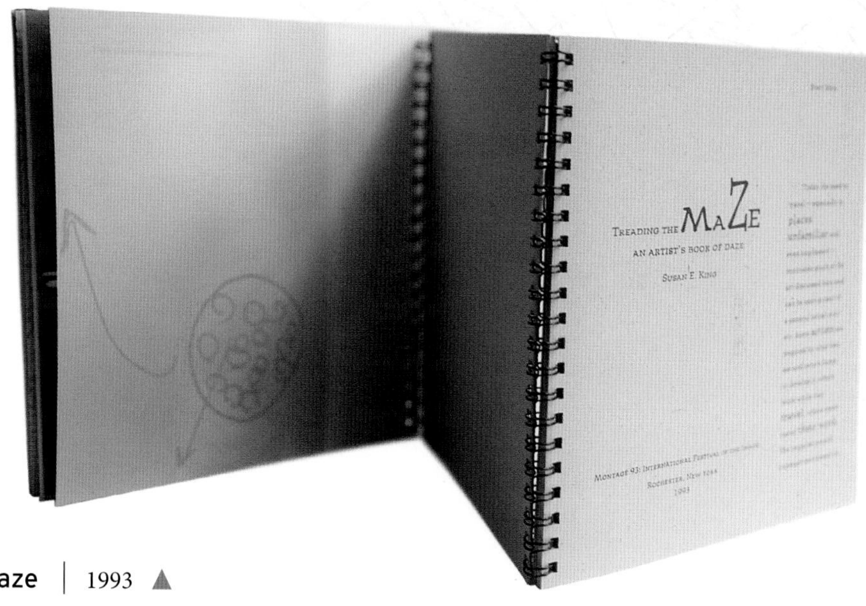

Treading the Maze: An Artist's Book of Daze | 1993 ▲

7⁵⁄₁₆ x 8¼ inches (18.6 x 21 cm)

Commercial paper, transparencies, UV Ultra II cover stock, museum board, plastic; double spiral binding, offset printed

Photos by John Kiffe

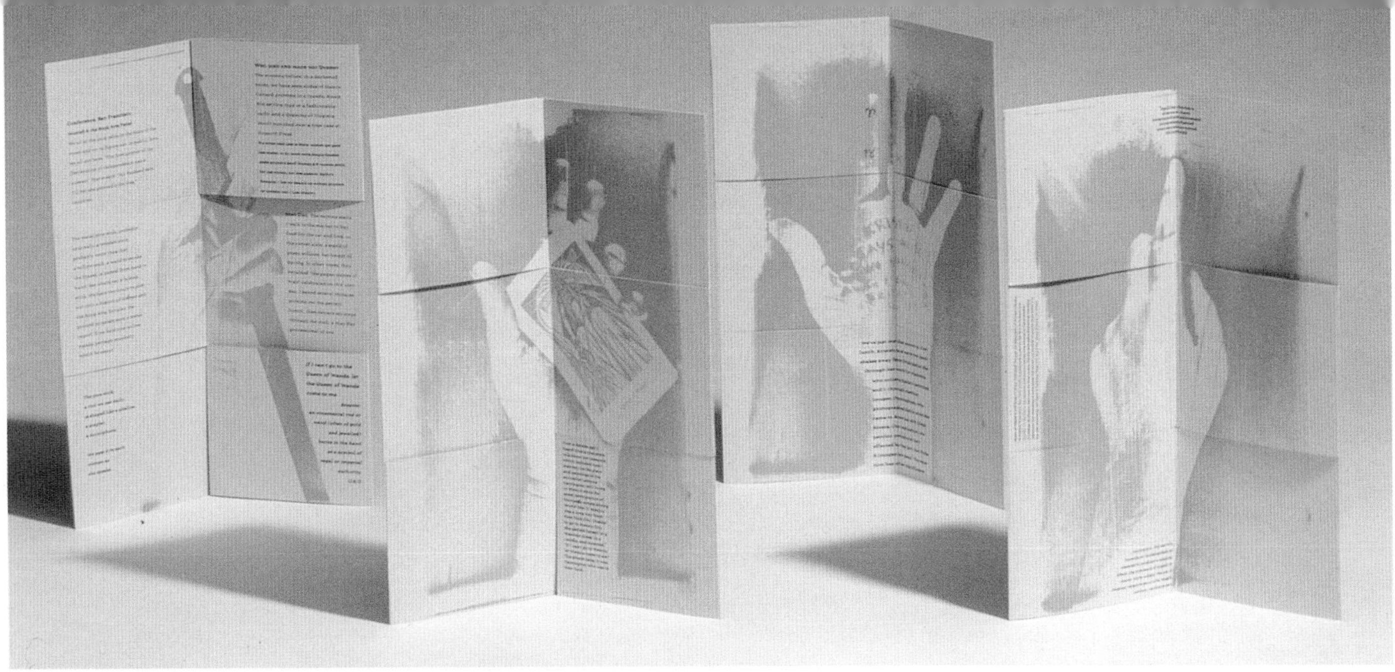

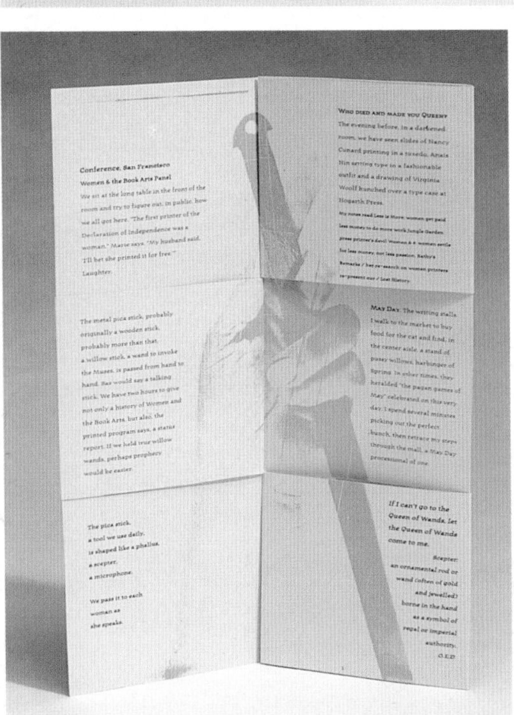

▲ The Queen of Wands | 1993

12½ x 9½ inches (31.8 x 24.1 cm)
Cover stock; die-cut tetratetra-flexagon binding, foil stamped, offset printed from Haloid Xerox image

Photos by John Kiffe

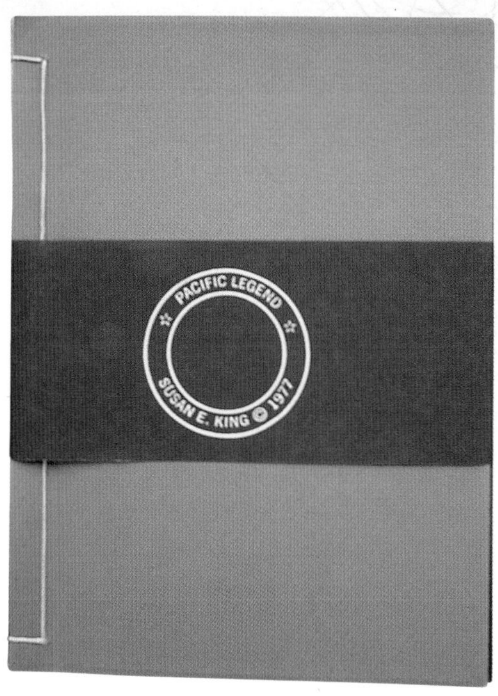

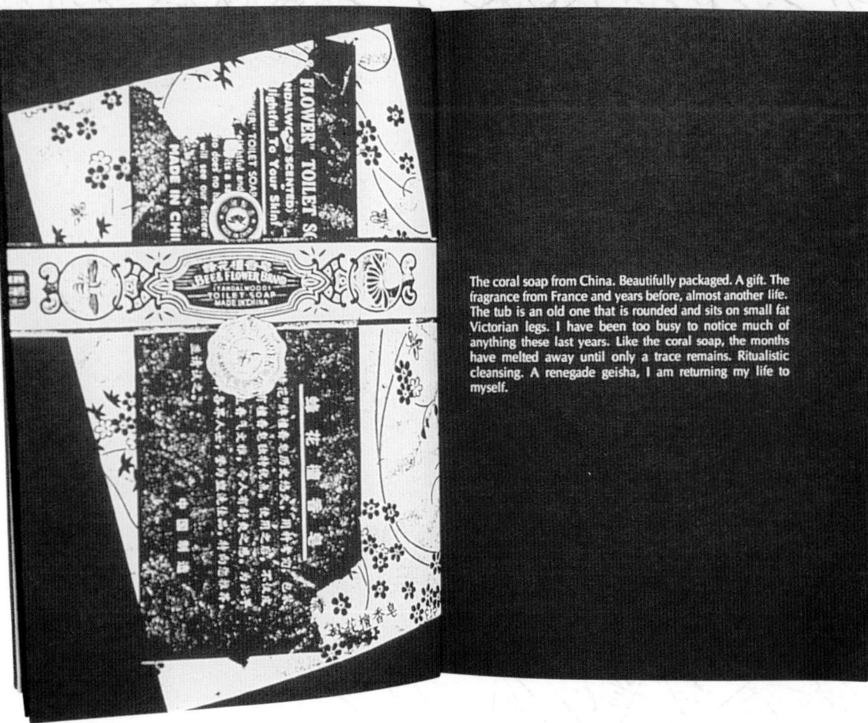

▲ **Pacific Legend** | 1977

8 x 6 inches (20.3 x 15.2 cm)
Blueprint paper, art paper; sidestab binding with paper band

Photos by artist

" I'm interested in letting the content of the book determine the form. Although this approach can be anxiety-provoking, the end result produces stronger work—work that goes beyond the perfection of craft alone. "

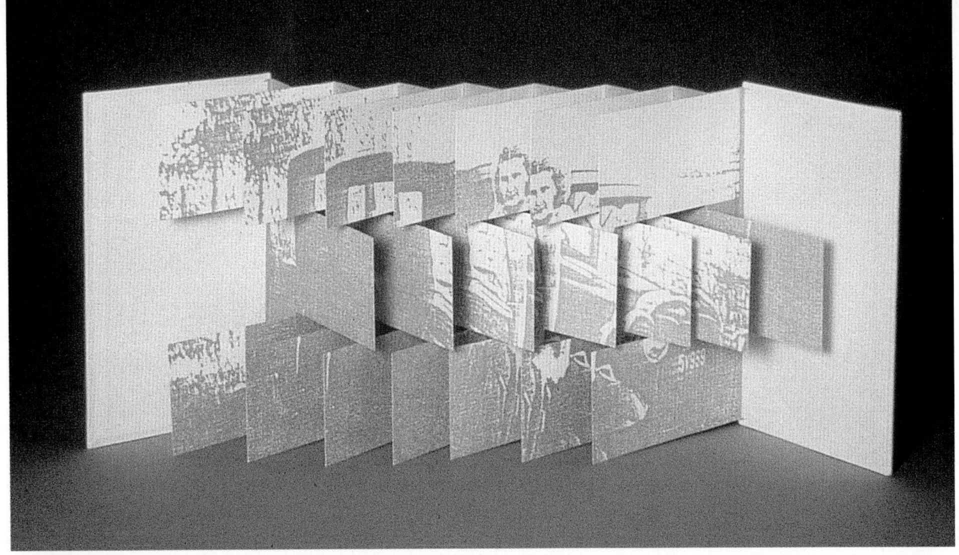

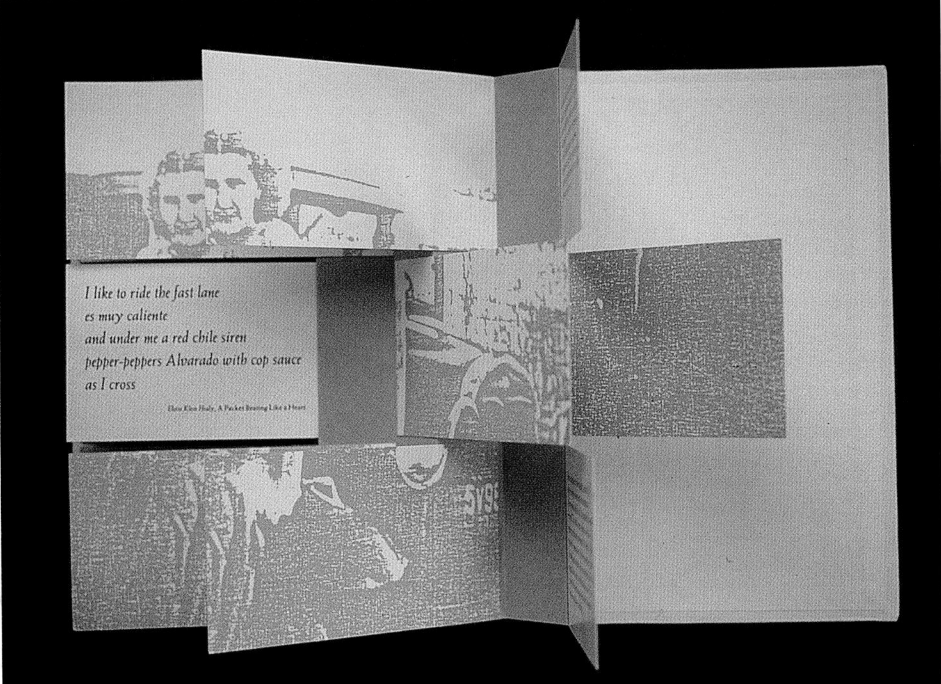

" My interest in printing goes back to the camp meetings I attended as a kid in Kentucky. I sat in the large wooden tabernacle staring at the New Testament my grandmother had given me and wondered how they printed Jesus' words in red. "

◀ **Women and Cars** | 1983

8⅛ x 5⅛ inches (20.6 x 13 cm)
Cardstock, Mohawk Superfine paper; hardbound flag-book binding, offset printed, letterpress printed

Photos by John Kiffee

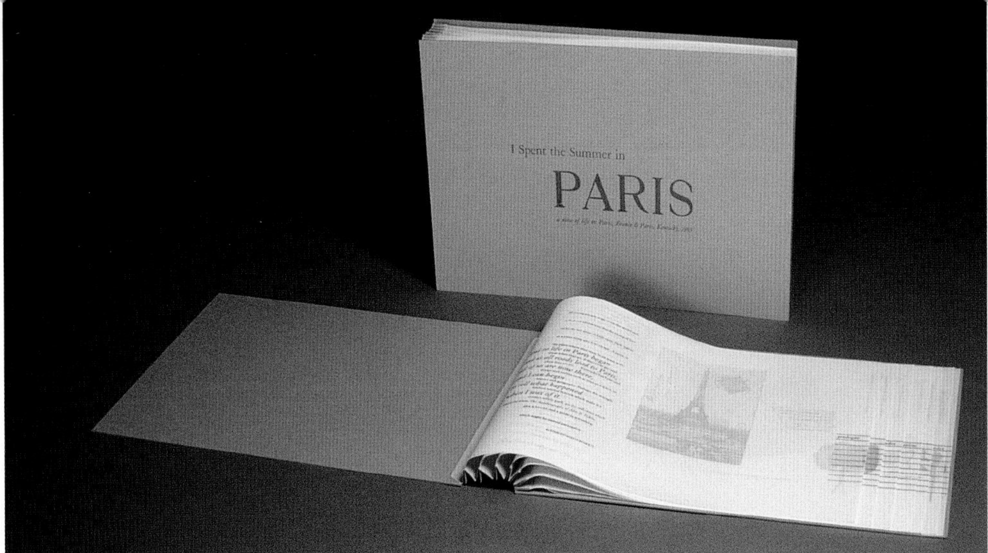

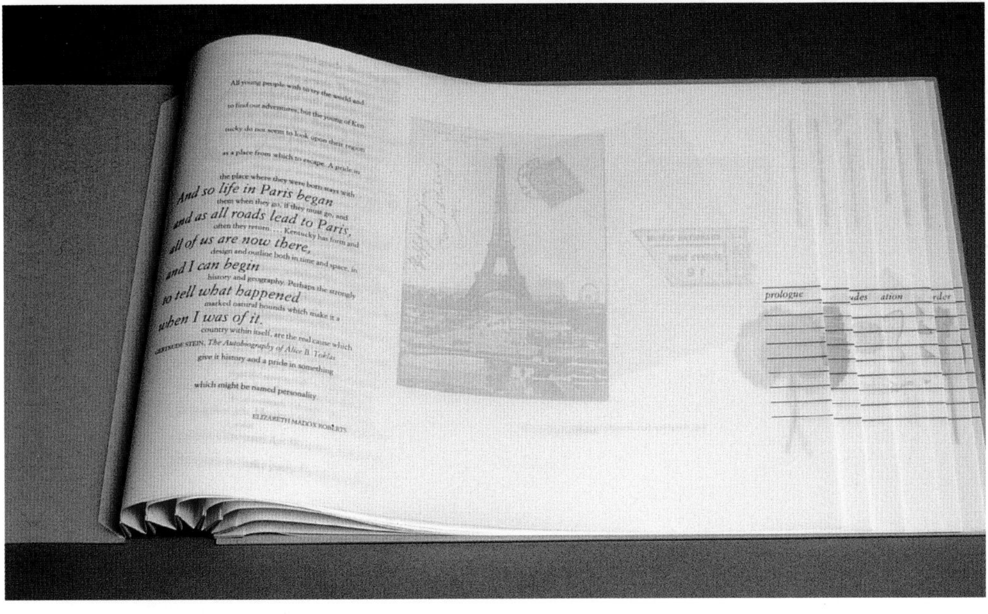

▲ **I Spent the Summer in Paris: A View of Life in Paris, France, and Paris, Kentucky** | 1984

9³⁄₁₆ x 12⅛ inches (23.3 x 30.8 cm)
UV Ultra II paper, Canson paper, Archivart museum board; accordion binding, offset printed, letterpress printed

Photos by John Kiffe

" The idea that the personal is political, a slogan from the Women's Liberation Movement, has always inspired me to explore territory outside the mainstream. "

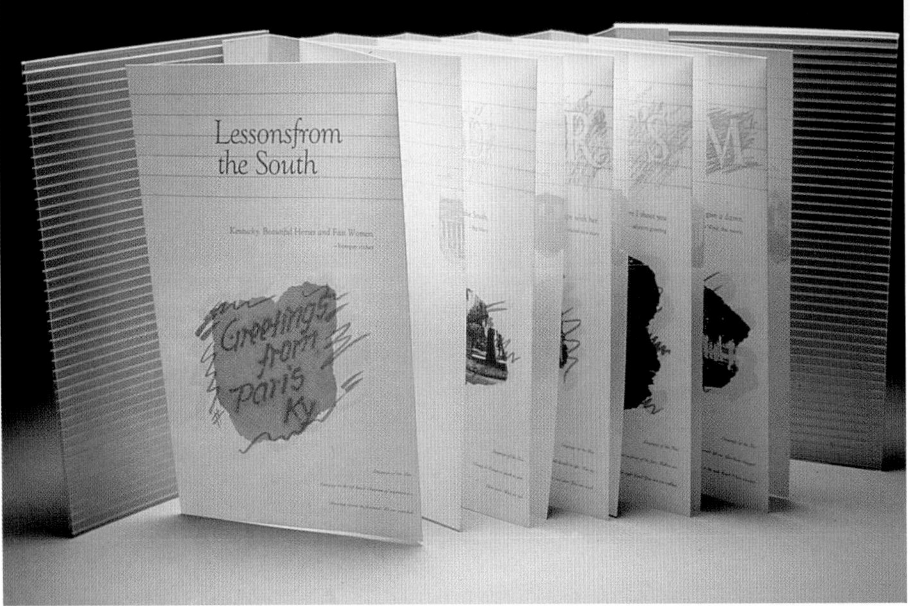

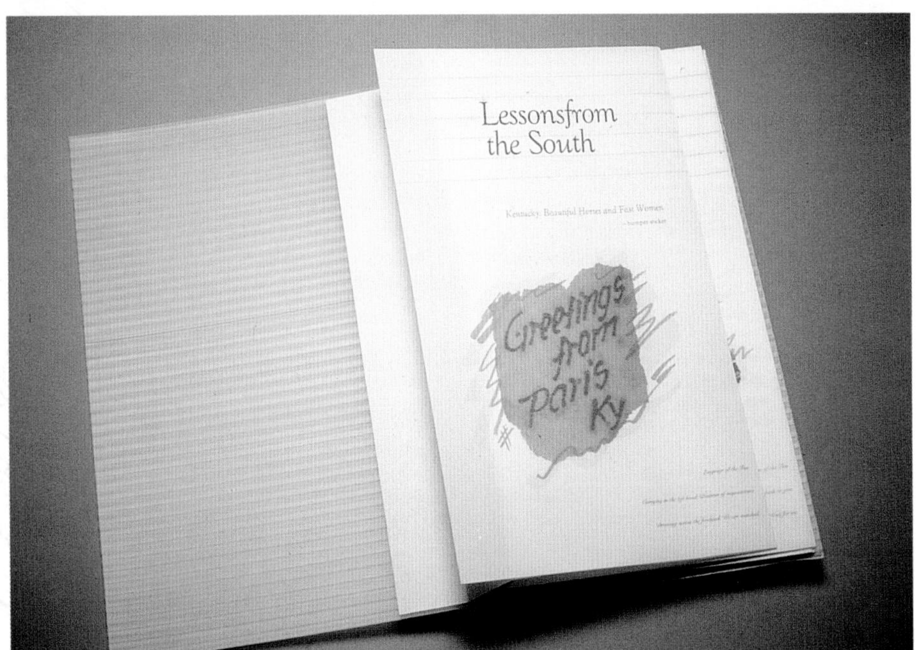

Lessons from the South | 1986

10¾ x 7 inches (17.8 x 27.3 cm)
UV Ultra II, corrugated plastic, commercial cover stock; die-cut accordion binding, offset printed

Photos by John Kiffe

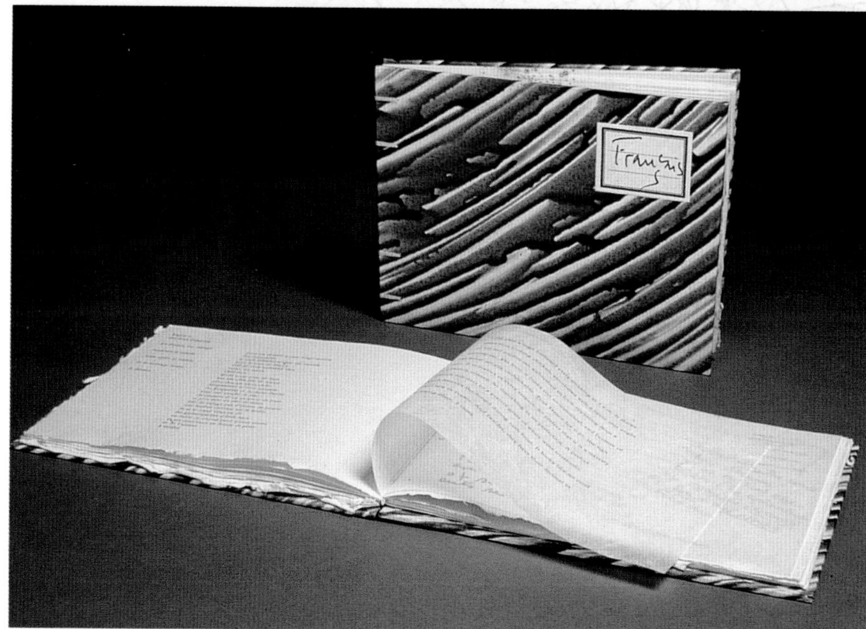

Say, See, Bone, Lessons from French | 1986

5½ x 7½ inches (14 x 19.1 cm)
St. Armand handmade paper, paste papers, Japanese paper, French label; Coptic binding

Coptic binding by Shelley Hoyt
Photo by John Kiffe

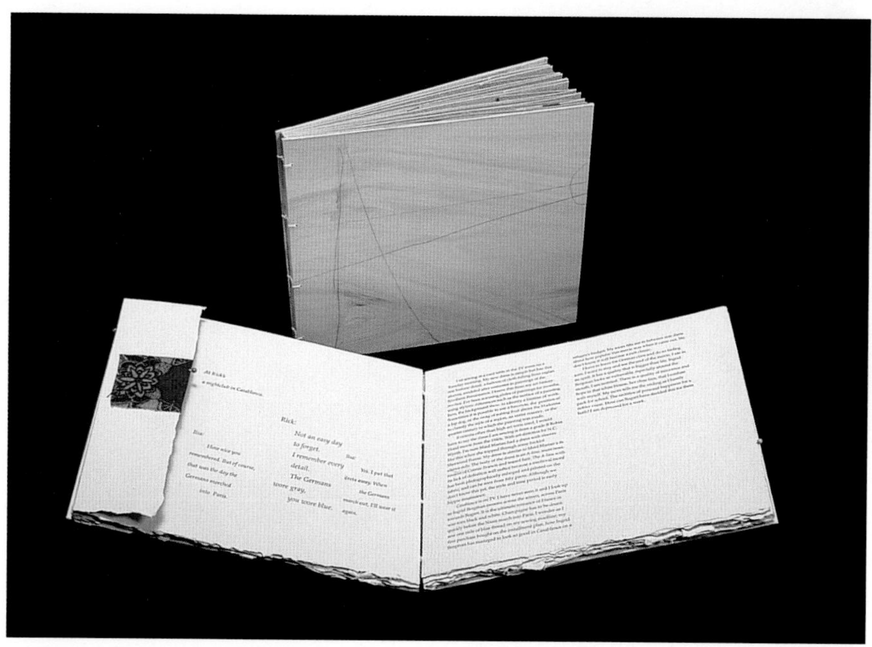

Redressing the Sixties: Art Lessons à la Mode | 2001

9⅛ x 10¾ inches (23.2 x 27.3 cm)
St. Armand handmade paper, vintage clothing, sewing notions, sandpaper, Chinese stick ink; Coptic binding, letterpress printed

Photo by John Kiffe

Barbara Tetenbaum

INSPIRED COMBINATIONS OF LAYERED VISUAL IMAGERY and a highly refined sense of design characterize the work of Barabara Tetenbaum. Thanks to her technical fluency and ingenuity with the printing press, Tetenbaum's rhythmic narratives, both visual and textual, flow over the pages of her books as though accompanied by some internal music. Tetenbaum works intuitively and spontaneously at the press, building images in response to each print run. Her work displays a frankness of execution and a sensitivity to the balance and geometry inherent in each page.

Known for her inventive use of non-traditional printing surfaces, Tetenbaum skillfully integrates formal and informal letterpress traditions into work that's vibrant, playful, and dynamic. Tetenbaum has received numerous awards for her books, which are held in public collections throughout the United States, Canada, and Europe. She lives in Portland, Oregon.

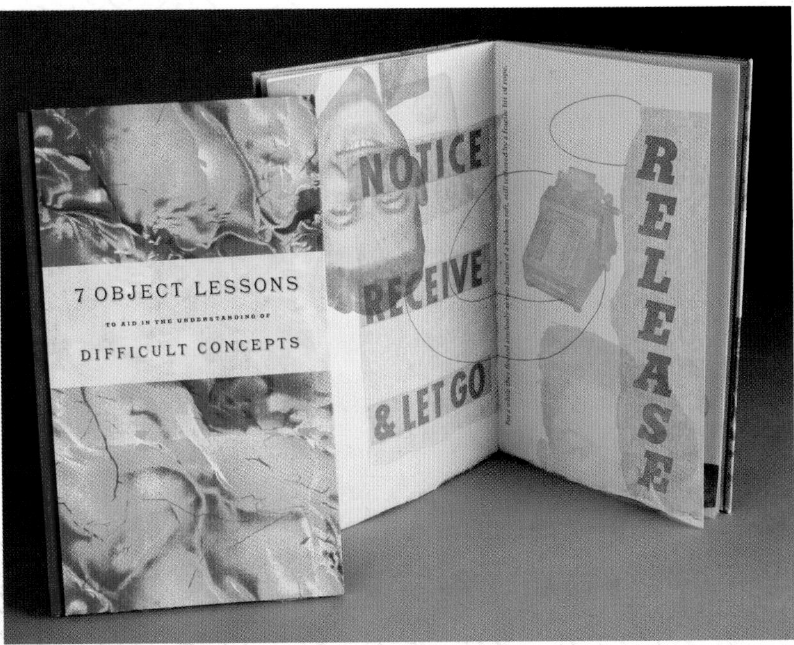

▲ **Seven Object Lessons to Aid in the Understanding of Difficult Concepts** | 2007

Closed: 8½ x 5 inches (21.6 x 12.7 cm)
Japanese paper; butterfly binding, letterpress printed from various materials
Photo by Stephen Funk

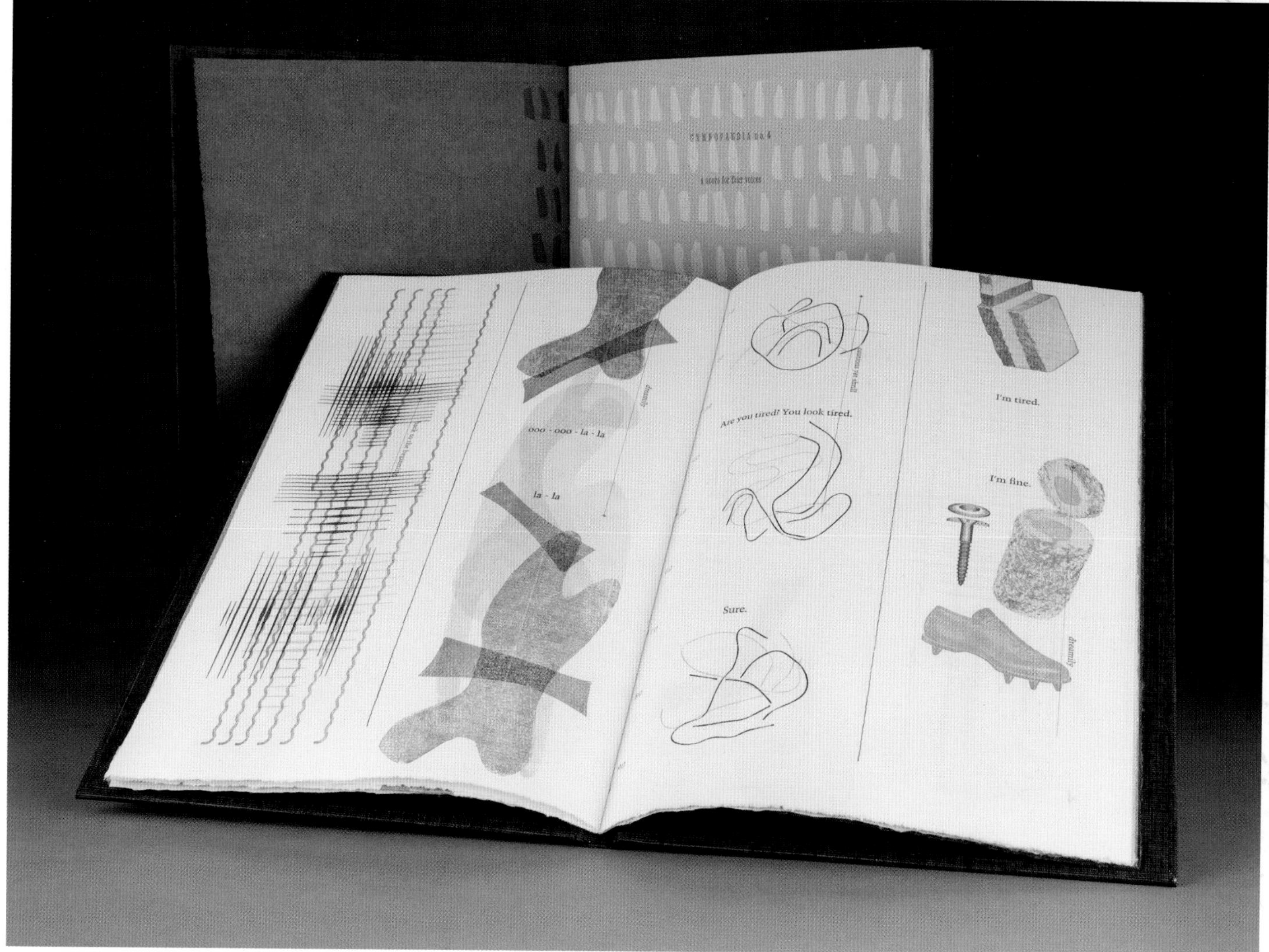

▲ **Gymnopaedia #4: A Piece for Four Voices** | 2005

Open: 11 x 14 inches (27.9 x 35.5 cm)
Mold-made paper; pamphlet German-case binding, letterpress printed from various materials
Photo by Stephen Funk

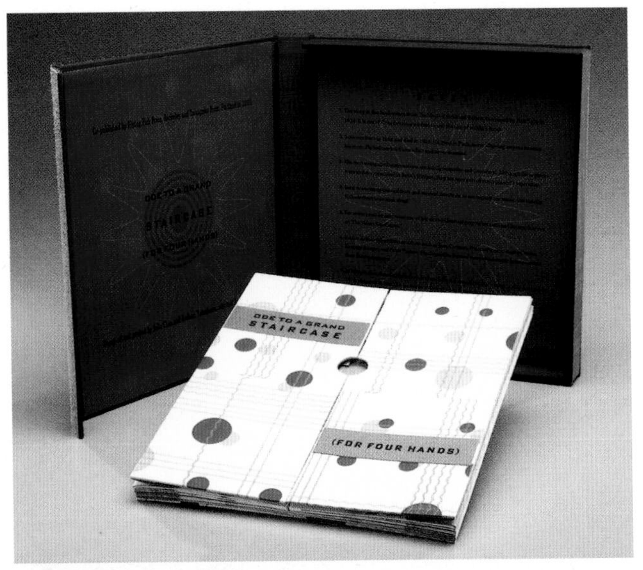

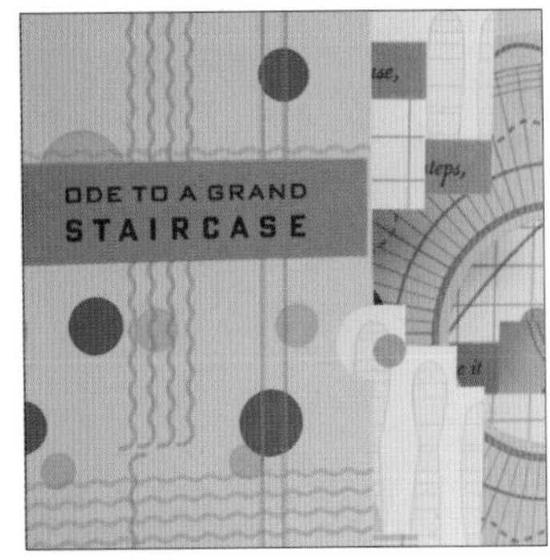

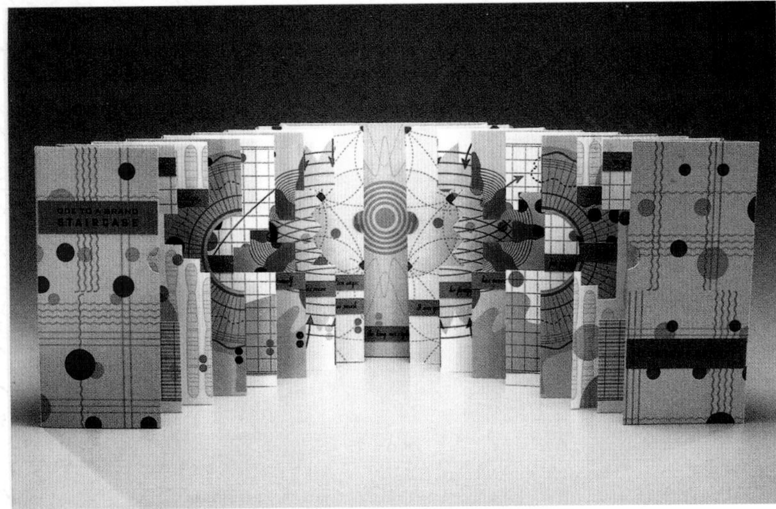

Ode to a Grand Staircase (for Four Hands) | 2001

5¾ x 7¾ x 2½ inches (14.6 x 19.7 x 6.4 cm)
Paper; double-sided accordion, letterpress printed

Photos by Gene Faulkner

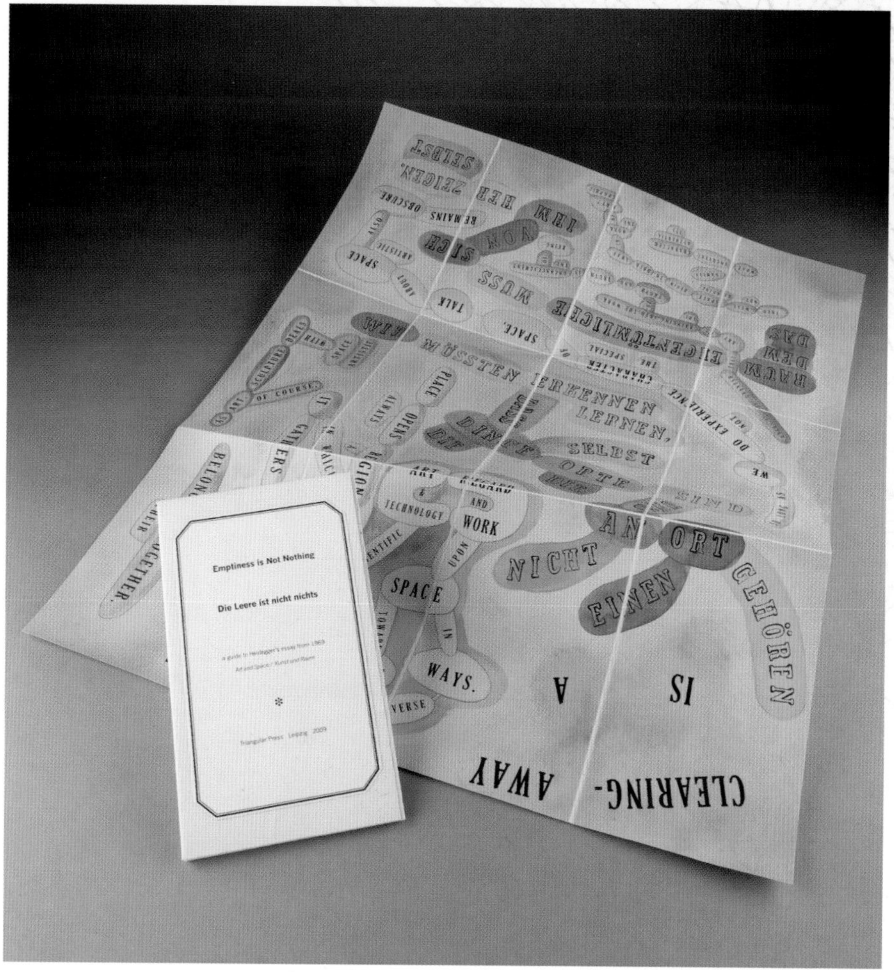

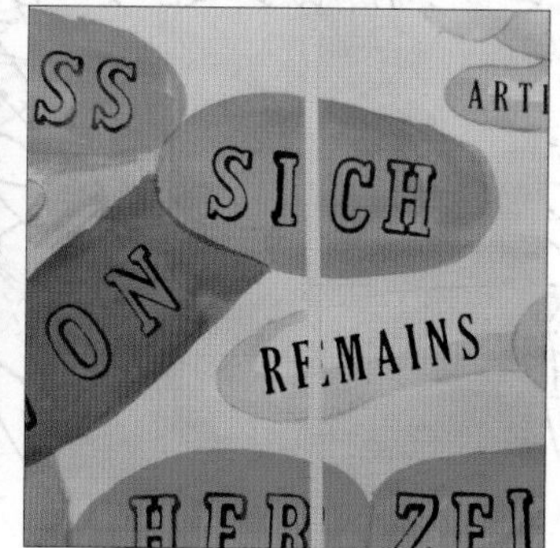

▲ **Emptiness Is Not Nothing/Die Leere Ist Nicht Nichts** | 2009

24 x 20 inches (61 x 50.8 cm)

Linen-backed paper, map structure; silk-screened, hand painted

Photos by Stephen Funk

" Like moveable type, I reuse images for different projects. They've become a vocabulary that unifies my work. "

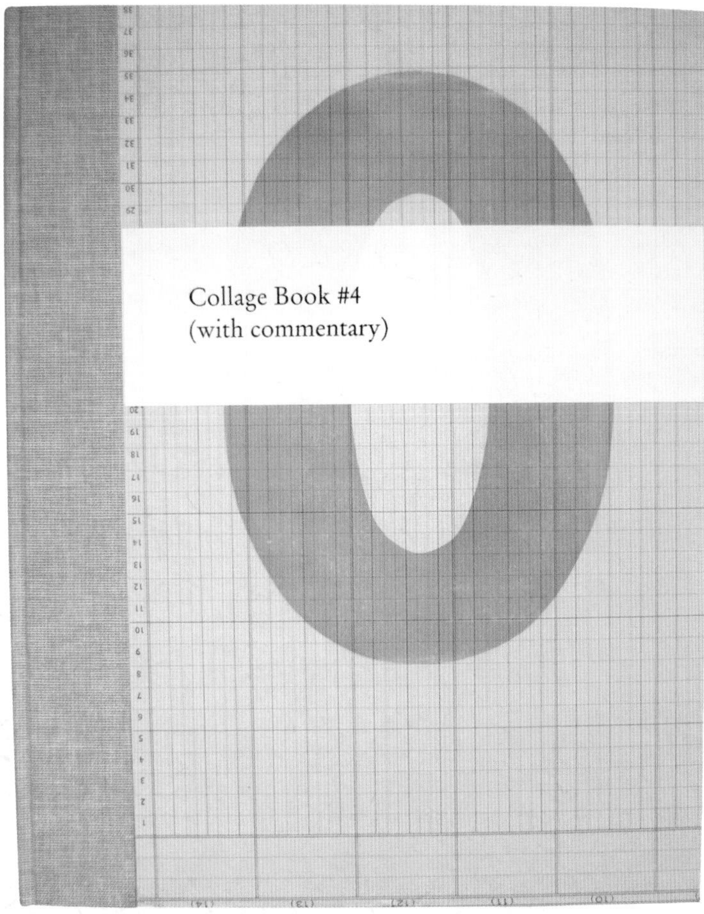

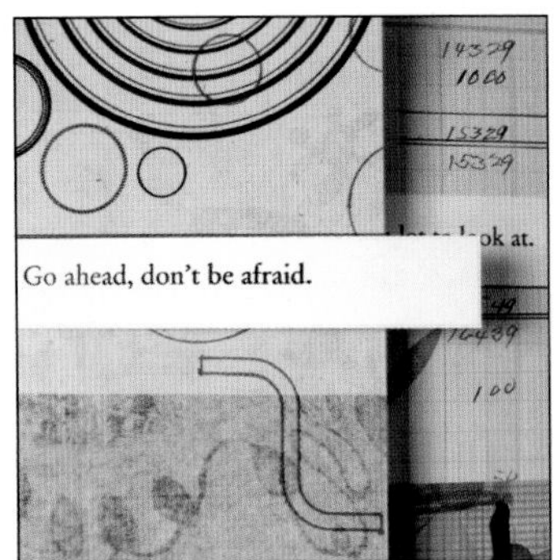

▲ **Collage Book #4 (with Commentary)** | 2008

9 x 6½ inches (22.9 x 16.5 cm)
Various papers and found materials, pencil; pamphlet binding, photocopied, collage
Photos by Gene Faulkner

" The slow processes of hand typesetting, hand printing, and binding give me time to respond to the work at hand, to consider the next move as well as the next project. Creative insights often arrive during these seemingly mechanical moments of work. "

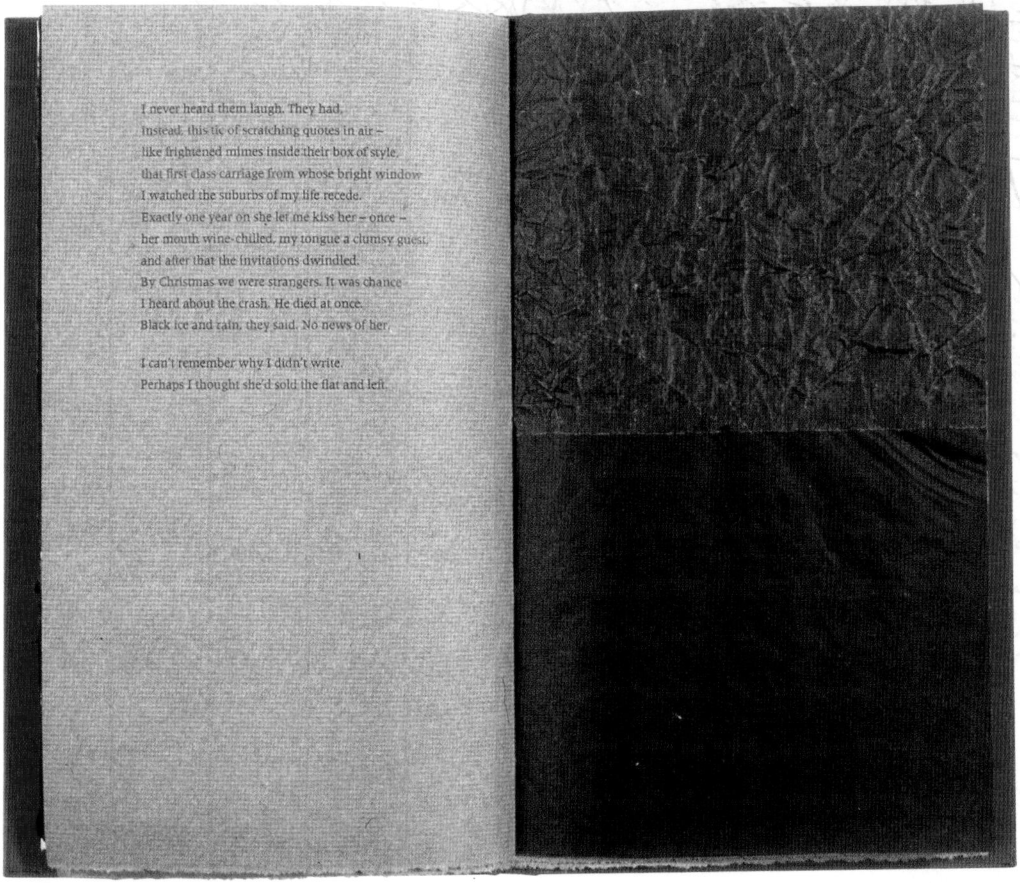

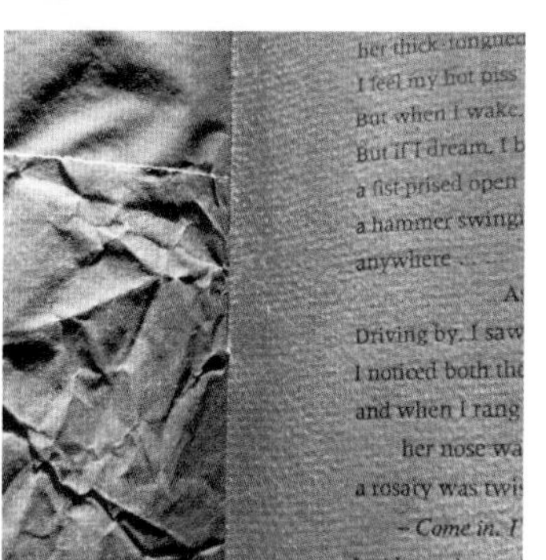

▲ Black Ice and Rain: Psalms 6:6
by Michael Donaghy | 2002

9¼ x 5½ inches (23.5 x 14 cm)
Mold-made paper, dyed abaca paper;
pamphlet-case binding, letterpress printed

Photos by artist

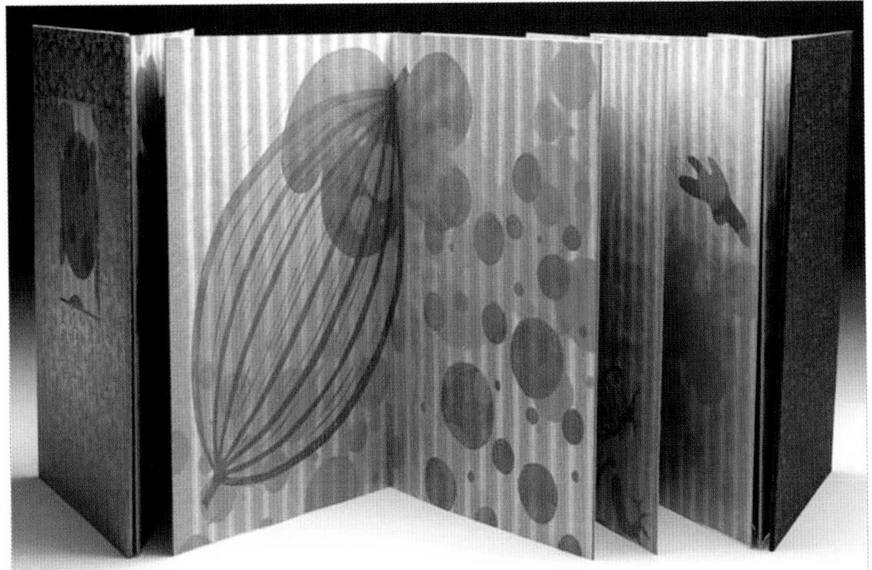

◀ **Cumbia Cumbia** | 1998

10¾ x 7½ inches (27.3 x 19.1 cm)
Decorative Japanese paper; accordion binding, linoleum printed
Photo by Gene Faulkner

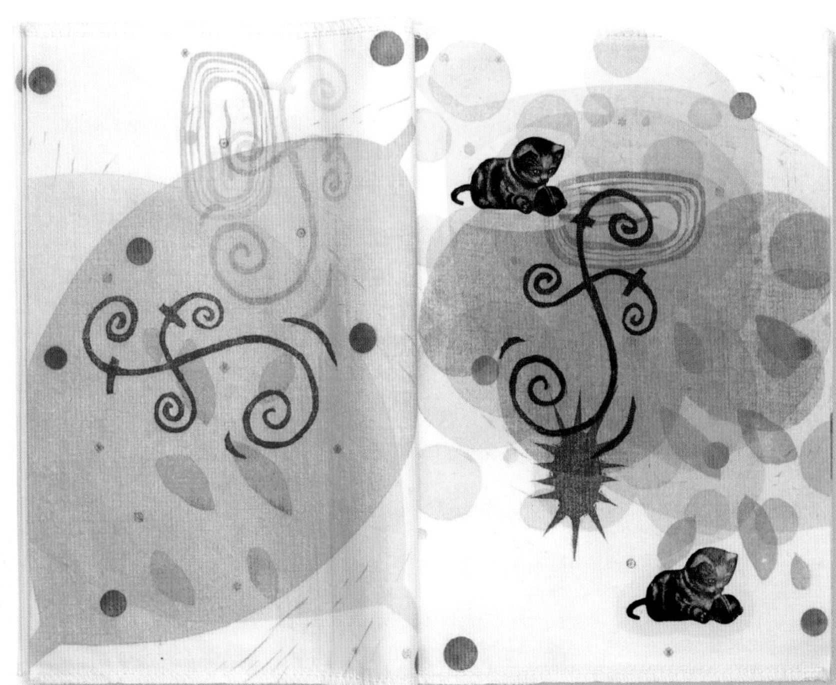

The Playtime Book of Fun | 1998 ▶

13 x 10 inches (33 x 25.4 cm)
Linen cloth; Japanese stab binding, linoleum and letterpress printed
Photo by Gene Faulkner

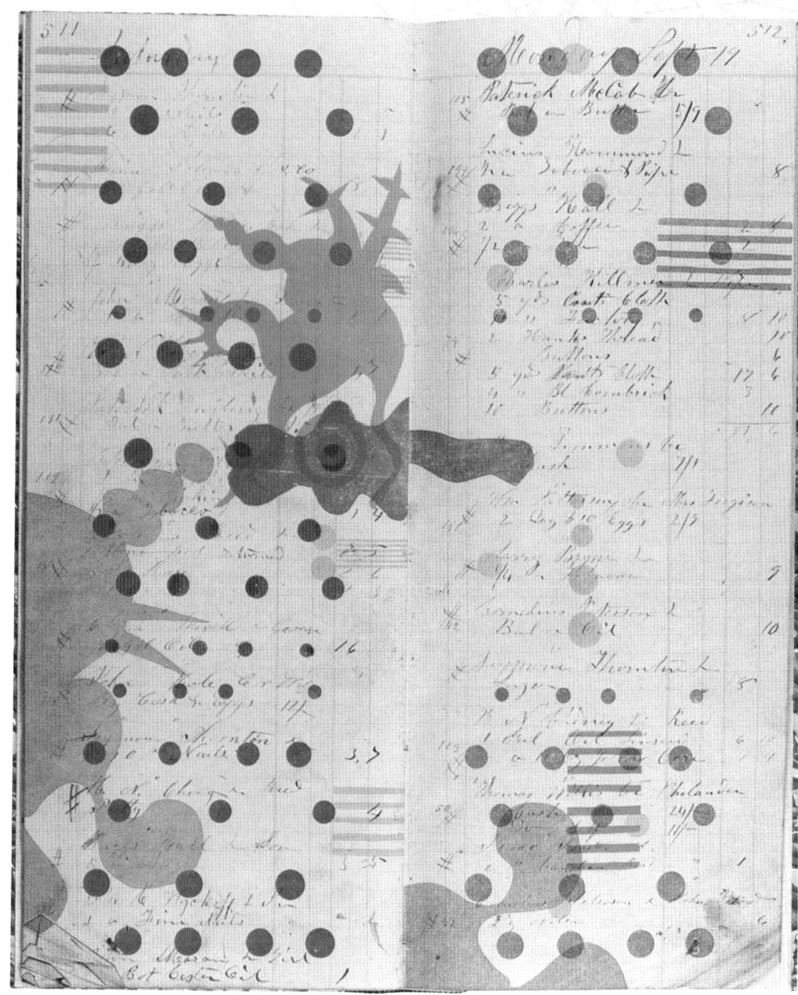

▲ **Gymnopaedia #2 (Second Movement)** | 1997

15½ x 6½ inches (39.4 x 16.5 cm)
Disbound ledger from 1851; pamphlet binding, letterpress printing
Photo by Gene Faulkner

" Setting type and fussing with letter spacing are not processes that appeal to me. As a result, the look of my books comes from my attempts to turn my printing press into a paint brush. "

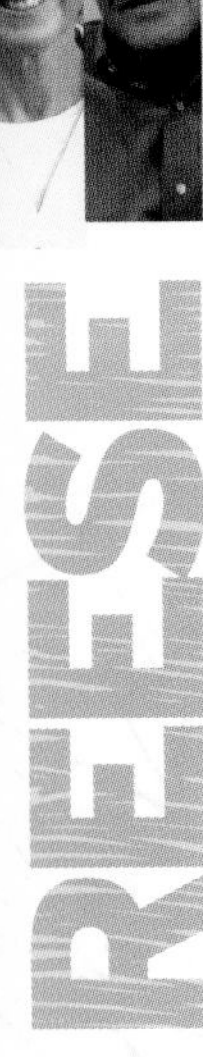

Harry Reese & Sandra Liddell Reese

FOR THE PAST THREE DECADES, Harry and Sandra Liddell Reese have published books that reflect a sophisticated vision of the form. Viewing the book as a repository for ideas and a conveyor of human emotion, they incorporate experimental texts and original art into their books. Each of their works is like a portable art exhibit, with new discoveries in store each time the pages are turned.

Bold and painterly illustrative elements, creative adaptations of binding structures, and new techniques, primarily the "sandragraph" (named for Sandra herself)—a method of creating low-relief printing surfaces—characterize the Reeses' work. Ultimately, their dynamic literary and visual books are a testament to the fulfillment that comes from the shared experience of making—not only between themselves but with the authors and artists with whom they collaborate. Through enterprising experimentation and inventive design solutions, they produce unforgettable works. The Reeses live in Isla Vista, California, where they operate the Turnkey Press.

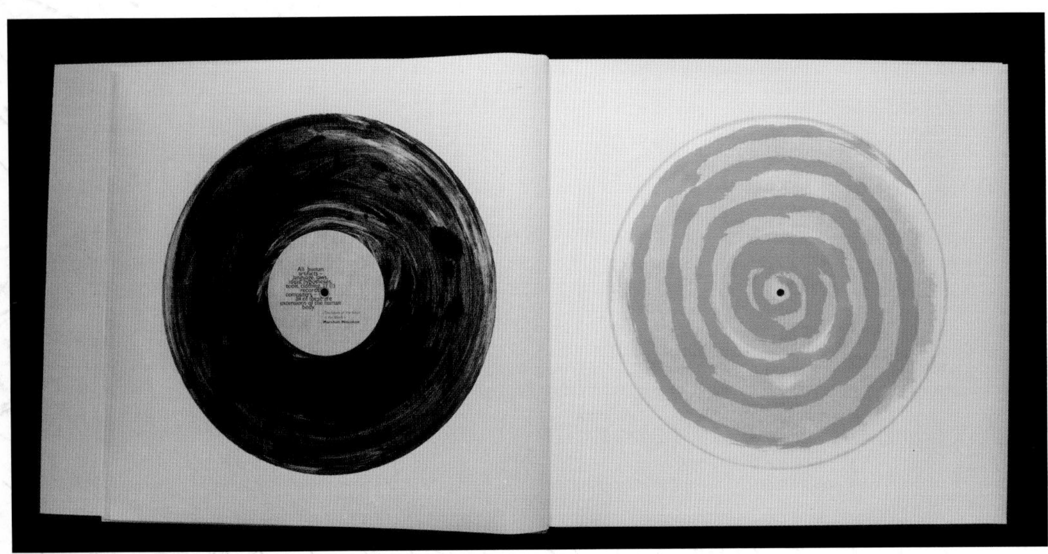

▲ **33⅓: Off the Record** | 2009

16½ x 17½ inches (41.9 x 44.5 cm)
Commercial papers, vinyl record, Mylar, oil paint, tape; handmade, mold made, laser printed, letterpress printed, collage, drawing, rubbed, screw-post exhibition-style binding
Photo by artists

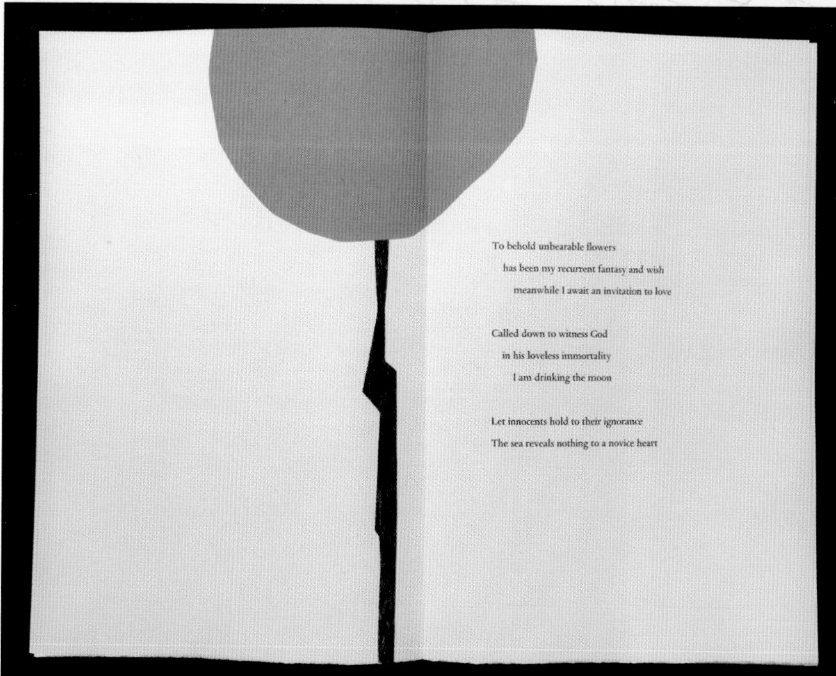

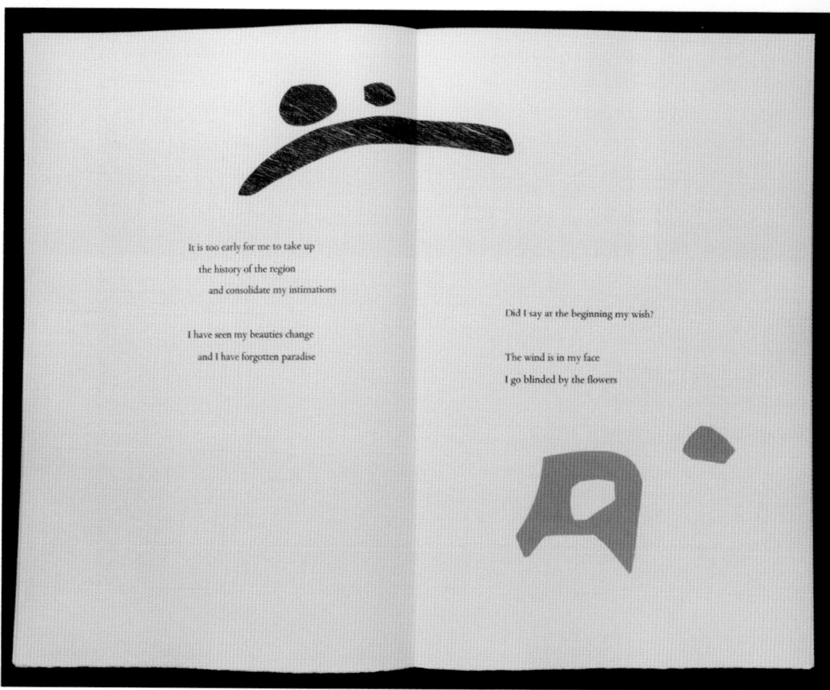

◀ **The Sea Gazer** | 2007

14½ x 9½ inches (36.8 x 24.1 cm)
Turkey Press handmade paper, Hahnemühle Biblio and Kitakata papers, clear plastic, woodcuts, monoprints; handset in Dante type, letterpress printed, cut, inkjet printed

Poem by Michael Hannon
Photos by Tony Mastres

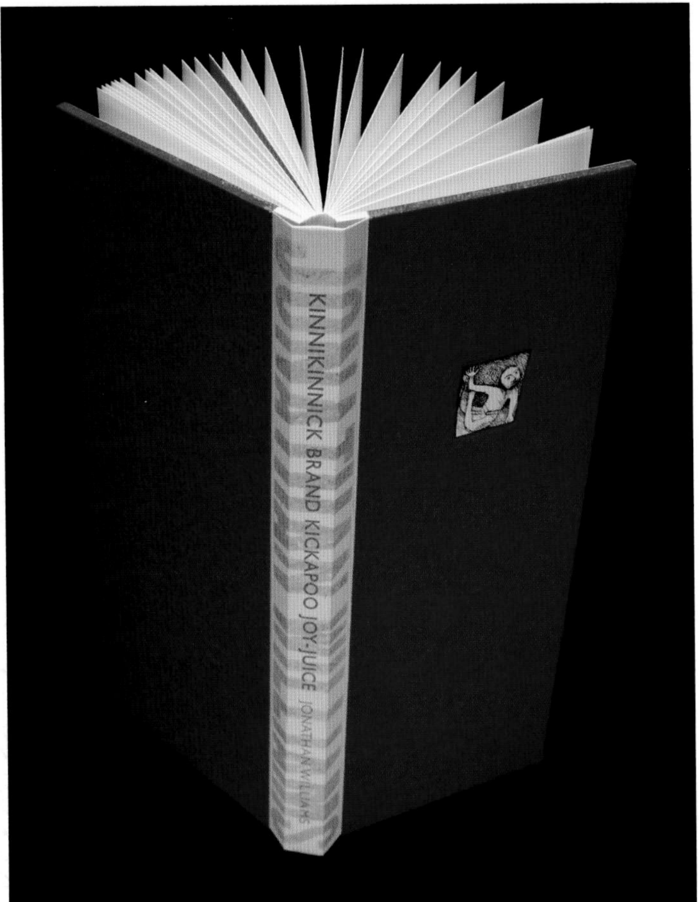

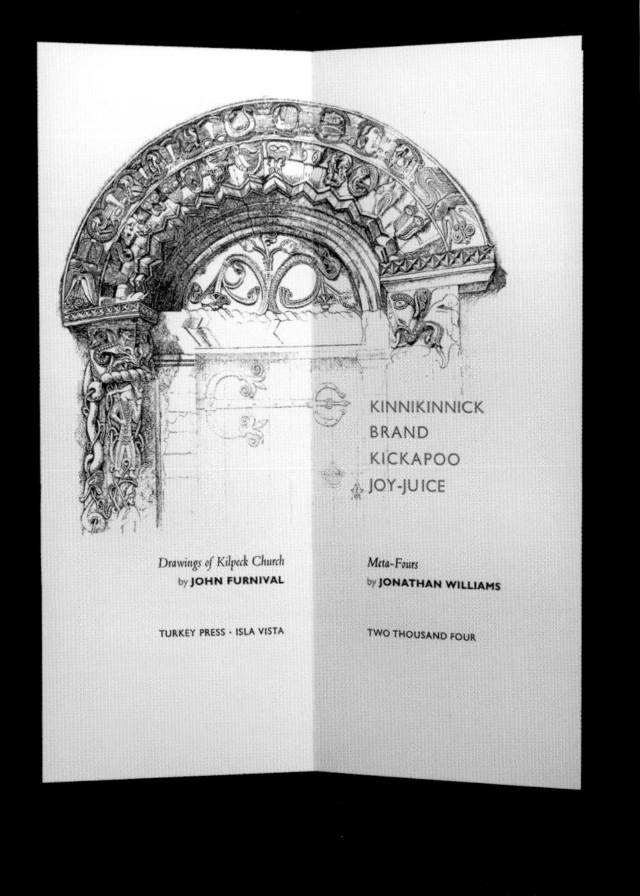

▲ **Kinnikinnick Brand Kickapoo Joy-Juice** | 2004

10½ x 4 inches (26.7 x 10.2 cm)

Monadnock Dulcet paper, handmade paper, acrylic paint, line drawing printed from polymer plates, hand-inked highlights, monoprints; handset in Narrow Bembo type, letterpress printed, hybrid false-accordion-sewn boards binding, hand-colored

Poems by Jonathan Williams
Drawings by John Furnival
Photos by Tony Mastres

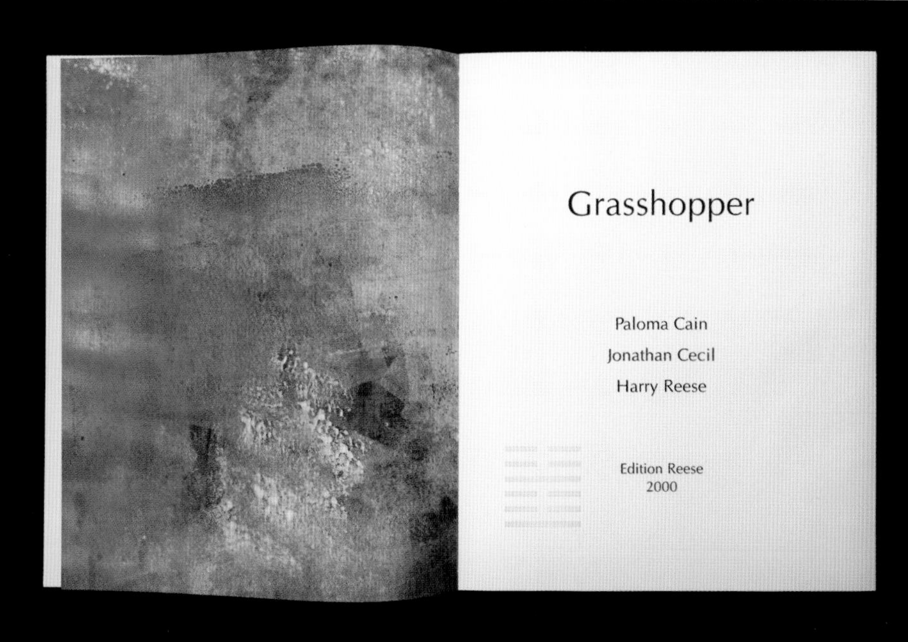

"The design and production of our books is a weaving process. The two of us offer our own experiences: visual, literary, technical. Front and back, back and forth, the book emerges."

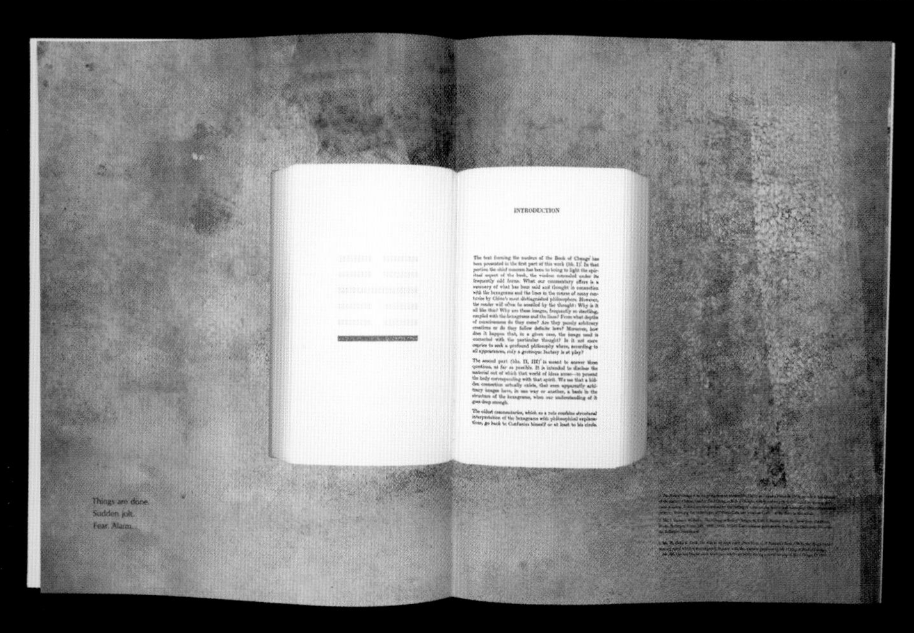

◀ **Grasshopper** | 2000

15 x 12 inches (38.1 x 30.5 cm)
Monadnock Dulcet paper, copper penny, monotype prints; letterpress, laser, and inkjet printed, handset in Optima type, hybrid sewn-boards binding

Photos by Tony Mastres

(Bababadalgharaghtakamminarronnkonnbronntonne
rronntuonnthunntrovarrhounawnskawntoohoohoordenen
thurnuk!)(Perkodhuskurunbarggruauyagokgorlayorgrom
gremmitghundhurthrumathunaradidillifaititillibumul
lunukkunun!)(Klikkaklakkaklaskaklopatzklatschabatta
creppycrottygraddaghsemmihsammihnouithappluddyap
pladdypkonpkot!)Bladyughfoulmoecklenburgwhurawhoras
cortastrumpapornanennykocksapastippatappatupperstrip
puckputtanach,eh?Thingcrooklyexineverypasturesixdix
likencehimaroundhersthemaggerbykinkinkankanwithdown
mindlookingated**Funagainstawake**Lukkedoerenduna
ndurraskewdylooshoofermoyportertooryzooysphalnabor
tansporthaokansakroidverjkapakkapukBothallchorac
torschumminaroundgansumuminarumdrumstrumtruminah
umptadumpwaultopoofoolooderamaunsturnup!Pappappap
parrassannuaragheallachnatullaghmonganmacmacmacw
hackfalltherdebblenonthedubblandaddydoodled(Husstenhas
stencaffincoffintussemtossemdamandamnacosaghcusaghh
obixhatouxpeswchbechoscashlcarcarcaract)Ullhodturden
weirmudgaardgringnirurdrmolnirfenrirlukkilokkibaugiman
dodrrerinsurtkrinmgernrackinarockar!Thor'sforyo!

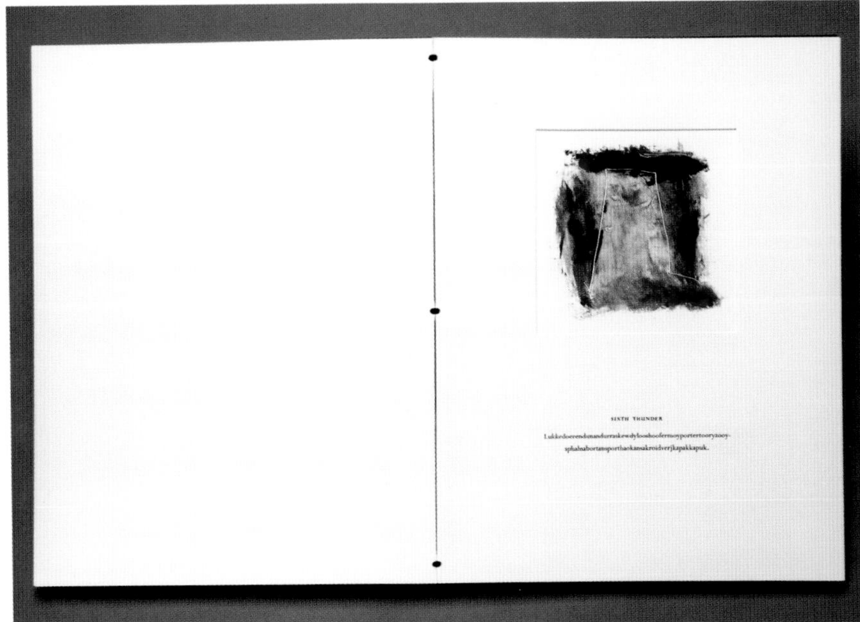

▲ **Funagainstawake** | 1997

12 x 9 inches (30.5 x 22.9 cm)
Magnani Italia paper, photoengraved relief print over hand-painted cover paper, monotype prints; letterpress printed, handset in Perpetua type, wire-edge hinging binding

Binding by Daniel E. Kelm
Text from *Finnegan's Wake* by James Joyce
Photos by Tony Mastres

" To make books by hand is to opt for slowness, rumination, patience, and length. "

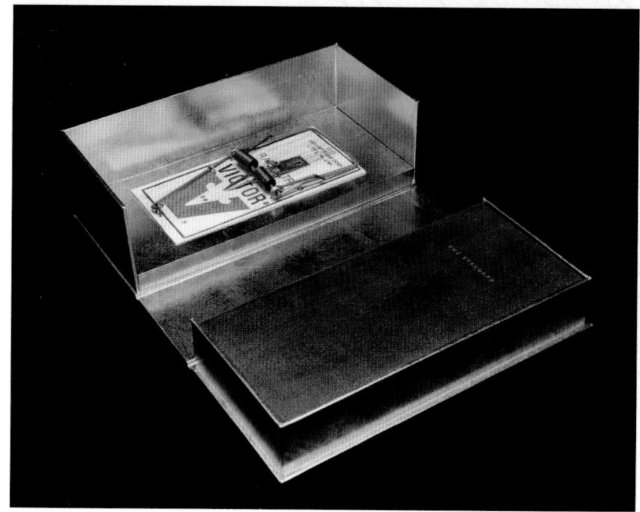

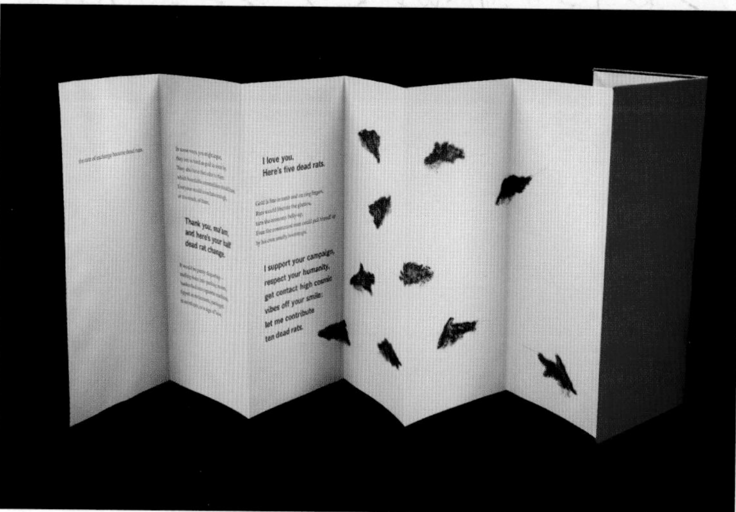

▲ **The Standard** | 1997

11 x 5 x 4 inches (27.9 x 12.7 x 10.2 cm)
MacGregor handmade paper, drawing, acrylic paint, split-leather binding over boards enclosed in a faux-gold brick box with a Victor-brand rattrap; letterpress printed, handset in Times New Roman and Franklin Gothic type

Photos by Tony Mastres

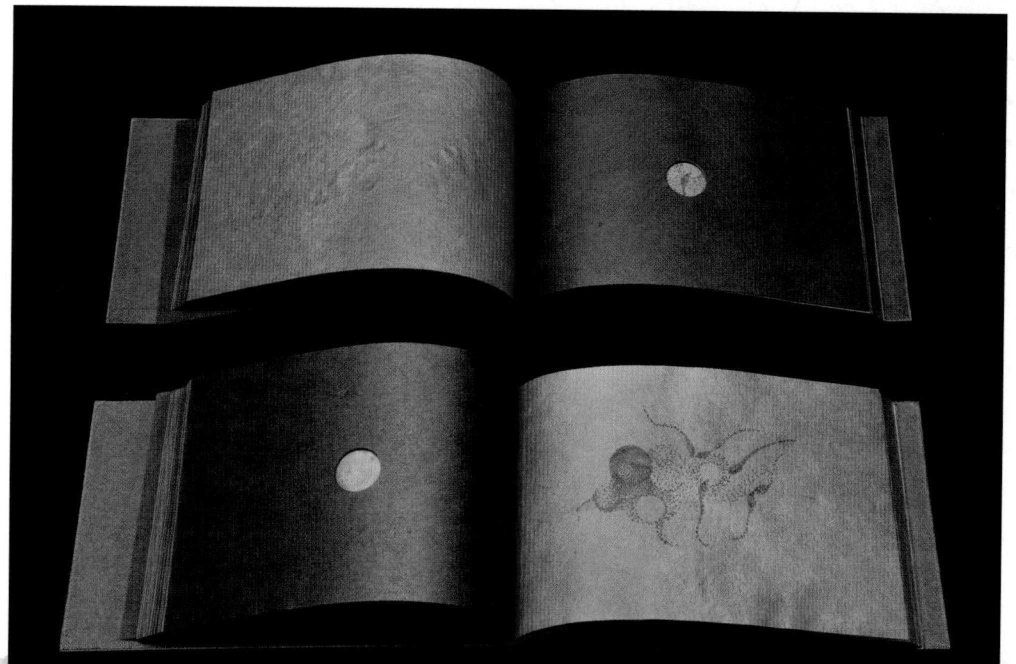

Pennyviews | 1995 ▶

4½ x 7¼ inches (11.4 x 18.4 cm)
Kakishibu and Moriki papers, acrylic paint, letterpress-printed drawings from polymer plates, letterpress-printed spine; die-cuts, side sewing

Drawings and book concept by Yoko Ono
Photo by Tony Mastres

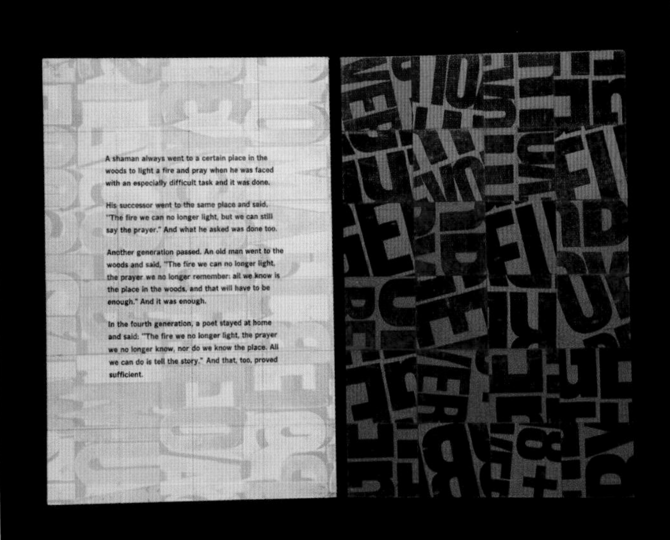

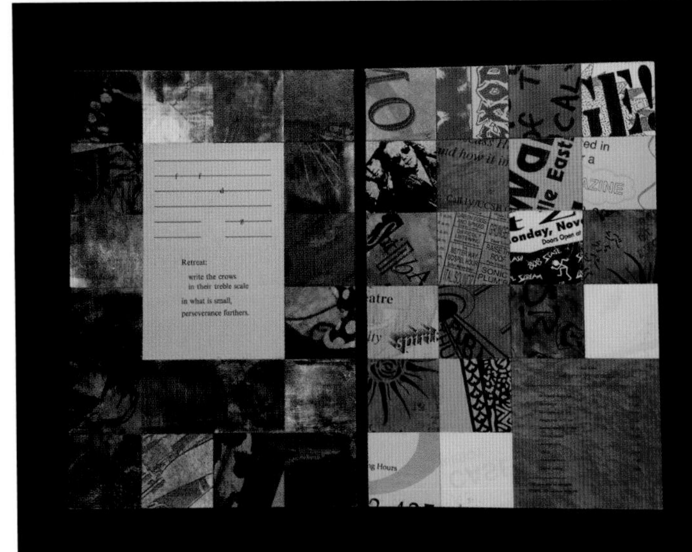

▲ **Near Goleta but Closer** | 1991

15 x 10 inches (38.1 x 25.4 cm)
Laminated paper tiles, handmade eucalyptus paper, found papers, photographs, photocopies, paintings, monotypes, transcribed conversations; letterpress printed

Photos by Tony Mastres

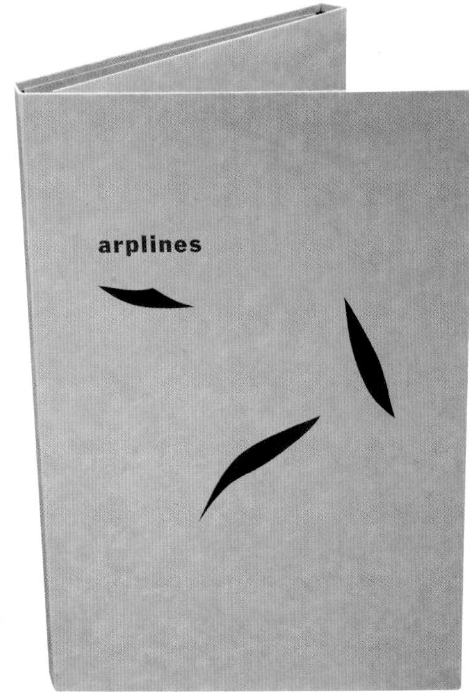

Arplines | 1989 ▶

13 x 8 inches (33 x 20.3 cm)
Drawings, relief prints, collages, paintings, letterpress-printed text, Arches cover

Photo by Tony Mastres

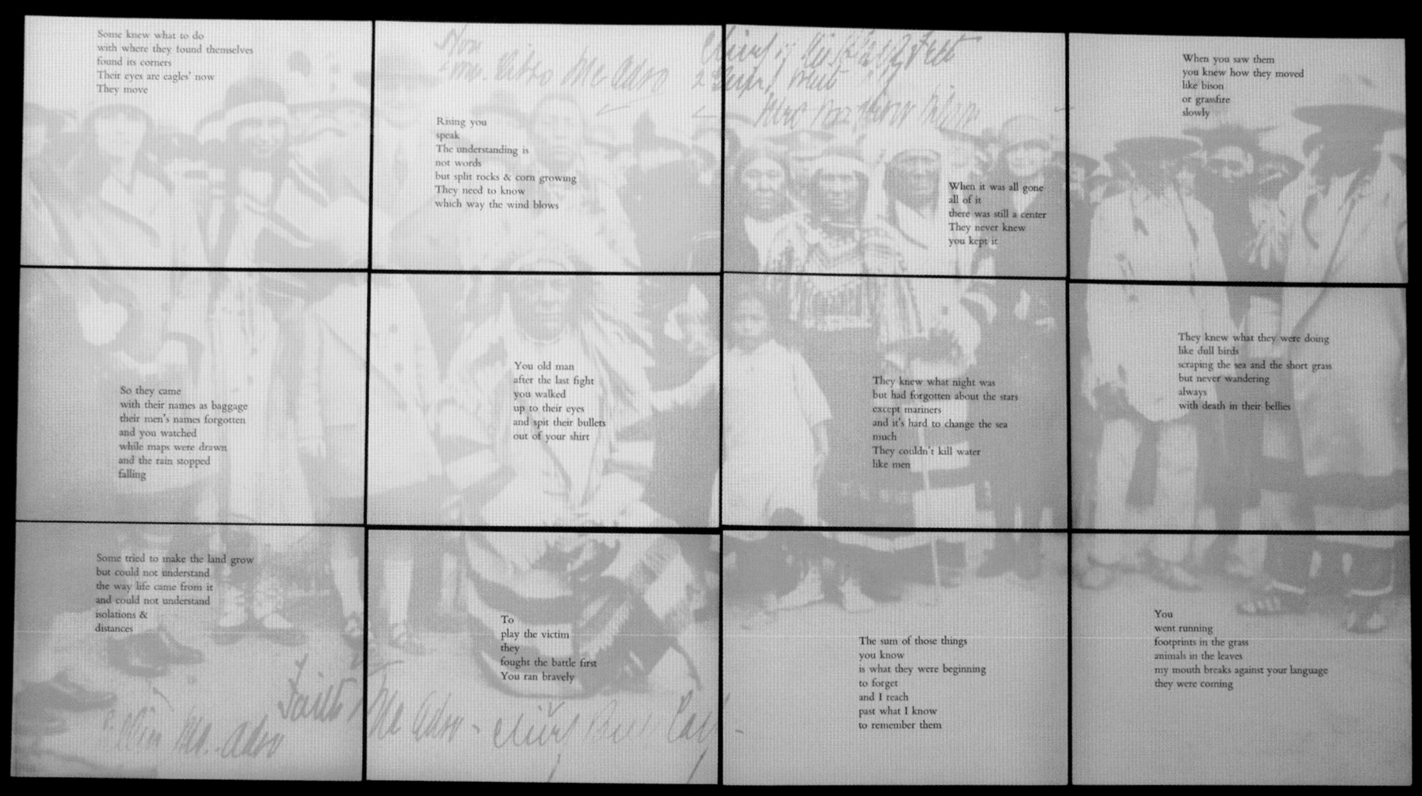

▲ **Hopi Set** | 1985

5 x 5 x ½ inches (12.7 x 12.7 x 1.3 cm)
Photographic image, postcards in paper wrapper with full-bleed "sandragraph" print; handset in Bembo type, letterpress printed, cut

Poems by David Ossman
Offset printing by Graham Mackintosh
Photo by Tony Mastres

" Our work orbits around the imaginative possibilities of the book as a container of thought, emotion, visual space, and beauty. "

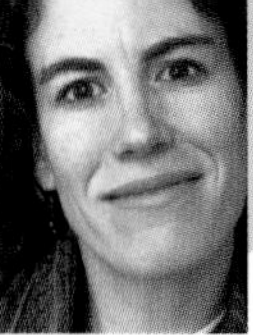

Sarah Bryant

IN CONSTRUCTING BOOKS THAT DISPLAY a crispness of impression, precise imagery, and an effective use of color, Sarah Bryant makes it clear that she delights in the process of letterpress printing. Bryant, who generally works in editions of 50 or 100, excels at producing identical multiples. Exhibiting meticulous attention to detail and exceptional ingenuity, her work is complex and intricate yet devoid of superfluous distractions. The page spreads Bryant creates may often stand alone, but her skillful integration of them into cohesive wholes ensures that each turn of the page is transformational.

Bryant is inspired by the ability she has as a bookmaker to guide viewers through a work along her intended path. Flipping through one of her books is a process of discovery, as the reader uncovers layers of information and meaning. Bryant lives in Aurora, New York, and issues her books under the imprint of Big Jump Press. Her work has been acquired by numerous special collections libraries, including the Yale University Arts Library in New Haven, Connecticut; the Atelier Vis-à-Vis in Marseille, France; and the New York Public Library in New York City.

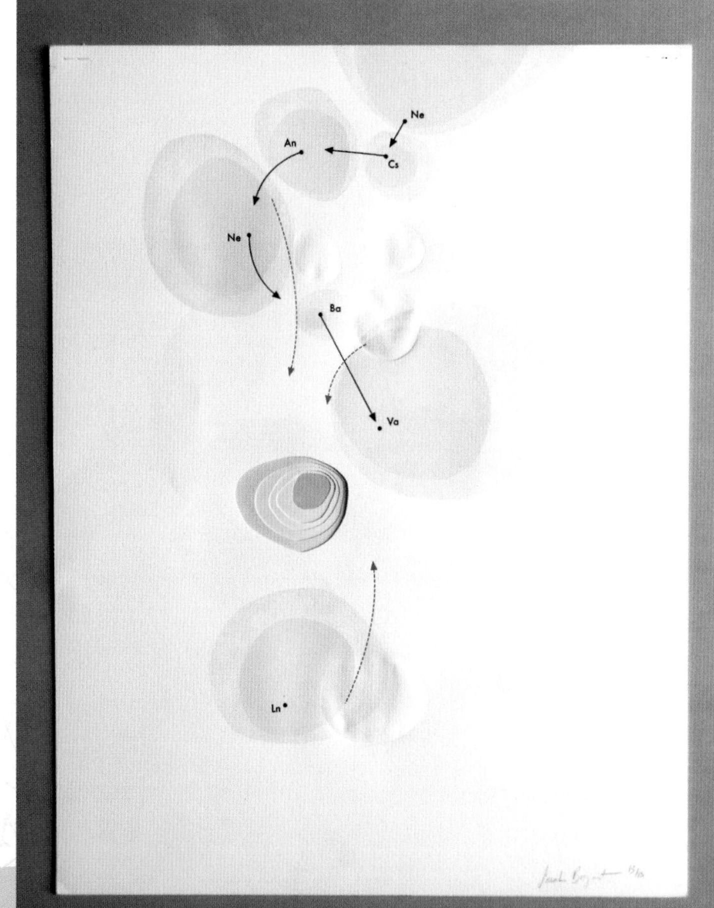

Untitled | 2009 ▶

14 x 11 inches (35.6 x 27.9 cm)
Arches paper; letterpress printed from polymer plates, pressure printed, hand cut
Photo by artist

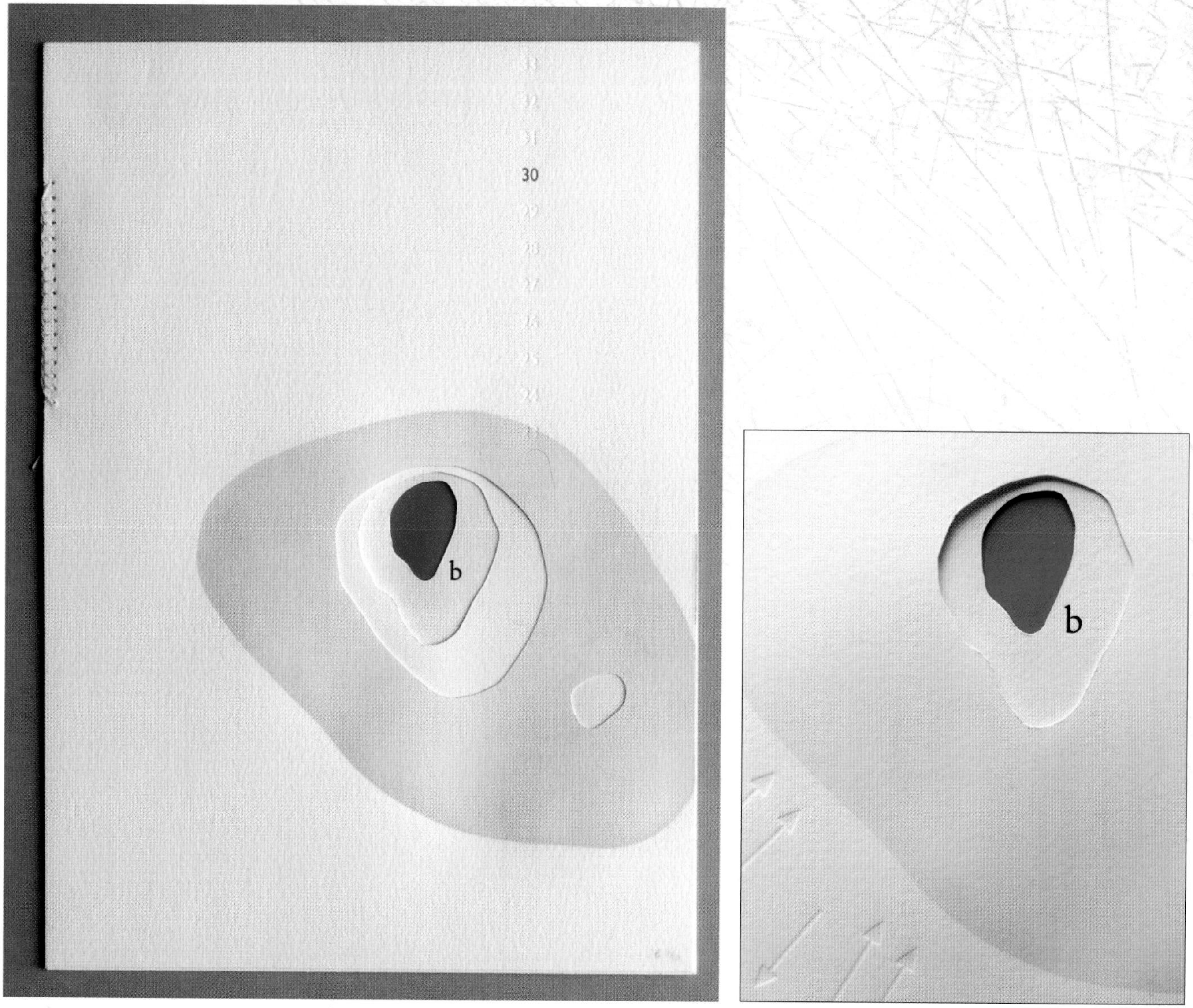

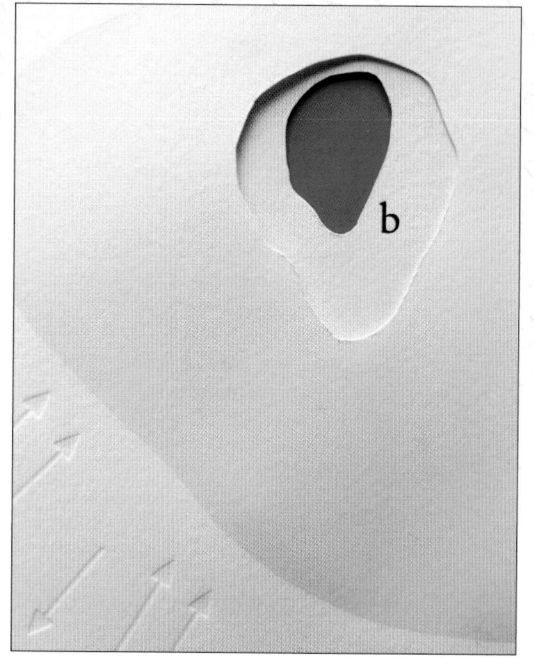

▲ **Untitled (b)** | 2009

8½ x 6 inches (21.6 x 15.2 cm)
Arches paper, thread; letterpress printed and blind stamped from linoleum, polymer plates, and metal type

Photos by artist

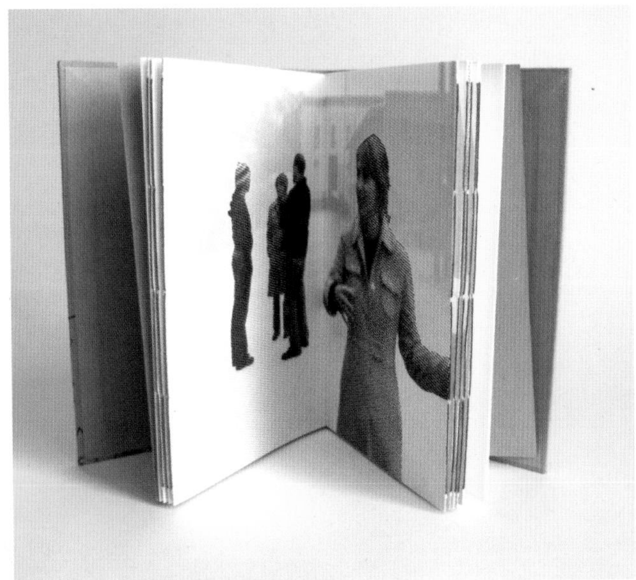

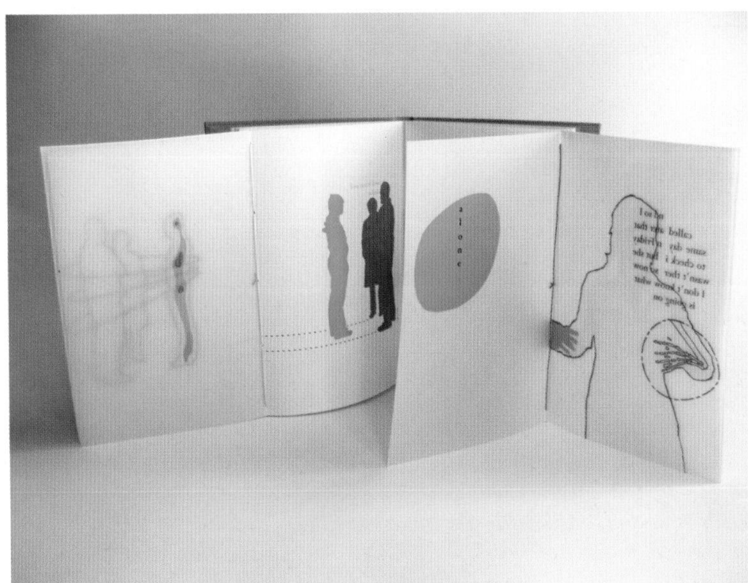

▲ **Point of View** | 2008

7¼ x 5⅛ x ½ inches (18.4 x 13 x 1.3 cm)
Arches paper, Wyndstone vellum; letterpress printed from polymer plates and metal type

Photos by artist

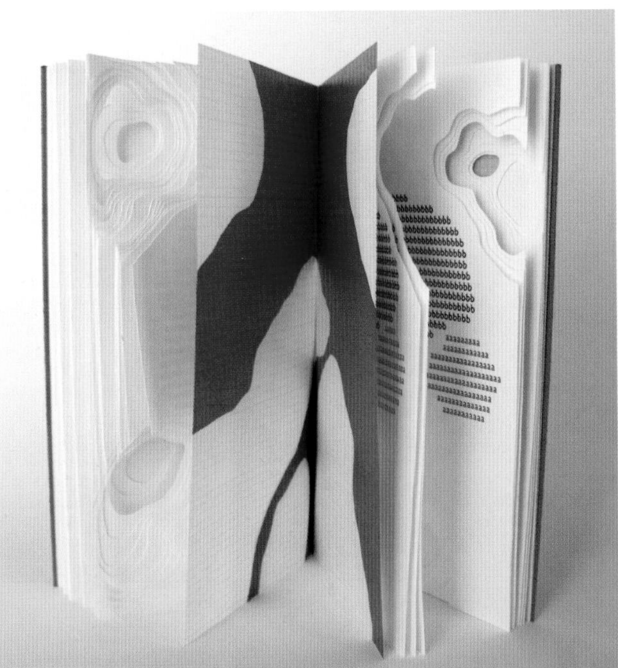

ab [landmass] | 2009 ▶

8 x 4½ x ⅜ inches (20.3 x 11.4 x 1 cm)
Bugra board, graph paper, machine-made paper; laser printed, letterpress printed, hand cut

Photo by artist

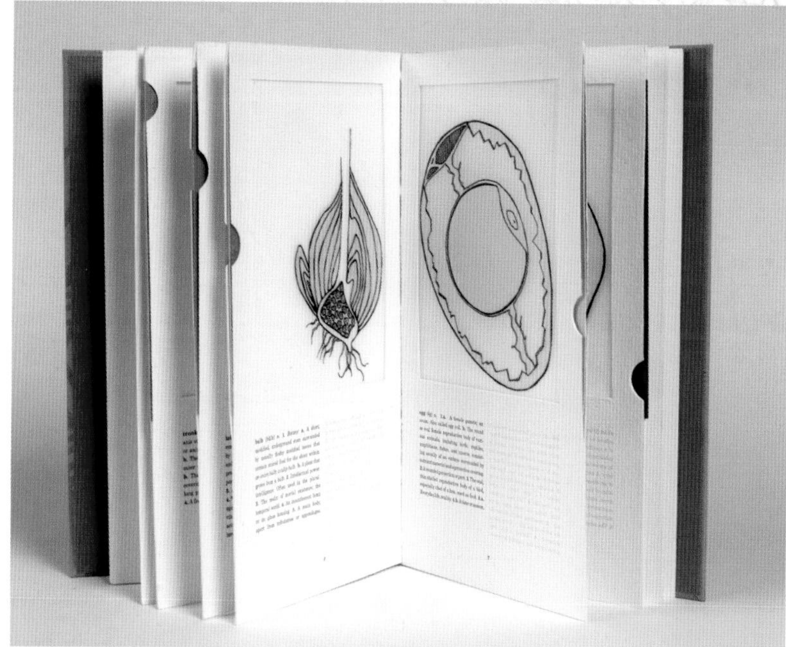

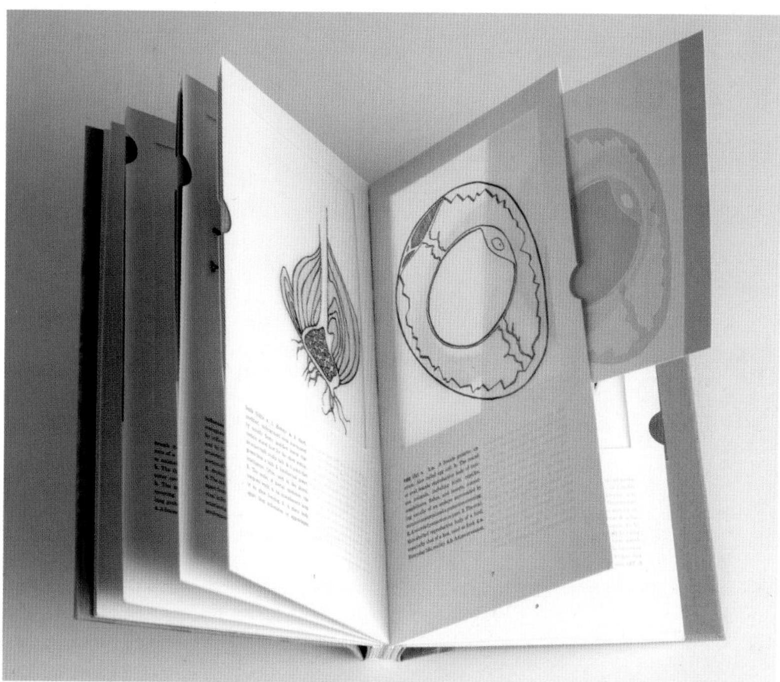

"My books are usually connected to the idea of hidden information. I use imagery relevant to this theme, including anatomical charts and cross sections, as well as structural elements such as layered pages that force the viewer to actively explore the book."

◀ **Cutaway** | 2007

8 x 5¼ x ¾ inches (20.3 x 13.3 x 1.9 cm)
Hahnemuhle Copperplate paper, Rives BFK paper, Mylar; letterpress printed from polymer plates

Photos by Laura Shill

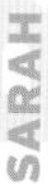

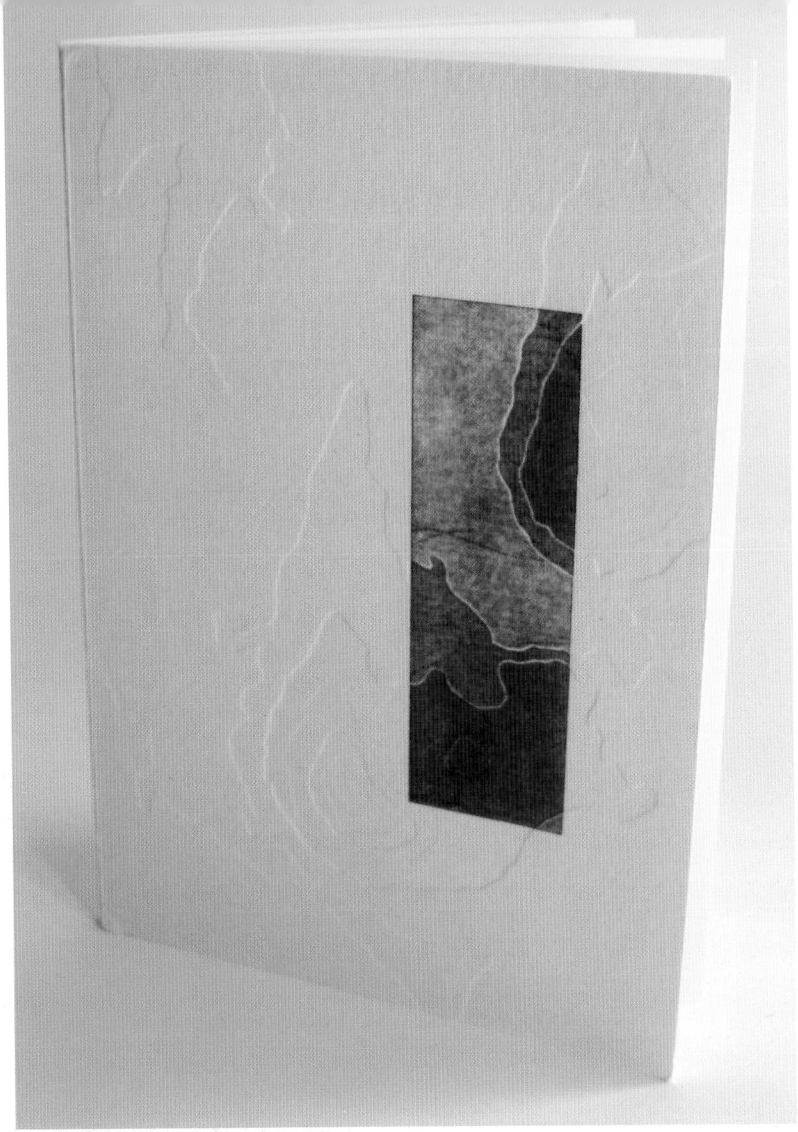

"When designing a new book, I make mockup after mockup in order to develop the content and structure simultaneously. I want these two critical parts of the book to work cohesively."

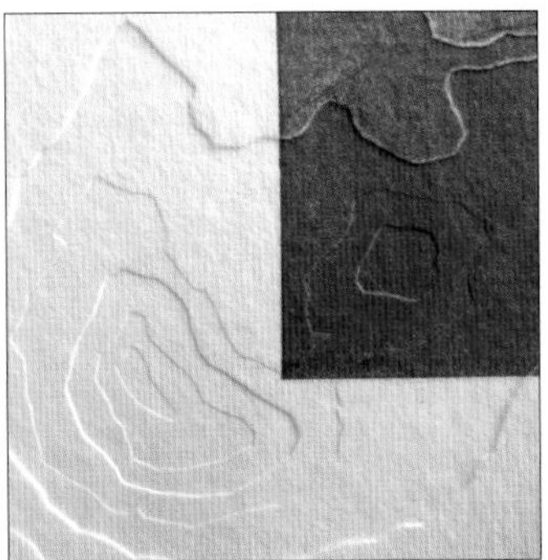

▲ **1:50000** | 2009

6½ x 4¾ x ¼ inches (16.5 x 12.1 x 0.6 cm)
Zerkall paper, acrylic paint; drum-leaf binding, printed from matt board and carbon paper, stenciled

Photos by artist

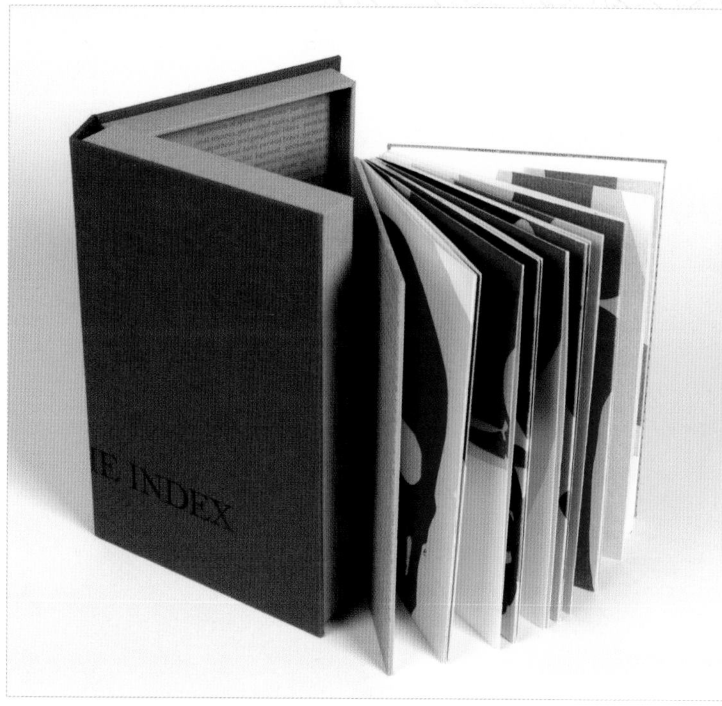

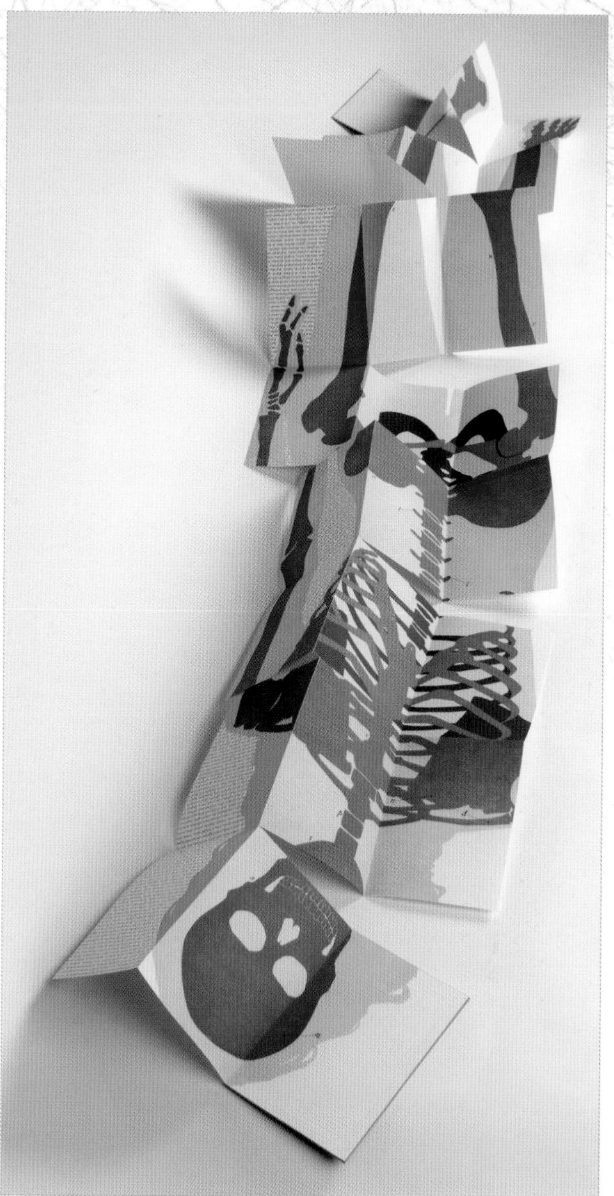

▲ **The Index** | 2006

Folded: 8¼ x 5½ x 1¼ inches (21 x 14 x 3.2 cm)
Rives Heavyweight paper; hinged map fold enclosed in a clamshell box, letterpress printed from polymer plates and linoleum reduction

Photos by Laura Shill

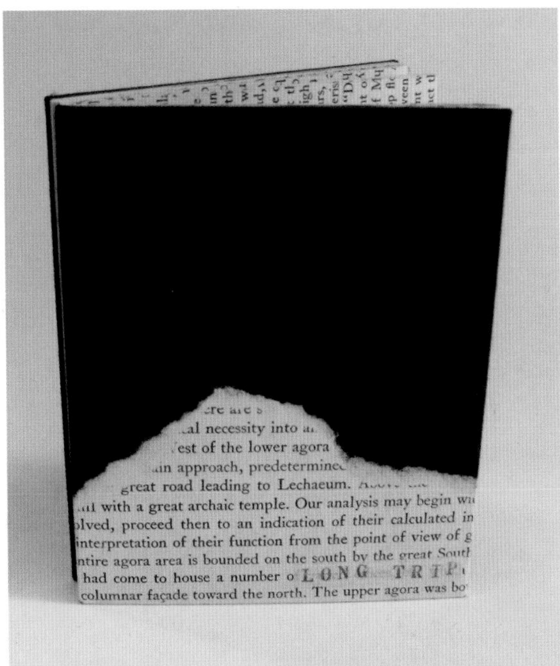

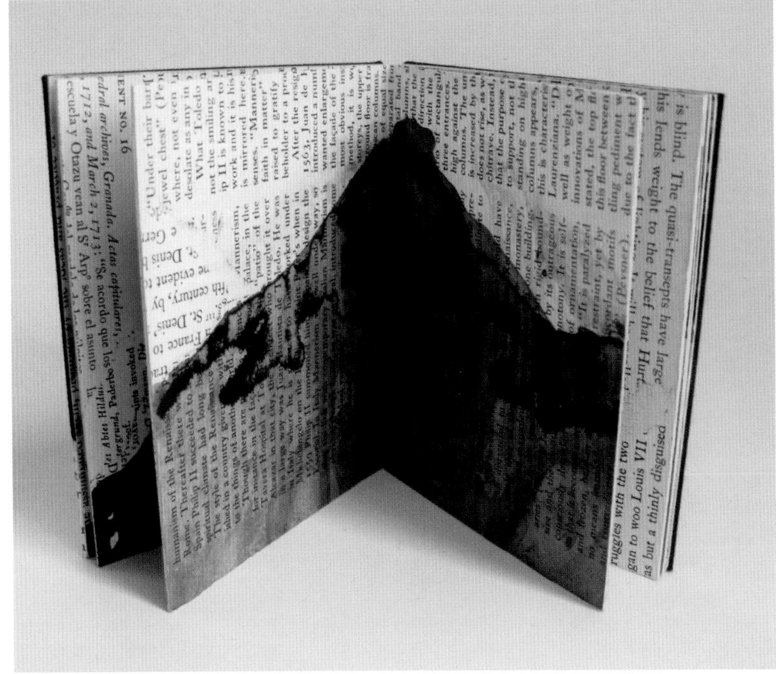

▲ **Long Trip** | 2007

5⅞ x 3⅞ x ½ inches (14.9 x 9.8 x 1.3 cm)
Old magazines, binder's board, sumi ink, walnut dye; stiff-leaf binding, collage
Photos by artist

> "It isn't important to me that viewers understand everything I'm trying to do. I give them clues to my intentions and hope that my content is compelling enough to lure them in for a second or third viewing."

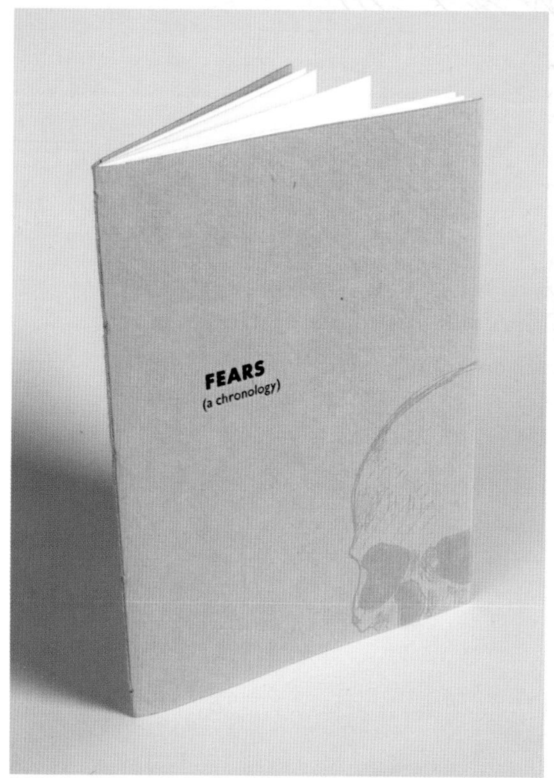

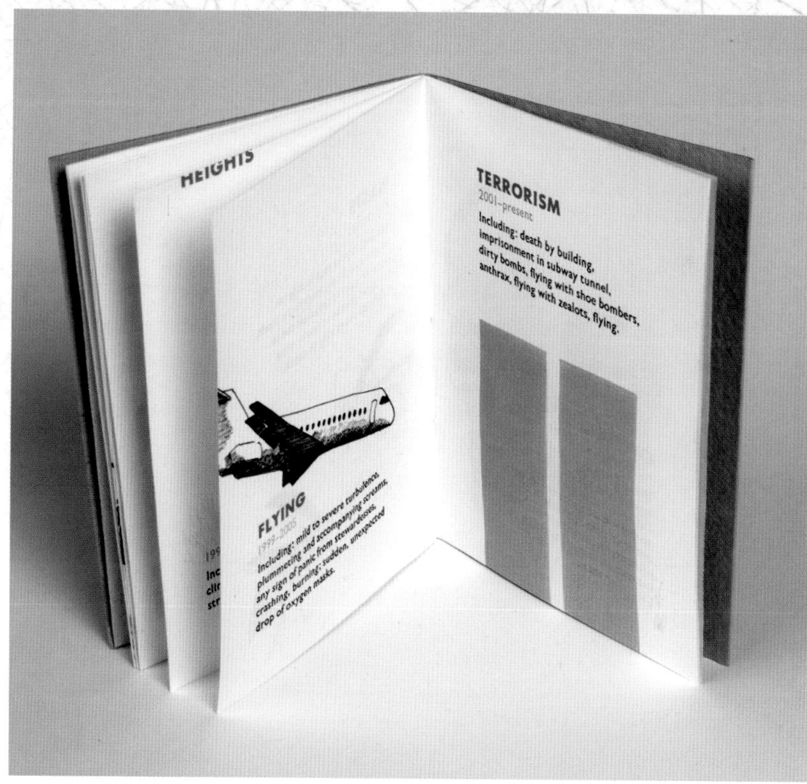

▲ **Fears (a chronology)** | 2006

6 x 4½ x ⅛ inches (15.2 x 11.4 x 0.3 cm)
Frankfurt paper, Indian Khadi; pamphlet binding, letterpress printed from linoleum, polymer plates, and metal type
Photos by Laura Shill

CAMPBELL

Susan Goethel Campbell

IN HER INGENIOUSLY DESIGNED BOOKS, Susan Goethel Campbell explores the intersection of the natural world and the built environment. She candidly juxtaposes images of built structures with natural, irregular forms that become the pages of a book. She also imposes images of nature onto rigid, gridded book panels, forcing the viewer to examine the impact that these discordant elements have on each other. The physical structure and movement of her innovative books reflect her ideas about suburban sprawl and the loss of undeveloped land.

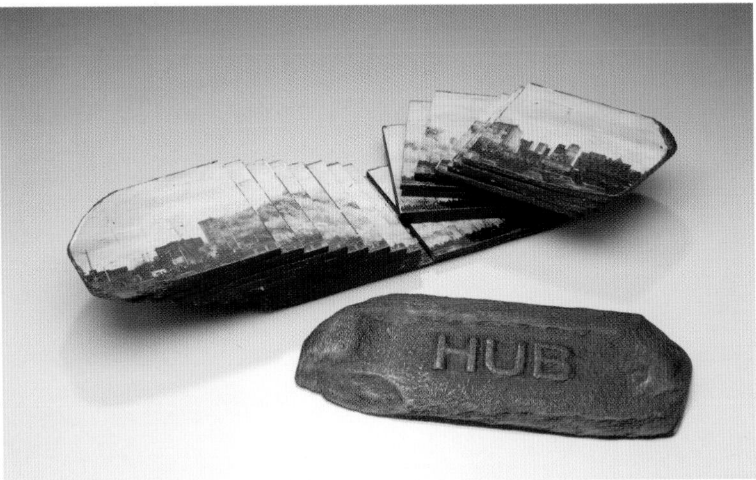

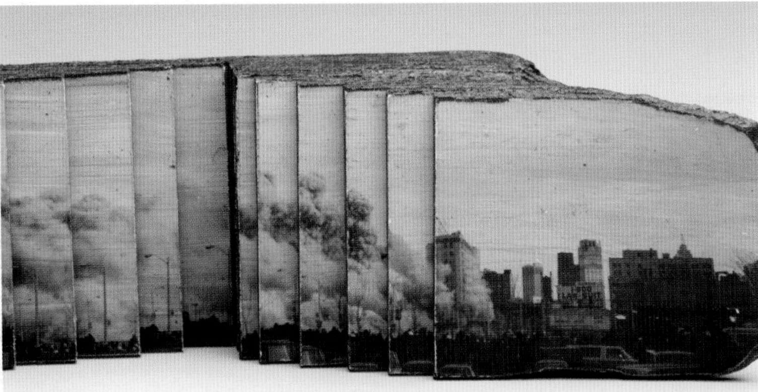

In her work Campbell uses inventive formats in order to speak about the irony of mankind's attempts to control the natural world. She uses nontraditional structures and materials that encourage viewers to reevaluate their own definitions of the book. Campbell's work can be found in major public and private collections, including the National Museum of Women in the Arts in Washington, D.C.; the New York Public Library in New York City; and the Detroit Institute of Arts in Detroit, Michigan. She lives in Ferndale, Michigan.

◀ HUB | 2000
Open: Dimensions variable
Closed: 2½ x 8 x 3 inches (6.4 x 20.3 x 7.6 cm)
Photograph, mixed media on magnetic sheeting
Photos by Tim Thayer

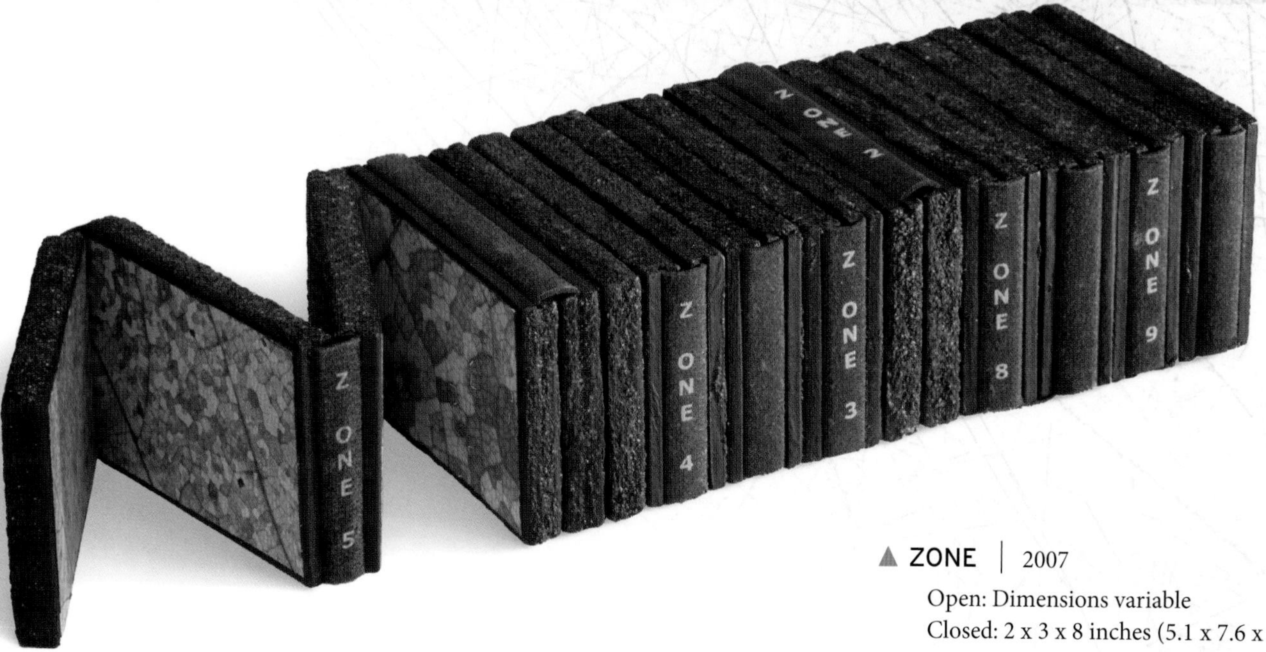

▲ **ZONE** | 2007

Open: Dimensions variable
Closed: 2 x 3 x 8 inches (5.1 x 7.6 x 20.3 cm)

Digital print, mixed media; silk-screened on magnetic sheeting

Photos by Tim Thayer

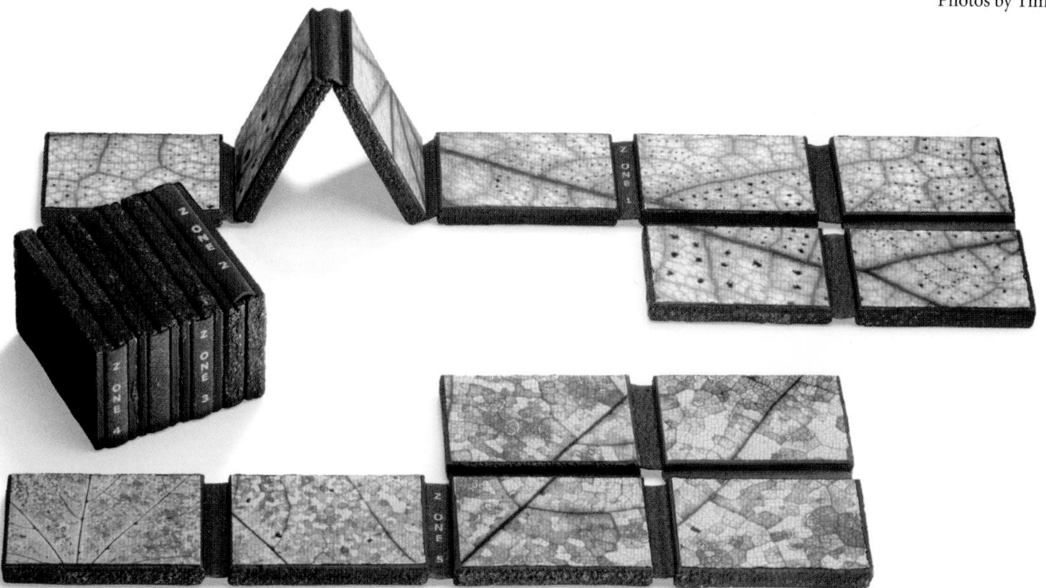

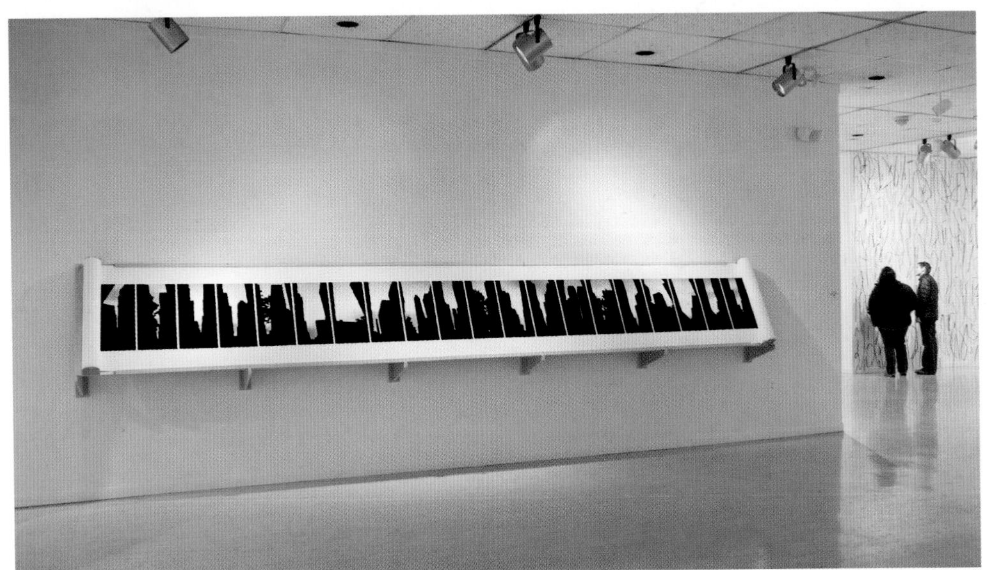

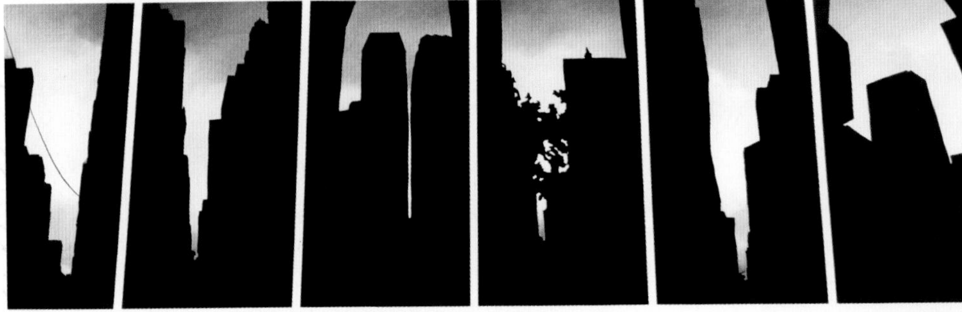

▲ **Between 40 + 60** | 2004

2½ x 20 feet (0.7 x 6.1 m)
Brushed ink and stencil on paper;
scroll format
Photos by Tim Thayer

" I hate to sew—a fact that's prompted my explorations of alternative materials and methods of binding. "

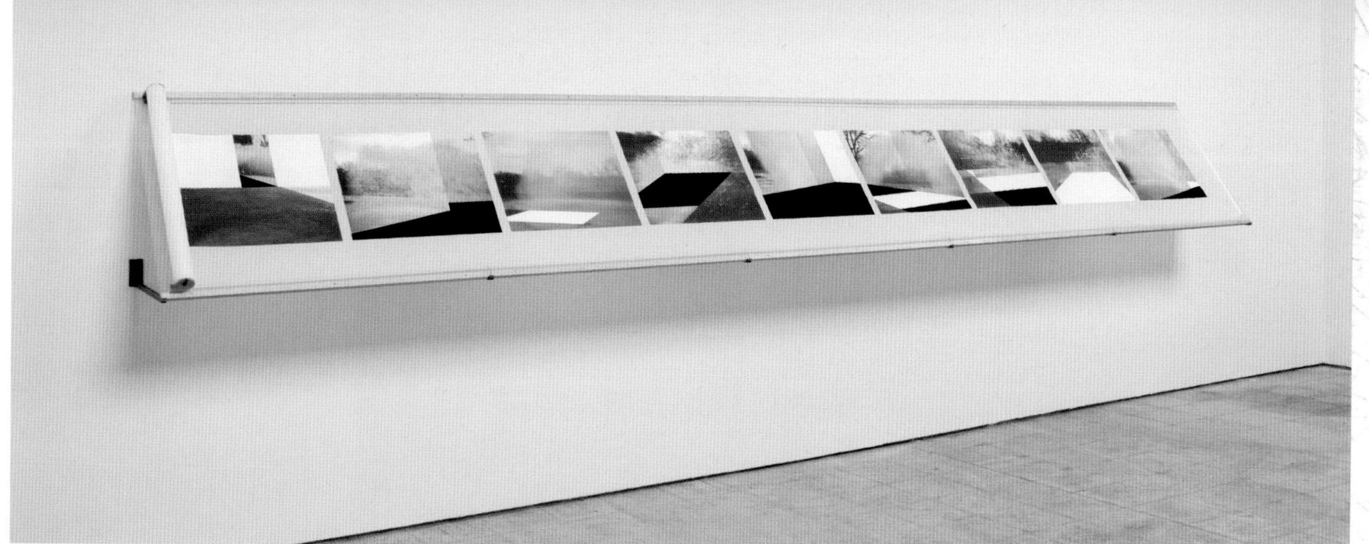

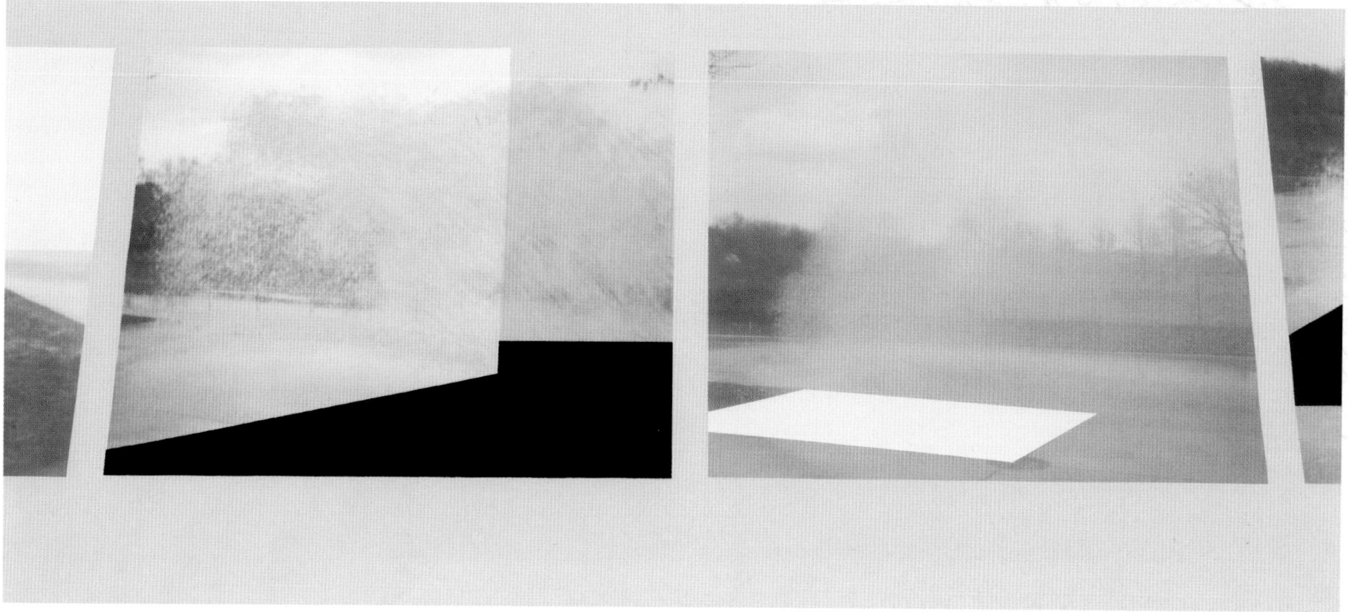

▲ **House Weather** | 2005

2 x 15 feet (0.6 x 4.5 m)
Digital print, acrylic paint, plastic sheeting;
scroll format

Photos by Tim Thayer

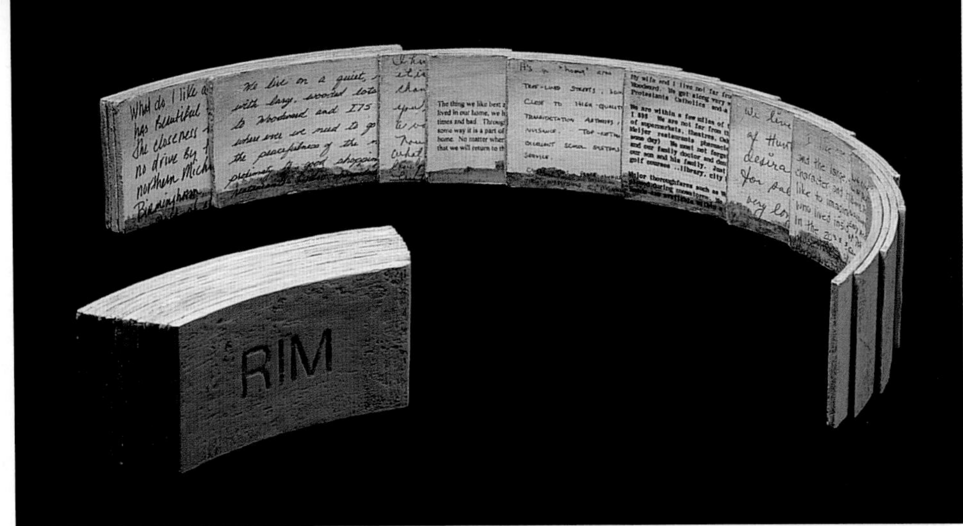

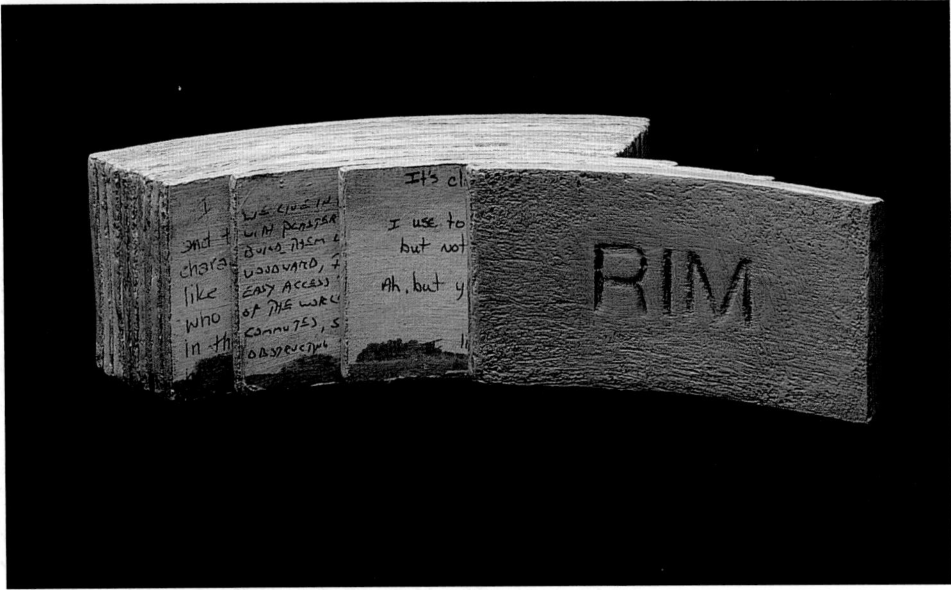

"I'm fascinated by the ways in which information and images can be ambiguous, defying classification and representation."

▲ RIM | 2000

Open: Dimensions variable
Closed: 2½ x 8 x 3 inches (6.4 x 20.3 x 7.6 cm)

Transfer print on silk tissue, mixed media on magnetic sheeting

Photos by Chuck Cloud

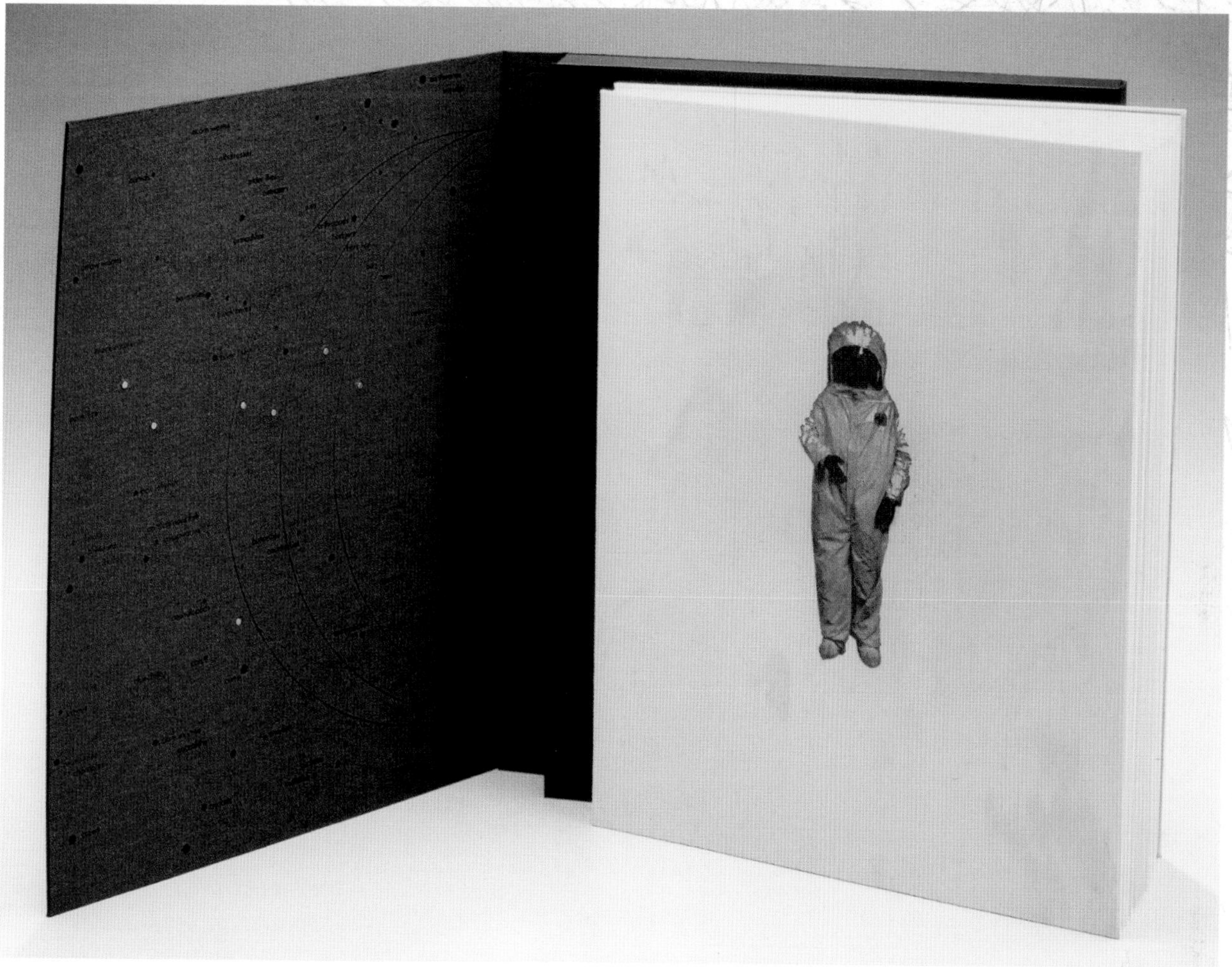

▲ **After the Deluge: The Post-Ark Report** | 2002

14 x 11 x 1 inches (35.6 x 27.9 x 2.5 cm)
Photo etching, photopolymer, tea stains; chine collé, board book binding, wrap-around cover

Photos by Tim Thayer

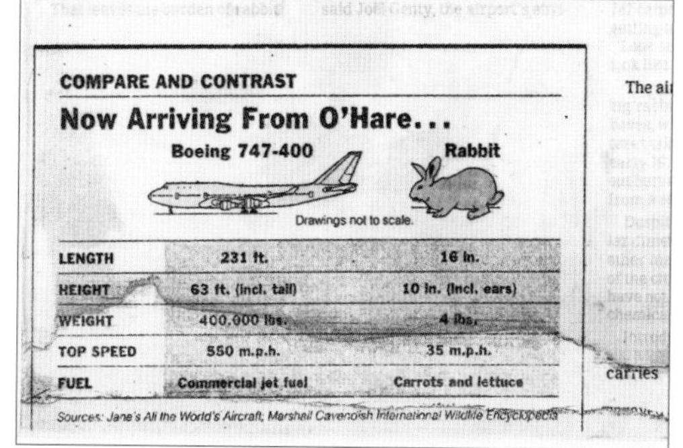

COMPARE AND CONTRAST

Now Arriving From O'Hare...

	Boeing 747-400	Rabbit
LENGTH	231 ft.	16 in.
HEIGHT	63 ft. (incl. tail)	10 in. (incl. ears)
WEIGHT	400,000 lbs.	4 lbs.
TOP SPEED	550 m.p.h.	35 m.p.h.
FUEL	Commercial jet fuel	Carrots and lettuce

Drawings not to scale.

Sources: Jane's All the World's Aircraft, Marshall Cavendish International Wildlife Encyclopedia

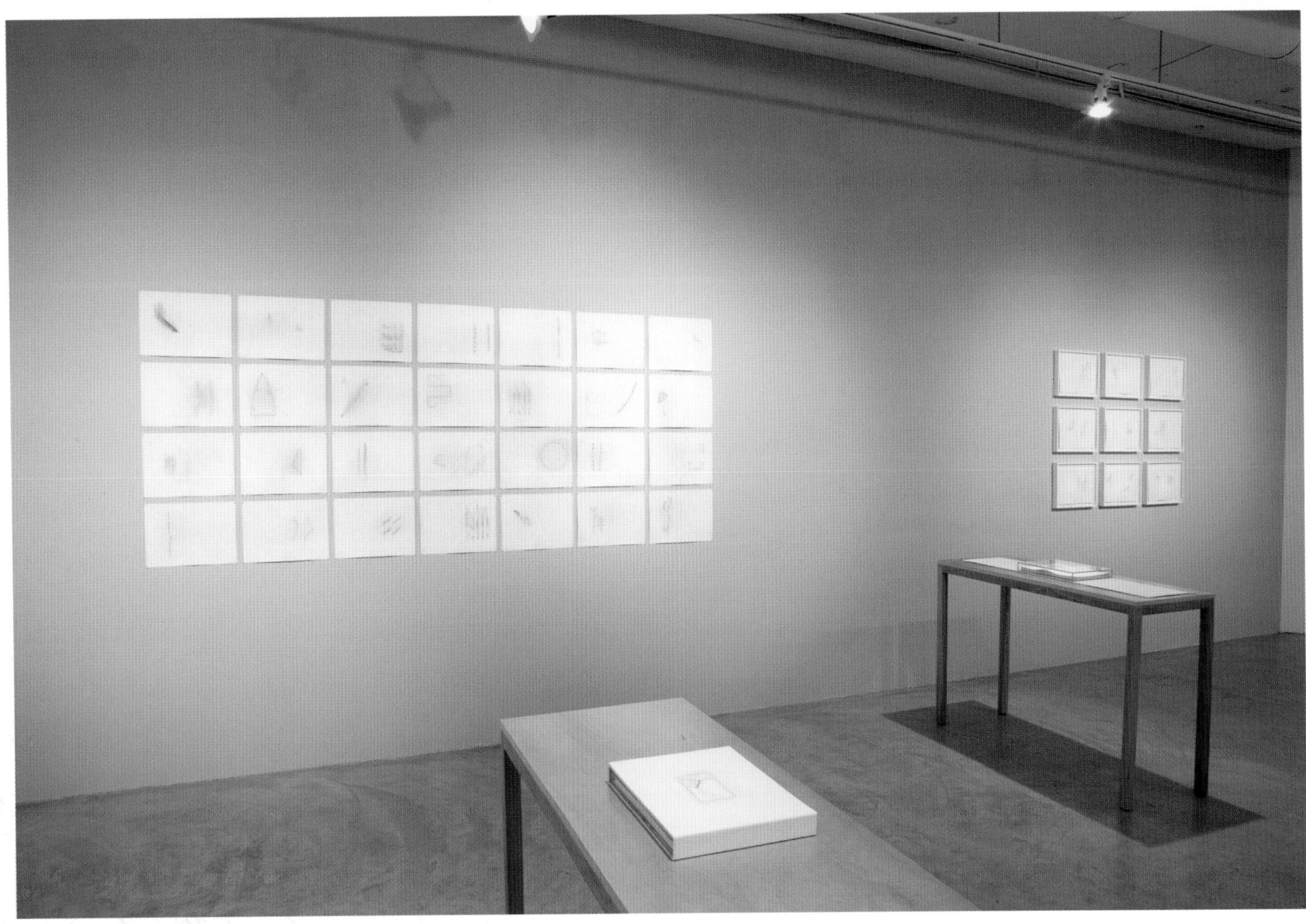

▲ **Control of Seedling Overconfidence (on table) and Peculiar Weather Explanation (on wall)** | 2007

Dimensions variable

Gesso on book pages, acrylic box; wrap-around cover

Photo by Tim Thayer

" My concept of artist's books is very broad. Every two or three years I make a work that might formally be considered a book. "

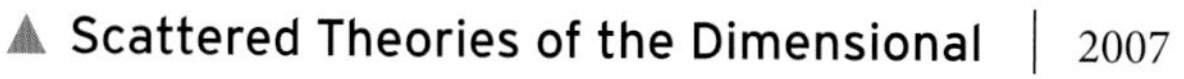

▲ **Scattered Theories of the Dimensional** | 2007

Box: 1 x 17½ x 11½ inches (2.5 x 44.5 x 29.2 cm)
Gesso on book pages, acrylic box; wrap-around cover
Photo by Tim Thayer

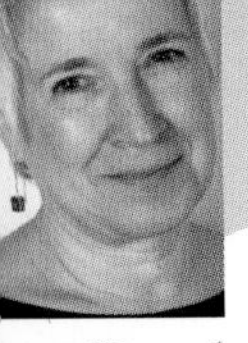

STAHLECKER

Bonnie Stahlecker

AN INTEGRATOR OF DIVERSE INFLUENCES, including sculpture, historical book structures, and typography, Bonnie Stahlecker operates on the edge of the bookbinding tradition. She started out making limited-edition books of poetry that were bound traditionally, but with contemporary quirks. She now focuses on the sculptural potential of her medium, giving herself the freedom to forget about the functionality of structure and to express the essence of a book as an object. The innovative use of materials such as piano keys, nails, beads, and twigs gives her books a sense of whimsicality.

Drawing inspiration from ancient writing systems such as Chinese oracle bones, cuneiform script, and the Ogham alphabet, Stahlecker unites her interest in early book forms with a uniquely personal style. By approaching the book as a three-dimensional object with multiple layers, both physical and mental, she creates unforgettable works that never fail to engage the viewer. Stahlecker lives in Plainfield, Indiana. Her books and book sculptures are held in major collections throughout the United States.

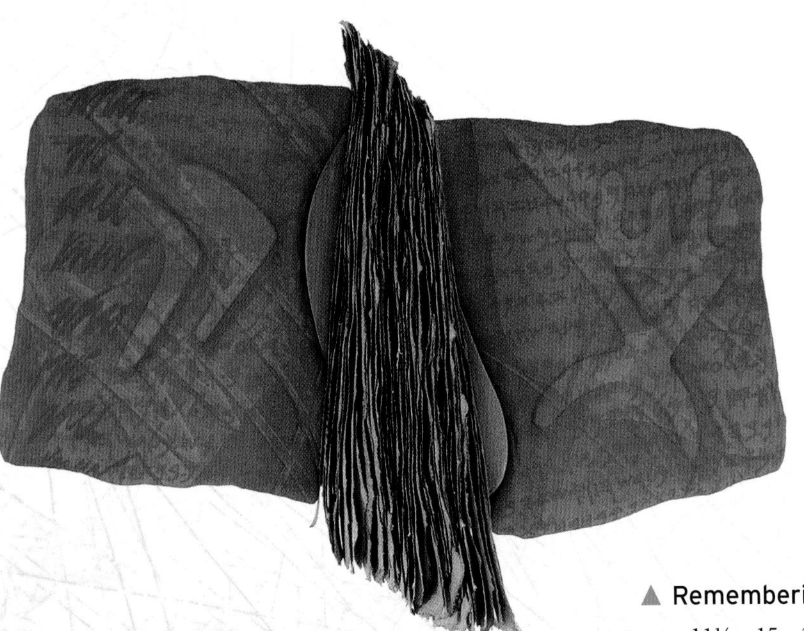

▲ **Remembering What We Once Knew** | 2009
11½ x 15 x 3 inches (29.2 x 38.1 x 7.6 cm)
Pigskin, basswood, torn paper; relief printed, painted, stained
Photo by artist

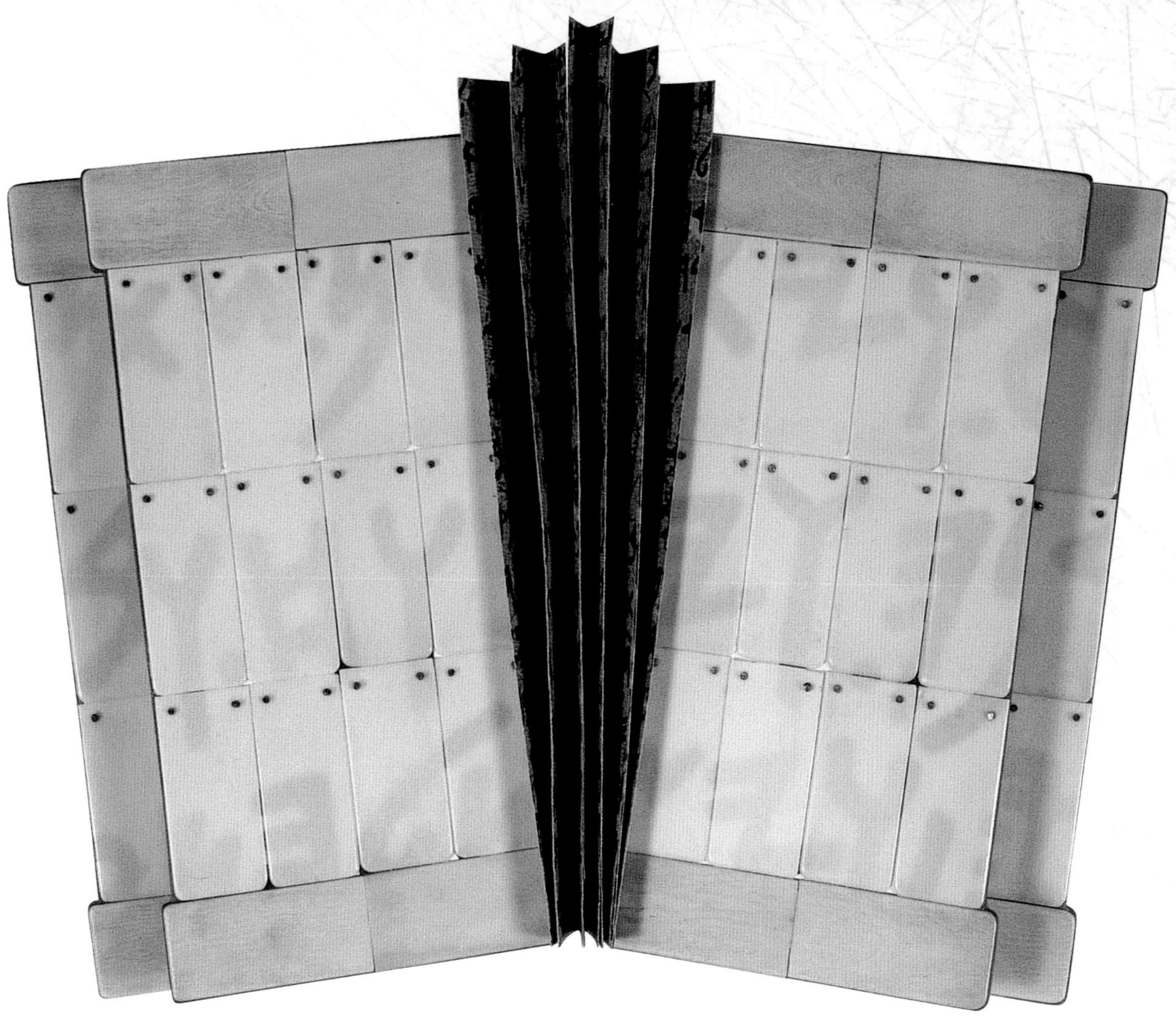

▲ **Sacred Authority** | 2008

9 x 11 x 2 inches (22.9 x 27.9 x 5.1 cm)
Piano keys, brass nails, handmade paper, drawing; letterpress printed

Photo by artist

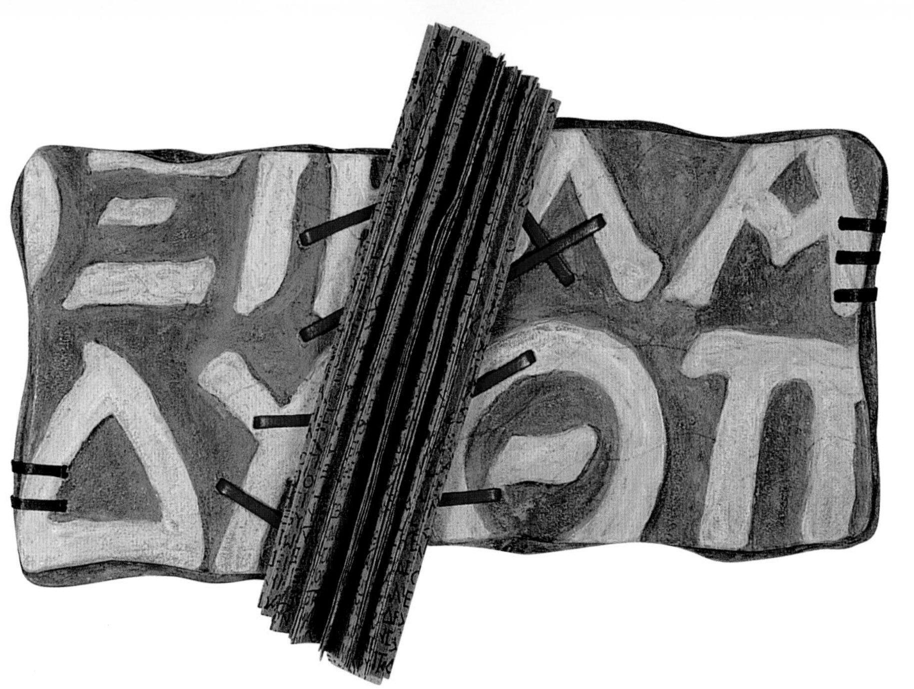

▲ **Connecting with the Disconnect** | 2006

8 x 11 x 1 inches (20.3 x 27.9 x 2.5 cm)
Binder's board, Cave paper, leather thong; painted, inkjet printed

Photo by artist

> " After making traditional books for years, I've finally allowed myself the freedom to forget about the functionality of the book structure and to express the essence of the book object. "

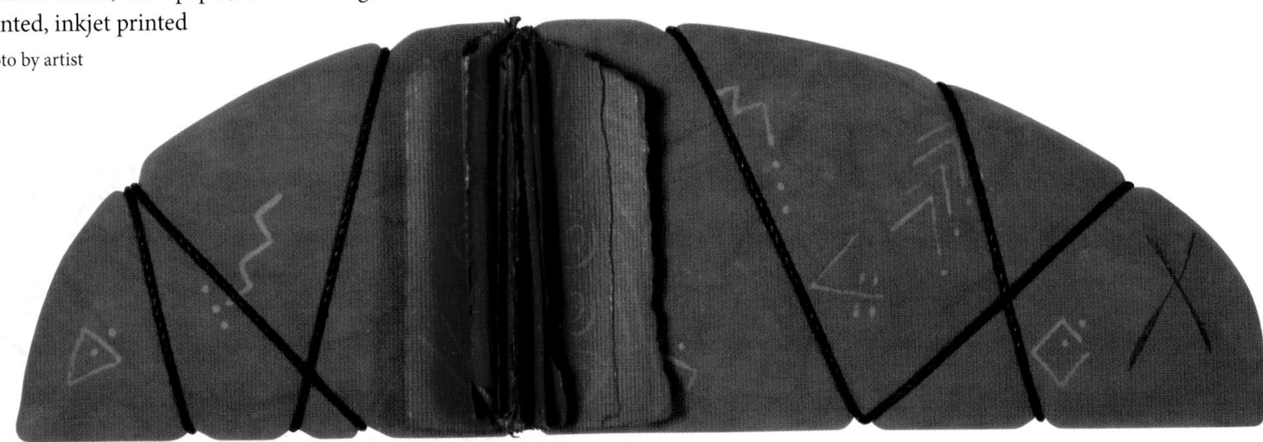

▲ **Stone Vessels** | 2006

4 x 12¼ x 2 inches (10.2 x 31.1 x 5.1 cm)
Suede leather, leather and cotton cord, handmade paper; painted

Photo by Rebecca Clune

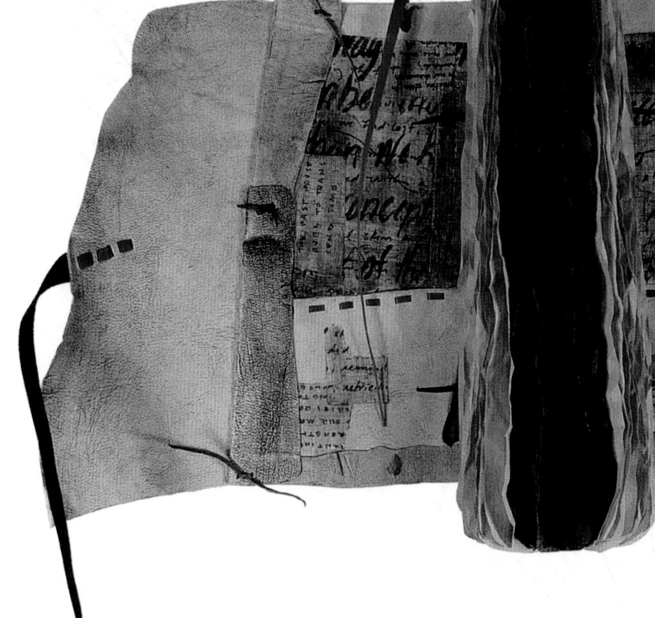

Vessels of the Forgotten | 2007 ▶

9 x 14¼ x 2 inches (22.9 x 35.2 x 5.1 cm)
Doe kidskin, leather thong, ink drawings, papyrus; dyed, stained
Photo by artist

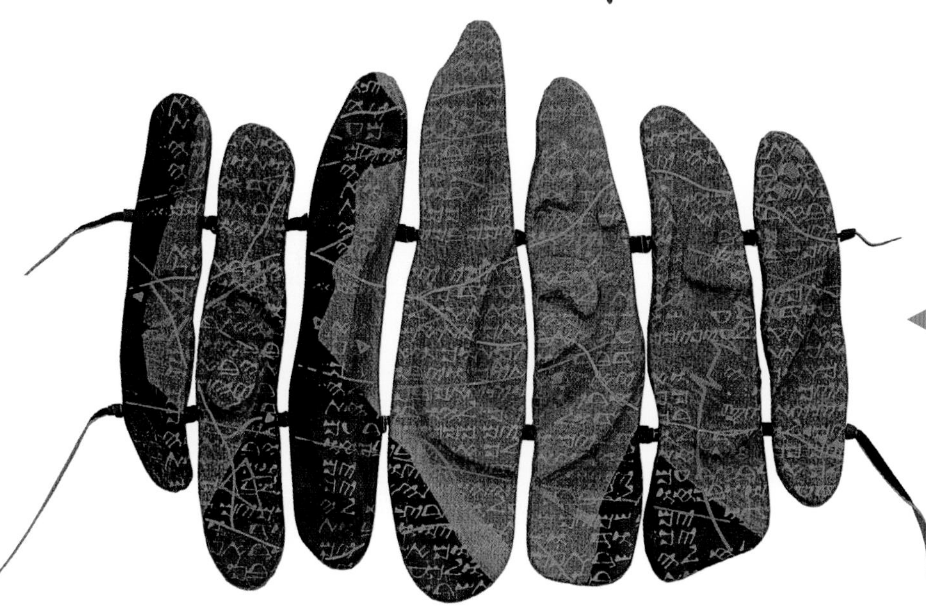

◀ **Finding the Source** | 2009

7½ x 10 x ½ inches (19.1 x 25.4 x 1.3 cm)
Pigskin, leather beads, leather thong; relief printed, painted
Photo by artist

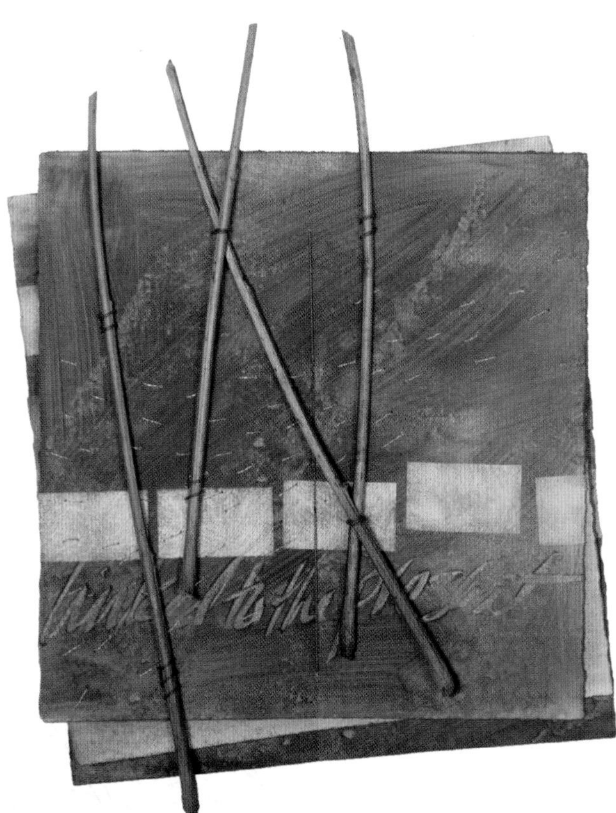

▲ **Time Links—Present** | 2003

11½ x 8½ x ½ inches (29.2 x 21.6 x 1.3 cm)
Arches paper, catalpa twigs, gold thread; paste painted, stitched

Photo by Rebecca Clune

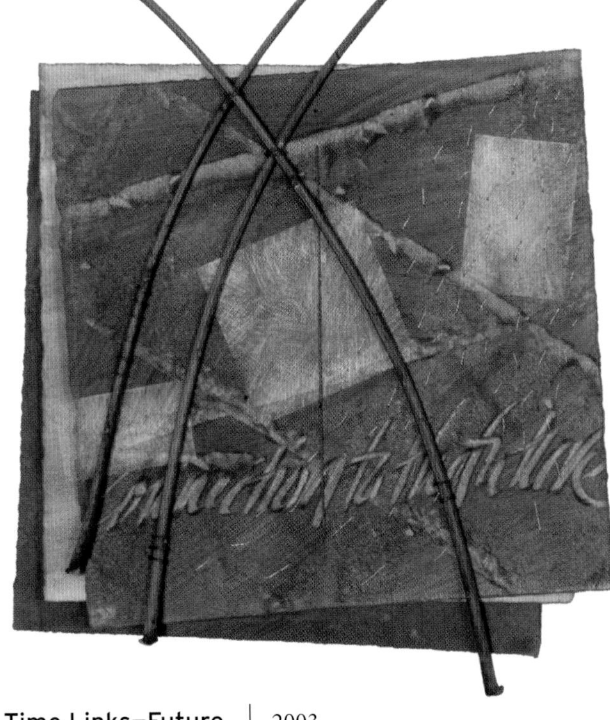

▲ **Time Links—Future** | 2003

11½ x 9½ x ½ inches (29.2 x 24.1 x 1.3 cm)
Arches paper, catalpa twigs, gold thread; paste painted, stitched

Photo by Rebecca Clune

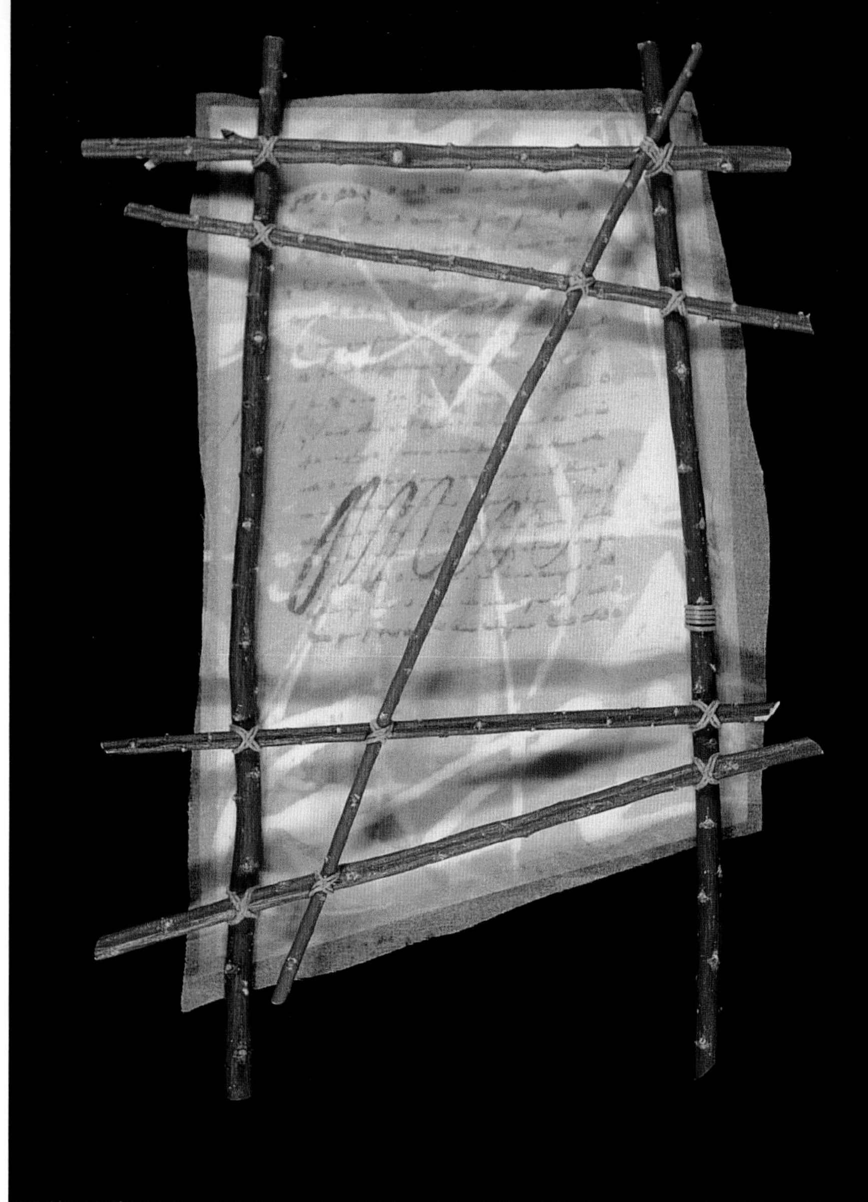

▲ **Omen Charts, No. 4** | 2005

10 x 7 x ½ inches (25.4 x 17.8 x 1.3 cm)
Silk, organza, twigs, waxed thread; batik dyed, fiber-reactive dyed, hand lettered
Photo by artist

" I have a love affair with early book objects such as clay tablets, Chinese slip books, and single-quire manuscripts. These artifacts are vessels of information that have carried secrets and treasures to us. "

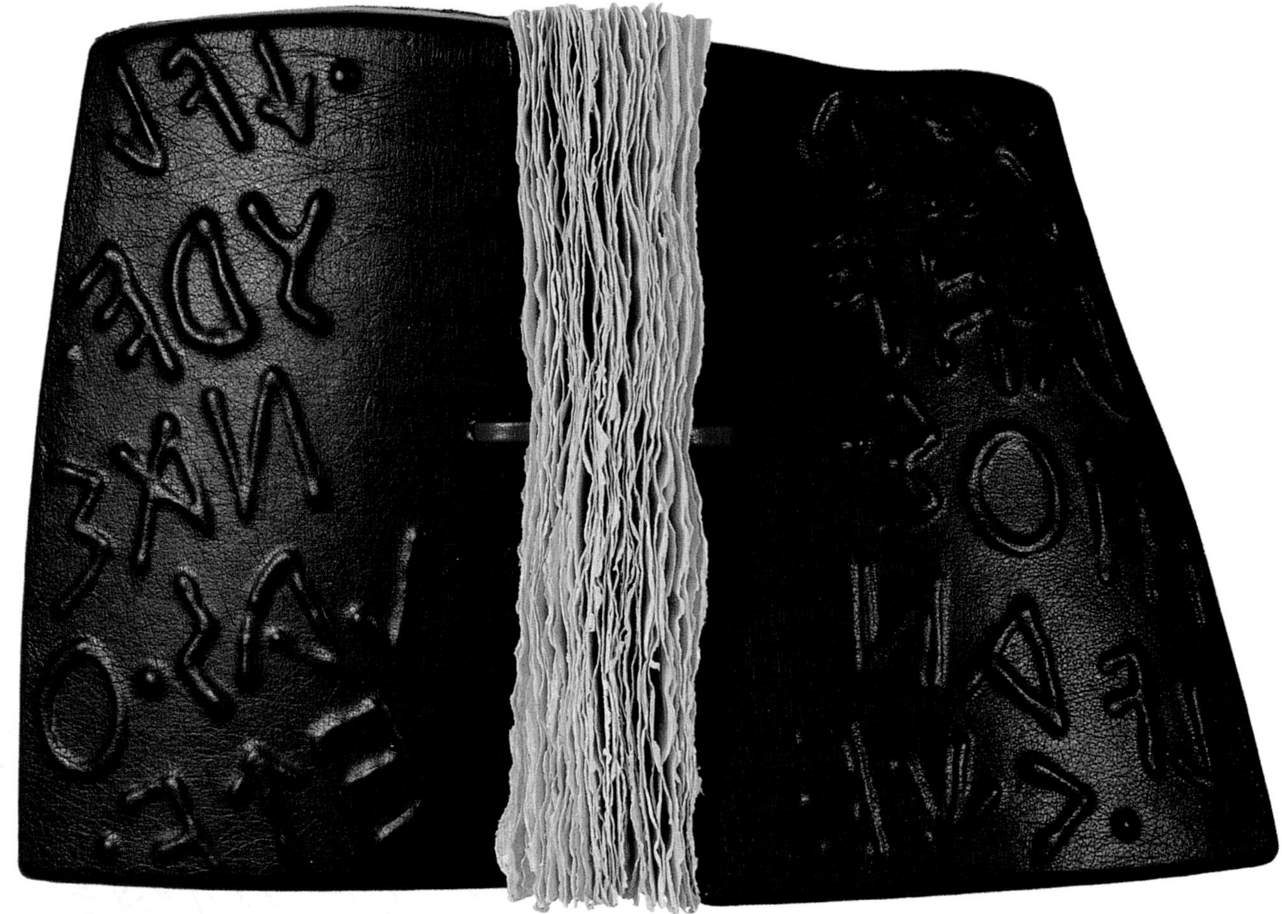

▲ **The Story of Thought** | 2007

6½ x 10 x 2 inches (16.5 x 25.4 x 5 cm)
Kidskin, handmade paper, leather thong, gesso drawing; molded over raised letterforms
Photo by artist

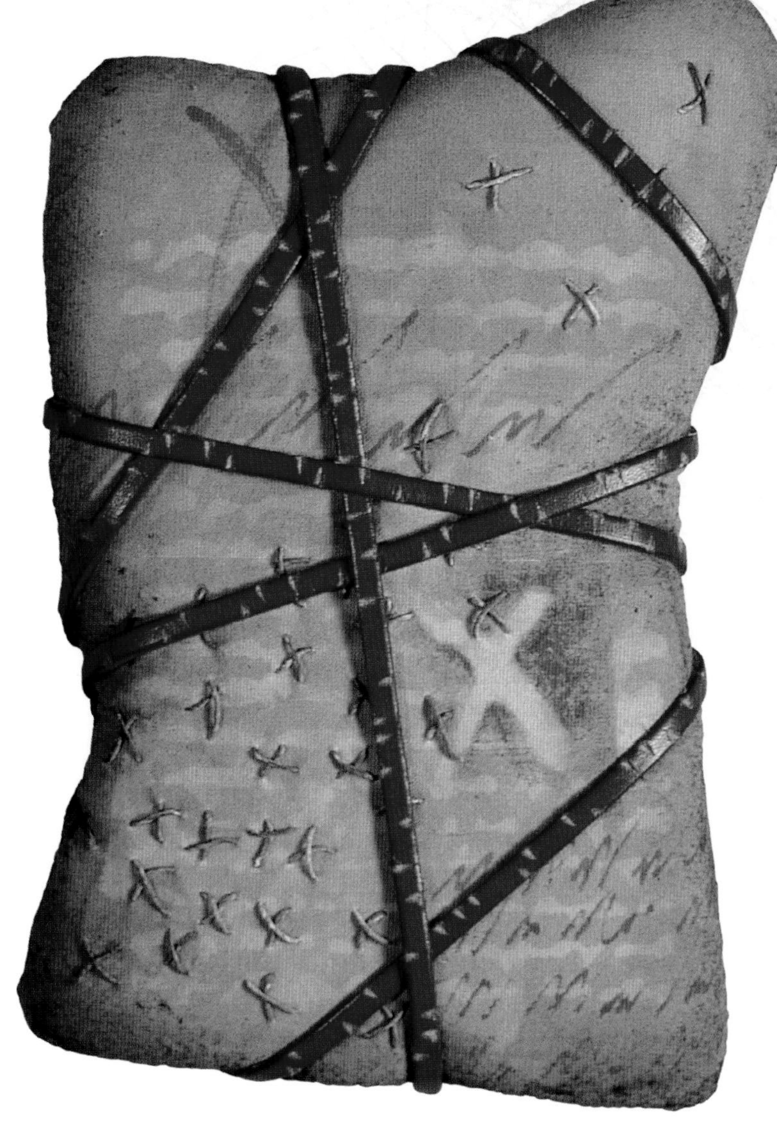

▲ **Memory Bundle, No. 6** | 2004

6½ x 4½ x ½ inches (16.5 x 11.4 x 1.3 cm)
Cotton cloths, leather thong, waxed thread;
fiber-reactive dyed, painted, stitched

Photo by artist

" When working on my pieces I find satisfaction in using materials like papyrus, ivory, and clay. Used by early bookmakers, these materials are historically significant. "

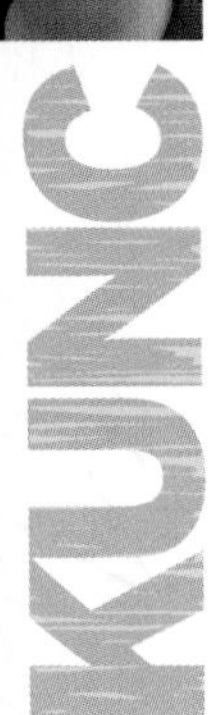

Karen Kunc

A FULL SPECTRUM OF SATURATED COLOR and dynamic imagery fills the pages of Karen Kunc's books. A recognized master of the woodcut, she deftly moves between prints and books, using a sophisticated vocabulary of abstract forms. Kunc's books investigate a multiplicity of themes. She expertly guides the reader through each piece by developing complex narratives—stories that require connections and interpretations on the part of viewers based on their personal experiences.

Kunc's aesthetic blends the humorous with the edgy. Her work addresses life issues and the perennial cycle of birth and renewal, offering rich allusions and compositional juxtapositions that are politically charged and poetically meaningful. Kunc has participated in exhibits around the world. Her work is in the Museum of Modern Art in New York City; the Smithsonian American Art Museum in Washington, D.C.; and the Machida Museum of Graphic Art in Tokyo, Japan. She lives in Avoca, Nebraska.

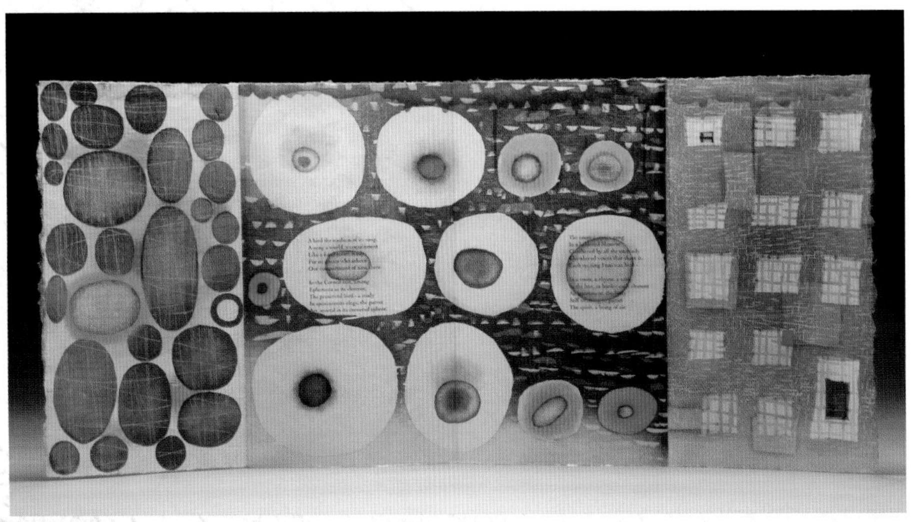

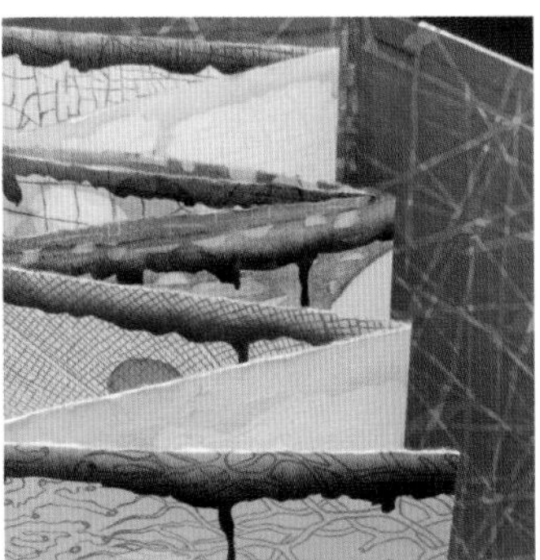

▲ **Ephemera** | 2009

Unfolded: 10 x 42 inches (25.4 x 106.7 cm)
Japanese paper, covered boards, leather; accordion binding with gatefold, woodcut, letterpress printed

Photos by Larry Ferguson

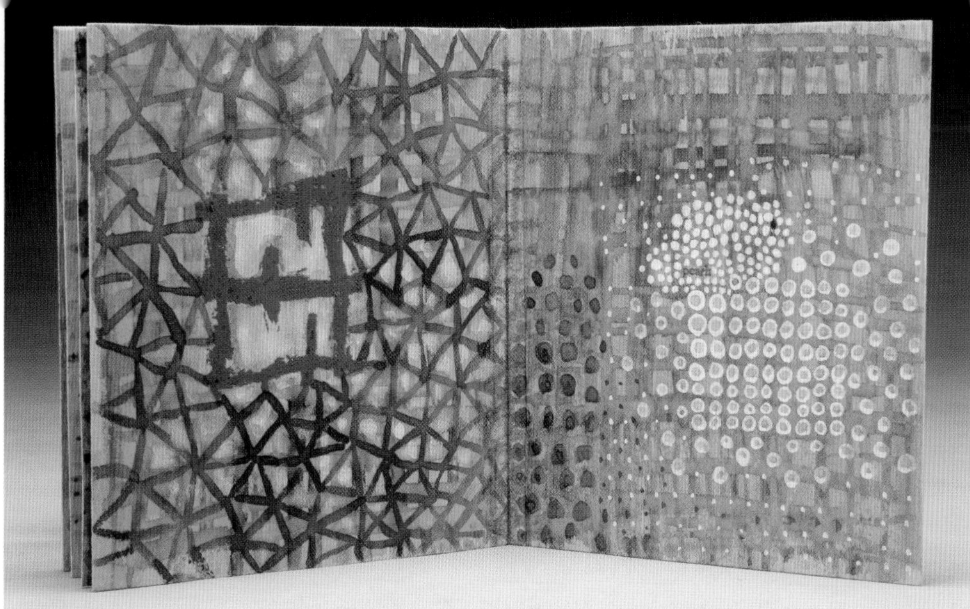

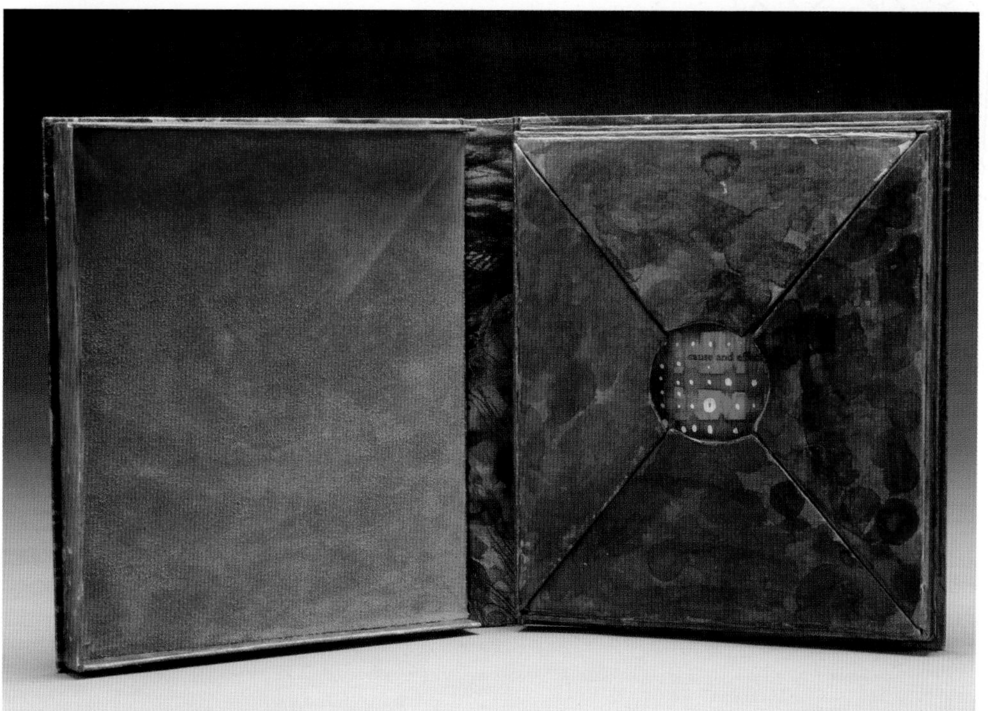

◀ **Cause and Effect** | 2006

7 x 6 x ¼ inches
(17.8 x 15.2 x 0.6 cm)
Wood veneer, covered box, leather, watercolor; pasted binding, screen-printed

Photos by Larry Ferguson

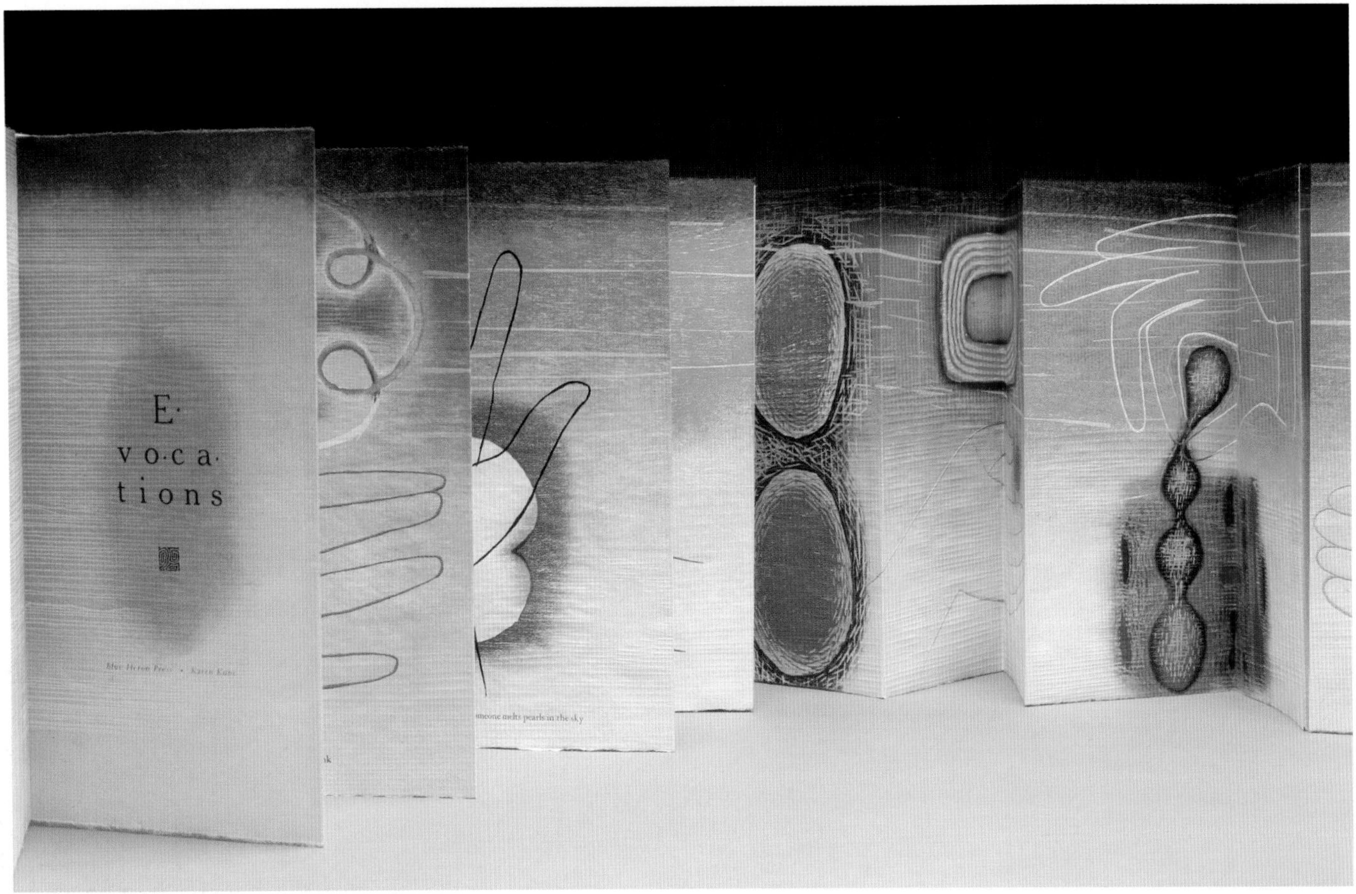

▲ **Evocations** | 2006

Unfolded: 9¼ x 108 inches (23.5 x 274.3 cm)
Japanese paper, covered board, book cloth, wax; woodcut, etched, letterpress printed, accordion binding

Photos by Larry Ferguson

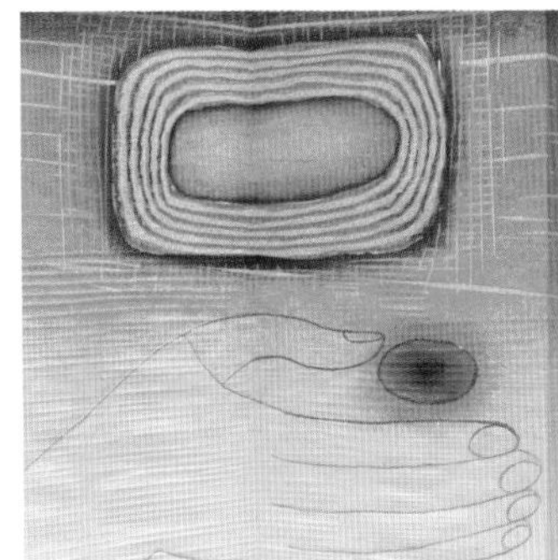

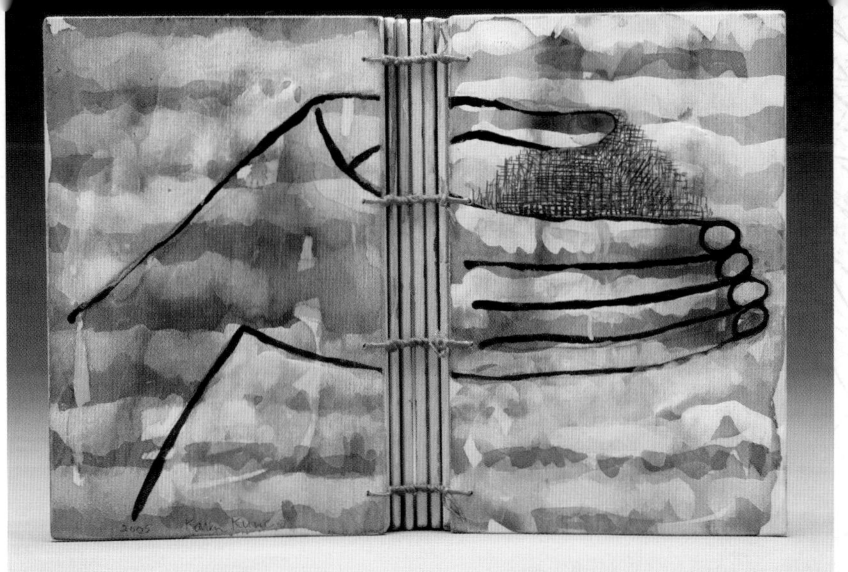

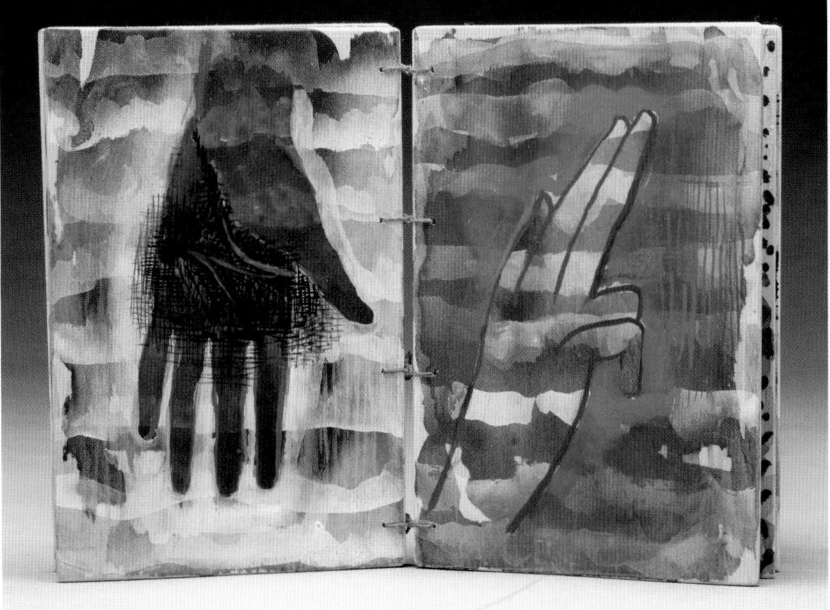

▲ **Gesture** | 2005

6 x 4 x 1 inches (15.2 x 10.2 x 2.5 cm)
Basswood, watercolor, decorative box; sewn binding
Photos by Larry Ferguson

" The relationship of word and image is a driving force for me. Finding the right words—words that will flow across the pages and fit my visual elements—challenges me. "

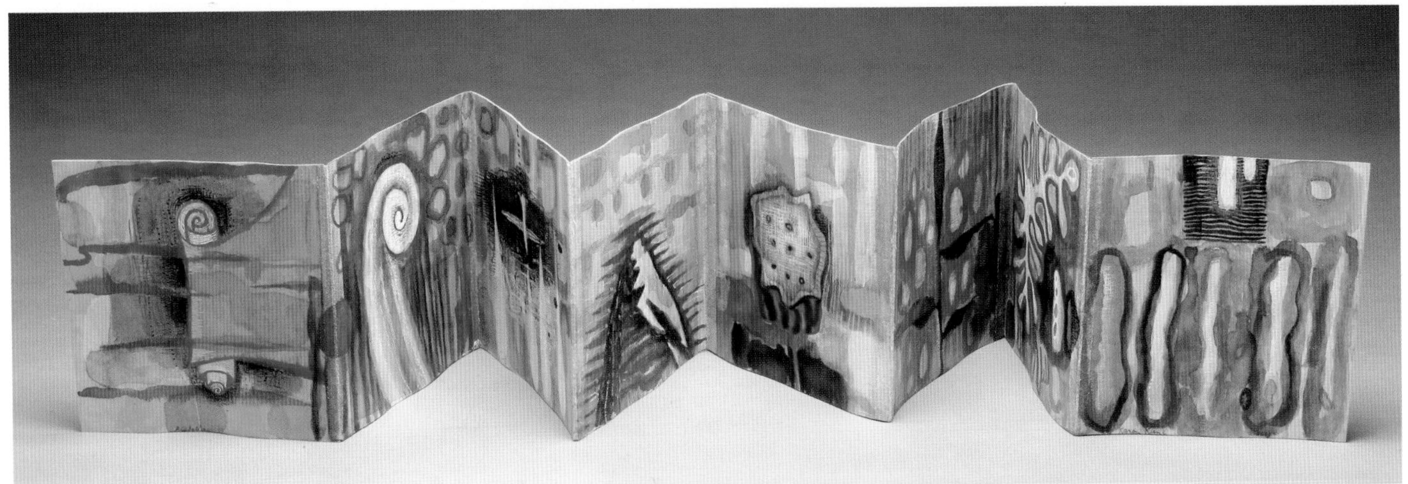

▲ **Predella** | 2003

Unfolded: 6 x 48 inches (15.2 x 121.9 cm)
Wood veneer, watercolor; accordion binding
Photos by Larry Ferguson

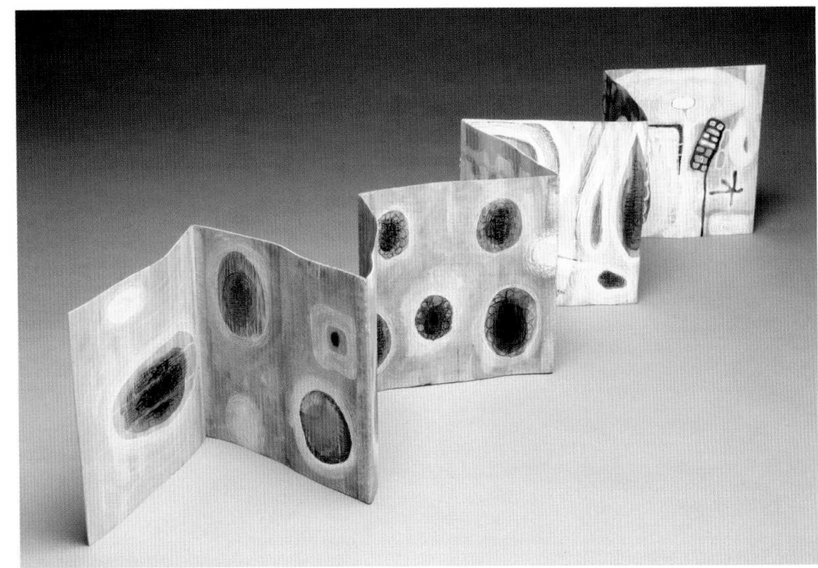

" Many of my books rely on the expansive, workable format of the accordion structure, with its flowing, horizontal orientations, fold-outs, and gatefolds. I use the horizontal flow to create a sort of visual-sensory threshold across the printed pages. "

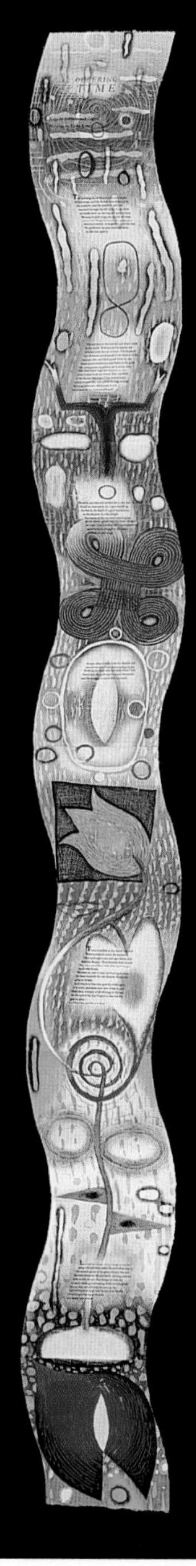

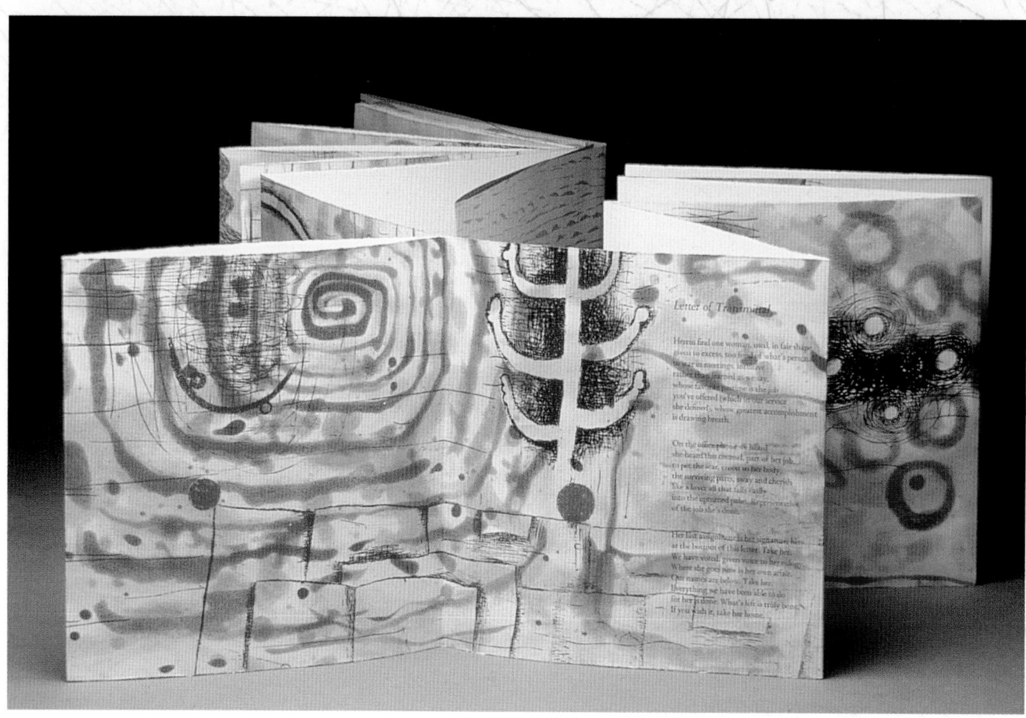

▲ **Truly Bone** | 1998

Folded: 7½ x 7½ inches (19.1 x 19.1 cm)
Unfolded: 7½ x 150 inches (19.1 x 381 cm)

Italian Alcantara paper; accordion binding, etched, spit-bite aquatint, drypoint, letterpress printed

Photo by Larry Ferguson

◀ **Offering Time** | 2001

Folded: 6¾ x 8 inches (17.1 x 20.3 cm)
Unfolded: 6¾ x 78 inches (17.1 x 198.1 cm)

Japanese paper, covered boards; accordion folded, woodcut, letterpress printed

Photo by Larry Ferguson

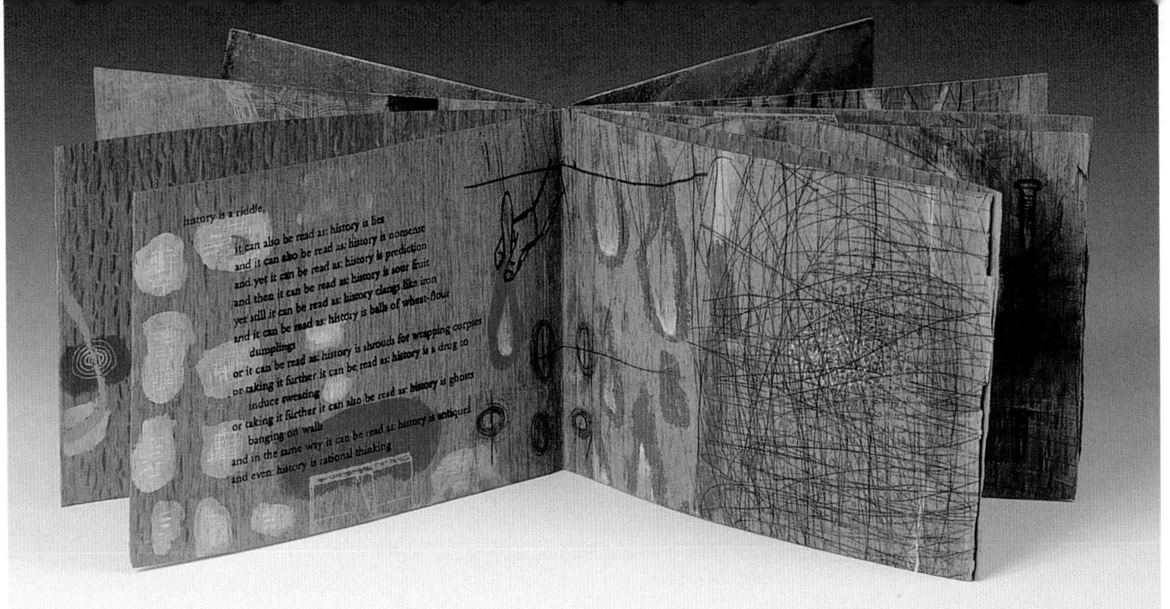

▲ **History Book** | 2002

5¼ x 7¼ x ½ inches (13.3 x 18.4 x 1.3 cm)
Brazilwood veneer, gampi paper, wax, altered found box; pasted binding, screen-printed, etched, collage

Photo by Larry Ferguson

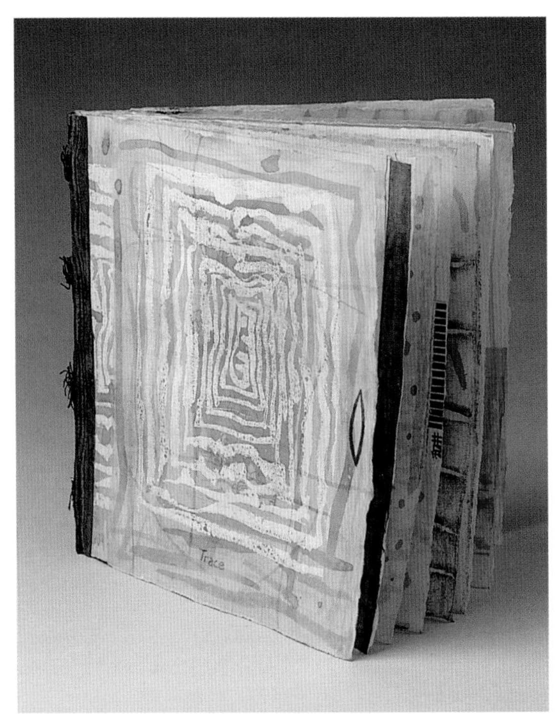

Trace | 2002 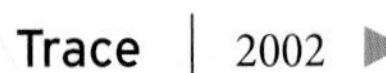

12 x 12 x ½ inches (30.5 x 30.5 x 1.3 cm)
Japanese paper, beeswax, found papers, powdered pigments; sewn binding, screen-printed, collage

Photo by Larry Ferguson

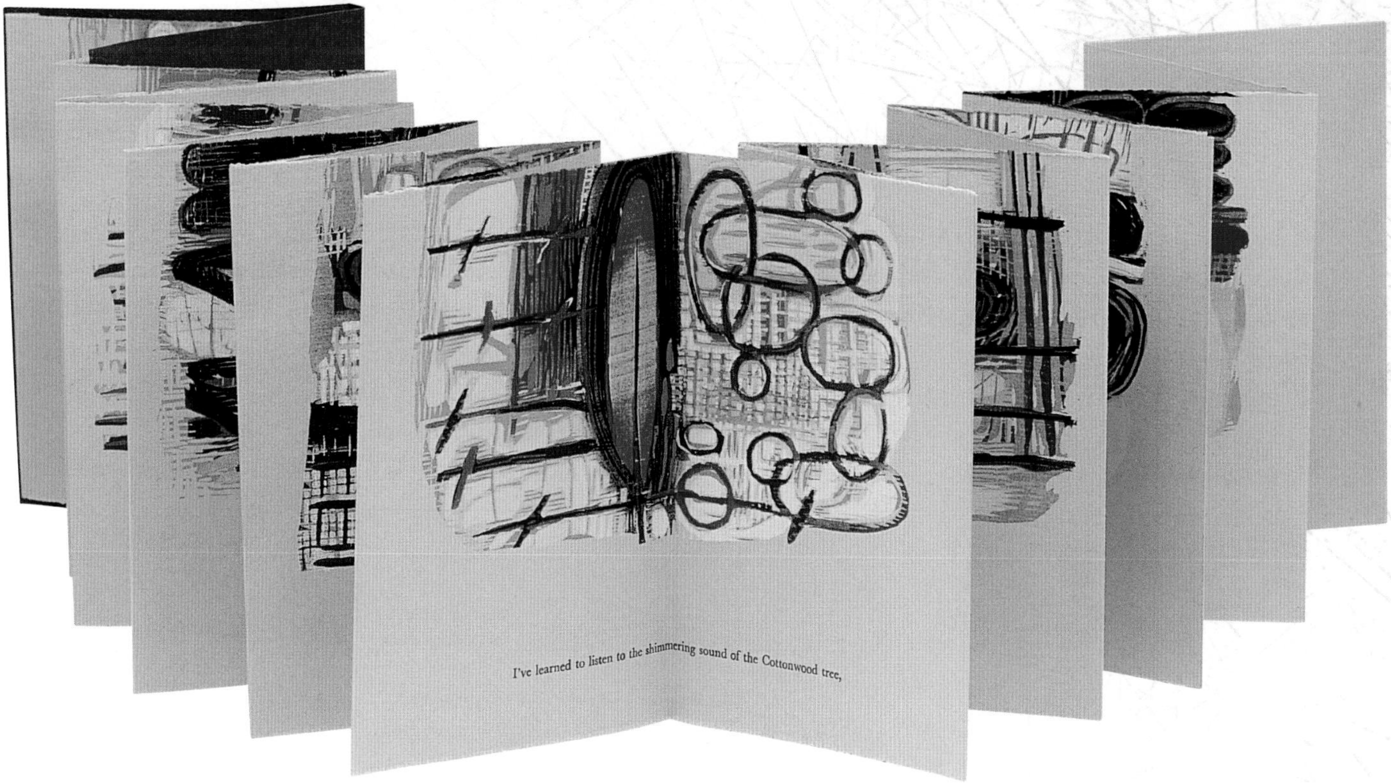

▲ **On This Land** | 1996

Unfolded: 7½ x 102 inches (19.1 x 259.1 cm)
Nideggen paper, linen paper; accordion binding, woodcut, letterpress printed
Photo by Larry Ferguson

> " My books are explorations into how we make things, into questions of creativity. How do we move from chaos to order, from chance to meaningfulness? "

MADDEN

Peter Madden

JOURNEYS TO EXOTIC DESTINATIONS AND ORDINARY walks around the block are celebrated equally in the travelogue books of Peter Madden. Reminiscent of pieced quilts and hand-stitched textiles, his work has an appealing simplicity that reflects a scaled-back aesthetic and a low-tech approach to the creative process. His books are inspired by the human need to record memories, share experiences, and connect with the natural world.

Madden often takes traditional book structures and adapts them to unusual materials, such as copper, wood, and burlap. A frequent experimenter, he uses the formal components of a book—the spine, end pages, and title page—in playful ways. His expressive, irregular stitching serves as both a structural and a decorative element. Madden divides his time between Portland, Maine, and Boston, Massachusetts. His work is owned by numerous institutions, including the Institute of Contemporary Art in Boston Massachusetts; the Houghton Library at Harvard University in Cambridge, Massachusetts; and Bowdoin College in Brunswick, Maine.

▲ **Little Blue Italy Book** | 2009

Closed: 6 x 4 x 3 inches (15.2 x 10.2 x 7.6 cm)
Open: 6 x 24 inches (15.2 x 61 cm)

Copper, wood, cyanotypes; accordion binding

Photo by Clements/Howcroft

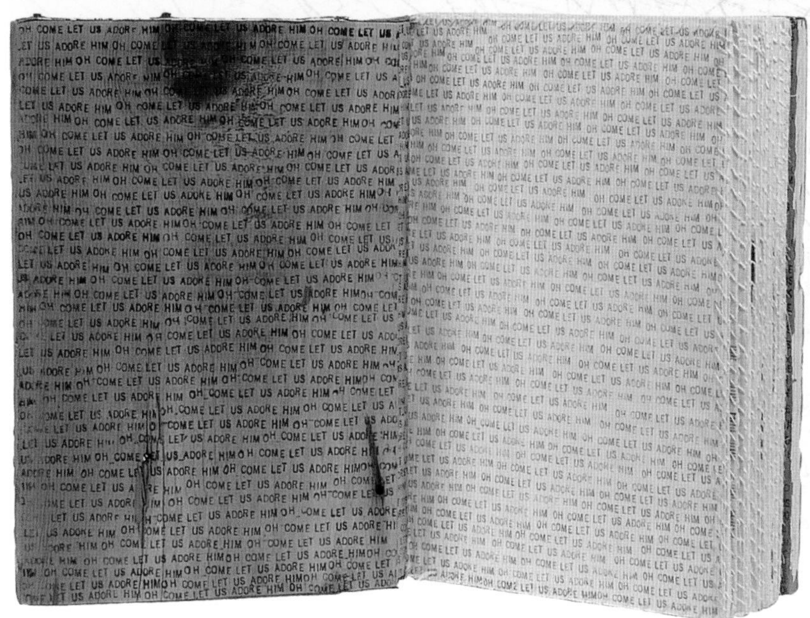

Oh Come Let Us Adore Him | 2007
11 x 8 x 4 inches (27.9 x 20.3 x 10.2 cm)
Found scrap wood, cotton, rubber stamping
Photo by Clements/Howcroft

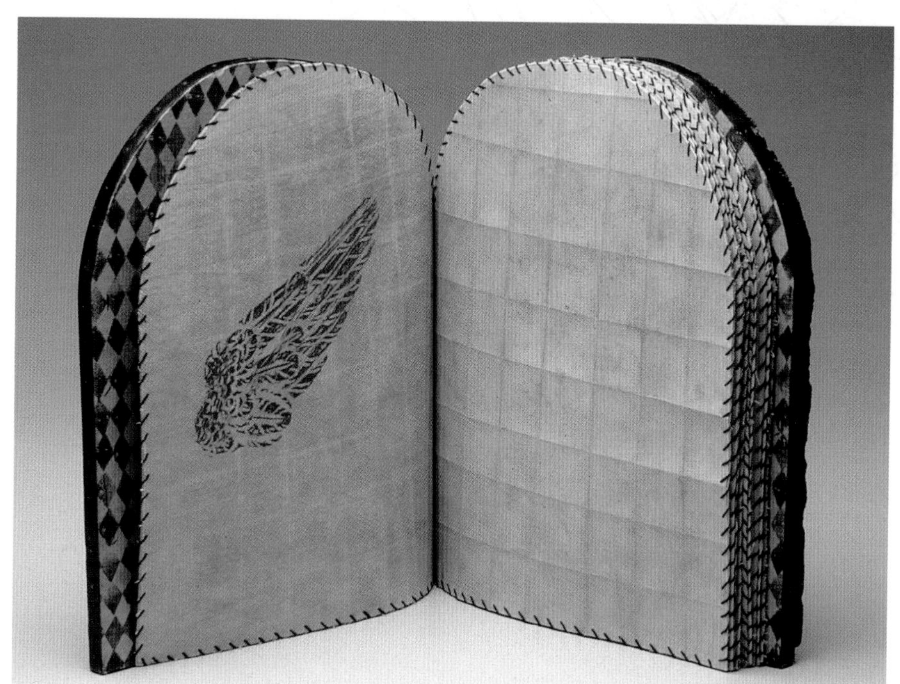

Misguided Angels | 2004
16 x 11 x 3 inches (40.6 x 27.9 x 7.6 cm)
Slate roof tile, copper, wood, gravestone rubbings on cotton and paper
Photo by Dana Salvo

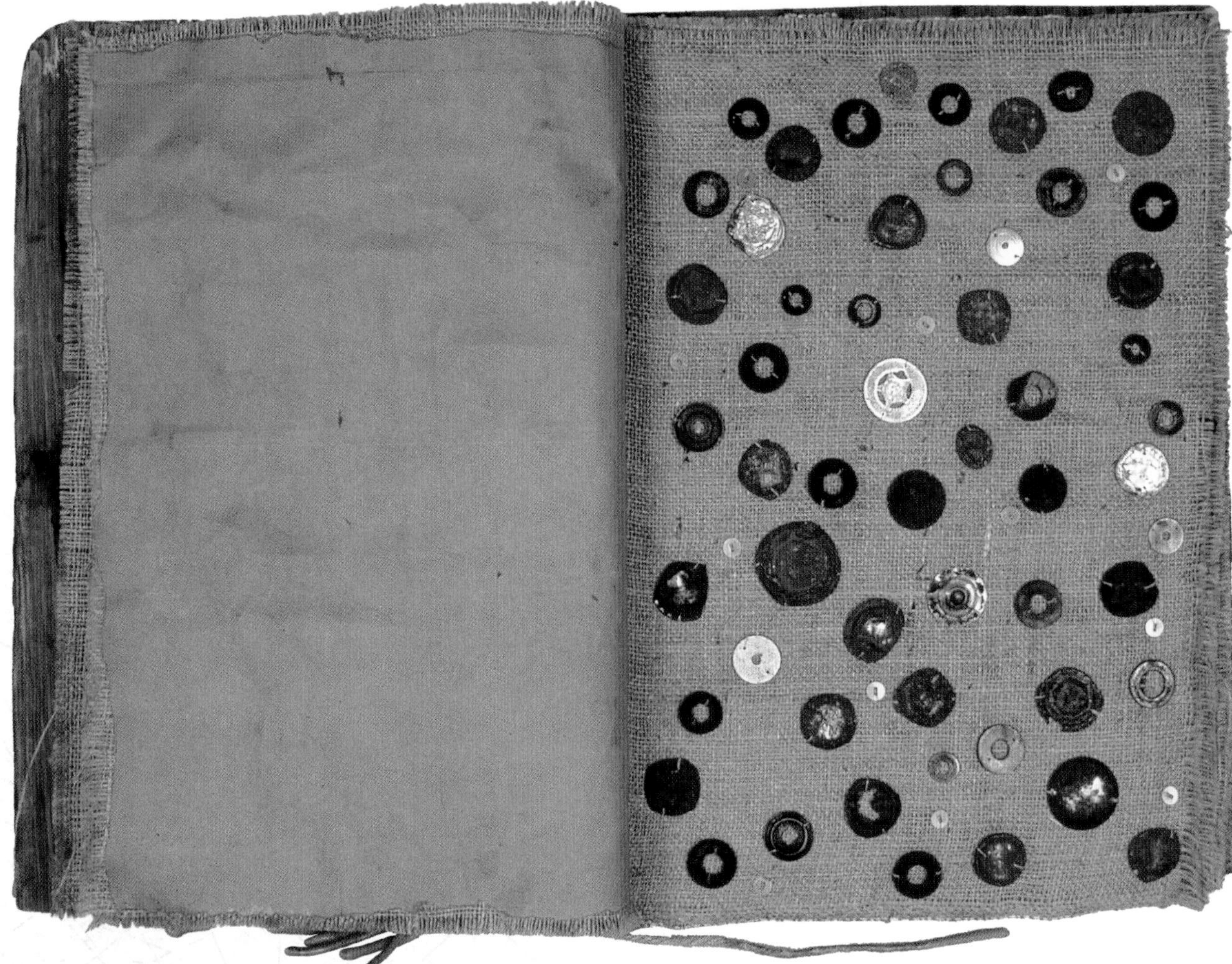

▲ **Scrap Book #1** | 2000

26 x 17 x 3 inches (66 x 43.2 x 7.6 cm)
Found scrap wood, packing twine, beeswax, burlap, brown paper bag, scrap metal; modified Japanese side-sewn binding

Photo by Dana Salvo

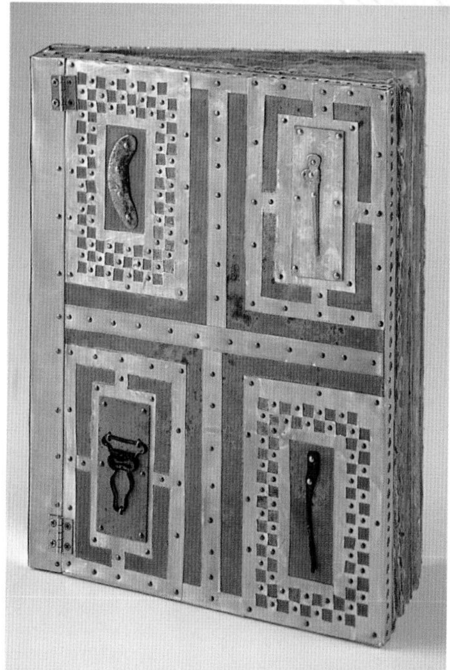

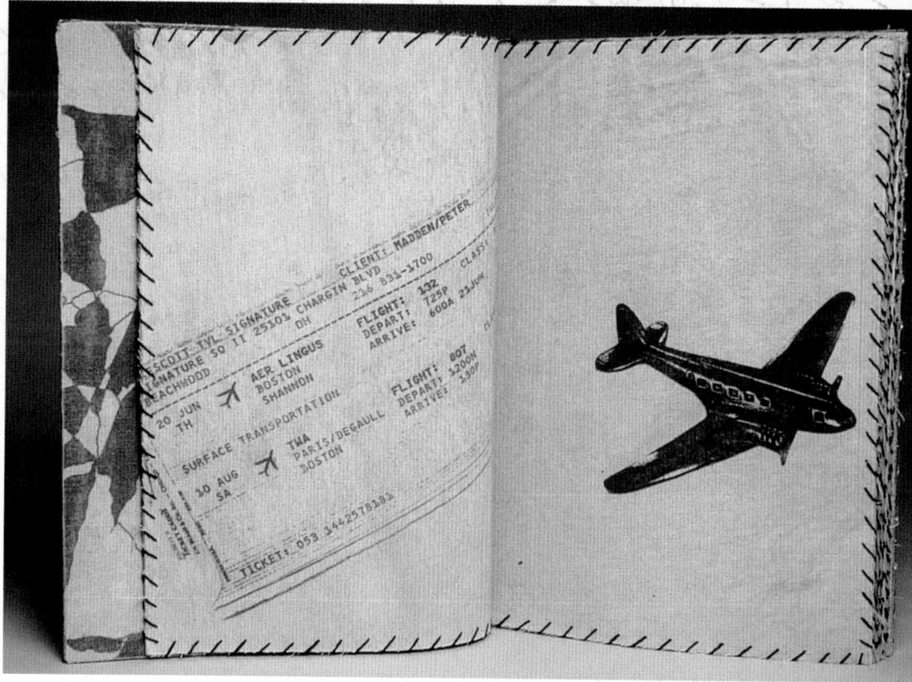

▲ **Ireland Journal** | 2000

9 x 11 x 3 inches (22.9 x 27.9 x 7.6 cm)
Copper, wood, aluminum, found objects, cotton paper, solvent transfers; modified Japanese side-sewn binding
Photos by artist

" I'm inspired by volumes that were made during the Middle Ages and the Renaissance, when books were considered precious objects. For this reason, I exclusively make one-of-a-kind or small-edition books. "

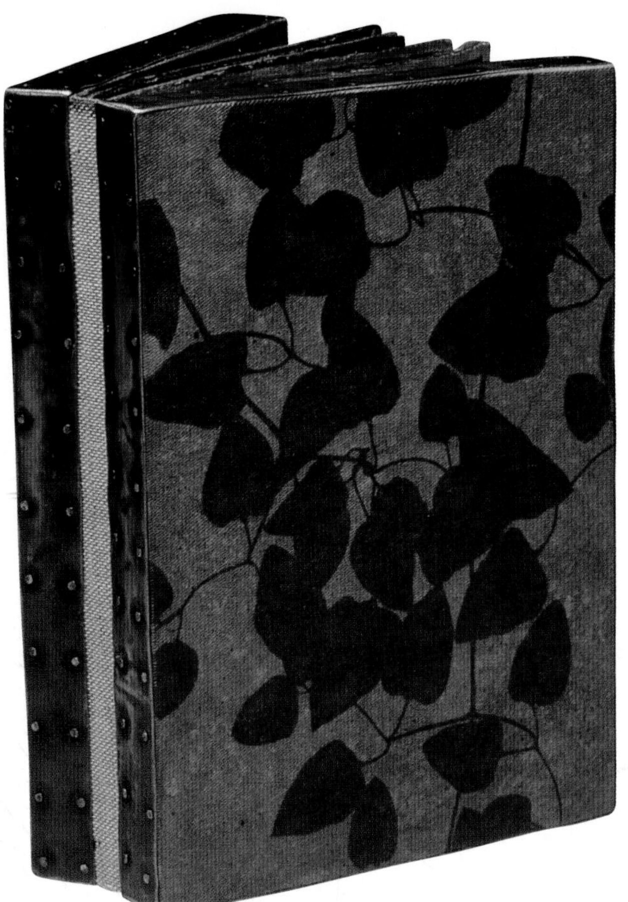

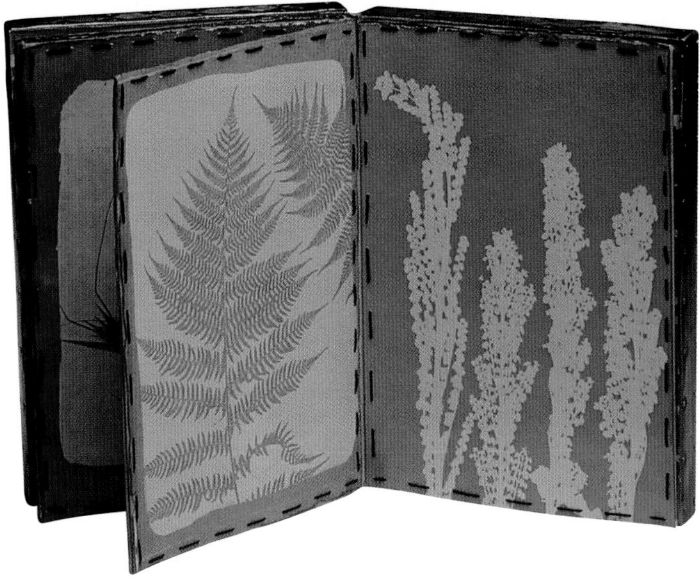

◀ **Garden Book** | 2009

9 x 6½ x 3 inches (22.9 x 16.5 x 7.6 cm)
Wood, cotton paper, linen, copper; dyed cyanotypes
Photos by Clements/Howcroft

" I've made books in one form or another since I was a kid. One of my first creations featured dayglow paintings of caves and Martians. It was bound with pink thread and yellow electrical tape. I still have it. "

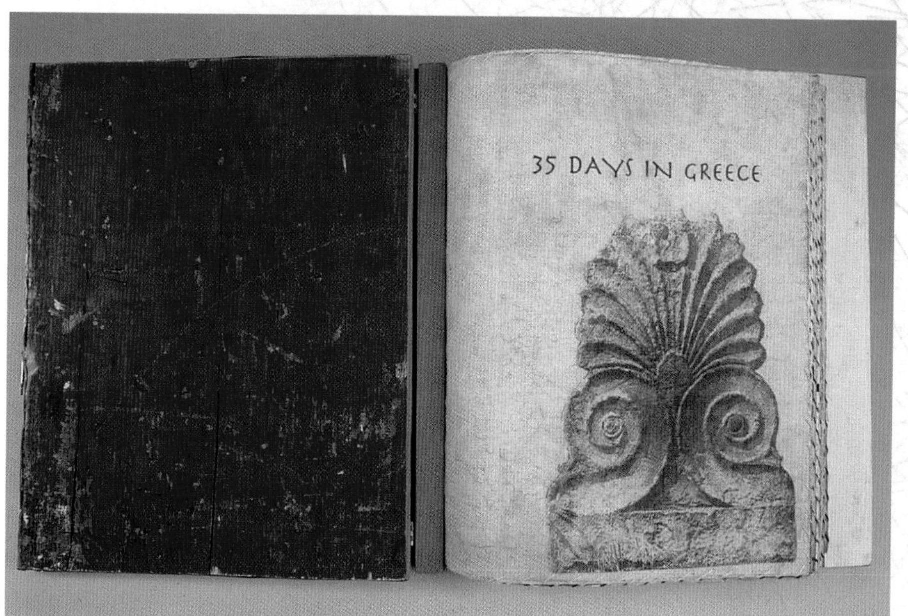

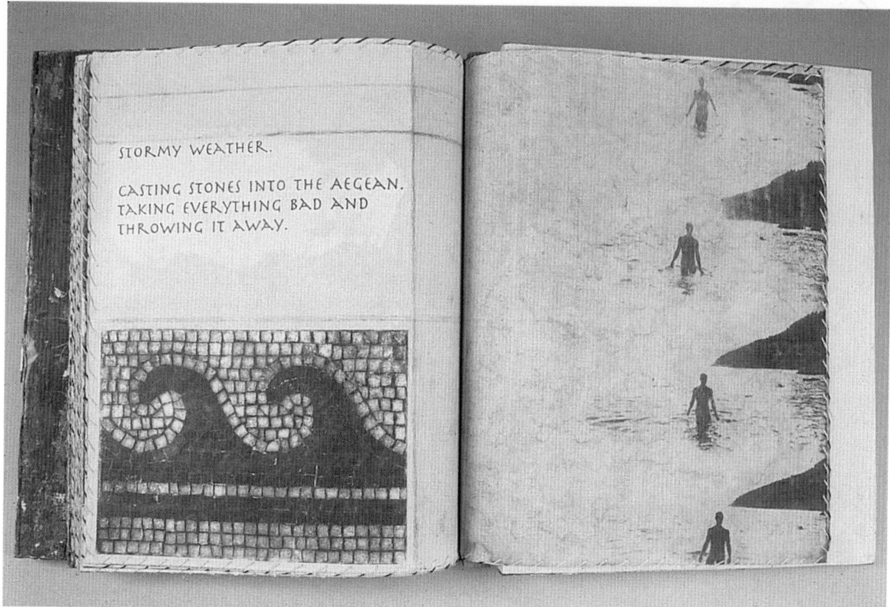

◀ **35 Days in Greece** | 2001

21 x 17 x 4 inches (53.3 x 43.2 x 10.2 cm)
Found wood, cotton, paper, copper, solvent transfers

Photos by Clements/Howcroft

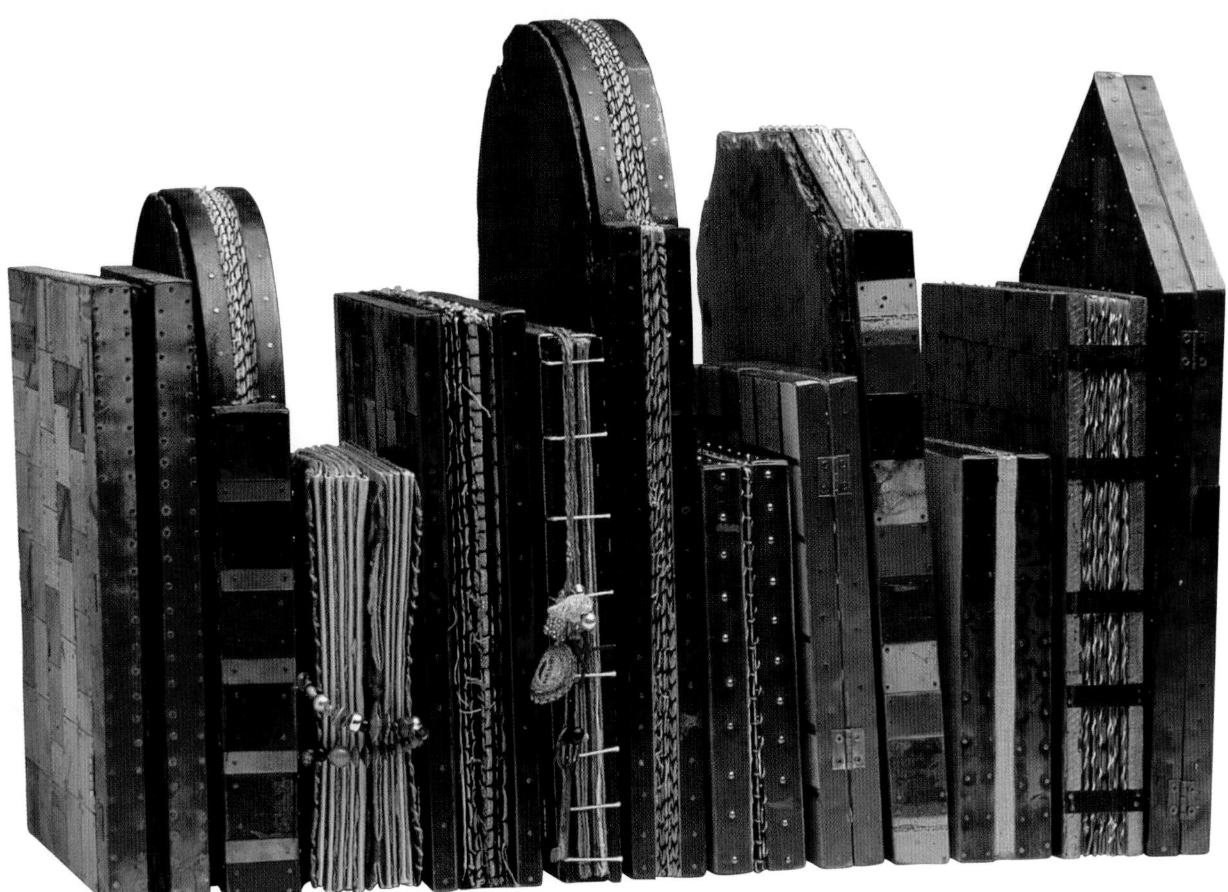

▲ **Various Bindings** | 2009

Various dimensions
Wood, copper, brass, slate, leather, handmade paper, found objects, wax
Photo by Clements/Howcroft

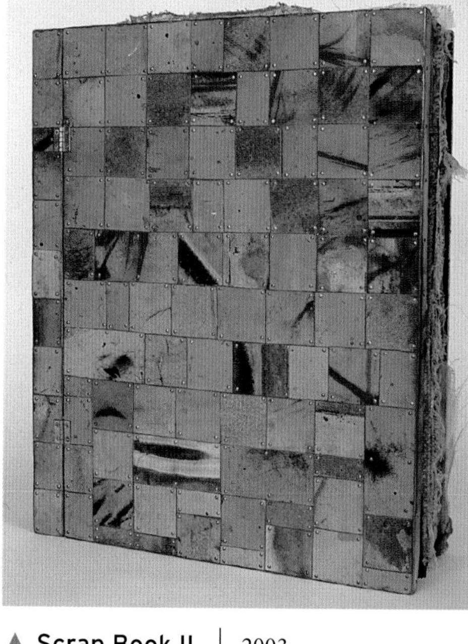

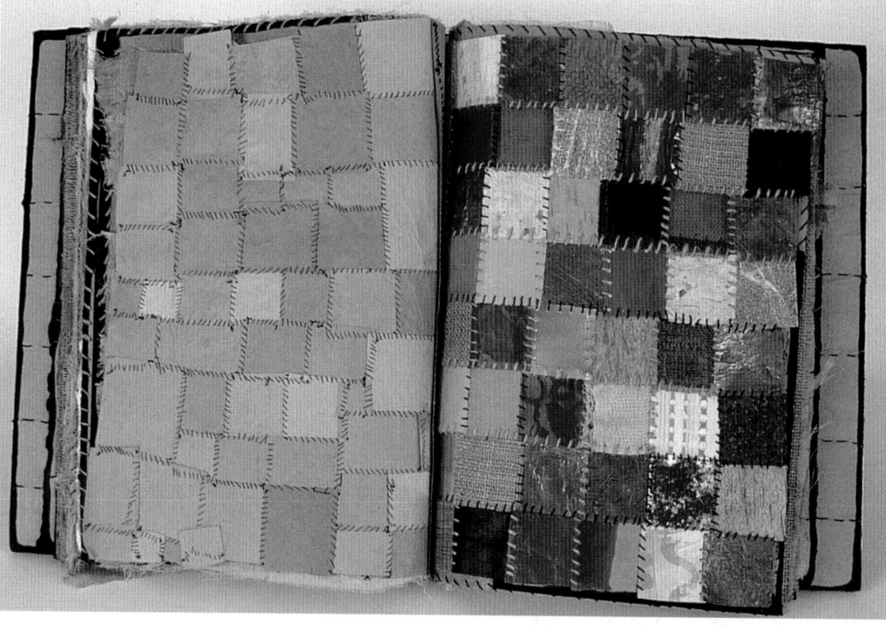

▲ **Scrap Book II** | 2003

16 x 14 x 3½ inches (40.6 x 35.6 x 8.9 cm)
Wood, copper, brass nails, brown paper bag, mixed media; modified Japanese side-sewn binding

Photos by Clements/Howcroft

" One of the many reasons that I love this medium is that it gives me the flexibility to include almost anything in my work. Over the years, I've fallen in love with and incorporated so many materials—everything from my grandmother's crocheting from the early 1900s to cherry and olive pits and broken furniture. "

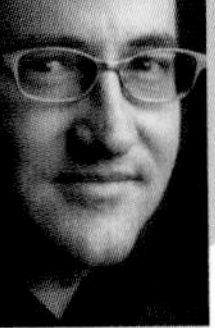

Wilber Schilling

THE COMPLEX, BEAUTIFULLY EXECUTED books made by Wilbur Schilling blend creative adaptations of traditional design with inspired embellishment. With meticulous attention to detail and great technical fluency, Schilling considers each facet of a book during the creative process, focusing on content and making typographic and structural choices that support his conceptual premises. His works are always cohesive.

Schilling's pieces are deeply rooted in the time-honored traditions of printing and bookbinding, yet they also beautifully incorporate new technologies and materials. While maintaining the integrity of the handmade book, he offers a creative vision for the future. Schilling lives in Minneapolis, Minnesota. His work has been collected by the British Library in London, England; the Library of Congress, in Washington, D.C.; and the Whitney Museum of American Art in New York City.

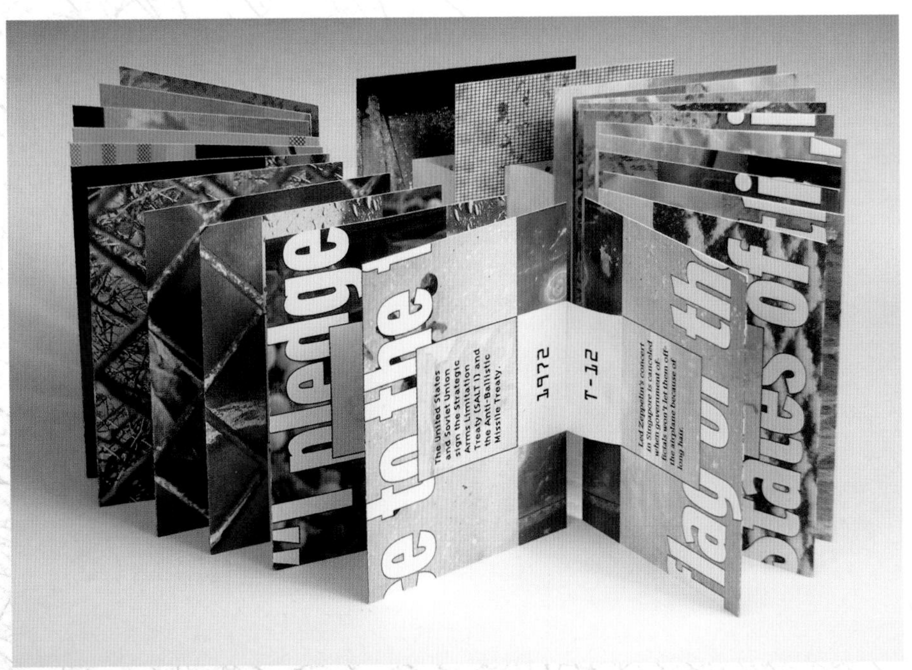

Half Life/Full Life | 2009

4 x 5 x ¾ inches
(10.2 x 12.7 x 1.9 cm)
Epson paper, Tyvek; woven-structure binding, inkjet printed, letterpress printed
Photo by artist

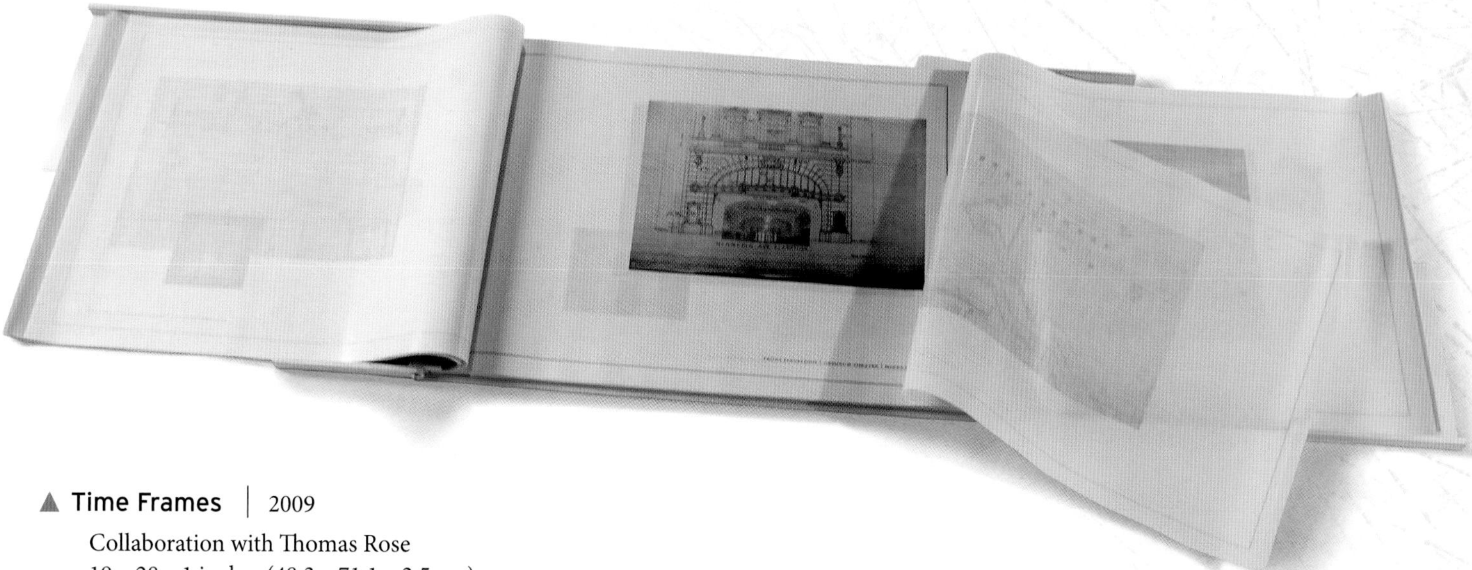

▲ **Time Frames** | 2009

Collaboration with Thomas Rose
19 x 28 x 1 inches (48.3 x 71.1 x 2.5 cm)
Antique drafting vellum, aluminum-machined covers; sandblast etched, inkjet printed with UV inks

Photo by artist

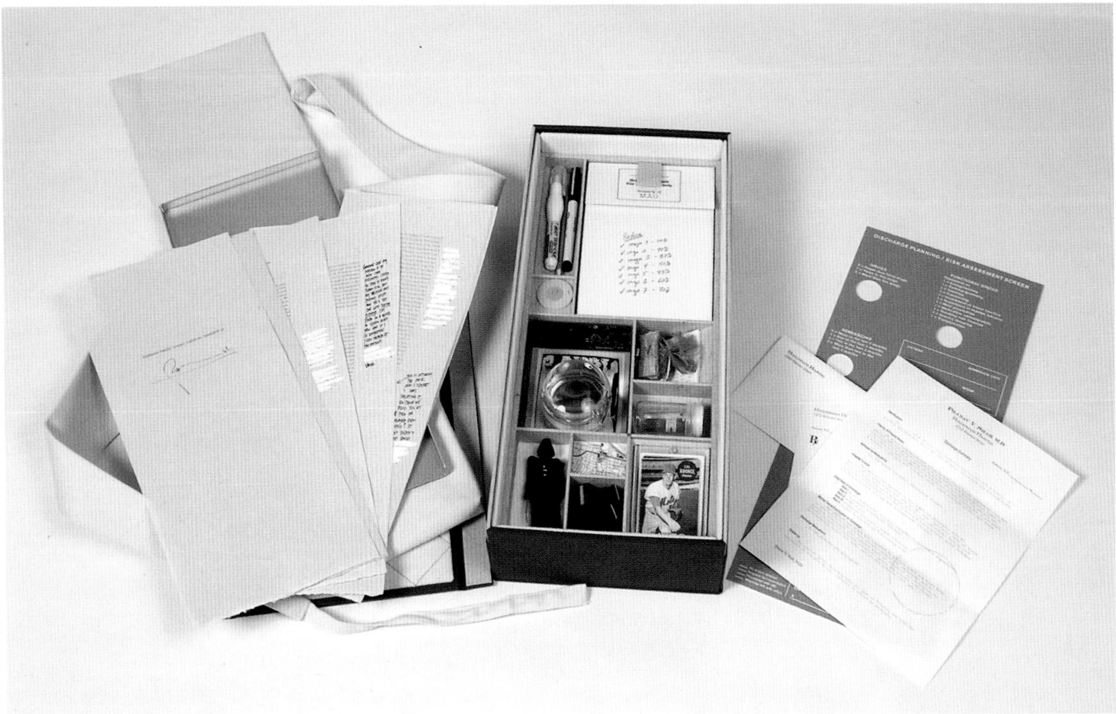

▲ Surplus Value Books #13 (Deluxe Edition) | 2004

Collaboration with Daniel E. Kelm
19 x 9 x 4½ inches (48.3 x 22.9 x 11.4 cm)
Cave handmade flax paper, found objects, various papers, fabric, canvas, correction fluid; laser cut, straight jacket binding, letterpress printed

Written by Rick Moody
Illustrated by David Ford
Binding by Daniel E. Kelm
Photo by artist

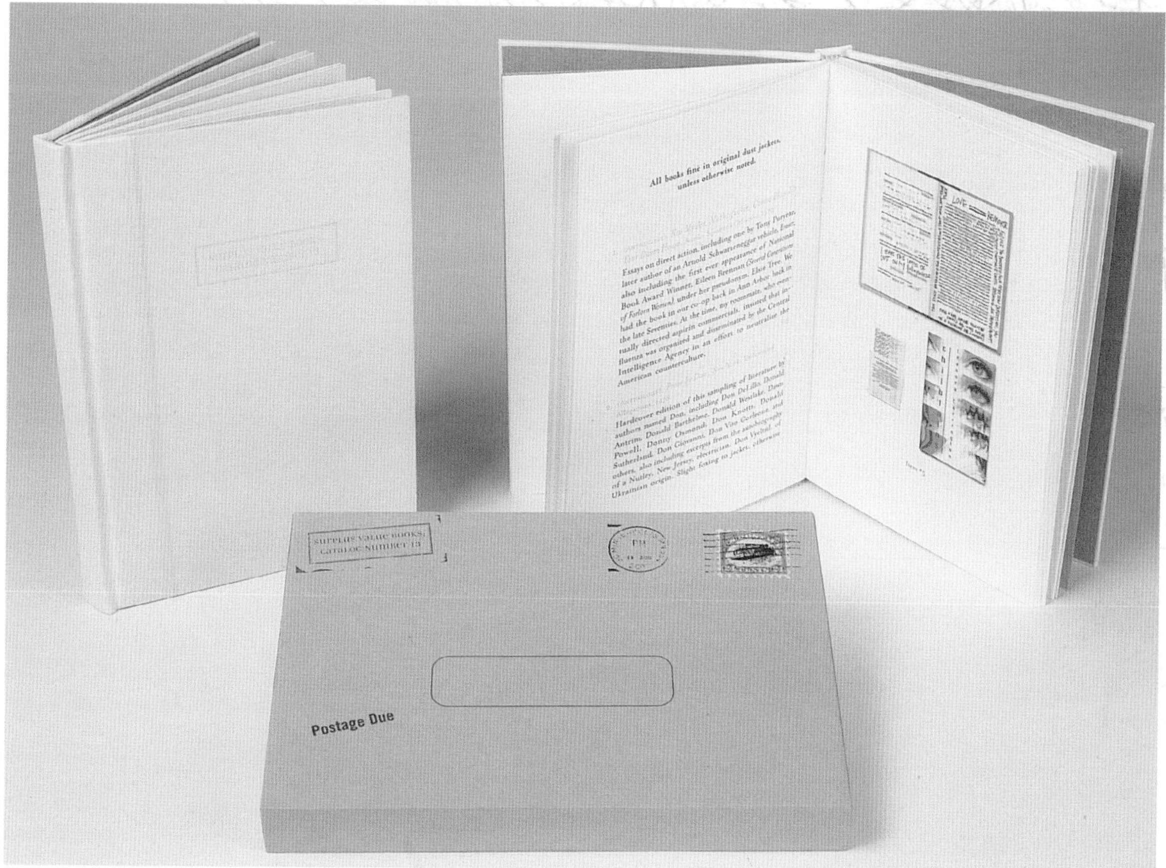

▲ **Surplus Value Books (Standard Edition)** | 2003

8 x 5 x 1 inches (20.3 x 12.7 x 2.5 cm)
Somerset paper, leather; case binding, inkjet printed, letterpress printed

Written by Rick Moody
Illustrated by David Ford
Photo by artist

" Book arts is a field of infinite learning, joy, and discovery. I'm constantly challenged by the craft. "

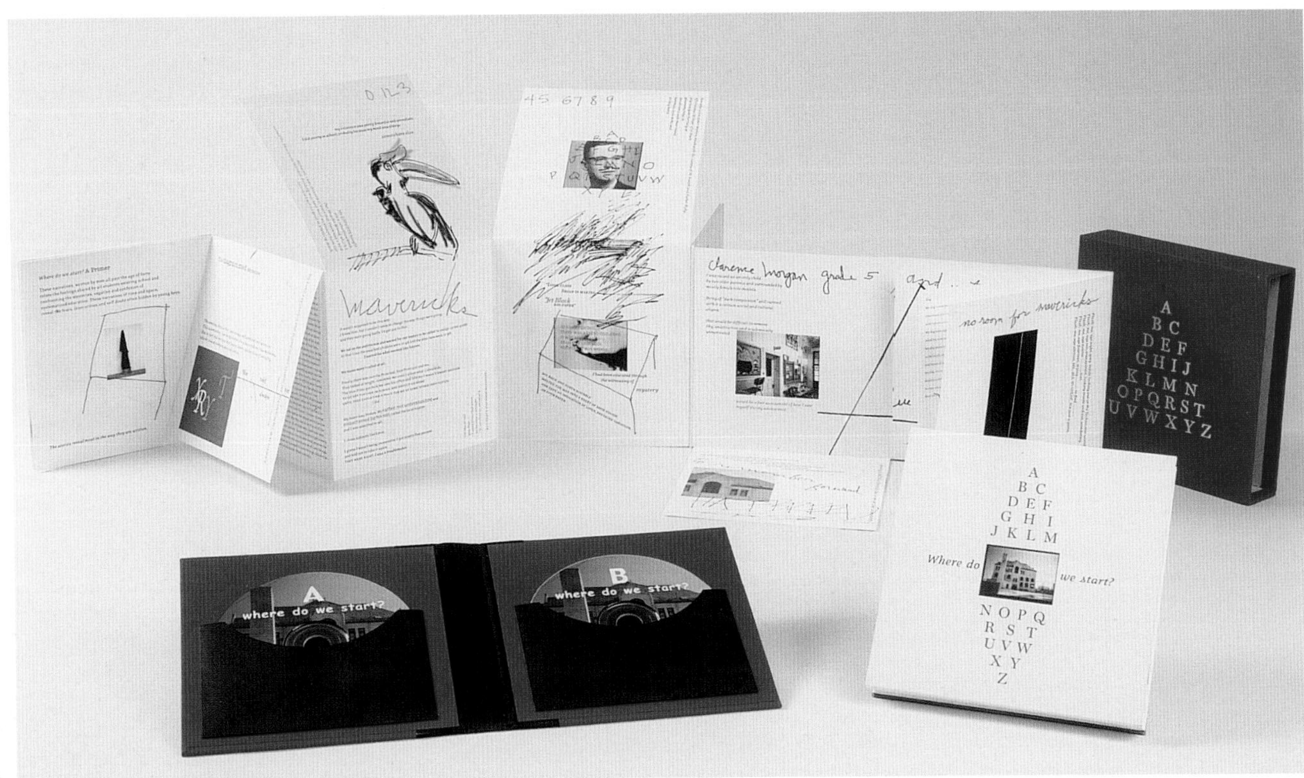

▲ **Where Do We Start?** | 2002

Collaboration with Thomas Rose
6½ x 6½ x 1½ inches (16.5 x 16.5 x 3.8 cm)
Hahnemühle Photo Rag Duo paper, book cloth, binder's board; twisted dos-à-dos binding, inkjet printed, letterpress printed
Illustrated by Thomas Rose
Photo by artist

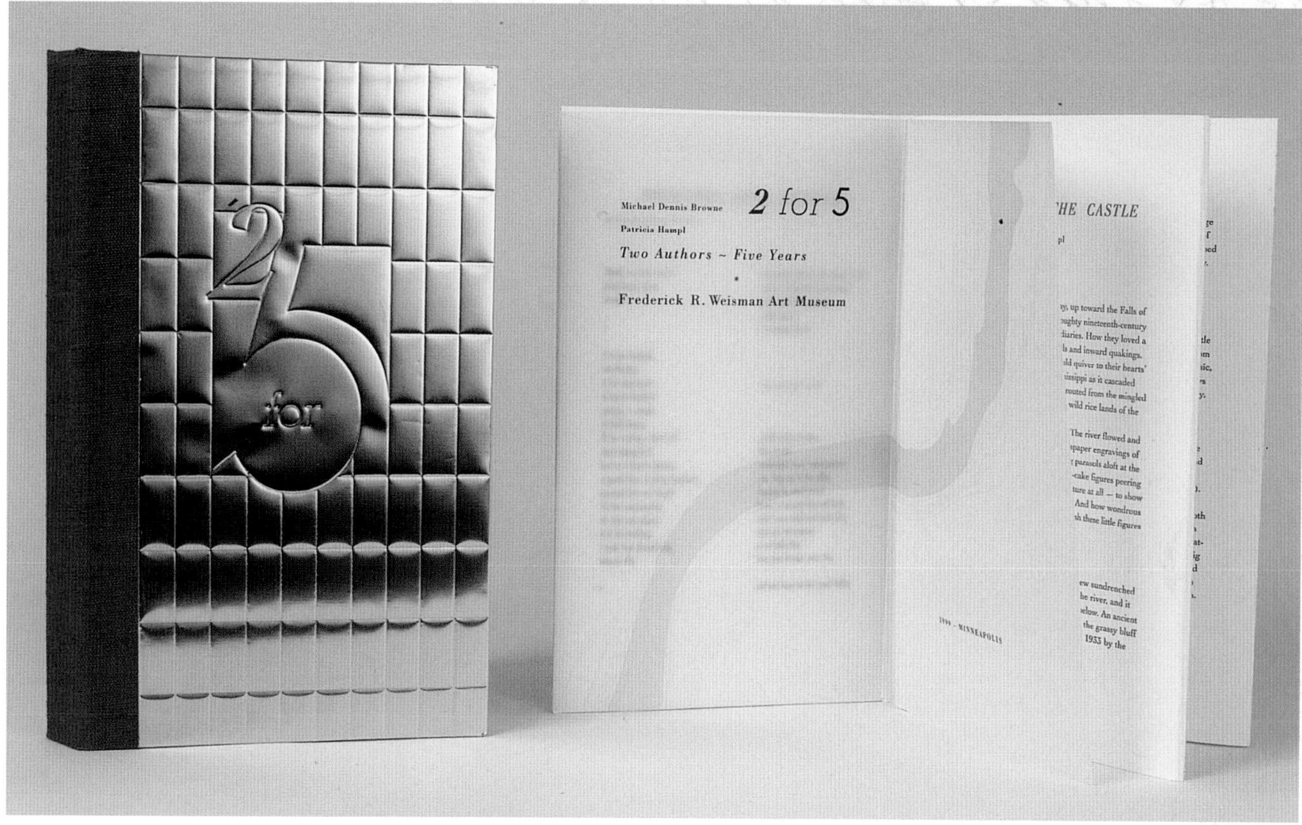

▲ **2 for 5** | 1999

9 x 6 x 1 inches (22.9 x 15.2 x 2.5 cm)
Stonehenge paper, UV Ultra paper, stainless steel, galvanized steel, binder's board, book cloth; non-adhesive binding, letterpress printed
Written by Michael Dennis Brown and Patricia Hemple
Photo by artist

" I believe artist's books should engage the reader on multiple levels, so I add physical and psychological twists to my works. I want the reader to see content in a new way. "

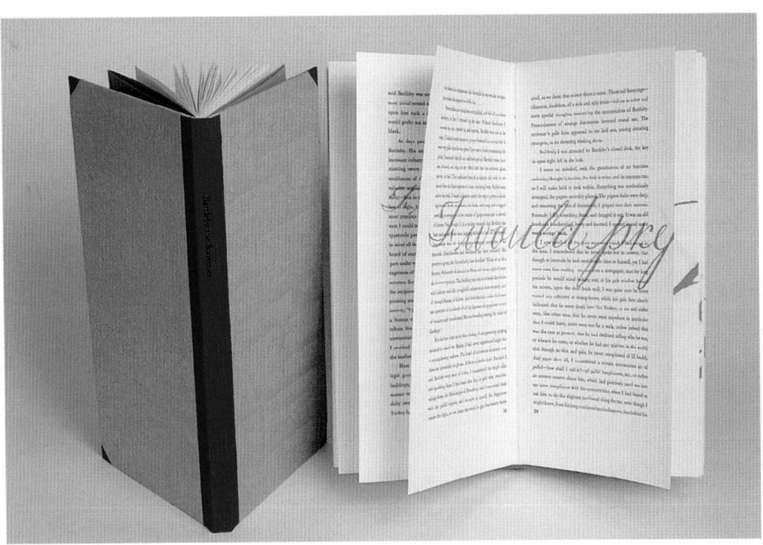

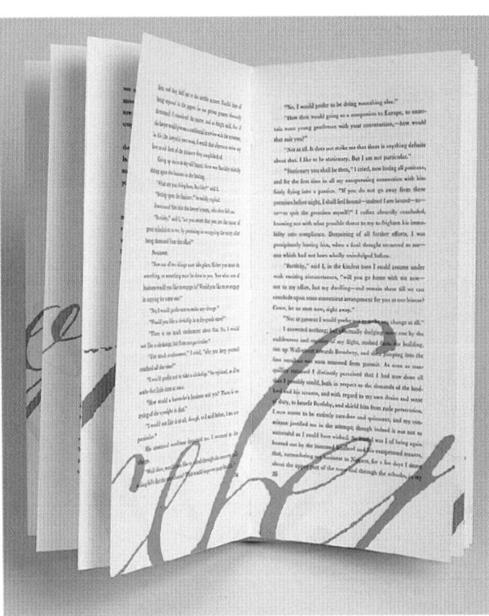

▲ **Bartleby, the Scrivener** | 1995

12 x 6 x ½ inches (30.5 x 15.2 x 1.3 cm)
Arches MBM paper, Canapetta book cloth; sewn-boards binding, Kallitype print, letterpress printed

Written by Herman Melville
Lettering by Suzanne Moore
Photos by artist

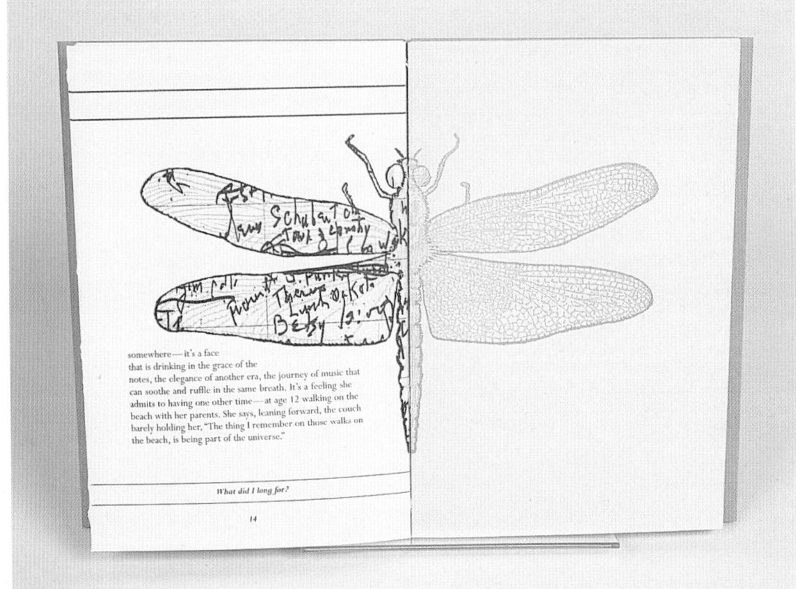

Jane—the Jazz Years | 2000 ▶

9 x 6 x ½ inches (22.9 x 15.2 x 1.3 cm)
Rives paper, Fabriano paper; non-adhesive binding, offset printed, letterpress printed

Written by Kira Obolensky
Photo by artist

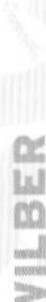

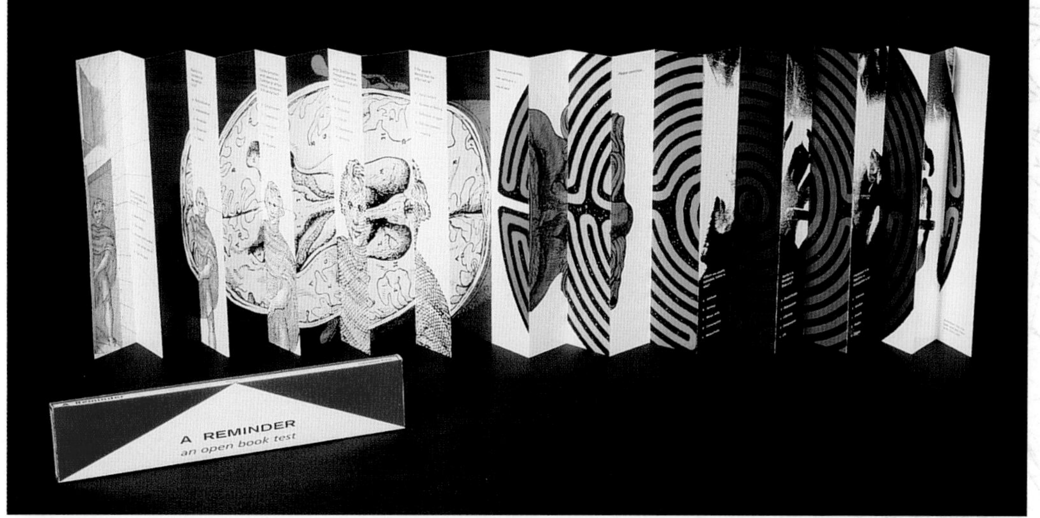

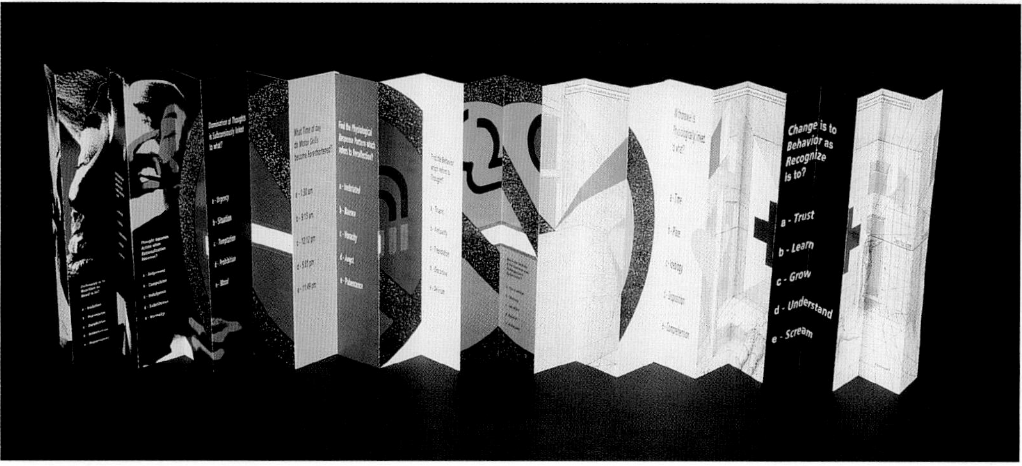

▲ **A Reminder** | 1993

12 x 2 x ¾ inches (30.5 x 5.1 x 1.9 cm)
Mohawk paper; accordion fold structure, offset printed

Printed by Lori Spencer
Photos by artist

" The combination of all the elements that go into a book—paper, printing, bookbinding, words—and how they work together to create a seamless whole is what keeps me excited about this medium. "

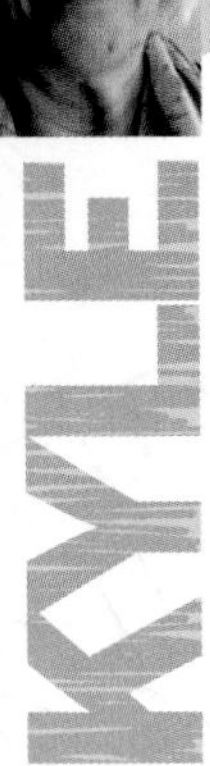

Hedi Kyle

ACKNOWLEDGED AS A MASTER OF INVENTION in the development of innovative book structures, Hedi Kyle has taught and inspired a countless number of book artists. She uses expressive structures as catalysts for giving form to ideas. Skillful and inventive in the use of unexpected materials, Kyle consistently pushes the limits of what can work within the parameters of a book. The transformation and manipulation of materials are key parts of her bookmaking process.

Kyle uses a range of techniques in her books, including collage, stenciling, and stitching, all of which work together to form imaginative compositions. Juxtaposing text and image, she fluently integrates structure, content, and intent in her work.

Kyle's one-of-a-kind book constructions have been exhibited internationally and are in private and public collections around the world. She lives in Philadelphia, Pennsylvania.

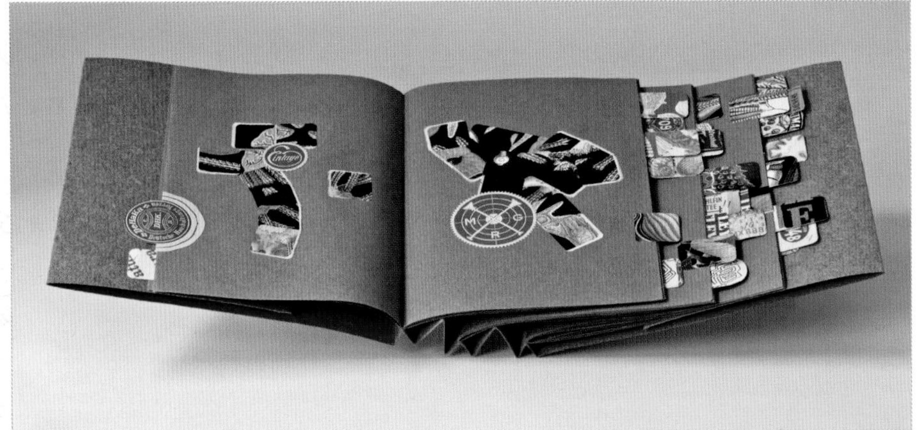

▲ **Sammelsurium I** | 2009

7¼ x 6¾ x 1¼ inches (18.4 x 17.1 x 3.2 cm)
Case handmade paper, Japanese paper, advertising stamps, stickers; inkjet printed, sewn, collage
Photos by Paul Warchol

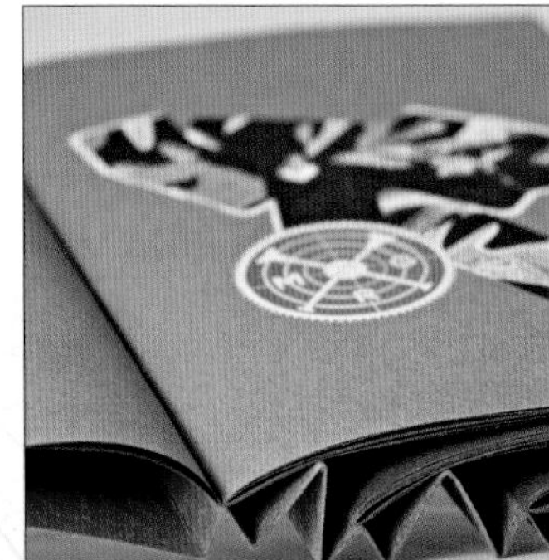

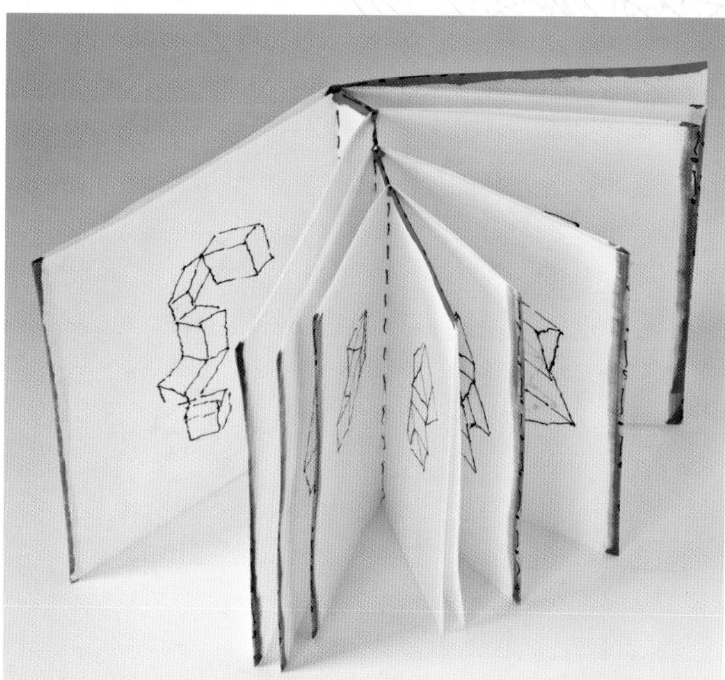

◀ **Three-Dimensional Sketch** | 2008

6 x 4 x ⅛ inches (15.2 x 10.2 x 0.3 cm)
Paper, drawings; fishbone folded
Photo by Paul Warchol

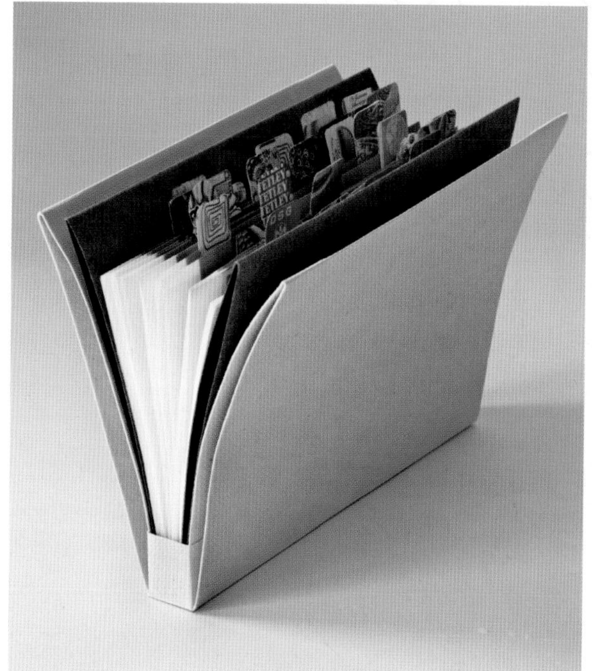

Sammelsurium II | 2009 ▶

8¼ x 6 x ½ inches (21 x 15.2 x 1.3 cm)
Zaan paper, sticker tabs; inkjet printed
Photo by Paul Warchol

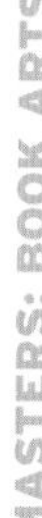

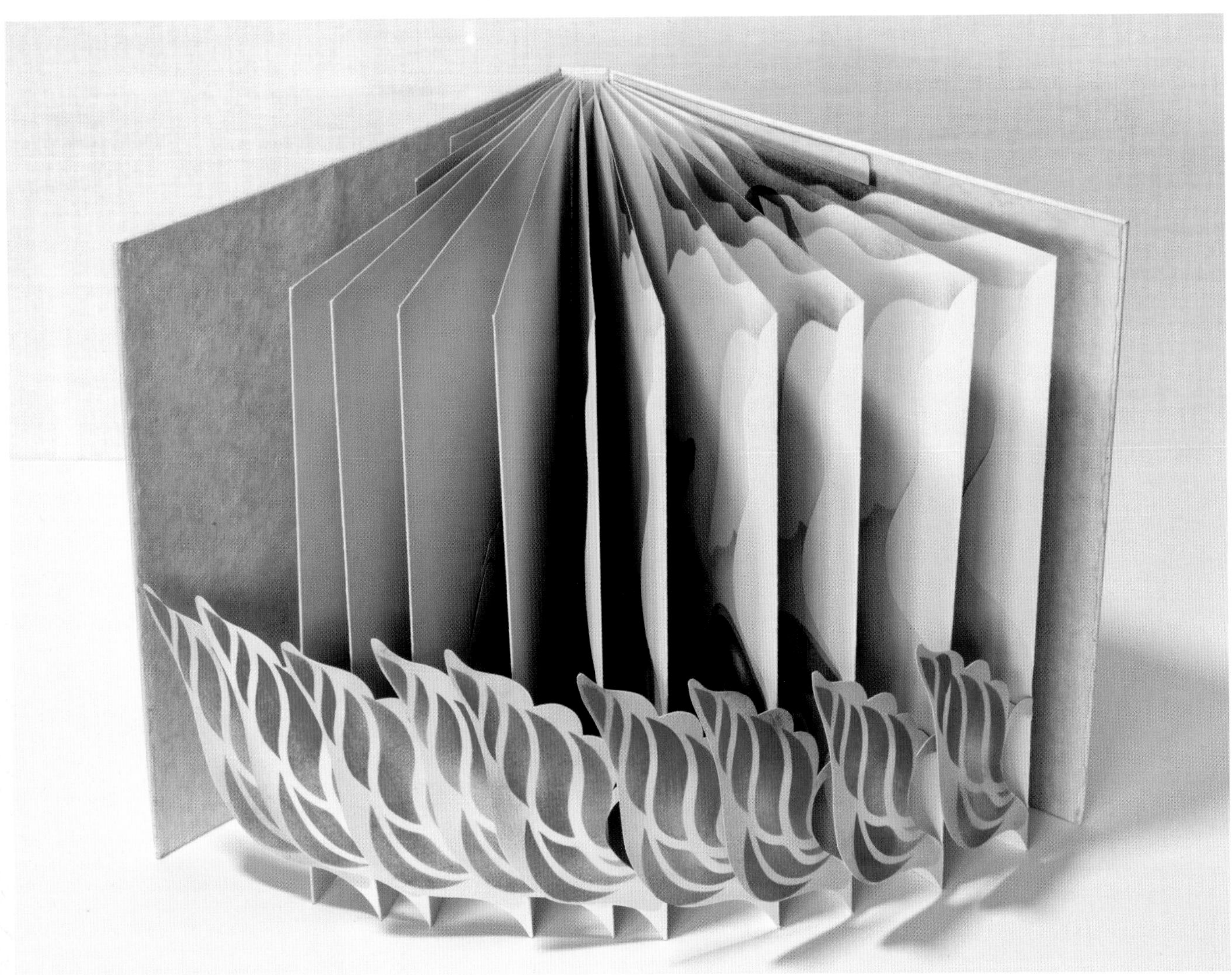

▲ **Listen to the Sound** | 1982

12 x 12⅜ x 1 inches (30.5 x 31.5 x 2.5 cm)
Board, book cloth, handmade paper; case binding, stenciled

Photo by Paul Warchol

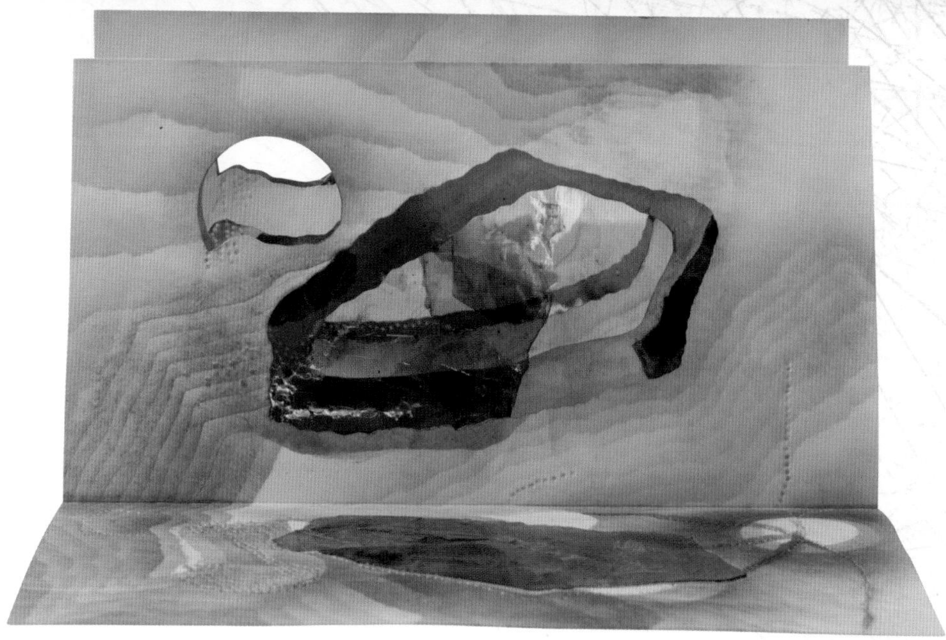

"I aim to achieve a state in which words can be viewed as images and images be seen as words."

▲ **Mica Lakes** | 1995

4½ x 6½ x ¼ inches (11.4 x 16.5 x 0.6 cm)
Tyvek, mica; accordion binding, stenciled, pierced
Photo by Paul Warchol

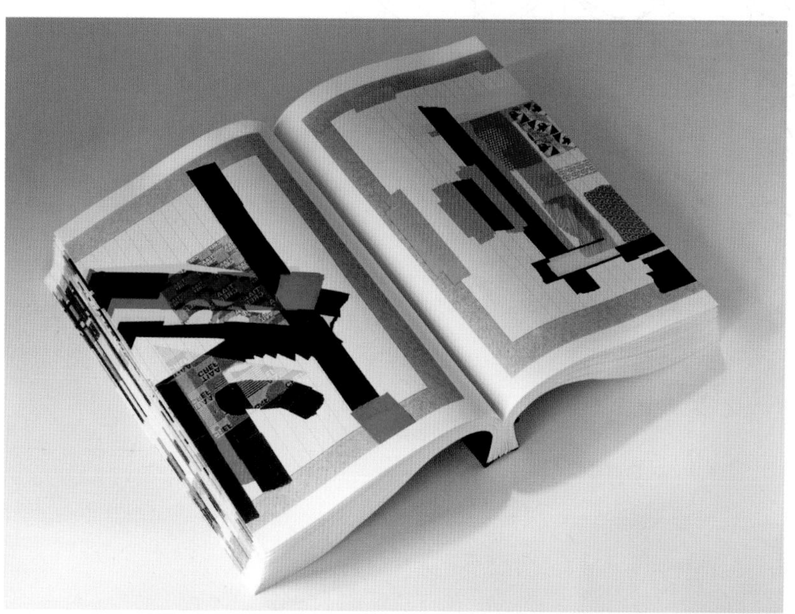

Bold Tape | 1995 ▶

11 x 8½ x 1 inches (27.9 x 21.6 x 2.5 cm)
Reeves paper; clamped binding, gocco printed, photocopied
Photo by Paul Warchol

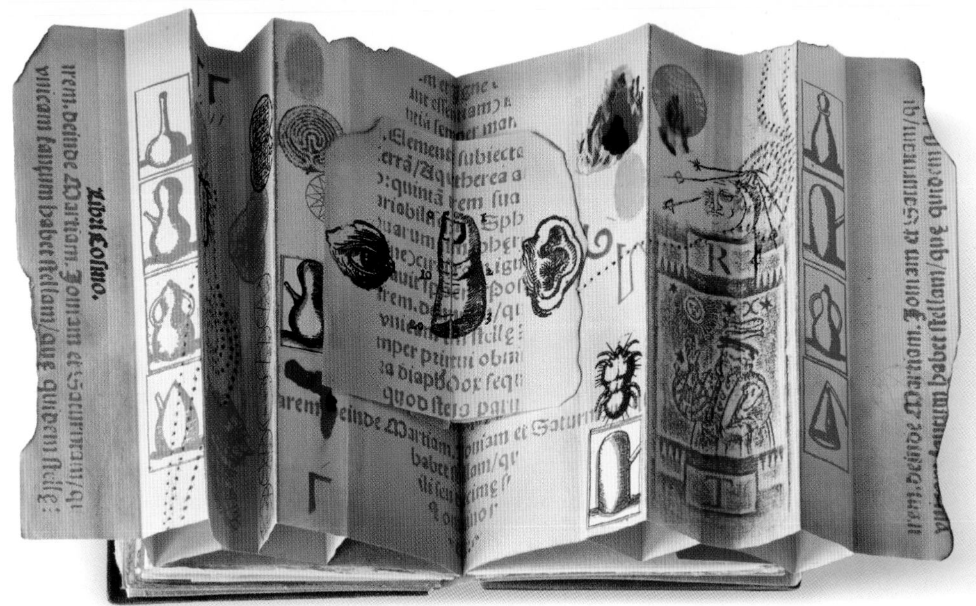

> "I marvel over the ways in which a flat sheet of paper can be transformed into a three-dimensional object."

▲ **In Praise of Dusting** | 2001

7 x 4¼ x 1 inches (17.8 x 10.8 x 2.5 cm)
Painted board, vellum, various papers; long-stitch binding, gocco printed, hand stamped, rubbed, burned, stenciled
Photo by Paul Warchol

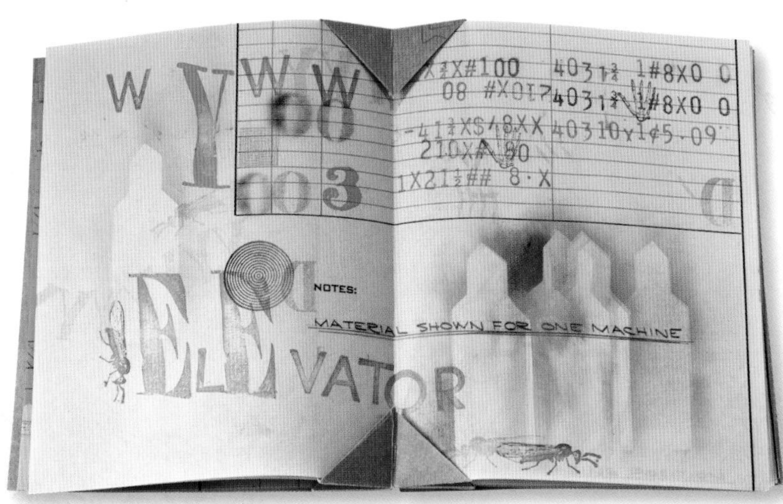

azard | 2003 ▶

7⅛ x 5⅞ x ½ inches (18.1 x 14.9 x 1.3 cm)
Vintage butcher paper, recycled plans; pamphlet binding, stenciled, hand stamped
Photo by Paul Warchol

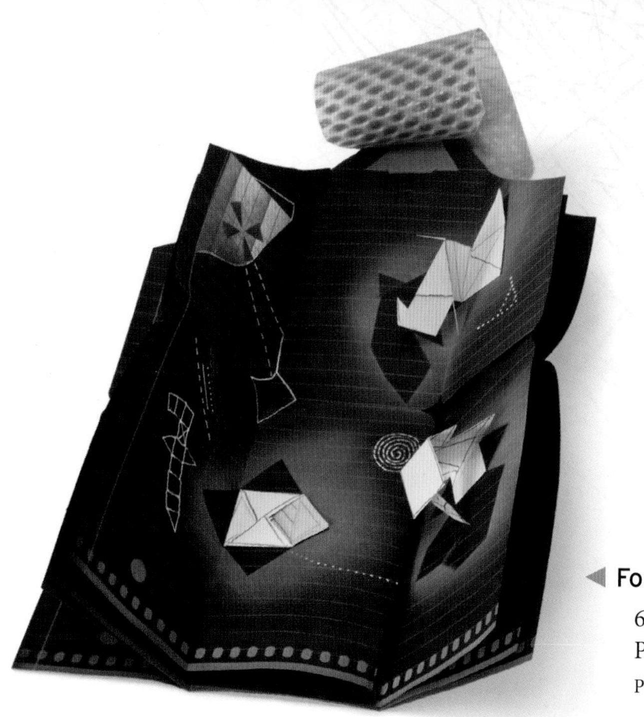

" I find the mechanism of the fold irresistible. It has the potential to generate book forms that delight me. "

◀ **Fold-Out Geometry** | 2003

6½ x 2½ x 1½ inches (16.5 x 6.4 x 1.3 cm)
Plastic, paper; stenciled, drawing, collage
Photo by Paul Warchol

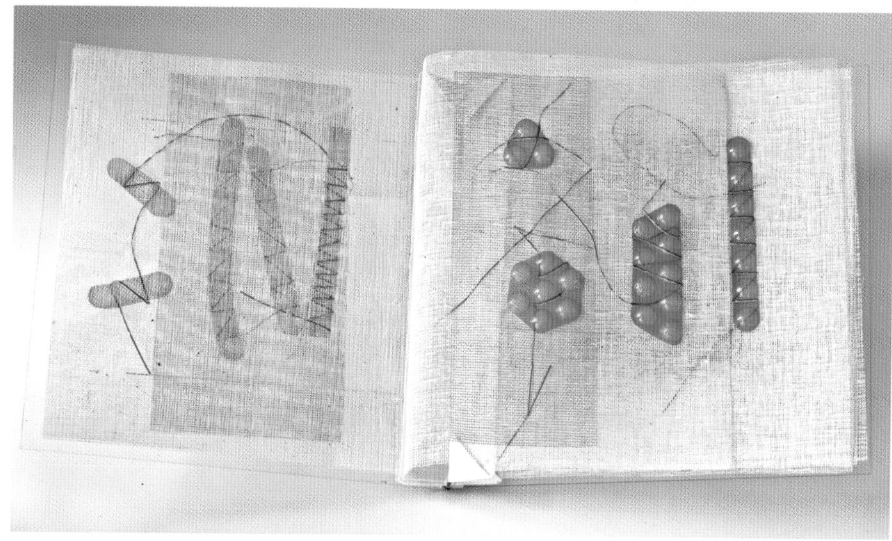

Blue Bubble | 2004 ▶

8 x 8 x ⅞ inches (20.3 x 20.3 x 2.2 cm)
Vivak, Tyvek, starched gauze, bubble wrap, plastic thread; collage, sewn
Photo by Paul Warchol

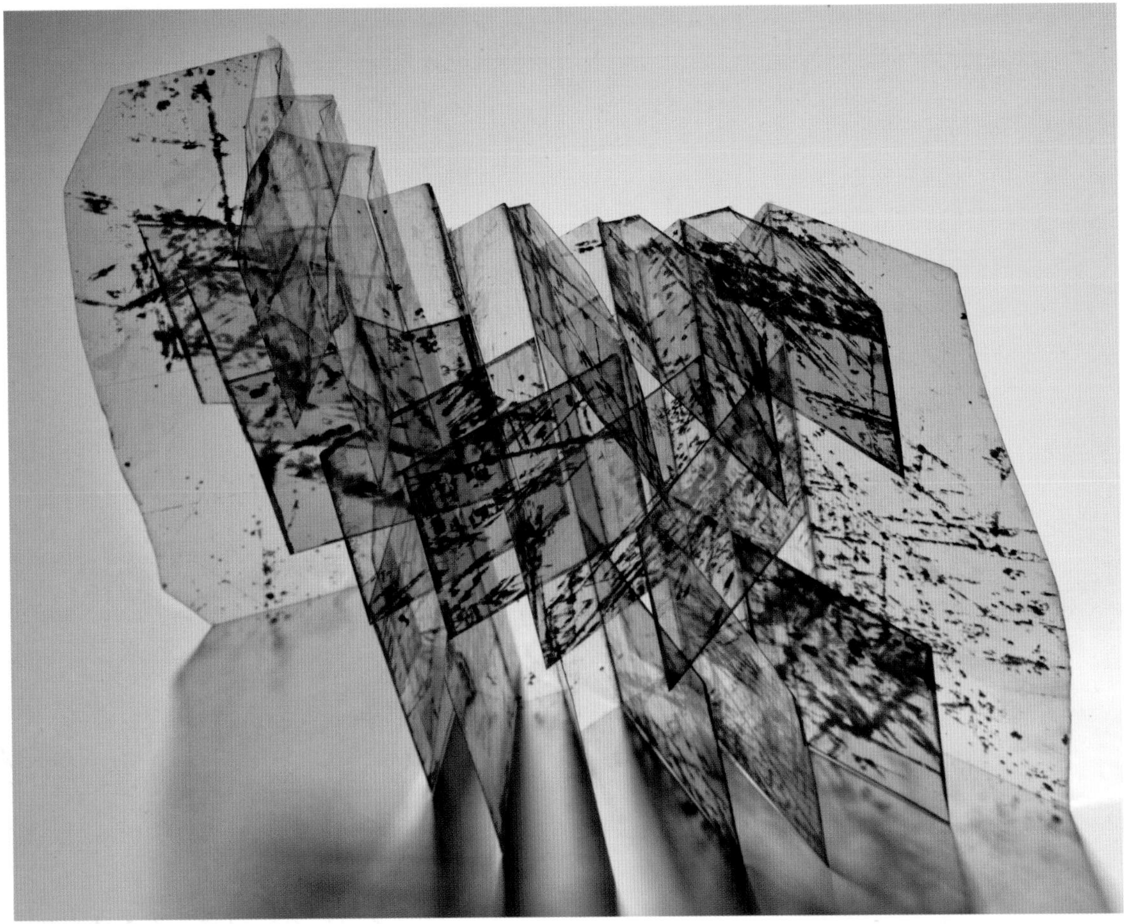

▲ **Mica Flags** | 2006

9 x 4 x ¾ inches (22.9 x 10.2 x 1.9 cm)

Mica, flag book, natural markings

Photos by Paul Warchol

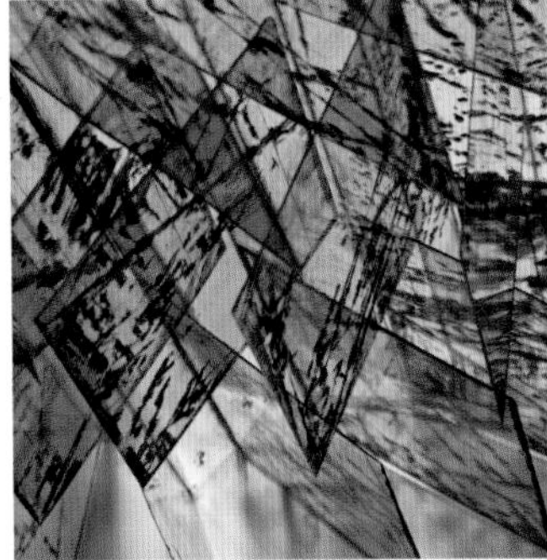

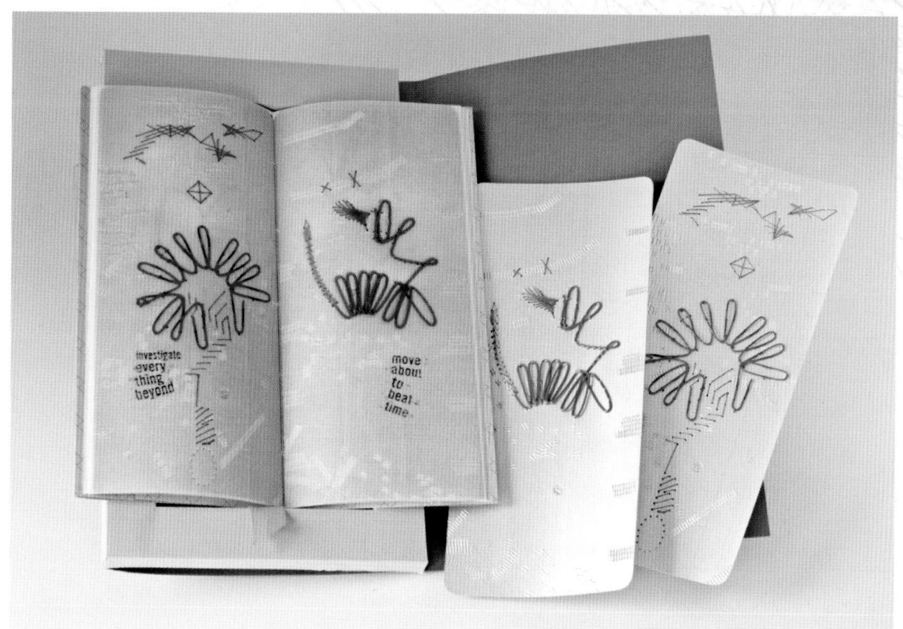

Roadmaps | 2006

8¾ x 4¼ x ¼ inches (22.2 x 10.8 x 0.6 cm)
Printed French paper, UV Ultra paper; inkjet printed, pamphlet binding

Photo by Paul Warchol

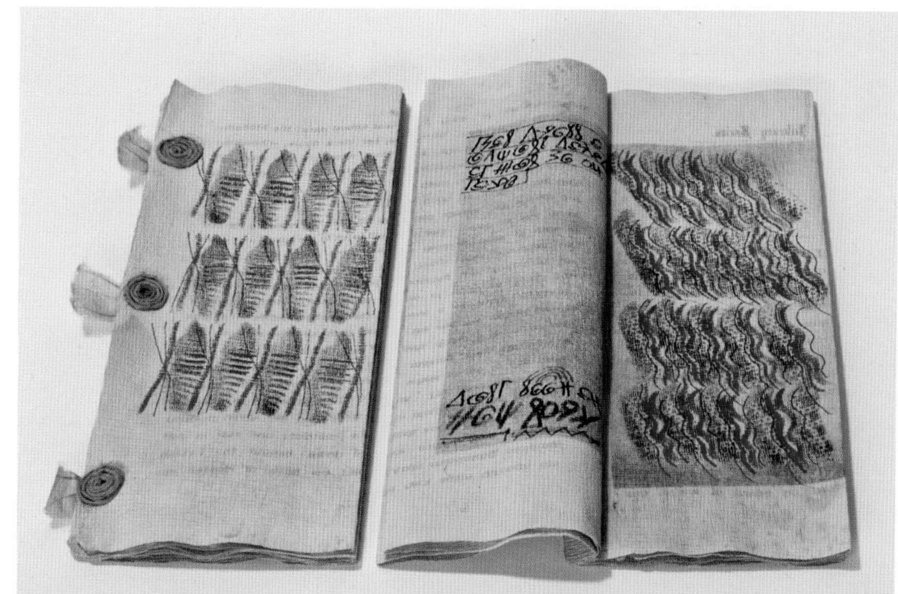

Pattern Trilogy (2 of 3) | 2008

7⅞ x 3¼ x ¼ inches (20 x 8.3 x 0.6 cm)
Recycled Japanese paper, stencils; drawing, stab binding

Photo by Paul Warchol

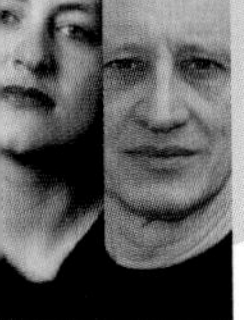

Ines von Ketelhodt & Peter Malutzki

ARTISTS WHOSE BOOKS REFLECT FRESH WAYS OF WORKING with traditional tools and materials, collaborators Ines von Ketelhodt and Peter Malutzki have their own personal, distinctive styles. Each masterfully extracts fragments of both text and image, then recontextualizes and assembles those disparate components into unexpected narratives. Von Ketelhodt and Malutzki blend the time-honored with the contemporary, drawing on both old and new printing techniques, and using experimental typography and photography. Their books radiate energy and refinement.

From 1997 until 2006, von Ketelhodt and Malutzki collaborated on a monumental project that was inspired by a short story called "Tlön, Uqbar, Orbis Tertius," written by Argentinean author Jorge Luis Borges. Their goal was to reconstruct the *Zweite Enzyklopädie von Tlön (Second Encyclopaedia of Tlön)*, a fictitious reference work that played a role in the story. Over the course of a decade, von Ketelhodt and Malutzki created fifty volumes—a breathtaking series representing their own version of Borges' encyclopedia. The consummation of their talents in typography and design, the work established a benchmark for achievement in the field of book arts.

Von Ketelhodt and Malutzki have received numerous awards for their work. Their books are in institutions around the world, including the Bibliothèque Nationale de France in Paris, and the Victoria and Albert Museum in London, England. They live in Flörsheim, Germany.

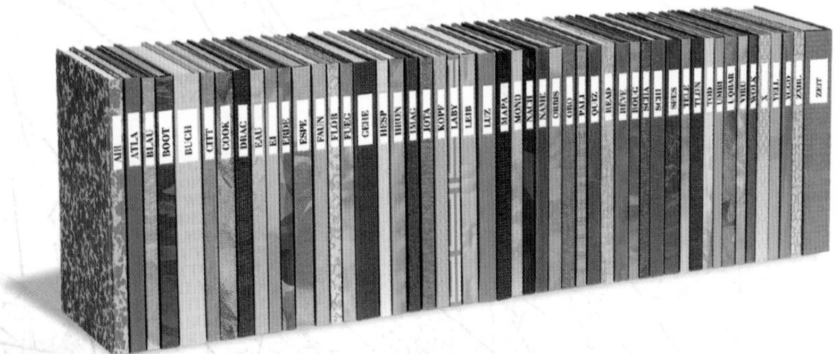

▲ **Zweite Enzyklopädie von Tlön** | 1997–2006

Each volume: 7 7/8 x 4 15/16 inches (20 x 12.5 cm)

Cloth, paper

Photo by Dieter Bachert

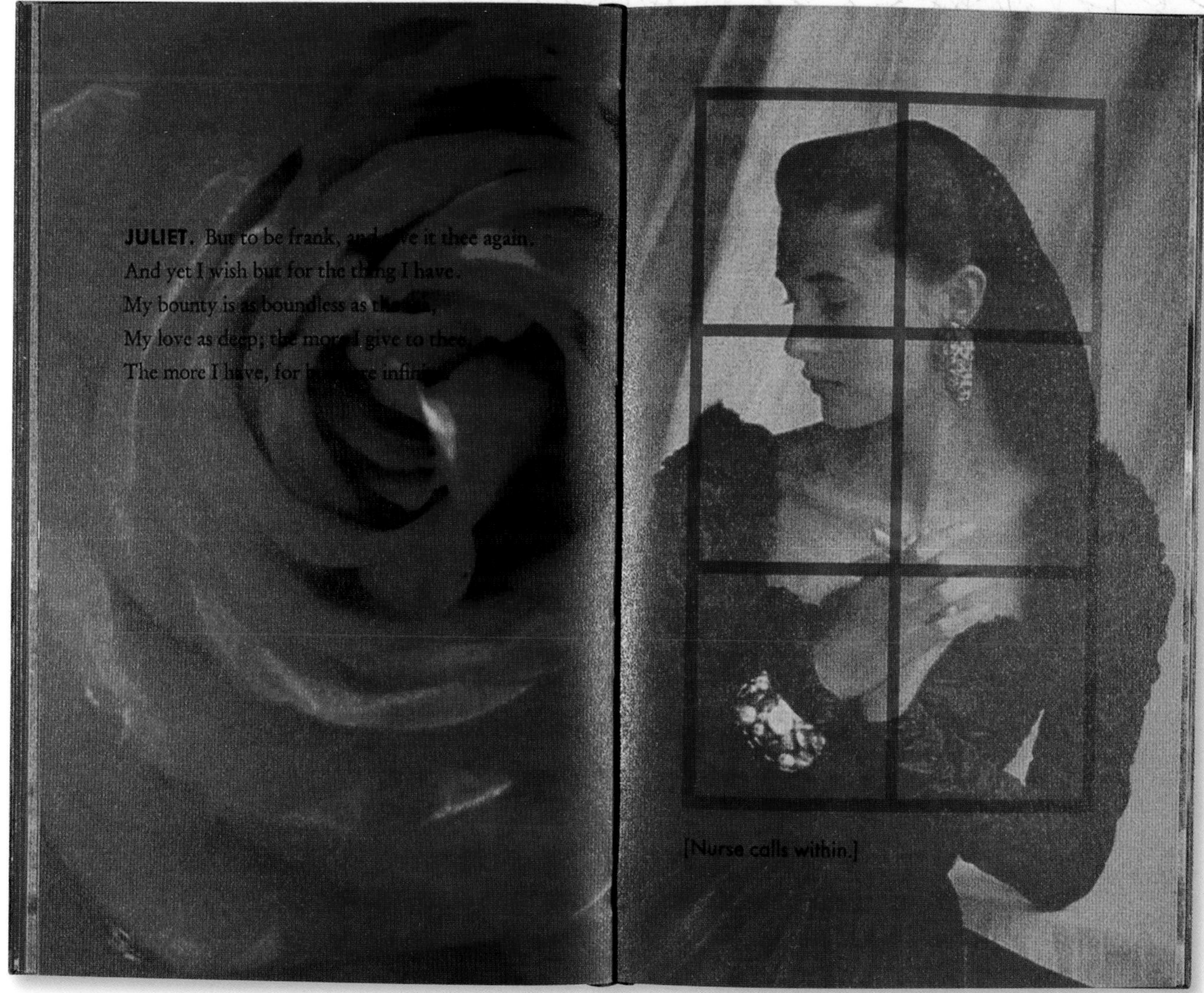

▲ Volume from Zweite Enzyklopädie von Tlön: ROUGE | 2001

7⅞ x 4 15⁄16 x ⅜ inches (20 x 12.5 x 1 cm)
Bookprinting and glassine paper, linen-over-board cover, photographs; offset printed, letterpress printed
Text by William Shakespeare
Photo by Dieter Bachert

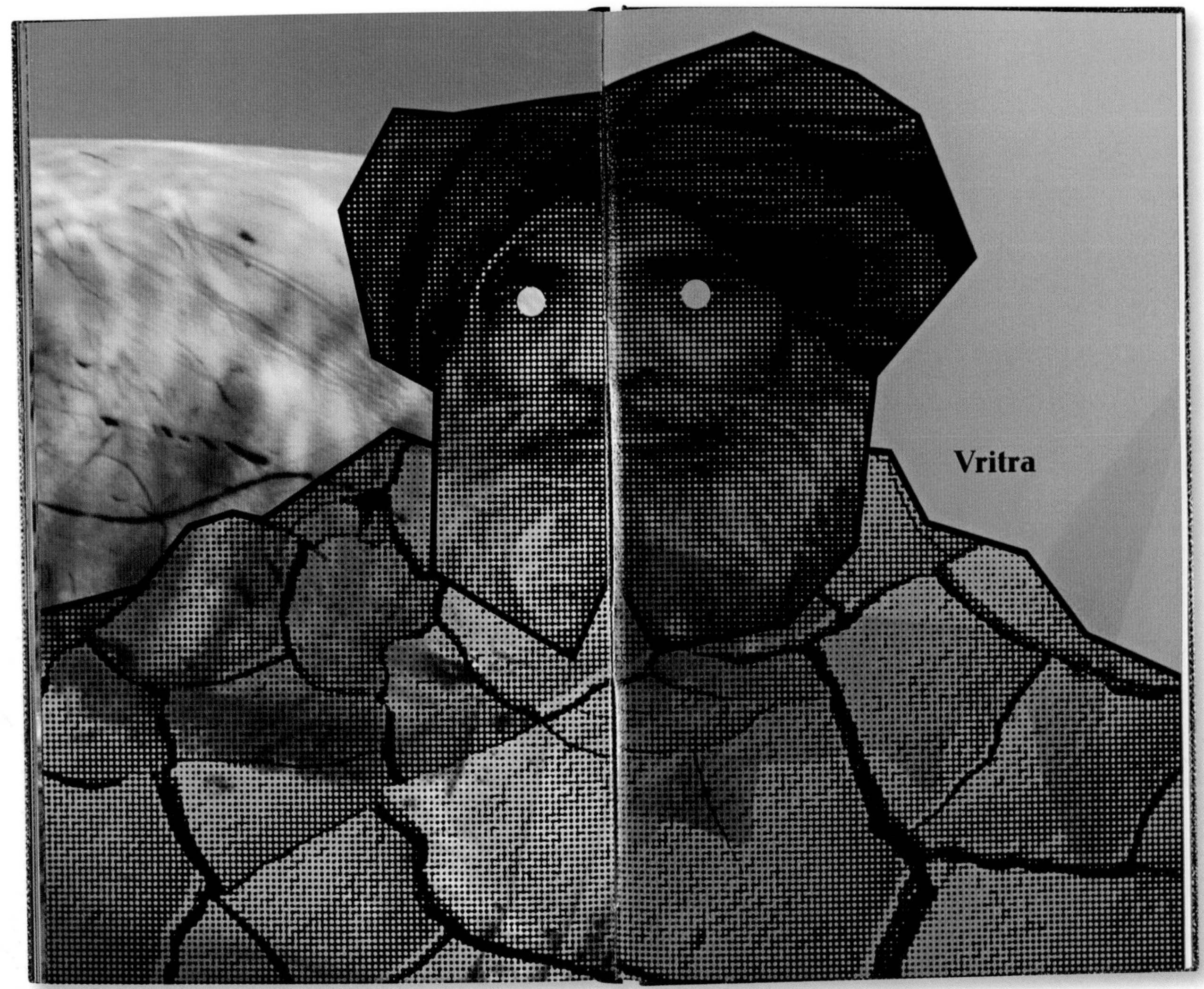

▲ Volume from Zweite Enzyklopädie von Tlön: DRACHE | 2002

7⅞ x 4$^{15}/_{16}$ x $^{7}/_{16}$ inches (20 x 12.5 x 1.2 cm)

Found spreads from animal books, linen-over-board cover, illustrations created on computer and printed with polymer plates; letterpress printed, handset

Dragon texts by Jorge Luis Borges
Illustrations by Peter Malutzki
Photo by Dieter Bachert

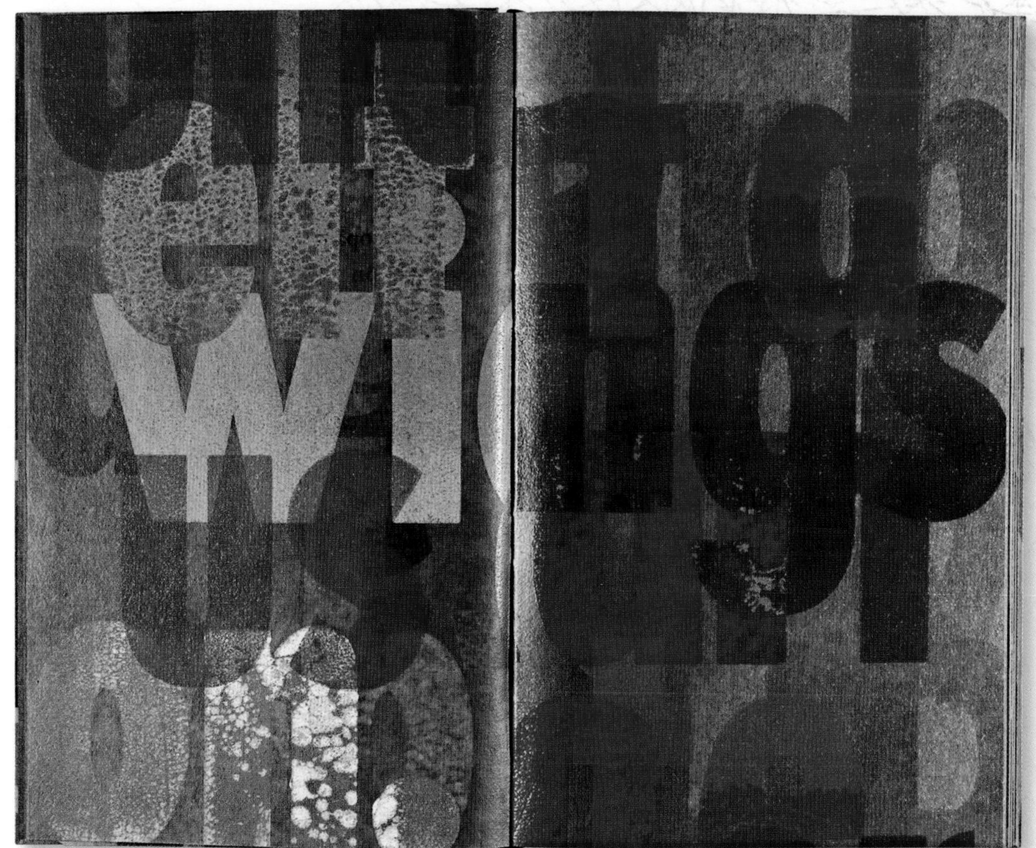

▲ **Volume from Zweite Enzyklopädie von Tlön: ERDE** | 2006

7⅞ x 4$\frac{15}{16}$ x ⅜ inches (20 x 12.5 x 1 cm)
Oil paper, printed paperboard; letterpress, handset

Text by Olga Tokarczuk
Typography by Ines von Ketelhodt
Photo by Dieter Bachert

" We view the *Zweite Enzyklopädie von Tlön* as a tiny part of a huge iceberg that's really a book-berg. The project is connected to a multitude of other books, and we're happy that, by its incorporation into public collections, it's now literally close to an enormous number of other books. "

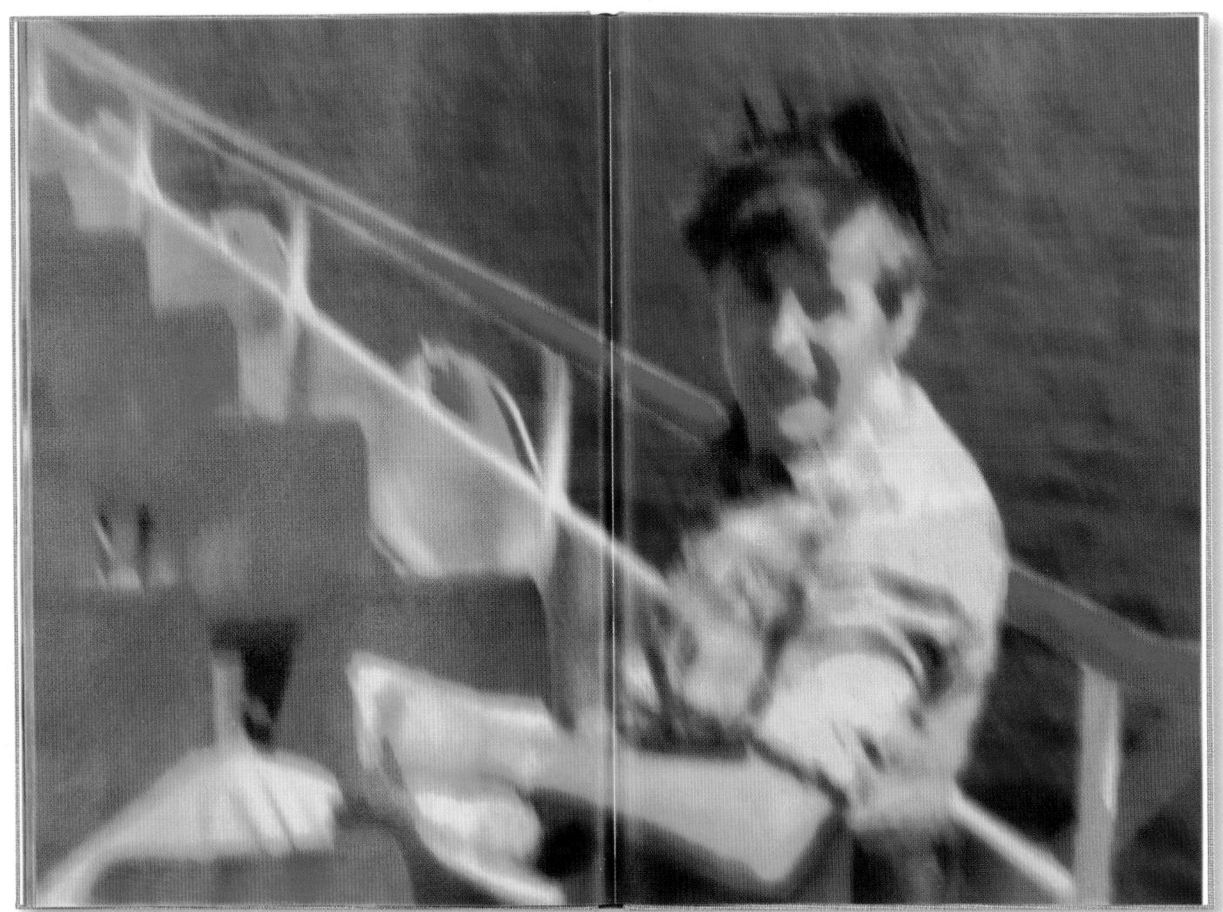

▲ **Album** | 2009

11 13⁄16 x 8 3⁄16 x 3⁄8 inches (30 x 20.8 x 1 cm)
Parchment paper, printed linen-over-board cover, family photographs from the artists; digital printed, letterpress printed, handset
Photo by Dieter Bachert

" My books often bring together text and photography, but the photos don't illustrate the text. They evoke an atmosphere. "

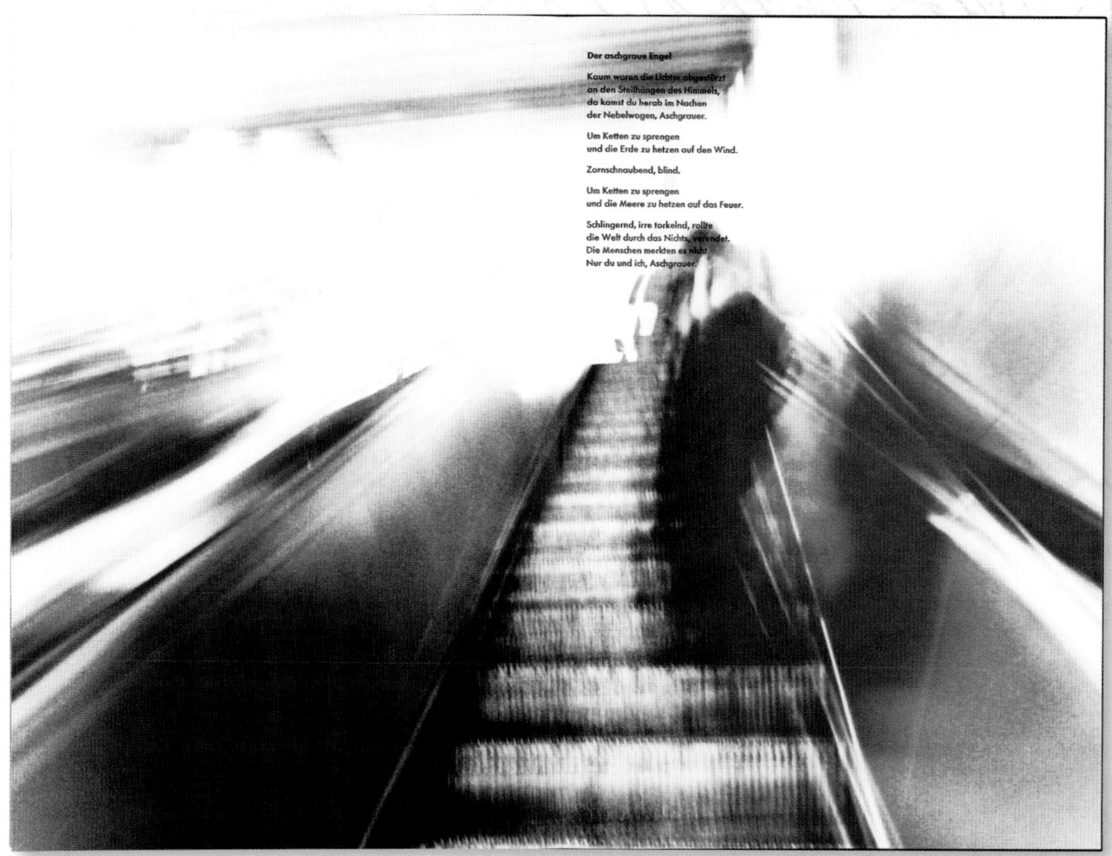

▲ **Engel** | 1995

15¾ x 10⁷⁄₁₆ x ⁹⁄₁₆ inches (40 x 26.5 x 1.4 cm)
Zerkall Werkdruckbütten paper, photographs; accordion binding, offset printed, letterpress printed, handset

Photos by Ines von Ketelhodt
Poems by Rafael Alberti
Photo by Dieter Bachert

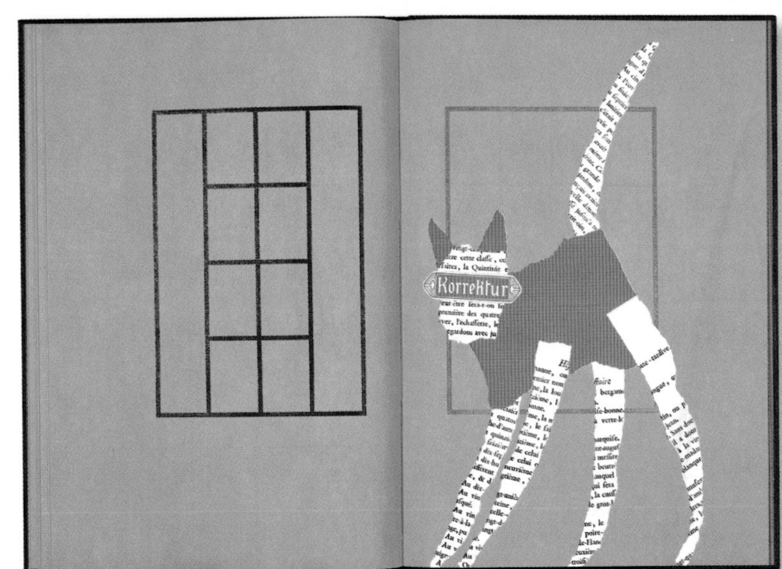

Collagebuch 1 | 2008 ▶

11 3/16 x 7 7/8 x 7/16 inches (28.4 x 20 x 1.2 cm)
Lunabütten paper, found pages from old French books, correction labels, linen-over-board cover in slipcase; letterpress printed, collage

Photo by Dieter Bachert

“ Although I often work with handset type and letterpress illustrations, I don’t try to make books that look as though Gutenberg had been peering over my shoulder. My work is a contemporary reaction to the world of today. ”

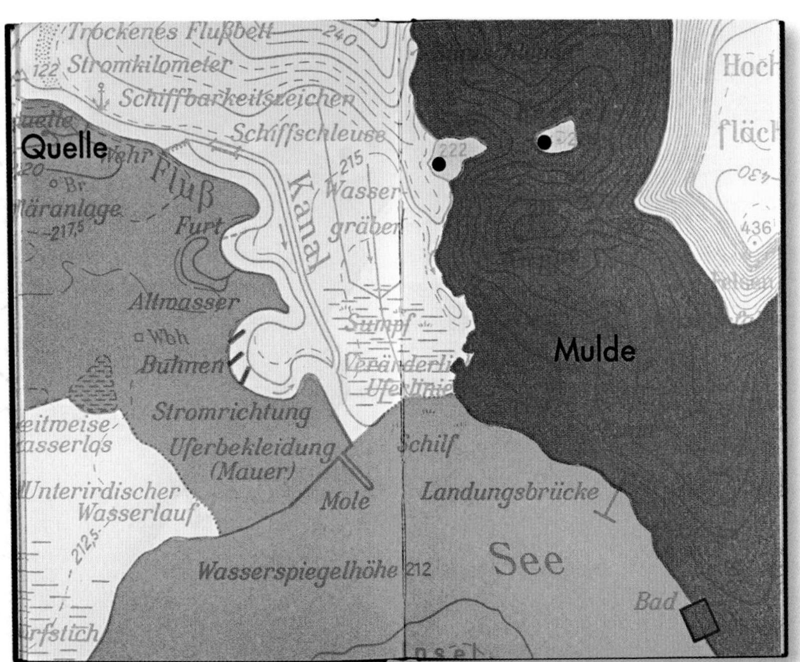

◀ **Volume from Zweite Enzyklopädie von Tlön: ATLAS by Peter Malutzki** | 1997

7 7/8 x 4 15/16 x 7/16 inches (20 x 12.5 x 1.2 cm)
Book-printing paper, linen-over-board cover, linocuts; letterpress printed, handset

Photo by Dieter Bachert

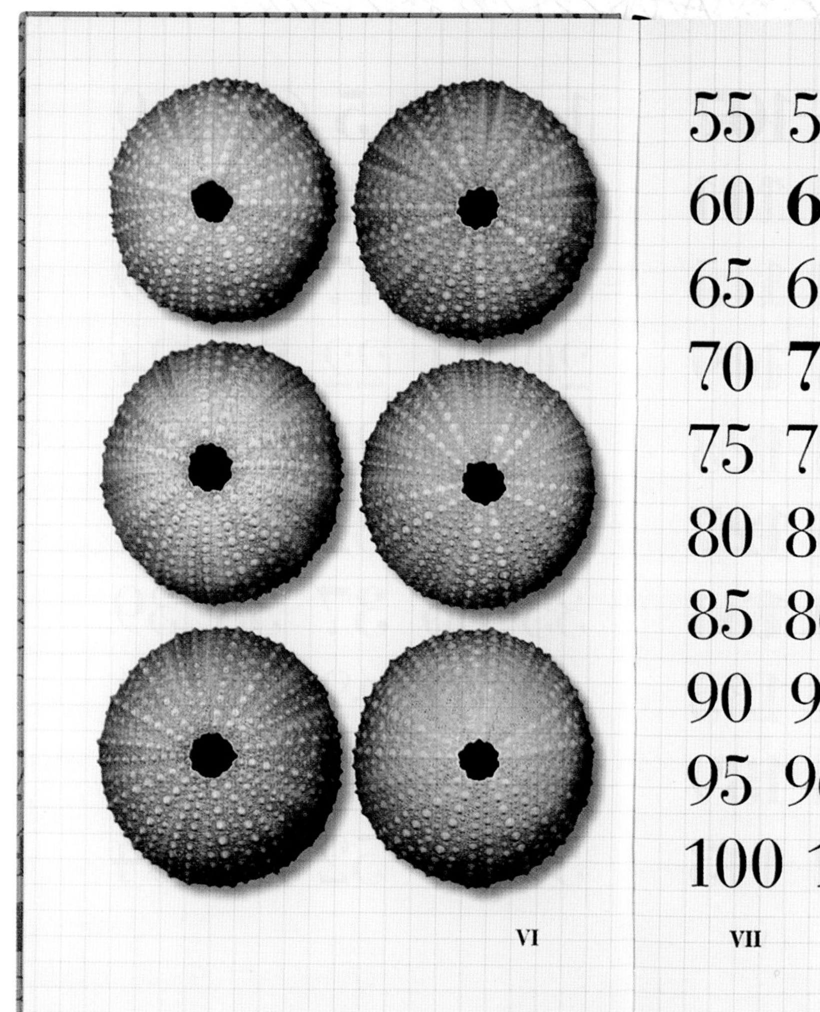

▲ **Volume from Zweite Enzyklopädie von Tlön: ZÄHLEN** | 2001

$7\frac{7}{8}$ x $4\frac{15}{16}$ x $\frac{7}{16}$ inches (20 x 12.5 x 1.1 cm)
Arithmetic paper, printed linen-over-board cover; offset printed, letterpress printed, handset, scanned

Text by various authors
Design by Peter Malutzki
Photo by Dieter Bachert

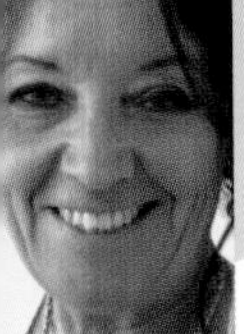

Adèle Outteridge

ALTHOUGH SHE OFTEN PRODUCES BOOKS USING traditional materials, Adèle Outteridge is best known for the gorgeous transparent book structures she makes from unconventional components such as acrylic sheet, acetate, and tracing paper. Through experimentation, Outteridge developed a special method for sewing single, see-through leaves together into a book form. Her luminous transparent books provide an elegant solution to the limitations of the medium, as each piece can be seen and read by the viewer in its entirety at once, whether open or closed.

Over the years, Outteridge has assembled a body of unforgettable work that includes beautifully bound journals and drawing books, as well as what she calls "feral" creations—pieces made from discarded materials such as teabags, old envelopes, junk mail, and metal. Outteridge pushes boundaries and plays with traditional definitions of the form while maintaining the highest level of craftsmanship. Based in Brisbane, Australia, she conducts workshops frequently in the United States.

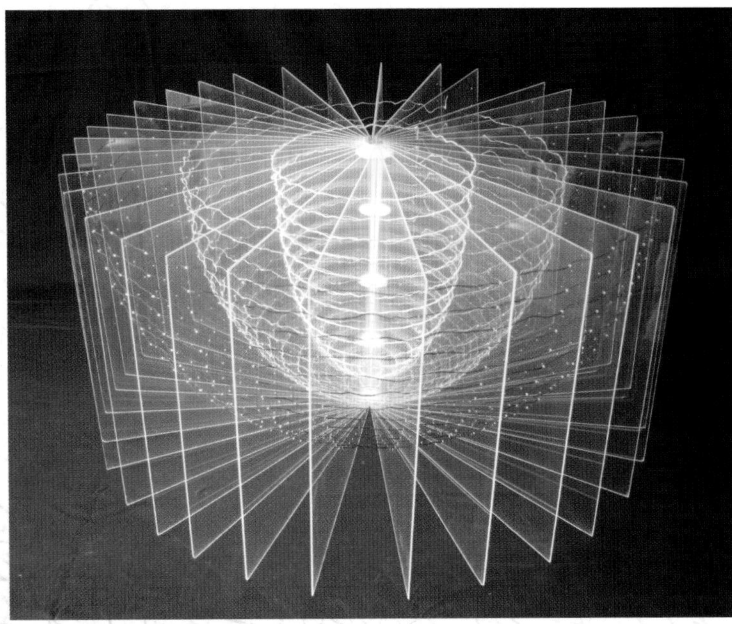

▲ **Vessels** | 2004

Closed: 11 13/16 x 11 13/16 x 2 9/16 inches (30 x 30 x 6.5 cm)
Acrylic sheet, linen threads; single-sheet Coptic binding
Photo by artist

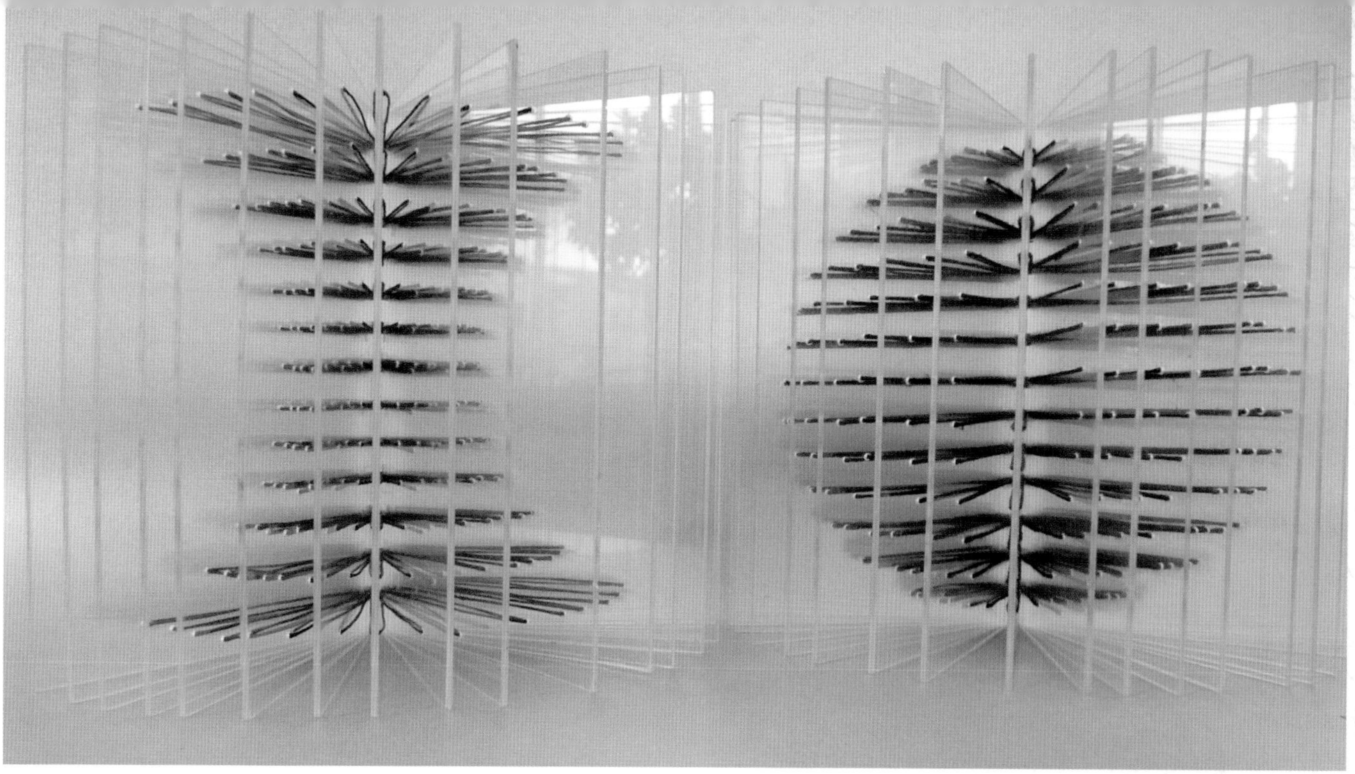

▲ **Gaia (Diptych)** | 2005

Each: 5½ x 3$\frac{9}{16}$ x 1$\frac{3}{16}$ inches (14 x 9 x 3 cm)
Acrylic sheet, linen thread; single-sheet Coptic binding

Photos by artist

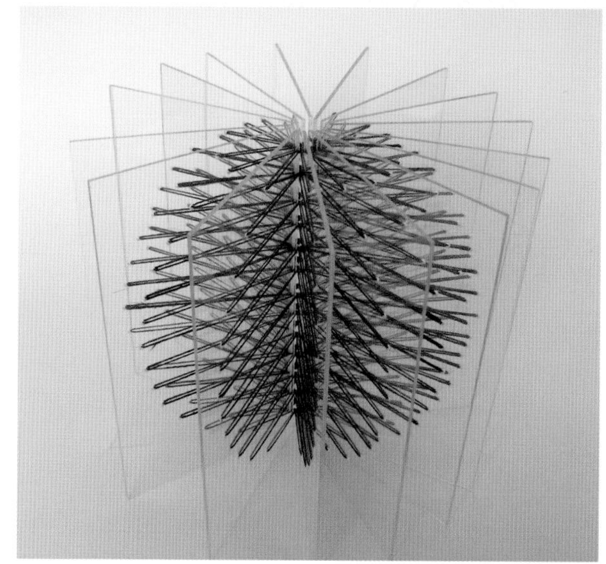

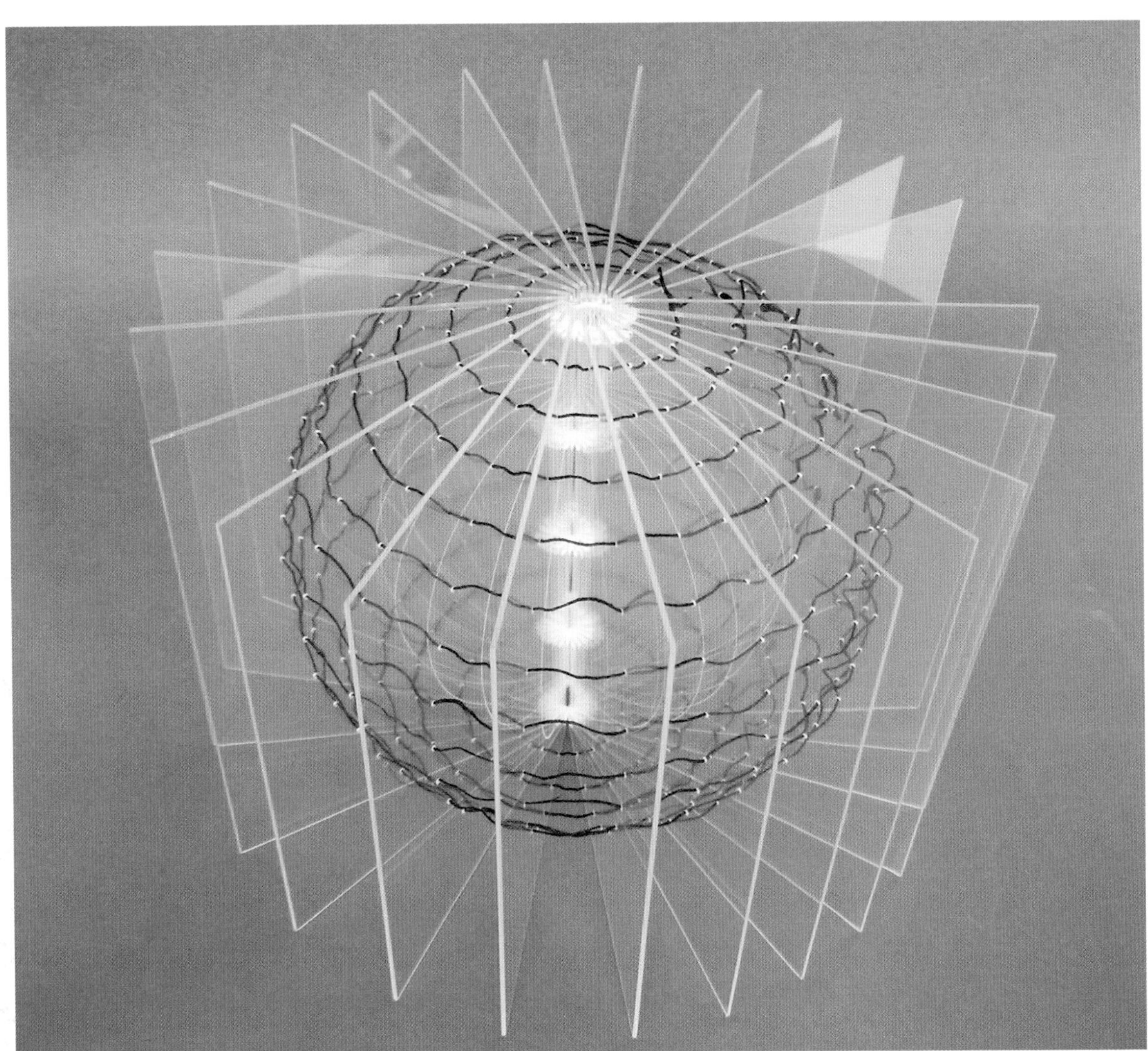

▲ **Saturn** | 1997

Closed: 7⁷⁄₁₆ x 5⅛ x 1¾ inches (19 x 13 x 4.5 cm)
Acrylic sheet, linen threads; engraved, Coptic binding
Photo by artist

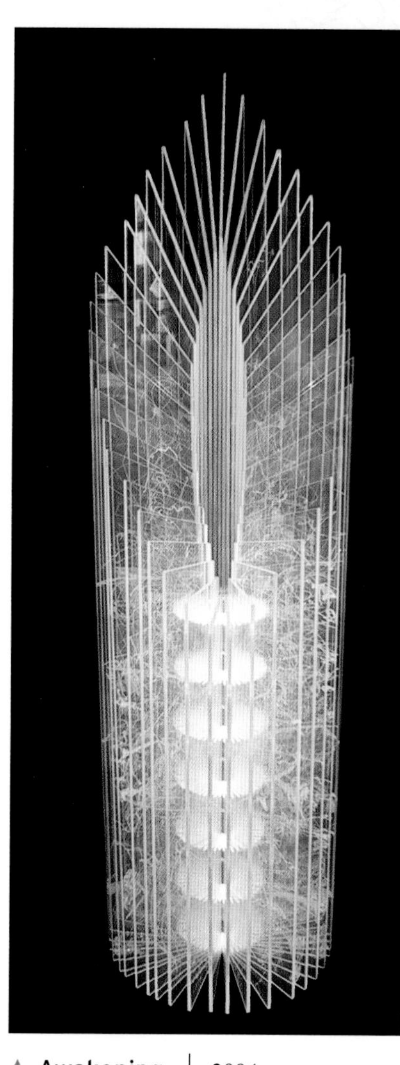
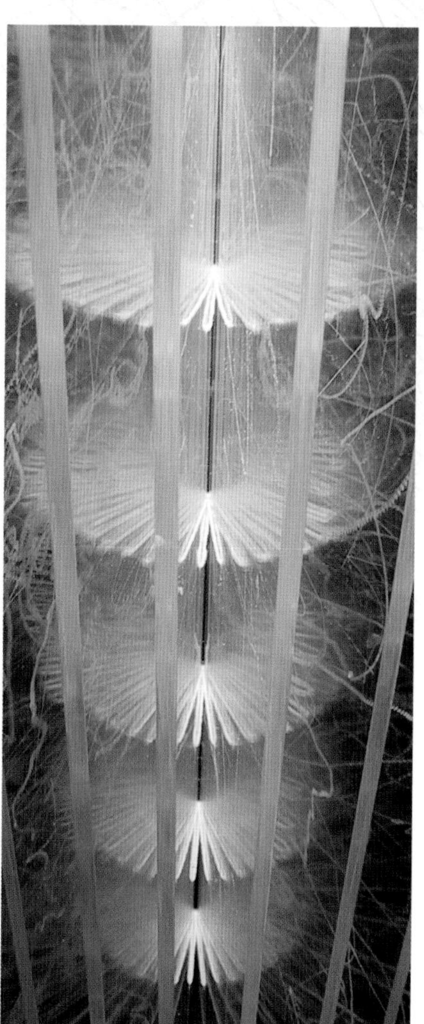

▲ **Awakening** | 2004

Collaboration with Wim de Vos
Open: 43 x 12 inches (110 x 32 cm)
Acrylic sheet, linen threads; engraved, single-sheet Coptic binding
Photos by artist

" The beauty of making books with transparent media is that all of the pages are visible simultaneously. The image or text appears to be suspended in space. "

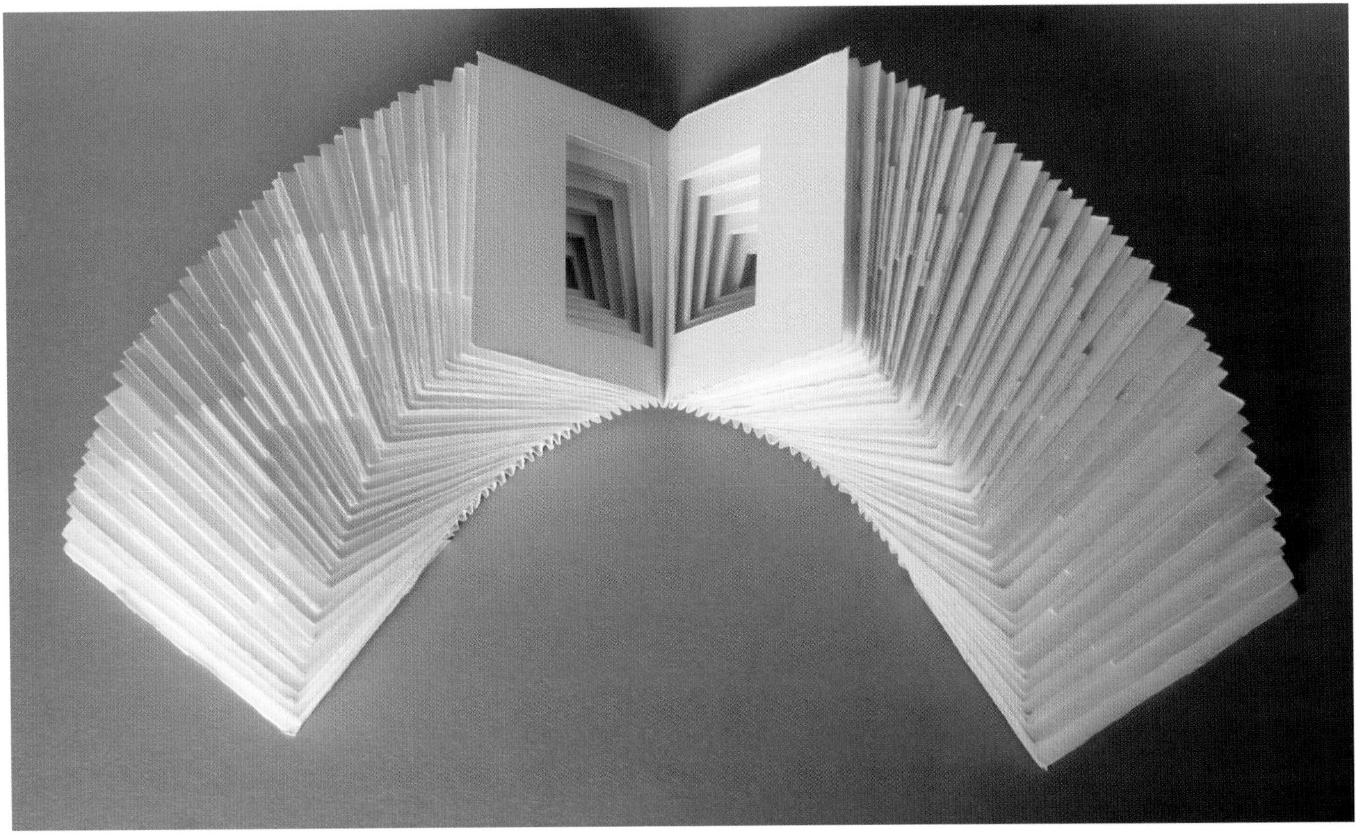

▲ **Stairs and Windows** | 2004

Closed: $3\frac{15}{16}$ x $3\frac{1}{8}$ x $7\frac{1}{16}$ inches (10 x 8 x 18 cm)
Watercolor paper, linen thread; cut folios, pamphlet stitching to concertina spine-fold

Photos by artist

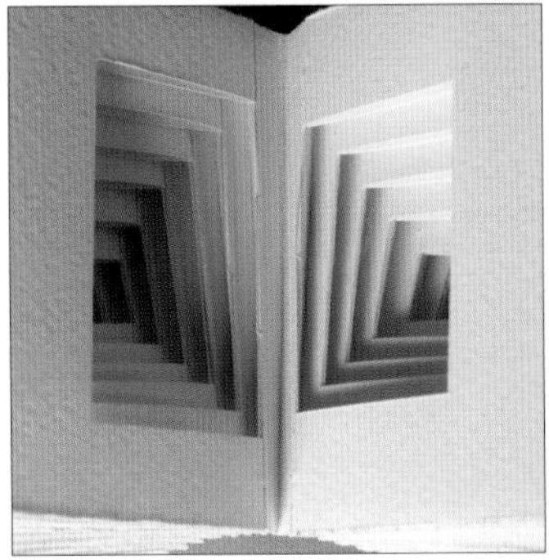

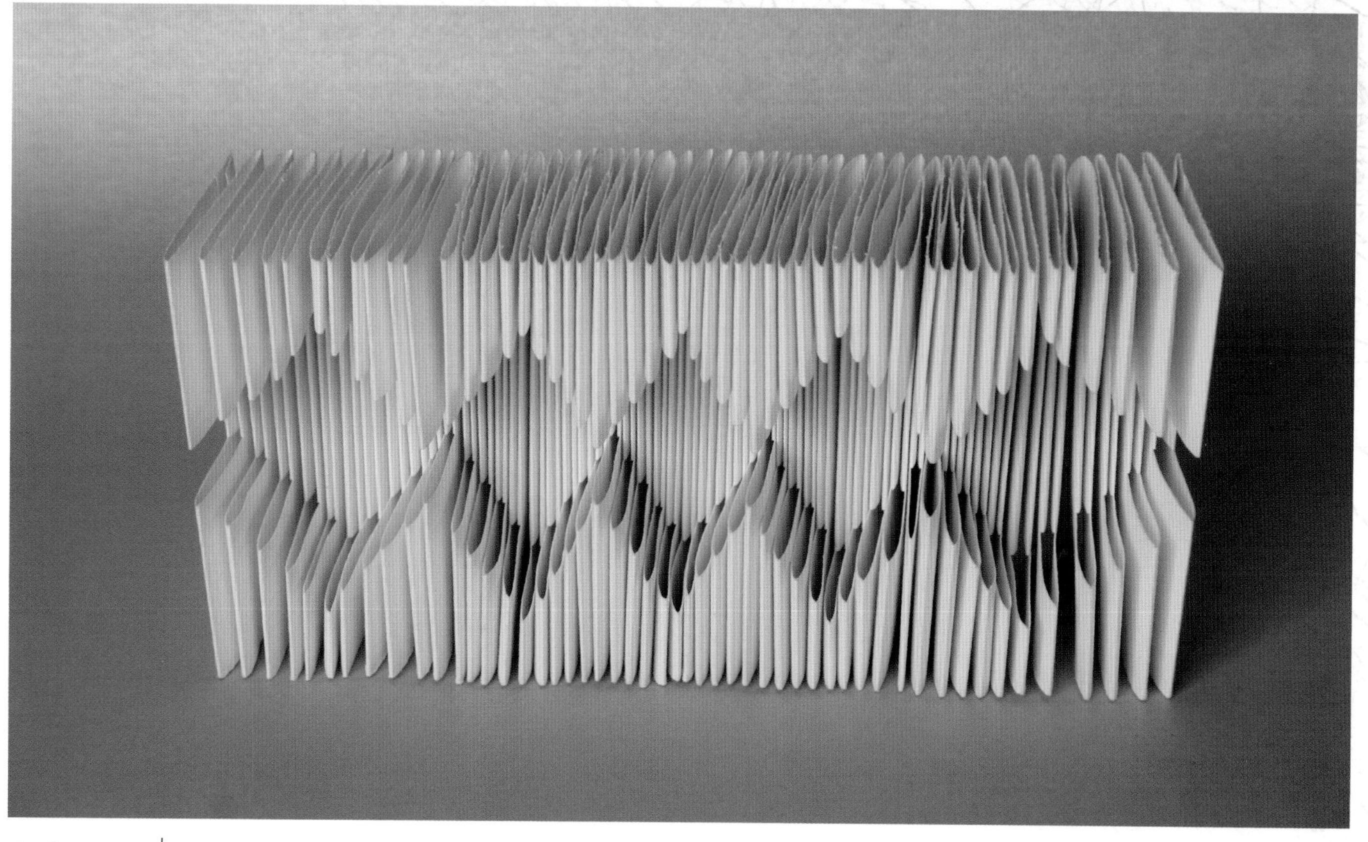

▲ **Caverns** | 2004

Closed: 3 15/16 x 2 15/16 x 7 1/16 inches (10 x 7.5 x 18 cm)
Watercolor paper; concertina folds, cut
Photo by artist

" Working with threads allows me to draw in three dimensions. The threads can be left to their own devices to make lovely scribbles in the air, or they can be stretched to make straight, geometric lines, with many different aerial marks in between. "

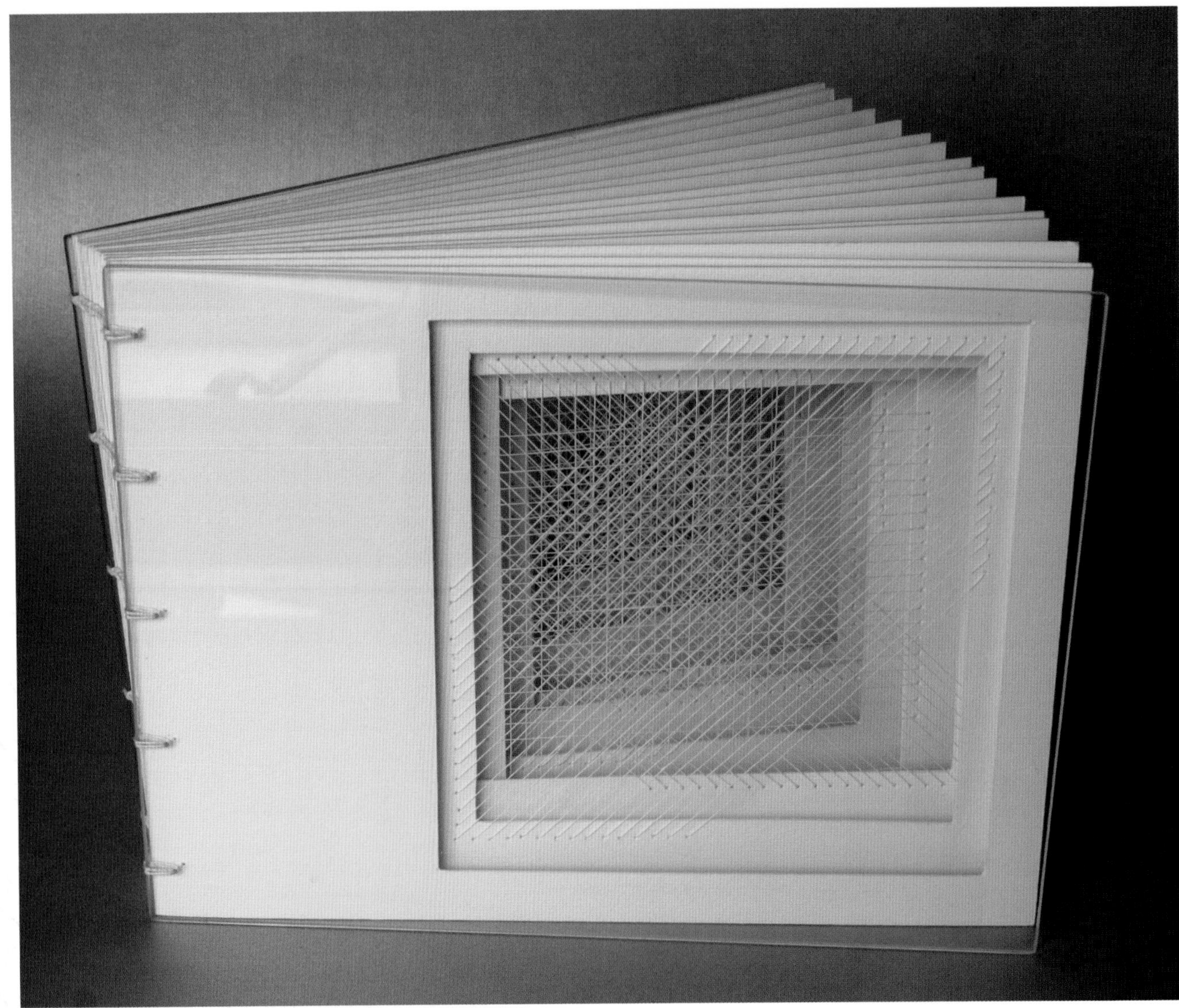

▲ **Between the Lines, White** | 2006

8$\frac{1}{16}$ x 10$\frac{13}{16}$ x 1$\frac{3}{16}$ inches (20.5 x 27.5 x 3 cm)
Watercolor paper, linen thread, acrylic sheet; cut, suspended, single-sheet Coptic binding

Photo by artist

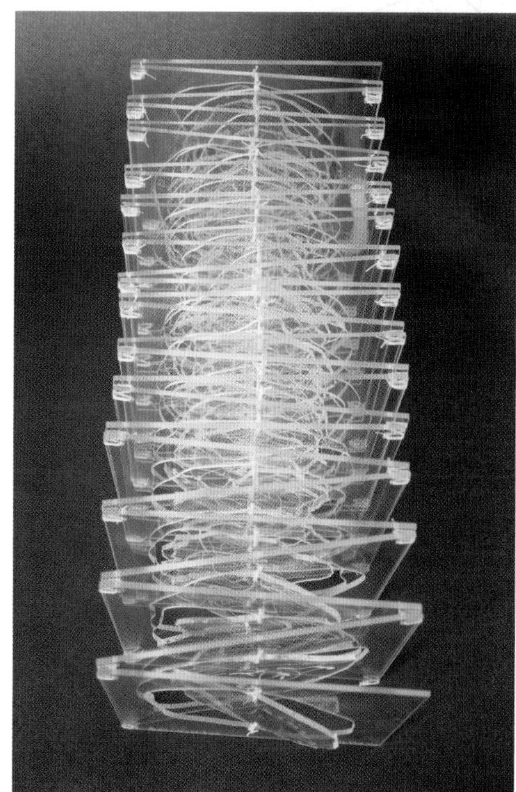

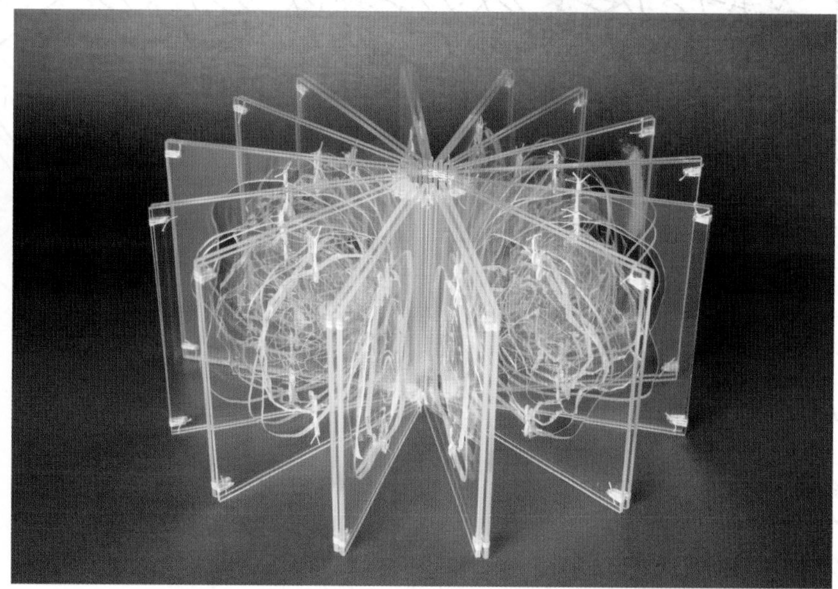

▲ **Small Sound Book** | 2005

Collaboration with Wim de Vos

Closed: 4⅛ x 4⅛ x 2¾ inches (10.5 x 10.5 x 7 cm)

Acrylic sheet, linen thread; engraved, suspended

Photos by artist

" Many of my books have no text or imagery at all. Thus, there may be little or no distinction between the container (the book) and the contents (text or images). The book itself tells the story. "

BOYDEN

Ian Boyden

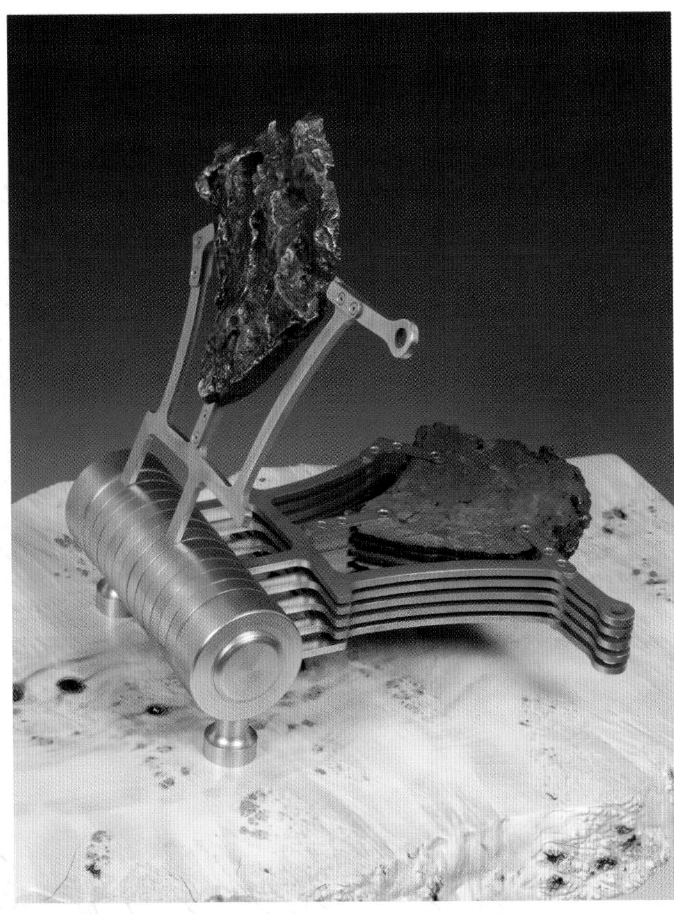

▲ **Field of the Sky** | 2010

9 x 12 x 4 inches (22.9 x 30.5 x 10.2 cm)
Nickel-iron meteorite, stainless steel, chrome, bronze, maple; single-pivot binding, polished, etched, laser engraved

Photo by artist

UNUSUAL MATERIALS such as shark's teeth, freshwater pearls, and meteorite dust are transformed from raw ingredients into paints and inks in the capable hands of Ian Boyden. The special relationship he forms with these materials is beautifully expressed in the exquisite paintings that fill the pages of his books. Wooden boards, calligraphy, and delicate illustrations with poetry and letterpress printing often appear in his pieces. Formal typographic elements provide contrast to his fluid illustrations, bringing a wonderful tension to his work.

Boyden is inspired by the ways in which writing occupies and is shaped by surfaces such as paper or stone, and the opposition that exists between surface and text is a recurring theme in his work. His interest in East Asian aesthetics complements his respect for his materials and methods—craft traditions that he has brought into modern practice with great sensitivity and skill. Boyden lives in Walla Walla, Washington, and publishes under the imprint Crab Quill Press.

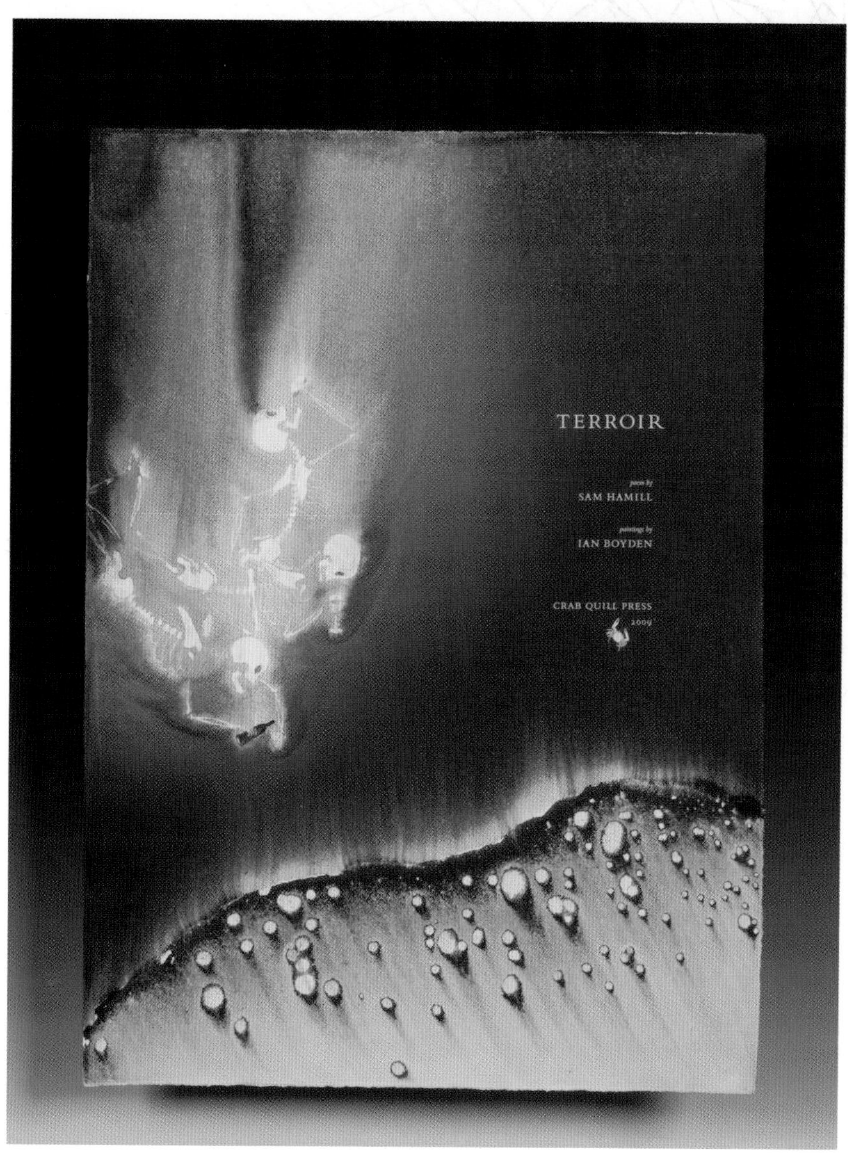

◀ **Terroir** | 2009

Collaboration with Sam Hamill
31 x 11½ x 1¼ inches (78.7 x 29.2 x 3.2 cm)
Paper, pigments, catalpa boards with walnut inlay, original paintings, silk; drum-leaf binding, laser engraved

Photo by artist

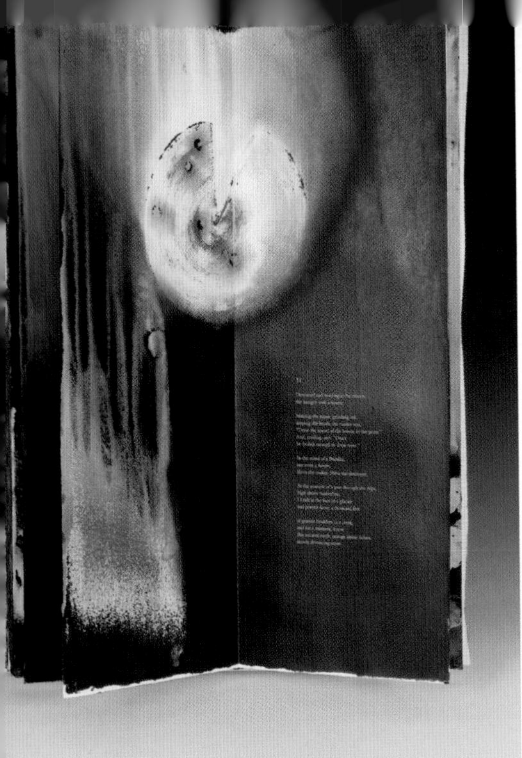

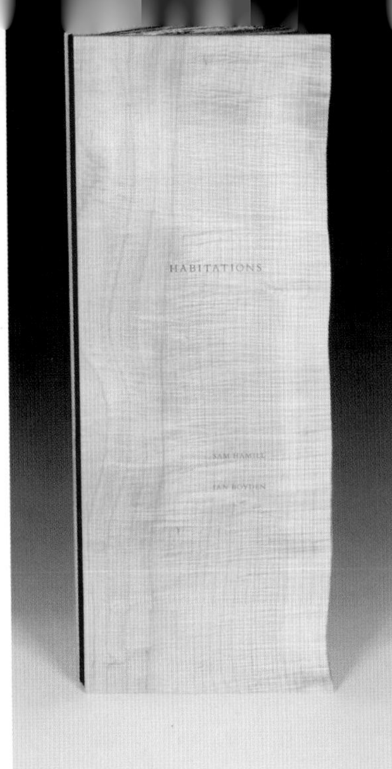

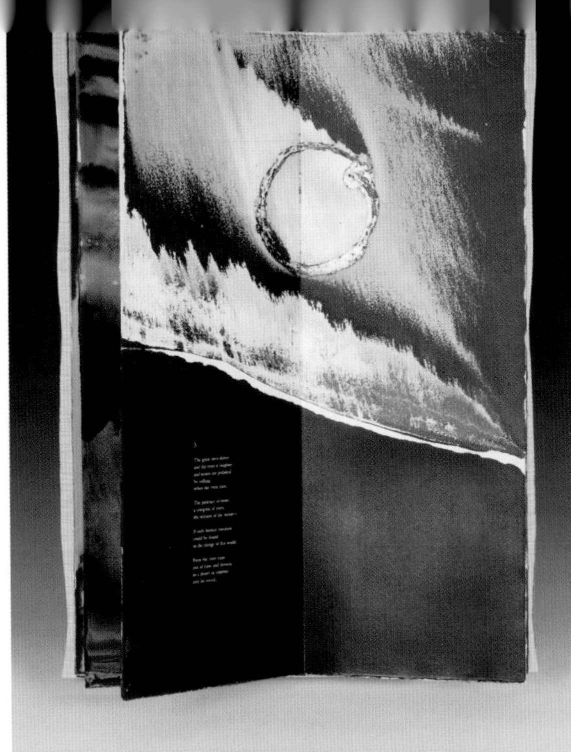

▲ **Habitations** | 2008

Collaboration with Sam Hamill
31 x 11½ x 1¼ inches (78.7 x 29.2 x 3.2 cm)
Paper, pigments, maple boards, original paintings, silk; drum-leaf binding, laser engraved
Photos by artist

" In my work I explore how the book can grow from and inform the information it contains. Instead of viewing the book as a structure that houses words or pictures, I view it as a sophisticated system that actually gives shape to ideas and images. "

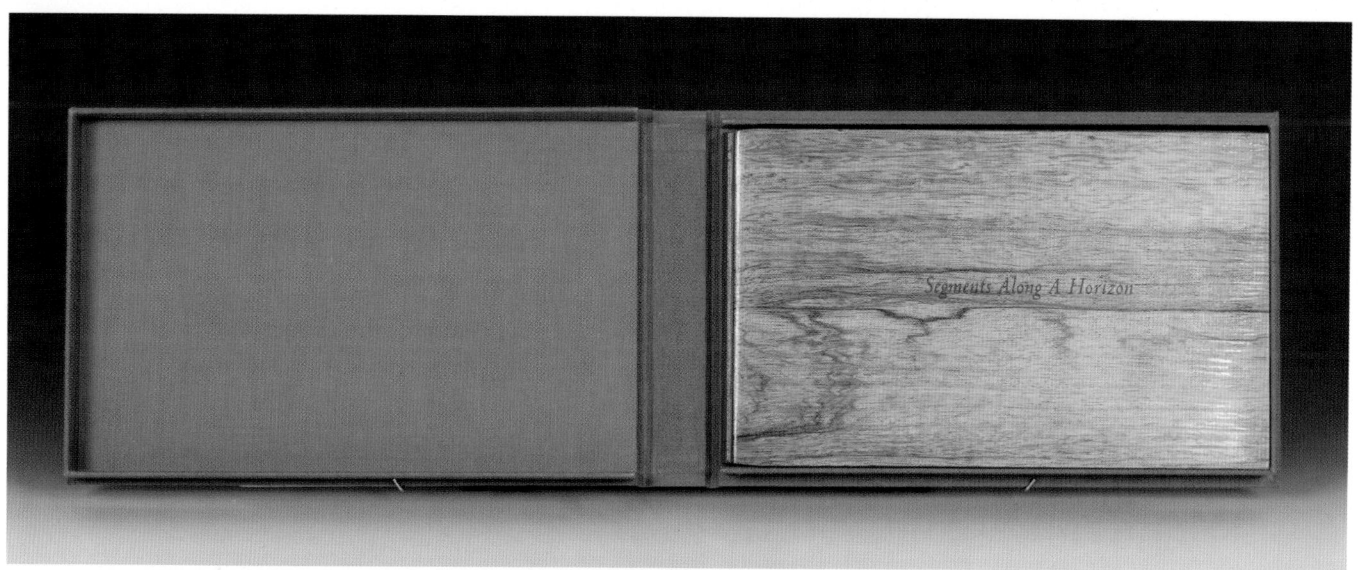

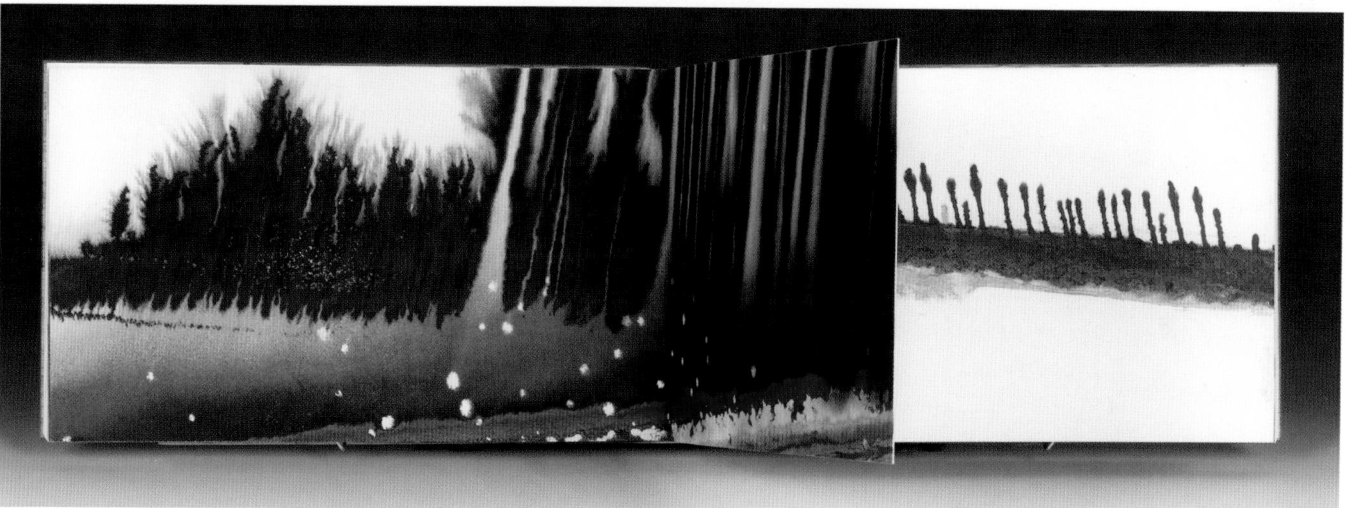

▲ **Segments Along a Horizon** | 2005

9 x 15 x 1 inches (22.9 x 38.1 x 2.5 cm)
German paper, pigments, polished goatskin, original paintings, black limba boards; drum-leaf binding, letterpress printed

Photos by artist

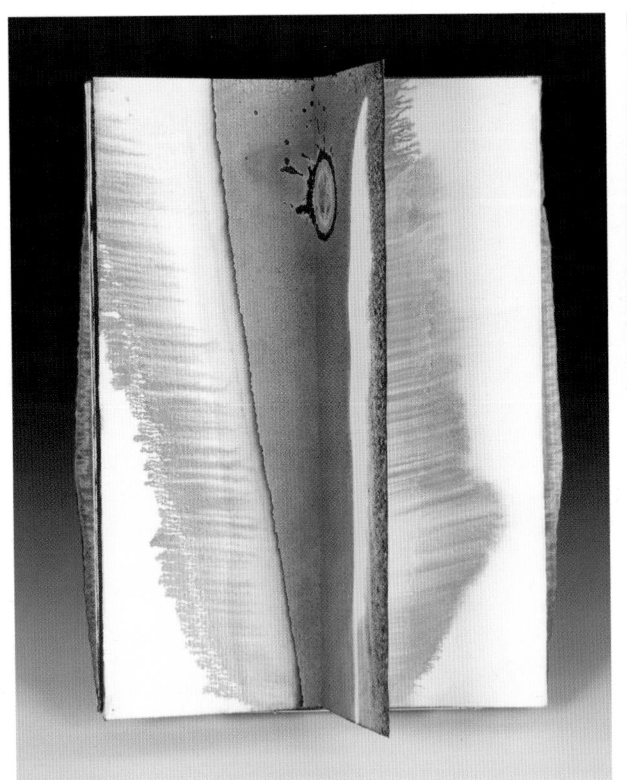

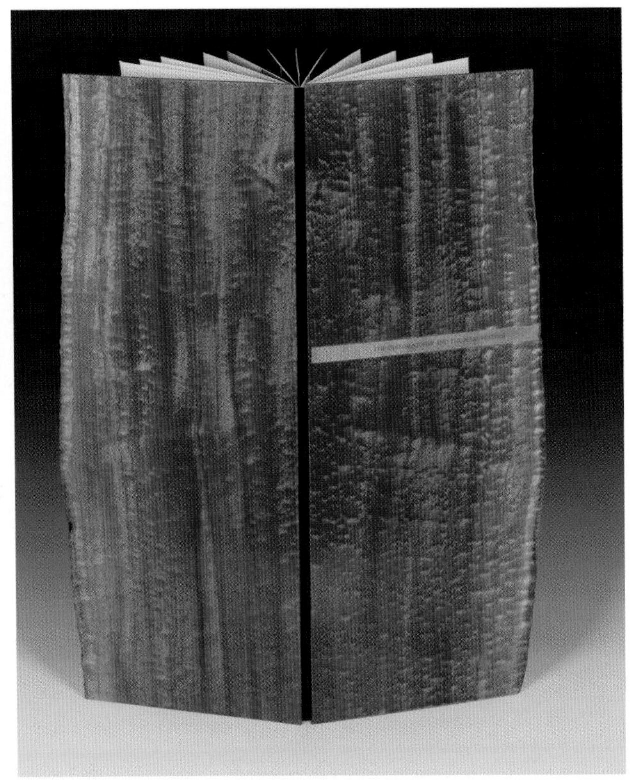

▲ **The Oystercatcher and the Pearl Feather** | 2006

30 x 11 x 1 inches (76.2 x 27.9 x 2.5 cm)
Paper, pigments, pomelle sapele boards with cork inlay, original paintings, silk; drum-leaf binding, letterpress printed

Photos by artist

" There is an intimate relationship between the book and the body. As an artist, I try to make books that engage people through multiple levels of perception. "

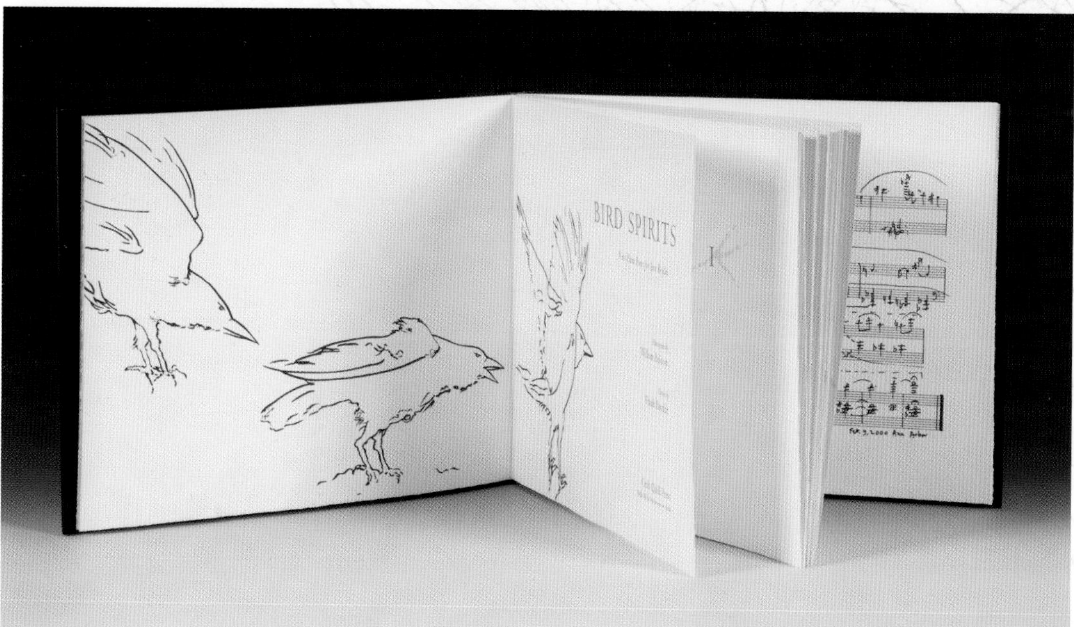

▲ Bird Spirits | 2000

Collaboration with William Bolcom and Frank Boyden
11¼ x 14⅜ x 1 inches (28.6 x 36.5 x 2.5 cm)
German papers, lacquered boards, silk; sewn-boards binding, intaglio printed, letterpress printed
Photo by artist

Evidence of Night | 2003 ▶

Collaboration with Jennifer Boyden and Frank Boyden
15 x 8½ x 1 inches (38.1 x 21.6 x 2.5 cm)
German and Japanese papers, goatskin, pomelle sapele boards; sewn-boards binding, intaglio printed, letterpress printed
Photo by artist

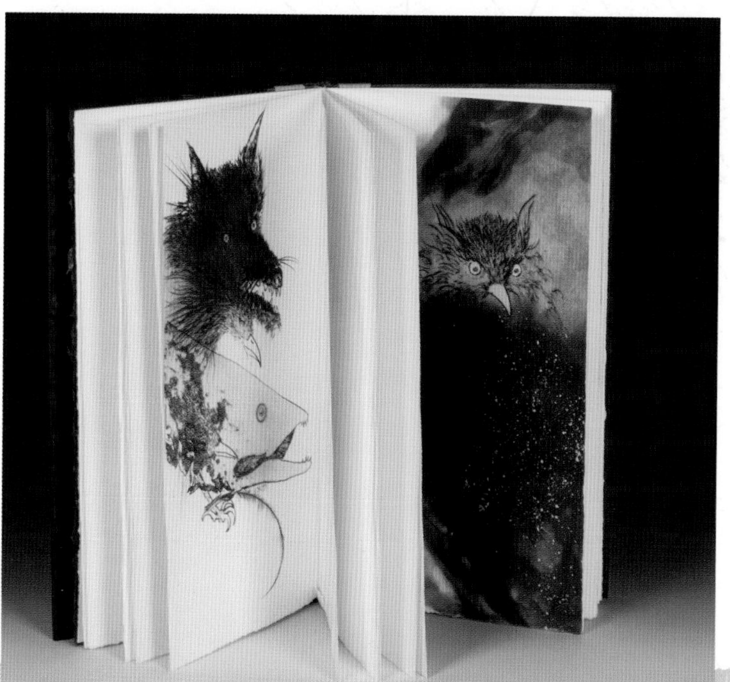

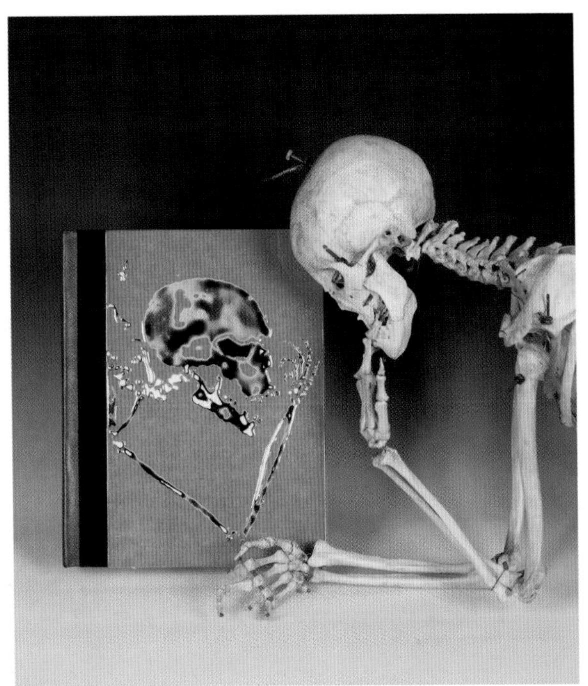

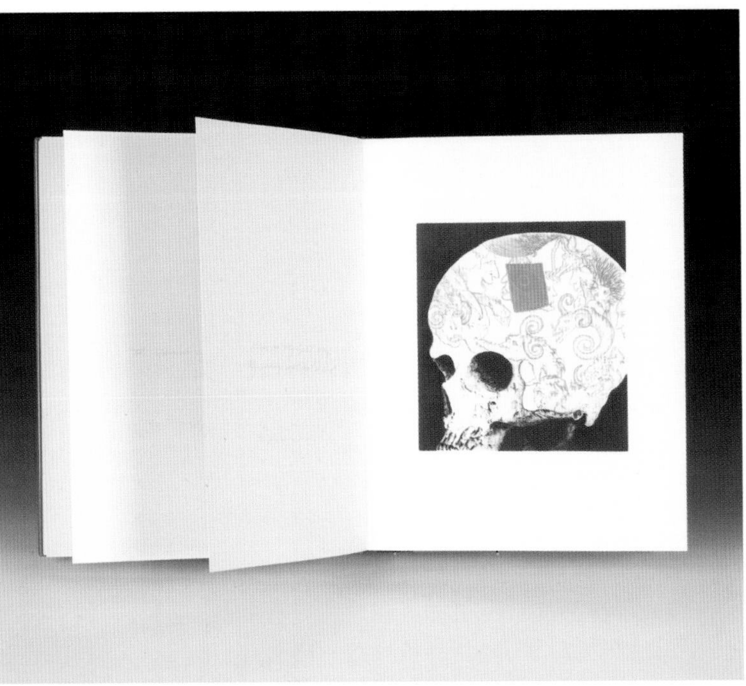

▲ **The Irreverences, Provocations, and Connivances of Uncle Skulky** | 2004

Collaboration with Frank Boyden
14⅜ x 11¾ x 1¾ inches (36.5 x 29.8 x 4.4 cm)
German paper, lacquer mahogany boards, original drawings, goatskin;
drum-leaf binding, intaglio printed, letterpress printed
Photos by artist

" I love the almost visceral quality of momentum that a book can lend to its content. When I begin to make a book, this quality of momentum is at the forefront of my thoughts. "

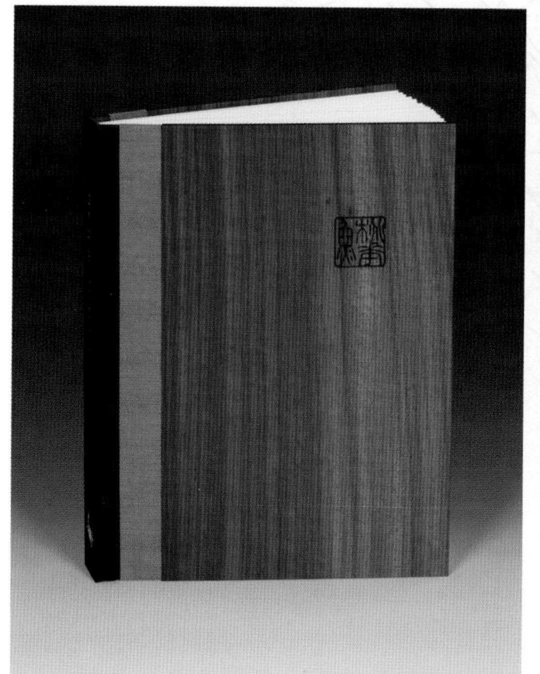

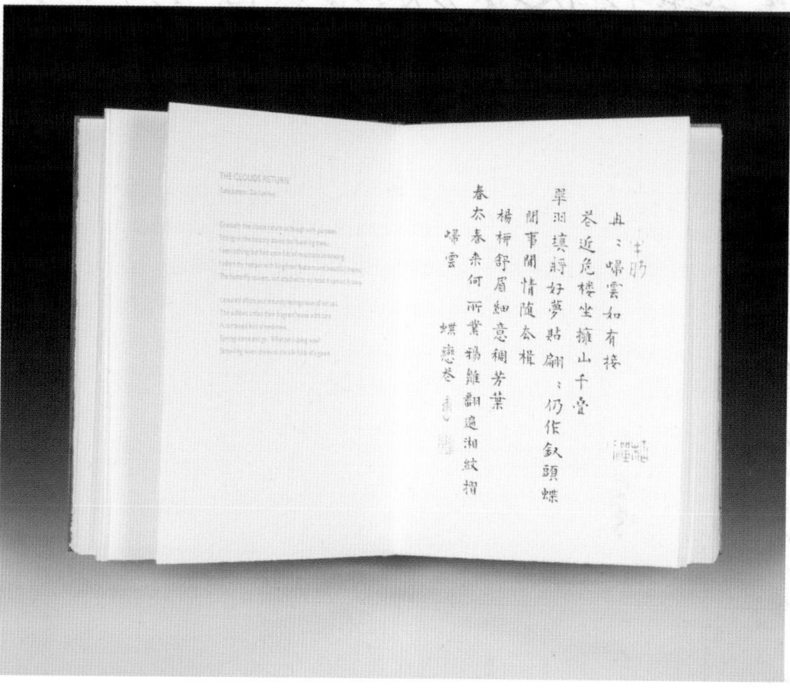

▲ **Peach Blossom Fish: Selected Poems Composed and Calligraphed by Chang Ch'ung-ho** | 1999

11 x 8½ x 1 inches (27.9 x 21.6 x 2.5 cm)

German papers, silk, padauk boards; sewn-boards binding, letterpress printed

Photos by artist

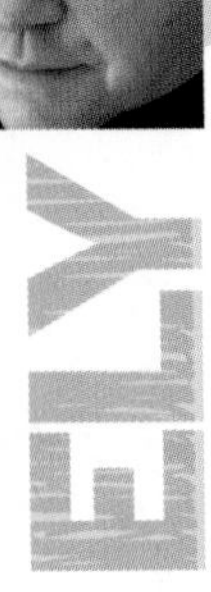

Timothy Ely

USING A COMPLEX VISUAL VOCABULARY, Timothy Ely creates elaborate and intriguing narratives, imaginative compositions that assimilate his interest in geometry and cartography. His content—orchestrated intersections of the abstract and the pictographic, enigmatic writings, and mysterious landscapes—embodies both precision and freedom. With a commitment to impeccable craftsmanship in all aspects of book production, Ely evaluates and adapts binding techniques as he works—a creative habit that led him to develop drum leaf binding. This structure, now widely used by other book artists, allows a book to lie flat when open, so that imagery can flow uninterrupted across the fold.

Ely's skills and creative vision have earned him a fellowship from the National Endowment for the Arts. His one-of-a-kind manuscript books are held in numerous public and private collections, including the Boston Athenaeum in Boston, Massachusetts; the Library of Congress in Washington, D.C.; and the New York Public Library in New York City. He lives in Colfax, Washington.

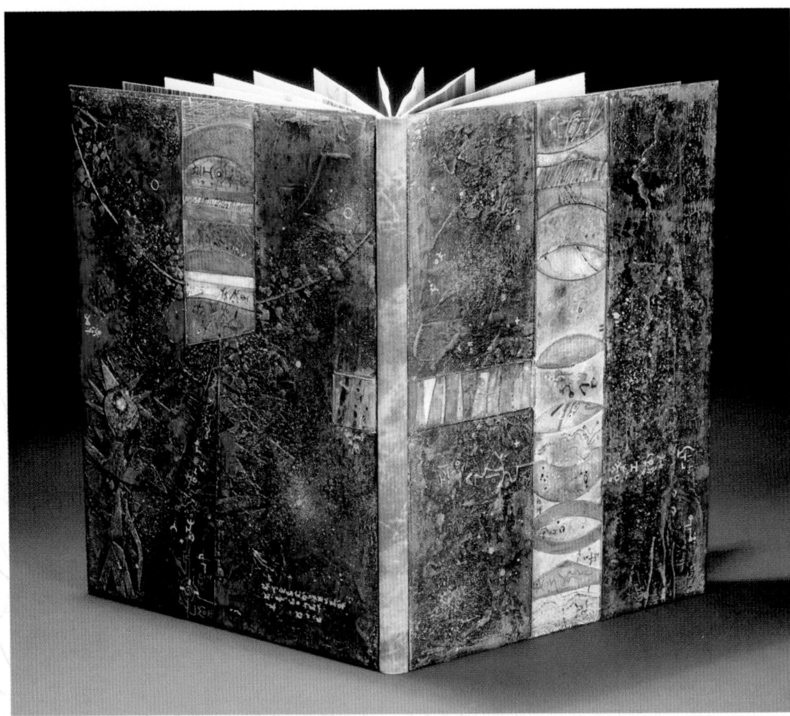

Observatory | 2008 ▶

15 x 11 x ½ inches (38.1 x 27.9 x 1.3 cm)
Acrylic resins, Japanese tissue, pigments, cotton fabric, ink, watercolor, graphite, Magnani paper; drum leaf binding
Photo by Jonathan Billing

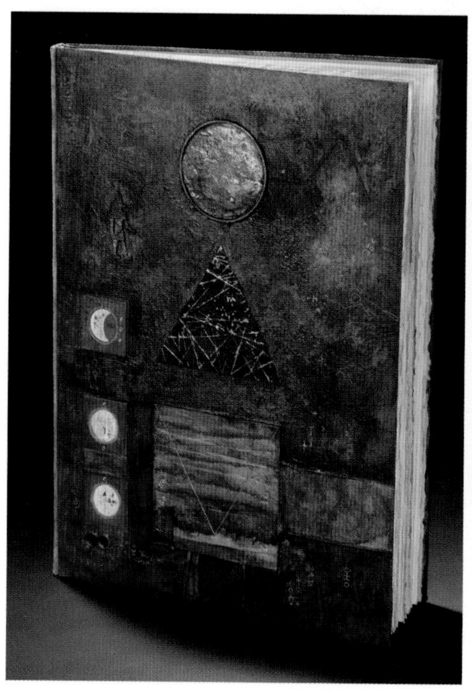

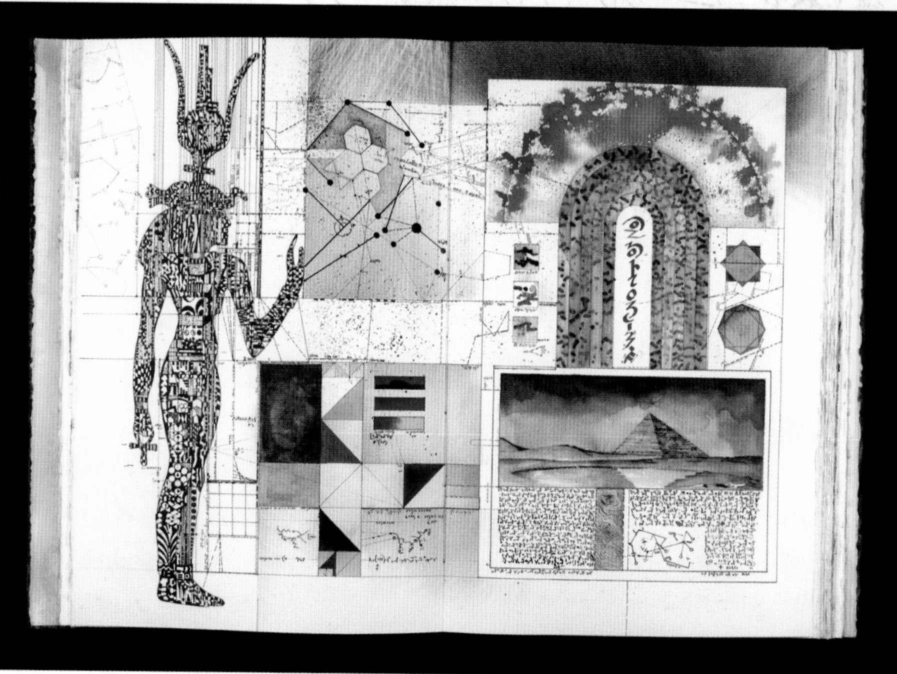

▲ **The Flight into Egypt: The Third Magnitude** | 2009

17 x 12 x 1 inches (43.2 x 30.5 x 2.5 cm)
Leather, resins, linen, papyrus, metals, glass, Egyptian soil, copper, ink, graphite, watercolor, anodized foils, paper, Egyptian cotton two-tier endbands; return-guard sewn binding

Photos by Jonathan Billing

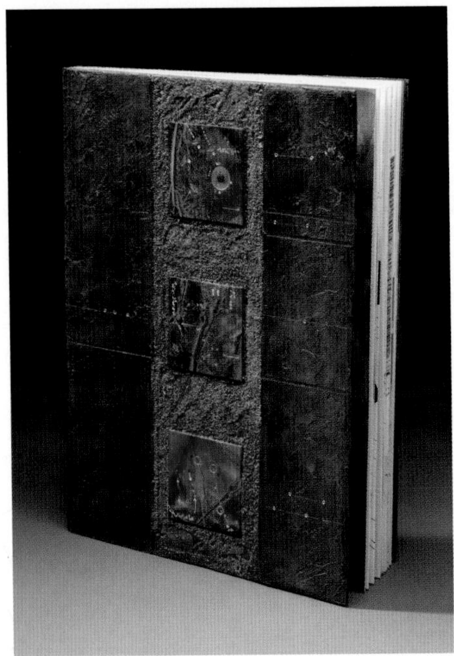

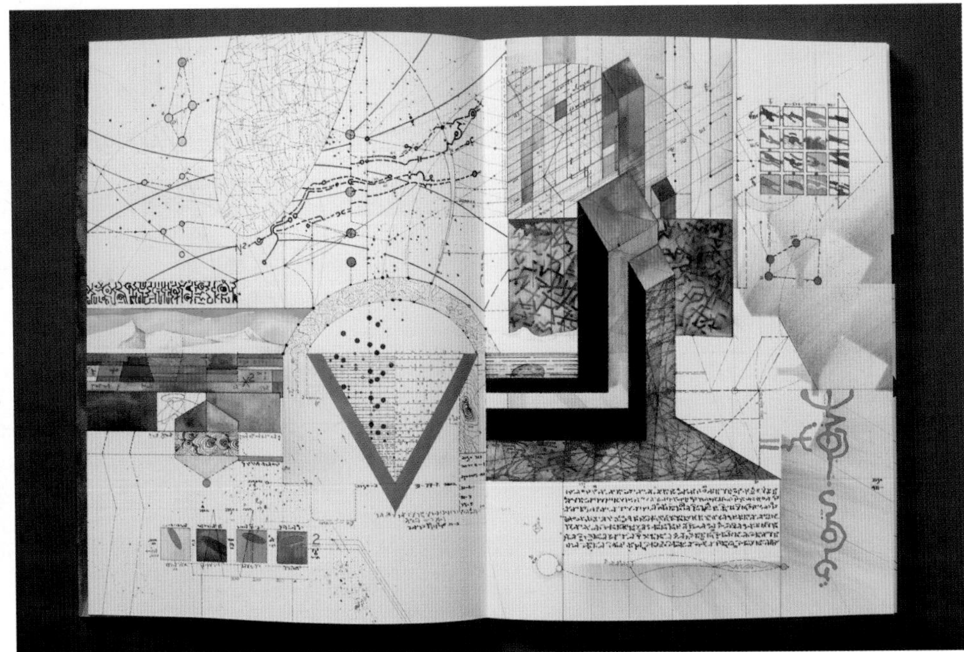

▲ **Index** | 2009

15 x 11 x 1 inches (38.1 x 27.9 x 2.5 cm)
Leather, gold, oolitic sand, carborundum, acrylics, paper, copper rivets, ink, graphite, watercolor, anodized foils, resin, pumice; drum leaf binding

Photos by Paul Foster

" I make books because I'm intrigued by the spatial compression provided by the form. "

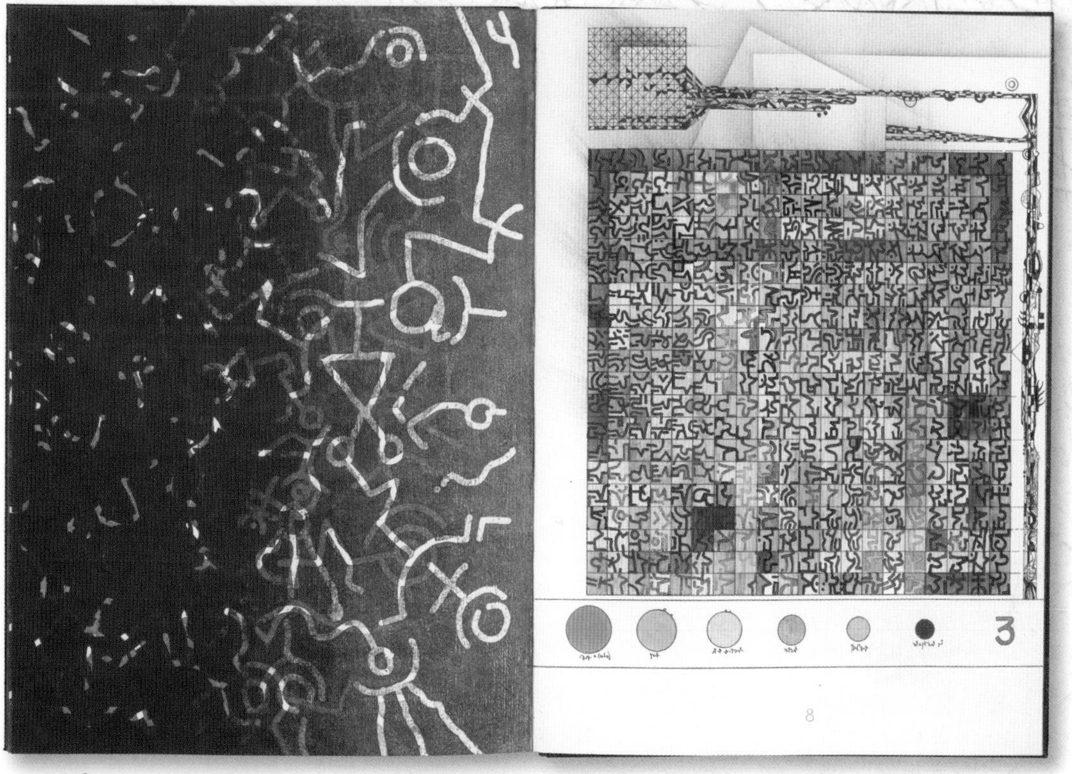

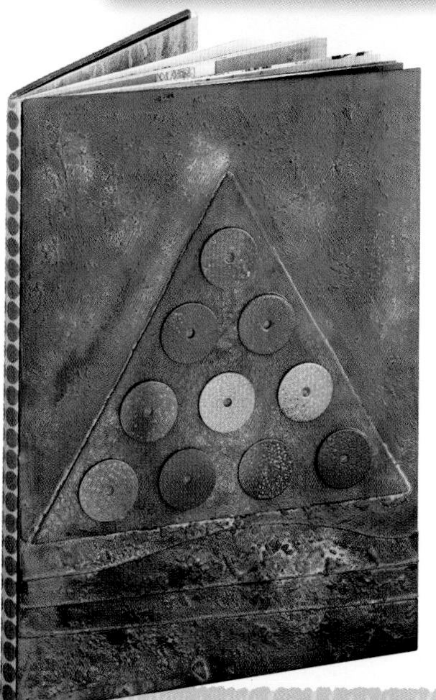

▲ **Dark Material** | 2008

15 x 11 x ½ inches (38.1 x 27.9 x 1.3 cm)
Enameled steel, acrylic resins, sand, commercial cotton fabric, ink, graphite, watercolor, paper, sand; drum leaf binding, woodcut monoprints

Photos by Jerry McCollum

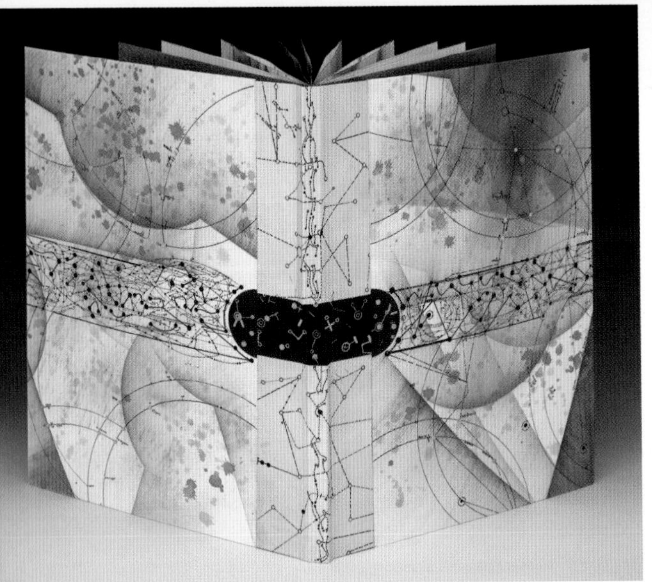

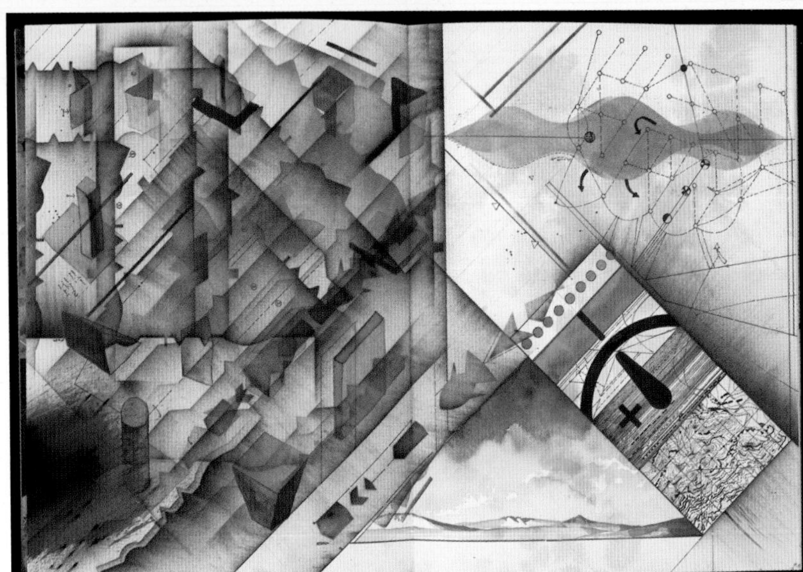

The Secret Books of Natural Philosophy: Time | 2008

14½ x 10½ x ½ inches (36.8 x 26.7 x 1.3 cm)
Leather, vellum, paper, anodized foils, ink, graphite, watercolor, paper; tooled, drum leaf binding
Photos by Jerry McCollum

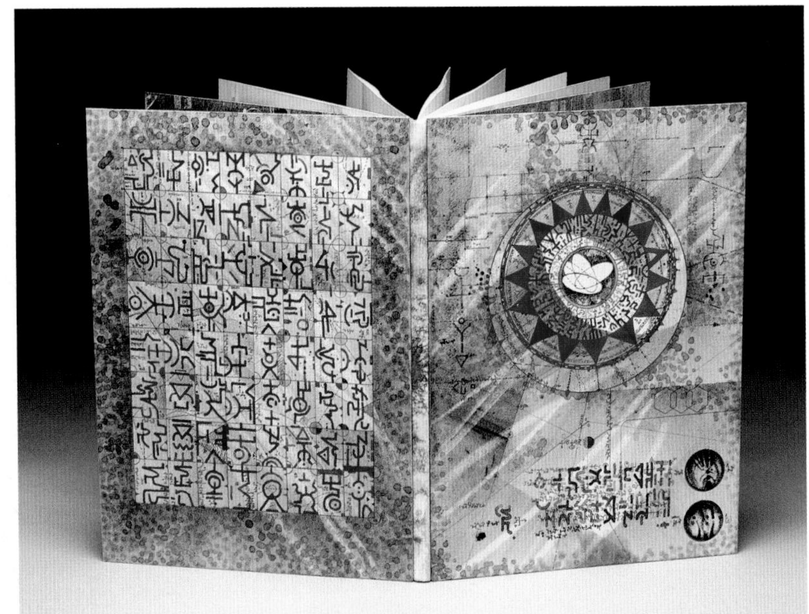

Halo Chalice | 2005

15 x 11 x ½ inches (38.1 x 27.9 x 1.3 cm)
Ink, resins, wax, graphite, watercolor; drum leaf binding
Photo by Mark LaMoreaux

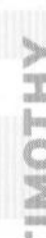

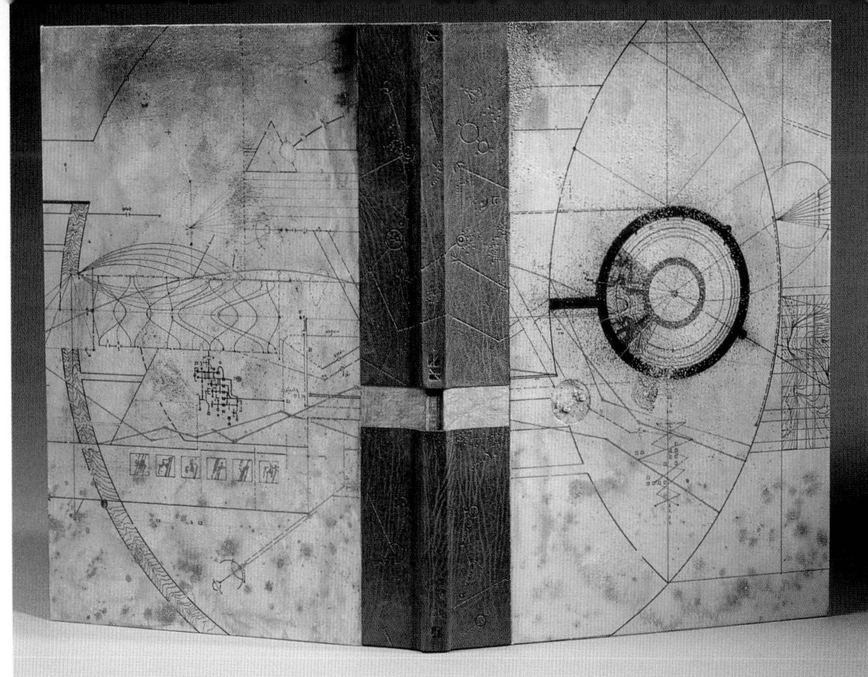

"My books are about the co-mapping of personal experiences with history and geography, at both conscious and unconscious levels. This merger provides visual metaphors out of which a complicated life might be understood."

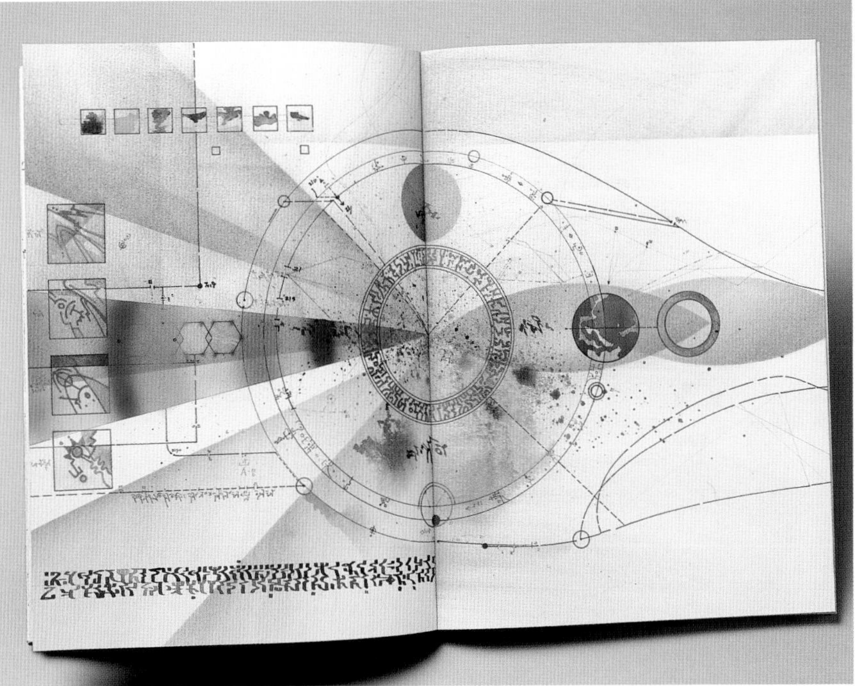

◀ **Folium** | 2000

15 x 11 x ½ inches (38.1 x 27.9 x 1.3 cm)
Ink, pigments, leather, paper, graphite, watercolor; drum leaf binding

Photos by Paul Foster

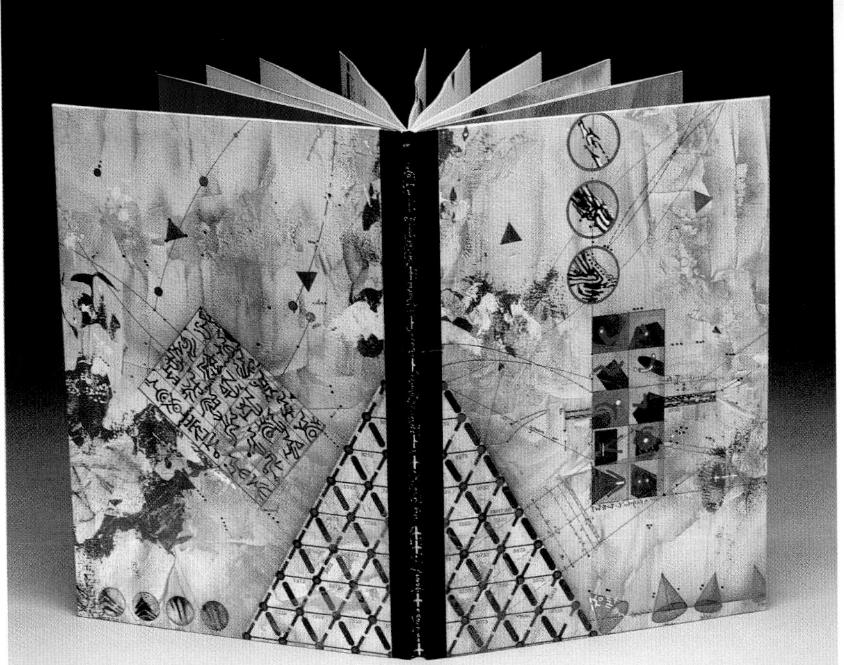

"I'm interested in how the artifacts of history help us invent our own personal stories."

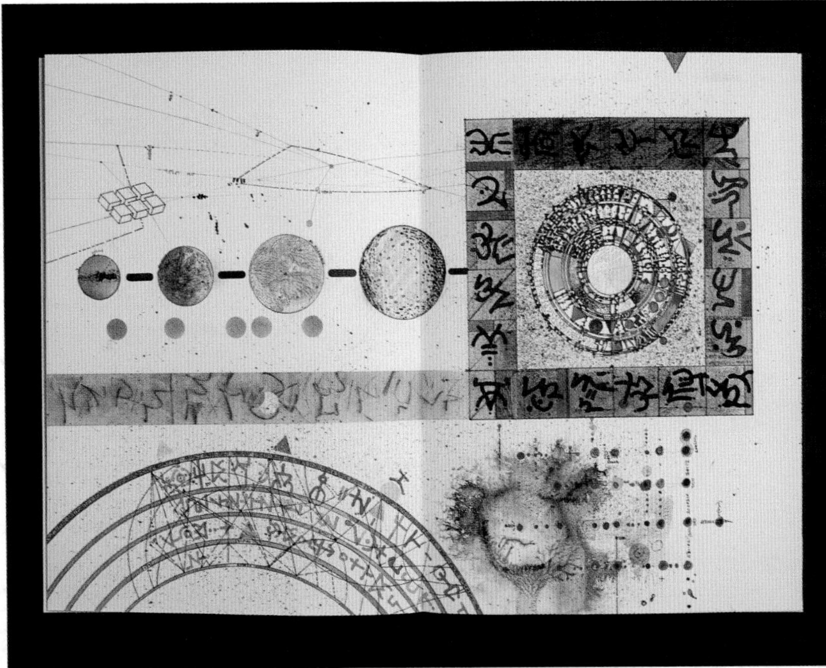

◀ **Trajections** | 2007

15 x 11 x ½ inches (38.1 x 27.9 x 1.3 cm)
Ink, graphite, watercolor, paper, leather, metals; drum leaf binding

Photos by Mark LaMoreaux

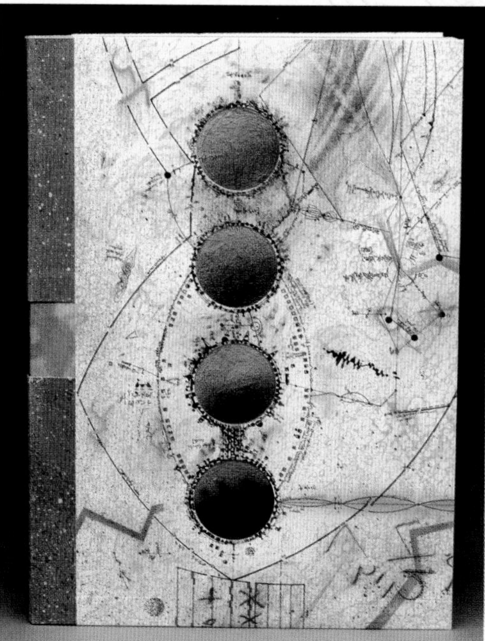

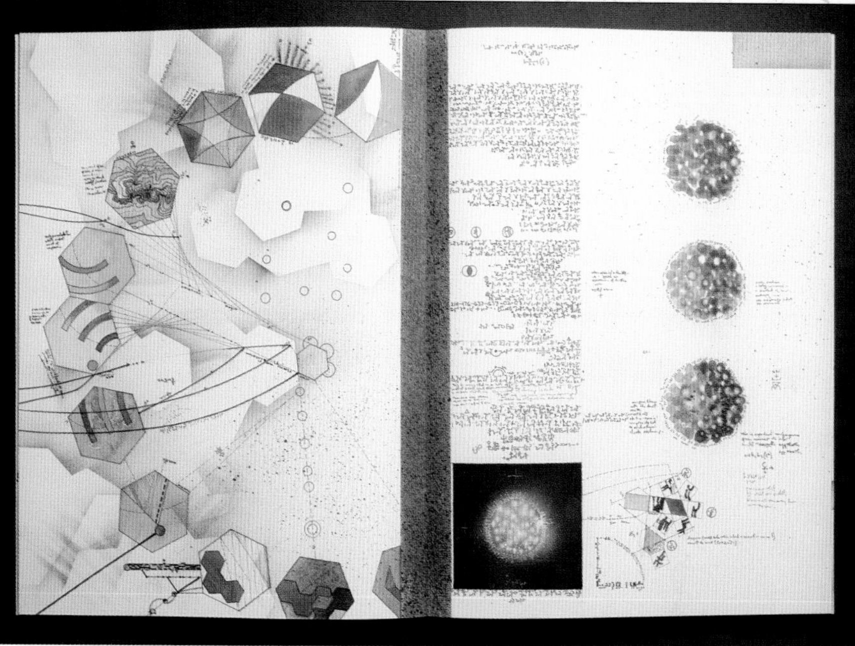

▲ **The Secret Books of Natural Philosophy: Dust** | 2007

14½ x 10½ x ½ inches (36.8 x 26.7 x 1.3 cm)
Dust, pigments, marble, resin, acrylics, silk, paper, wax, ink, graphite, watercolor, paper; drum leaf binding

Photos by Mark LaMoreaux

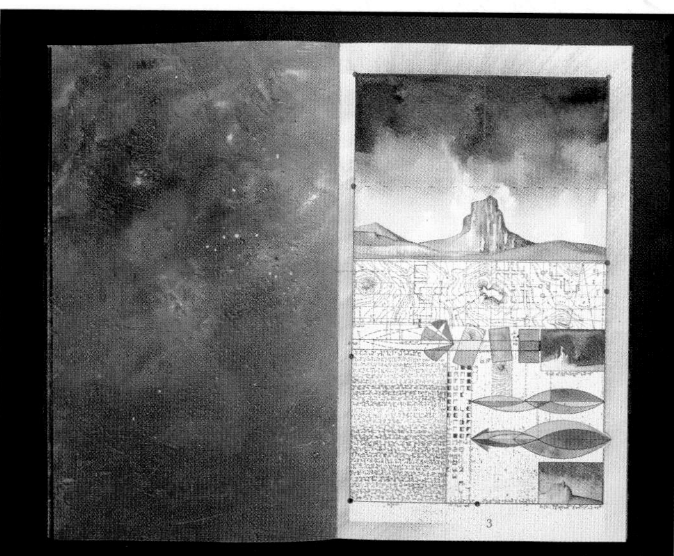

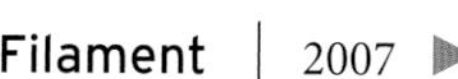

Filament | 2007 ▶

14½ x 9 x ¾ inches (36.8 x 22.9 x 1.9 cm)
Oolitic sand from the Great Salt Lake, resin, iron-oxide pigment, varnish, copper, ink, graphite, watercolor, paper; drum leaf binding

Photo by Mark LaMoreaux

Jody Alexander

THE QUIRKY CHARACTERS THAT INHABIT THE pages of Jody Alexander's books come to us fully developed. She nurtures them for months—sometimes years—developing complex lives for each personality and using them as the foundations for her work. Alexander skillfully breathes new life into discarded books and found objects, imbuing her work with layers of meaning and authenticity. Her pieces are carefully contained within timeworn boxes, and the intricacy of these structures echo the multifaceted lives of her characters.

Delicately rendered, Alexander's monochromatic, repetitive stitching both binds and reveals. Her sensitive layering of castoff book pages, textiles, and photographs lends depth, texture, and a sense of history to each book, a quality that reinforces her storytelling. Alexander, who lives in Santa Cruz, California, describes herself as an artist, bookbinder, papermaker, librarian, and teacher. She teaches book arts workshops throughout the United States.

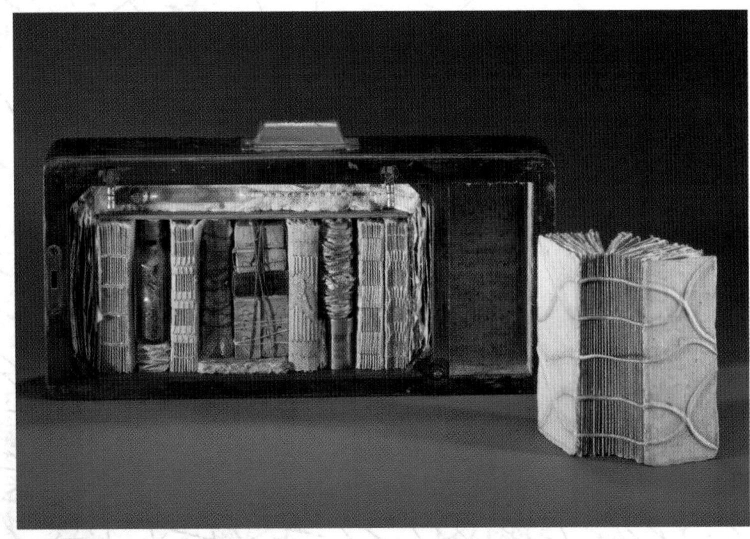

Miss Sook's Dropsy Cure Drawer Remained Unbeknownst to Most | 2009

9 x 17 x 3 inches (22.9 x 43.2 x 7.6 cm)
Wooden sewing machine base, handmade kozo/gampi paper, found objects, encaustic; packed sewing over cords, Ethiopian Coptic binding, long stitch

Photo by r.r. jones

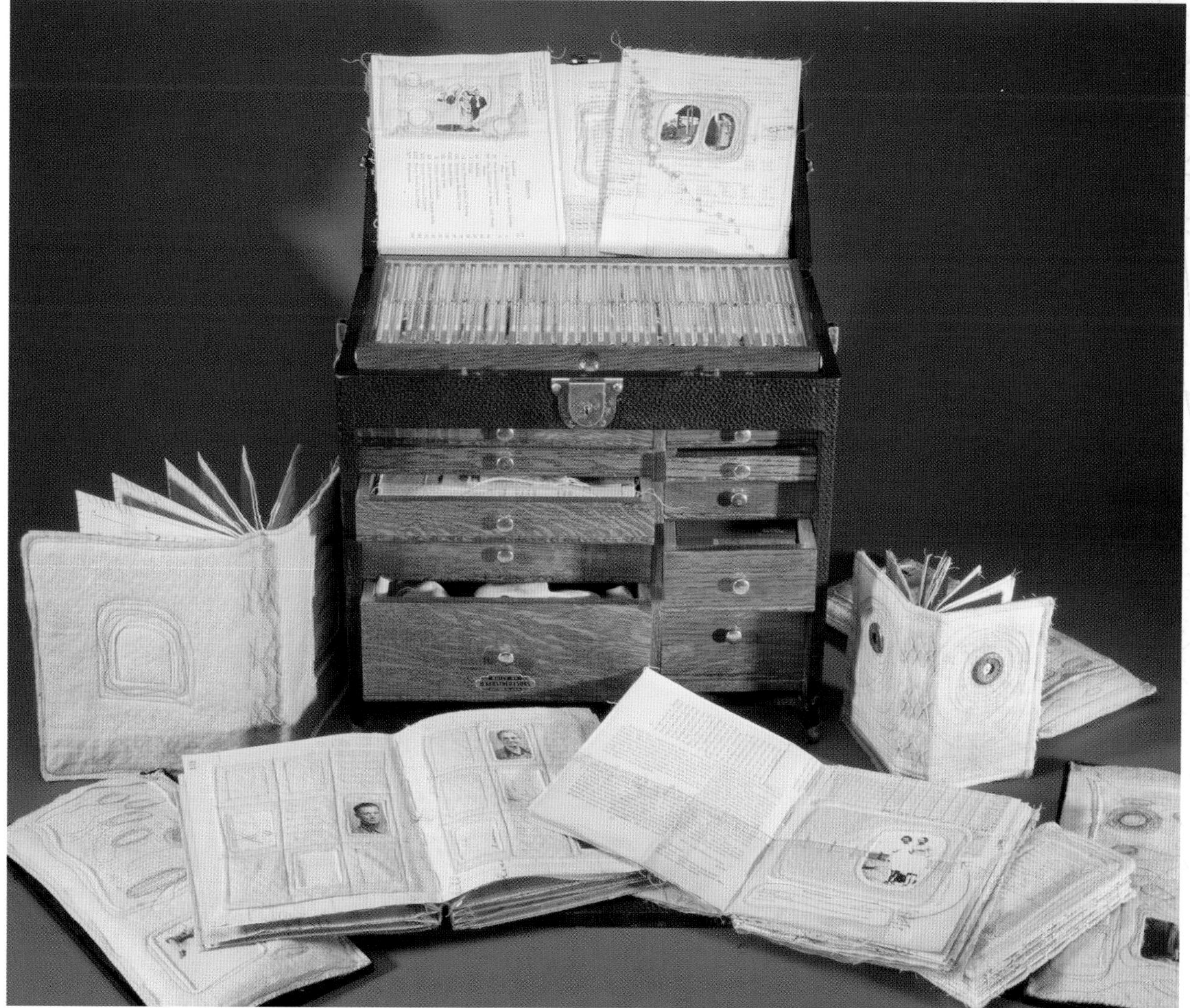

▲ **The Odd Volumes of Ruby B. (Boxed Set)** | 2009

Various dimensions

Portable dental case, test tubes, altered book pages, cotton batting, mull, old photographs; various bindings

Photo by r.r. jones

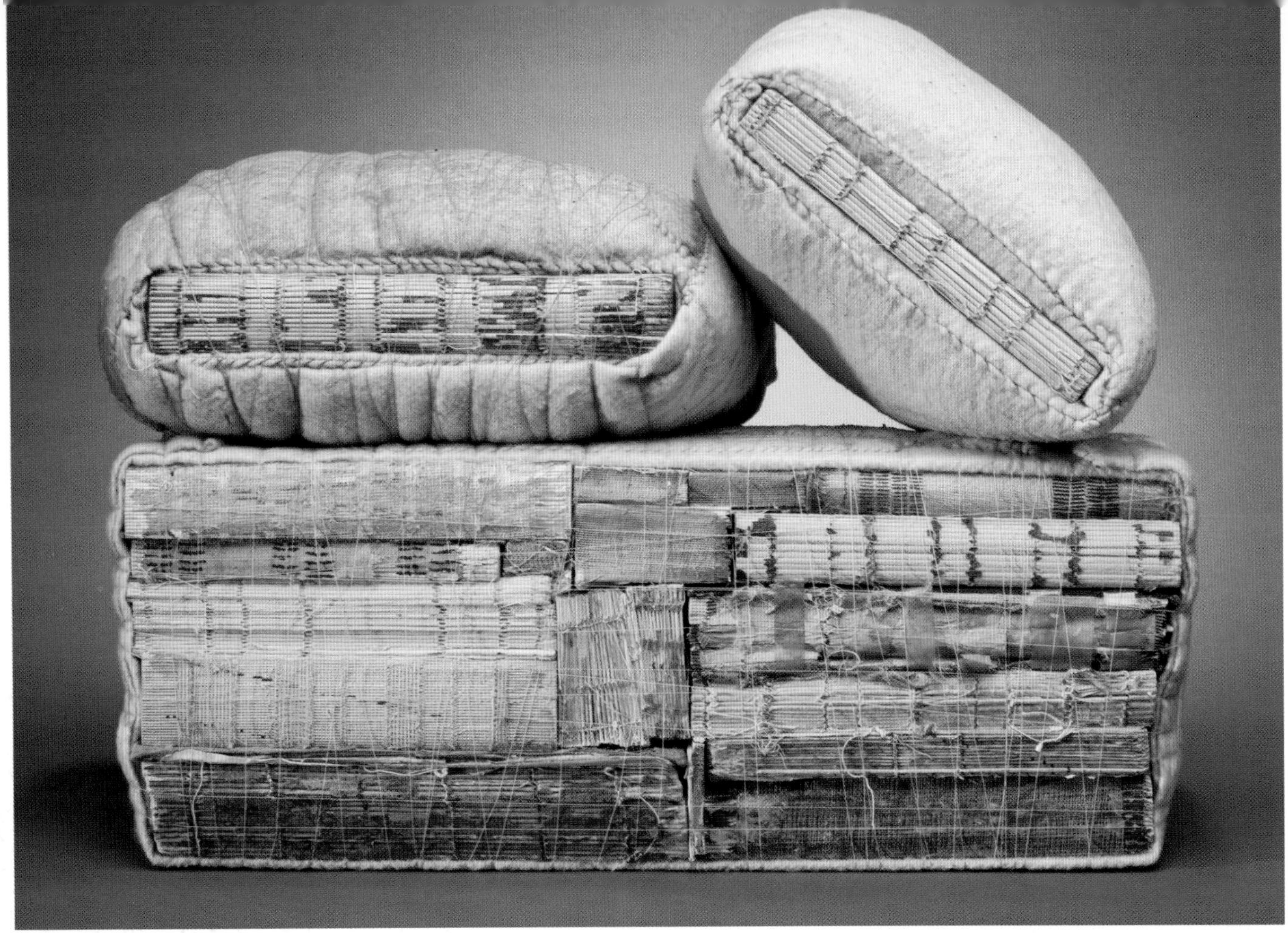

▲ **Exposed Spines** | 2009

23 x 18 x 8 inches (58.4 x 45.7 x 20.3 cm)
Old books, cotton batting, thread

Photos by r.r. jones

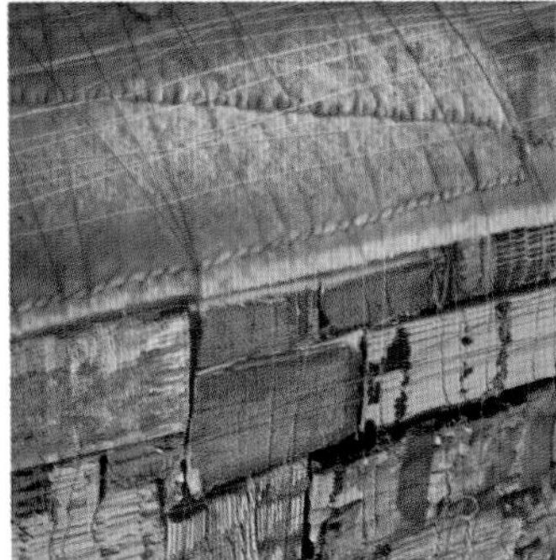

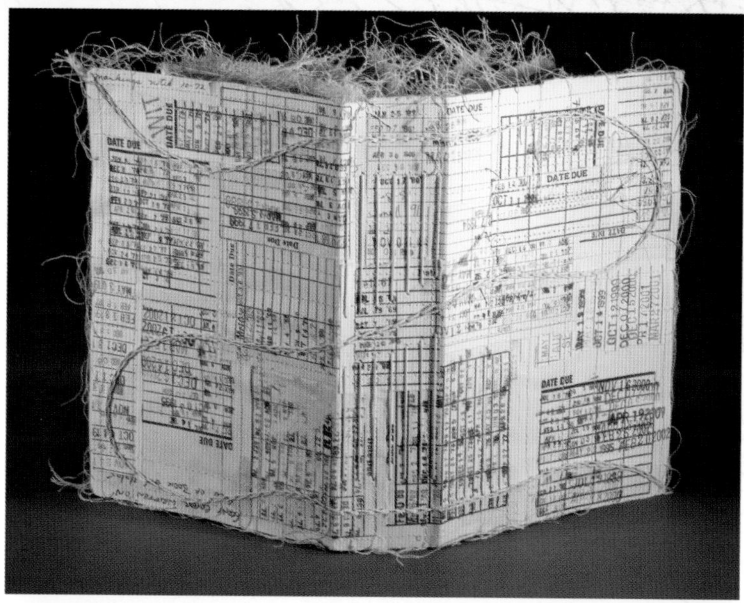

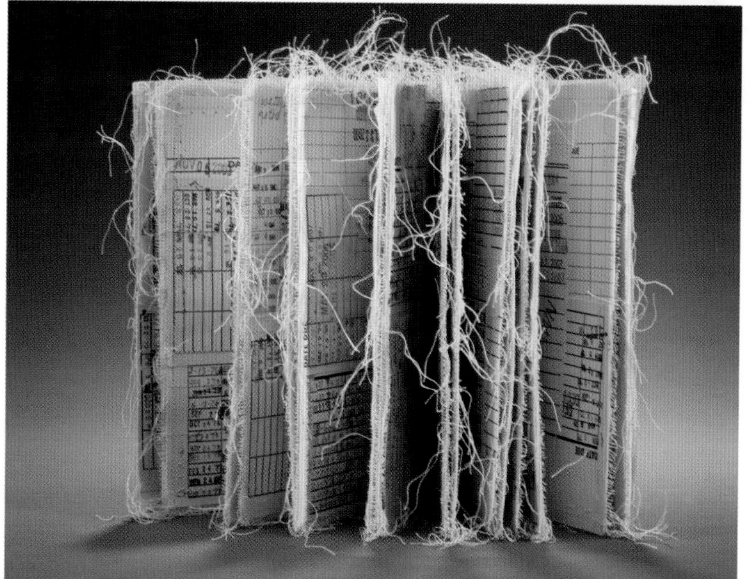

▲ **Date Due: It's Not a Popularity Contest** | 2008

7 x 5 x 1¾ inches (17.8 x 12.7 x 4.4 cm)
Date-due pockets from withdrawn library books, mull, thread; decorative long-stitch binding

Photos by r.r. jones

"If I make a piece of art that doesn't have a book in it, that piece just doesn't feel right. Using books, whether they're volumes that I've bound or old discards, somehow gives my work the depth that I'm looking for."

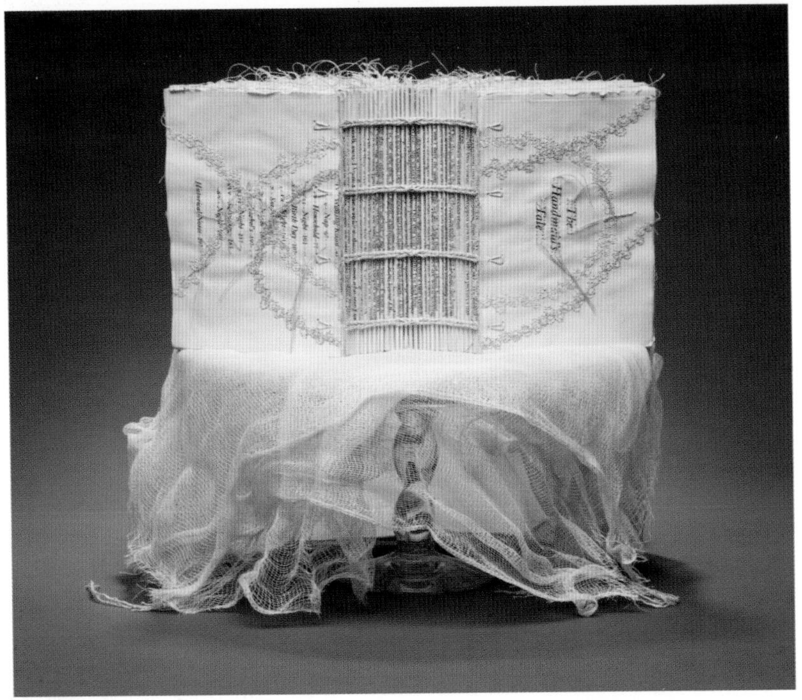

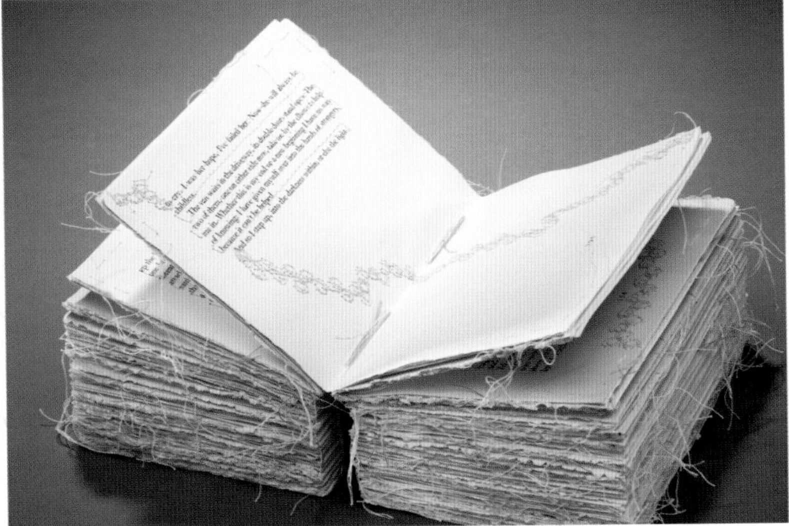

" As a librarian and book artist, I see that many books have a lifespan, and that often their lives, as they were originally intended, come to an end. I like to give these books new life in my art pieces. "

◀ **Wrapped Words** | 2008

12 x 12 x 12 inches (30.5 x 30.5 x 30.5 cm)
Book pages, thread, cheesecloth, glass cake stand;
Greek Coptic binding

Photos by r.r. jones

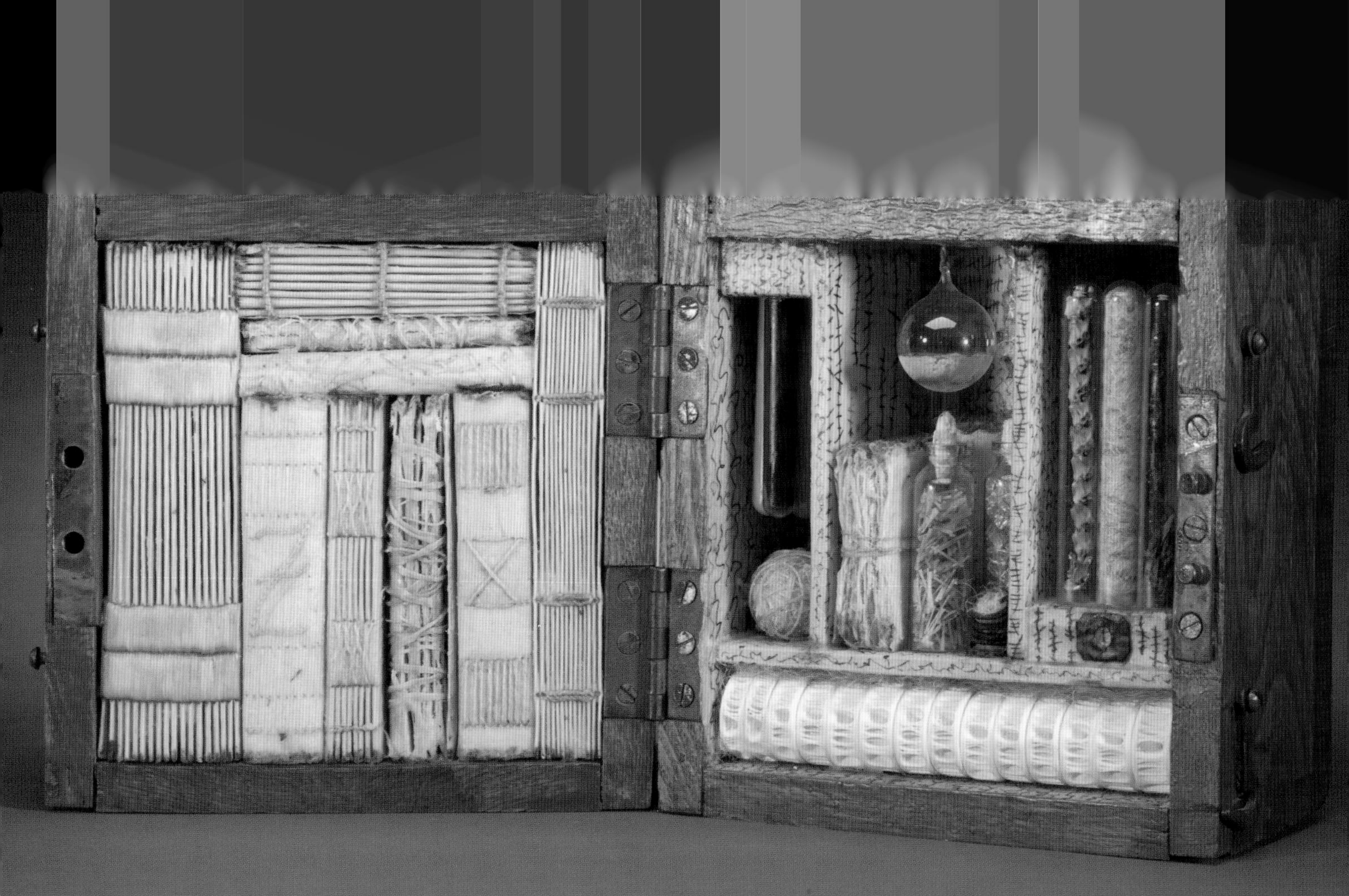

▲ **If She Thought It Would Help, Zelda Would Use Her Antediluvian Curse Cache to Attain Her Revenge** | 2004

7 x 17 x 5 inches (17.8 x 43.2 x 12.7 cm)

Wooden box, handmade kozo/gampi paper, wax, found objects; Ethiopian Coptic binding, long stitch, packed sewing over cords

Photo by r.r. jones

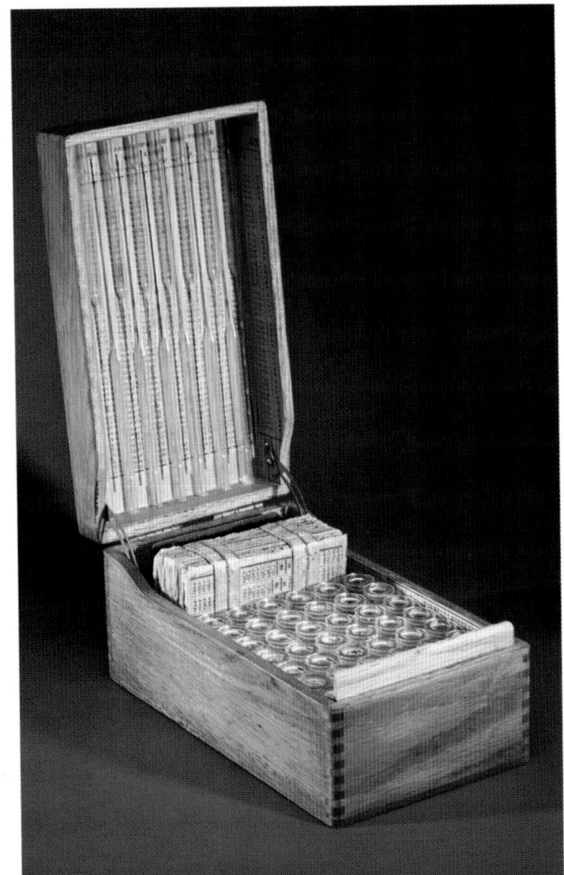

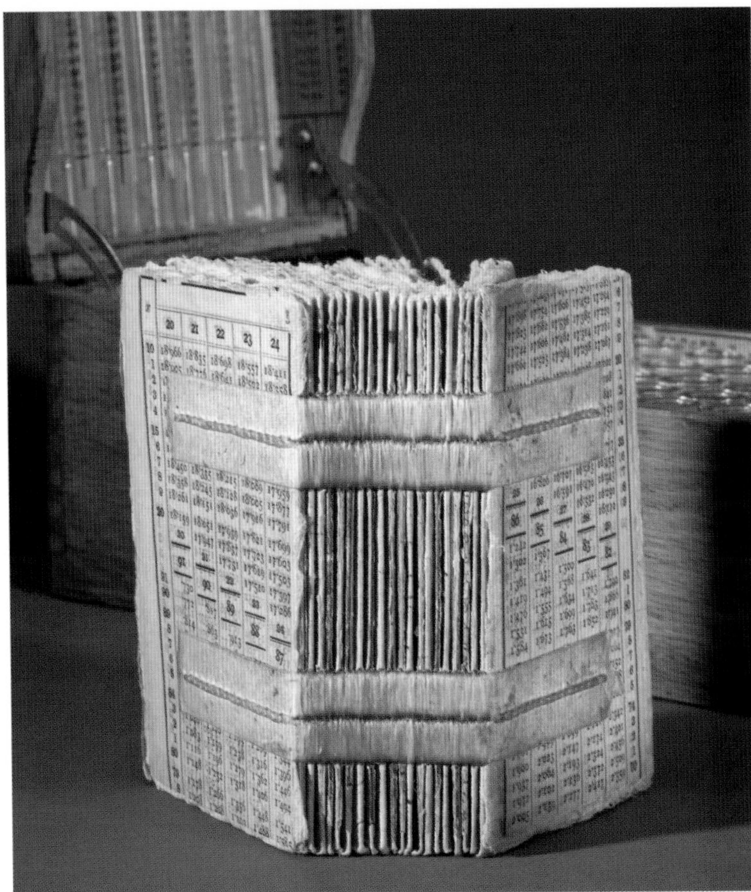

▲ **He Thought He Might Beat the Odds if Only He Applied Himself** | 2005

13 x 6 x 11 inches (33 x 15.2 x 27.9 cm)
Wooden box, handmade gampi/kozo paper, encaustic, chemistry glass, etched brass; packed sewing over split thongs binding

Photos by r.r. jones

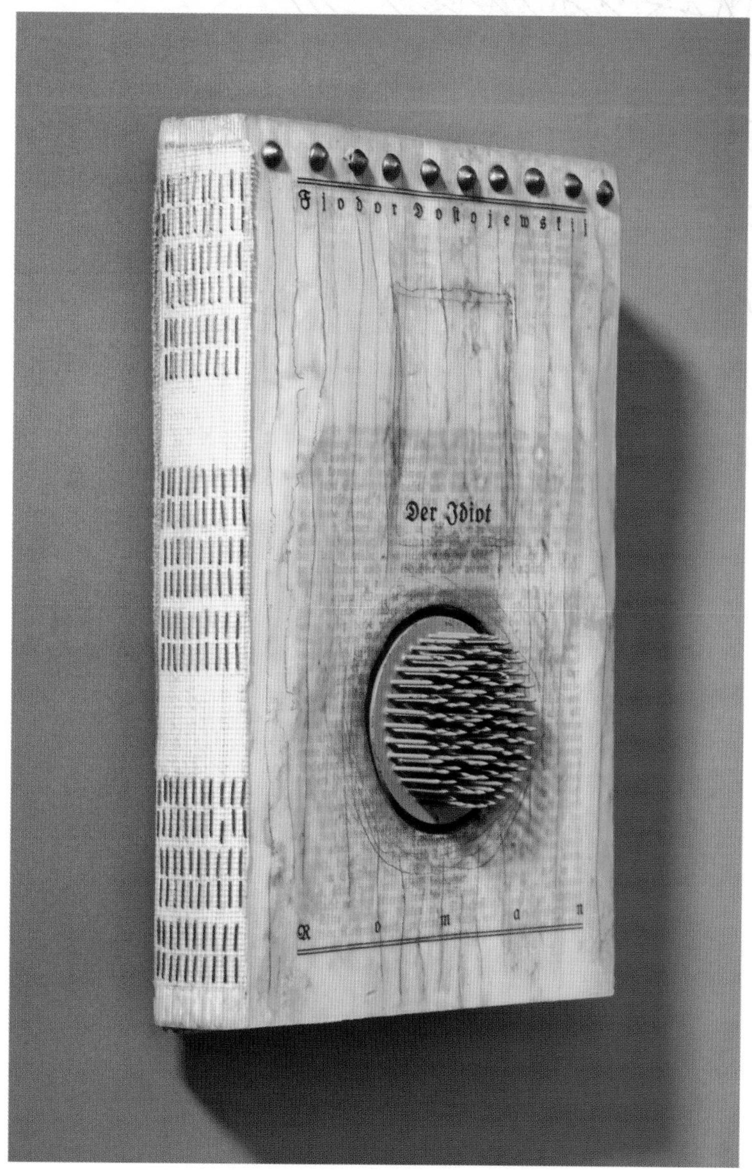

▲ **Der Idiot** | 2008

7 x 5 x 1 inches (17.8 x 12.7 x 2.5 cm)
Altered book, encaustic, tacks, frog
Photo by r.r. jones

" Revenge, mortality, isolation–these are some of the human issues with which the characters in my artwork are dealing. "

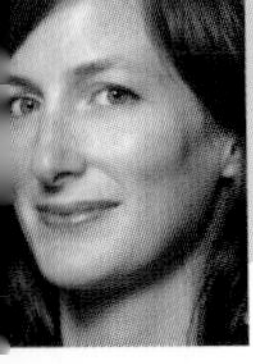

CHADWICK

Macy Chadwick

CONNECTIONS BOTH HUMAN AND CONCEPTUAL are at the core of the provocative books made by Macy Chadwick. Often featuring tangled layers of pattern and text, her work employs a sensitive use of color and line. She creates sparse but meaningful narratives that allow readers room to breathe and reflect as they flip through each book's atmospherically printed pages. Chadwick, who publishes under the imprint of In Cahoots Press, is an avid collaborator who produces books that adeptly reflect the dynamic of an evolving dialogue.

Employing a range of printing processes, Chadwick's expertly crafted books retain an ethereal spontaneity that communicates her passion and joy in the process of making. She lives in Oakland, California. Her work is included in many prominent collections in the United States and abroad, including the Victoria and Albert Museum in London, England; the Yale University Library in New Haven, Connecticut; and the University of Washington-Seattle.

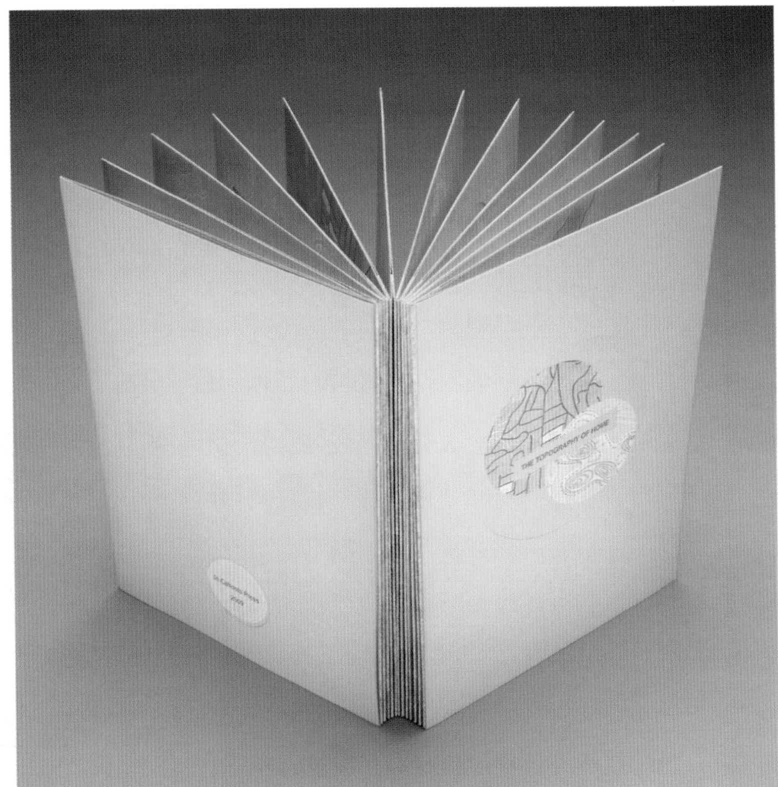

The Topography of Home | 2009 ▶

10½ x 7 x ¾ inches (26.7 x 17.8 x 1.9 cm)
Mohawk Superfine paper, Butcher paper, silk tissue; storage book binding, letterpress printed with pressure prints and polymer plates, pochoir
Photo by Sibila Savage

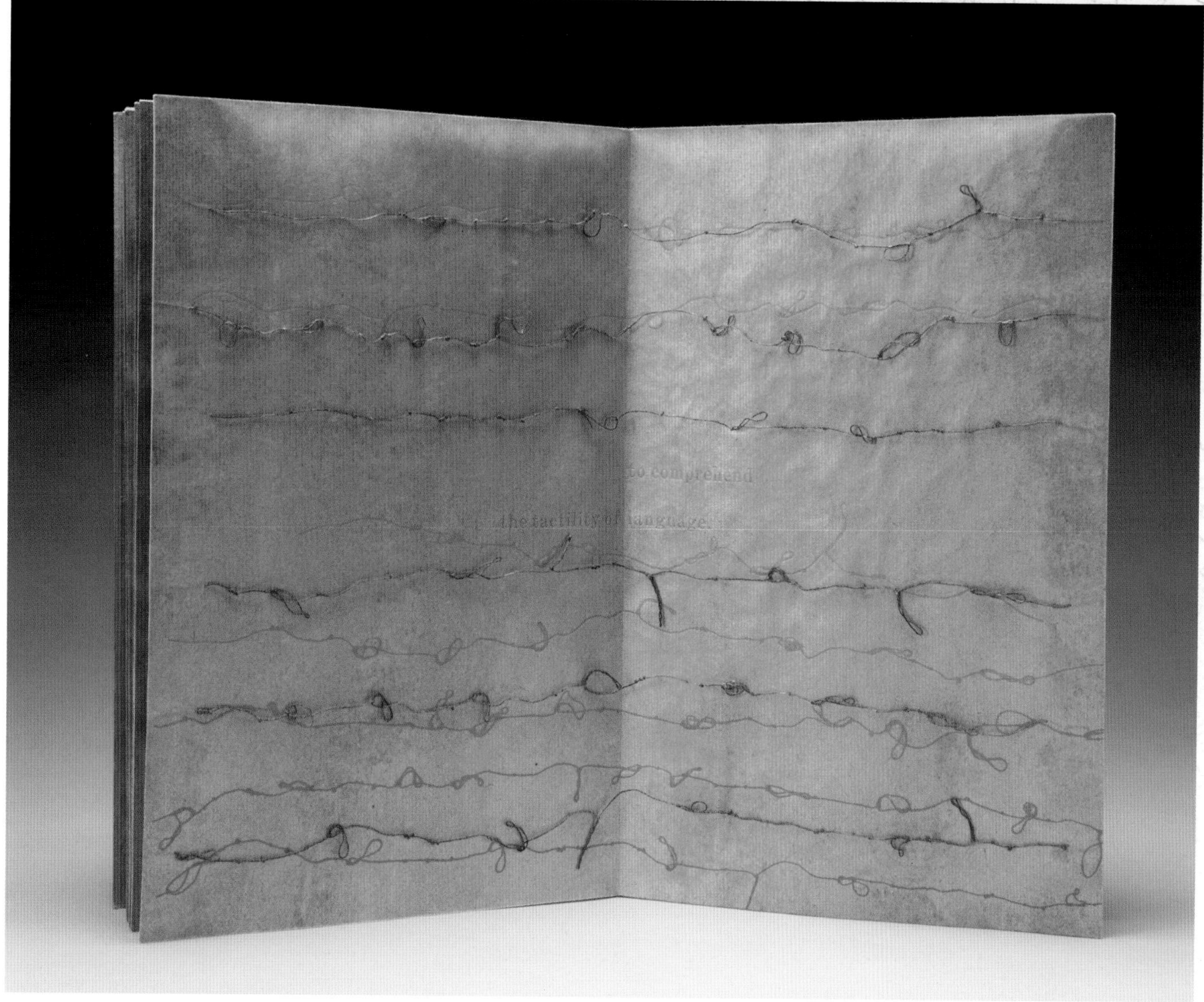

▲ **Letter by Letter** | 2008

10 x 7 x ½ inches (25.4 x 17.8 x 1.3 cm)
Mulberry paper treated with persimmon dye, linen thread;
letterpress printed with handset type and polymer plates

Photo by Sibila Savage

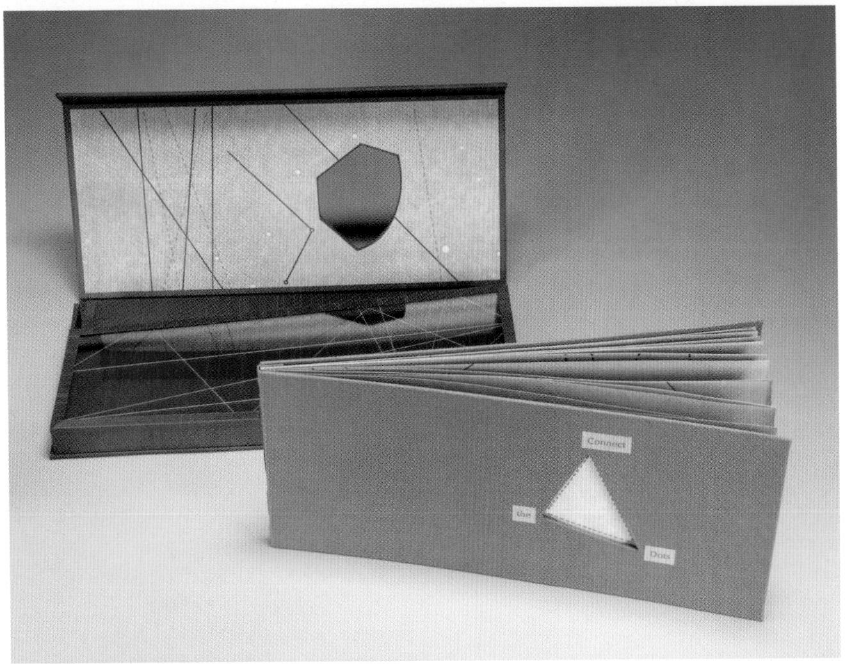

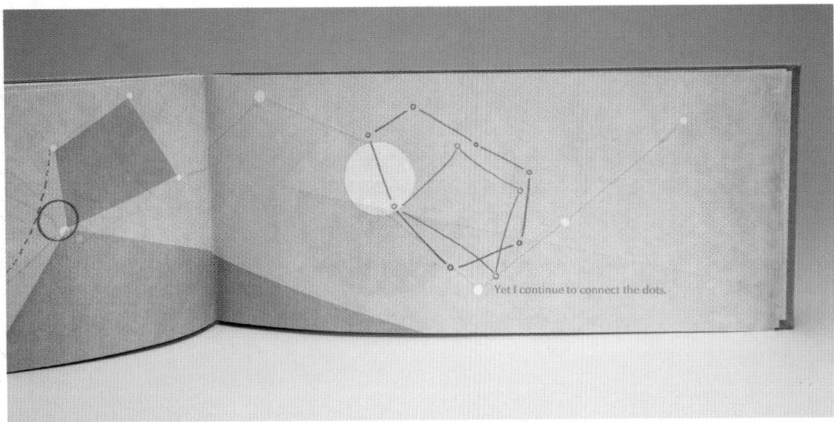

"I intentionally start printing before my artistic ideas have been fully resolved, because I want to leave room for the happy accidents that often occur at the press. The printing process keeps my creativity alive."

▲ **Connect the Dots** | 2007

Book: 4¼ x 10¼ x ¼ inches (10.8 x 26 x 0.6 cm)
Box: 4¾ x 10¾ x 1 inches (27.3 x 12.1 x 2.5 cm)

Kitakata paper, plastic sheeting, thread, book cloth; longstitch binding, letterpress printed with pressure prints, relief prints, polymer plates, and handset text

Photos by Sibila Savage

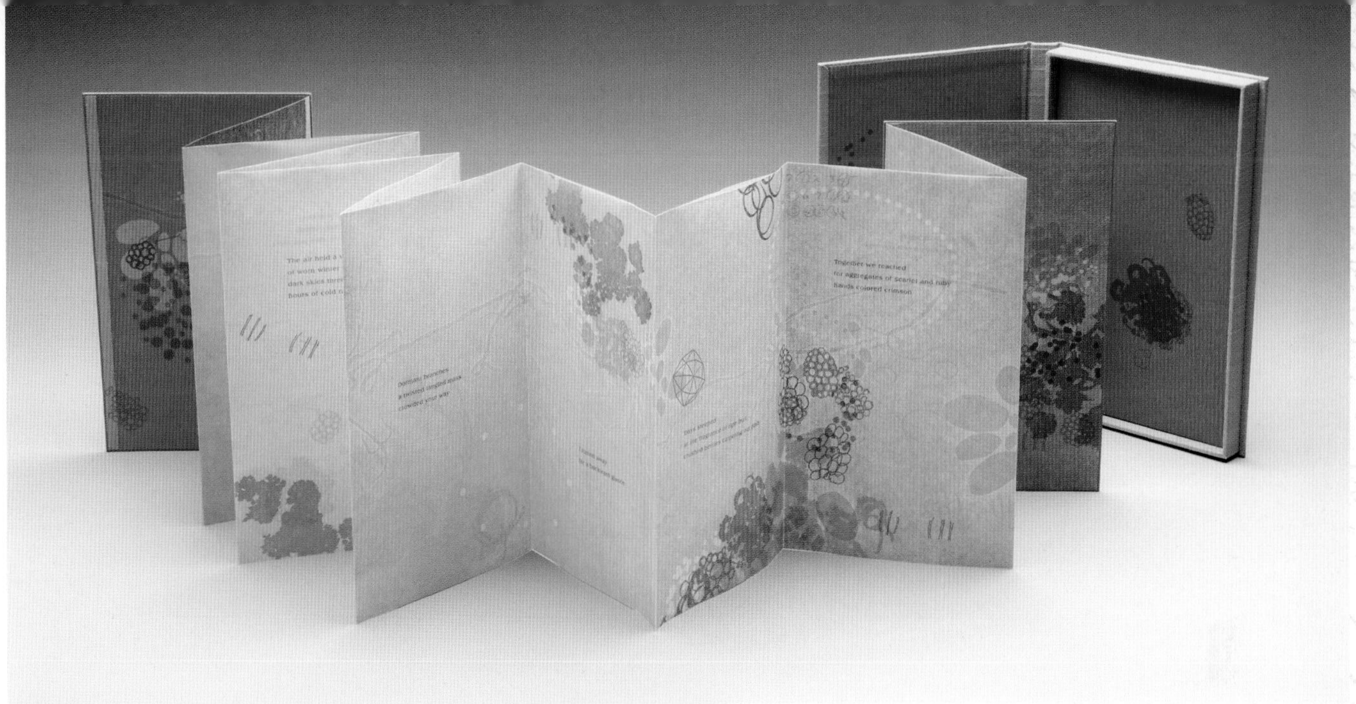

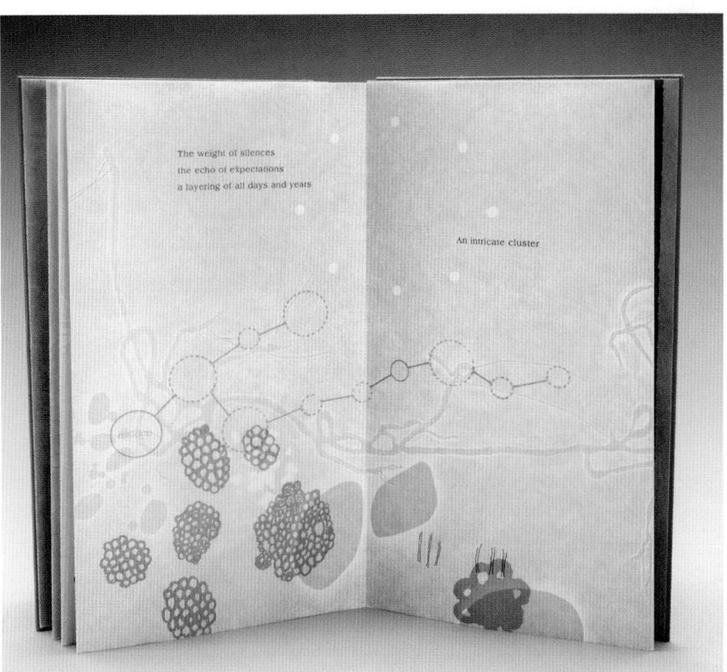

▲ **Aggregate Memory** | 2005

Collaboration with Lisa Onstad
8½ x 5 x ¼ inches (21.6 x 12.7 x 0.6 cm)
Gasen and Hanji papers; leporello binding, letterpress printed with pressure prints, relief prints, and polymer plates

Photos by Sibila Savage

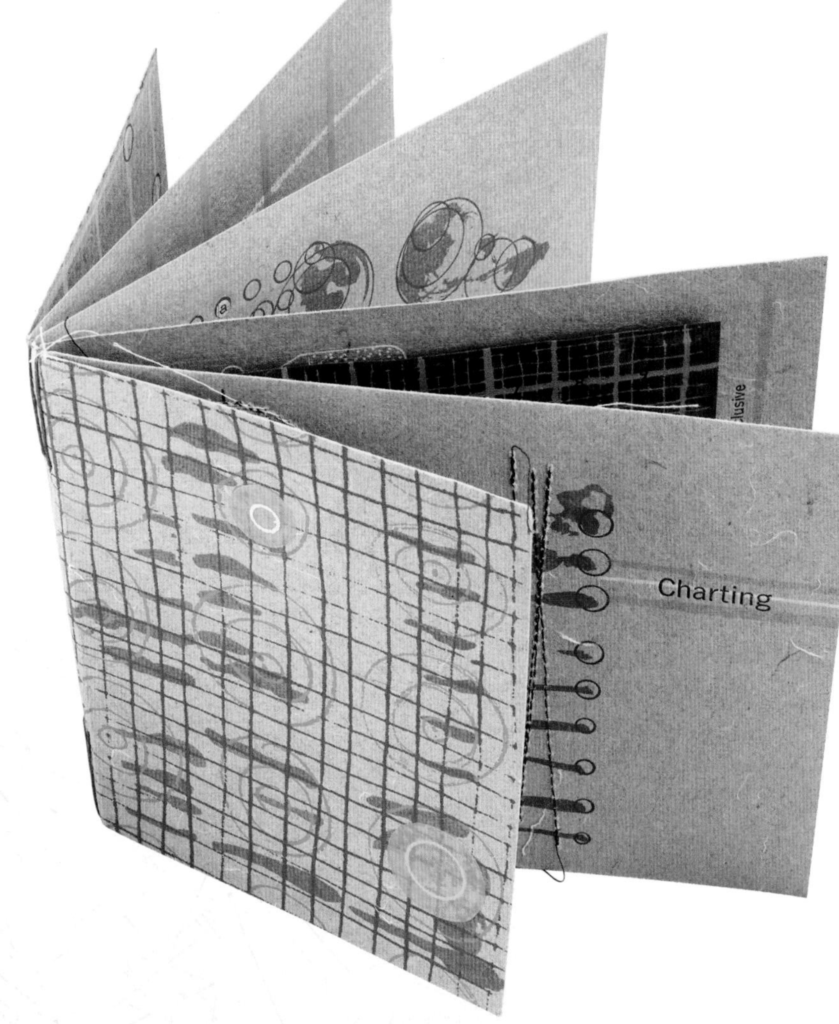

"The magic of book arts, for me, is in the structure—physically housing my ideas inside the interactive pages of a book."

▲ **Charting** | 2005

Collaboration with Lisa Hasegawa
5½ x 6¾ x ¼ inches (14 x 17.1 x 0.6 cm)
Handmade papers; longstitch binding, letterpress printed, silk-screened, drawing, collage, machine stitched

Photo by Sibila Savage

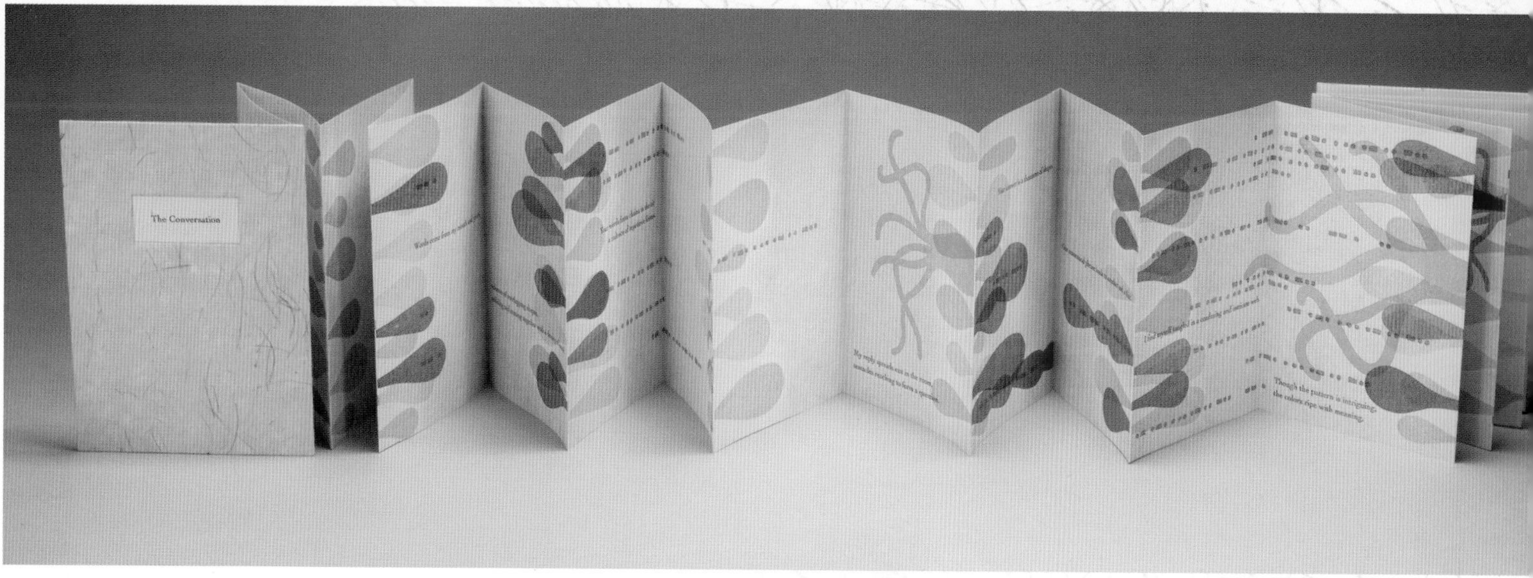

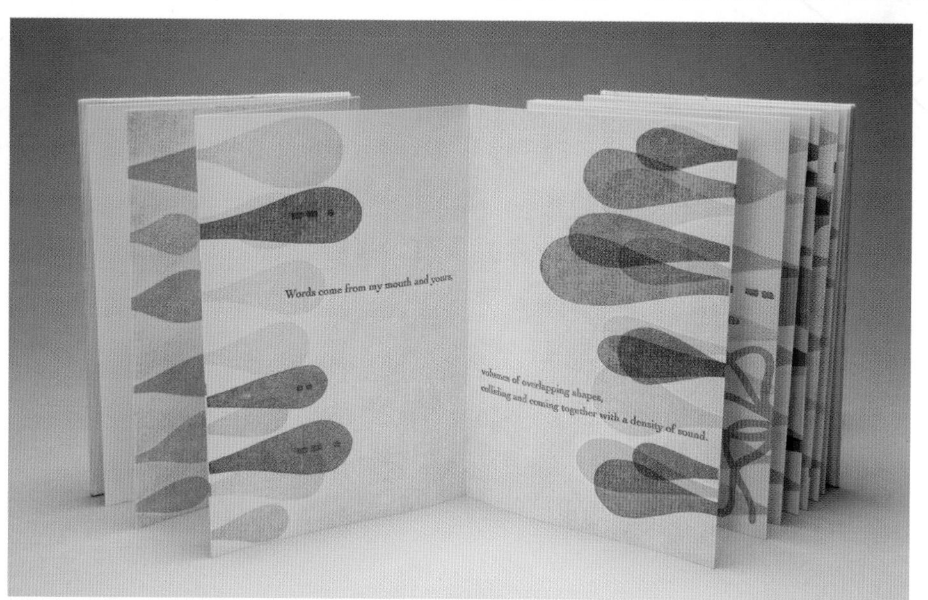

▲ **The Conversation** | 2004

5 x 7 x ¼ inches (12.7 x 17.8 x 0.6 cm)
Ingres paper, handmade paper; accordion binding, letterpress printed with polymer plates, relief, and pressure printing

Photos by Sibila Savage

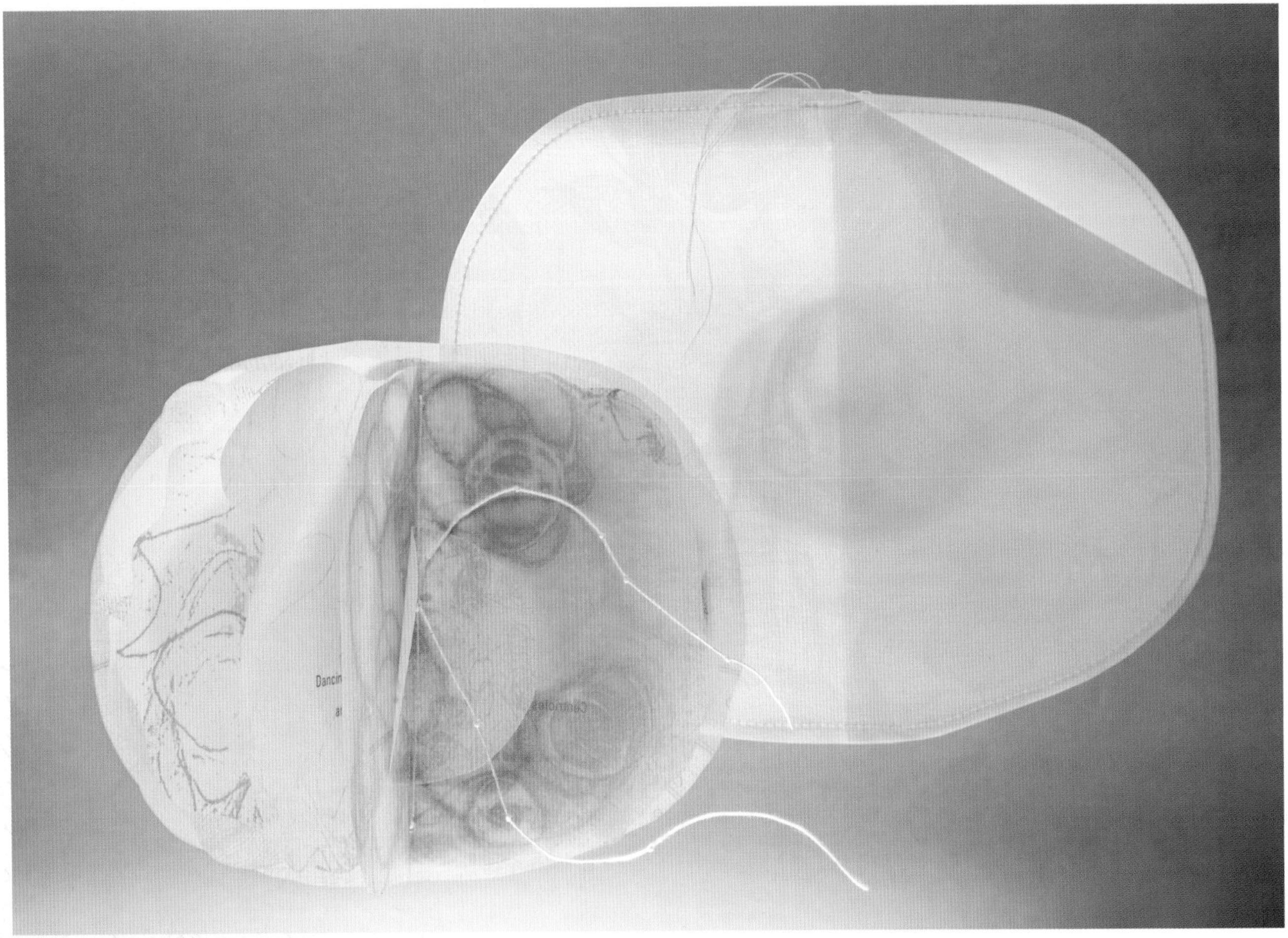

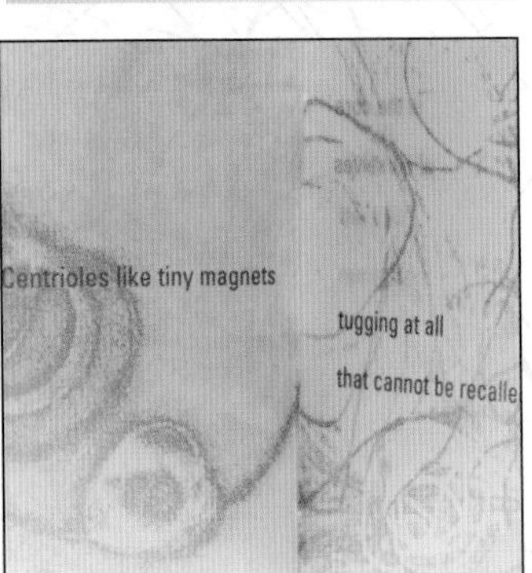

Cell Memory | 2002

Book: 6 x 7¾ inches (15.2 x 19.7 cm) open
Envelope: 7½ x 9½ inches (19.1 x 24.1 cm)

UV Ultra paper, linen thread, cheesecloth; pamphlet binding, offset lithography

Lithography printed by Lori Spencer
Photos by Sibila Savage

" Without a doubt, there's an element of performance to a book. Pacing is everything. "

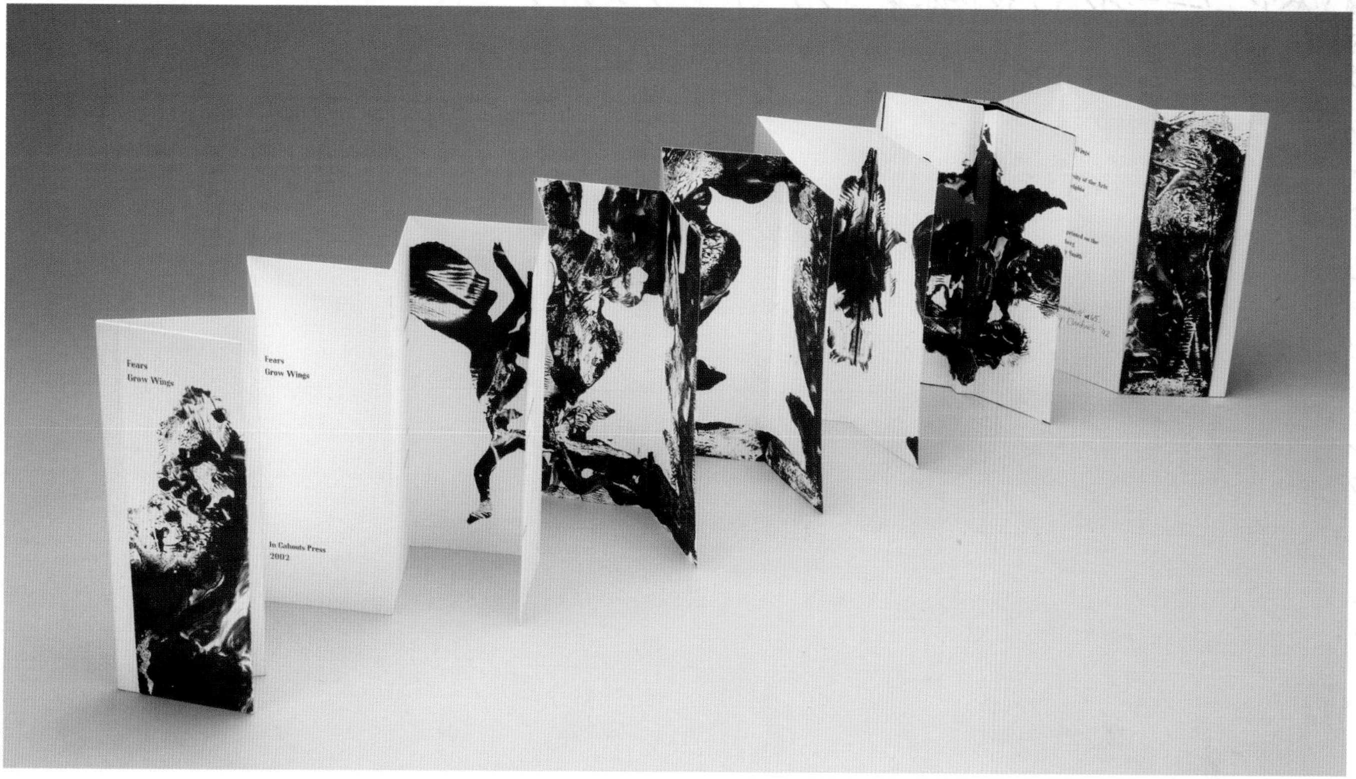

▲ **Fears Grow Wings** | 2002

8 x 3 x ½ inches (20.3 x 7.6 x 1.3 cm)
Mohawk superfine paper; leporello binding, offset lithography, letterpress printed, handset type

Lithography printed by Patty Smith
Photos by Sibila Savage

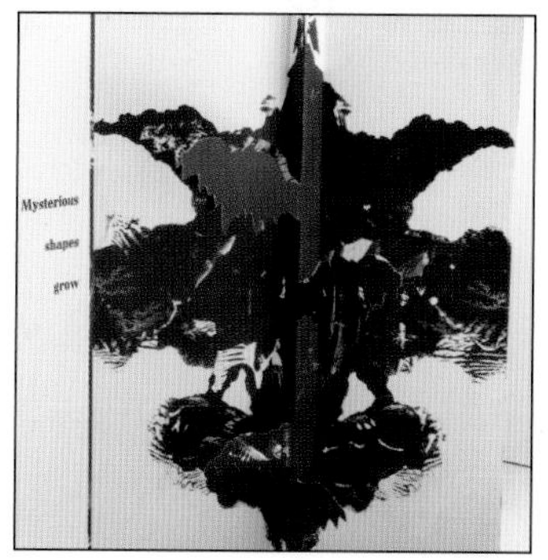

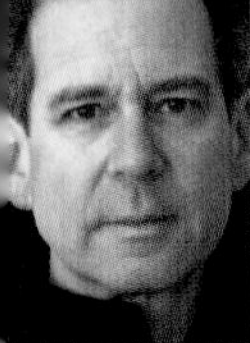

BOTNICK

Ken Botnick

EARLY TRAINING IN LANDSCAPE ARCHITECTURE instilled in Ken Botnick a sense of the page as a landscape, an invaluable instinct that has guided his masterful work from the beginning. Smartly conceived and consistently innovative, his pieces display attention to both design and content. Text and visuals bear equal weight in his books. From subtle gradations to vivid, vibrating hues, he uses color discerningly and with finesse to augment content. He employs language as a material, shaping words on the page with a keen awareness of paper, ink, and form.

Over the years, Botnick has printed works by Allen Ginsberg, William S. Burroughs, and William Faulkner. While possessing a strong design aesthetic, his remarkable books elude categorization. Botnick lives in St. Louis, Missouri. His work can be found in numerous collections, including the Library of Congress in Washington, D.C.; the Getty Center for Humanities in Los Angeles, California, and the Newberry Library in Chicago, Illinois.

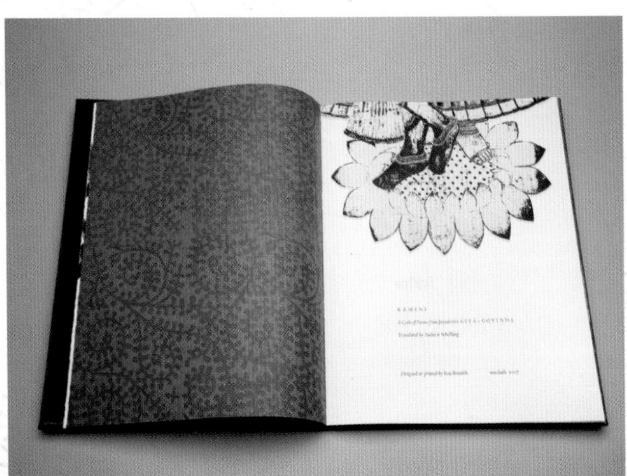

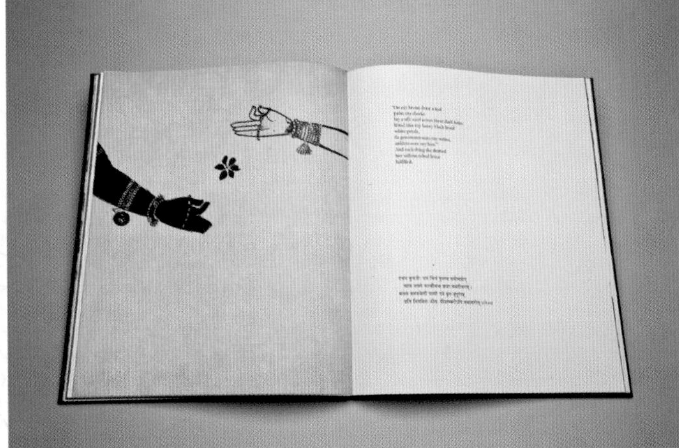

▲ **Kamini: Selections from The Gita Govinda of Jayadeva** | 2007

11¼ x 9¼ inches (28.6 x 23.5 cm)

Bugra paper, gold leaf, monoprint; letterpress printed, sewn, quarter-cloth binding

Photos by artist

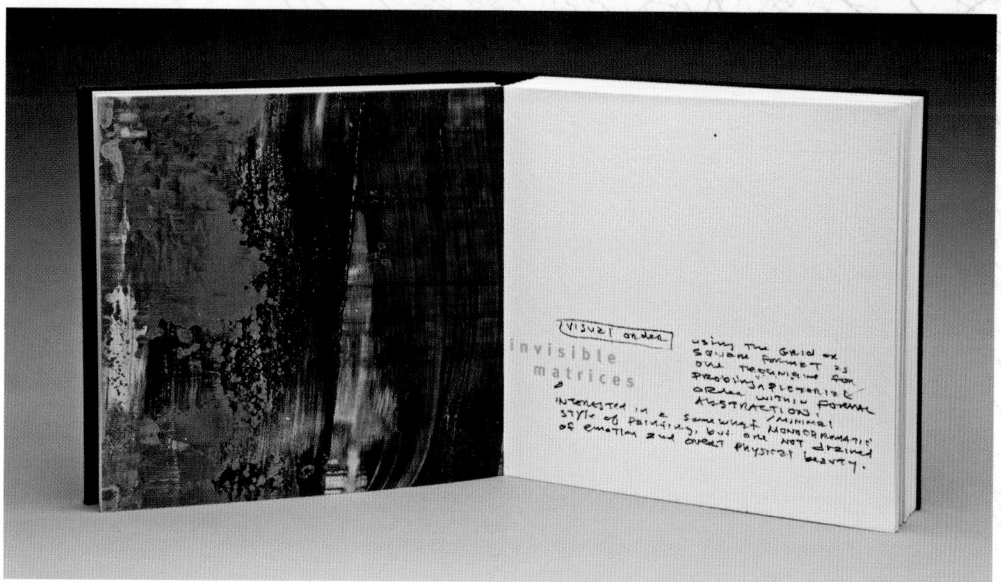

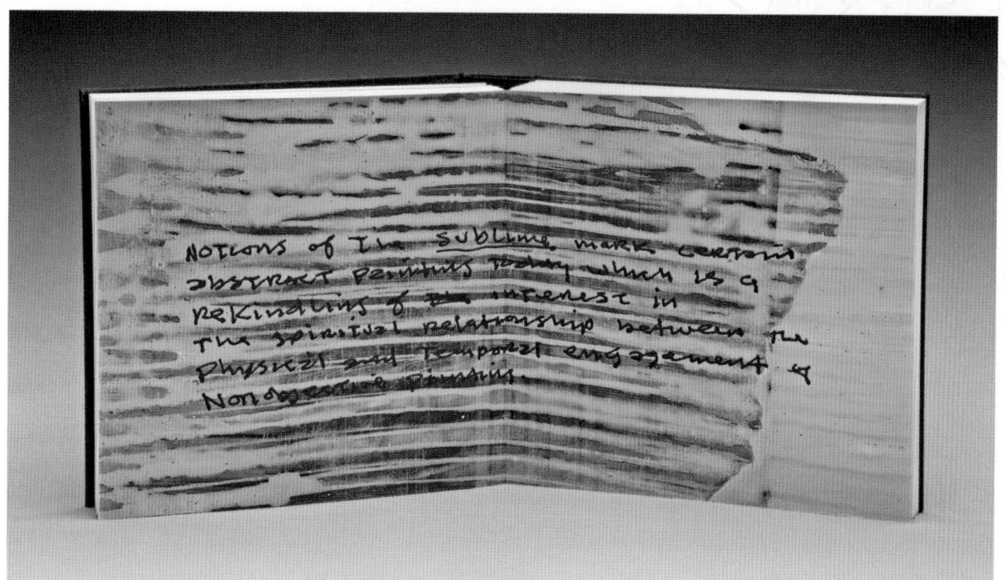

▲ **Clarence Morgan: Sketchbooks** | 2000

7½ x 7½ inches (19.1 x 19.1 cm)

Somerset paper, cloth-covered boards; digital printed, letterpress printed, accordion binding

Photos by artist

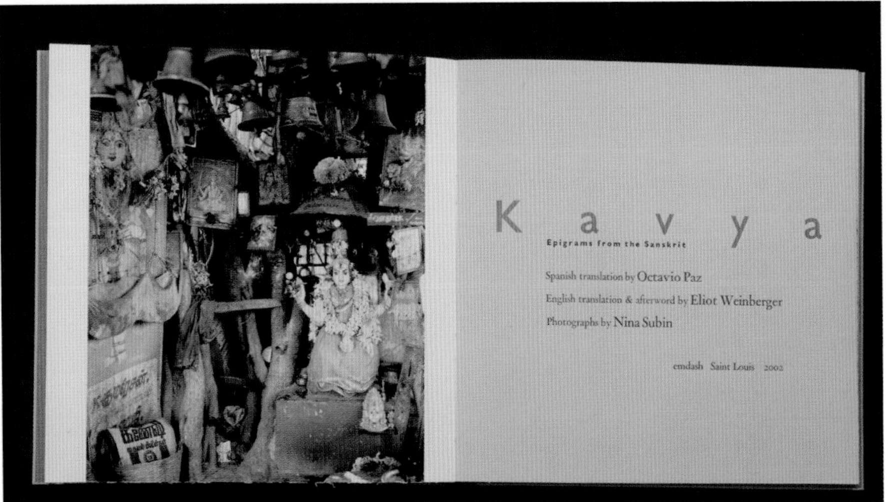

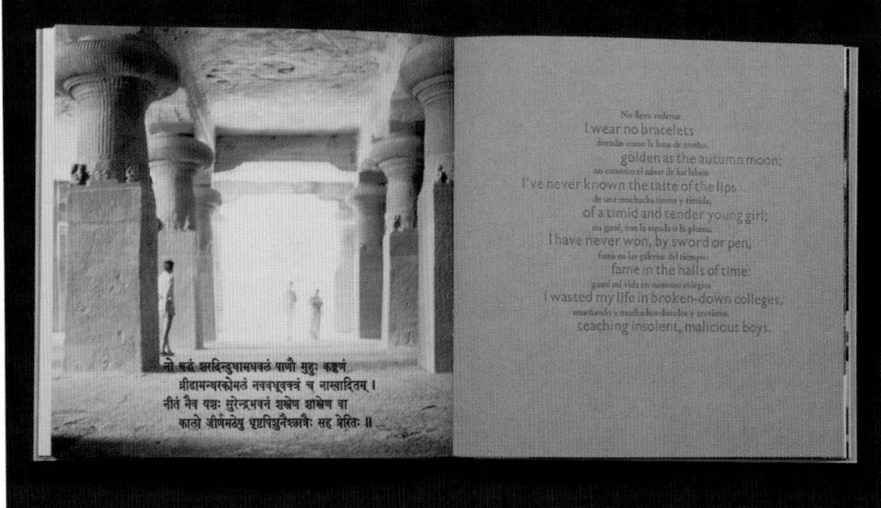

▲ **Kavya: Epigrams from the Sanskrit** | 2002

8½ x 8½ x ⅜ inches (21.6 x 21.6 x 1 cm)
Bugra and Concorde paper, painted and printed paper over boards; letterpress printed, inkjet printed, sewn in signatures

Spanish translation by Octavio Paz
English translation by Eliot Weinberger
Photographs by Nina Subin
Photos by artist

" My projects often take a long time to complete, and this is something I savor. Slowing down gives me time to study and interpret the meaning of words on a page. "

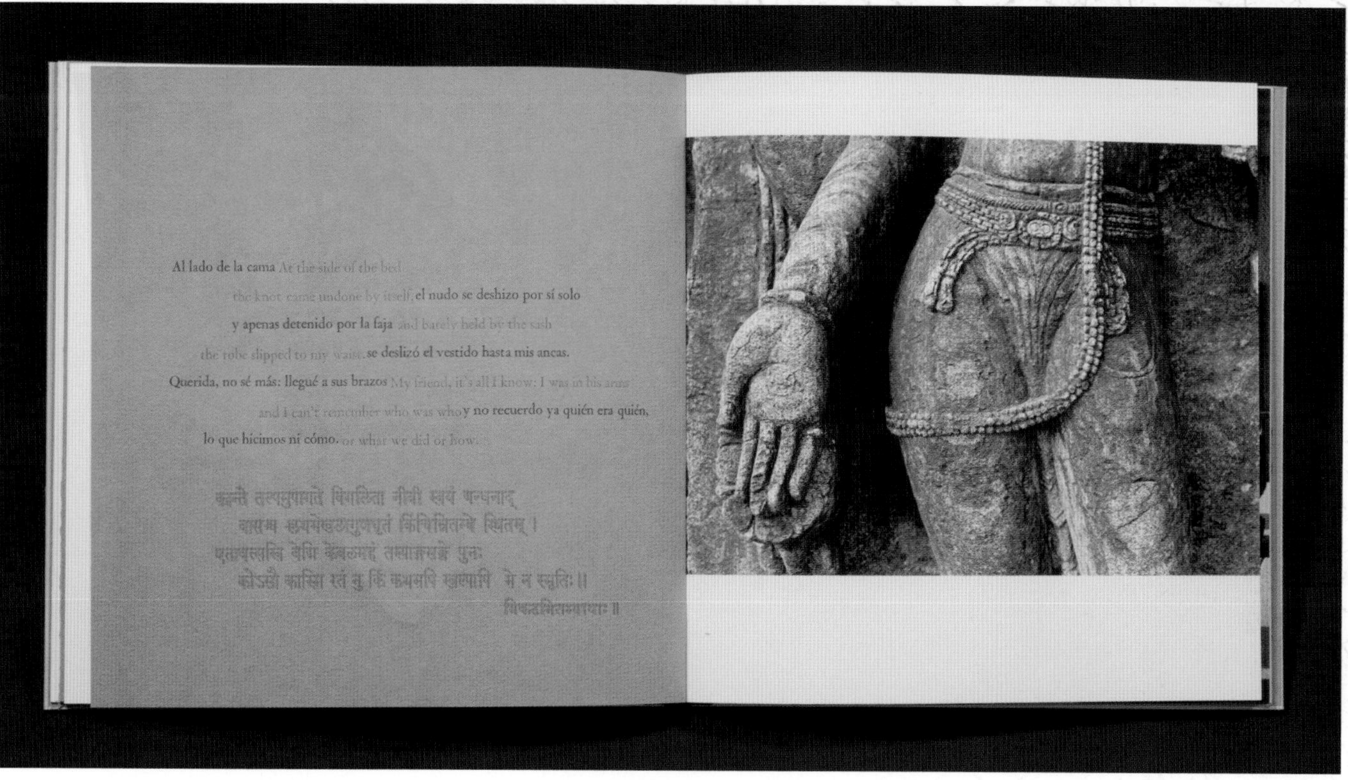

▲ **Kavya: Epigrams from the Sanskrit** | 2002

8½ x 8½ x ⅜ inches (21.6 x 21.6 x 1 cm)

Bugra and Concorde paper, painted and printed paper over boards; letterpress printed, inkjet printed, sewn in signatures

Spanish translation by Octavio Paz
English translation by Eliot Weinberger
Photographs by Nina Subin
Photo by artist

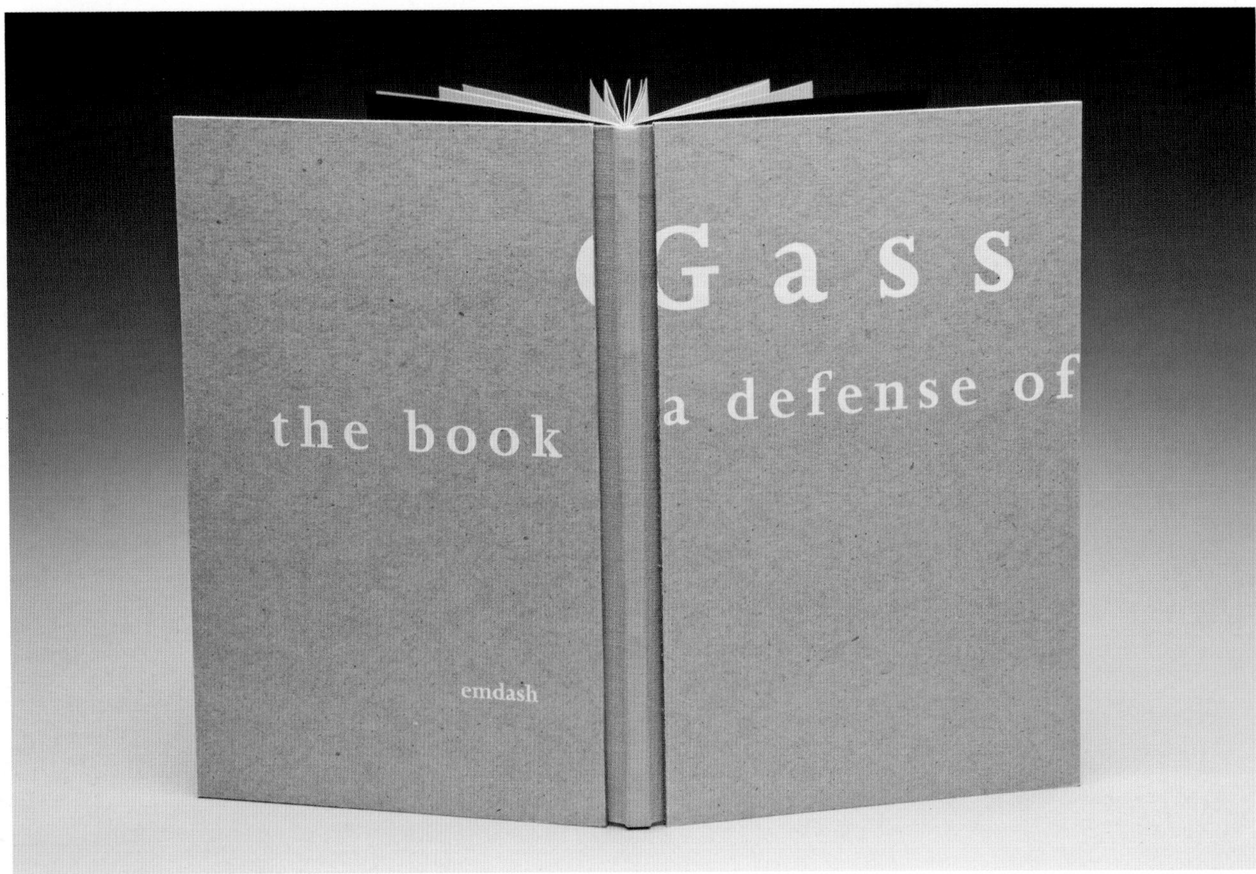

▲ A Defense of the Book by William Gass | 2001

9 x 6 x ¼ inches (22.9 x 15.2 x 0.6 cm)
Bugra paper, boards with cloth spine, digitally generated letter forms; letterpress printed, sewn, bound

Photo by artist

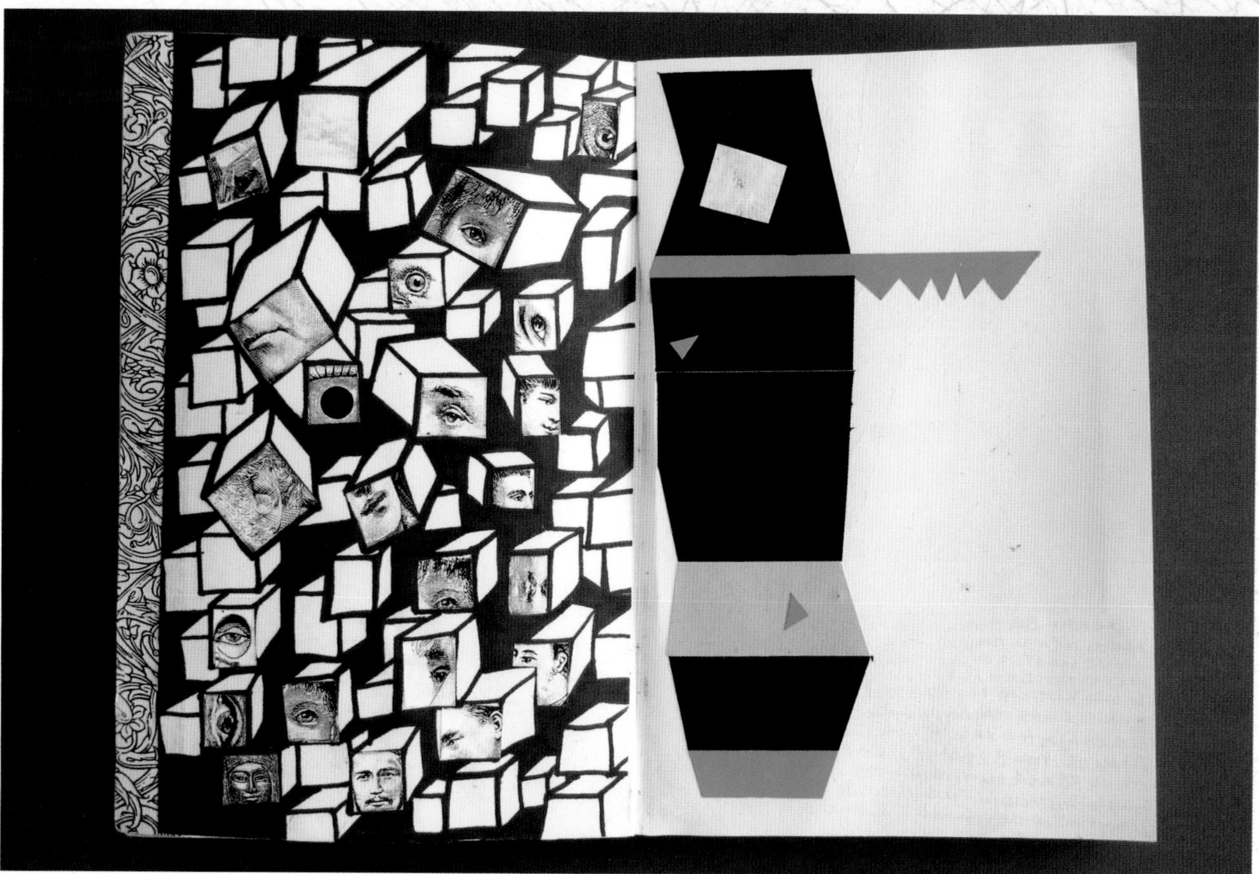

▲ **Sketchbook with Bob Ebendorf** | 2004

Collaboration sent back and forth through the mail
6½ x 9½ inches (16.5 x 24.1 cm)

Drawing, collage, tape

Photo by artist

" On any given day, I find myself working as editor, designer, typographer, publisher, printer, illustrator, and binder. "

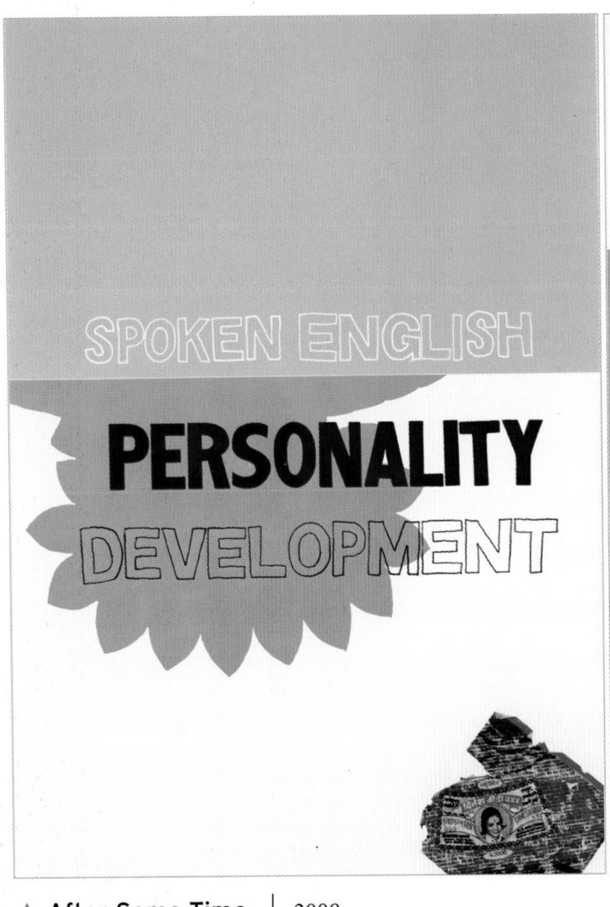

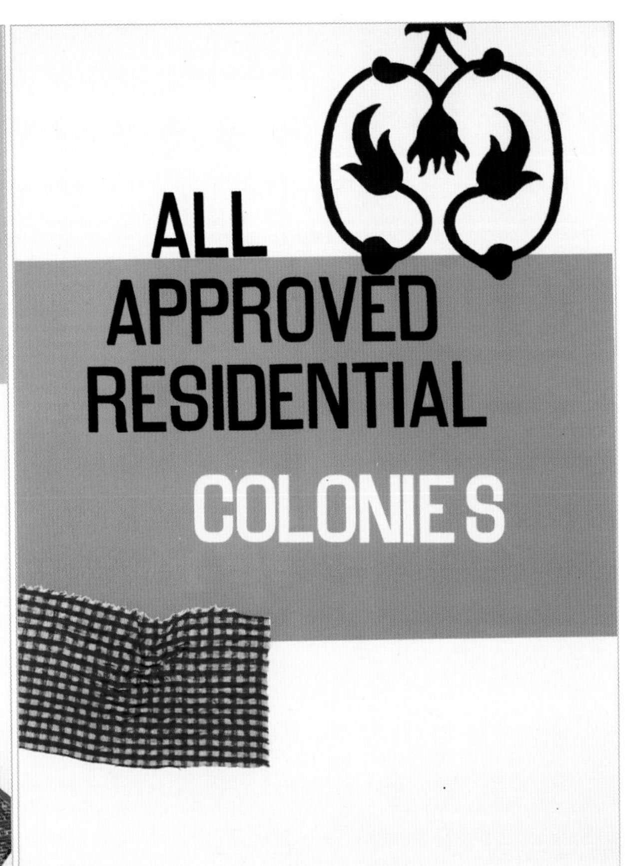

▲ **After Some Time** | 2008

Collaboration with Diana Guerrero-Macia
17¼ x 12½ x ⅜ inches (43.8 x 31.8 x 1 cm)
Somerset paper; inkjet and letterpress printed
Photo by artist

" Book arts involves many repetitive tasks that could be considered boring. But I enjoy those parts of the process, because they remind me that making is not only thinking but feeling. "

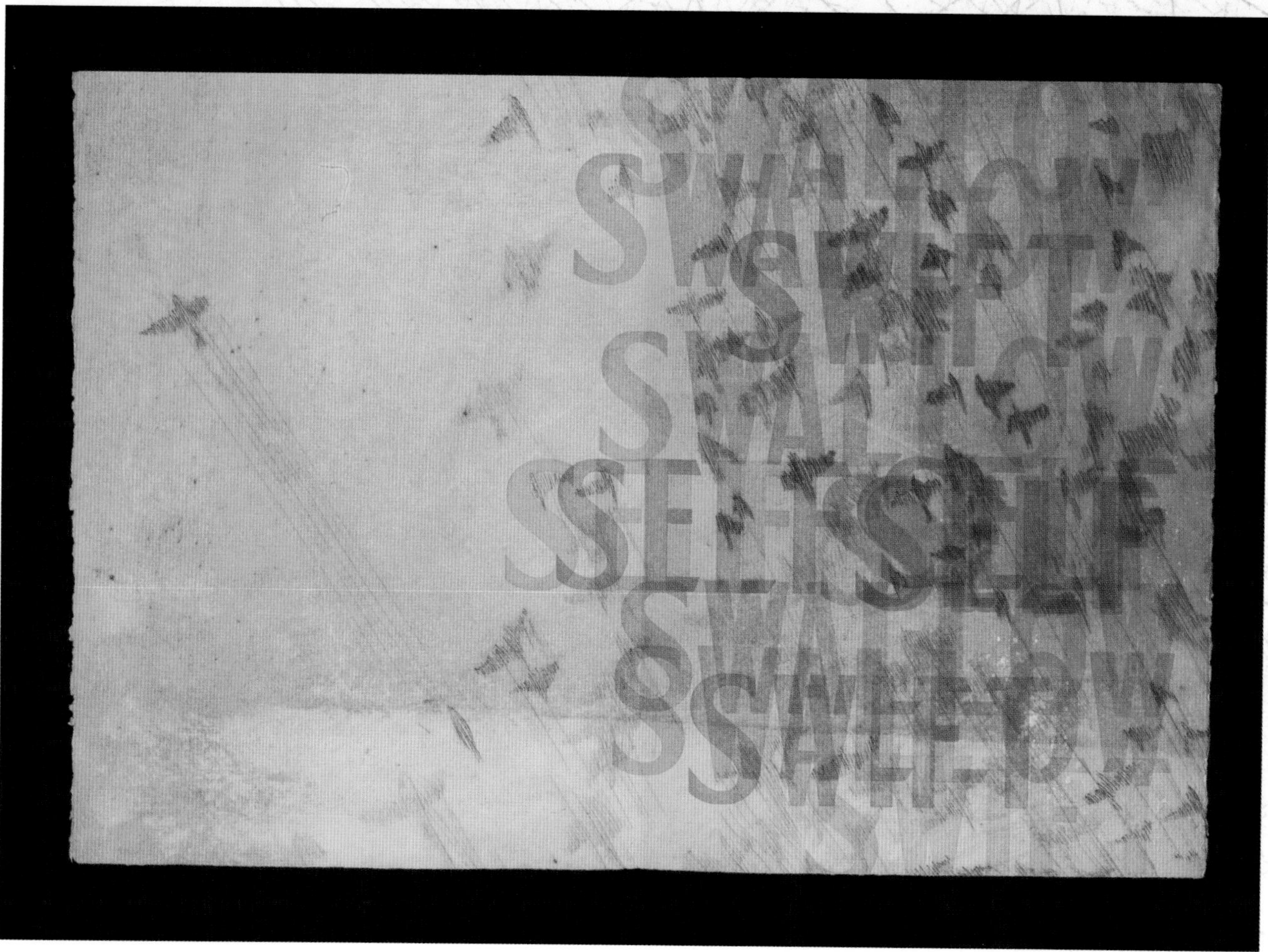

▲ **Earth, Sea, Sky** | 2006

Collaboration with Jana Harper
15¼ x 11¾ x ¾ inches (38.7 x 29.8 x 1.9 cm)
Rives paper, Japanese cloth-covered portfolio, monotype; letterpress printed, etched, chin collé
Photo by artist

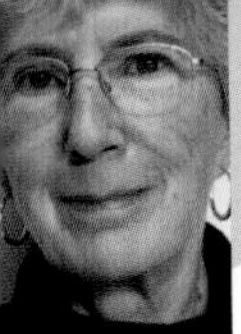

SHENK

Genie Shenk

DENSELY COMPOSED ASSEMBLAGES OF VISUAL iconography populate Genie Shenk's books. Inspired by her own dreams, which she records in a journal, Shenk creates books that serve as visual representations of emotions and themes. Using a range of techniques, she suffuses each page with symbolic narratives on the physical and emotional complexities of human existence.

Meaningful content is most often the impetus for Shenk's intimate books, but she occasionally works on a large scale—a shift that allows her to consider the book as a purely sculptural form. Regardless of scale or content, her works are always beautiful and engaging. Shenk lives in Solana Beach, California. Her work is held in galleries throughout the United States, including the Long Beach Museum of Art in Long Beach, California; the National Museum of Women in the Arts in Washington, D.C.; and the University of California–San Diego.

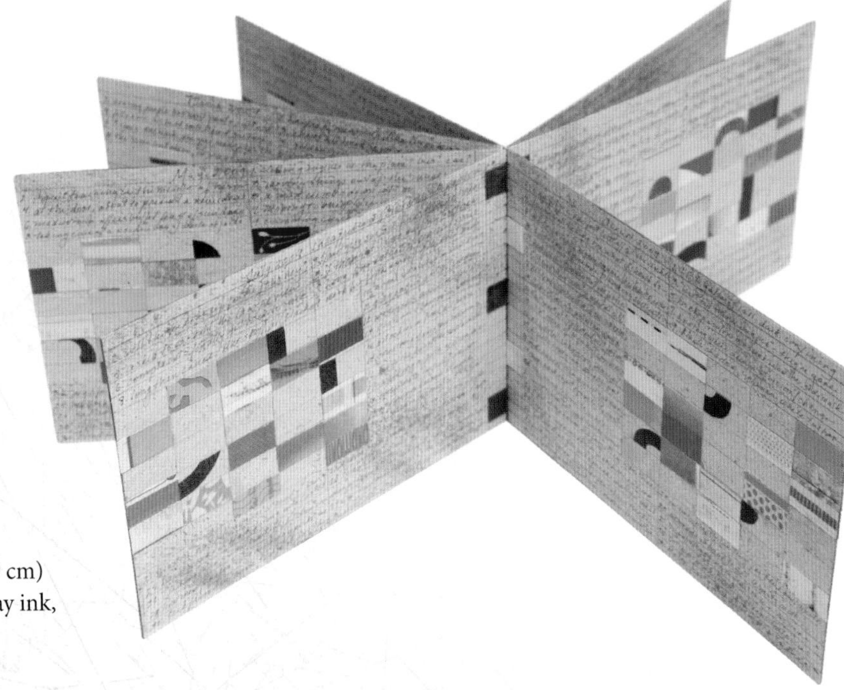

Dreams 2009 | 2010 ▶

5½ x 8½ x ⅓ inches (14 x 21.6 x 0.9 cm)
Board, mulberry paper binding, gray ink, pencil, newsprint collage
Photo by artist

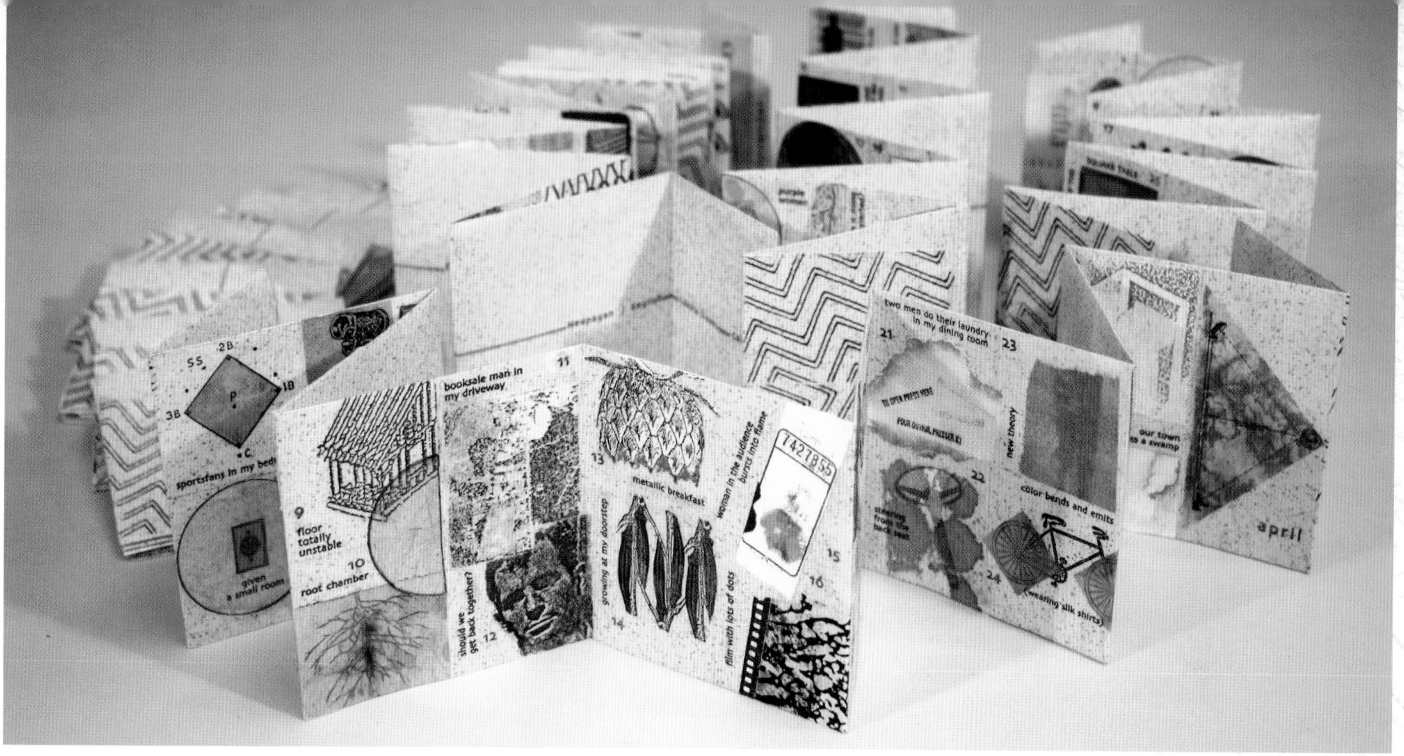

▲ **Dreams 2007** | 2008

Each book: 4½ x 4 x ¼ inches (11.4 x 10.2 x 0.6 cm)

Tea-dyed Japanese paper; accordion structure, transfer print, collage, pigment

Photos by artist

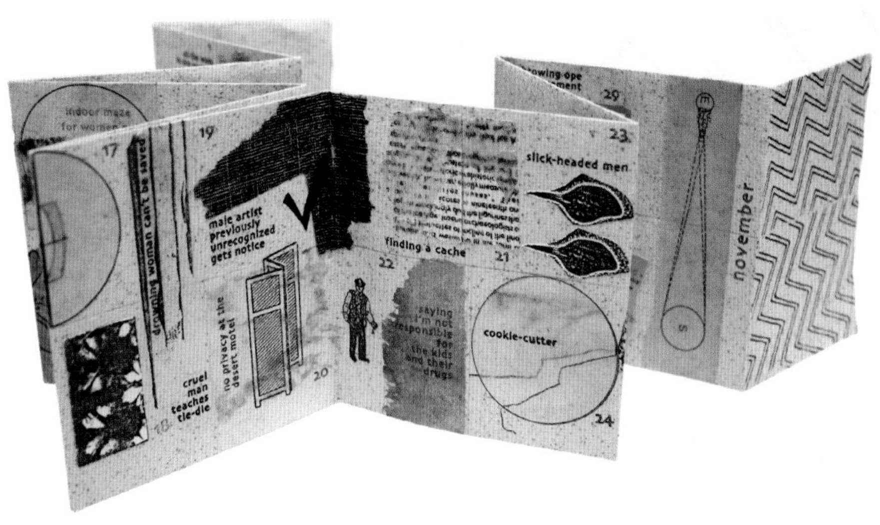

MASTERS: BOOK ARTS

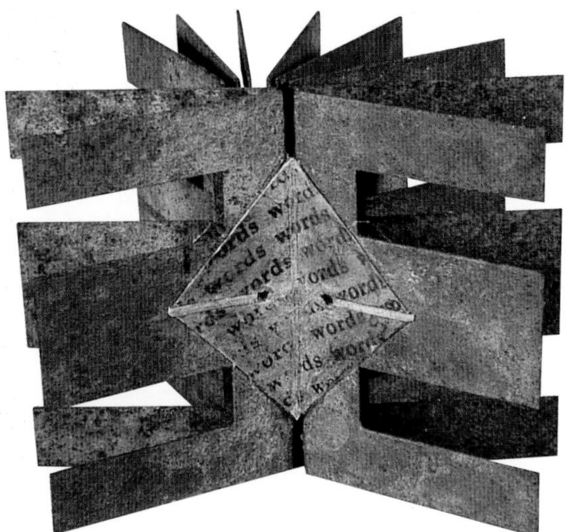

▲ **Enemy** | 2004

Open: 3½ inches (8.9 cm) in diameter
Found metal, paper; inkjet printed

Photo by artist

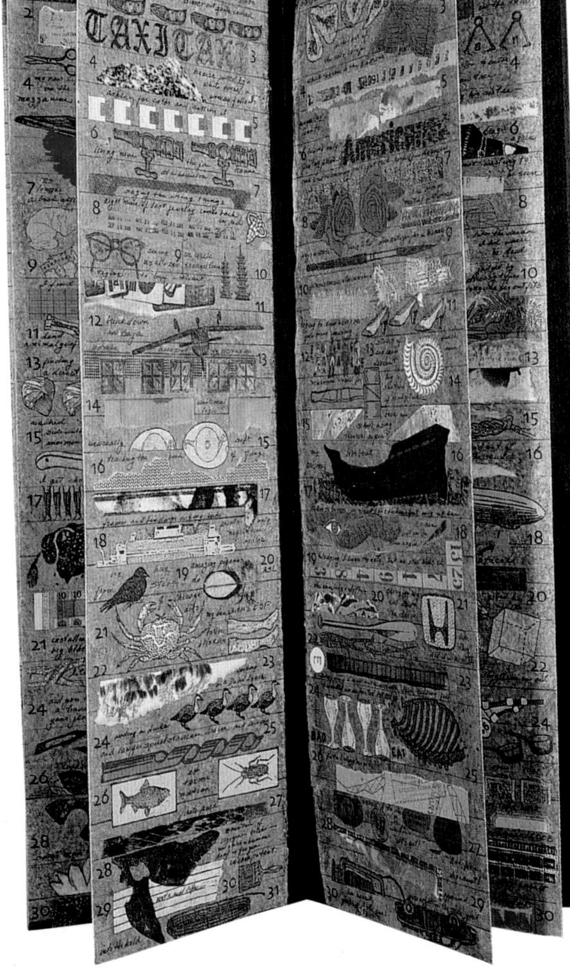

Dreams 2004 | 2005 ▶

Open: 28 x 16 inches (71.1 x 40.6 cm)
Painted Indian paper, board, hinged structure, ink; transfer print, pigment

Photo by artist

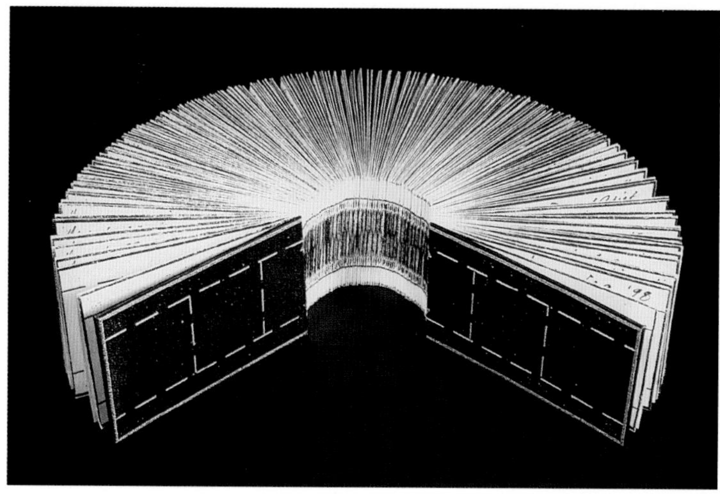

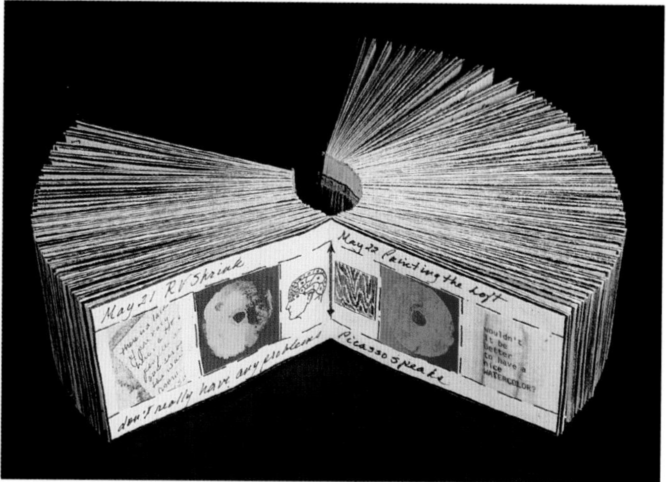

▲ **Dreamlog 1998** | 1998–1999

2½ x 10 inches (6.4 x 25.4 cm)
Mulberry paper, boards; sewn link-stitch with silk suture, photocopy, collage, pigment
Photos by artist

" I enjoy the haiku-like craft of putting as much meaning as I can into a few words. It's a delight when viewers are able to immerse themselves in this combination of text and image. "

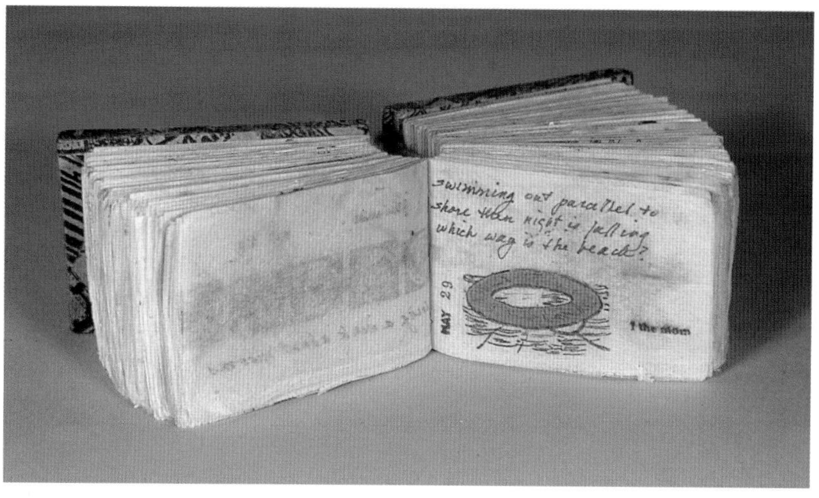

Dreamlog 2002: I the Dreamer | 2003 ▶

2½ x 3 x 6 inches (6.4 x 7.6 x 15.2 cm)
Teabag paper, linen, hemp, board, cork with collage; Coptic stitch, pigment, transfer print
Photo by artist

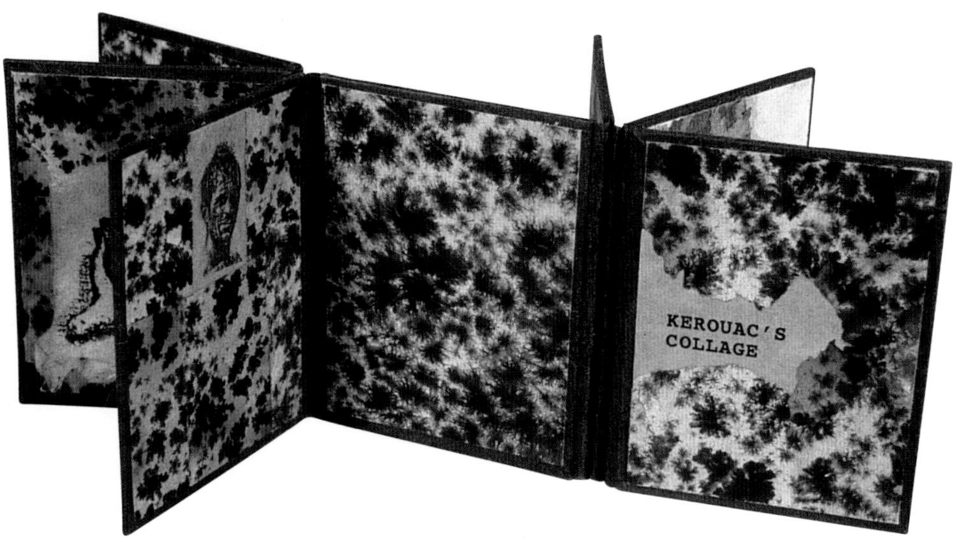

◀ **Dreams of Kerouac** | 2000

3½ x 3 x 1 inches (8.9 x 7.6 x 2.5 cm)
Restructured wood box, paper, antique paper; dos-à-dos binding, photocopy

Photo by artist

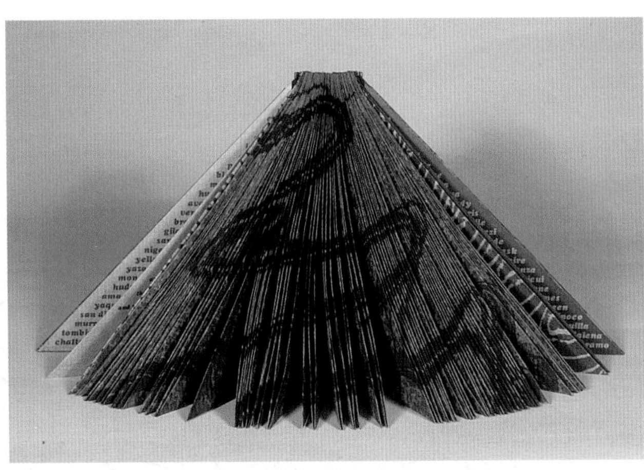

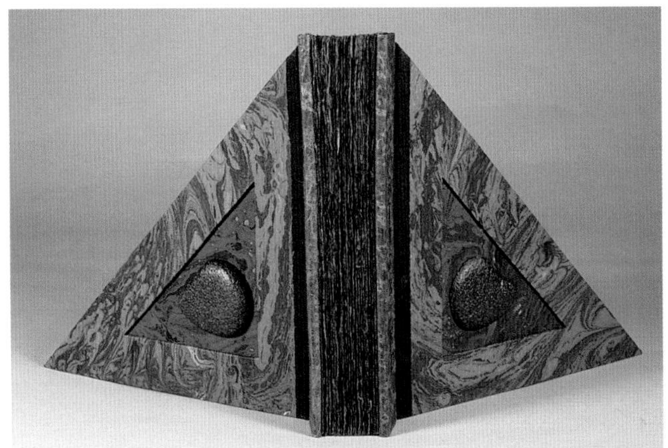

▲ **Riverine** | 2002

7½ x 9 x 2½ inches (19.1 x 22.9 x 6.4 cm)
Board, paper, marbled papers, patterned Asian paper; Asian binding modified for flip-book, photocopy

Photos by artist

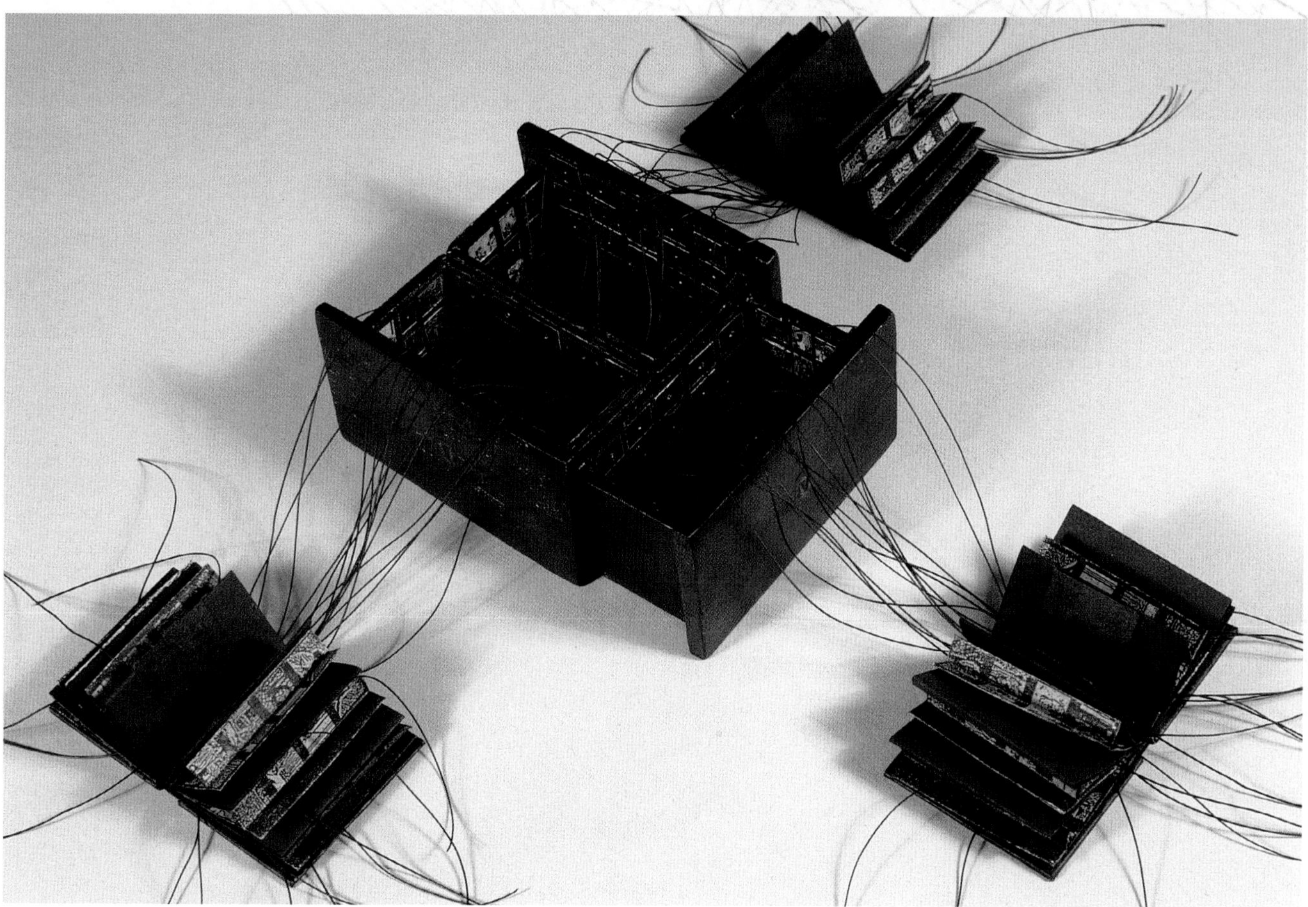

▲ **The Slow Ties of Love and Pain** | 1993

2½ x 10 x 14 inches (6.4 x 25.4 x 35.6 cm)
Found wooden drawers, board, paper, paint, mica, ink; sewn with silk suture and thread
Photo by artist

" Art has changed me over the years, opening an intuitive door to an inner world, a path to the spirit. It has made me more resourceful, more adventurous, and much more patient! "

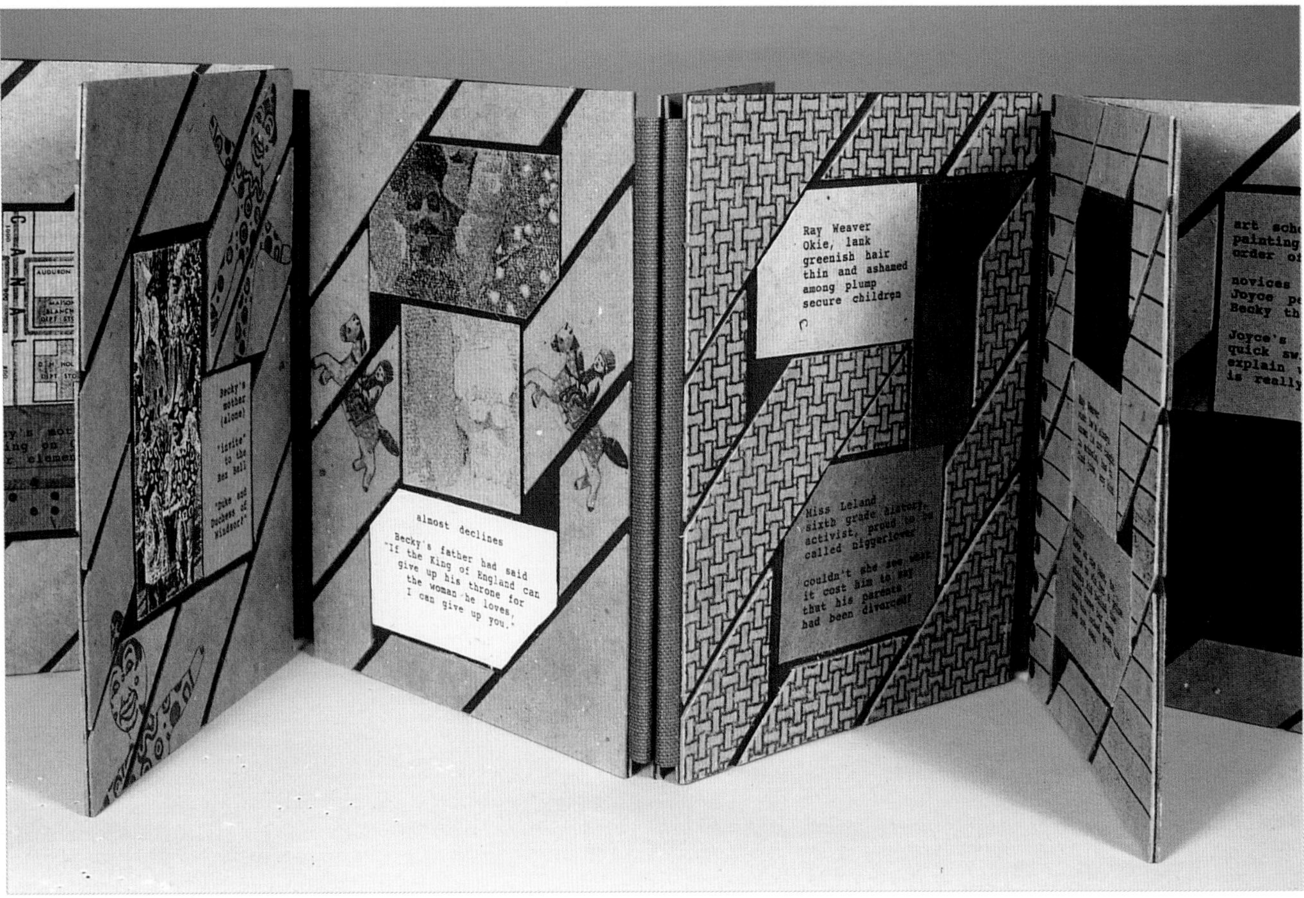

▲ **Bias** | 1997

7¼ x 6 x 2 inches (18.4 x 15.2 x 5.1 cm)
Book cloth, board, paper, antique bias tape on original board; modified accordion, photocopy, laser printed

Photo by artist

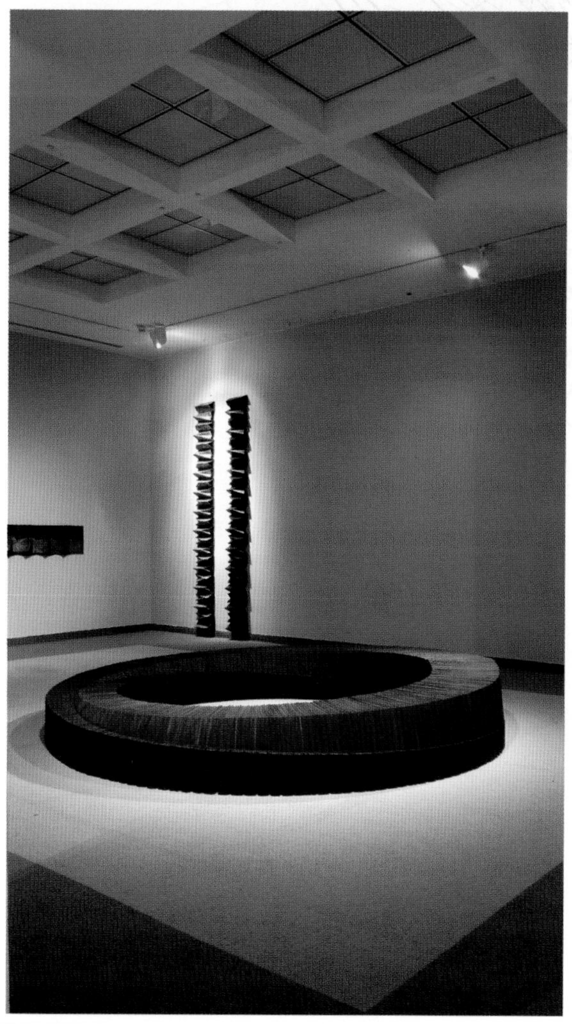

" My intial vision is never a complete vision. As I become involved with a project, it reveals itself to me. I pay a lot of attention to mistakes—they often tell me that I haven't yet understood all of the possibilities. "

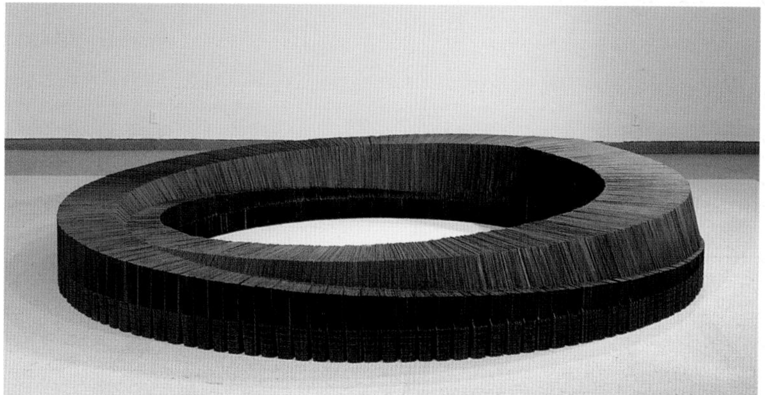

▲ **Ring** | 1999

20 x 132 inches (50.8 x 335.3 cm) in diameter
Tarpaper, linen; cut, folded, Coptic bound
Main photo by artist
Detail photo by Sandra Williams

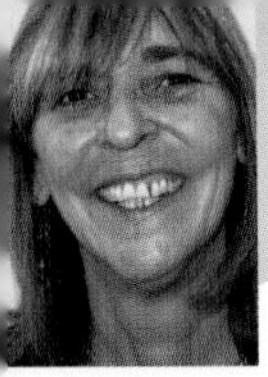

LEONARD

Julie Leonard

WHETHER UTILITARIAN IN INTENT OR CONCEPTUALLY driven, the book works of Julie Leonard exemplify pride in the well-crafted object. Within the pages of her traditionally formatted books, themes of memory and nostalgia appear like moments of recall—selective, fluid, and out of sequence. Leonard uses botanical illustrations and texts to support the personal remembrances she weaves into the pages. Concealing and revealing, layering and unfolding, her books awaken emotion in the viewer while avoiding sentimentality.

Leonard's journals and sketchbooks feature traditional sewn bindings based on historic book structures that look delicate but are durable. Handmade decorative papers, collages, and hand-painted silks serve as her cover materials. As she searches for new ways to use structures and decorative processes, Leonard produces work that has wonderful richness and depth. Leonard lives in Iowa City, Iowa. Her work has been exhibited internationally and is in numerous public collections, including the Sackner Archive of Visual and Concrete Poetry in Miami, Florida; and the Ringling College of Art and Design in Sarasota, Florida.

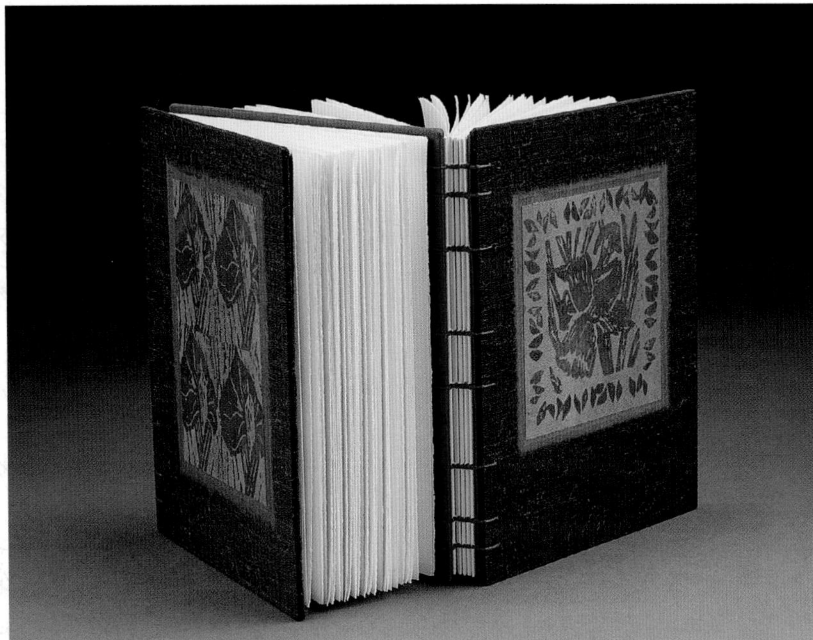

Journal (Dos-à-Dos) | 1997 ▶

5 x 4 x 2 inches (12.7 x 10.2 x 5.1 cm)
Silk, book cloth, binder's board, thread, text paper; hand stamped, painted, dos-à-dos binding, link-stitch binding
Photo by Tom Mills

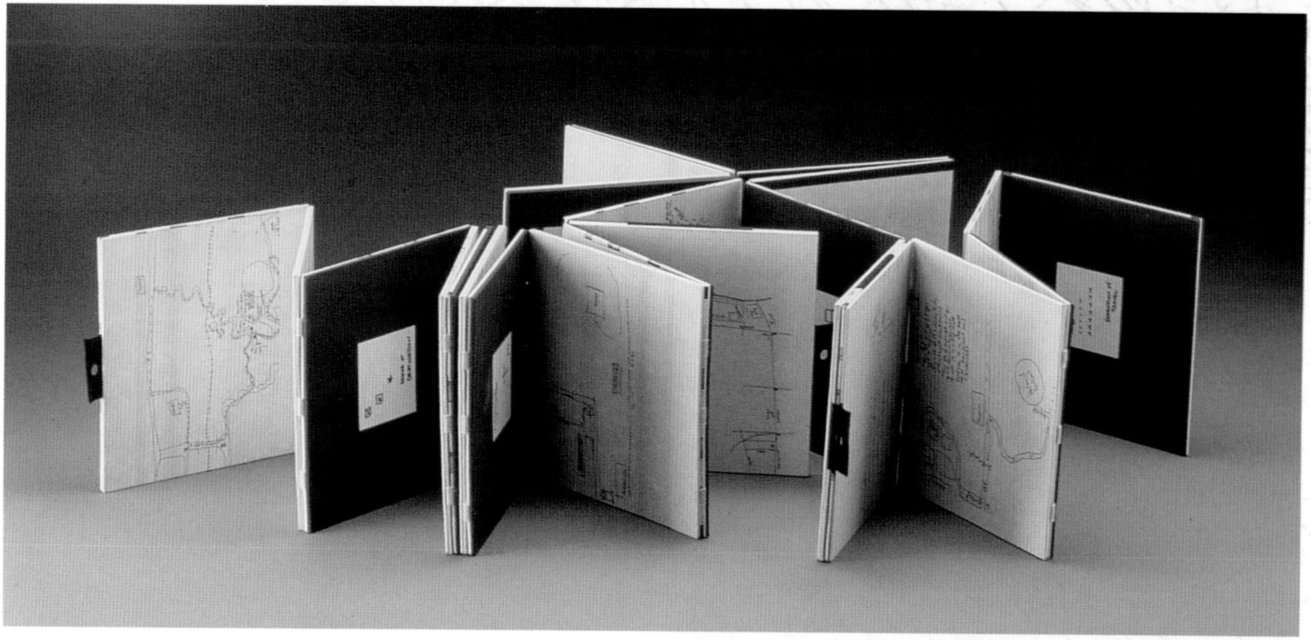

▲ **Mapping Symbols** | 1997

Closed: 5 x 5 x 5 inches (12.7 x 12.7 x 12.7 cm)
Open: 25 x 25 x 1/8 inches (63.5 x 63.5 x 0.3 cm)

Drawings, paper, binder's board, line tapes; hinged map-folded

Photos by Tom Mills

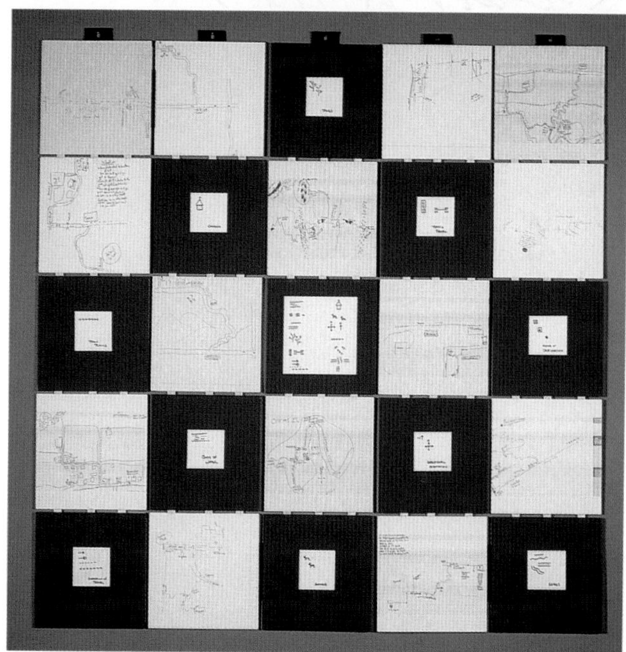

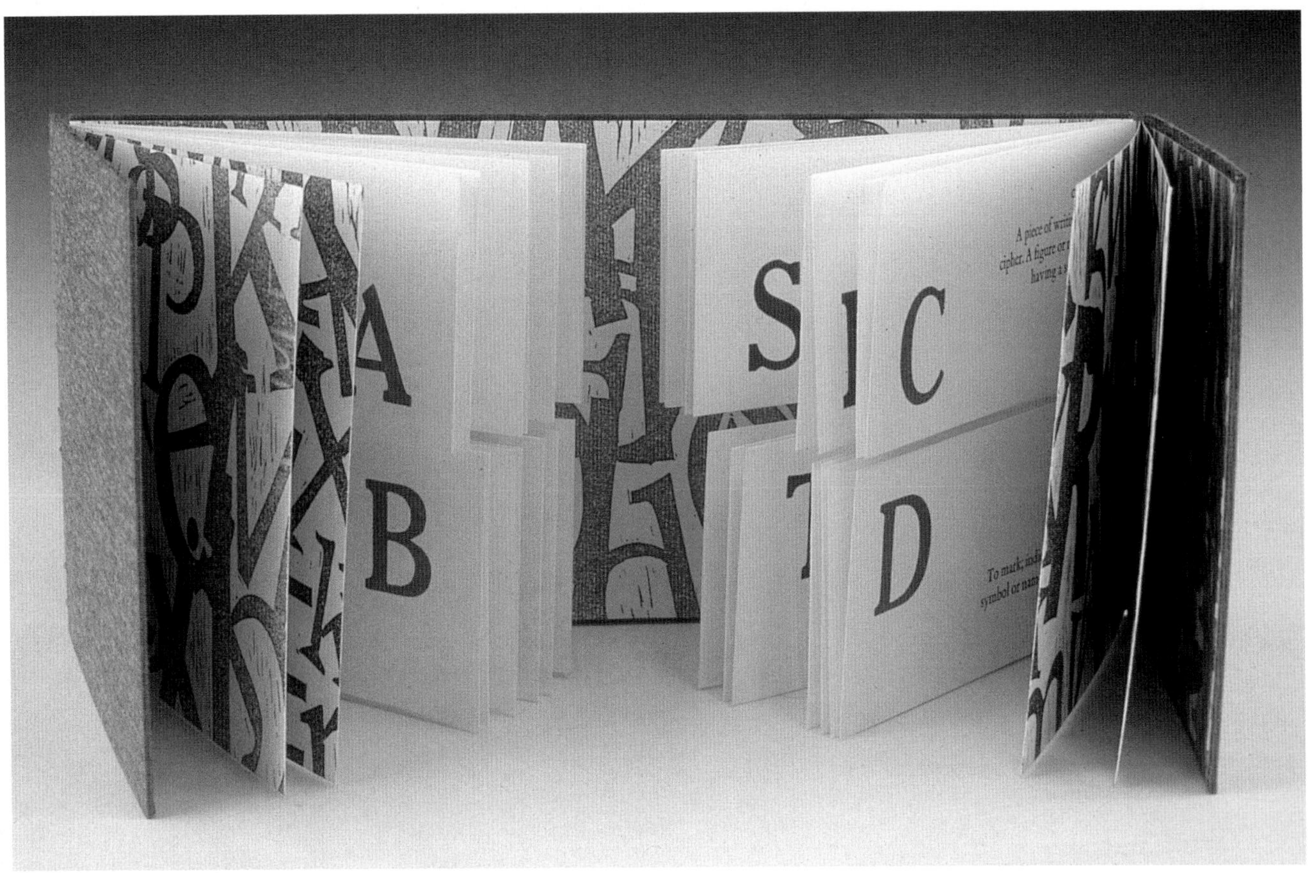

▲ **al · pha · bet** | 1998

5½ x 9 x ¼ inches (14 x 22.9 x 0.6 cm)
Watercolor paper, cloth, binder's board, thread; letterpress printed from wood and metal types, linoleum cut, French-door link-stitch binding

Photo by Tom Mills

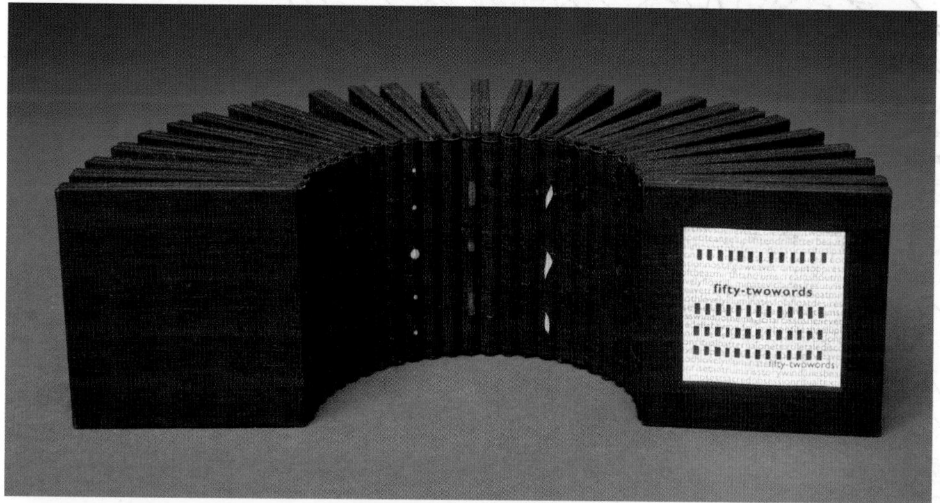

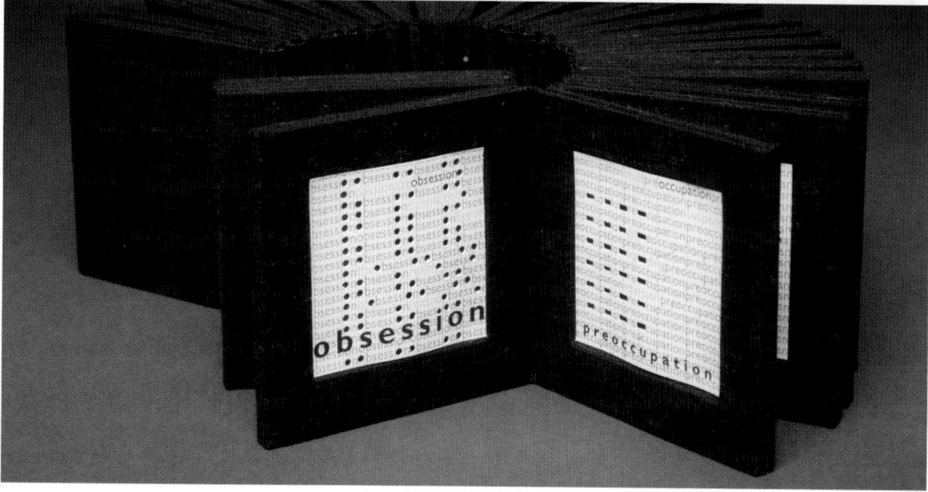

▲ **fifty-two words** | 2001

Closed: 4 x 10 x 4 inches (10.2 x 25.4 x 10.2 cm)
Cloth over boards, domestic etching paper, Japanese dyed papers; stiff-leaf binding, laser printed

Photos by Thomas Langdon

" I'm fascinated by how books work, by the myriad ways in which they can be constructed and in which they function. "

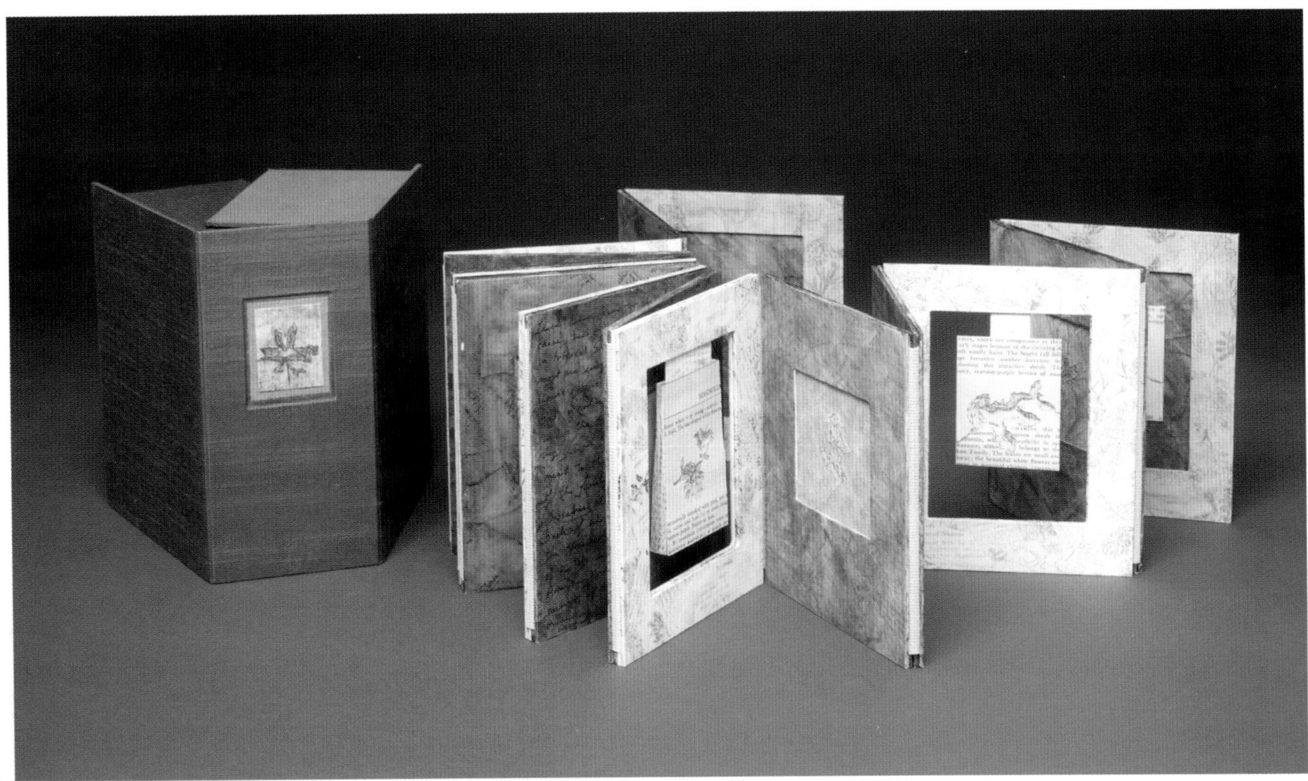

▲ **Fragments** | 2002

Closed: 6 x 5 x 3 inches (15.2 x 12.7 x 7.6 cm)
Open: 6 x 30 inches (15.2 x 76.2 cm)

Found botanical book pages, binder's board, linen tapes, watercolor, gesso, ink; hinged accordion binding, handwritten text, collage, cut, suspended

Photo by Thomas Langdon

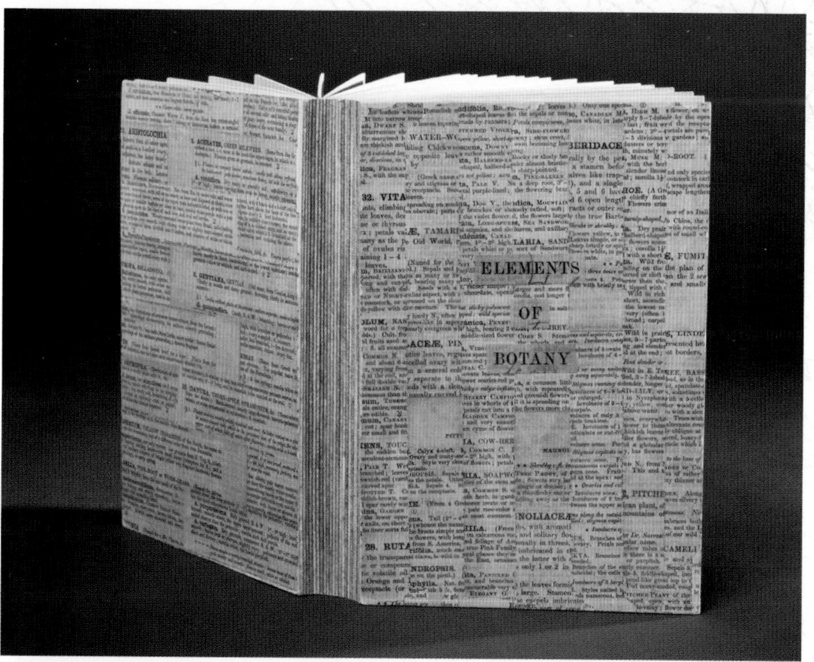

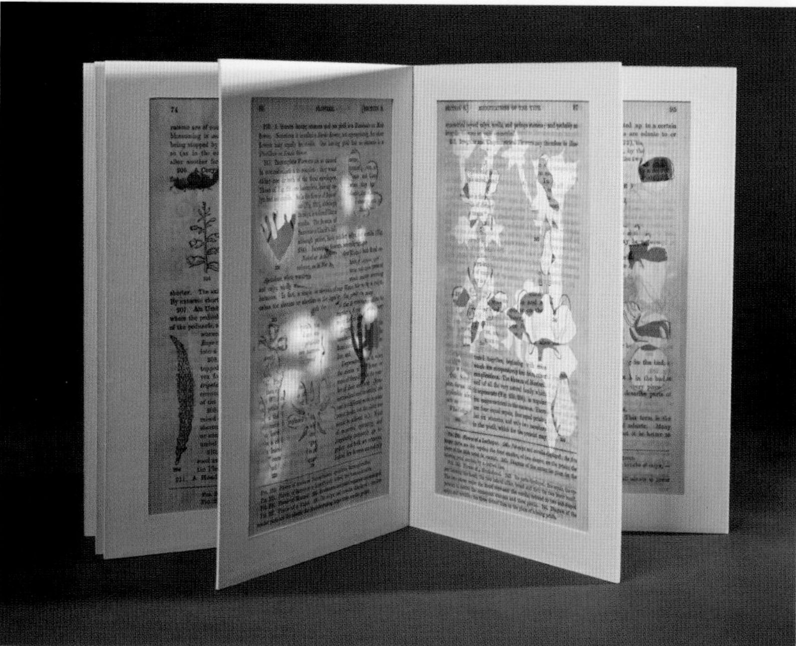

"I want to make books that function in a manner we associate with traditional book forms, but I also want play within the traditional form—to toy with the viewer's expectations about reading or receiving a story."

◀ **Elements of Botany** | 2001

8½ x 5½ x 1½ inches (21.6 x 14 x 3.8 cm)
Found book pages, varnish, graphite, museum board; cut, varnished, layered, stiff-leaf binding structure, collage
Photos by Thomas Langdon

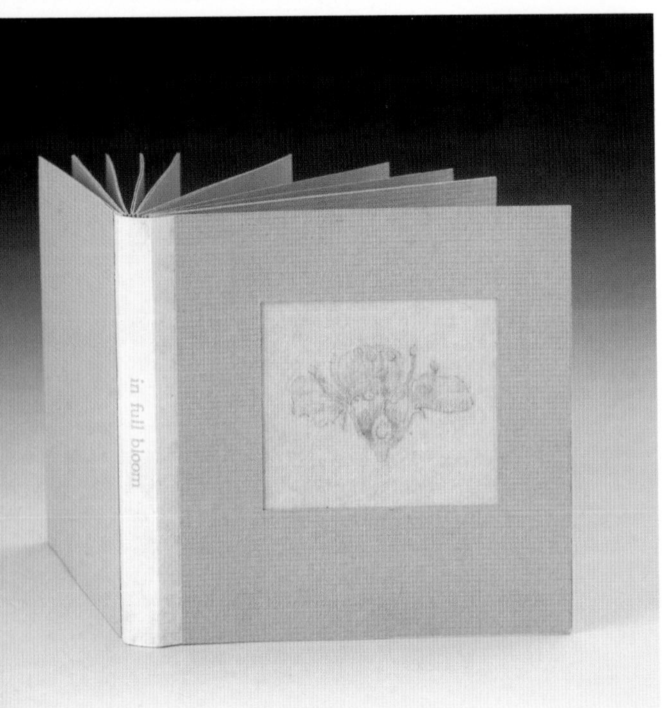

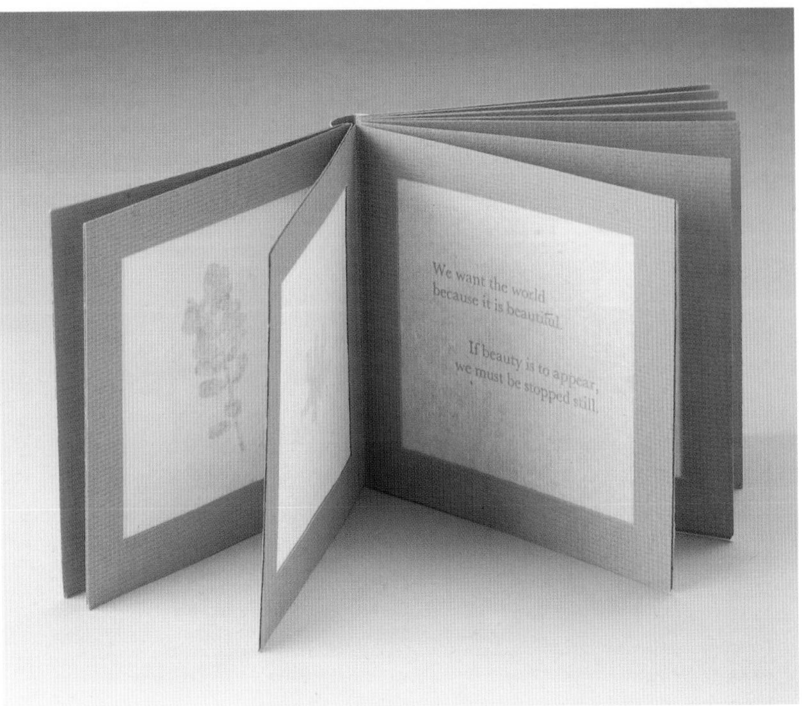

▲ **In Full Bloom** | 2003

3 x 3 x ¼ inches (7.6 x 7.6 x 0.6 cm)
Handmade papers, Ingres paper; letterpress printed from metal types, stiff leaf structure binding
Photos by Jill Tobin

" As I cut into pages, removing parts and creating openings, I layer those pages together, watching the shapes that appear. The translucency that results makes new patterns, letting light through and further illuminating the shape of words on paper. "

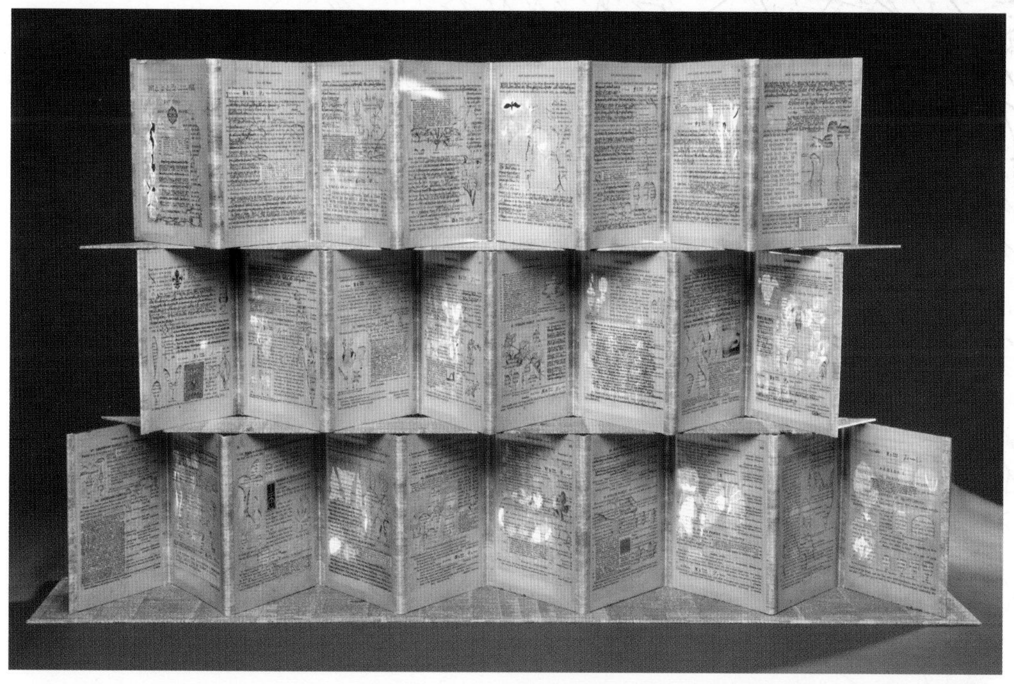

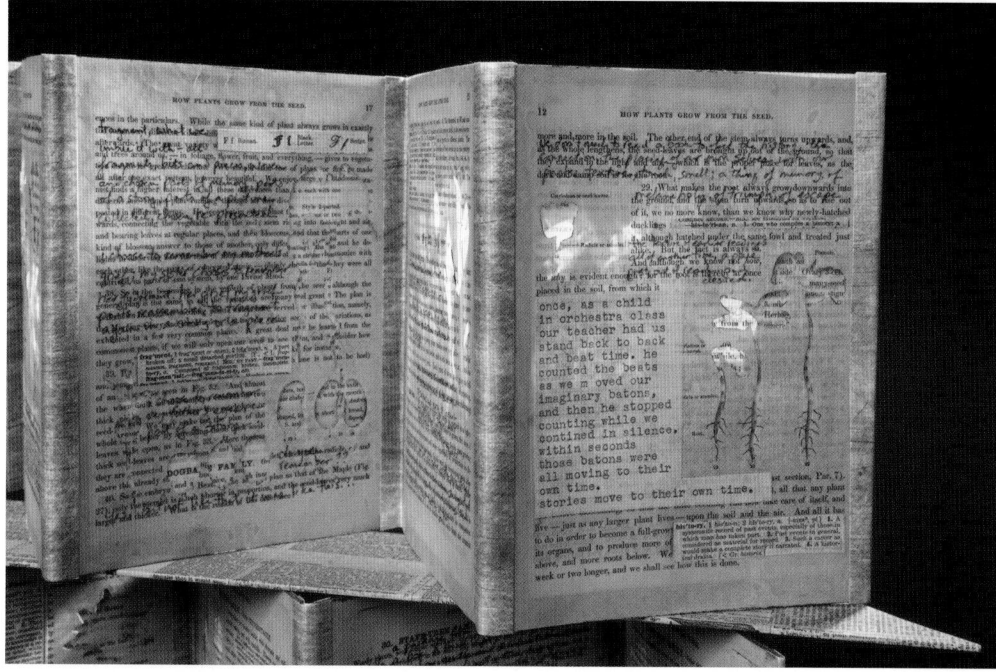

◀ **Palimpsest** | 2008

Closed: 7 x 5 x 5 inches
(17.8 x 12.7 x 12.7 cm)
Open: 21 x 25 x 7 inches
(53.3 x 63.5 x 17.8 cm)

Found book pages, Tyvek, card stock; three-tiered accordion binding, cut, varnished, layered, collage, typewritten text

Photos by Thomas Langdon

DEZSÖ

Andrea Dezsö

CITYSCAPES, INSECTS, AND WHIMSICAL FIGURES feature prominently in the tunnel books and journals of Andrea Dezsö. Often macabre in tone, Dezsö's books are windows into fantastical worlds that compel viewers to reflect on their own feelings about the transitory nature of life. For Dezsö, the tunnel-book format serves as a sort of stage, as it enables each of her scenarios to be viewed in its entirety, thereby maximizing the impact of her singular vision and remarkable virtuosity.

Dezsö creates her tunnel books from layers of paper. She draws and paints on each sheet, then cuts out forms individually. She then arranges the layers in a stack, one in front of the other, to form a collapsible unit—a tiny, precisely imagined scene with dimension and depth. Dezsö brings a range of skills to her intriguing work, including expertise as a painter and illustrator. Many of the drawings that embellish her beautifully bound books have a wonderful childlike simplicity. Dezsö's work has received coverage in numerous media outlets, including *NPR, The New York Times, The Wall Street Journal,* and the *Village Voice.* A native of Romania, she lives in New York City.

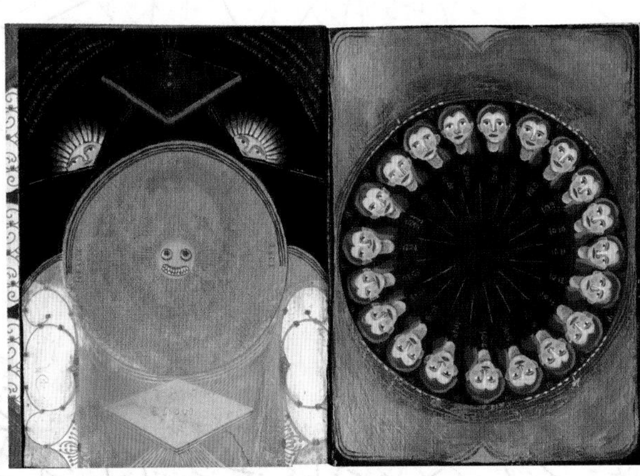

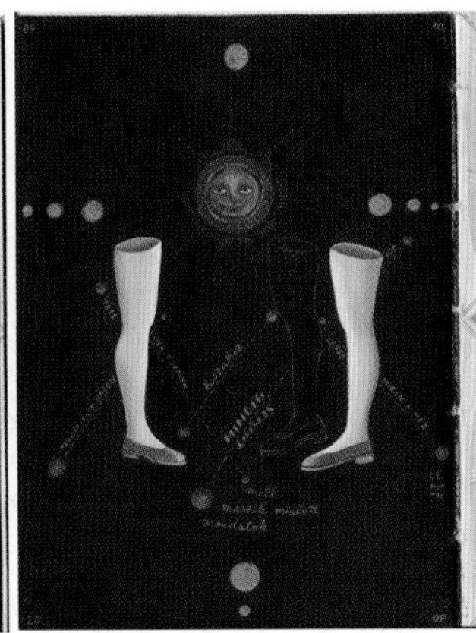

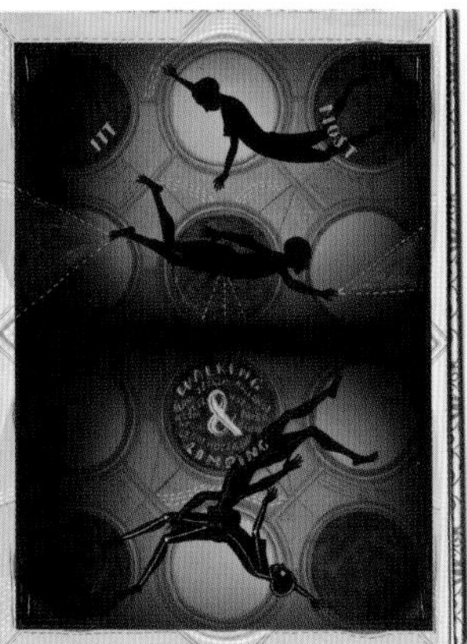

▲ **Candyland WY** | 2005

14 x 5 inches (35.5 x 12.7 cm)

Paper, linen thread; Coptic binding, mixed media

Photos by artist

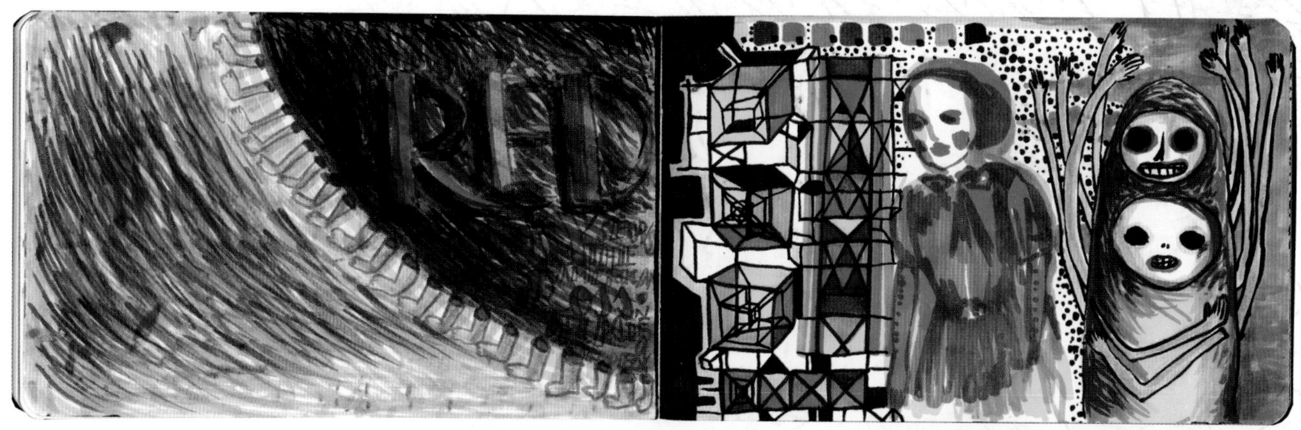

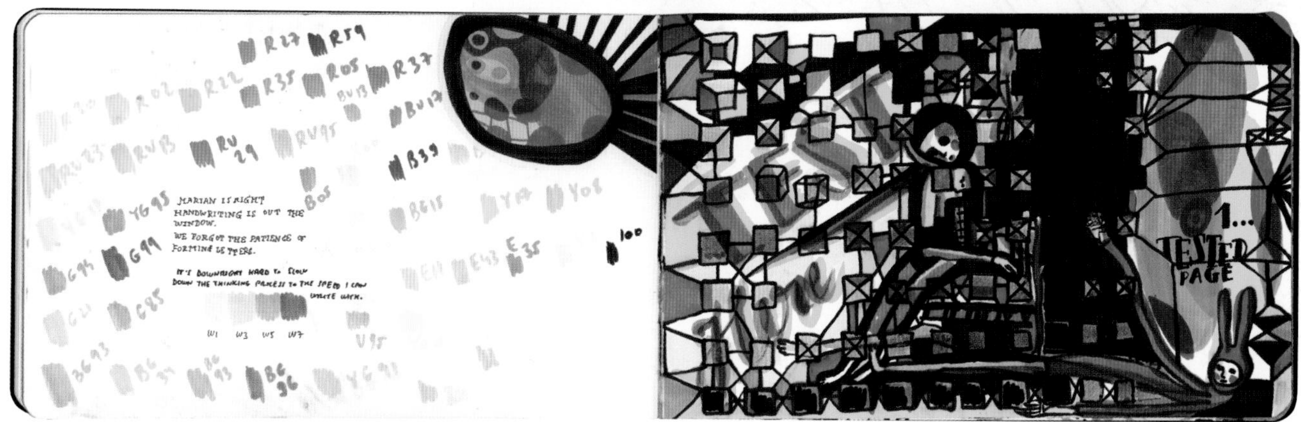

▲ **Vitamin D Sketchbook** | 2010

5 x 16½ inches (12.7 x 42 cm)

Watercolor sketchbook, alcohol markers

Photos by artist

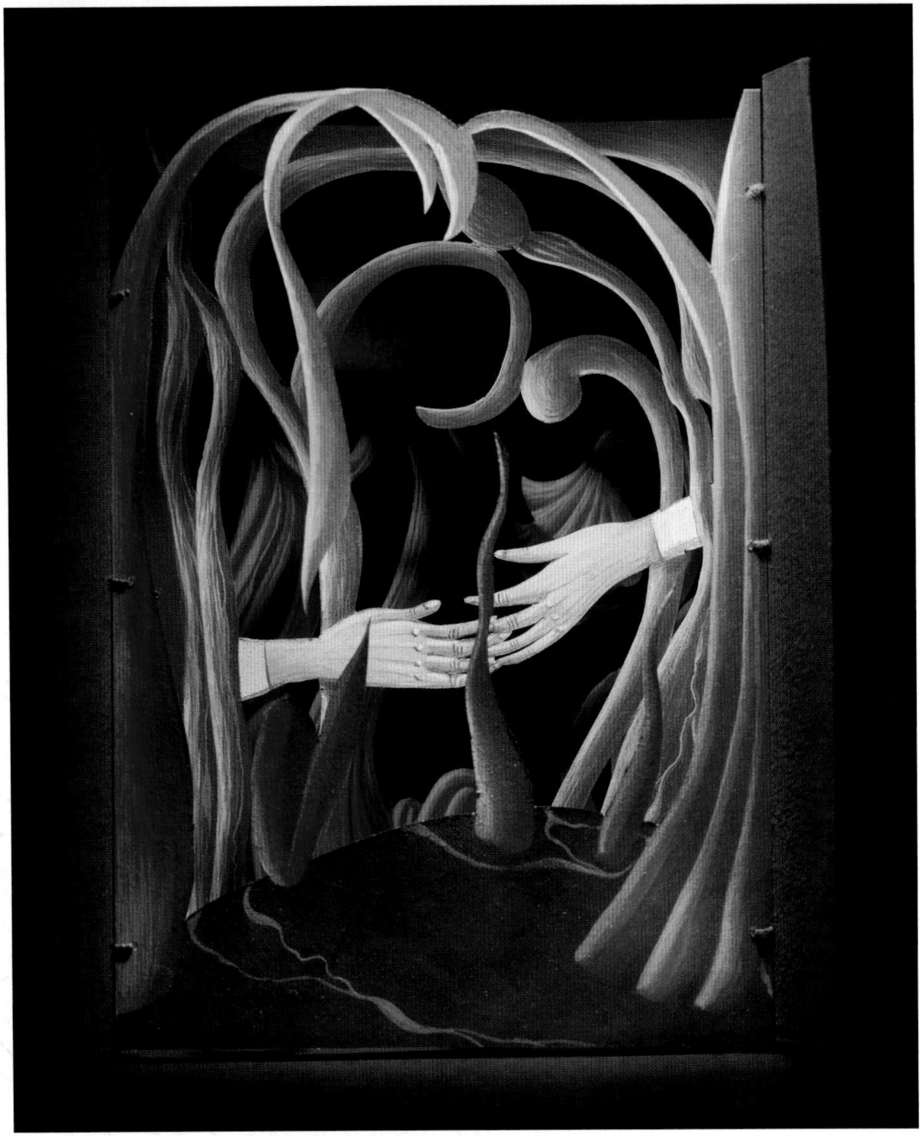

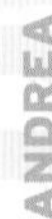

" My three-dimensional tunnel books allow glimpses into small, self-contained, magical worlds in which viewers can make their own narratives. "

▲ **Tunnel Book from the Living Inside Series** | 2009

6 x 7 x 8 inches (15.2 x 17.8 x 20.3 cm)
Hand-cut paper, linen thread, acrylic mixed media
Photo by Péter Hapák

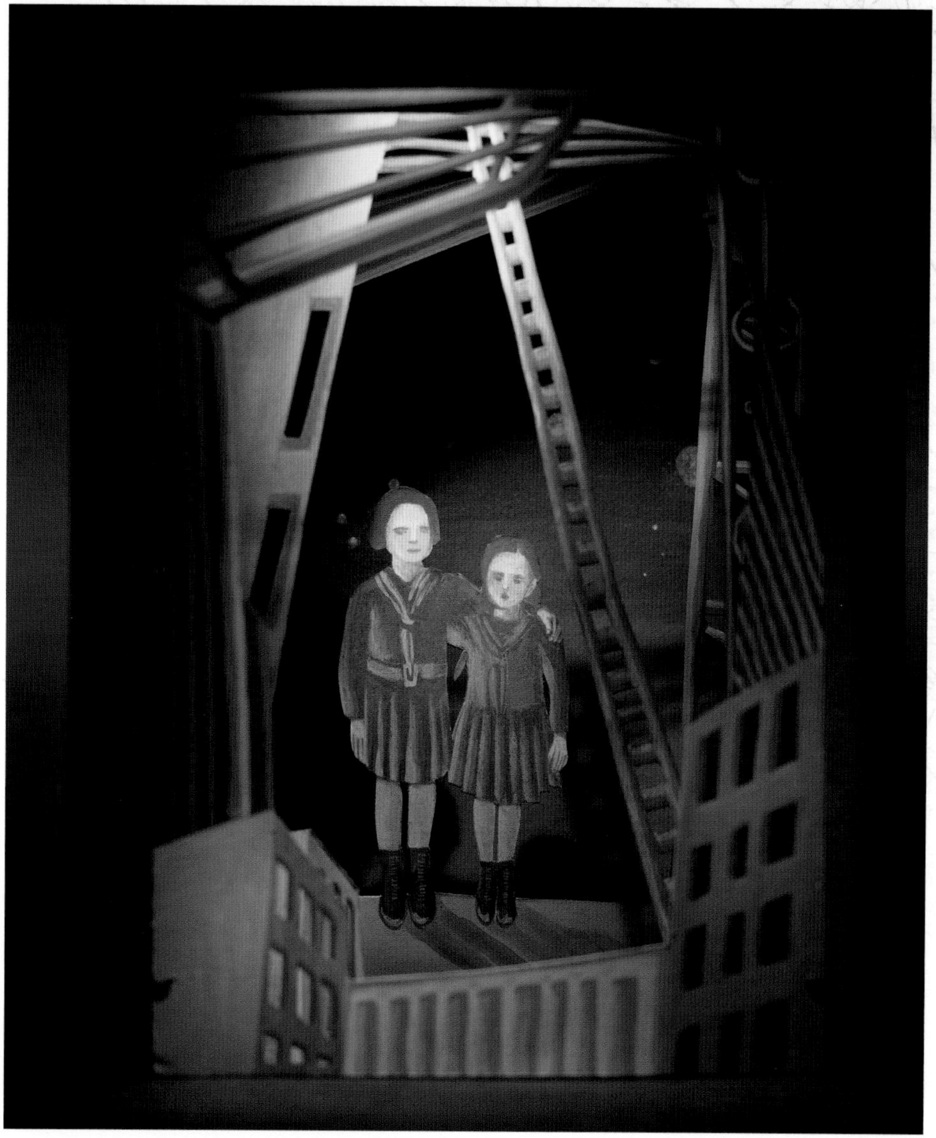

▲ **Tunnel Book from the Living Inside Series** | 2009

6 x 7 x 8 inches (15.2 x 17.8 x 20.3 cm)
Hand-cut paper, linen thread, acrylic mixed media
Photo by Péter Hapák

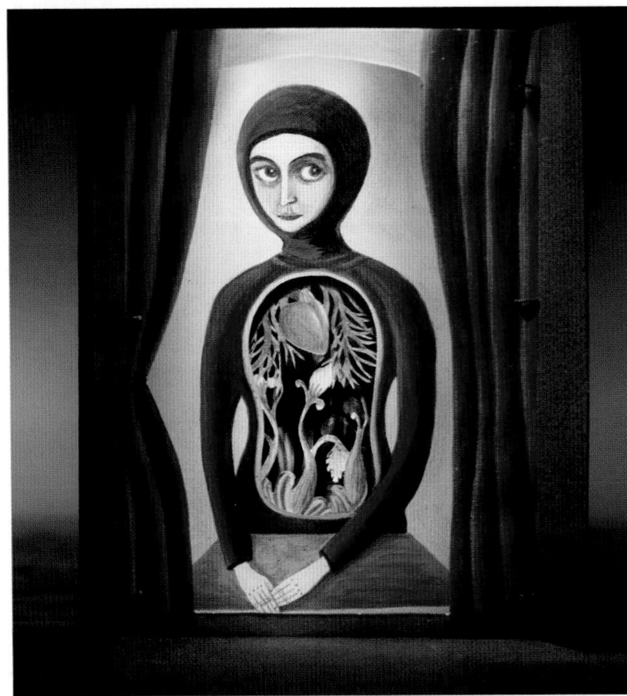

▲ **Tunnel Book from the Living Inside Series** | 2009

6 x 7 x 8 inches (15.2 x 17.8 x 20.3 cm)
Hand-cut paper, linen thread, acrylic mixed media
Photo by Péter Hapák

" Many of my recent books play with dimensionality, symbolism, and revelation. "

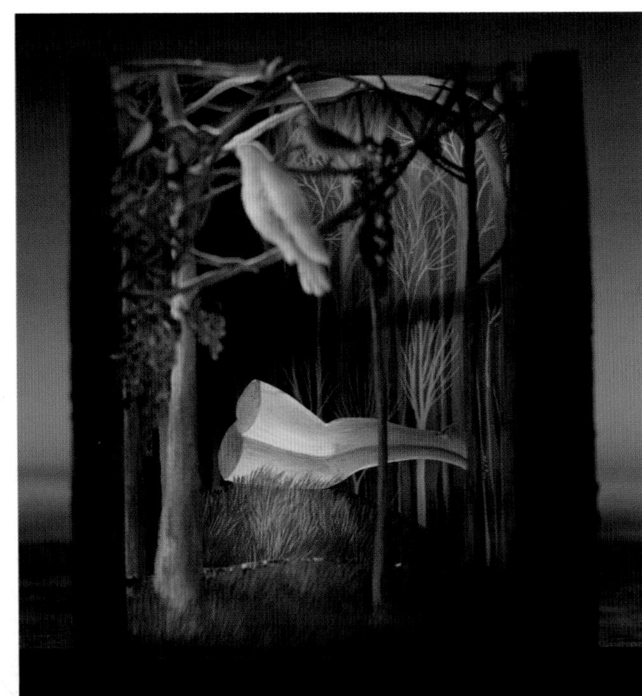

Tunnel Book from the Living Inside Series | 2009 ▶

6 x 7 x 8 inches (15.2 x 17.8 x 20.3 cm)
Hand-cut paper, linen thread, acrylic mixed media
Photo by Péter Hapák

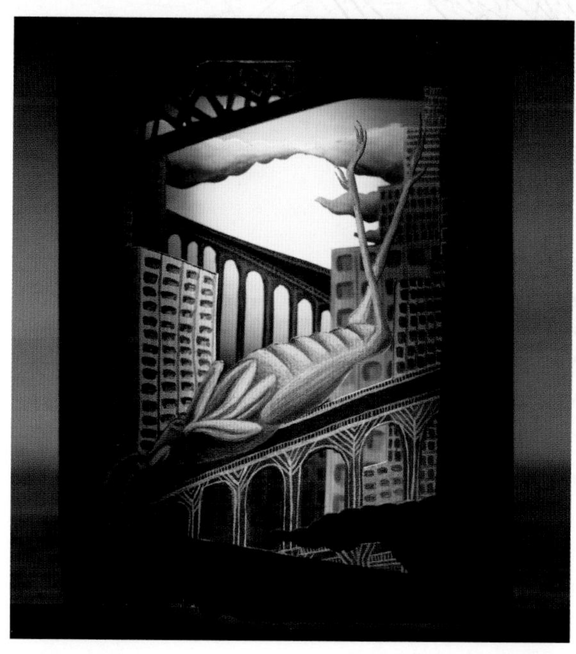

Tunnel Book from the Living Inside Series | 2009

6 x 7 x 8 inches (15.2 x 17.8 x 20.3 cm)
Hand-cut paper, linen thread, acrylic mixed media
Photo by Péter Hapák

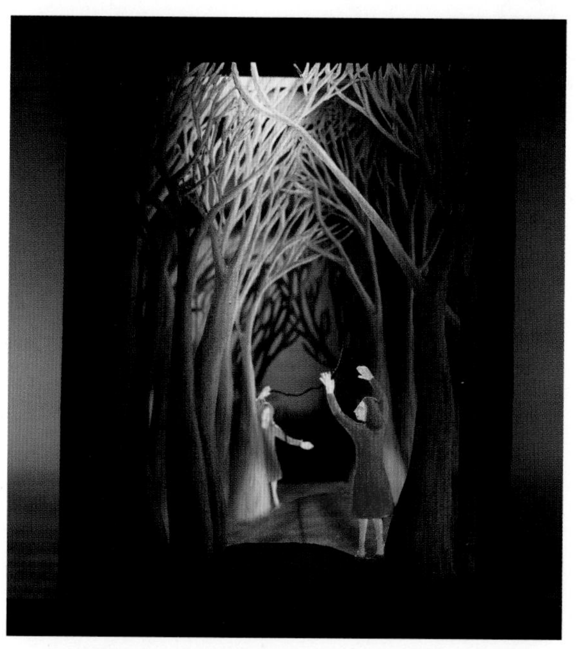

Tunnel Book from the Living Inside Series | 2009

6 x 7 x 8 inches (15.2 x 17.8 x 20.3 cm)
Hand-cut paper, linen thread, acrylic mixed media
Photo by Péter Hapák

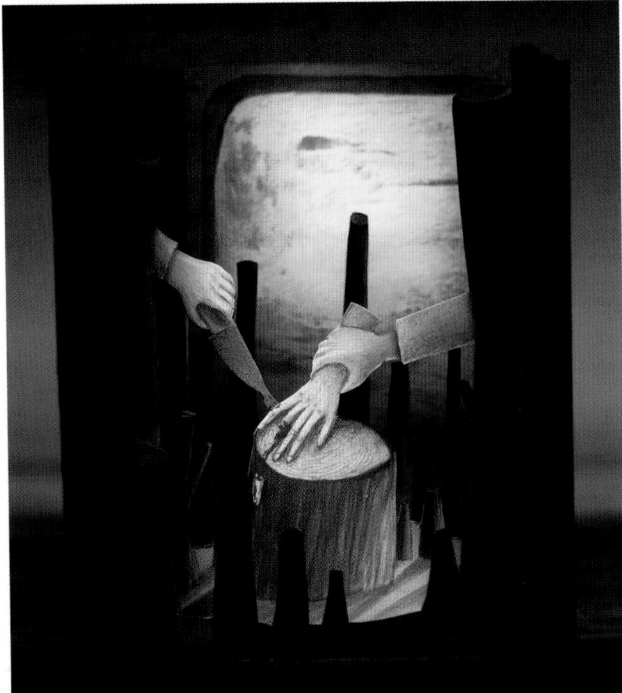

▲ **Tunnel Book from the Living Inside Series** | 2009
6 x 7 x 8 inches (15.2 x 17.8 x 20.3 cm)
Hand-cut paper, linen thread, acrylic mixed media
Photo by Péter Hapák

" I'm drawn to the aesthetically unusual, to the odd and the strange. "

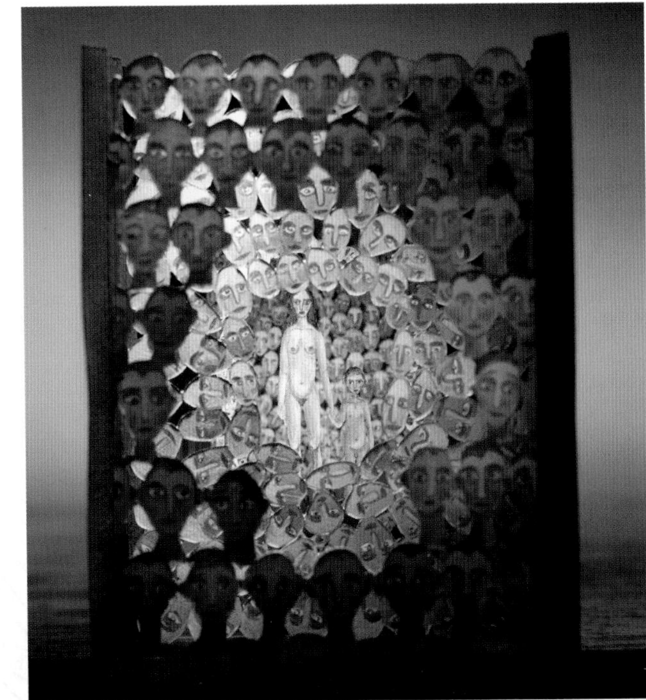

Tunnel Book from the Living Inside Series | 2009 ▶
6 x 7 x 8 inches (15.2 x 17.8 x 20.3 cm)
Hand-cut paper, linen thread, acrylic mixed media
Photo by Péter Hapák

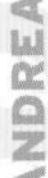

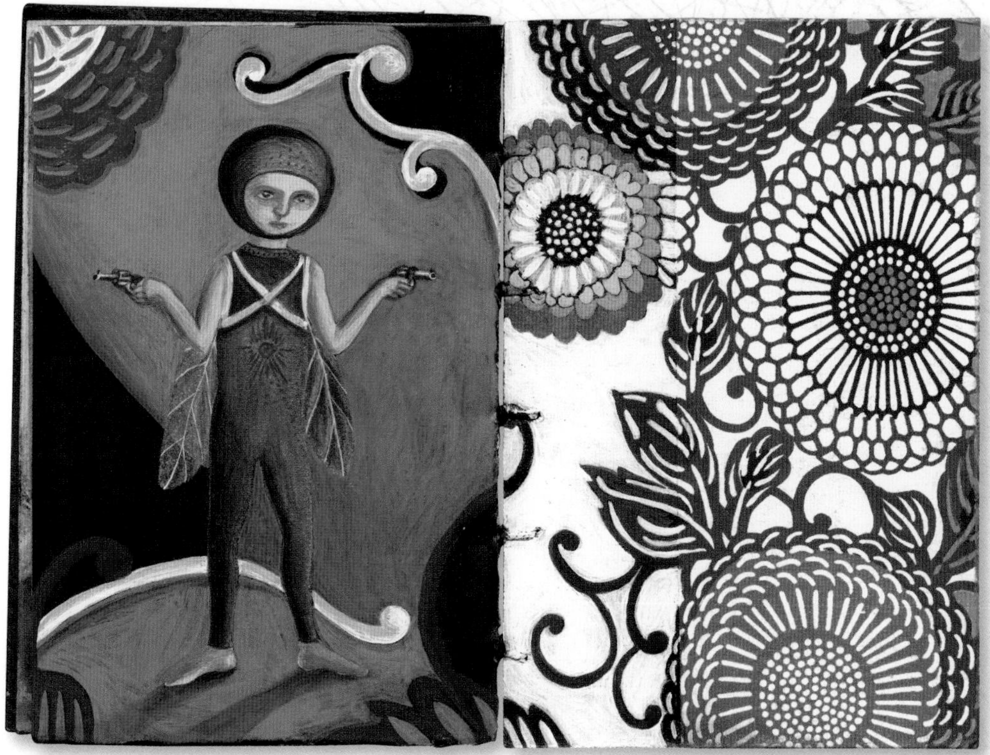

◀ **Insectmen** | 2005

12 x 4 inches (30.5 x 10.2 cm)
Paper, linen thread; Coptic binding, mixed media
Photo by artist

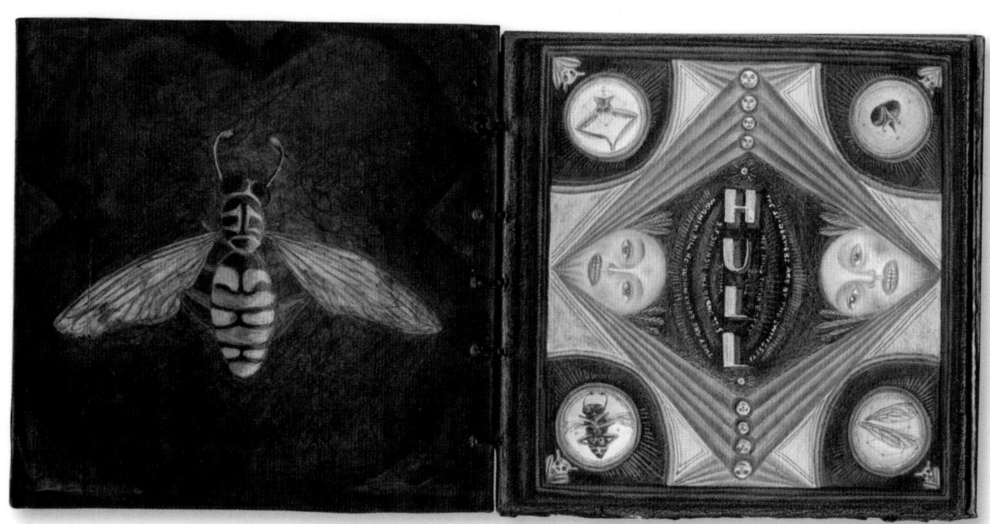

◀ **Hull** | 2004

5 x 10 inches (12.7 x 25.4 cm)
Paper, linen thread; Coptic binding, mixed media
Photo by artist

BODMAN

Sarah Bodman

AT ONCE STARTLING AND CAPTIVATING, THE WORK of Sarah Bodman features subject matter that at first glance feels innocuous—familiar topics such as nature, romance, and history. But closer inspection by the viewer reveals the ominous spirit of Bodman's narratives. She excels at synthesizing historical and contemporary texts with traditional and modern bookmaking techniques, creating distinctly identifiable work that prompts readers to think about subjects from various angles.

Bodman plays up the menacing nature of plants and flowers to create her own visual vocabulary, which she uses to probe layers of meaning and develop keen metaphors. Her beautifully evocative work engages the reader with multiple interpretations. Bodman exhibits her work regularly throughout Europe and the United States. Her work is held in the permanent collections of the Victoria and Albert Museum in London, England; the Museum of Modern Art in New York City; and the Bibliotheca Alexandria in Alexandria, Egypt. She lives in Bristol, England.

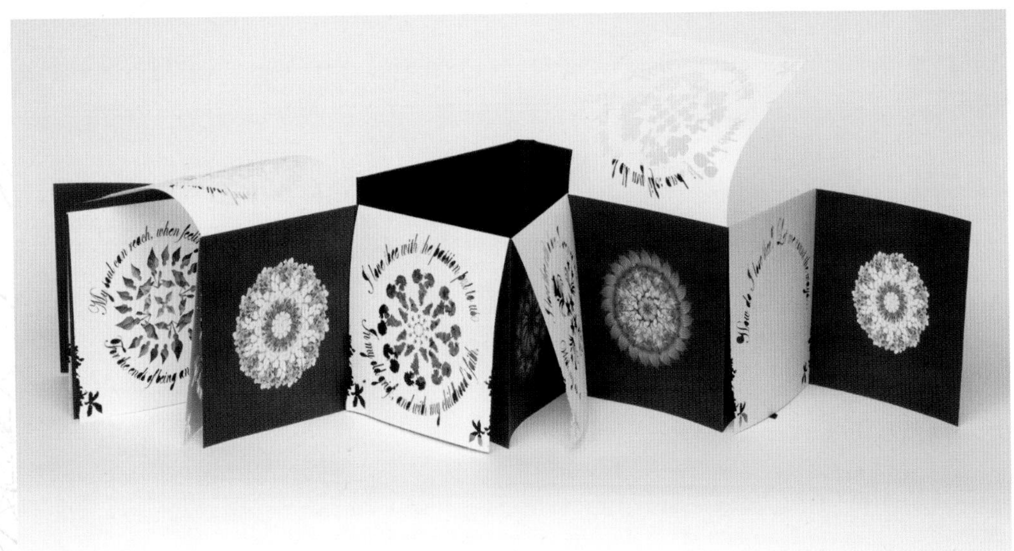

How Do I Love Thee? | 2009 ▶

Collaboration with J. P. Willis

5⅞ x 5⅞ x ⅜ inches (15 x 15 x 1 cm)

Japanese paper, ribbon, book cloth, archival digital-pigment print; screen-printed, laser cut, image overlay, clothbound

Photo by Melissa Olen

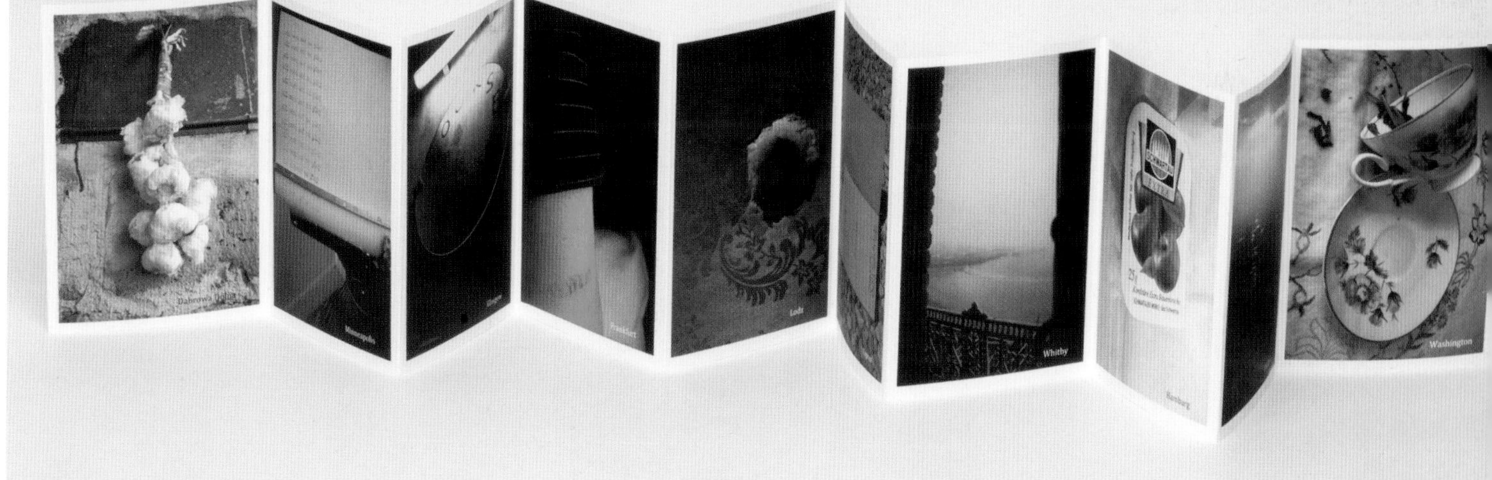

▲ **Flowers in Hotel Rooms, Volume IV** | 2009

Open: 2 feet (0.6 m) wide
Woodstock Superfine paper, six-sheet card, archival digital-pigment print, ribbon; screen-printed
Photo by Melissa Olen

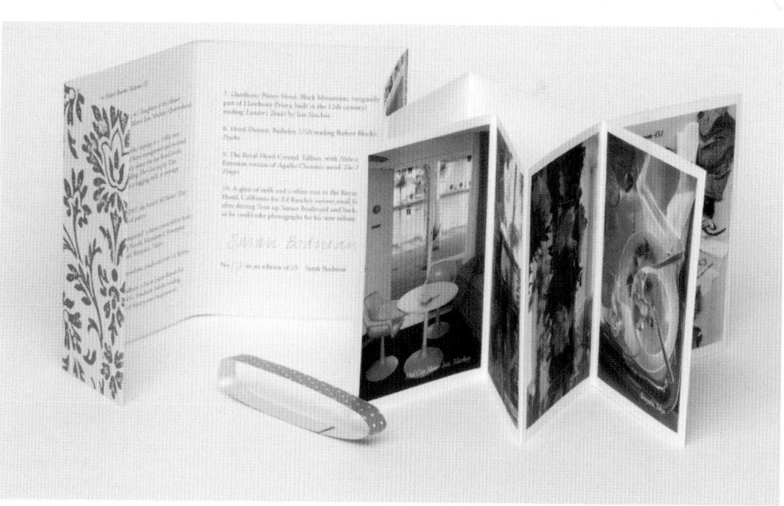

Flowers in Hotel Rooms, Volume III | 2008 ▶

Open: 2 feet (0.6 m) wide
Woodstock Superfine paper, six-sheet card, wallpaper, ribbon, archival digital-pigment print; screen-printed, wallpaper cover
Photo by Melissa Olen

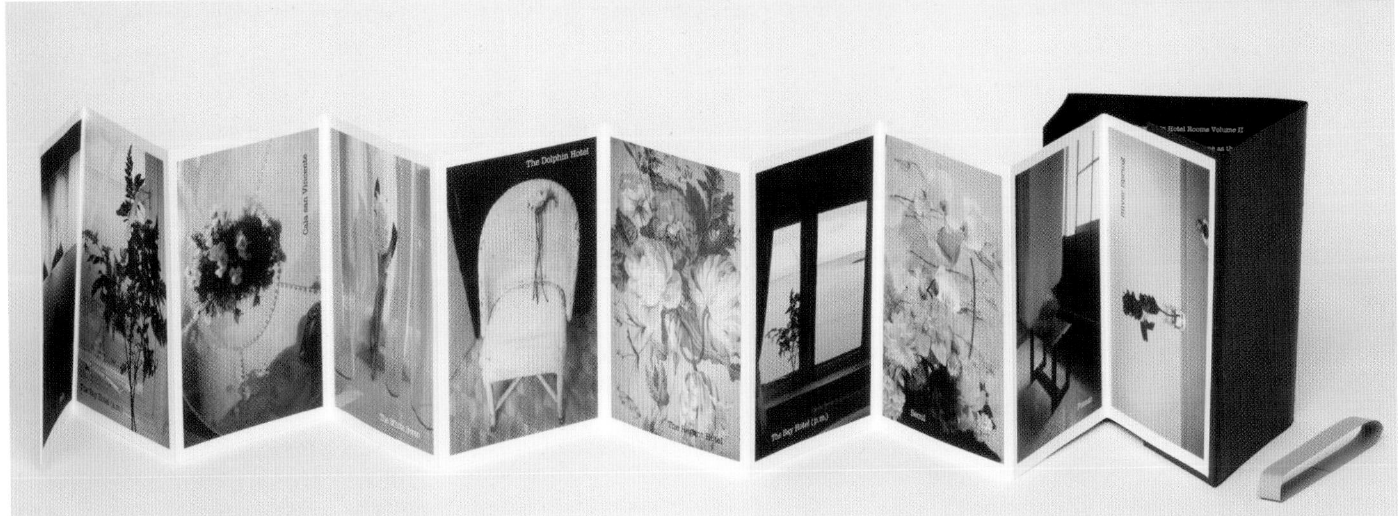

▲ **Flowers in Hotel Rooms, Volume II** | 2005

Open: 2 feet (0.6 m) wide
Artist's paper, six-sheet card, ribbon, archival digital-pigment print; screen-printed
Photos by Melissa Olen

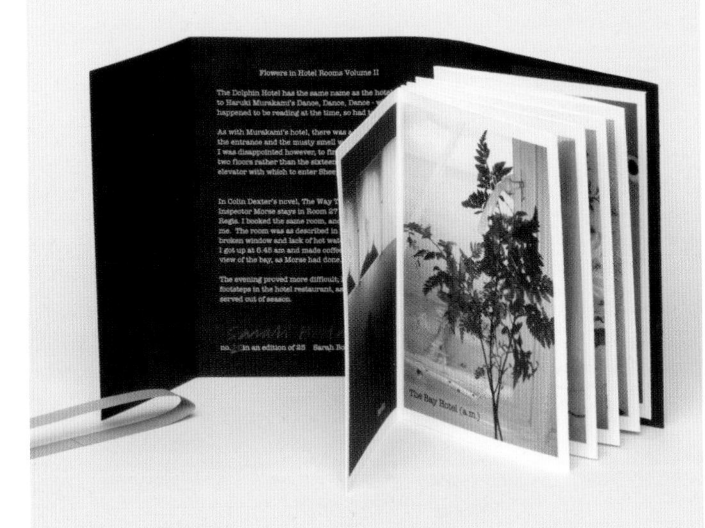

" Found objects frequently inspire my books. Old pharmacy bottles, glass slides, and rusty tools often match the eras of the historical characters I've been studying and end up in my pieces. "

SARAH BODMAN

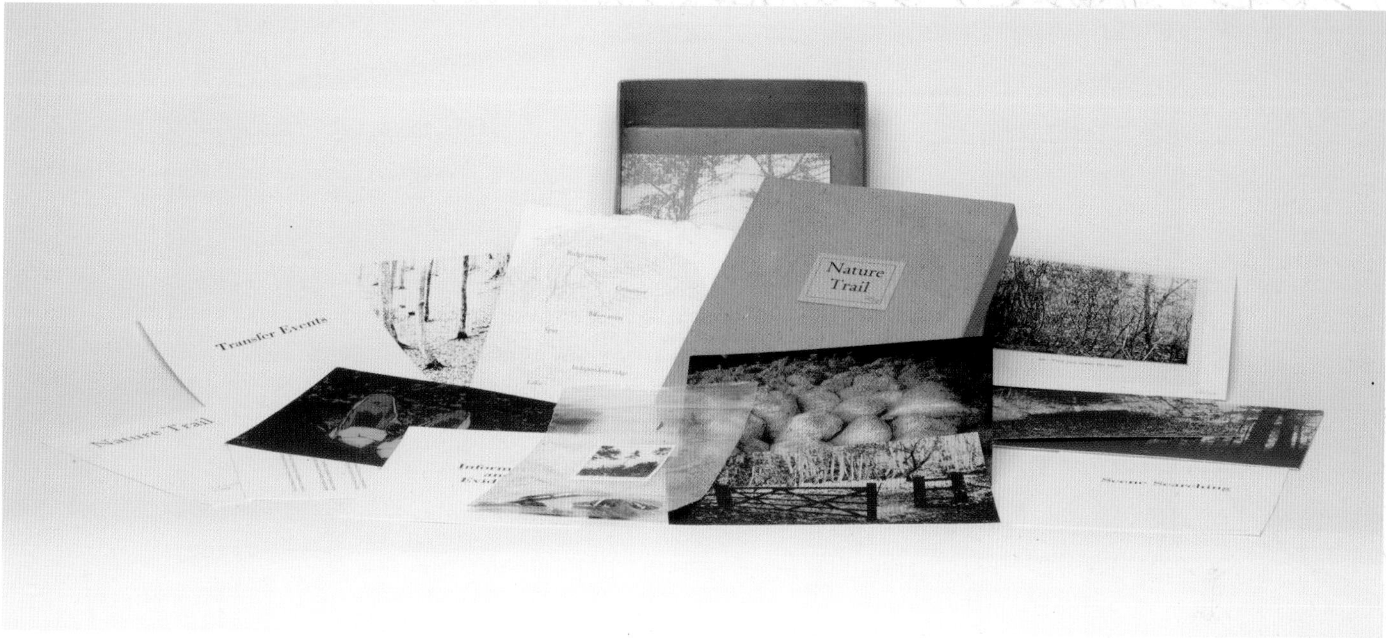

▲ **Nature Trail** | 1998

8¼ x 5⅞ x 1 5/16 inches (21 x 15 x 5 cm)
Moulin de Gue and Somerset Satin papers, remains of a pink orchid, tree bark, tweezers, ribbon, box, watercolors, pencil, paint; screen-printed, letterpress printed, photocopied, hand tinted
Photo by Melissa Olen

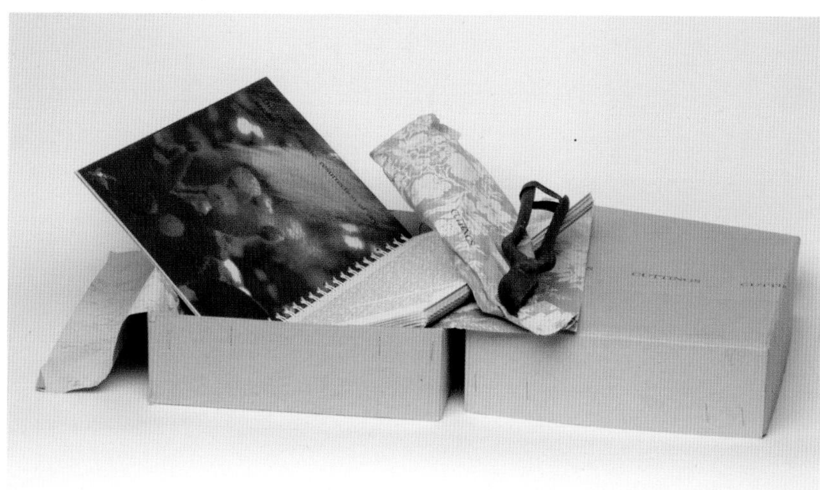

◀ **Cutting** | 1994

11⅜ x 7⅞ x 2¾ inches (29 x 20 x 7 cm)
Card box, printed wrap, assorted papers, heavy board covers, film overlay, old gardening tool, watercolors, crayon, ink, pencil; metal full-ring binding, screen-printed
Photo by Melissa Olen

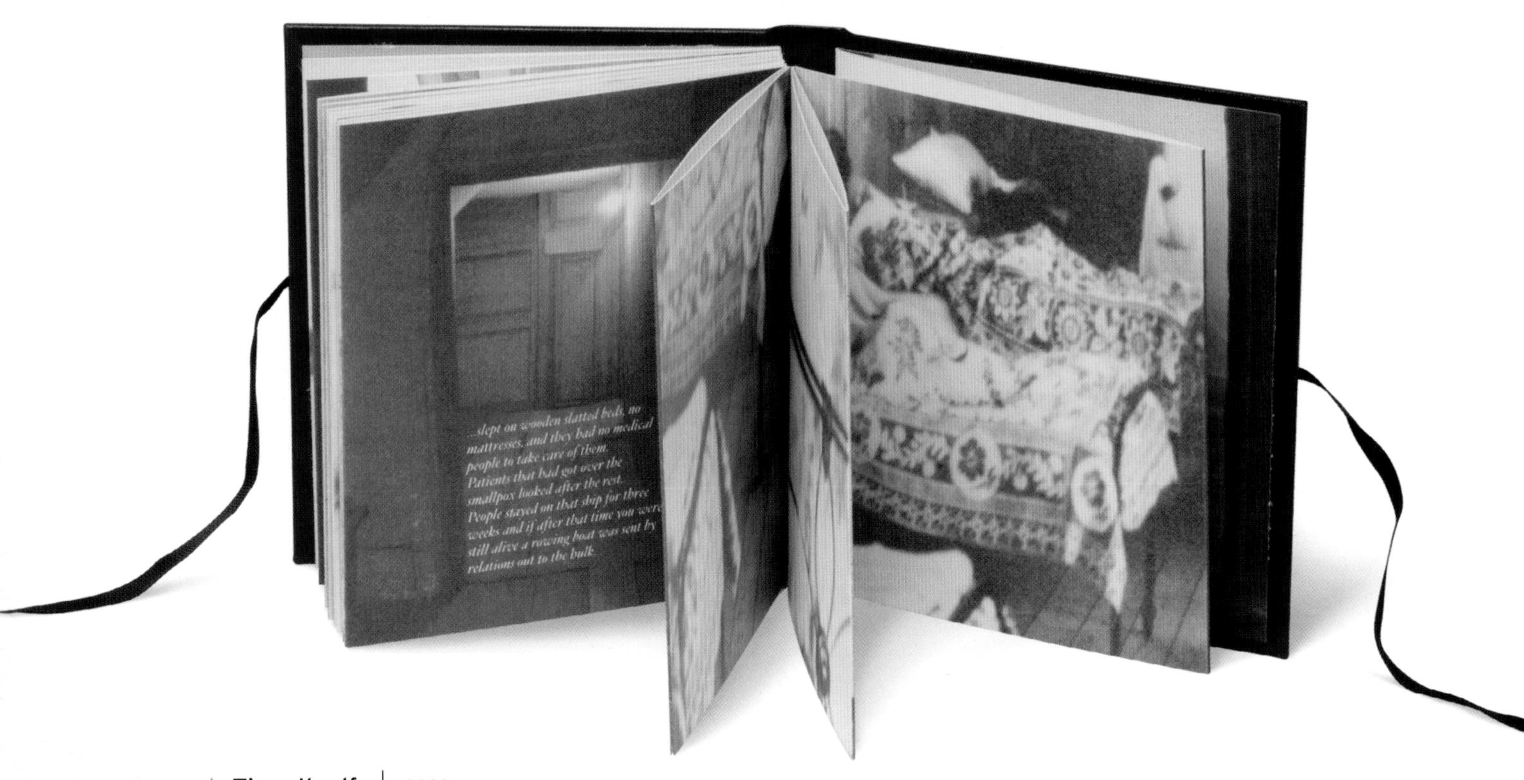

▲ **Time Itself** | 2002

6 5/16 x 5 7/8 x 3/4 inches (16 x 15 x 2 cm)
Velin Arches Blanc paper, ribbon, book cloth, archival digital-pigment print, buckram; bound, tooled
Photo by Melissa Olen

" I try to make my books appealing, so that viewers pick them up. Each one contains a surprise—a hidden element tucked behind a photo or inside a pocket. "

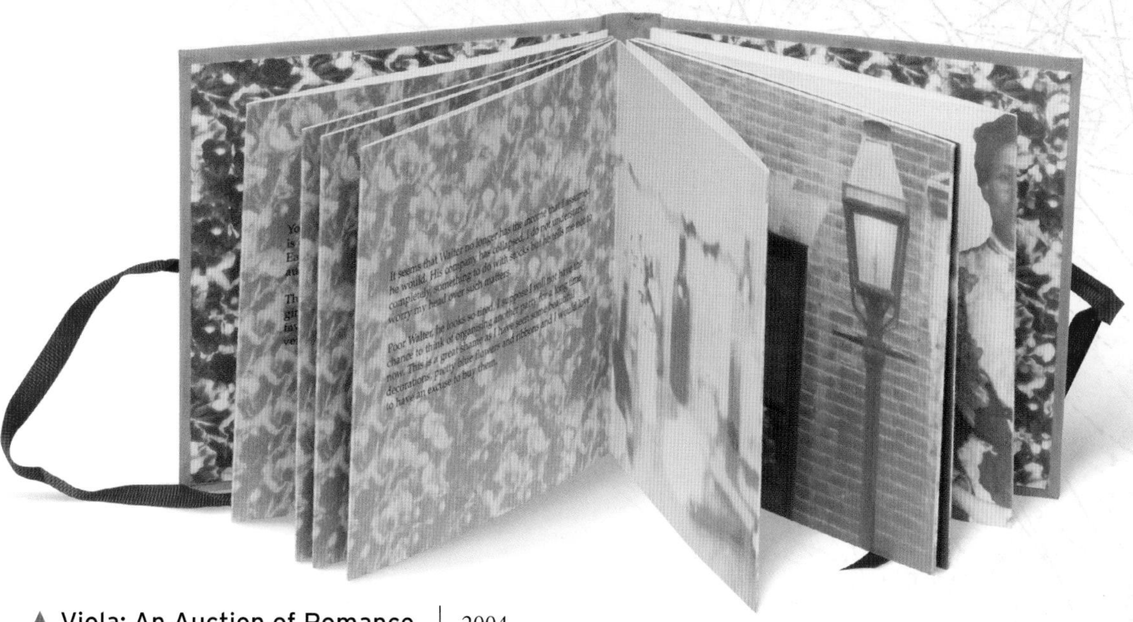

▲ **Viola: An Auction of Romance** | 2004

5⅞ x 5⅞ x 1 inches (15 x 15 x 2.5 cm)
Velin Arches Blanc paper, ribbon, suedette book cloth, archival digital-pigment print; bound, embossed

Photo by Melissa Olen

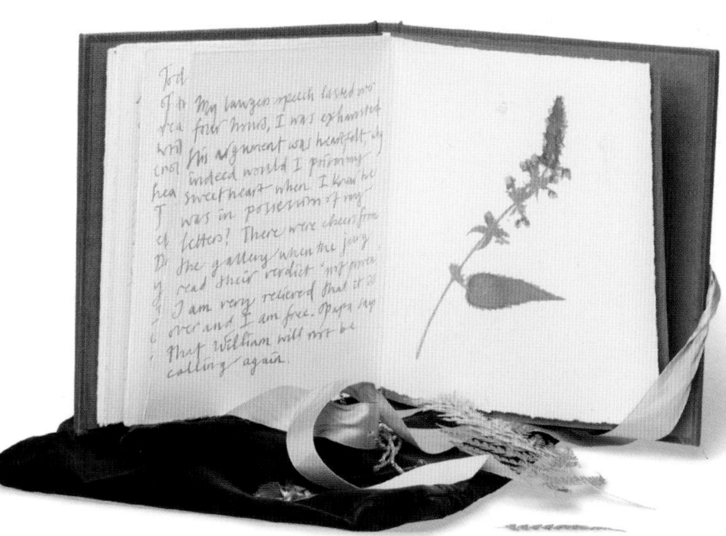

Angelier | 2000 ▶

$6\frac{5}{16}$ x $6\frac{5}{16}$ x ⅜ inches (16 x 16 x 1 cm)
Somerset Satin paper, book cloth, ribbons, pressed leaves, Victorian glass crusher, velvet bag and pouch, found embroidered material, watercolors; screen-printed, hand tinted, hand bound

Hand bound by Guy Begbie
Photo by Melissa Olen

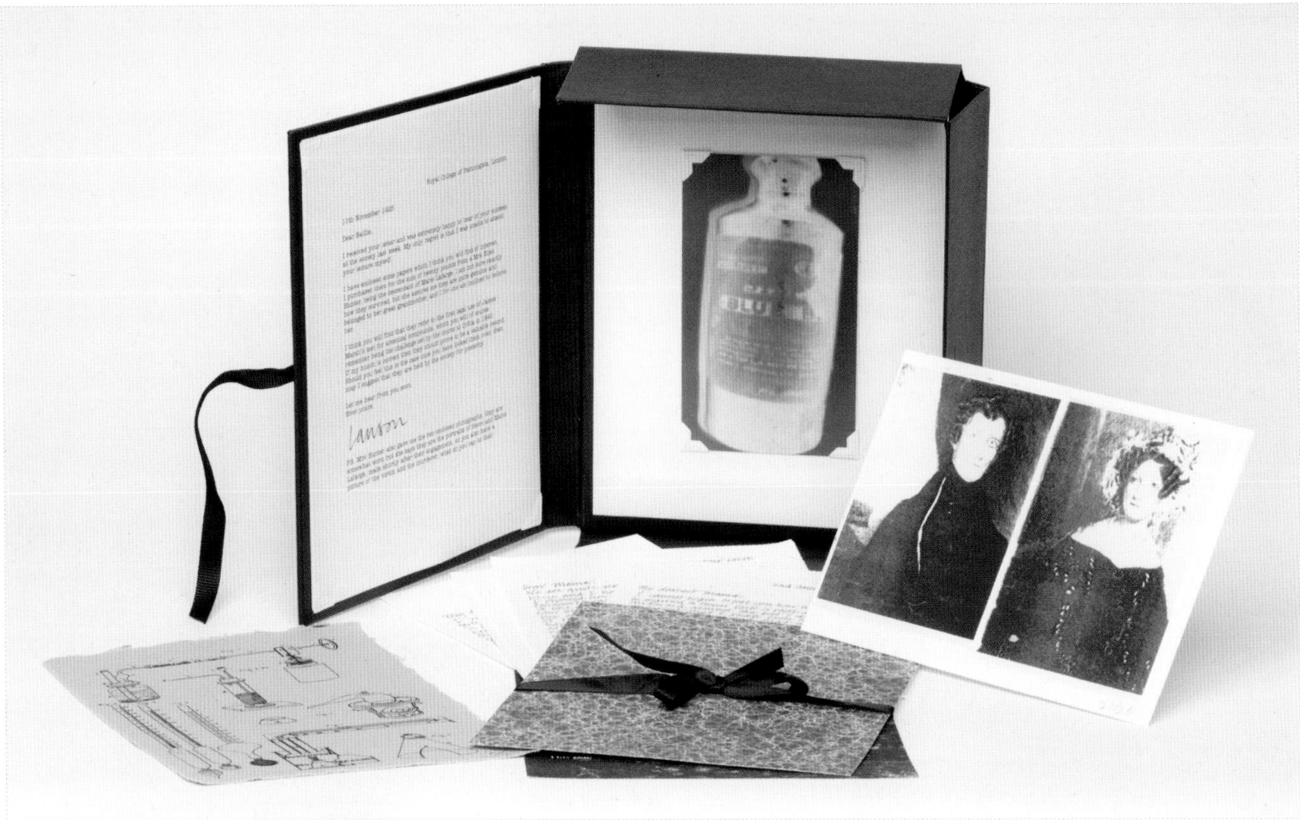

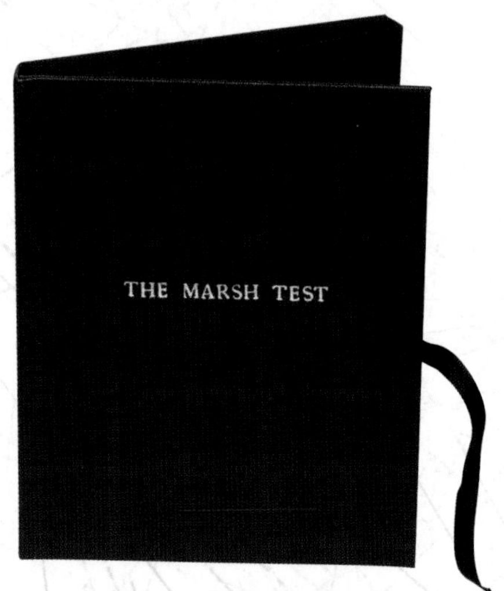

▲ **The Marsh Test** | 2002

6$\frac{5}{16}$ x 7$\frac{7}{16}$ x $\frac{1}{2}$ inches (16 x 19 x 1.3 cm)
Velin Aches Blanc and Somerset Satin papers, ribbon, buckram folio, facsimiles of handwritten letters, typed letter, flysheets, photographic images, color diagram, etching; bound, tooled

Photos by Melissa Olen

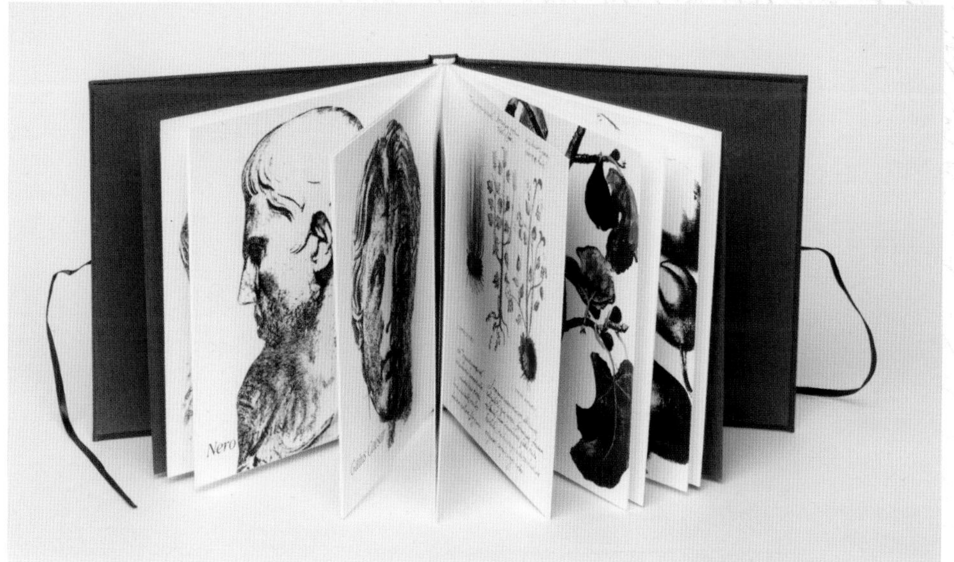

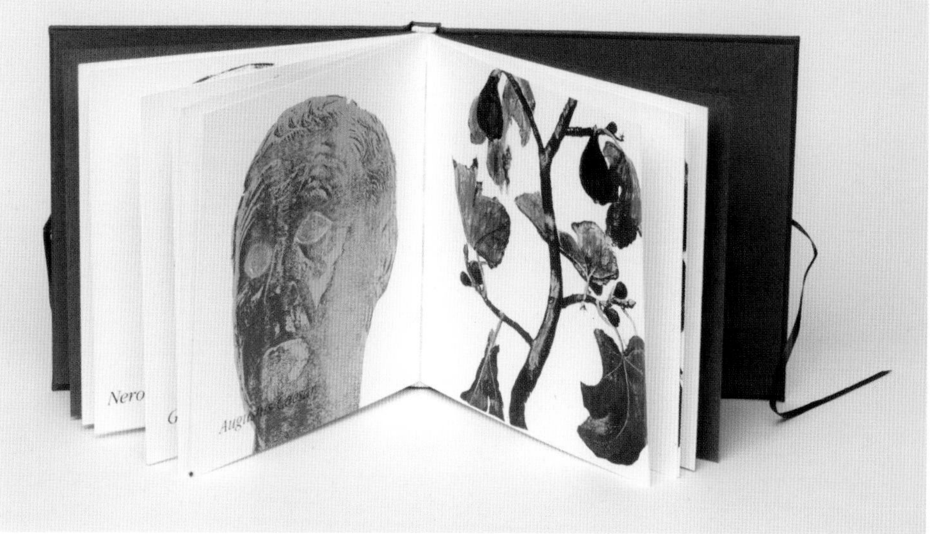

▲ **Livia's Garden** | 1997

$6\frac{5}{16}$ x $6\frac{5}{16}$ x $\frac{7}{16}$ inches (16 x 16 x 1.2 cm)
Somerset Satin paper, ribbon, book cloth, hardback cloth covers, watercolors; screen-printed, hand tinted, hand bound

Hand bound by Guy Begbie
Photos by Melissa Olen

" I manipulate images in order to reinterpret the traditional notions of nature as something beautiful and safe. Nature can also be deadly and poisonous, and I find that fascinating. "

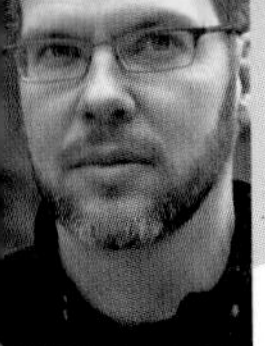

ESSIG

Daniel Essig

BLURRING BOUNDARIES AND DEFYING CATEGORIZATION, Daniel Essig is a sculptor, painter, and woodworker whose allegiance as an artist lies with the book. Like artifacts from antiquity, Essig's works feel monumental in their complexity. To make his remarkable assemblages, he incorporates a multitude of components, including mica, nails, shells, old gears, and thorns. These comprise what Essig calls visual diaries—collections of found objects and totems of memory that ultimately honor the importance of the book.

Nuanced with shallow textures, carved, painted, and layered, Essig's sublime surfaces appear softened by time. His unforgettable pieces challenge traditional ideas about the medium as they straddle the line between book and sculpture.

Based in Asheville, North Carolina, Essig makes work that is unrivaled in conceptual style and accomplishment. His pieces are held in numerous private and public collections, including the Smithsonian American Art Museum's Renwick Gallery in Washington, D.C., and the University of Iowa in Iowa City.

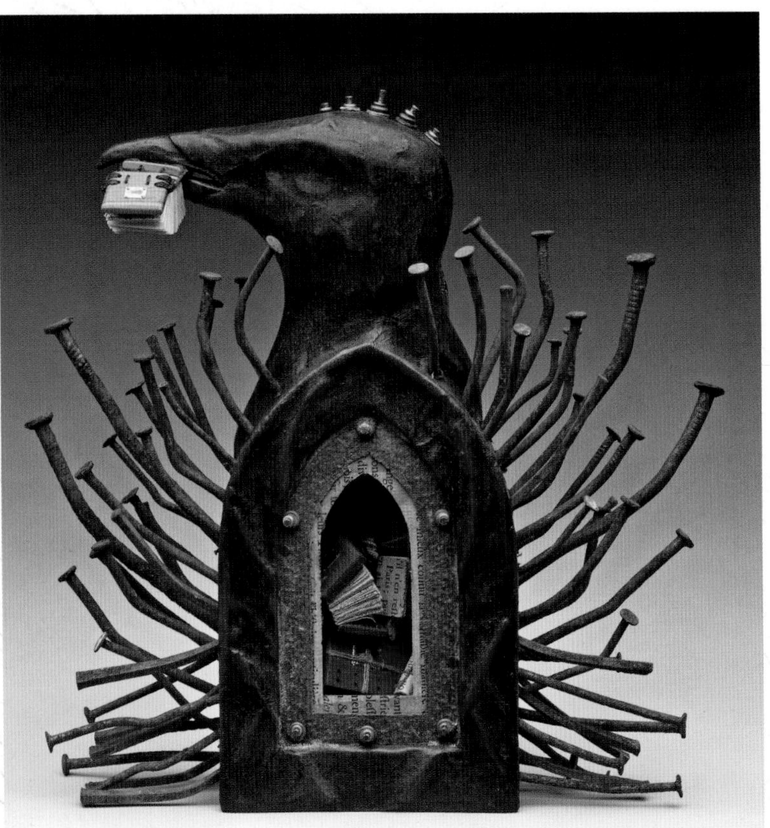

◀ **Bower Bird** | 2009

9 x 9 x 2½ inches (22.9 x 22.9 x 6.4 cm)

Yew, mahogany, handmade paper, milk paint, nails, mica, tin, scrolls; accordion and Ethiopian binding

Photo by Walker Montgomery

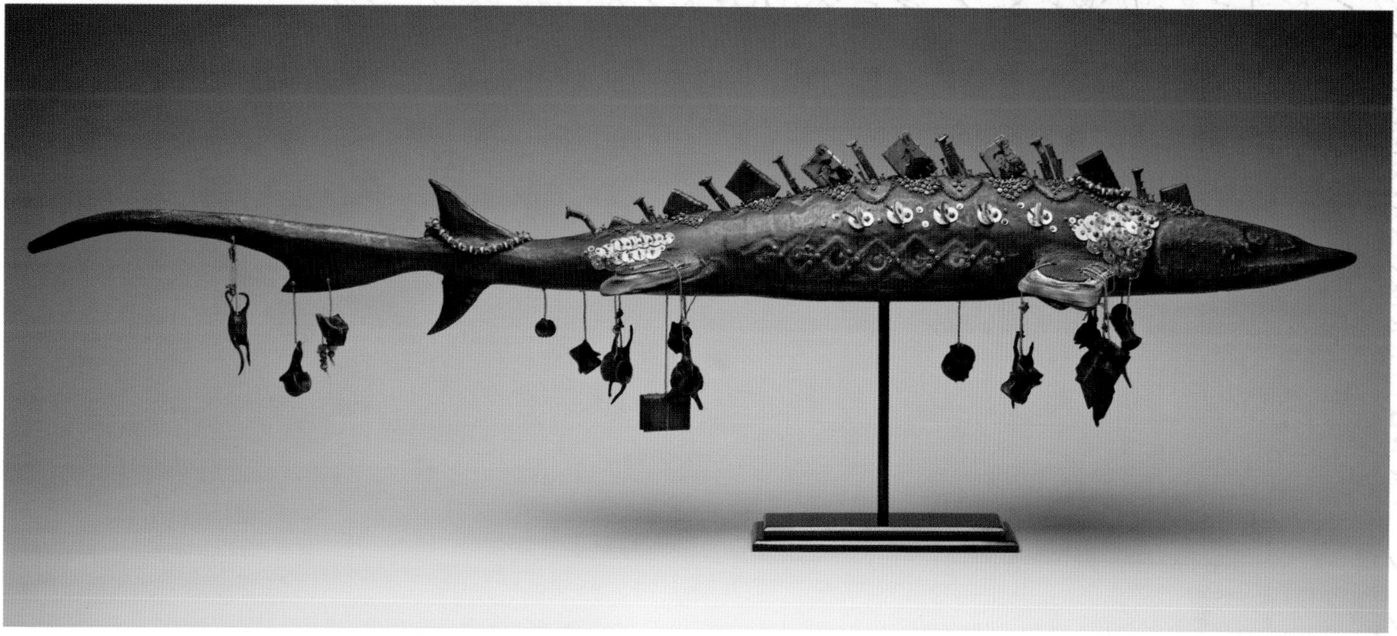

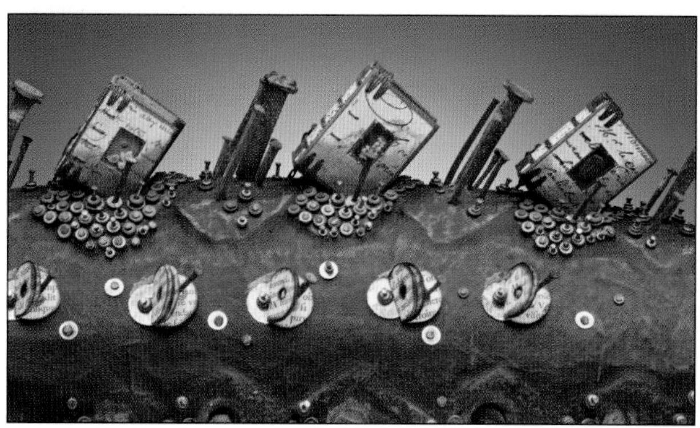

▲ N'Kisi Bricolage–Sturgeon | 2009

13 x 59 x 14 inches (33 x 149.9 x 35.6 cm)
Mahogany, handmade paper, milk paint, mica, antique text papers, found natural nails, found object, tintypes, linen cord; Ethiopian binding

Photos by Walker Montgomery

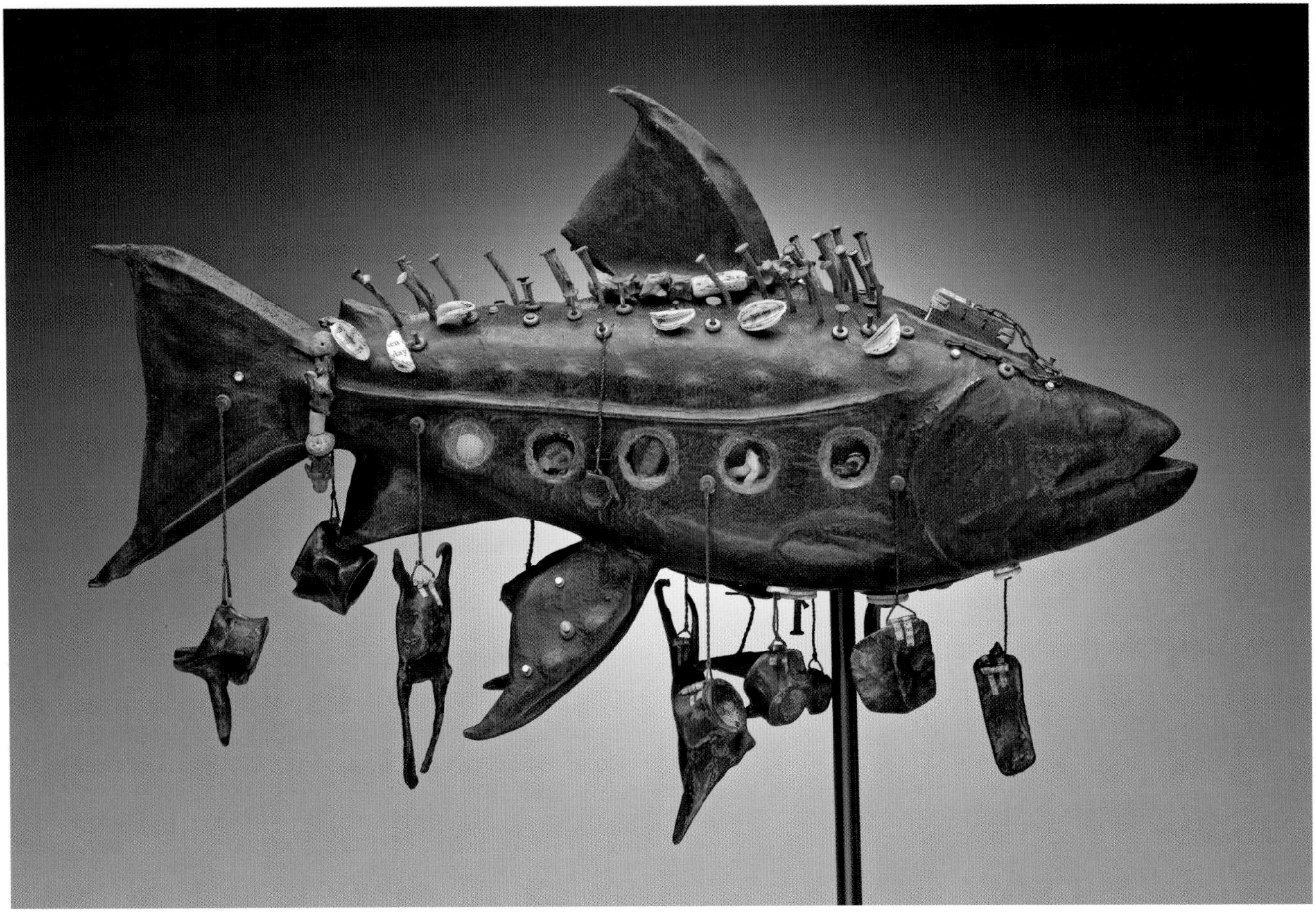

▲ **N'Kisi Bricolage—Trout** | 2008

12 x 16 x 3½ inches (30.5 x 40.6 x 8.9 cm)
Mahogany, handmade paper, milk paint, mica, nails, fossils, bones; carved, Ethiopian binding

Photos by Walker Montgomery

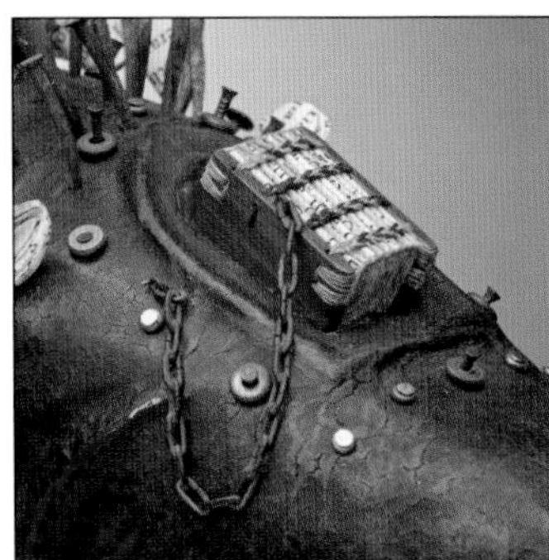

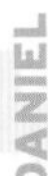

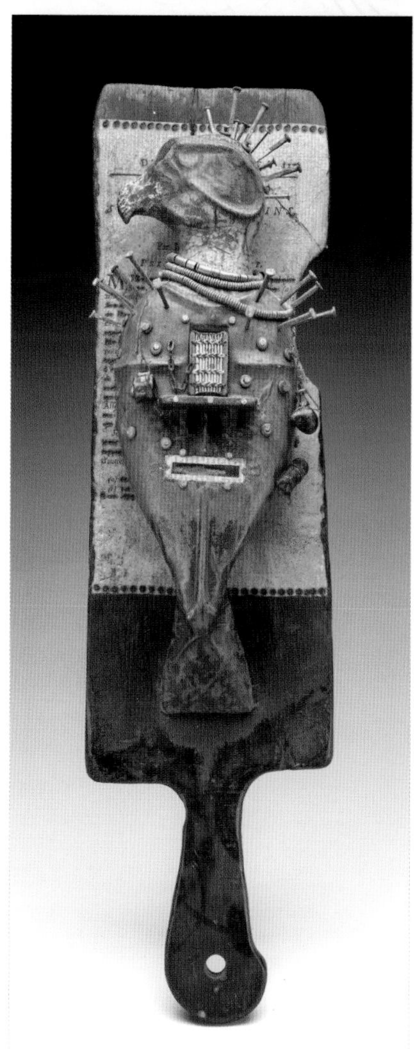

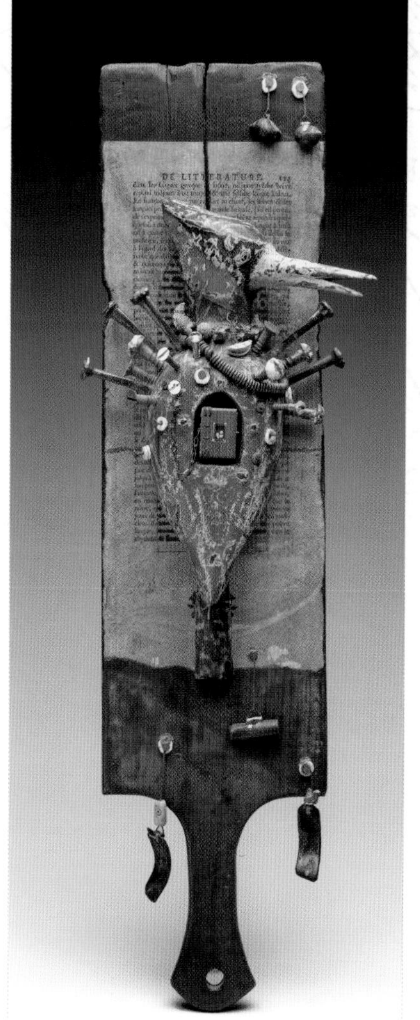

> "I'm inspired by history and by traces of the past—ancient binding styles, altered books, distressed finishes, and found objects."

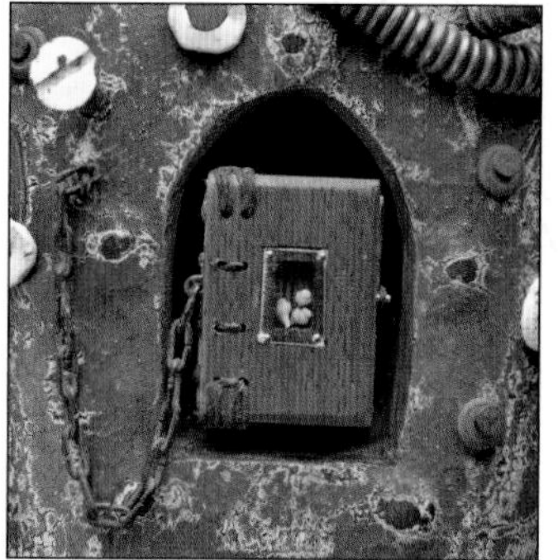

▲ **Horn Book—Falcon** | 2008

18 x 6 x 5 inches (45.7 x 15.2 x 12.7 cm)
Mahogany, cherry, handmade paper, antique text paper, milk paint, nails, mica, fulgarite; carved, burned, painted, Ethiopian binding

Photo by Walker Montgomery

▲ **Horn Book—Fisher** | 2008

20 x 7 x 5 inches (50.8 x 17.8 x 12.7 cm)
Mahogany, cherry, handmade paper, antique text paper, milk paint, nails, mica, shells; carved, burned, painted, Ethiopian binding

Photos by Walker Montgomery

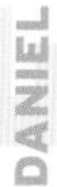

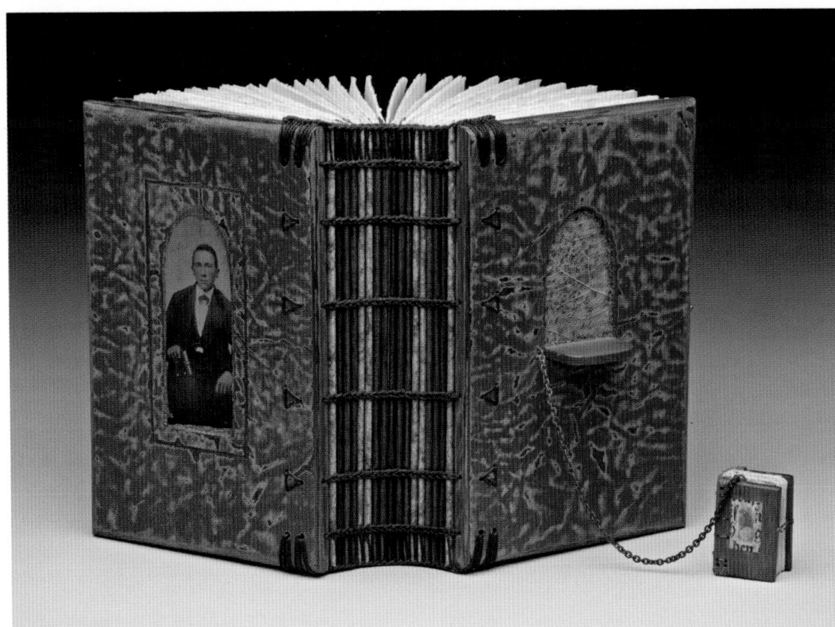

▲ **Chained Book** | 2008

6 x 4 x 3 inches (15.2 x 10.2 x 7.6 cm)
Mahogany, handmade paper, milk paint, tintype, mica, shell; Ethiopian binding

Photo by Walker Montgomery

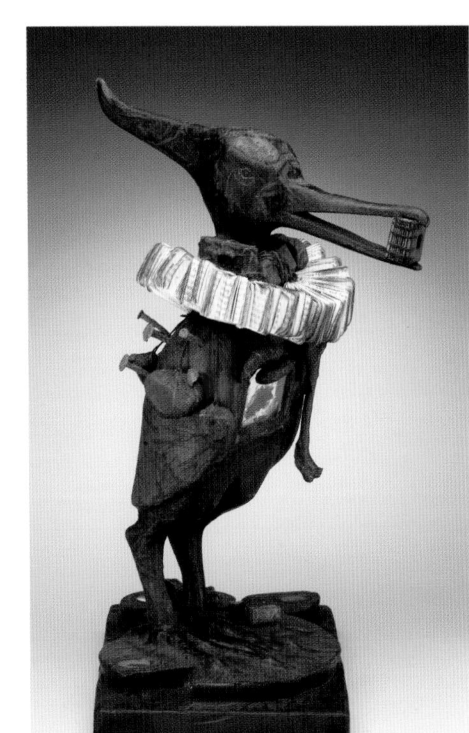

N'Kisi Bricolage | 2006 ▶

15 x 10 x 10 inches (38.1 x 25.4 x 25.4 cm)
Mahogany, cherry, handmade paper, milk paint, antique text paper, mirror, shell, nails; carved, burned, painted, Ethiopian binding

Photo by Walker Montgomery

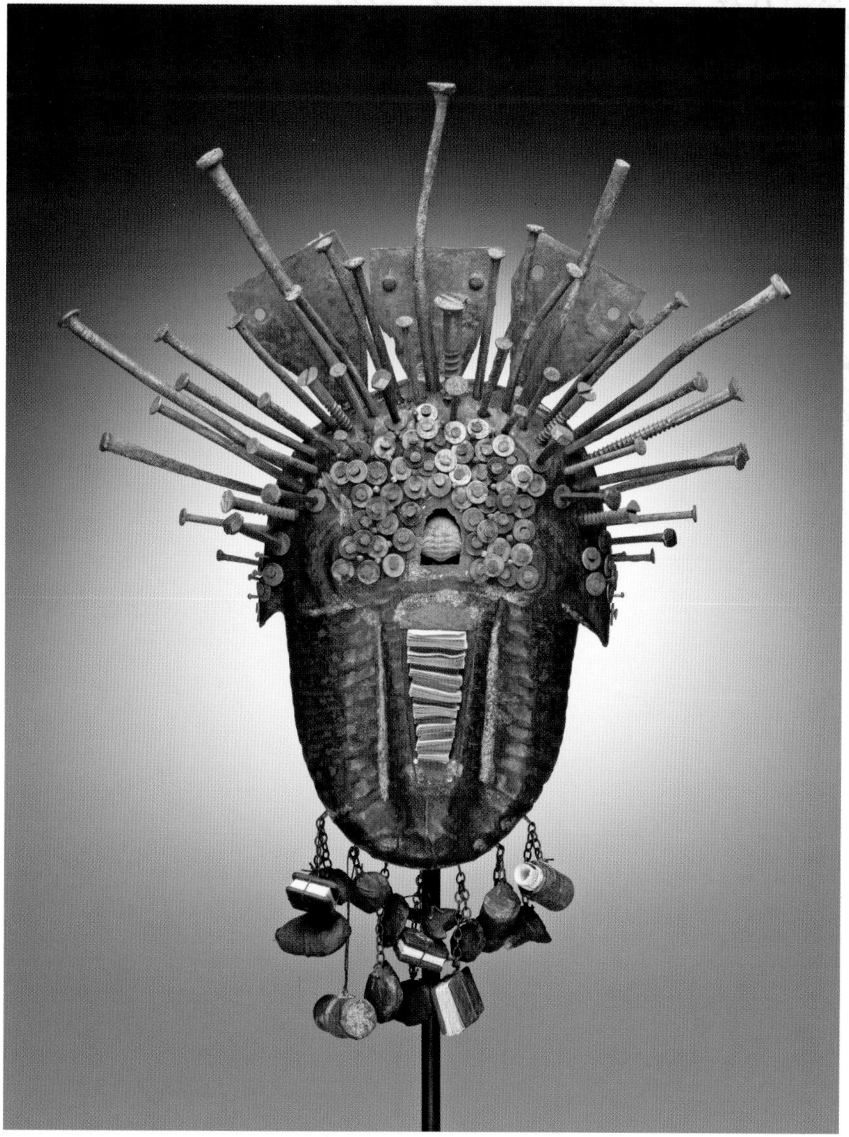

" N'kisi nkondi nail figures—wooden sculptures made by the Kongo peoples of central Africa—served to protect villages, cure illnesses, and settle disputes. In my interpretations of these figures, I see the nails as a form of defense—they protect the tiny book at the center of the sculpture. "

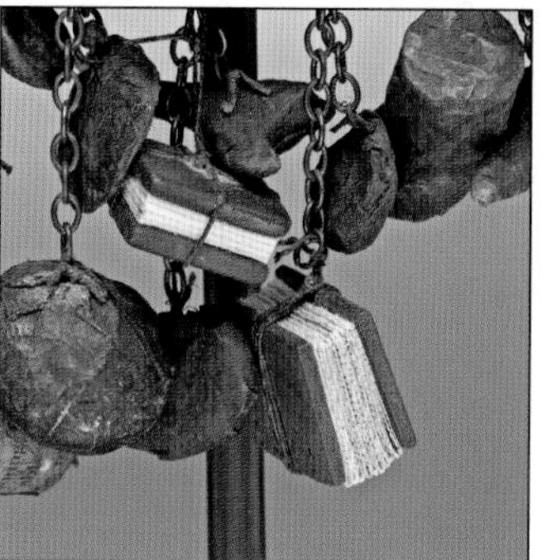

▲ **N'Kisi Bricolage–Trilobite** | 2007

15 x 12 x 2 inches (38.1 x 30.5 x 5.1 cm)
Mahogany, handmade paper, milk paint, antique text paper, nails, found metal, trilobite fossil; carved, painted, accordion binding, Ethiopian binding

Photos by Walker Montgomery

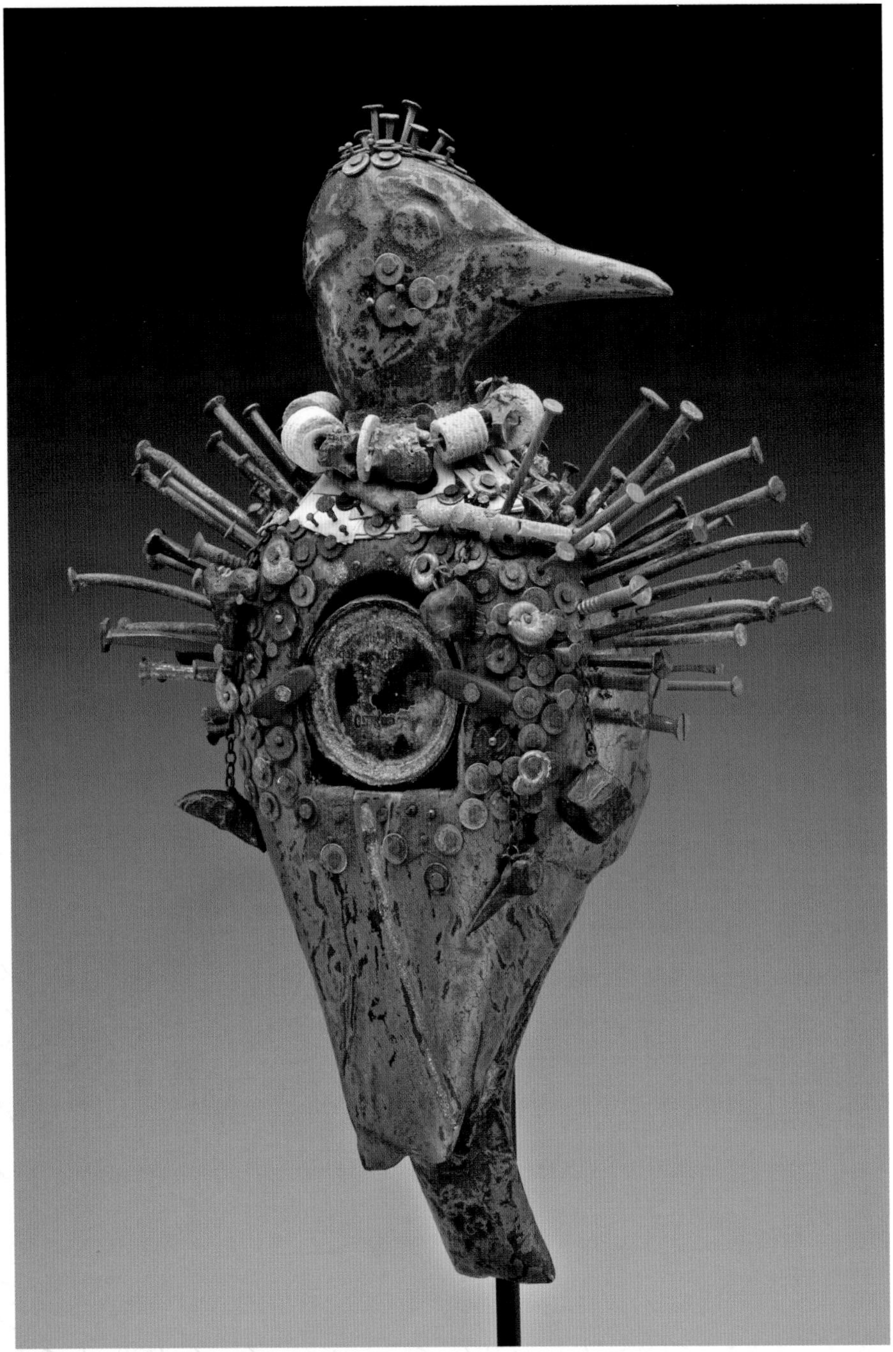

◀ **Flicker For Vicki** | 2007

14 x 10 x 4½ inches
(35.6 x 25.4 x 11.4 cm)
Mahogany, handmade paper, milk paint, nails, fossils, lens; carved, painted, Ethiopian binding

Photos by Walker Montgomery

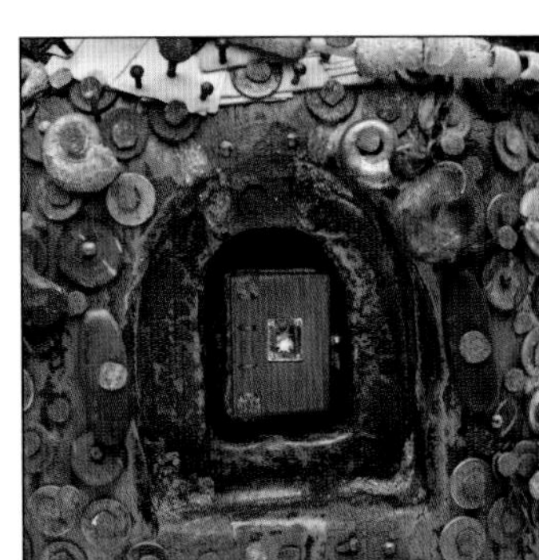

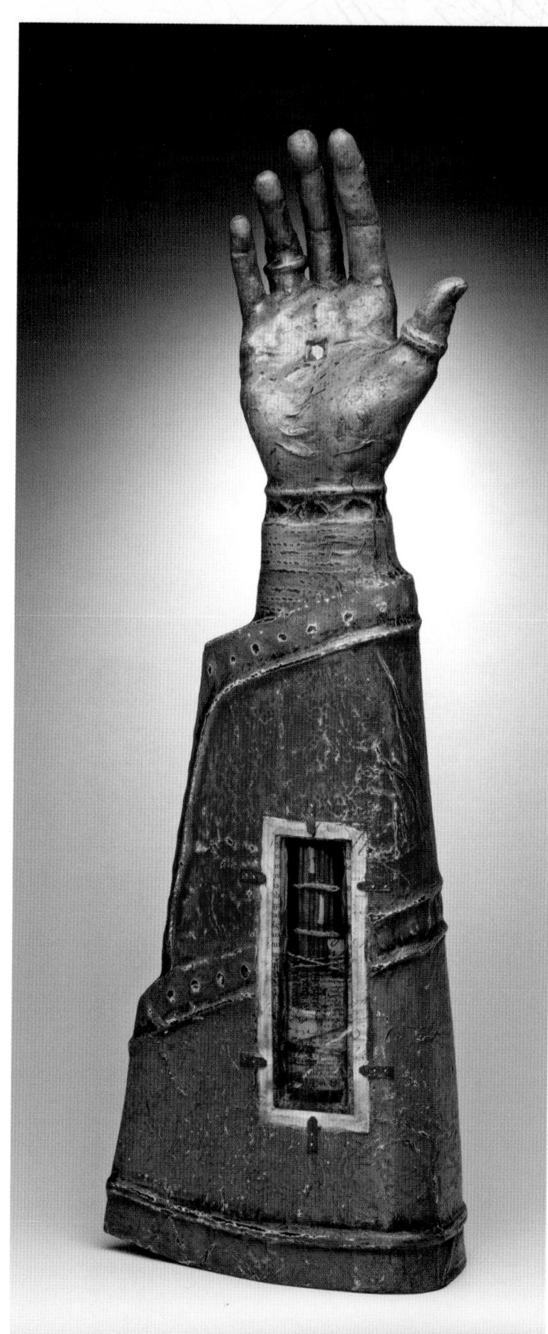

" An old typesetter's cabinet sits in my basement. Instead of lead type the tiny drawers hold fossils, shells, and other found objects. Just as type impressed meaning onto the pages of traditional books, the objects in my cabinet help my books speak. "

◀ **Reliquary** | 2007

Collaboration with Melissa Cadell
20 x 8 x 6 inches (50.8 x 20.3 x 15.2 cm)
Wood, clay, handmade paper, milk paint, mica, tin, antique text paper; carved, painted, Ethiopian binding
Photos by Walker Montgomery

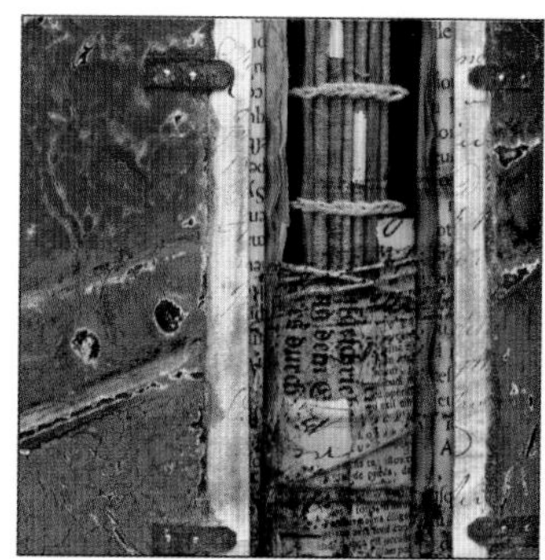

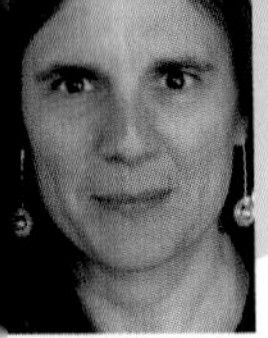

HANMER

Karen Hanmer

MEMORY, NOSTALGIA, SCIENCE, AND POLITICS are among the diverse themes that appear in Karen Hanmer's smartly constructed, beautifully conceived books. Hanmer's gift lies in recognizing the relationships that exist between seemingly disparate elements and presenting those relationships to readers, who gain a fresh awareness of their nature. Featuring fragments and layers of text and image, Hanmer's books are often designed on an intimate scale that evokes the experience of looking through a photo album or diary.

Hanmer carefully considers the multiple ways in which a reader might encounter her books, scrupulously adjusting and editing until she's satisfied that a piece can be successfully navigated. This flawless integration of content and structure is a hallmark of her work. Hanmer lives in Glenview, Illinois. Her books are in private and public collections around the world, including the Tate Britain in London, England; the Library of Congress in Washington, D.C.; and the National Museum of Women in the Arts in Washington, D.C.

Mirage | 2009
7 x 5 x ½ inches (17.8 x 12.7 x 1.3 cm)
Pigment inkjet prints; drum-leaf binding
Photo by artist

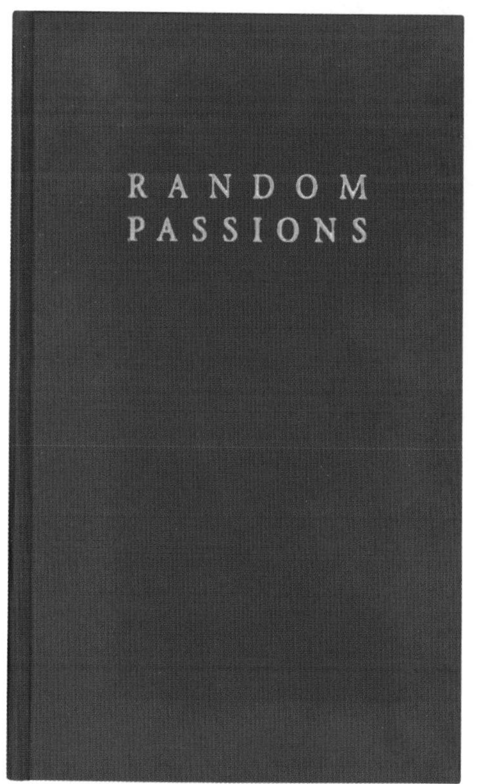

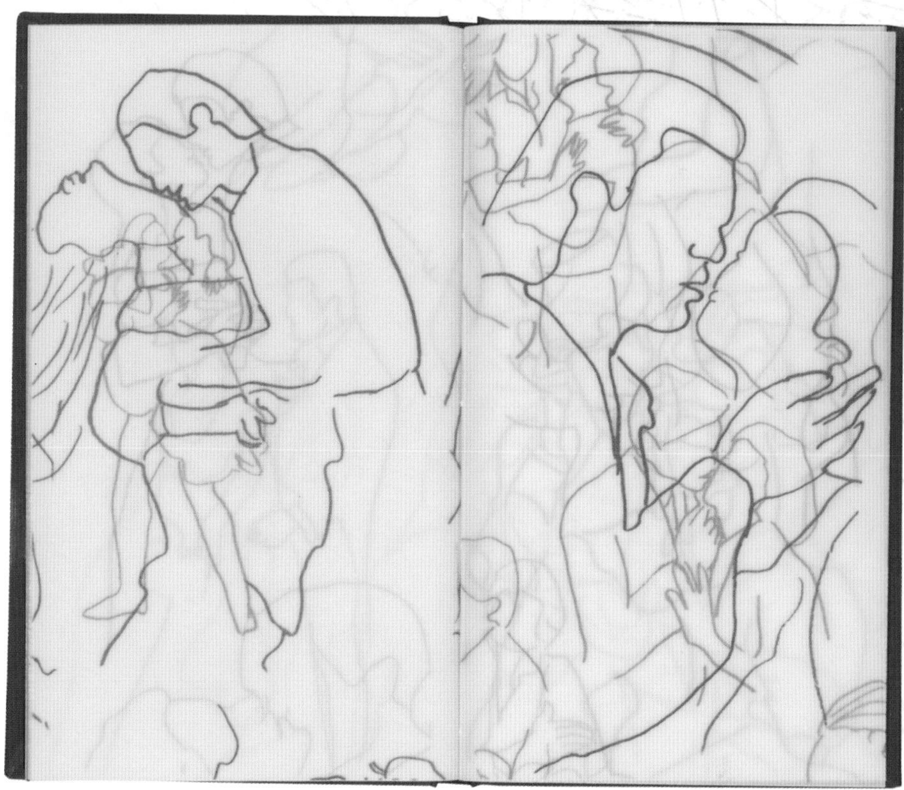

▲ **Random Passions** | 2008

7 x 4 x ¼ inches (17.8 x 10.2 x 0.6 cm)
Book cloth, laser prints, translucent paper; pamphlet in case binding

Photos by artist

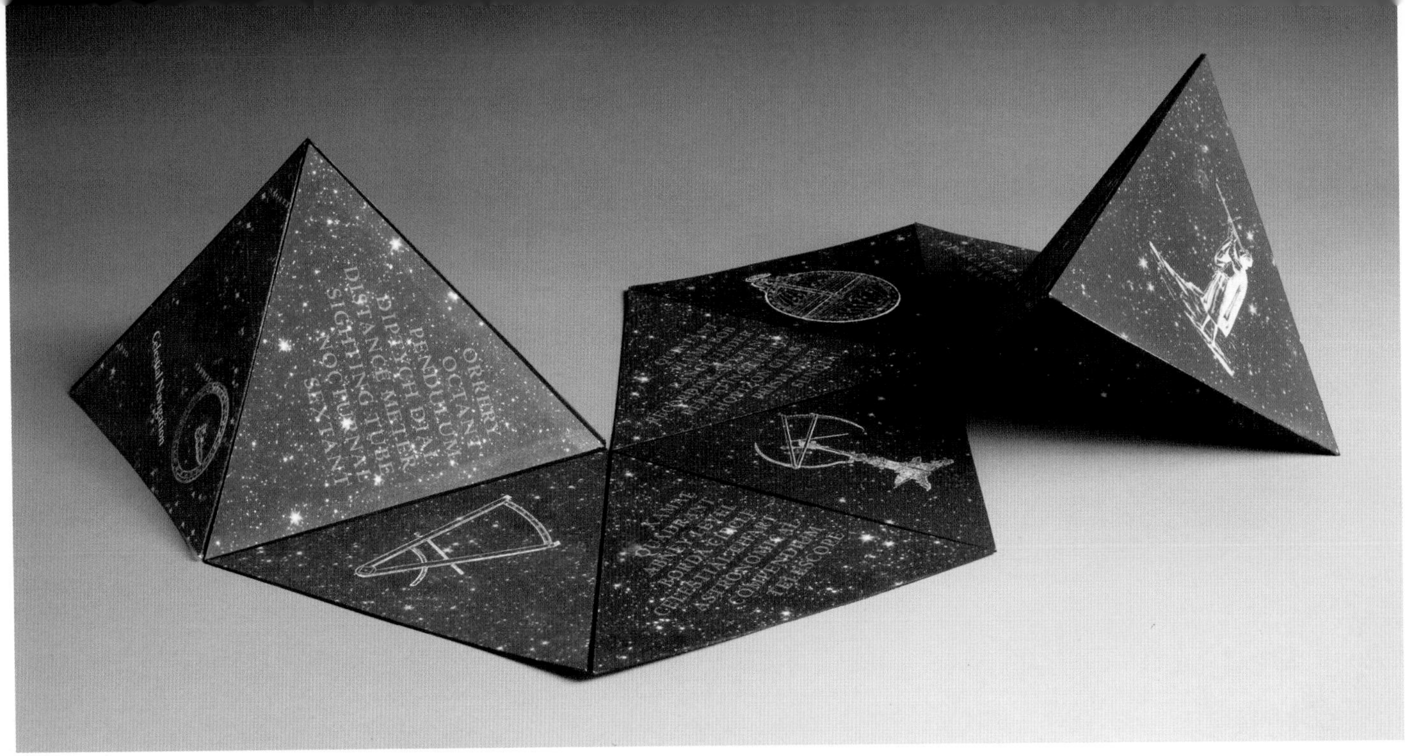

▲ **Celestial Navigation** | 2008

Open: 17½ x 30 inches (44.5 x 76.2 cm)
Closed: 6¾ x 5¾ x ½ inches (17.1 x 14.6 x 1.3 cm)
Pigment inkjet prints, book cloth; hinged

Main photo by Jerry Mathiason
Detail photo by artist

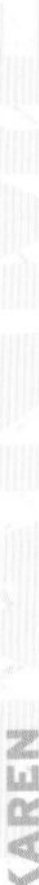

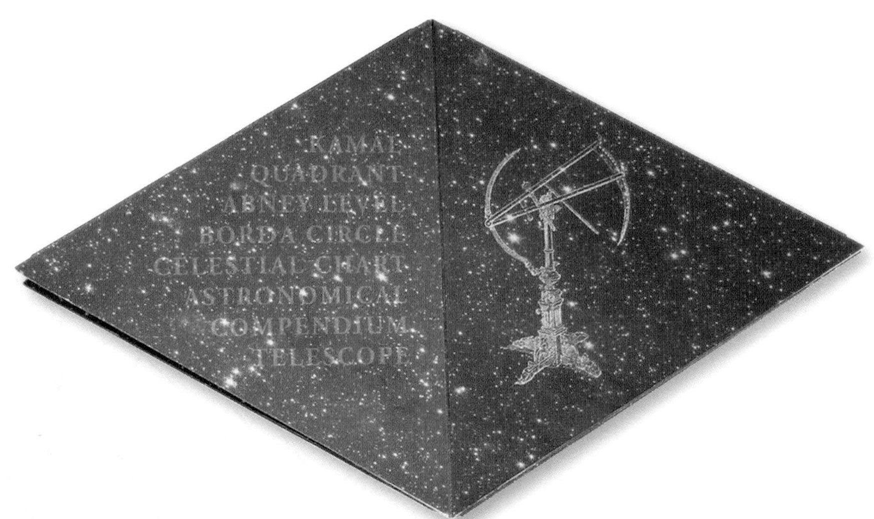

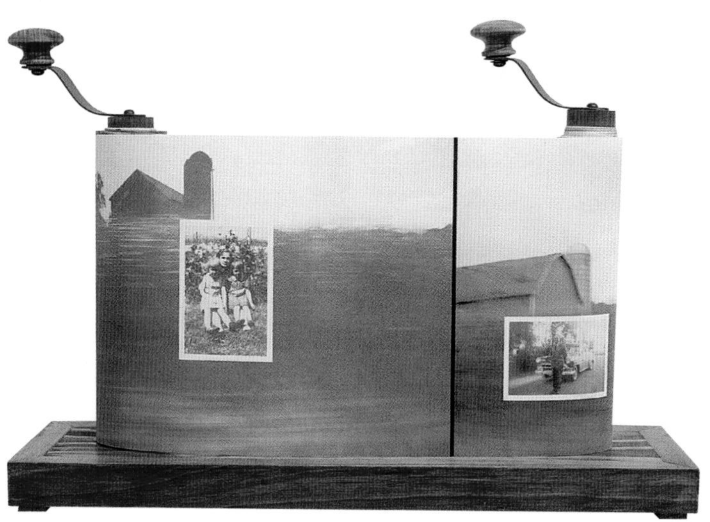

"Using archival photographs and artifacts, I link my work as an artist to that of the inventor, explorer, or scientist."

▲ **Homestead** | 2001

12 x 17½ x 5½ inches (30.5 x 44.5 x 14 cm)
Wood, metal, Japanese paper; inkjet printed, scroll
Photo by artist

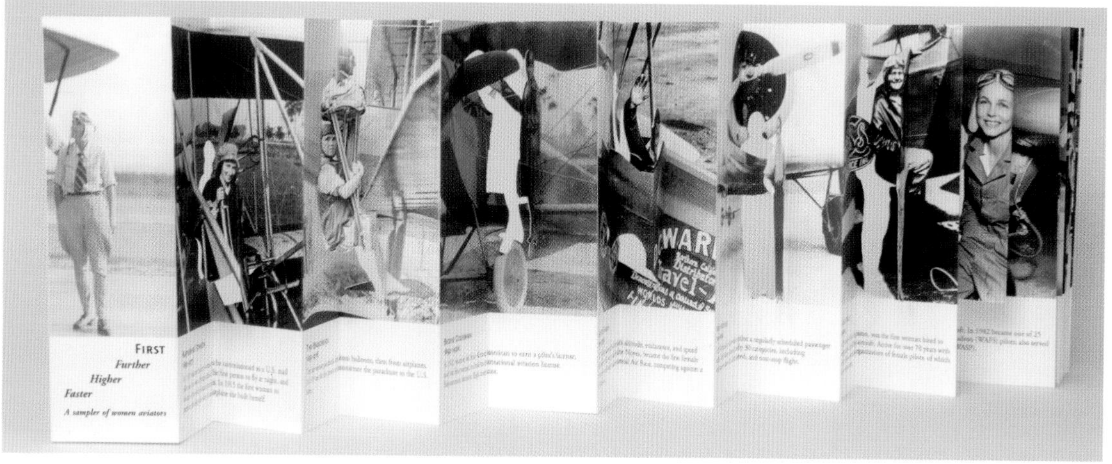

▲ **Faster Higher Further First: A Sampler of Women Aviators** | 2005

Open: 8 x 56 x 5 inches (20.3 x 142.2 x 12.7 cm)
Pigment inkjet prints; accordion fold with pop-ups
Photo by artist

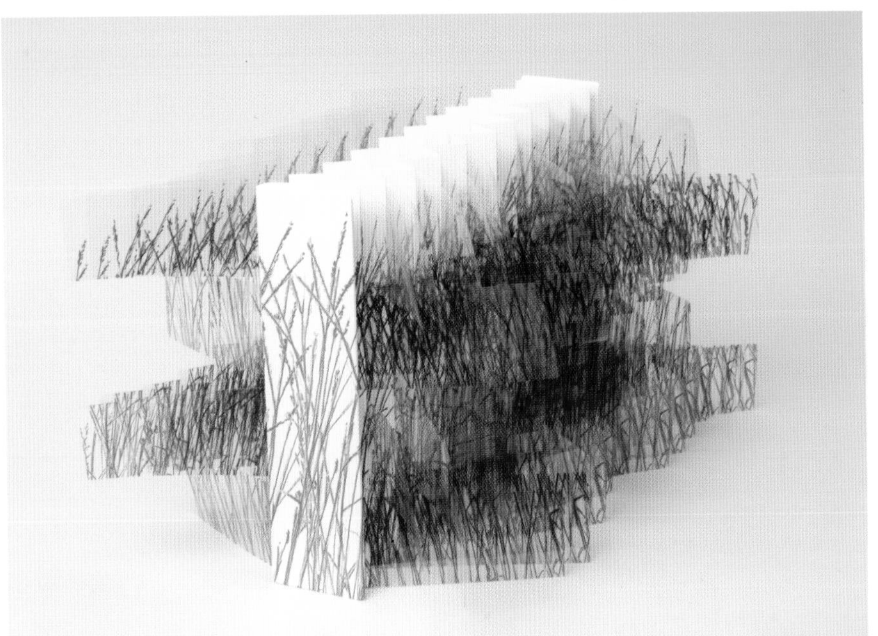

▲ **Bluestem** | 2006

Closed: 8 x 10 x ½ inches (20.3 x 25.4 x 1.3 cm)
Pigment inkjet prints on polyester film; double-sided variation of flag book

Photos by artist

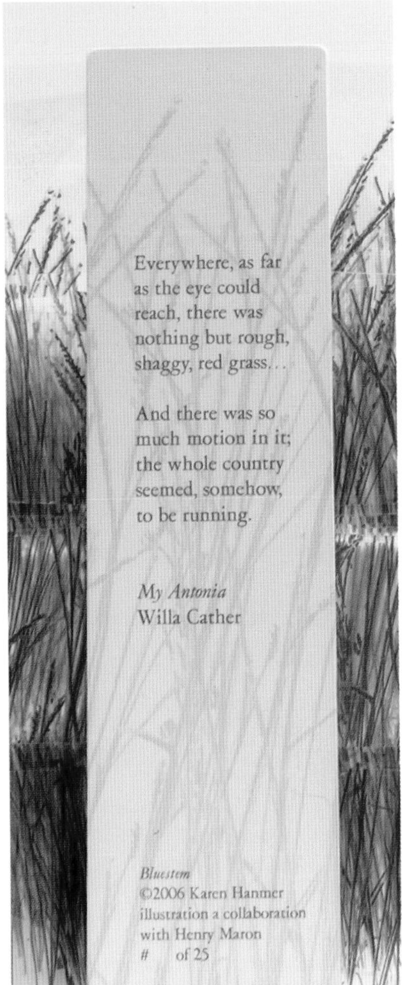

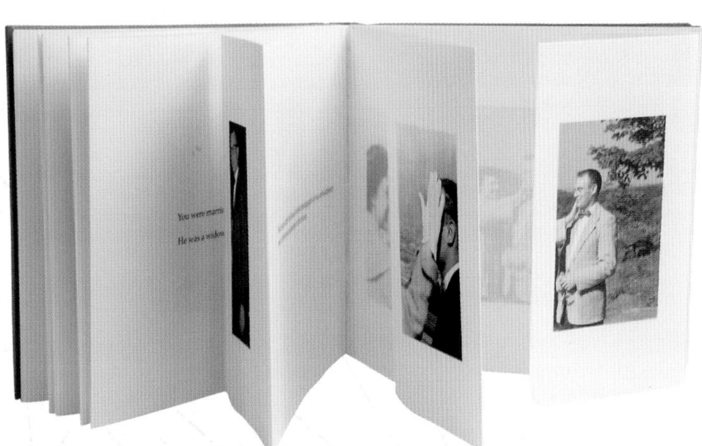

◀ **Reunion** | 2006

7 x 7½ x ½ inches (17.8 x 19.1 x 1.3 cm)
Pigment inkjet prints, silk brocade, goatskin spine; sewn-boards binding

Photo by artist

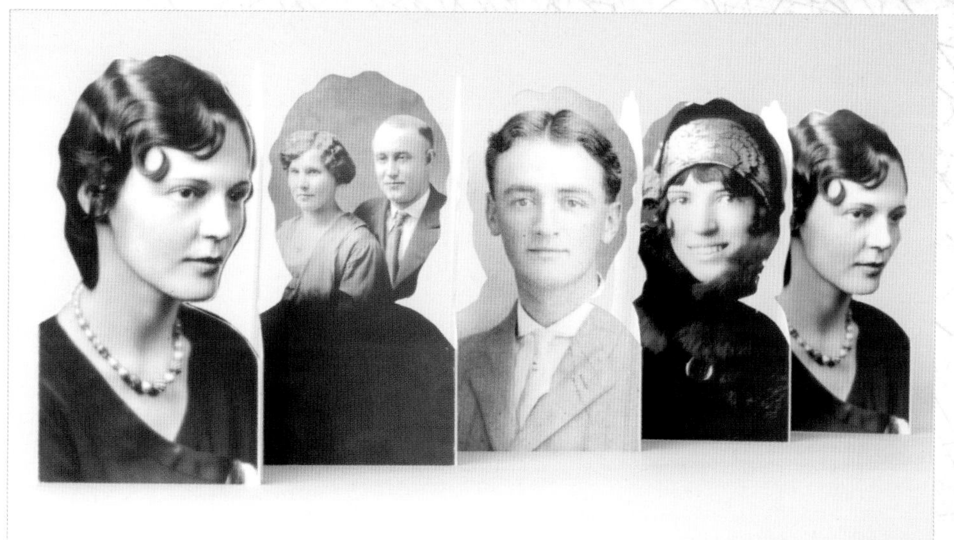

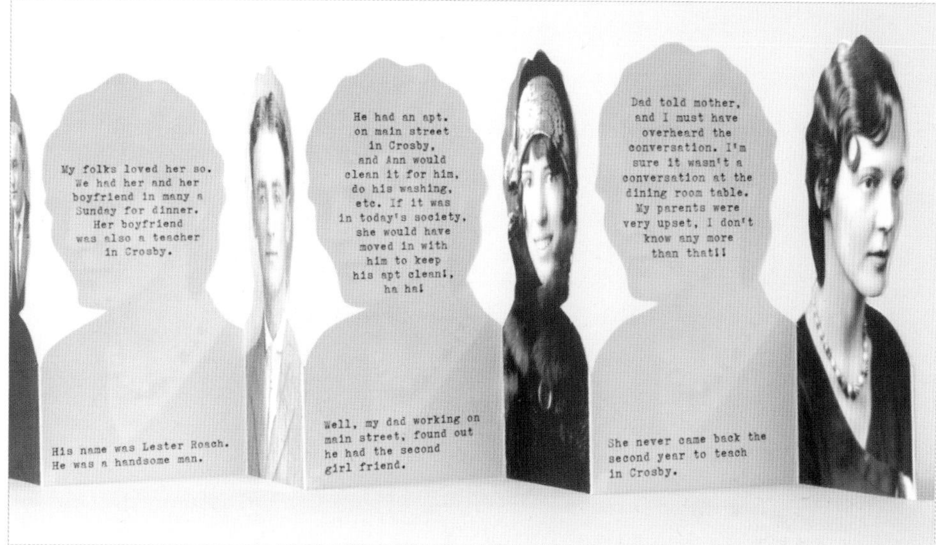

▲ **Ann Black** | 2003

Open: 6½ x 20 x 3 inches (16.5 x 50.8 x 7.6 cm)
Pigment inkjet prints; hand-cut and hand-shaped accordion
Photos by artist

" I want each of my books to function well on several levels—as a work to be read, as a sculpture, and as a delightful object to play with. "

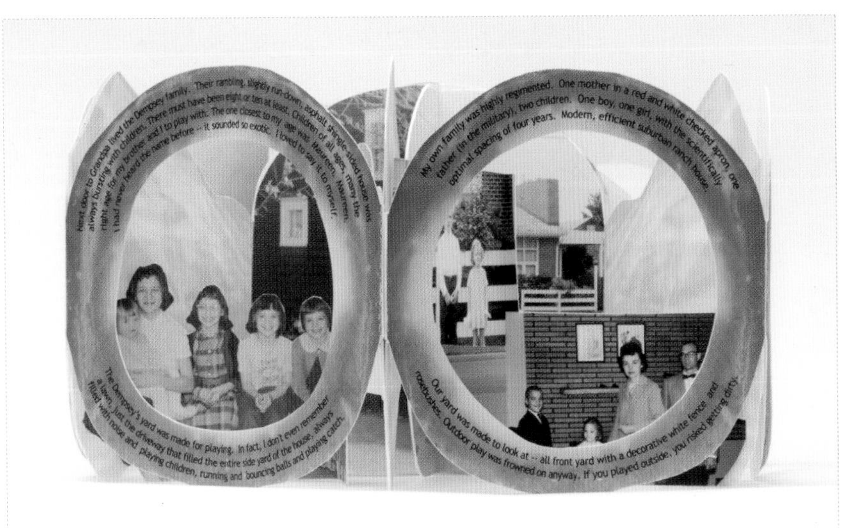

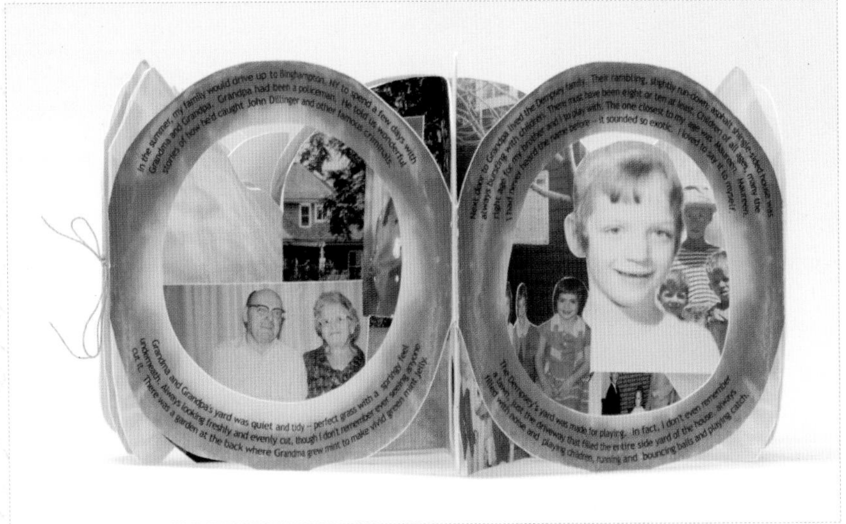

"When I'm working on a new book I'll ask for feedback on my prototypes. People don't always navigate through a piece in the way I planned, and sometimes they manipulate the structure in ways I never imagined. Sometimes I'm stubborn and think they're 'doing it wrong,' and sometimes I make the modifications they suggest."

◀ **Crystals** | 2000

Open: 7 x 14 x 7 inches (17.8 x 35.6 x 17.8 cm)
Pigment inkjet prints; carousel book
Photos by artist

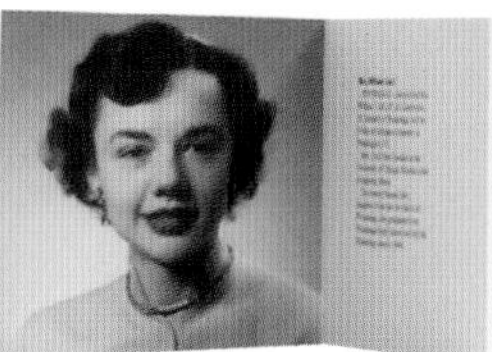
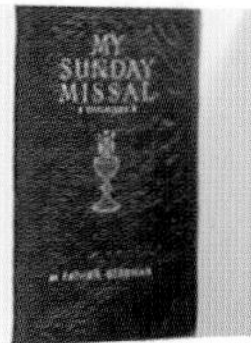

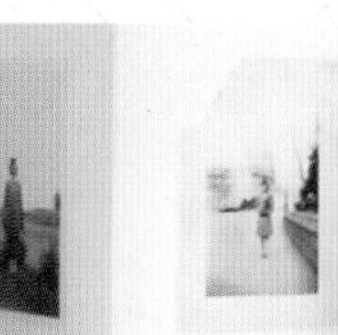
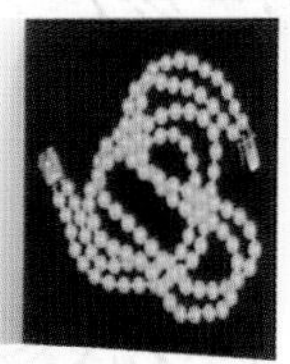
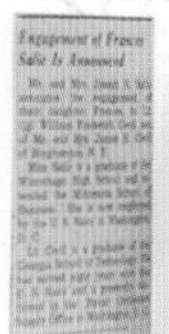
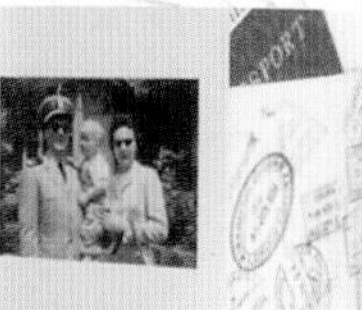
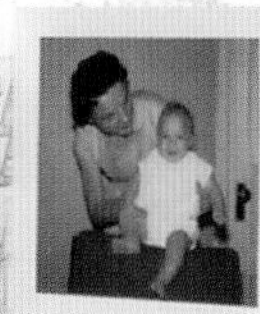
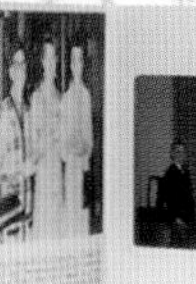
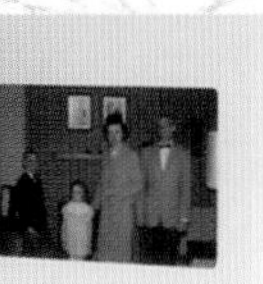
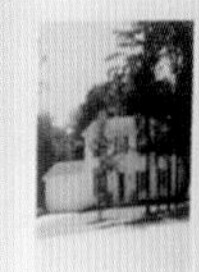
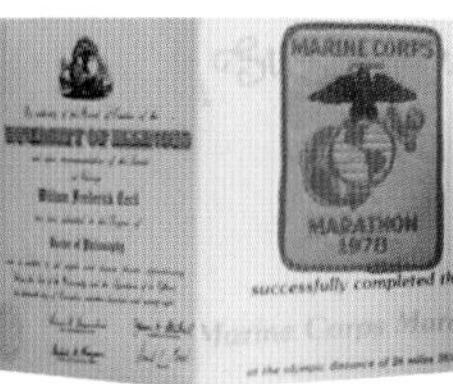
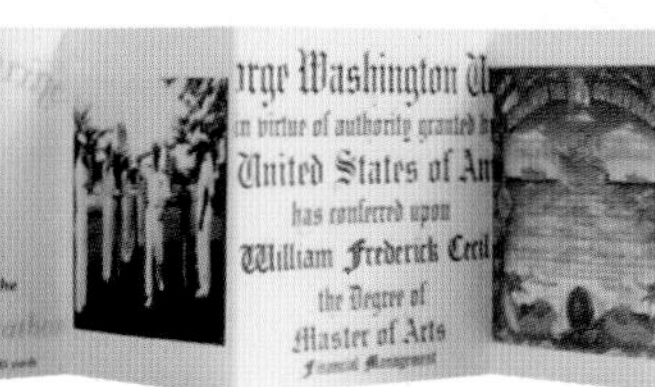

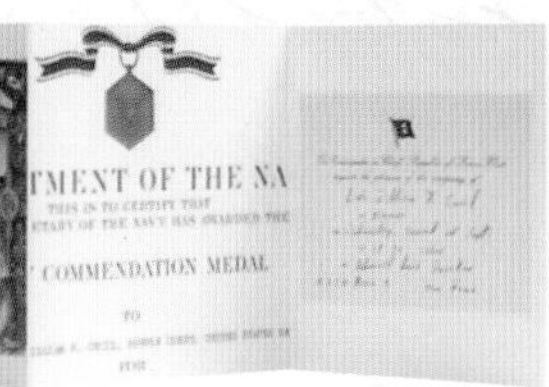

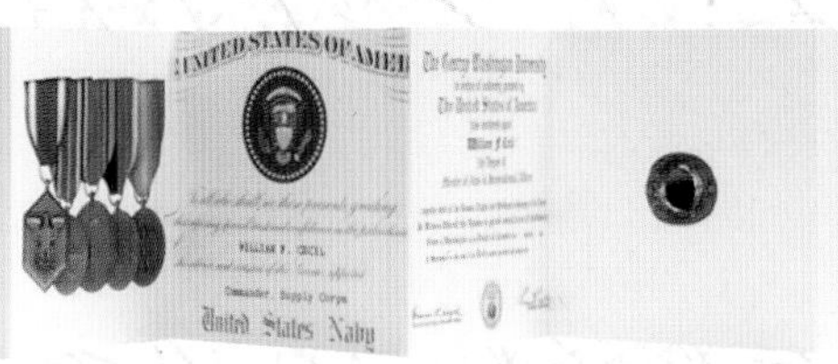

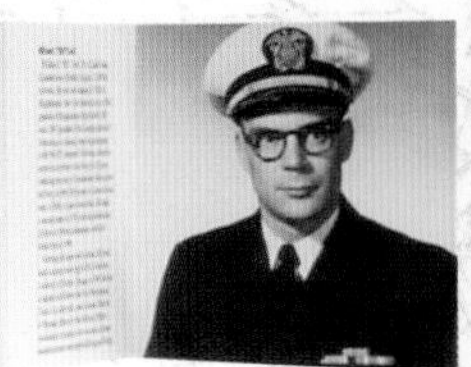
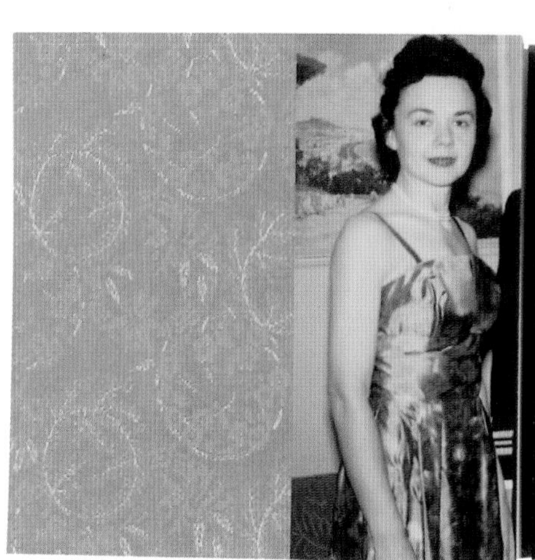
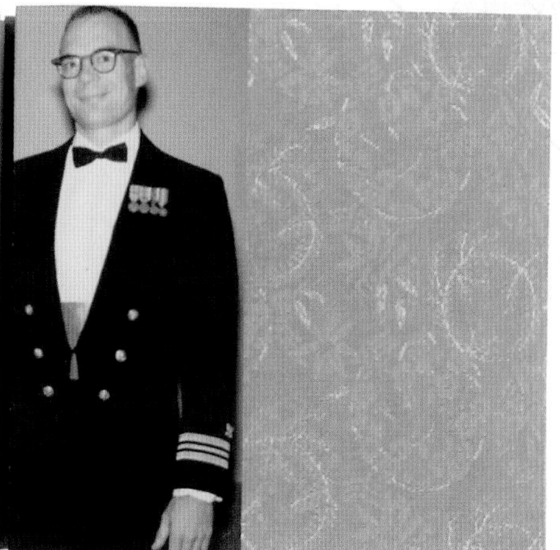

▲ **Decoration** | 2006

Open: 9 feet (2.7 m) long

Closed in dust jacket: 5 x 10½ x ¼ inches (12.7 x 26.7 x 0.6 cm)

Pigment inkjet prints; gatefold opening, double accordion

Photos by artist

SMITH

Keith Smith

SINCE HE GOT HIS START IN THE 1960s, Keith Smith has written nine textbooks on bookmaking and devised more than 200 new bindings. Yet his generous technical contributions to the field of book arts are overshadowed by the significance of his creative endeavors. Smith's visionary artist's books are studies in innovation and skill. By setting up simple and evocative juxtapositions or creating a collage-like effect through a mix of photos, drawings, and text, he finds rich new ways to tell stories. Each of his books has a clear sense of progression, as the pages work together to form a cohesive whole.

Under the name Ivarykeith, Smith collaborates with South Korean artist Kim Myong Soo to produce imaginative and vibrant book works. They combine perspectives, languages, and cultures in cleverly conceived pieces that often feature spliced-together images and off-the-wall humor. The recipient of two Guggenheim Fellowships and a grant from the National Endowment for the Arts, Smith lives in Rochester, New York. His work is in the permanent collections of the Museum of Modern Art in New York City; the Victoria and Albert Museum in London, England; and the National Gallery of Canada in Ottawa.

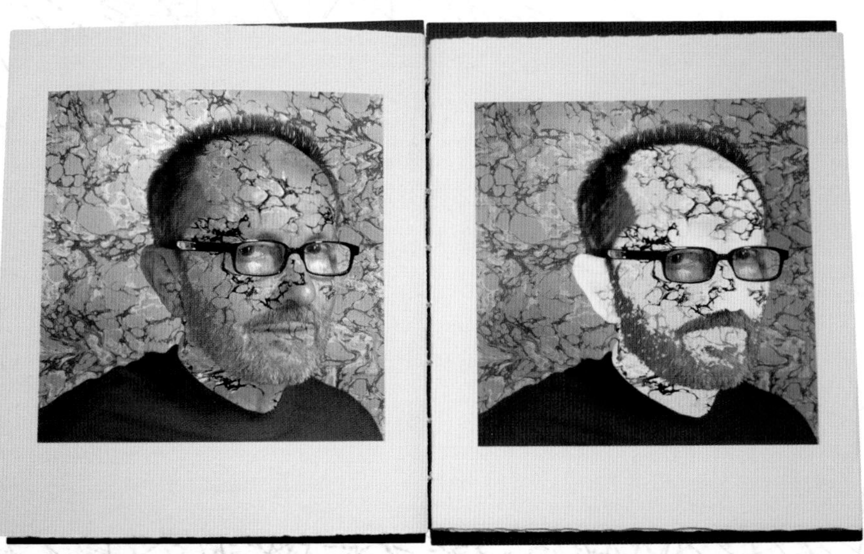

◄ **Book Number 251, Getting Acquainted with a Picture** | 2006

8¾ x 7½ x 2 inches (22.2 x 19.1 x 5.1 cm)
Digital prints; Coptic sewing
Photo by artist

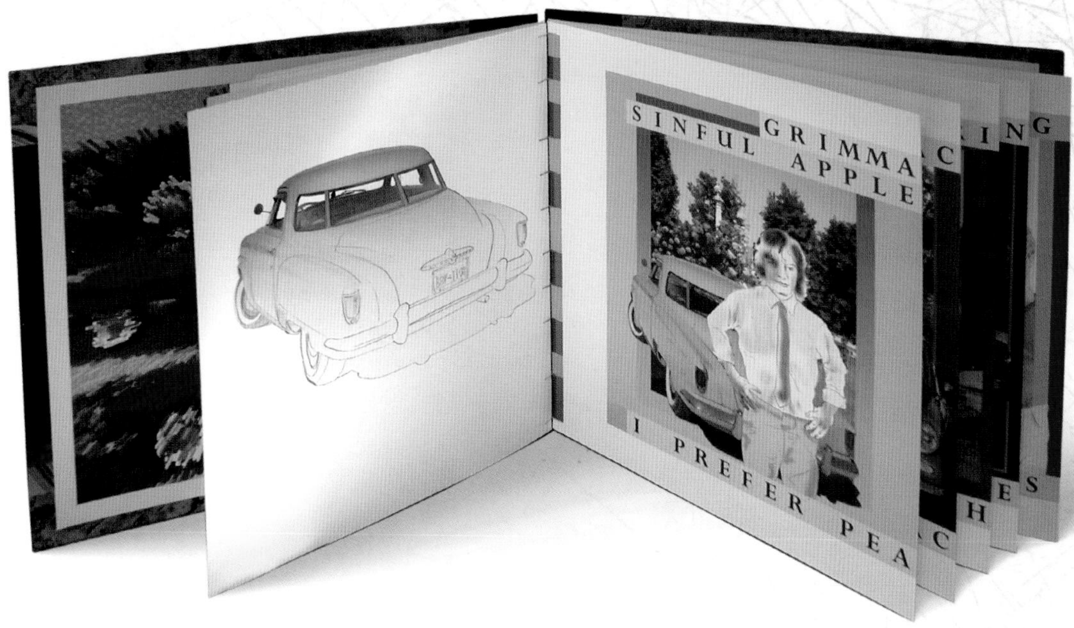

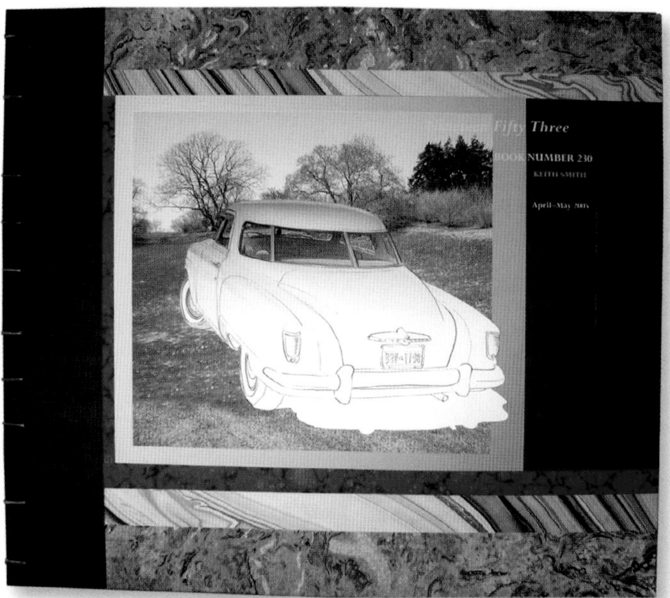

▲ **Book Number 230, Nineteen Fifty-Three** | 2005

17¾ x 19½ x 1½ inches (45.1 x 49.5 x 3.8 cm)
Digital prints; Coptic sewing
Photos by artist

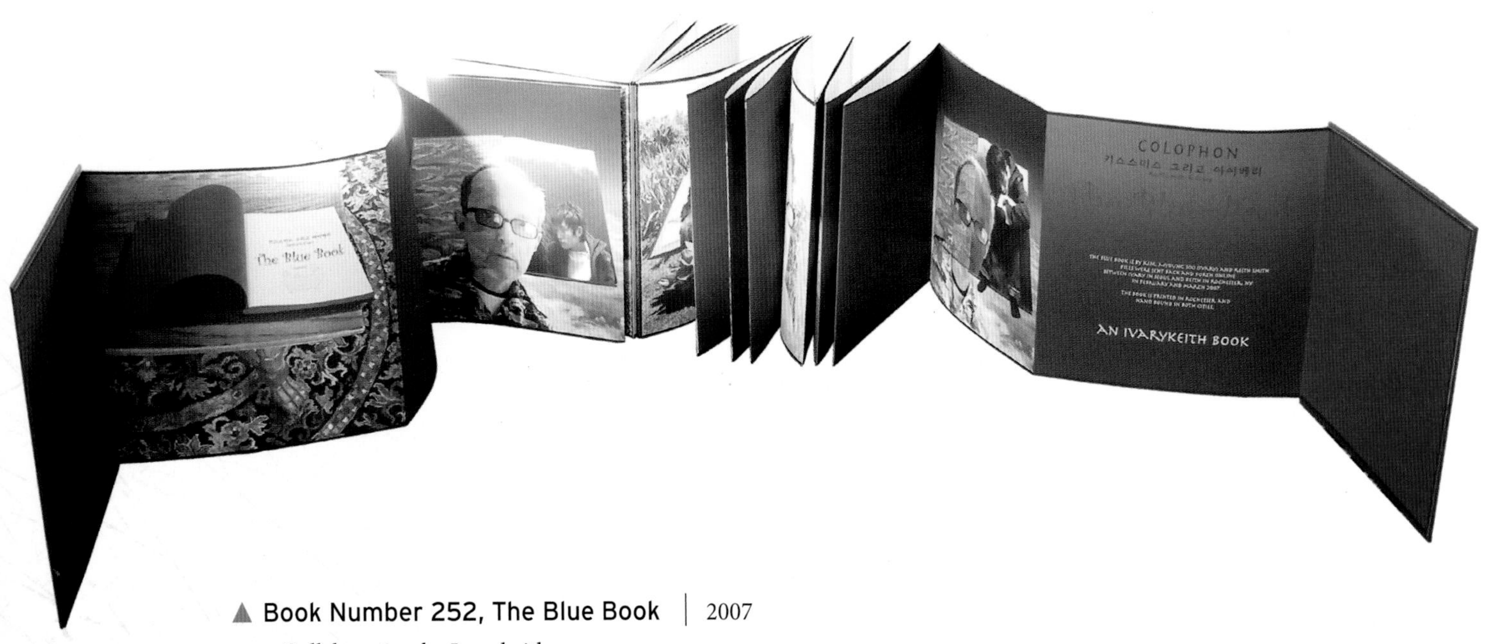

▲ **Book Number 252, The Blue Book** | 2007

Collaboration by Ivarykeith
Each page: 15 x 15 inches (38.1 x 38.1 cm)
Digital print; fold book
Photo by artist

" My books don't lend themselves to art exhibitions. In order for viewers to discover the different layers of structure and levels of meaning in my work, they need to turn pages and take multiple looks. "

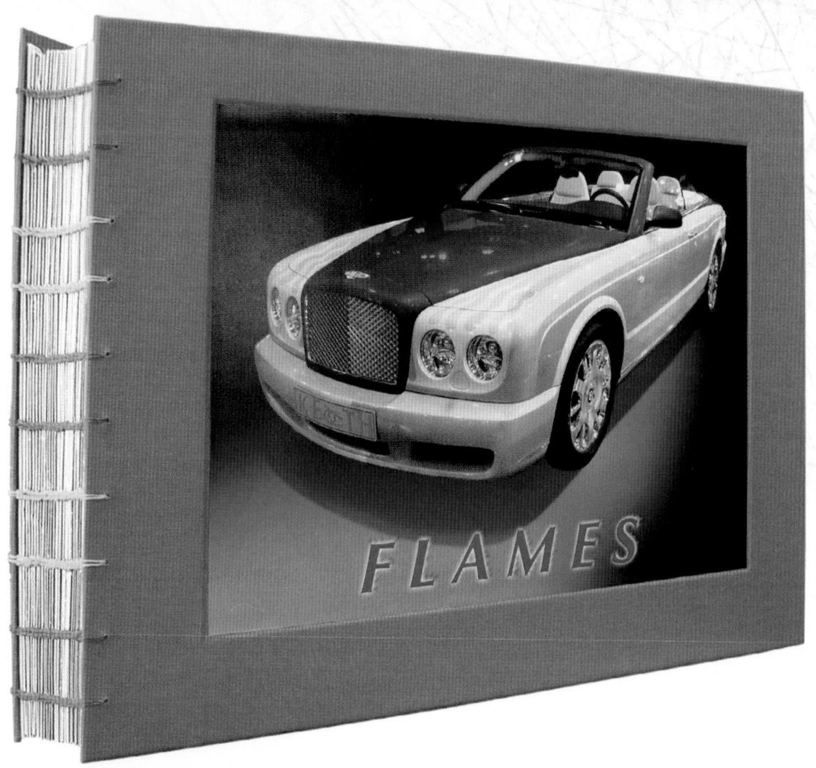

Book Number 253, Flames | 2007

12 x 15¾ x 2 inches (30.5 x 40 x 5.1 cm)
Digital prints; Coptic sewing
Photos by artist

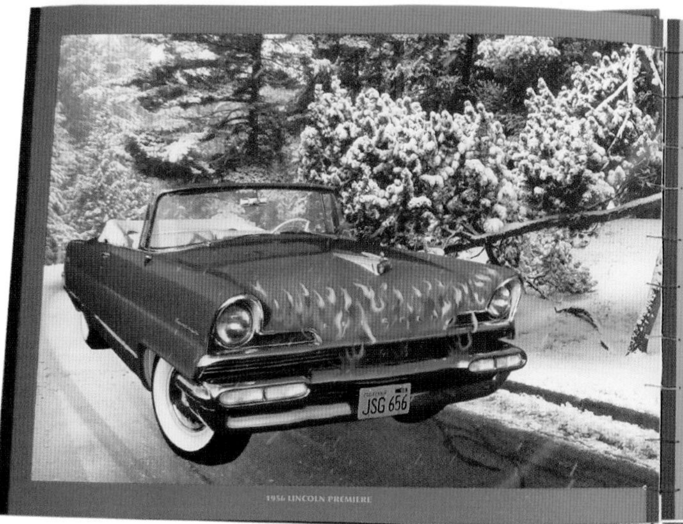

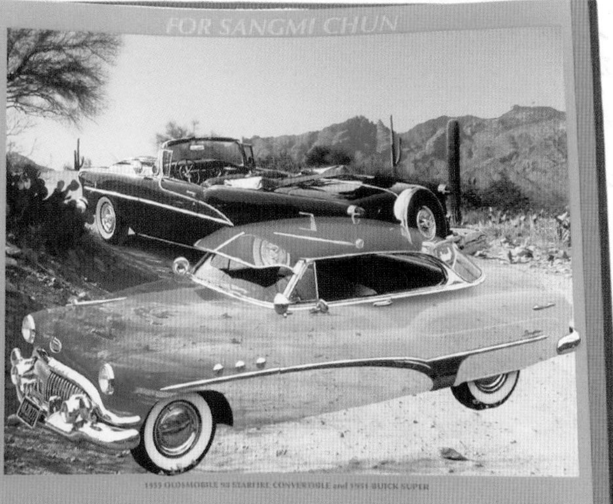

KEITH SMITH

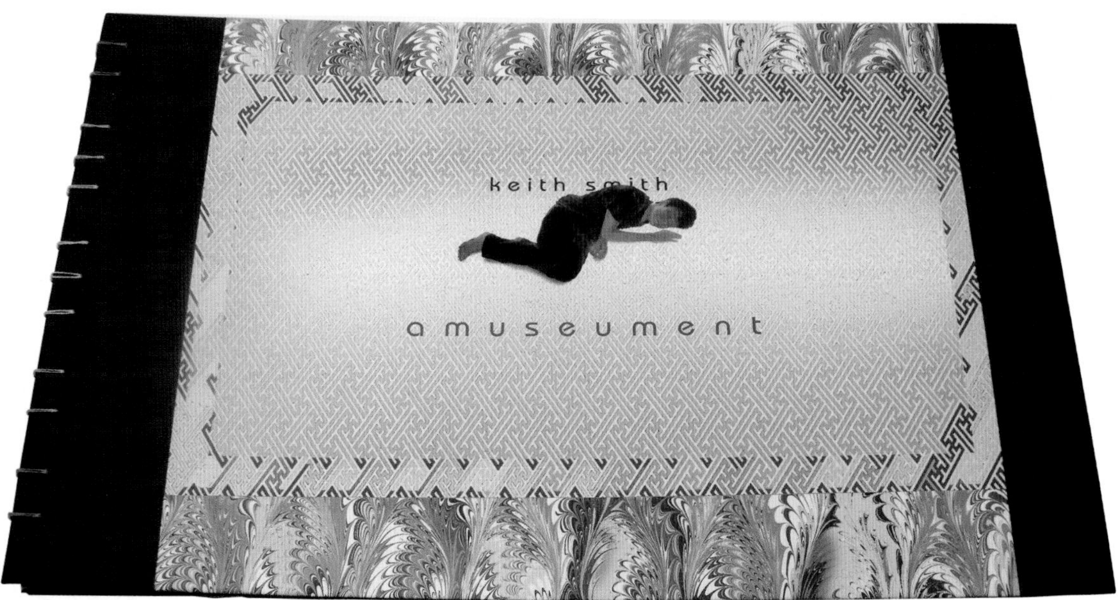

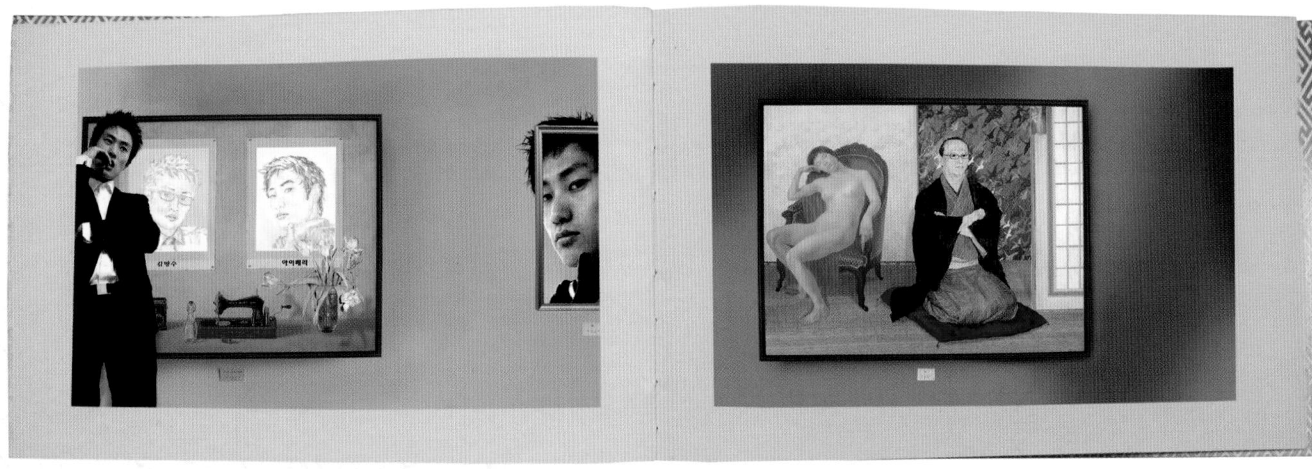

▲ **Book Number 260, Amusement** | 2008

12½ x 21¾ x 1½ inches (31.8 x 55.2 x 3.8 cm)
Digital prints; Coptic sewing
Photos by artist

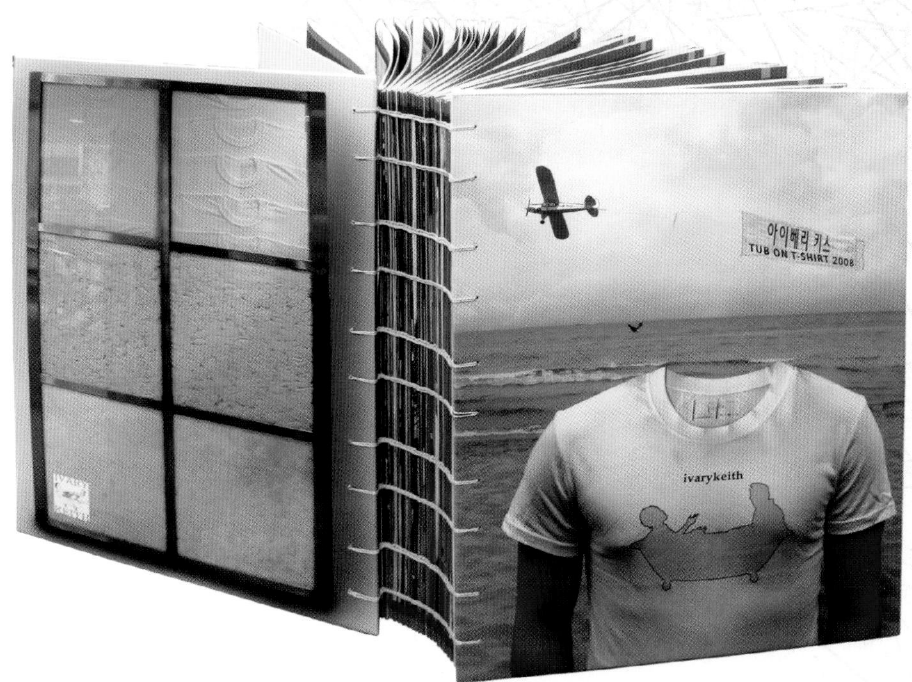

" One of my creative influences is classical music. It's taught me a great deal about pace and how to use rhythm from page to page. "

▲ **Book Number 261, Clothes Friends** | 2008

Collaboration by Ivarykeith
12 x 9 x 2¼ inches (30.5 x 22.9 x 5.7 cm)
Digital prints; Coptic sewing
Photos by artist

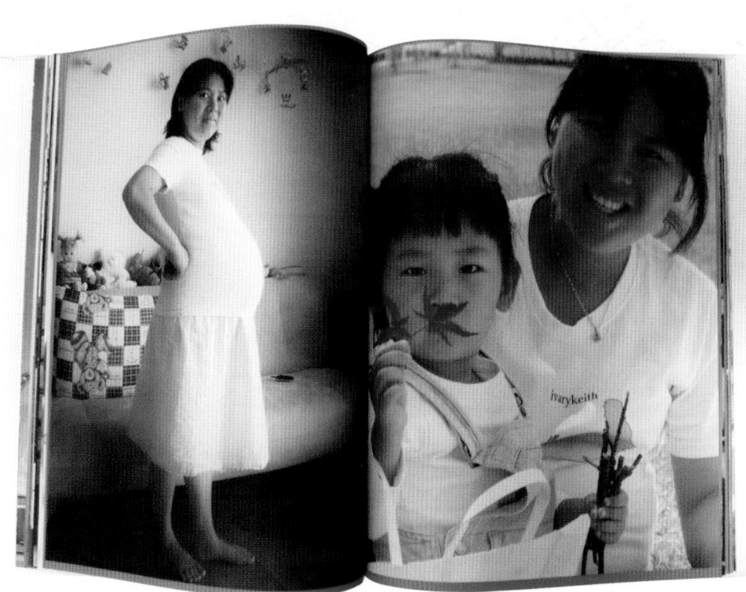

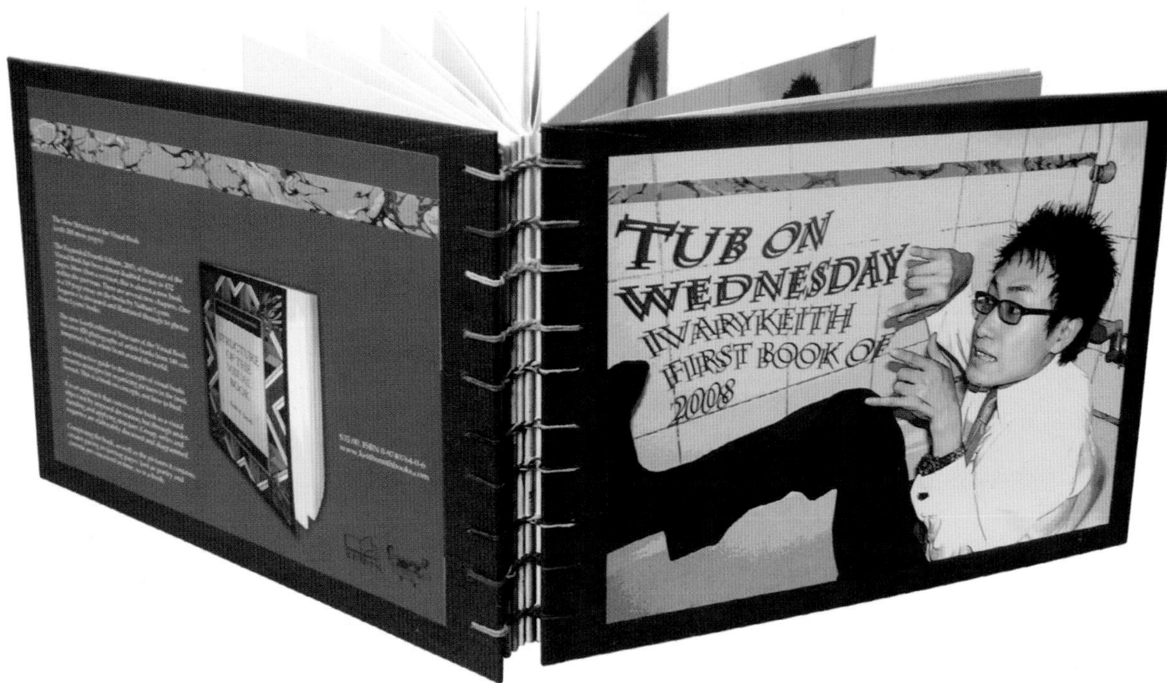

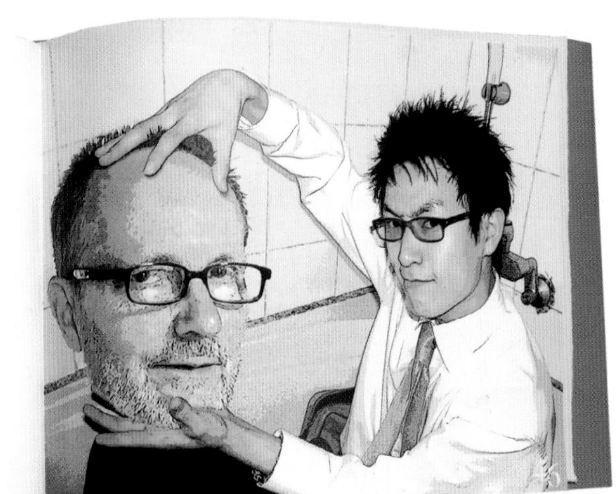

▲ **Book Number 262, Tub on Wednesday** | 2008

Collaboration by Ivarykeith
7 x 9 x ½ inches (17.8 x 22.9 x 1.3 cm)
Digital prints; Coptic sewing
Photos by artist

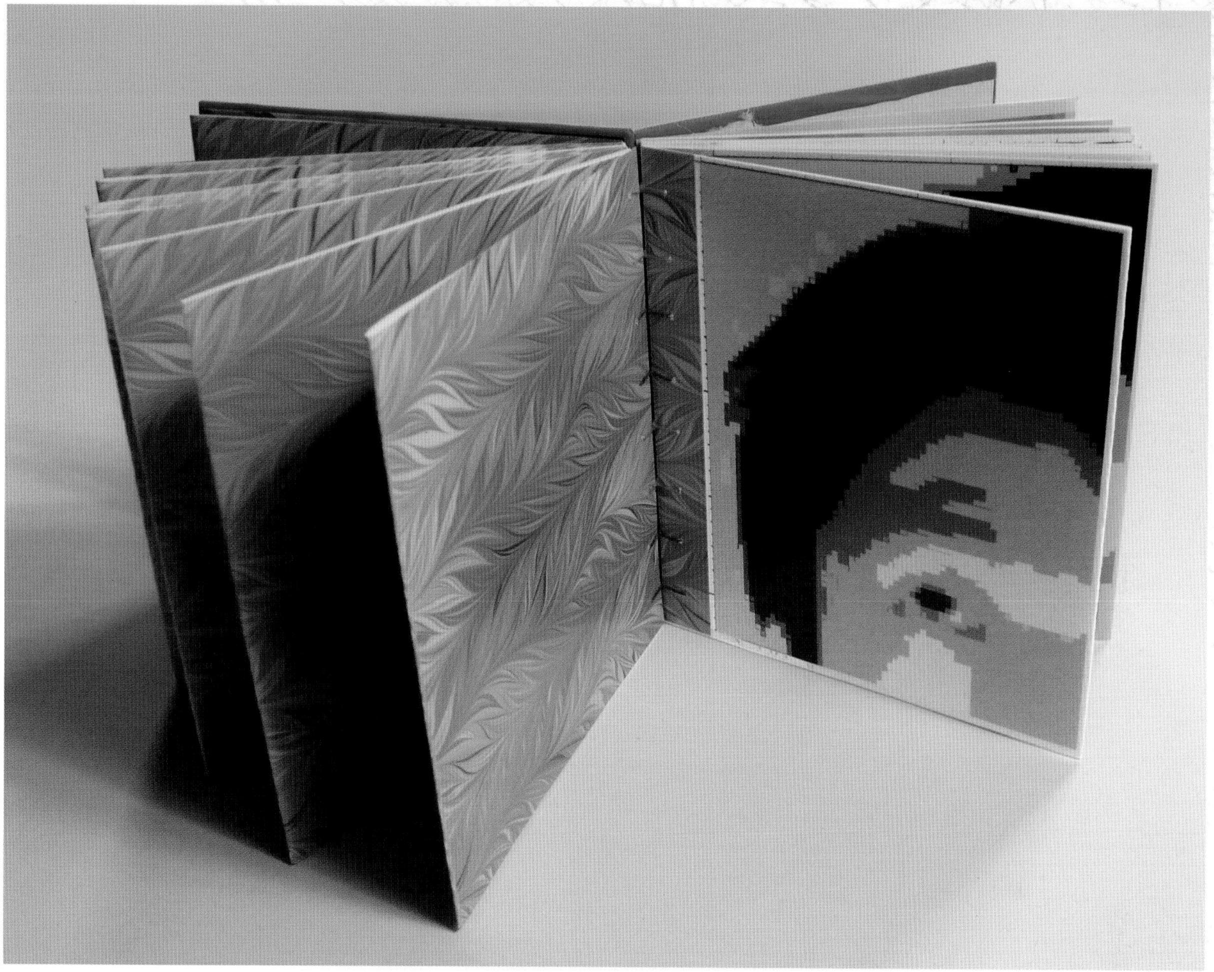

▲ **Book Number 263, Screen Capture** | 2008

6 x 5¾ x 1½ inches (15.2 x 14.6 x 3.8 cm)
Digital prints; Coptic sewn
Photo by artist

" I don't write poems to fit each book in the conventional sense. Instead, I write texts that are dependent upon the turning of pages. "

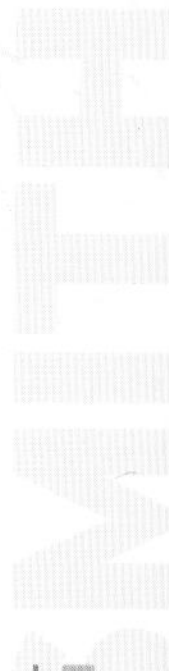

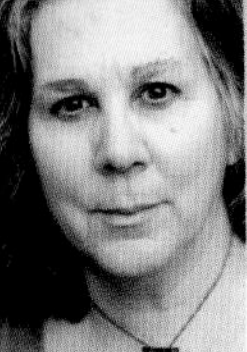

MAURIELLO

Barbara Mauriello

STRONG PATTERNS AND JOYFUL, BOLD COLORS reflect the energy and enthusiasm that Barbara Mauriello brings to the creation of her books and boxes. Often conceptually driven and grounded in research, Mauriello's pieces have a playfulness that complements the logic. In works honoring writers and visual artists, she constructs ingenious miniature houses, distilling the essence of her iconic subjects—Virginia Woolf, Jane Austen, and Harper Lee—into the walls, doors, and windows of each structure and inviting the viewer to interact with the work.

Mauriello is a pioneer in her use of the box. Elevating it from its traditional supporting role as protection for a precious object, she puts it front and center and uses it to tell a story in the same way she would a book. Her quirky explorations of architecture reveal that boxes can be manipulated as thoughtfully and as playfully as any other medium. Constructed with impeccable technique, Mauriello's pieces never fail to engage the viewer. The author of *Making Memory Boxes*, she lives in Hoboken, New Jersey.

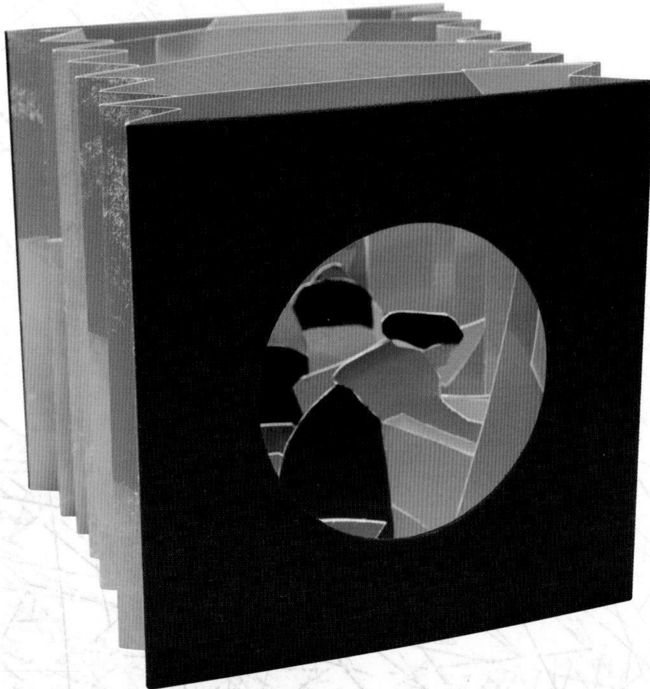

◀ **Ricordo d'Italia** | 2005

8⅝ x 8¾ x 11 inches (21.9 x 22.2 x 27.9 cm)
Gouache, paper, cloth, boards; tunnel book with die-cut peephole

Photo by Jeffrey Vock

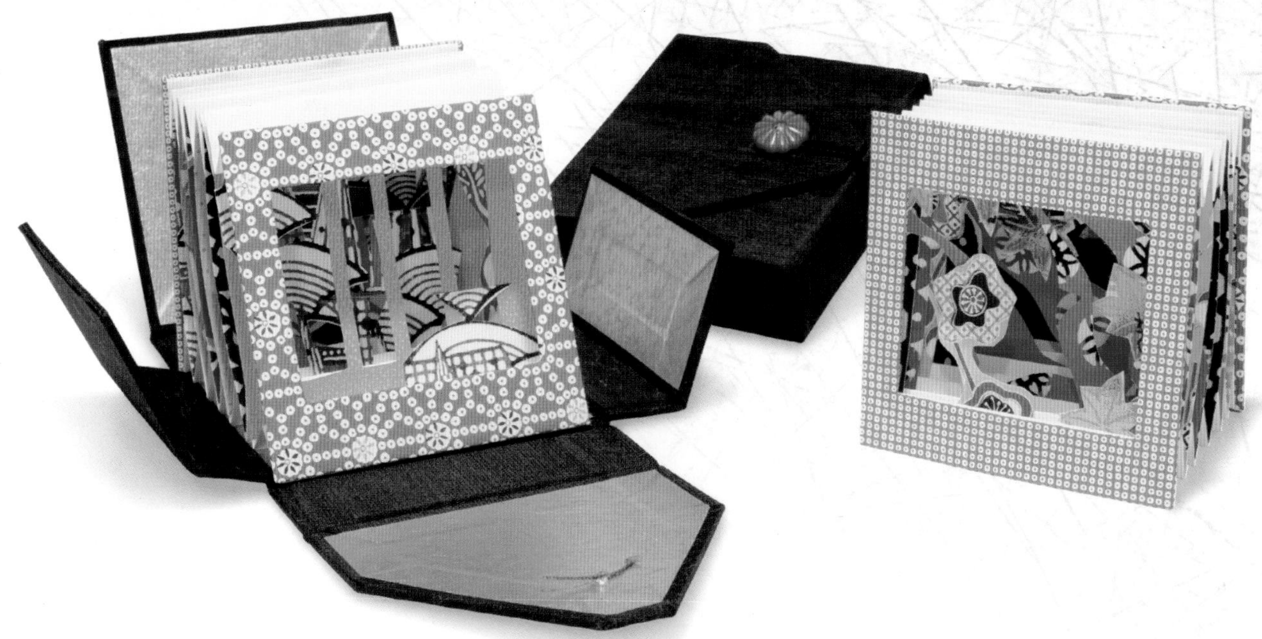

▲ **Wonder Worlds** | 2007

Open: 3⅞ x 3⅞ x 6 inches (9.8 x 9.8 x 15.2 cm)
Japanese printed papers, cloth over boards; tunnel book, collage

Photo by Jeffrey Vock

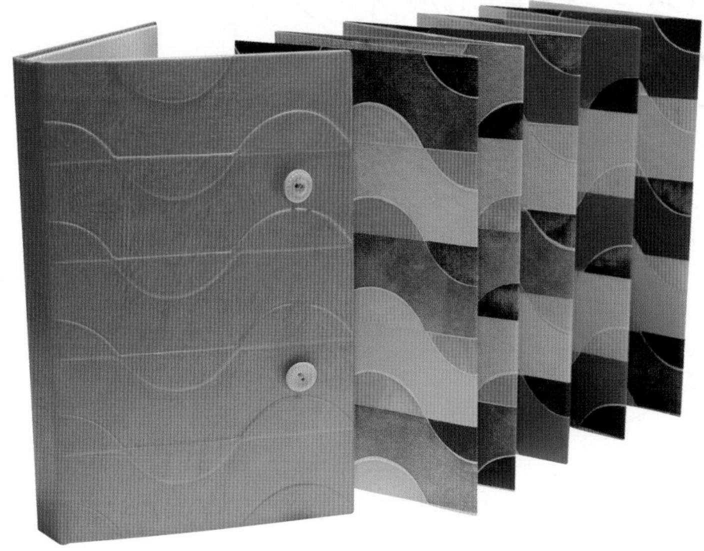

Moon over the Mountain | 2004 ▶

Open: 11 x 7⅛ x 70 inches (27.9 x 18.1 x 177.8 cm)
Leather, boards, plastic buttons, oil-based ink, handmade paper; accordion binding, collagraph printed

Photo by Jeffrey Vock

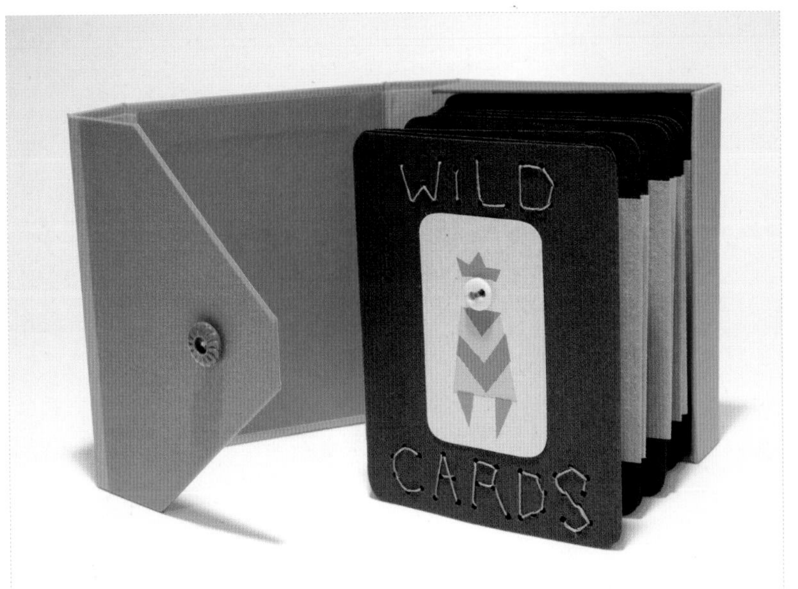

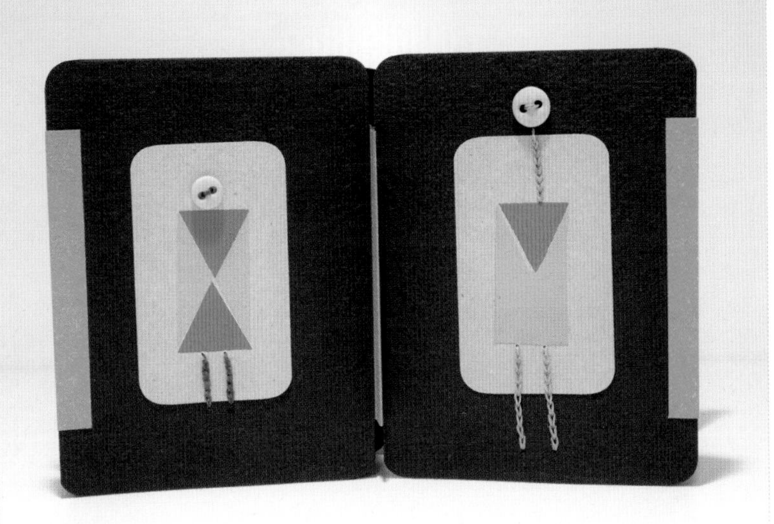

"I love bits and pieces of things: a fragment of cloth rather than an entire yard of it; a handful of mismatched buttons; a single playing card gone astray from its deck. Out of context, incomplete, and mysterious, these types of items are often the starting points for my books."

▲ **Wild Cards** | 2007

Open: 6½ x 5 x 53 inches (16.5 x 12.7 x 134.6 cm)
Handmade paper, buttons, linen thread, cloth over boards, gouache; accordion binding, stencil-printed cards

Photos by Jeffrey Vock

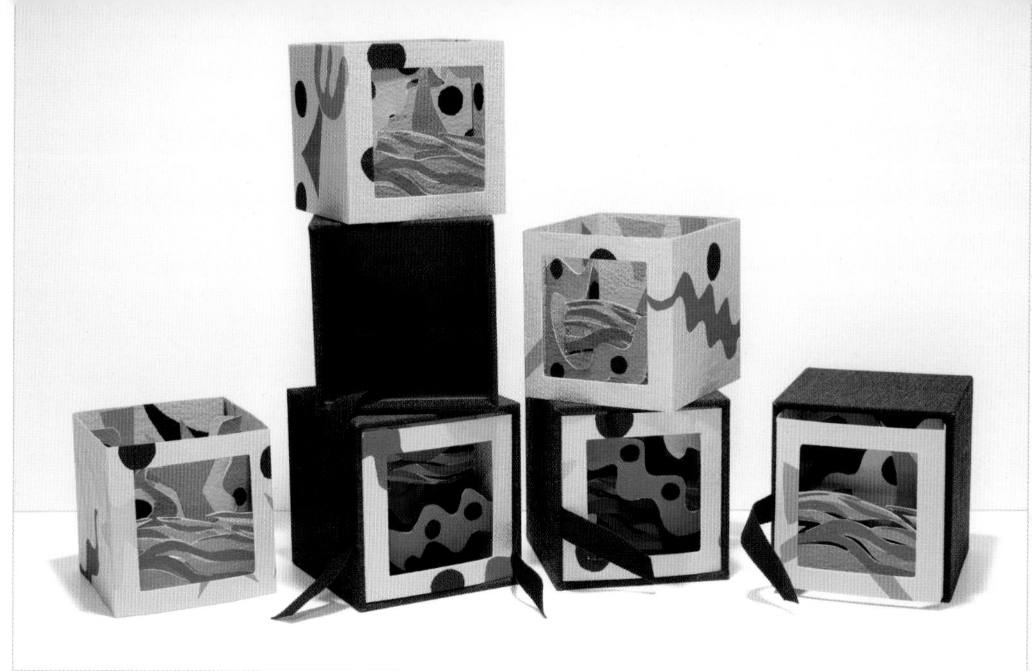

◀ **Painted Cubes** | 2008

Each: 4⅜ x 4⅜ x 4½ inches (11.1 x 11.1 x 11.4 cm)
Gouache, handmade paper, ribbon, cloth over boards; tunnel books in slipcases
Photo by Jeffrey Vock

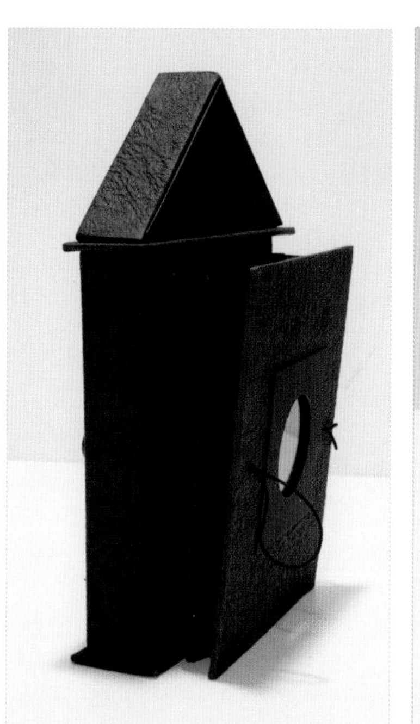

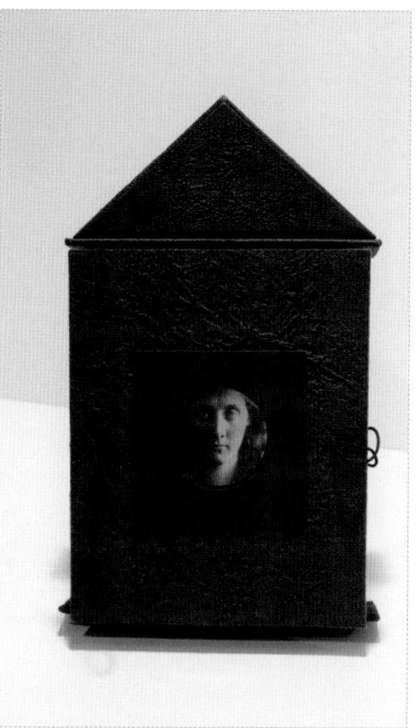

◀ **Artists' Housing: For Julia Margaret Cameron** | 2004

Open: 9½ x 5¾ x 3 inches (24.1 x 14.6 x 7.6 cm)
Momi paper over boards, plastic, photo
Photos by Jeffrey Vock

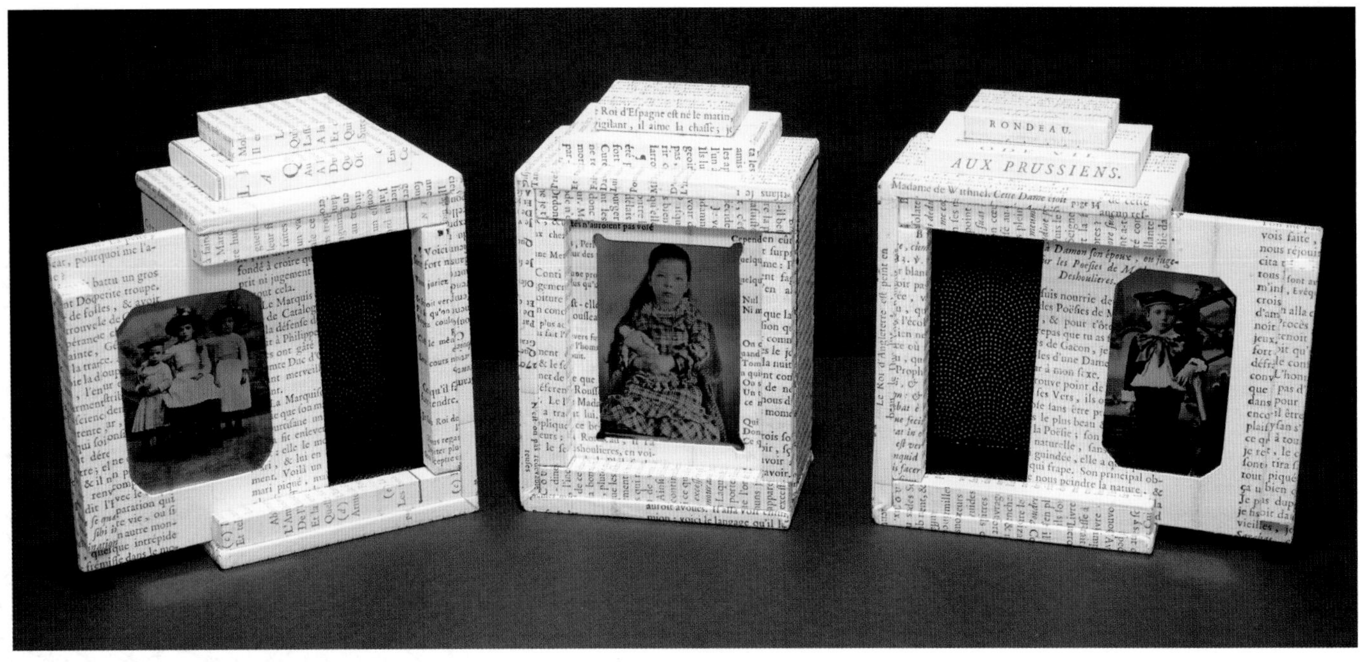

▲ **Tinytype Boxes** | 2009

Each: 5½ x 3¾ x 2½ inches (14 x 9.5 x 6.4 cm)
Nineteenth-century book pages, tintypes, boards; boxes with sliding doors

Photo by Jeffrey Vock

" I want viewers to respond physically to my books. They should peer down the tunnels, open the doors, play with the paper dolls, and work the accordions. I want those kinds of reactions. "

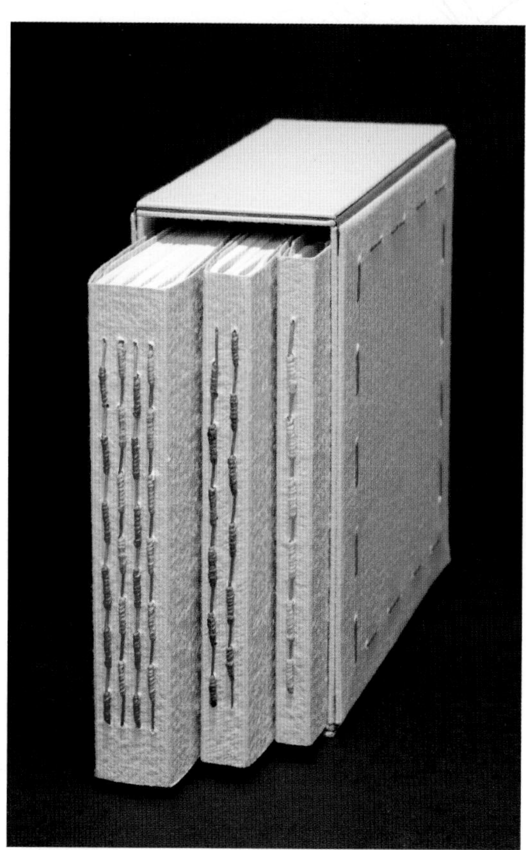

▲ **Tacket Bindings, Boxed** | 2009

5½ x 5½ x 2¼ inches (14 x 14 x 5.7 cm)
Handmade paper, linen thread; tacket binding in slipcase
Photo by Jeffrey Vock

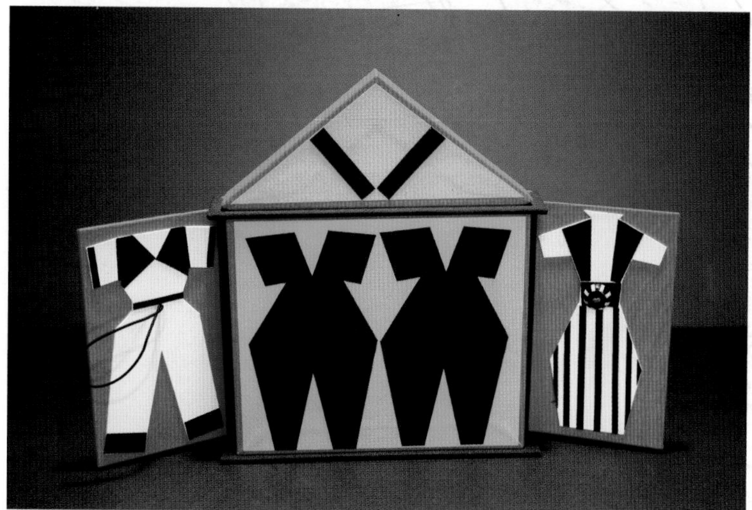

▲ **Artists' Housing: For Liubov Popova** | 2004

Open: 8¼ x 13 x 1½ inches (21 x 33 x 3.8 cm)
Book cloth, colored paper, museum board; button and elastic loop closure
Photo by Jeffrey Vock

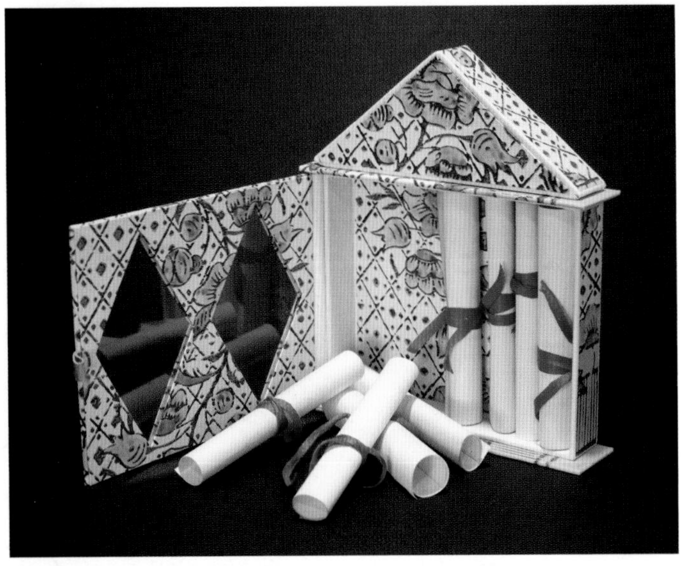

◀ **Artists' Housing: For Emily Dickinson** | 2004

Open: 8¼ x 13 x 1½ inches (21 x 33 x 3.8 cm)
Nineteenth-century wallpaper over boards, cotton ribbon, plastic windows

Photo by Jeffrey Vock

> " I'm inspired by paper theaters, peep shows, and souvenir books. I love the conciseness of their structures and the density of their picture-making. "

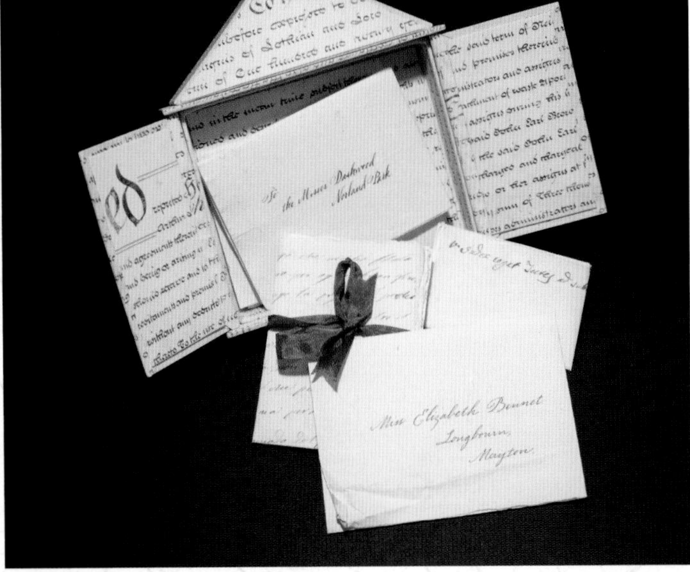

◀ **Artists' Housing: For Jane Austen** | 2004

Open: 8¼ x 13 x 1½ inches (21 x 33 x 3.8 cm)
Nineteenth-century parchment and paper, letters

Photo by Jeffrey Vock

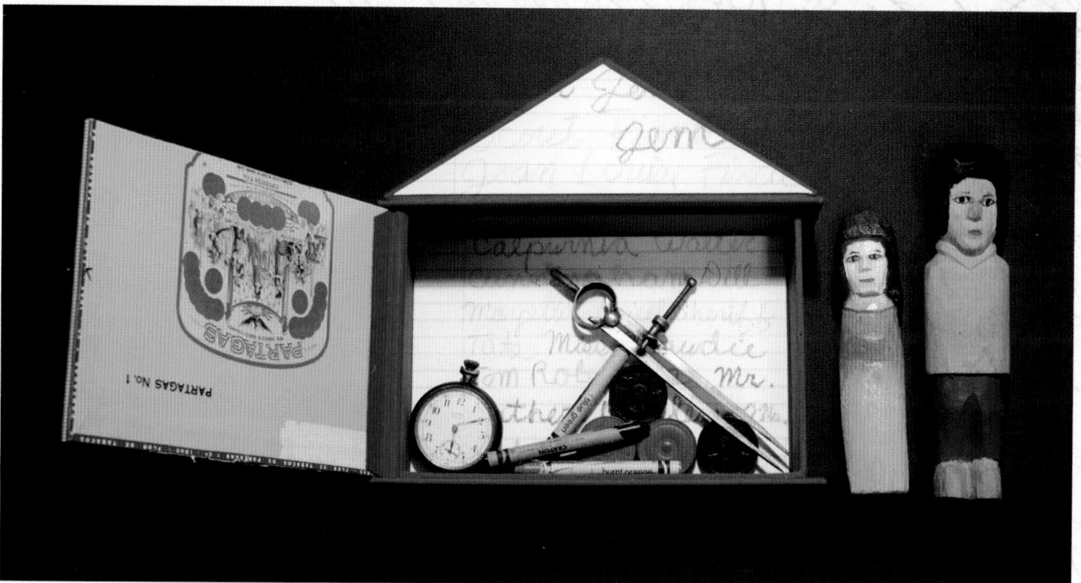

▲ **Artists' Housing: For Harper Lee** | 2004

Open: 8½ x 15½ x 2½ inches (21.6 x 39.4 x 6.4 cm)
Cigar-box lid, ruled paper with crayon drawings and writing; box holds Jem's found treasures

Photo by Jeffrey Vock

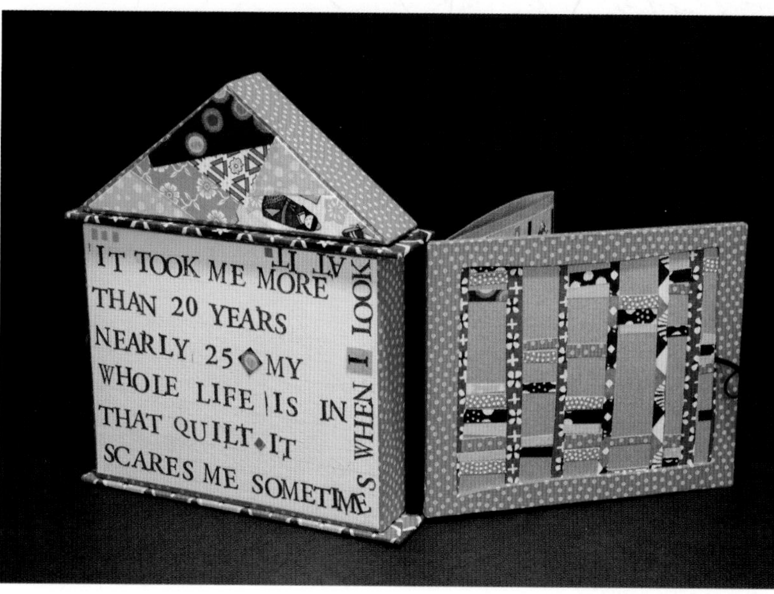

Artists' Housing: For Anonymous | 2004 ▶

Open: 8¼ x 13 x 1¼ inches (21 x 33 x 3.2 cm)
Assorted patterned papers, cloth, boards; rubber stamped, collage, accordion fold

Photo by Jeffrey Vock

Veronika Schäpers

THE CHALLENGES OF LIVING IN A FOREIGN country serve as both an inspiration and a point of departure for Veronika Schäpers. A native of Germany who has lived in Tokyo, Japan, since 1997, Schäpers embraces cultural barriers to produce elegant books that often focus on societal differences. Her work reminds readers that the success of a book depends not only on meticulous craftsmanship and functional form, but also on well-developed content.

For Schäpers, the binding is the unifying factor of a book, and her meticulously designed pieces reflect this attitude. In some of her most exceptional works, she uses nuance of color, translucent paper, and refined illustrative elements to elucidate intricate narratives. Finding the appropriate structures to enhance poignant, meaningful content, she creates intriguing, delightful books. Schäpers has participated in solo and group exhibitions throughout Europe, Asia, and the United States. Her work is owned by many prestigious institutions, including the Museum of Modern Art in New York City; the Pratt Library in Brooklyn, New York; and the Library of Congress in Washington, D.C.

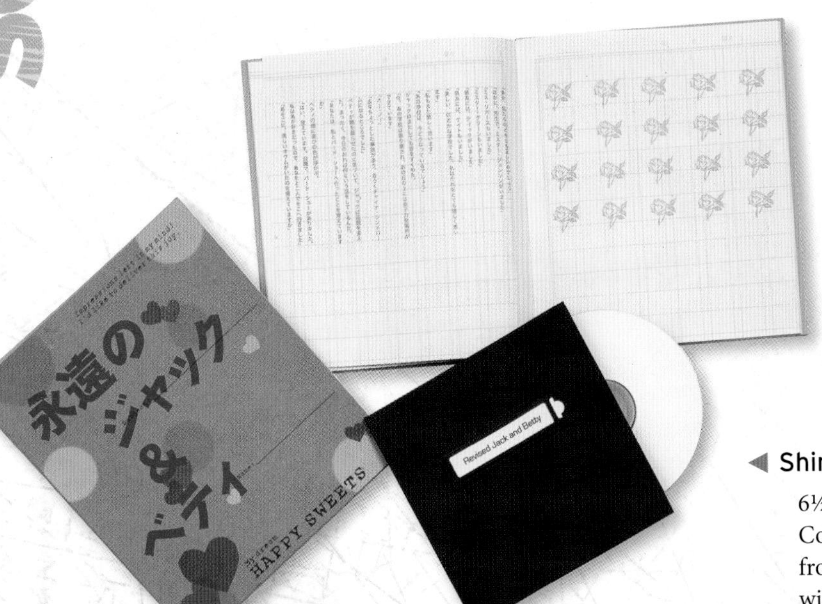

◀ **Shimizu Yoshinori: Jack and Betty Forever** | 2005

$6\frac{1}{2}$ x $7\frac{7}{16}$ inches (16.5 x 19 cm)

Covers from Japanese notebooks, CD with old recordings from the textbook *Revised Jack and Betty*; letterpress printed with zinc clichés, linocut on notebook paper, cover made by GA-File

Photos by Keizo Kioku

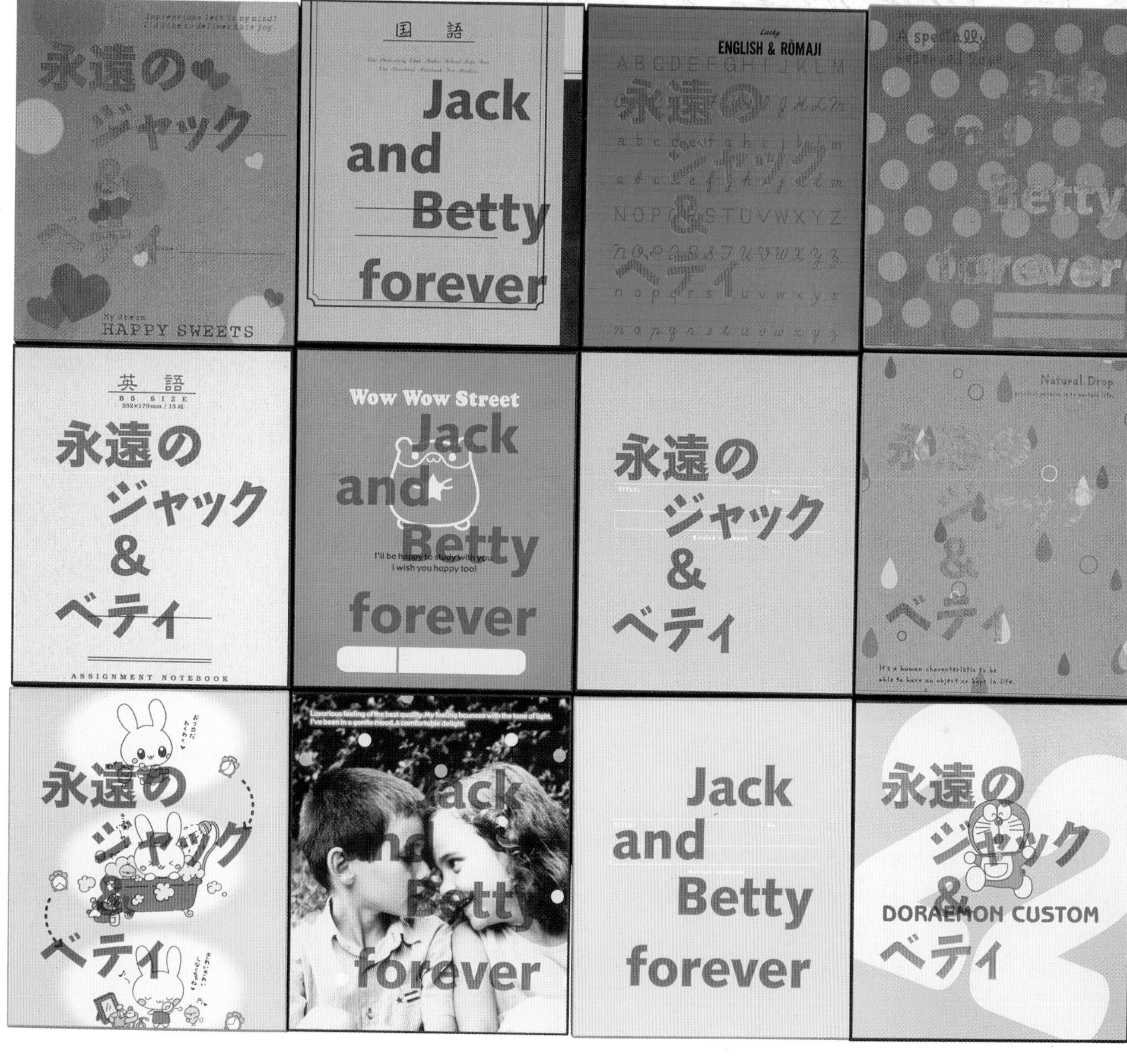
Impressions left in my mind!
I'd like to deliver this joy.
永遠の
ジャック
&
ベティ
My dream
HAPPY SWEETS
国語
Jack
and
Betty
forever
ENGLISH & RÔMAJI
永遠の
ジャック
&
ベティ
Betty
forever
英語
B5 SIZE
永遠の
ジャック
&
ベティ
ASSIGNMENT NOTEBOOK
Wow Wow Street
Jack
and
Betty
forever
I'll be happy to study with you.
I wish you happy too!
永遠の
ジャック
&
ベティ
Natural Drop
&
ベティ
It's a human characteristic to be
able to have an object or hope in life.
永遠の
ジャック
&
ベティ
Luxurious feeling of the best quality.My feeling bounces with the tone of light.
I've been in a gentle mood.A comfortable delight.
forever
Jack
and
Betty
forever
永遠の
ジャック
&
DORAEMON CUSTOM
ベティ

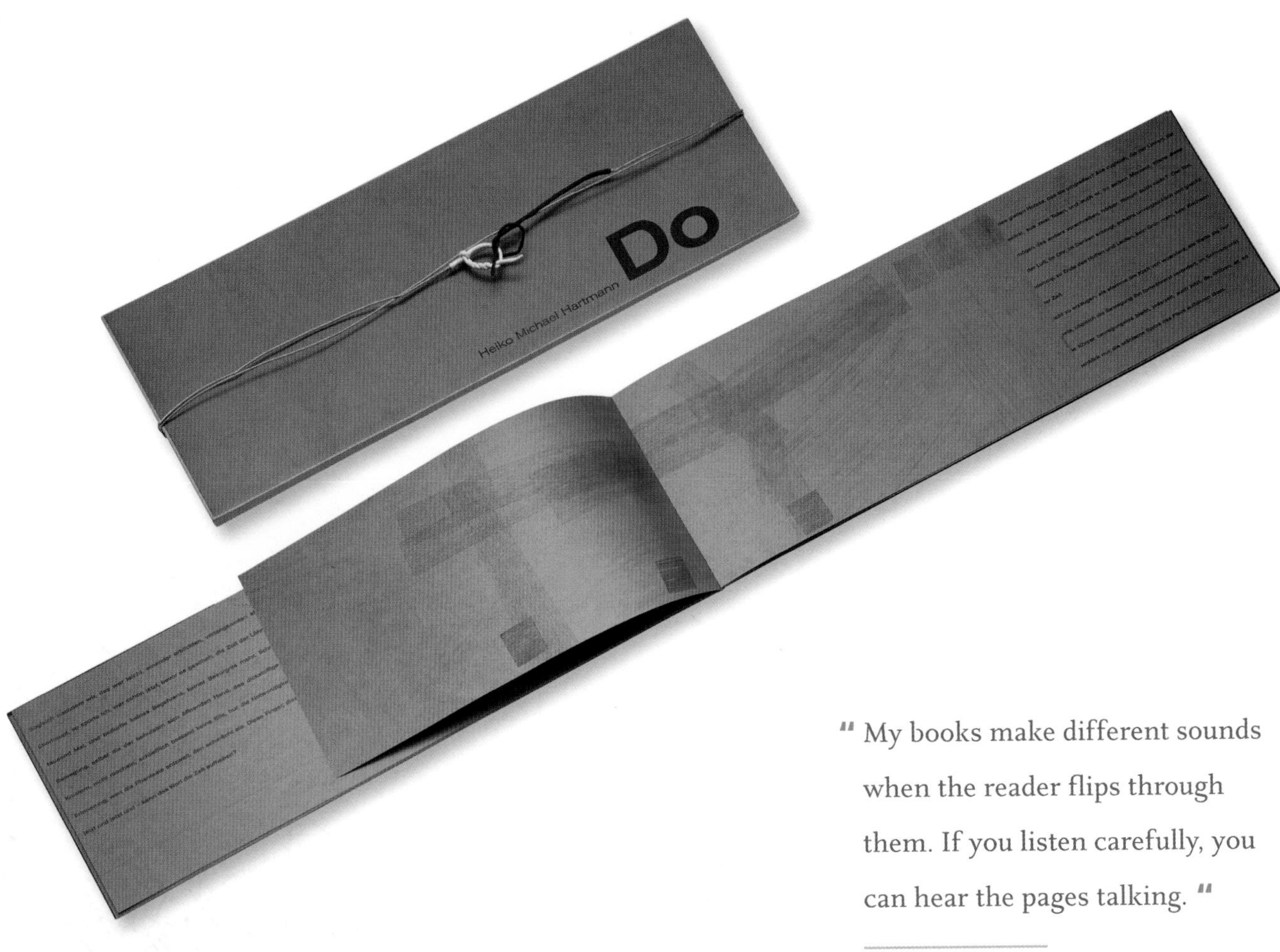

" My books make different sounds when the reader flips through them. If you listen carefully, you can hear the pages talking. "

▲ **Heiko Michael Hartmann: Do** | 2005

20 7/16 x 6 7/8 inches (52 x 17.5 cm)
Japanese katajigami paper, mitsumata paper, multi-colored illustrations printed with strips of bamboo, bow string; letterpress printed with zinc clichés
Photo by Keizo Kioku

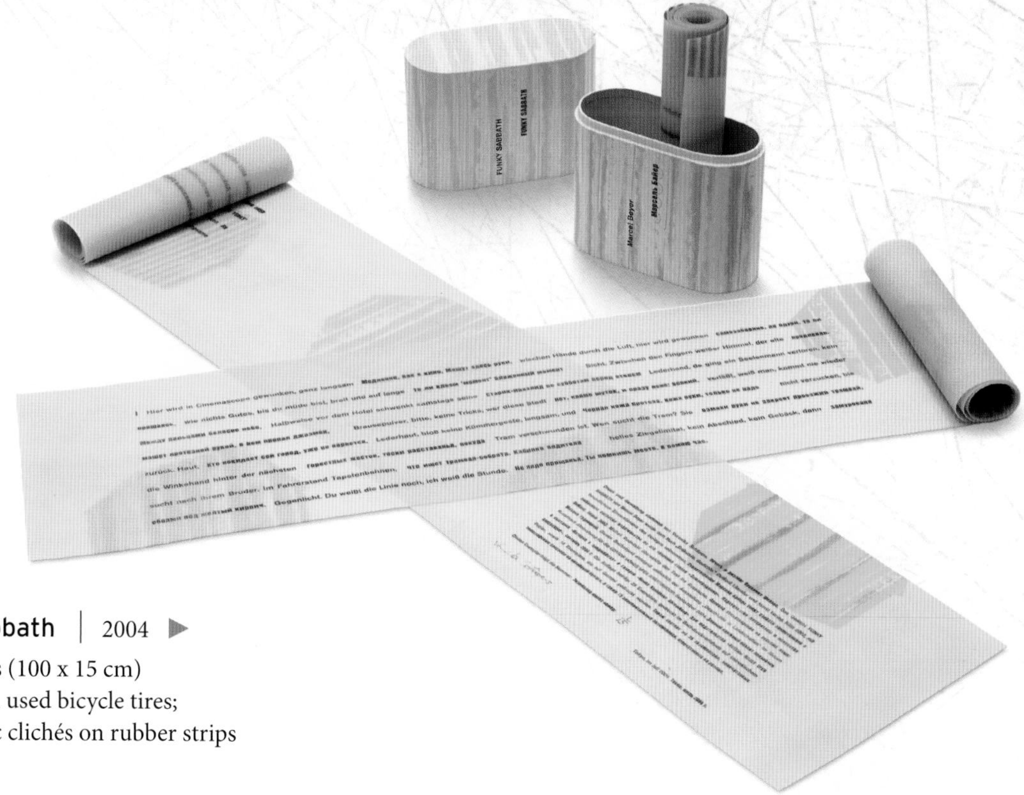

Marcel Beyer: Funky Sabbath | 2004 ▶

Each strip: 39⅜ x 5⅞ inches (100 x 15 cm)
Multicolored frottages from used bicycle tires;
letterpress printed with zinc clichés on rubber strips

Photo by Keizo Kioku

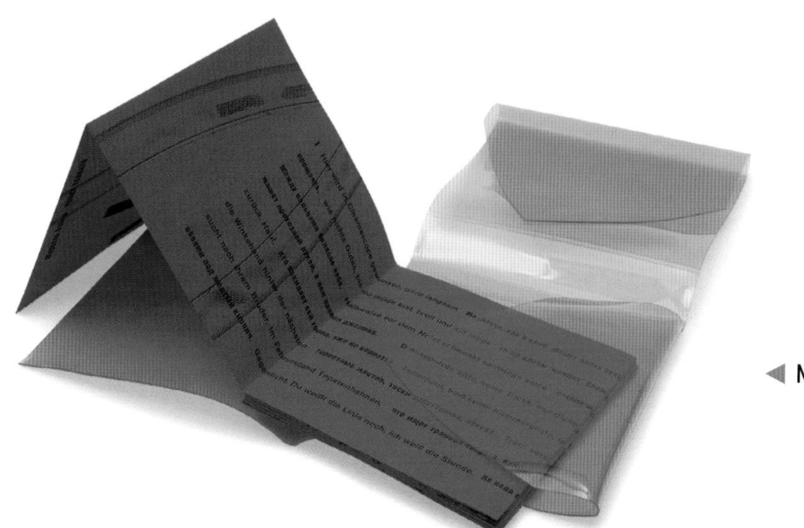

◀ **Marcel Beyer: Funky Sabbath** | 2004

59 1/16 x 11 13/16 inches (150 x 30 cm)
Chinese paper, pattern printed from used bicycle tires;
letterpress printed from zinc clichés

Photo by Keizo Kioku

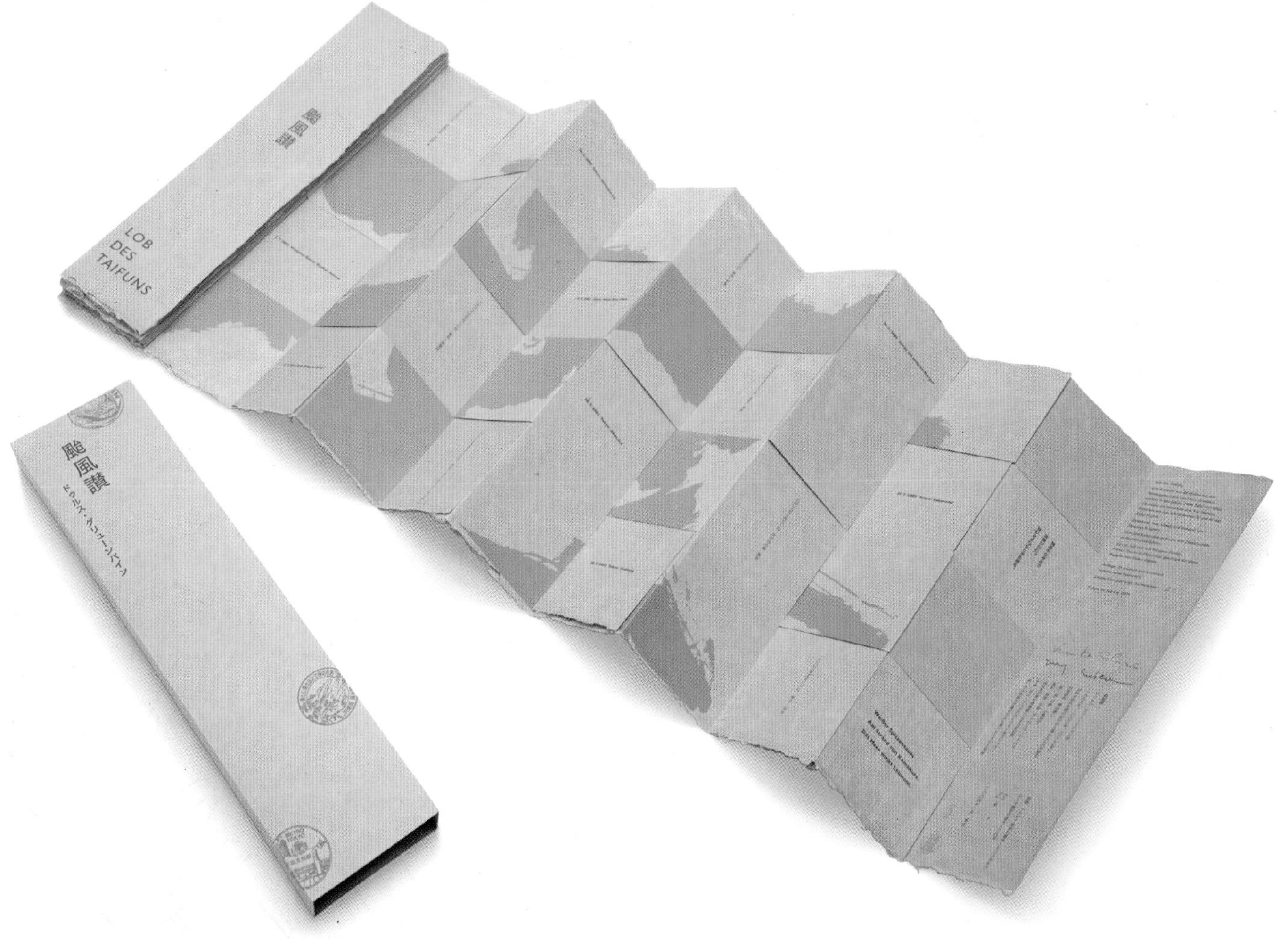

▲ **Durs Grünbein: Lob des Taifuns** | 2004

Open: 8½ feet (2.5 m) wide
Handmade mitsumata-tsuchi-iri-paper, slipcase with printed title, clear vinyl, calligraphy; concertina folded, letterpress printed with zinc clichés

Handmade paper by Hideo Ogawa
Calligraphy by Akiko Kojima
Photos by Keizo Kioku

" I always try to make the construction of my books obvious to readers. Sometimes I give them the opportunity to take a book to pieces and re-assemble it. "

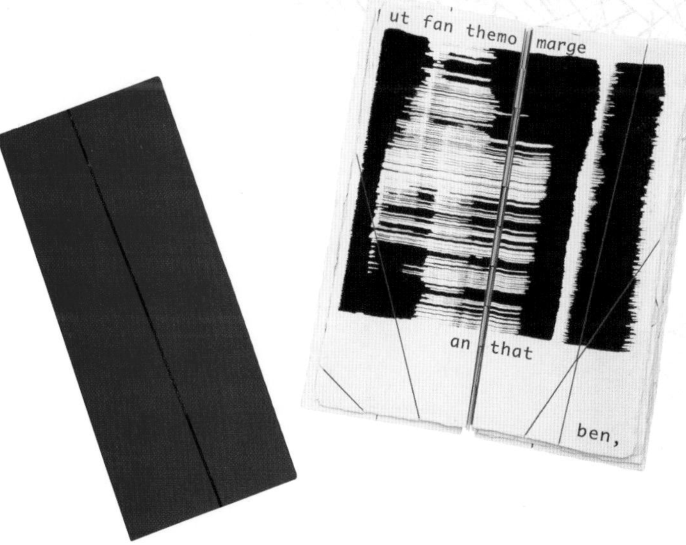

▲ **Wurmzauber** | 2002

5⅛ x 13 3/16 inches (13 x 33.5 cm)
Torinoko paper, kozo paper, shoen ink, gum label and gum stripes, Torinoko cardboard, slipcase covered with red polyester cotton fabric; stitched, letterpress printed with zinc clichés

Photo by Keizo Kioku

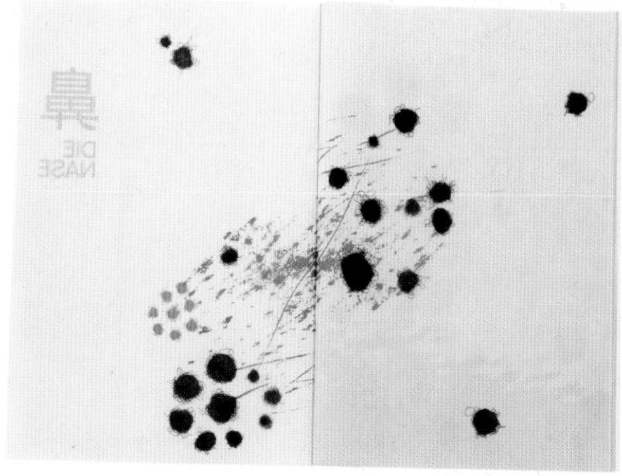

Ryunosuke Akutagawa: The Nose | 2009 ▶

13 9/16 x 18⅞ inches (34.5 x 48 cm)
Mitsumata paper, photographs, hair, vellum, kozo-ganpi cardboard, Jellyfilm, vinyl cords, Neodym-magnets; Japanese binding, letterpress printed with polymer plates

Photos by Keizo Kioku

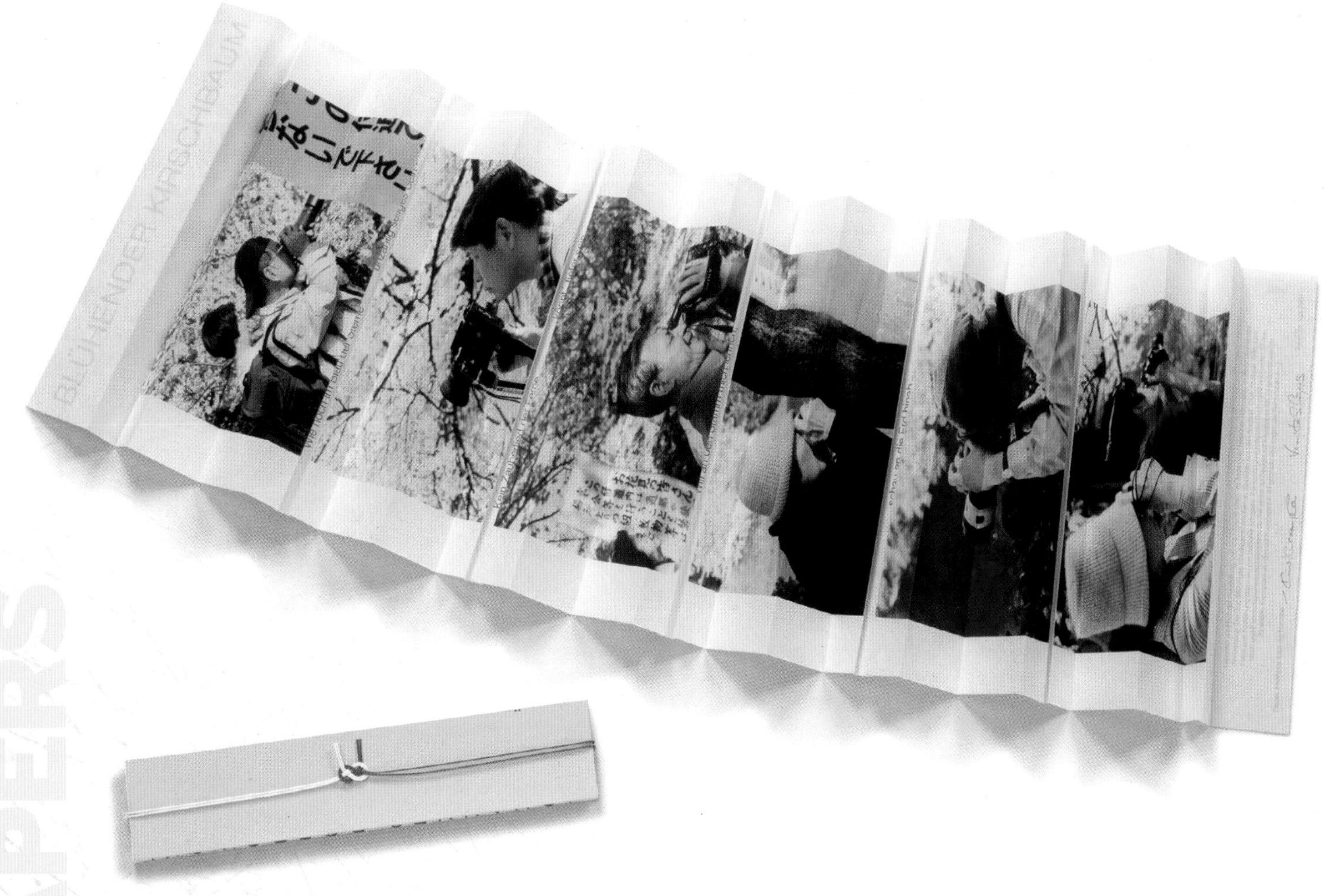

▲ **Johannes Bobrowski: Blühender Kirschbaum** | 2000

Open: 9⁷⁄₁₆ x 37 inches (24 x 94 cm)
Kozo paper, photographs, ganpi boards and paper, mizuhiki papercord; inkjet printed, concertina folded

Photo by Keizo Kioku

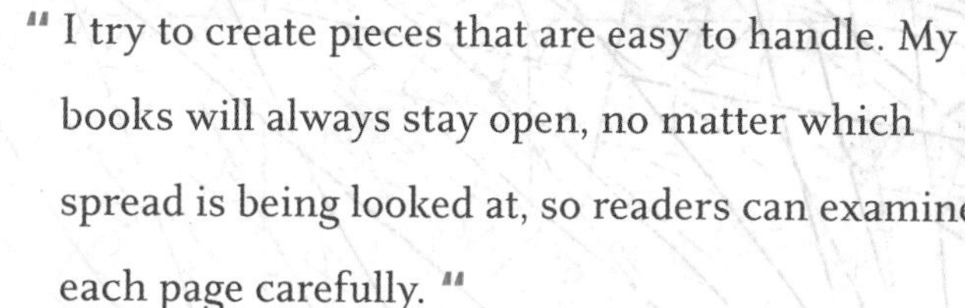

" I try to create pieces that are easy to handle. My books will always stay open, no matter which spread is being looked at, so readers can examine each page carefully. "

▲ **Helmut Heißenbüttel: Von Liebeskunst** | 2000

13¾ x 7⅟₁₆ inches (35 x 18 cm)

Mitsumata-gasen and mitsumata-hakuai papers, mitsumata pasteboard cover, photographs, carbon rods; inkjet printed, stitched, concertina folded

Photo by Keizo Kioku

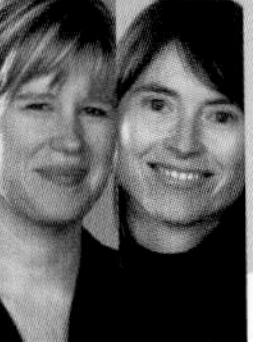

Daniela Deeg & Cynthia Lollis

WORKING COLLABORATIVELY SINCE THE 1990s, Daniela Deeg and Cynthia Lollis create structurally integrated books that feature provocative imagery and a masterful use of layering. Charting their friendship and mutual interests over the years, their work exhibits a sensitivity to materials and dexterity with multiple techniques. Travel, foreign cultures, and language all play a role in their skillfully conceived and executed works.

Often relying on photography to portray their narrative themes, Deeg and Lollis design intriguing travelogue books. Printed text is a critical aspect of their work, but it's usually subordinate to the visual elements of a piece. Capturing the mystery and wonder that characterize the discovery of new places, their books convey emotion without evoking sentimentality.

As a collaborative team, Lollis and Deeg publish under the ETC Press imprint. Deeg lives in Ludwigsburg, Germany, while Lollis is based in Atlanta, Georgia. Their work is held in collections throughout Europe, the United States, and South Africa.

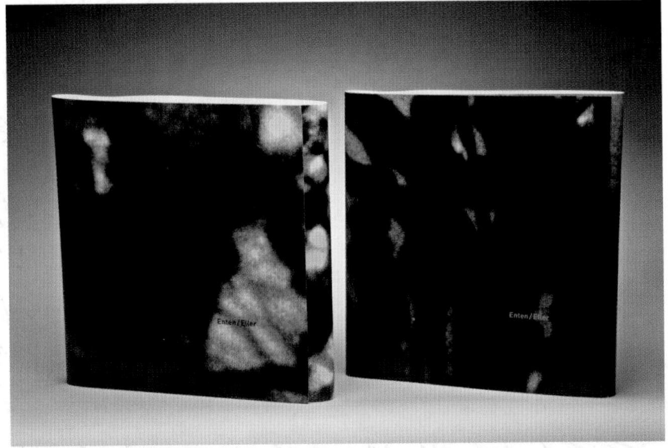

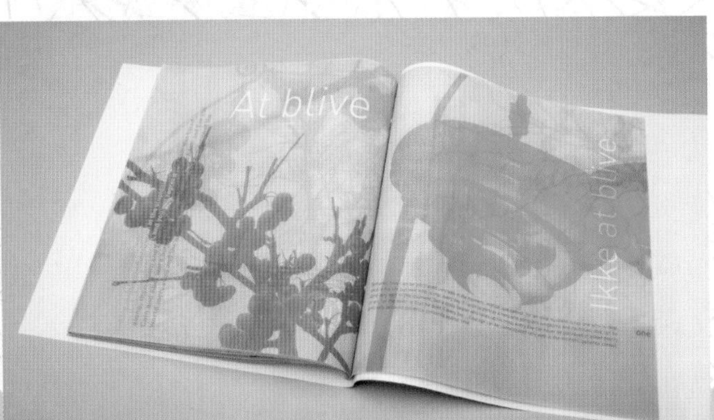

◄ **Enten/Eller** | 2009

Each book: 11⅝ x 12 x ¾ inches (29.5 x 30.5 x 2 cm)
Glama Natural paper, bookscrews, custom-printed tarpaulin, grey-board box; stab binding, screen-printed
Photos by Walker Montgomery

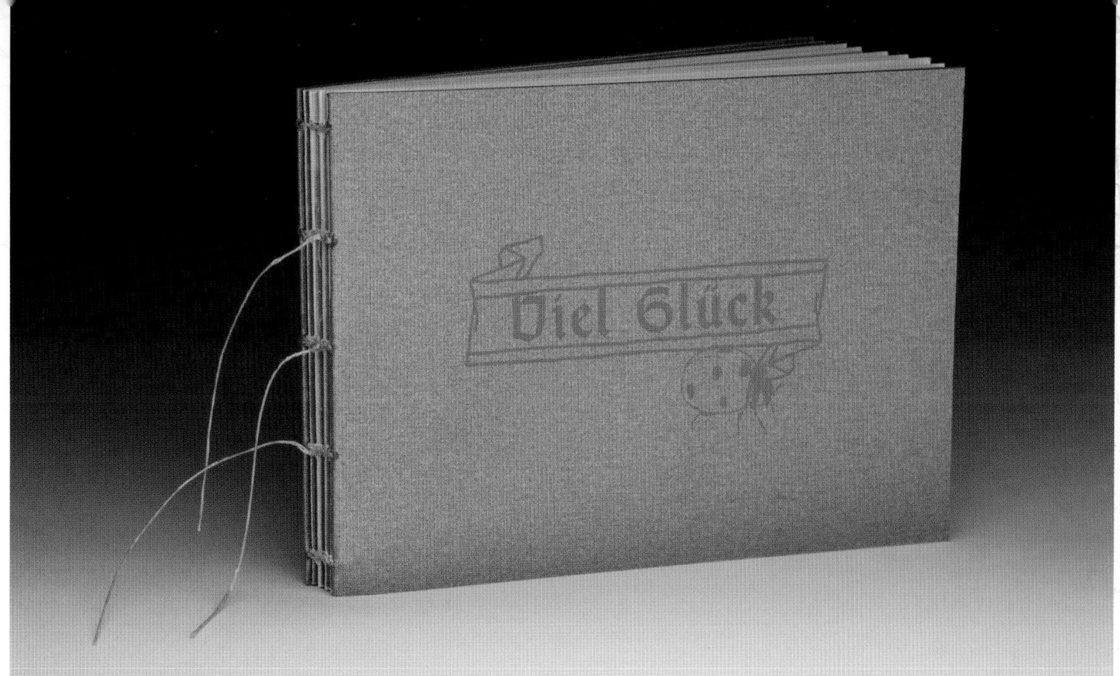

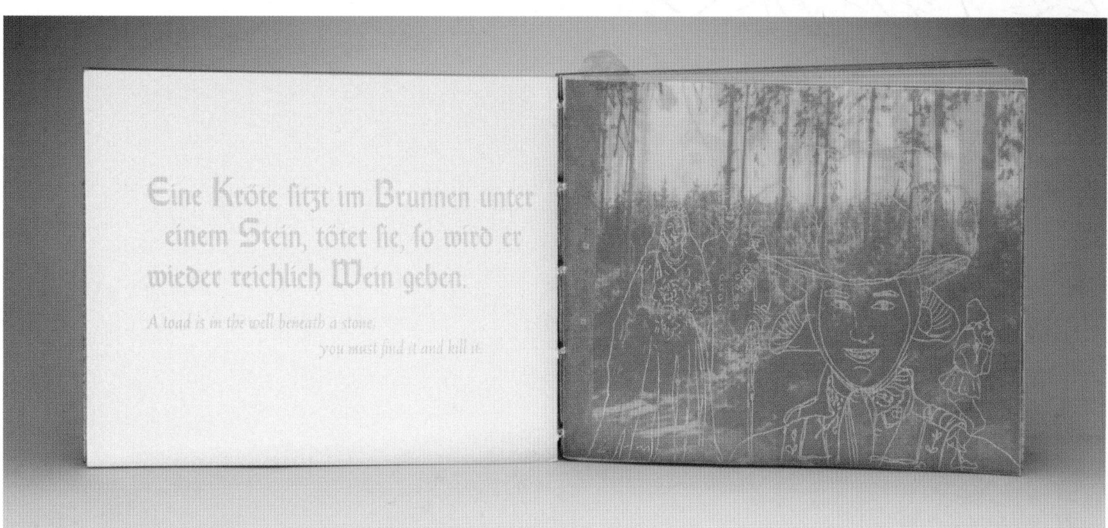

▲ **Viel Glück** | 2007

4⅛ x 5⅞ x ¾ inches (10.5 x 15 x 2 cm)
Gmund Reaction, Curious Translucents, and Zanders Gohrsmühle papers, waxed linen thread, grey-board box; Coptic binding, screen-printed, laser printed

Photos by Walker Montgomery

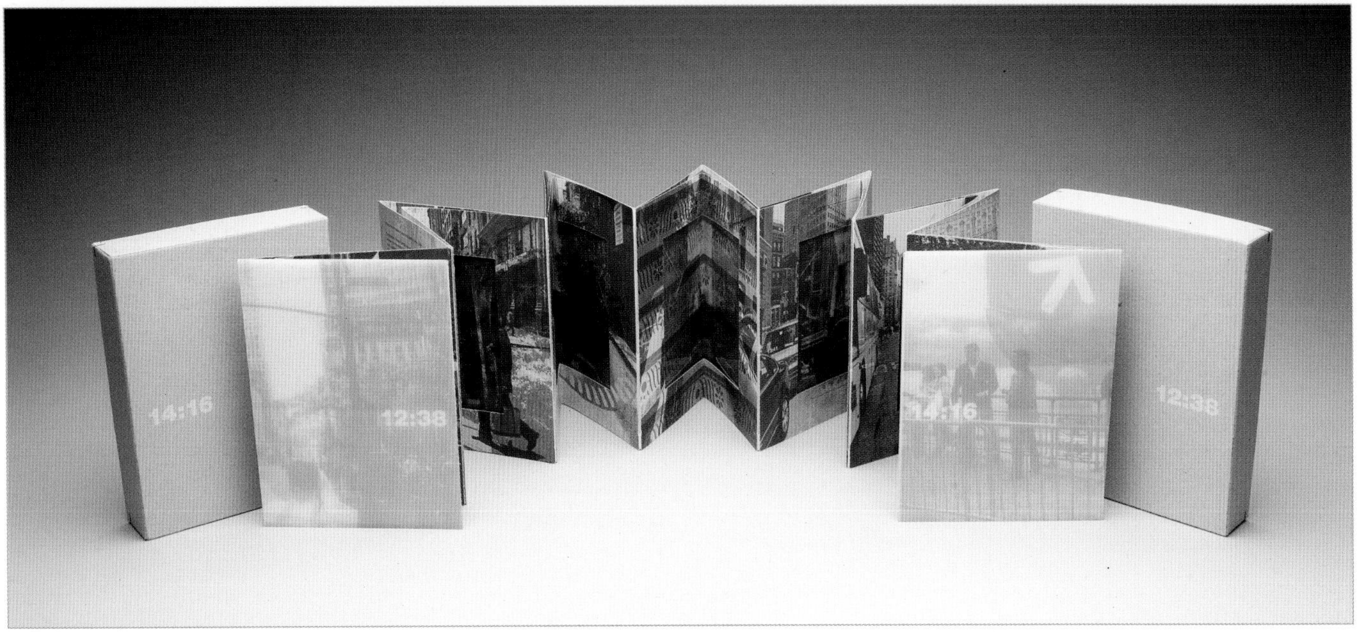

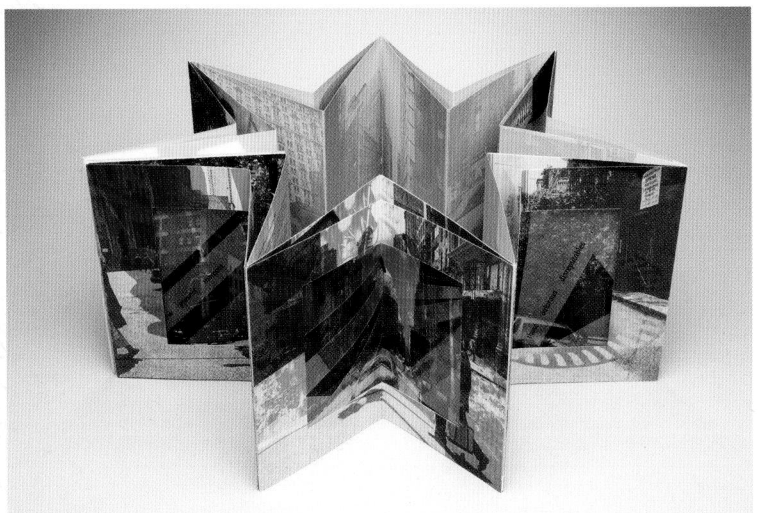

◀ **12:38–14:16** | 2006

Closed: $7\frac{7}{8}$ x $5\frac{7}{8}$ x $1\frac{9}{16}$ inches (20 x 15 x 4 cm)
Gmund Color paper, acetate, linen thread, acrylic sheeting, grey-board box; star accordion binding, screen-printed, die cuts

Photos by Walker Montgomery

" We challenge each other to create work that goes beyond what either of us could have imagined independently. "

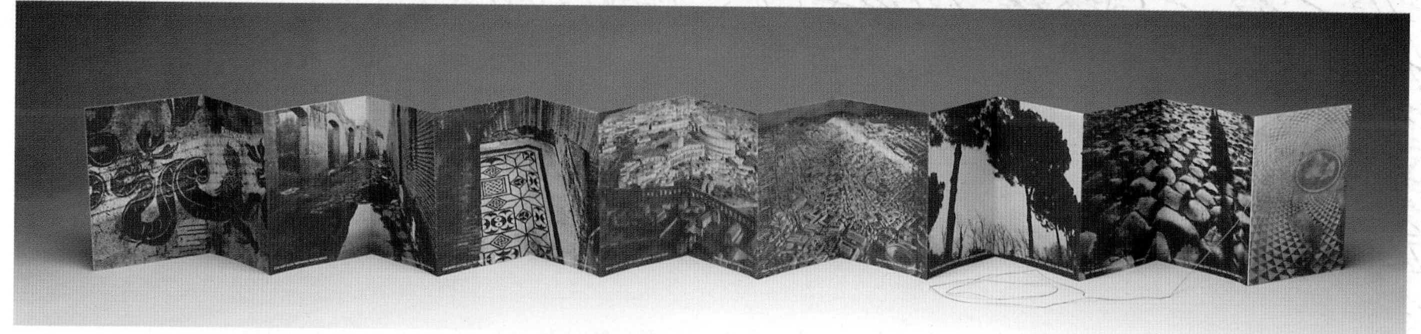

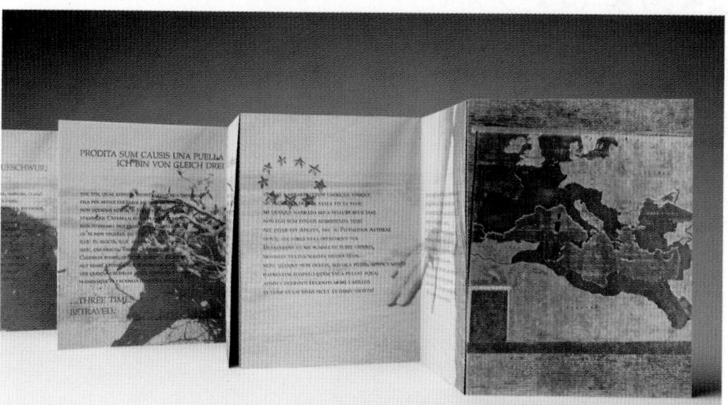

▲ Relinquo | 2005

9¼ x 7¼ x 1 inches (23.5 x 18.5 x 2.5 cm)
Yatsuo Moriki paper, medium-density fiberboard, cold wax medium, waxed linen thread, grey-board box; accordion binding, screen-printed

Photos by Walker Montgomery

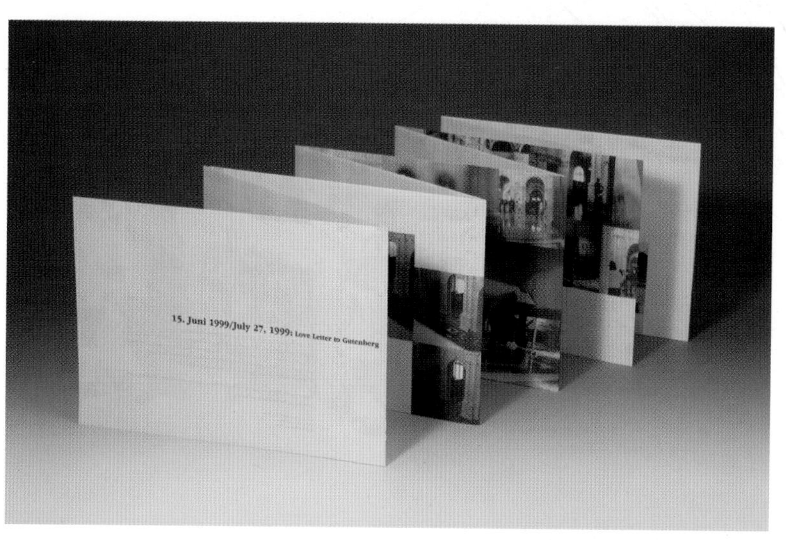

15 Juni 1999/July 27, 1999: Love Letter to Gutenberg | 2000 ▶

11¼ x 15$\frac{15}{16}$ x ⅜ inches (28.5 x 40.5 x 1 cm)
Kaschmir paper, grey-board envelope; accordion binding, offset printed, letterpress printed, embossed

Photo by Thilo Schmid

" Making books collaboratively is always surprising. In the end, the book has a life of its own, and its needs are what matter most. "

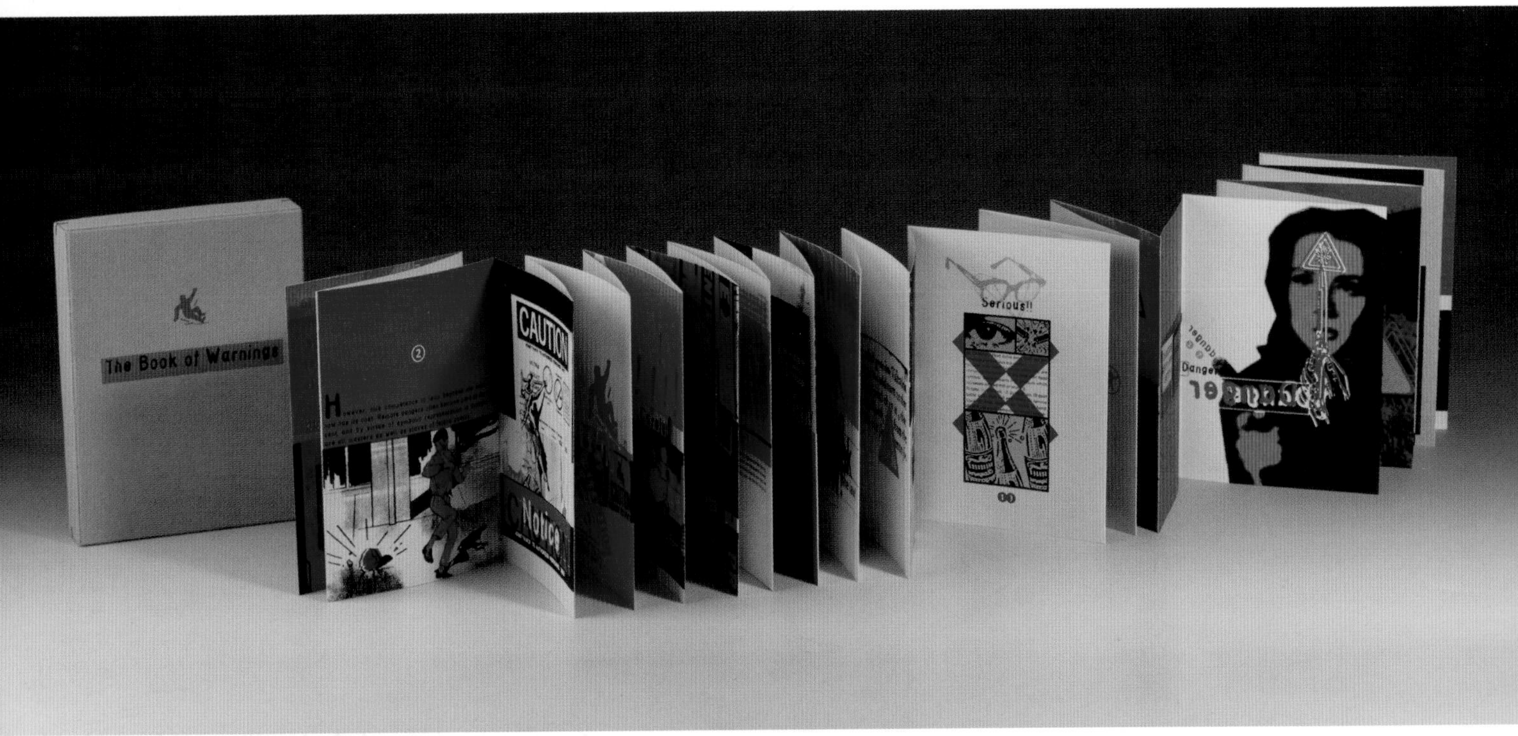

▲ **The Book of Warnings** | 2001

Designed by Daniela Deeg
Closed: 8 1/16 x 6 1/8 x 1 3/16 inches (20.5 x 15.5 x 3 cm)
Rives BFK lightweight paper, grey-board box; accordion binding, screen-printed
Photo by Thilo Schmid

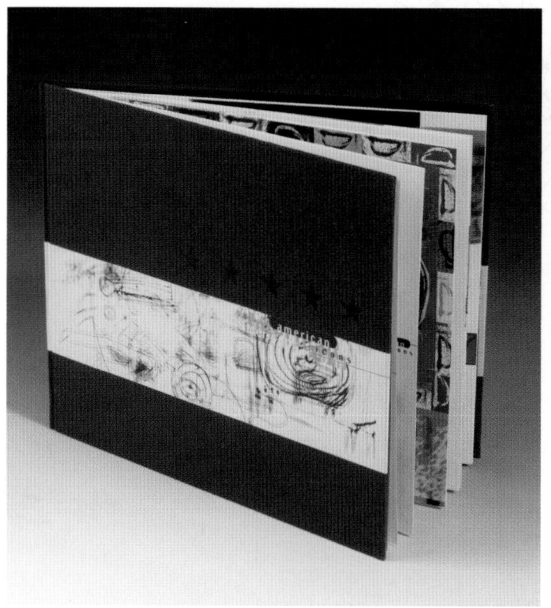

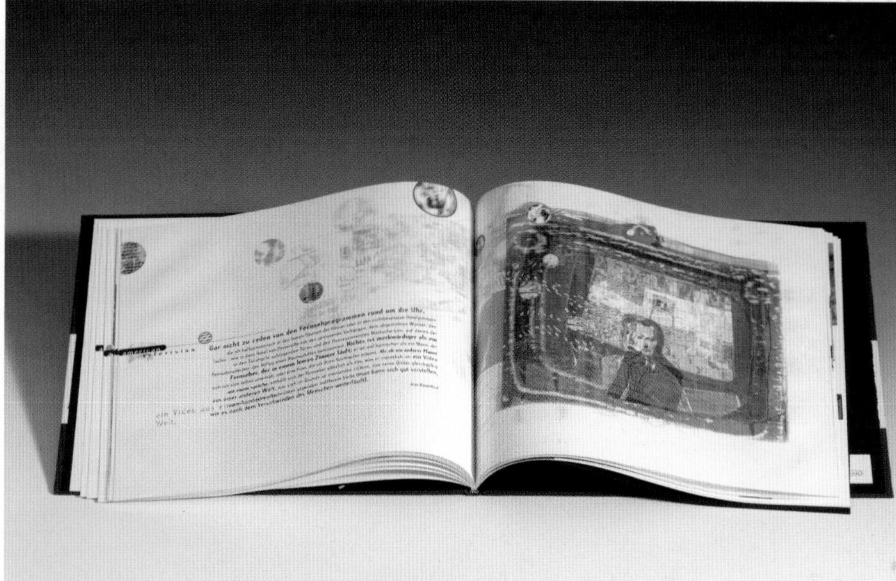

▲ **American Icons** | 1995

Designed by Daniela Deeg
10¼ x 12⅜ x ⅜ inches (26 x 31.5 x 1 cm)
Munken Pure paper, book cloth; western-style binding, laser printed, embossed
Photos by Thilo Schmid

" We spend most of the year apart but meet each winter and summer for concentrated time together. In the winter, we gather images and focus on text. In the summer, we finalize layouts, screen-print, and bind. During each stage of our bookmaking process, there is dialogue. "

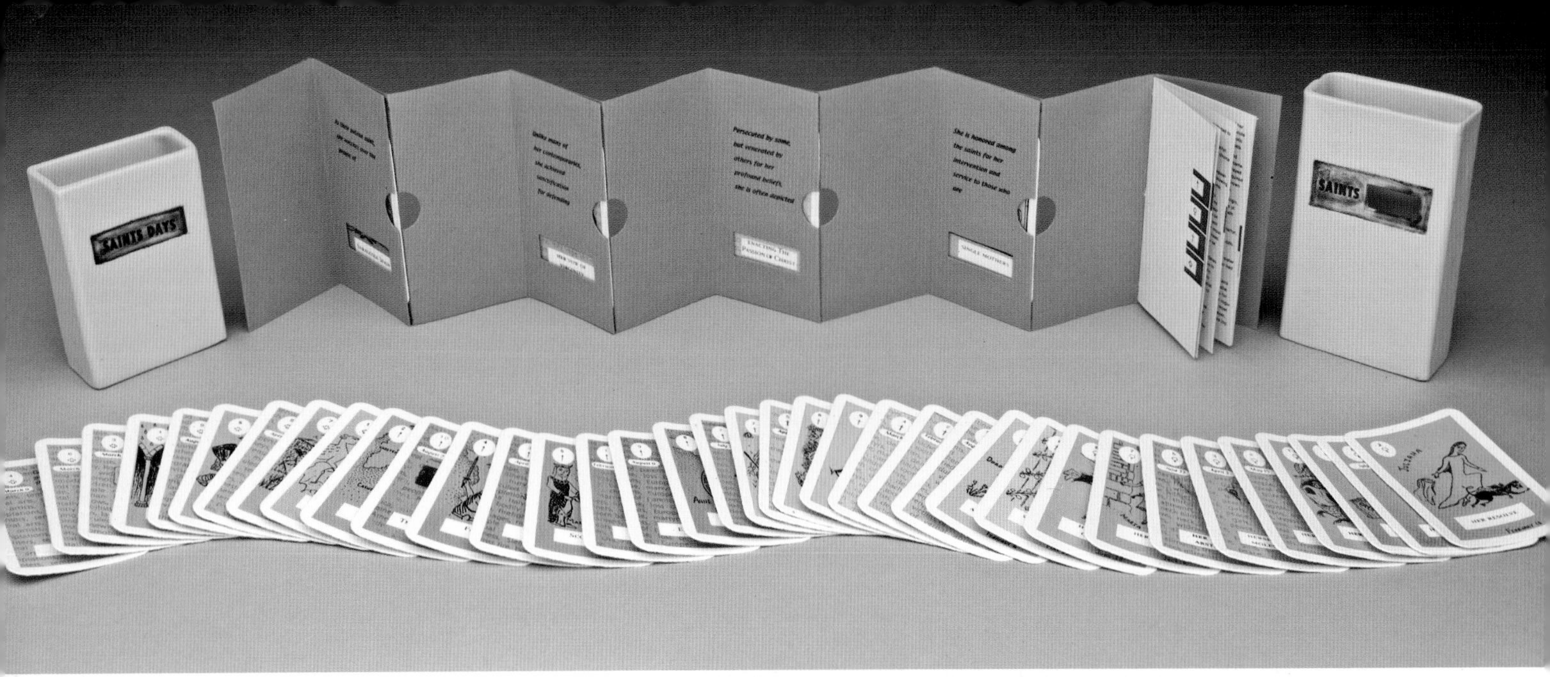

▲ Saints' Days | 2002

Designed by Cynthia Lollis in collaboration with Annette Gates
$4\frac{11}{16}$ x $2\frac{3}{4}$ x $1\frac{3}{16}$ inches (12 x 7 x 3 cm)
French construction, French Smart White, and French Dur-o-Tone papers, linen thread, slip-cast porcelain slipcase; accordion binding, screen-printed, letterpress printed, die cut
Photos by Walker Montgomery

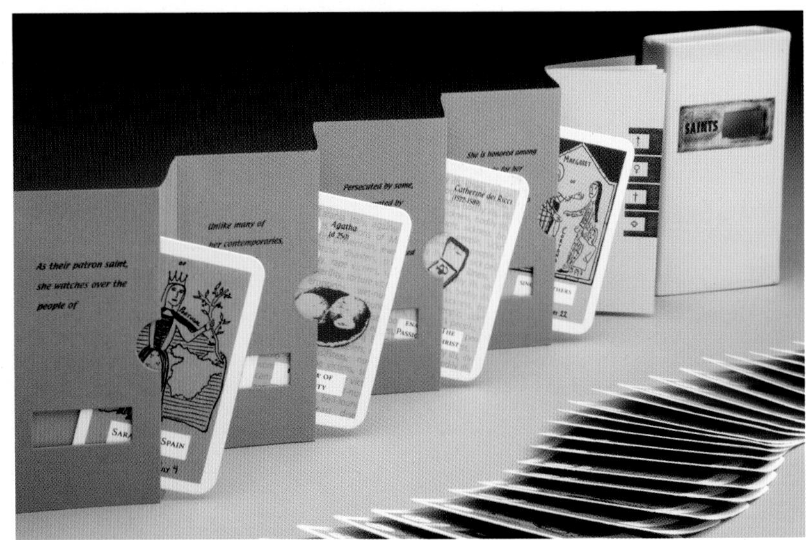

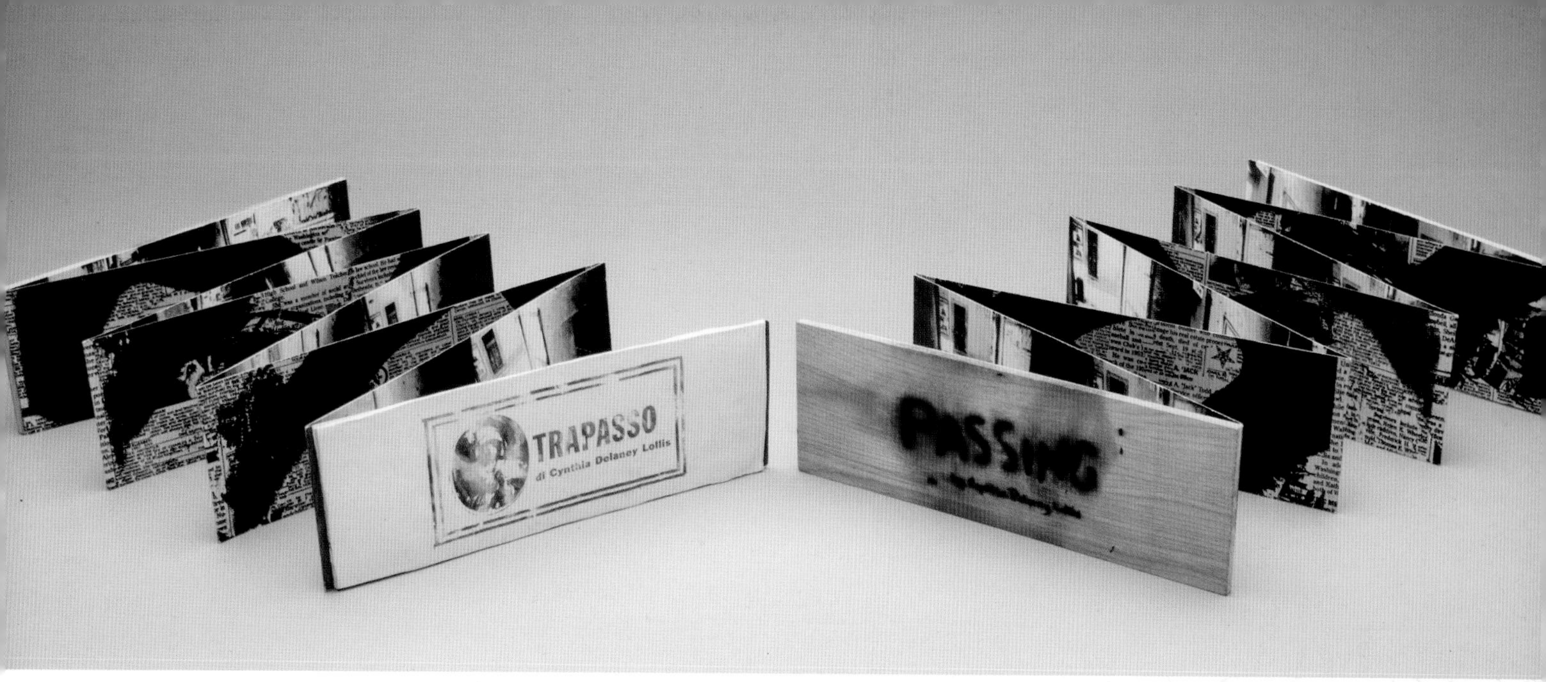

▲ **Trapasso/Passing** | 1998

Designed by Cynthia Lollis
3¼ x 9⅜ x 1 inches (8.3 x 23.8 x 2.5 cm)
Rives Heavyweight paper, linen tape, fire-heated iron-branded wood, glazed ceramic with screen-printed ceramic stain pigment; accordion binding, screen-printed

Photo by Walker Montgomery

AVADENKA

Lynne Avadenka

REFINED AND BEAUTIFULLY CONSTRUCTED, the books of Lynne Avadenka demonstrate an elegant restraint. Avadenka excels at expressing the essence of an idea without using superfluous embellishment. Operating under the imprint of Land Marks Press, she gracefully combines harmonious palettes with hand lettering, mark making, and abstracted lines to create books that display an astute understanding of her subject matter. Carefully considered visual elements elucidate meaning in the texts, while Avadenka's purely visual books employ an efficiency of line and atmospheric delicacy in counterbalance to the profundity of her message.

Avadenka, who lives in Huntington Woods, Michigan, has received grants from the National Endowment for the Arts and the Michigan Council for Arts and Cultural Affairs. Her work is included in collections around the world, including the British Library in London, England; the Cleveland Museum of Art, in Cleveland, Ohio; and The Jewish Museum in New York City.

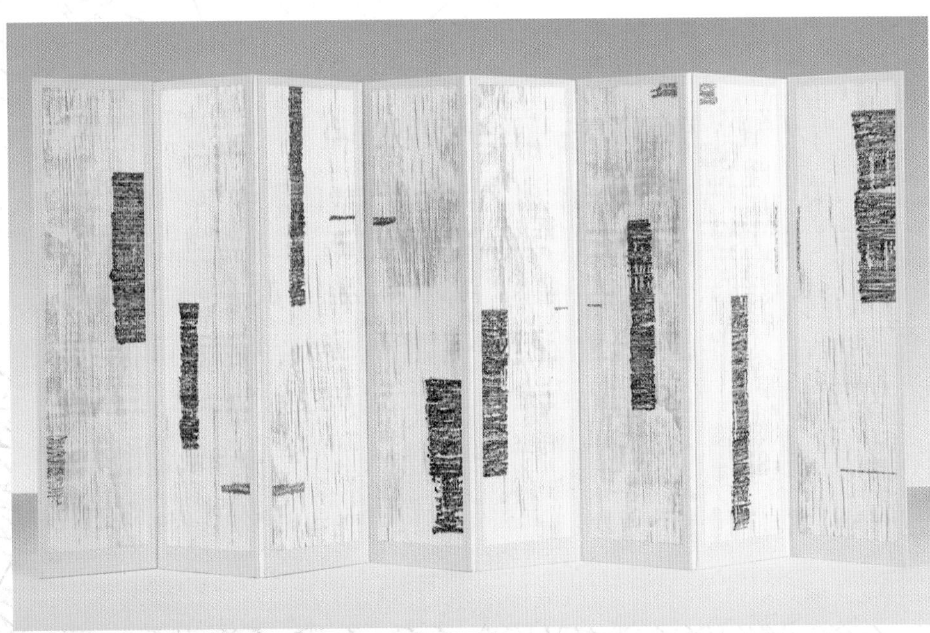

◀ **Under the Sun** | 2009

26 x 54 inches (66 x 137.2 cm)
Paper, Tyvek, board; folding screen, relief printed, typing
Photo by R. H. Hensleigh

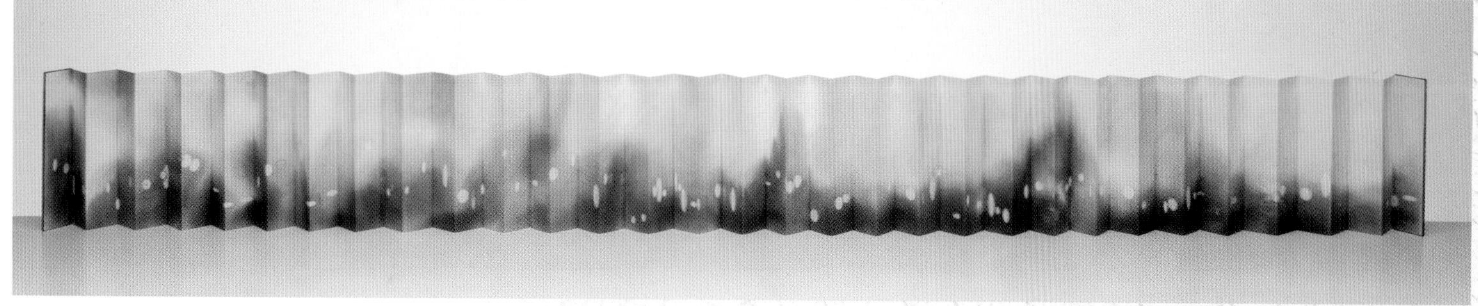

▲ **Silent Reading** | 2009

11 x 96 inches (27.9 x 243.8 cm)
Powdered graphite, pencil, paper, board, book cloth; drawing, unique accordion book

Photos by R. H. Hensleigh

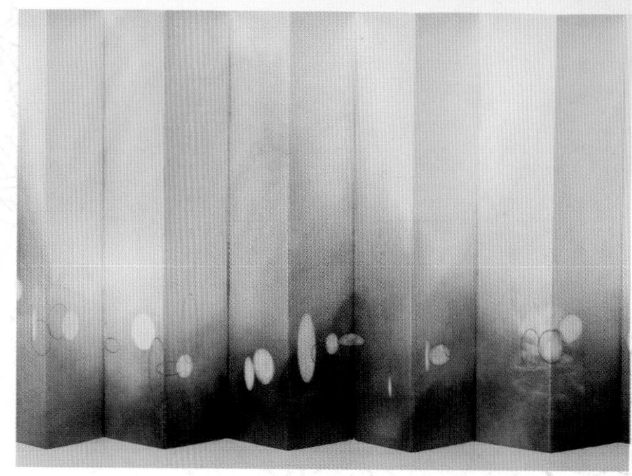

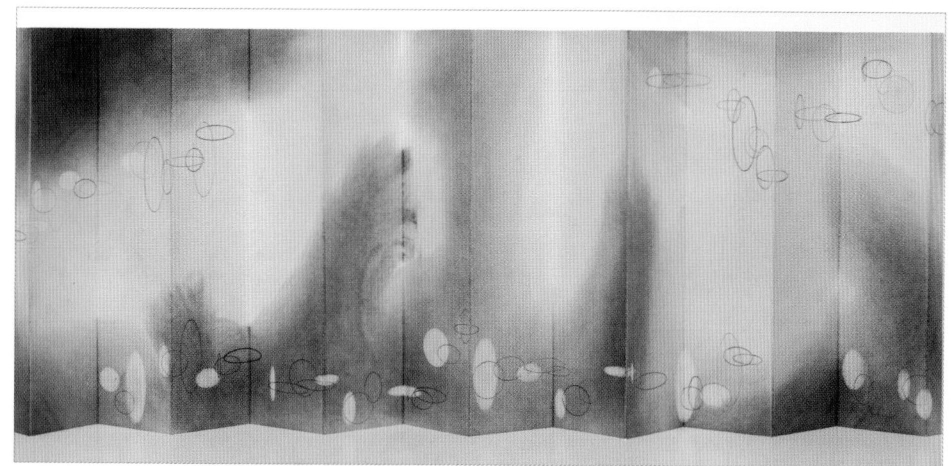

◀ **Futile Beauty** | 2009

8 x 60 inches (20.3 x 152.4 cm)
Powdered graphite, pencil, paper, book board, book cloth; drawing, unique accordion book

Photo by R. H. Hensleigh

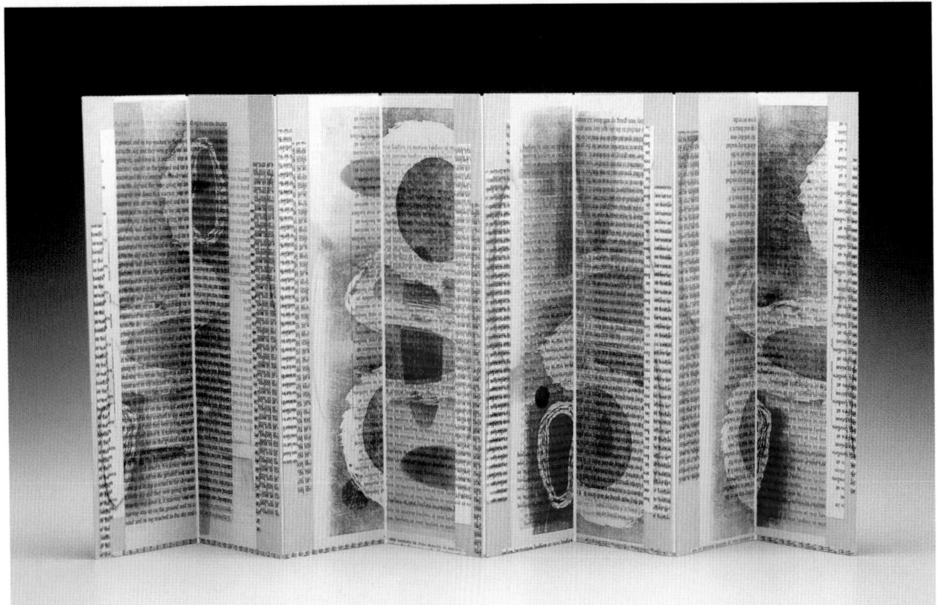

Aftermath I | 2003

12⅜ x 29 inches (31.4 x 73.7 cm)
Paper, Tyvek, book board; unique accordion book, letterpress printed, woodcut, collage, drawing

Photo by R. H. Hensleigh

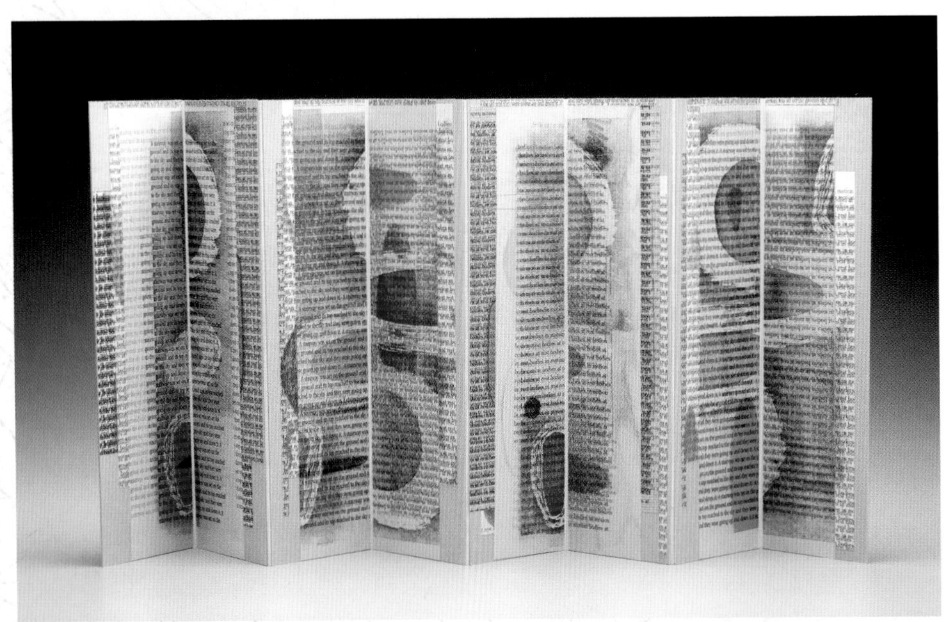

Aftermath II | 2003

12⅜ x 29 inches (31.4 x 73.7 cm)
Paper, Tyvek, book board; unique accordion book, woodcut, letter-press printed, collage, drawing

Photo by R. H. Hensleigh

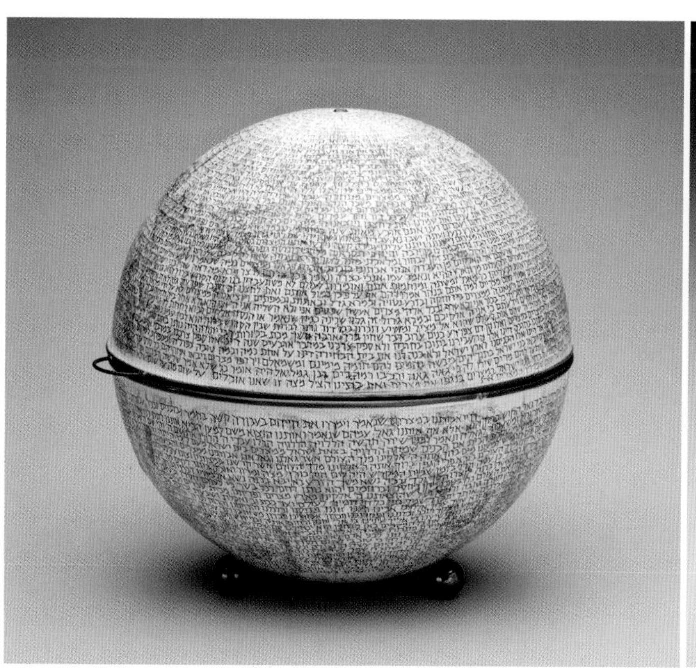

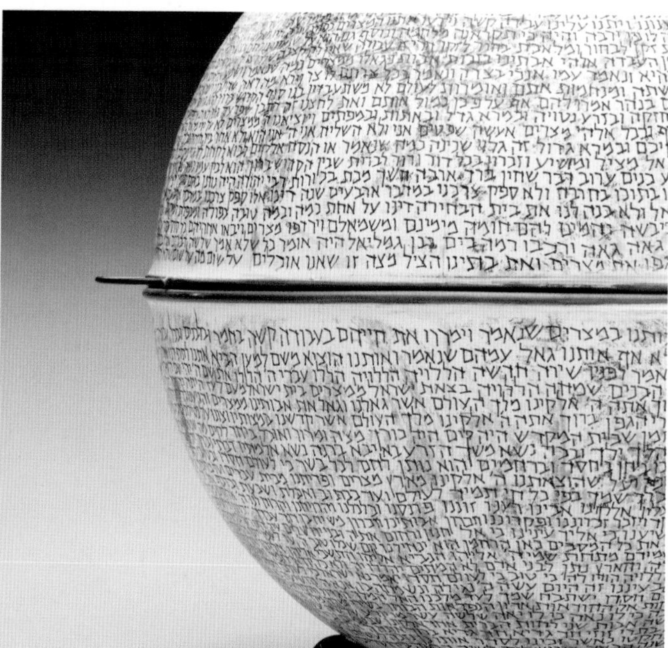

▲ **World Book** | 2008

12 inches (30.5 cm) in diameter
Paper globe, ink; hand lettering
Photos by R. H. Hensleigh

" I'm guided by the original concept of the book as a repository of memory and loss, as a vehicle for transmitting transcendent information, and as a singular object that binds together a multiplicity of meanings and ideas. "

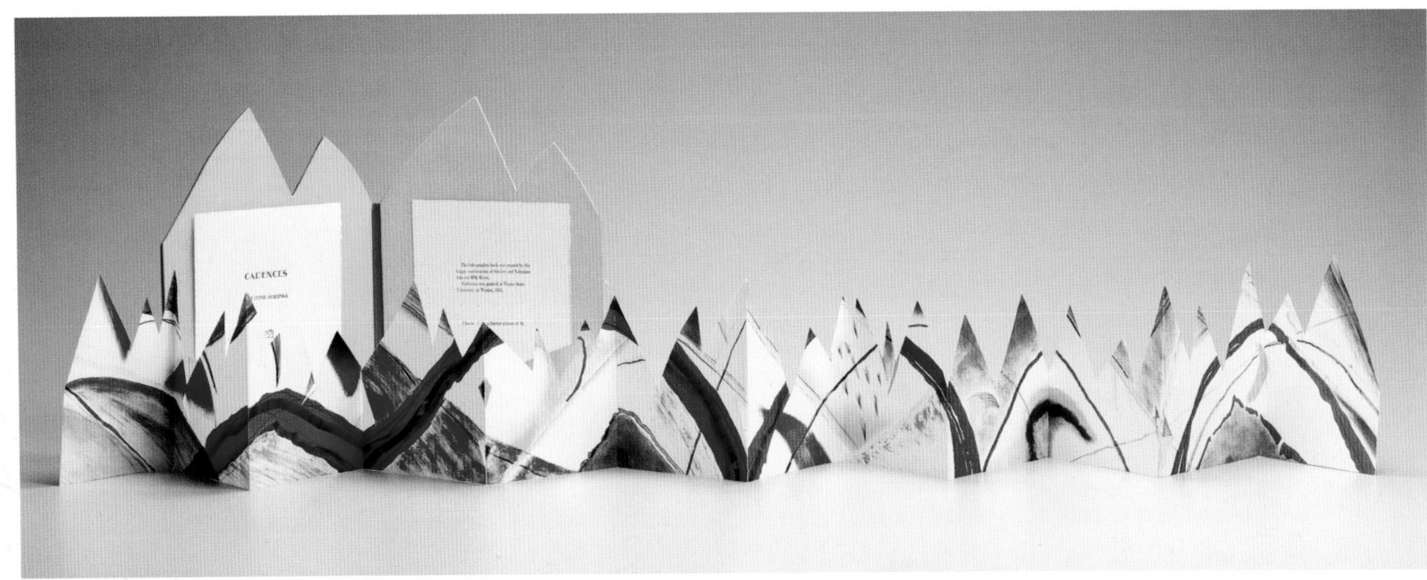

▲ **Cadences** | 1981

7½ x 56 inches (19.1 x 142.2 cm)
Paper, book cloth, board; color lithography, letterpress printed

Photo by R. H. Hensleigh

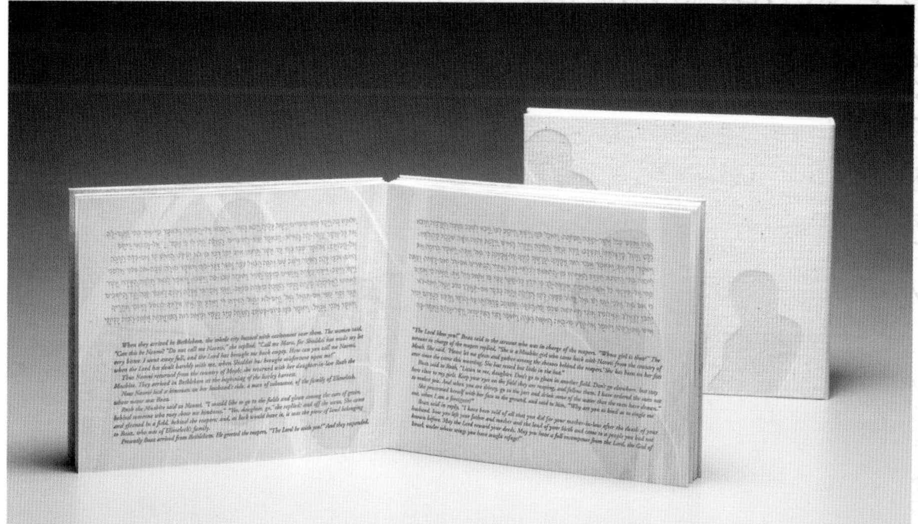

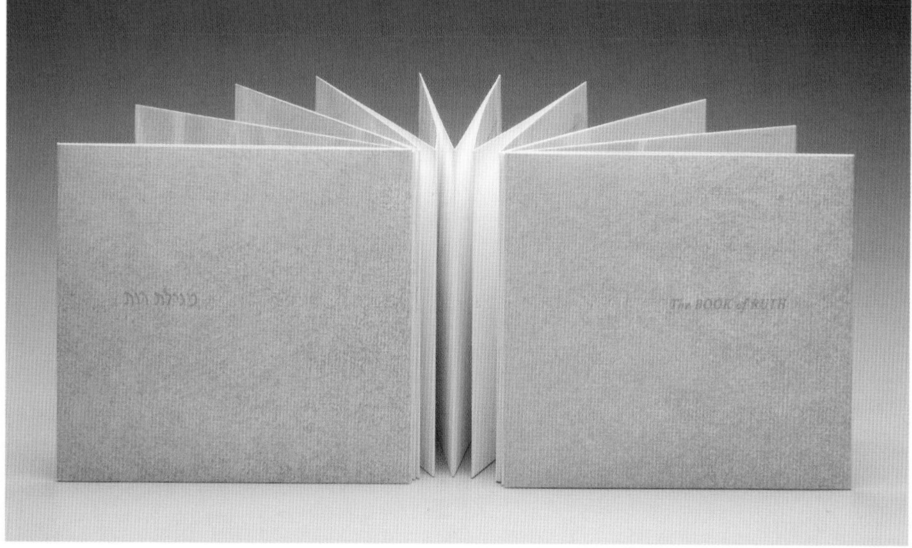

▲ **The Book of Ruth** | 2004

6¾ x 15½ inches (17.1 x 39.4 cm)
Paper, acrylic paint; letterpress printed from photopolymer, pressure printed, relief printed

Photos by R. H. Hensleigh

" Many years ago, when I realized I was giving the same serious consideration to the titles of my work as I was to the work itself, I invited words into my art. The combined power of word and image is now integral to my art. "

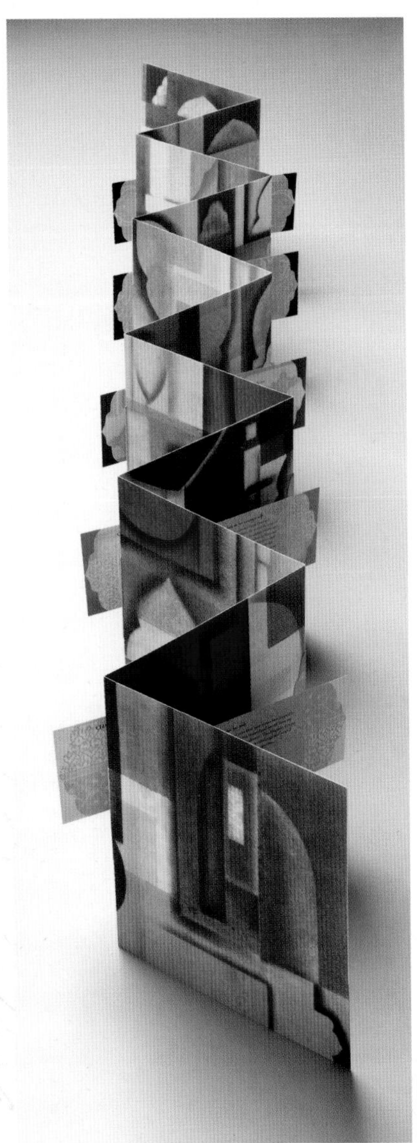

▲ **By a Thread** | 2006

8 x 64 inches (20.3 x 162.6 cm)
Paper; offset-color lithography, die cut
Photo by R. H. Hensleigh

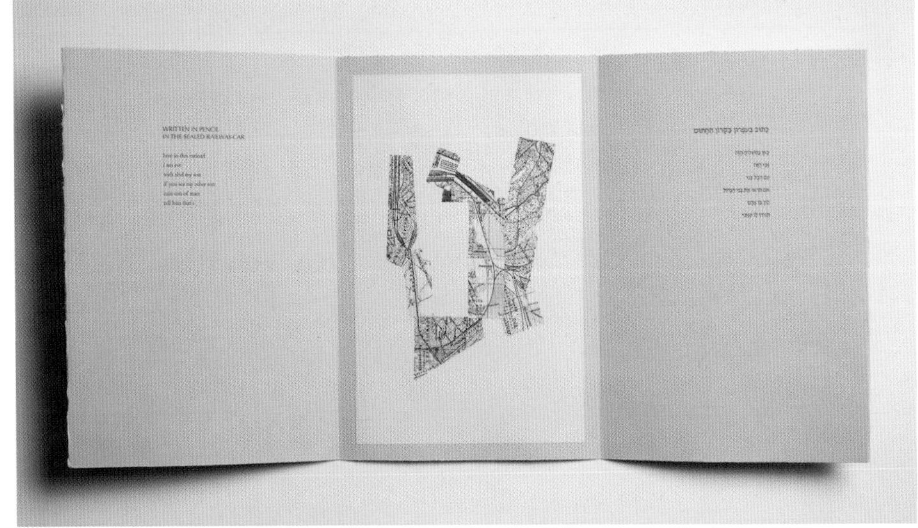

▲ **Dan Pagis: Ein Leben** | 2007

11 x 22 inches (27.9 x 55.9 cm)
Paper; letterpress printed from photopolymer, lithography, gouache
Photo by R. H. Hensleigh

" The interplay of text and visual elements is a rich one. It propels me to explore reading and seeing on multiple levels. "

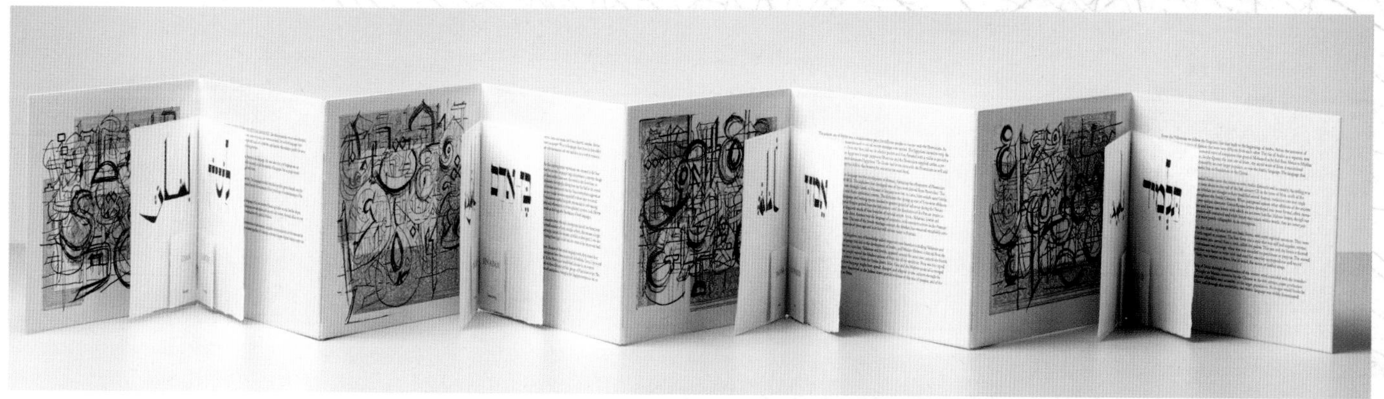

▲ **Root Words** | 2001

12 x 77 inches (30.5 x 195.6 cm)

Paper, board, thread; letterpress printed from photopolymer plates, lithography

Photo by R. H. Hensleigh

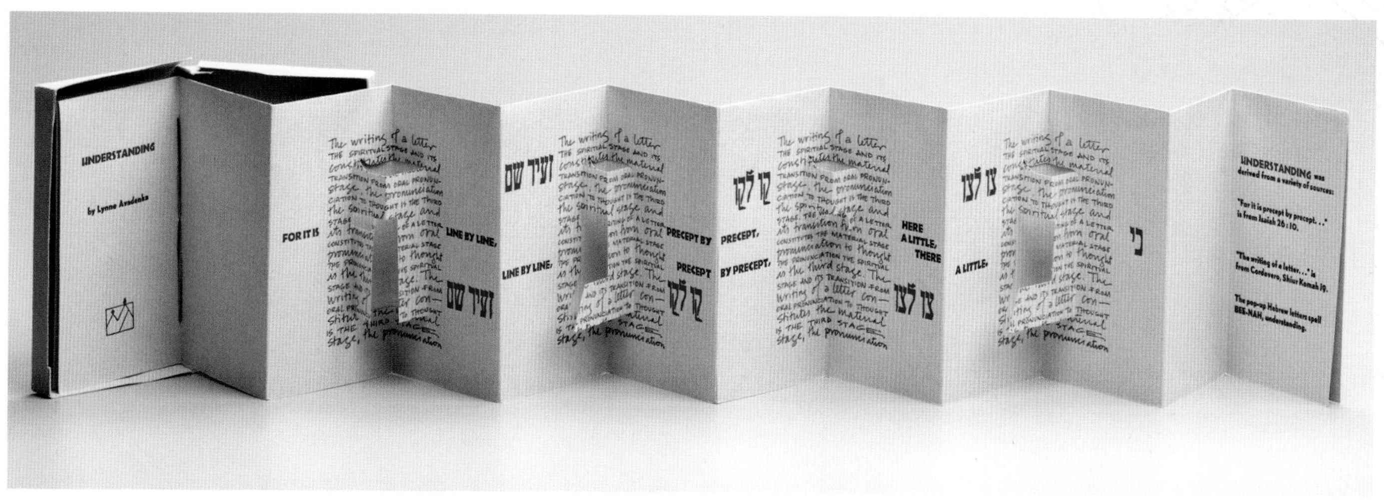

▲ **Understanding** | 1988

5 x 27 inches (12.7 x 68.6 cm)

Paper; letterpress printed from metal type and engravings, die cut

Photo by R. H. Hensleigh

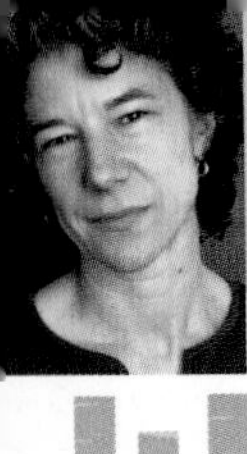

PRICE

Robin Price

AN ARTIST WHO PURSUES DIVERSITY IN HER WORK, Robin Price consistently displays virtuosity in the midst of tenacious experimentation with both form and content. Price willingly embraces chance occurrences in the conceptual development and production of her book structures, remaining open to spontaneous creative opportunities. Her work has a wonderful liveliness as a result. In her collaborations with artists and writers, she approaches each project with a new perspective, producing books that reflect a multiplicity of techniques and styles.

The impressive range of Price's output makes it difficult to interpret her work by a specific set of defined attributes. Her ability to integrate sophisticated literary content with elegant imagery results in lively, well-paced books—works that exemplify her expertise as a designer and printer. Price lives in Middletown, Connecticut. Her works are in collections around the world, including those of the British Library in London, England; the Württembergische Landesbibliothek in Stuttgart, Germany; and the Princeton University Library in Princeton, New Jersey.

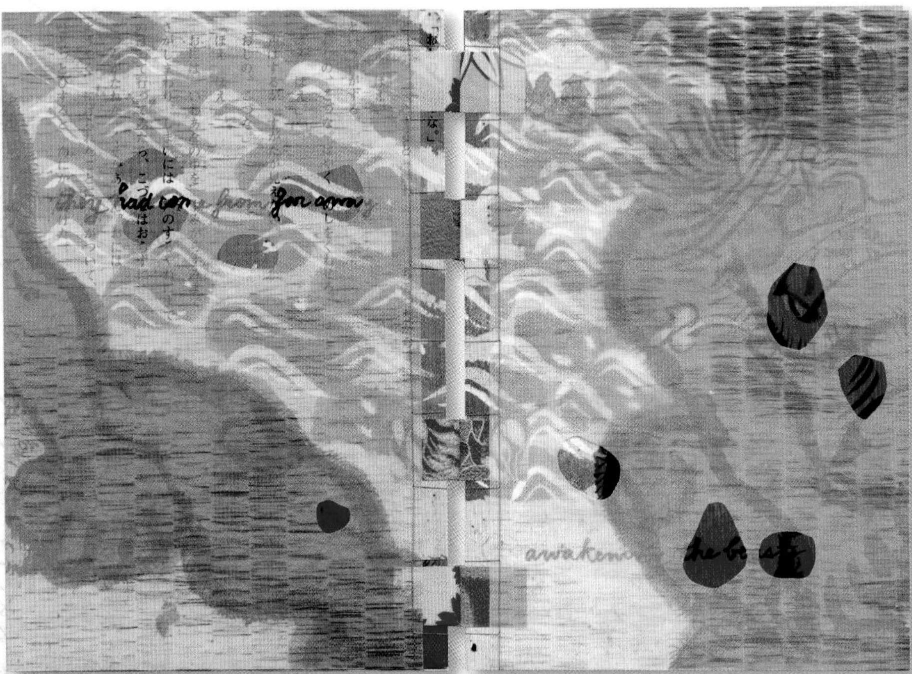

More Joy | 2004 ▶

9¼ x 6½ x ½ inches (23.5 x 16.5 x 1.3 cm)
Altered Japanese children's book, tracing vellum, fabric hinges, colored pencils, sumi ink, paper cut-outs
Photo by artist

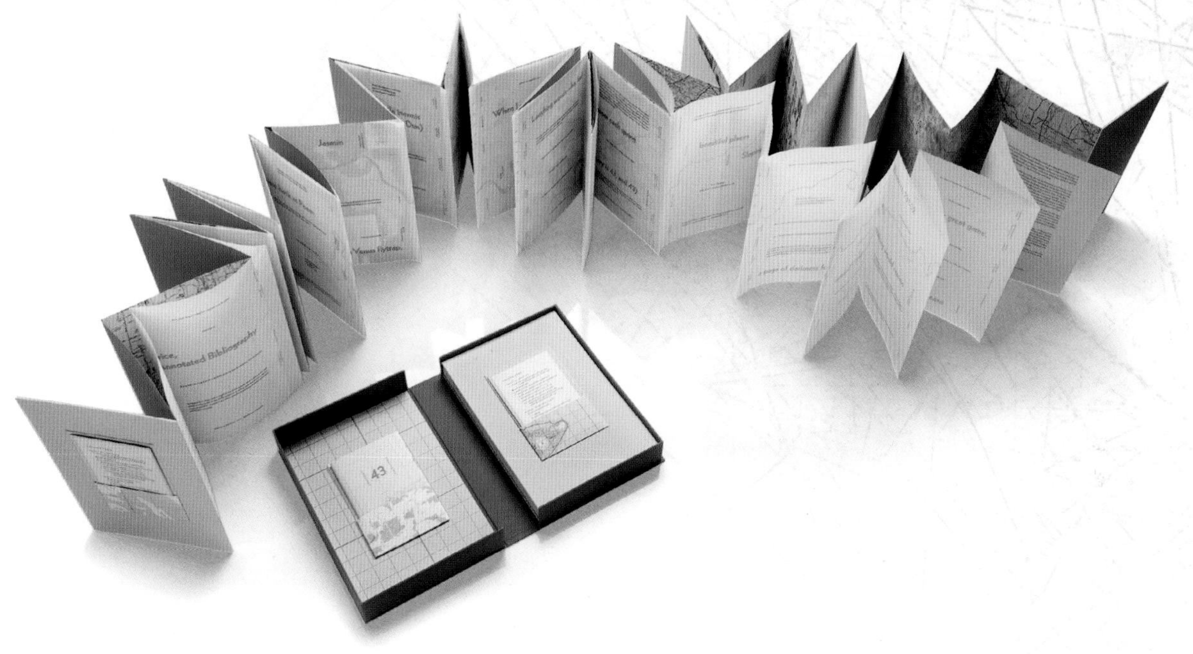

▲ **43, According to Robin Price, with Annotated Bibliography (Standard Edition)** | 2008

Collaboration with Daniel E. Kelm
Closed: 12 x 8 x 1½ inches (30.5 x 20.3 x 3.8 cm)
Open: 20 feet (6.1 m) wide
Graph paper, maps, handmade cover paper; double-layer accordion, letterpress and laser printed
Photo by Derek Dudek

John Cage loved numbers. And his music was never without them. He used them to generate notes and silences & sounds and rhythmic structures and compositional forms. He loved their rationality and used them to integrate all the above. He loved their irrationality and used them to remove his likes and dislikes from his music, but not, of course, from the compositional process. He even loved them for their superrationality; he found the discipline of laboriously obtaining numbers—whether throwing dice to get random numbers out of the *I Ching* for his chance works, or making charts & calculations, or measuring and splicing recording tape—useful 'to sober and quiet the minD/so that It/iS/in aCcord/wIth/what haPpens.'‡ He used numbers to pose aesthetic questions & to solve musical problems. He used them, at times, to name pieces and to give them character. He found them a jumping off place for exploring the unknown. He made himself slave to numerological systems to free the spirit. *Mark Swed*

‡The strange capitalization comes from the mesostic:

to sober and quiet the minD
so that It
iS
in aCcord
wIth
what haPpens
the worLd
around It
opeN
rathEr than

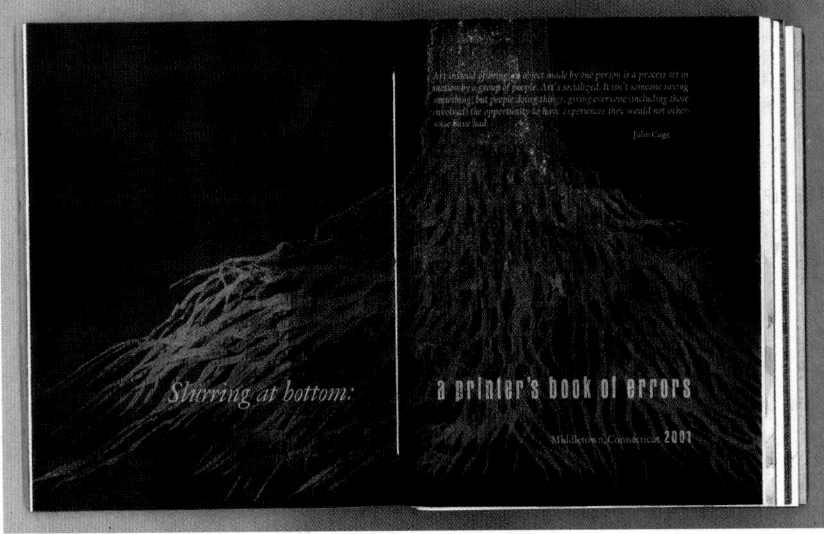

"I've become increasingly attracted to the unique-book format as a place for working out ideas relatively quickly. The format gives me greater flexibility than I have with edition work."

▲ **Slurring at Bottom: A Printer's Book of Errors** | 2001

Collaboration with Emily K. Larned
7 x 5½ x ¾ inches (17.8 x 14 x 1.9 cm)
Plastic covers, paper from previous press books; sanded, painted, letterpress printed with mixed media by ten invited artists

Photos by artist

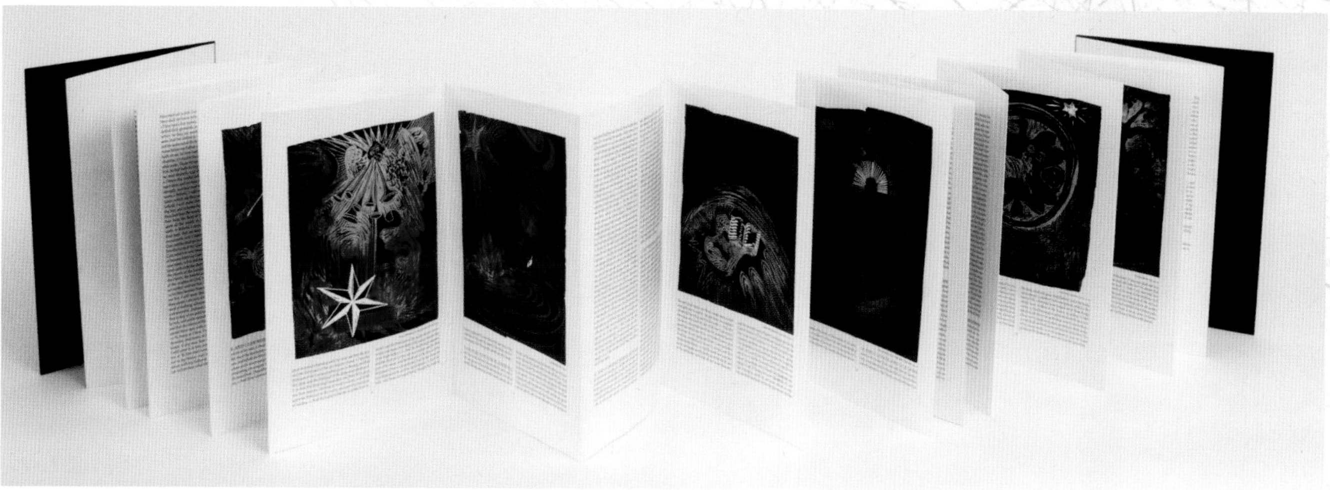

▲ **The Book of Revelation** | 1995

Open: 20 feet (6.1 m) wide
Closed: 15½ x 11 x 1 inches (39.4 x 27.9 x 25.4 cm)
Velké Losiny and De Ponte Tamayo handmade papers, linoleum cuts; accordion structure, letterpress printed

Linoleum cuts by Barbara Benish
Photo by artist

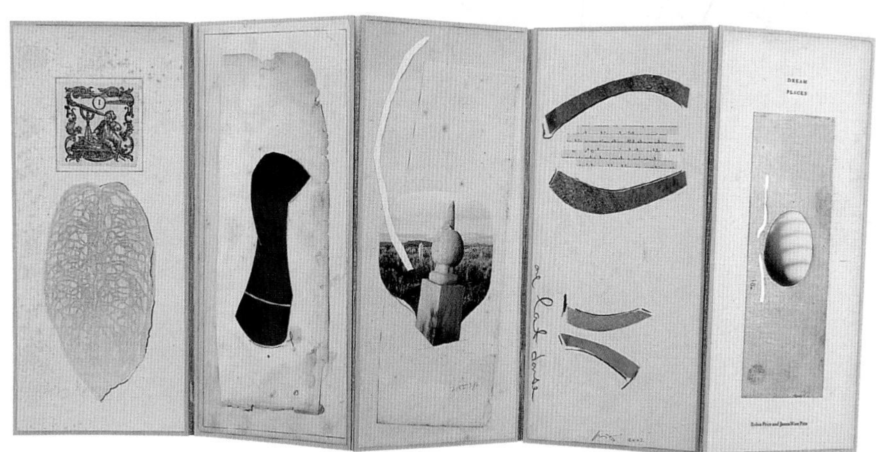

Dream Places | 2002 ▶

Blind collaboration with James W. Pitts
10¼ x 4½ x ½ inches (26 x 11.4 x 1.3 cm)
Nineteenth-century papers, cheesecloth, board; accordion structure, letterpress printed, palladium print, collage, drawing

Photo by artist

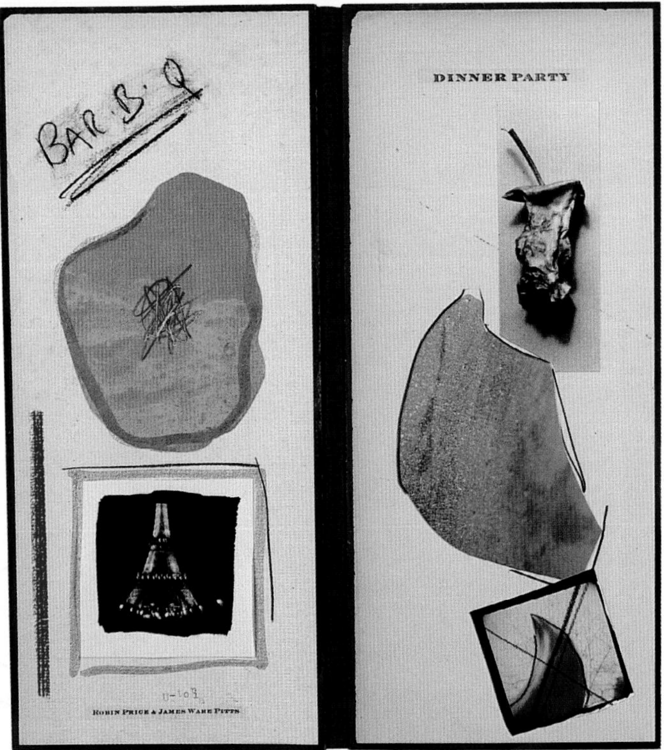

▲ **Dinner Party** | 2002

Blind collaboration with James W. Pitts
10¼ x 4½ x ¼ inches (26 x 11.4 x 0.6 cm)
Nineteenth-century papers, cheesecloth, board; accordion structure, letterpress printed, palladium print, collage, drawing

Photo by artist

> " For my recent books, I've reached out to contemporary artists, writers, and artisans, asking them to collaborate. Together, we strive to create synergistic books with extensive diversity in content and form. "

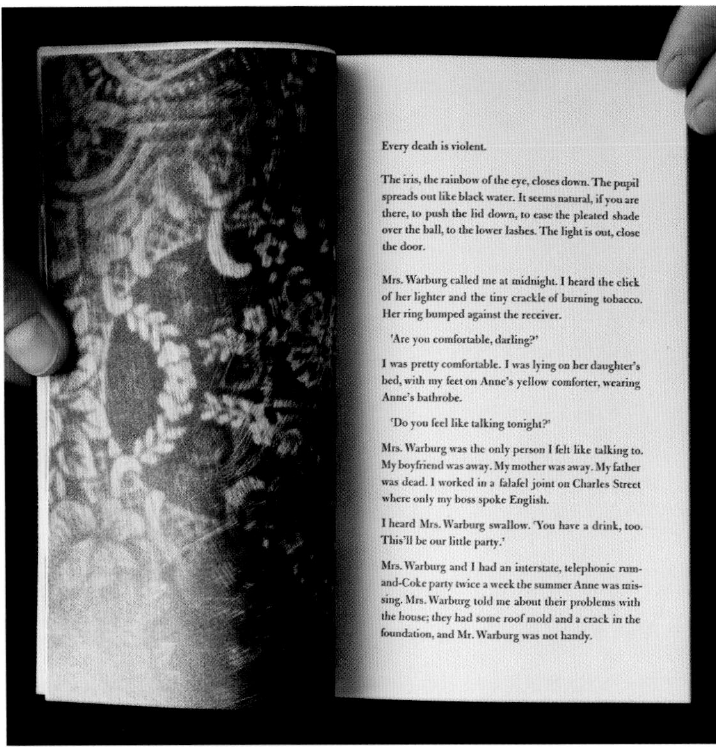

Every death is violent.

The iris, the rainbow of the eye, closes down. The pupil spreads out like black water. It seems natural, if you are there, to push the lid down, to ease the pleated shade over the ball, to the lower lashes. The light is out, close the door.

Mrs. Warburg called me at midnight. I heard the click of her lighter and the tiny crackle of burning tobacco. Her ring bumped against the receiver.

'Are you comfortable, darling?'

I was pretty comfortable. I was lying on her daughter's bed, with my feet on Anne's yellow comforter, wearing Anne's bathrobe.

'Do you feel like talking tonight?'

Mrs. Warburg was the only person I felt like talking to. My boyfriend was away. My mother was away. My father was dead. I worked in a falafel joint on Charles Street where only my boss spoke English.

I heard Mrs. Warburg swallow. 'You have a drink, too. This'll be our little party.'

Mrs. Warburg and I had an interstate, telephonic rum-and-Coke party twice a week the summer Anne was missing. Mrs. Warburg told me about their problems with the house; they had some roof mold and a crack in the foundation, and Mr. Warburg was not handy.

▲ **By-and-By** | 2005

7½ x 5 x ½ inches (19.1 x 12.7 x 1.3 cm)
Japanese handmade papers, acetate, doilies, original rubbings, Denril, Johannot, Clearprint, Quinel, and Suedel Luxe papers; side-stitch binding, pyrography, letterpress printed, photocopied

Artwork by M. Jordan Tierney
Short story by Amy Bloom
Photo by Derek Dudek

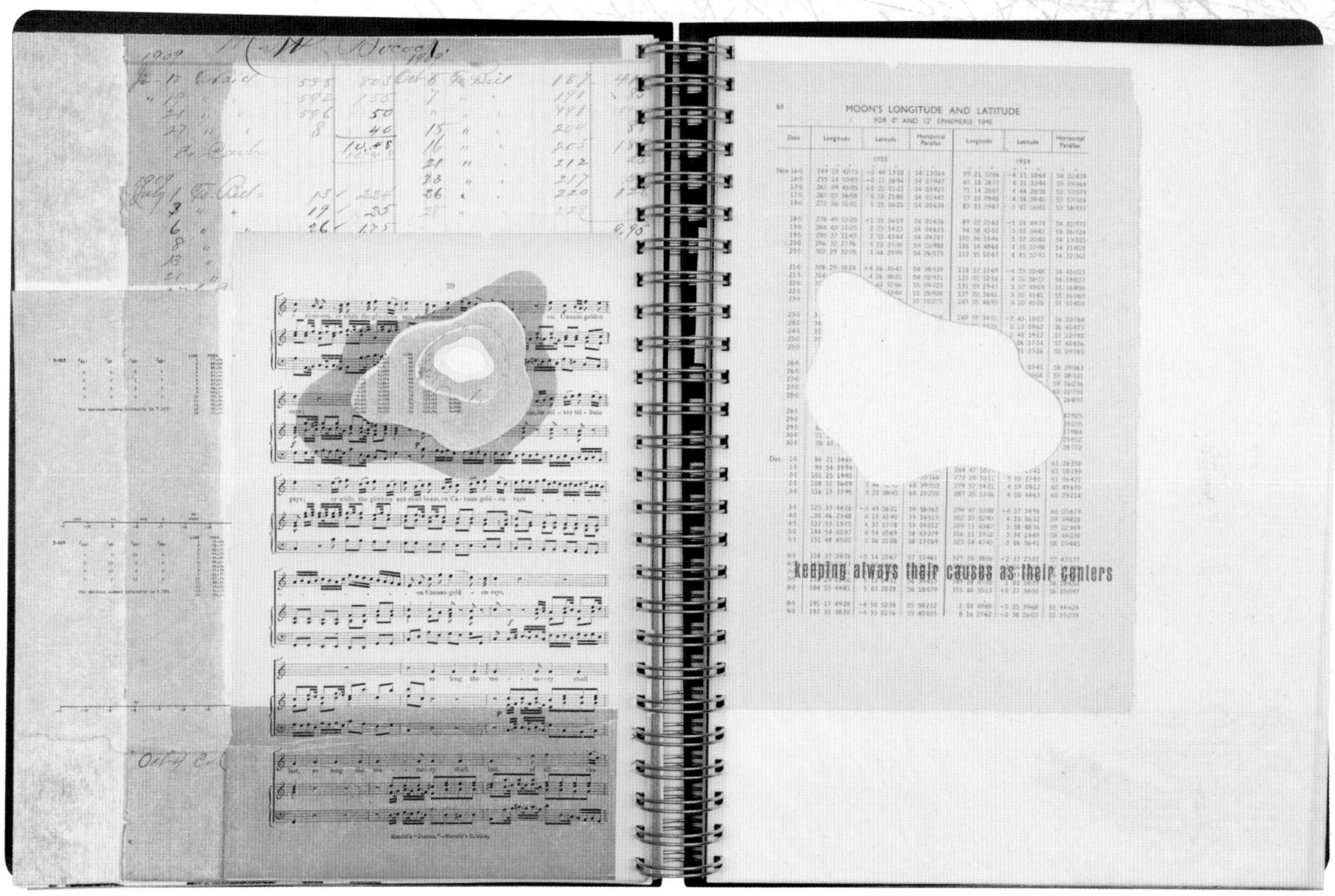

▲ **The Impetus Generated in Still Water (A Section of Periodic Tableau Field Report #1)** | 2007

Collaboration with M. Jordan Tierney
13 x 10 x ⅛ inches (33 x 25.4 x 0.3 cm)
Historic USGS maps, antique account-book pages, pages from various library discards; letterpress printed, paper cut-outs
Photo by artist

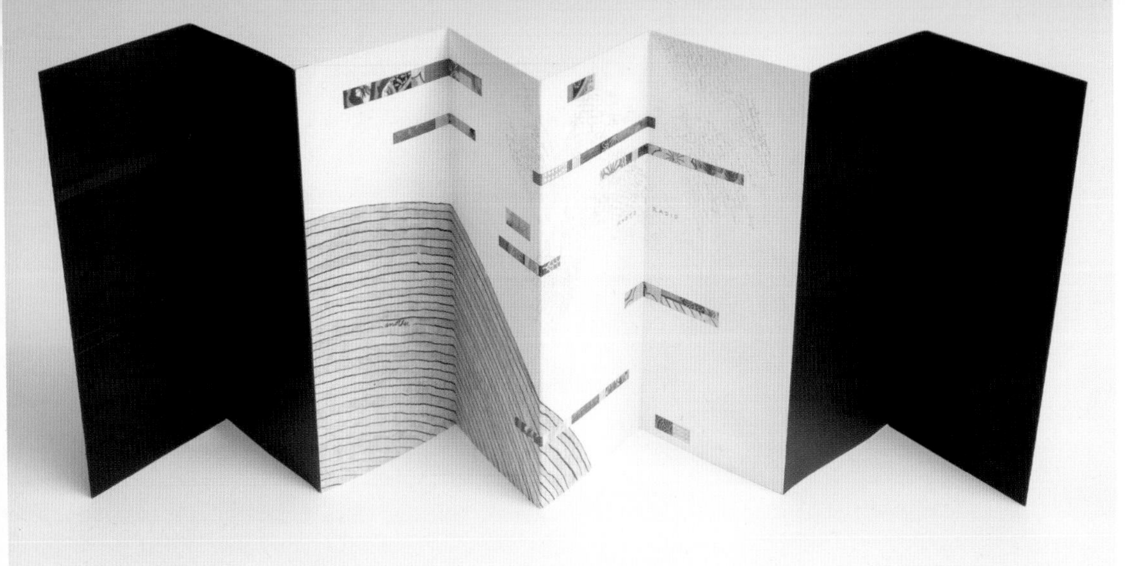

Kyoto Radio | 2004

Open: 20 feet (6.1 m) wide
Closed: 9¾ x 4½ x ¼ inches (24.8 x 11.4 x 0.6 cm)
Japanese handmade papers, fabric, Japanese children's book pages; drawing, painted, stained, collage

Photo by artist

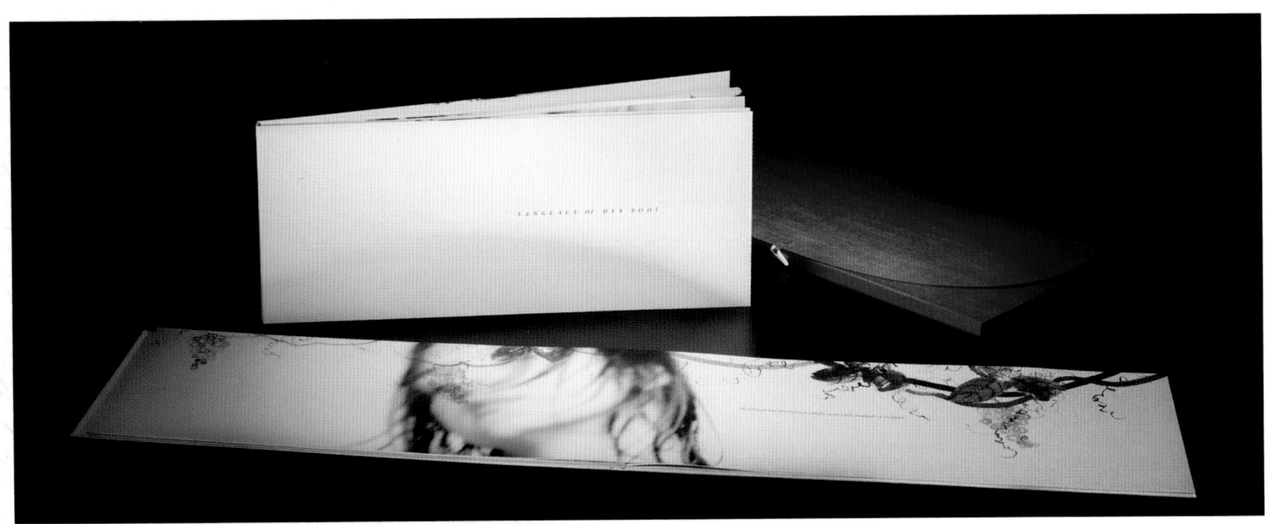

Language of Her Body | 2003

Collaboration with Claudia Cohen
8 x 18 x ½ inches (20.3 x 45.7 x 1.3 cm)
Tosa hanga paper, silk cloth, original sumi painting; ink-jet printed, letterpress printed, modified concertina binding housed in silk enclosure

Sumi-e by Keiji Shinohara
Photo by Derek Dudek and artist

" For the past few years, a major wellspring of inspiration for me has been the purposeful use of chance in creative work. "

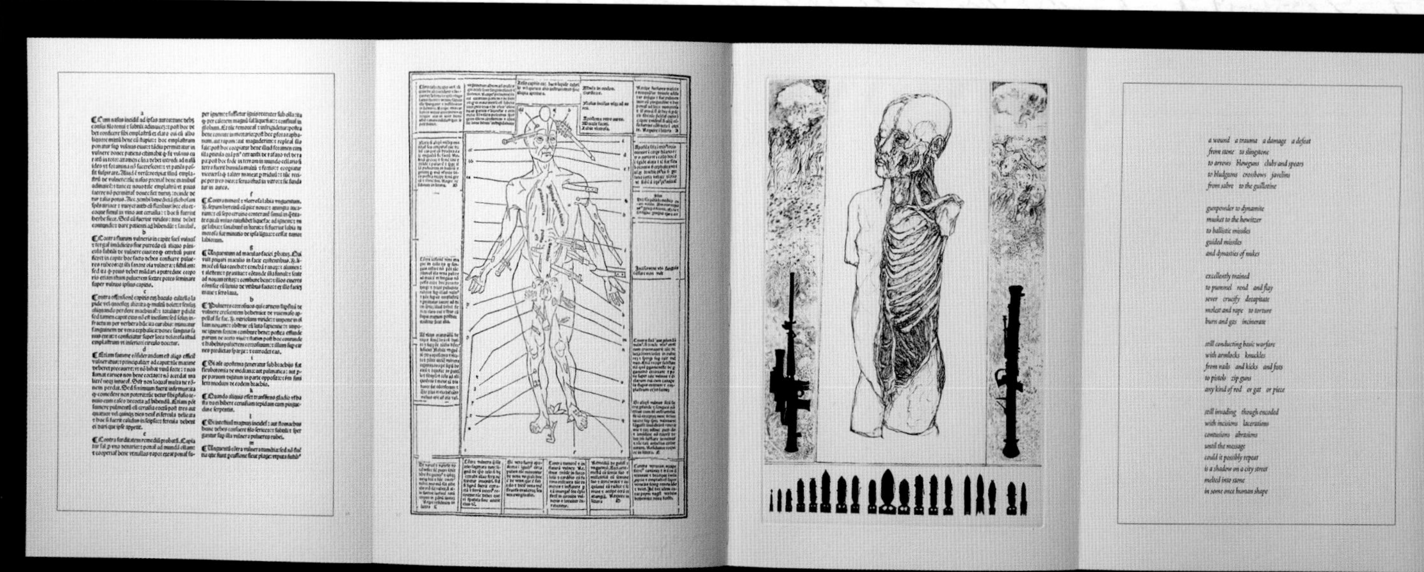

▲ **The Anatomy Lesson** | 2004

Open: 40 feet (12.2 m) wide
Closed: 14 x 10 x 1½ inches (35.6 x 25.4 x 3.8 cm)

Hologram, handmade paper, stainless-steel case; concertina binding, photogravure, letterpress printed, engraved

Contemporary artwork by Joyce Cutler Shaw and various authors
Binding co-designed with Daniel E. Kelm
Photo by Derek Dudek

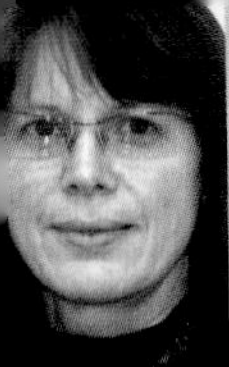

VASSDAL ELLIS

Elsi Vassdal Ellis

NARRATIVE STRUCTURES RICH WITH SYMBOLISM and politically charged content frequently fill the pages of Elsi Vassdal Ellis' remarkable books. Addressing topics that some readers may find disturbing—from war and genocide to economics and politics—Vassdal Ellis' work serves as a record of human behavior during important moments in history. Pointed, provocative, and poignant, her books challenge society's tendency to accept the status quo. The profundity of her message is amplified by her mastery of design and flawless technique, which add a disarming beauty and an intriguing duality to her work.

Vassdal Ellis uses the intimate book format to its fullest, creating eclectic works that display her skills with binding and typography. Sensuality of form, control of sequencing, and a gift for storytelling all come together in her compelling work. Vassdal Ellis lives in Bellingham, Washington. Her books are owned by numerous institutions, including the National Museum of Women in the Arts in Washington, D.C., and the New York Public Library in New York City.

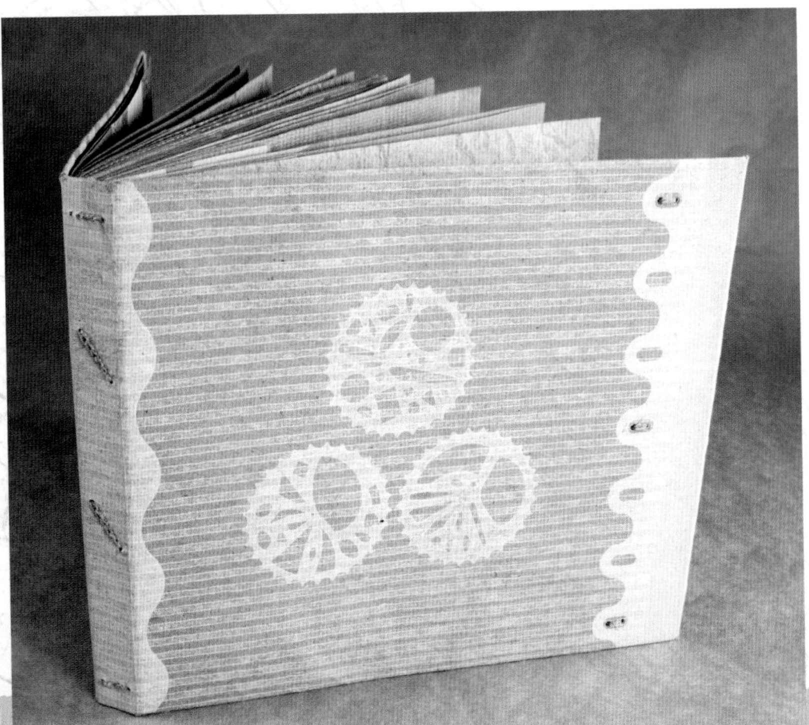

◀ **Fusion Frottage (One)** | 2008

8⅛ x 10½ x 1¼ inches (20.6 x 26.7 x 3.2 cm)
Soy black and opaque white printing inks, Aquabee Bogus drawing paper, hemp thread, recycled make-ready; German medieval linking-stitch binding, found objects mounted type, letterpress printed, handset
Photo by artist

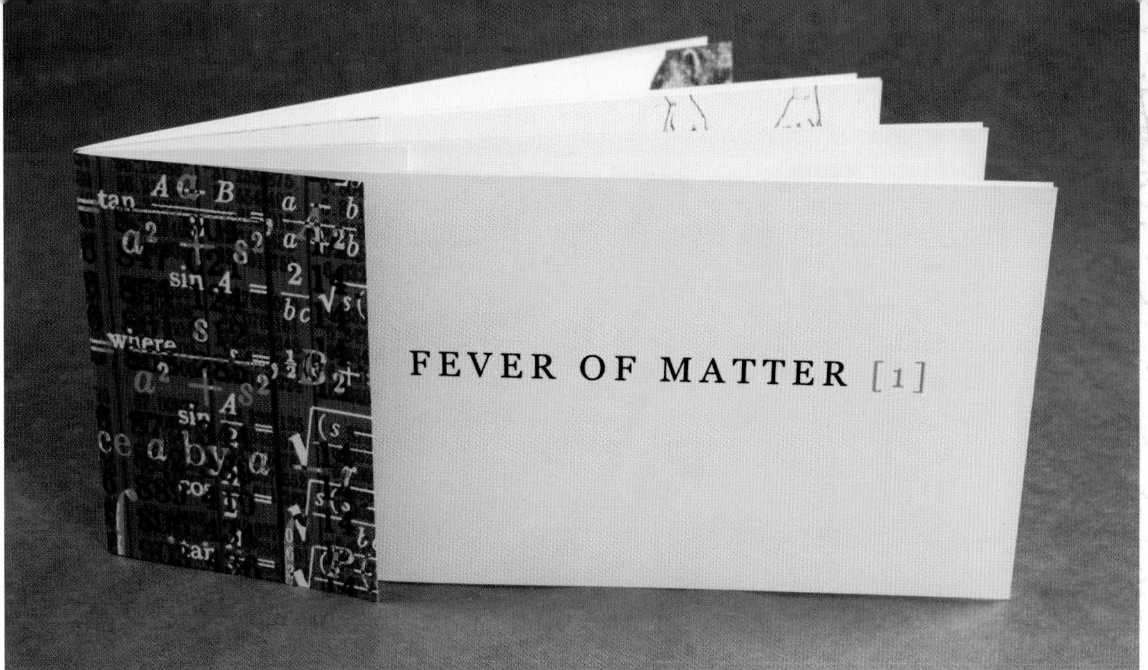

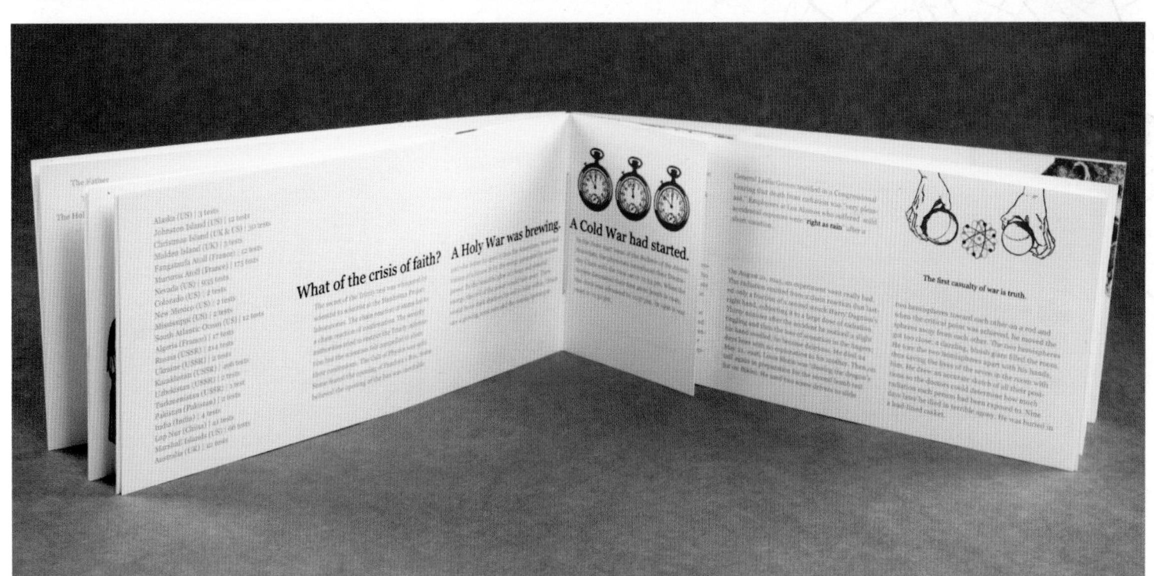

▲ **Fever of Matter [1]** | 2008

4 x 9 x ¼ inches (10.2 x 22.9 x 0.6 cm)

Mohawk Superfine text with eggshell finish, linen thread; Ethiopian sewing, inkjet printed

Photos by artist

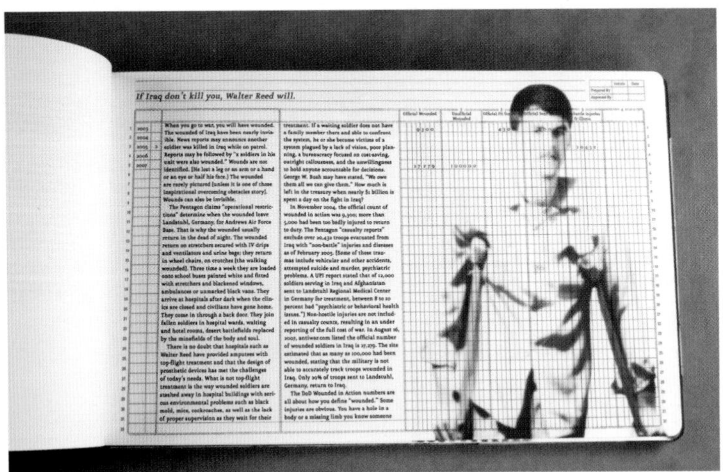

"Sometimes I feel I'd be better off not focusing on war and genocide in my work, but I tell myself that someone must stand as a witness. My books are my street corner, my soapbox."

▲ **Iraq War Ledger** | 2007

8¼ x 14 x ¾ inches (21 x 35.6 x 1.9 cm)
Book cloth, binder's board, brass-plated card frame and screw posts, amate, Mohawk Superfine text with eggshell finish; album binding, rounded corners, inkjet printed

Photo by artist

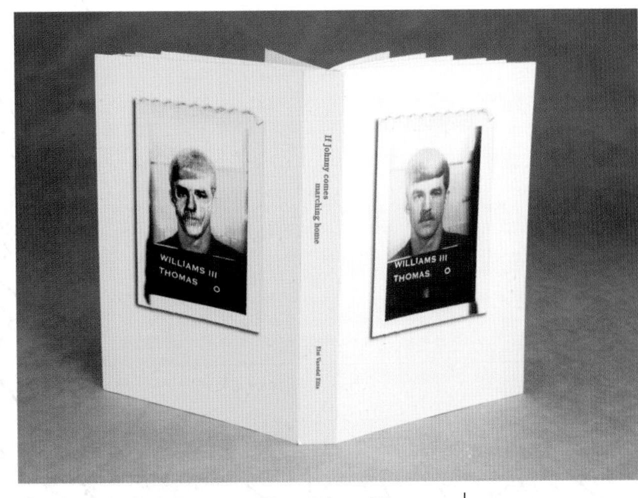

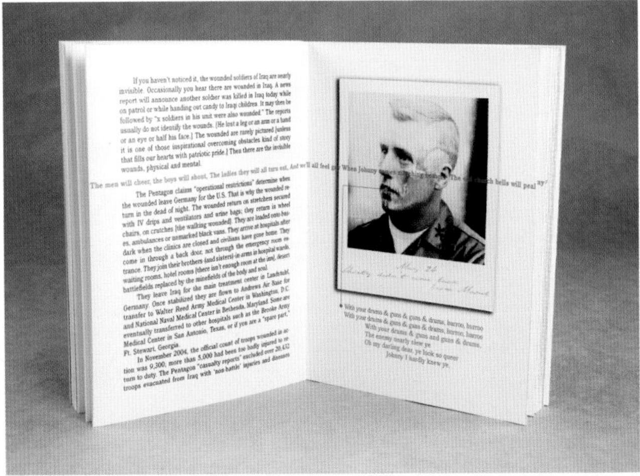

▲ **If Johnny Comes Marching Home** | 2006

7 x 5 x 1 inches (17.8 x 12.7 x 2.5 cm)
Cougar Opaque cover, Filare linen red text; circle accordion binding with red tabs, inkjet printed

Photos by artist

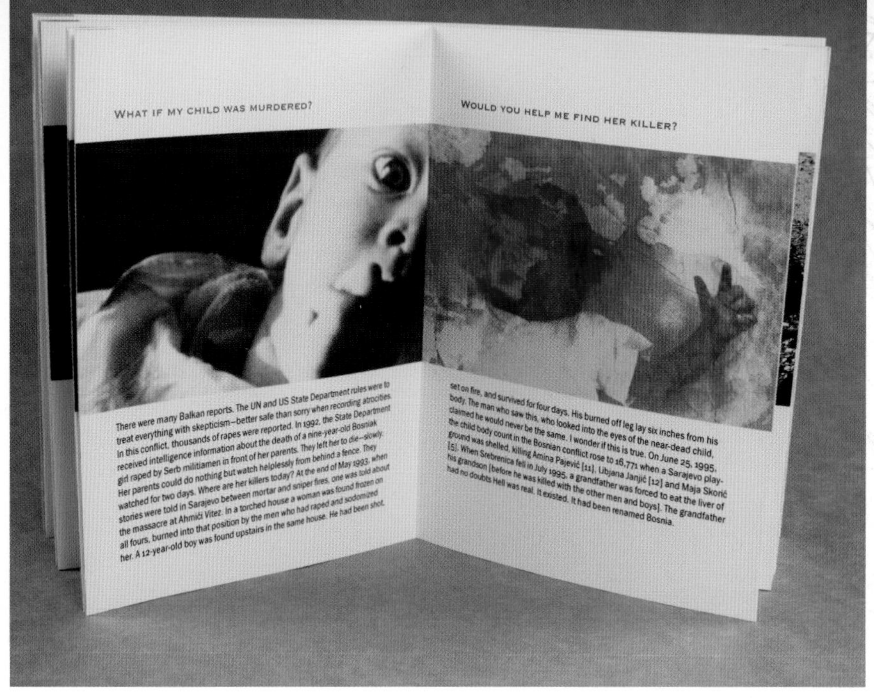

◀ **What if It happened Here?** | 2006

7 x 5 x 1 inches (17.8 x 12.7 x 2.5 cm)
Cougar Opaque cover, Filare linen red text;
circle accordion binding with red tabs,
inkjet printed

Photo by artist

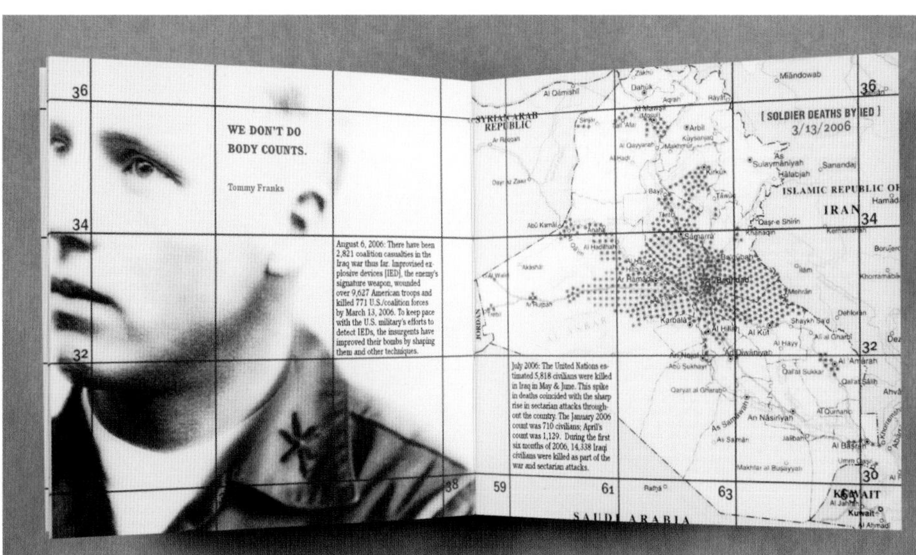

◀ **This Land** | 2006

5½ x 5⅝ x ½ inches (14 x 14.3 x 1.3 cm)
Recycled Icarus press sheets, Cougar
Opaque Natural text, linen thread;
Coptic sewn flat back case binding,
inkjet printed

Photo by artist

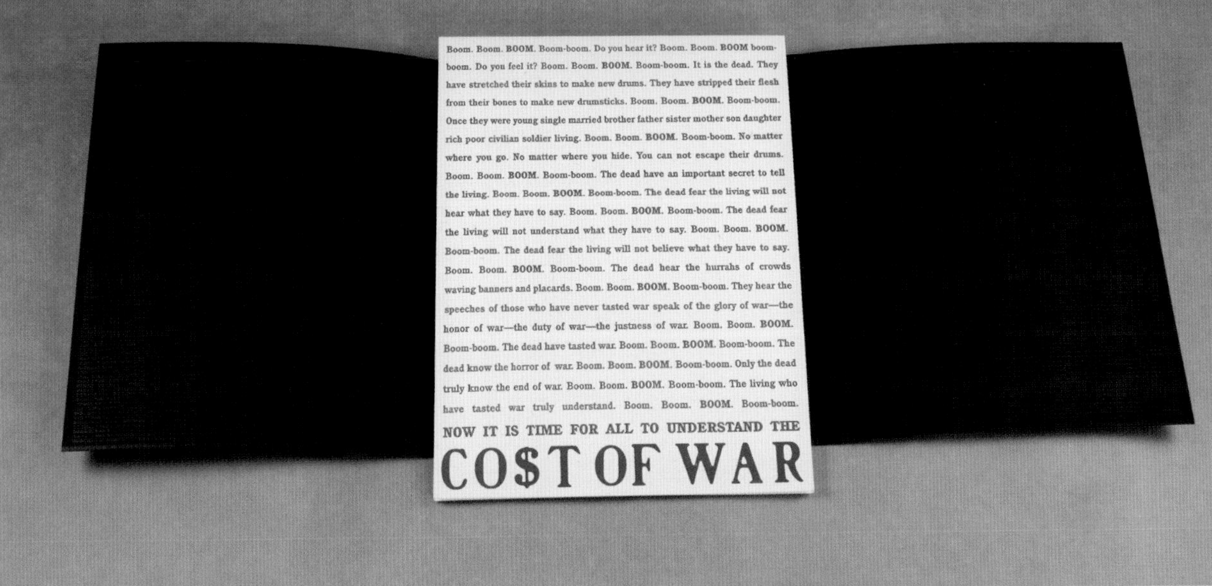

▲ **Cost of War** | 2005

Closed: 12 x 9 x ⅛ inches (30.5 x 22.9 x 0.3 cm)
Royal Complements black cover, Cougar Opaque white cover, soy metallic black, red, and blue inks; letter-fold wrap, top single-fold broadside, wood type, photopolymer plate type and art

Photos by artist

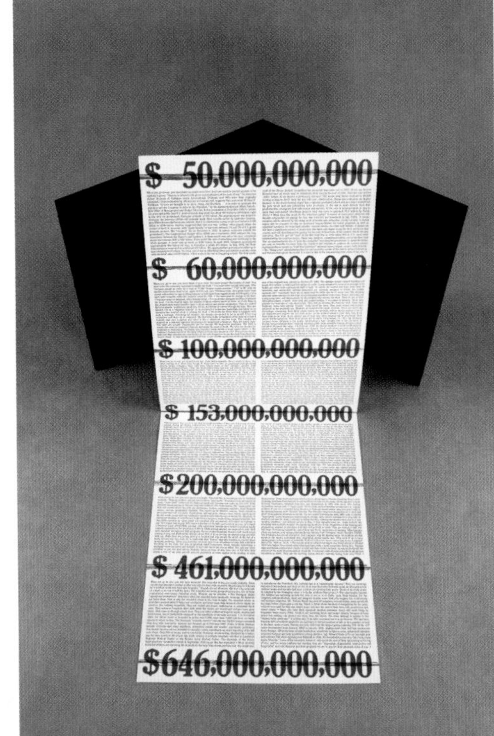

" Some of my books are the products of a challenge I give myself: Take a box of newspaper and magazine clippings, lists, notes, and photographs and work them all into a new book in 24 hours or one week. "

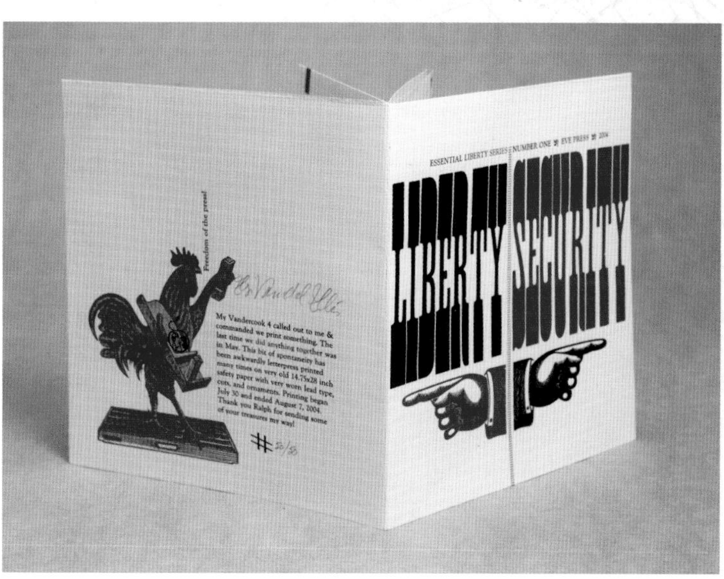

◀ LIBERTY | SECURITY | 2004

7 x 6¾ x 1⁄16 inches (17.8 x 17.1 x 0.2 cm)
Antique check paper, stickers, soy printing inks; accordion French fold with slit, wood, and lead type, wood ornaments, copper and magnesium cuts, brass borders

Photos by artist

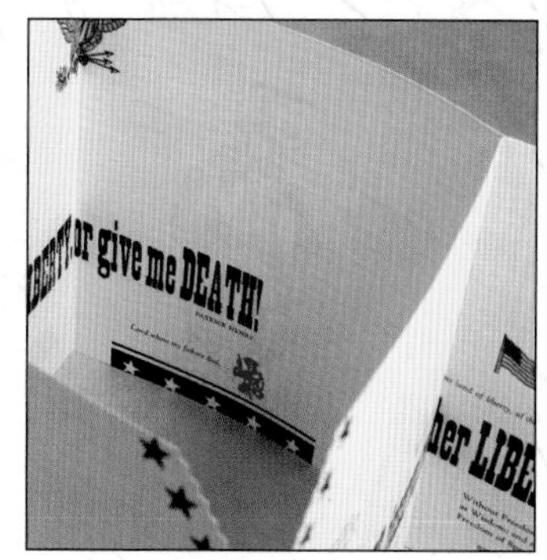

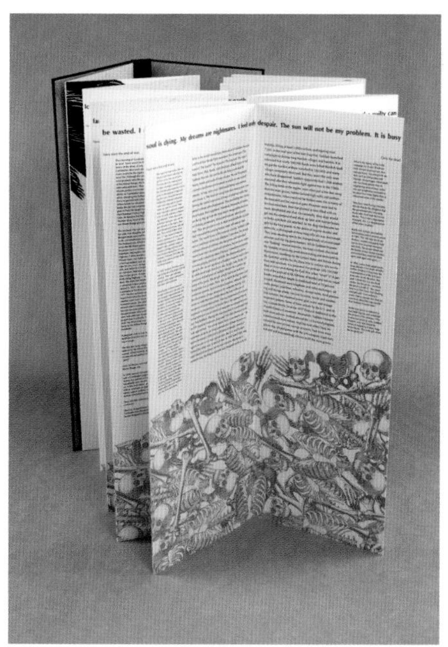

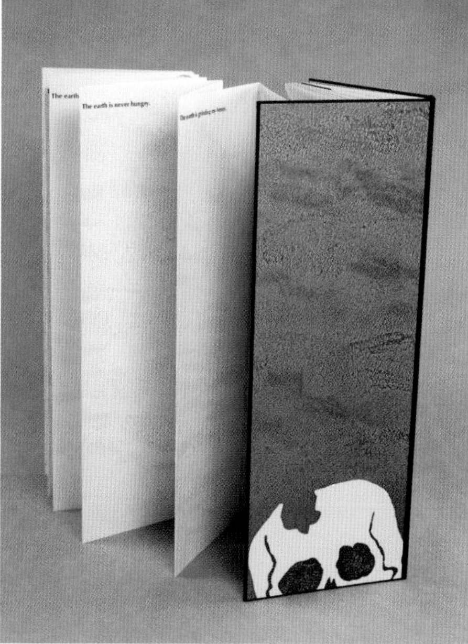

◀ Icarus | 2003

15⅝ x 5¾ x ¾ inches
(39.7 x 14.6 x 1.9 cm)
Book cloth, binder's board, Cougar Opaque cover, soy printing inks; hard case binding, accordion textblock, photopolymer, handset type, linoleum cuts, sandragraphs

Photos by artist

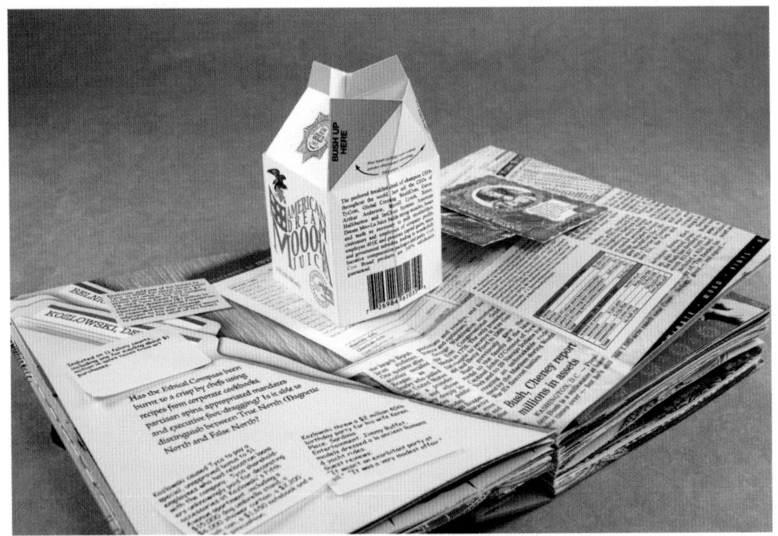

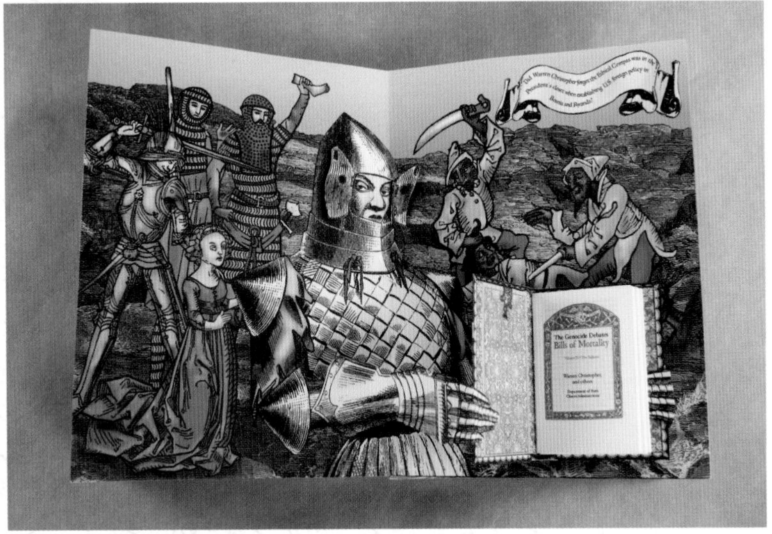

" When I began making books I saw the process as a continuation of the temptation Eve faced in the Garden of Eden. Eve's apple was inviting; it imparted knowledge, and it was forbidden. I want my books to be today's apple. "

◀ **The Quest for the Ethical Compass** | 2004

2⅝ x 2⅛ x 1 inches (6.7 x 5.4 x 2.5 cm)
Book cloth, binder's board, compass, brass-plated fleur-de-lis, Cougar Opaque text and cover; inkjet printed, hand cut pop-ups

Photos by artist

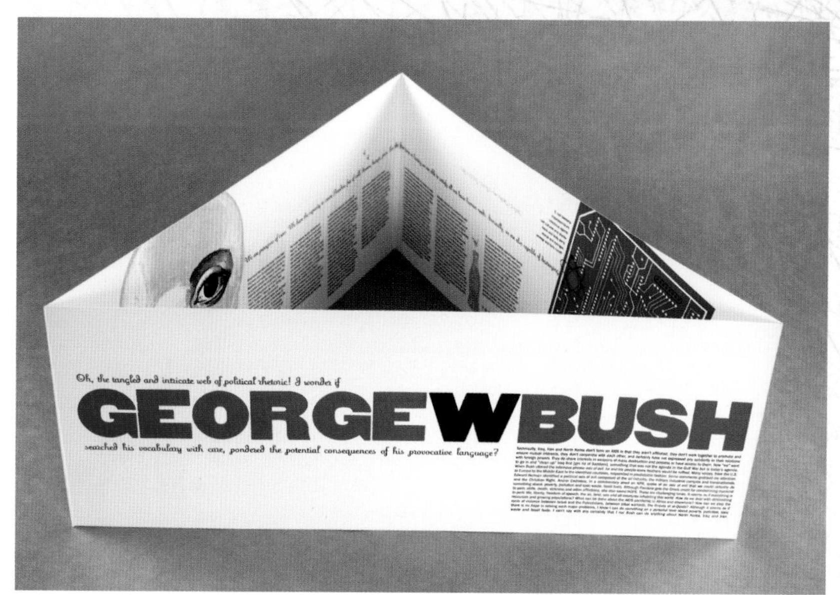

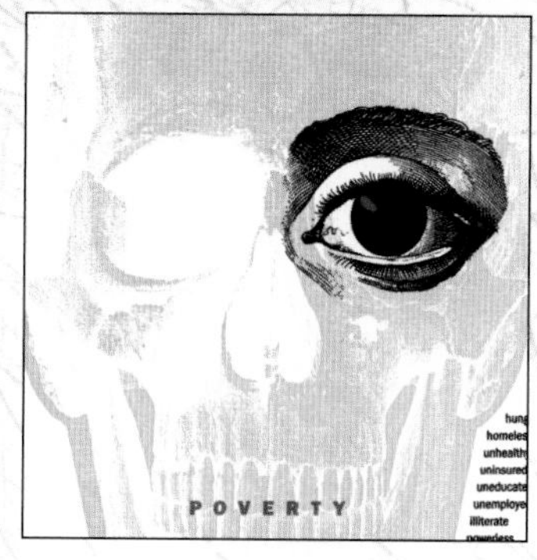

◀ **Axis of Evil** | 2002

Closed: 6 x 16 x ⅛ inches (15.2 x 40.6 x 0.3 cm)
Nekoosa Solutions cover, soy printing inks; attached panels, letterpress printed with photopolymer plates, handset type, antique cuts

Photos by artist

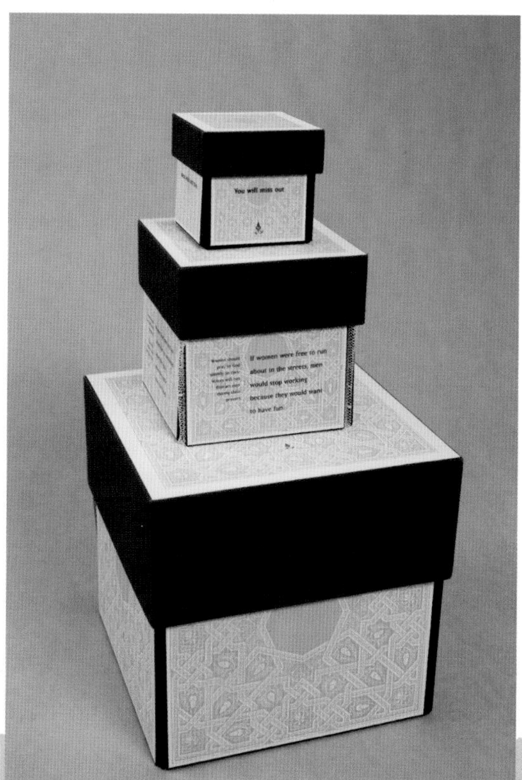

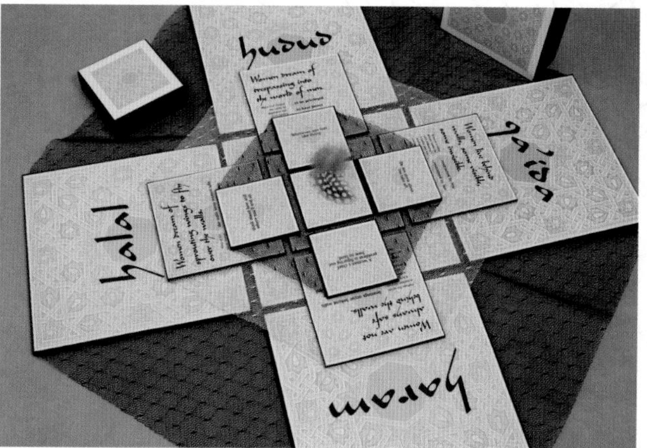

◀ **Women Dream** | 2001

6 x 6½ x 6½ inches (15.2 x 16.5 x 16.5 cm)
Nekoosa Solutions cover, soy printing inks, cream and black netting, black book cloth, feather; nested collapsible boxed with lids, photopolymer plates, letterpress

Photos by artist

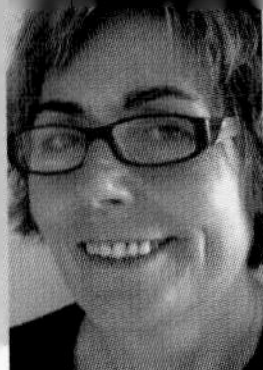

CORON

Béatrice Coron

WORKING FROM A POINT OF VIEW THAT'S AT ONCE detailed and monumental, Béatrice Coron creates mesmerizing artist's books filled with what she calls cut stories. With total control of her knife, Coron cuts away negative spaces, balancing content and form to create multiple, independent worlds within a single plane of paper. Coron is inspired by words and books and how they shape our perceptions of the world. She uses her medium as a mise-en-scène for complex narrative ideas.

Whether featured within the traditional book format or installed vertically in a gallery, Coron's intricately rendered silhouettes invite viewers to take a close look. Despite the meticulous planning required for these remarkable scenes, they retain a sense of spontaneity and feature an animated liveliness. Coron's acclaimed work is held in major collections worldwide, including the Metropolitan Museum of Art in New York City and the Walker Art Center in Minneapolis, Minnesota. Her public art installations can be seen on subways, in airports, and in sports facilities across the United States.

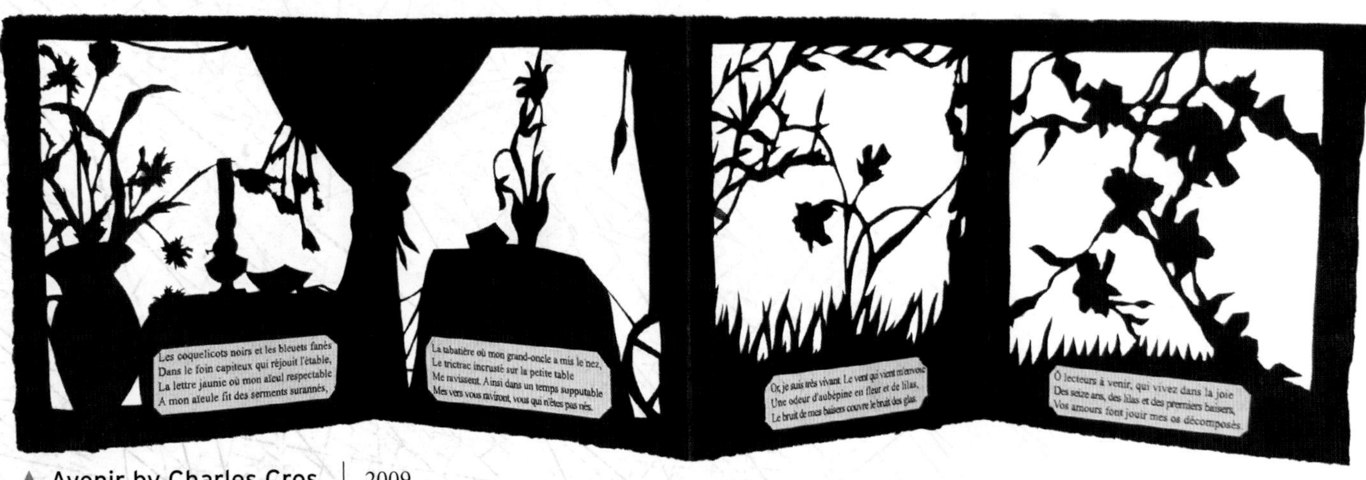

▲ **Avenir by Charles Cros** | 2009

6 x 22 inches (15.2 x 55.9 cm)
Handmade paper; cut, inkjet printed
Photo by artist

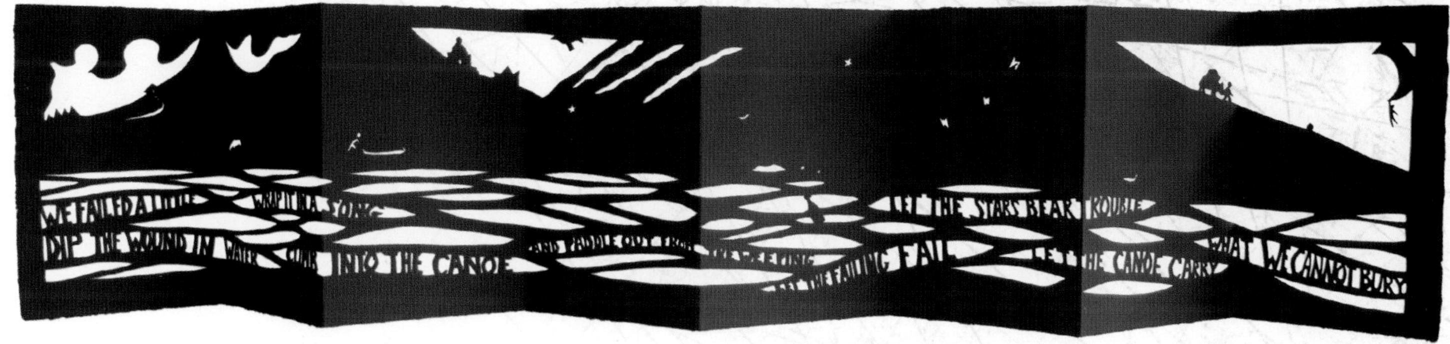

▲ **Evening Song by Joy Harjo** | 2009

7½ x 44 inches (19.1 x 111.8 cm)

Arches paper; cut

Photo by artist

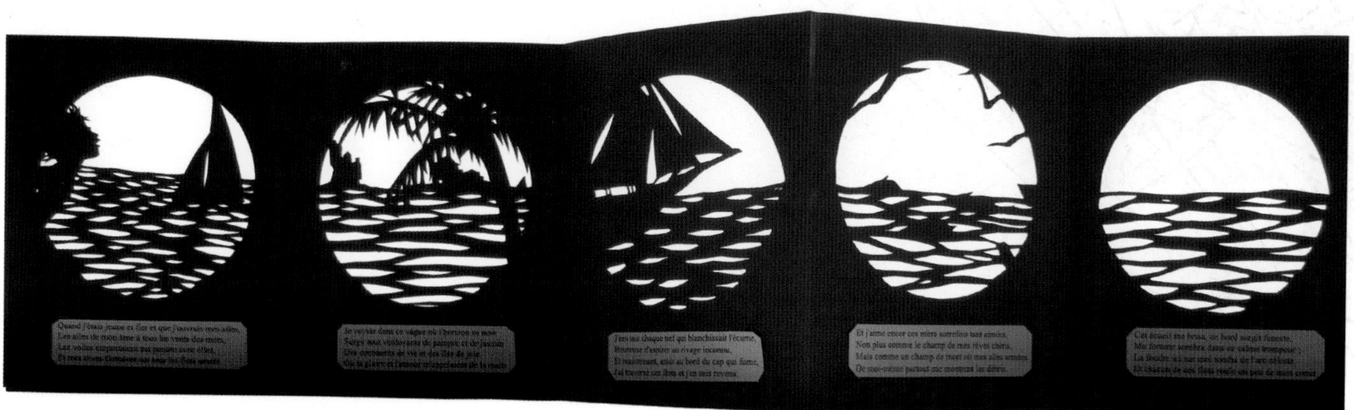

▲ **Les Voiles by Alphonse de Lamartine** | 2009

6 x 27 inches (15.2 x 68.6 cm)

Arches paper; cut, inkjet printed

Photo by artist

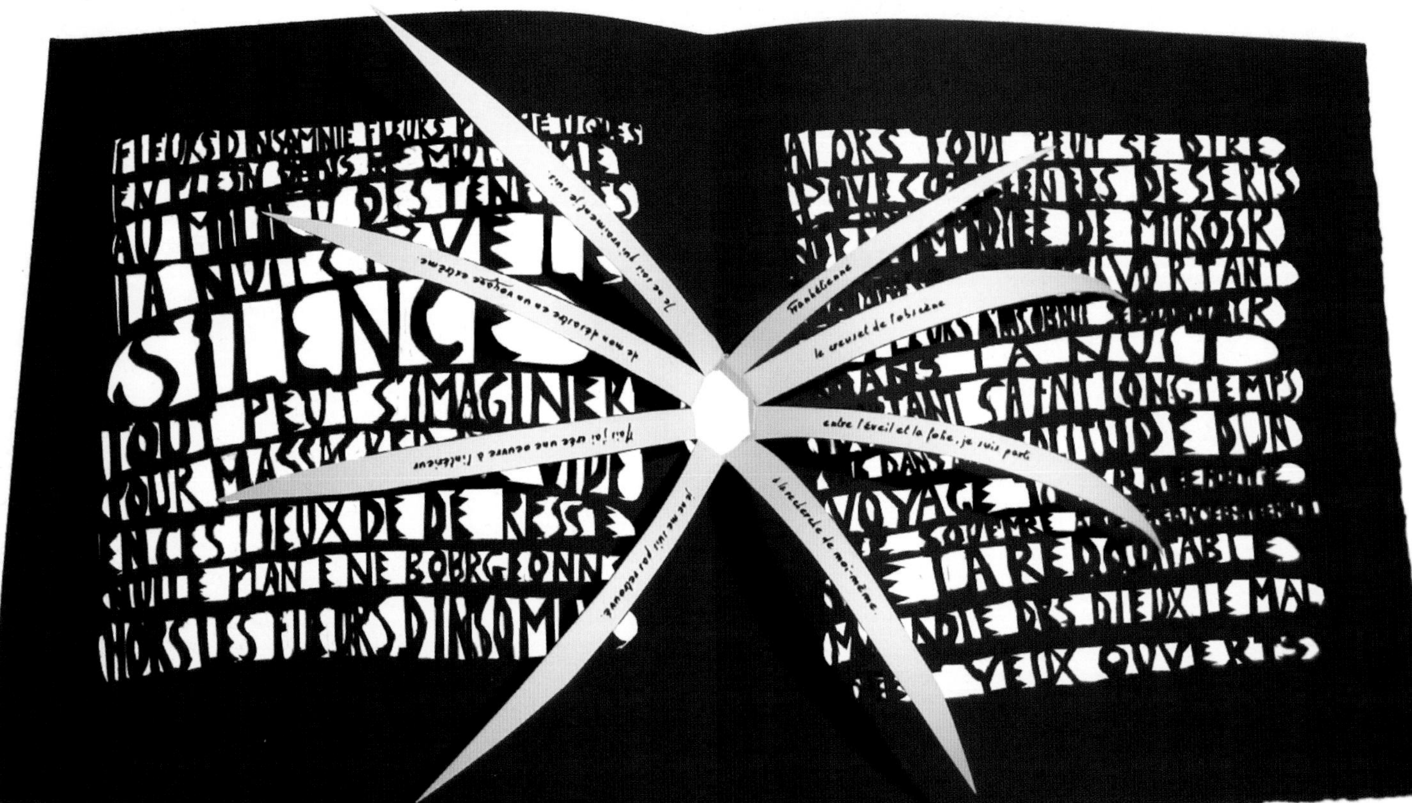

▲ Fleurs d'Insomnie by Frankétienne | 2005

12 x 22 inches (30.5 x 55.9 cm)

Arches paper; cut

Photo by artist

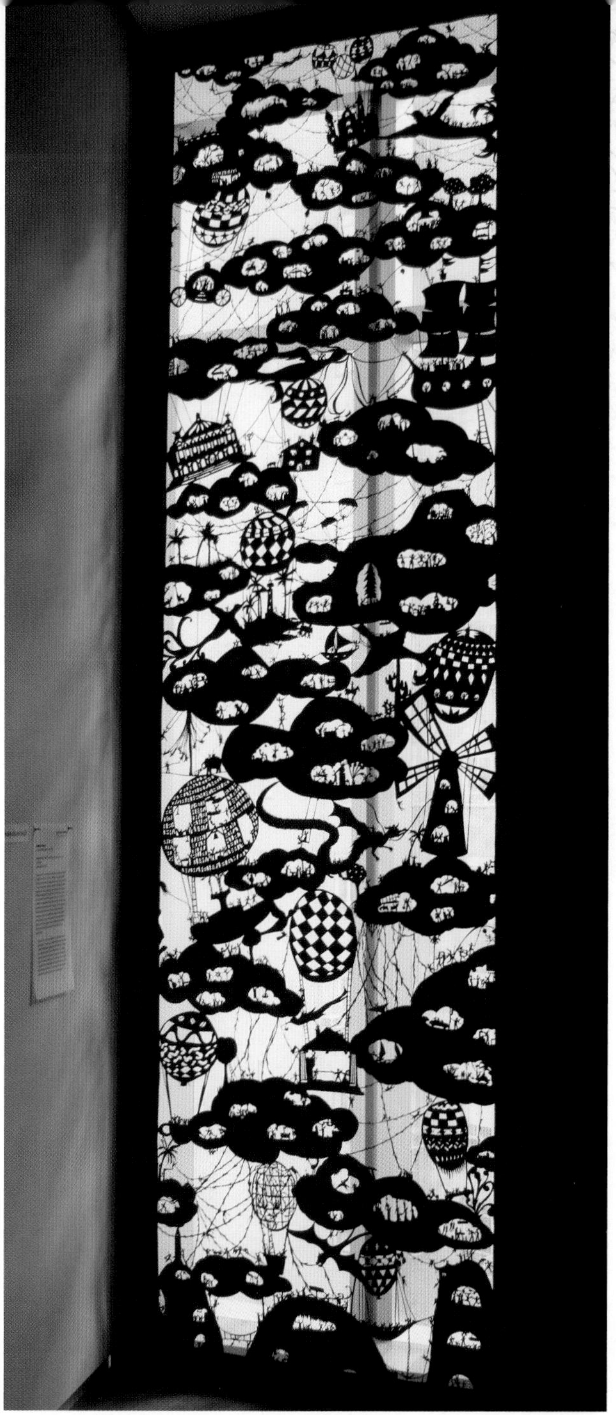

" My silhouettes are a language I've developed over the years. I cut them from a single piece of material, yet they result in a profusion of individual stories. "

◀ **Hells and Heavens** | 2009
13 x 3¼ feet (3.9 x 1.1 m)
Tyvek; cut
Photos by artist

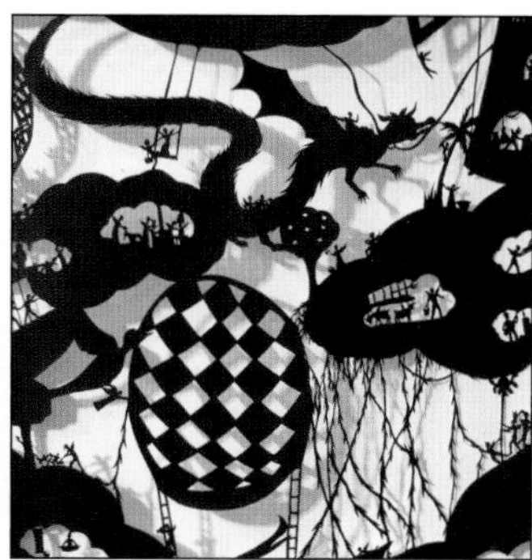

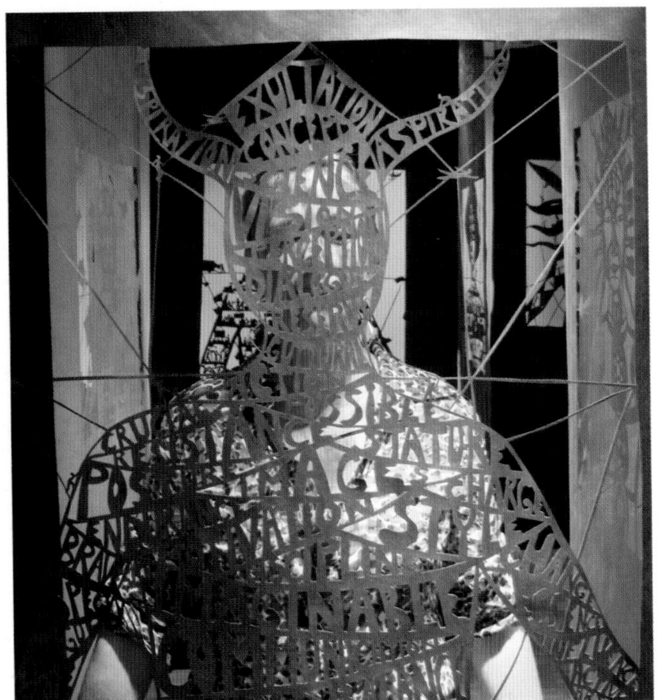

" Using metaphorical, poetic, or fantastic accumulations of images, I invite the viewer to daydream and imagine different layers of realities. "

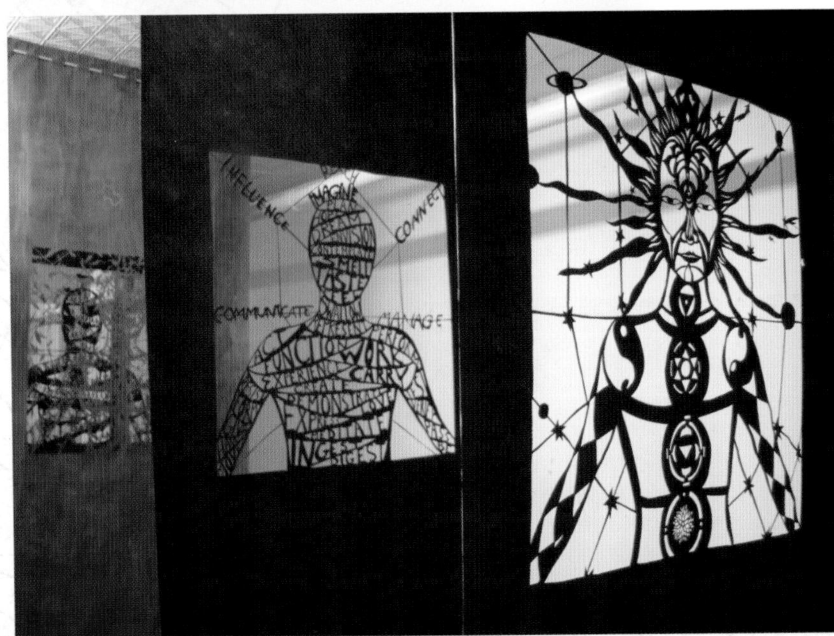

◀ **Identities** | 2009

Each page: 8 x 3¼ feet (2.4 x 1.1 m)
Tyvek; cut
Photos by artist

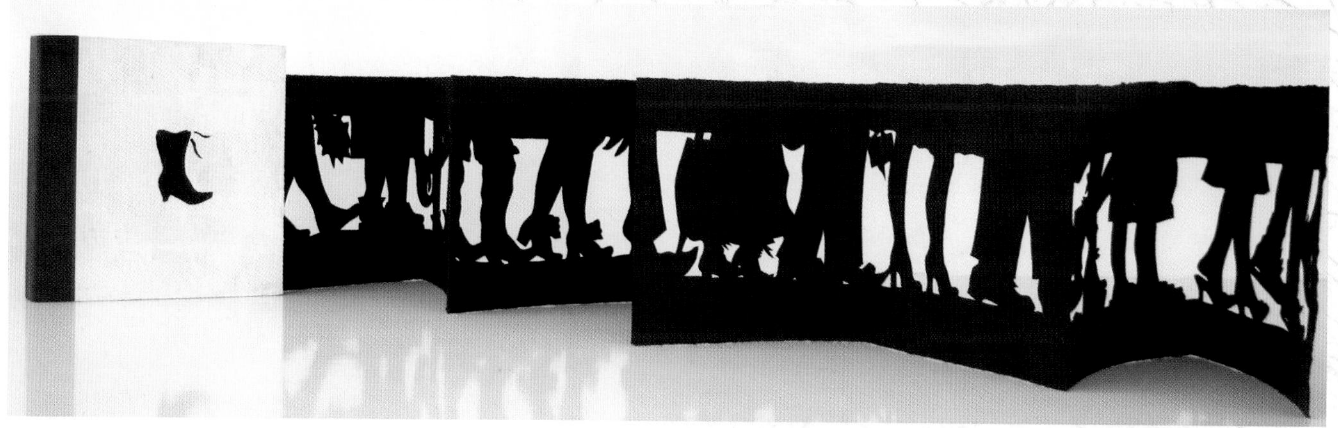

▲ **All Walks of Life** | 2008

6 x 44 inches (15.2 x 111.8 cm)
Arches paper; cut
Photo by artist

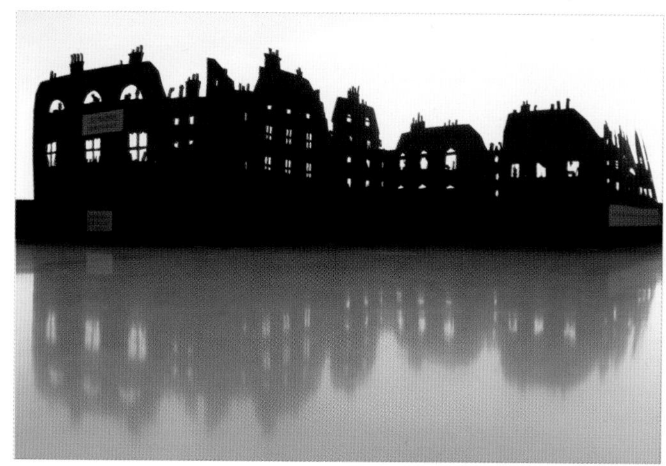

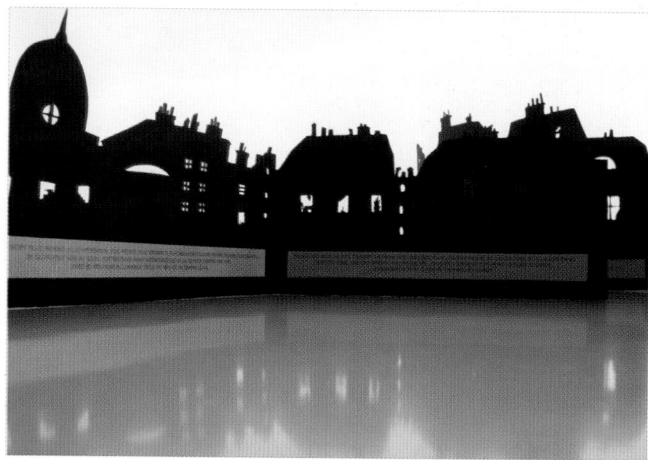

▲ **Une Femme à sa Lenêtre by Charles Baudelaire** | 2007

8 x 50 inches (20.3 x 127 cm)
Arches paper; cut, inkjet printed
Photos by artist

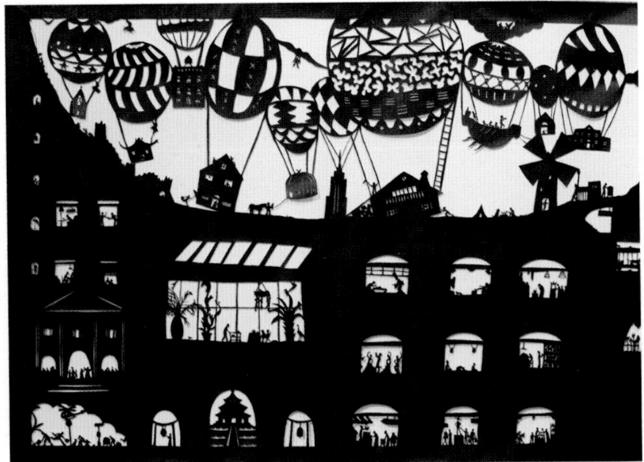

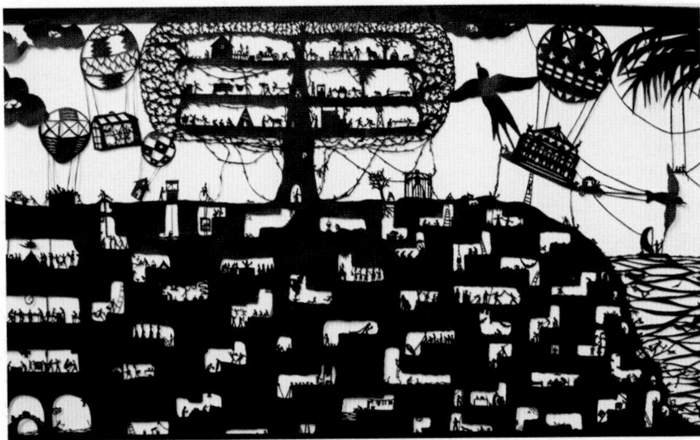

"Reminiscent of film noir and voyeurism, shadows leave room for multiple interpretations. Silhouettes can be read in numerous ways."

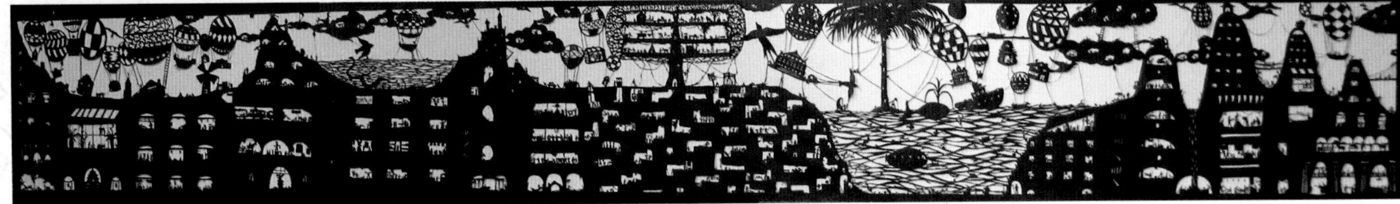

▲ **The Whole Nine Yards Series: Habitats and Vagabonds** | 2007

3¼ x 27 feet (1.1 x 8.23 m)
Tyvek; cut
Photos by Antoine Tempé

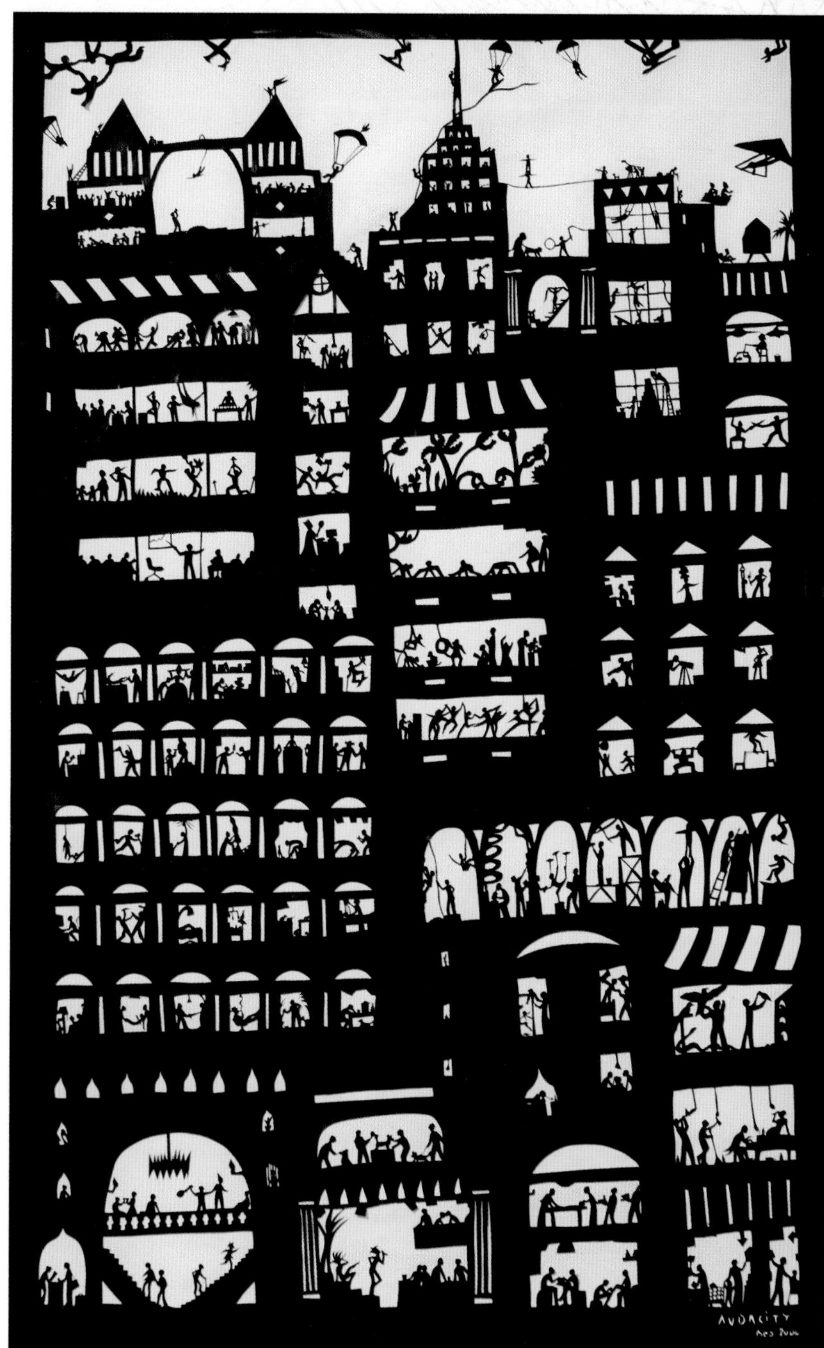

◀ **Auda City** | 2004

7 x 4½ feet (2 x 1.3 cm)

Tyvek; cut, painted

Photo by Antoine Tempé

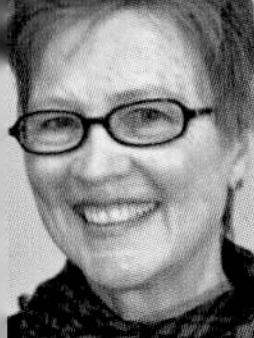

Pati Scobey

FLUID NARRATIVES COMPOSED OF DYNAMIC IMAGERY swirl across the pages of Pati Scobey's books. Using positive and negative shapes, intersections, and overlaps to develop complex layered images, she infuses her work with wonderful energy. Scobey's printing process involves combining plates that depict narratives and patterns with stencils of shapes and characters. By manipulating these elements, she instills her books with a sense of movement and geography.

Through the thoughtful sequencing of imagery, Scobey establishes momentum in her work, letting levels of information open up to other levels and allowing for an understory to come through in each book. Her attention to design is reflected in her selection of book structures—forms that beautifully reinforce her creative content. Scobey lives in Concord, Michigan. Her books are owned by the Getty Center in Los Angeles, California, and the British Library in London, England, among other institutions.

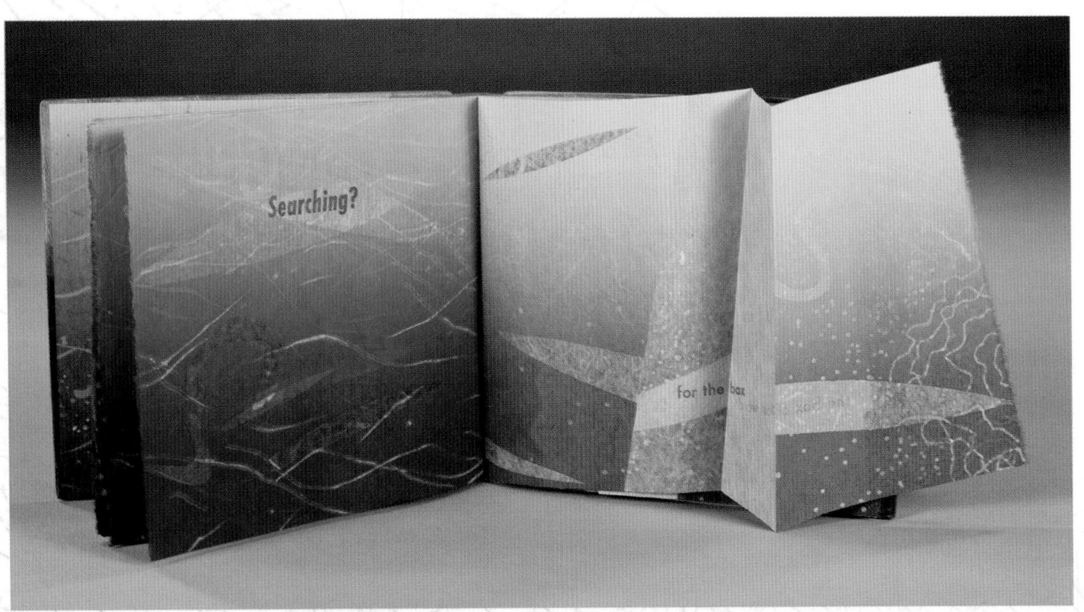

◀ **Morning** | 2008

Open: 4¼ x 11 inches (10.8 x 27.9 cm)
Gambi paper, book cloth, board, acrylic paint; relief printed, letterpress pamphlet binding

Photo by J. Wayne Jones

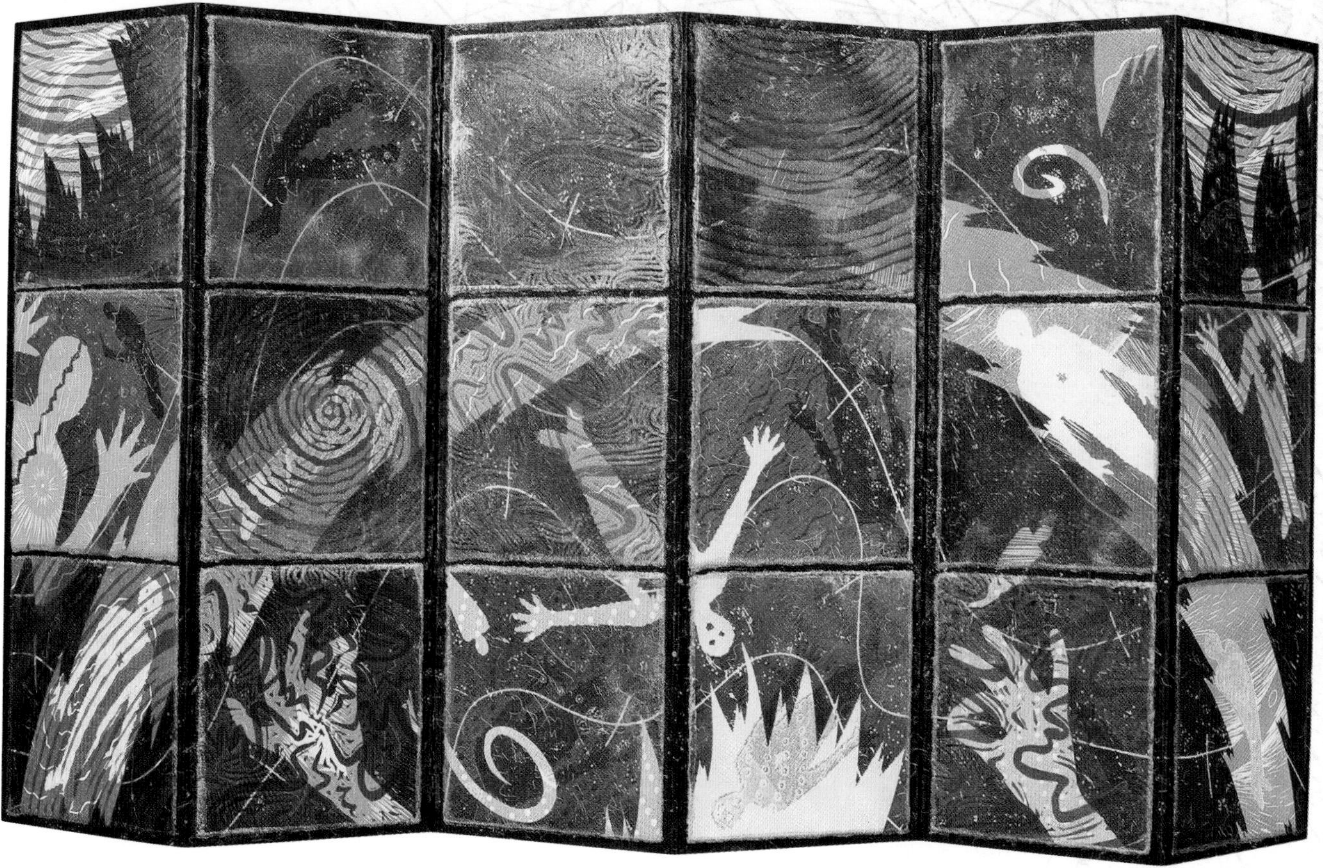

▲ **Broken Time** | 1997

Open: 9½ x 18 inches (24.1 x 45.7 cm)
Rives BFK paper, Tyvek, board, acrylic paint, watercolor; relief etched, linocut with stencils, accordion with wrapper, letterpress printed

Photo by J. Wayne Jones

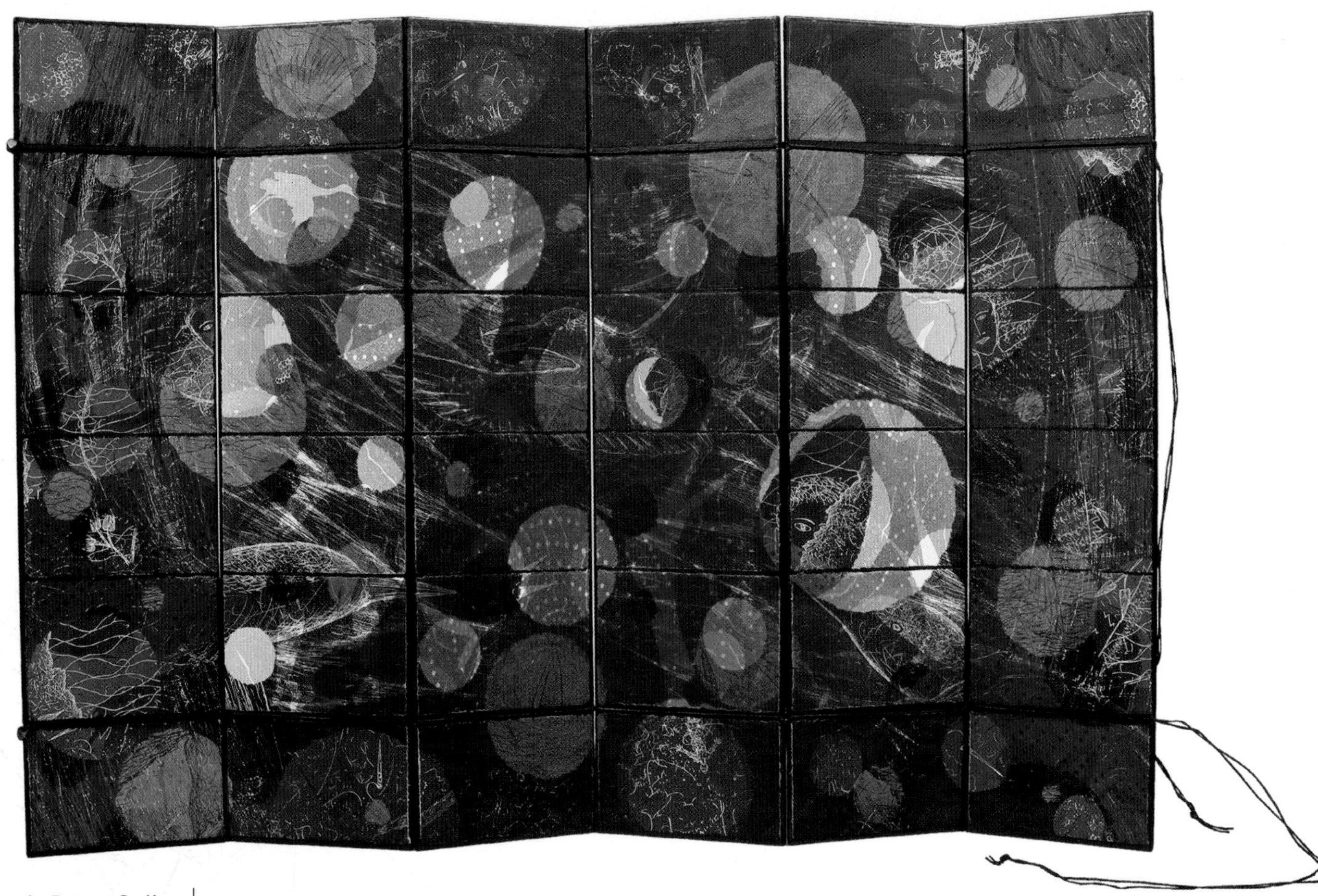

▲ **Deep Calls** | 2006

Open: 12½ x 18 inches (31.8 x 45.7 cm)
Lana Royal paper, binder's board, embossed Rives Lightweight paper, acrylic paint; relief etched, linocut with stencils, slip book binding

Photo by J. Wayne Jones

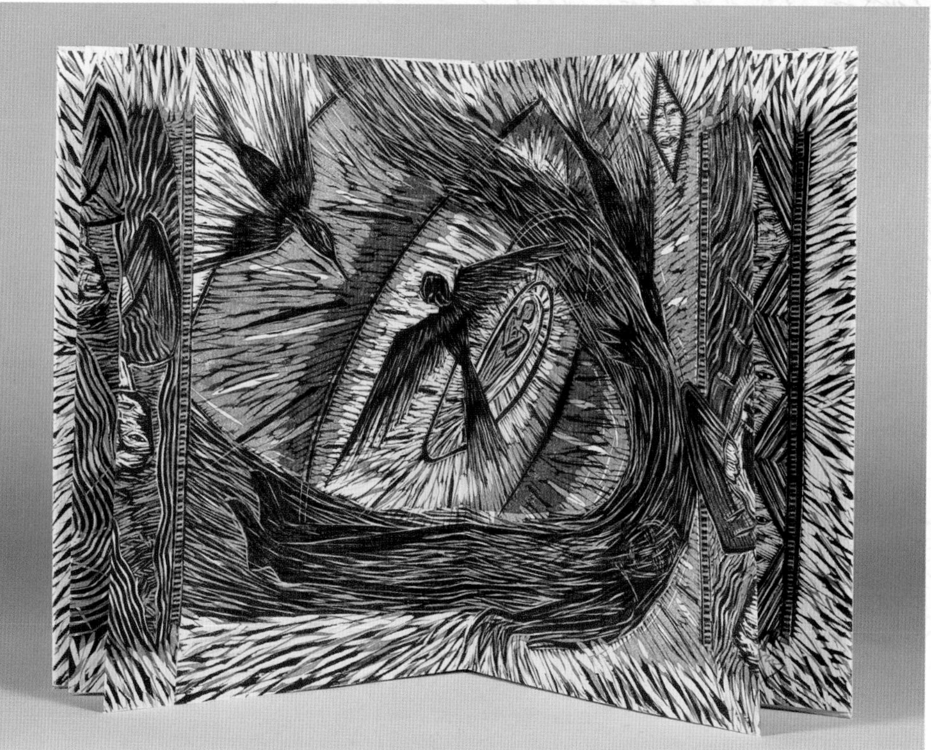

" The book is the perfect medium for me. It allows me to investigate the interaction of concept, structure, image, and sequence. "

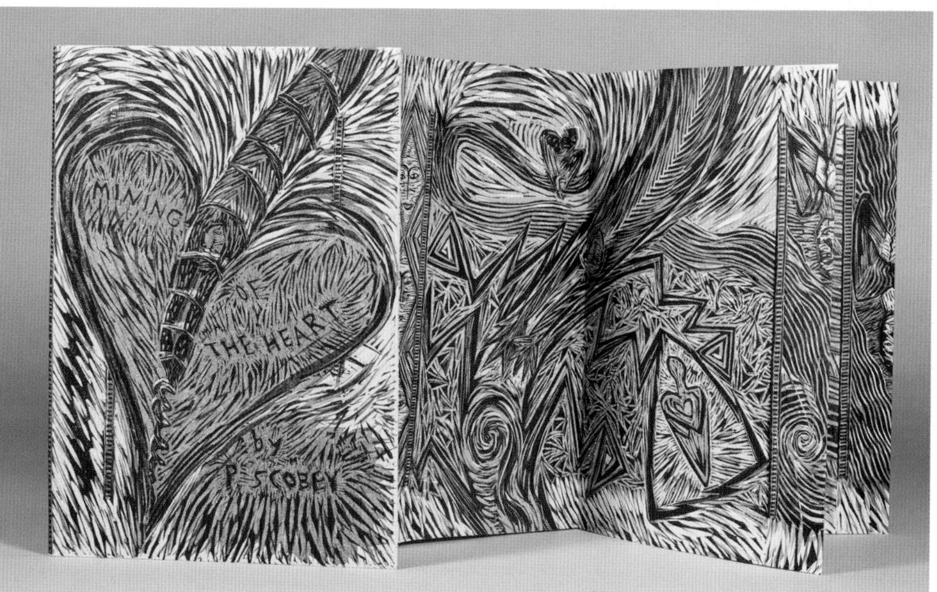

◀ **Mining of the Heart** | 1988

Open: 10 x 14 inches (25.4 x 35.6 cm)
Twinrocker handmade paper; woodcut, linocut, accordion binding

Photos by J. Wayne Jones

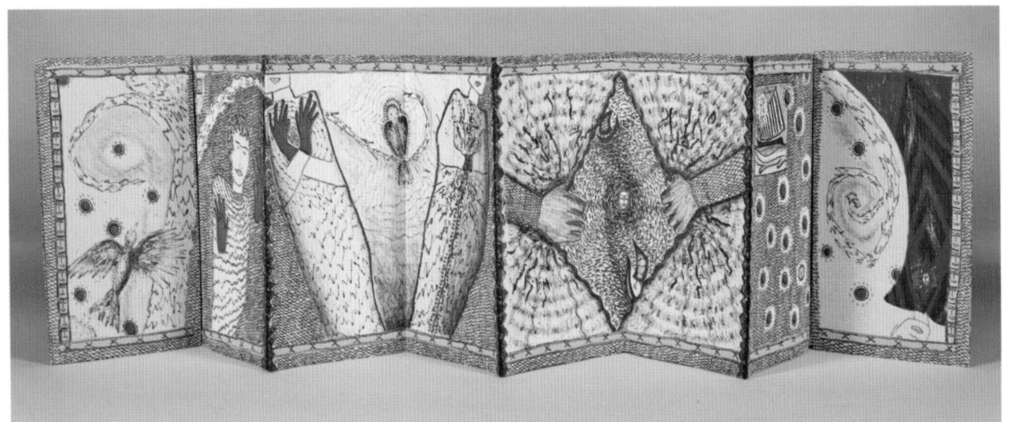

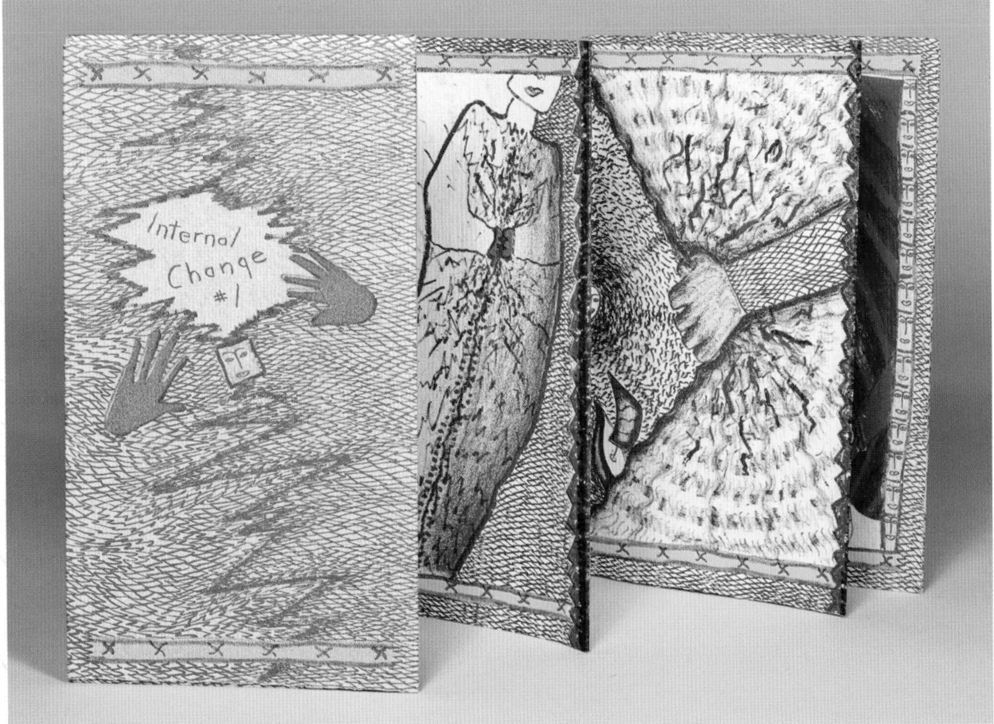

▲ **Internal Change #1** | 1988

Open: 7 x 24 inches (17.8 x 61 cm)
Handmade paper; lithography, accordion binding
Photos by J. Wayne Jones

" To examine a book, the viewer must hold, touch, and look at it closely. This is a private, intimate experience. The opportunity to communicate with viewers in this way is what compels me to make books. "

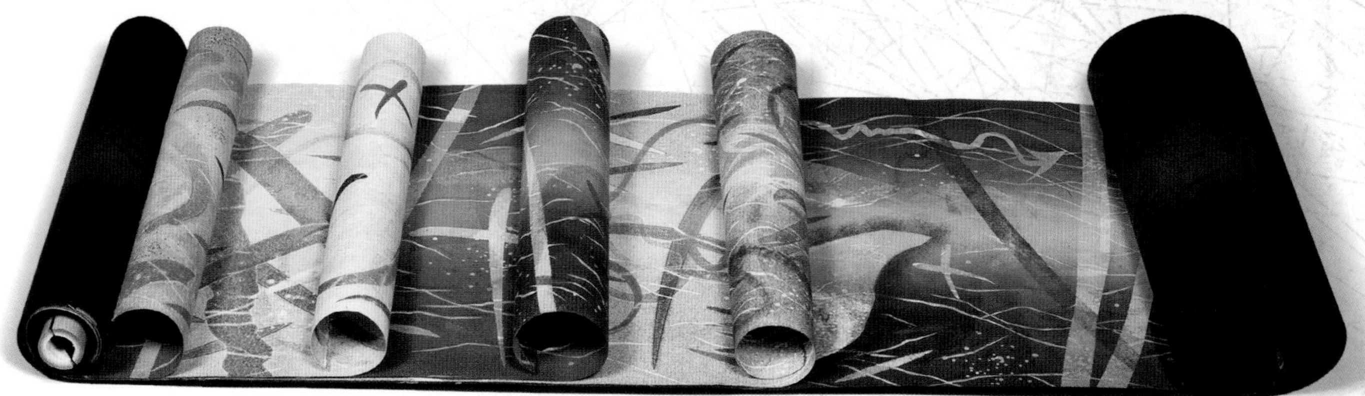

▲ **Evening Susurrus** | 2005

6 x 24 x 2½ inches (15.2 x 61 x 6.4 cm)
Kitakata paper, book cloth, bamboo, watercolor; linocut with stencils, whirlwind binding

Photo by J. Wayne Jones

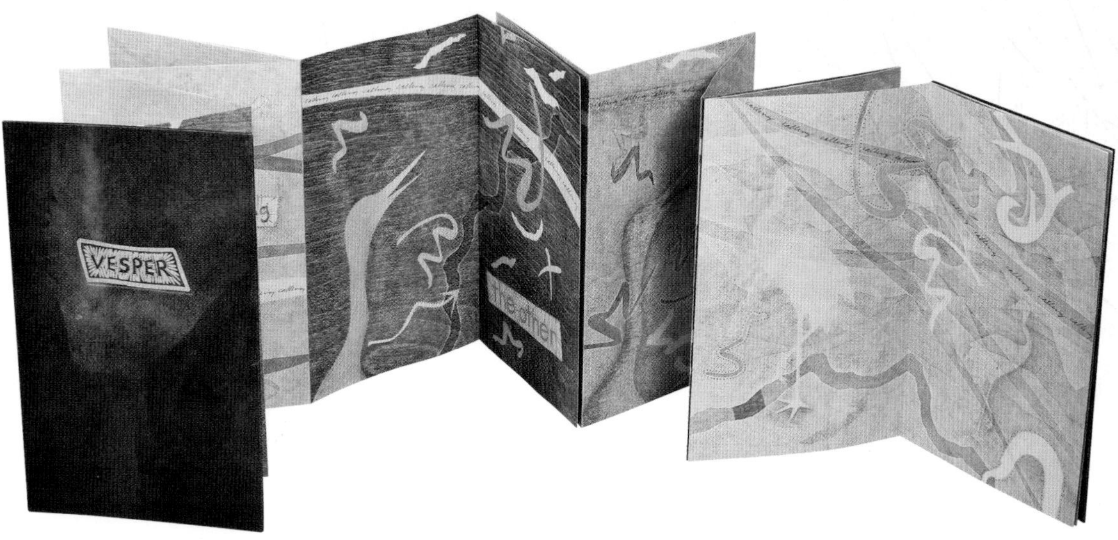

▲ **Vesper** | 2004

Each page spread: 8 x 10 inches (20.3 x 25.4 cm)
Kitakata paper, Cave handmade paper, colored pencil, pen and ink; relief printing with birch plywood and stencils, Leporello binding

Photo by J. Wayne Jones

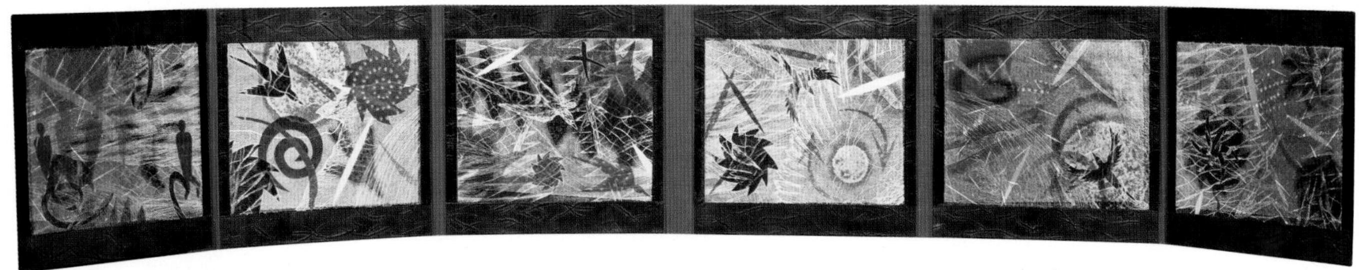

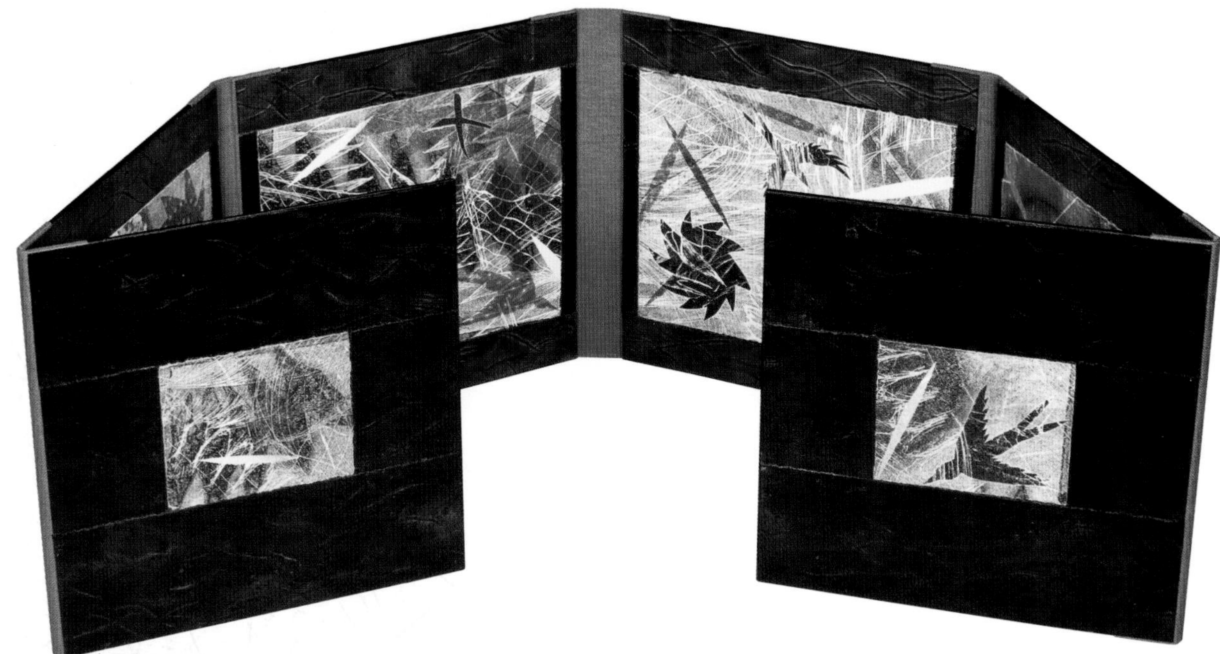

▲ **Waiting** | 2006

Open: 5⅝ x 30 inches (14.3 x 76.2 cm)
Rives paper, book cloth, embossed Arches paper, acrylic paint; relief etched with stencils

Photos by J. Wayne Jones

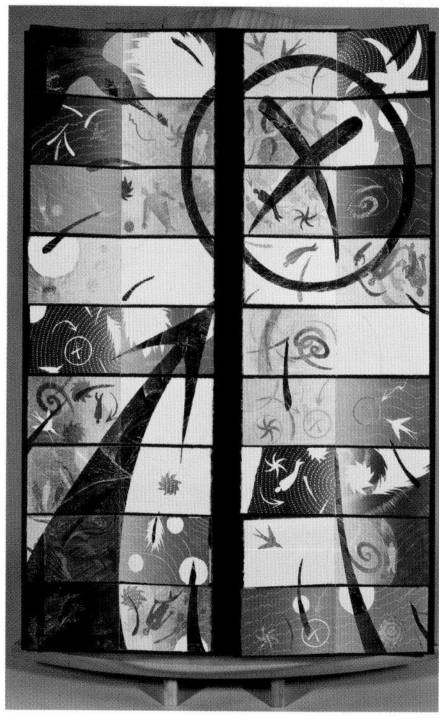

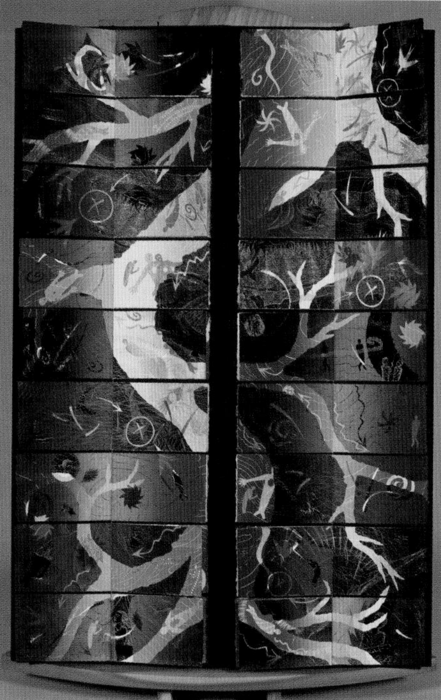

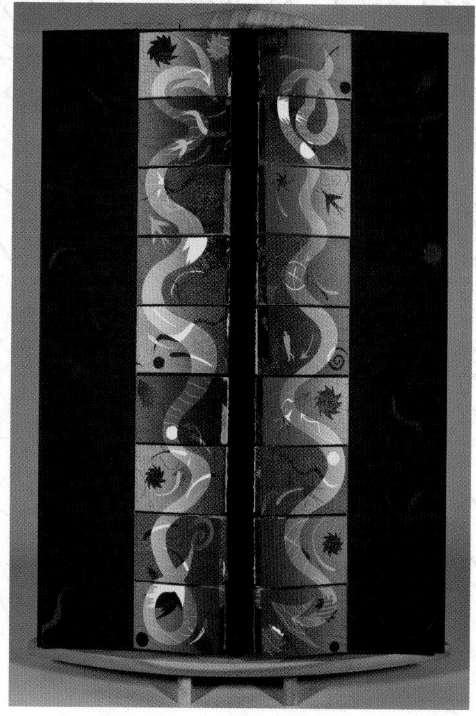

▲ X | 2000

Open: 37½ x 25½ inches (95.3 x 64.8 cm)
Rives Heavyweight paper, book cloth, binder's board; relief etched, linocut with stencils, pamphlet stitched

Photos by J. Wayne Jones

" Books can be vessels of possibility. Like seeds, they contain potential for expansion and transformation. "

KELM

Daniel Kelm

MASTERFUL CONNECTIONS—BOTH LITERAL AND FIGURATIVE—that merge binding and content are quintessential features of Daniel Kelm's innovative books. Long interested in ancient alchemical symbols and imagery, Kelm uses both in his work with rich thematic and visual results. His interest in the alchemical lexicon is also reflected in his passion for the literal transformation of the materials used in book construction. His books, book sculptures, and interpretive fine bindings combine traditional and new materials in inventive and delightful ways.

Kelm embraces the interdependence of each component of a book through a seamless integration of lyrical content and ingenious structure. Known for the development of wire-edge binding, a technique that has been enthusiastically adopted by the book arts community, he lives in Easthampton, Massachusetts, where he directs the Garage Annex School for Book Arts with his wife, artist Greta Sibley.

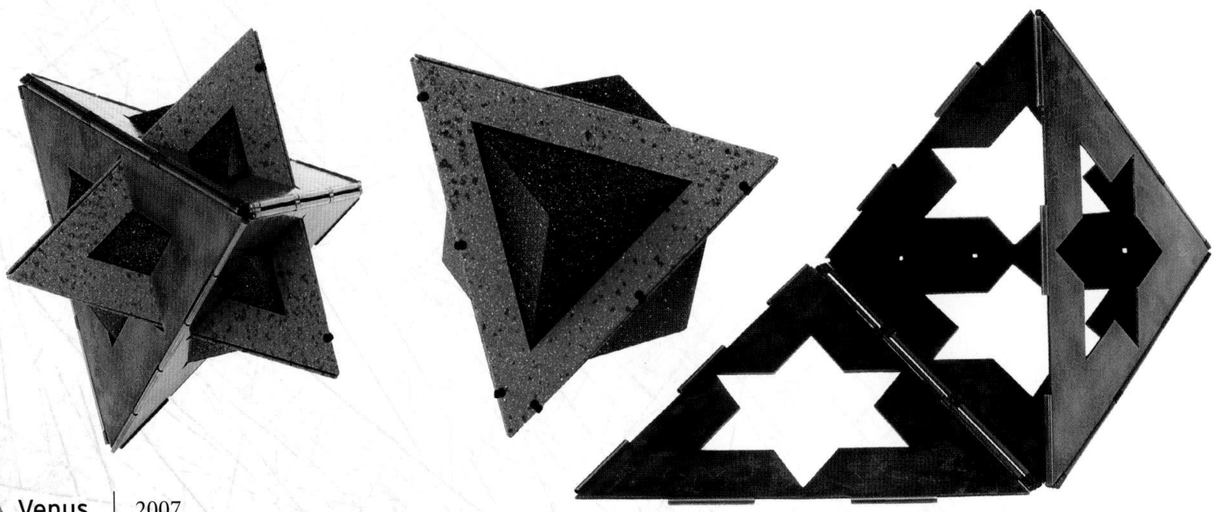

▲ **Venus** | 2007

6 x 6 x 6 inches (15.2 x 15.2 x 15.2 cm)
Paper, paper board, copper sheet, rod and tubing, brass hinges, patina, acrylic paint; wire-edge binding, etched, spattered, soldered

Photos by Jeff Derose

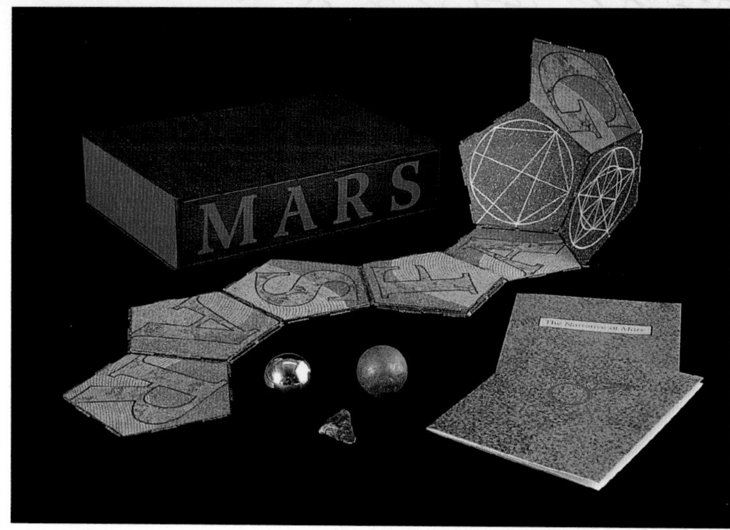

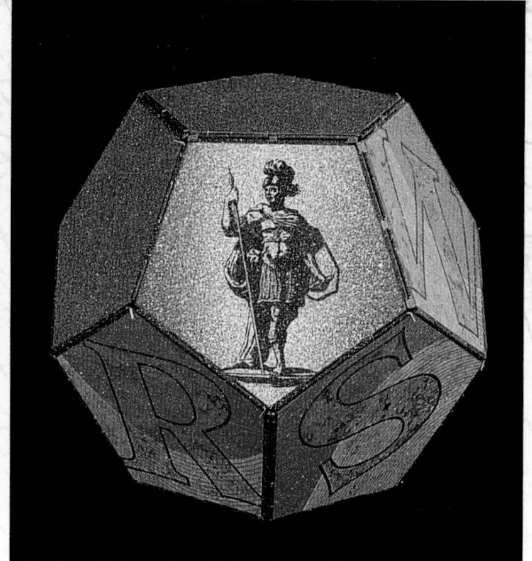

▲ **Mars** | 2005

Closed box: 11½ x 8 x 3 inches (29.2 x 20.3 x 7.6 cm)

Paper board, paper, acrylic paint, thread, stainless-steel wire, dry-mount adhesive, iron nickel meteorite, chrome steel ball bearing, Civil War iron canister ball, felt, paste paper, fiber board, cloth; wire-edge binding, painting, photocopy transfer, airbrushed, silk-screened, letterpress printed, cast, spattered

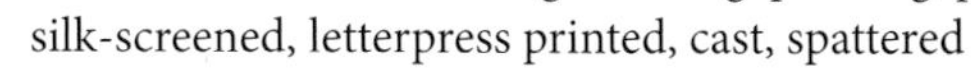

Photos by artist

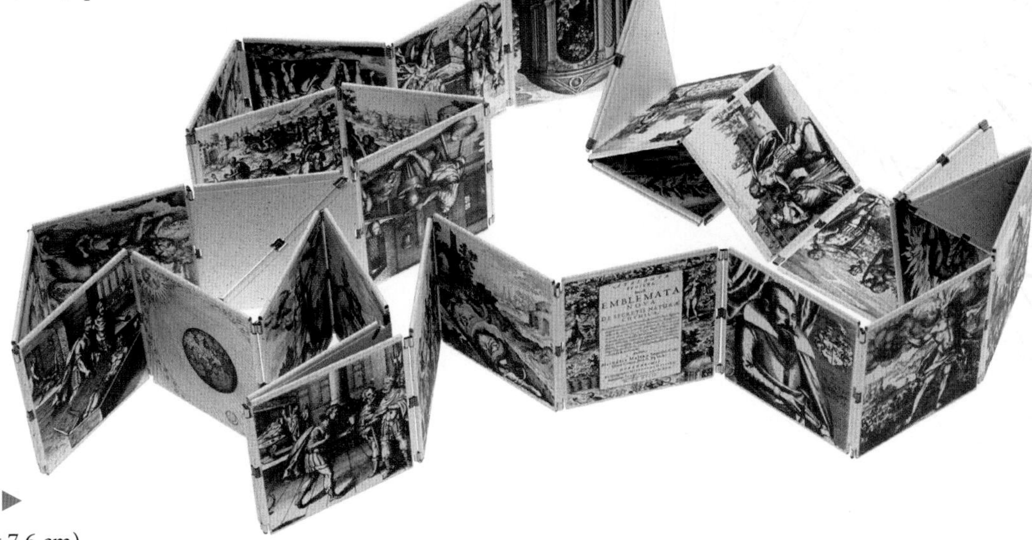

Neo Emblemata Nova | 2005 ▶

Closed: 3 x 3 x 3 inches (7.6 x 7.6 x 7.6 cm)

Paper, paper board, iron wire, brass tubing, brass and stainless steel hinges, acrylic paint; wire-edge binding, offset printed, soldered, laser welded, spattered

Photo by Jeff Derose

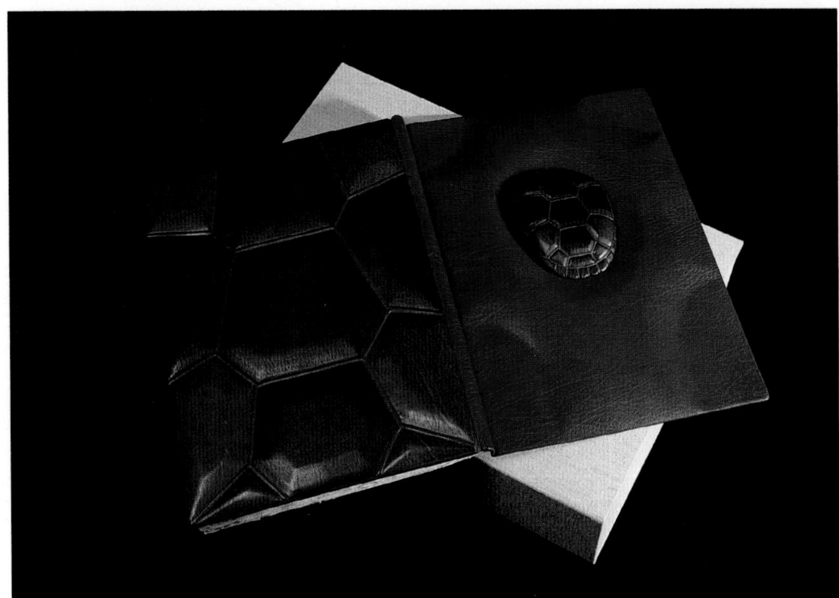

Tortoises | 1983

11¼ x 8 x 1¼ inches (28.6 x 20.3 x 3.2 cm)
Vegetable-tanned goatskin leather, sculpted balsa wood, paper, linen thread and cord, book board, cloth; English-style leather binding with sculpted boards, letterpress printed with engravings

Photo by Lionel Delevingne

"The concept of the book as material object has inspired my work for thirty years."

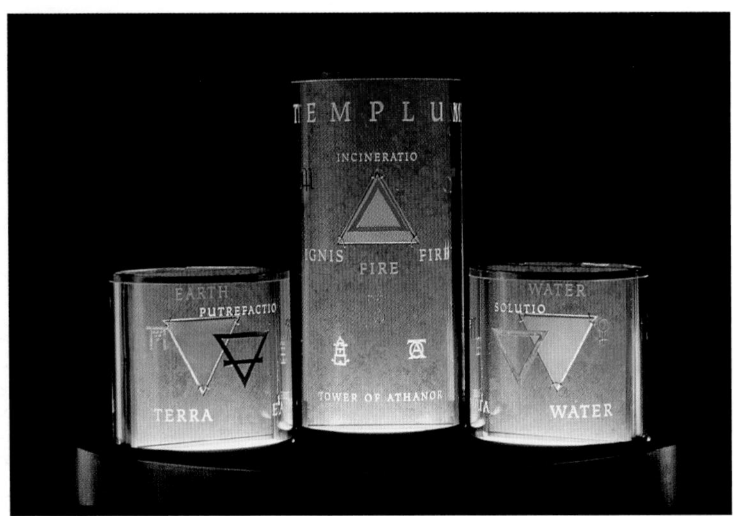

Templum Elementorum | 1995–Ongoing

22 inches (55.9 cm) in diameter
Paper, paper board, stainless steel wire, brass sheet and tubing, thread, lead, copper, tin, iron, glass, wood, acrylic paint, patina, felt, gold leaf; wire-edge binding, sandblasted, soldered, stenciled, spattered, gilded, soldered

Photo by artist

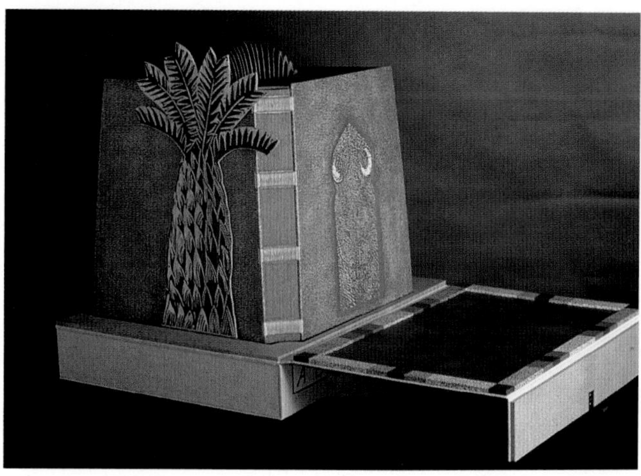

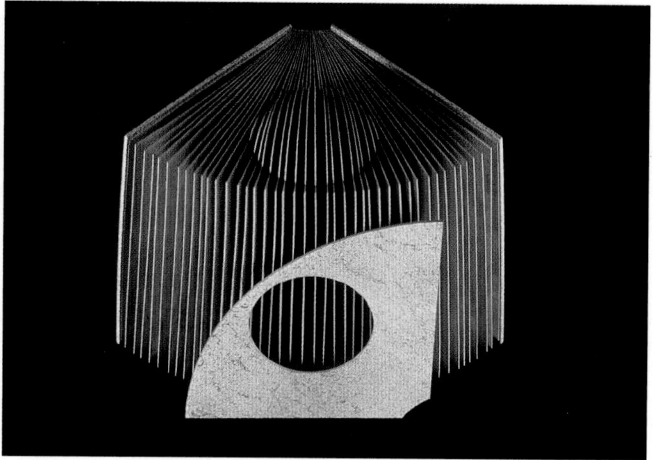

▲ **A Dog Story** | 1988

15 x 12¾ x 2 inches (38.1 x 32.4 x 5.1 cm)

Vegetable-tanned goatskin suede, paper, linen thread and tape, brass wire, magnets, cloth, paint; exposed spine-wire edge binding of rigid page panels, letterpress printed, relief images, photocopy transfer

Photos by artist

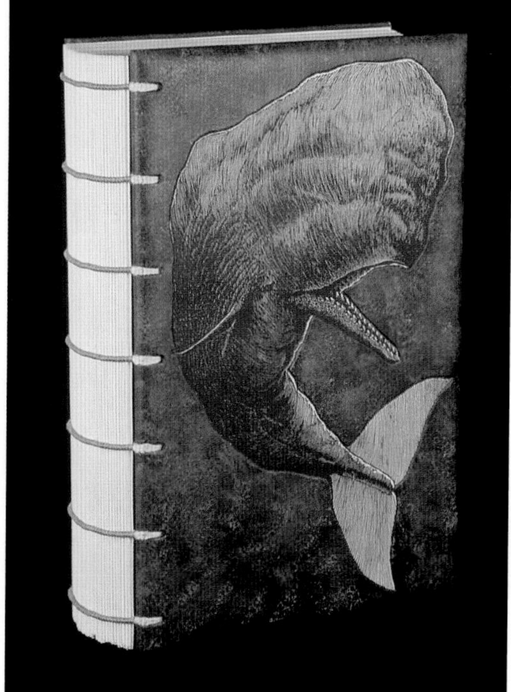

Moby-Dick | 1990 ▶

16¼ x 10½ x 3 inches (41.3 x 26.7 x 7.6 cm)

Vegetable-tanned goatskin suede, alum tawed pigskin suede, paper, linen thread and cord, brass wire, magnets, cloth, acrylic paint; exposed spine-wire edge binding, letterpress printed, photocopy transfer

Photo by artist

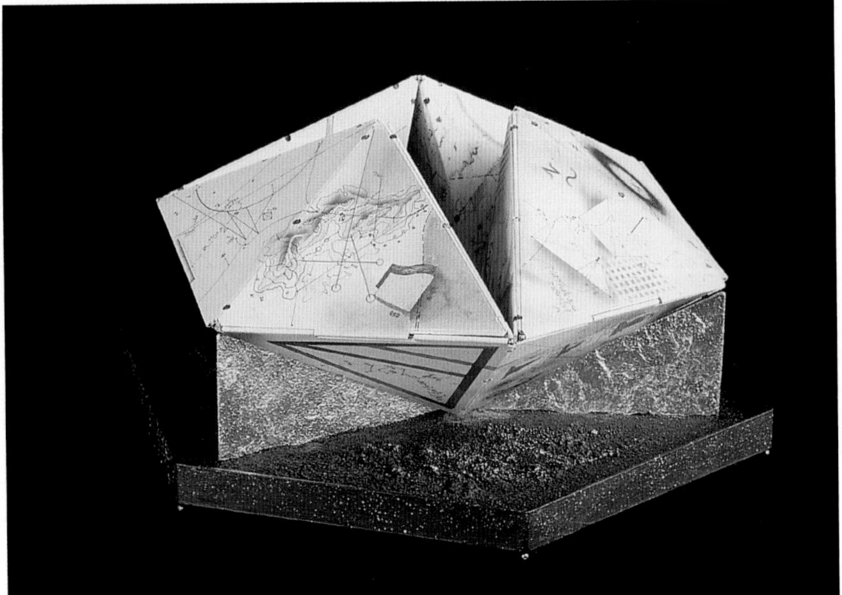

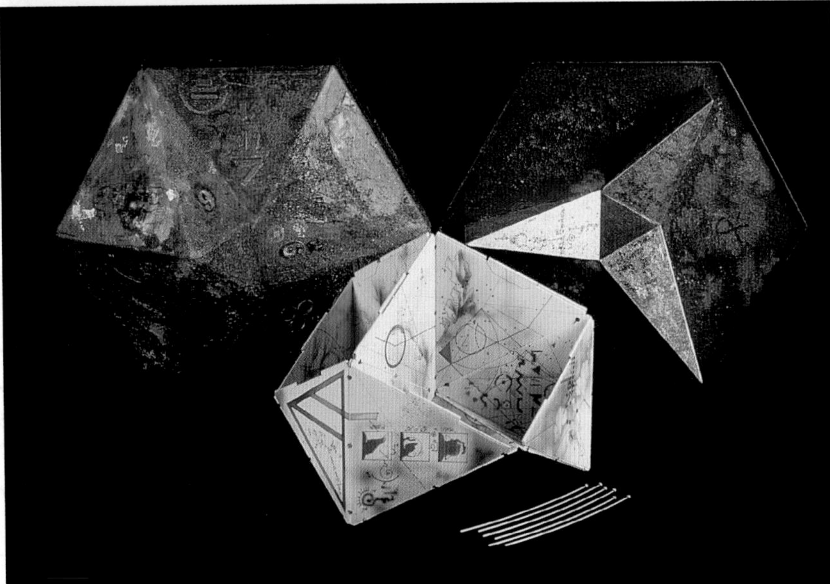

" The deep, expressive traits of a binding are to be found not just on its surface, but in its form, material, and movement. When these integrally support the text and imagery of a book, a synergistic quality results. The impact can be potent. "

◀ **Rubeus** | 1990

Book sculpture: 5 x 10 x 10 inches (12.7 x 25.4 x 25.4 cm)
Paper board, fiber board, paper, acrylic paint, polymer medium, ink, thread, stainless-steel wire, silver leaf, dry-mount adhesive, sand; wire-edge binding, painting, drawing, airbrushed
Photos by artist

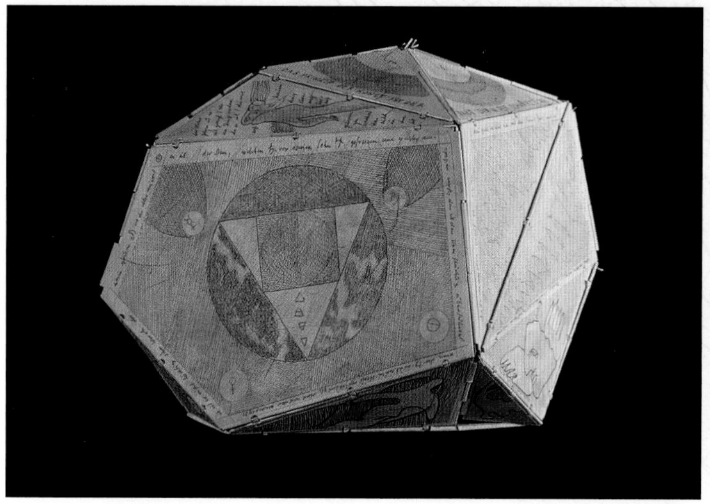

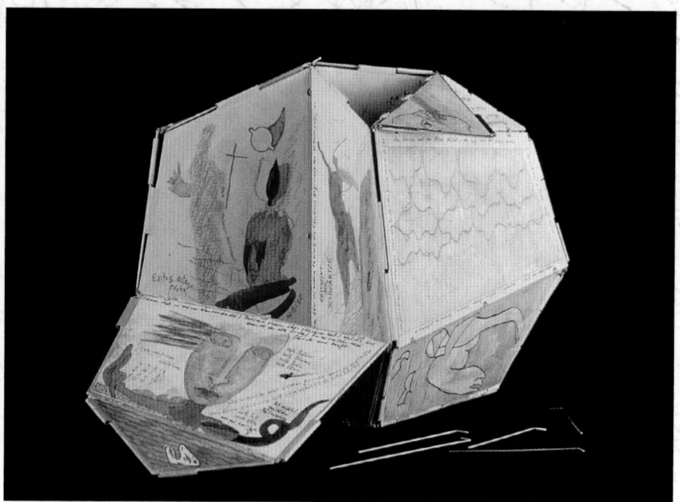

▲ **The Philosopher's Stone** | 1993

5½ x 8 x 6½ inches (14 x 20.3 x 16.5 cm)
Paper board, paper, pencil, ink, acrylic paint, thread, stainless-steel wire, dry-mount adhesive, brass tubing; wire-edge binding, drawing

Photos by artist

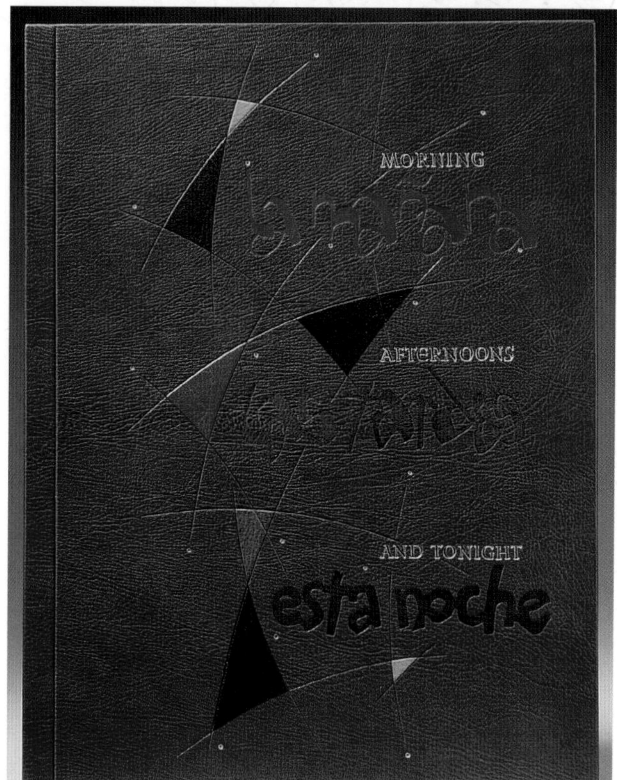

Mornings, Afternoons, and Tonight | 2004 ▶

18½ x 14¾ x 1¼ inches (47 x 37.5 x 3.2 cm)
Goatskin leather, paper, silk thread and cord, stainless-steel wire, gold and palladium leaf; wire-edge binding combined with English-style leather flatback cover, raised cord sewing, calligraphy, drawing, leather onlay and tooling with leaf

Photo by M. Lee Fatherree

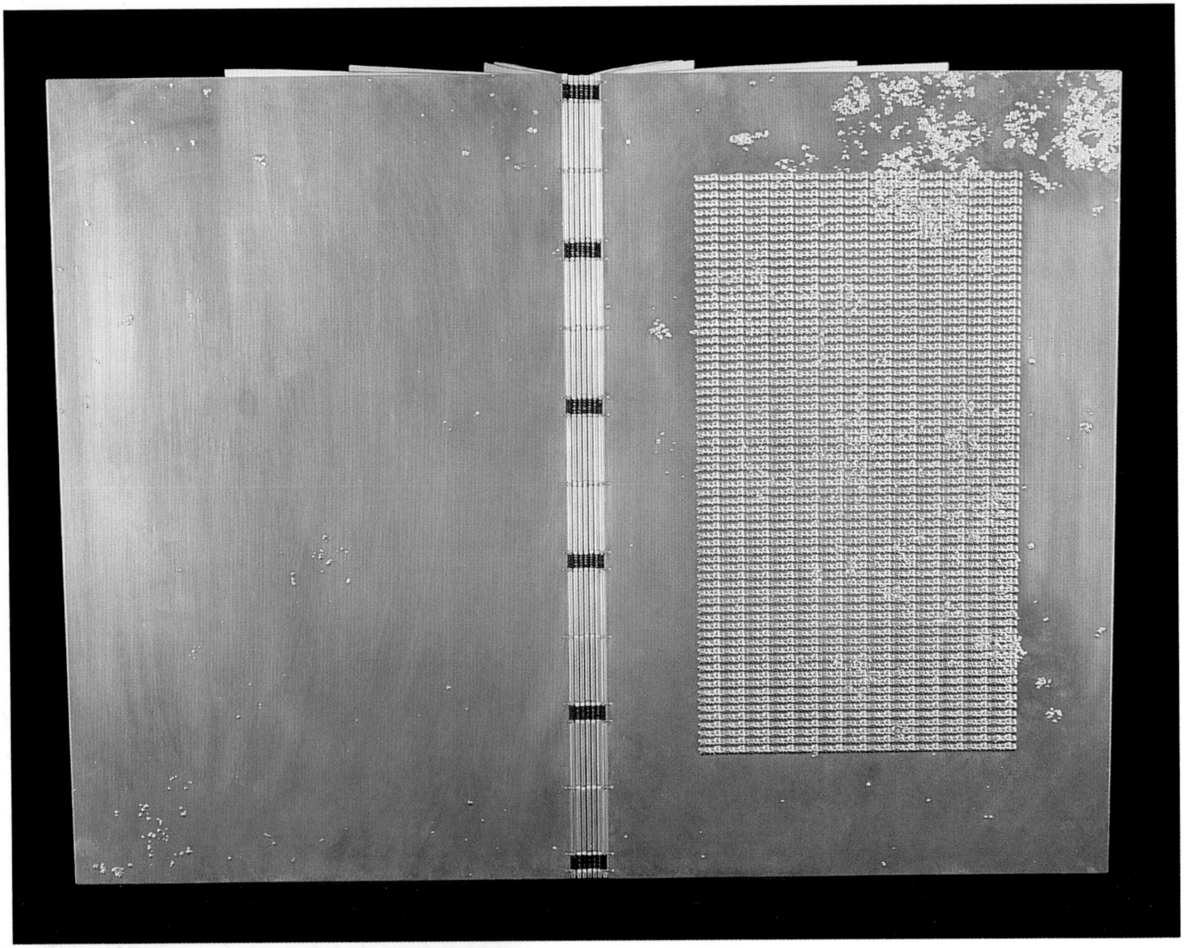

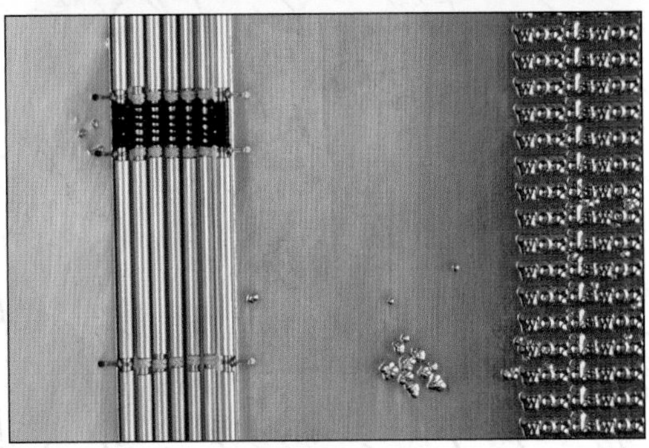

▲ Ur-text (Volume 3) | 1994

16 x 10½ x 1 inches (40.6 x 26.7 x 2.5 cm)
Zinc sheet, aluminum tubing, paper, acrylic paint, patina, thread, brass wire and sheet; wire-edge binding, photo etched, airbrushed, letterpress printed

Photos by artist

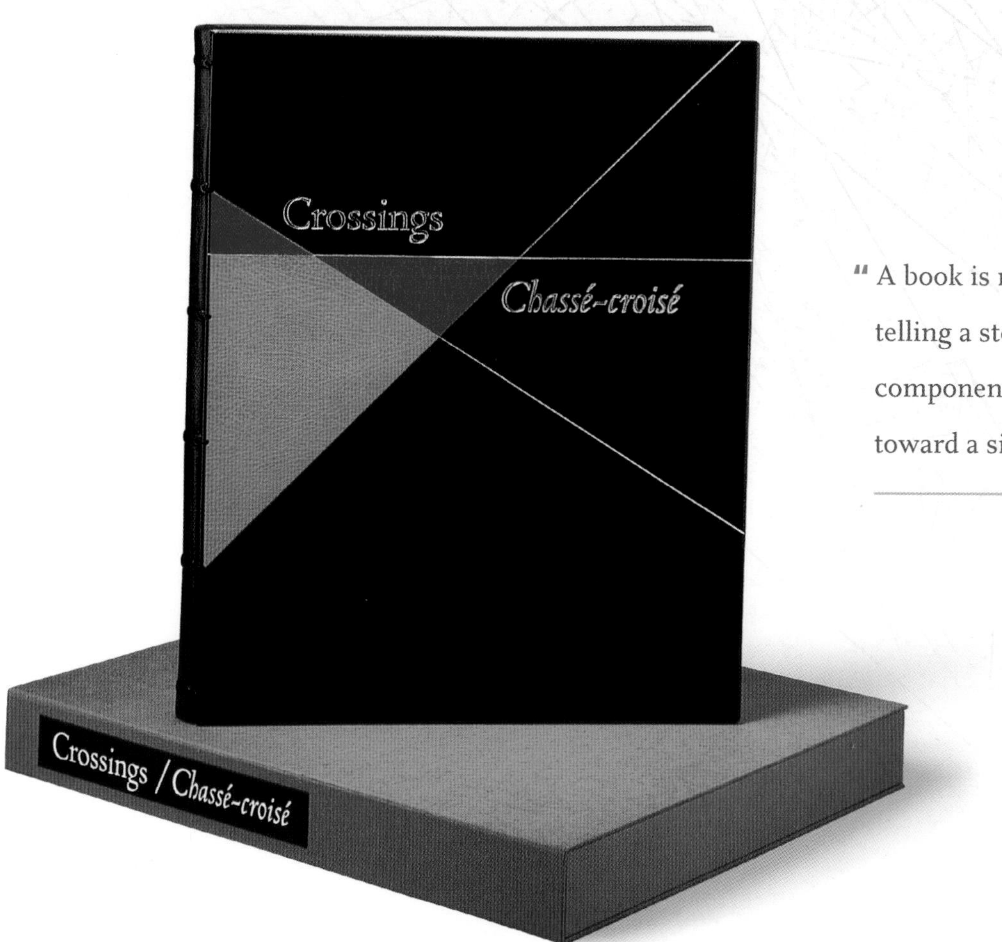

" A book is most successful at telling a story when all of its components work together toward a single effect. "

▲ **Crossings/Chassé-croisé** | 2002–2003

17¼ x 14½ x 1½ inches (43.8 x 36.8 x 3.8 cm)
Goatskin leather, paper, linen thread and cord, stainless-steel wire, cloth, photographs, palladium leaf, paint; wire-edge binding combined with English-style leather cover, raised cord sewing, letterpress printed, leather onlay and tooling with leaf
Photo by M. Lee Fatherree

Laura Wait

RHYTHMIC BRUSHSTROKES OF ABSTRACTED LETTERFORMS and symbols punctuate the pages of Laura Wait's books. Her images are lavishly rendered in rich color, the shapes at once delicate and strong, subtle and saturated. Employing a range of media, including paint, encaustic, and woodcut, and working in a fluid, painterly fashion, Wait creates surfaces that appear to be softened by time.

Wait's beautifully complex books are often composed of monoprints, with layers of writing, painting, and printing. Reformatted images and scraps left over from old books sometimes find their way into her new pieces. Referencing ancient wall inscriptions and hieroglyphics, Wait strives for dense fresco-like surfaces in her work. She blends antique and contemporary elements with gorgeous results. Based in Steamboat Springs, Colorado, Wait exhibits her work regularly. Her books are in many public and private collections, including the Library of Congress in Washington, D.C.

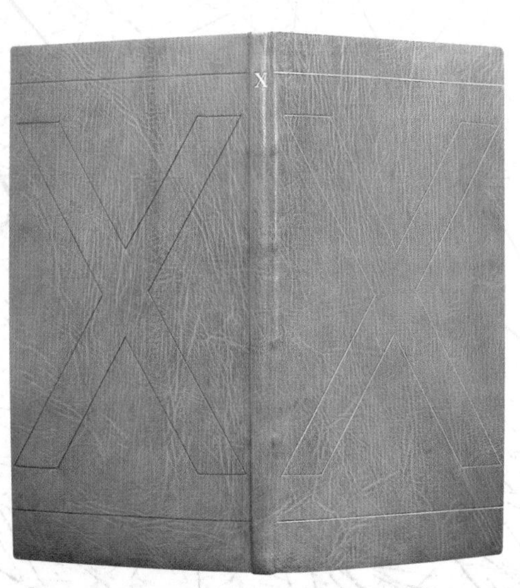

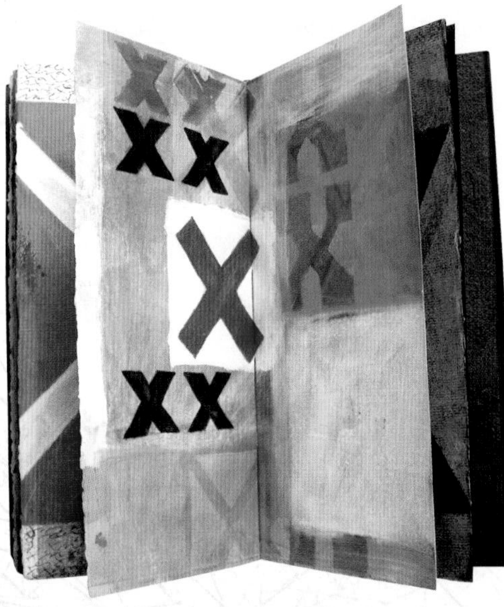

X, Letter of Danger, Sex, and the Unknown: Vol. VI | 2006

14¾ x 7½ x ⅝ inches (37.5 x 19.1 x 1.6 cm)
Rives BFK paper, Cave paper, Harmatan goat leather, ink, Akua color, acrylic, gold, woodcuts, collographs, paste paintings, handwriting; English-style fine binding, hand tooled
Photos by artist

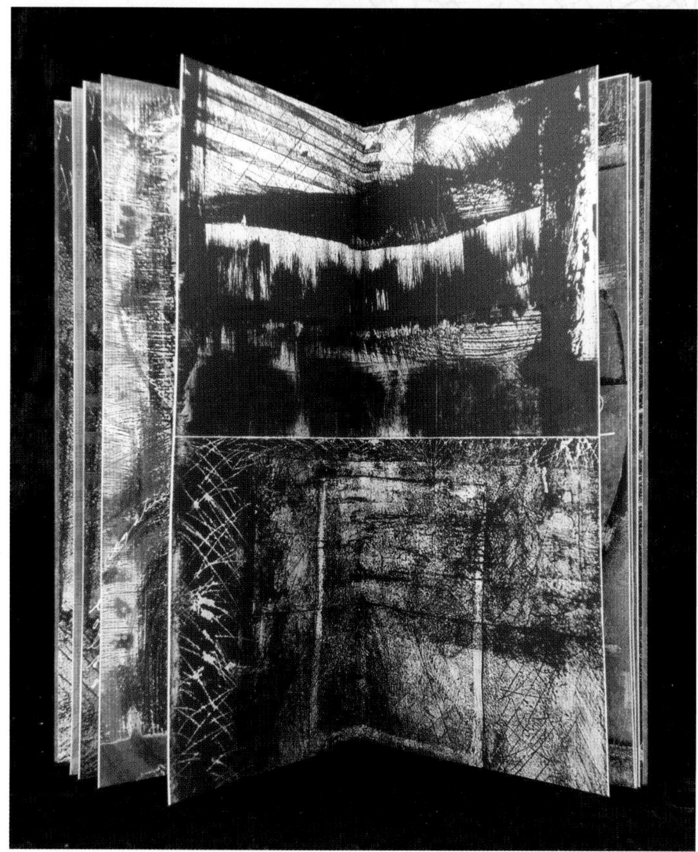

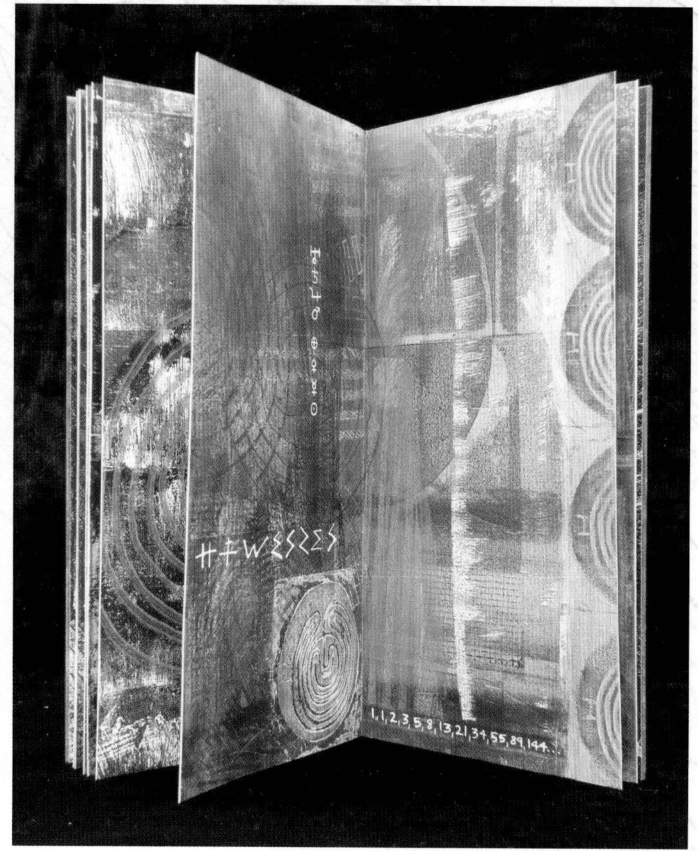

▲ **Volute, No. 1** | 2008

13½ x 6¾ x ⅝ inches (34.3 x 17.1 x 1.6 cm)
Leather, Rives BFK paper, acrylic paint, ink, Akua color, woodcuts, collographs, paste painting, handwriting; solar-plate intaglio, stenciled, drum leaf-style binding, embossed

Photos by artist

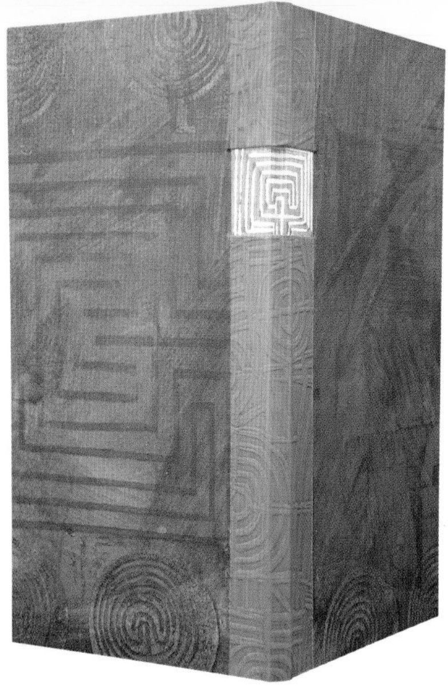

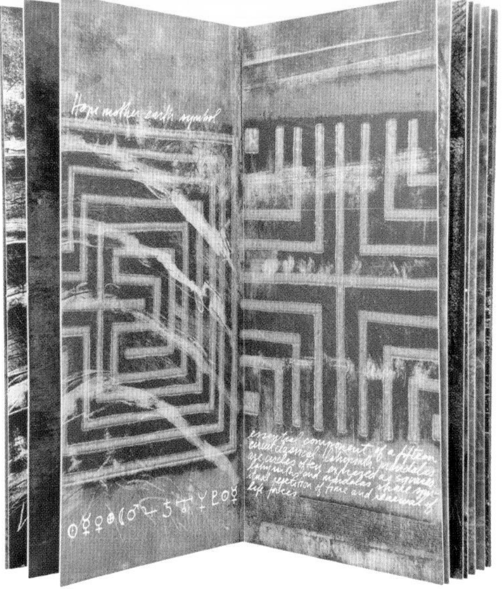

> " My work is inspired by abstract expressionism, Japanese calligraphy, and the idea that art is not perfect. "

▲ **Volute, No. 4** | 2008

13½ x 6¾ x ⅝ inches (34.3 x 17.1 x 1.6 cm)
Leather, Rives BFK paper, acrylic paint, ink, Akua color, woodcuts, collographs, paste painting, handwriting; solar-plate intaglio, stenciled, drum leaf-style binding, embossed
Photos by artist

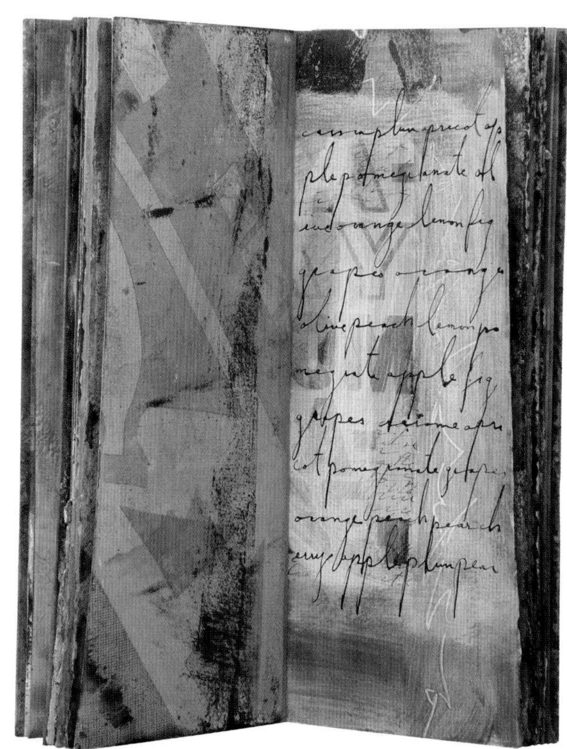

Monumentum Arbusti: A Celebration of Trees, AP | 2008 ▶

14⅞ x 5⅞ x ⅞ inches (14.9 x 37.8 x 2.2 cm)
Rives BFK paper, Mylar, acrylic, ink, linen thread, cord, copper, woodcuts, paste painting, handwriting; stenciled, raised-cord sewing with sewn boards
Photo by artist

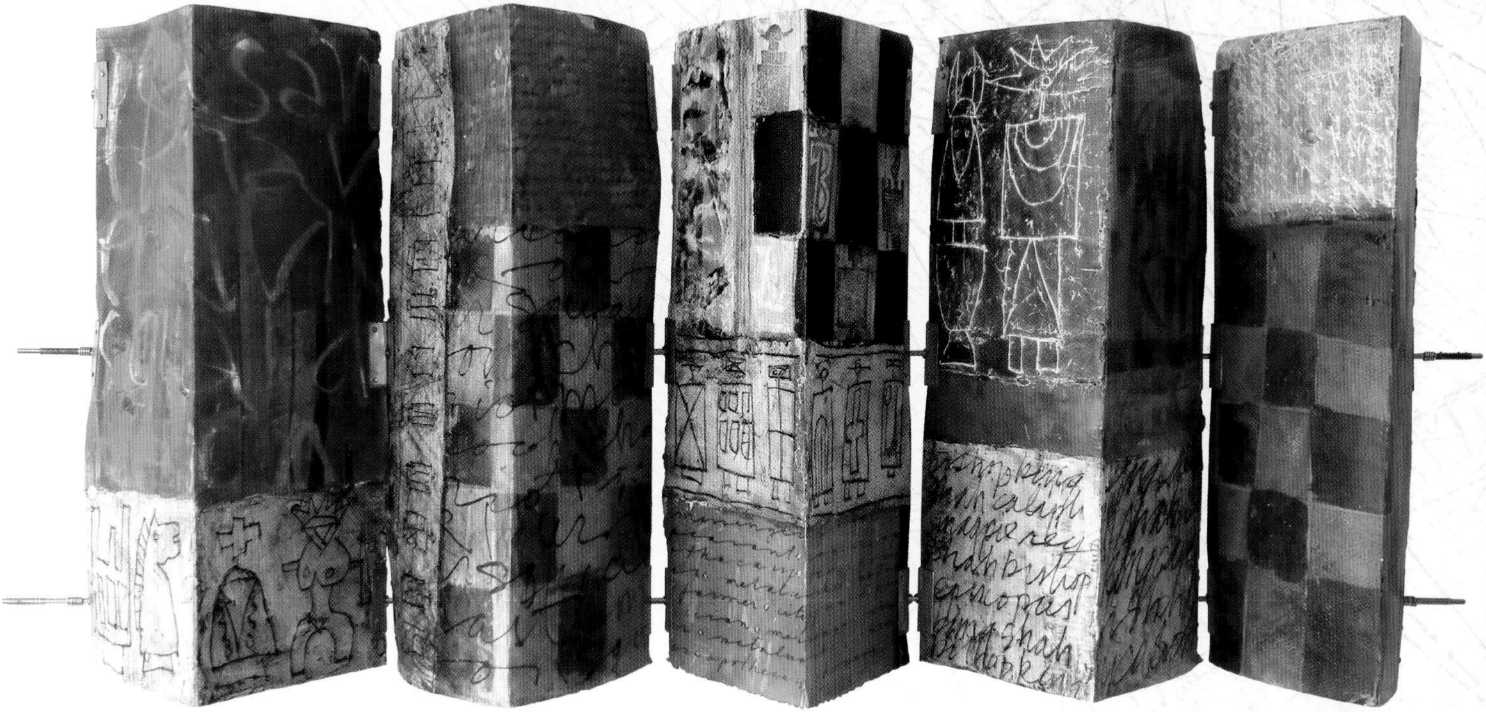

▲ **Middlegame** | 2008

15 x 33 x 6½ inches (38.1 x 83.8 x 16.5 cm)
Encaustic, paint, inks, copper, brass, Japanese paper, Rives BFK paper, handwriting; riveted, hand stamped

Photos by artist

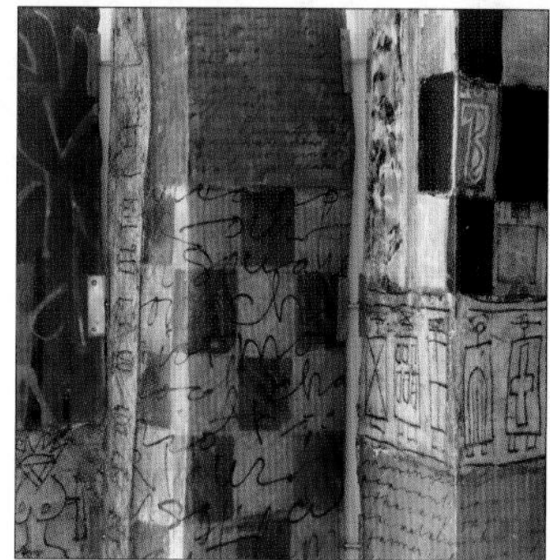

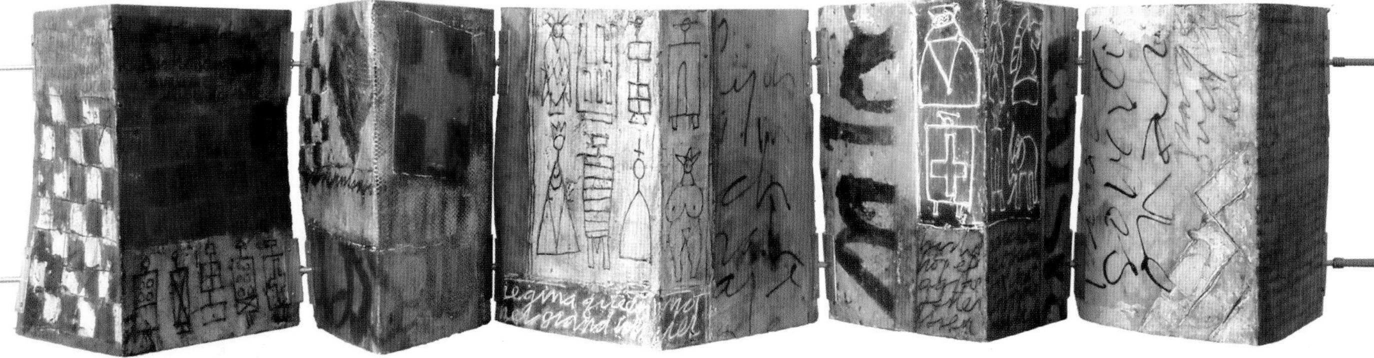

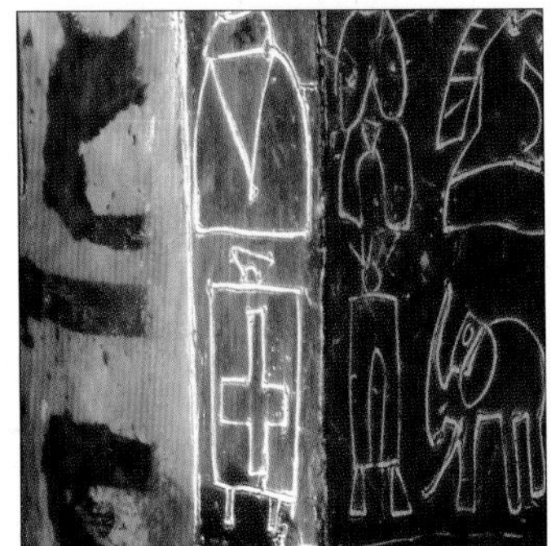

▲ **Chessmen** | 2008

7 x 33 x 6½ inches (17.8 x 83.8 x 16.5 cm)
Encaustic, paint, inks, copper, brass, Japanese paper, Rives BFK paper, handwriting; riveted, hand stamped

Photos by artist

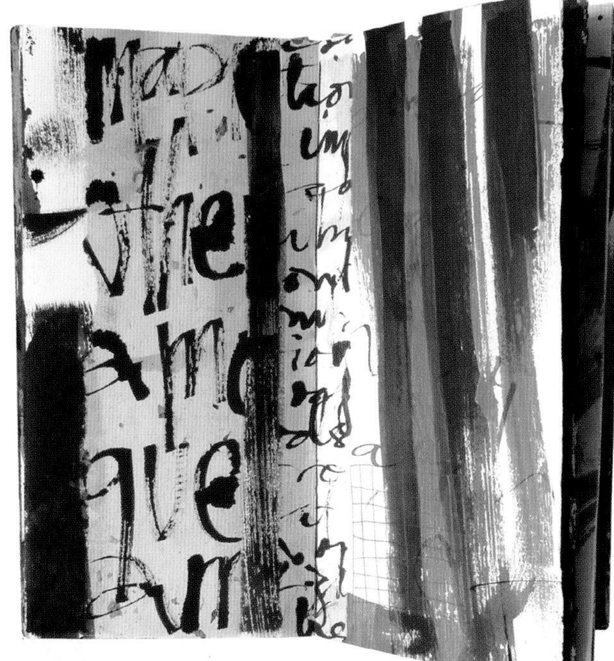

Unspoken Promises | 2009 ▶

15 x 7¾ x ⅞ inches (38.1 x 19.7 x 2.2 cm)
Rives BFK paper, various Japanese papers, ink, pencil, acrylic, aircraft plywood, handwriting, paste; raised-cord sewing with laced-on boards

Photo by artist

" I use the fluidity of handwriting as a way to create energy and concentrate on the abstract nature of letters as symbols. "

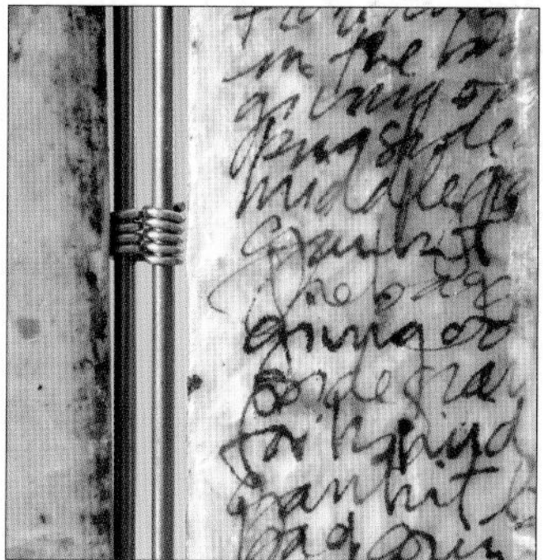

▲ **Hostilities** | 2009

10 x 4½ x 1 inches (25.4 x 11.4 x 2.5 cm)
Copper, brass, aircraft plywood, encaustic, ink, Japanese paper, oil stick, handwriting; metalwork

Photos by artist

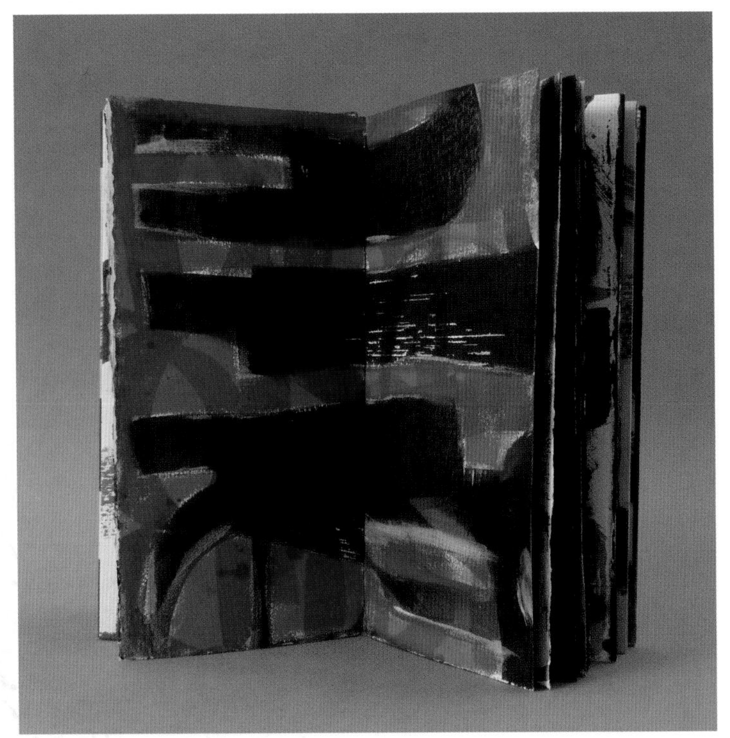

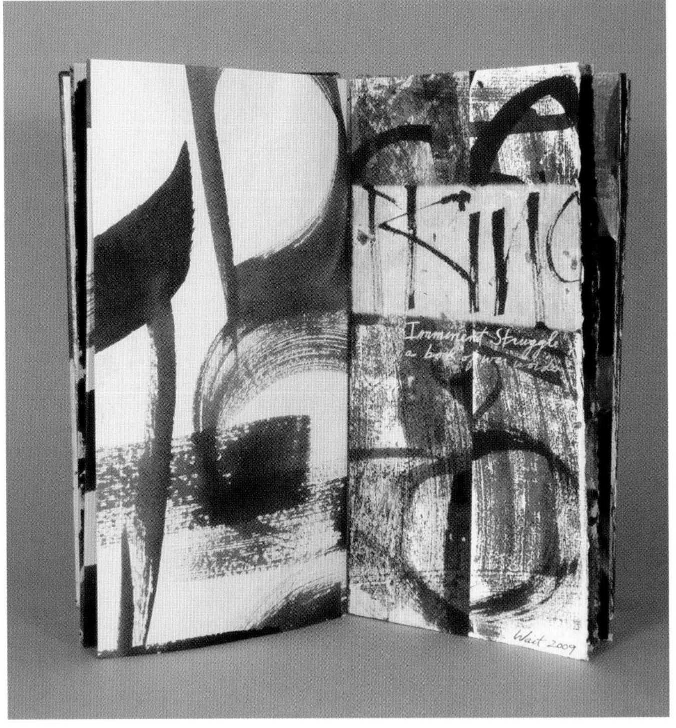

▲ **Imminent Struggle** | 2009

15 x 7¾ x ⅞ inches (38.1 x 19.7 x 2.2 cm)
Rives BFK paper, various Japanese papers, ink, pencil, acrylic, aircraft plywood, handwriting, paste; raised-cord sewing with laced-on boards

Photos by artist

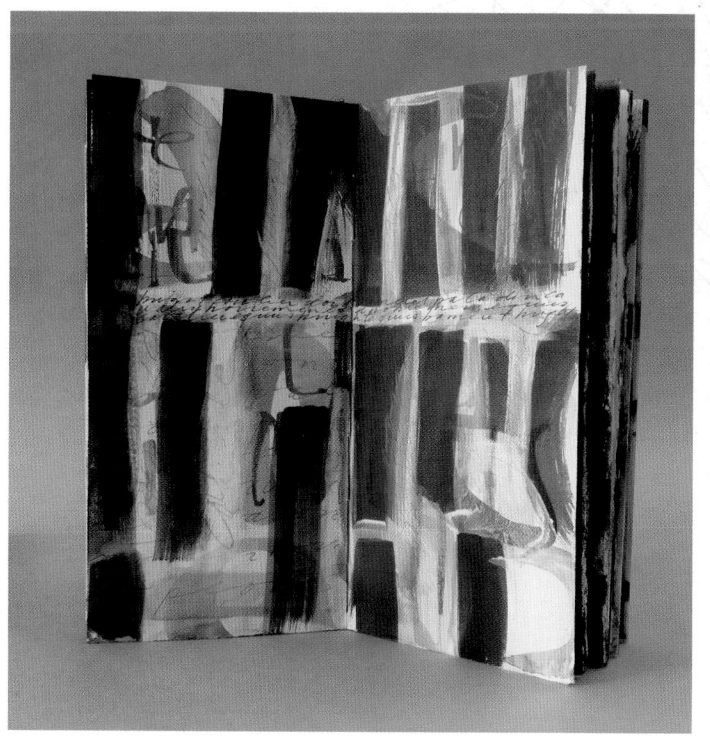

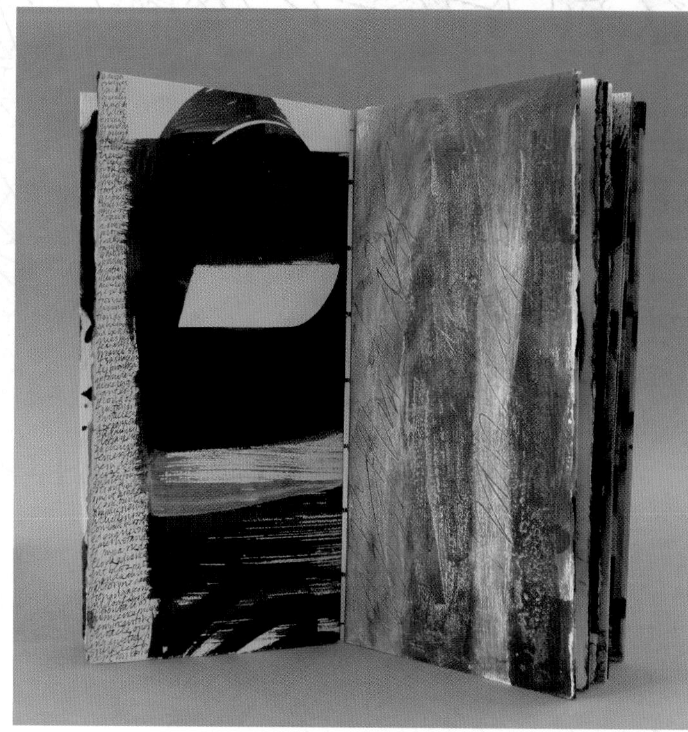

▲ **Warmongering** | 2009

15 x 7¾ x ⅞ inches (38.1 x 19.7 x 2.2 cm)
Rives BFK paper, various Japanese papers, ink, pencil, acrylic, aircraft plywood, handwriting, paste; raised-cord sewing with laced-on boards

Photos by artist

" Words play an important part in all my work. They serve as images and help to establish patterns and textures. "

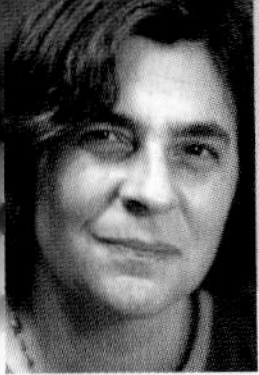

Julie Fremuth

EVOCATIVE OF EARLY AMERICAN FOLK-ART PORTRAITURE, Julie Fremuth's sublimely painted books combine humor and eccentricity in revelatory scenarios that comment on the complexity of the human condition. Her hand-written texts are suggestive but intentionally vague, providing the backdrop for figures that are tenderly rendered. Her characters are anxious and slightly uneasy, yet they possess a quiet dignity and fortitude.

Fremuth successfully utilizes book structures that reinforce the dialogue between her characters. She sets up stories that embrace the efforts of ordinary people to create works that celebrate the universality of mankind's triumphs, challenges, and fears. Fremuth has participated in many juried shows and art fairs. In 2009, she was one of ten American artists invited to Yokohama, Japan, where she served as an ambassador at the Yokohama International Open-Air Art Fair, the first outdoor fair of its kind in Japan.

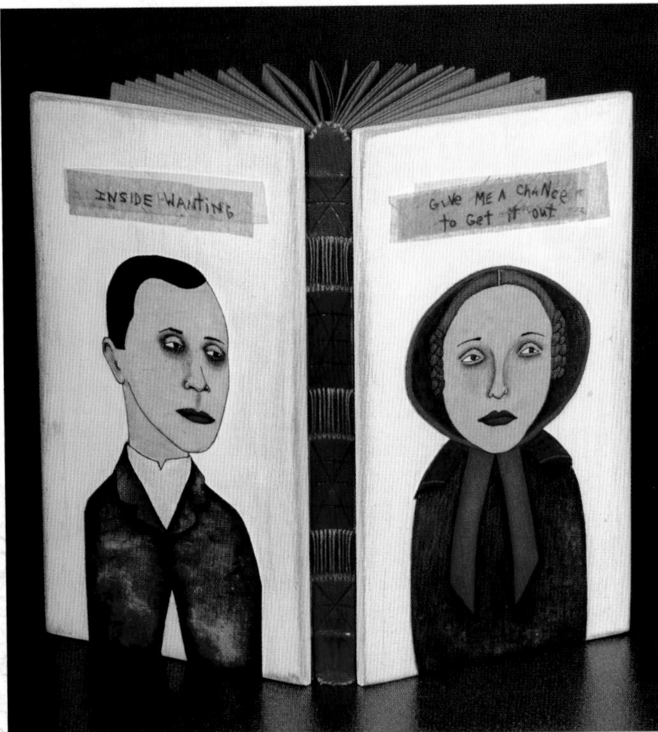

Give Me a Chance to Get It Out | 2008

8 x 4½ x 1¼ inches (20.3 x 11.4 x 3.2 cm)
Wood, paper, cloth, thread, gouache, paint, ink; hand-sewn binding, drawing, collage

Photo by Lon Horwedel

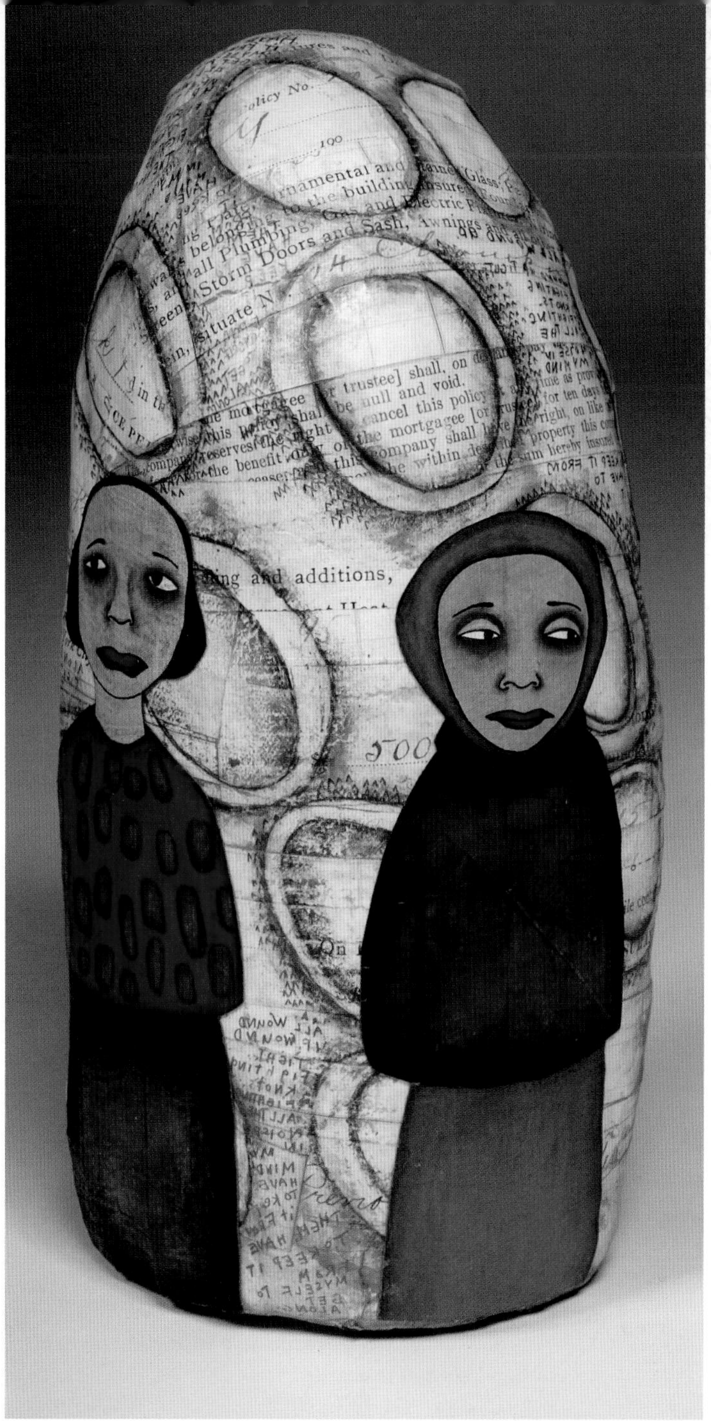

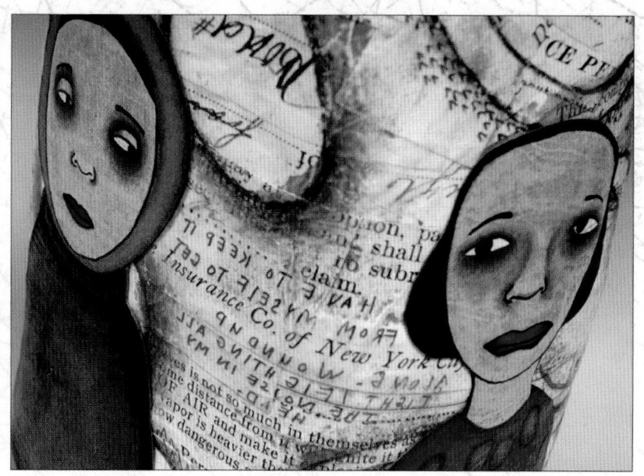

◀ **Have to Keep It from Myself to Get Along** | 2008

7½ x 3¾ inches (19.1 x 9.5 cm)
Paper, paste, paint, watercolor, pencil, papier-mâché; collage, drawing

Photos by Lon Horwedel

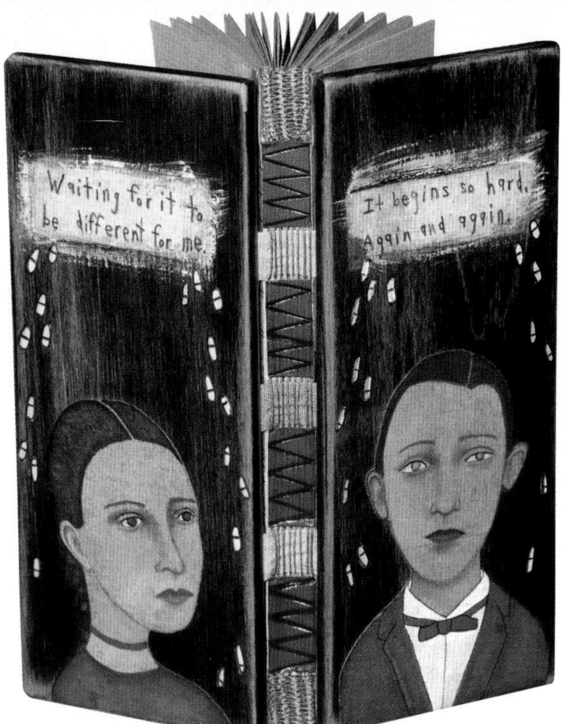

◀ **It Begins So Hard** | 2005

7 x 3½ x 1½ inches (17.8 x 8.9 x 3.8 cm)
Wood, paper, cloth, leather, gouache, ink, paint, thread; hand-sewn binding, drawing, collage
Photo by Lon Horwedel

" I've found solace in using portraiture as my subject matter. The figures often share my anxieties, fears, and passions. Portraiture is a release for me. "

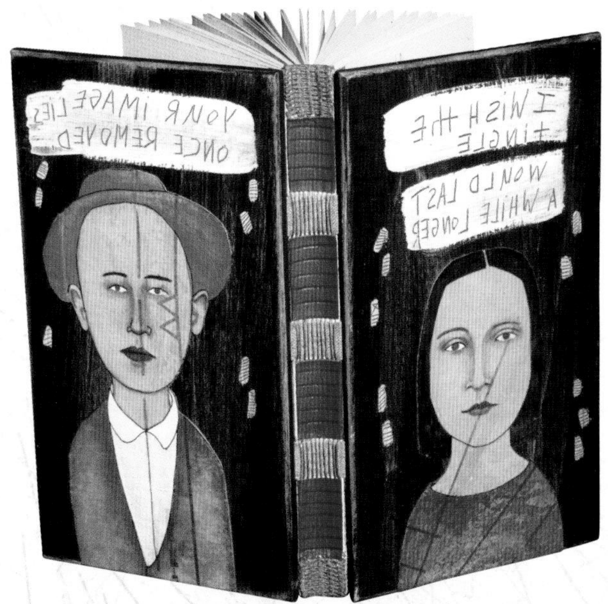

◀ **I Wish the Tingle Would Last a While Longer** | 2005

7 x 4 x 1¼ inches (17.8 x 10.2 x 3.2 cm)
Wood, paper, cloth, leather, gouache, ink, paint, thread; hand-sewn binding, drawing, collage
Photo by Lon Horwedel

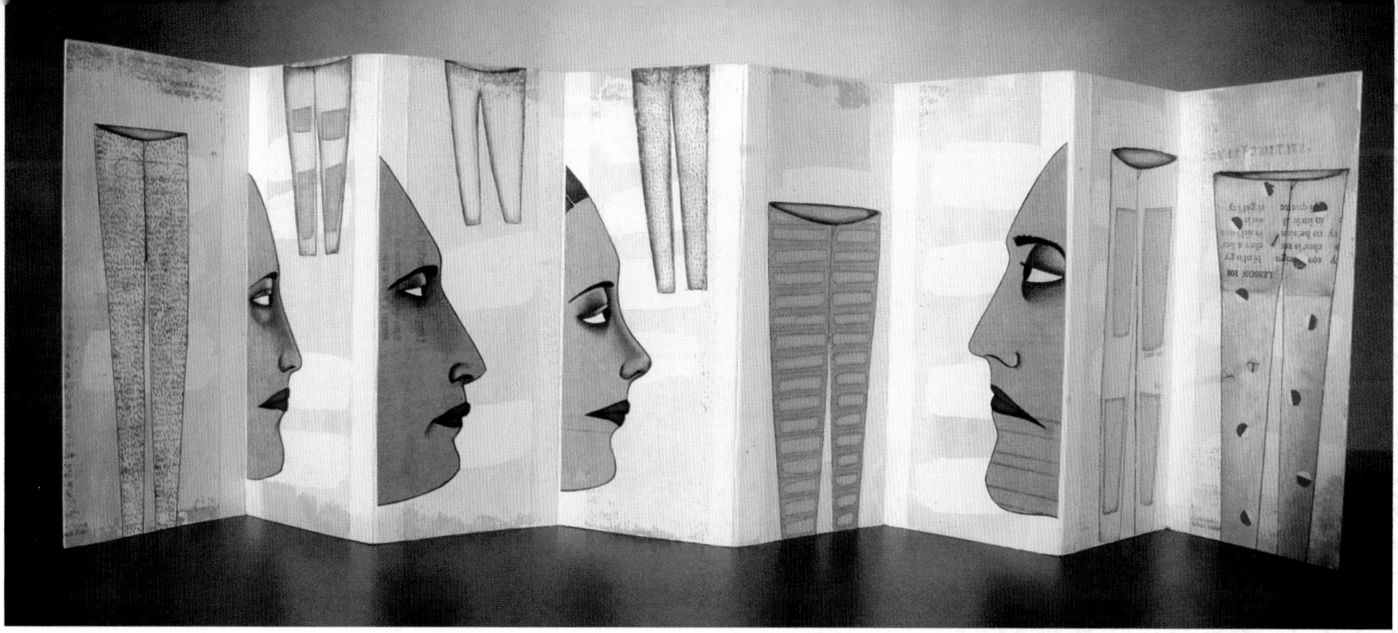

▲ **Untitled** | 2009

Open: 7¼ x 24¼ inches (18.4 x 61.6 cm)
Mat board, paper, cloth, gouache, paint, pencil, ink; accordion binding, drawing, collage
Photo by Lon Horwedel

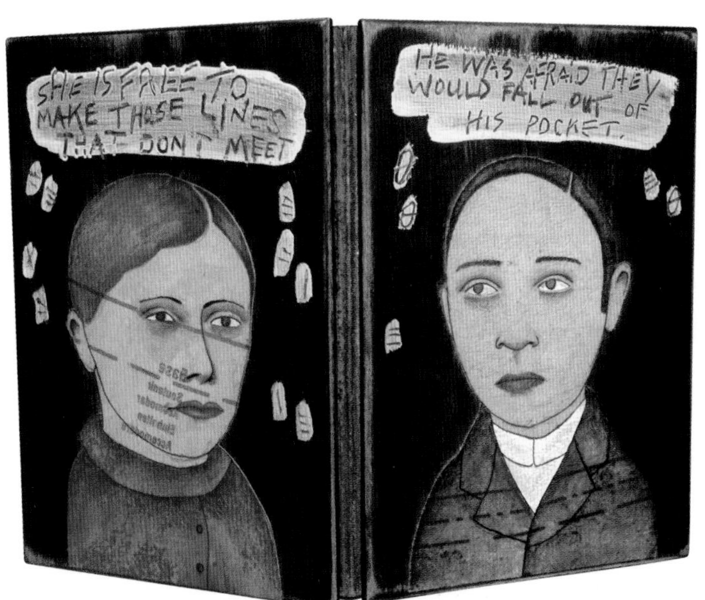

◀ **She Is Free** | 2007

5 x 3½ x ½ inches (12.7 x 8.9 x 1.3 cm)
Wood, paper, paint, gouache, pencil, ink; diptych binding, drawing, collage
Photo by Lon Horwedel

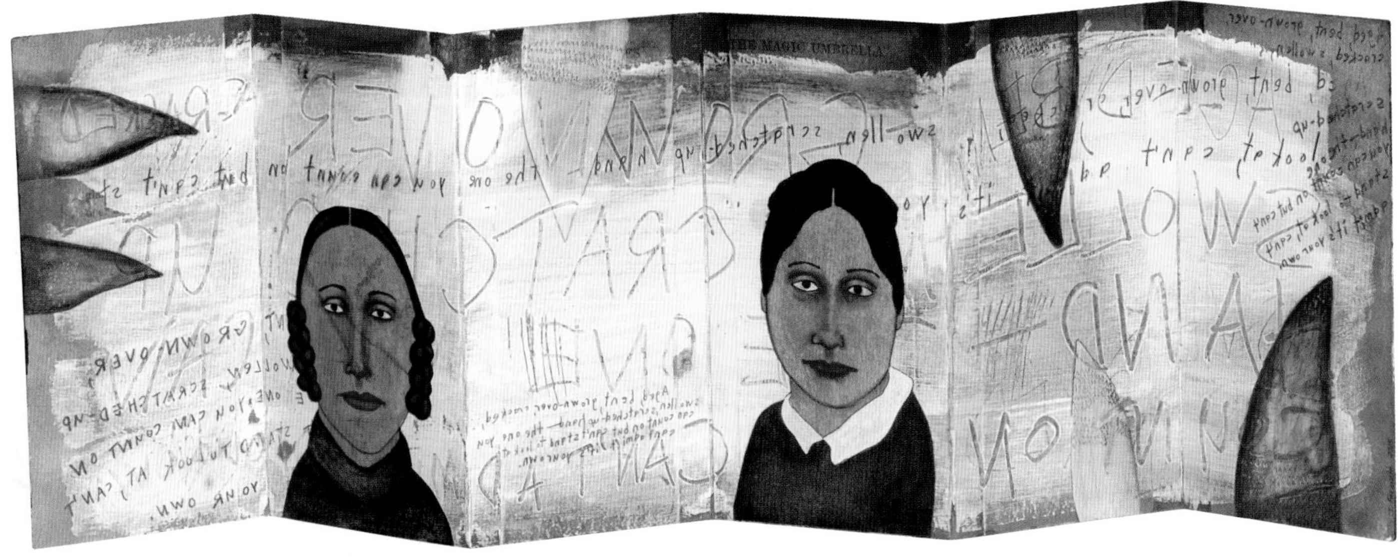

▲ **Aged, Bent, and Grown over** | 2005

Open: 7¾ x 28 inches (19.7 x 71.1 cm)
Mat board, paper, cloth, gouache, paint, ink;
accordion binding, drawing, collage

Photos by Lon Horwedel

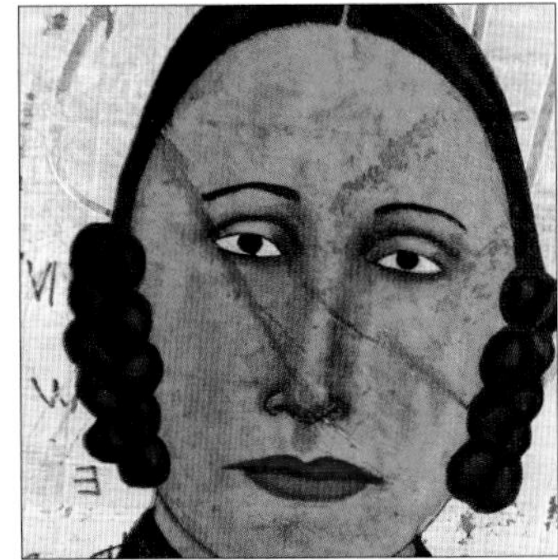

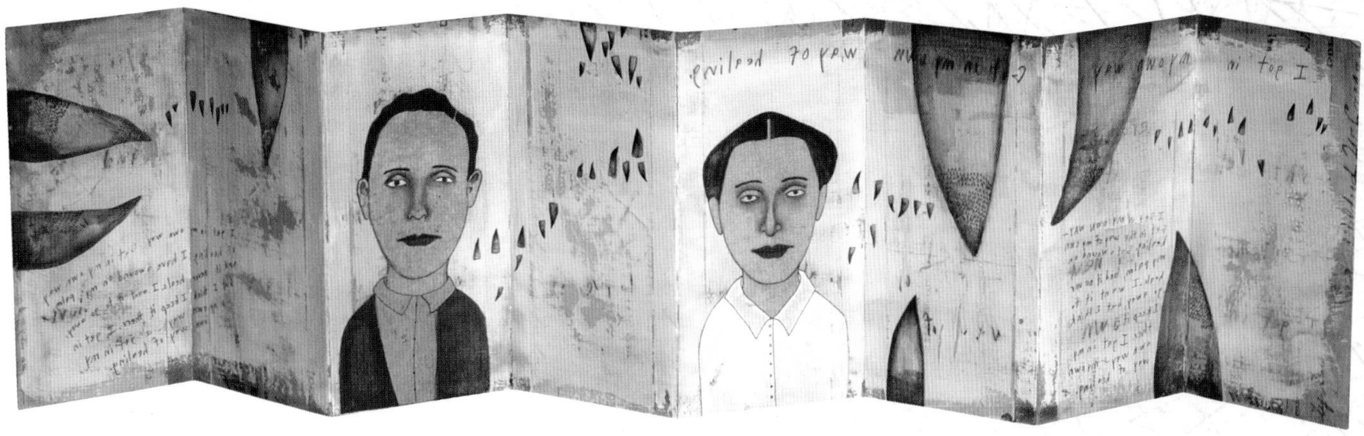

▲ **I Get in the Way of My Own Healing** | 2005

Open: 6¼ x 26½ inches (15.9 x 67.3 cm)
Mat board, paper, cloth, gouache, paint, ink; accordion binding, drawing, collage
Photo by Lon Horwedel

" I view books as containers for thought and emotion. They reveal traces of human existence and the human spirit. "

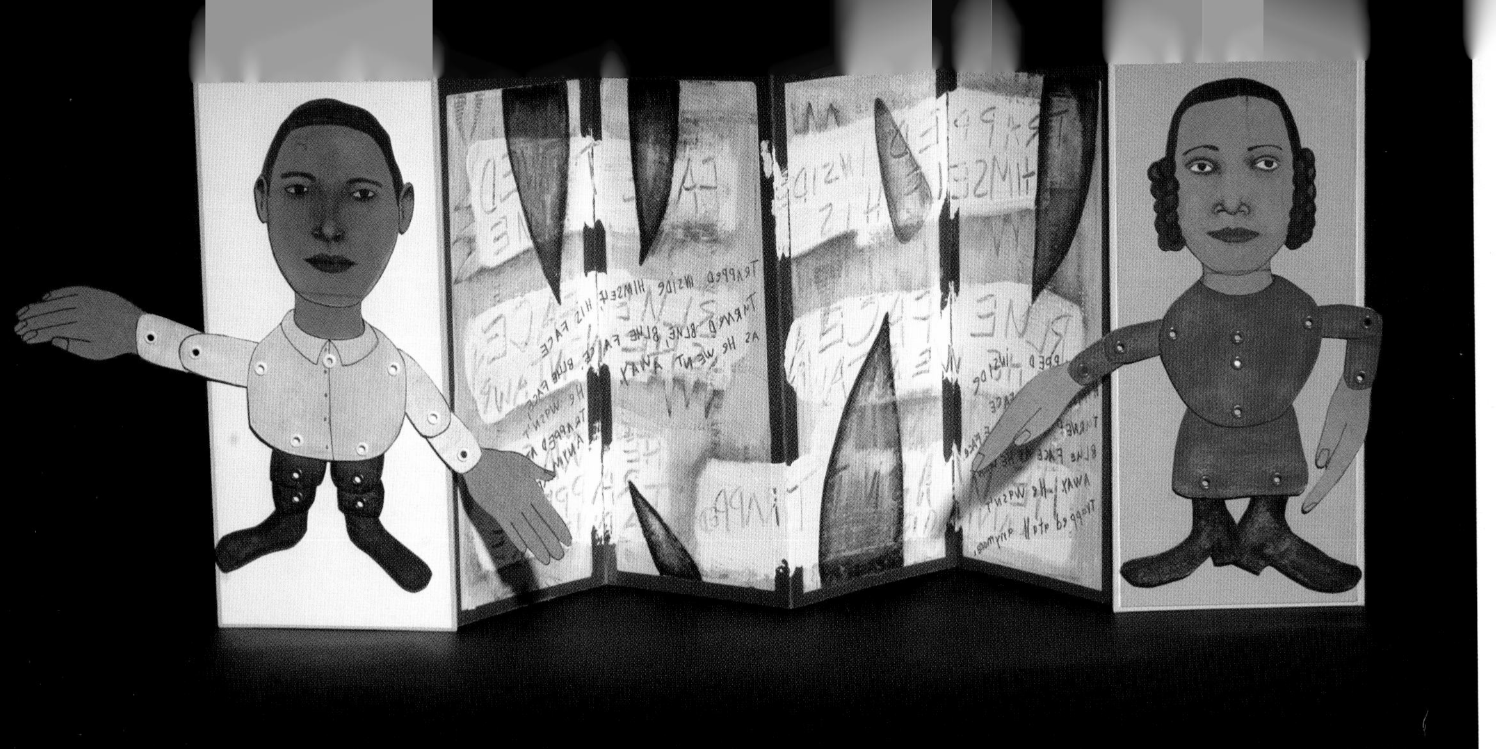

▲ **Trapped inside Himself** | 2004

8 x 3¼ x ½ inches (20.3 x 8.3 x 1.3 cm)
Mat board, paper, paint, gouache, pencil, ink, rivets; accordion binding, drawing, collage
Photo by Lon Horwedel

" When I was very young I discovered that I could write backwards. Now I like to incorporate backwards writing into my work because it has a graphic nature and creates texture. "

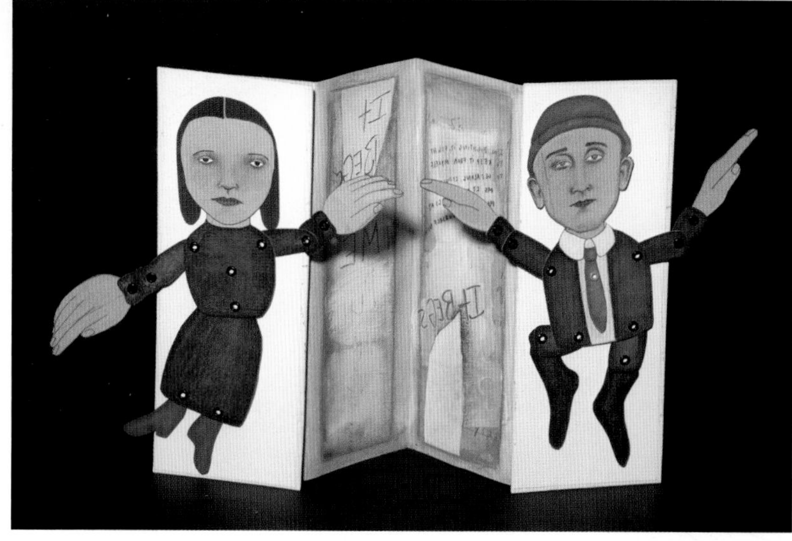

It Begs at Me | 2006

8 x 3½ x ½ inches (20.3 x 8.9 x 1.3 cm)
Mat board, paper, paint, gouache, pencil, ink; accordion binding, drawing, collage

Photo by Lon Horwedel

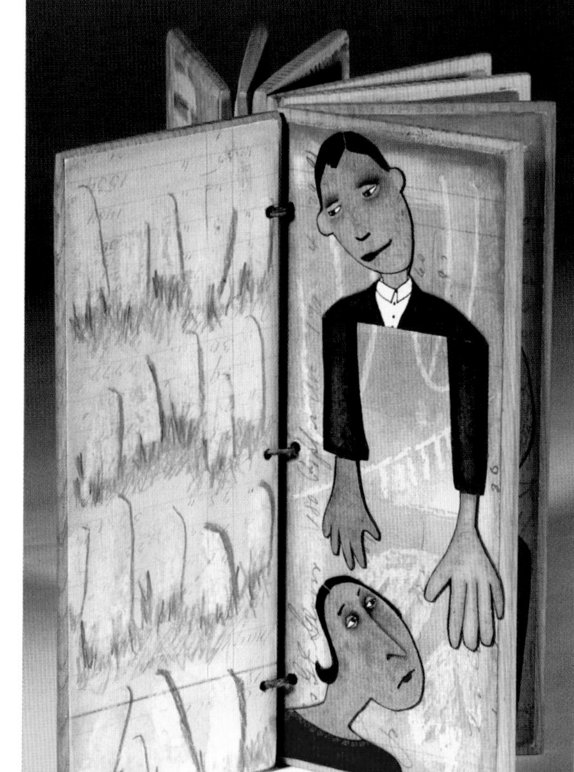

Tombstone Book Series #1: Pieces Saved in a Box | 2003

7¼ x 3 x 2¼ inches (18.4 x 7.6 x 5.7 cm)
Wood, paper, thread, sheet metal, gouache, pencil, oil crayon, wooden slats, fans; collage, painted, drawing

Photo by Lon Horwedel

About the Curator

Eileen Wallace is a letterpress printer and bookbinder specializing in custom printing and box-making. In addition to maintaining a private studio, she teaches workshops across the country and is a visiting assistant professor in printmaking and book arts at the University of Georgia. Wallace recently co-curated The Artist's Hand: Dard Hunter and the American Arts and Crafts Movement, an exhibit held at the Decorative Arts Center of Ohio in Lancaster, Ohio. She is on the board of directors of *Hand Papermaking* magazine and has served as a co-director for the Paper & Book Intensive since 1996. Wallace lives in Chillicothe, Ohio, where she assists in maintaining the archives and studio of renowned papermaking scholar Dard Hunter.

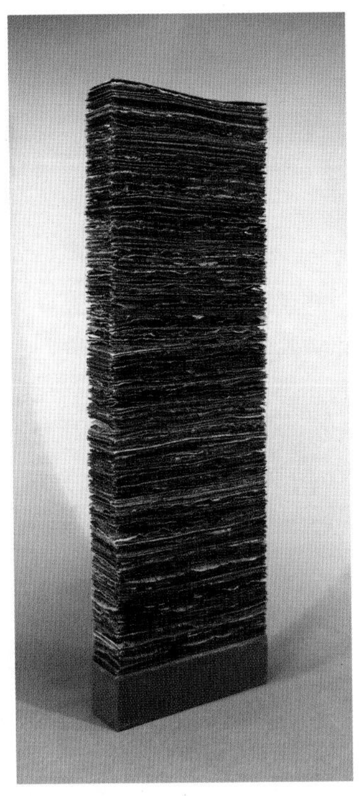

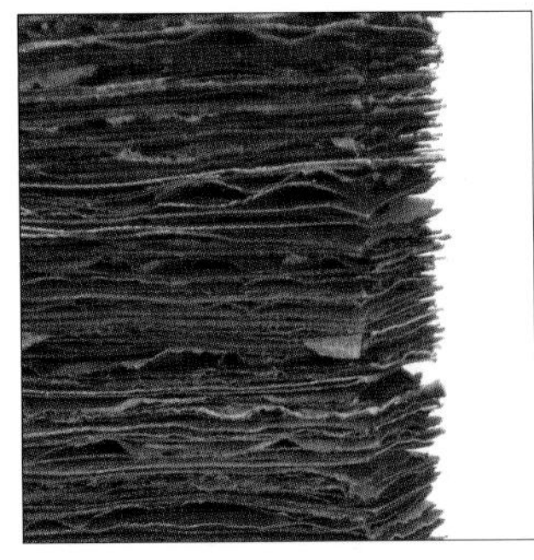

◀ **Field Trip: Good Dirt** | 2010
36 x 7 x 1 inches (91.4 x 17.8 x 2.5 cm)
Handmade paper, pigment and walnut dye
Photos by artist

Acknowledgments

To curator Eileen Wallace, whose knowledge and discerning eye gave shape to this wonderful volume, we extend our sincere appreciation. A special thanks goes to the artists who submitted work for the book. We're also indebted to Dawn Dillingham for her first-class editorial support, and to Shannon Yokeley and Maegan Zigarevich for their art production expertise. Proofreader Susan Kieffer also provided invaluable assistance, and art director Travis Medford produced a beautiful layout. Our thanks to all.

—Julie Hale and Beth Sweet, editors

Portrait Photographers

Thank you to the photographers whose portraits of the artists appear in this book:

Macy Chadwick, photo by Von Span
Karen Hanmer, photo by John Kim
Susan King, photo by Allwyn O'Mara
Peter Madden, photo by Mass Art
Peter Malutzki, photo by Ines von Ketelhodt
Barbara Mauriello, photo by Jeffery Vock
Wilber Schilling, photo by Marc Norberg
Bonnie Stahlecker, photo by Rebecca Clune
Elsi Vassdal Ellis, photo by Greg Ellis
Ines von Ketelhodt, photo by Bärbel Högner

The photos of Jody Alexander, Lynne Avadenka, Sarah Bodman, Ken Botnick, Ian Boyden, Sarah Bryant, Julie Chen, Susan Goethel Campbell, Margaret Couch Cogswell, Béatrice Coron, Daniela Deeg, Brian Dettmer, Andrea Dezsö, Timothy Ely, Julie Fremuth, Daniel Essig, Daniel Kelm, Karen Kunc, Hedi Kyle, Shanna Leino, Julie Leonard, Cynthia Lollis, Adèle Outteridge, Robin Price, Harry Reese, Sandra Liddell Reese, Veronika Schäpers, Pati Scobey, Genie Shenk, Keith Smith, Barbara Tetenbaum, Claire Van Vliet, and Laura Wait are self-portraits.

Artist Index

Our American Century

★

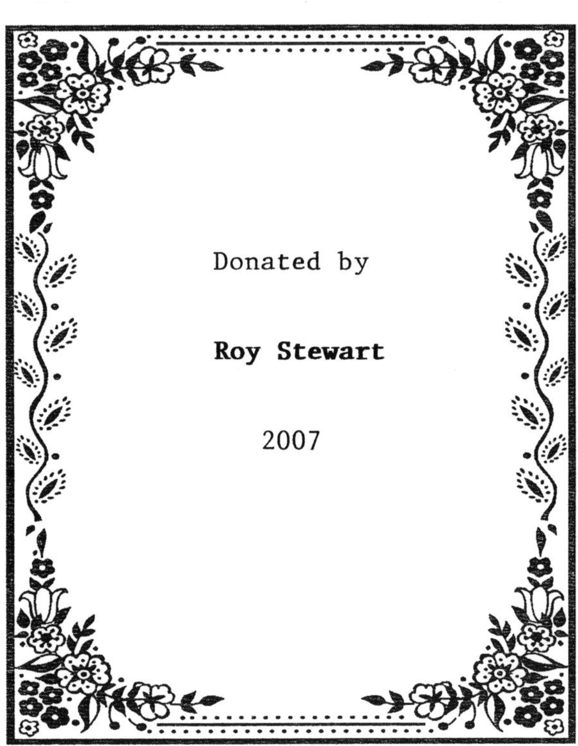

100 Years of Hollywood

★

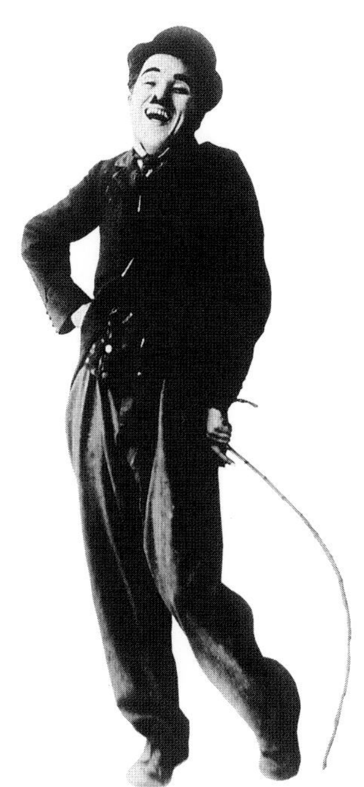

By the Editors of Time-Life Books, Alexandria, Virginia

Contents

Lauren Bacall

Cultivating Fantasy: Movies and Their Stars

From the earliest years to the present, the movies have traded on people's appetite for fantasy. Always a key to the industry's success, the making of dreams reached its peak in the "golden age" of Hollywood, the era between the 1920s and the late 1940s when the big studios held unchallenged power over stars and directors and their movies enjoyed an unrivaled hold on the public's imagination. Moviegoing then was such a way of life that during an average week in 1938, America's population of 120 million bought 80 million movie tickets.

Audiences were drawn to particular films primarily because of the stars featured in them. And the stars' appeal was fueled by ubiquitous publicity photographs gazing out from magazine covers and movie posters, the faces entirely familiar but still impossibly, irresistibly romantic.

Star portraits were a specialized form of Hollywood art. Studio photographers like the renowned George Hurrell adopted a dramatic lighting style that set their subjects brilliantly aglow against a background of shadow. The effect transformed already beautiful men and women into icons. Like the stars shown on these pages, some radiated elegance, others had a wise-guy swagger, still others an all-American appeal. Sometimes they were simply breathtakingly gorgeous, but always they seemed larger than life.

Lauren Bacall, at right, represented the very stuff of such fantasy. At age 20, the former Betty Joan Perske made her film debut opposite Humphrey Bogart in 1944's *To Have and Have Not,* creating an instant sensation with her striking looks, husky voice, and tough charm. This 1946 publicity portrait for *The Big Sleep,* which again paired the two stars, conveyed the film's hard-boiled flair and Bacall's own distinctive magnetism while stoking the public's fascination with her recent marriage to Bogart. To the studio publicity machines, the stars' real lives were additional fodder for fantasy.

For decades the great studios made an art of cultivating star appeal, but their days of absolute power could not last. Television began competing for viewers. A new crop of actors and directors demanded and got more control over their own careers. A trend toward greater realism sent moviemakers off studio lots and out on location. Yet through these and all the other changes of its first 100 years, Hollywood has remained the film capital of the world, and its movies and stars retain their power to fascinate.

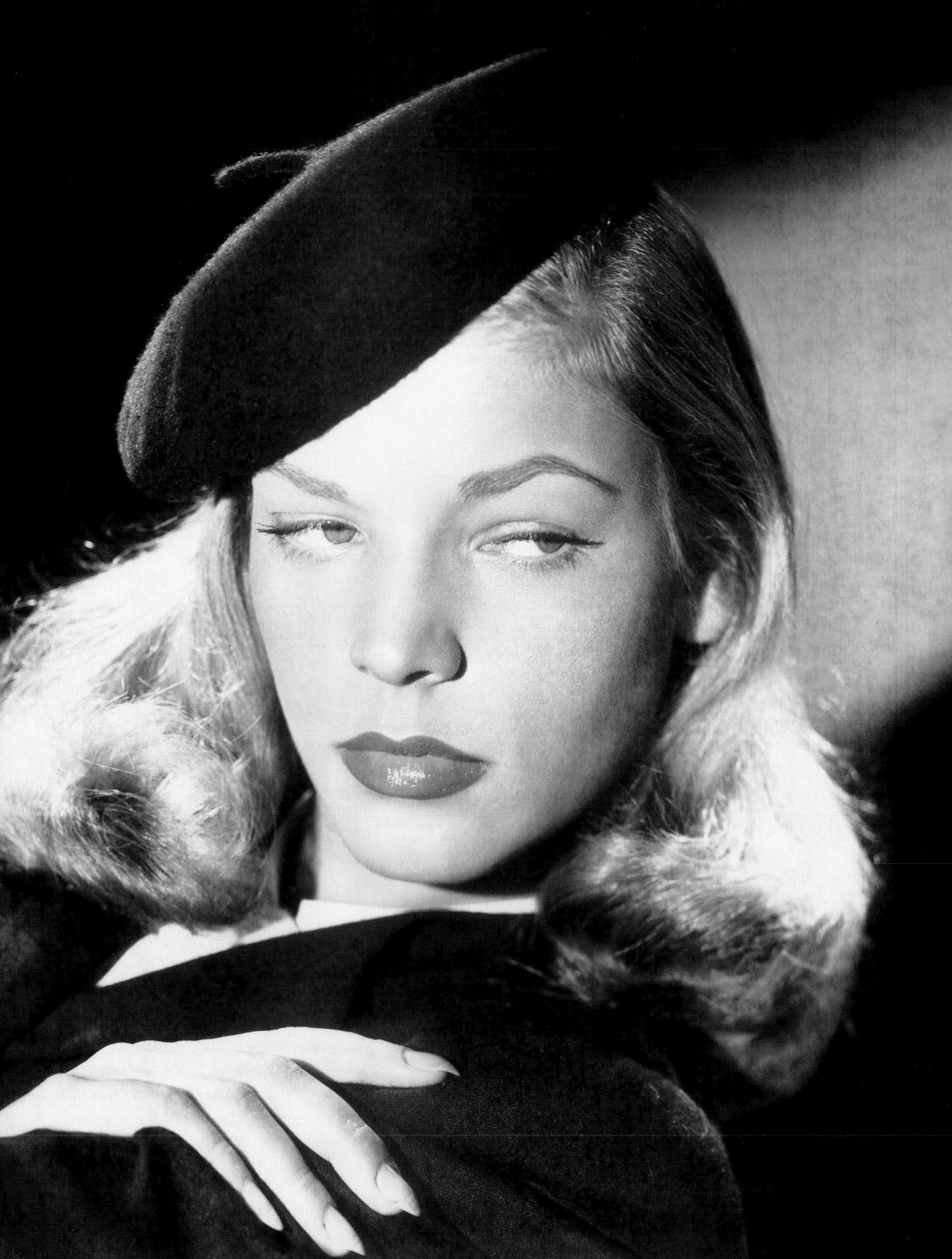

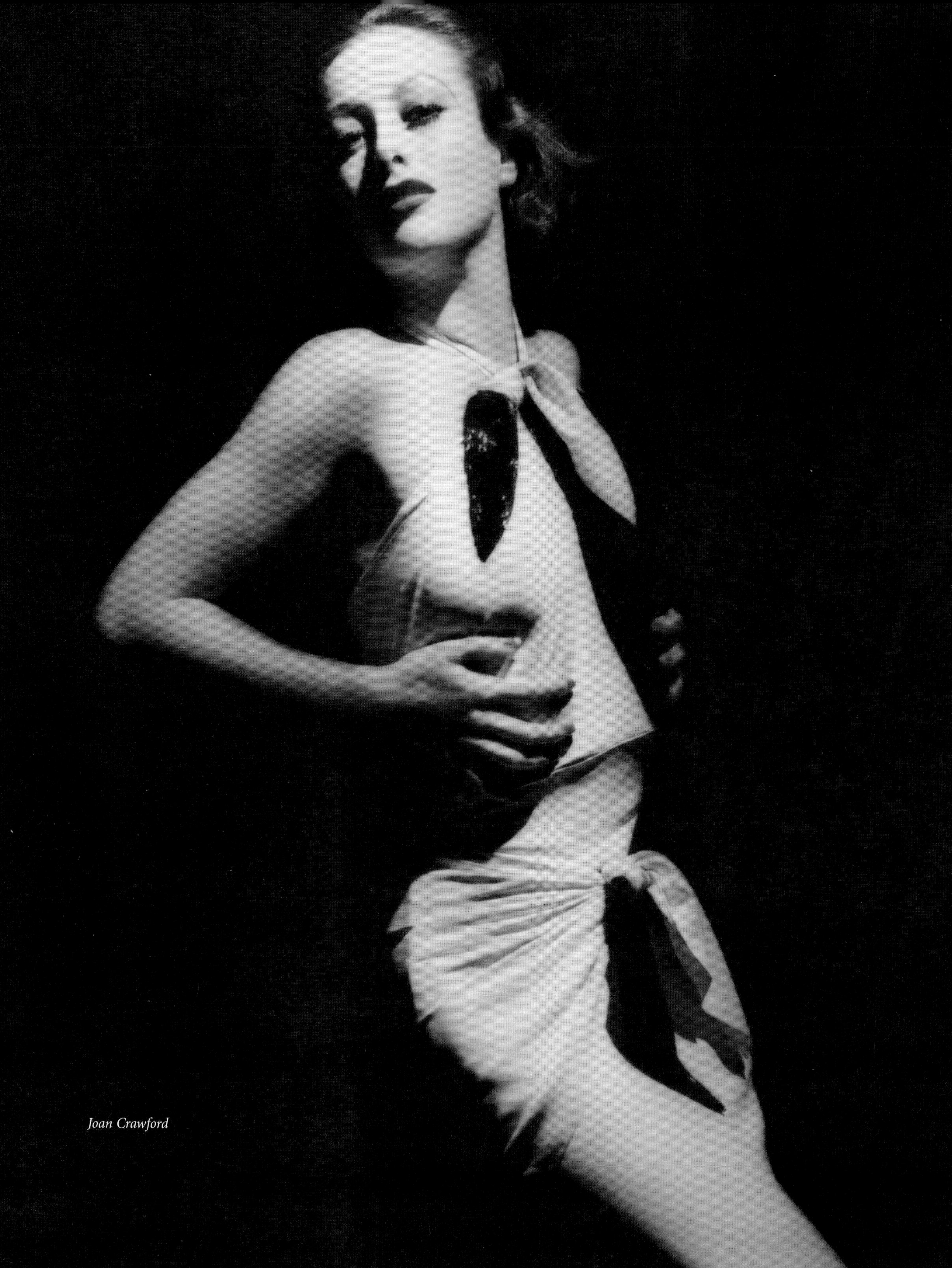

Joan Crawford

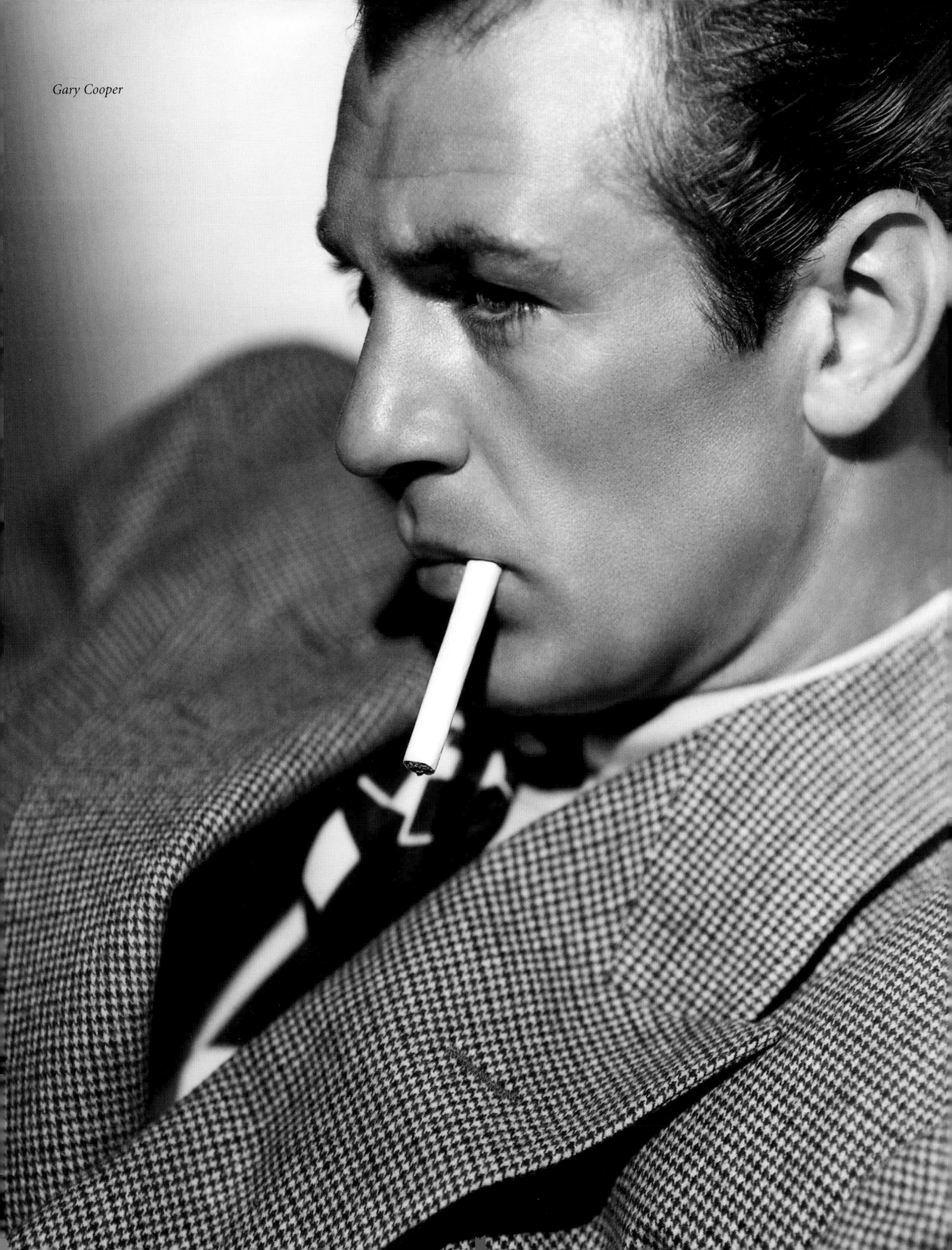
Gary Cooper

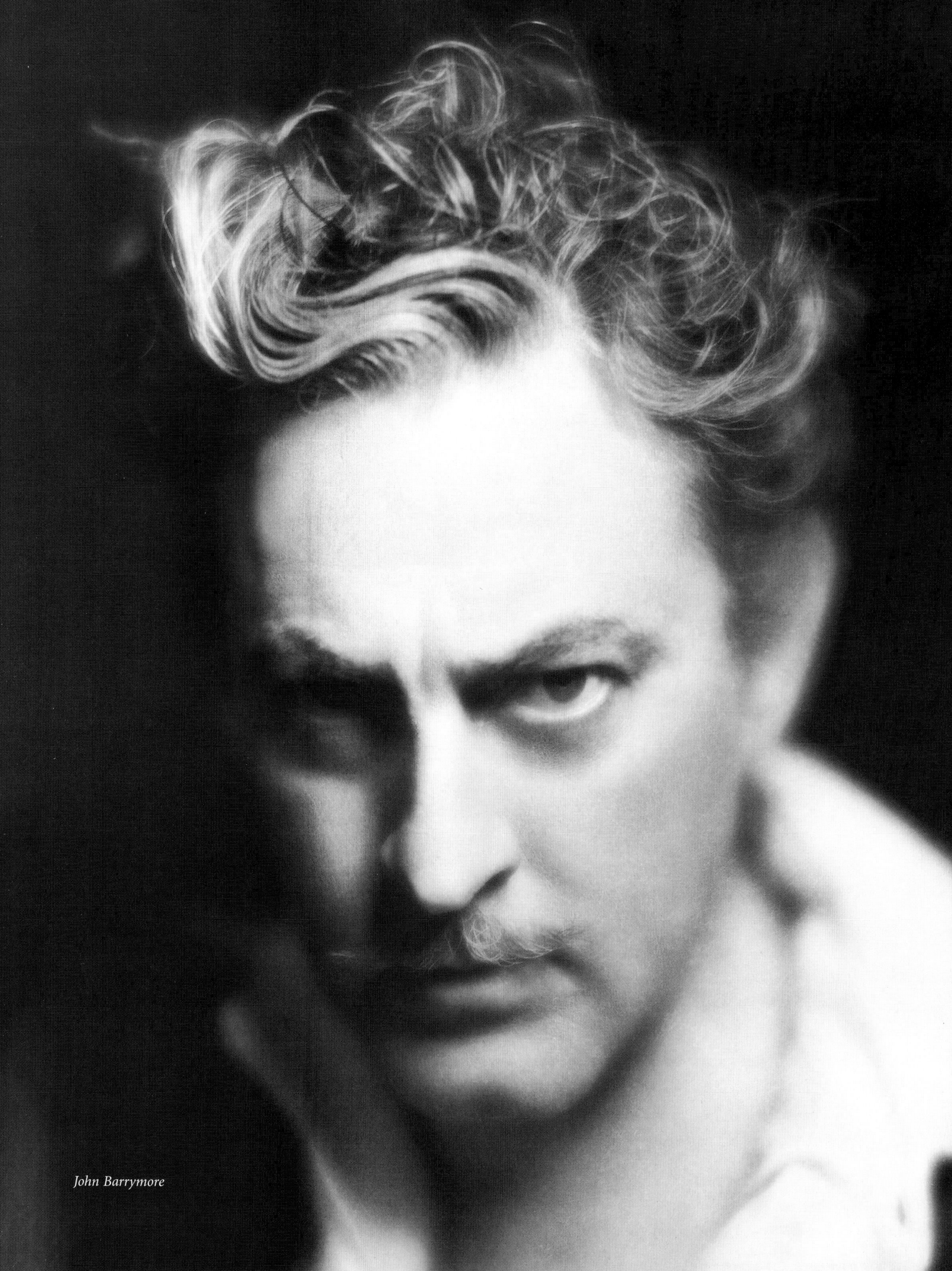

John Barrymore

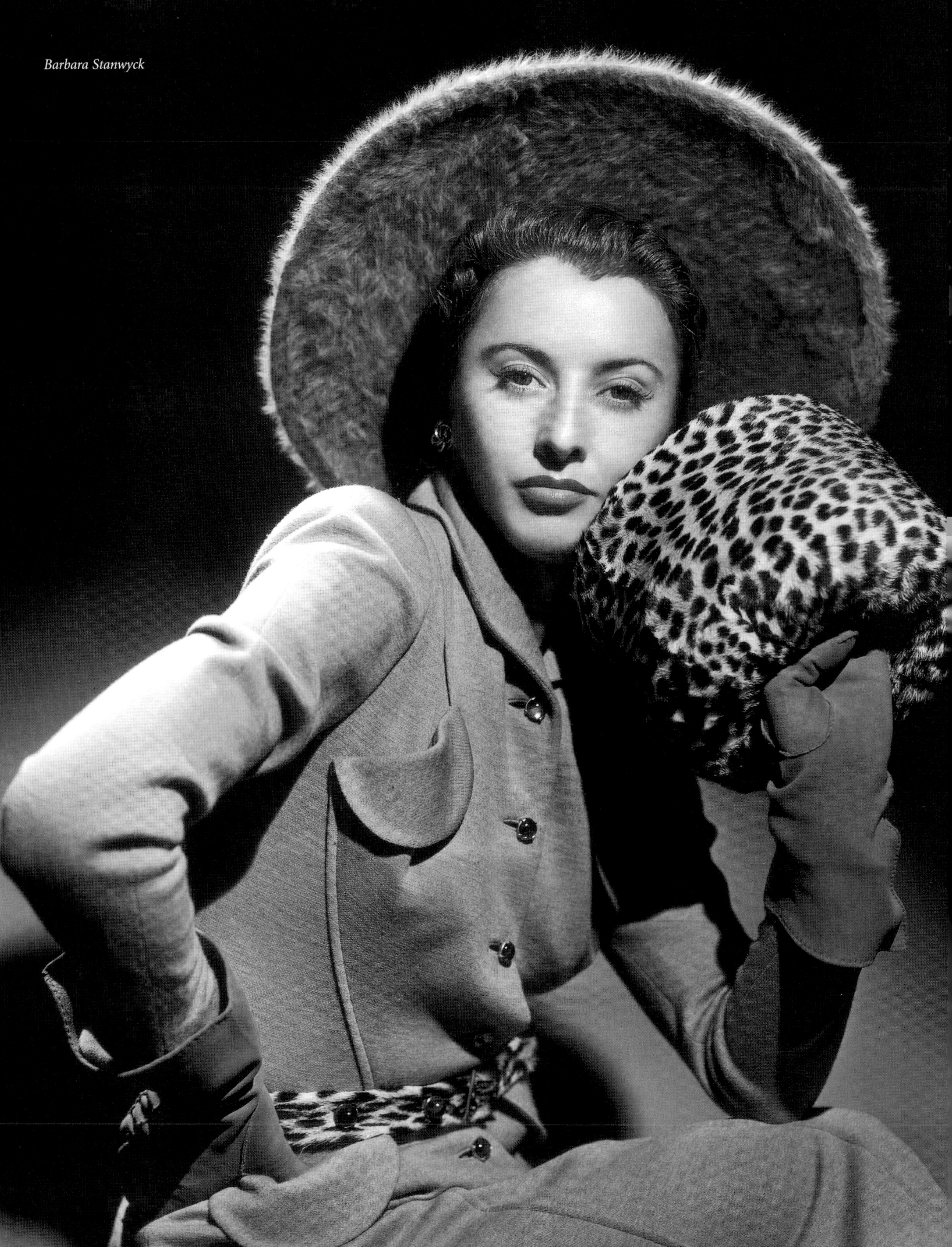
Barbara Stanwyck

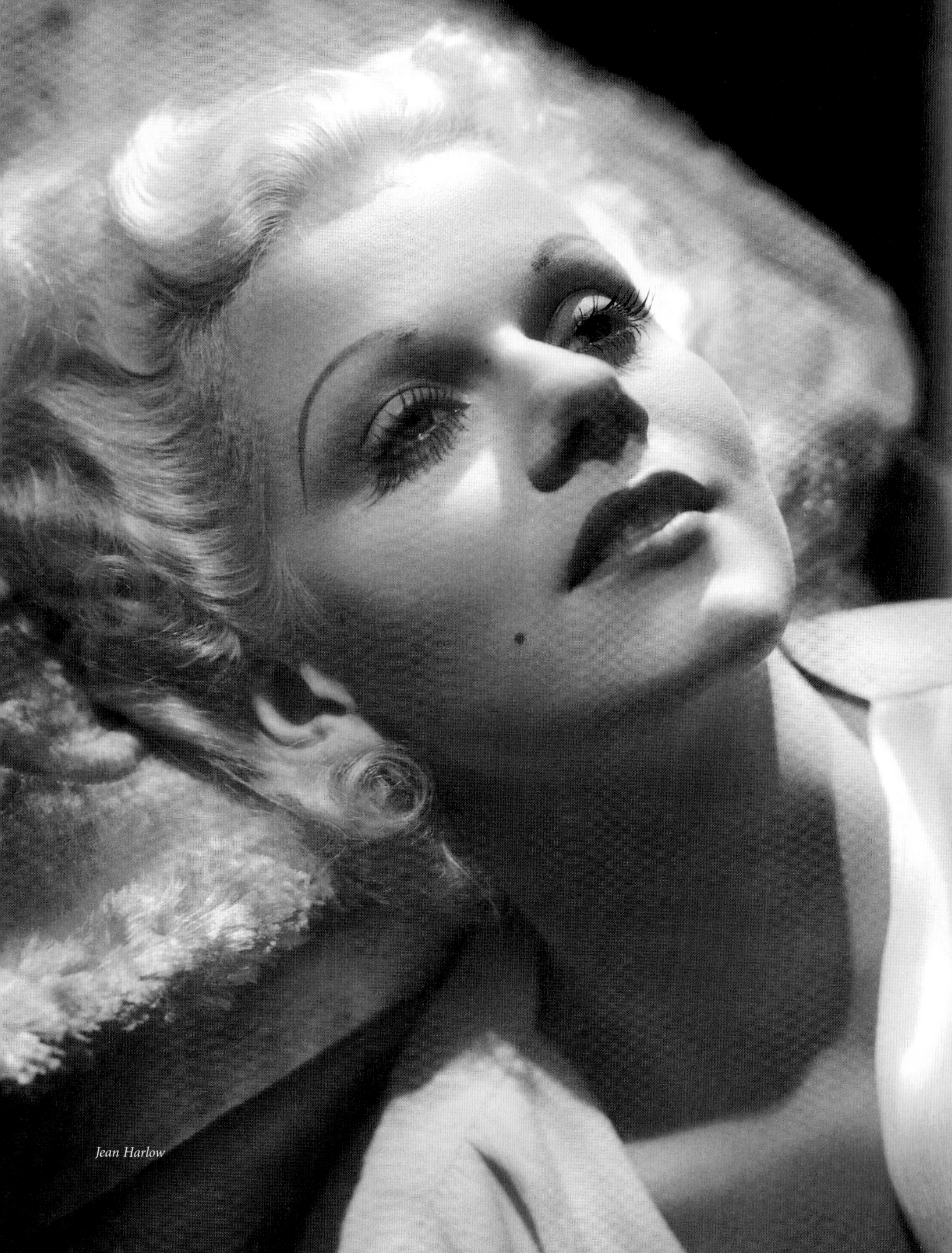

Jean Harlow

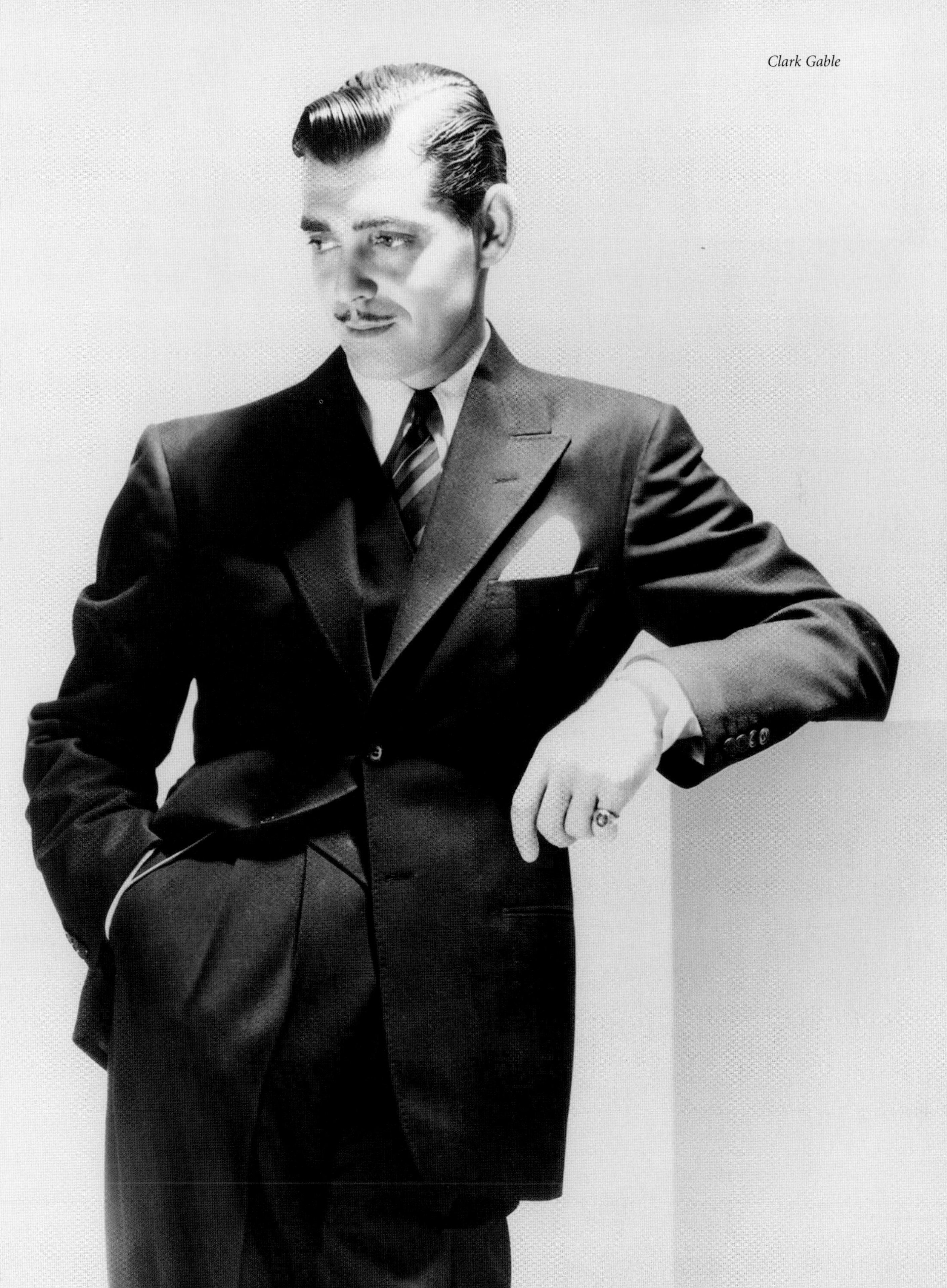

Clark Gable

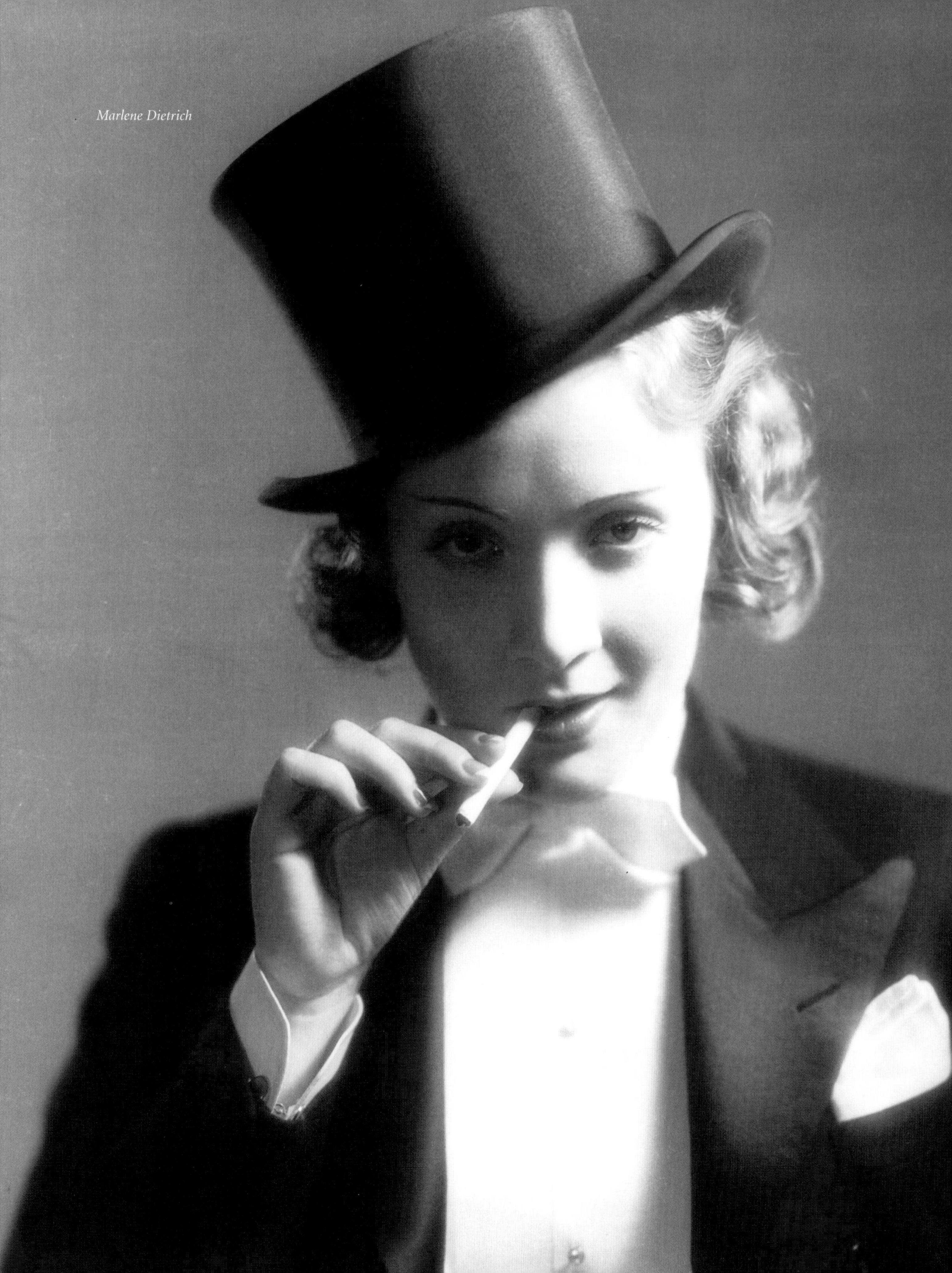
Marlene Dietrich

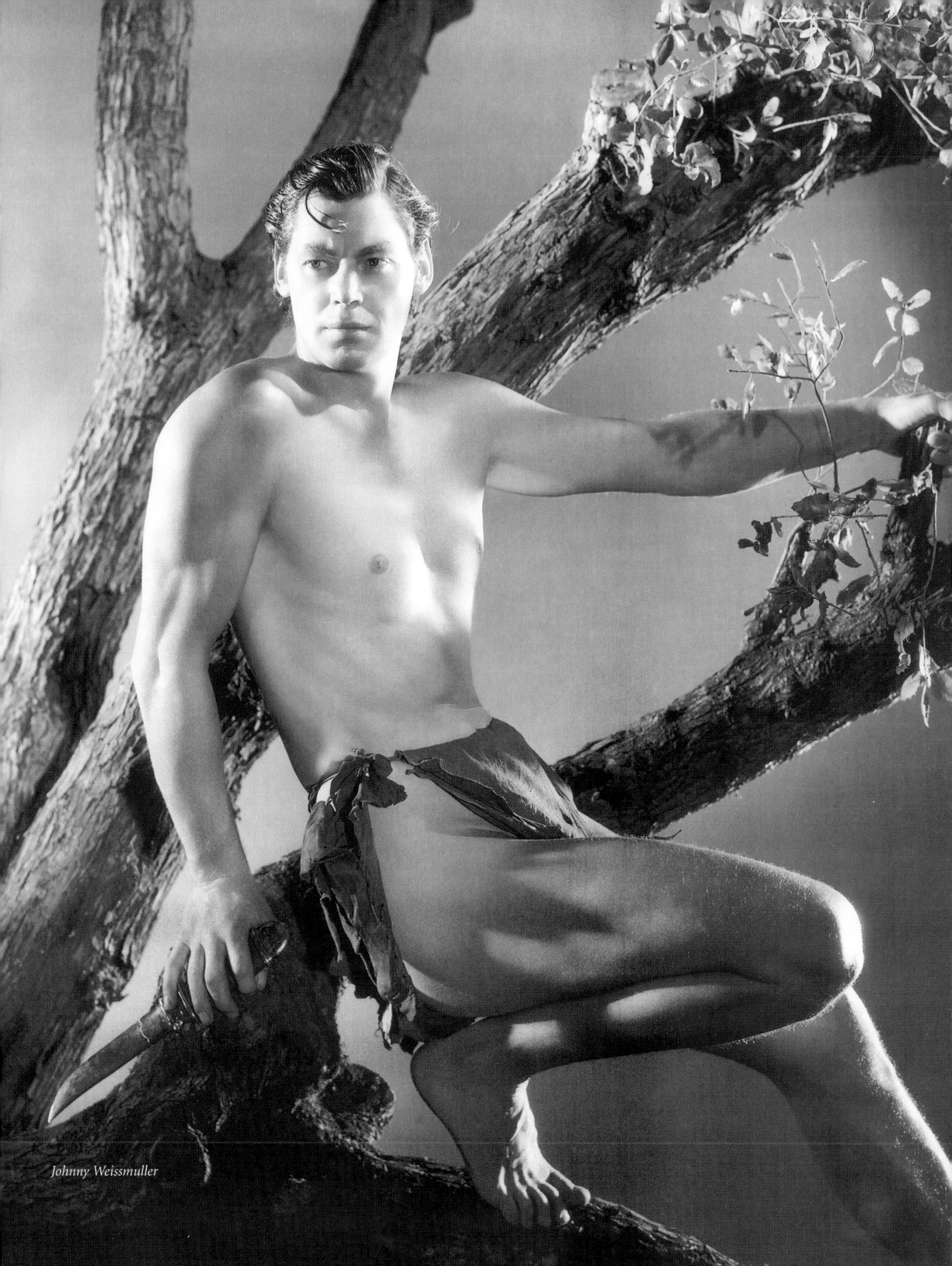

Johnny Weissmuller

Greta Garbo

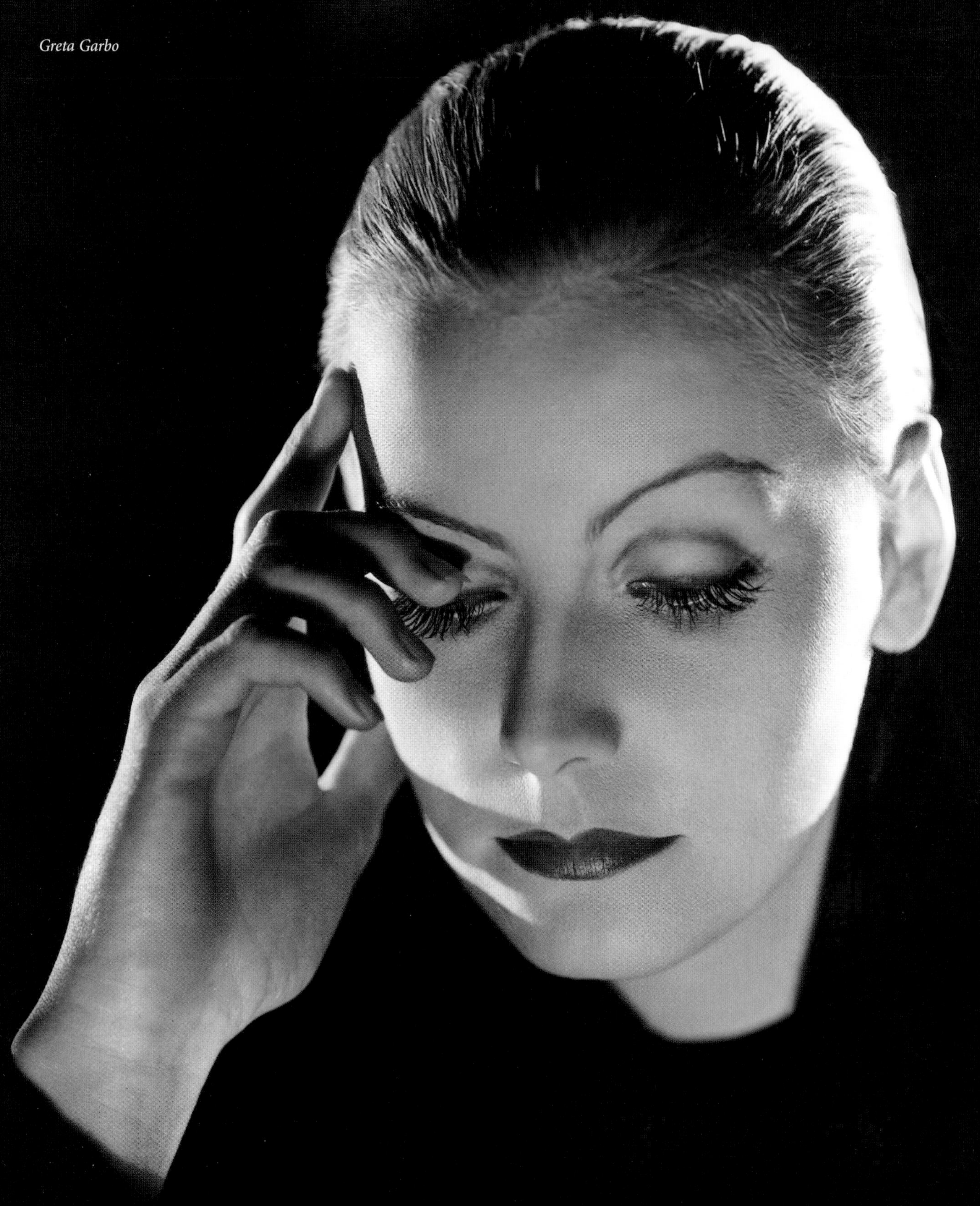

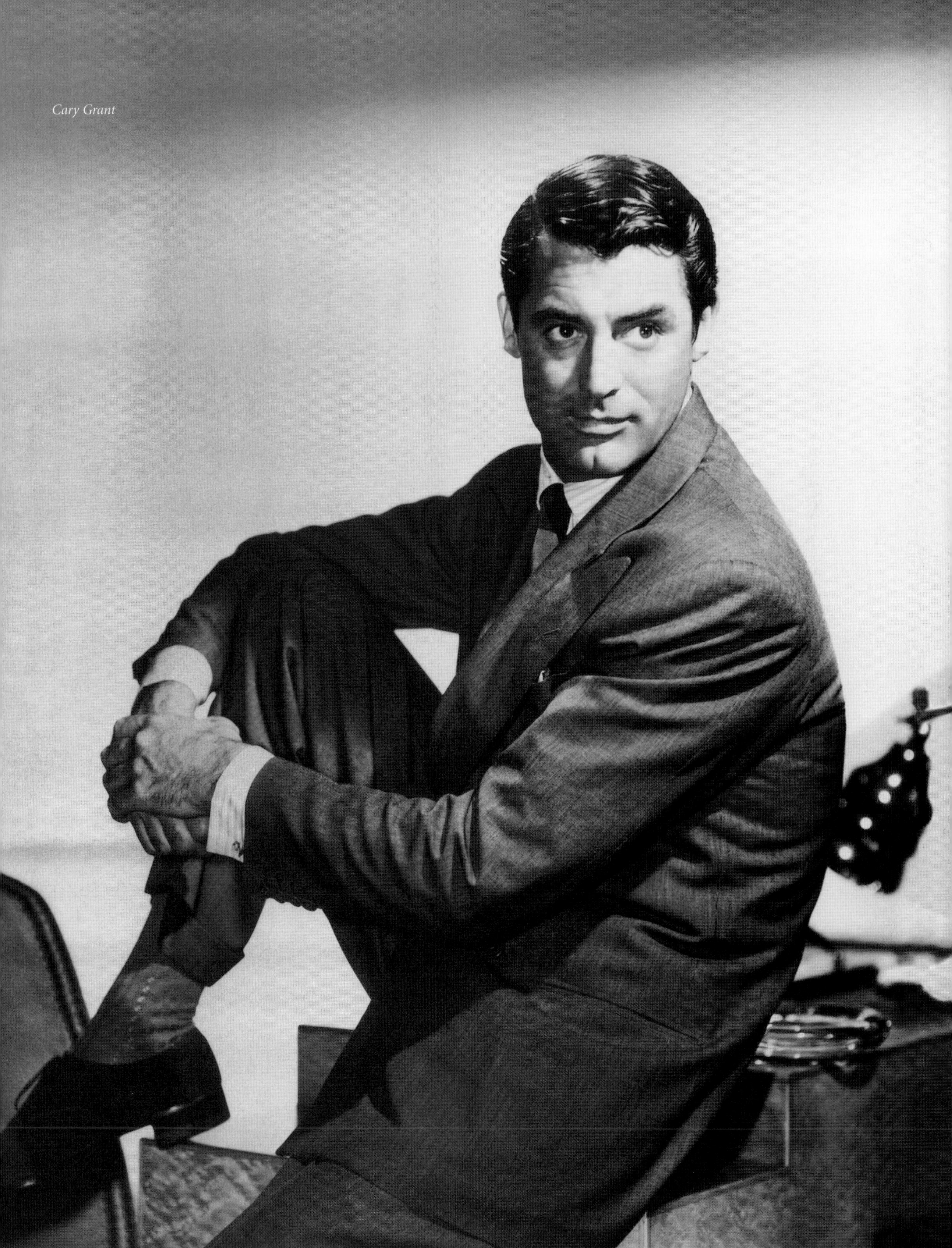

Cary Grant

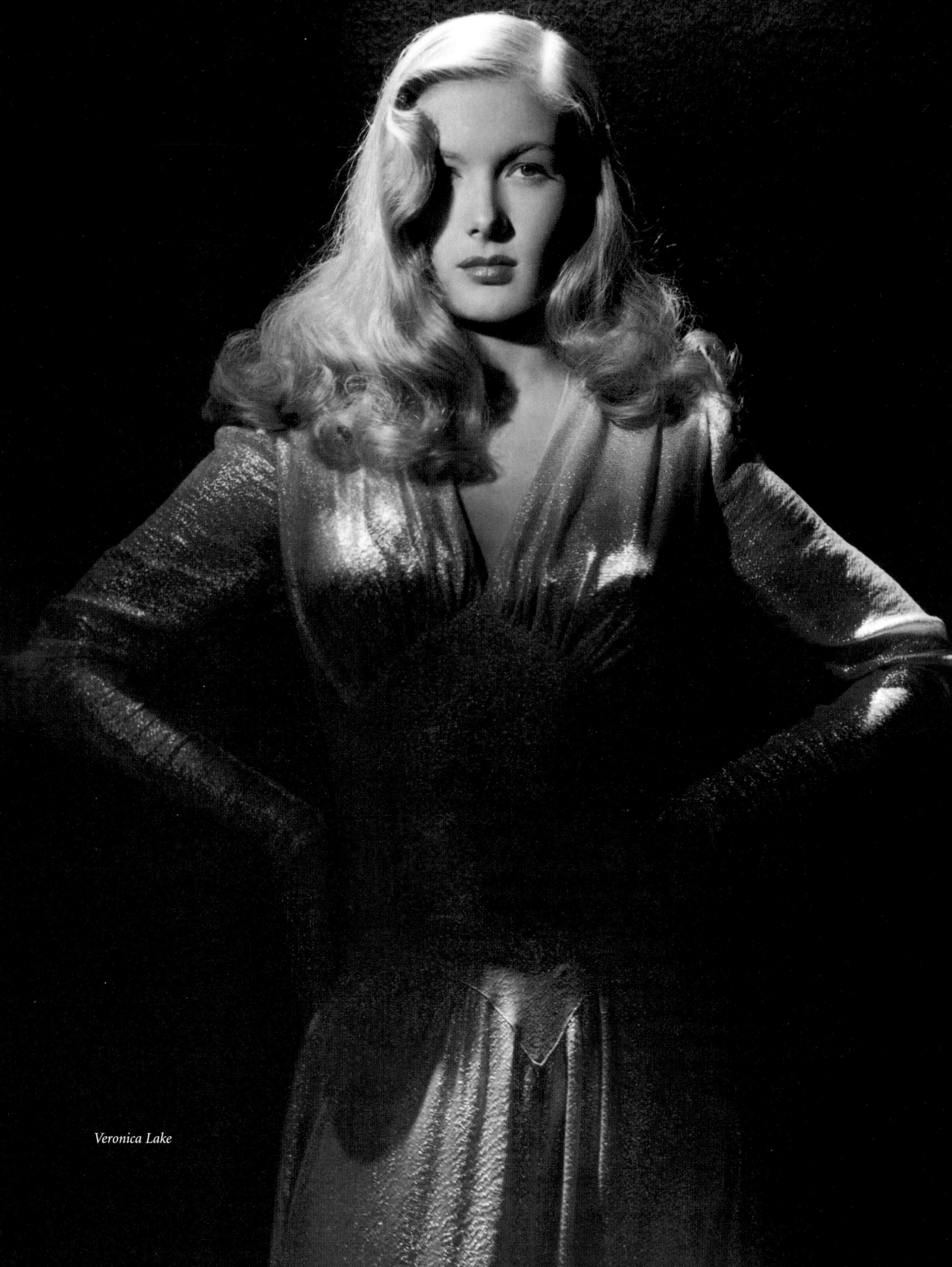

Veronica Lake

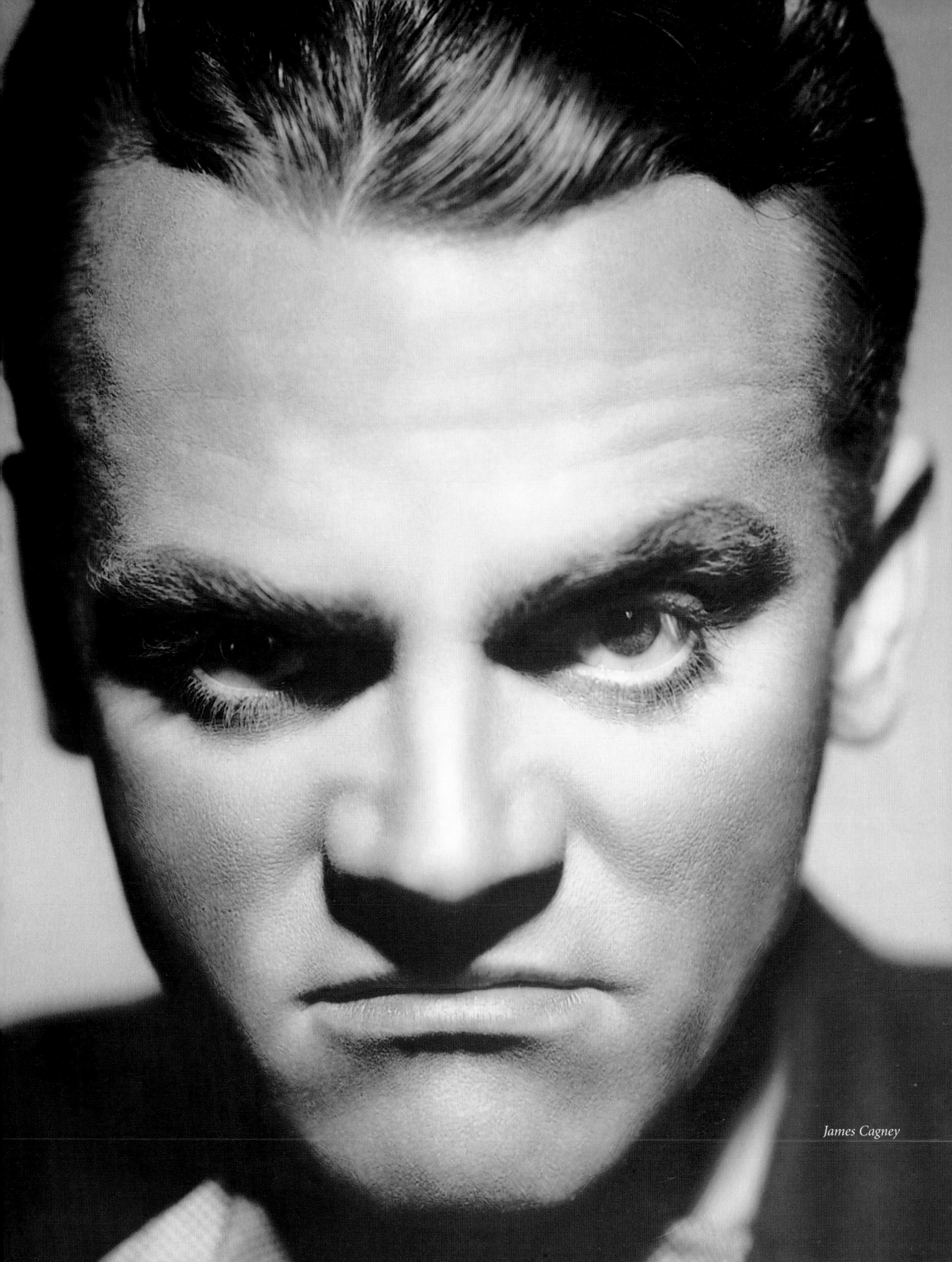

James Cagney

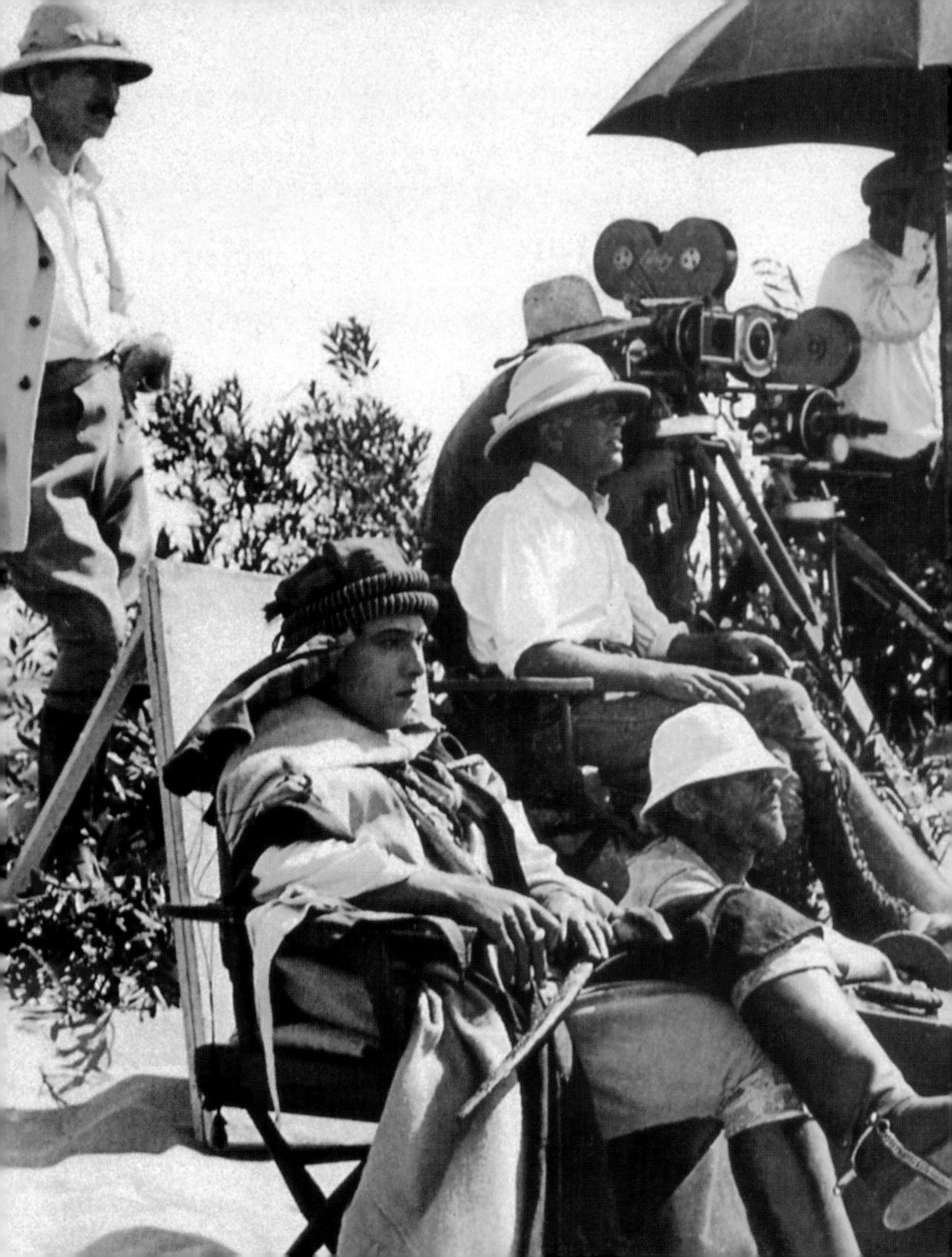

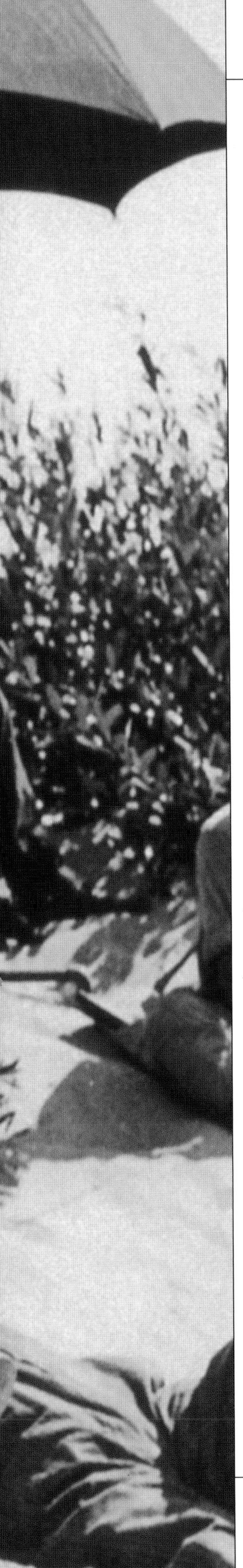

The Birth of American Film

★

PHOTOGRAPHS SPRING TO LIFE

In 1896 a short motion picture of waves crashing onto a beach debuted at a New York music hall—and viewers in the front rows squirmed at the prospect of being drenched. An audience in Paris panicked and fled as the screen filled with the image of an onrushing locomotive. The mixture of reality and illusion produced by photographs that suddenly became moving pictures contained a potent magic. The pioneers who understood that magic best made movies into an instant industry.

From humble beginnings in "peep-show" machines, motion pictures took only about two decades to evolve into complex, feature-length spectacles shown in palatial theaters seating thousands. In the eyes of ordinary moviegoers and critics the cinema rapidly came into its own as a distinct form of art. And while this growth was taking place, film production migrated from the East Coast to southern California, where the climate let dream factories run year round.

Appearing almost as quickly as the films themselves, movie magazines let fans read all about Hollywood's emerging nobility: stars like lovely Mae Murray, adorning a 1924 magazine *(inset),* or smoldering Rudolph Valentino *(left, foreground);* moguls such as MGM's Louis B. Mayer or Paramount's Adolph Zukor; and brilliant directors like D. W. Griffith. By the early 1920s movies had become America's fifth most lucrative industry.

A pith-helmeted production crew shoots a scene for the 1921 desert epic The Sheik. In costume for the title role, silent-era heartthrob Rudolph Valentino awaits his turn in front of the camera.

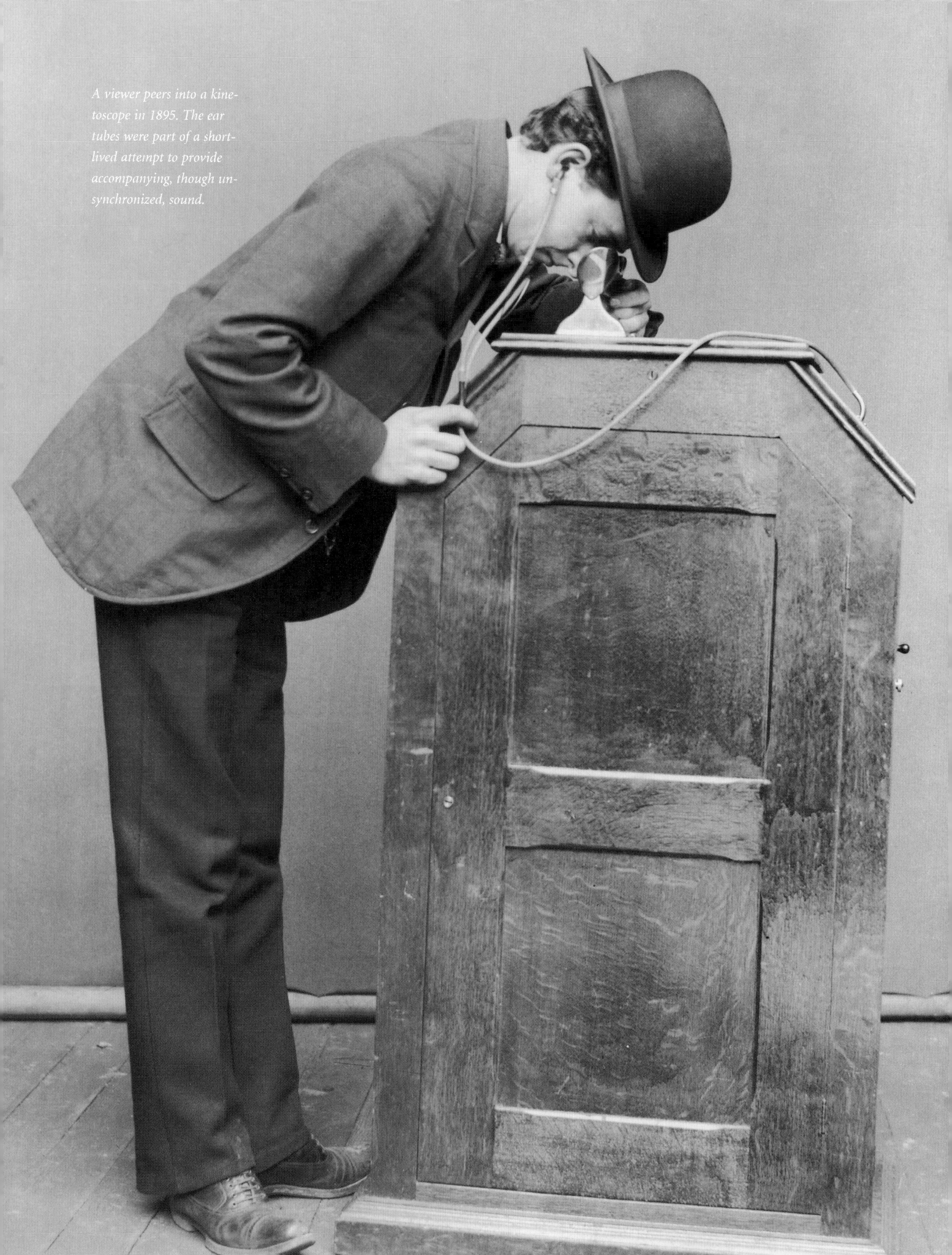

A viewer peers into a kinetoscope in 1895. The ear tubes were part of a short-lived attempt to provide accompanying, though unsynchronized, sound.

East Coast Origins

In 1888 the New Jersey laboratory of America's leading inventor, Thomas Alva Edison *(below, right),* developed the kinetograph, the world's first motion-picture camera. Though Edison got the credit, the invention was primarily the work of one of his assistants, W. K. Laurie Dickson.

Six years later the Edison Company introduced another marvel—the kinetoscope *(left),* the first commercial system for showing motion pictures. To use the boxlike contraption, a customer put in a penny, gazed through a viewer, and watched some postage stamp-size action play out as a 50-foot loop of film unrolled over a period of a few seconds.

The content of the films was as rudimentary as the peep-show machine itself: Pretty women danced, terriers worried rats, trains rushed by, and contortionists twisted into knots. Viewers, however, were stunned and

> "If we make this screen machine that you are asking for, it will spoil everything."
>
> Thomas Edison, arguing against the development of a motion-picture projector

delighted at the experience of seeing still photographs erupt into motion. Kinetoscopes quickly began operating in arcades, bars, and stores throughout North America and Europe.

The obvious next step was to liberate motion pictures from their tiny existence in the box and project them large on a screen. Edison at first did not approve, believing that one-at-a-time viewing meant bigger profits. But in 1896 he introduced a projector called the vitascope. (He had acquired it from its creator, Thomas Armat, who went unnoticed as Edison, again, accepted praise for someone else's work.) The vitascope was an instant hit, and soon audiences were gathering before screens in makeshift theaters across the land.

Having patented all these devices, Edison hoped to control the world of cinema. But some filmmakers and exhibitors defied him by using cameras and projectors imported from Europe, where he had not registered his

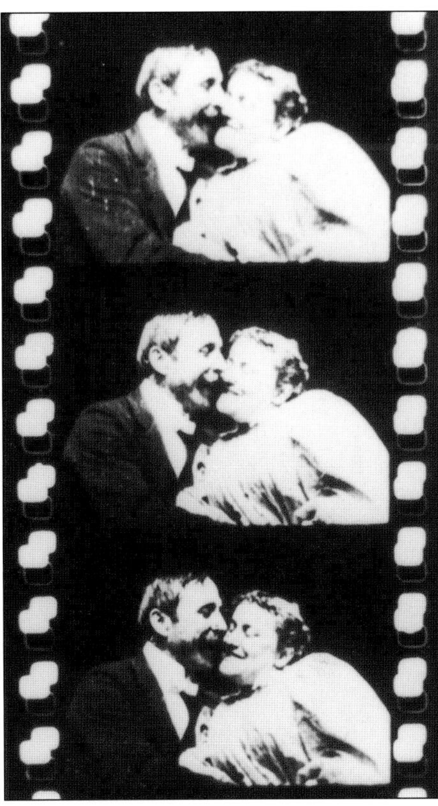

In an 1896 Edison film, May Irwin and John Rice reenact a scene from a stage play, creating a cinematic first and sparking moral indignation.

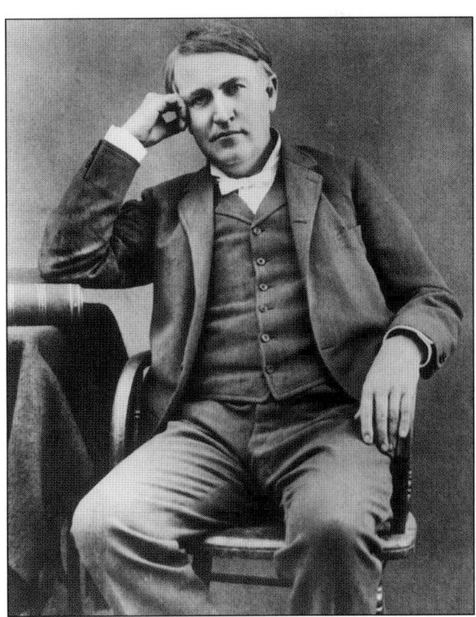

Thomas Edison (above, in 1889) was as ferocious in business as he was ingenious in the lab, spending big money to enforce his patents.

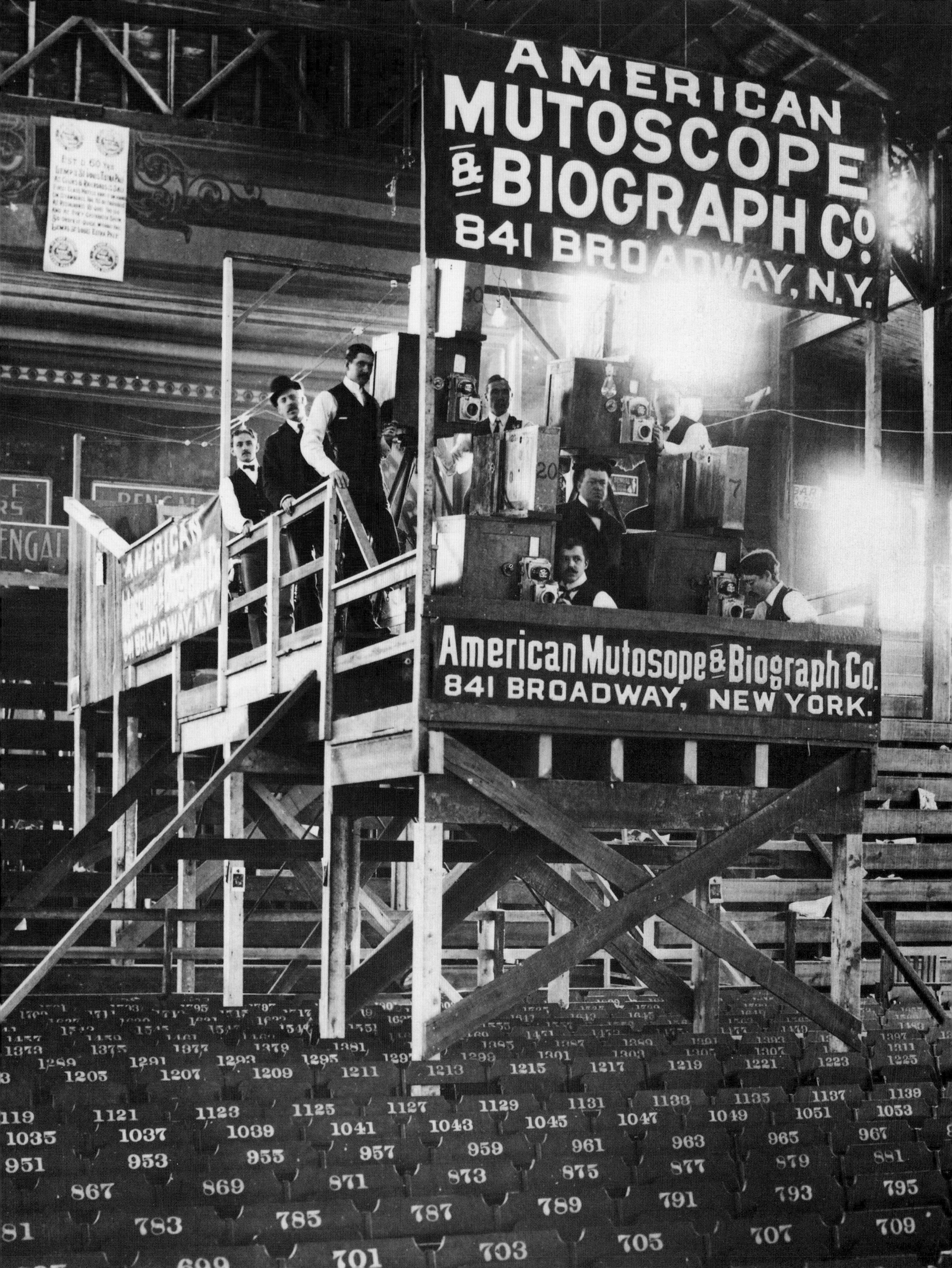
AMERICAN
MUTOSCOPE
& BIOGRAPH Co.
841 BROADWAY, N.Y.
American Mutosope & Biograph Co.
841 BROADWAY, NEW YORK.

patents. Meanwhile, a rival system emerged. Since Edison's patents were based on the sprocket holes in motion-picture film, an outfit called the American Mutoscope and Biograph Company devised a camera that used unperforated film.

Edison filed suit, but the courts sided with Biograph, which then suggested a partnership. In 1908 Edison, Biograph, and several other companies joined forces as a would-be monopoly, the Motion Picture Patents Company (MPPC). They attempted to close down every studio, distributor, and exhibitor that refused to honor their patents by paying licensing and other fees. They also sent thugs to steal the negatives or destroy the cameras of maverick studios.

But the independents proved more resourceful. They fought the Edison trust in court. They also headed for southern California, which got them away from the trust's patent enforcers back east and offered better weather. In the end, the independents won: The U.S. government filed a successful antitrust suit against the MPPC in 1912.

Even before most studios relocated to the obscure Los Angeles community called Hollywood, another big change was taking place in the industry—the birth of the star system. Biograph's top attraction was a comely young woman known to the public only as the Biograph Girl. Like other studios, Biograph was leery of giving its actors and actresses the financial leverage that would come with celebrity. In 1910 newspapers reported that the Biograph Girl had died in a streetcar accident. In fact, she had been lured away by the rival Independent Motion Picture Company, run by budding mogul Carl Laemmle, who most likely dreamed up and circulated the story of her death himself—possibly filmdom's first instance of a planted publicity item. Laemmle then ran advertisements blasting the lie "circulated by enemies" of his company, revealed his new player's identity as Florence Lawrence, and reaped enough publicity to make her a household name. The era of anonymous actors was ending; from now on there would be movie stars.

A Biograph crew (left) prepares to film an 1899 match between boxers Jim Jeffries and Tom Sharkey. Fights were a popular film subject.

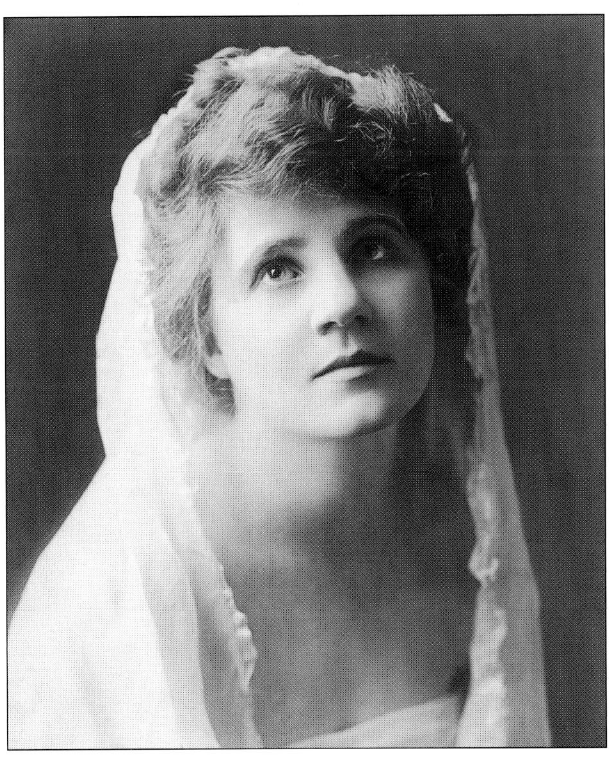

When Florence Lawrence (above) was the Biograph Girl, a review praised her acting but lamented, "We do not know the lady's name."

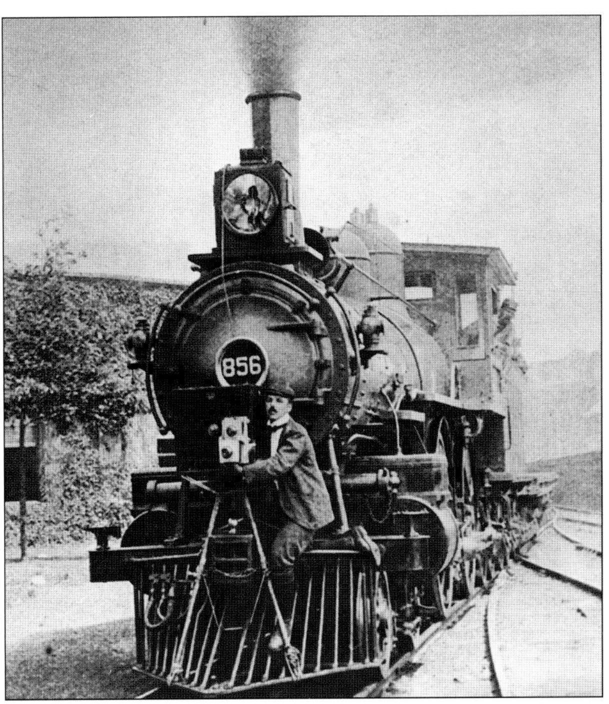

Billy Bitzer (above), one of the first masters of cinematography, uses a Biograph camera to take footage from a moving train in 1898.

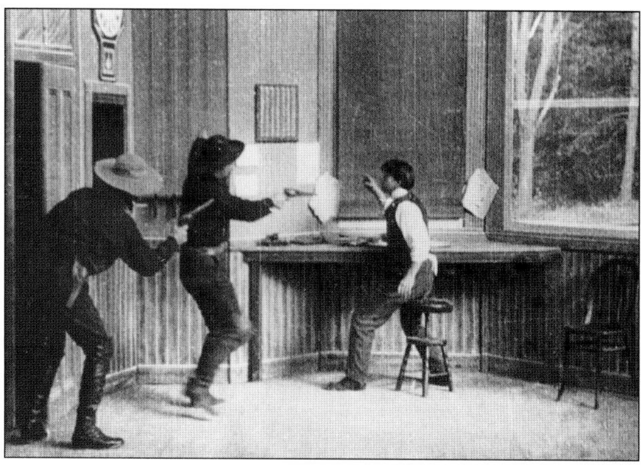

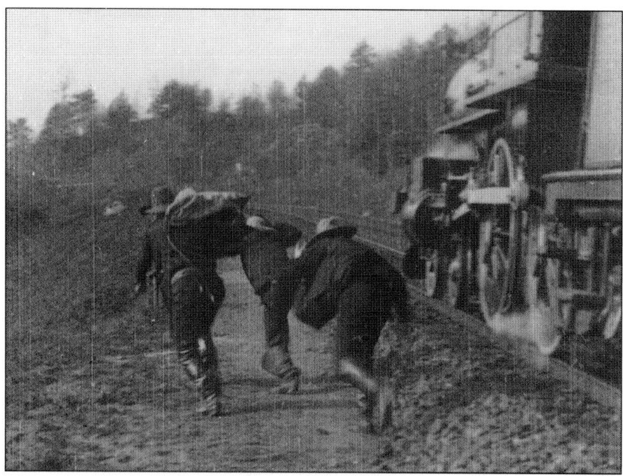

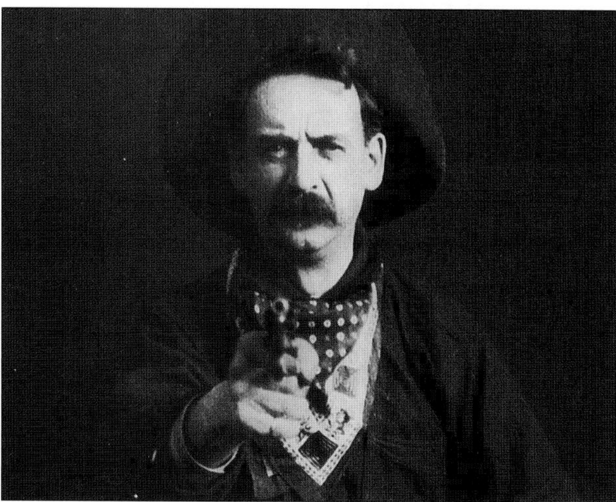

Scenes from The Great Train Robbery, directed by Edwin S. Porter, include (from top) two bandits threatening the depot agent; the robbers fleeing with their loot; and, in a thrilling if inexplicable final note, a character firing his pistol at the audience. Some audiences saw the film in a version hand tinted with bright colors.

Nickel Madness

As late as 1908 the average movie was just one reel long. A reel contained about a thousand feet of film that was good for 10 to 12 minutes' running time, cost a few hundred dollars to produce, and was shot in a single day. But if films were still brief, they had grown more sophisticated in both plot and technique.

The first clear sign of the new medium's storytelling potential was a 10-minute microepic titled *The Great Train Robbery (left),* a western shot in urban New Jersey. Made for the Edison Company in 1903, it offered something new in film, a suspenseful drama that was played out in a series of tightly knit scenes: the holdup, a chase, a dance hall episode, and an escape. At the first showing, viewers were so caught up in the tale that some of them yelled, "Catch 'em! Catch 'em!" as the thieves fled. Afterward the audience demanded that the projectionist run it again. Within five years the film brought in a staggering two million dollars in profits.

With such rewards beckoning, the movie business drew entrepreneurs of every stripe. In Kansas City, former fire chief George Hale created a new type of theater in 1904. The audience, seated in a replica of a railroad car *(near right, top),* watched travelogues that had been shot from an actual train. The concept of illusory railway journeys, dubbed Hale's Tours, became franchised internationally *(far right, top).*

Movie exhibitors soon struck pay dirt with other variations of the nickelodeon, so named because admission initially cost five cents. Nickelodeons occupied every sort of space, from cramped shops to ballrooms. Customers were mostly working class, and they loved what their nickel bought—a few short films with piano accompaniment, often interspersed with vaudeville acts, songs, or lectures.

Nickelodeons quickly became a national mania—"nickel madness," one observer called it. By 1907 there were more than 3,000 of the rough-and-ready theaters across the country, and average daily attendance had soared to the two million mark.

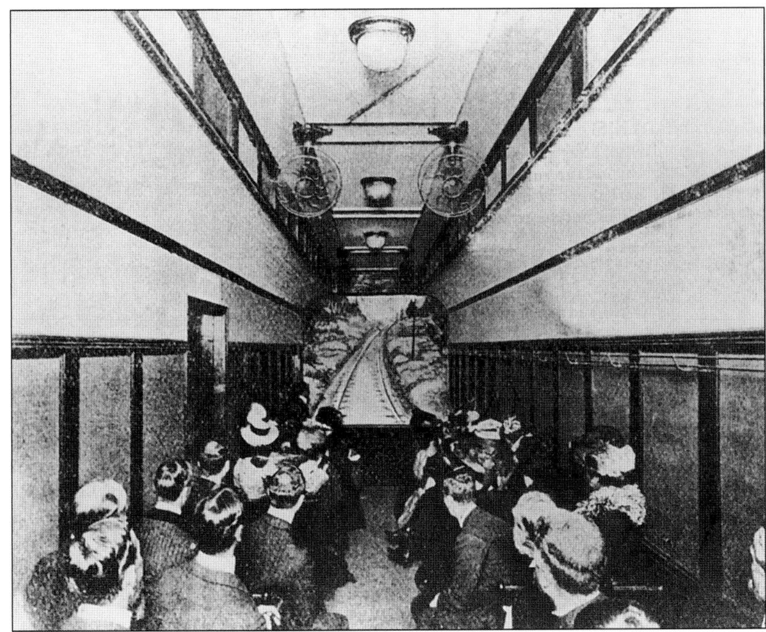

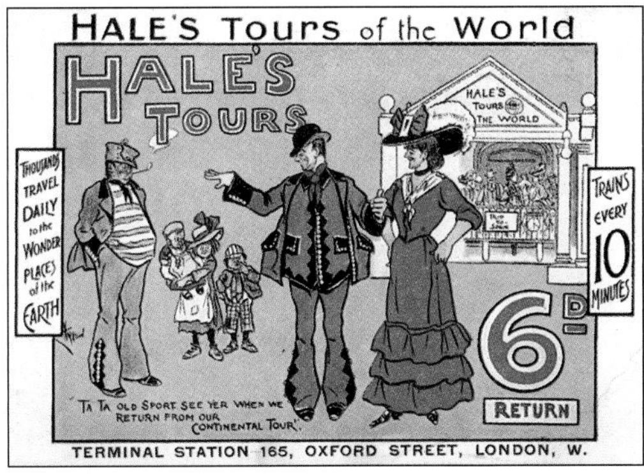

Seated in a Hale's Tours theater built to resemble a Pullman car (left), an audience takes a virtual trip by watching a film that replicates the view from a train. Such make-believe journeys were popular as far afield as London (above). To add to the illusion, the theaters were sometimes equipped with machinery that mimicked the noise and swaying motions of a real train ride.

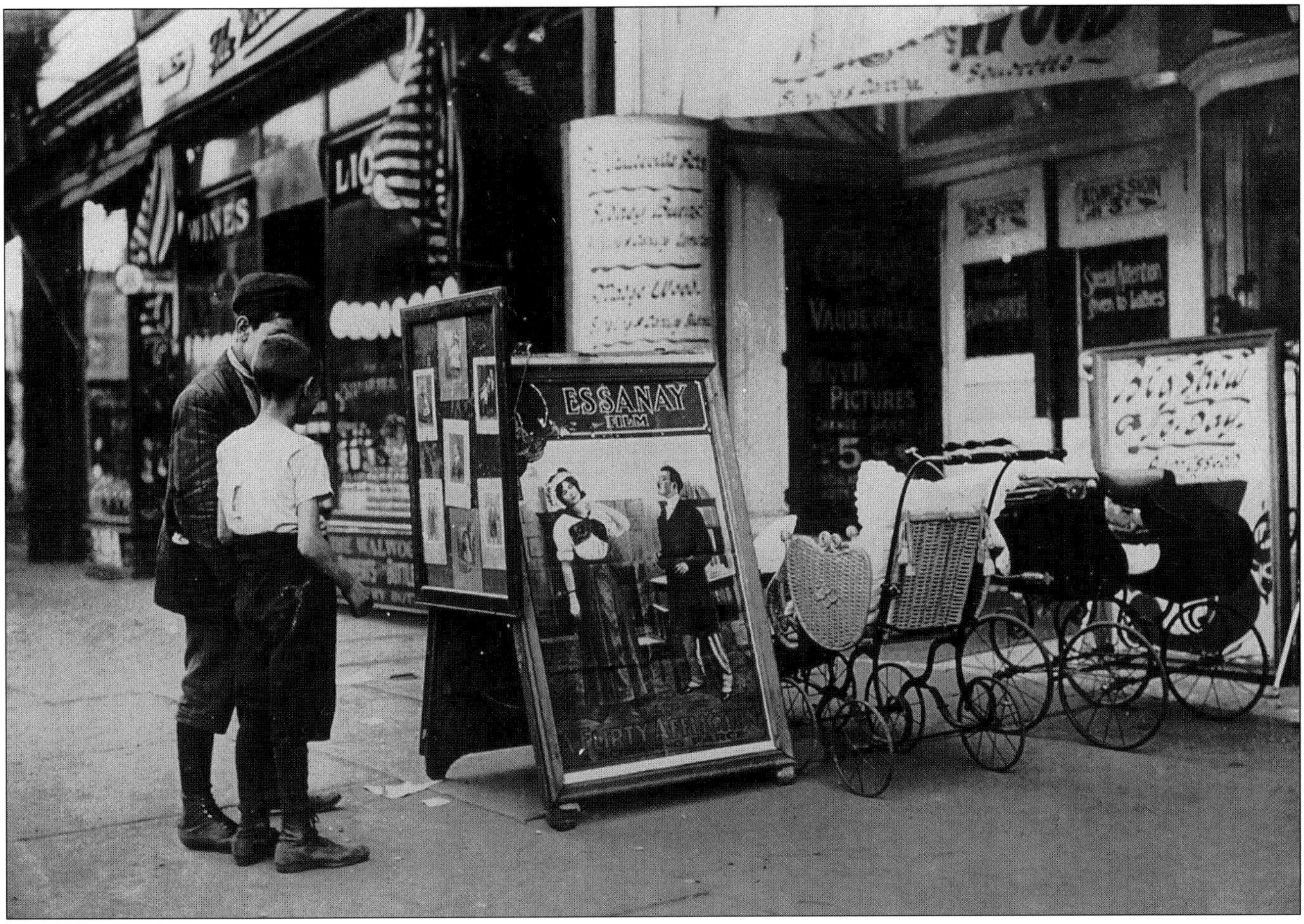

A magistrate assailed nickelodeons as "dens of iniquity," but the baby carriages outside this theater suggest that some upstanding ladies disagreed.

The First Moguls

During the second decade of the 20th century, a handful of entrepreneurs pushed aside Edison and his allies to conquer the motion-picture industry. They were ambitious, hard-charging Jewish immigrants or sons of immigrants who started by running nickelodeons, then followed the golden vein to its source—the movies themselves.

These were street-smart men attuned to the dreams of the working-class Americans who made up their first audiences. They saw the new medium's possibilities before anyone else did. The film industry had been open to them in part because it was considered a slightly disreputable novelty business. What they now wanted was to achieve culture as well as profit. They perceived that this meant moving away from the kinds of cheap one-reelers the Edison trust turned out. Paramount chief Adolph Zukor said of the trust, "They put some brains into their mechanical devices and into their sales department, but never by any chance into their films."

Under these moguls, studios acquired stables of producers, directors, writers, and stars. Production moved to balmy California, films became longer and better, and theaters grew bigger and more luxurious. It was a time of rapid evolution, steered by risktakers who started small but thought very, very big.

Key figures in building Paramount Pictures Corporation were Adolph Zukor, seen above as a 23-year-old furrier; Jesse Lasky, who performed in vaudeville with his sister Blanche (below) before becoming a producer; and Samuel Goldfish (right), later Goldwyn, who had been a glove salesman but, after marrying Blanche, helped form the Jesse L. Lasky Feature Play Company.

Paramount Pictures. Adolph Zukor was a 15-year-old orphan when he left Hungary for New York in 1888. He made good, first in furs, then in nickelodeons. But despite his success with the movies, he recalled, "These short films, one-reelers or less, didn't give me the feeling that this was something that was going to be permanent."

In 1912 Zukor bought distribution rights to a four-reel French film, *Queen Elizabeth,* starring stage legend Sarah Bernhardt. It was a success, showing that there was a market for sophisticated, feature-length movies. Since the Edison trust insisted the "time is not ripe for feature pictures, if it ever will be," Zukor chose to join the ranks of independent filmmakers, establishing a studio that he called, hopefully, the Famous Players Film Company. For distribution, he signed up with an outfit called Paramount.

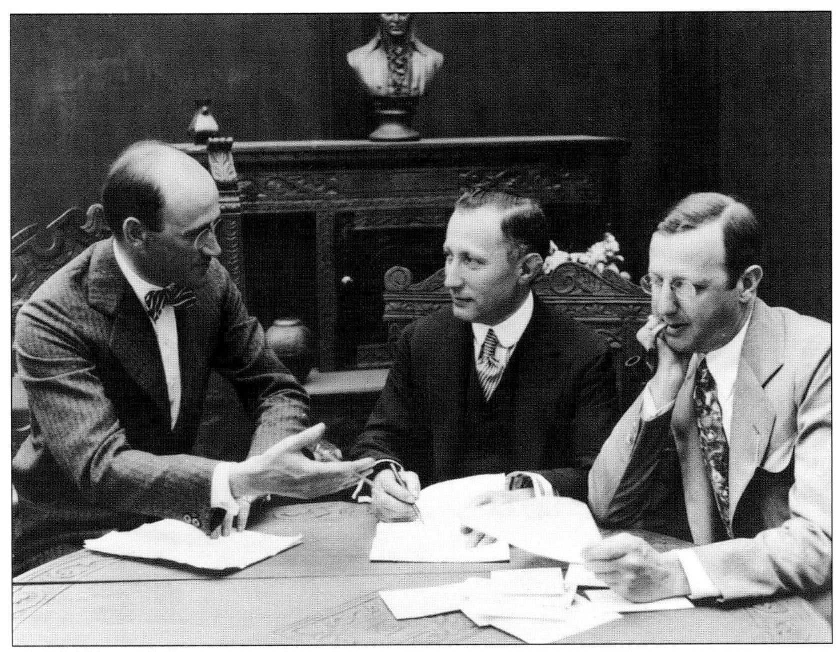

"[His] mind works with all the swiftness and certainty of the mind of a Napoleon."

Newspaper description of Adolph Zukor, 1912

Left: Sam Goldfish, Adolph Zukor, and Jesse Lasky confer in 1916. Below: Gunplay looms in The Squaw Man, Lasky's first film. The director, Cecil B. DeMille, reported death threats from the Edison trust and kept a revolver and a pet wolf on location.

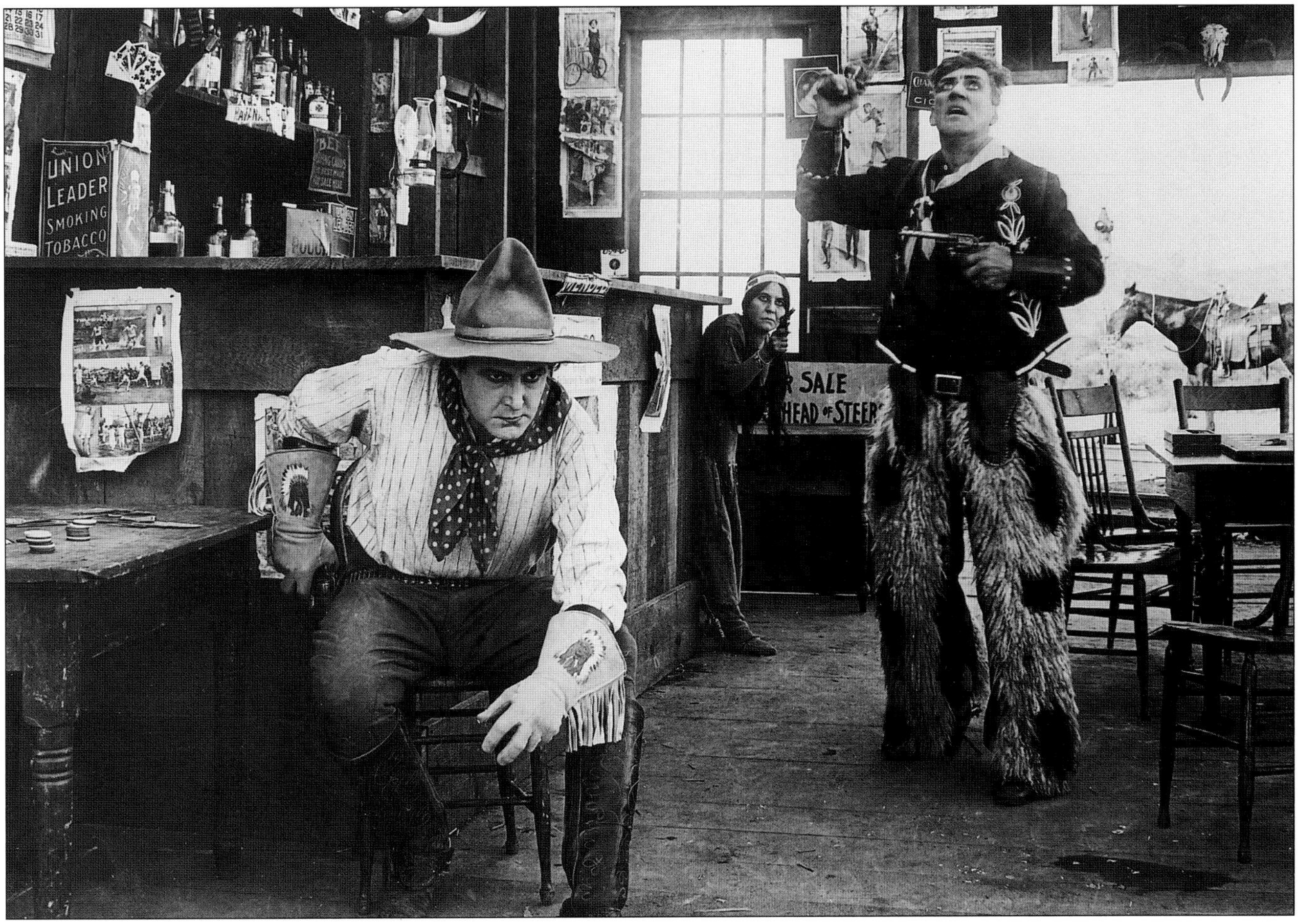

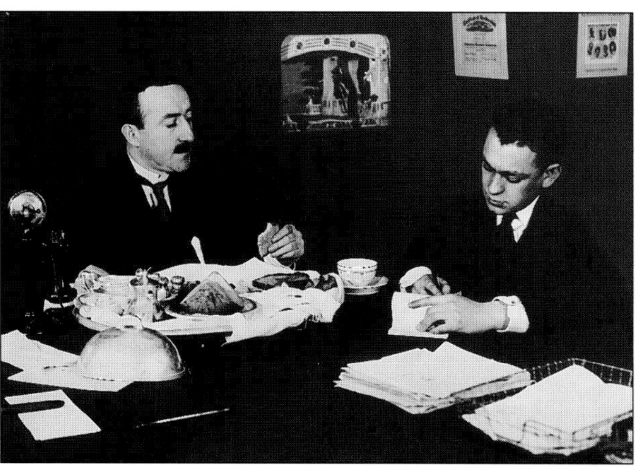

His attention on business even during meals, mogul William Fox (left) slept little and would often work for 24 hours at a stretch.

In 1916 Zukor merged his studio with the Jesse L. Lasky Feature Play Company—whose 1914 hit *The Squaw Man* was the first feature-length western made in Hollywood and marked the debut of director Cecil B. DeMille. Zukor soon clashed with and forced out Lasky's brother-in-law and partner, Samuel Goldfish, winning control first of the studio and then of the distributor, Paramount.

Under the overall name Paramount, Zukor built the nation's largest movie company. One acquaintance called him "the shark, the killer." He dominated almost all the other early moguls—and then outlived them, going into the office every morning until his final years and dying in 1976 at 103.

Fox. The brash, overbearing, and indefatigable founder of the Fox Film Corporation was William Fox, the oldest of 13 children of Hungarian immigrants. He had to leave school at age 11 to support the family, since his hard-drinking father did not, and when the elder Fox died, William spat on his coffin. In 1903, when he was 24, he and a friend bought a penny arcade. It proved so lucrative that thereafter he trained all his energies on the entertainment business.

Fox went on to buy and build fancy theaters designed to expand the appeal of movies beyond working-class audiences. He also, in 1914, embarked on film production. His studio put out dozens of westerns starring cowboy Tom Mix. Another big box-office draw for Fox was Theda Bara *(left),* the original vamp, who steamed up the screen with a predatory eroticism. As the studio's success grew, so did Fox's ambition. According to his biographer, the novelist Upton Sinclair, Fox, like a latter-day Edison, "planned to get all the moving picture theaters in the United States under his control . . .

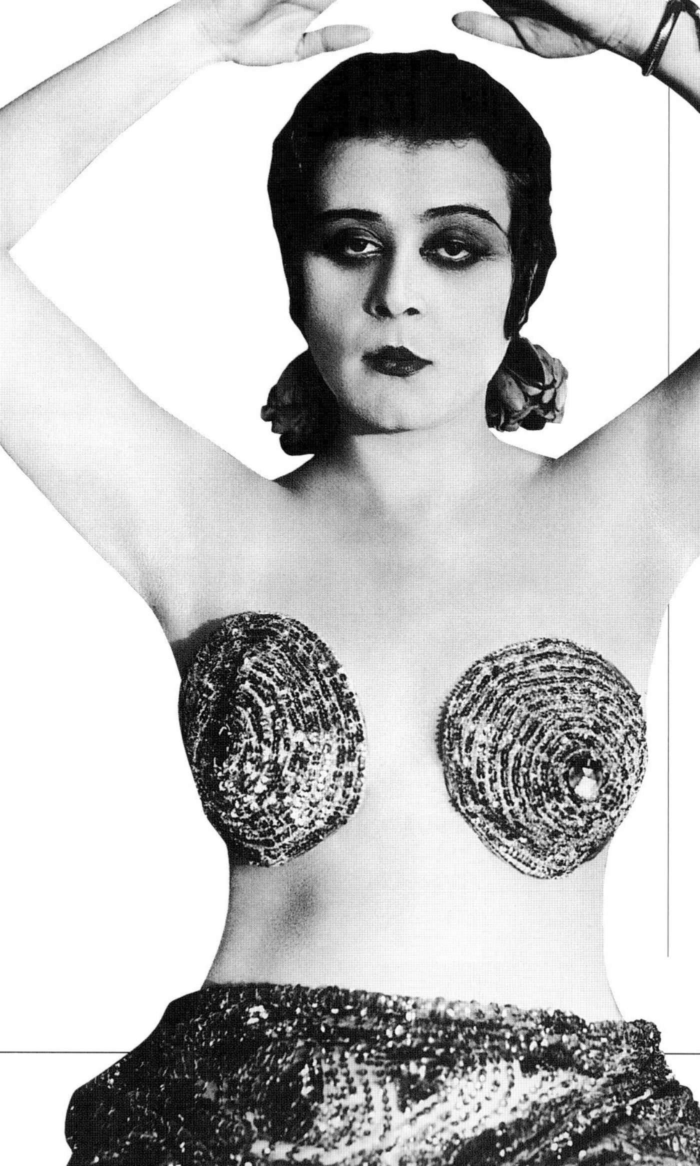

Fox star Theda Bara, in risqué costume for the 1917 film Cleopatra, played alluring sirens who seduced men, then destroyed them.

I think also that he planned to have the making of motion pictures entirely in his own hands."

But in 1929 Fox overreached. He took out colossal loans to acquire another big movie company, Loew's Inc., and its Metro-Goldwyn-Mayer studio. Just as negotiations were closing, Fox was gravely injured in an auto accident and did not recover for three months. Meanwhile, three ruinous things happened: The Justice Department decided that a merger of the two studios would violate antitrust law, the stock market crashed, and Fox's loans came due. He lost his shot at MGM as well as control of his own company.

Universal. The man who established Universal Pictures was already middle-aged before he encountered much success in life. Carl Laemmle had come to America from Germany as a teenager and for many years went from one lowly job to another. He finally rose to manager of a clothing store in Oshkosh, Wisconsin, but then he quarreled with the owner and, at 40, found himself jobless again.

One night in Chicago, however, he discovered his true calling. "I dropped into one of those hole-in-the-wall five-cent motion picture theaters," Laemmle later remembered. "The pictures made me laugh, though they were very short and the projection jumpy. I liked them, and so did everybody else. I knew right away that I wanted to go into the motion picture business."

In 1906 Laemmle started a company that rented films to exhibitors. When the formation of the Edison trust in 1908 threatened to ruin him, he decided to begin producing his own films, forming the Independent Motion Picture Company—IMP, for short. Laemmle proved to be the most feisty of the independents, lambasting Edison's group in a vigorous advertising campaign while fighting off 289 separate legal actions it filed against him. Meanwhile he enticed "Biograph Girl" Florence Lawrence to join IMP—and then lured her replacement at Biograph, young Mary Pickford.

In 1912 Laemmle merged his studio with several others to form Universal, then drove off his new partners to gain full control of the company. Universal was successful from

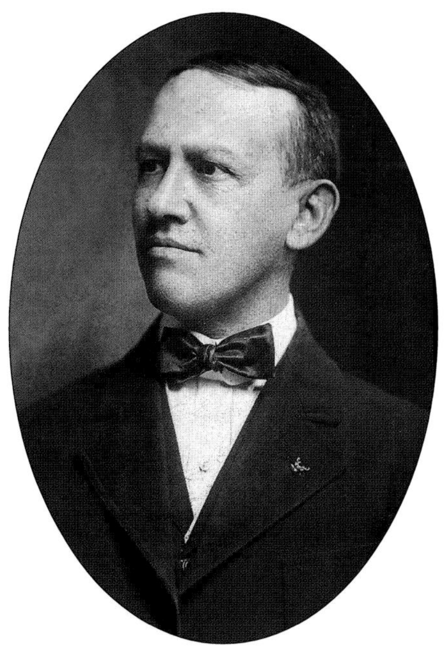

Carl Laemmle—known to everyone at Universal as Uncle Carl—had a lighthearted manner but was a fierce business competitor.

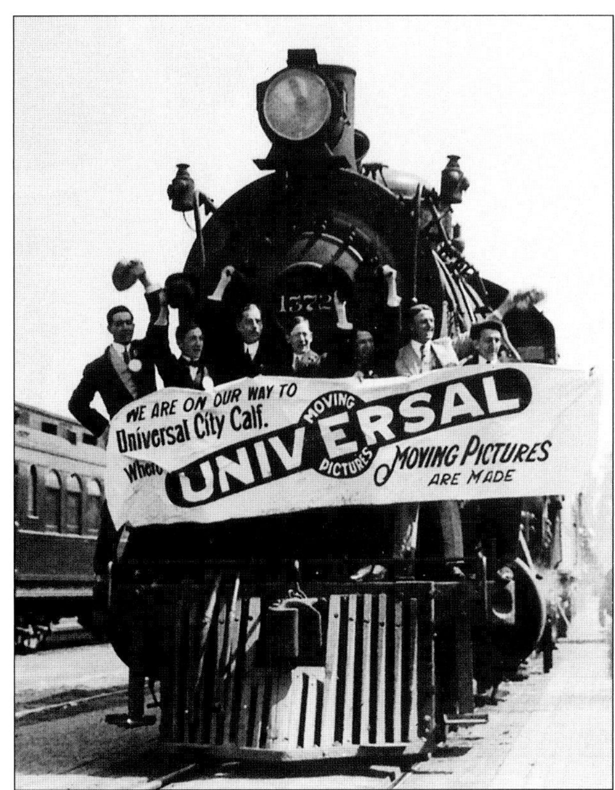

Universal executives publicized the 1915 opening of their new California studio by arriving from the East on this banner-draped train.

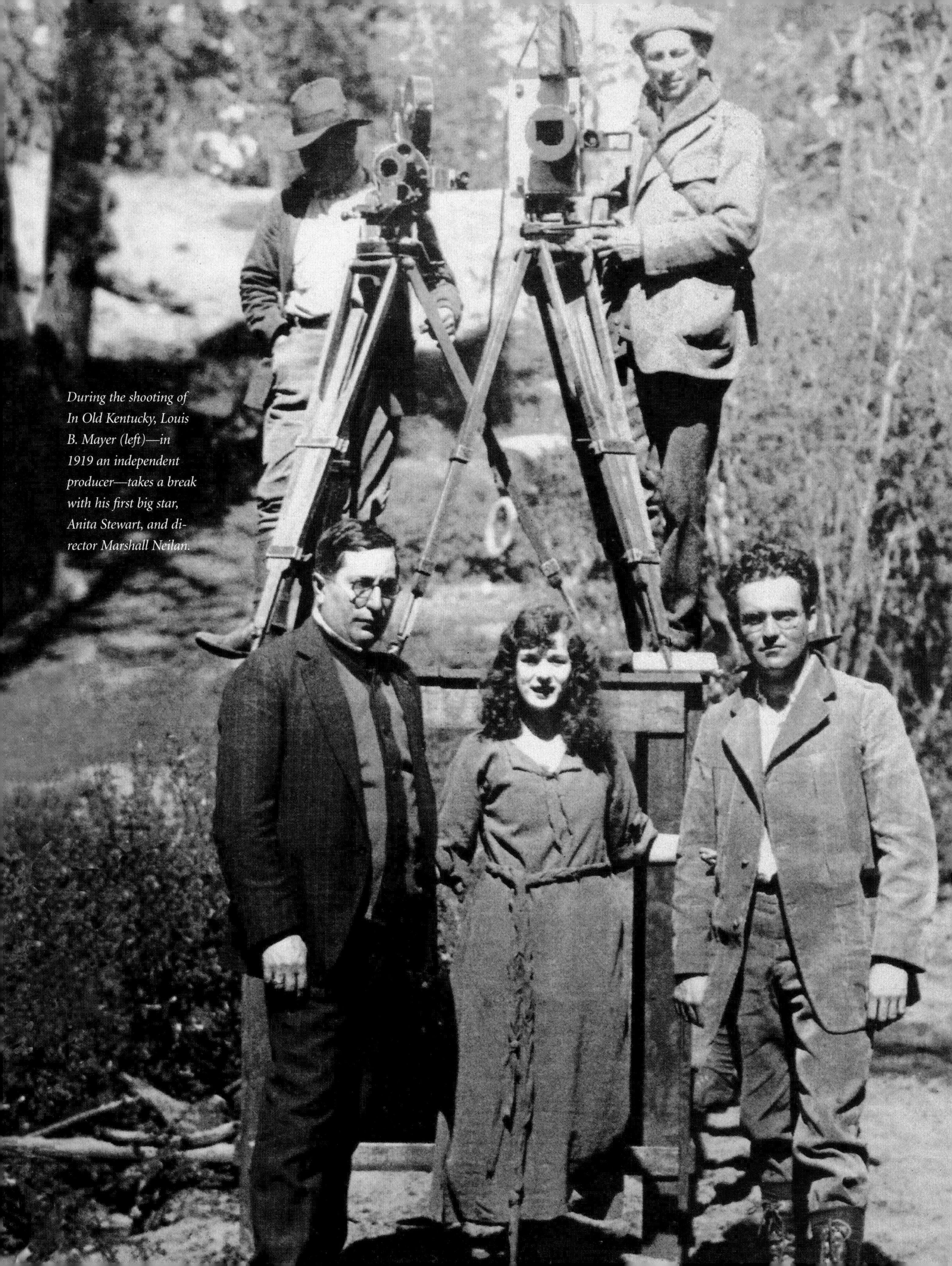

During the shooting of In Old Kentucky, Louis B. Mayer (left)—in 1919 an independent producer—takes a break with his first big star, Anita Stewart, and director Marshall Neilan.

the beginning, and in 1915 it established a state-of-the-art studio north of Hollywood. Sprawling over 230 acres, Universal City was large enough to be granted its own post office and voting precinct. Without question, Carl Laemmle had taken his place among the studio moguls.

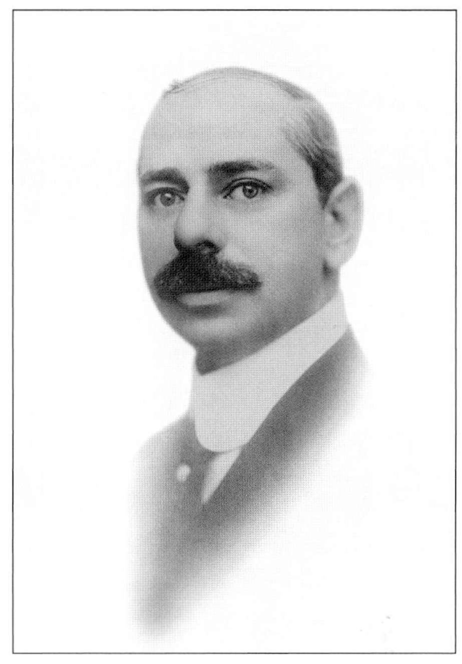

Theater magnate Marcus Loew was a superb manager, whose operations one journalist likened to "the maneuvers of a crack army division."

MGM. Like the other big studios, Metro-Goldwyn-Mayer was the product of the moguls' compulsion to take over rival companies. MGM's dominant force was Marcus Loew, who had been born into poverty on New York's Lower East Side. Ambition to achieve his goal was a byword for Loew. "You must be as ravenous to reach it," he said, "as the wolf who licks his teeth behind a fleeing rabbit."

As a young man Loew joined fellow furrier Adolph Zukor in running penny arcades, then in 1904 launched what grew to be a mighty chain of theaters. To increase the supply of high-quality films, he decided to go into movie production himself.

The second key figure at MGM was Louis B. Mayer. An immigrant from Russia, Mayer got his start in the movie business by converting a run-down Massachusetts burlesque house into a handsome cinema. In 1915 he helped form Metro Pictures Corporation, then left for California and began making films on his own. Mayer became a Hollywood legend: so sentimental that *Lassie* made him weep; so foul-tempered that he more than once punched a star in the snoot; so given to pomp and excess that he declared the Fourth of July his own birthday, claiming he could not remember his exact birthday back in Russia, and every year led all of MGM in a massive celebration—whether primarily of America's birthday or his own was never certain.

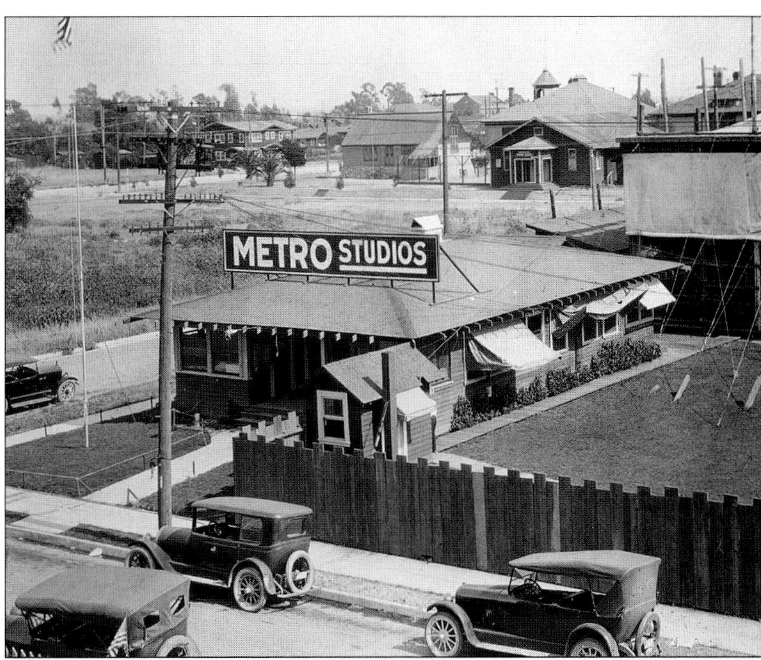

The sleepy look of Metro's front office in 1918—and its coming years of box-office torpor—belie the studio's eventual destiny as part of moviemaking giant Metro-Goldwyn-Mayer.

Completing MGM's pedigree was the irrepressible Samuel Goldfish, who had gone on from Famous Players-Lasky to start a new studio in 1916. He and his partner, Edgar Selwyn, combined their last names to call it the Goldwyn Pictures Corporation, and Goldfish liked the name so well that he gave it to himself. Although he built up an impressive roster of talent at Goldwyn Pictures, he was forced out of that company as well, and he spent the rest of his career as an independent producer, famous for films such as *Wuthering Heights* and *The Pride of the Yankees*—and for such mangled metaphors, dubbed Goldwynisms, as accusing

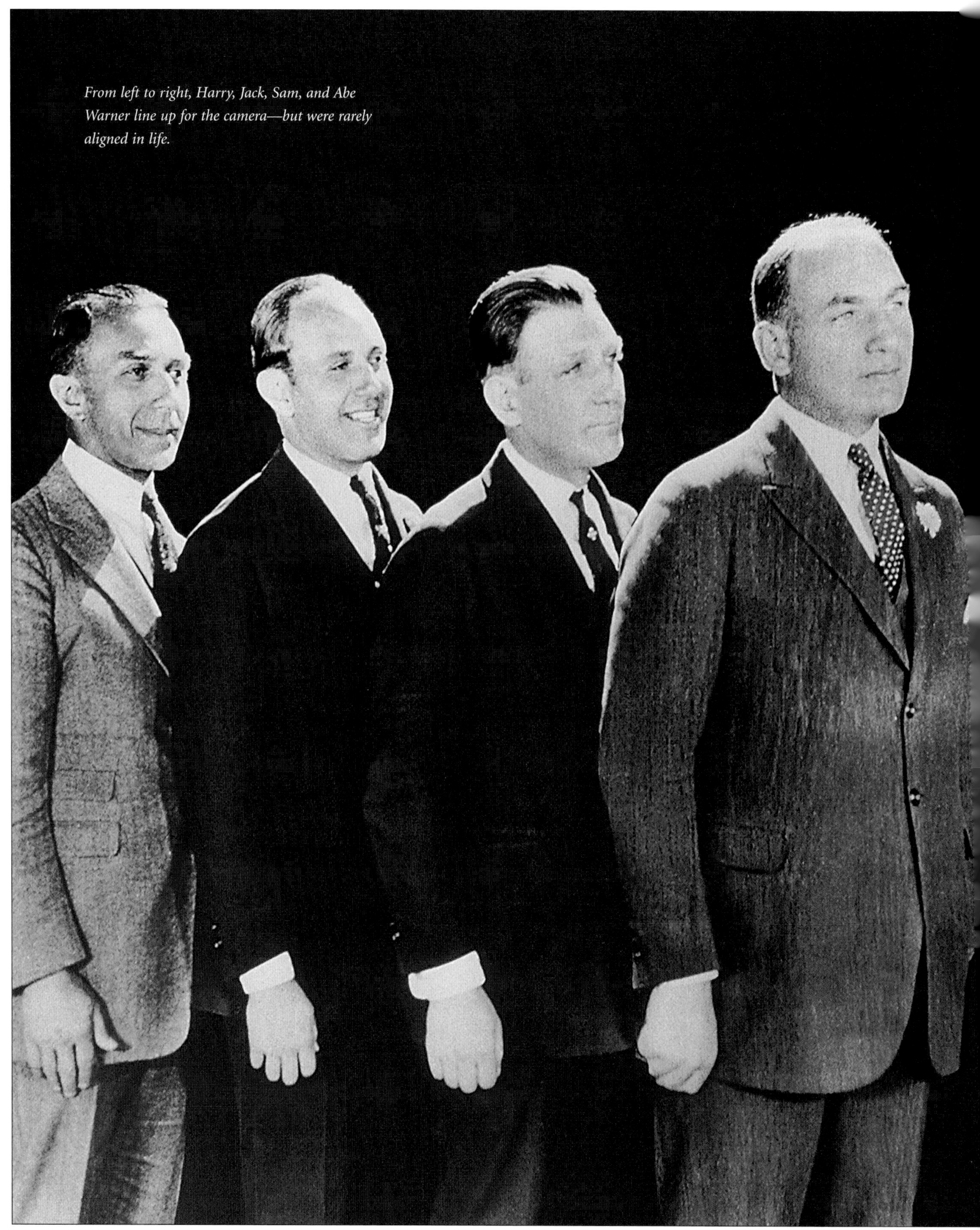

From left to right, Harry, Jack, Sam, and Abe Warner line up for the camera—but were rarely aligned in life.

directors of "biting the hand that laid the golden egg" and nixing a project with "Include me out!"

In 1919 Loew purchased Metro Pictures Corporation. Five years later he folded in Goldwyn Pictures and made Mayer head of filmmaking operations for the huge new studio, soon renamed Metro-Goldwyn-Mayer. In 1927 Loew died of heart disease, before the studio reached its glory days. But Mayer went on to make MGM Hollywood's most prestigious film studio.

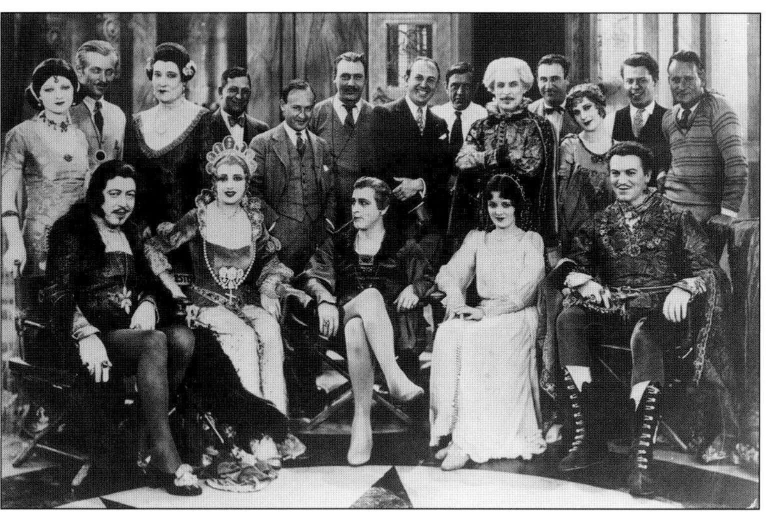

With leading man John Barrymore seated in the center, the cast of Don Juan—the 1926 Warner Bros. film that pioneered the use of sound in the movies—assembles for a celebratory portrait.

Warner Bros. There was often little brotherly love among Harry, Abe, Sam, and Jack Warner. The four sons of a Polish immigrant first decided to try the motion-picture business in 1903. They showed films in a tent in their Youngstown, Ohio, backyard, then opened a nickelodeon where Harry and Abe sold tickets, Sam cranked the projector, and Jack sang between screenings.

They ventured into film distribution, but the Edison trust forced them out of business, so in 1910 they began producing inexpensive movies. Profits were often elusive, but the brothers refused to throw in the towel, and after 15 years of scrambling they had accumulated enough capital to try a revolutionary breakthrough—melding film with synchronized sound. They obtained the major rights to a system called Vitaphone and used it in a 1926 John Barrymore feature, *Don Juan*. Although the movie had no talk, just music and sound effects, the audience was amazed.

"Without a doubt the biggest stride since the birth of the industry."

The Warners' assessment of the talkie

The following year, the Warners included fragments of dialogue in *The Jazz Singer,* starring Al Jolson. Harry reportedly had doubts; "Who the hell wants to hear actors talk?" he said. But the movie proved a sensation. Warner Bros. Pictures rapidly built itself into a giant.

But as success arrived, what little fraternal harmony there was disappeared. The day before *The Jazz Singer* debuted, Sam, the family mediator, suddenly died. Somewhat later Abe pulled out of the business, and tensions grew so fierce that Harry once chased Jack around the studio lot with a lead pipe. By the end the two active Warners, men who had launched the talkies, were no longer speaking to each other.

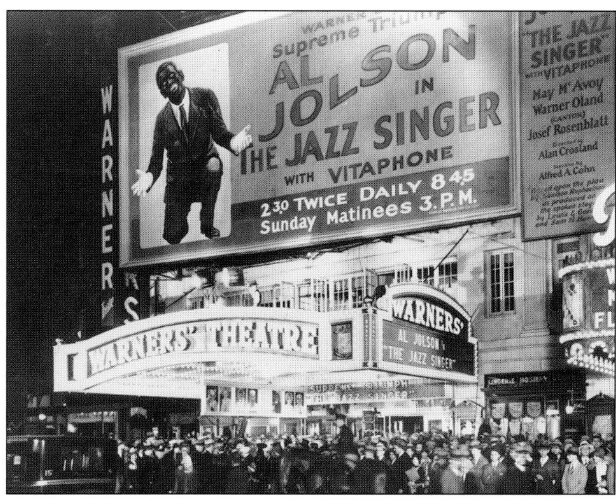

Beneath an image of Al Jolson in blackface, New Yorkers swarm the theater where the first talkie, The Jazz Singer, premiered in 1927.

Ince the Innovator

While the budding moguls at the top of the movie industry assembled mammoth corporations, filmmaking at the nuts-and-bolts level was becoming increasingly sophisticated. Much of the pioneering work in production was done by Thomas Harper Ince, an easterner who gained fame as a maker of westerns.

Born in Newport, Rhode Island, in 1882, Ince gave up playing the rear end of a horse onstage to join Biograph in 1910 as an actor, later becoming a writer and director. The next year, he struck out for California to supervise the operations of the Bison Company, a studio specializing in the popular but still crude genre of westerns. Bison leased 18,000 acres of land near Santa Monica, where Ince created the standard industry practice of shooting from detailed scripts. Bison also signed up an entire Wild West show wintering in the area. The show had authentic cowboys and Indians, horses, steers, and wagons. The cowboys not only served as extras in Ince's oaters but also patrolled the lot's fences, ready to run off any Edison trust detectives.

His face a picture of determination, Thomas Ince was a trailblazer as a manager of studio operations and creator of cinematic atmosphere.

Ince brilliantly exploited these assets. He had a water supply system installed so his employees could keep on shooting pictures right through the blistering summer. His studio buildings were designed so they could double as exterior sets. Within a few years he was overseeing eight directors and had more than 500 people on his payroll, and the Bison complex became known as Inceville.

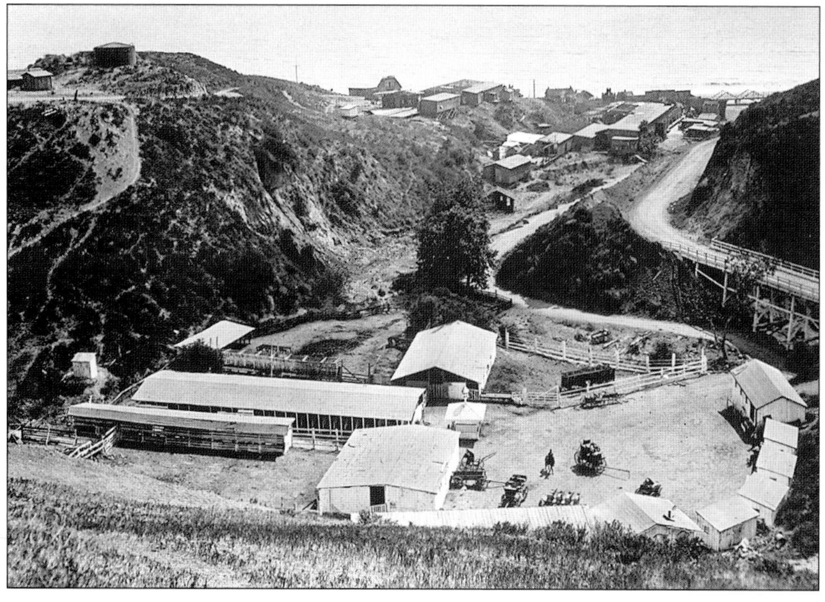

This 1918 view shows the filmmaking kingdom Ince ruled—studio buildings and sets spread across a southern California landscape.

In 1914 Ince launched the film career of William S. Hart, a trained Shakespearean actor who loved the Old West and was committed to re-creating it as authentically as possible. Handling a pair of six-shooters with panache, Hart went on to star in westerns until 1925. But the hard-driving Ince had pushed himself too far: He had died of an apparent heart attack a year earlier.

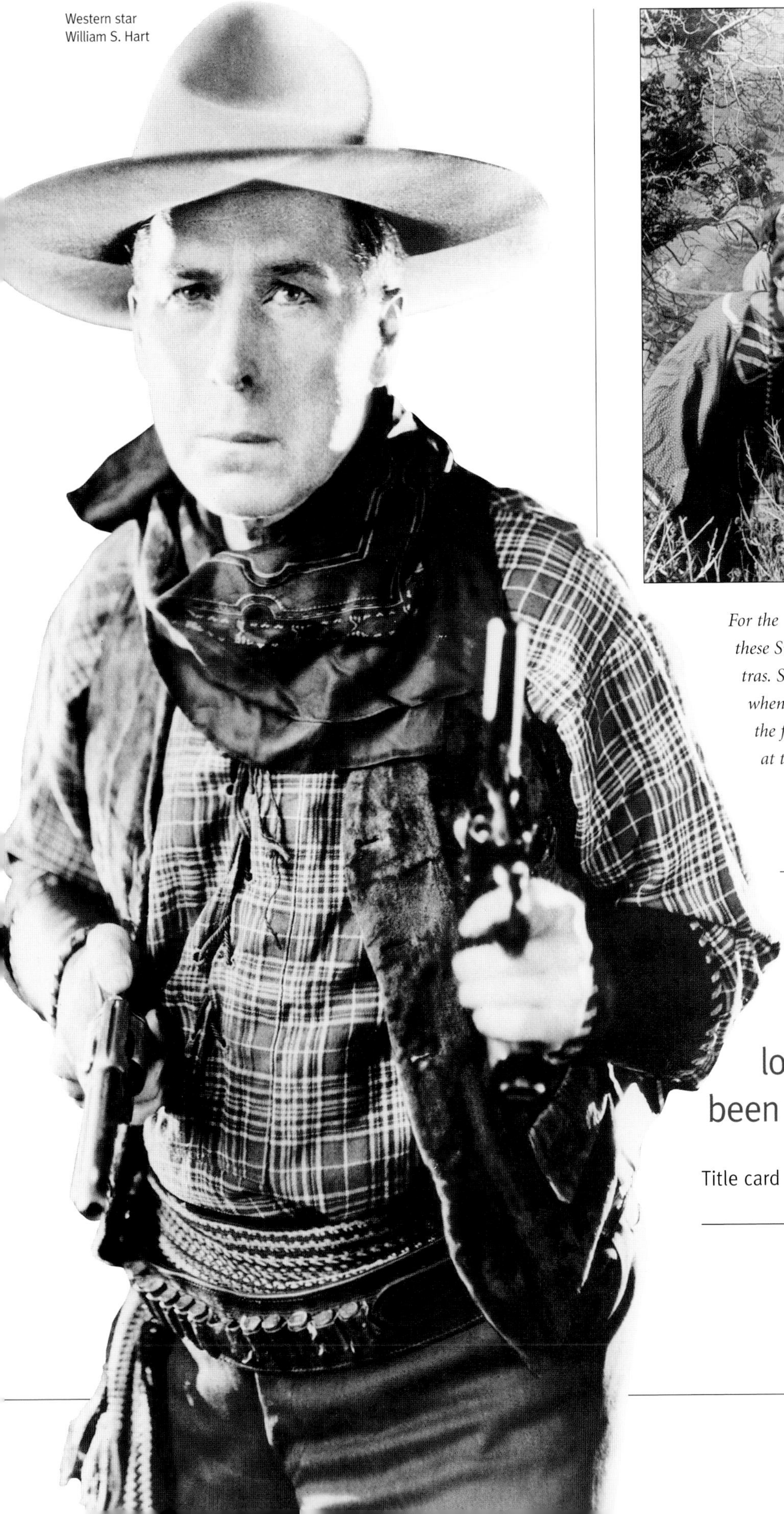

Western star William S. Hart

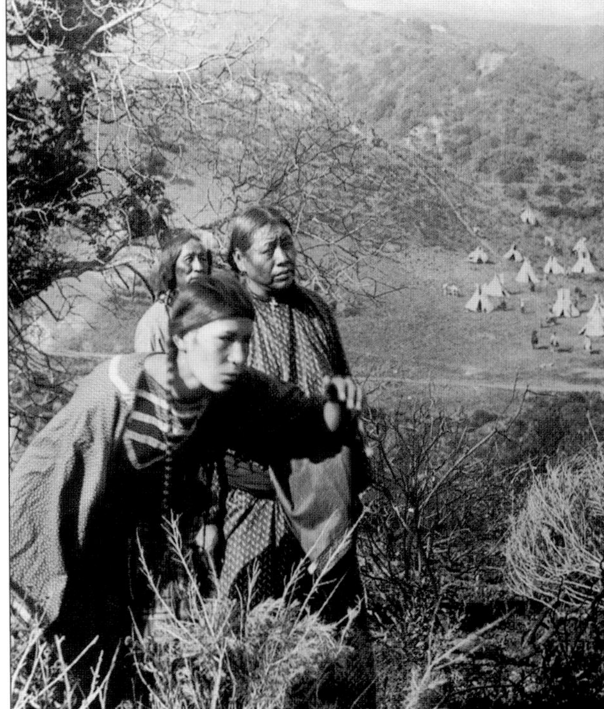

For the 1912 film Custer's Last Raid, Ince employed these Sioux and more than a hundred others as extras. Some had actually been present as young boys when, in 1876, Sioux and other warriors wiped out the force led by General George Armstrong Custer at the Little Bighorn.

"I reckon God ain't wantin' me much, ma'am, but when I look at you, I feel I've been ridin' the wrong trail."

Title card dialogue for William S. Hart's character

Mack Sennett (above, right)—famous as the director and producer of the hilarious Keystone Kops films—here appears in a comic acting role, doubtfully contemplating a matchmaking agency's services.

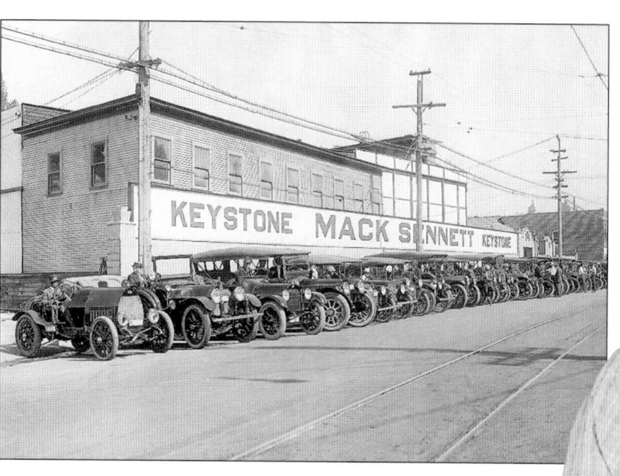

Lined up outside the Los Angeles studio of Keystone Pictures in 1915 are the rolling props of some of Mack Sennett's funniest scenes. The automotive mayhem was murder on the cars and risky for the actors, but audiences loved it.

> "Go hire some girls, any girls, so long as they're pretty, especially around the knees."
>
> Mack Sennett, on finding potential bathing beauties

The Silent Clowns

No one did more to tickle the funny bone of early moviegoers than a one-time vaudevillian named Mack Sennett. Sennett gave up the New York stage for the movie business in 1908, set out for Hollywood two years later to work with director D. W. Griffith at Biograph, and tried his hand at directing comedy for the company. He showed a genius for it, so he went out on his own in 1912 and founded Keystone Pictures. At Keystone he would turn out some 900 films, working with a whole galaxy of major comic talents—among them Fatty Arbuckle *(below),* Mabel Normand *(far right, bottom),* Ben Turpin *(page 41, bottom),* and Charlie Chaplin *(page 45, top).*

Like Thomas Ince, Sennett was a production whiz, supervising numerous one- and two-reel films simultaneously. In the early days he worked with rudimentary scripts, encouraging his cast to improvise physical hilarity on camera. Later he began to plan out his films in more detail. The essence of Sennett's comic style was slapstick—pies in the face, manic escapades with cars, and other sorts of madcap goings-on. According to Hollywood lore, the pie-throwing gimmick originated one day when the irrepressible Mabel Normand grabbed a pie from some workmen who were having lunch and chucked it at Turpin to loosen him up. Sennett found the prank so funny that he made it a staple of his comedies.

Policemen were also a regular source of laughs. Sennett realized that portraying them as self-important figures of authority made them wonderfully

Roscoe "Fatty" Arbuckle

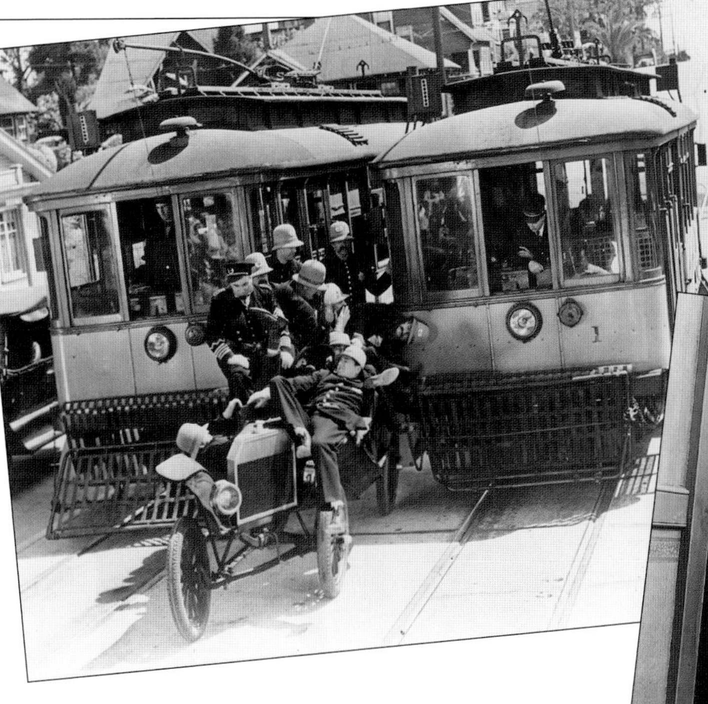

In a typical moment of delightful madness, a car full of Keystone Kops (left) is mashed between two trolleys. Every Sennett actor made his first appearance as one of the bumbling officers.

Sennett's female extras, like those at right, sported bathing attire that was daringly skimpy for its time. Keystone bathing beauties were the pinup choice of many World War I soldiers.

In the 1919 film Up in Alf's Place, card playing takes a turn toward gunplay (left). In movie slapstick, bullets could fly furiously without injury to any of the characters.

A deliciously villainous Ford Sterling—another Keystone star—drives in a stake to pin Mabel Normand to the railroad tracks, while Mack Sennett himself secures her legs (right).

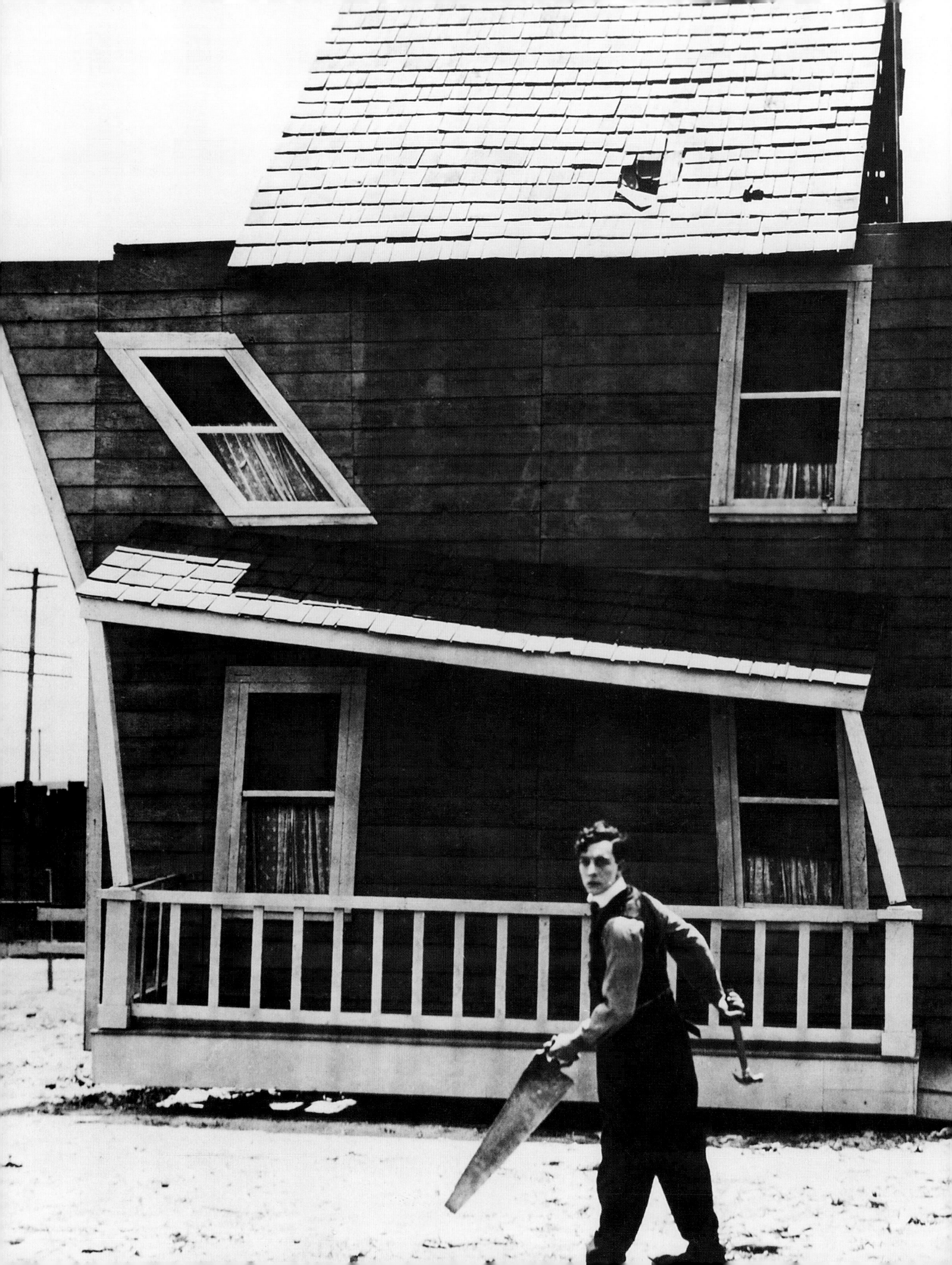

ridiculous: "Wherever there is dignity, comics can embroil it, embarrass it, flee from it, and thumb their noses at it," he said. The entertainingly inept Keystone Kops *(page 39, top left)* endured mishaps, collisions, and pratfalls of every kind. Keystone films also featured a host of bathing beauties *(page 39, top right)*, who were, in Sennett's words, "around to be looked at while the comics are making funny."

An alternative to slapstick was pioneered by Charlie Chaplin, who learned his trade in British music halls. He went to work for Sennett in 1913 at $125 a week and, like all Sennett actors, served a brief studio apprenticeship as a Keystone Kop. But the slapstick-loving Sennett was, fundamentally, out of tune with Chaplin's style of comedy—subtle characterizations and a wistful sadness that, as Normand said, "made your heart ache." So although Chaplin eventually was allowed to deviate from the stock Sennett roles, he didn't last long at Keystone. By 1916, having developed his trademark character the Little Tramp, he was making $10,000 a week at the Mutual Film Corporation.

If other silent-era comic actors couldn't quite reach Chaplin's level of genius, they came close. Buster Keaton *(left)*, a veteran of vaudeville, created dazzling sight gags in which he endured bizarre and often threatening situations with gloomy aplomb: In various films he soared skyward atop a runaway balloon, played solitaire in a sinking rowboat, and lived inside a steamboat's paddle wheel.

Harold Lloyd gave comedy a note of realism. Horn-rimmed glasses were the trademark of his usual role as an earnest but hapless young man. Lloyd specialized in predicaments that were extreme yet believable, such as the harrowing scene at right. He had a reputation—somewhat exaggerated—for doing all his own stunts. In reality, as a valuable box-office draw, at times surpassing even Chaplin, he was held out of the riskier scenes in favor of a stunt man.

In the film One Week, Buster Keaton (left) follows instructions for putting up a prefabricated house, persevering in his long-suffering way even though the components of the kit are mismarked.

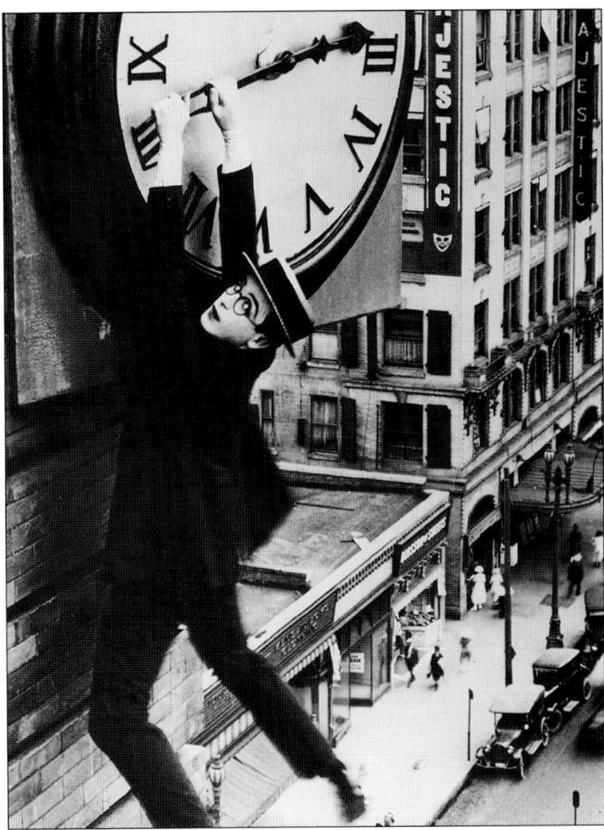

Things have somehow gone wrong again for Harold Lloyd, as he hangs on for dear life in a famous scene from the 1923 film Safety Last.

Diminutive Ben Turpin—whose eyes were insured against uncrossing—was a regular in Mack Sennett's stable of comics.

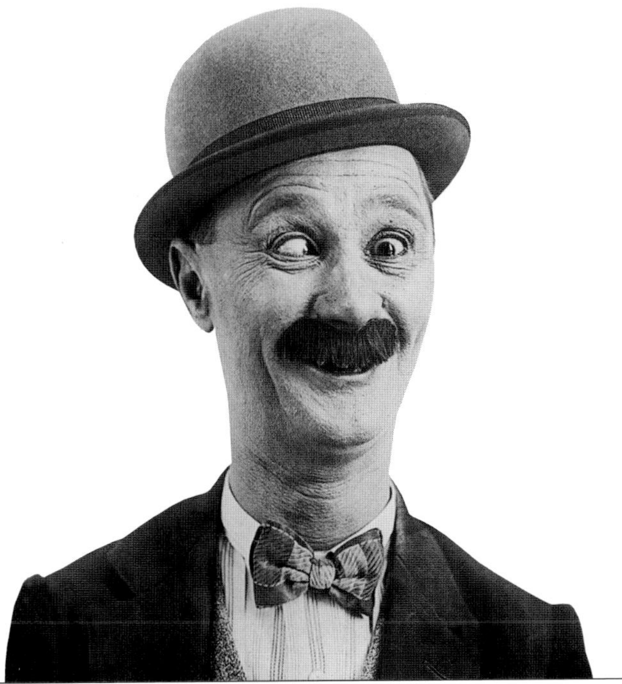

D. W. Griffith and *The Birth of a Nation*

"He gave us the grammar of filmmaking. He understood the psychic strength of the lens." So said actress Lillian Gish of David Wark Griffith, who directed her in his controversial 1915 masterpiece *The Birth of a Nation* and many other pictures. Griffith did not invent such techniques as closeups or crosscutting, but in *The Birth* he used them to more compelling effect than any American filmmaker had before.

The son of a former Civil War Confederate colonel, Griffith joined Biograph as a director in 1908. Over the next five years he made 400 films, mostly one-reelers, for the studio, until its lack of interest in feature-length films prompted him to go out on his own. Within months, he began shooting *The Birth*.

Blending grandeur and intimacy, the film followed two families, one Northern and one Southern, through the Civil War and Reconstruction eras. At 12 reels, it was the longest movie yet made in America. Its scale, its narrative complexity, and especially its nuances of emotion were unprecedented.

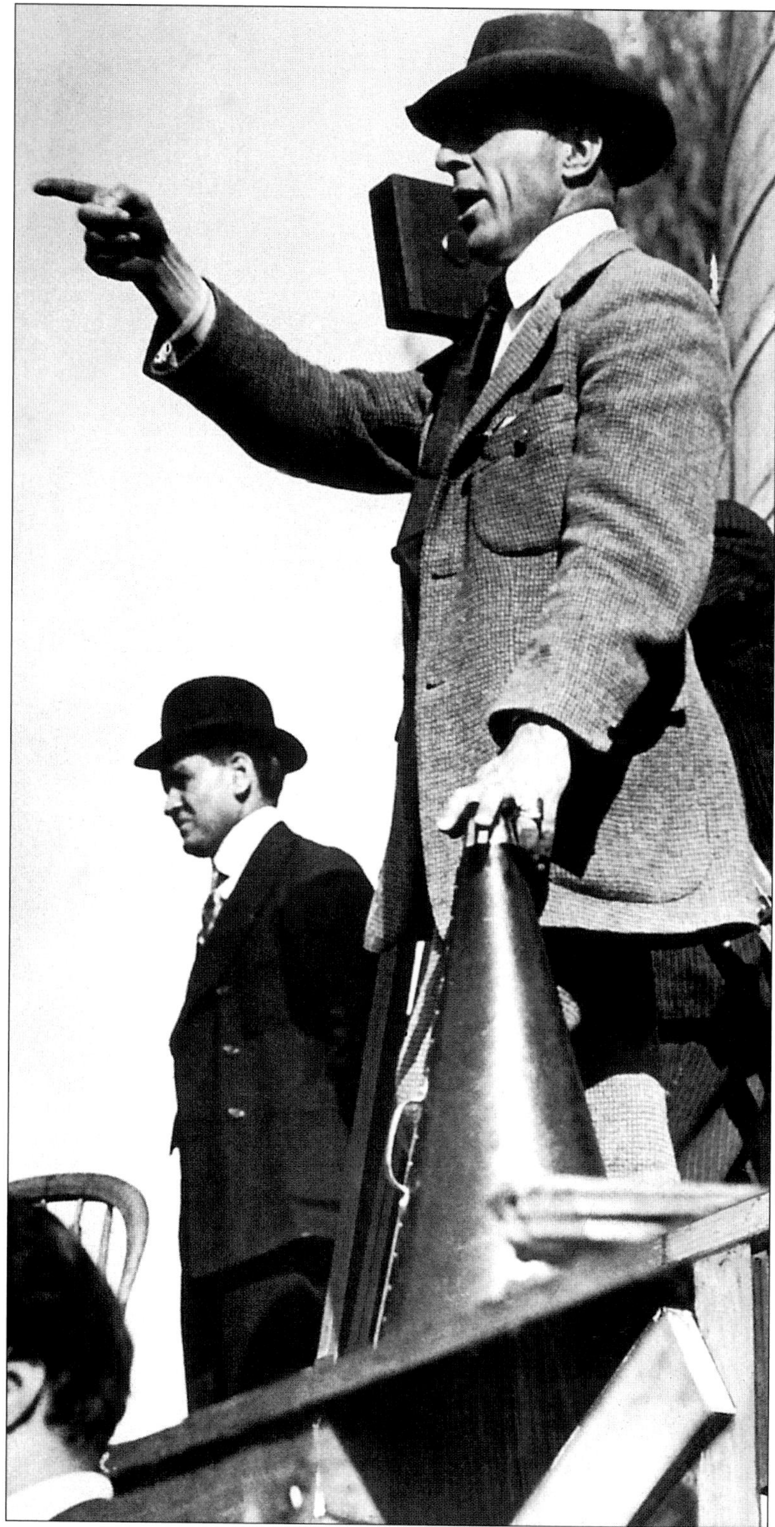

D. W. Griffith gives instructions on the set of The Birth of a Nation. During the shooting of some of the battle scenes, his voice couldn't be heard over the noise even through a megaphone, so he controlled the action by waving color-coded flags.

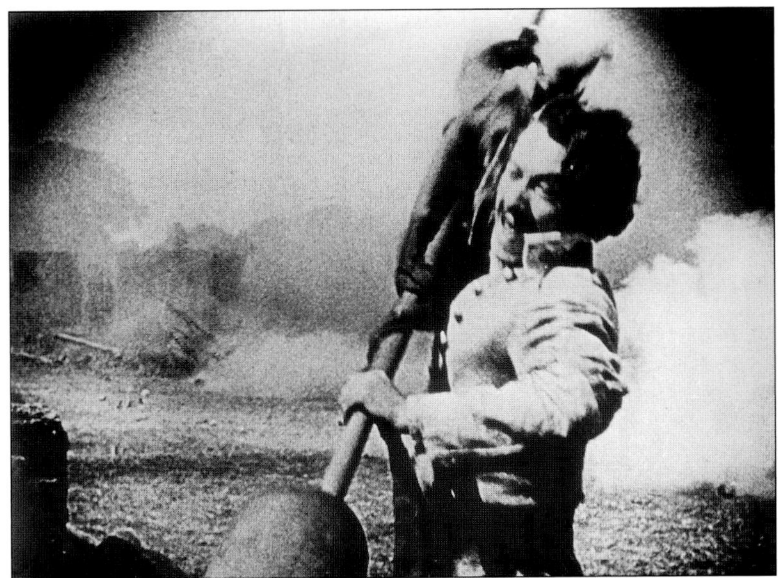

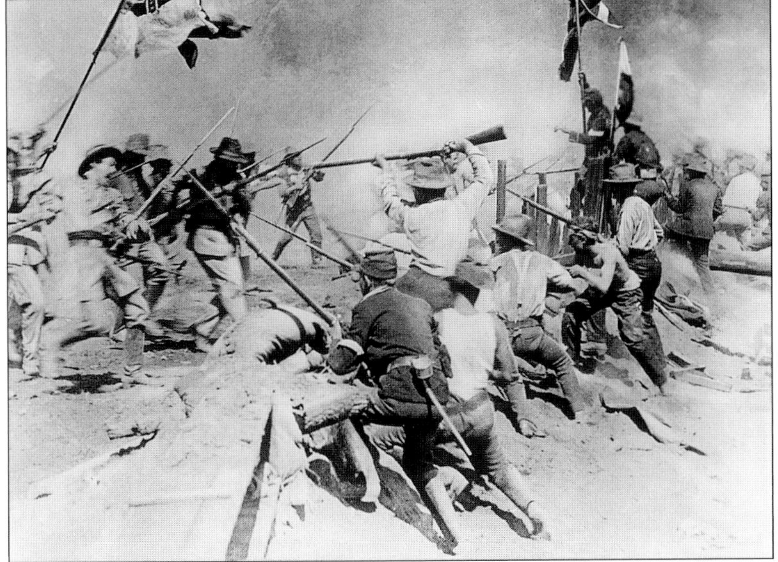

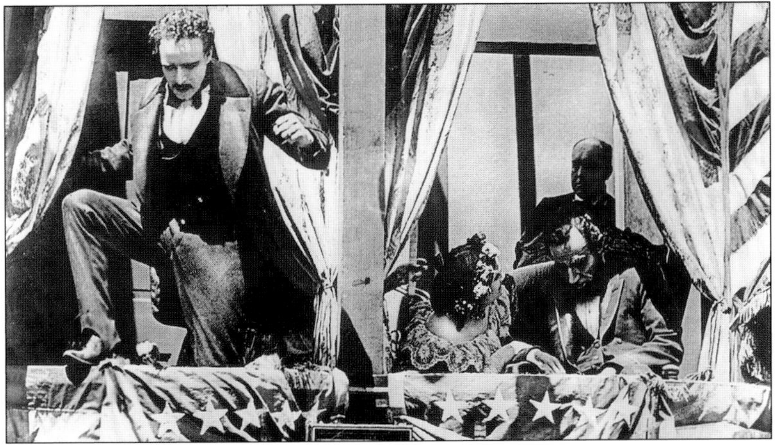

Acclaim came swiftly—and so did outrage. Griffith presented equal rights for blacks as dangerous and showed the Ku Klux Klan *(inset opposite)* in a heroic light. So powerful was the film's impact that the KKK, defunct since 1869, came back to malignant life in 1915 in Atlanta, using the premiere of *The Birth* as its inspiration.

The National Association for the Advancement of Colored People and prominent figures like reformer Jane Addams spoke out against the film. But most viewers were simply awestruck. It opened on Broadway in New York, playing to full houses at live-theater ticket prices, and ran for 44 weeks. It persuaded Americans to think of films as an art form, not just an amusing novelty.

The next year Griffith produced an even more complex film, *Intolerance.* The lavish three-hour-and-15-minute epic used settings varying from ancient Babylon to modern America to dramatize the title theme, although one form of intolerance it failed to address was antiblack racism. Box-office results, although impressive, did not match production costs, a problem that dogged Griffith's career until he was finally forced out of the business in the 1930s.

Three moments from Griffith's The Birth of a Nation *demonstrate the director's mastery of action and his careful composition of shots: a battlefield closeup of the "Little Colonel," played by Henry B. Walthall (top); Confederate and Union forces clashing (center); and John Wilkes Booth leaping from a box at Ford's Theatre after shooting President Lincoln. Griffith spent $100,000 on* The Birth of a Nation, *a figure that seemed enormous until the next year, when his costs for producing* Intolerance *ballooned to two million dollars.*

The Talent Takes Over

Early filmmakers refused to credit actors by name, fearing that fame could lead to demands for higher salaries. When the cloak of anonymity was removed, their fears were realized—and then some. A leader of the upward salary spiral was golden-curled Mary Pickford, who began performing in theaters at age six and went on to a blockbuster career in film roles of innocent adorability. So powerful was her childlike image that even at age 27 she played a 10-year-old, the illusion aided by the use of oversize furniture on her sets. In real life, Pickford was canny and iron willed, and she negotiated her pay rate to a stratospheric $10,000 a week by 1915. Charlie Chaplin soon reached the same heights, as did Douglas Fairbanks, an acrobatic swashbuckler and Pickford's future husband.

In 1919, to thwart a possible salary squeeze by the big studios acting in unison, Pickford, Chaplin, and Fairbanks banded together with director D. W. Griffith to form their own company, United Artists. Continuing to make big money wasn't a bad idea, and the new operation succeeded. But there was also something to the stars' claim that United Artists' mission was to maintain the integrity of the filmmaking art without interference from greedy moguls. Chaplin was free to spend several years on a single production and to resist talkies, making silent films until 1940. And Griffith, at least for a time, was permitted his runaway budgets.

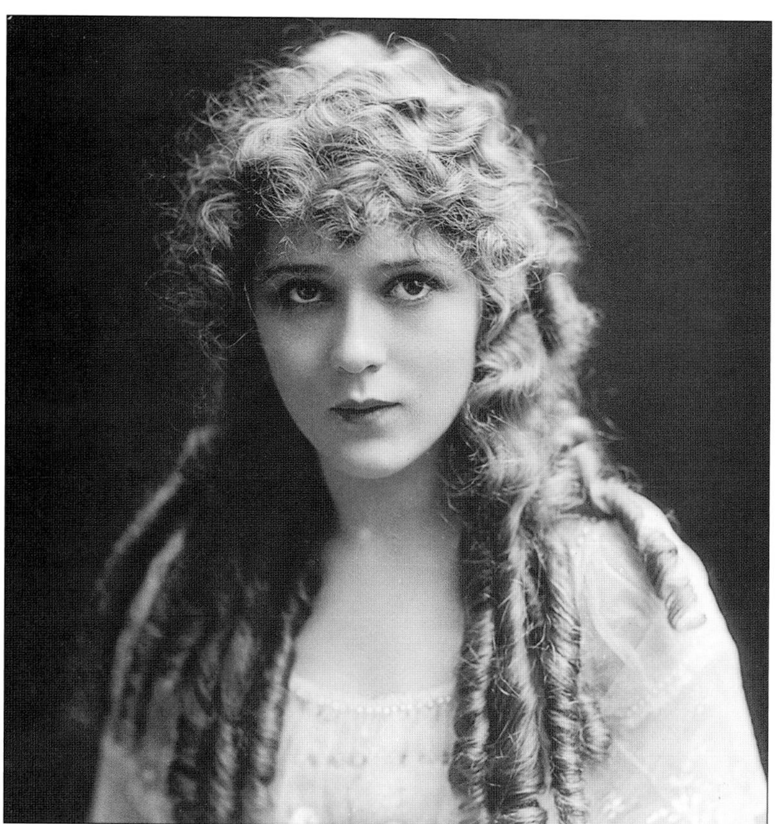

Born Gladys Smith in Toronto, Mary Pickford became known as America's Sweetheart. Her famous ringlets were augmented with hair bought from Los Angeles prostitutes.

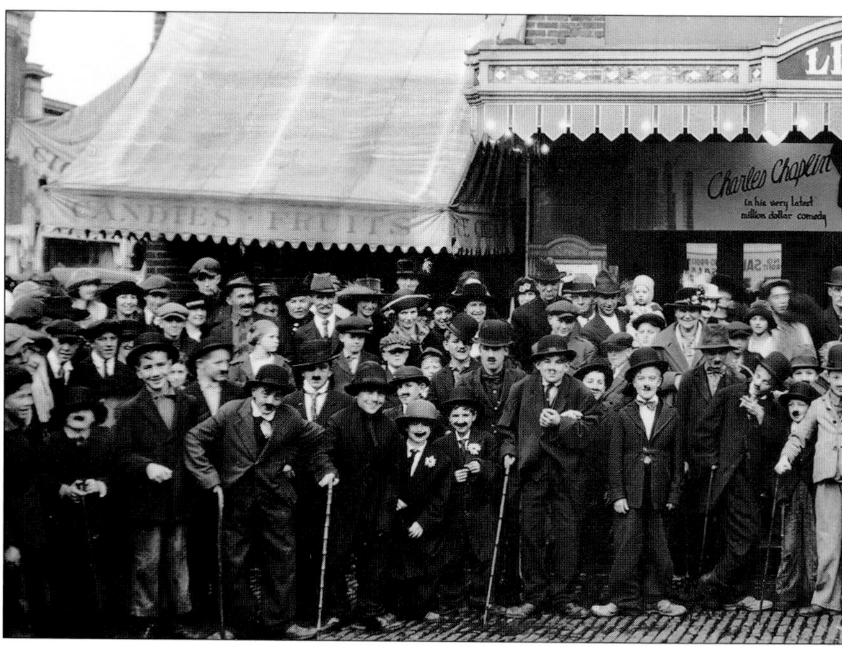

A 1917 look-alike contest in Bellingham, Washington, testifies to Charlie Chaplin's

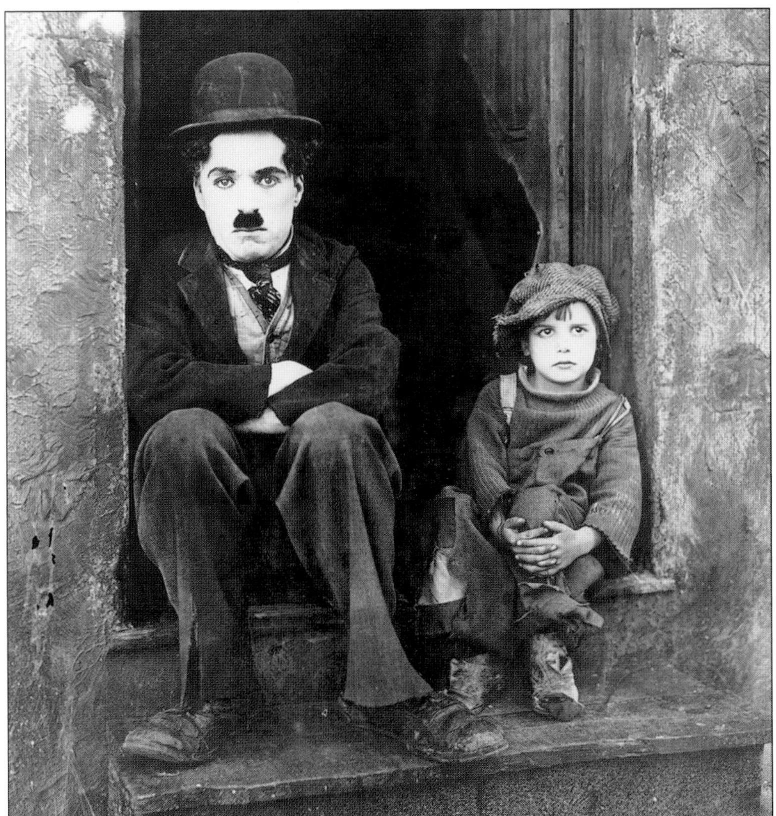

Sad-faced Charlie Chaplin sits in a doorway with Jackie Coogan, a waif whom the Little Tramp adopts in The Kid. Chaplin wrote and directed the poignant 1921 comedy.

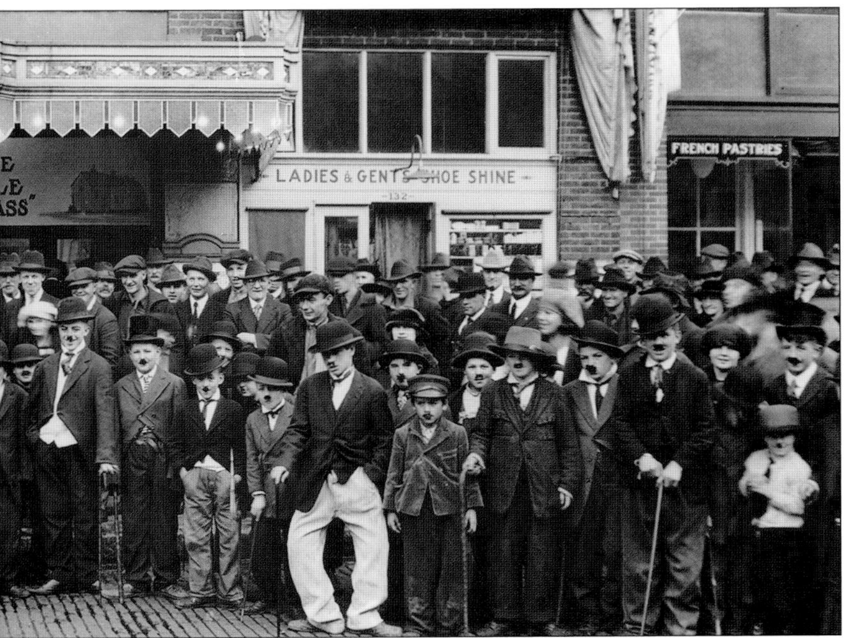

immense popularity. His Little Tramp role was widely imitated by other actors.

"So the lunatics have taken charge of the asylum."

An executive's remark about United Artists

Douglas Fairbanks, the agile hero of numerous historical dramas, embraces a swooning Julanne Johnston in The Thief of Bagdad, a 1924 hit.

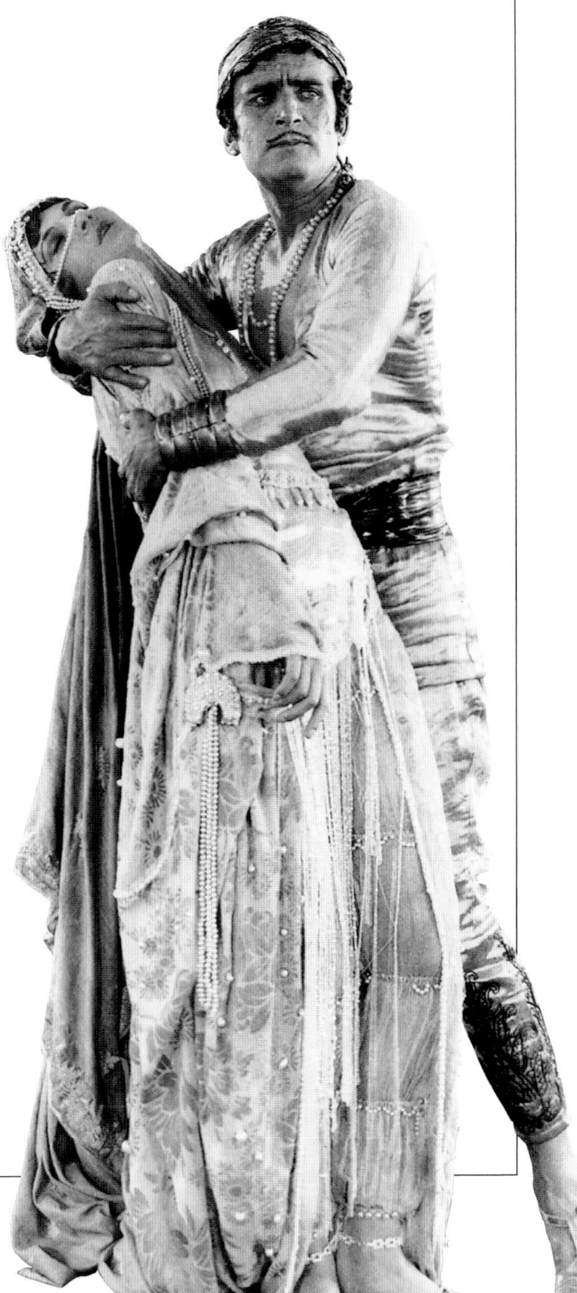

An Evening at the Movies

As salaries and studios grew to monumental proportions, movie theaters were doing the same. A move toward opulence was in evidence by 1910, as exhibitors in big cities began fitting out their theaters with marble, oak panels, mirrors, and deep carpeting to attract upscale audiences. A sumptuous 3,000-seat picture palace called the Strand, for example, opened in New York in 1914. But its manager, Samuel "Roxy" Rothapfel *(inset),* had even grander visions.

In 1927 the city witnessed the debut of the Roxy *(right)*—named for Rothapfel, who had spent $10 million building what he proclaimed to be the largest theater in the world. The Roxy seated more than 6,000 viewers in air-conditioned comfort on red plush seats monogrammed with the letter *R.* It housed a 110-piece symphony orchestra, a mammoth pipe organ that was played from three separate consoles, and a fully equipped hospital in case any patrons were taken ill. Sightlines and acoustics had received meticulous attention, and a retired marine colonel trained the ushers. The Cathedral of the Motion Picture, as it was dubbed, even possessed its own set of cathedral bells. A greater contrast to the old-time nickelodeon—with its dingy storefront, smoky interior, and wooden benches—could hardly have been

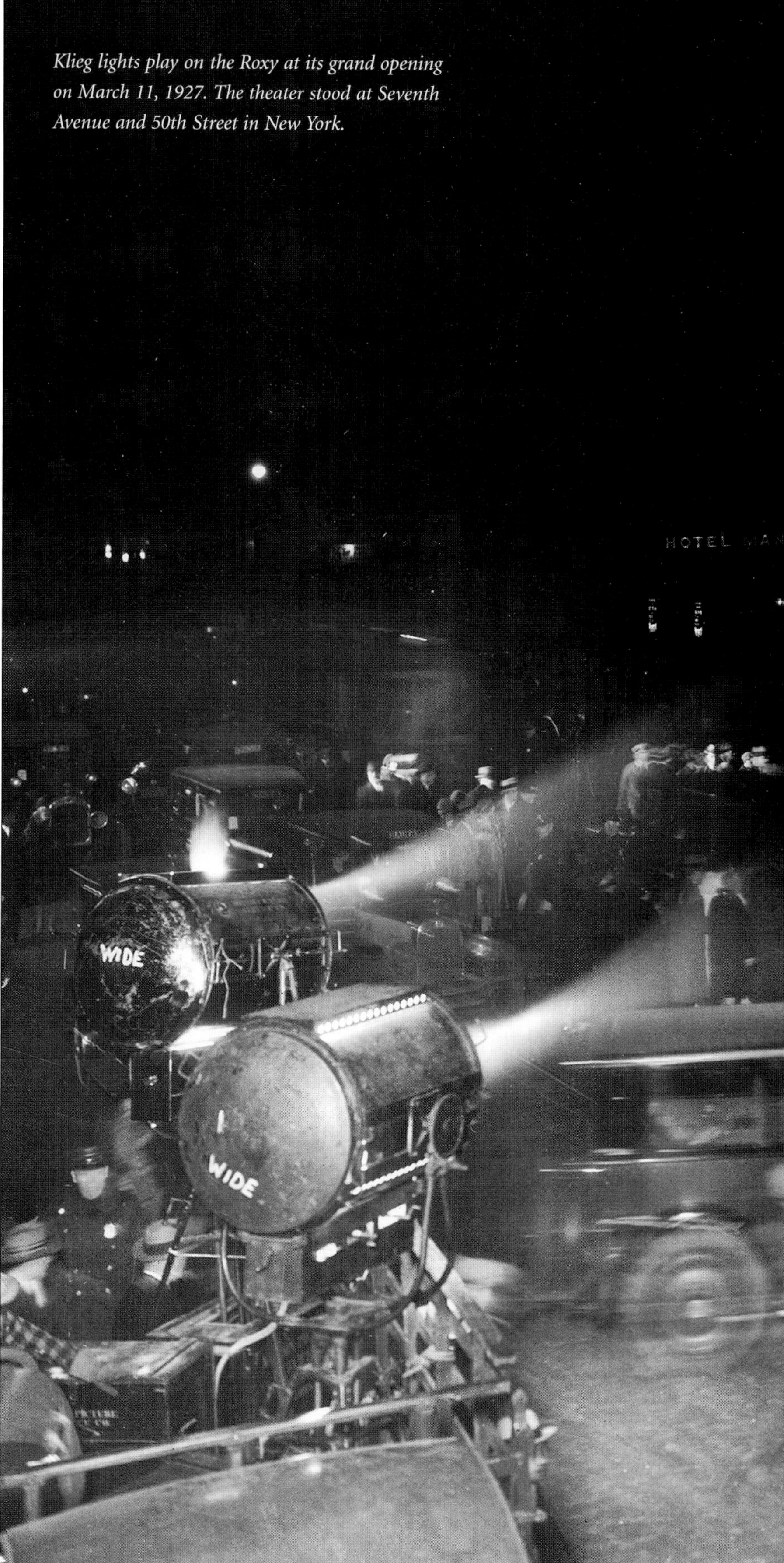

Klieg lights play on the Roxy at its grand opening on March 11, 1927. The theater stood at Seventh Avenue and 50th Street in New York.

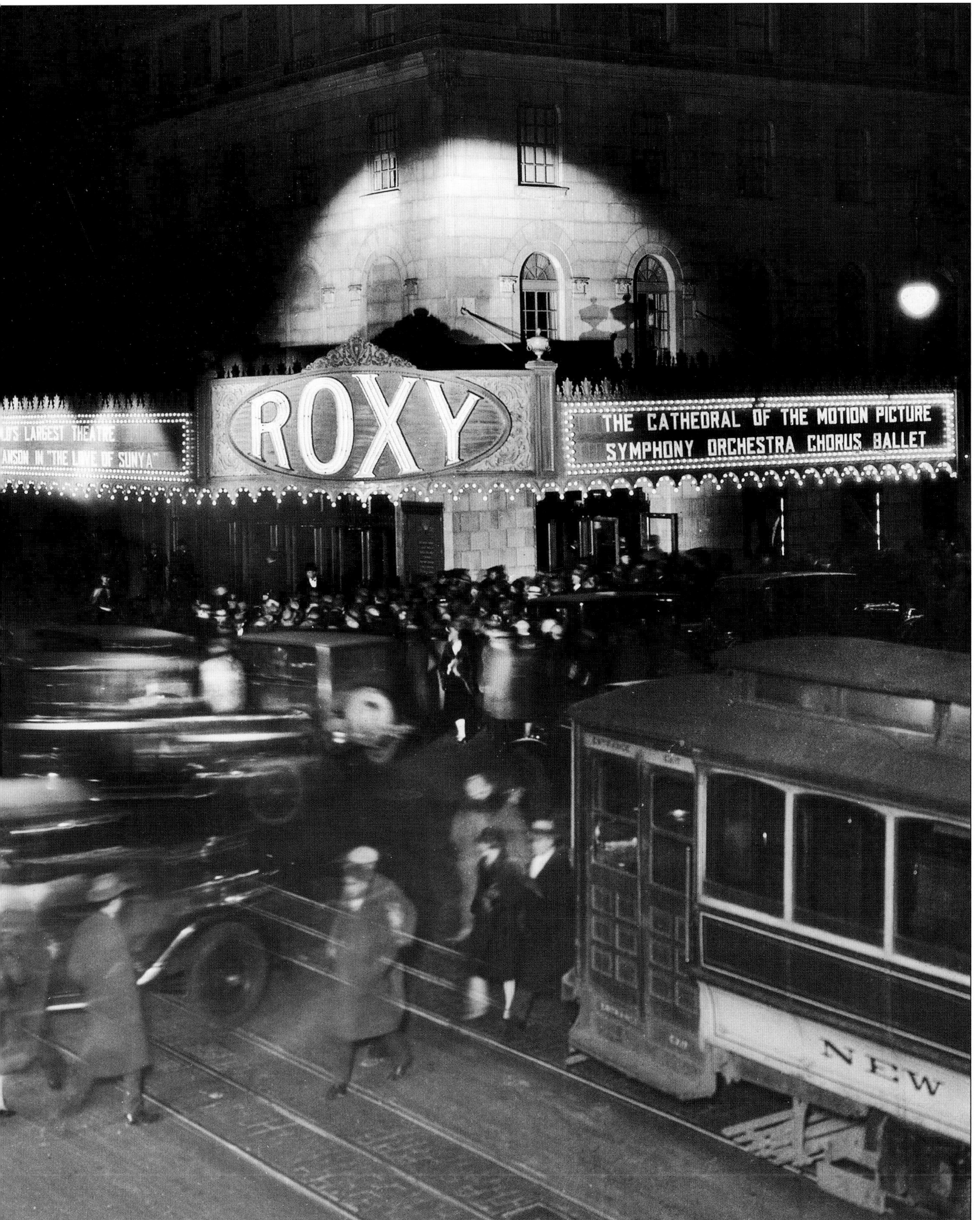
LARGEST THEATRE
IN "THE LOVE OF SUNYA"
ROXY
THE CATHEDRAL OF THE MOTION PICTURE
SYMPHONY ORCHESTRA CHORUS BALLET
NEW

imagined. Roxy, one journalist declared, had given the movies "a college education."

Glorious excess was breaking out all over. In Los Angeles Sid Grauman *(opposite, bottom left)* chose Spanish and Byzantine design touches in 1918 for the Million Dollar Theater. He built an Egyptian-style venue in 1922, then in 1927 created his masterpiece, the stunning 2,258-seat Chinese Theater on Hollywood Boulevard.

A Seattle movie palace *(opposite, top)* was modeled on the royal quarters of the Chinese emperors. The firm of Balaban & Katz gave Chicago theaters like the Tivoli, an imitation Versailles, and advertised the "intricacies of Eastern magnificence" on display at the Oriental. Balaban & Katz theaters were adorned with towering electric signs that could be seen for miles. Inside were awe-inspiring mazes of vestibules, waiting rooms, promenades, lounges, and lobbies—the latter embellished, as in all picture palaces, with vivid lobby cards advertising the latest Hollywood productions *(right)*. Each of the theaters offered a playground for children with a staff of nurses to watch them while their parents enjoyed the movie.

This escalation of extravagance did not always add up to sound financial practice, and many of the theater palaces were absorbed by the big studios. Adolph Zukor pulled Balaban & Katz into Paramount in 1925; William Fox took control of the overextended Roxy Theaters Corporation in 1926, before Rothapfel could even complete his great showplace; and by 1930 Sid Grauman was a Fox employee. But that was the movie industry—a business battlefield that resembled nothing so much as a big-screen epic.

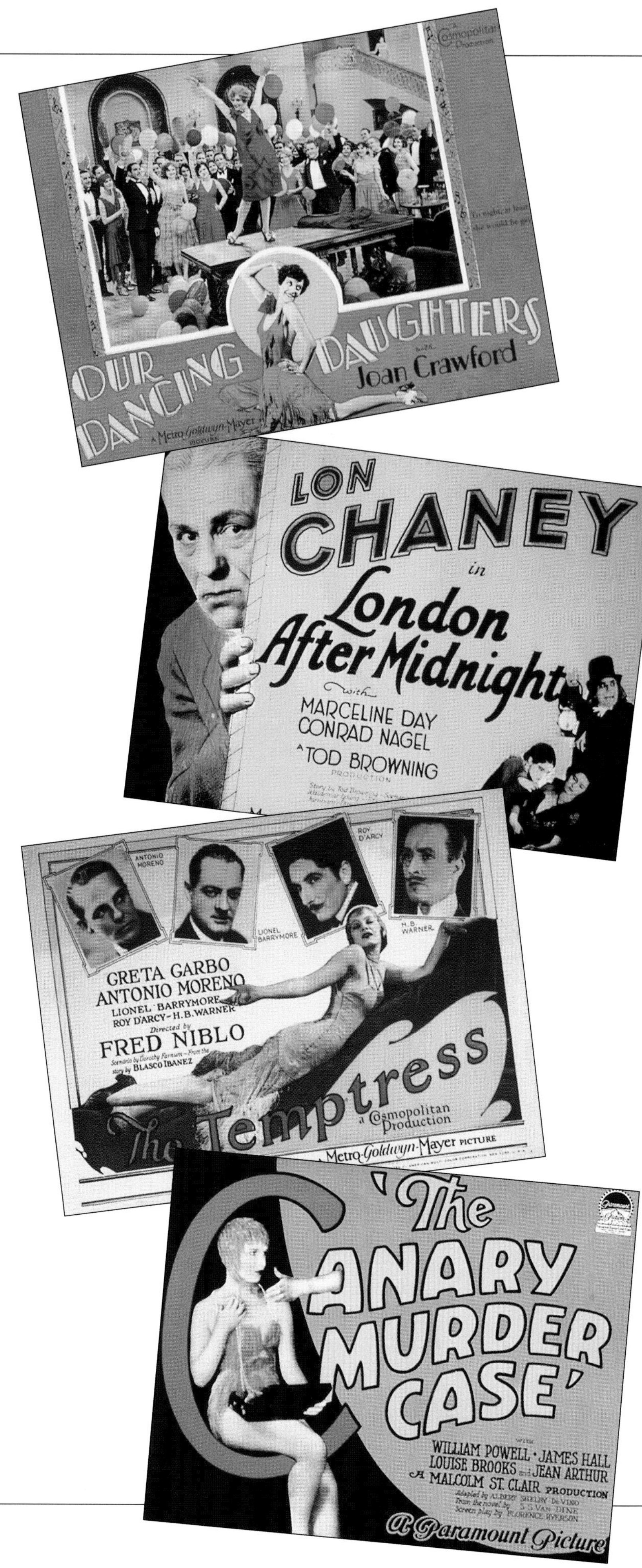

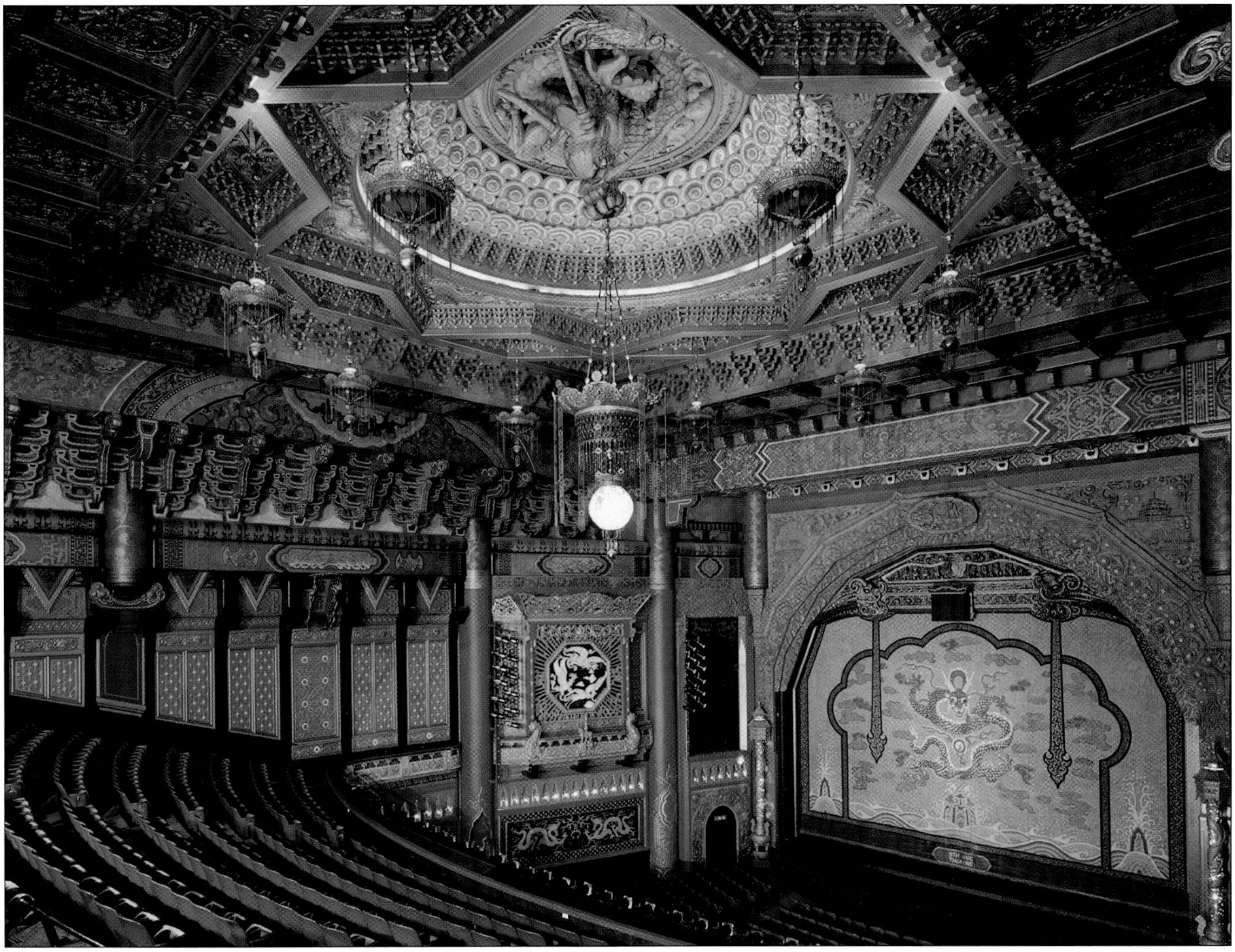

The ceiling of the Fifth Avenue Theatre in Seattle copied—at double the size—the vault of the imperial throne room in Beijing's Forbidden City.

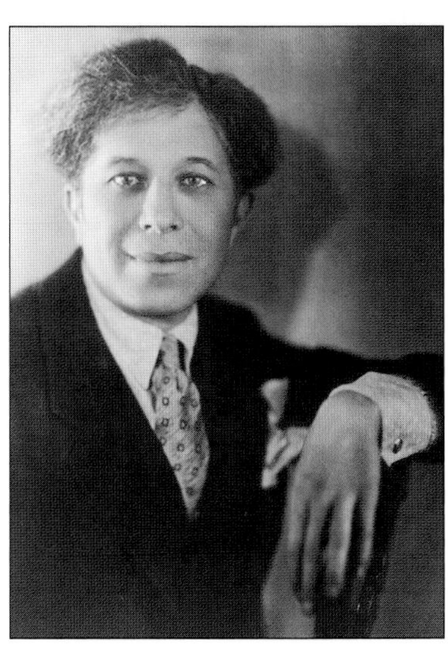

Impresario Sid Grauman (left) created one gaudy movie palace after another, culminating in the world-famous Chinese Theater. A Los Angeles Times columnist wisecracked, "Sid may go in for barbaric splendor, but, anyway, it's splendor." A tradition at the Chinese was for stars to leave their prints and autographs in wet cement in front of the theater (right).

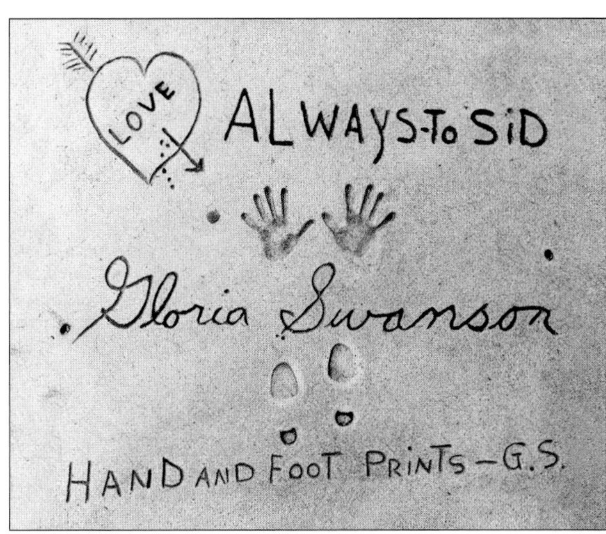

Stars of the Silent Screen

The key to a silent film's box-office success, studios eventually realized, was star power. "You could take 1,000 feet of Norma Talmadge in a chair," said a director, "and her fans would flock to see it." In the eyes of the public, movie stars—images hyped by press agents—enjoyed near-mythic status. Two of the greatest, adored in America and Europe alike, lived in a palatial Hollywood home. Mary Pickford and Douglas Fairbanks struck Britain's Lord Louis Mountbatten as fellow nobility: "At the time of their reign in Pickfair," Mountbatten said, they were "treated like royalty, and in fact they behaved in the same sort of dignified way that royalty did."

The public's fascination with stars extended to their off-screen lives, giving rise to movie magazines, tabloid coverage, and gossip columns. But not every star's behavior could stand up to such scrutiny, and many a reputation suffered lethal damage. Clara Bow, for example, was immensely popular, but her wild private life led Paramount to fire her. Even Pickford and Fairbanks, both already married when they fell in love, feared the consequences of divorce and remarriage.

No silent-era star could match the public adulation lavished on Rudolph Valentino. This Italian immigrant made a living playing stereotypical gangsters and cads until his sinuous tango scene in 1921's *The Four Horsemen of the Apocalypse* transfixed female audiences. His next film, *The Sheik,* established him as the screen's first great "Latin lover."

Valentino blended dark good looks, physical grace, and erotic force in a way that made women swoon—and men snort in derision. Mocking his bracelets and cosmetics, one writer termed him a "pink powder puff." And in his private life the great screen paramour proved less than commanding. His first wife refused to consummate their marriage, which endured all of six hours. His next, set and costume designer Natacha Rambova, demanded the lion's share of artistic control of his films.

But all sniping ceased in 1926, when Valentino, 31 and at the peak of his fame, died suddenly of peritonitis. Among the 30,000 mostly female mourners who swarmed his funeral in New York, the outpouring of grief was so rampant that police lost control of the crowd and many were trampled. There were also reports that at least a dozen overwrought fans committed suicide. Valentino's death marked the first appearance of the phenomenon of mass hysteria over a show-business idol, demonstrating the power a flickering face on a silent screen could have.

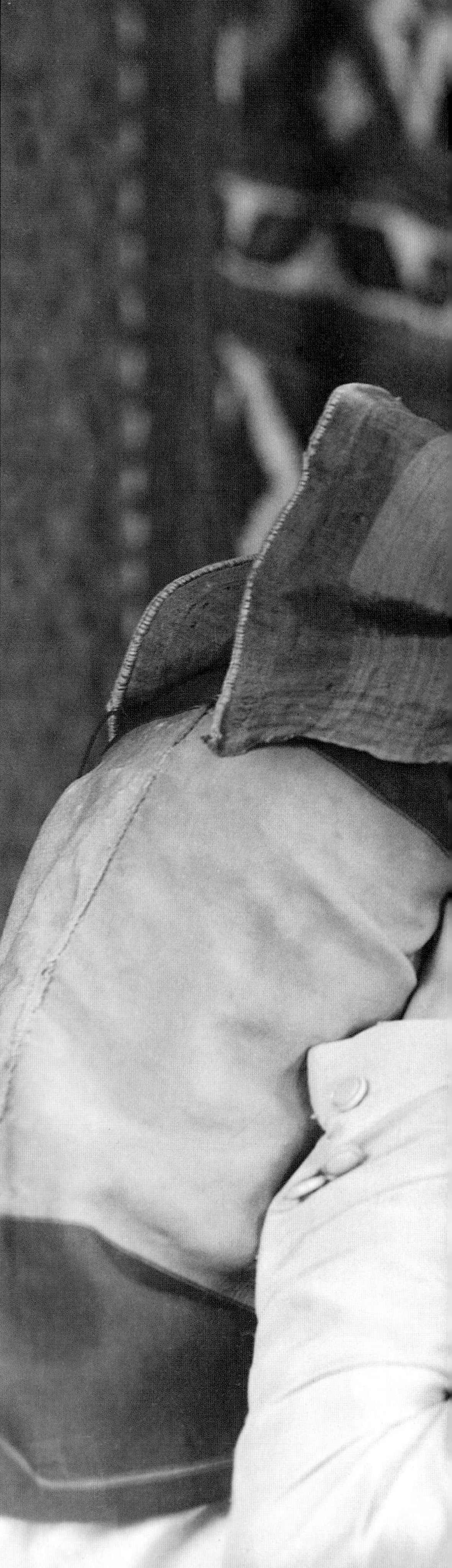

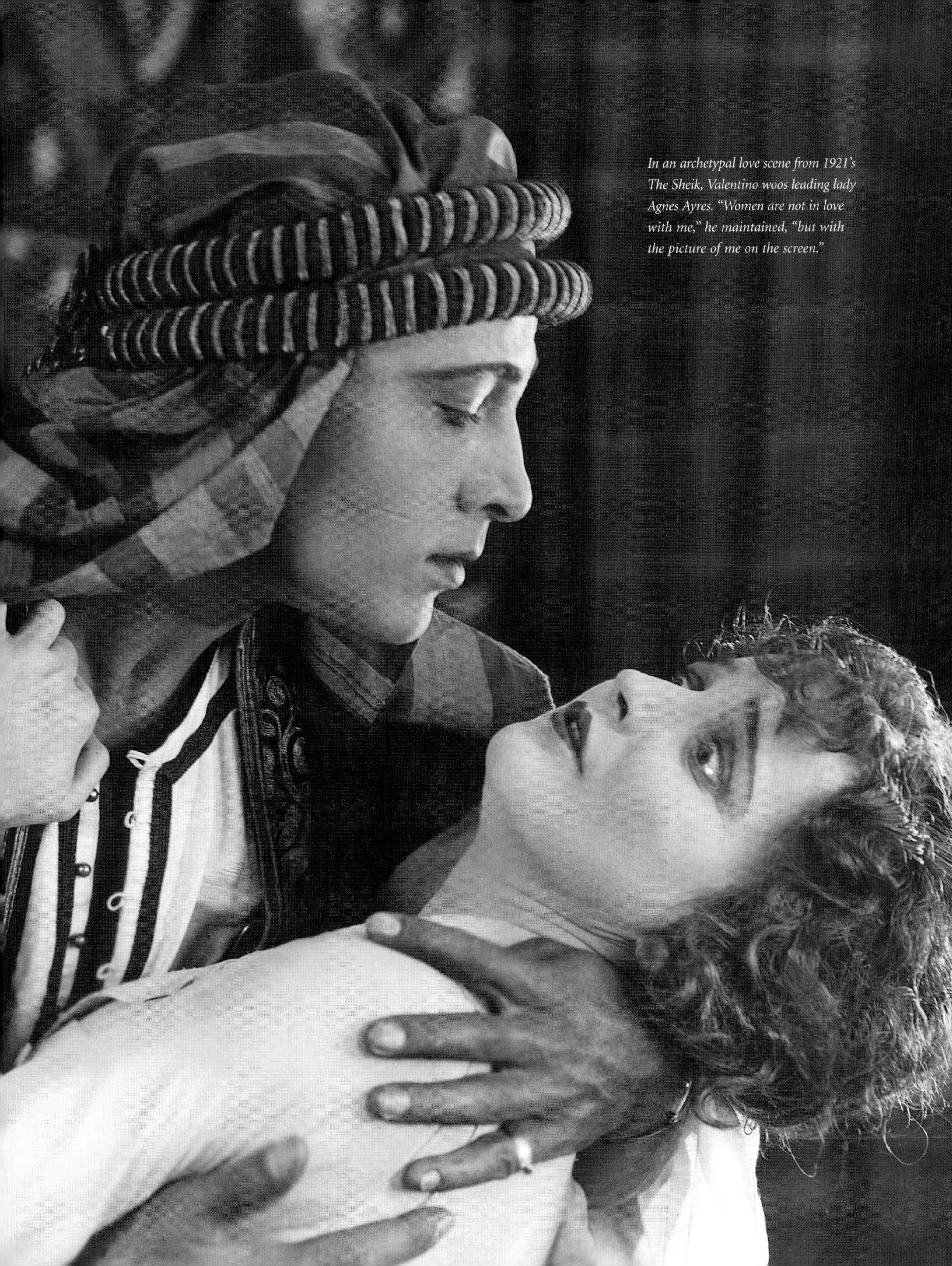

In an archetypal love scene from 1921's The Sheik, Valentino woos leading lady Agnes Ayres. "Women are not in love with me," he maintained, "but with the picture of me on the screen."

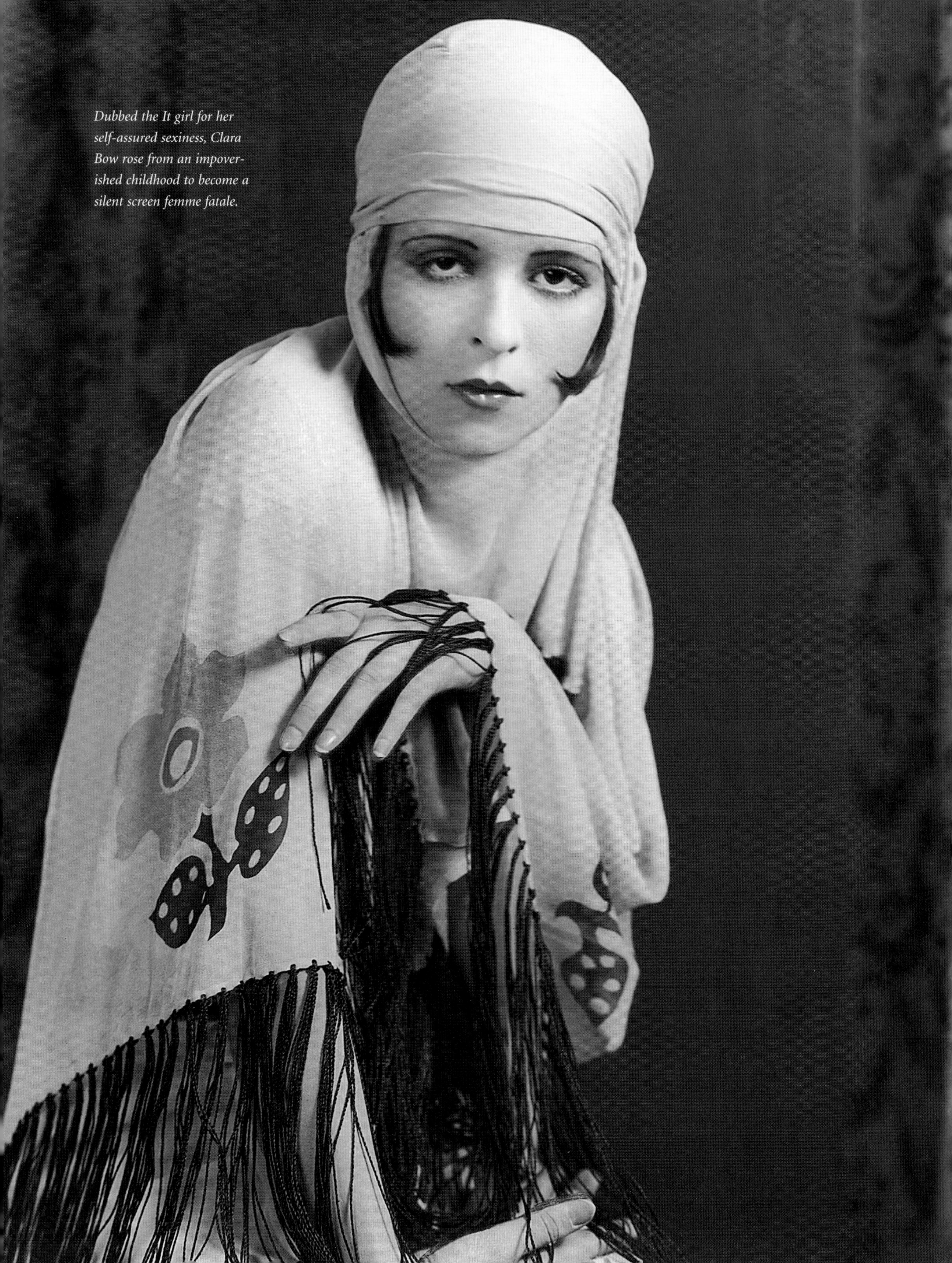

Dubbed the It girl for her self-assured sexiness, Clara Bow rose from an impoverished childhood to become a silent screen femme fatale.

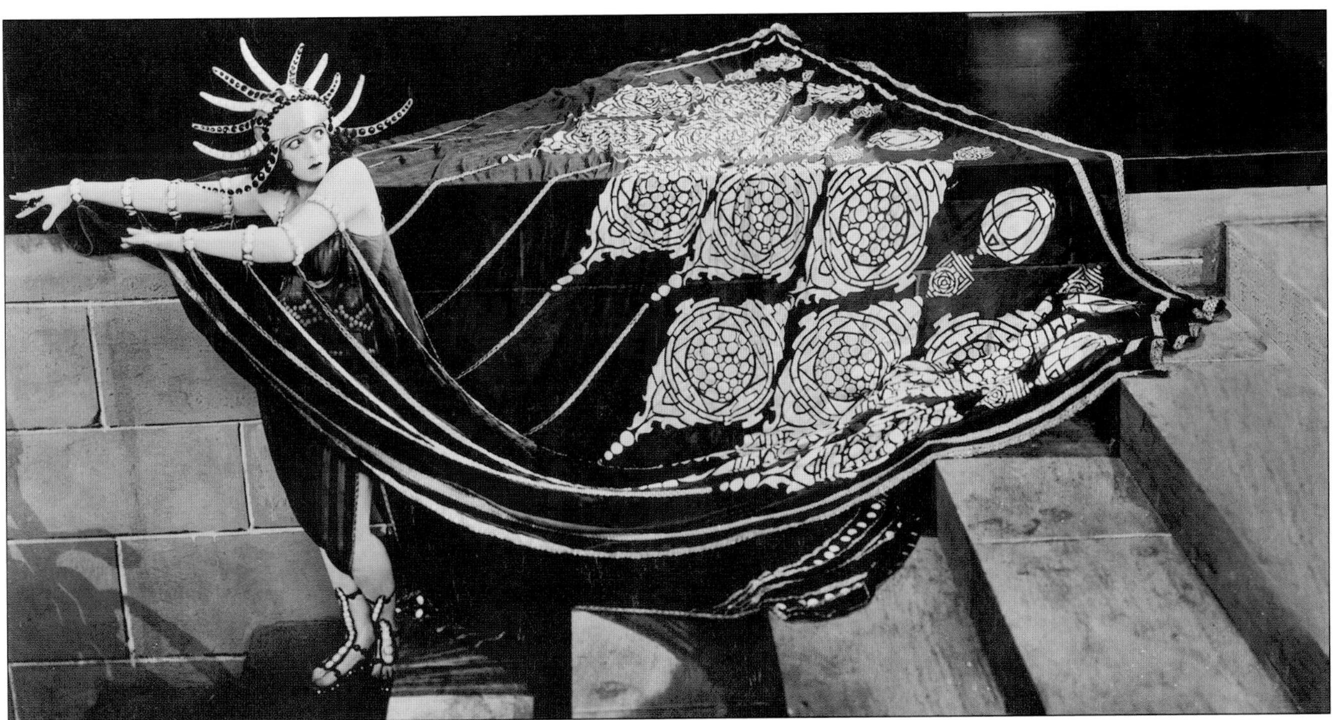

Bebe Daniels displays an extravagant costume from Cecil B. DeMille's 1919 melodrama Male and Female, which juxtaposed ancient and modern scenes.

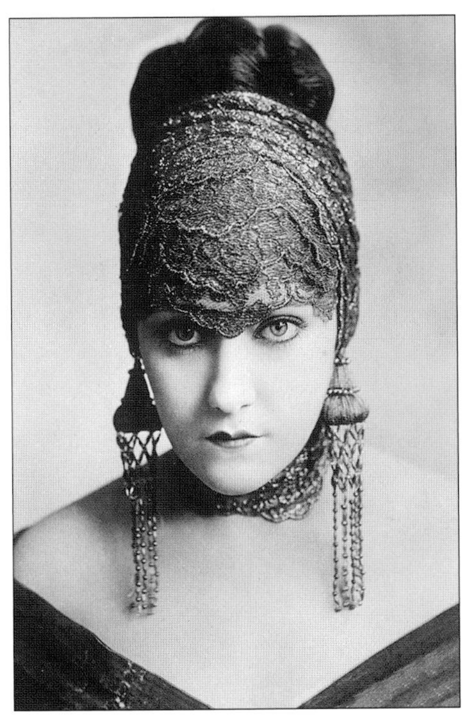

Fans copied the lavish on-screen wardrobe and hairstyles of movie queen Gloria Swanson. Marriage to a French marquis added to her glamour.

Sisters Lillian (left) and Dorothy Gish won critical acclaim in Orphans of the Storm.

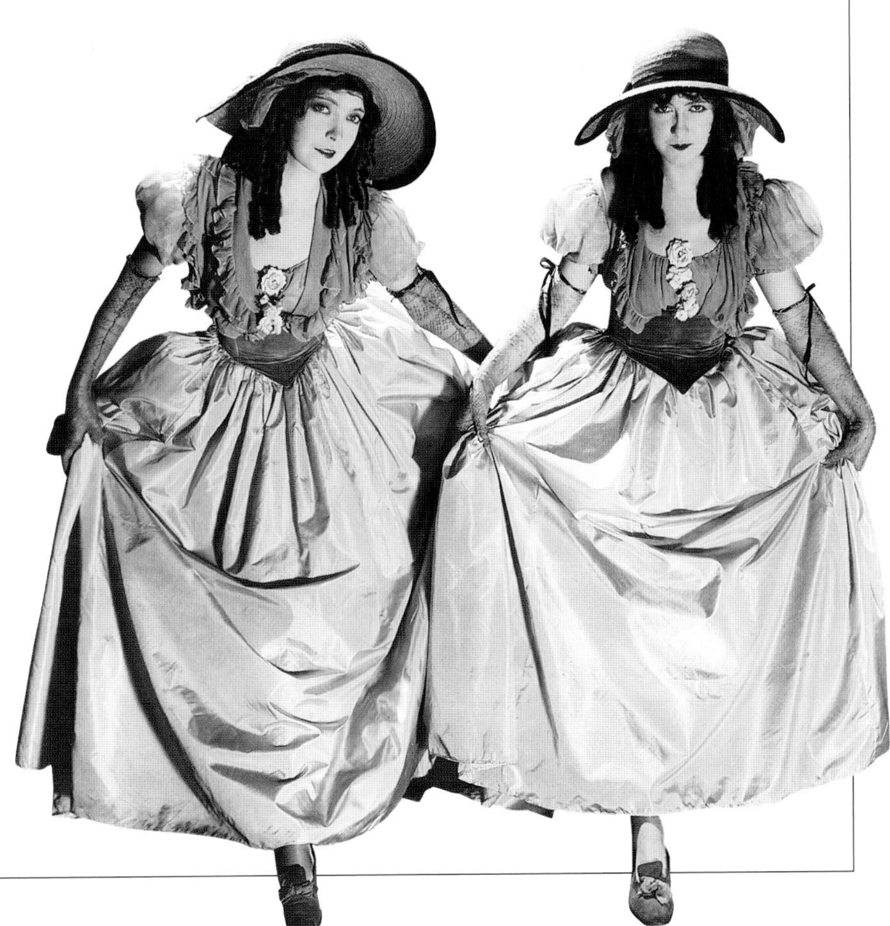

Lon Chaney, the "Man of a Thousand Faces," appears as a tragic clown in the film He Who Gets Slapped (right). Chaney portrayed a series of grotesque but sympathetic outcasts, most notably in The Hunchback of Notre Dame and The Phantom of the Opera.

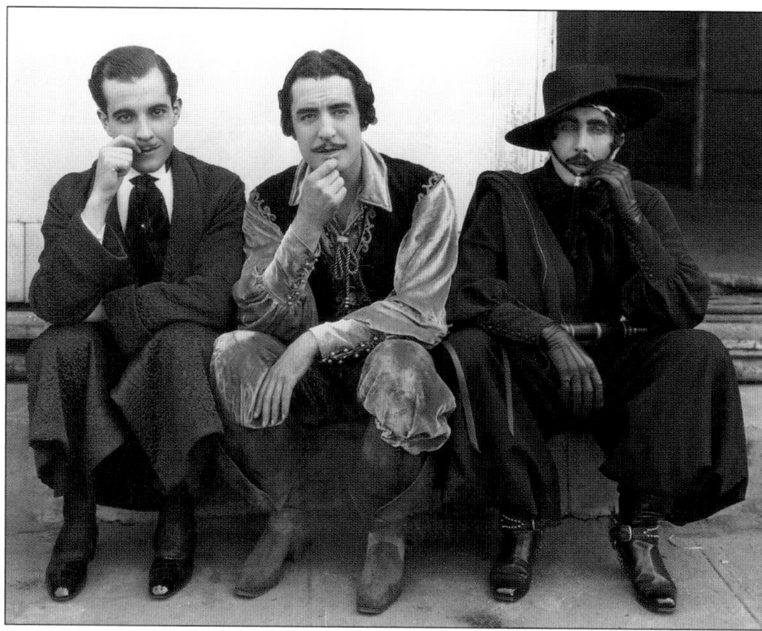

Three screen heartthrobs—Ramon Novarro, John Gilbert, and Roy D'Arcy, costumed for three different movies—relax between scenes on the MGM studio lot in this 1926 photo.

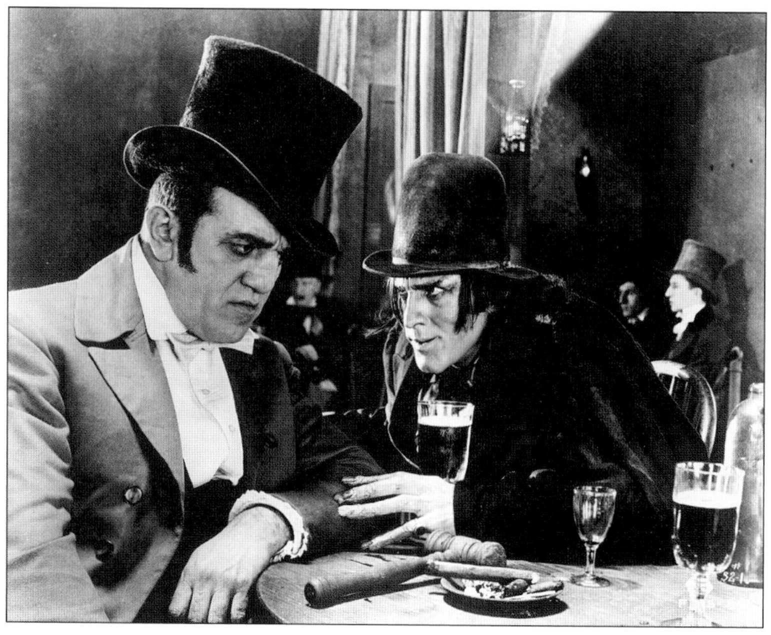

In the 1920 version of Dr. Jekyll and Mr. Hyde, John Barrymore—member of a distinguished acting clan—played both the doctor and (above, right) his evil alter ego.

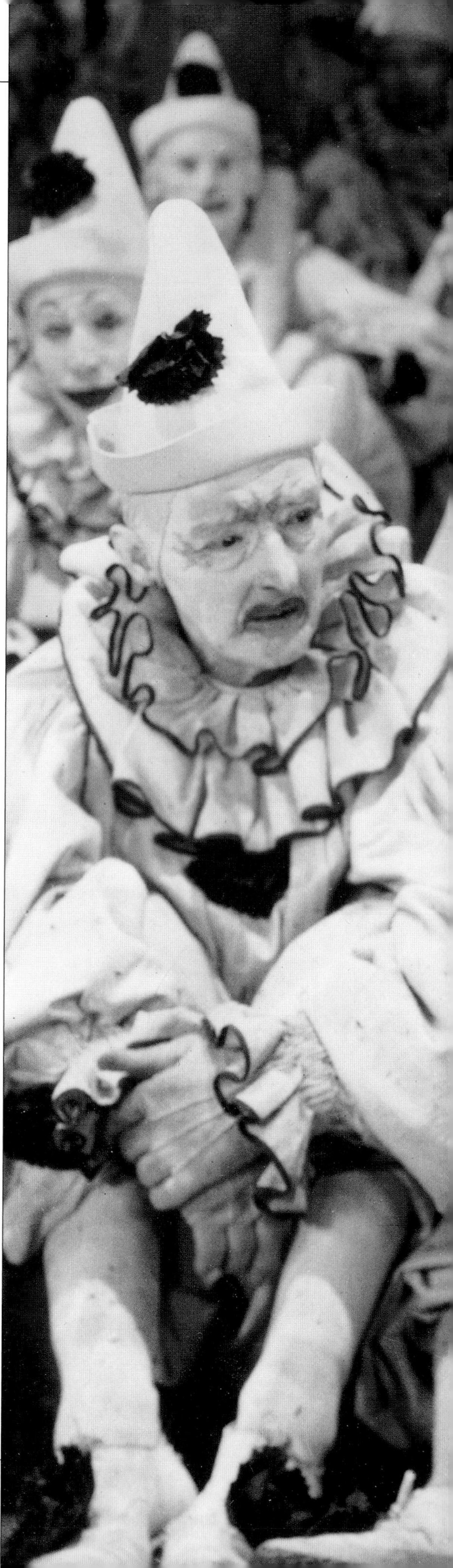

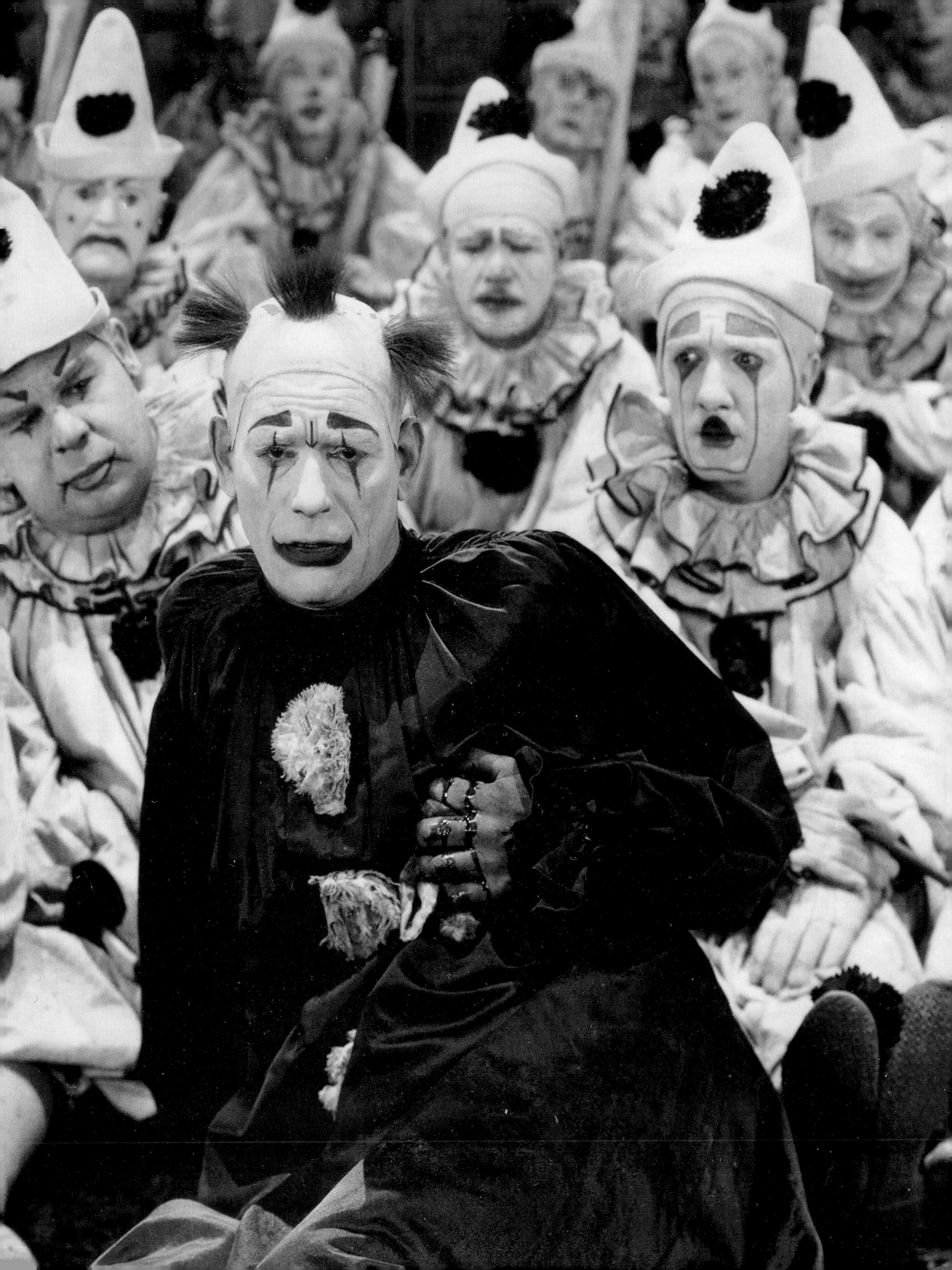

Shaping Worlds on Film

★

THE HOLLYWOOD DIRECTOR

"What is drama, after all," Alfred Hitchcock once remarked, "but life with the dull bits cut out?" There was some truth in that, but as a movie director, Hitchcock also knew that building drama on film was anything but easy. In the decades following D. W. Griffith's *Birth of a Nation*, the 1915 masterpiece that demonstrated the evocative power of the camera *(page 42)*, movies grew into an immensely expressive art, with the director positioned at the very center of the creative process. Although approaches to the job varied somewhat, directors typically played a major role in casting, hired technicians, coached actors, made decisions about lighting and camera angles, and took a hand in the final editing.

So pivotal a role naturally drew strong personalities. Cecil B. DeMille, Hollywood's longtime maestro of epics, popularized the image of the director as despot. On the set he wore riding boots and wielded a crop, and he once told his staff, "You are here to please me. Nothing else on earth matters." Otto Preminger gained notoriety for his tirades during shooting; at the slightest provocation, he would subject an offending actor or crew member to a highly public tongue-lashing. Hitchcock referred to actors as being "like cattle."

The demanding ways of some directors seemed to know no bounds. Austrian-born Erich von Stroheim, the silent era's ultimate perfectionist, became known for his wars with studio executives over budgets, schedules, and content. For his 1922 film *Foolish Wives* he

A superb cinematic technician and an unrelenting taskmaster on the set, British-born director Alfred Hitchcock adopts an imperious look in a publicity shot for his 1960 classic of terror.

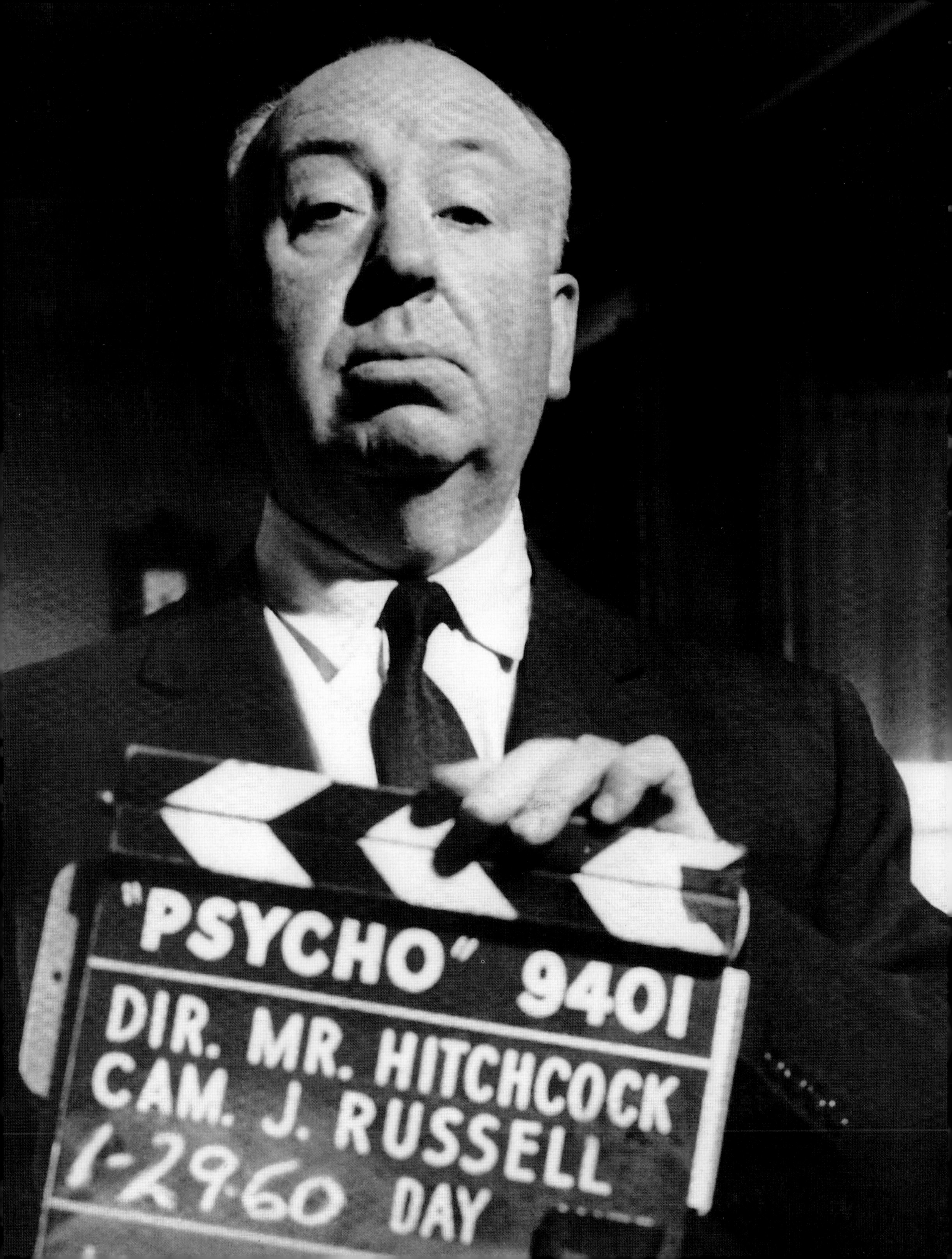

"PSYCHO" 9401
DIR. MR. HITCHCOCK
CAM. J. RUSSELL
1-29-60 DAY

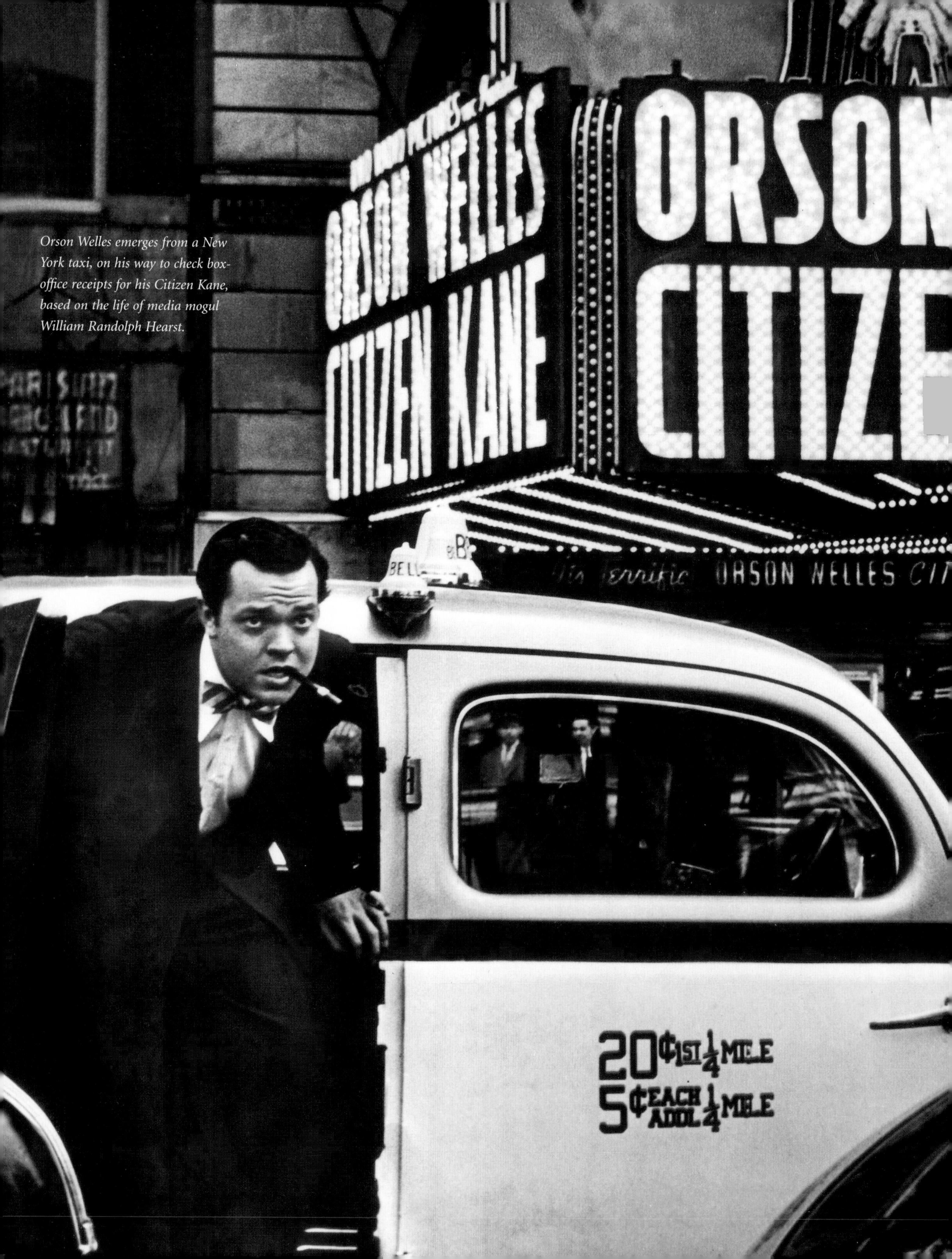

Orson Welles emerges from a New York taxi, on his way to check box-office receipts for his Citizen Kane, based on the life of media mogul William Randolph Hearst.

insisted that a full-size replica of the casinos of Monte Carlo be built on the Universal lot. He then had a second version erected on the California coast to show the same casinos from the ocean side. The film took a year to shoot and ran 400 percent over budget. After a colossal fight in 1922 with Universal's boy-wonder producer Irving Thalberg about those excesses, von Stroheim transferred his talents to MGM and began work on his trailblazing film *Greed (right)*. Two years later he handed the studio what he thought was the final product—eight hours long. MGM promptly gave it to a $30-a-week film cutter, who chopped it by three quarters. "It was like seeing a corpse in a graveyard," moaned von Stroheim, though the film as released is considered one of the silent era's greatest.

In the heyday of the studio system, the all-powerful moguls were generally able to keep their top directors in check. Executives mustered the creative package of script, stars, and director, and films flowed out the studio doors with businesslike efficiency. Michael Curtiz, a Hungarian recruited by Jack Warner in 1926, directed more than a hundred pictures for Warner Bros. in almost every imaginable genre. Though he complained that "Hollywood is money, money, money, and the nuts with everything else," Curtiz managed to create some of the finest pictures of the studio era, including *The Charge of the Light Brigade* (1936), *Angels With Dirty Faces* (1938), *The Adventures of Robin Hood* (1938), and 1942's immortal *Casablanca (right)*.

Other gifted directors—Howard Hawks, Frank Capra, John Ford, and John Huston to name a few—were also able to achieve creative greatness despite the constraints of the studio system. All were skilled at navigating the shark-infested Hollywood waters, and each had a strong personal style, although they didn't like to talk about it. When asked about "the John Huston style," that master scoffed, "I myself haven't the vaguest idea." John Ford would not go along

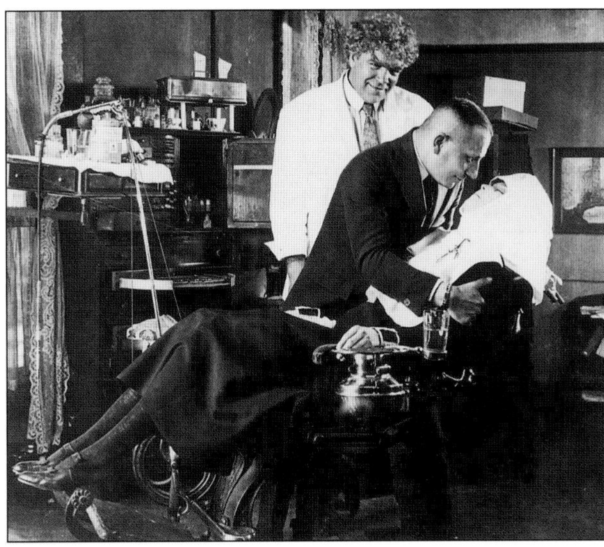

In his 1925 film Greed, based on the Frank Norris novel McTeague, director Erich von Stroheim shows an actor playing the title character, a dentist, how to ravish a drugged patient. To achieve the realism he wanted, von Stroheim shot on location in a boardinghouse in San Francisco and in 120-degree midsummer heat in Death Valley.

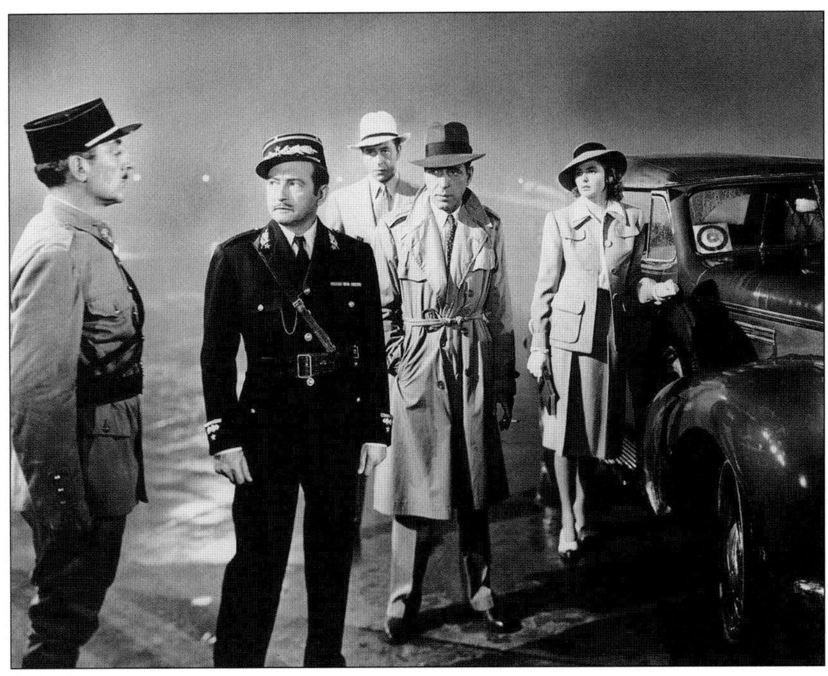

The main characters in Michael Curtiz's Casablanca—Rick (Humphrey Bogart), Ilsa (Ingrid Bergman), Victor Lazlo (Paul Henreid), and Captain Renault (Claude Rains)—gather for the film's stirring climax. Rick manfully persuades his true love, Ilsa, to forget about him and fly off with her Resistance-leader husband, Victor.

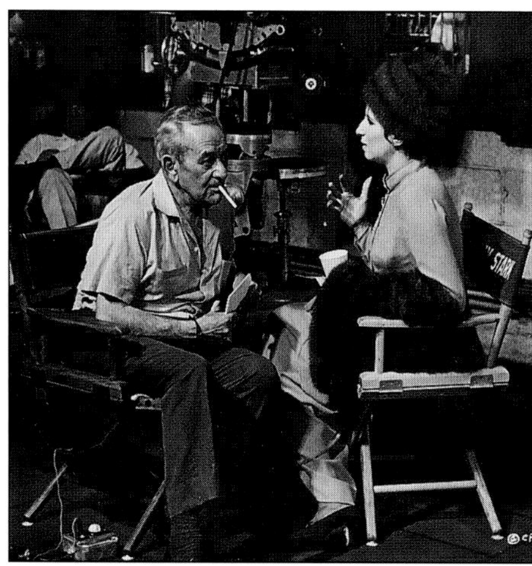

William Wyler huddles with his star, Barbra Streisand, while shooting a movie version of the musical Funny Girl (1968). In a directorial career spanning almost five decades, Wyler adapted many stage productions to film. "I consider the first function of a director to be the acting," he said.

with anyone who tried to coax out of him an explanation or even an admission of his genius. But his colleagues in the industry recognized that Ford's work was a virtual encyclopedia of the film medium. "Almost anything that any of us has done you can find in a John Ford film," said director Sidney Lumet. Frank Capra described Ford as a kind of apotheosis of the profession: "half-tyrant, half-revolutionary; half-saint, half-satan; half-possible, half-impossible . . . but all director."

Orson Welles watched Ford's groundbreaking western *Stagecoach* 40 times before starting his own film-directing career with *Citizen Kane* in 1941 *(page 58)*. Welles was just 26 at the time but already a legend in the worlds of theater and radio. Three years earlier, in a Halloween eve broadcast based on the H. G. Wells novel *The War of the Worlds*, his dramatization of Martians landing in New Jersey was so convincing that it caused a nationwide panic. For his baptismal film effort, Welles was given almost unprecedented artistic freedom by RKO, and he used it to the fullest, describing the situation as "the biggest electric train set any boy ever had." Functioning as writer, performer, and daring cinematographic experimentalist, he crafted a film that combined newsreel techniques with the drama of a detective mystery. Press magnate William Randolph Hearst, who took offense at the lead character, an obvious—and unflattering—version of himself, ordered his newspapers to snub the film. Thus it was a box-office disappointment, but it would be ranked by many critics the finest American movie ever made.

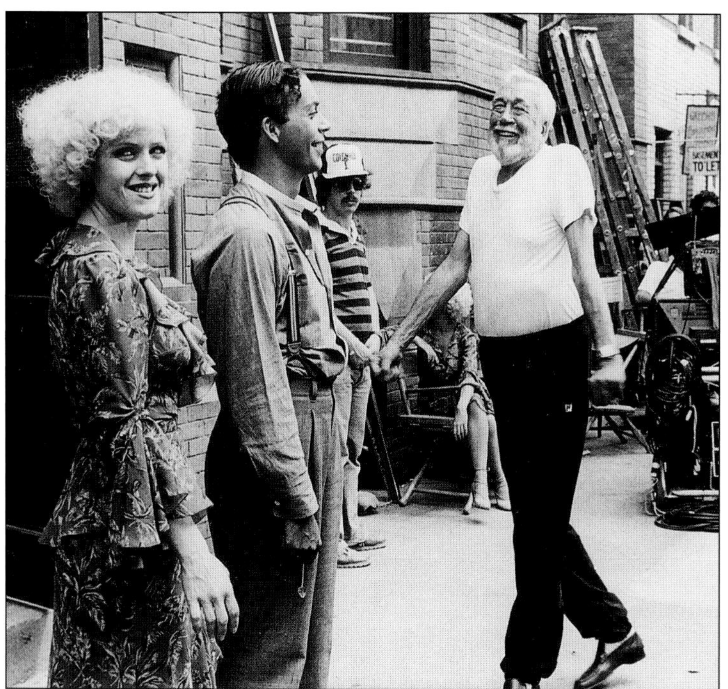

Helping dispel tension, John Huston mugs to his cast during the filming of the 1982 musical Annie. Before joining the ranks of Hollywood directors, Huston—the son of a film actor—worked as a journalist, tried prizefighting, and briefly served as a cavalryman in the Mexican army.

In the mid- and late 1940s many leading directors, resentful of studio control, began trying to produce films independently. It was often a draining experience. As one critic later wrote, "the studio chiefs created a magnificent support system for directors," freeing them from worries about financing and arranging for them to work with familiar actors and crew.

As a new generation of directors came of age outside the studio system, creativity surged. Arthur Penn took one of the oldest Hollywood genres, the gangster picture, into new and more brutal territory with his stunning 1967 film *Bonnie and Clyde*. Sam Peckinpah did the same for the western two years later with *The Wild Bunch*. In terms of sheer range, no one outdid Stanley Kubrick, who filmed the cast-of-thousands Roman epic *Spartacus* (1960), the stinging antiwar film *Paths of Glory* (1957), the blackly humorous, end-of-the-world classic *Dr. Strangelove* (1964), the breakthrough science fiction film *2001: A Space Odyssey* (1968), and the hair-raising social satire *A Clockwork Orange* (1971).

In the 1970s and '80s directors emerged as superstars in their own right. The names Steven Spielberg *(right)* and George Lucas became synonymous with "blockbuster" after Spielberg's phenomenal success with *Jaws* (1975), *Raiders of the Lost Ark* (1981), and *E.T.* (1982), and Lucas's with *Star Wars* (1977) and its sequels. And film audiences eagerly awaited each new work by Woody Allen, Robert Altman, Brian De Palma, Francis Ford Coppola, and Martin Scorsese.

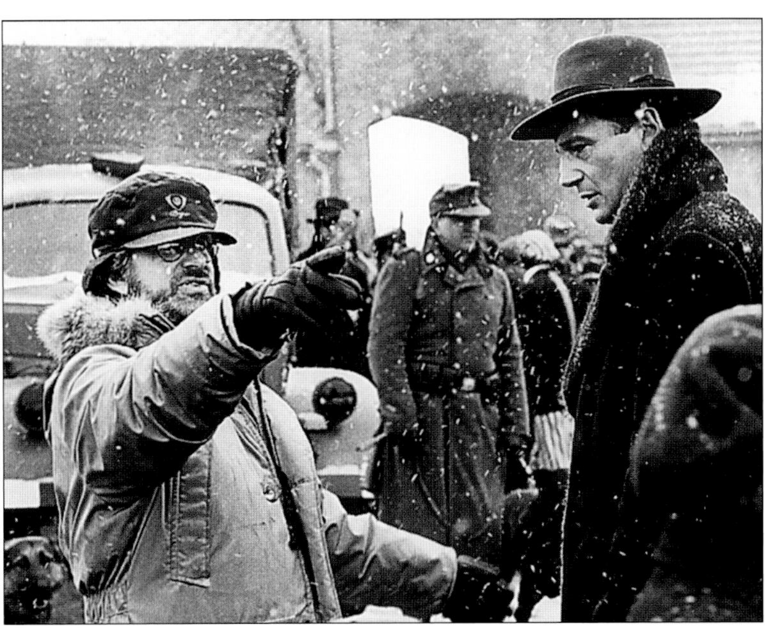

On location in Poland, Steven Spielberg directs Liam Neeson in the 1993 drama Schindler's List, which recounted the story of a German industrialist who shielded more than a thousand Jews from the Nazis by employing them in his factory.

In Hollywood's early days, at a time when one studio executive gave a director his first job because "he yells good," women hardly stood a chance. But Dorothy Arzner defied convention and masculine prejudice, working her way up from script supervisor to editor to screenwriter, then directing a comedy called *Fashions for Women* in 1927. She went on to direct Clara Bow and Fredric March in Paramount's first sound release, *The Wild Party* (1929), and subsequently worked with Claudette Colbert, Sylvia Sidney, Katharine Hepburn, Rosalind Russell, and Joan Crawford. Much later, Barbra Streisand, Penny Marshall *(right)*, and Jodie Foster were able to use their clout as actors to make forays into directing. In 1976 Italian filmmaker Lina Wertmuller became the first woman to be nominated for a Best Director Oscar, for the harrowing World War II drama *Seven Beauties*, and New Zealand-born Jane Campion was nominated in 1993 for her haunting *The Piano*. Neither won, but Campion's script earned her a screenwriting award.

Despite changing tastes and the challenges of mastering new film technology, one of the legendary directors of the 1940s and '50s, John Huston, made a brilliant comeback with *The Man Who Would Be King* (1975), *Prizzi's Honor* (1985), and *The Dead* (1987). The title of his last film was all too fitting, since Huston did not live to see its release. Earlier he had remarked on the intimate connection between directors and their work: "Each picture," he said, "is a world unto itself. Picture makers lead dozens of lives—a life for each picture. And, by the same token, they perish a little when each picture is finished and that world comes to an end."

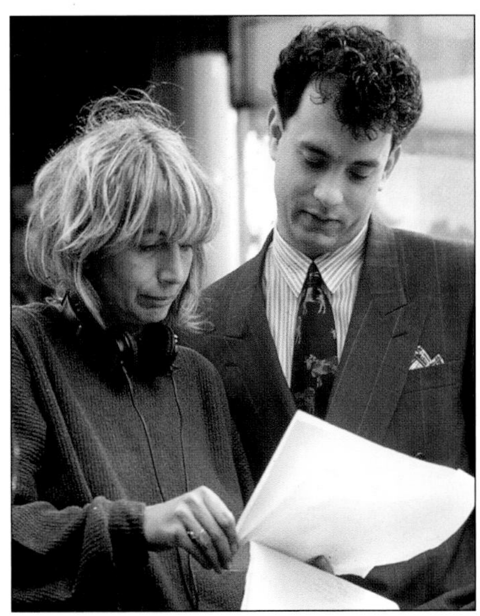

Penny Marshall reviews the script with Tom Hanks on the set of the 1988 comedy Big, which grossed more than $100 million. A former television sitcom actress, Marshall launched her directing career two years earlier with Jumpin' Jack Flash, starring comedienne Whoopi Goldberg.

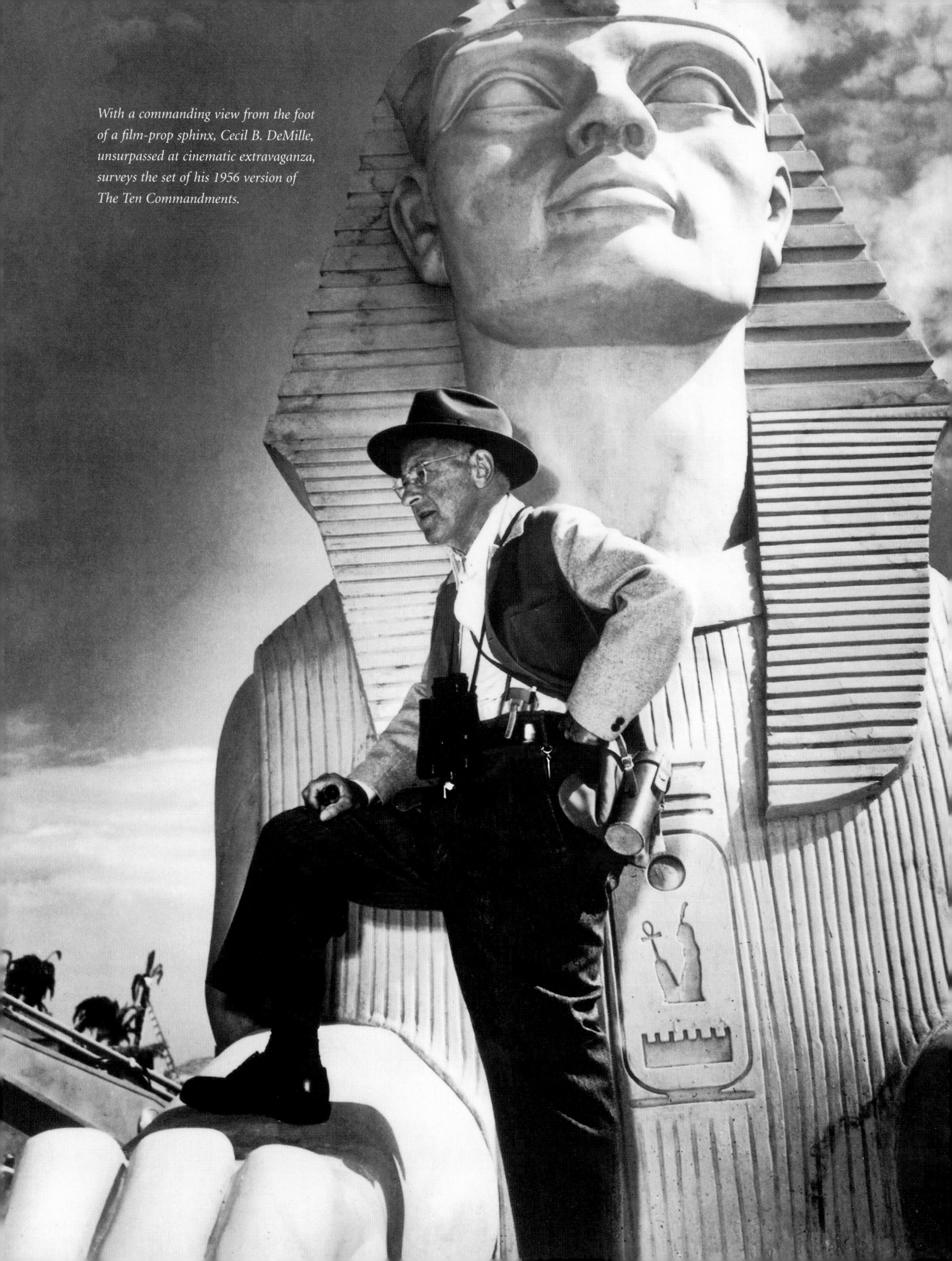

With a commanding view from the foot of a film-prop sphinx, Cecil B. DeMille, unsurpassed at cinematic extravaganza, surveys the set of his 1956 version of The Ten Commandments.

Masters of the Big-Budget Epic

A taste for spectacle showed itself early among filmmakers, with Cecil B. DeMille setting the pace for sheer directorial grandiosity. Pharaoh-like, he ordered the construction of the largest set in movie history for his 1923 Technicolor epic *The Ten Commandments.* In a California desert rose an ersatz ancient Egyptian city—100 feet tall, 700 feet wide, and studded with a million pounds of statuary. He also had craftsmen build 300 chariots for the film and assembled 3,500 extras and 5,000 animals for the shooting. Studio executives were appalled, but the film became the biggest moneymaker of its time. Through the silent era and for decades afterward, DeMille continued to create epics—invariably spiced with romance and violence but often neatly wrapped in the cloak of a historical or Biblical event.

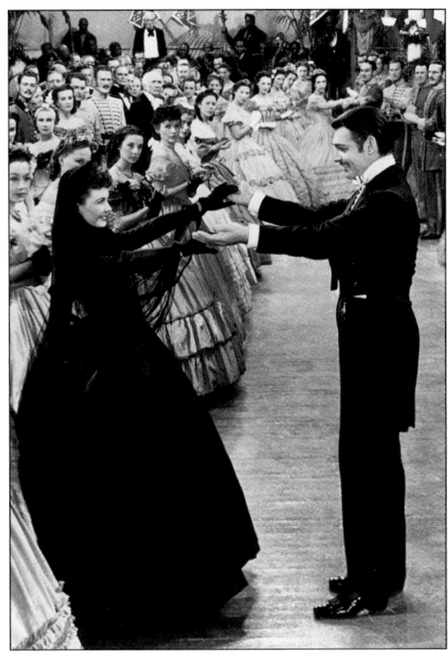

Rhett Butler (Clark Gable) scandalizes Southern aristocrats by leading the recently widowed Scarlett O'Hara (Vivien Leigh) in the Virginia reel in Victor Fleming's Gone With the Wind.

In 1939 director Victor Fleming followed the same general recipe in making *Gone With the Wind (right).* For a scene of Scarlett O'Hara wandering amid wounded and dying soldiers in Civil War-ravaged Atlanta, Fleming had 1,600 bodies—800 extras and 800 dummies being rocked discreetly by the extras—arrayed in front of the meticulously re-created Atlanta train station.

In the 1950s and '60s, Hollywood, competing with TV, rolled out new wide-screen formats such as CinemaScope and VistaVision. Lavish productions like *Around the World in Eighty Days* wowed audiences, as did a spate of Biblical and Roman epics, including *The Robe* (1953), *Ben-Hur* (1959), *Spartacus* (1960), *Cleopatra* (1963), and DeMille's final film, a wildly popular remake of *The Ten Commandments.* But there was art, too. In 1962's *Lawrence of Arabia (right),* director David Lean captured the mystery and majesty of the desert with a nearly silent, three-minute sequence: A tiny speck on the horizon grows into a swirl of dust that draws closer and closer until it reveals itself as a man on a camel galloping toward the viewer—pure cinematic magic.

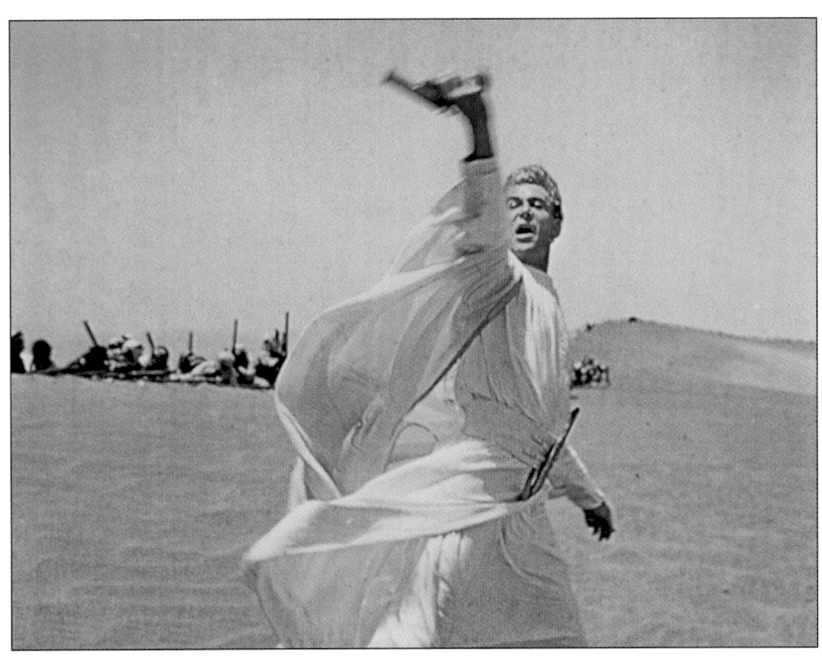

Peter O'Toole as Lawrence of Arabia leads a charge across the desert. Director David Lean's choice of the little-known Irish actor for the role was seen as risky but proved brilliant.

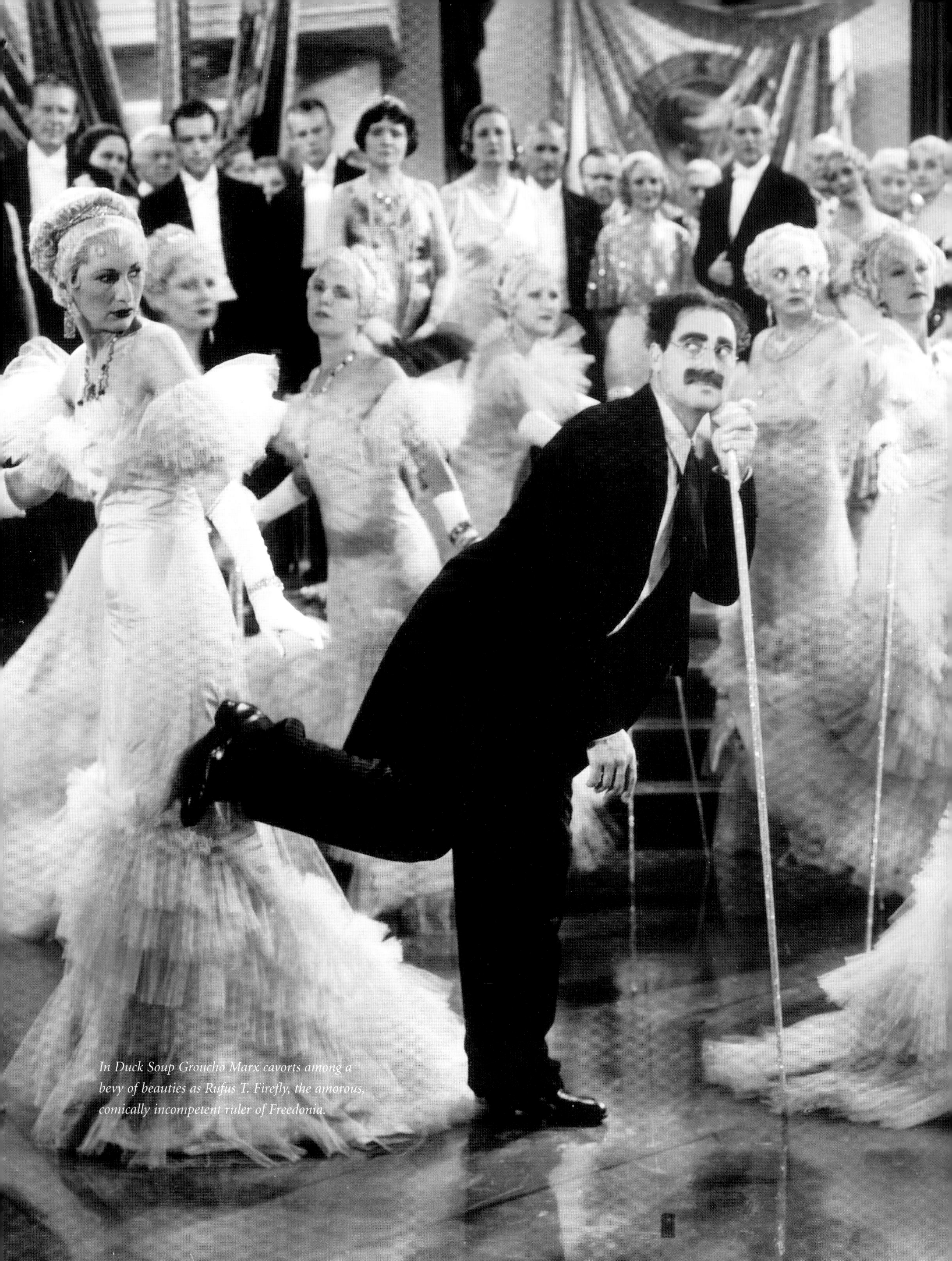

In Duck Soup Groucho Marx cavorts among a bevy of beauties as Rufus T. Firefly, the amorous, comically incompetent ruler of Freedonia.

A Range of Comic Flavors

In the depths of the Depression, a comedy came along to sweep all the major Oscars. Frank Capra's *It Happened One Night* (1934) featured Clark Gable as a tough-as-nails reporter in pursuit of a runaway heiress played by Claudette Colbert. The reporter thinks he wants the story, not the girl, but Cupid launches his arrow at the mismatched couple, and hilarity reigns as the sexes battle against the inevitable. Capra's romp put several scenes into the Hollywood pantheon—including one in which Gable makes a mocking nod toward modesty by hanging a blanket on a clothesline to separate his bed from Colbert's in the cabin they're forced to occupy, and a hitchhiking sequence in which Colbert shows that a leg works better than a thumb—if it's on a comely female.

It Happened One Night inaugurated the genre of comedy described as "screwball"—a term drawn from a baseball pitch that darts and dips in unexpected ways and in a movie refers to zany goings-on. These celluloid cocktails combined fast-paced banter with themes as old as Shakespeare—mistaken identities, the battle of the sexes, and abrupt reversals of fortune. The genre reached a peak in 1938 with Howard Hawks's *Bringing Up Baby (right, top and center).* Cary Grant played a tweedy paleontologist who finds himself mixed up, much against his will, with Katharine Hepburn as a ditzy socialite. In the ensuing romantic melee, cars are stolen, clothing torn, a lawyer is beaned by a rock, and the reluctant Grant ends up chasing a leopard through the Connecticut woods.

The Marx Brothers perfected their own inimitable brand of comedy in chaotic confections such as 1933's *Duck Soup.* In this send-up of diplomacy and saber-rattling, Groucho played the newly appointed ruler of a country called Freedonia, with brothers Chico as minister of war, Harpo as his chauffeur, and Zeppo as his secretary.

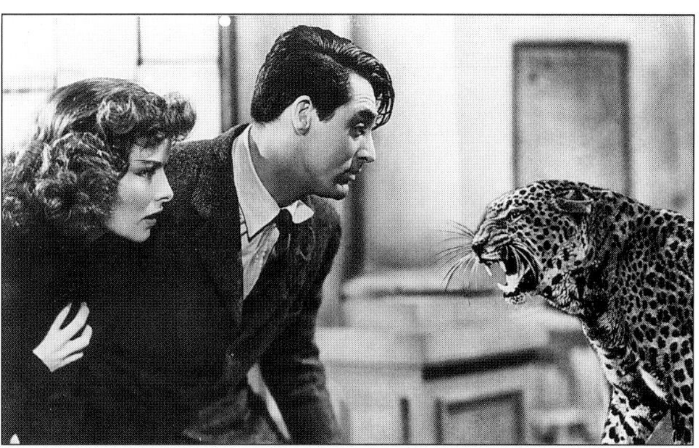

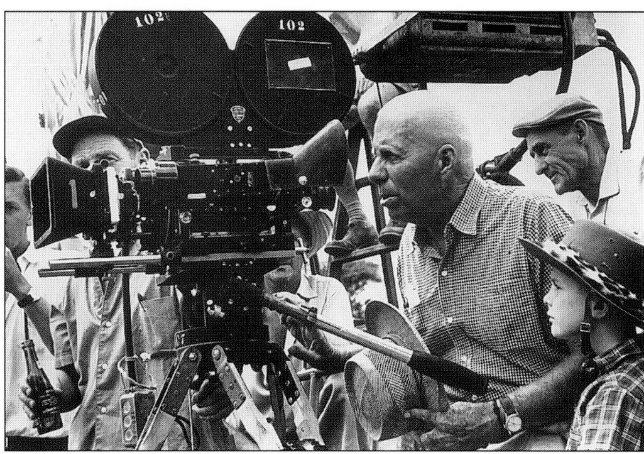

In Bringing Up Baby, Katharine Hepburn and Cary Grant (top) find themselves facing an ill-tempered double of the tame leopard they have been pursuing. Their director, Howard Hawks (above), created westerns, thrillers, and war films as well as comedies.

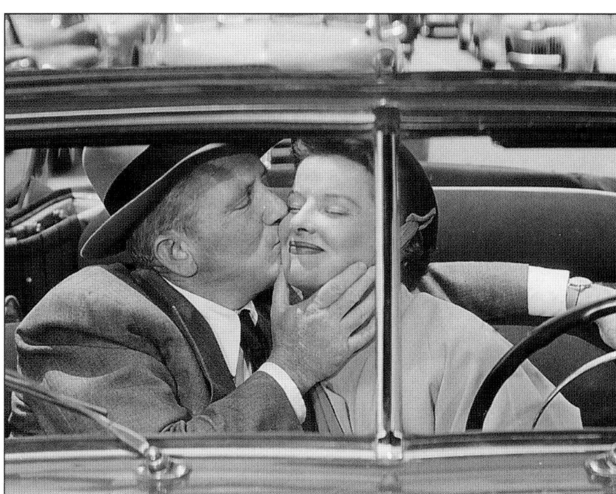

Spencer Tracy busses Katharine Hepburn in George Cukor's witty romance Adam's Rib, which locked them, as prosecuting and defense attorneys, in a courtroom battle of the sexes.

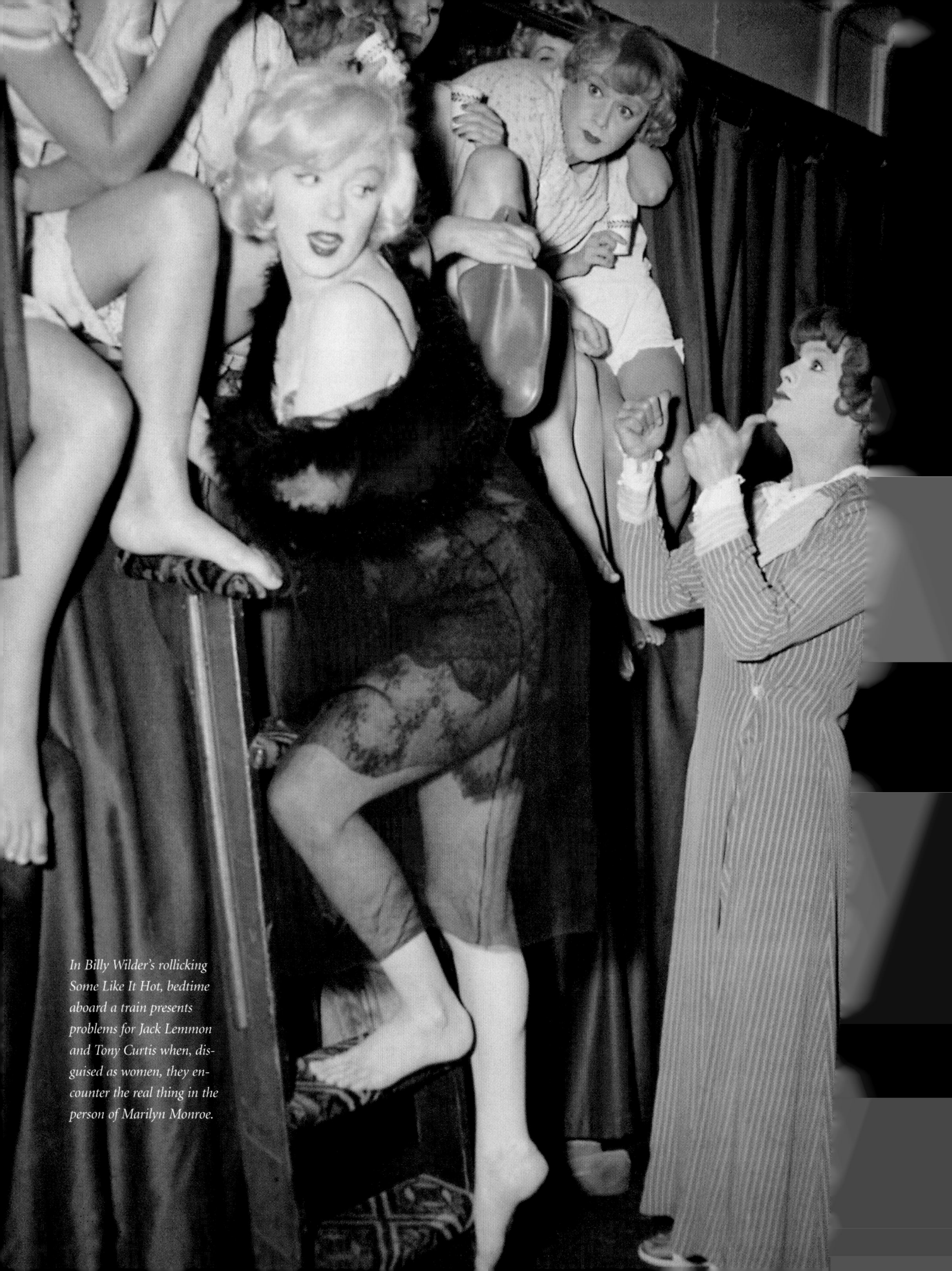

In Billy Wilder's rollicking Some Like It Hot, bedtime aboard a train presents problems for Jack Lemmon and Tony Curtis when, disguised as women, they encounter the real thing in the person of Marilyn Monroe.

As Freedonia lurches into war with its fictional neighbor, Sylvania, Groucho relaxes with a game of jacks. In a classic sequence that required perfect comic timing, Harpo dresses up like Groucho and tries to convince the fearless leader that he's gazing into a mirror. *Duck Soup*'s director, Leo McCarey, also worked with such icons of comedy as Harold Lloyd, Laurel and Hardy, Mae West, and W. C. Fields.

Comedies directed by Preston Sturges wryly toyed with American dreams of wealth and fame. In *Christmas in July* (1940), young Dick Powell believes his life has changed forever when he wins $25,000 in a contest, only to discover—after a wild spending spree—that he's not the winner he thought he was. Sturges's bubbly *Palm Beach Story* (1942) starred Claudette Colbert as a beautiful young wife disappointed by the failures of her inventor husband, played by Joel McCrea. Fleeing to Florida, Colbert encounters a trainful of wacky millionaires, including the ultrawealthy but penny-pinching oil king J. D. Hackensacker, played by crooner Rudy Vallee. Just when it seems that Colbert might snag the rich hubby of her dreams, love-starved McCrea shows up, and she has second thoughts about joining the ranks of the lunatic rich.

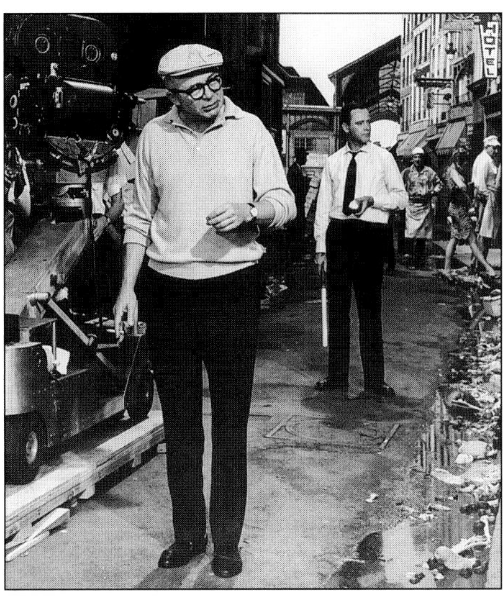

Preparing to shoot a scene with Jack Lemmon, Billy Wilder strolls the set of Irma La Douce, a 1963 comedy about a Paris prostitute and her gendarme lover, who has to wear disguises because he is also her pimp. In a long career, the Vienna-born Wilder won two Best Director Oscars.

Some of Hollywood's greatest actors—Katharine Hepburn and Spencer Tracy among them—did their best comic turns under the direction of George Cukor. Despite the success of *Bringing Up Baby*, the outspoken, independent-minded Hepburn was regarded as box-office poison until Cukor helped rehabilitate her career with *Holiday* (1938) and *The Philadelphia Story* (1940). In 1949 Cukor paired Hepburn with Tracy as a battling couple of married attorneys in *Adam's Rib* *(page 65)*, and three years later they returned as a top female athlete and her manager in *Pat and Mike.* Their on-screen chemistry, sparked by an off-screen romance, became the stuff of film legend.

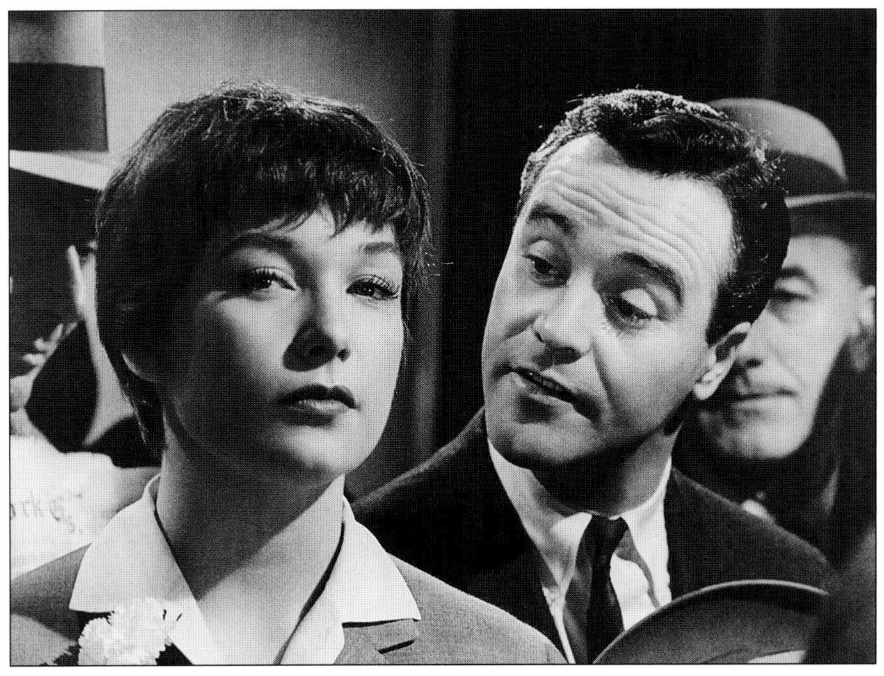

Co-workers on a bumpy road to love in Billy Wilder's The Apartment, Jack Lemmon rides with elevator operator Shirley MacLaine. Ambitious Lemmon lends his apartment to his bosses for trysts—until one of them uses it with MacLaine.

Billy Wilder *(right, top),* known for such dark dramas as *Double Indemnity* and *The Lost Weekend,* also wrote or directed some sparkling comedies from the 1930s to the '60s—*Ninotchka* (1939), *The Major and*

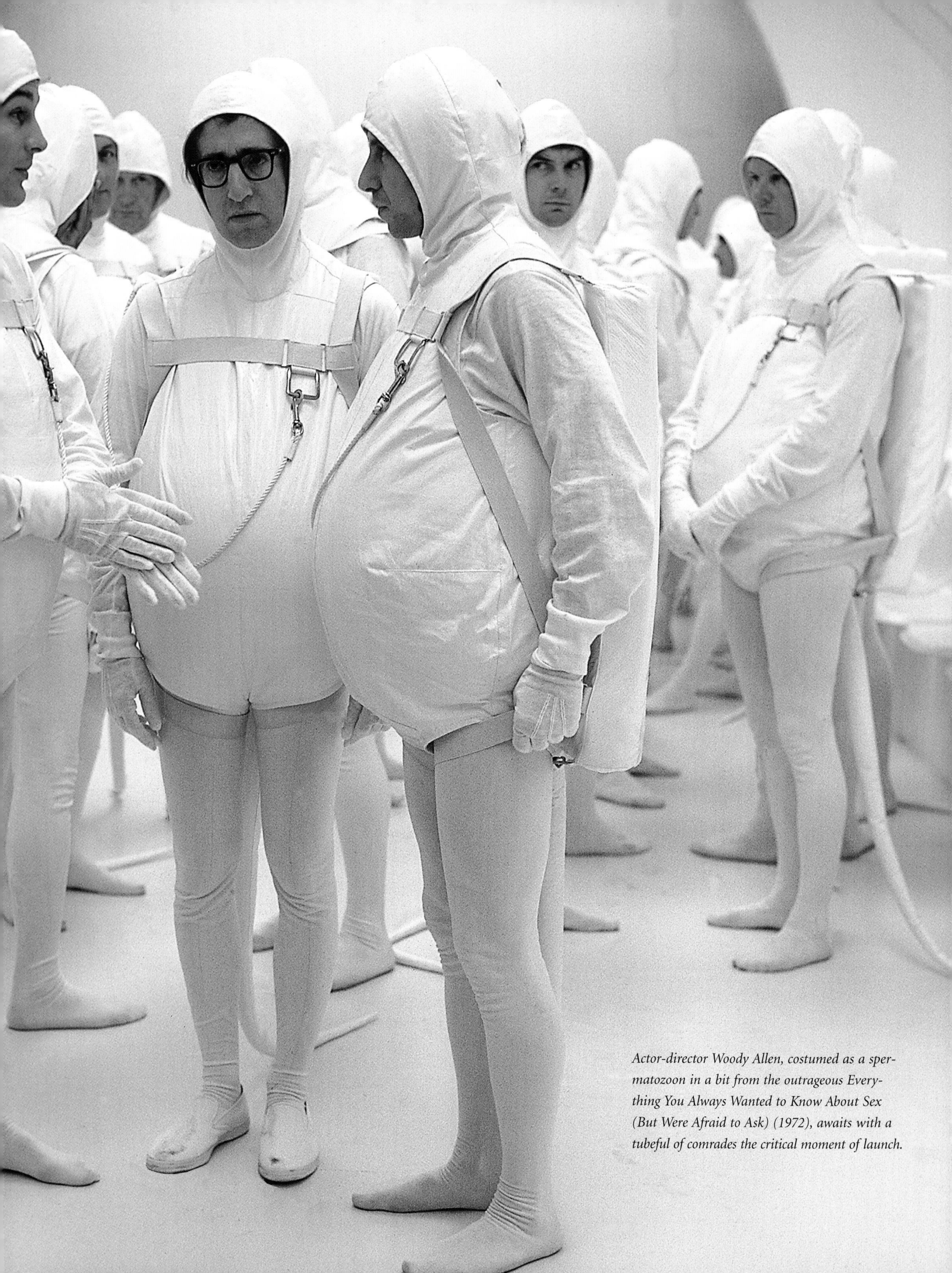

Actor-director Woody Allen, costumed as a spermatozoon in a bit from the outrageous Everything You Always Wanted to Know About Sex (But Were Afraid to Ask) (1972), awaits with a tubeful of comrades the critical moment of launch.

the Minor (1942), *Stalag 17* (1953), *The Seven Year Itch* (1955), and 1960's *The Apartment (page 67)*. His 1959 smash *Some Like It Hot (page 66)*, set in the Roaring Twenties, featured Tony Curtis and Jack Lemmon as jazz musicians who, to elude mobsters, disguise themselves as women and join an all-girl band, where they encounter the ravishing Marilyn Monroe.

The cross-dressing theme, which made sport of the definition of sexuality itself, reached full comic flower in 1982 with Sydney Pollack's *Tootsie (right)*, in which Dustin Hoffman plays an obnoxiously touchy actor who dons women's clothes to get a TV soap opera part. He proceeds to fall in love with his female costar, who does not know, and can't be told, that he's really a man—while her father, equally ignorant of the masquerade, falls in love with him.

Just as screwball comedies humorously reflected Depression-era concerns with money, class, and status, the comedies of Woody Allen *(left)* captured the big-city neuroses of the late 20th century. His *Annie Hall* won the Best Picture Oscar for 1977 (along with Best Director and Best Screenplay) with its bittersweet tale of two angst-afflicted New Yorkers, played by Allen and Diane Keaton, who meet, fall in love, and split up. Allen's *Manhattan* (1979) played the same themes in a more poignant—but still hilarious—way, and his *Hannah and Her Sisters* (1986) delved even deeper into the urban psyche without losing any of the laughs. Hip but worried, smart but self-absorbed, forever obsessed with sex, Allen's leading characters—often just reflections of himself—inhabited a sophisticated terrain of Manhattan restaurants, loft apartments, art galleries, and, perhaps most important, psychoanalysts' offices. Though far from the mainstream, these urbanites, like the heiresses and plutocrats of the screwball 1930s films, struck a chord with viewers as they acted out their version of the universal human comedy.

> "Life is divided into the horrible and the miserable. . . . So you should be thankful you're miserable."
>
> Woody Allen, in *Annie Hall*

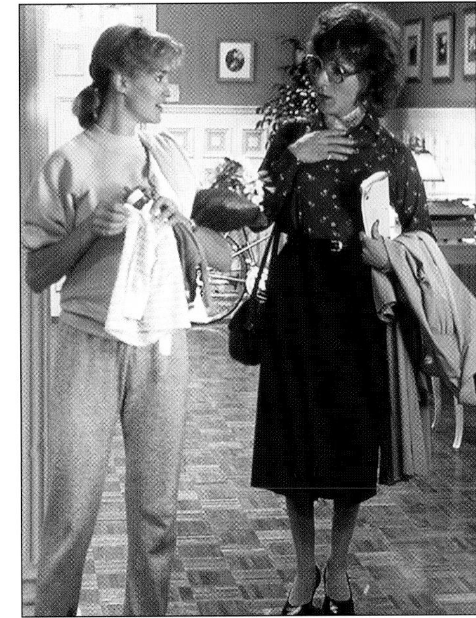

In drag as soap opera star "Dorothy" in Tootsie, Dustin Hoffman (above, right) chats with Jessica Lange, playing an actress friend. The director, Sydney Pollack (below), worked in television for years before trying his hand at movies.

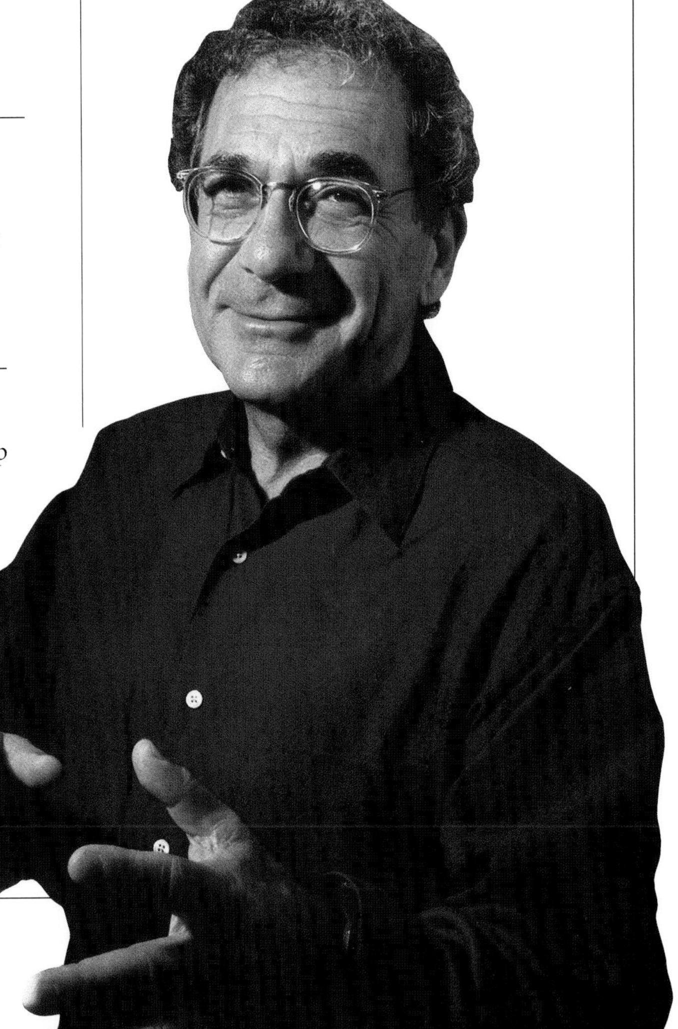

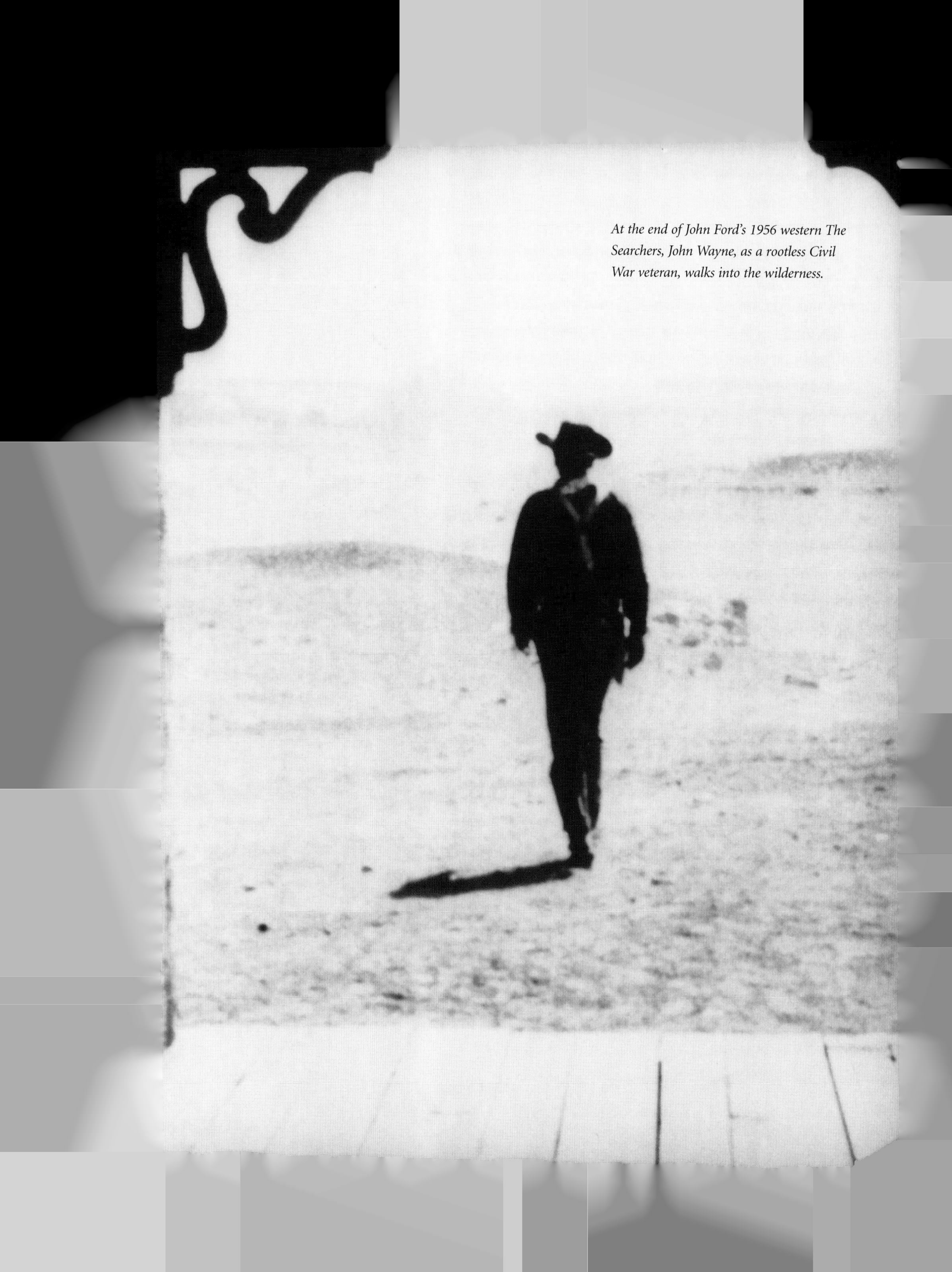

At the end of John Ford's 1956 western The Searchers, John Wayne, as a rootless Civil War veteran, walks into the wilderness.

Taut Tales of the Frontier

More than any other film genre, westerns seemed quintessentially American, harking back to the pioneers who built a civilization in a vast, challenging landscape—and wiped out ancient native societies in the process. These movies helped create an archetypal American male hero: laconic, self-reliant, good with a gun but using it only when necessary. In George Stevens's 1953 film *Shane*, for example, Alan Ladd plays a nomadic former gunfighter who reluctantly takes up arms to rescue homesteaders from a vicious gang, then moves on. Western female leads, by contrast, were often schoolmarms or other gentle tamers, bringing order to the unruly male world.

Director Fred Zinnemann explored these male and female archetypes in his starkly drawn 1952 classic, *High Noon* *(page 72)*. Gary Cooper is a sheriff about to hang up his guns and marry a beautiful Quaker, Grace Kelly. When he learns a gang of killers is gunning for him, he must choose, as the film's hit theme song put it, " 'tween love and duty."

The director most responsible for the look and feel of the classic western was John Ford, creator of *My Darling Clementine* (1946) and *Fort Apache* (1948). Ford established his style in *Stagecoach (inset),* shot in 1939 in Monument Valley, Utah, where outsize geological formations dwarfed the characters while giving their struggles an epic scale.

Stagecoach featured John Wayne, whose gruff strength suited Ford so well that the pair *(right)* worked together for decades.

Wayne also teamed up with another master of the genre, Howard Hawks, lending an unsettling dimension to Hawks's *Red River* (1948) as the ruthless leader of a cattle drive.

Several directors have been fascinated by the theme of the end of the Old West. George Roy Hill's *Butch Cassidy and the Sundance Kid* *(pages 72-73)* romanticized the two outlaws as knights of a dying frontier realm. Amid the turmoil of the late 1960s, Sam Peckinpah upended the western's conventional morality with *The Wild Bunch* *(page 72)*. The hyper-violent film—set in 1913, long after the frontier had been tamed—depicted some 200 killings. In 1992 Clint Eastwood's unflinching *Unforgiven* offered no heroes, only killers dueling to the death.

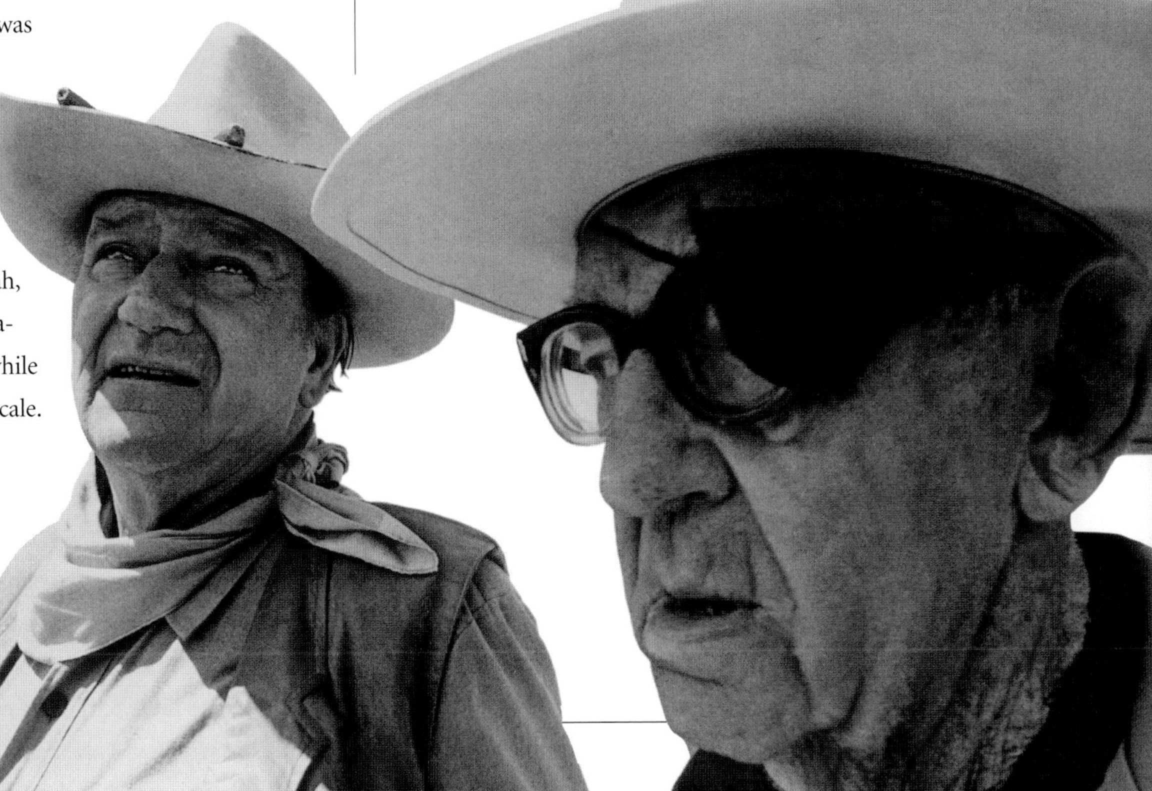

Film icon John Wayne stands with the master of the western, John Ford, during the shooting of The Man Who Shot Liberty Valance *(1962). Ford directed his first western back in 1917—and played the lead.*

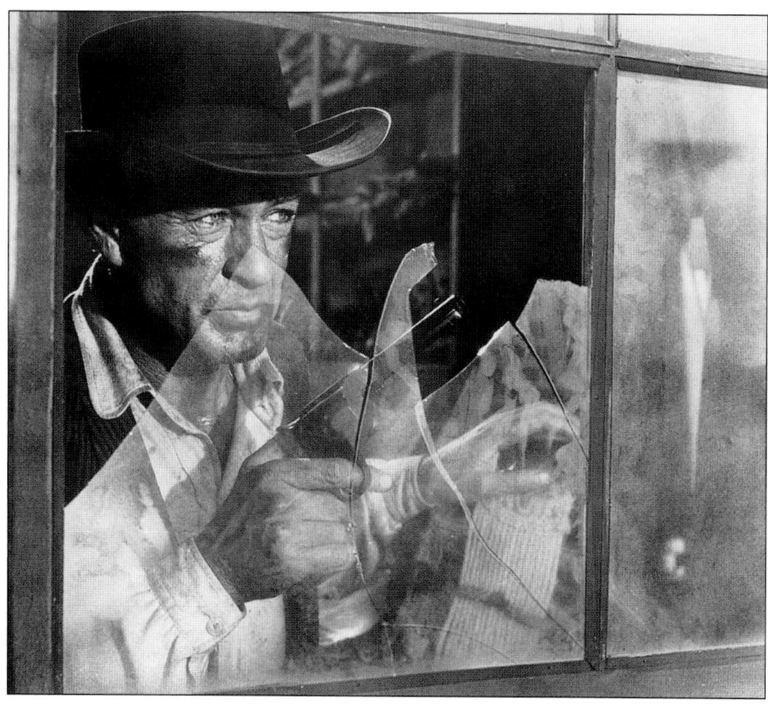

Abandoned by fearful townspeople, Sheriff Will Kane (Gary Cooper) faces a gang of desperadoes in High Noon. The story reflected the travails of the screenwriter, Carl Foreman, who had been a victim of the anti-Communist purge in Hollywood in the 1950s.

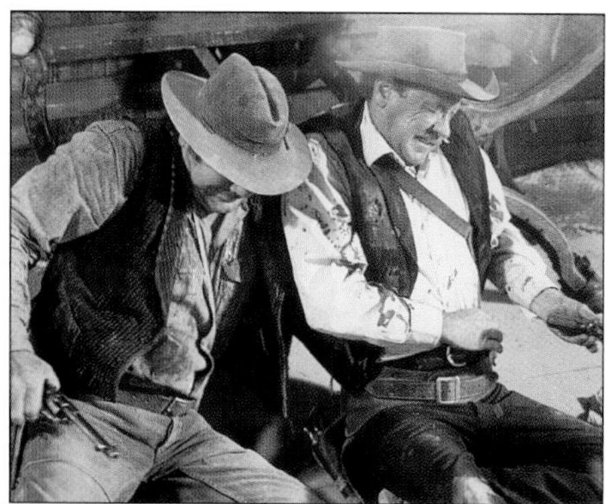

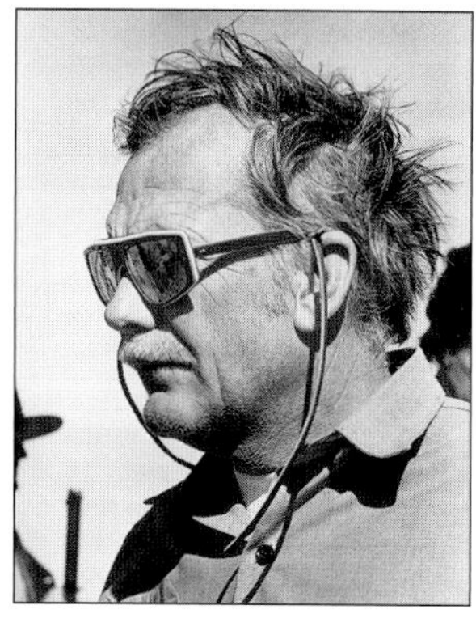

Blood-spattered Ernest Borgnine and William Holden take cover during a gunfight in Sam Peckinpah's grim, gory western The Wild Bunch (1969). Peckinpah (right) portrayed the West as the domain of amoral antiheroes who lived and died by the gun.

Surrounded by Bolivian troops, outlaws Butch Cassidy (Paul Newman) and the Sundance Kid (Robert Redford) go out in a blaze of glory. George Roy Hill's deft 1969 mixture of humor, romance, and adventure became a popular and critical hit.

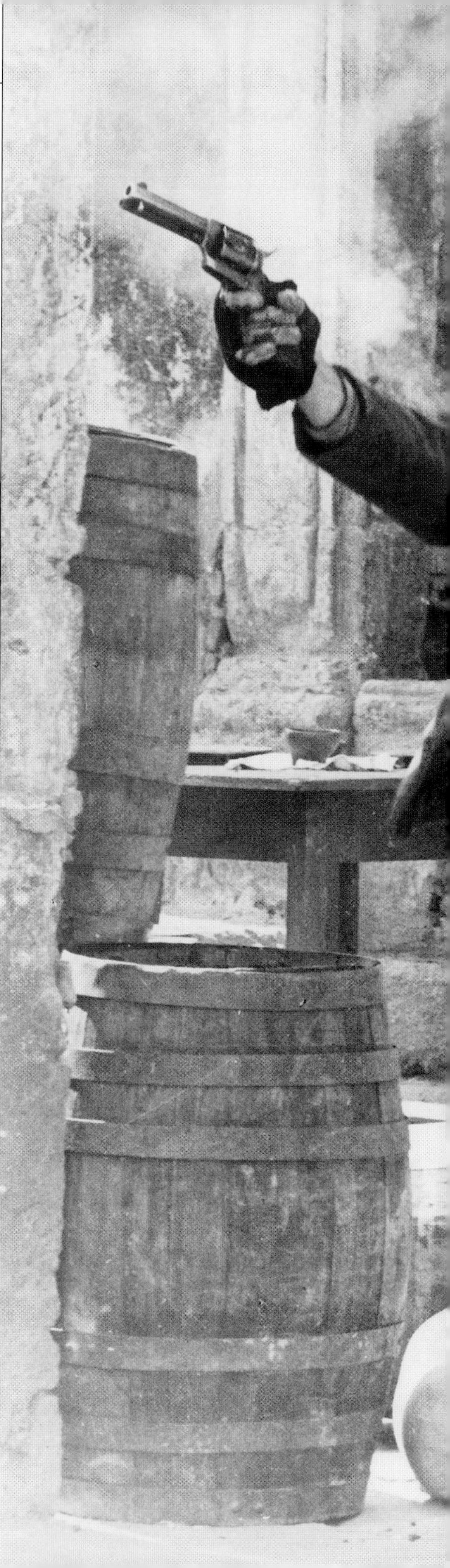

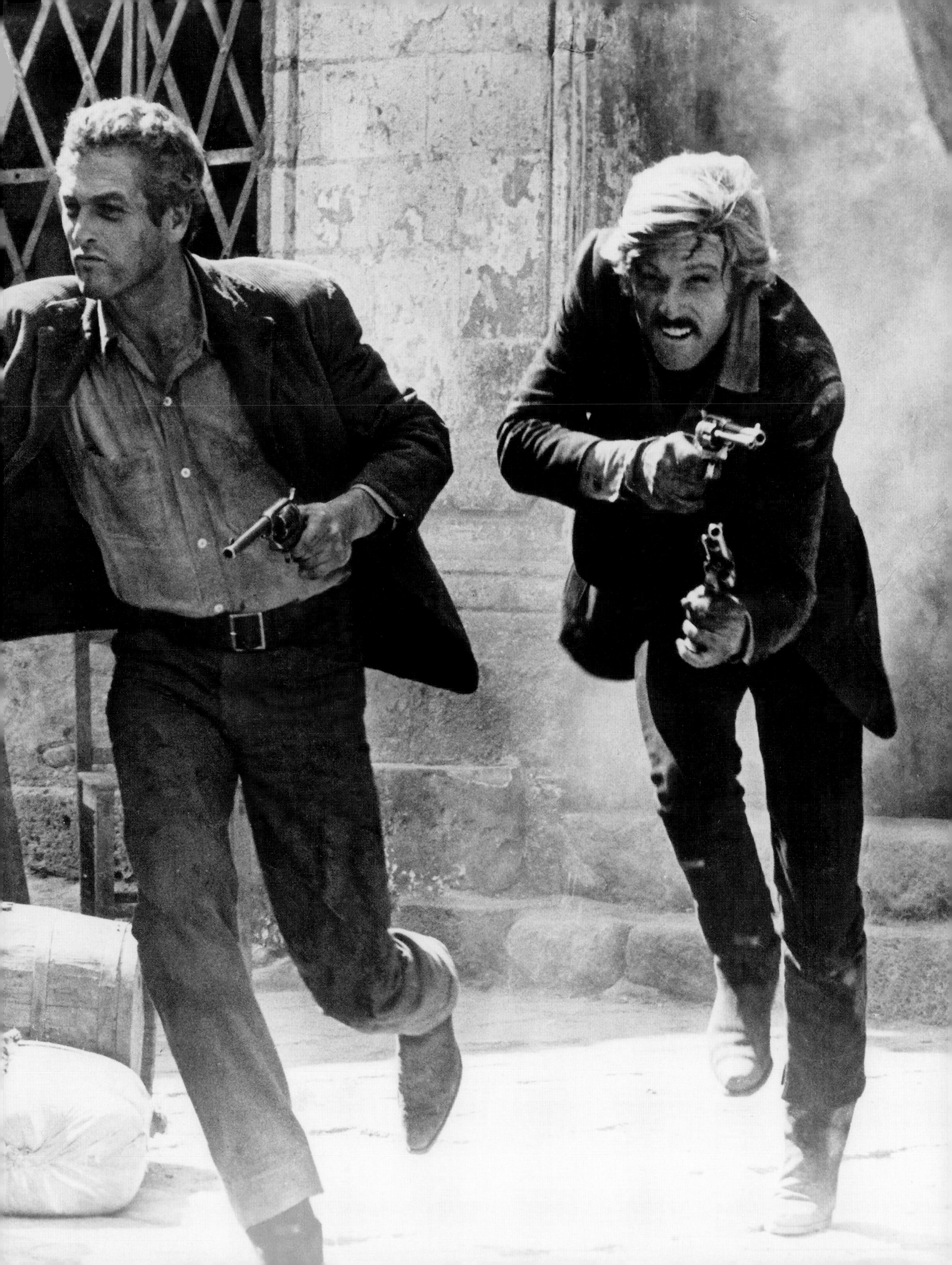

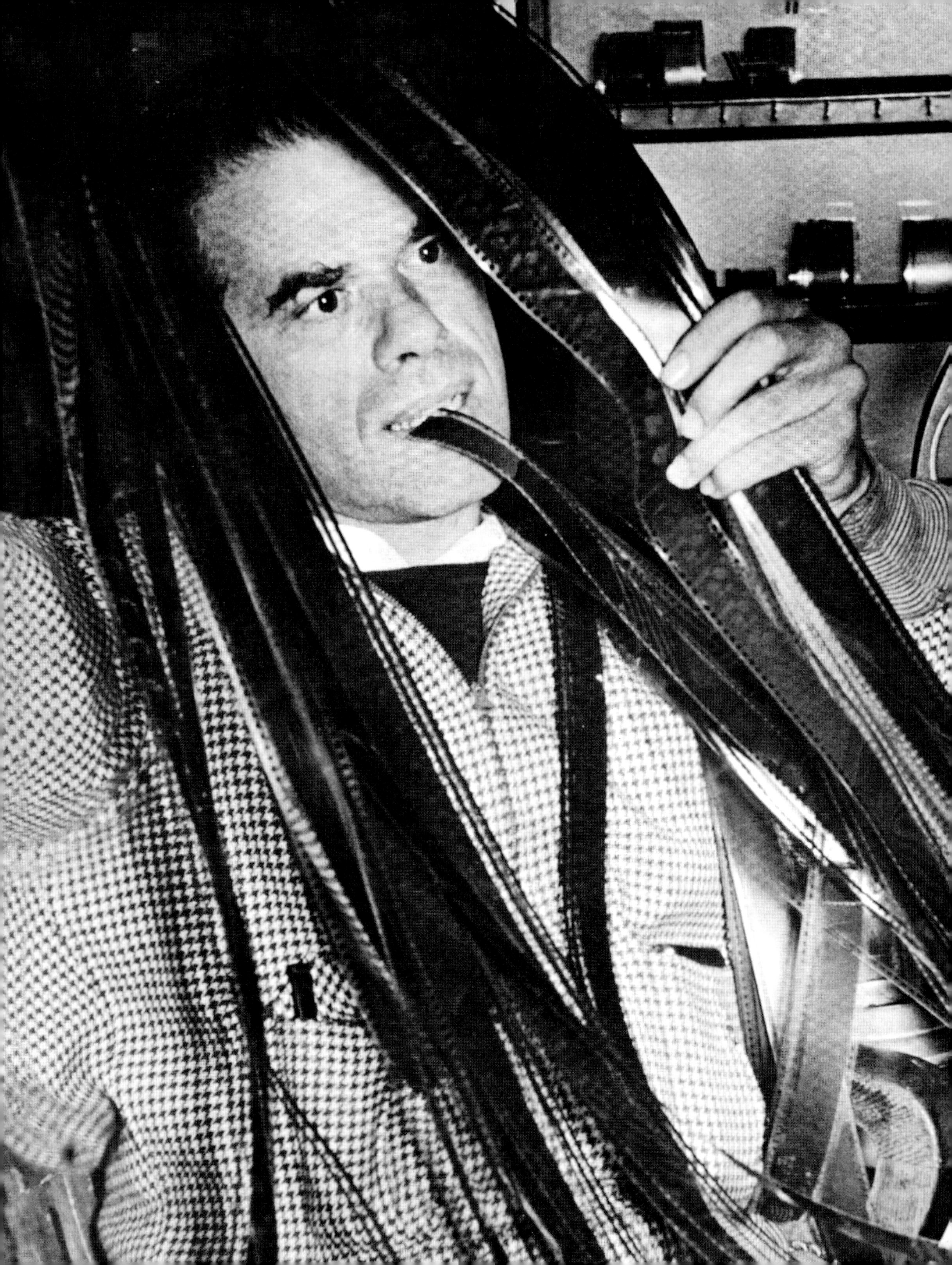

The Common Man as Hero

The string of memorable movies made by Frank Capra *(left)* in the 1930s and '40s—including *Mr. Deeds Goes to Town, Meet John Doe,* and *It's a Wonderful Life (right)*—bore such a strikingly original style and personal stamp that the director's own name became an adjective: The term "Capraesque" (or, as some critics and even a self-mocking Capra put it, "Capracorn") was used to describe triumph over long odds by an ordinary citizen.

Capra himself might have represented the American dream. He arrived in California from Italy in 1903 at age six, later supported his immigrant family with odd jobs, put himself through college, got into movies as a lowly film processor, and went on to become the most popular director of his day, winning three Oscars.

Idealism was a Capra signature, perhaps seen at its purest in his 1939 film *Mr. Smith Goes to Washington.* When Jimmy Stewart, playing a scoutmaster turned freshman senator, filibusters on the floor of the U.S. Senate *(right)* to the point of physical collapse —and to ultimate victory over government corruption—it was one of the most unabashedly patriotic, sentimental, and emotionally powerful scenes in movie history. Capra had evoked an America where the little guy can, by decency and strength of will, prevail over the powers of greed and venality. The Depression-era audience, dabbing away tears, loved it, as did the critics.

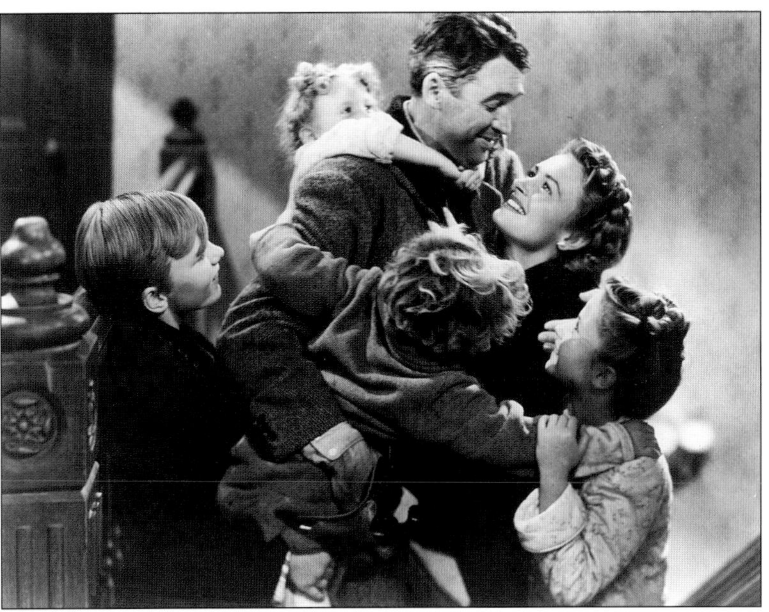

Dissuaded from suicide by an angel after a business disaster, George Bailey (James Stewart) rediscovers the joys of his family in It's a Wonderful Life. The heartwarming 1946 fable about the goodness of the common man did poorly when first released, but it was Capra's favorite film and eventually became a Christmastime staple on TV.

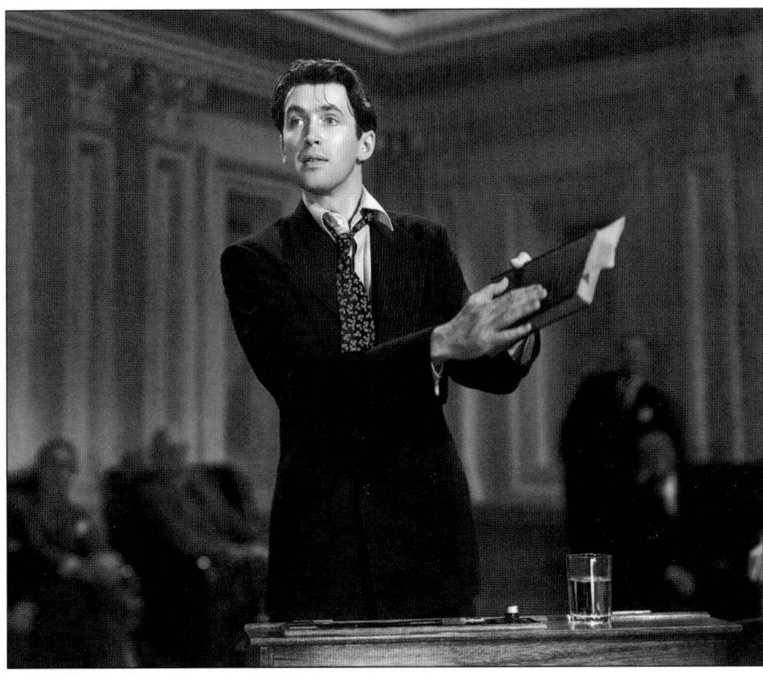

Gesturing with a book containing the Declaration of Independence, Jimmy Stewart as a youthful, idealistic newcomer holds the floor of the U.S. Senate during his climactic filibuster scene in Mr. Smith Goes to Washington. Stewart had a doctor swab his vocal cords with a caustic solution so his voice would be suitably raspy.

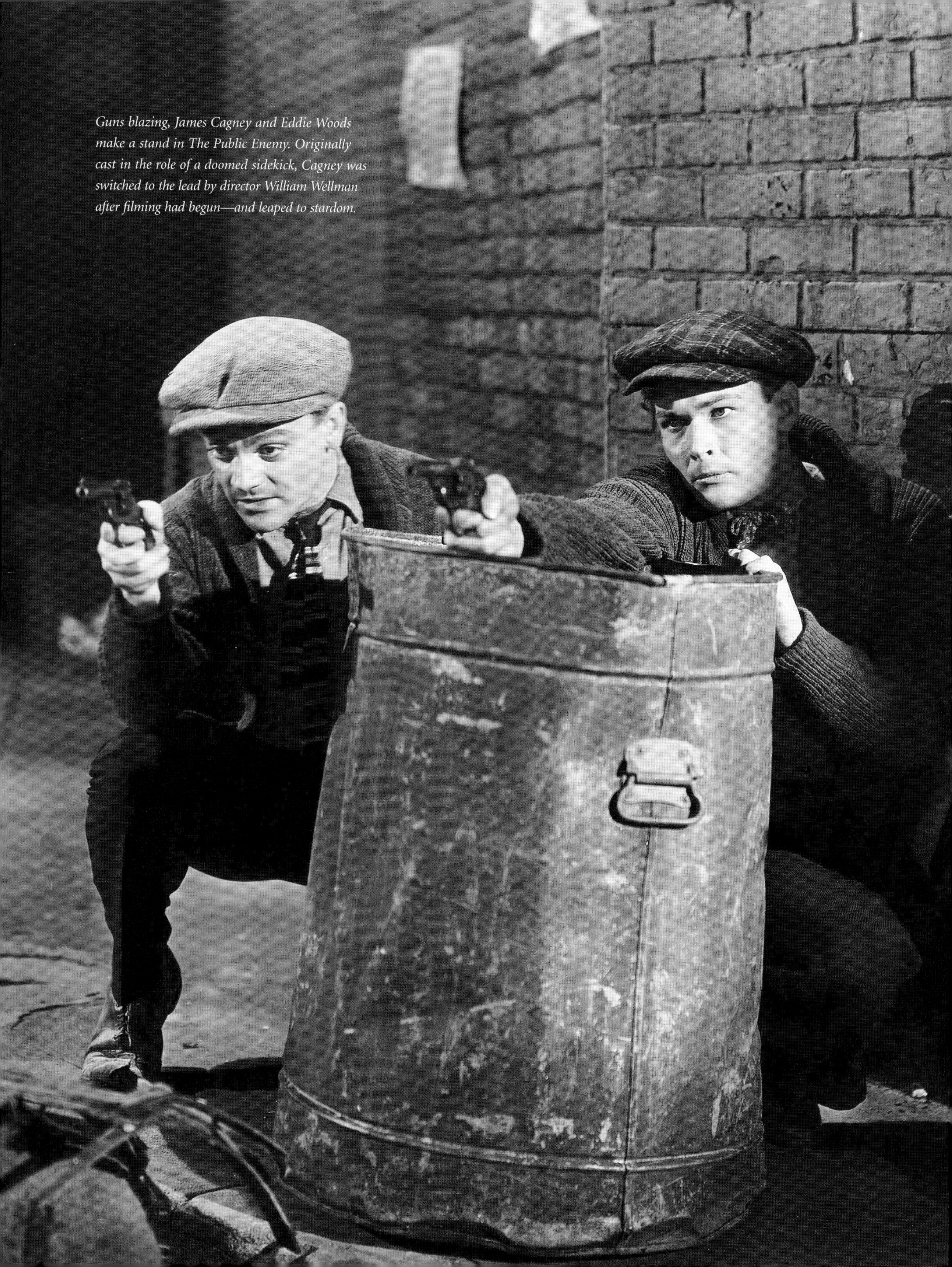

Guns blazing, James Cagney and Eddie Woods make a stand in The Public Enemy. Originally cast in the role of a doomed sidekick, Cagney was switched to the lead by director William Wellman after filming had begun—and leaped to stardom.

Journeys into Gangland

Growled threats, storms of gunplay, and the screech of sirens terrified and thrilled audiences in the early 1930s as a wave of gangster films took America on a tour of the underworld. Warner Bros. led the way when production chief Darryl F. Zanuck took note of newspaper stories about big-city gang wars and called for pictures based on the headlines. To lend authenticity to their productions, Warner Bros. and other studios hired streetwise crime reporters—the illustrious Ben Hecht among them—to spin out scenarios and fast-paced dialogue.

The most violent picture of the period, *Scarface,* directed by Howard Hawks, was modeled after the life of Chicago mobster Al Capone, with Paul Muni in the lead role. Another Hollywood tough guy, George Raft, appeared as Muni's henchman. But the two actors most responsible for defining the image of the screen gangster were Edward G. Robinson *(right, top)* and James Cagney. With his swagger and his flair for tough talk, Cagney ignited the screen when, in 1931, he appeared in *The Public Enemy (left),* directed by William Wellman *(right, bottom).* It recounted how Cagney's youthful character, Tom Powers, fell into a life of crime and thrived at it, at one point ridiculing his hardworking brother thus: "Aw, that sucker—he's too busy going to school. He's learning how to be poor."

Though crime ultimately did not pay in these films, Depression-era audiences, buffeted by economic forces beyond their control, often cheered the bad guys who outsmarted the law and polite society to get fancy cars, fancy clothes, fancy apartments, and fancy dames. Gangster films, in fact, represented a low point in Hollywood's depiction of women. Cagney, for example, became famous for the scene in *The Public Enemy* in which he angrily grinds a grapefruit half into the face of his moll, played by Mae

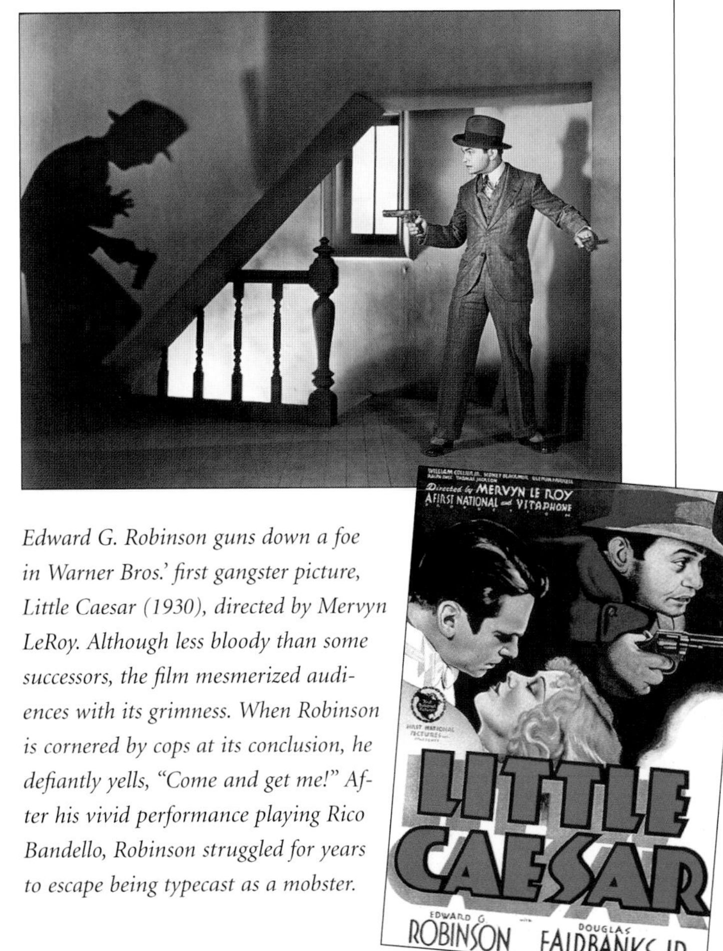

Edward G. Robinson guns down a foe in Warner Bros.' first gangster picture, Little Caesar (1930), directed by Mervyn LeRoy. Although less bloody than some successors, the film mesmerized audiences with its grimness. When Robinson is cornered by cops at its conclusion, he defiantly yells, "Come and get me!" After his vivid performance playing Rico Bandello, Robinson struggled for years to escape being typecast as a mobster.

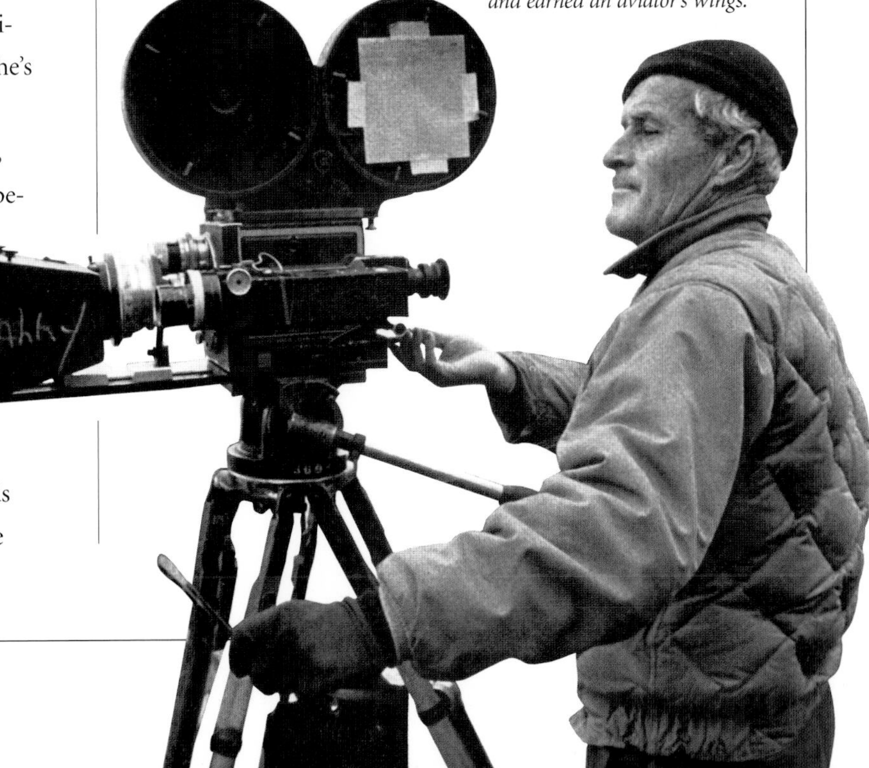

William Wellman, director of The Public Enemy, had tough-guy credentials himself. A former professional hockey player, he joined the French Foreign Legion in World War I and earned an aviator's wings.

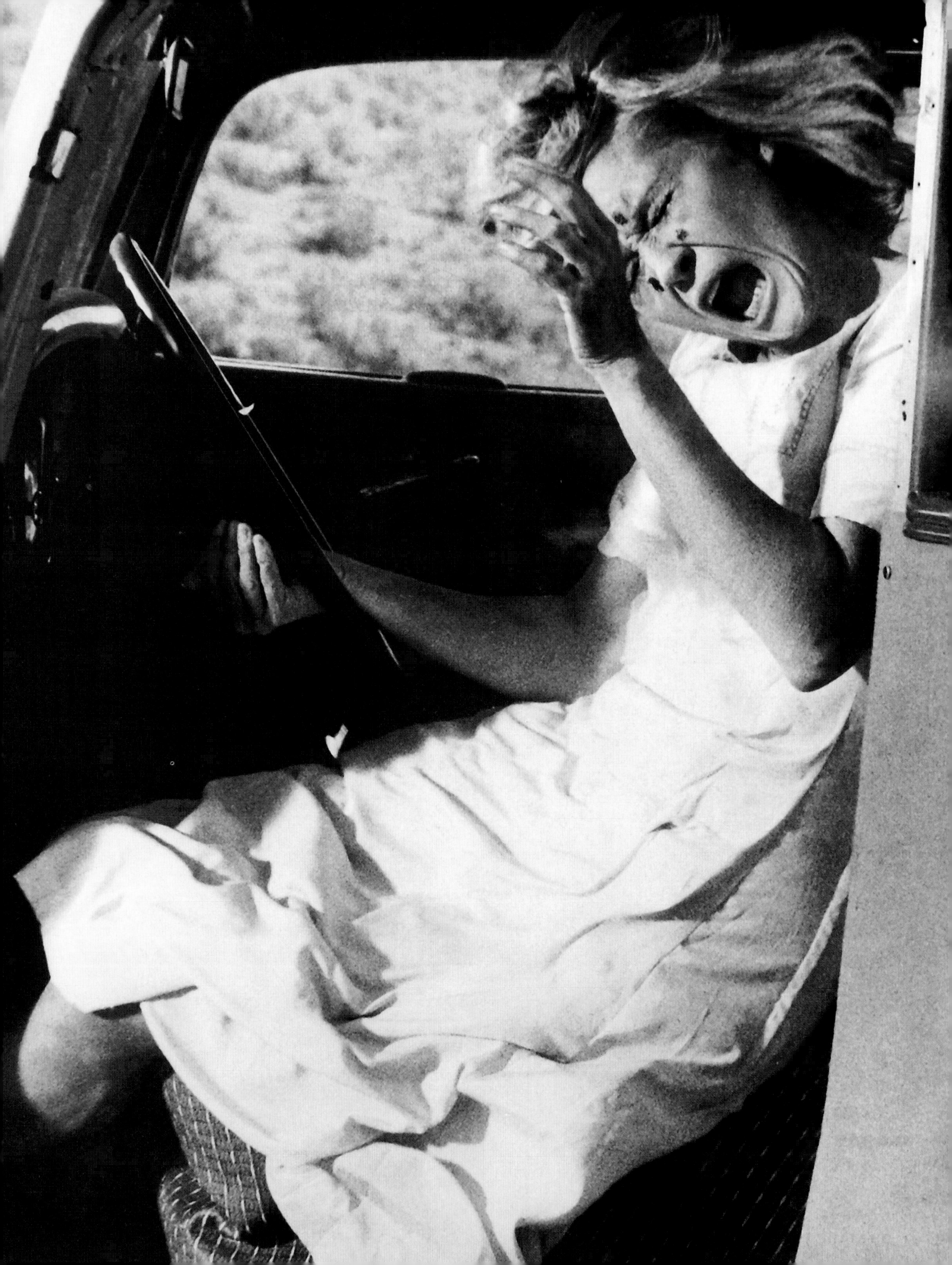

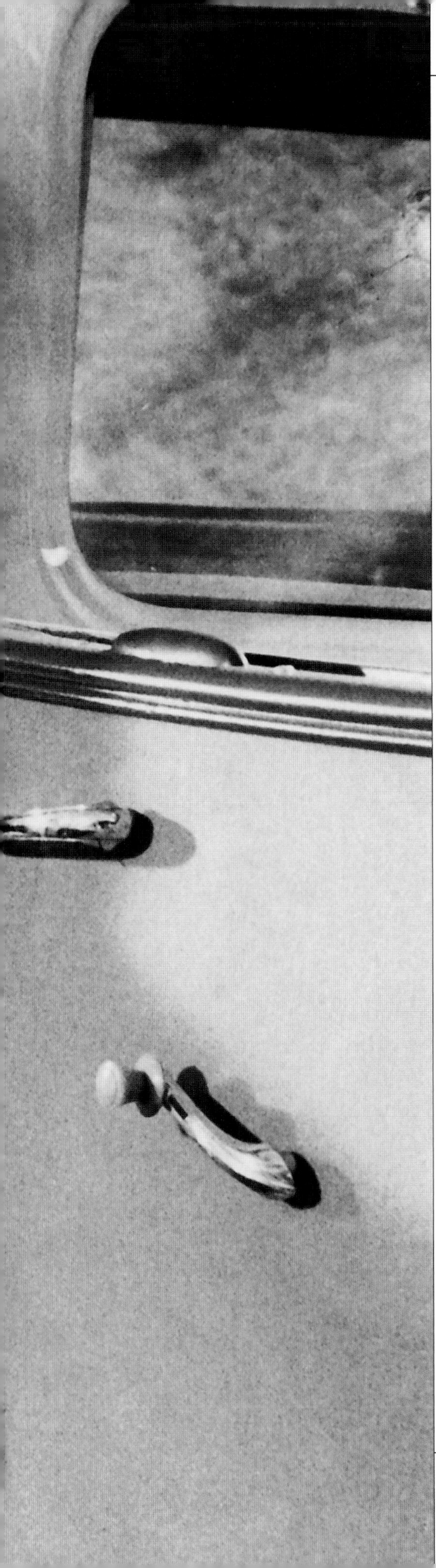

Clarke, who endured slaps, kicks, and shoves in other gangster movies as well.

The films drew criticism from censors, sociologists, and politicians, who feared that they were influencing young people toward criminality. Under this pressure the studios altered course and began to emphasize the virtues of hard work over the appeal of the tough-guy lifestyle. In films such *as "G" Men* (1935), the cops became all-American good guys in a life-and-death struggle against the evil underworld. In 1938 Cagney and Warner Bros. cinematically atoned with the Michael Curtiz film *Angels With Dirty Faces.* Cagney played the vicious mobster Rocky Sullivan, regarded as a hero by the boys in his old slum neighborhood—to the dismay of Catholic priest Jerry Connelly (Pat O'Brien), Rocky's boyhood pal. When Rocky is condemned to die in the electric chair, Father Connelly makes a death-row plea to the killer. Taking the priest's appeal to heart, the sneering, cocky Cagney marches toward the execution chamber, then suddenly pretends to break down, transforming himself into a sniveling, weeping coward. His supposed emotional collapse is witnessed by assembled reporters, who do not know of its redemptive purpose. The next day the kids in the slums read the headline "ROCKY DIES YELLOW" and realize that crime not only doesn't pay, it doesn't make heroes.

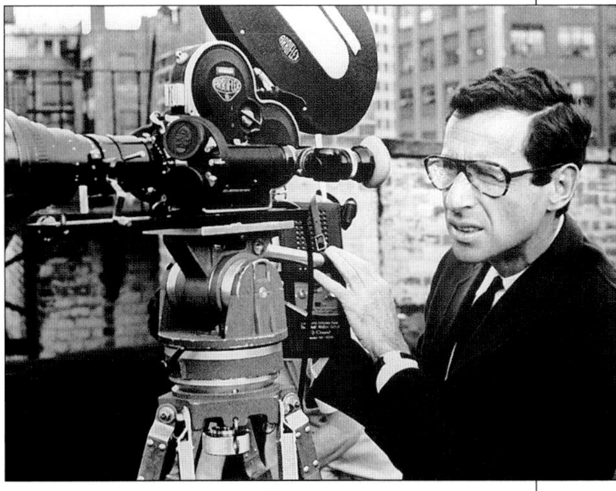

During the next decade, the gangster picture gave way to the murky world of film noir *(page 80),* but in 1967 director Arthur Penn *(inset)* revived the genre for a hyperviolent farewell in *Bonnie and Clyde*, based on the real-life robbery-and-murder spree of Clyde Barrow and Bonnie Parker. Starring Warren Beatty and Faye Dunaway *(left),* the film brimmed with old-style movie star allure, and then seemed to wash it away in a tide of blood—though some viewers felt that Penn, intentionally or not, had glamorized crime all over again.

Faye Dunaway writhes under the impact of bullets in the harrowing climax of Bonnie and Clyde. Arthur Penn (above) filmed the scene as a slow-motion dance of death.

Dark Films About Dark Deeds

Above: *Noir posters promise gritty atmosphere and tawdry sex.*
Below: In Laura, Dana Andrews as a homicide detective interrogates the suspicious but alluring title character (Gene Tierney).

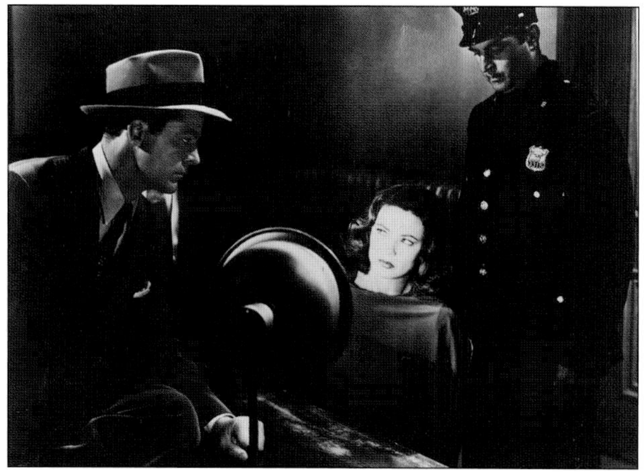

Film noir—a genre whose name, meaning "black," came from French critics—was soaked in cynicism born of the Depression and World War II. Populated by cigarette-puffing hoods and sensuous femmes fatales, its domain of cheap hotels and nighttime city streets promised little more than disappointment and the double cross.

Noir directors created a style that featured deep shadows, stark angles, and a sense of menace. An early example of the form was *This Gun for Hire* (1942), directed by Frank Tuttle and starring Alan Ladd in a hallmark tough-guy role. A pair of 1944 noir classics featured Fred MacMurray playing against type as a slick insurance salesman lured into murder in Billy Wilder's *Double Indemnity* and a hard-as-nails Dana Andrews *(left, bottom)* in *Laura,* by Otto Preminger. Novelist James M. Cain's steamy *The Postman Always Rings Twice* was the basis for Tay Garnett's 1946 masterpiece. French-born Jacques Tourneur's *Out of the Past* (1947) starred the inherently noir Robert Mitchum.

Nothing was straightforward in the noir world. Time was fractured into frequent flashbacks, and plots were filled with red herrings and unexpected twists that often left the audience off-balance and uneasy. In John Huston's *The Maltese Falcon (right),* hard-boiled detective Sam Spade, played by Humphrey Bogart, acts not out of heroism but according to some world-weary private code: "When a man's partner is killed he's supposed to do something about it. It doesn't make any difference what you thought of him, he was your partner and you're supposed to do something about it." The meaning of it all, in true noir fashion, remains impenetrable.

As gumshoe Sam Spade in John Huston's 1941 noir tour de force The Maltese Falcon, Humphrey Bogart vies with ponderous Sydney Greenstreet and sniveling Peter Lorre over a gem-studded statuette.

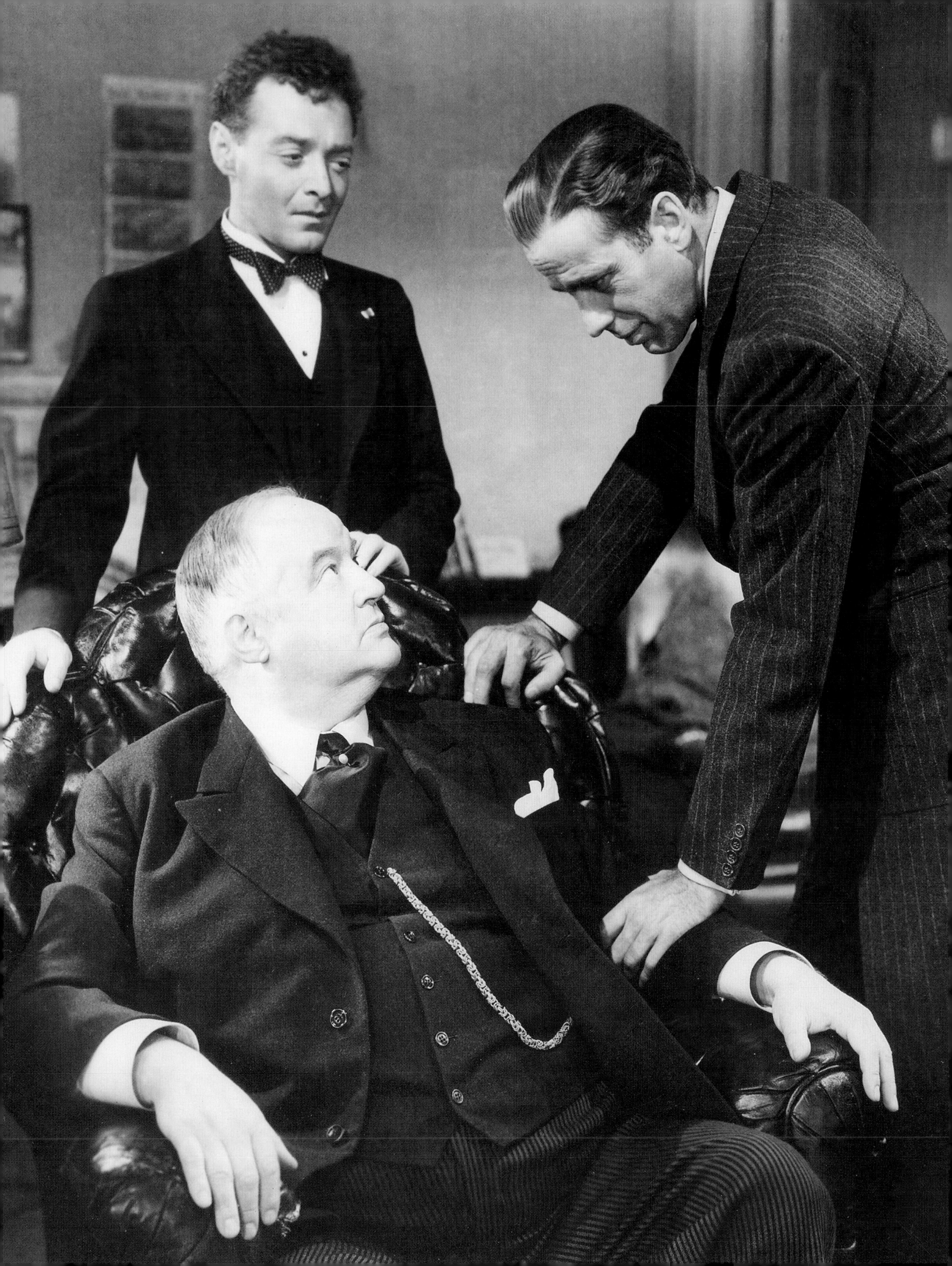

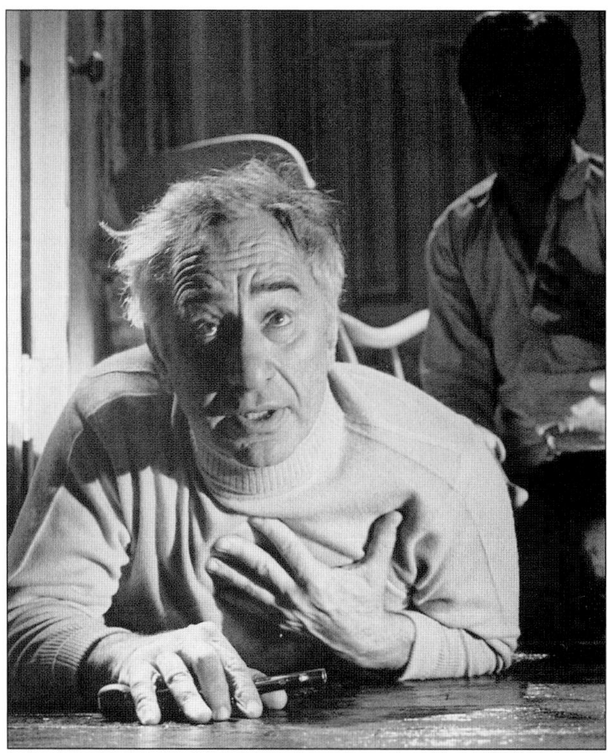

Elia Kazan demonstrates emotion on a set. A master at bringing out the best in his cast, Kazan directed 21 actors in performances that drew Academy Award nominations, resulting in nine Oscars.

"The camera is more than a recorder, it's a microscope. It penetrates, it goes into people and you see their most private and concealed thoughts."

Elia Kazan, 1981

Gritty Portrayals of City Life

As America grew increasingly urbanized after World War II, directors turned their attention to cities as the settings, and sometimes even the subjects, of their films. They expanded genres like gangster movies and film noir into works that were more realistic, more richly textured, and often far more violent than the movies of the 1930s. Their goal, as director Elia Kazan *(left)* put it, was "to get poetry out of the common things of life."

Kazan was the pioneer of a new naturalism based on location shooting, on long shots and takes, and, especially, on the psychological exploration demanded by Method acting. This technique, derived from the work of Russian stage director Konstantin Stanislavsky, was taught at New York's Group Theatre and Actors Studio in the 1930s and '40s, when Kazan was working on Broadway. A genius at inspiring actors, Kazan brought the Method to Hollywood in the late 1940s and changed film acting styles forever.

Kazan himself, however, soon became a pariah among many theater and movie people. He had been a member of the Communist Party in the early 1930s but had quit when party bosses ordered a Communist takeover of the Group Theatre. Much later, during the controversial red-hunting days of the Cold War, he appeared before the infamous House Un-American Activities Committee, admitting his own past party membership and naming former Communist colleagues, some of whose careers were ruined as a result. Excoriated as one who had betrayed friends to a witch hunt, he said, "Any time you hurt people, and I did hurt some people, you don't like it." But then he pointed to those friends' continuing silence in the face of Stalin's murderous dictatorship and said, "I'm glad I was on the other side."

Perhaps because of this experience, Kazan's 1954 masterpiece, *On the Waterfront (right),* is a study in the

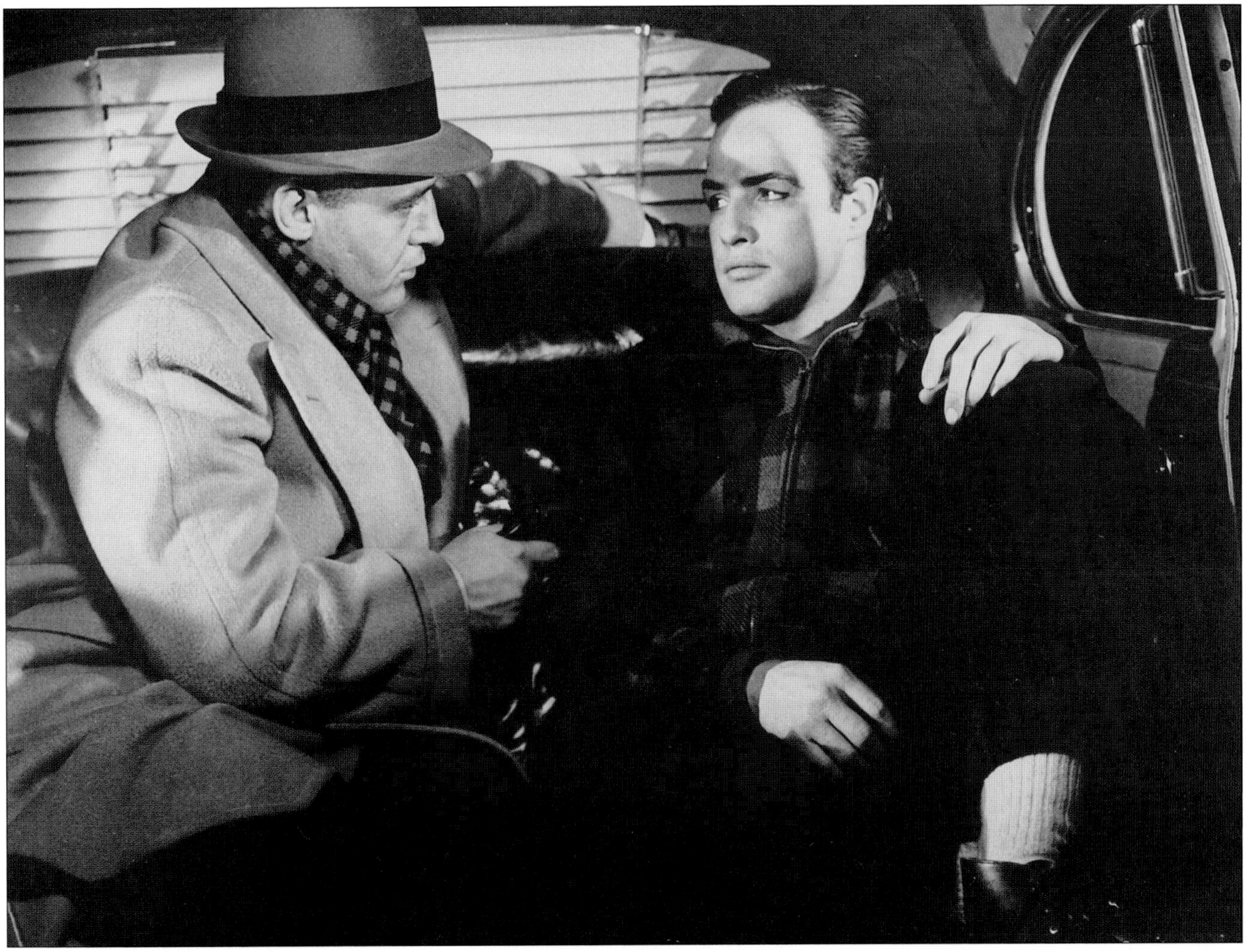

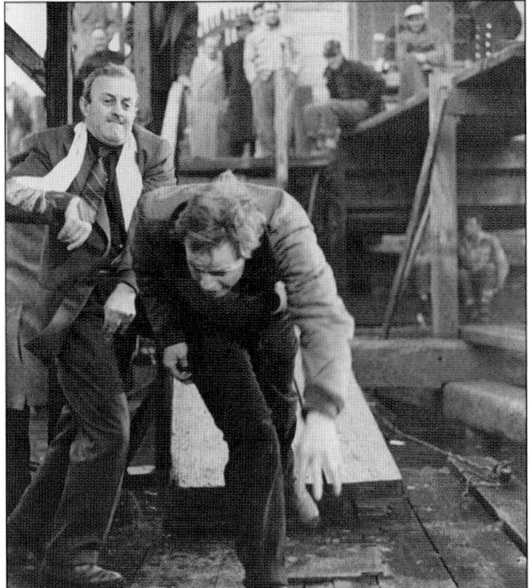

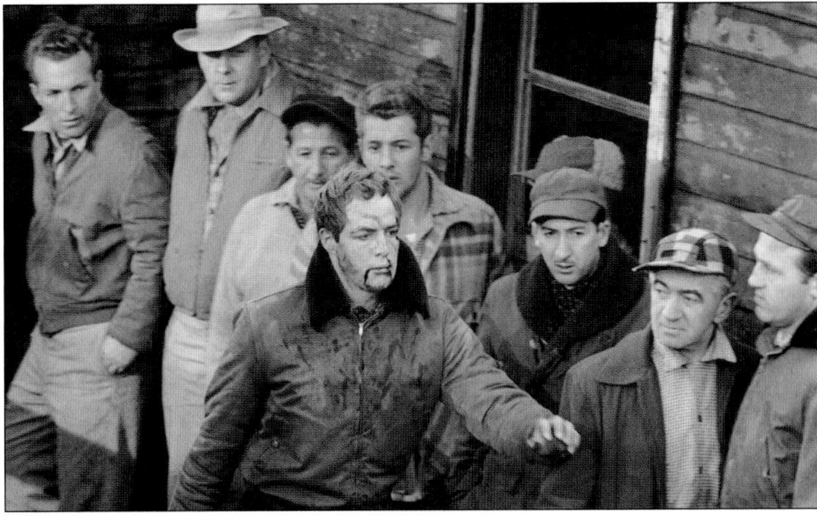

In scenes from Elia Kazan's On the Waterfront, ex-boxer Terry Malloy (Marlon Brando) hears his brother, Charlie (Rod Steiger), confess his own corruption and betrayal (top); staggers under a mob beating (bottom left); and strides past once hostile fellow dockworkers (bottom right).

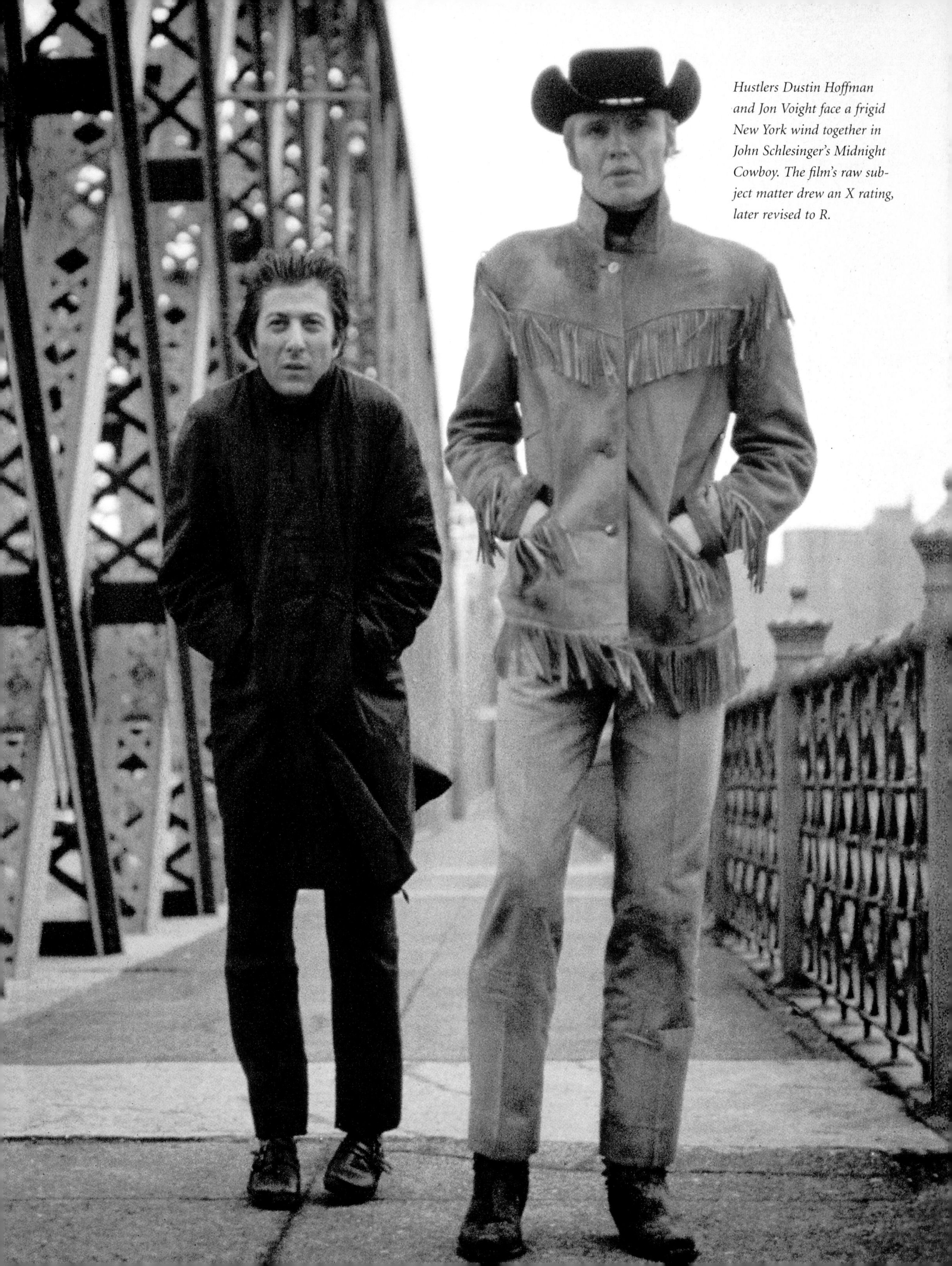

Hustlers Dustin Hoffman and Jon Voight face a frigid New York wind together in John Schlesinger's Midnight Cowboy. The film's raw subject matter drew an X rating, later revised to R.

ambiguities of betrayal. The black-and-white film, which won eight Academy Awards, explores gangster control of dockworkers' unions around New York harbor. Its inarticulate longshoreman hero, Terry Malloy, played by Marlon Brando, faces an agonizing crisis of conscience: whether to inform on his gangster acquaintances, when doing so would be anathema among his peers, even those being exploited by the crooks. He makes his choice under pressure from a priest, but only after several mob murders—one victim the brother of the girl he loves, another his own brother. His punishment for informing is ostracism; his reward is belief in his own integrity. "They always tell me I'm a bum," he says. "Well, I ain't a bum."

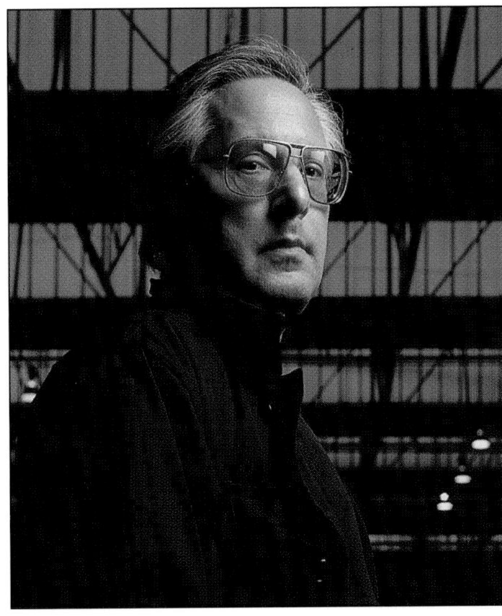

Chicago-born William Friedkin began working in TV while still in his teens. He later directed more than a dozen films, ranging from the fluffy rock-and-roll flick Good Times to the daring film about gay life The Boys in the Band.

Kazan would go on to make more superb movies, but because of his own act of informing in 1952, even a special award given him by the Academy of Motion Picture Arts and Sciences almost half a century later was controversial. Yet all admitted he was one of Hollywood's greatest directors, a man who had forged a new acting style that, as Martin Scorsese would later say, "revealed something in the natural behavior of people that I hadn't seen on the screen before: the truth behind the posture."

The new style permeated urban films of the '60s and '70s, such as British director John Schlesinger's first Hollywood movie, *Midnight Cowboy.* This was the tale of a Texas drifter, played by Jon Voight, who arrives in New York to hustle rich women and is hustled himself—for $20—by a sickly, repulsive, streetwise con man with the memorable name of "Ratso" Rizzo (Dustin Hoffman) *(left).* The young Texan, instead of getting revenge, develops a protective affection for the doomed Ratso. The layered, sensitive performances Schlesinger drew from his stars, evoking both laughter and tears, earned the film three Academy Awards.

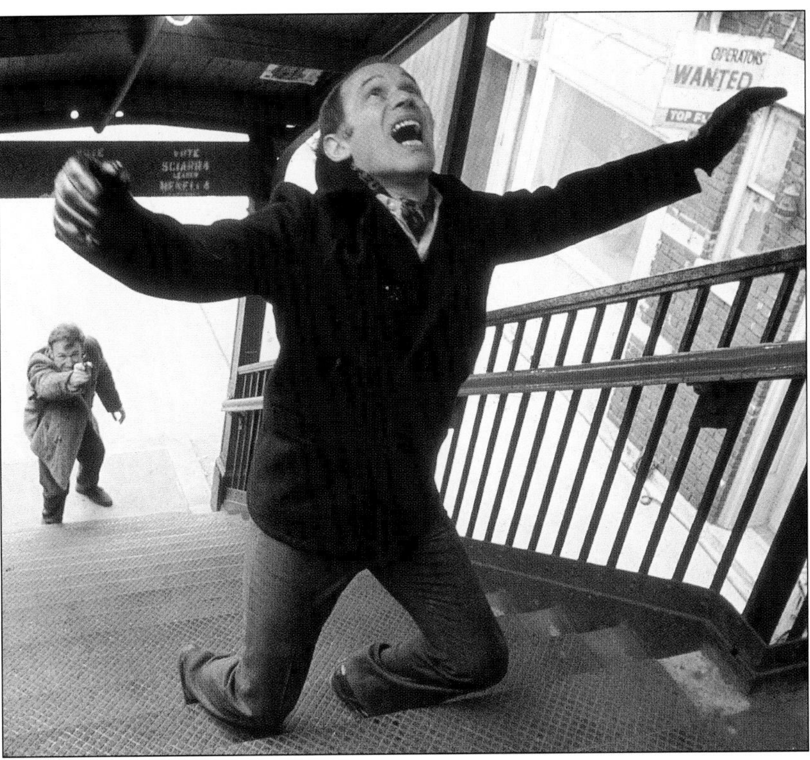

A Marseilles hit man is gunned down by New York cop Popeye Doyle (Gene Hackman) after a spectacular car chase in The French Connection.

A fast-moving documentary style and a lengthy, pulse-pounding car chase won William Friedkin *(right, top)* a Best Director Oscar for the 1971 thriller *The French Connection (right),* which pitted New York cop Popeye Doyle against an urbane European heroin smuggler, Alain Charnier. Friedkin's direction

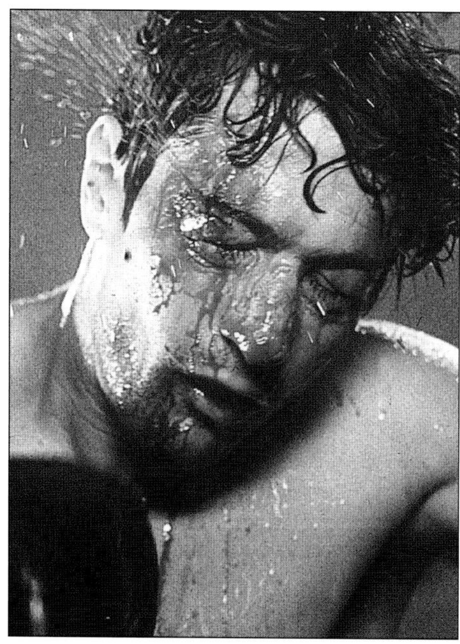

Robert De Niro as Jake LaMotta takes a punch in Martin Scorsese's Raging Bull (above). Below, actor and director confer on the set of Taxi Driver; De Niro played a Vietnam veteran driven homicidally over the edge by the corruption of New York life.

helped evoke a superb performance from Gene Hackman as Popeye, despite the liberal actor's disgust for the bigoted, racist, dishonest but dedicated character he portrayed. But the film, as Friedkin said and showed, was about "that thin line between the policeman and the criminal."

Although Friedkin would have another hit with the horror thriller *The Exorcist* (1973), he was eclipsed during the decade by a group of young new directors, including George Lucas *(page 132)* and Steven Spielberg *(page 108)*. All had been fascinated by film since childhood, all possessed encyclopedic movie knowledge, and most trained at university film schools. The two most attuned to the harsh urban American scene were Francis Ford Coppola and Martin Scorsese.

In Hollywood Coppola was a man of many parts. By the time he directed his first big-budget movie he had already shared a Best Screenplay Oscar for *Patton,* produced George Lucas's first science fiction film—*THX-1138*—and founded his own production company. His big breakthrough as a director was *The Godfather* (1972). With a large cast of future stars and Marlon Brando in the title role *(right),* it became an overnight classic, effortlessly balancing the vicious world of organized crime, the ethnic family values within it, and the deeply realized, tragic characters of those who shared those values.

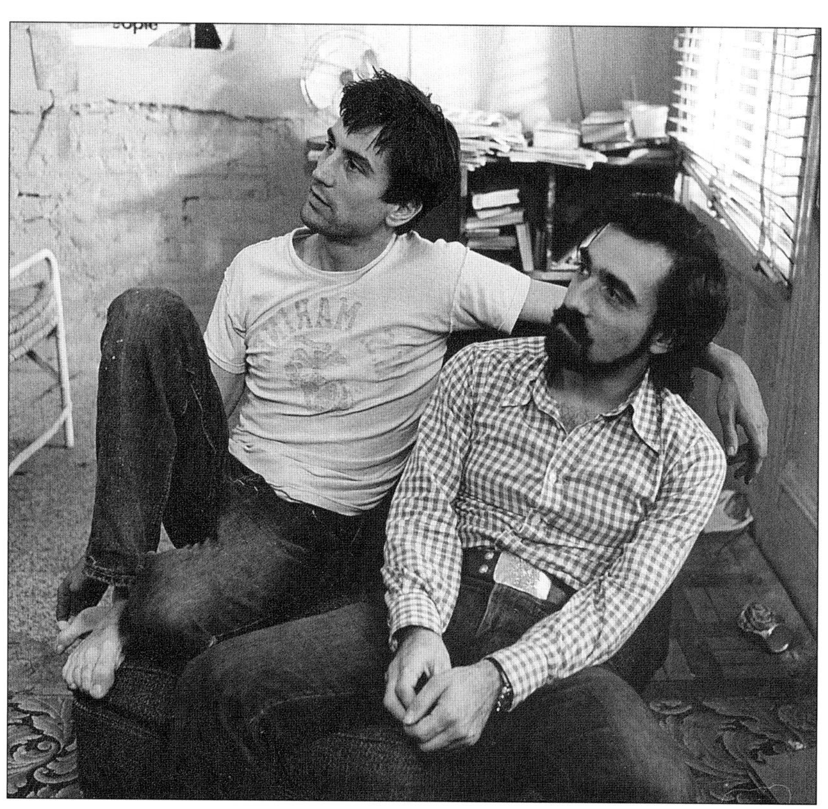

Of this almost mythic film and its sequels, Coppola's colleague Martin Scorsese said, "It's like epic poetry, like *Morte d'Arthur.* My stuff is like some guy on the street corner talking." Scorsese grew up in New York's Little Italy. Inspired by the power and honesty of films like Kazan's and by the new-wave style of director-conceived, or auteur, movies arriving from Europe in the 1960s *(page 107),* he wanted, he said, "to create images that reflected the life around me: what I saw in the streets, at home and, in particular, in my church. There I found the images very powerful, transcendent and, at times, lurid and erotic."

Scorsese formed a famous and enigmatic partnership with Method actor Robert De Niro *(left).* Together they made a string of tough, gritty, big-city films, including *Mean Streets* (1973), *Taxi Driver* (1976), *Raging Bull* (1980),

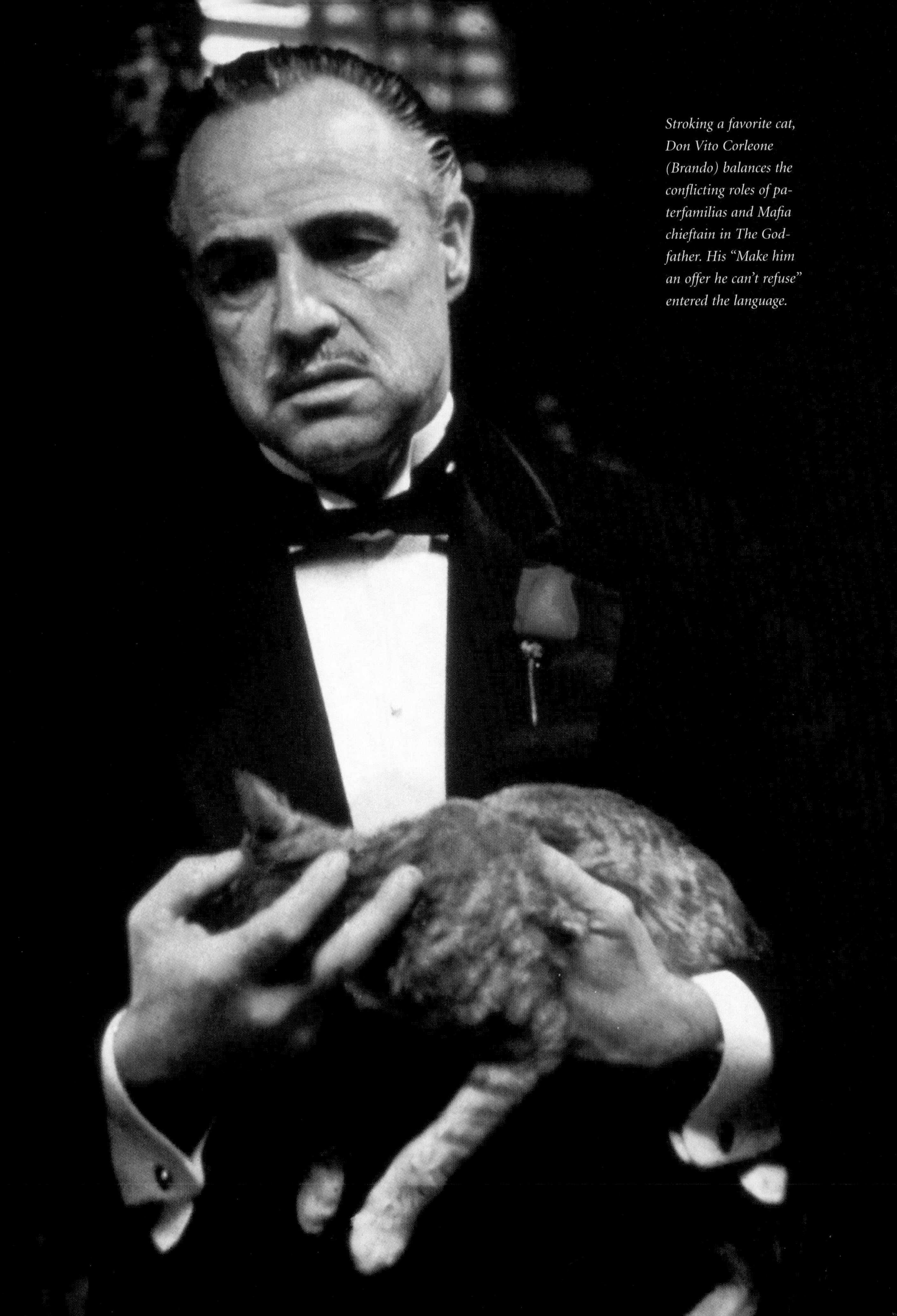

Stroking a favorite cat, Don Vito Corleone (Brando) balances the conflicting roles of paterfamilias and Mafia chieftain in The Godfather. His "Make him an offer he can't refuse" entered the language.

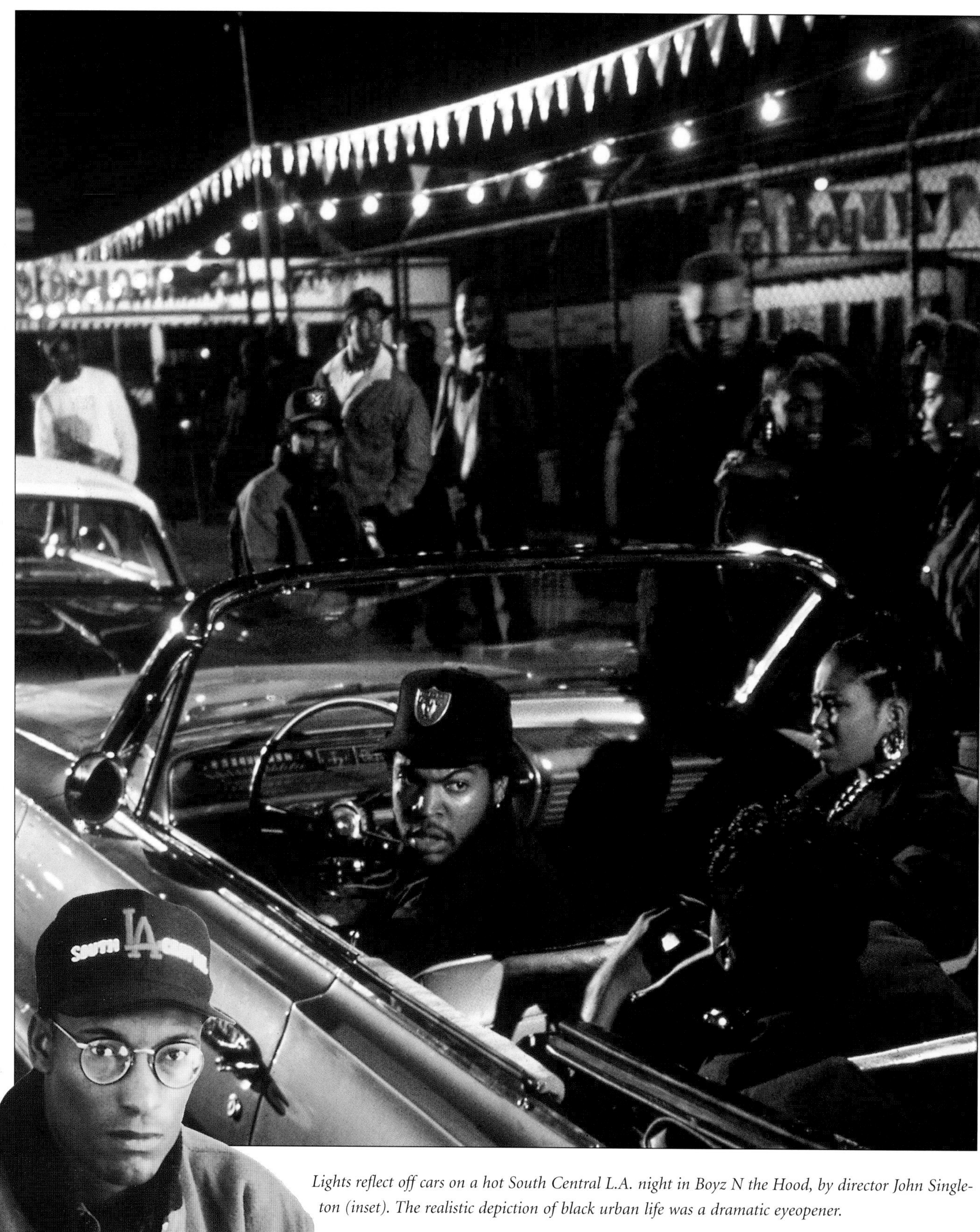

Lights reflect off cars on a hot South Central L.A. night in Boyz N the Hood, by director John Singleton (inset). The realistic depiction of black urban life was a dramatic eyeopener.

and *GoodFellas* (1990). Dark though Scorsese's stories were, by using staccato camera work and editing he re-created the pulsing energies of New York. He found poetry in rock music, traffic lights, neon signs, shiny cars, street noise, and (as in *Taxi Driver*) demented, often improvised voice-overs.

Revolutionary and iconoclastic in their time, Scorsese and his fellow upstart directors of the '70s paved the way for, and helped support, an even younger generation of filmmakers. These newcomers sometimes lacked the formal training of their mentors, but they were self-taught and well taught.

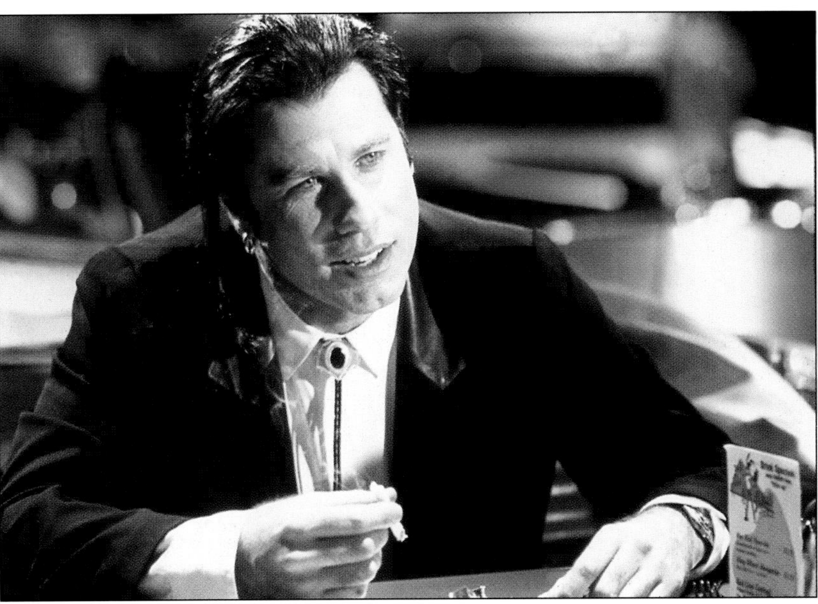

John Travolta, as the unintellectual hit man Vincent Vega, struggles with a thought-provoking situation in Quentin Tarantino's Pulp Fiction. The film showcased Travolta's remarkable acting skills and restored his long-moribund career.

Among them were African American directors, almost nonexistent in Hollywood until the 1970s, when Melvin Van Peebles created *Sweet Sweetback's Baad Asssss Song,* evoking the realities of black urban life. His famous successors included Spike Lee *(page 102)* and wunderkind John Singleton *(inset, opposite)*, the youngest filmmaker (at 24) to garner Academy Award nominations for both directing and screenwriting for his 1991 work *Boyz N the Hood (left).* This story about three young men struggling to grow up amid the gang violence of South Central Los Angeles was so thick with reality and so vibrantly acted that it reminded people, as one critic put it, that "a ghetto is also a home." Singleton followed up in 1993 with *Poetic Justice*, which showed South Central L.A. life from the women's point of view.

The body of new African American film work was one sign of the growing authority of independent filmmakers; another was the wild success enjoyed by such visceral, anti-intellectual writer-directors as Quentin Tarantino, whose film education came from working in a video store. His bloody first movie, *Reservoir Dogs* (1992), became a cult classic. He entered the mainstream in 1994 with the outrageously violent but darkly funny *Pulp Fiction.* Using every seedy urban reference and lashings of comic-book gore, the film intertwined the tales of small-time thieves with those of a pair of hit men. It was nominated for seven Academy Awards—and won for Tarantino's script. Its most obvious virtues, however, were the sterling performances the director drew from actors John Travolta *(top right),* Uma Thurman *(bottom right),* Samuel L. Jackson, and Bruce Willis.

"You name me any horrific thing, and I can make a joke out of it."

Quentin Tarantino, 1994

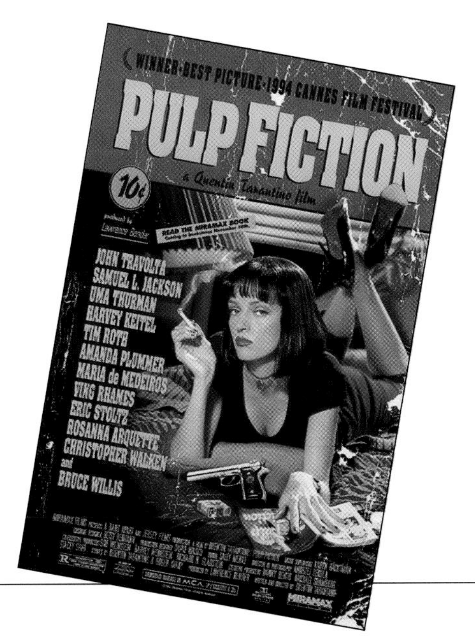

Directors as Music Men

The Hollywood musical was born with the introduction of sound movies—in Al Jolson's *The Jazz Singer* (1927)—and then languished. It took visionary film artists and moviegoers longing for escape from the Depression to make the musical a new American genre.

First credits go to Darryl F. Zanuck, who, despite the misgivings of Warner Bros., produced the hit *42nd Street* in 1933—with Broadway's Busby Berkeley as choreographer. Berkeley designed his numbers specifically for the screen and was the first to use a camera mounted overhead *(page 92)* or hidden beneath the stage. The result of *42nd Street*'s success was a series of extravagant Berkeley-choreographed films marked by kaleidoscopic chorus line formations.

A flood of song-and-dance flicks followed from other studios. At RKO, Fred Astaire danced through a series of comedies, mostly with Ginger Rogers. ("He gives her class and she gives him sex," Katharine Hepburn observed.) MGM set up a team that would dominate the genre, named the Freed Unit after its producer, lyricist Arthur Freed. He acquired *The Wizard of Oz (page 114)* for MGM and hired famed screenwriters like Betty Comden and Adolph Green, songwriters from Irving Berlin to Alan Jay Lerner, and directors like Vincente Minnelli.

After assisting Busby Berkeley on *Strike Up the Band* (1940), Minnelli directed the smash hit *Meet Me in St. Louis (left, top)*, a nostalgic family tale set in 1900 whose theme, like that of *The Wizard of Oz*, was "There's no place like home." Minnelli's characteristically brilliant use of color and design and his seamless working in of sentimental songs made the film a classic. Minnelli

Director Vincente Minnelli calms a high-strung Judy Garland, his future wife, on the set of 1944's Meet Me in St. Louis (left). The 21-year-old star was reluctant to play yet another teenage ingenue, but the film proved a vehicle for some of her classic numbers, including "The Trolley Song" and "Have Yourself a Merry Little Christmas."

Co-directors Gene Kelly and Stanley Donen confer on the set of Singin' in the Rain (1952). The pair, both dancers and choreographers, had already collaborated on Broadway and in Hollywood, most recently in 1949's On the Town.

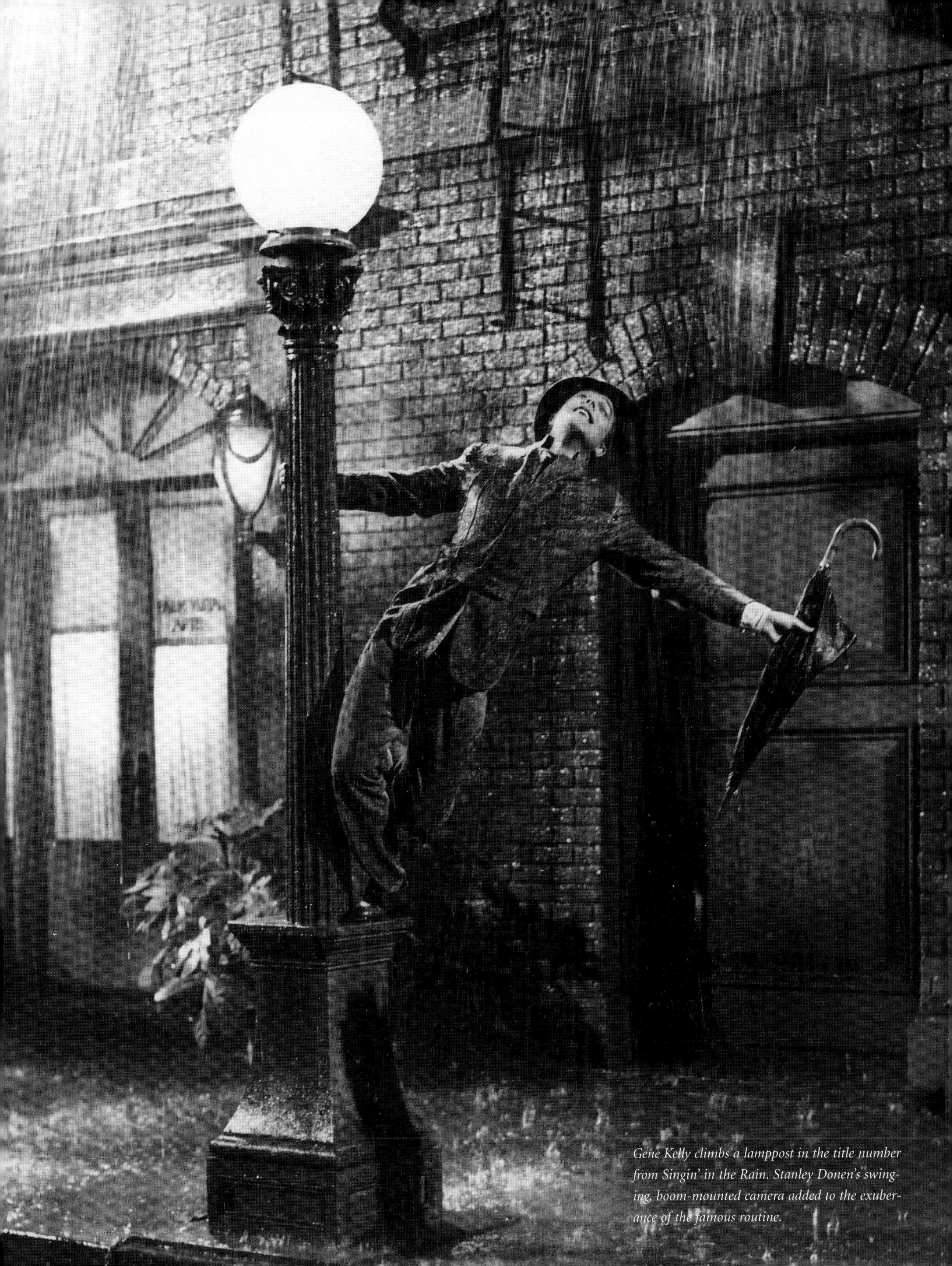

Gene Kelly climbs a lamppost in the title number from Singin' in the Rain. Stanley Donen's swinging, boom-mounted camera added to the exuberance of the famous routine.

would direct a Freed protégé from Broadway, dancer-choreographer Gene Kelly, in 1951's *An American in Paris,* based on a George Gershwin tone poem. The Freed-Kelly collaboration, with co-director Stanley Donen *(page 90),* reached its peak the following year with *Singin' in the Rain (page 91),* a blockbuster about "old" Hollywood written by Comden and Green around decades of Freed's own songs.

Traditional musicals remained popular in the 1950s and '60s, with such box-office smashes as *Guys and Dolls* (1955), *Gigi* (1958), *The Music Man* (1962), *My Fair Lady* (1964), and *The Sound of Music* (1965). But a newer, more edgy, more urban kind of musical was in the wings.

The first of these was a 1961 adaptation of Broadway's *West Side Story.* Choreographed by Jerome Robbins *(right),* the tale—*Romeo and Juliet* transferred to New York, with music by Leonard Bernstein and Stephen Sondheim—became cinematic in the hands of Robbins's co-director, Robert Wise. Spectacularly filmed on location, it won 10 Oscars.

A decade later came *Cabaret (opposite),* the inspired work of director-choreographer Bob Fosse, notorious for his risky lifestyle of drink, drugs, cigarettes, and women—which ended abruptly with a heart attack when he was 60. Fosse used Christopher Isherwood's *Berlin Stories* to create a new kind of musical—not surprisingly, about decadence. The songs and dances provided comment not only on the tale of Sally Bowles (Liza Minnelli) and her lovers, but on dissolute Weimar Germany and the approaching Nazi storm. The strands of story and song became one, thanks to Fosse's brilliant direction.

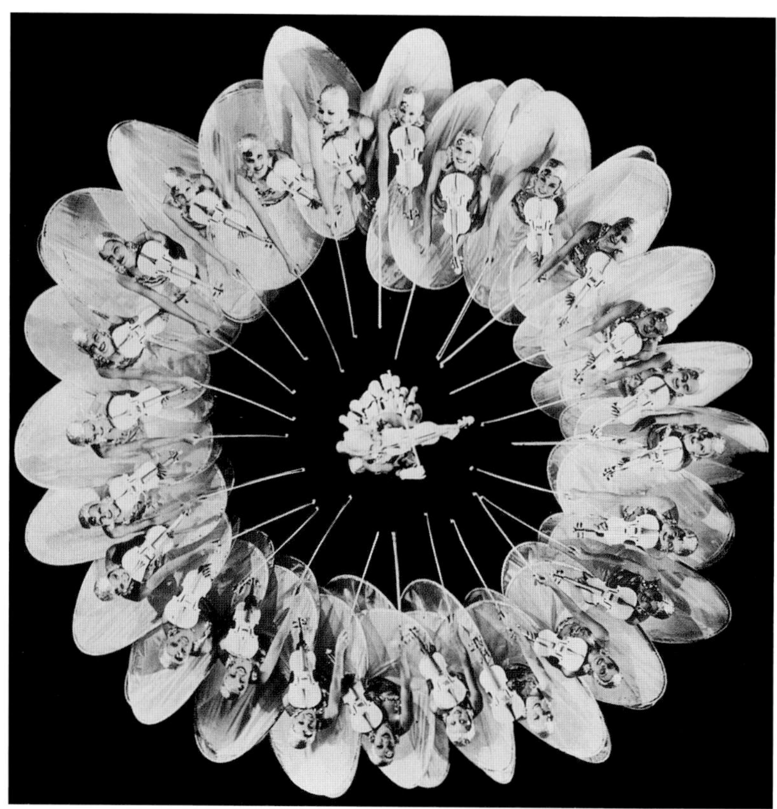

Chorines with neon-lighted violins form a flower in Gold Diggers of 1933. The lavish spectacle was a signature of Busby Berkeley musicals like this one.

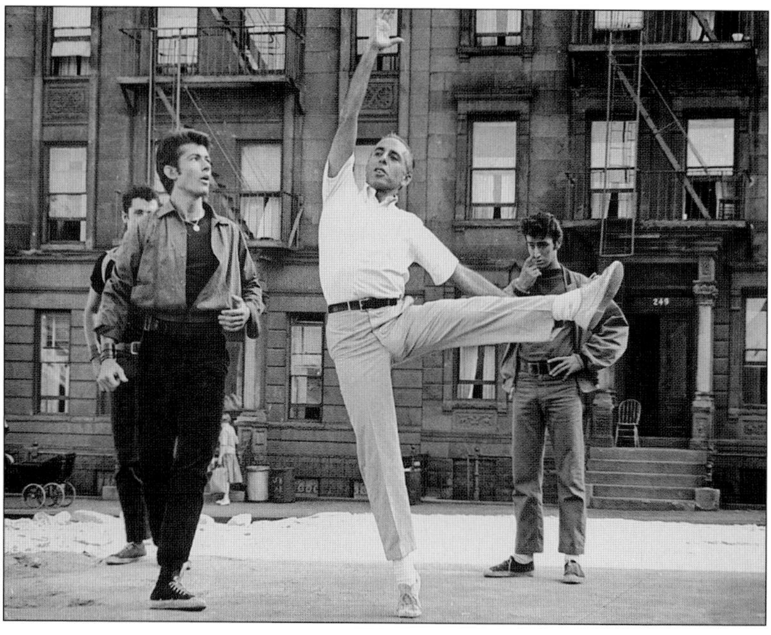

Choreographer Jerome Robbins demonstrates a move for West Side Story. "Dancers didn't always like him," co-director Robert Wise said, "but they respected him."

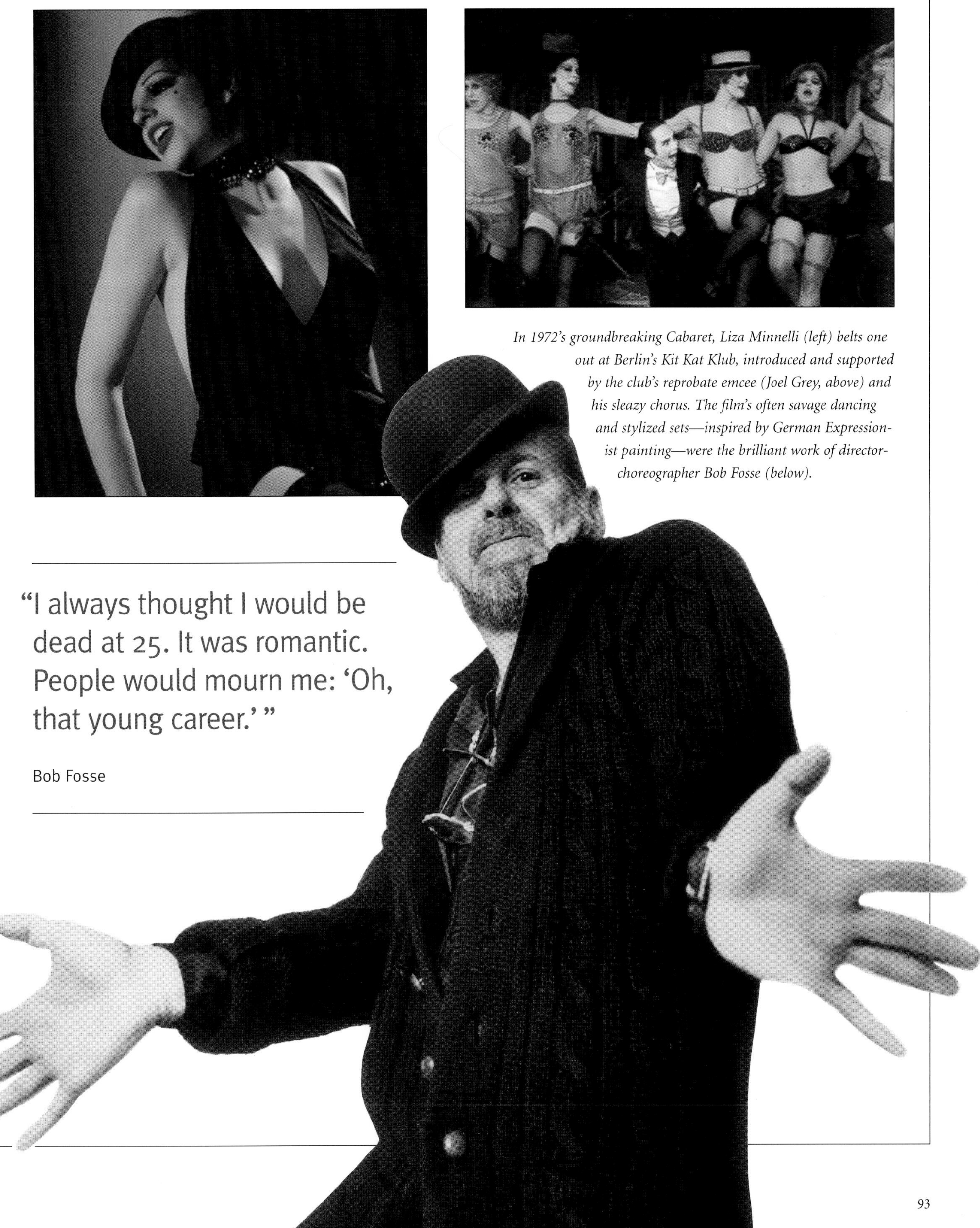

In 1972's groundbreaking Cabaret, Liza Minnelli (left) belts one out at Berlin's Kit Kat Klub, introduced and supported by the club's reprobate emcee (Joel Grey, above) and his sleazy chorus. The film's often savage dancing and stylized sets—inspired by German Expressionist painting—were the brilliant work of director-choreographer Bob Fosse (below).

"I always thought I would be dead at 25. It was romantic. People would mourn me: 'Oh, that young career.' "

Bob Fosse

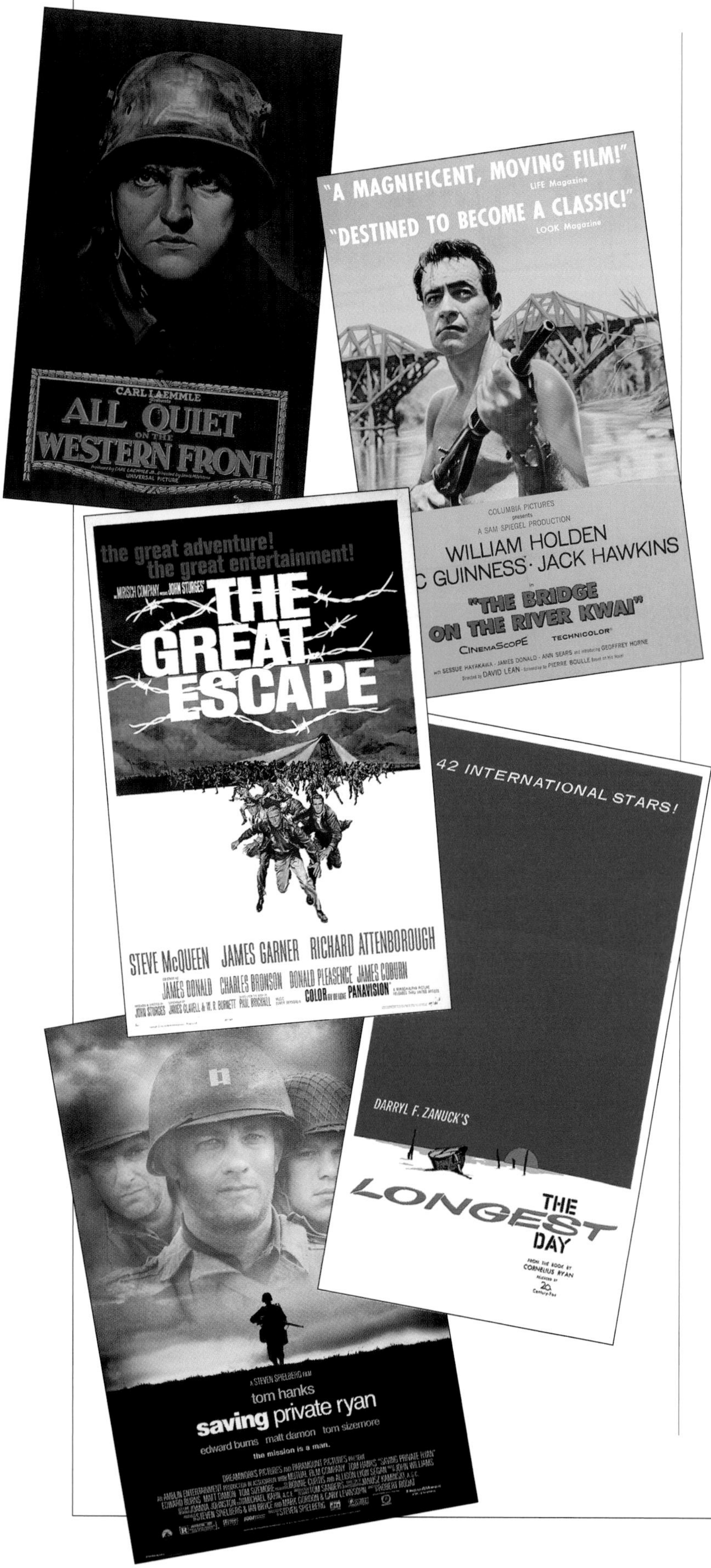

Bringing War to the Screen

War stories offer a wealth of cinematic possibilities to the director: high drama and low comedy; epic scope alongside the intimate; and tales of a cross section of American characters at the most challenging moments of their lives.

Combat films provide civilians their only view of war. What the films have shown them depends on both the director and his era. During and after World War II, for instance, war movies emphasized the courage of soldiers in battle. In many of these films, as one real-life soldier observed, "people sat in their trenches and had ideological discussions about the beauties of democracy at home." John Sturges's 1963 action adventure about Allied POWs, *The Great Escape,* was in this tradition; so was producer Darryl F. Zanuck's panoramic re-creation of D-Day, *The Longest Day* (1962). A much more grim and realistic look at war marked Steven Spielberg's 1998 masterpiece, *Saving Private Ryan (pages 124-125),* whose opening sequence of the American D-Day landing on

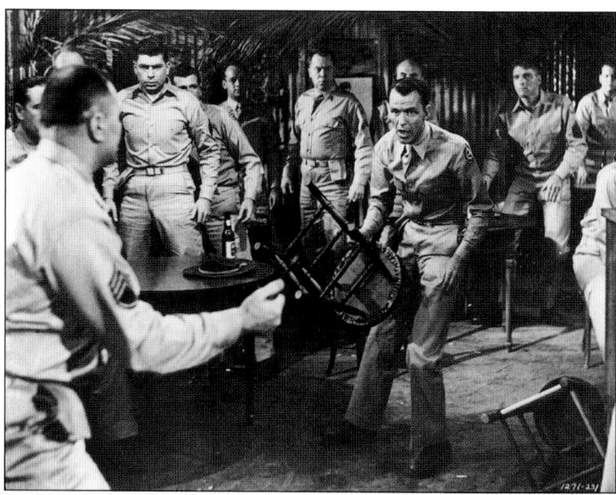

Private Maggio (Frank Sinatra) defies a sadistic sergeant (Ernest Borgnine) in 1953's From Here to Eternity. The film won eight Oscars.

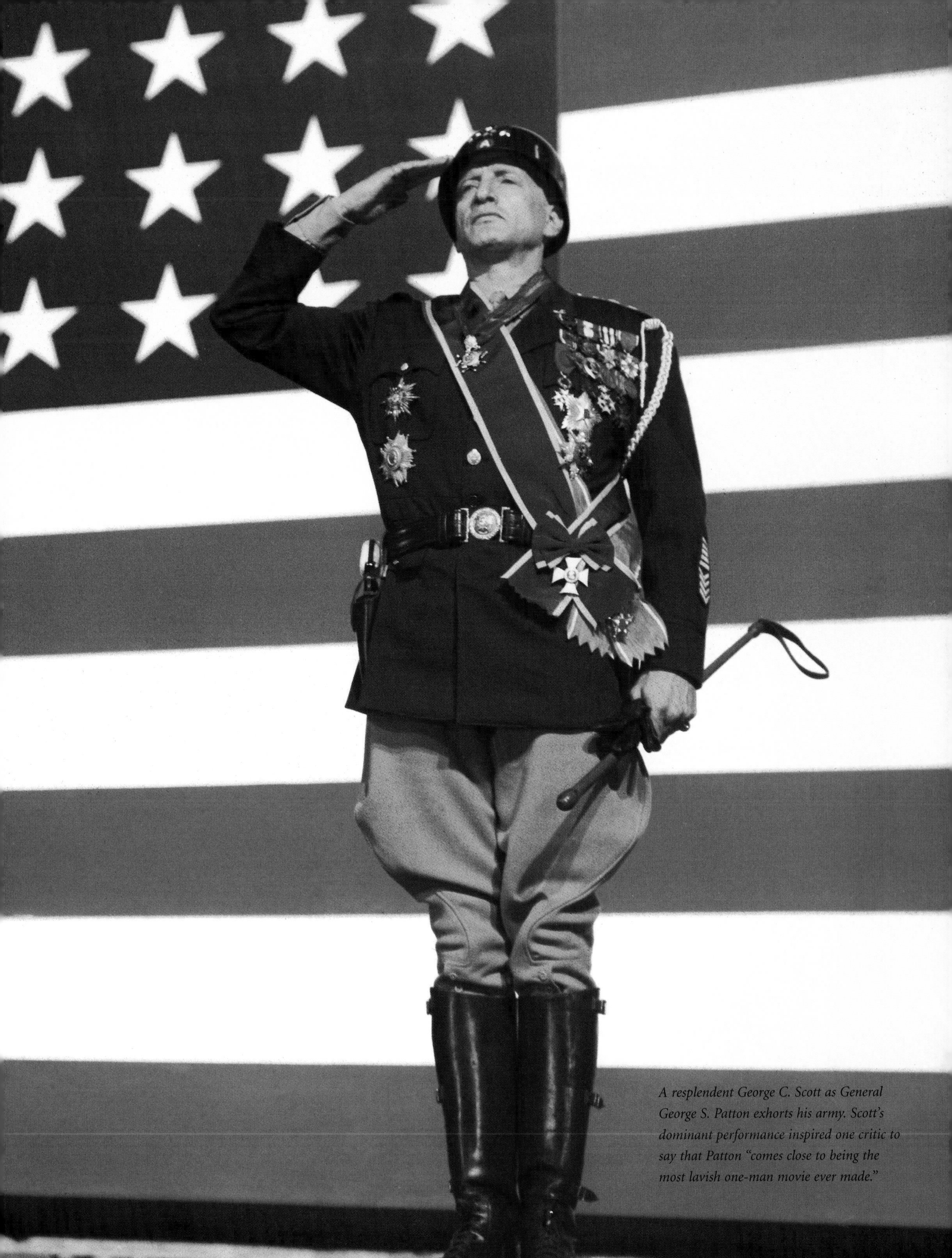

A resplendent George C. Scott as General George S. Patton exhorts his army. Scott's dominant performance inspired one critic to say that Patton "comes close to being the most lavish one-man movie ever made."

Omaha Beach constitutes perhaps the starkest and most terrifying cinematic look at combat ever offered to the moviegoing public.

Lewis Milestone's film of Erich Maria Remarque's World War I novel about idealistic young Germans caught in a wilderness of futile death, *All Quiet on the Western Front,* also offered a nightmare vision. Fine acting and unforgettable images—severed arms holding barbed wire, for instance—made the 1930 film a classic. A dramatic and many-sided tale of America's pre-World War II army was Fred Zinnemann's powerful *From Here to Eternity (page 94),* which culminated with the Japanese attack on Pearl Harbor. David Lean presented a look at the psychology of men in wartime situations in *The Bridge on the River Kwai* (1957), a tale of British POWs in a Japanese camp in which their brave and honorable commander proceeds blindly toward self-destruction.

America's Vietnam experience brought new ambiguity to combat movies, epitomized by Franklin Schaffner's 1970 World War II epic, *Patton (page 95).* George C. Scott's portrayal of the brilliant but flawed warrior and Schaffner's ruthless insistence on authenticity resulted in a film that pleased both hawks and doves.

A more typical response to Vietnam, however, was a series of passionately antiwar films in the 1970s and '80s. The funniest was 1970's *MASH (inset),* whose setting was actually the Korean conflict. Getting his first crack at a big-time movie, TV director Robert Altman broke every rule in the Hollywood book in filming *MASH*'s virtually plotless string of vignettes skewering the military.

The most chilling of the antiwar films was Francis Ford Coppola's phantasmagoric 1979 vision, *Apocalypse Now (right),* which followed GIs in Vietnam on a descent into madness during a mission to assassinate a Green Beret officer (Marlon Brando) gone off the deep end. The situation is so ugly that the commander of the team, played by Martin Sheen, is told by his superiors in military doublespeak that the mission "does not exist, nor will it ever exist." When Sheen reaches Brando's jungle enclave, he sees the irrelevance of right and wrong in the moral squalor of Vietnam. "Charging a man with murder in this place," he thinks to himself, is "like handing out speeding tickets at the Indy 500." The film was nominated for eight Academy Awards, winning two.

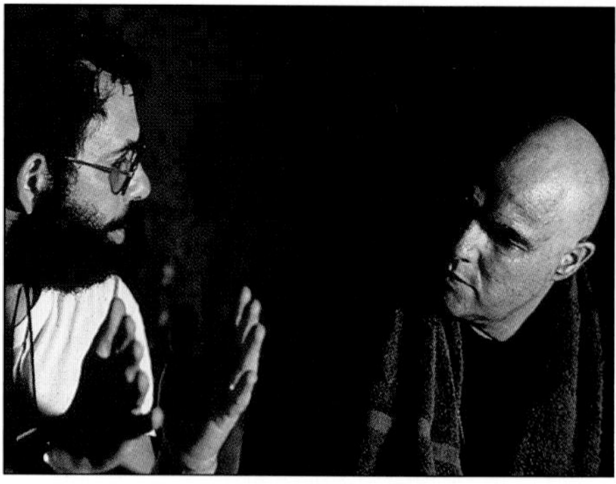

Producer-director Francis Ford Coppola, who lost 100 pounds during the arduous filming of Apocalypse Now, reviews a scene with Marlon Brando.

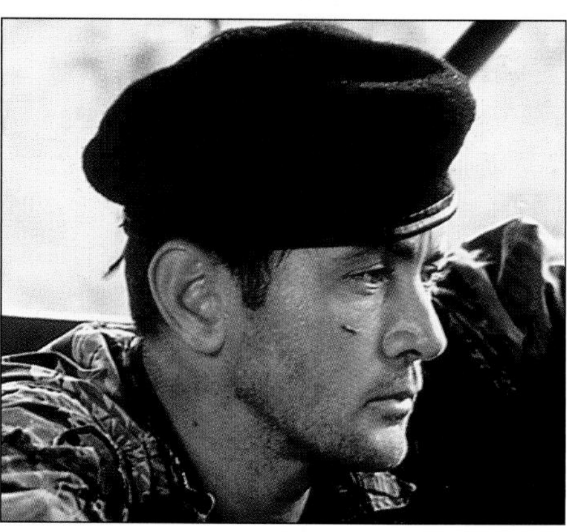

Captain Willard (Martin Sheen) searches for the maniacal, renegade Colonel Kurtz (Brando) with orders to "terminate with extreme prejudice."

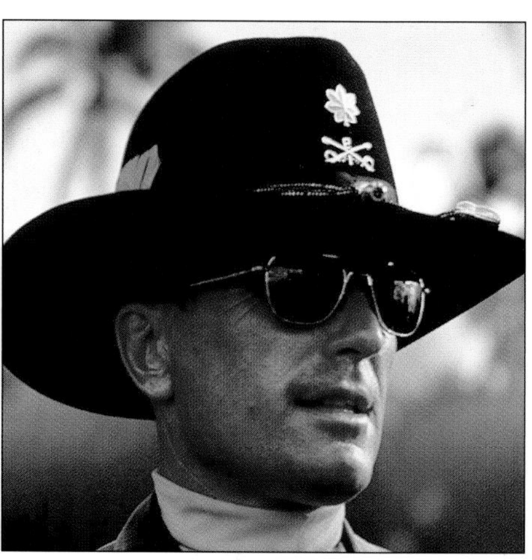

Lieutenant Colonel Kilgore (Robert Duvall), sporting a cavalry hat, uttered the immortal phrase "I love the smell of napalm in the morning."

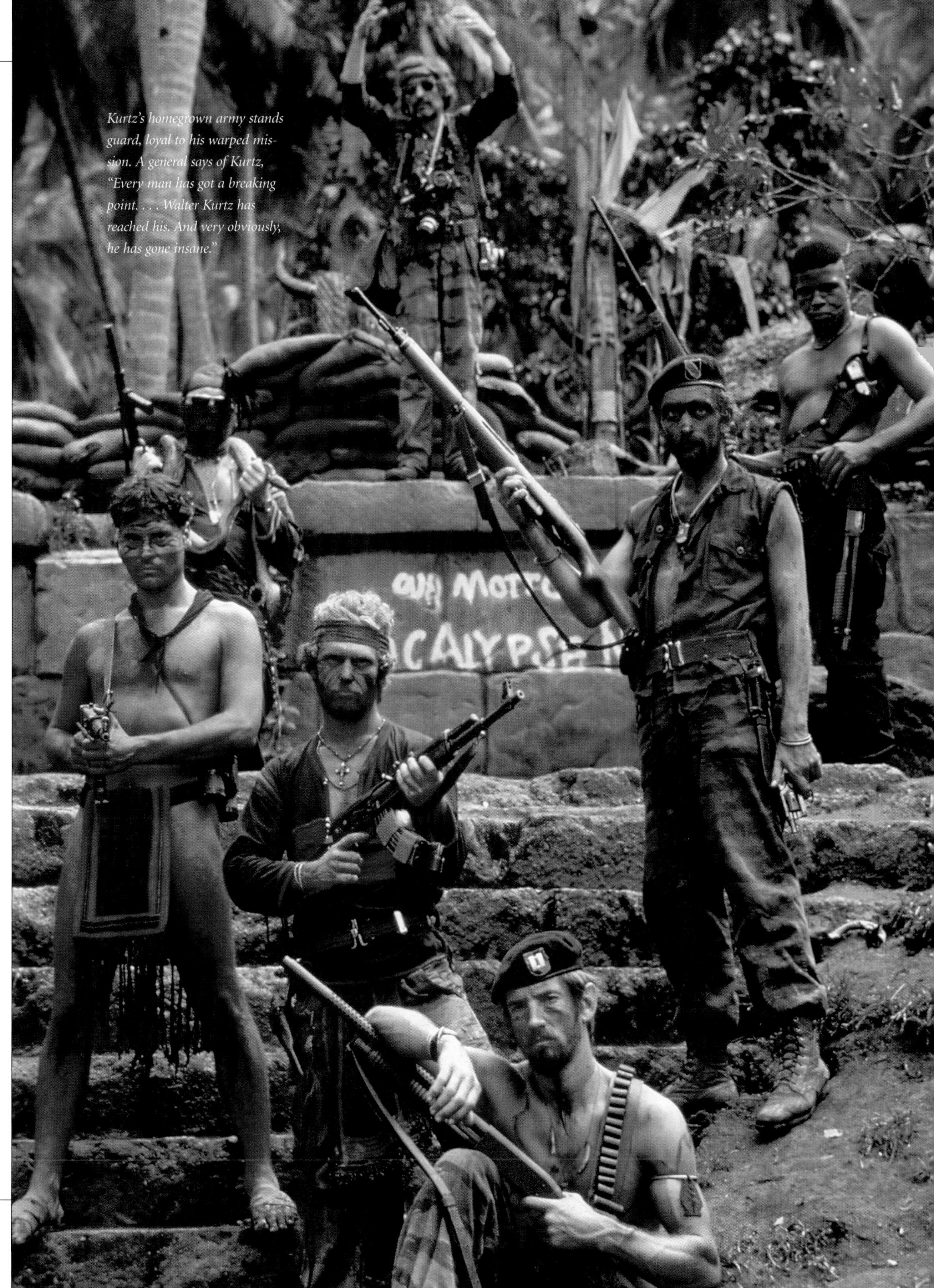

Kurtz's homegrown army stands guard, loyal to his warped mission. A general says of Kurtz, "Every man has got a breaking point. . . . Walter Kurtz has reached his. And very obviously, he has gone insane."

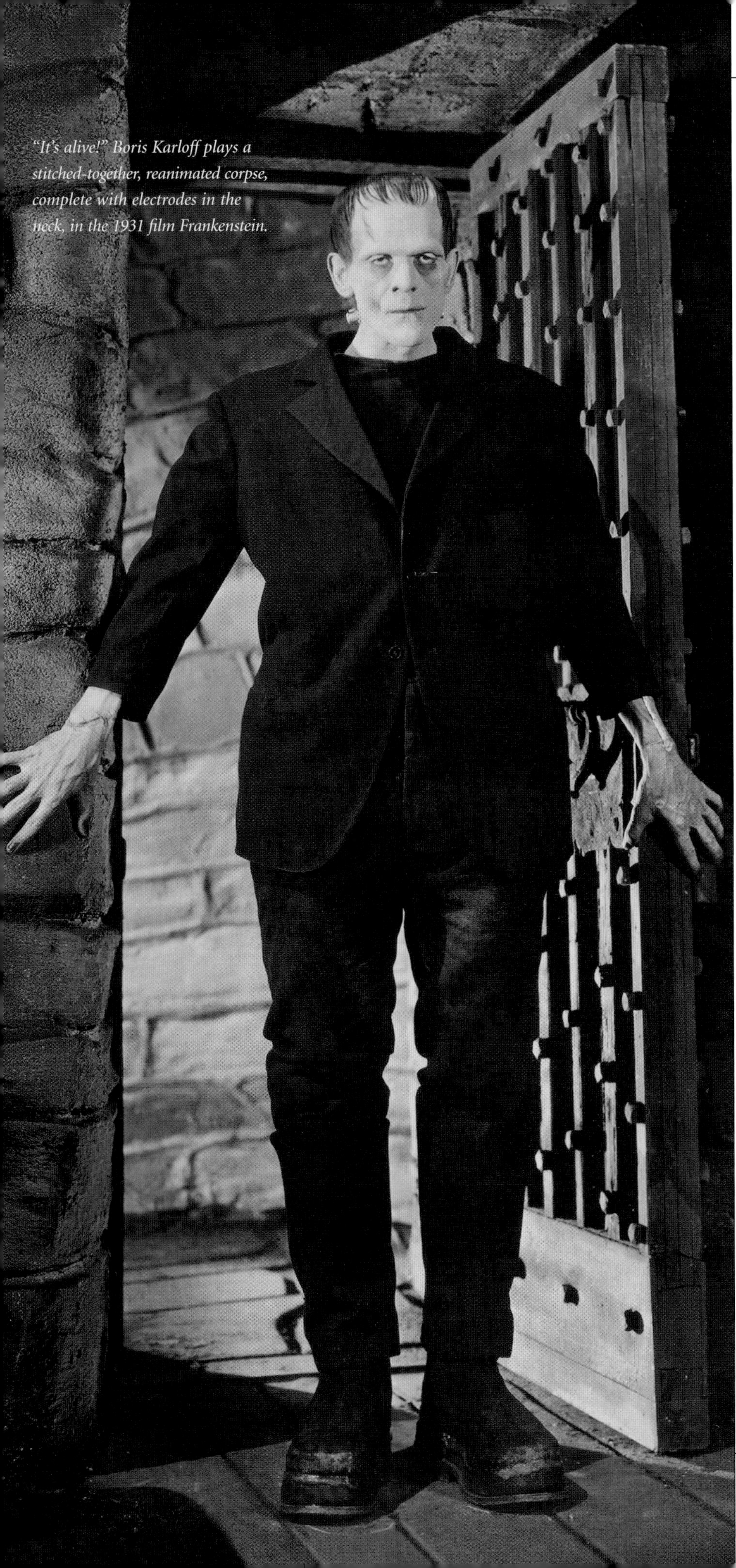

"It's alive!" Boris Karloff plays a stitched-together, reanimated corpse, complete with electrodes in the neck, in the 1931 film *Frankenstein.*

Films That Tweak Fears

Inspired by folklore about vampires, werewolves, and zombies, horror movies have thrilled audiences since Hollywood's early days. Director Tod Browning made a name for himself in the genre, filming Lon Chaney in a number of silents that capitalized on the actor's terrifying visages. In the talkie era Browning introduced a new sensation, Bela Lugosi, who starred in Universal's 1931 thriller *Dracula (right)* complete with creepy sound effects.

The same year Universal released director James Whale's *Frankenstein (left),* starring Boris Karloff. Four years later Whale followed up with the wildly eccentric *Bride of Frankenstein*, casting a weird-looking but sympathetic Elsa Lanchester *(inset)* as the monster's mate.

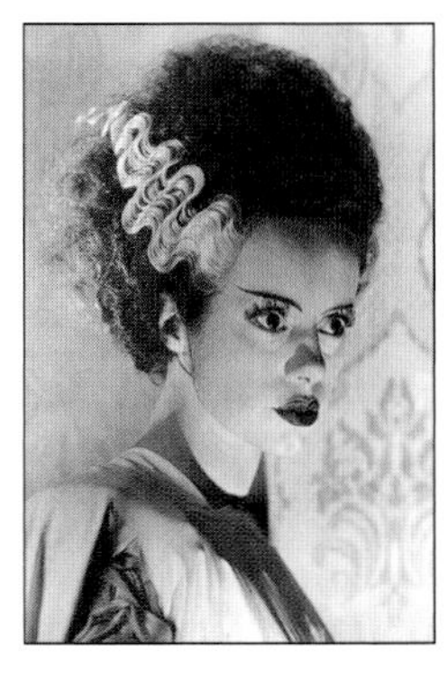

From *The Mummy* in 1932, which marked the directorial debut of *Dracula* cinematographer Karl Freund, through Roger Corman's low-budget '60s fright flicks based on Edgar Allan Poe stories, horror movies depicted little bloodletting. But John Carpenter's grisly 1978 hit *Halloween* and Wes Craven's 1984 slasher *A Nightmare on Elm Street* launched a trend toward graphic guts and gore.

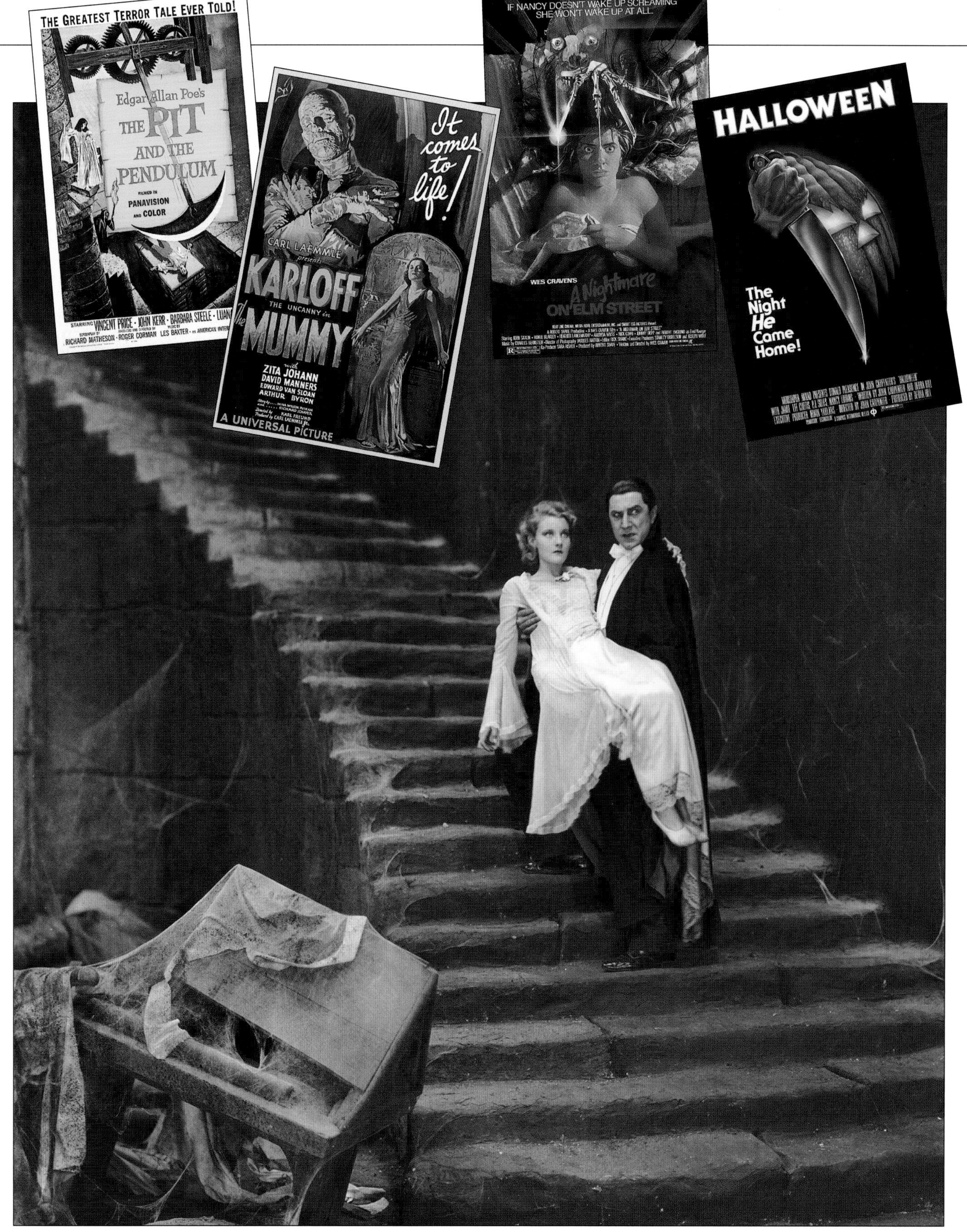

Top: Posters of early and new-generation horror flicks. Above: Bela Lugosi as Dracula carries a potential blood donor up the stairs of his castle.

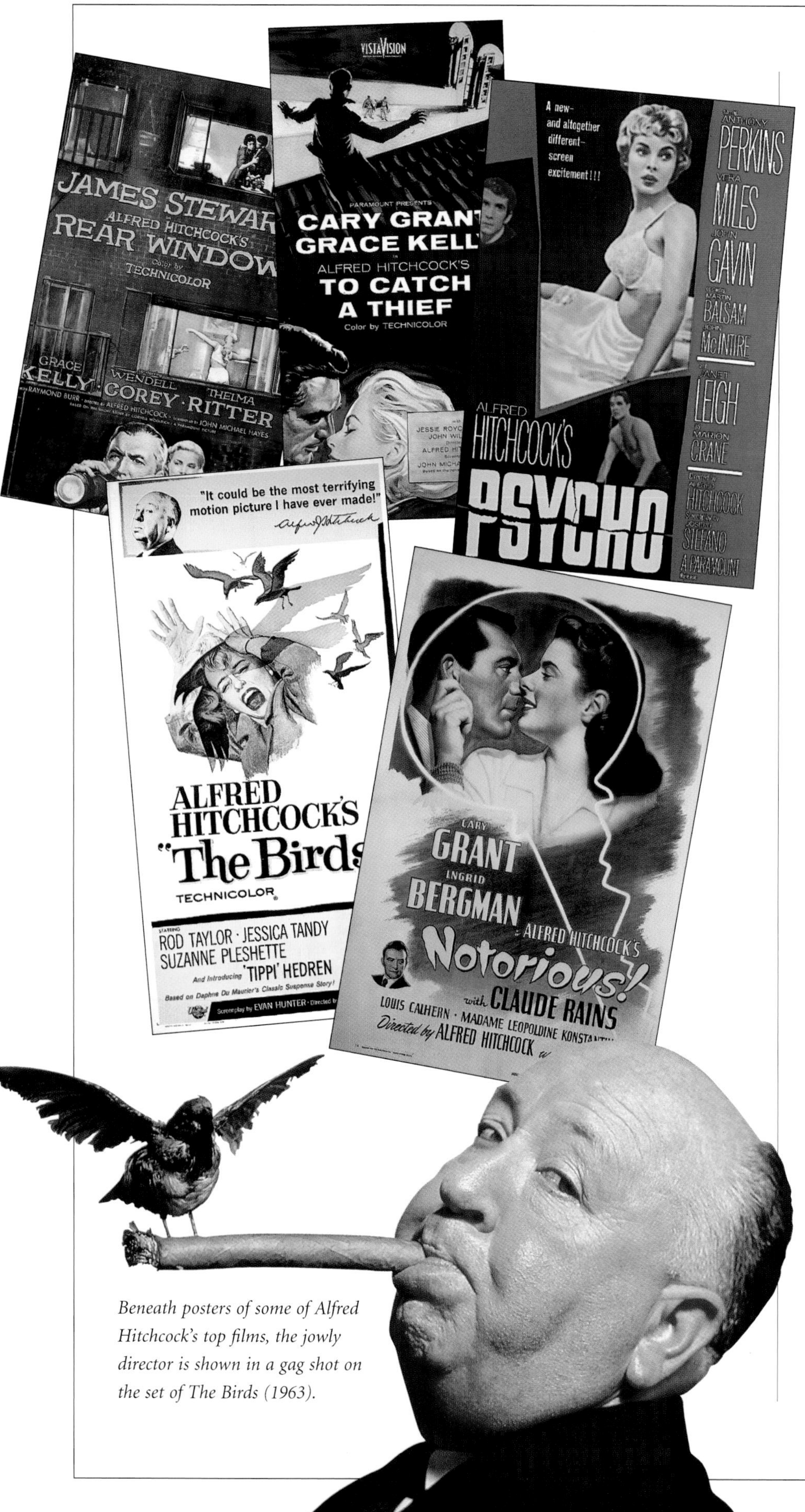

Beneath posters of some of Alfred Hitchcock's top films, the jowly director is shown in a gag shot on the set of The Birds (1963).

The Master of Suspense

With their blend of intrigue, smoldering sensuality, and dark humor, the films of maestro of menace Alfred Hitchcock held audiences spellbound for six decades. Classic Hitchcock plots placed some of Hollywood's most self-possessed blonde beauties, including Ingrid Bergman, Vera Miles, Grace Kelly, and Kim Novak, in perilous situations. "I had always heard that his idea was to take a woman—usually a blonde—and break her apart to see her shyness and reserve broken down, but I thought this was only in the plots of his films," said Tippi Hedren. She learned otherwise during her physically punishing attic scene in *The Birds,* which left her needing a week of medical treatment.

At his best in films such as the 1946 spy melodrama *Notorious*, the 1954 suspense story *Rear Window,* and the 1955 thriller *To Catch a Thief,* Hitchcock probed for the evil that lurks behind benign facades. Heralded for his cinematic expertise, he used inventive techniques such as complex camera movements, montage editing, and shifting points of view. Thanks to cameo appearances he made in the majority of his movies, the portly director's profile and image became an icon. His black-and-white masterpiece *Psycho (right),* which he slyly called a "fun picture," led one critic to call the mischievous director a "barbaric sophisticate."

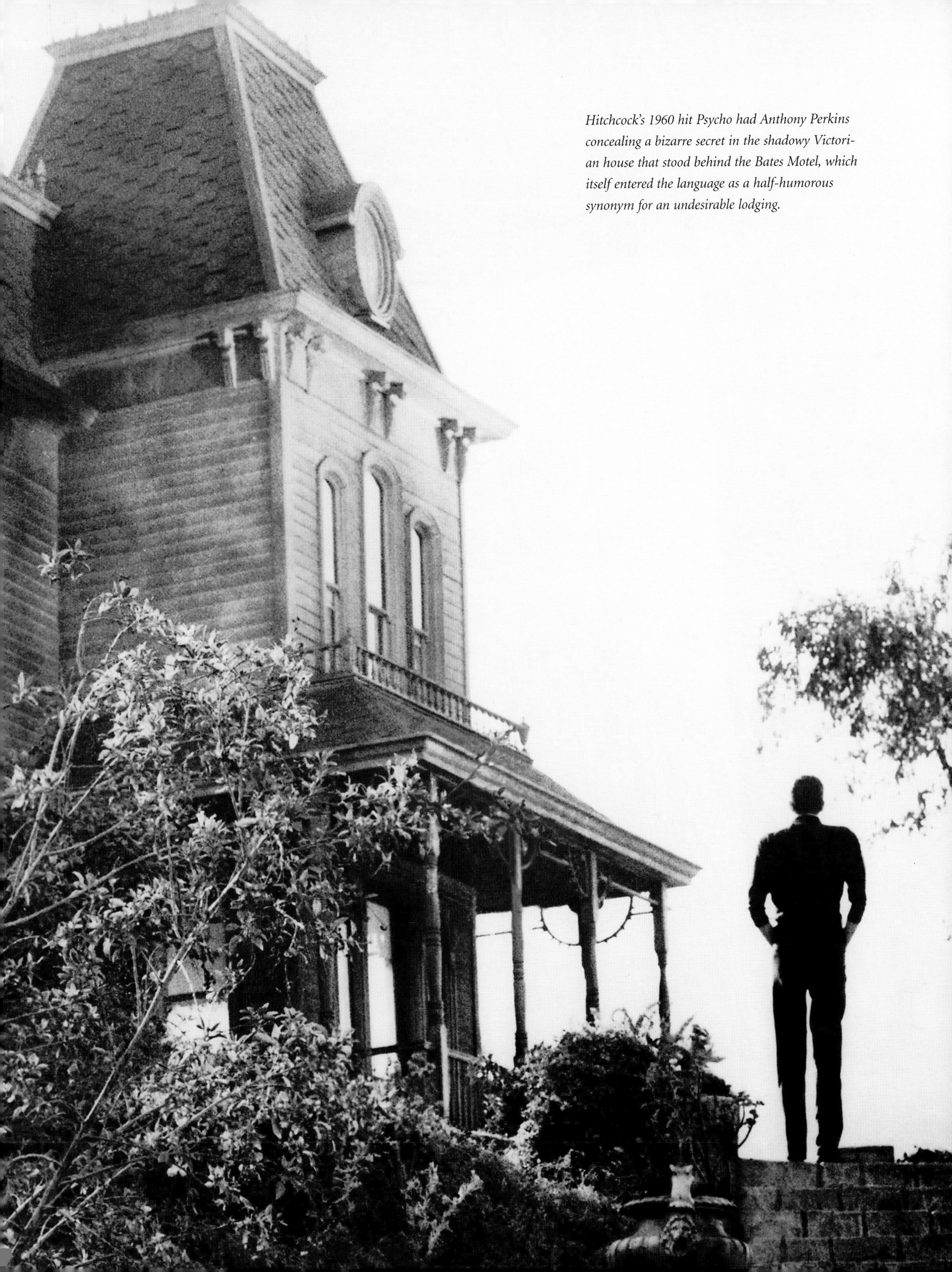

Hitchcock's 1960 hit Psycho had Anthony Perkins concealing a bizarre secret in the shadowy Victorian house that stood behind the Bates Motel, which itself entered the language as a half-humorous synonym for an undesirable lodging.

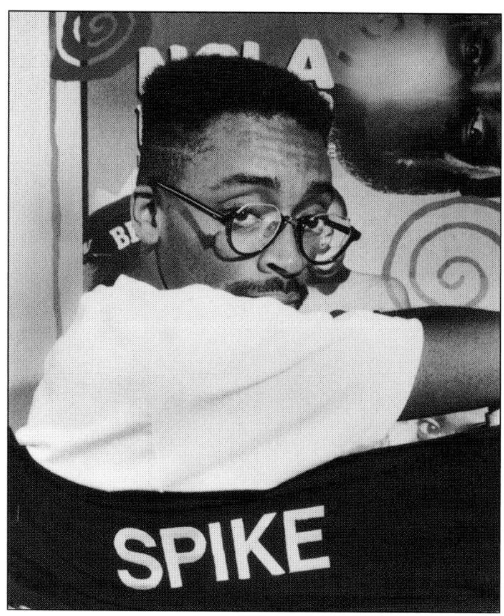

Beginning in the '80s, the films of director Spike Lee (above) offered a black perspective.

Mavericks of Moviedom

Director Spike Lee's surprise 1986 hit comedy *She's Gotta Have It* showed Hollywood that handling black urban themes could be profitable. A graduate of the film school at New York University, Lee offered scathing, often controversial social commentary in his movies, reaching a peak in 1989 with *Do the Right Thing,* which received an Oscar nomination for Best Screenplay. The film took a sledgehammer approach to the urban racial tensions surrounding an Italian-American pizza parlor located in a black neighborhood in Brooklyn.

In the 1992 film biography *Malcolm X (below),* Lee reexamined the life of the radical African-American political leader. Despite a running time of more than three hours, the movie showed Lee at the height of his directori-

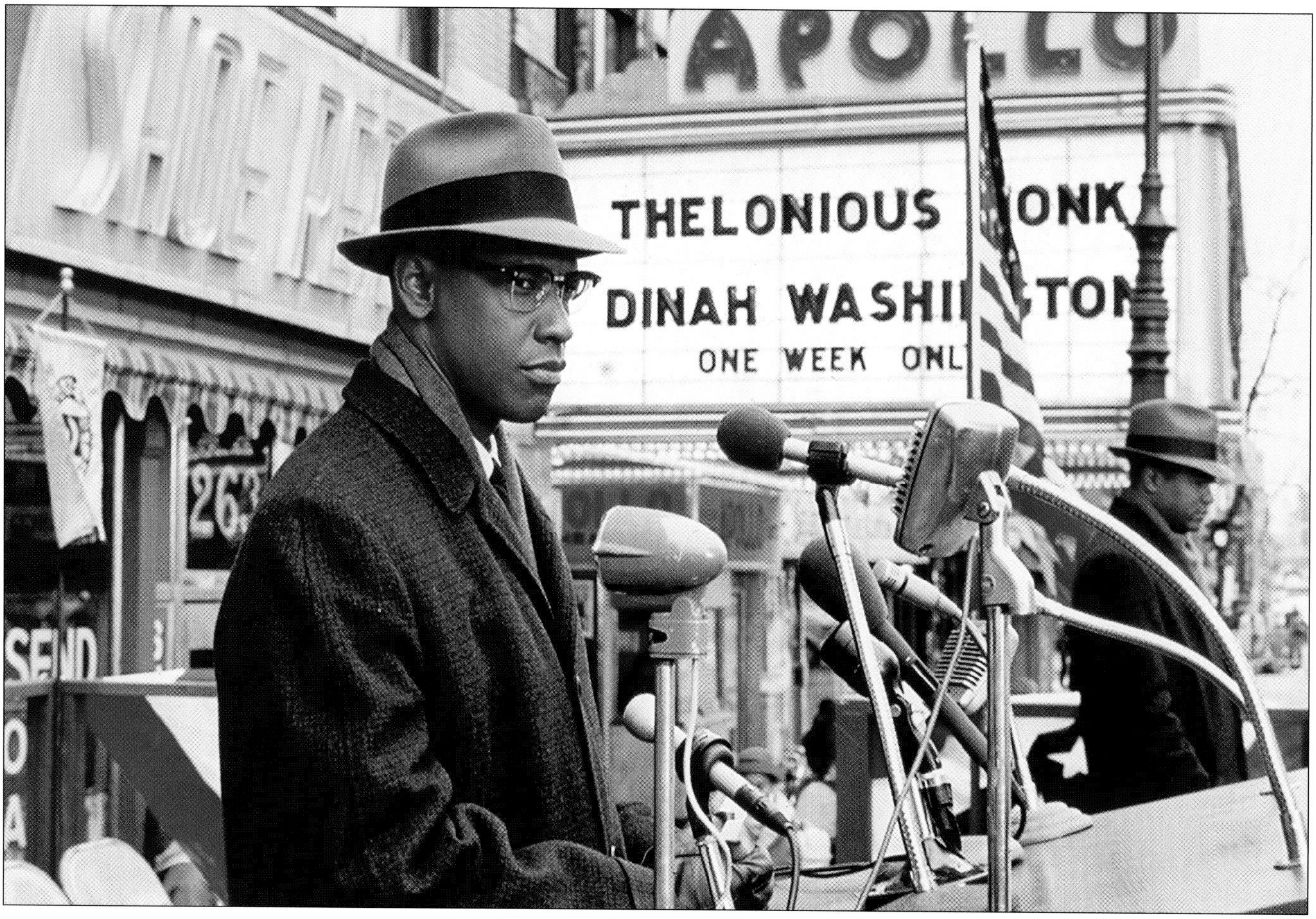

Denzel Washington, playing the title role in Spike Lee's powerful biopic Malcolm X, preaches to a crowd outside Harlem's Apollo Theatre.

al powers, combining complex camera angles with multiple story lines in a film of epic proportions.

Controversy of a different sort surrounded the work of director Oliver Stone *(right)*. He began his film career as a screenwriter, winning an Oscar for *Midnight Express* (1978). Stone's first commercial success as a director, *Salvador*, combined elements of brutality and politics in a 1986 tale of journalists caught in an insurrectionary cross fire in Central America. That same year Stone finished the smash hit *Platoon (below)*. This account of the horrors of the Vietnam War, in which Stone had served, earning a Bronze Star and a Purple Heart, depicted gut-wrenching action and moral degradation so true to life that many Vietnam veterans hailed the movie as Hollywood's most authentic picture of their war experience. *Platoon* received the Academy Award for Best Picture, and Stone won an Oscar for his directing.

He continued his hard-hitting filmmaking with the 1989 saga *Born on the Fourth of July*, starring Tom Cruise as a paraplegic Vietnam veteran, for

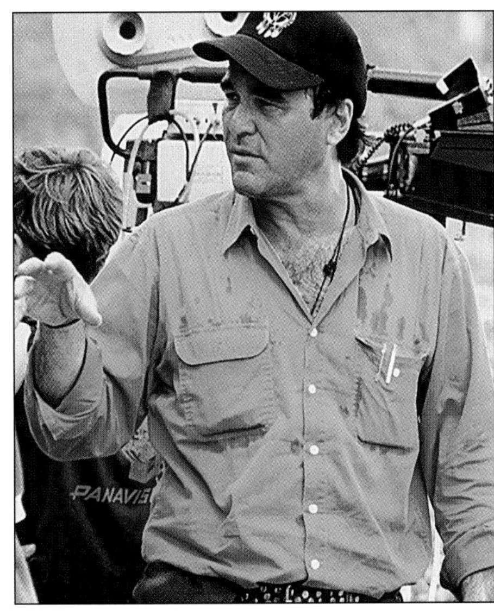

Oliver Stone (above) directs the action in his 1993 Vietnam film Heaven & Earth.

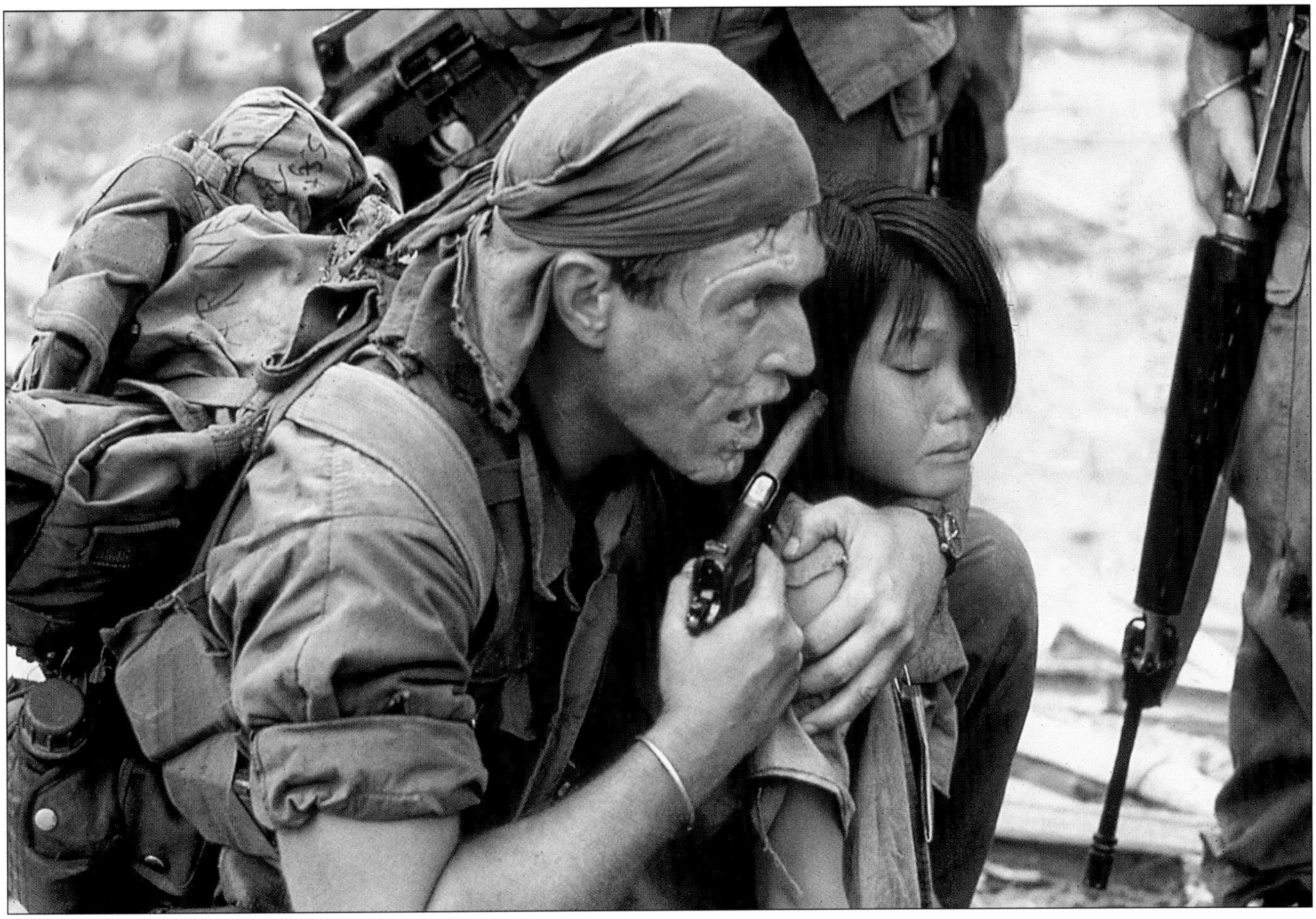

The psychotic Sergeant Barnes, played by Tom Berenger, threatens a Vietnamese child in Oliver Stone's grimly realistic war drama, Platoon.

which Stone won his second Best Director Oscar. *JFK,* a 1991 film in which Stone contended that the assassination of President Kennedy had been a conspiracy among high government officials, was widely criticized as a fanciful and biased version of that tragedy and prompted the U.S. Congress to open sealed files on the assassination.

Three thought-provoking hits placed Stanley Kubrick *(right)* squarely in the forefront of the screen's most inventive directors. The blackest of black comedies, 1964's *Dr. Strangelove (below, right)* starred Peter Sellers in three roles, including a lunatic German scientist and an English officer desperately trying to avert world catastrophe. The movie marvel of 1968, Kubrick's landmark science fiction epic *2001: A Space Odyssey,* took four years to make and featured elaborate visual and sound effects. Melding space travel with theology, philosophy, and allegories on the future of mankind, the film virtually reinvented the genre.

A Clockwork Orange (1971), perhaps Kubrick's most controversial movie, painted an unsettling portrait of a future steeped in senseless violence. Both praised and damned, the film contained seductive scenes of stylized mayhem and torture that astonished some viewers and offended others. His last work before his death in 1999 was the psychosexual thriller *Eyes Wide Shut,* with Nicole Kidman and Tom Cruise, who had only praise for the legendary director. "Suddenly he'll say something to you, or you'll see how he creates a shot, and you realize this man is different," said Cruise. "This man is profound."

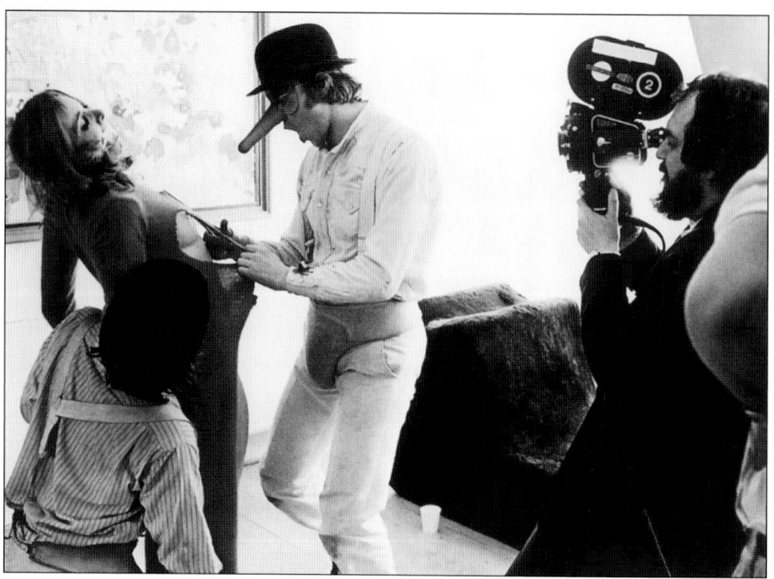

Director Stanley Kubrick (right) choreographs a savage rape scene carried out to the accompaniment of jaunty music to advance his cynical view of a world gone mad in A Clockwork Orange. Malcolm McDowell plays the sadistic hooligan Alex.

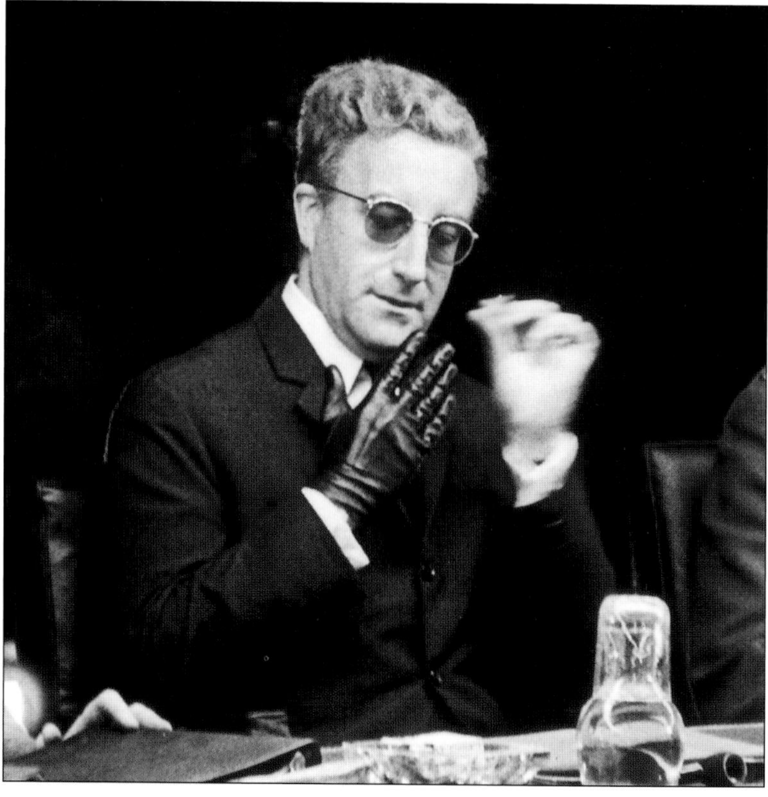

In Dr. Strangelove, Peter Sellers as the title character—one of three different roles he played—loses control over his ex-Nazi persona in Kubrick's dark comedy about military and political folly and the Cold War's dance with nuclear catastrophe.

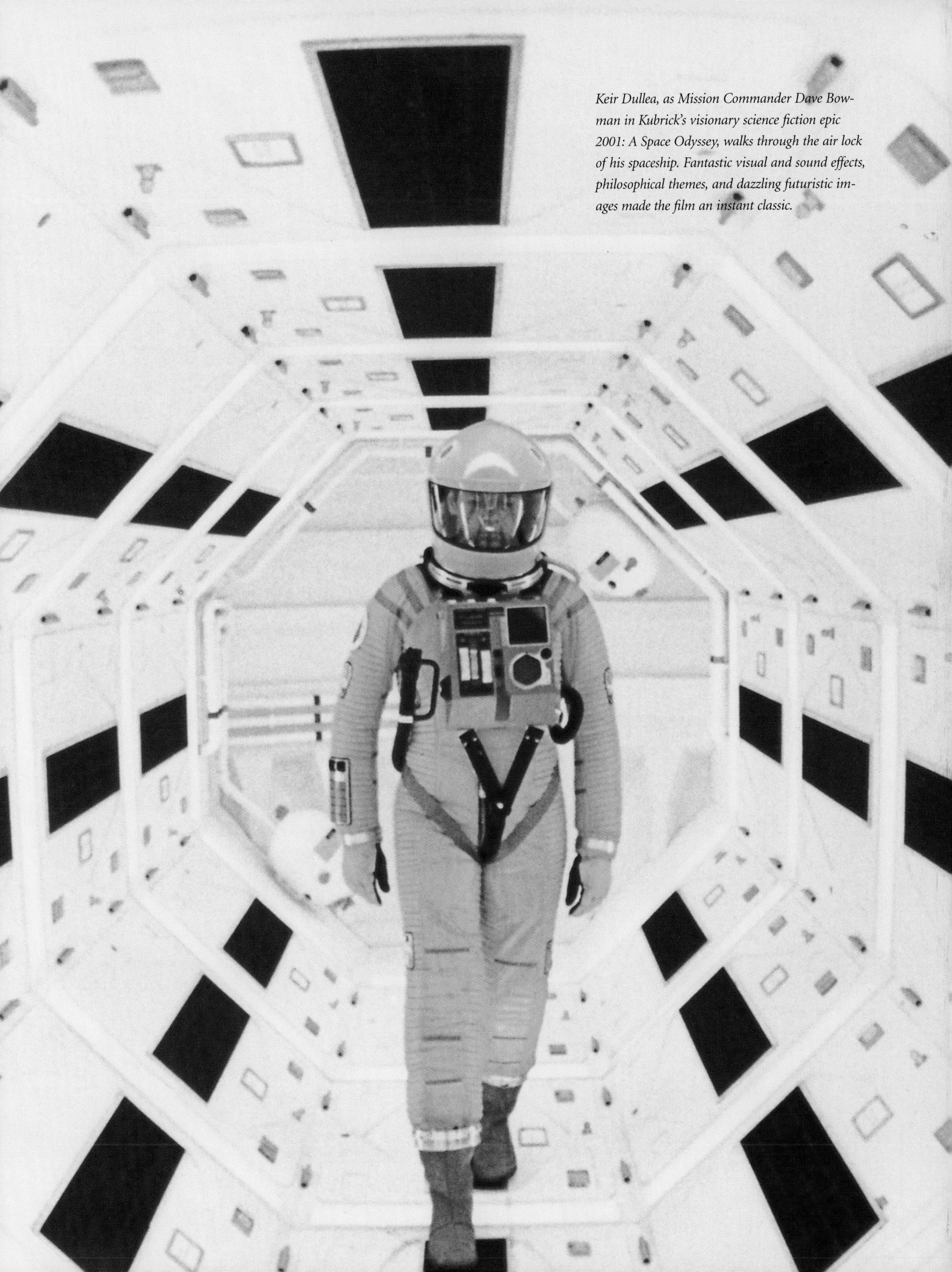

Keir Dullea, as Mission Commander Dave Bowman in Kubrick's visionary science fiction epic 2001: A Space Odyssey, walks through the air lock of his spaceship. Fantastic visual and sound effects, philosophical themes, and dazzling futuristic images made the film an instant classic.

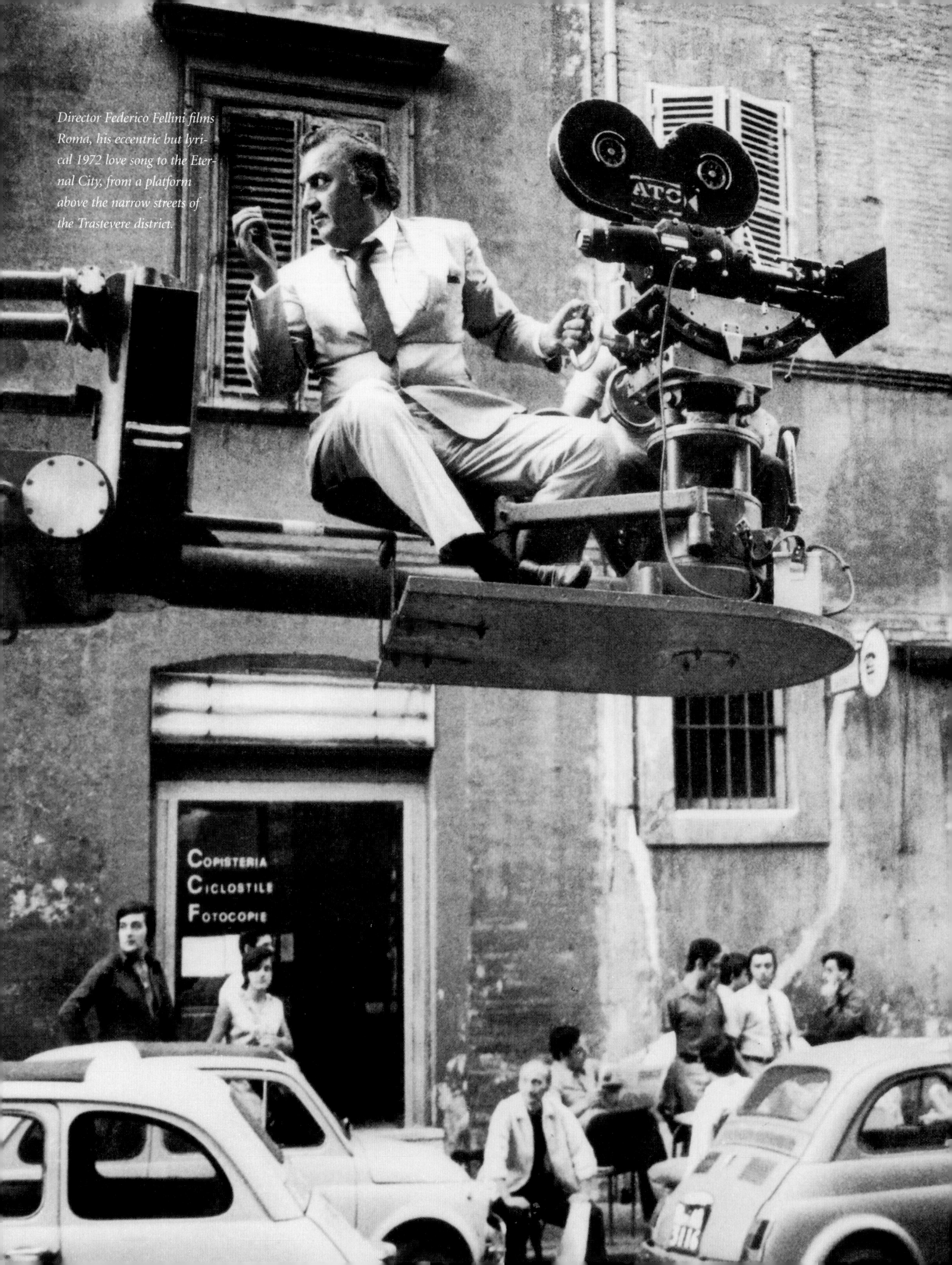

Director Federico Fellini films Roma, his eccentric but lyrical 1972 love song to the Eternal City, from a platform above the narrow streets of the Trastevere district.

Influences from Abroad

A group of imaginative foreign directors emerged from art house obscurity in the 1950s. Federico Fellini first made a splash with the international release of *La Strada,* a parable about lost innocence that won the Oscar for Best Foreign Film in 1956. With *La Dolce Vita* (1960), his bag of tricks spilled forth, releasing outrageous fantasies, sins, symbols, masks, and perversions. Cementing Fellini's stature as the director's director was *8½* (1963), about a director trying vainly to complete a film.

From Japan, Akira Kurosawa burst upon the scene with *Rashomon* (1950), a complex story of rape and murder. In 1954 Kurosawa directed the epic *The Seven Samurai,* and he scored again late in his career with *Ran* (1985), a colossal samurai version of Shakespeare's *King Lear.* Beginning in the 1950s French directors launched new-wave filmmaking, in which the director became an auteur, giving primacy to his own visual and cinematic creativity over the "literary" emphasis of screenwriters. Films such as Alain Resnais's *Last Year at Marienbad* (1961) and François Truffaut's 1973 Oscar winner *Day for Night* helped make the new wave famous. Swedish director Ingmar Bergman gained an international reputation upon the 1957 worldwide release of *The Seventh Seal* and *Wild Strawberries,* with their surreal treatment of the themes of faith, alienation, and death.

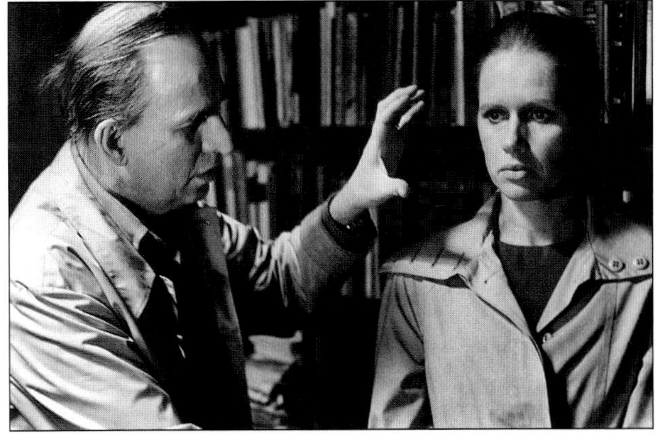

Liv Ullmann (above) plays a coldly analytical psychiatrist confronting her own breakdown in Ingmar Bergman's Face to Face *(1976).*

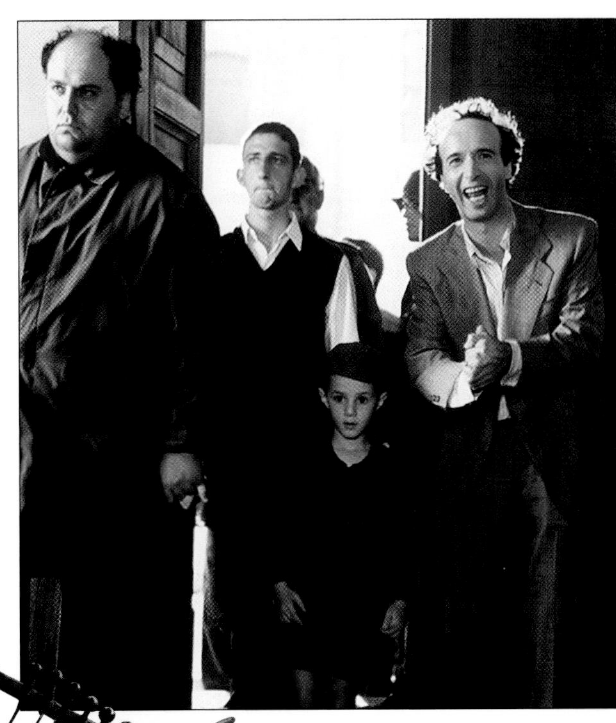

Roberto Benigni (right) directed, cowrote, and starred in the Oscar-winning 1997 fable Life Is Beautiful, *about a father who shields his son from the horrors of a concentration camp through humor, quick wits, and love.*

Fellini cast his wife, Giulietta Masina, as the impish and lovable Gelsomina (left) in La Strada, *his exquisitely touching tale of the relationship between a carnival strongman and a simpleminded waif.*

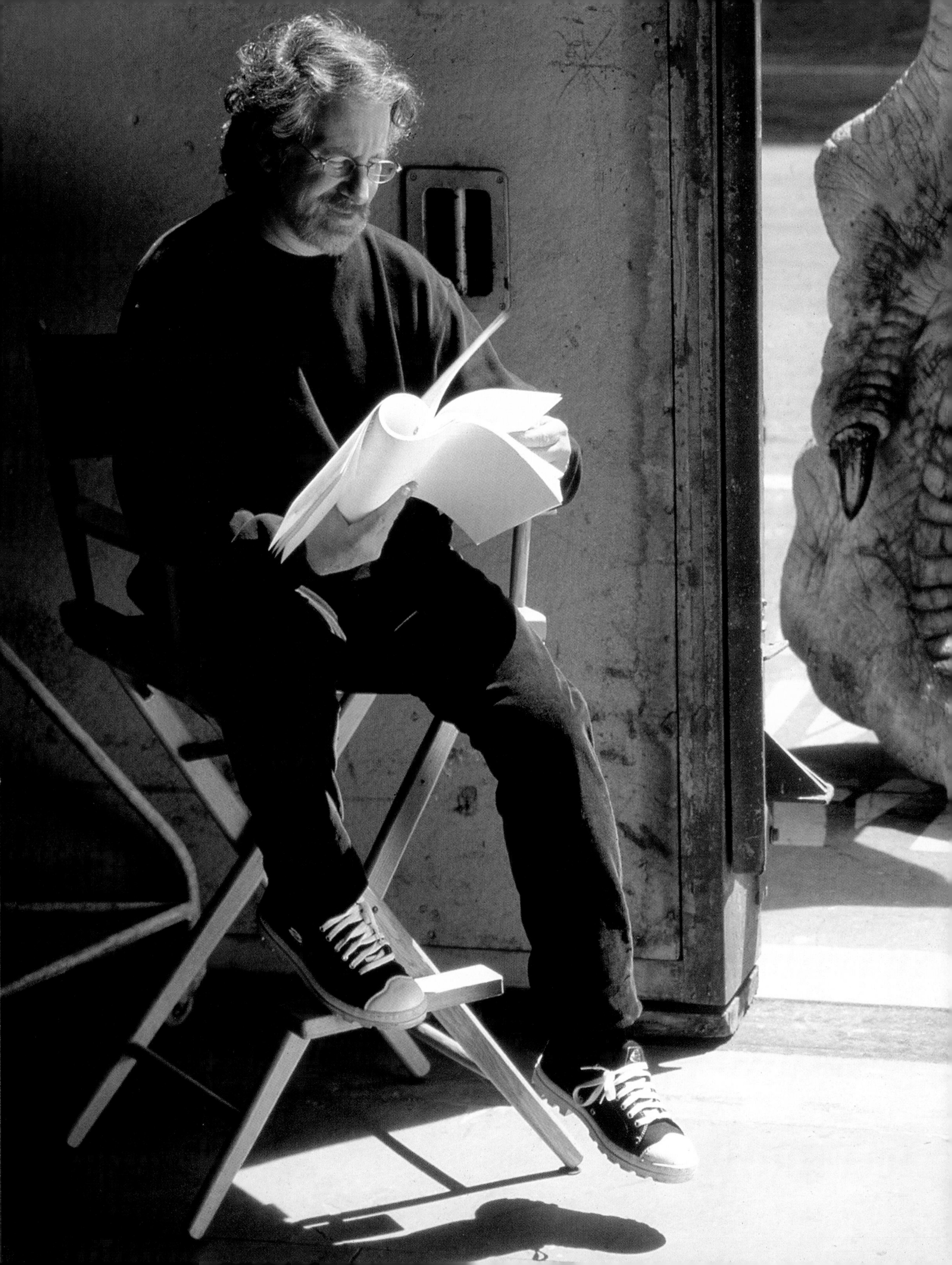

Manufacturing the Dream

★

BEHIND-THE-SCENES MOVIE MAGIC

I like to sweat the details," declared Steven Spielberg *(left),* Hollywood's most successful director and producer. On the set of fantasy blockbusters like *Raiders of the Lost Ark* and *E.T.: The Extra-Terrestrial* and dramas like *Schindler's List* and *Saving Private Ryan*, Spielberg earned a reputation for stepping in to make sure that the particulars came out exactly as he wanted. During the shooting of *Amistad* in 1997, he grabbed a crewman's lantern and held it himself at just the right angle to illuminate the tortured faces of a group of slaves.

Yet even filmmakers who take Spielberg's hands-on approach still depend upon the efforts of a multitude of specialists, such as screenwriters, set and costume designers, cinematographers, sound engineers, makeup artists, stunt performers, and special-effects technicians. Stars give films their faces and voices, directors receive the artistic accolades, and producers get credit for making the whole enterprise happen—but the people listed in the closing credits, whether they create sparkling dialogue or dizzying digital effects, are essential to a movie's success.

Savvy directors fully appreciate—even relish—the work of these experts. A computer-graphics designer said of the experience of bringing dinosaurs to life for Spielberg in *The Lost World: Jurassic Park*: "He'll howl with glee if something is exciting to him, say, a person getting attacked by a *T. rex.* He just can't contain himself."

Steven Spielberg works on the set of The Lost World: Jurassic Park*, undistracted by the immense model of a dinosaur's foot, a product of the vast off-camera effort required to create a movie.*

Mapping Out a Movie

This excerpt from the shooting script for Gone With the Wind choreographs action and camera movements, using abbreviations like b.g. for background and assigning a number to each shot.

252 LONG SHOT - WAGON AT RAILROAD TRACK
Burning buildings in b.g. Rhett gets out of wagon, goes to horse's head, starts to pull horse bridle.

253 MEDIUM CLOSE SHOT - RHETT AT HORSE'S HEAD

RHETT *(pulling at horse)* Come on! Come on! Throw me your shawl.
(he reaches out of scene)

254 MEDIUM CLOSE SHOT - SCARLETT
Prissy in back of wagon. Scarlett throws the shawl.

255 MEDIUM CLOSE SHOT - RHETT AT HORSE'S HEAD
He catches the shawl, ties it around the horse's head.

RHETT Sorry, but you'll like it better if you don't see anything.

256 LONG SHOT - WAGON AT R.R. TRACKS - (BURNING BUILDINGS IN B.G.)
Rhett finishes tying shawl over the horse's head.

257 MEDIUM CLOSE SHOT - EXPLOSIVES IN BOXCAR
The fire is in the background.

RHETT Come on, Come on!
He pulls the horse, turns the horse, and then leads him away from CAMERA.

259 LONG SHOT - EXPLOSIVES IN BOXCAR
The fire is nearer.

260 LONG SHOT
Slowly, pulling the reluctant horse, Rhett heads away from CAMERA toward the spot still clear of flame. A moment after they have disappeared through the opening, the flames reach their climax, the boxcars start to blow up, the largest building at the left end of the screen collapses, and the screen becomes a mass of flames.

Words on Paper Give Voice to a Film

The screenplay may be the most important element of a movie, providing not just memorable lines but, in the form of a shooting script *(left)*, a blueprint for filming. It is also, however, the most vulnerable element. Producers, directors, agents, and actors can all insist on changes, sometimes to strengthen a character or resolve a problem that arises during shooting, sometimes just because writing looks so easy: As screenwriter William Goldman put it, "Everybody knows the alphabet."

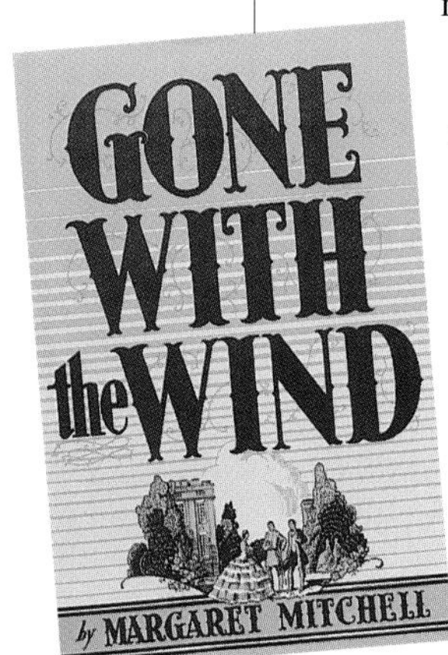

When producer David O. Selznick decided to make *Gone With the Wind,* he turned to playwright Sidney Coe Howard, who pared Margaret Mitchell's best-selling 1,037-page novel *(inset)* down to a cogent script. But Selznick went on to hire—and fire—a long series of other writers, including F. Scott Fitzgerald, to produce new versions of the screenplay, all the while constantly revising their work. The resulting mound of pages eventually filled an entire filing cabinet, yet when shooting began, only a fraction of the scenes existed in usable form.

For help, Selznick called in another screenwriter, the highly regarded Ben Hecht, who suggested they start again from Howard's version. The resulting effort won a posthumous Best Screenplay Oscar for Howard, who had died four months before the film's December 1939 release.

In the old Hollywood, writers rarely commanded much respect from studio executives. Jack Warner scornfully labeled them "schmucks with Underwoods," and most of them labored under contract to one studio or another, relegated to shabby, cramped offices. Their latter-day equivalents enjoy much higher prestige, as well as paychecks that can run to seven figures. And those who both direct and write, like Woody Allen and Francis Ford Coppola, wield enormous creative control.

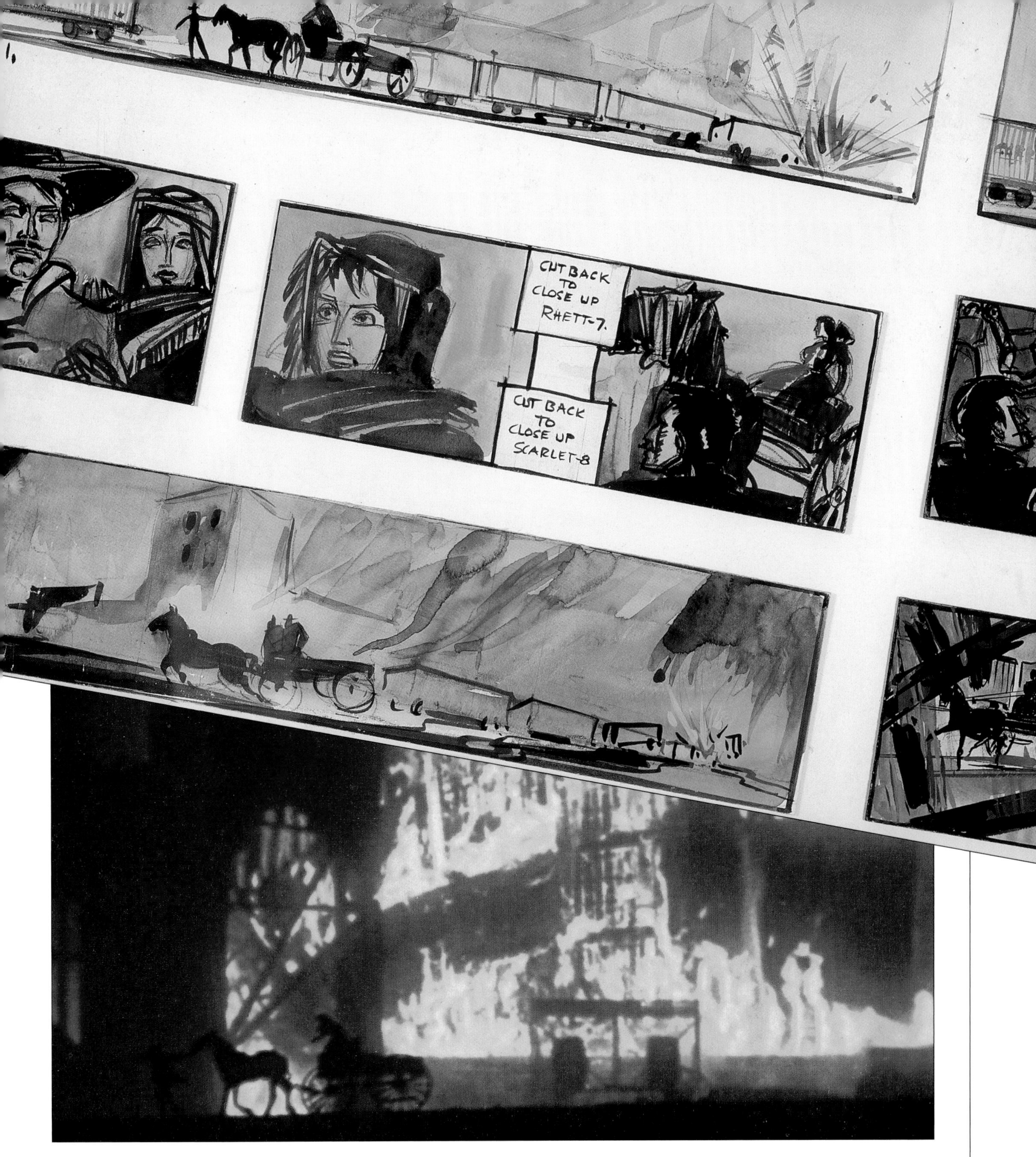

A storyboard of thumbnail sketches, based on the screenplay, allows the producer, director, and others to visualize each scene. The sequence of sketches at top by William Cameron Menzies, production designer for Gone With the Wind, depicts Scarlett and Rhett as they flee a burning Atlanta. To create the dramatic scene (bottom), the crew assembled and set ablaze old sets from Selznick's back lot—including some from 1933's King Kong.

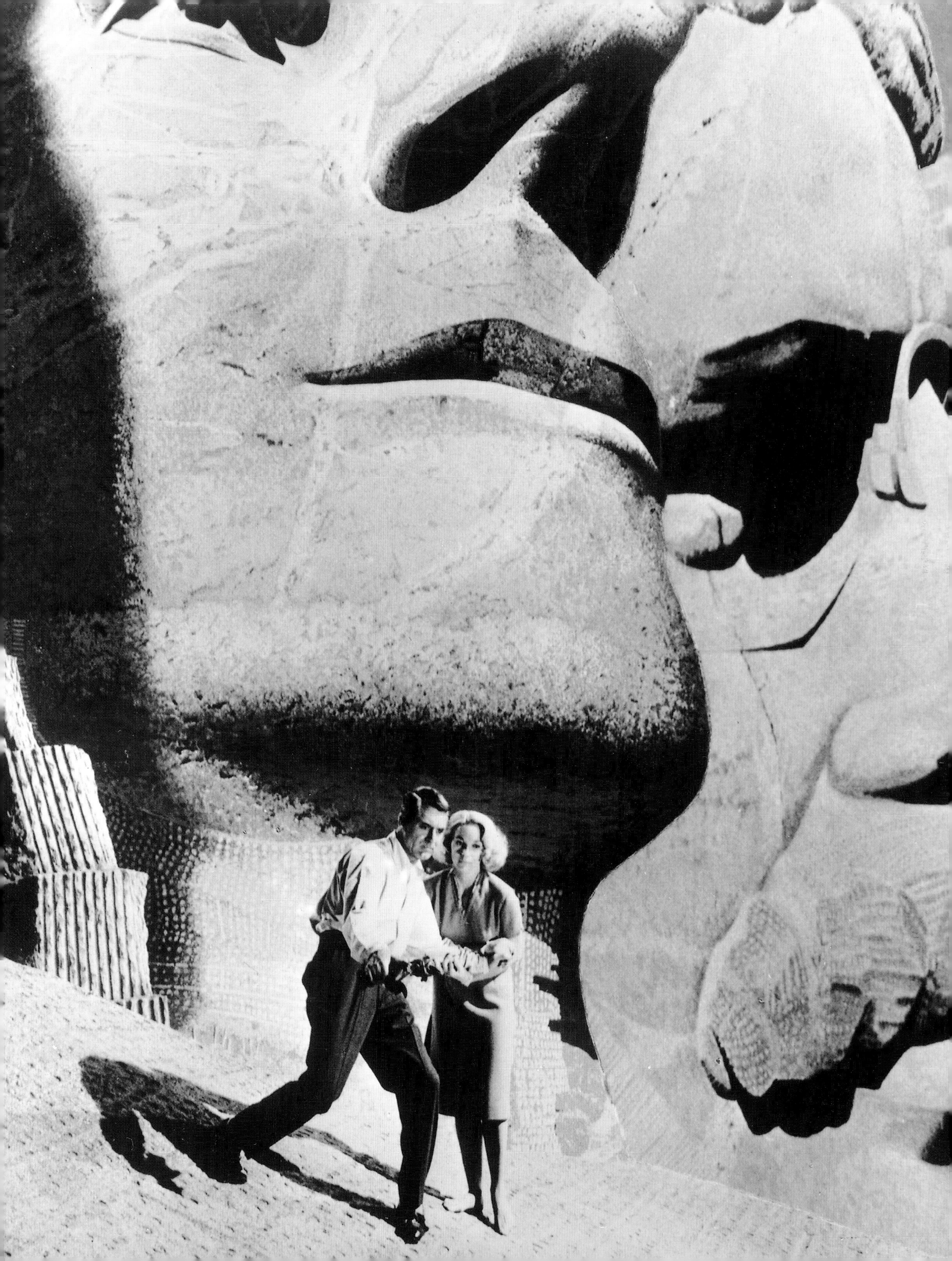

Designers Set the Scene

Robert Boyle, a top Hollywood production designer, was able to ply his trade because he knew, as he put it, "what a liar the camera can be." Boyle's job was to design the sets, select the locations, and create the right visual environment. He always sought "dramatic truth," but this, he noted, could be "very, very far from reality."

During the making of Alfred Hitchcock's classic 1959 thriller *North by Northwest,* Boyle helped the camera lie convincingly. The screenplay called for a spectacular chase across the Mount Rushmore National Memorial. But the U.S. Department of the Interior refused Hitchcock permission to film on site, and he felt in any case that he could better control the lighting on a studio set. So he had Boyle design scale-model plaster casts of the four presidents' faces instead, and viewers came away convinced they had seen the real monument.

Fooling the eye is all part of the job. A clever designer can create the illusion of a vast room while constructing only a small corner. The epic sea battle in 1959's *Ben-Hur* skillfully blends closeups of the actors in motion with footage of miniature ships floating on dyed water. Designers use such tricks of the trade whenever necessary, but their commitment to authenticity can also go to extraordinary lengths. For *All the President's Men* (1976), George Jenkins re-created not only the *Washington Post* newsroom but even the kinds of trash found in reporters' wastepaper baskets. For director Josef von Sternberg, the products of his imagination took on a certain authenticity. After creating his own sets for *Shanghai Express* in 1932, he visited China and declared the real thing disappointing.

In North by Northwest, Cary Grant and Eva Marie Saint pause under Thomas Jefferson's chin (left) as they flee from villains.

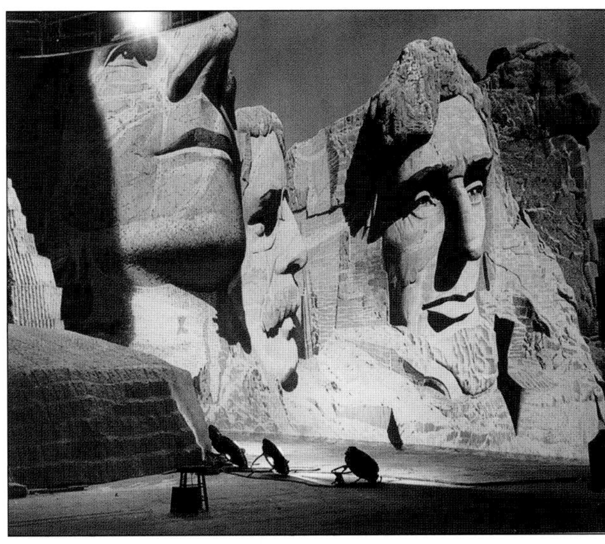

Lights illuminate a plaster replica of Mount Rushmore, built at the MGM studio after Hitchcock was denied use of the real thing.

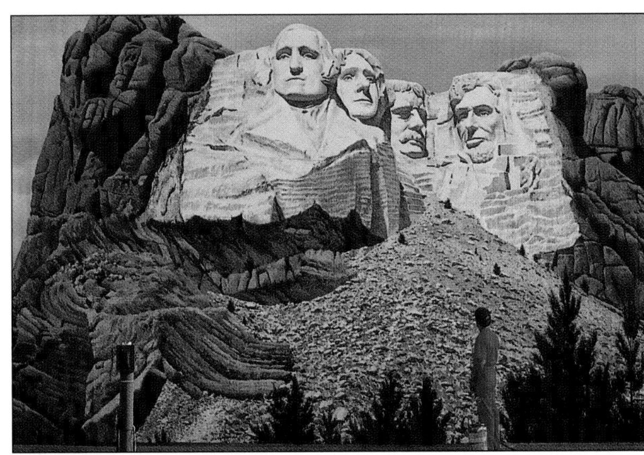

A painted backdrop depicts the carved stone faces of George Washington, Thomas Jefferson, Theodore Roosevelt, and Abraham Lincoln.

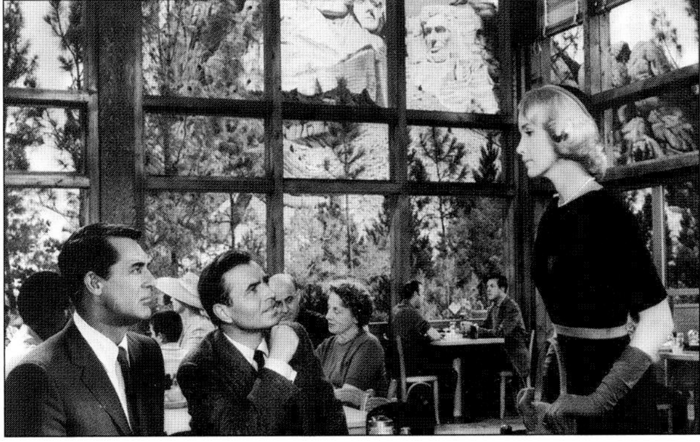

The real Rushmore makes its only appearance in this scene, filmed on location in South Dakota with Grant, James Mason, and Saint.

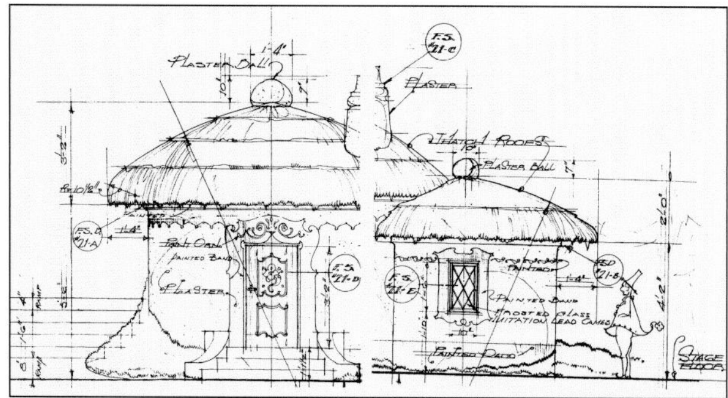

A drawing by artist Jack Martin Smith specifies the dimensions of Munchkin houses and the materials to be used in constructing them. The tiny mushroom-shaped cottages with thatched roofs were scaled to the size of the Munchkins—played by dwarfs in the film.

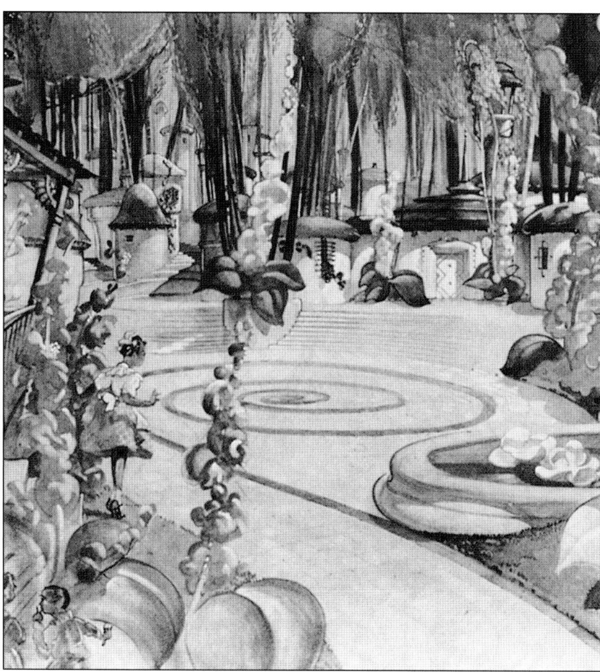

This sketch is an artist's conception of the set for Munchkinland. The mythical place consisted of 122 structures, built at one-fourth normal size and arrayed on terraces around a pool. Flowers towered 10 feet high to make the Munchkins appear even smaller.

Dorothy, played by Judy Garland, stands awestruck in Munchkinland (opposite). "I've a feeling we're not in Kansas anymore," she exclaims. The bridge, pool, and flowers are part of the constructed set, whereas the houses combine painted cutouts and a muslin backdrop.

A World That Wasn't. When work began on *The Wizard of Oz* (1939), the art department at MGM was considered by many the best in the business. For this movie it had to be. Although this was an era when films were shot much more often in the studio than on location—and painted sets did duty as Paris or the Himalaya—the scenery for *The Wizard of Oz* posed a special challenge: The world to be created had existed only in the imagination of author L. Frank Baum.

Bringing it to life was the task of designer William Horning, a qualified architect whom one of his assistants called "extremely practical, ferociously intelligent, and hard as nails." The original book contained no illustration of Munchkinland, so Horning had to dream the place up and then build it to the scale of its diminutive residents. Even harder was envisioning the Emerald City. As the home of the Wizard of Oz, it needed to surpass the rest of the settings in surreal magic. The head of MGM's art department, Cedric Gibbons, eventually came across an old German drawing of a fantasy city that looked like "test tubes upside down," one artist said.

Creating the sets was further complicated by the use of Technicolor. This process, still in its infancy, was cumbersome and unpredictable, and the art department had to learn a new color vocabulary. One employee spent a week finding a shade of paint for the yellow brick road that would not appear green on film. Another color-related problem, making the carriage horse in Oz turn every hue of the rainbow, was solved by using a succession of horses and sponging each one down with a different variety of Jell-O powder. The animals did, however, tend to lick off most of the Jell-O between shots.

In all, about 60 *Oz* sets were built on six different sound stages, as nearly 1,000 carpenters, painters, and other craftsmen labored frantically to stay a week ahead of the shooting schedule. On film the world they created was obviously imaginary—but still so vivid that when Dorothy gazes around and concludes, "We must be over the rainbow," generations of audiences have agreed.

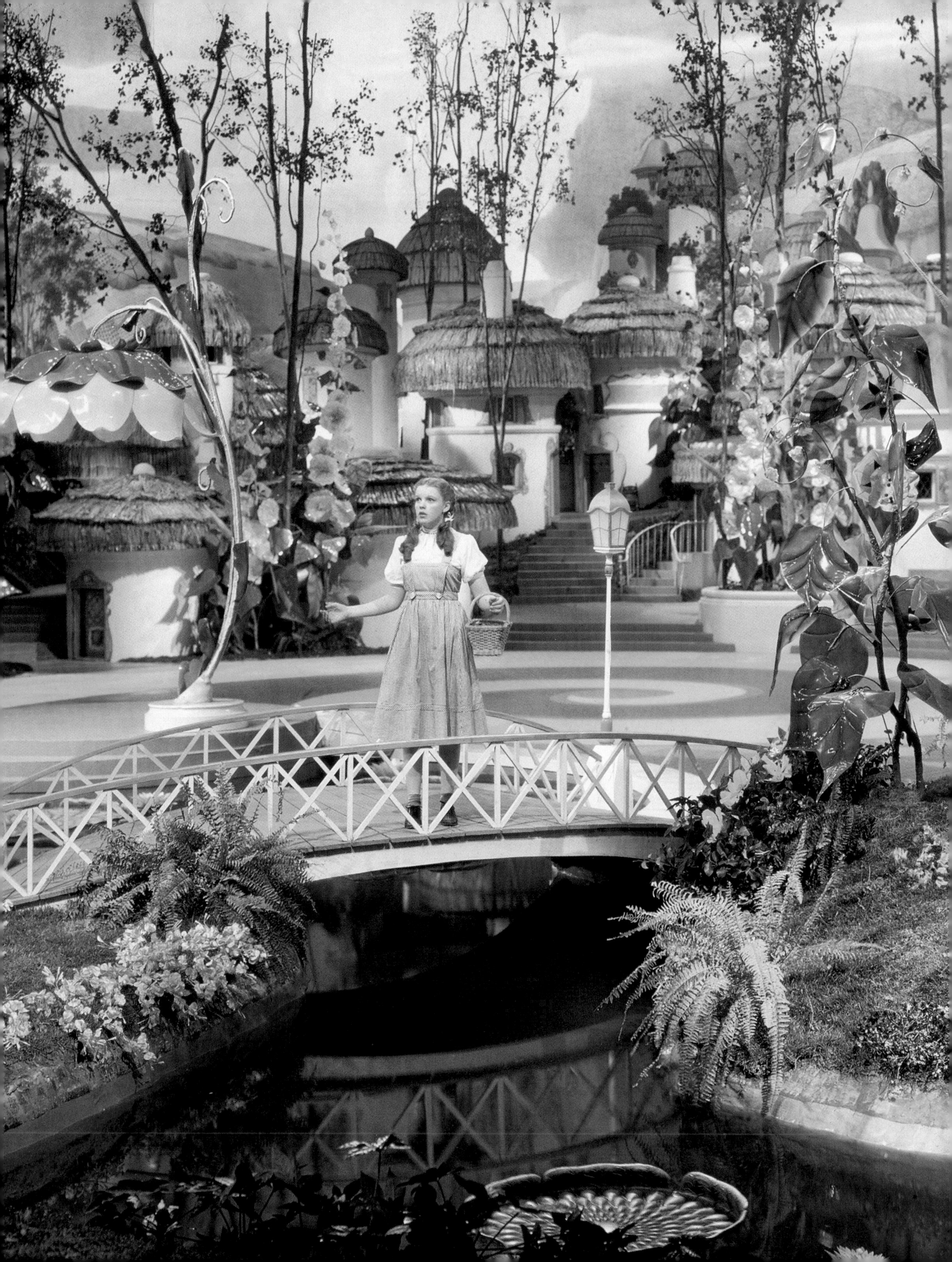

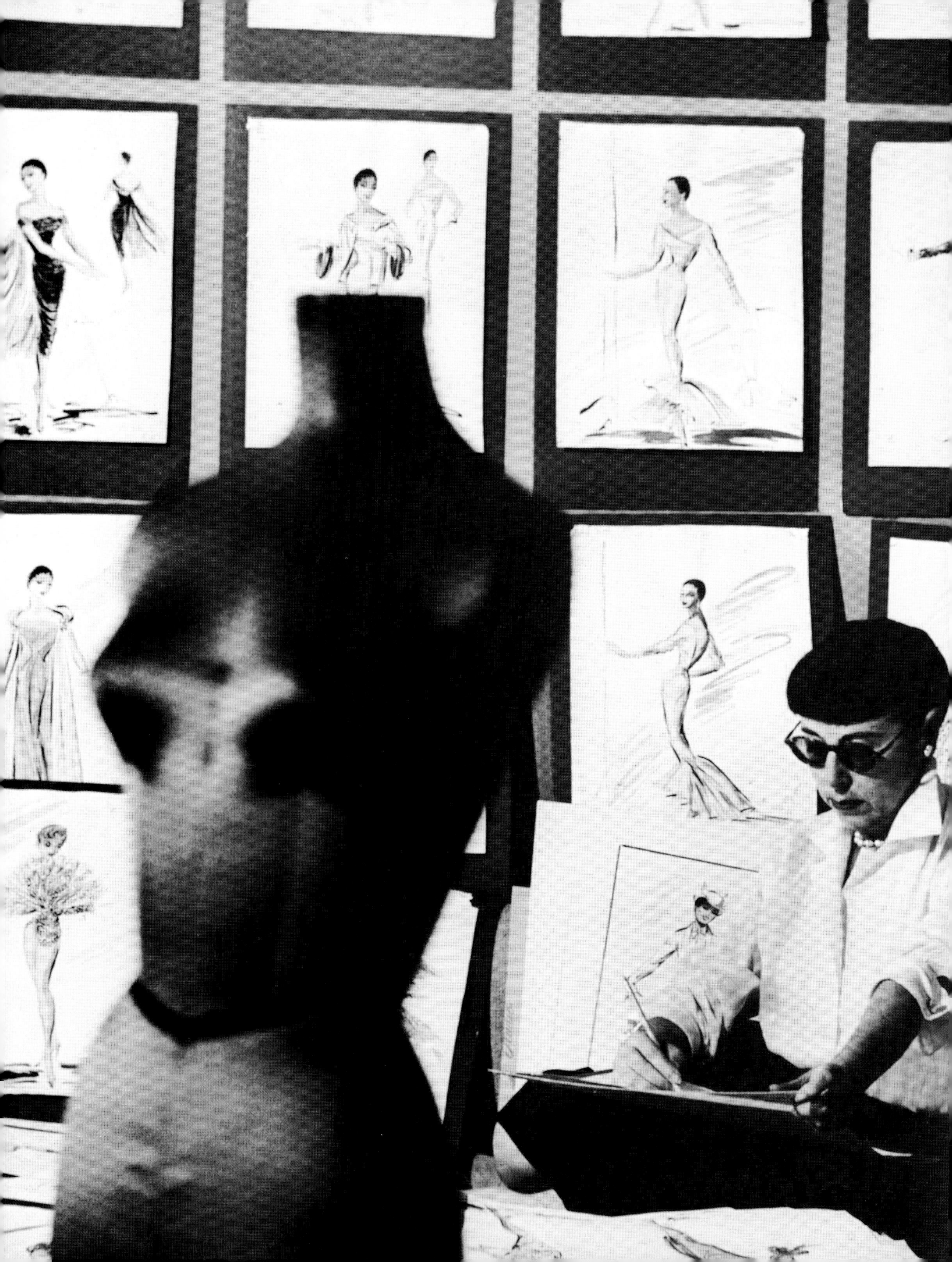

Dressing the Stars with Drama

I want my clothes loose enough to prove I'm a lady, but tight enough to show 'em I'm a woman," Mae West told the designer costuming her for 1933's *She Done Him Wrong.* Edith Head complied, outlining the star's voluptuous form to such effect that she helped make the film a smash. West praised "Edith's things" for being "allurin' without being vulgar." They had, she said, "just a little *insinuendo* about them."

In a career that spanned more than half a century, Head *(at left, sketching in her studio)* costumed the stars in more than 500 films. As Paramount's chief designer at the height of the studio era, she supervised dozens of fitters, cutters, seamstresses, and milliners. Few expenses were spared: Six or eight employees might spend weeks sewing beads onto a single gown. For *The Jungle Princess* (1936) she wrapped an unknown named Dorothy Lamour in a boldly patterned sarong that became Lamour's trademark and established a new fashion on American beaches. The $35,000 mink dress she created for Ginger Rogers in *Lady in the Dark* (1944) became a Hollywood legend for its extravagance. She was still working into the 1970s, doing polyester miniskirts and bell-bottom pantsuits for *Airport* and outfitting Paul Newman and Robert Redford as dapper 1930s con men in *The Sting.*

Head saw herself, she said, as "a combination of psychiatrist, artist, fashion designer, dressmaker, pincushion, historian, nursemaid, and purchasing agent." "In her dressing room," said actress Arlene Dahl, "you had no secrets—you were stripped bare." One of Head's own secrets was to never upstage the star. She kept her appearance so plain that she once made Hollywood's worst-dressed list.

No one else came near Head's record of 35 Academy Award nominations and eight Oscars. But British

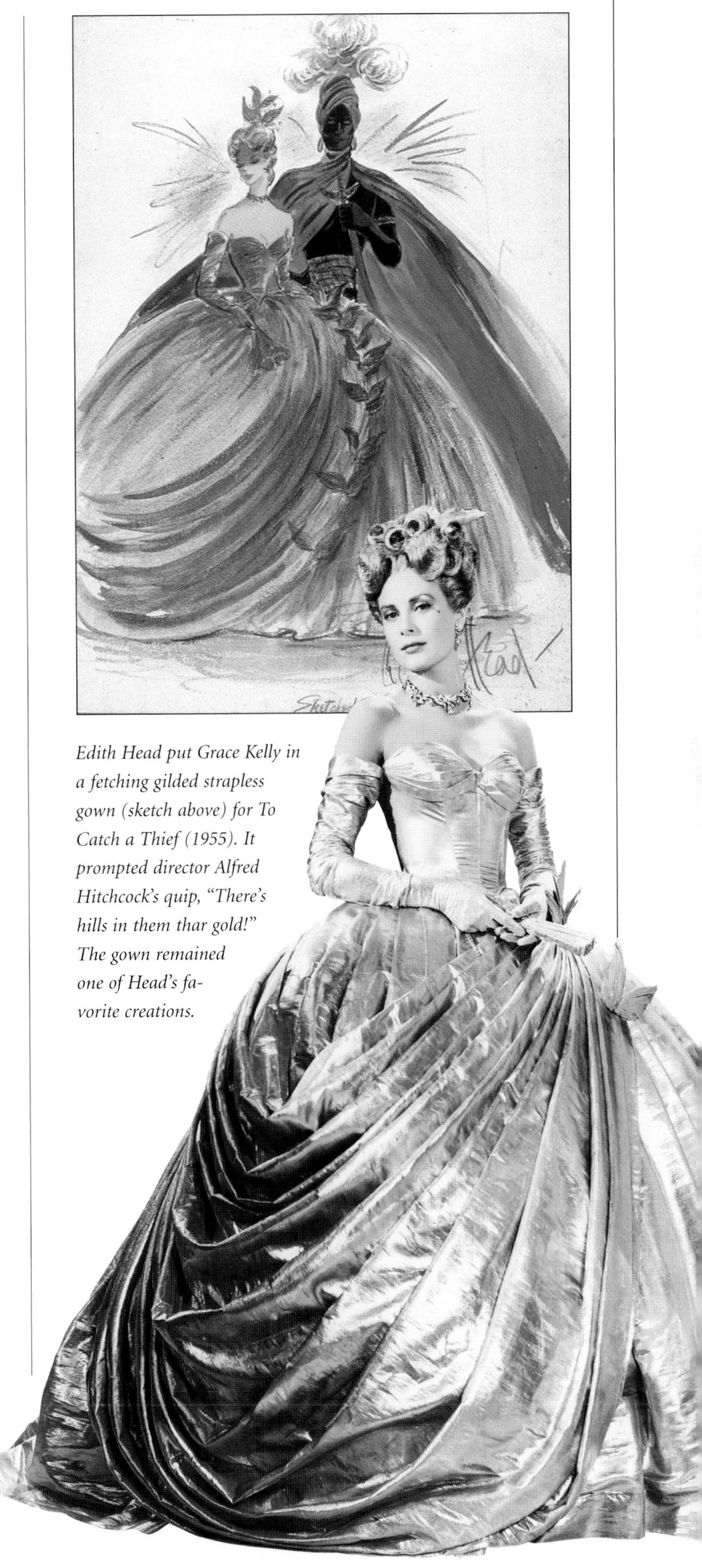

Edith Head put Grace Kelly in a fetching gilded strapless gown (sketch above) for To Catch a Thief (1955). It prompted director Alfred Hitchcock's quip, "There's hills in them thar gold!" The gown remained one of Head's favorite creations.

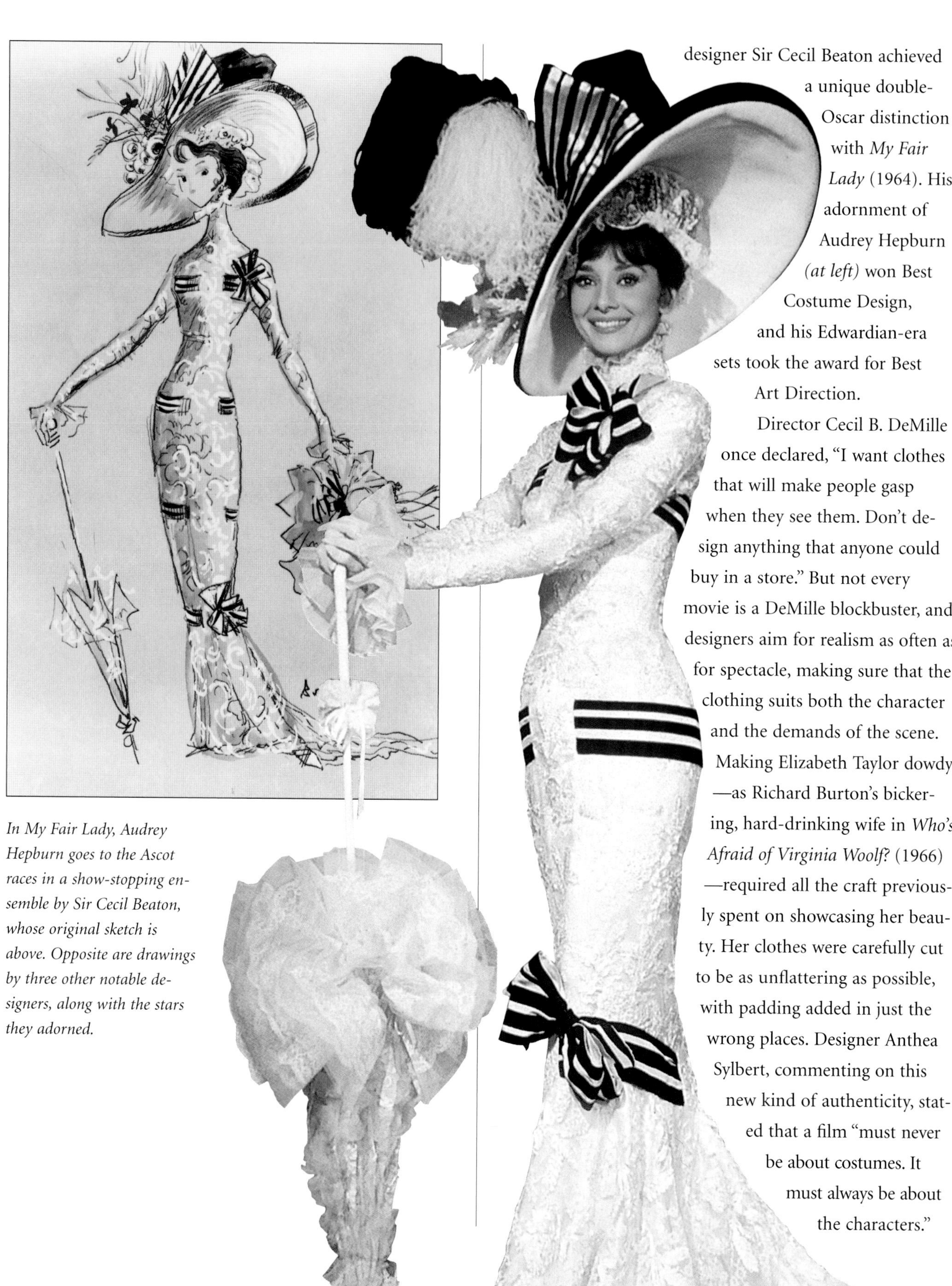

In My Fair Lady, Audrey Hepburn goes to the Ascot races in a show-stopping ensemble by Sir Cecil Beaton, whose original sketch is above. Opposite are drawings by three other notable designers, along with the stars they adorned.

designer Sir Cecil Beaton achieved a unique double-Oscar distinction with *My Fair Lady* (1964). His adornment of Audrey Hepburn *(at left)* won Best Costume Design, and his Edwardian-era sets took the award for Best Art Direction.

Director Cecil B. DeMille once declared, "I want clothes that will make people gasp when they see them. Don't design anything that anyone could buy in a store." But not every movie is a DeMille blockbuster, and designers aim for realism as often as for spectacle, making sure that the clothing suits both the character and the demands of the scene. Making Elizabeth Taylor dowdy—as Richard Burton's bickering, hard-drinking wife in *Who's Afraid of Virginia Woolf?* (1966)—required all the craft previously spent on showcasing her beauty. Her clothes were carefully cut to be as unflattering as possible, with padding added in just the wrong places. Designer Anthea Sylbert, commenting on this new kind of authenticity, stated that a film "must never be about costumes. It must always be about the characters."

Marilyn Monroe, *There's No Business Like Show Business* (1954)—William Travilla

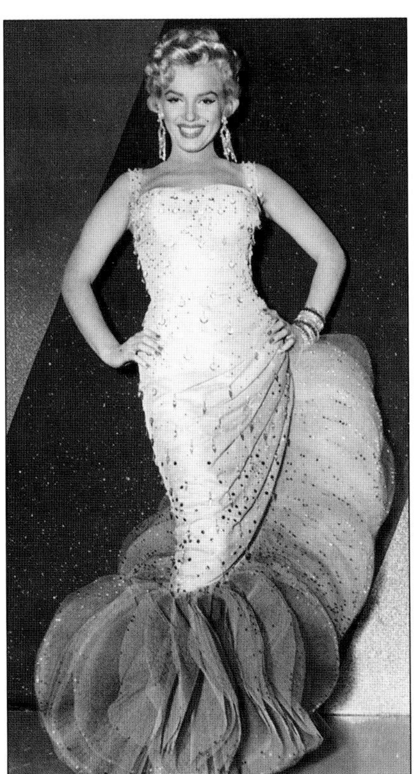

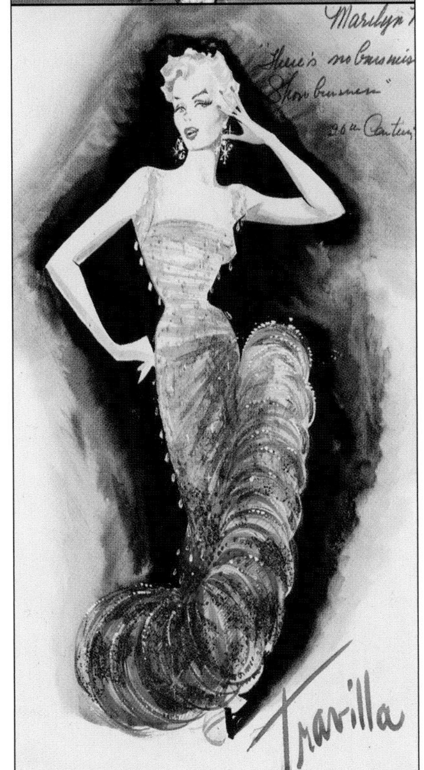

Faye Dunaway, *Bonnie and Clyde* (1967)—Theadora Van Runkle

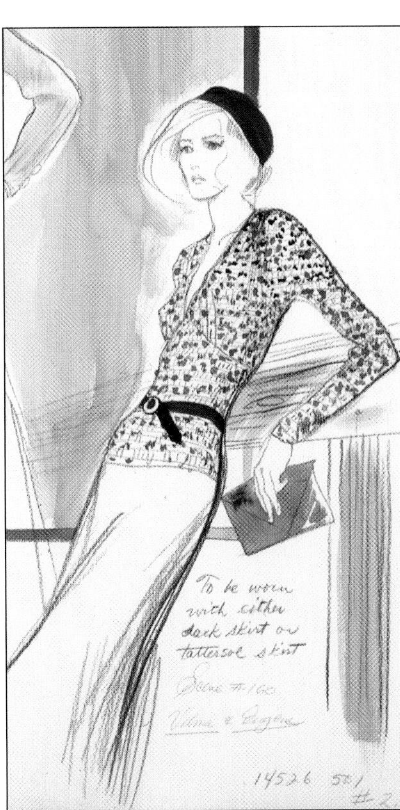

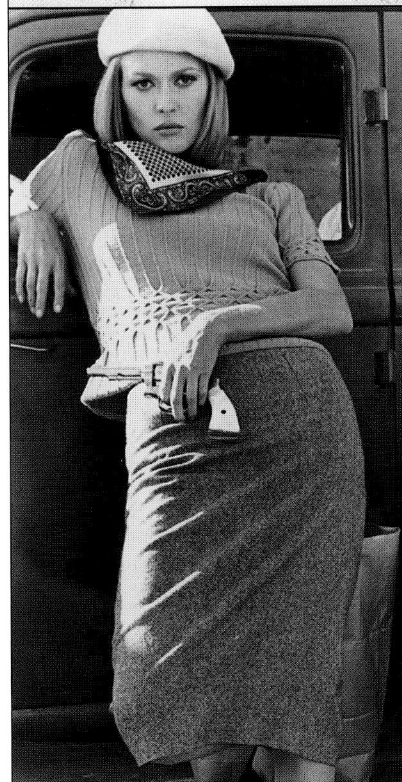

Kate Capshaw, *Indiana Jones and the Temple of Doom* (1984)—Anthony Powell

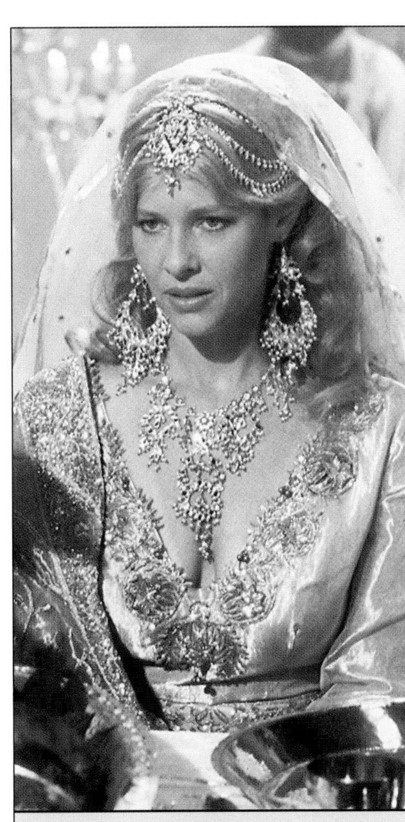

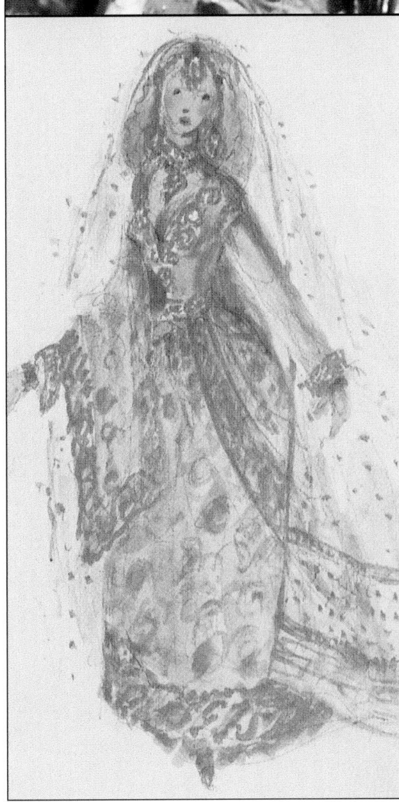

Makeup: The Magic of Transformation

The artists who apply movie makeup usually remain faceless. The exceptions are the remarkable Westmores, a four-generation makeup dynasty whose members have become Hollywood celebrities in their own right. In 1917 George Westmore, a former wigmaker, began beautifying silent-film stars. His six sons all followed in his footsteps, and during the 1930s the makeup department of every major studio was headed by a Westmore. Three of George's grandsons continued the Westmore tradition, as did several members of the next generation.

Since George Westmore's time, the task of writing a story on the tablet of the human face has grown increasingly complex. Modern movie makeup relies heavily on prosthetics—artificial features made out of rubbery material that can add dramatic scars or wrinkles or turn a human into an alien or a monster. For *Little Big Man* (1970), makeup artist Dick Smith had to change 33-year-old Dustin Hoffman *(inset)* into a 121-year-old survivor of the Old West. Smith began by studying the faces of old men. Then, using a plaster cast of Hoffman's head as a base, he sculpted wrinkled features in clay. Molds made from each of these clay features were filled with liquid latex, which hardened into the prosthetics. This method allowed Smith to produce a fresh set of prosthetics—painted with age spots and veins—for each day's filming. It took five hours to position and glue all the pieces onto Hoffman's face and then to paint more liquid latex around the edges to blend them with his skin. The final effect was so powerful that people on the set found themselves helping Hoffman out of his chair or offering him an arm as if he really were an old man.

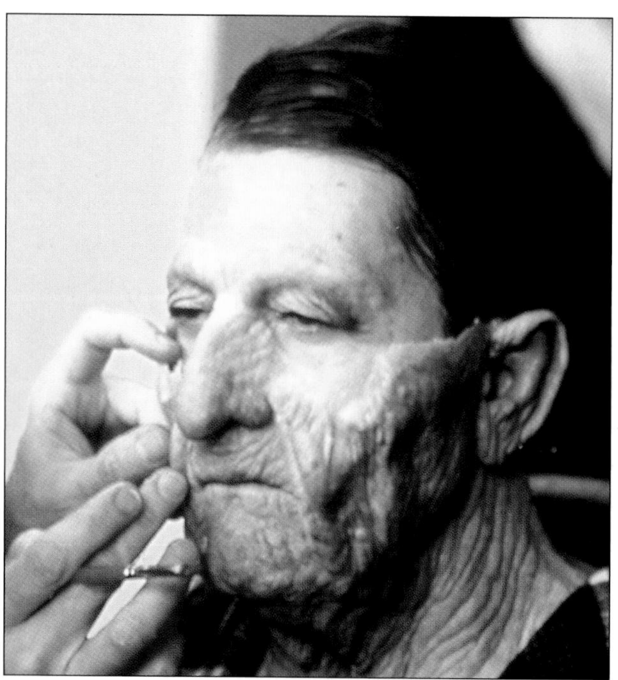

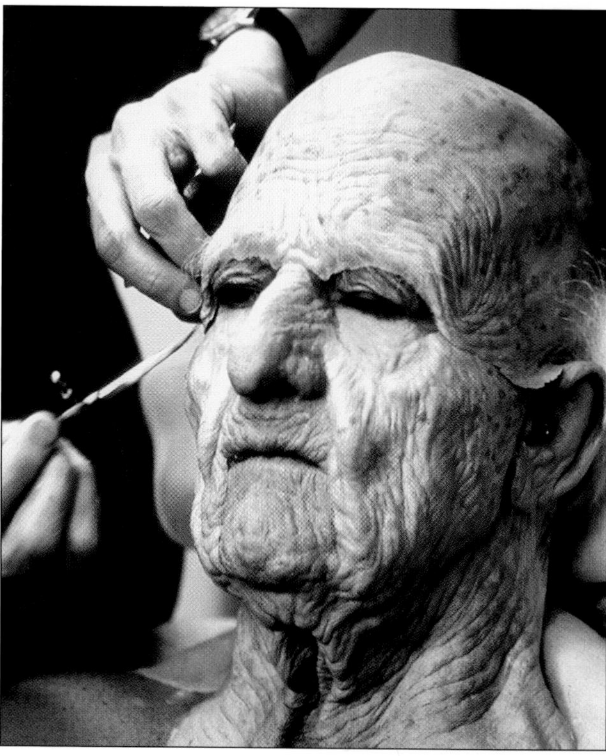

For his role in 1970's Little Big Man, Dustin Hoffman undergoes a lengthy makeup ordeal (above). The carefully crafted latex features that were applied to his skin weighed several pounds altogether—but the result was dramatic, convincingly turning Hoffman into a former frontiersman (right) who claimed to be 121 years old.

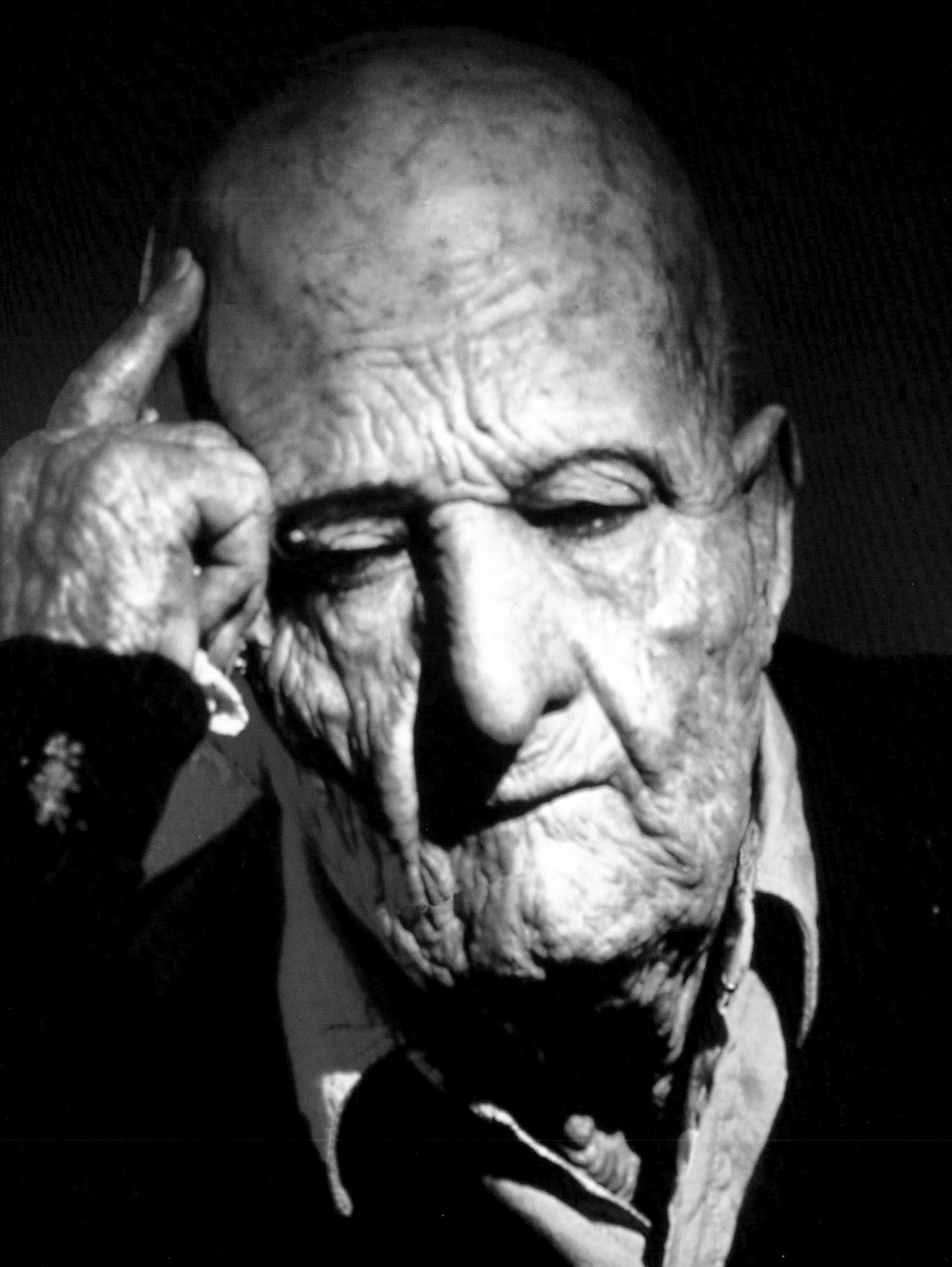

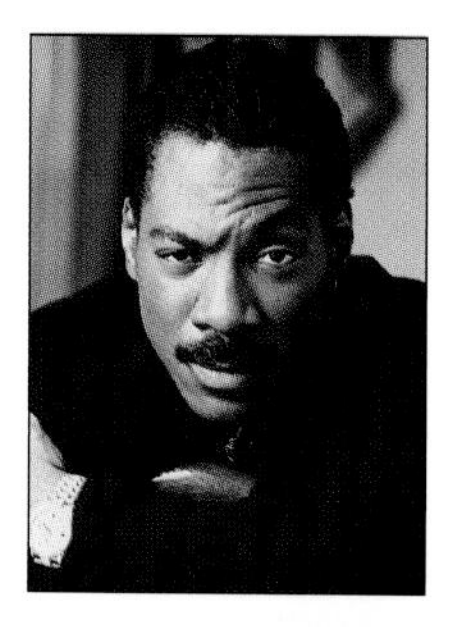

In 1996's The Nutty Professor, Eddie Murphy (left) played seven different roles. The title character is obese chemistry professor Sherman Klump, who tinkers with his own DNA and transforms himself into slim Buddy Love. These two characters were only the beginning for makeup artists Rick Baker and David LeRoy Anderson, who had to make Murphy over for five more parts—workout guru Lance Perkins and four other Klumps. The film won an Oscar for Best Makeup.

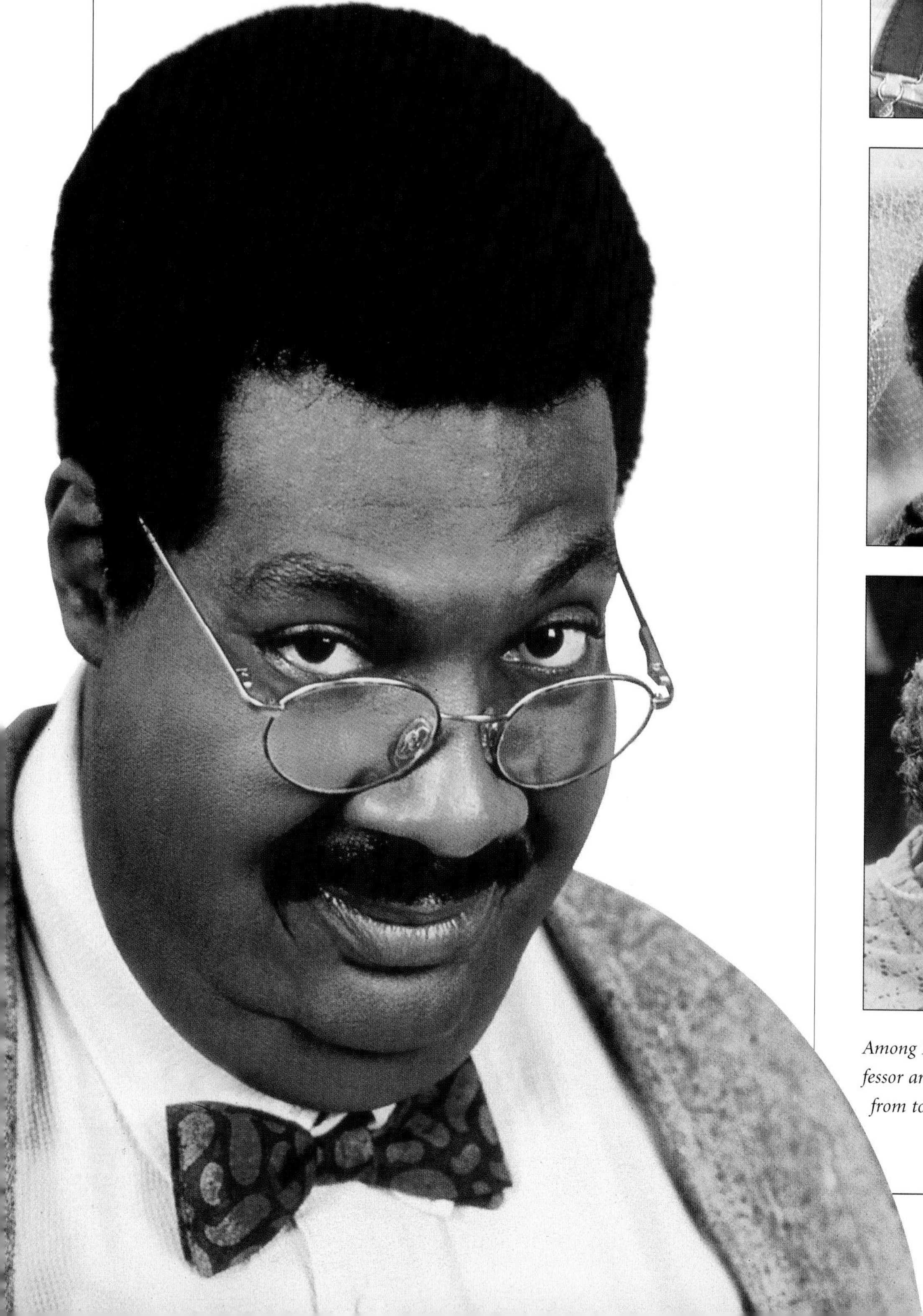

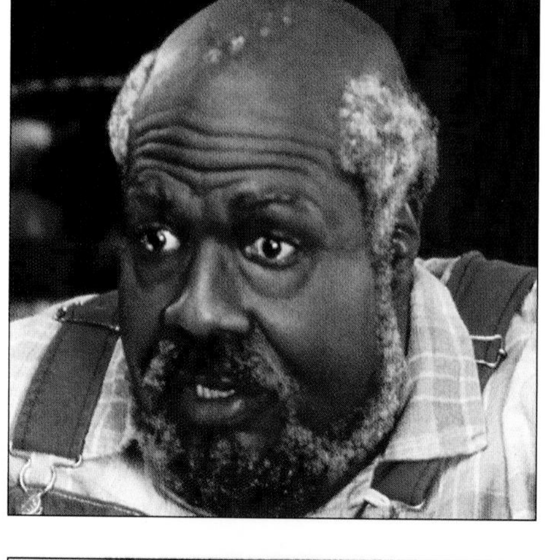

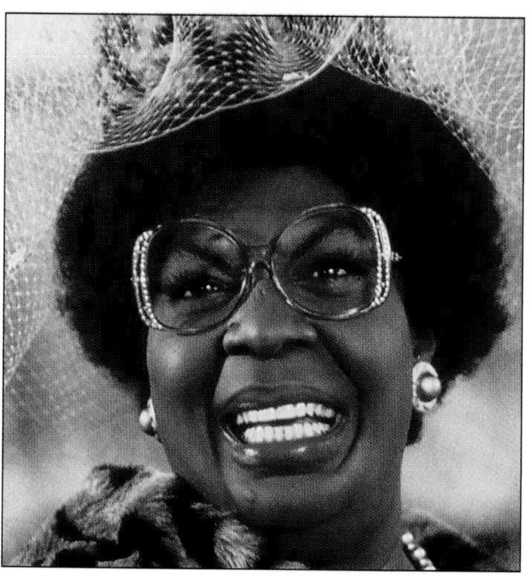

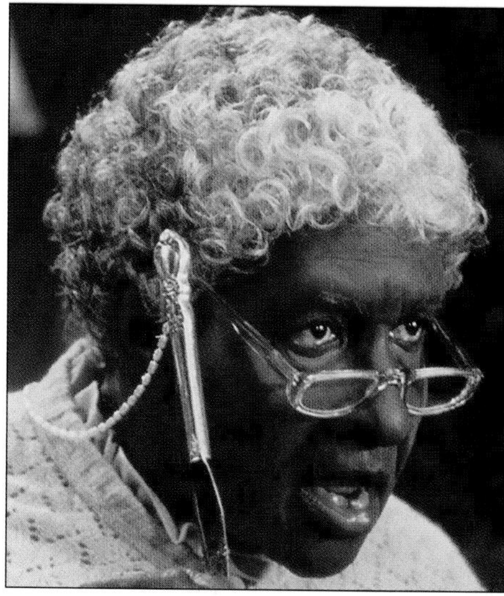

Among Eddie Murphy's roles in The Nutty Professor are, at left, Professor Sherman Klump and, from top, Papa, Mama, and Grandma Klump.

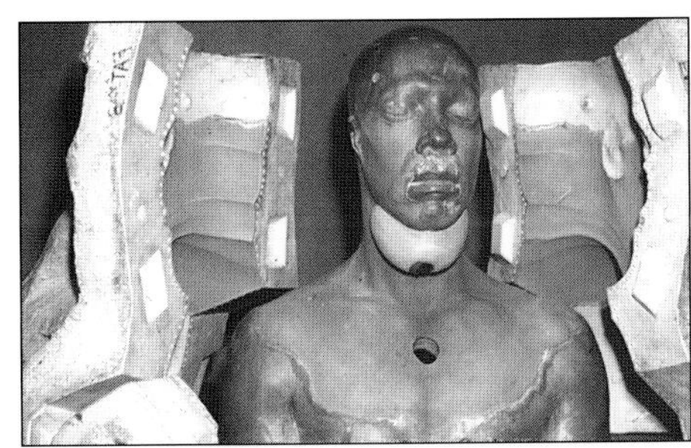

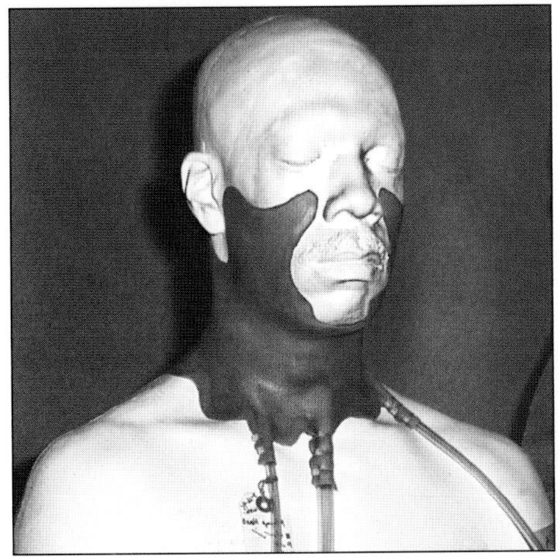

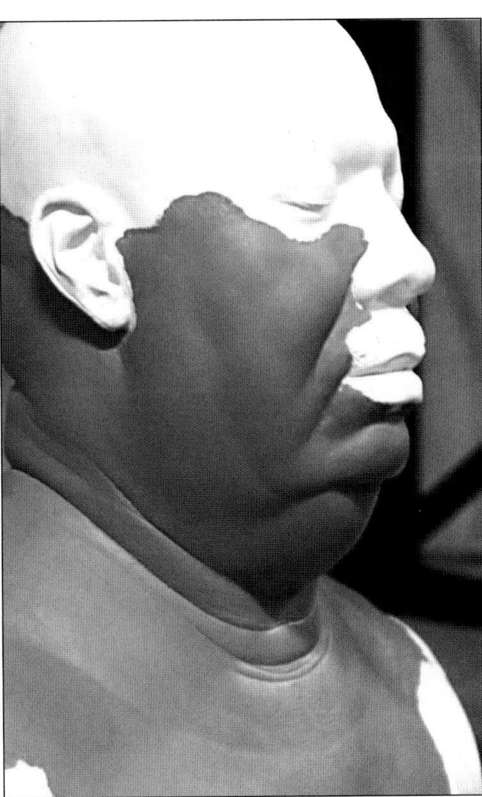

As makeup artists formed prosthetics for Eddie Murphy, they worked from a cast of his head and shoulders (left) and from concept sculptures of Sherman Klump's enormous body (below). One of the most daunting tasks was making the pieces of imitation fat "move and squish like flesh," as makeup artist Rick Baker put it. After a variety of experiments, Baker and his crew found that they could produce the desired effect by using condoms filled with water as one of the components of the "fat."

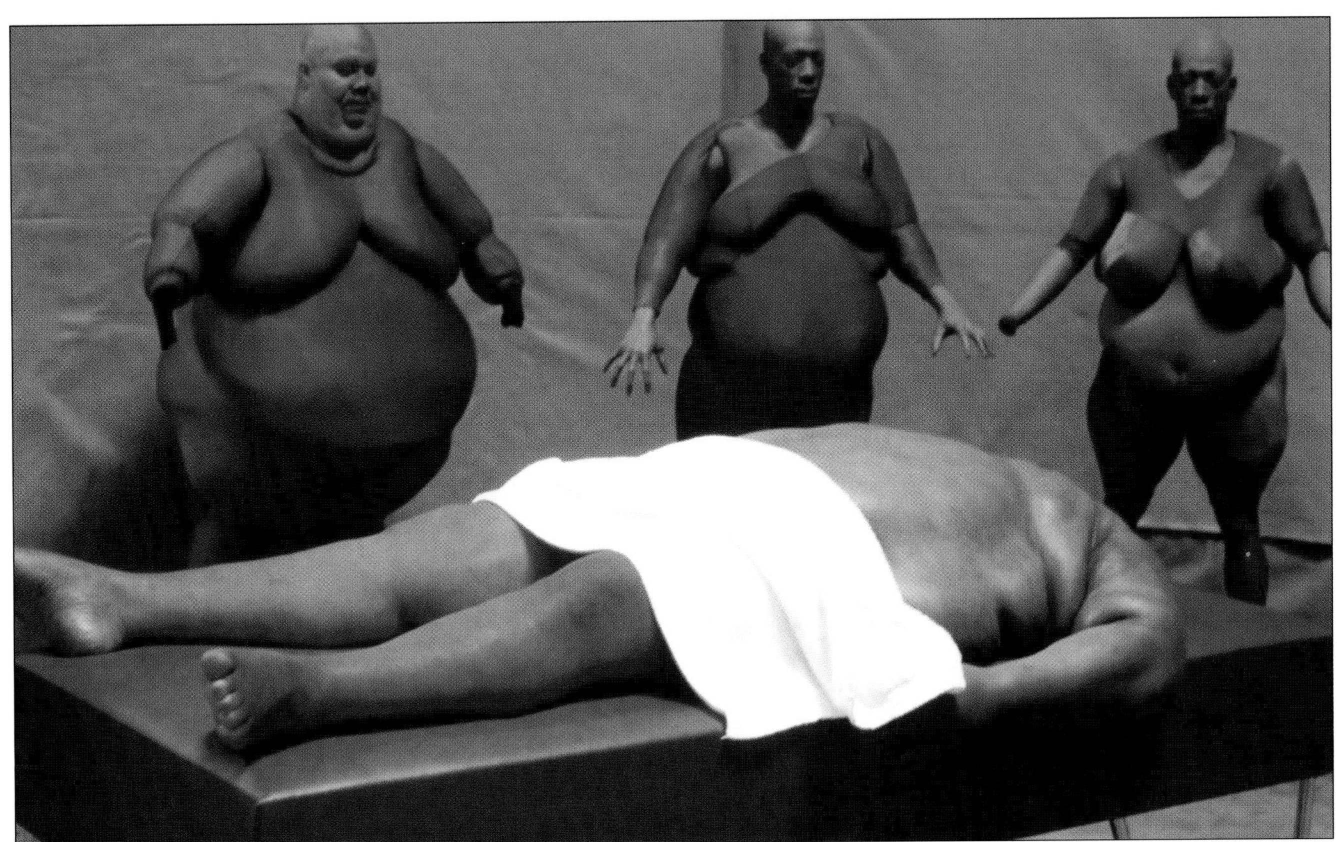

Capturing the Story in the Camera's Eye

When I read a script and like the story, I respond to it on an emotional level," cinematographer Janusz Kaminski said. "I then imagine how I can enhance the storytelling through visuals." As director of photography for *Saving Private Ryan* (1998), Kaminski had the challenge of making the camera translate filmmaker Steven Spielberg's vision into reality. For its first 25 minutes this powerful World War II drama focuses unrelentingly on the carnage and chaos of the Allies' D-Day landing on the Omaha Beach sector of France's Normandy coast. After studying actual combat footage and photographs, especially the work of legendary *Life* magazine photojournalist Robert Capa, Spielberg and Kaminski decided the film should, as Kaminski put it, "look like it was shot in 16 mm by a bunch of combat cameramen."

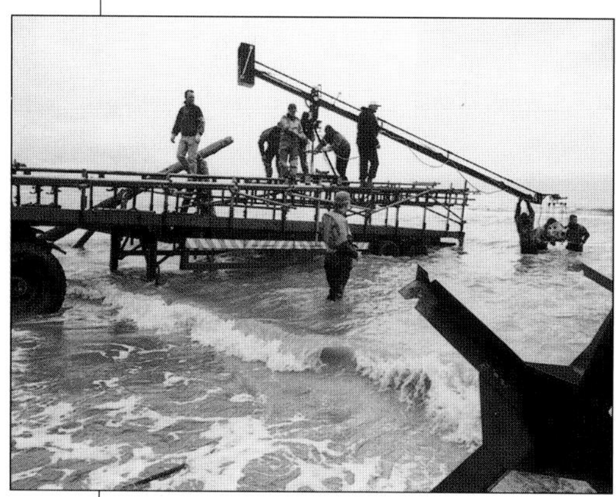

To achieve this sense of realism, Kaminski had his camera operators shoot mostly with hand-held cameras. They simulated the frenetic quality of combat with deliberately out-of-sync shutters and special devices that shook the cameras. If water or artificial blood splattered the lenses, Kaminski said, "we kept shooting because that's what we assumed would happen in reality."

Kaminski also manipulated the lighting. Because he wanted a "kind of burned-out, bleary sky," he had the protective coating stripped from lenses for flatter contrast. Overhead silk canopies and heavy black smoke helped diminish sunlight. And to enhance the documentary look, he extracted roughly 60 percent of the color from the final negative—creating muted tones. For making the camera "a real participant in the film," as a colleague put it, Kaminski received an Academy Award for Best Cinematography.

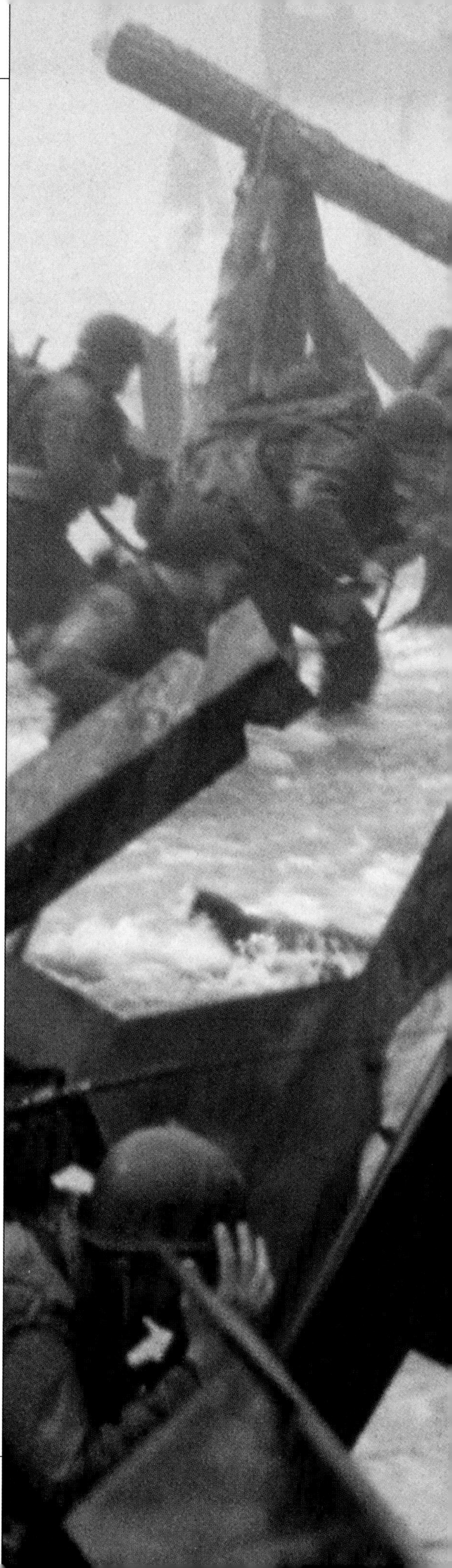

The GIs of Saving Private Ryan struggle through enemy obstacles on Omaha Beach (right). Above, the crew prepares to shoot with a crane-mounted camera.

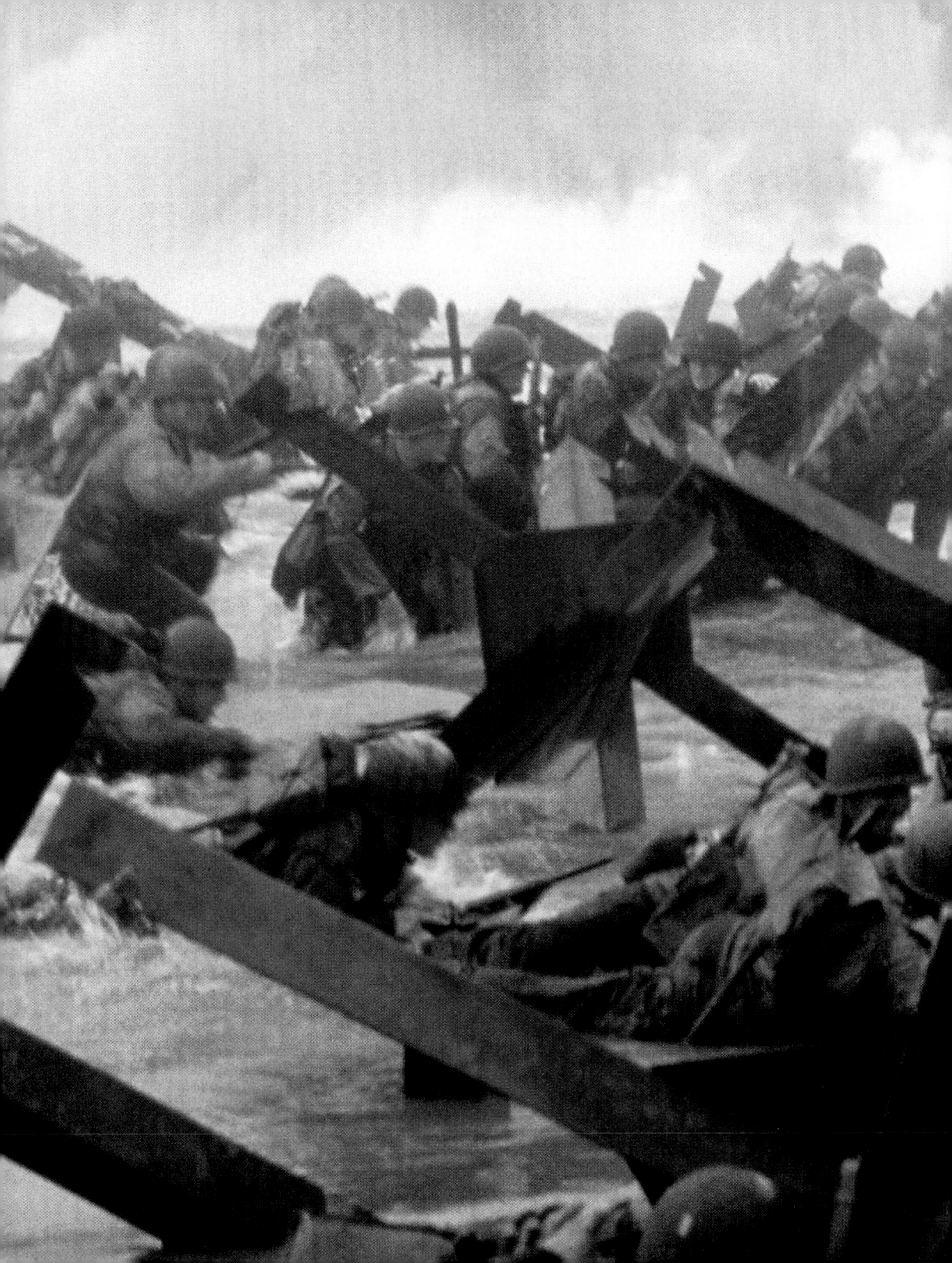

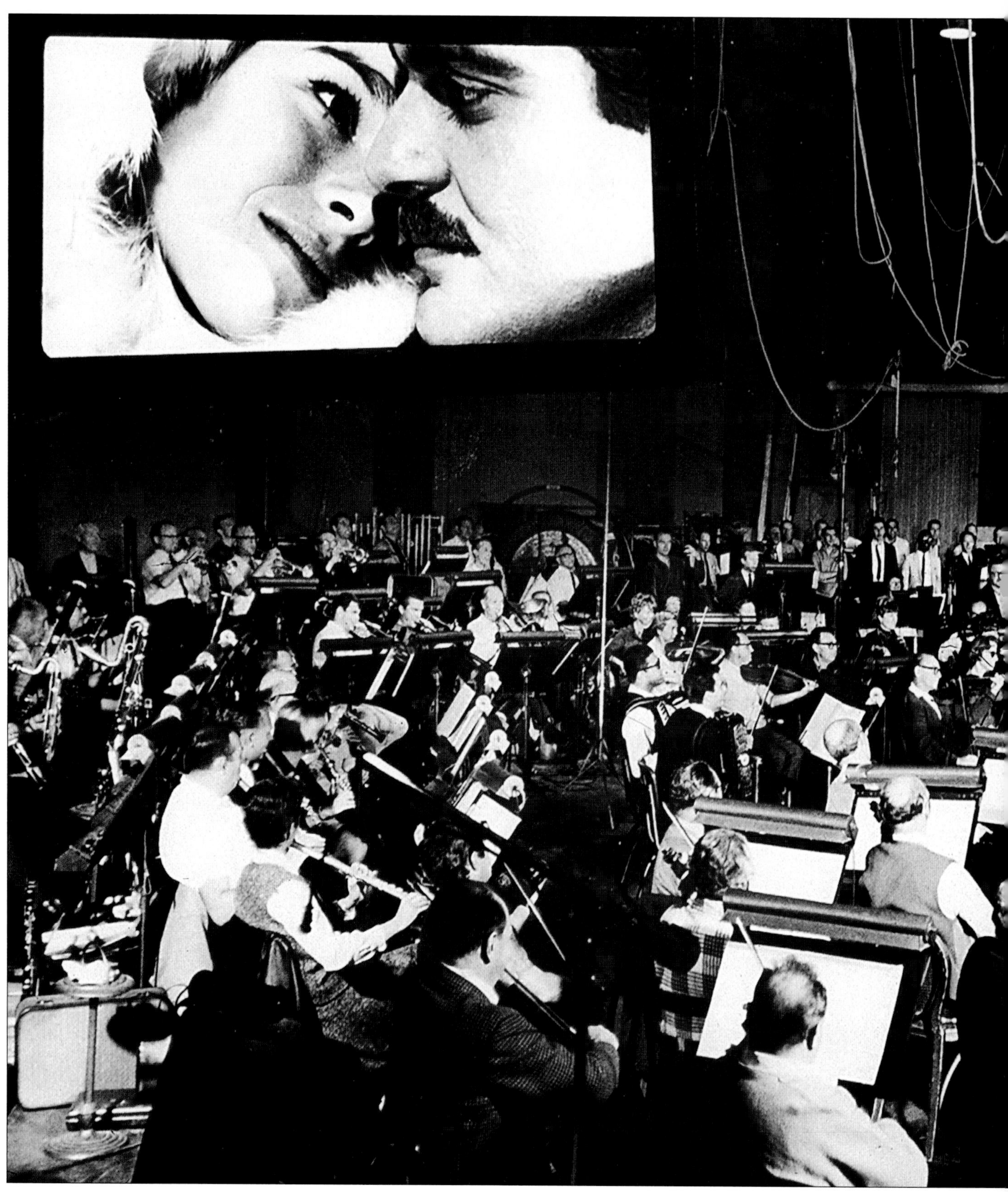

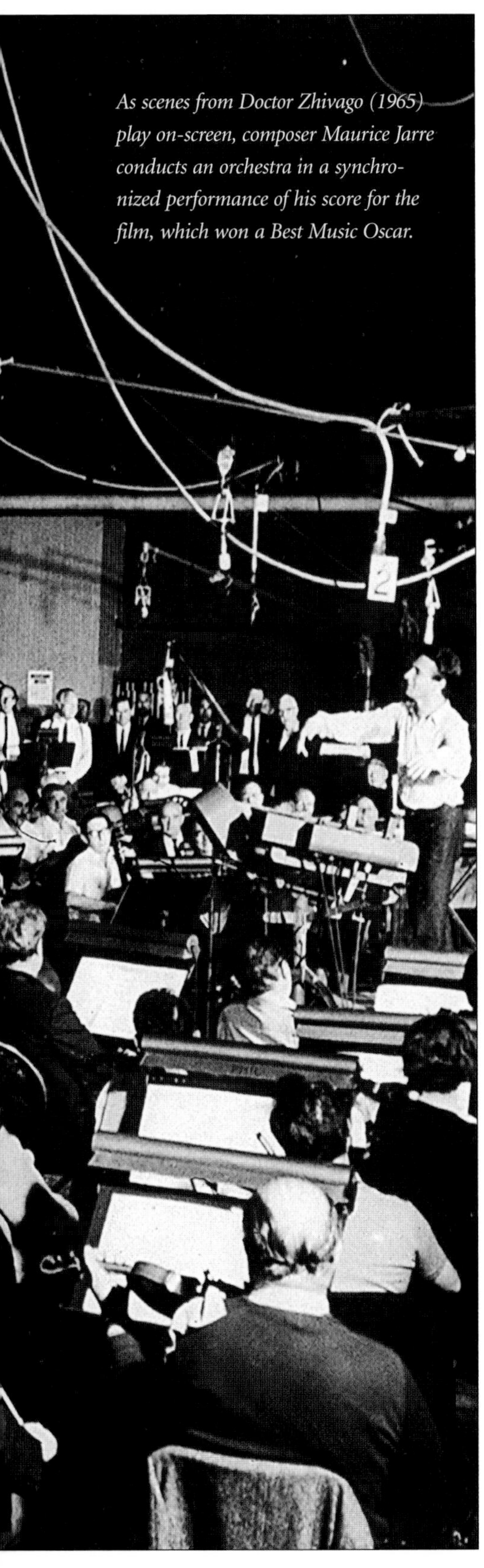
As scenes from Doctor Zhivago (1965) play on-screen, composer Maurice Jarre conducts an orchestra in a synchronized performance of his score for the film, which won a Best Music Oscar.

The Sound of Movies

In the days of silent film, live organ music added drama to the action on-screen. Since the advent of sound in 1927, movie scores have played the same role, enhancing the mood and sometimes providing a hit song that helps sell tickets.

The best-known modern scores are those of composer-conductor John Williams. In 1975 his ominous theme for *Jaws* sharpened the suspense of impending shark attacks—and paid tribute to Bernard Herrmann's music for the 1960 thriller *Psycho.* The sweeping orchestral odyssey Williams created for the Star Wars films almost single-handedly brought symphonic scores back into style.

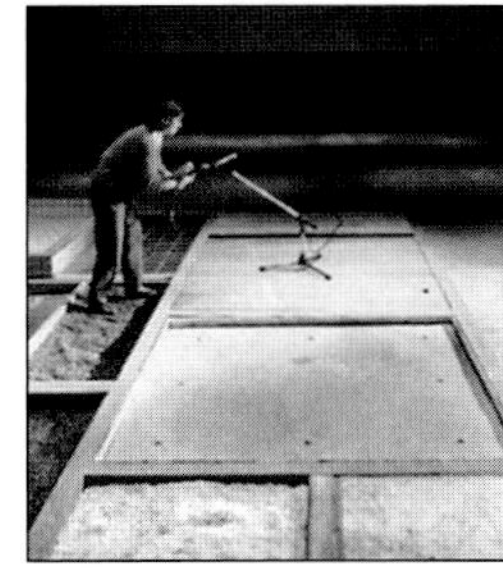
A Foley artist at work

During filming, microphones also capture dialogue, which actors may rerecord later as needed. Other noises, such as a gunshot, usually come from a library of recordings. A Foley stage *(inset)*—invented by movie sound pioneer Jack Foley—provides a variety of surfaces for creating sounds. There a "Foley artist" can reproduce, for example, the cadence of a woman's footsteps on a marble floor. On the set, microphones may have been arranged to catch dialogue more clearly at the expense of such sounds; adding them back in heightens realism. Foley artists also specialize in innovative sound effects—like squeezing an open bottle of dishwashing detergent to simulate the sound of a dinosaur egg hatching.

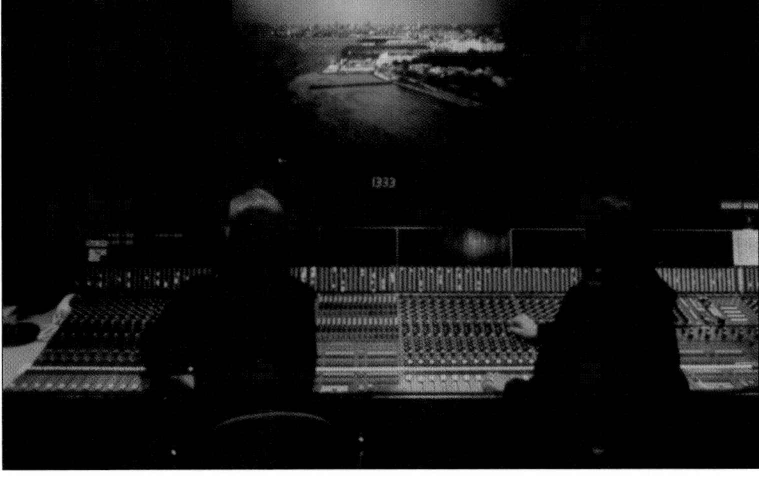
At the mixing board in a recording studio, specialists perfect the combination of music, dialogue, and sound effects that audiences will hear on a film's soundtrack.

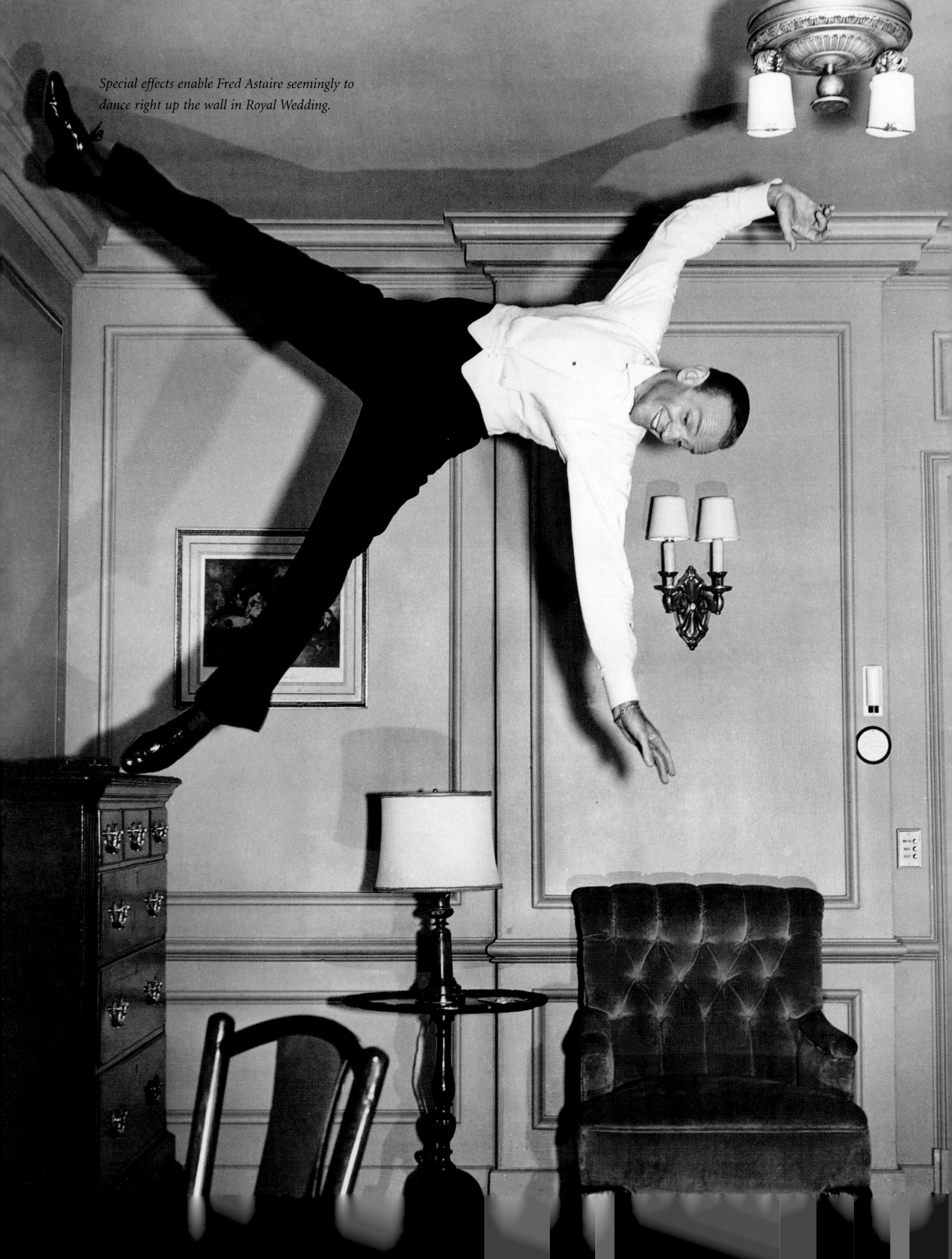

Special effects enable Fred Astaire seemingly to dance right up the wall in Royal Wedding.

Believable Make-Believe

Fred Astaire *(left)* was so high on love that he defied gravity in 1951's *Royal Wedding,* climbing the walls of his hotel room and tap-dancing across the ceiling. How did he do it? The room turned upside down, not the dancer. The set—with furniture, camera, and cameraman anchored to its floor—was placed in a revolving cage that turned while Astaire danced.

This trick was Astaire's own inspiration, but usually the ideas behind such illusions come from special-effects experts. The very first of them was Georges Méliès, a French magician turned filmmaker, who in *The Conjuror* (1899) made himself and his assistant disappear.

Over the next century special effects took on an ever higher level of sophistication. In *The Wizard of Oz,* MGM's legendary Arnold Gillespie "melted" the Wicked Witch of the West by standing actress Margaret Hamilton on a small patch of floor that could be lowered. As she descended, her clothing—pinned to the stationary floor around her—remained behind. Alfred Hitchcock staged frightening avian attacks in *The Birds* (1963) by blending separate footage of diving birds and shrieking actors for some scenes, using mechanical birds for others. Today's visual wizardry can make entire cities go up in fireballs, as they did when alien ships blasted earth in the 1996 blockbuster *Independence Day.*

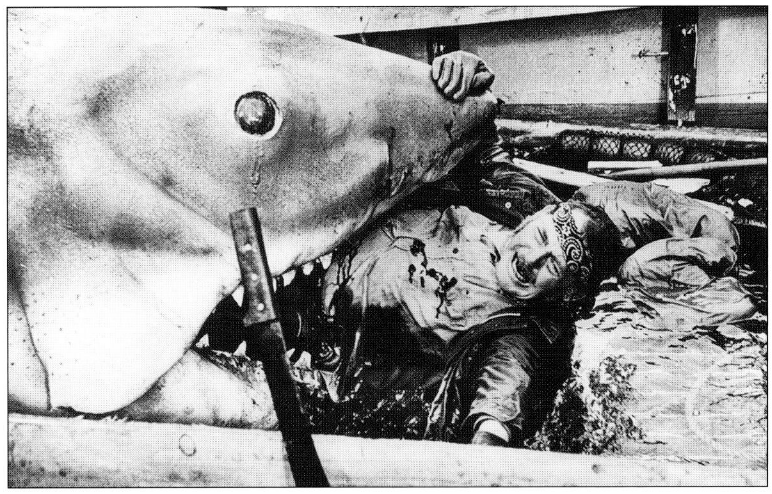

A mechanical shark operated by air pressure devours actor Robert Shaw in Jaws (1975). Three sharks were built, all named Bruce after director Steven Spielberg's lawyer.

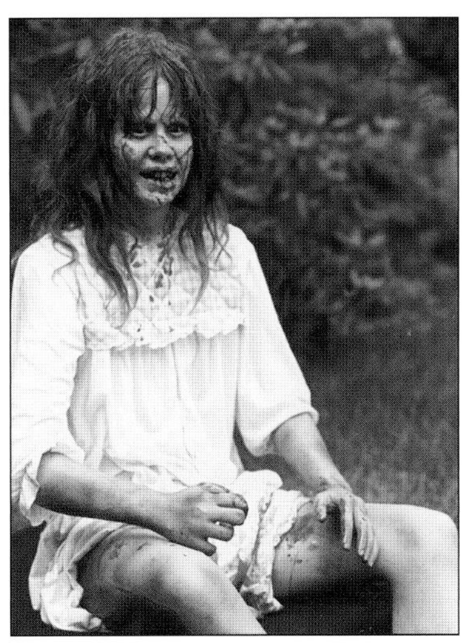

This lifelike dummy with a swivel neck performed the famous scene from The Exorcist (1973) in which Linda Blair's head appeared to turn 360 degrees.

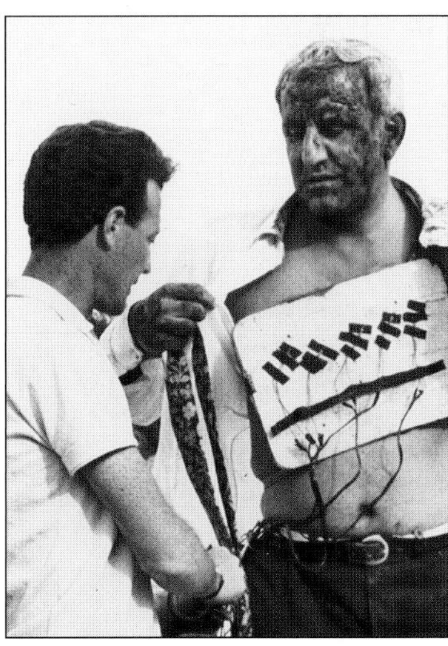

A crewman for Danger: Diabolik (1967) rigs an actor with a remote-controlled device that produces the illusion of bullet wounds. On cue, caps explode, burning bullet holes in the actor's shirt and rupturing sacs of fake blood.

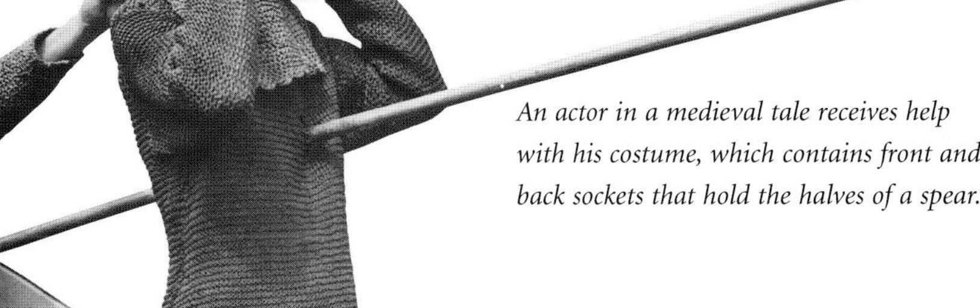

An actor in a medieval tale receives help with his costume, which contains front and back sockets that hold the halves of a spear.

Daredevils at Work

They hurtle through the air, catch fire, fly off cliffs in runaway automobiles, collapse under falling debris. It's all in a day's work for the men and women who perform the stunts. Modern filmmakers recall that silent-film comedian Buster Keaton did his own stunts but had a brush with death when he broke his neck in one of them—and they are rarely willing to take such risks with a star. When the scenes get dangerous, skilled daredevils step in.

Stunt coordinators try to maximize the illusion of danger on the screen while minimizing actual risk. Enormous air bags cushion falls. Special props called breakaways ease the impact of blows. The chair that crashes down on a character's head is made of soft balsa wood held together by toothpicks. Those whiskey bottles in barroom brawls are molded from paraffin. The glass window the hero smashes through is thin plastic, though for a long time the industry used sugar candy. The sound of shattering glass is added to reinforce the illusion.

Spectacular effects often result from clever tricks or optical sleight of hand *(box, opposite)* as well as human derring-do. When a car soars off a cliff, it gets an extra lift from a small ramp placed inconspicuously at the edge of the precipice. The soldier blown into the air by an exploding mine probably sprang off a hidden trampoline. The

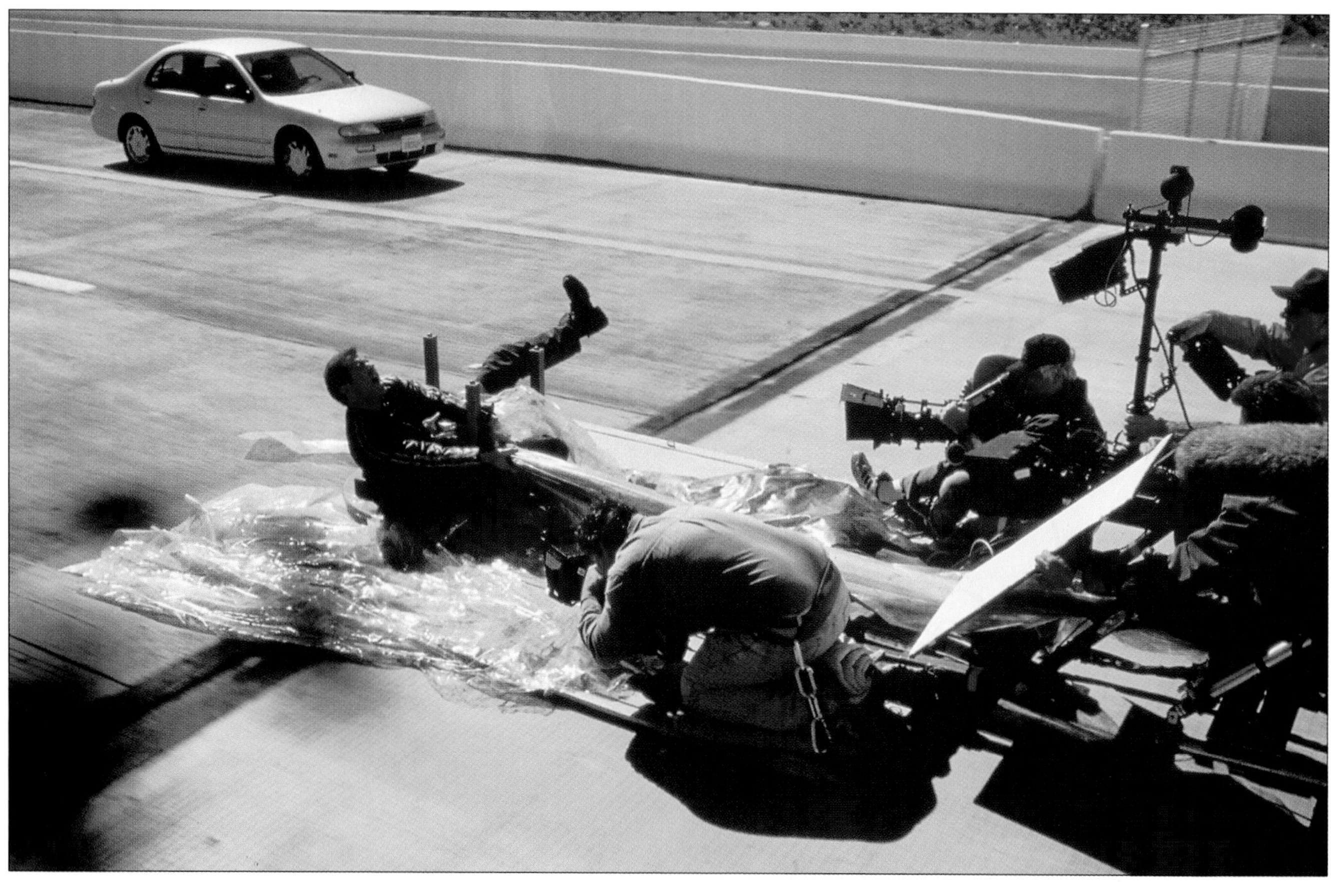

Star Mel Gibson perches atop an upside-down coffee table on a Nevada freeway, as part of a stunt created for Lethal Weapon 4 (1998). Gibson himself performed the scene—a wild chase in which his character, police detective Martin Riggs, is dragged through heavy traffic behind a trailer truck.

laws of physics also may lend a hand. When Keanu Reeves's stunt double, Brian Smrz, jumped from a moving car to a moving bus in *Speed* (1994), he knew he would not miss if both vehicles were going at the same velocity.

One of the most perilous feats is the stunt known as the full burn. Human torches typically wear fireproof garments and face masks designed both to protect them and to help them resemble the actors they double for. They may even carry concealed miniaturized breathing equipment. A combustible substance that burns at low temperatures is painted on the protective clothing and then set afire. Crew members stand by to hose it down with carbon dioxide. One over-the-top disaster film, *The Towering Inferno* (1974), contained enough fiery deaths and plunges from skyscrapers to require no fewer than 140 stunt artists.

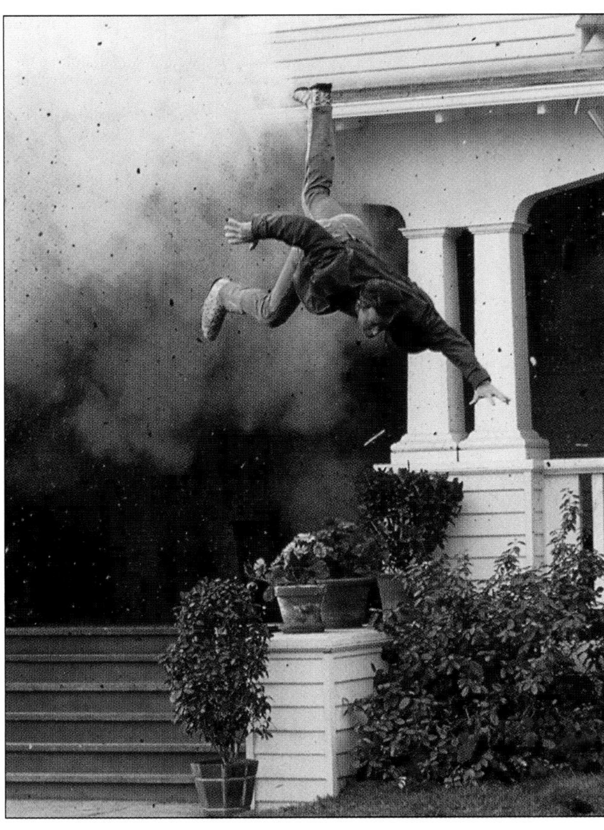

A stunt man hurtles from an exploding house in the Arnold Schwarzenegger thriller Last Action Hero (1993). His dramatic flight actually occurred with help from the compressed air in a hidden device, a hinged kicker ramp, which flipped him aloft.

Cut-and-Paste Action

Some of the most stunning effects stem from optical trickery rather than from a stunt man's courage. One scene that electrified viewers of Die Hard 2 (1990) was actually a photographic composite. Hero Bruce Willis, as policeman John McClane, besieged by enemies in the cockpit of a grounded military plane, escapes by strapping himself into an ejection seat and punching out. The shot was achieved by cinematic cut and paste. Below, Willis, in the ejection seat, was filmed against an illuminated blue screen. This allowed the isolation of the image of Willis alone, with no background. The film of Willis was then laid over a background image of the plane exploding, leading to the final composite shot shown at bottom.

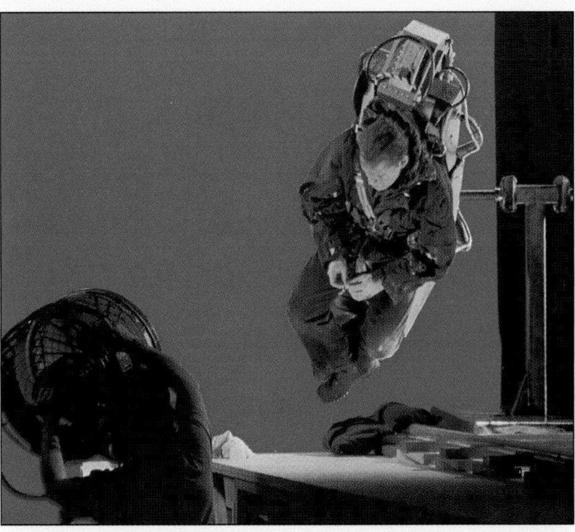

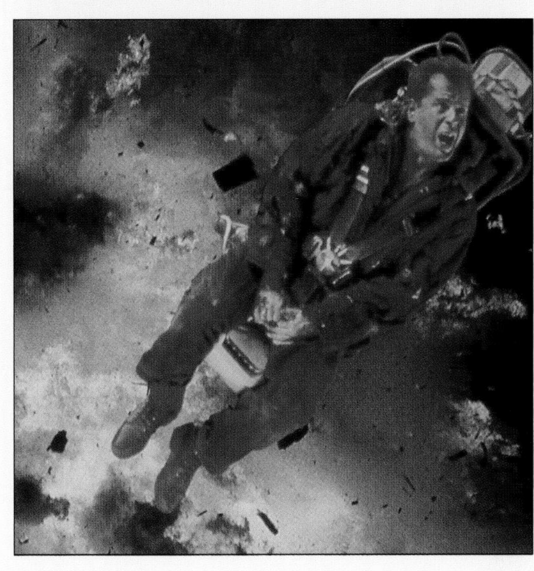

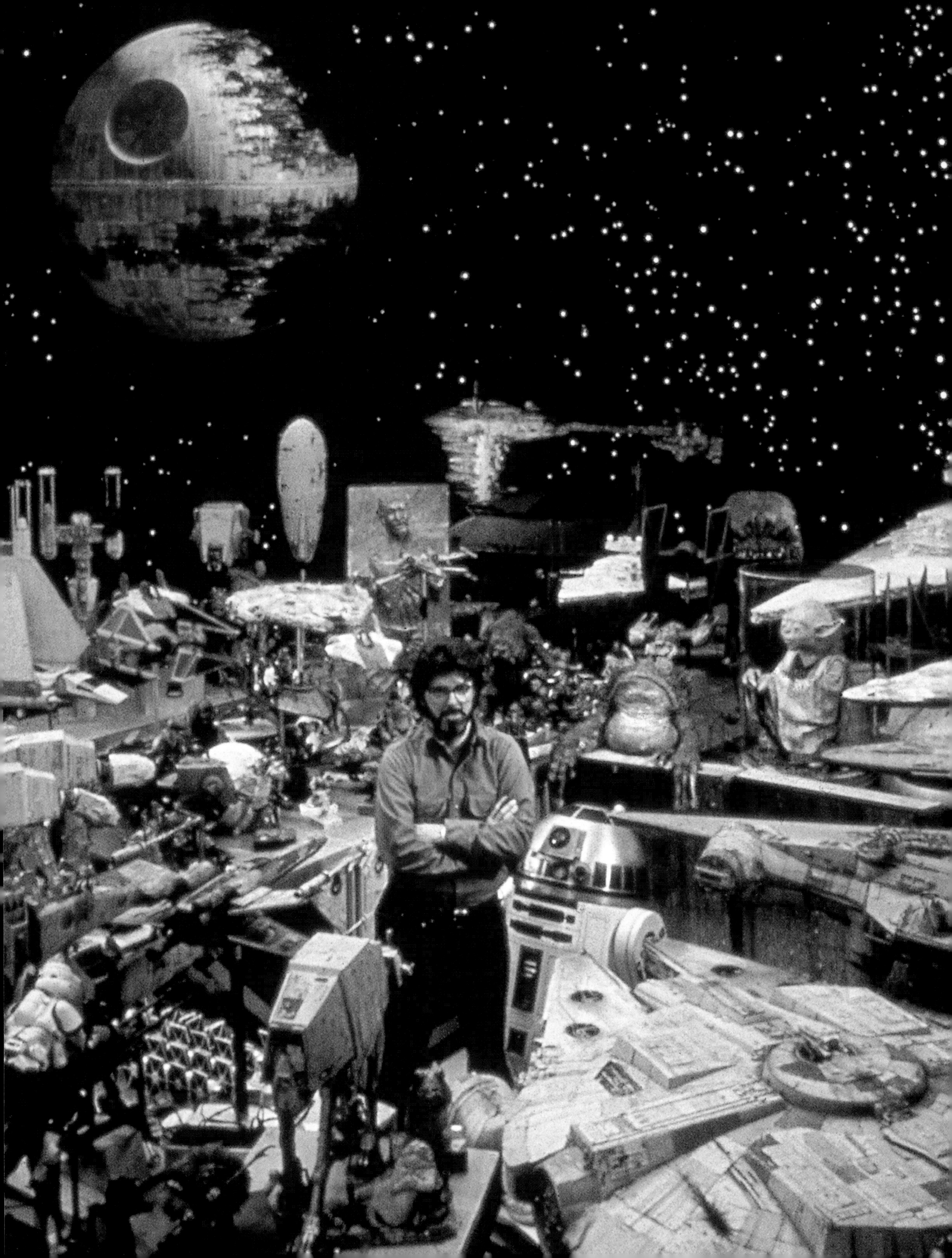

Industrial Light & Magic

Lucas's toy box"—that's what some employees called Industrial Light & Magic (ILM), the famed special-effects shop. George Lucas—shown at left among some of his models from the Star Wars series of films—started the firm in 1975 to generate effects for the original *Star Wars* movie. He set up shop in a warehouse north of Los Angeles and hired an energetic young staff, many barely out of college, who showed up for work at all hours wearing T-shirts, shorts, and flip-flops. It was a "hang-loose atmosphere," one of the pioneers recalled. "We were a bunch of hippies, really—but highly motivated."

There and later in a facility north of San Francisco, Lucas and his crew launched a revolution in movie effects. To populate the *Star Wars* cosmos—"a galaxy far, far away"—they designed, built, and brought to life robots and other wonderfully grotesque creatures. They constructed miniature spaceships flickering with thousands of tiny window lights. On-screen these craft zoomed at warp speed in intergalactic dogfights while actually sitting still—thanks to new computer-controlled camera systems perfected by the firm *(page 135)*.

Though ILM provided effects for more than 150 films, including the Indiana Jones trilogy and *Jurassic Park*—winning 14 Oscars in the process—the Star Wars flicks exerted a special magic. For the fourth in the series, *Star Wars: Episode I—The Phantom Menace* (1999), ILM special effects showed up in nearly 95 percent of the shots. Even before that release, Star Wars had become the most successful series ever made. Appealing across generations, through 1998 the Star Wars trilogy had grossed \$1.8 billion at the box office and more than \$4.5 billion in licenses for books, video games, apparel, and replicas of George Lucas's beloved toys.

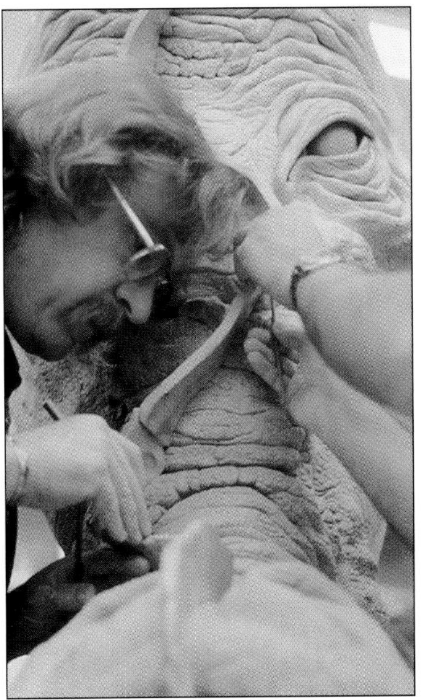

Artists at Industrial Light & Magic (left) shape a plaster mold for the giant head of the character in Return of the Jedi (1983) known as Ephant Man. From the final mold filled with latex rubber emerged the completed creature—below, with friend Salacious Crumb.

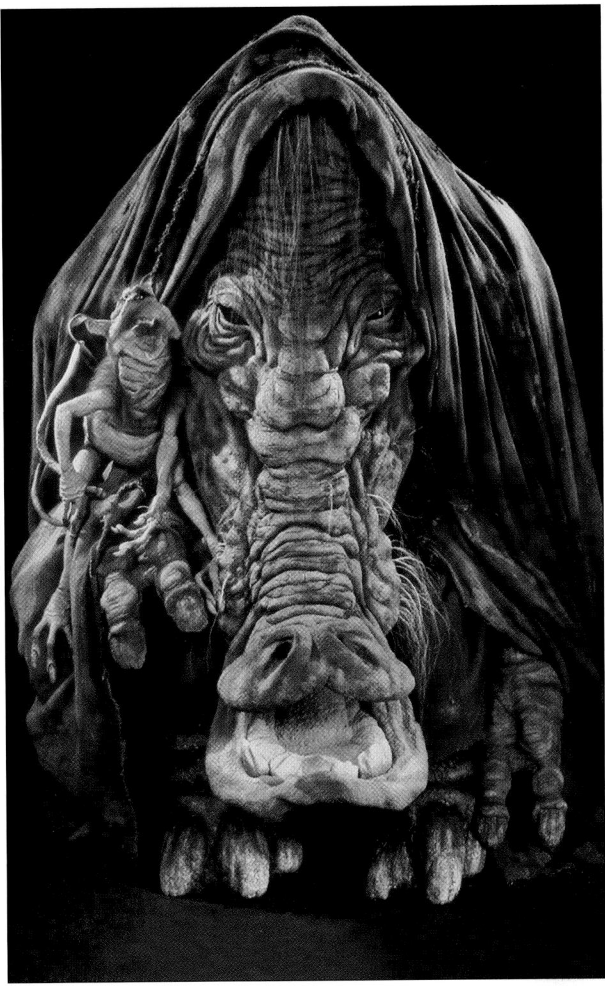

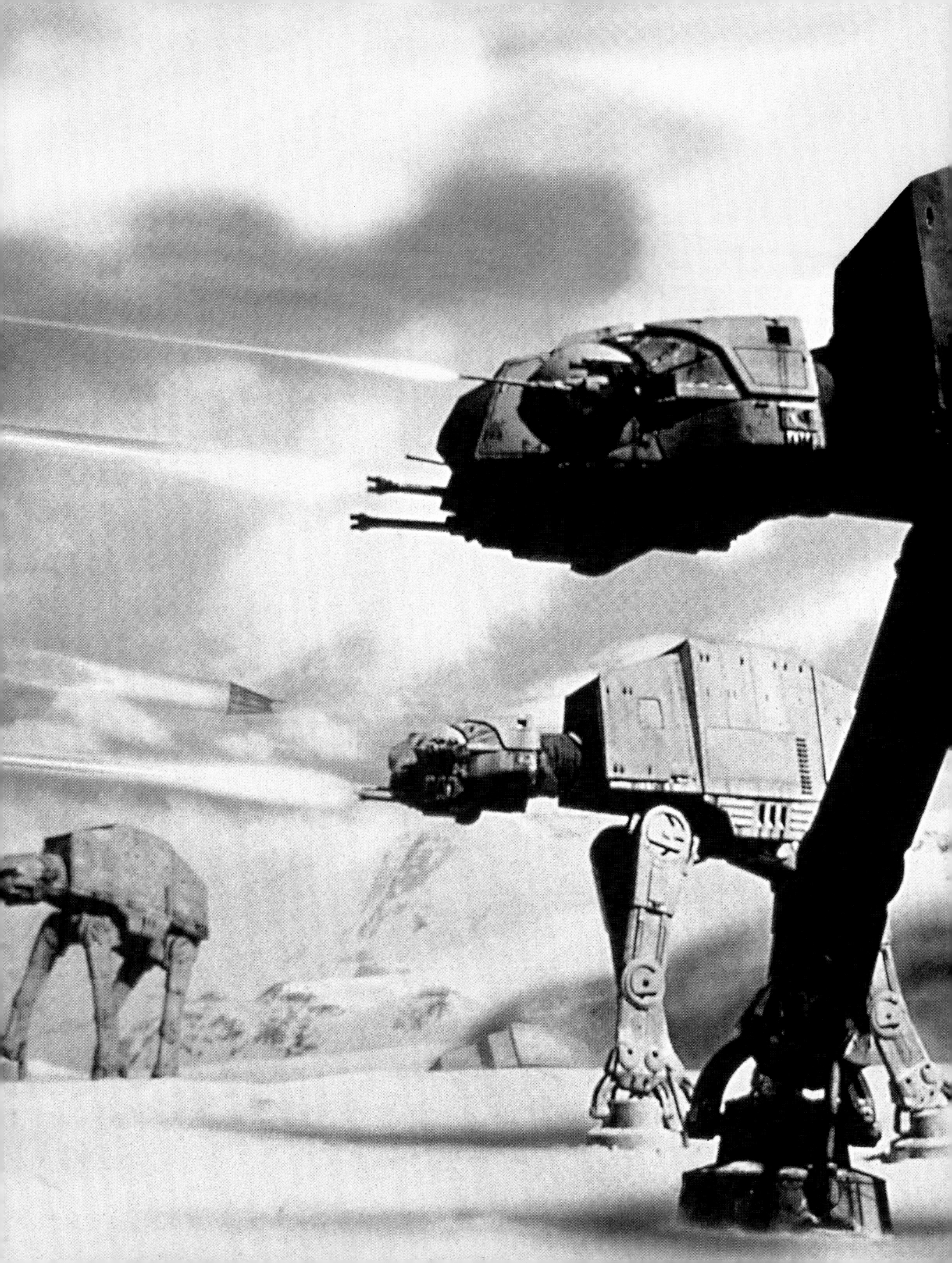

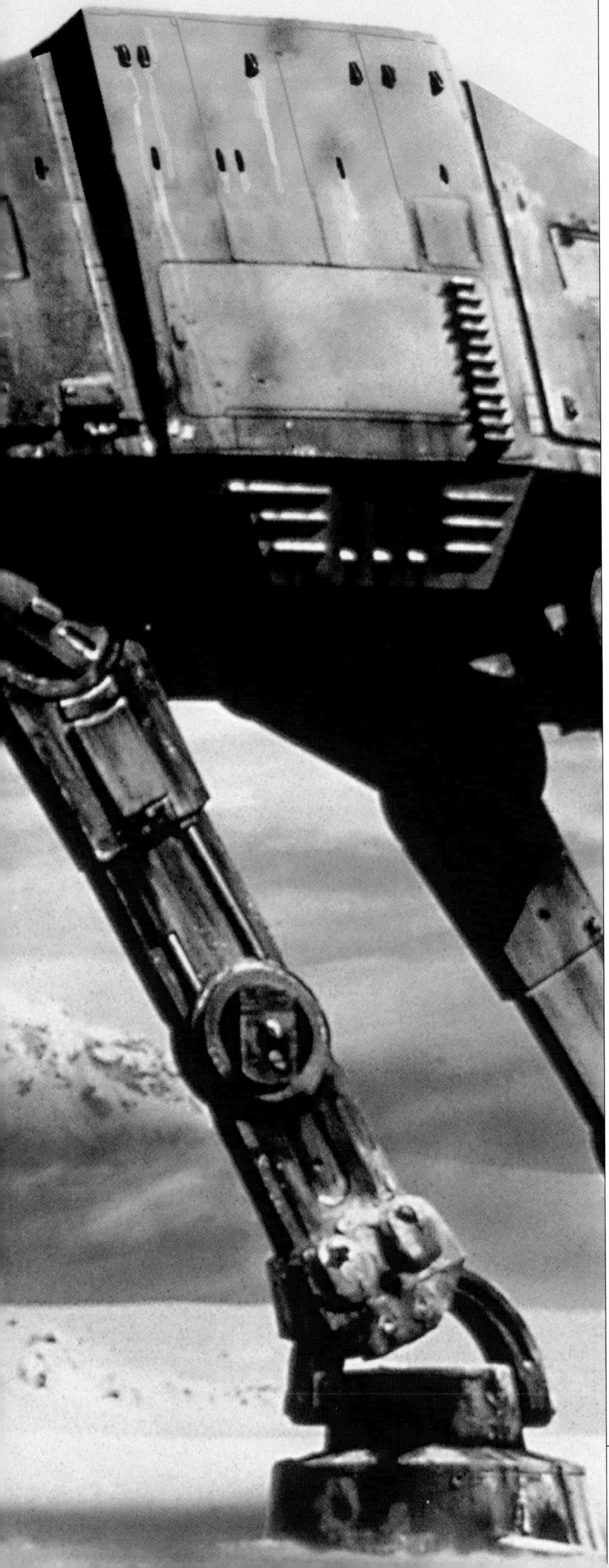

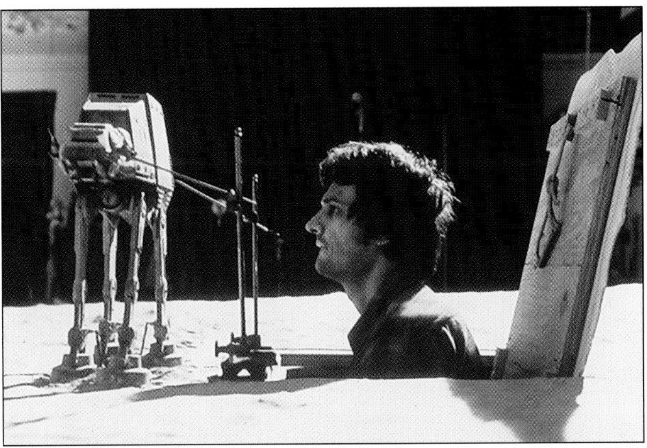

Popping up on the set through a trapdoor that conceals him during filming, animator Jon Berg adjusts the position of one of the snow walkers seen in The Empire Strikes Back (1980). In ILM's stop-motion technique, the illusion of movement was achieved by filming an object one frame at a time and moving it between exposures.

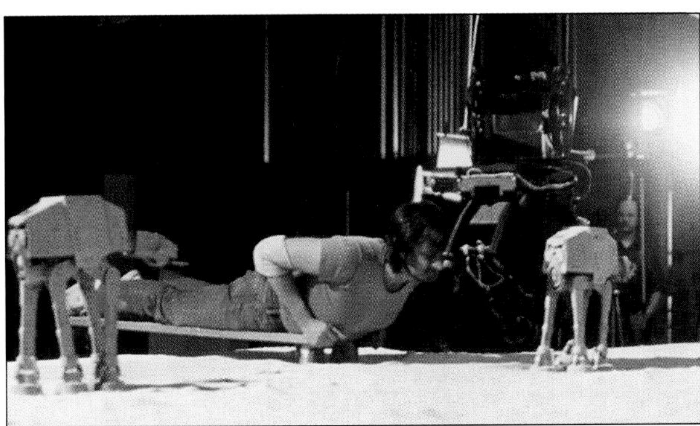

Jon Berg peers through the viewfinder of a motion-control camera to line up a shot of a snow walker. The computer-operated camera allowed filmmakers to impart the illusion of motion to stationary models and to make exact multiple copies of objects and movements for the purpose of building composite images.

In a masterpiece of ILM special effects, little snow walkers (left) look immense as they stride across the screen with guns blazing in The Empire Strikes Back. This image was the fruit of stop-motion technique, motion-control cameras, and compositing—the optical magic that permits various elements to be layered into one shot.

Breakthroughs in Digital Illusion

For all the spectacular special effects of the original Star Wars trilogy, George Lucas felt frustrated. Technology could not yet translate all his fantastic visions into realistic images. But that began to change dramatically in the late 1980s with the advent of ever more sophisticated computer graphics.

Major breakthroughs in digital effects started when ILM confronted an extraordinary challenge in *The Abyss* (1989). Director James Cameron envisioned the strangest of creatures, a snakelike "pseudopod" made totally of seawater that could transform its tip into various human faces. "It had to be living," said Mark Dippé of ILM. "You had to feel that it had a mind of its own and was moving and rippling purposefully."

To create it, ILM had to vastly expand its computer hardware capabilities and employ new software. Special programs modeled the beast, augmenting a basic tube shape with such intricacies as transparent ripples and luminous reflections. One vital tool was Photoshop, a program created primarily for publishing, which enabled ILM to resize, color-correct, and alter digitized images. Still, Lucas's crew needed nine months to complete the 75-second computerized sequence—and establish an Oscar-winning milestone in digital effects.

For his next film, *Terminator 2: Judgment Day* (1991), director Cameron asked ILM's computer specialists to summon forth an even more startling character, a cyborg named T-1000. The creature had to metamorphose through a series of stages, from gleaming metallic humanoid to amorphous blob of liquid metal to human form. Rapid increases in digital processing power and memory gave the technicians new possibilities for scanning existing images, composing new ones, and transferring them to film. In what one of them described as a "manic, energy-filled production with incredible dead-

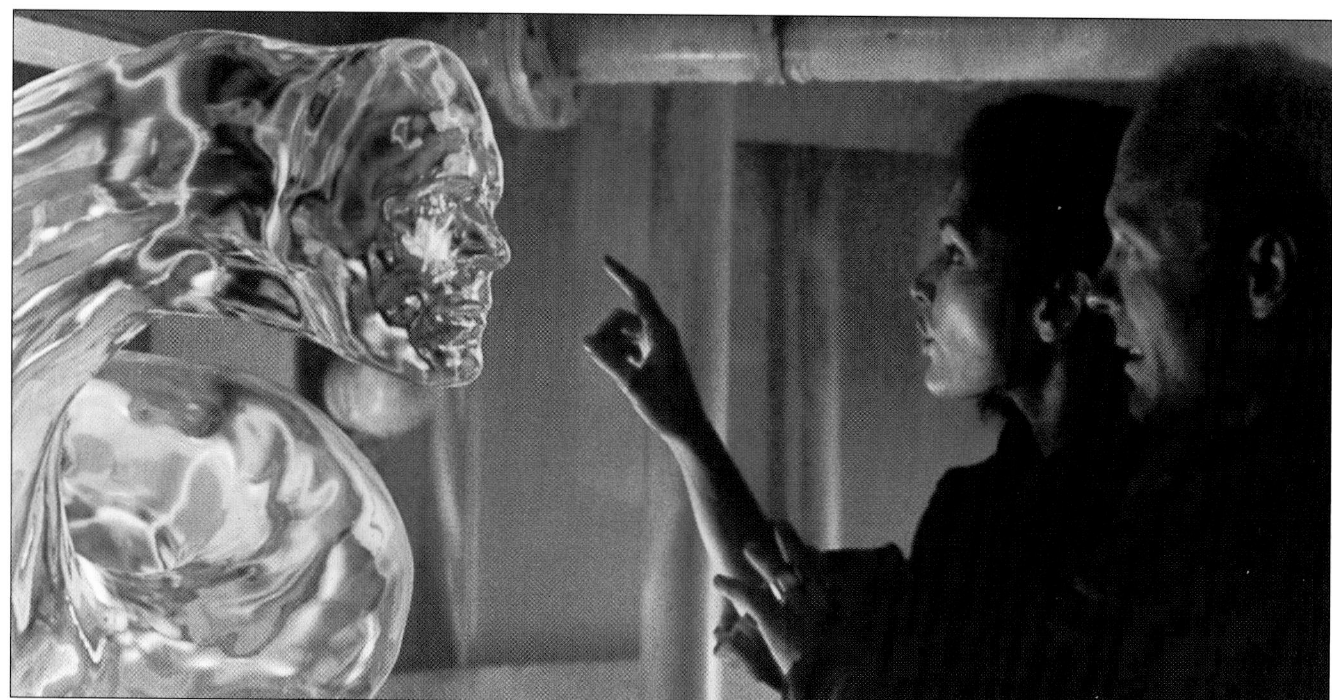

In The Abyss a computer-generated creature made of seawater changes into the likeness of Ed Harris, as Mary Elizabeth Mastrantonio reaches out.

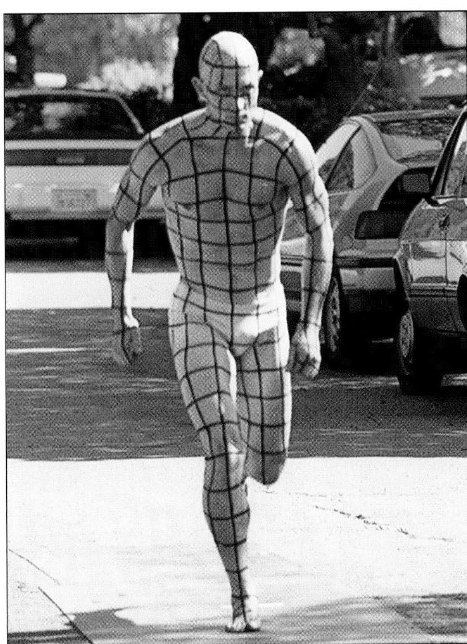

Preparing for the computerized birth of T-1000, actor Robert Patrick—painted with a black grid of reference points—runs for the camera.

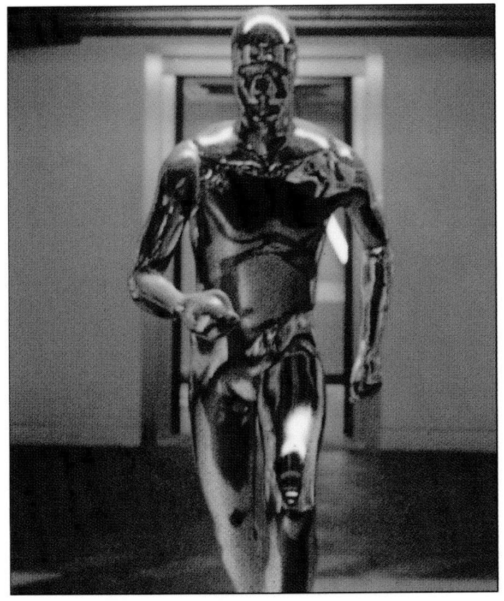

Given life by software using digitized images of Patrick, the gleaming T-1000 runs just like the actor, who limps slightly from an old injury.

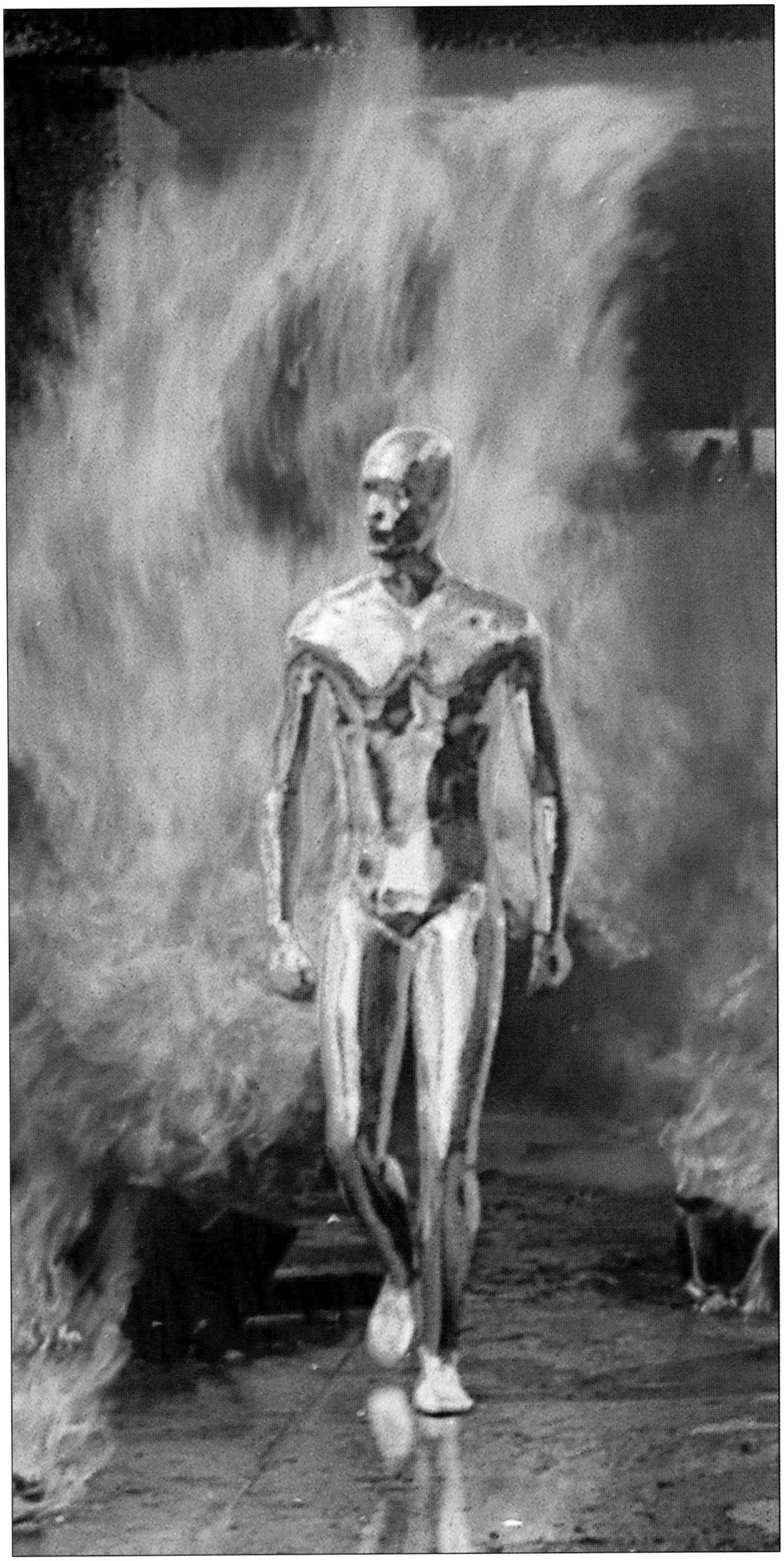

In a spectacular sequence from Terminator 2: Judgment Day, T-1000 emerges from a wall of fire as liquid metal, which then shifts into human shape.

lines and pressures," ILM brought to life Cameron's cyborg in nearly six minutes of computer-generated film.

When George Lucas's old associate, Steven Spielberg, planned his 1993 adaptation of the best-selling thriller *Jurassic Park,* he anticipated using only a bit of computer graphics. He intended to rely mostly on physical models. But ILM's computer whiz kids wanted to show him that they could generate a "full-screen, in-your-face *Tyrannosaurus rex.*" Their demonstration was so awe-inspiring that Spielberg wound up allotting six dramatic minutes to their digital dinosaurs, capped by the climactic battle between the *T. rex* and the velociraptors.

"The keys to filmmaking are all subliminal," said Mark Dippé. "You see a dinosaur walk by a tree and the tree shakes, you believe it's there." To get an idea of how dinosaurs moved, ILM animators observed large animals, consulted paleontologists, and even participated in dance and movement classes. With in-house software they captured the dinosaurs' every sway and jiggle, even such subtleties as the expansion and contraction of skin during breathing.

Some computer-graphics solutions brought with them new problems. The images frequently seemed too mechanical, so technicians had to add blur and grain for a more natural look. They also used electronic paintbrushes to touch up flaws in the final composites. But in one dramatic example of the power of digital effects, the head of a child actress was attached to the body of an adult stunt woman so that the child appeared to be performing the stunt. Not just animals but humans could now be built digitally.

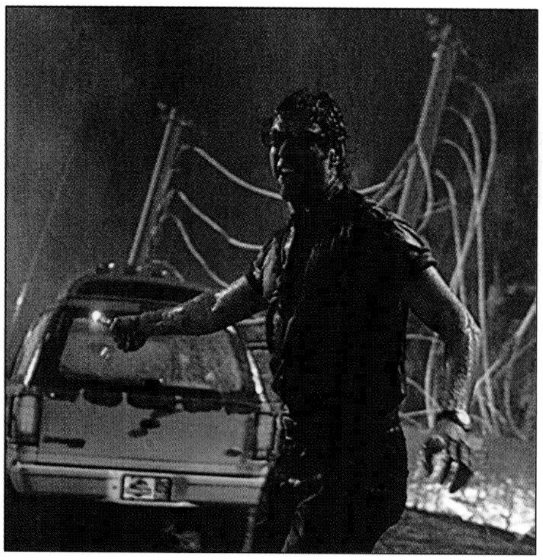

To set up a scene for Jurassic Park, actor Jeff Goldblum—in the role of mathematician Ian Malcolm—flees a charging Tyrannosaurus rex that he has to imagine is there. Before being inserted into the shot, the beast was built from scratch by computer.

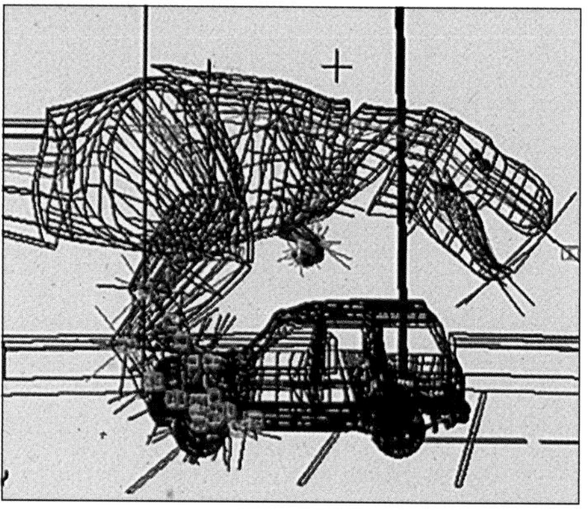

Beginning its creation of a T. rex, the computer produces an image representing a three-dimensional wire-frame skeleton of the six-ton beast. Using special software, the creators later added muscles, surface texture, and other features.

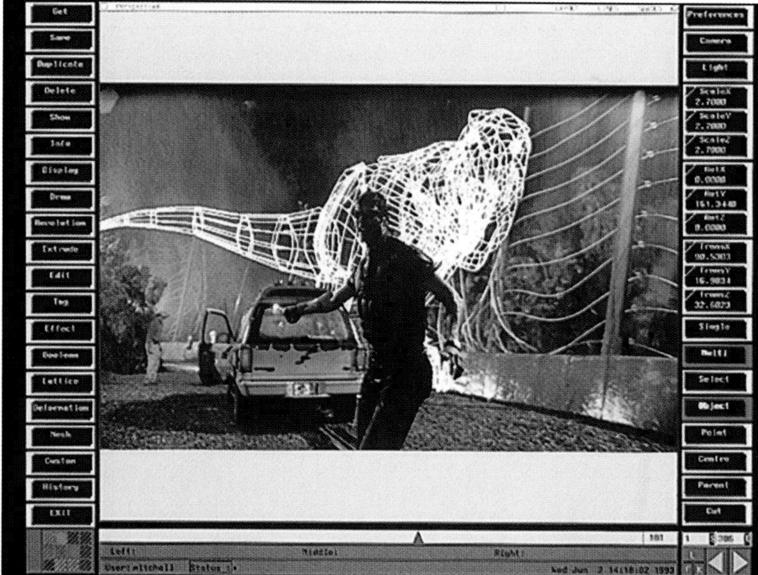

During film editing (above), the computer integrates the evolving digital creature with live action. This compositing process combines two separate images—the three-dimensional wire model and the so-called background plate of the fleeing actor.

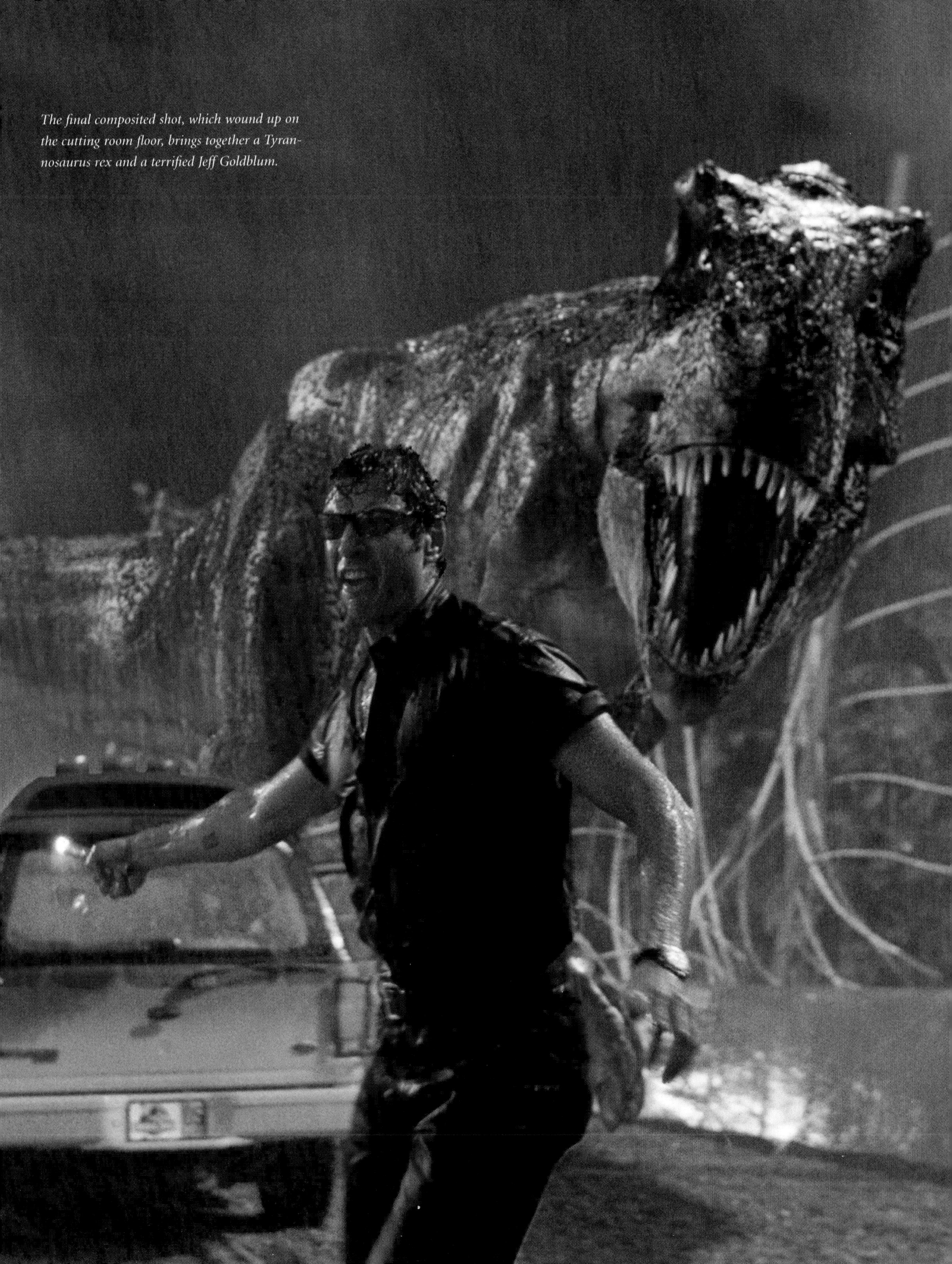

The final composited shot, which wound up on the cutting room floor, brings together a Tyrannosaurus rex and a terrified Jeff Goldblum.

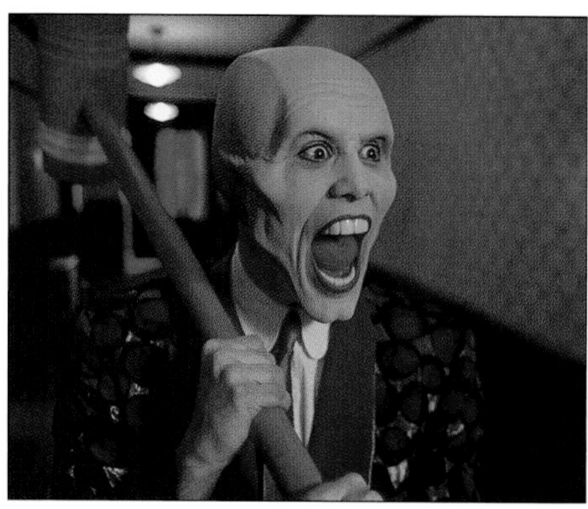

In The Mask (1994), Jim Carrey plays a bank clerk whose body changes to a kind of Silly Putty when he dons a mysterious mask. The filmed image above provides the background plate.

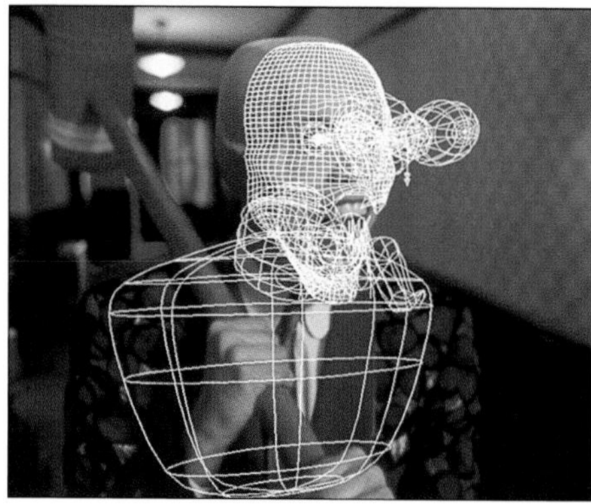

With eyes popping, a computer-generated wireframe figure is composited over the filmed background plate of Carrey. Computer images exaggerated the actor's own facial contortions.

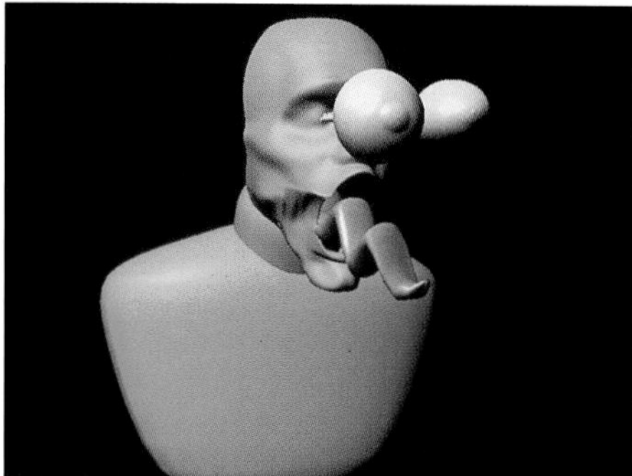

In the computerized figure, Carrey's tongue and eyeballs extend hugely. In other scenes, his figure explodes and—when commanded by a cop to "freeze"—drips with icicles.

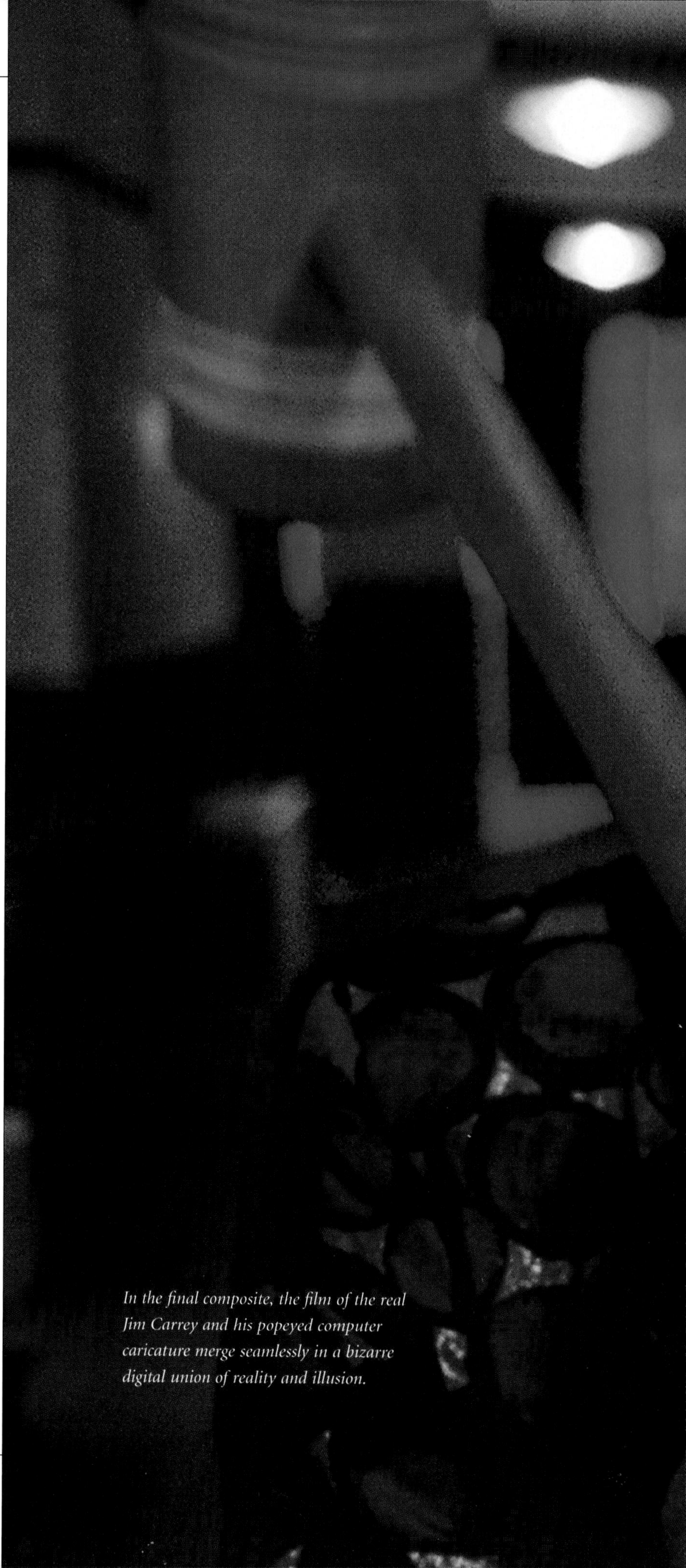

In the final composite, the film of the real Jim Carrey and his popeyed computer caricature merge seamlessly in a bizarre digital union of reality and illusion.

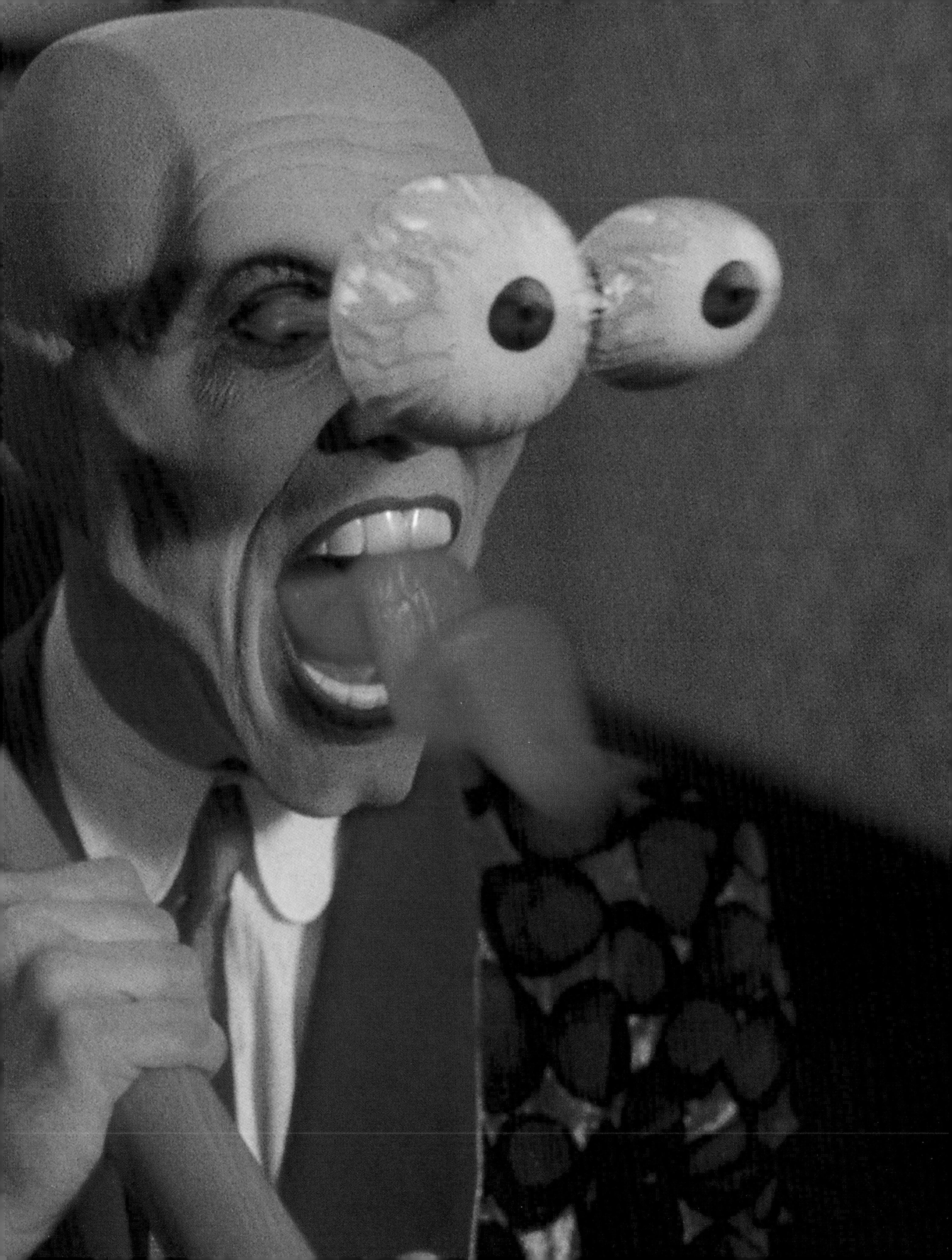

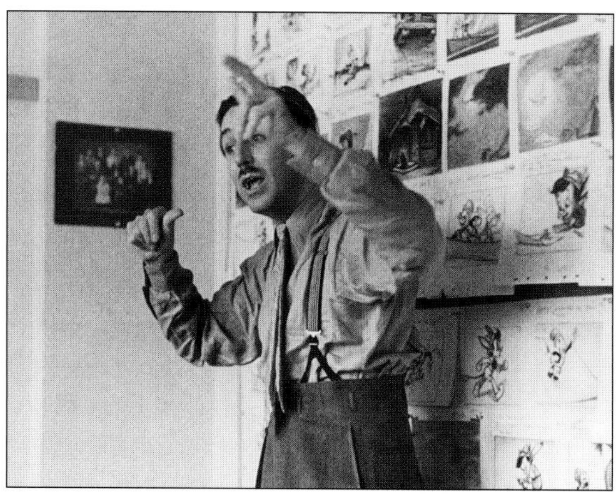

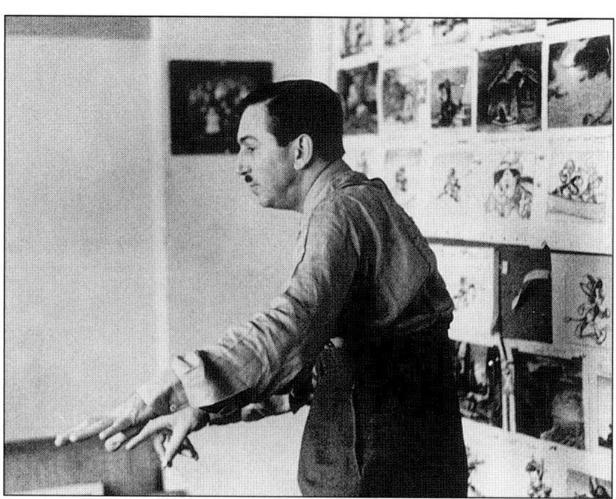

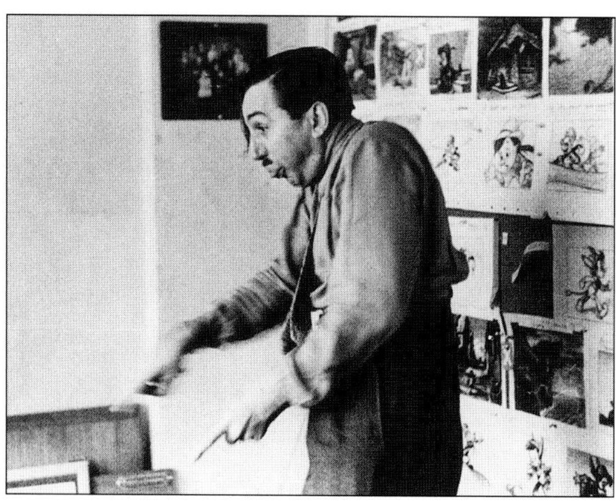

Walt Disney acts out a scene from Pinocchio (1940) for his staff. Disney routinely introduced ideas through such performances, which often, one animator said, would "kill you laughing, they were so funny." His presentation of the Snow White and the Seven Dwarfs story reportedly moved the room to tears.

Master of Animation

"It's not just a cartoon," Walt Disney once exclaimed about a project. "We have new worlds to conquer here." Animation was a primitive art in 1920 when Disney, then 18, got started. Eight years later he brought his chosen field into the age of sound with *Steamboat Willie*—the cartoon that launched Mickey Mouse *(right, bottom)*. By 30, Disney was one of Hollywood's biggest names, having won an Oscar in 1932 for *Flowers and Trees,* the first full-color cartoon. Competing animators were awed by his studio's beautifully executed work: "The giraffes ran like giraffes and the chipmunks and squirrels scampered like chipmunks and squirrels," one artist said admiringly.

In 1934 he began a three-year project that skeptics labeled Disney's Folly—the first feature-length animated film. Audiences nationwide were dazzled by *Snow White and the Seven Dwarfs*, with its enthralling story, winning characters, irresistible music, and lavish, unprecedented detail. Immense labor went into making Snow White move with realism and grace, determining how shadows should fall, and adding glistening effects to jewels and soap bubbles.

Disney's spare-no-expense approach carried over to the studio's later films. Lead characters like Dumbo *(inset, top)* and Bambi *(inset, bottom)* became part of the world's popular culture. Disney successfully turned his attention to television, live-action films, and amusement parks. After he died in 1966 the studio seemed to drift. But with *The Little Mermaid* in 1989 it began a new era of animated blockbusters, showing that the world Disney had created half a century earlier still held its magic.

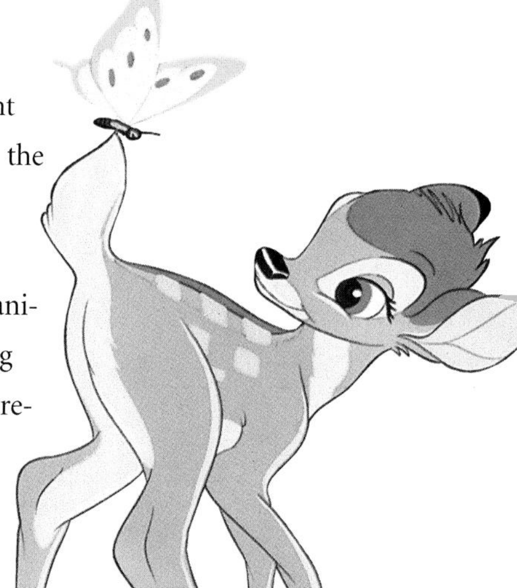

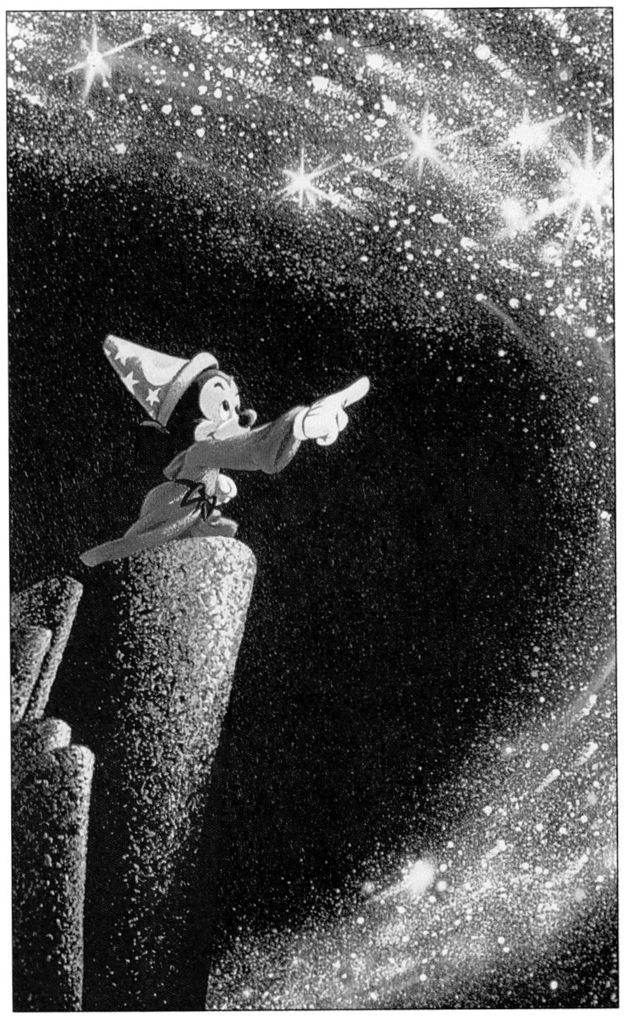

Fantasia, 1940

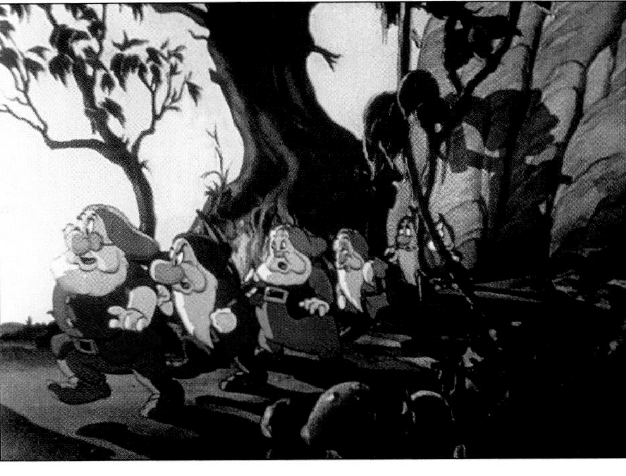

Snow White and the Seven Dwarfs, 1937

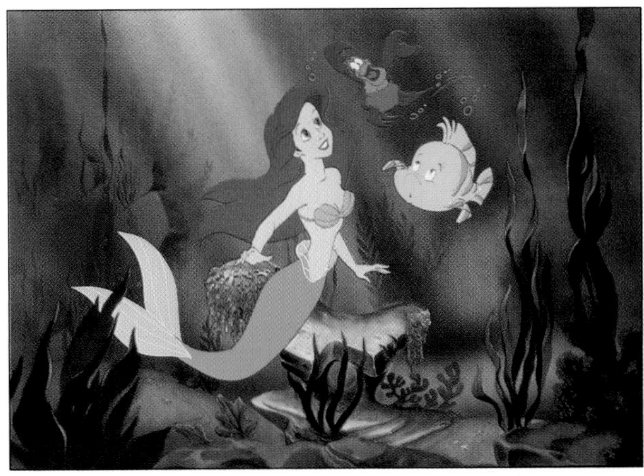

The Little Mermaid, 1989

Disney Classics

Mickey Mouse, as the Sorcerer's Apprentice, makes the stars dance in Fantasia; Snow White's dwarfs sing "Heigh Ho"; Ariel, the Little Mermaid, frolics in the sea; and a sacred ceremony marks the birth of Simba and Nala's cub in The Lion King.

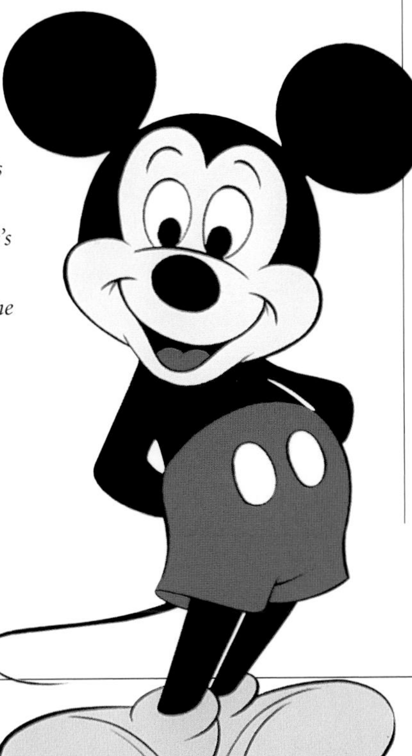

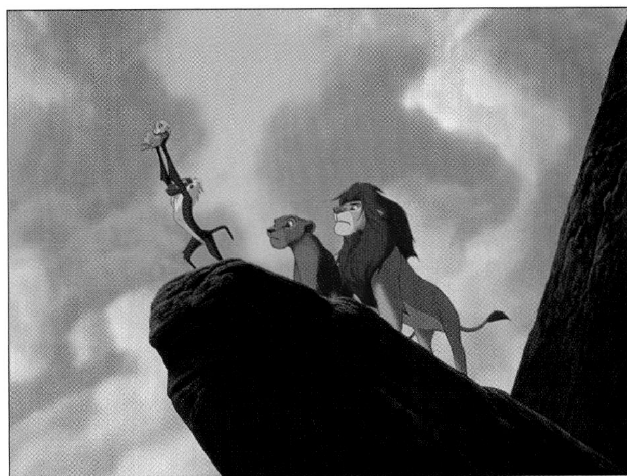

The Lion King, 1994

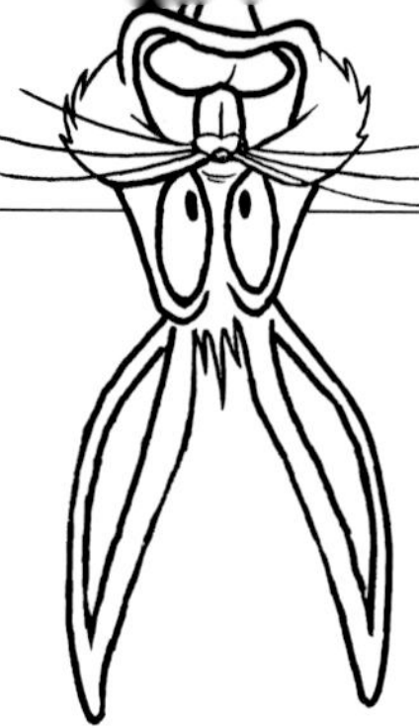

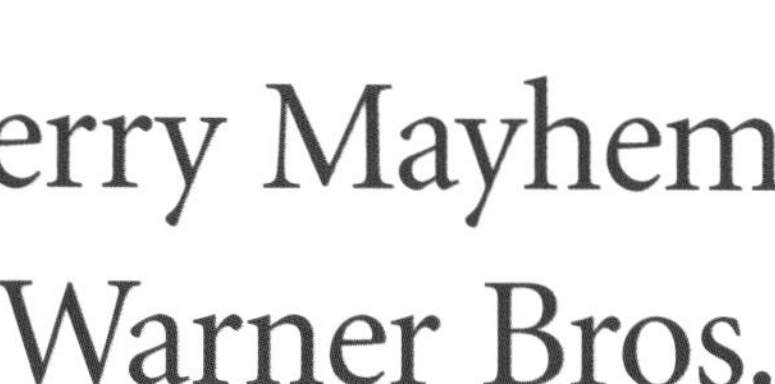

Merry Mayhem at Warner Bros.

For those who found Disney's world a little saccharine, there were Warner Bros. cartoons: fast, ferocious, and very funny, they had a wisecracking tone and relentless mayhem that nicely matched with Warner Bros. gangster flicks playing on the same bill. As storyman Michael Maltese recalled, "We wrote cartoons for grownups."

The Looney Tunes and Merrie Melodies series began in the 1930s, and by the next decade its anarchic, cheeky style was in full bloom: Anvils fell on heads, dynamite exploded while being held, and characters obliviously dashed off cliffs. Warner animators working on minuscule budgets produced some of the six- to seven-minute epics in a dilapidated, malodorous building fondly known as Termite Terrace. Yet gifted directors like Tex Avery, Friz Freleng, Chuck Jones, Bob Clampett, and Robert McKimson turned out a thousand-cartoon body of work that remains unmatched in animation history.

Warner Bros.' first enduring character was chubby pink Porky Pig *(inset)*. He was joined later by Bugs, the unflappable, smart-aleck bunny with the Brooklyn-Bronx accent. The "scwewy wabbit," always too much for befuddled Elmer Fudd, also made short but hilarious work of antagonists like Daffy Duck, the Tasmanian Devil, and pint-size, high-decibel Yosemite Sam, "the roughest, toughest, he-man stuffest hombre that ever crossed the Rio Grande."

Sylvester the cat's vain quest to make a meal of little Tweety sustained dozens of Warner Bros. cartoons, and Wile E. Coyote continually chased the Road Runner across stylized desert landscapes, betrayed time and again by Acme brand products and his own ever more crackpot schemes. The loquacious southern rooster Foghorn Leghorn was faced with a very different foe: a tiny young hawk, Henery, determined to catch his first chicken no matter what the disparity in their sizes.

Man of a Thousand Voices

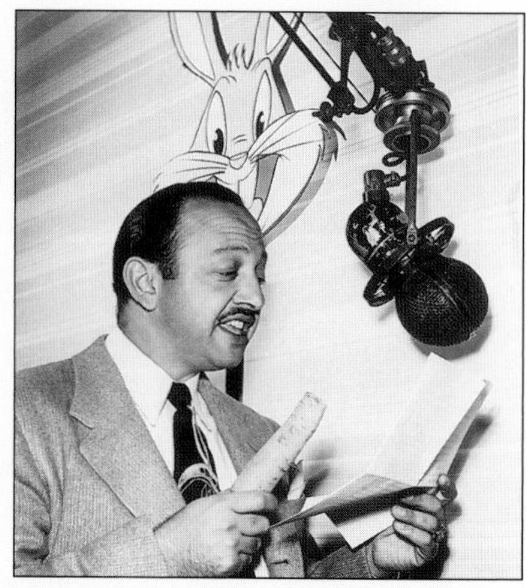

The legendary Mel Blanc (above, with a carrot for a Bugs Bunny sound effect) supplied the voices for almost all the major Warner cartoon characters. The most taxing was Yosemite Sam's holler, he said, and Sylvester's sputter left his scripts "covered with saliva." A medical specialist told Blanc that he had throat muscles like those of Enrico Caruso.

"Ehh, what's up, doc?"
—Bugs Bunny

"Th-th-that's all, Folks!"
—Porky Pig

"I tawt I taw a puddy tat!"
—Tweety Bird

"You're despicable!"
—Daffy Duck

"Be vewy, vewy quiet!"
—Elmer Fudd

"Ah say, Ah say, Son!"
—Foghorn Leghorn

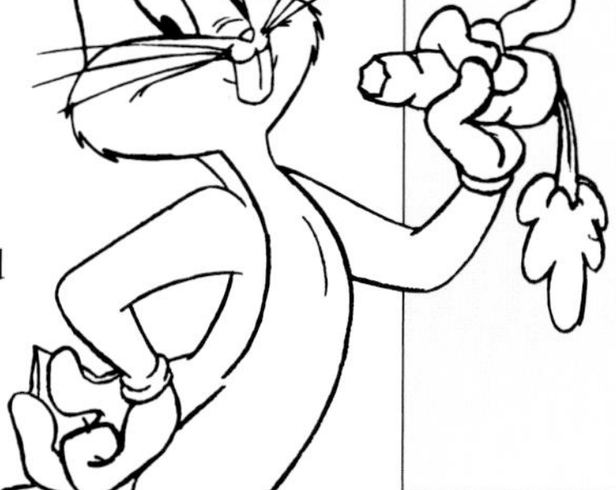

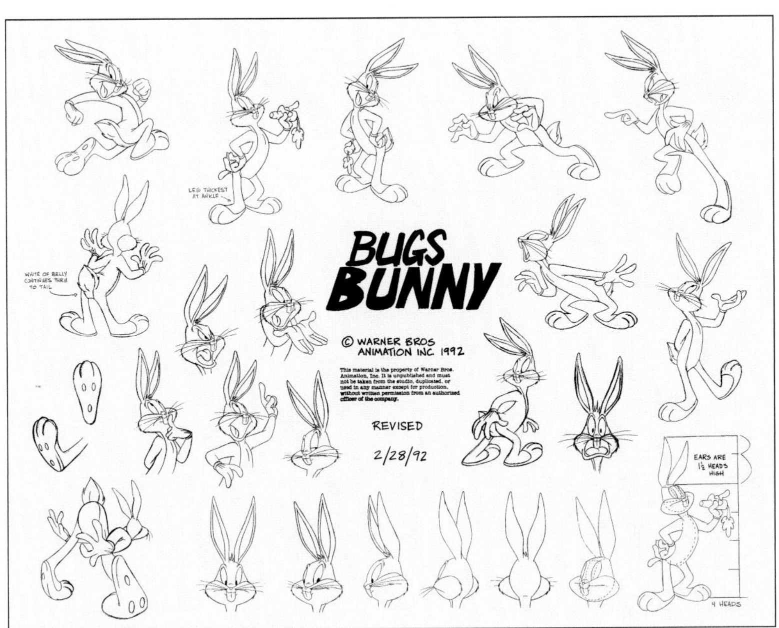

Model sheets like this one helped animators maintain a consistent look for each character. Bugs Bunny kept a consistent attitude as well. From his debut on, he was, Friz Freleng said, "so cocky he wasn't afraid of a guy with a gun who was hunting him."

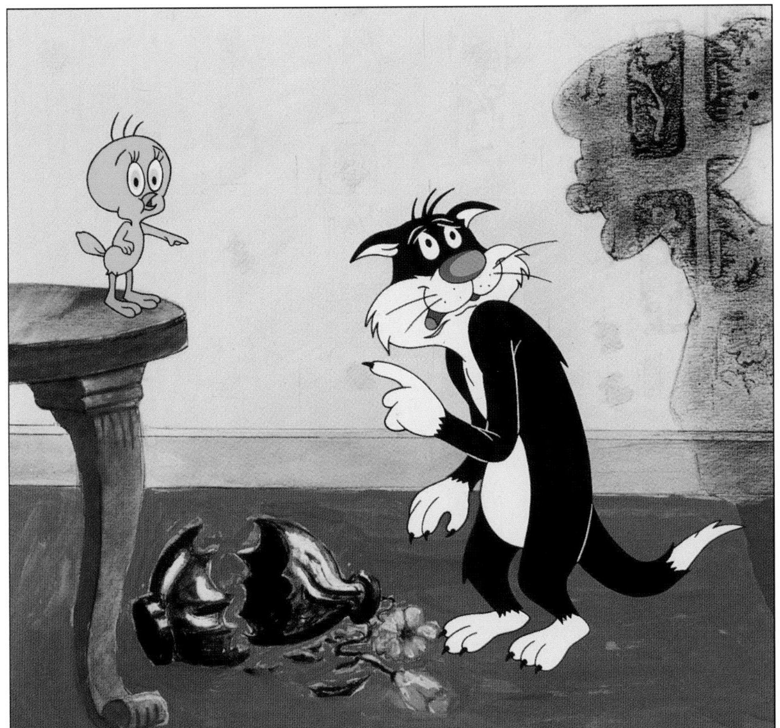

"Sufferin' Succotash!" Sylvester is in trouble with Granny again. Continually bested by Tweety, the cat also stood little chance against Speedy Gonzales, "the fastest mouse in all Mexico," or Hippety Hopper, the diminutive boxing kangaroo.

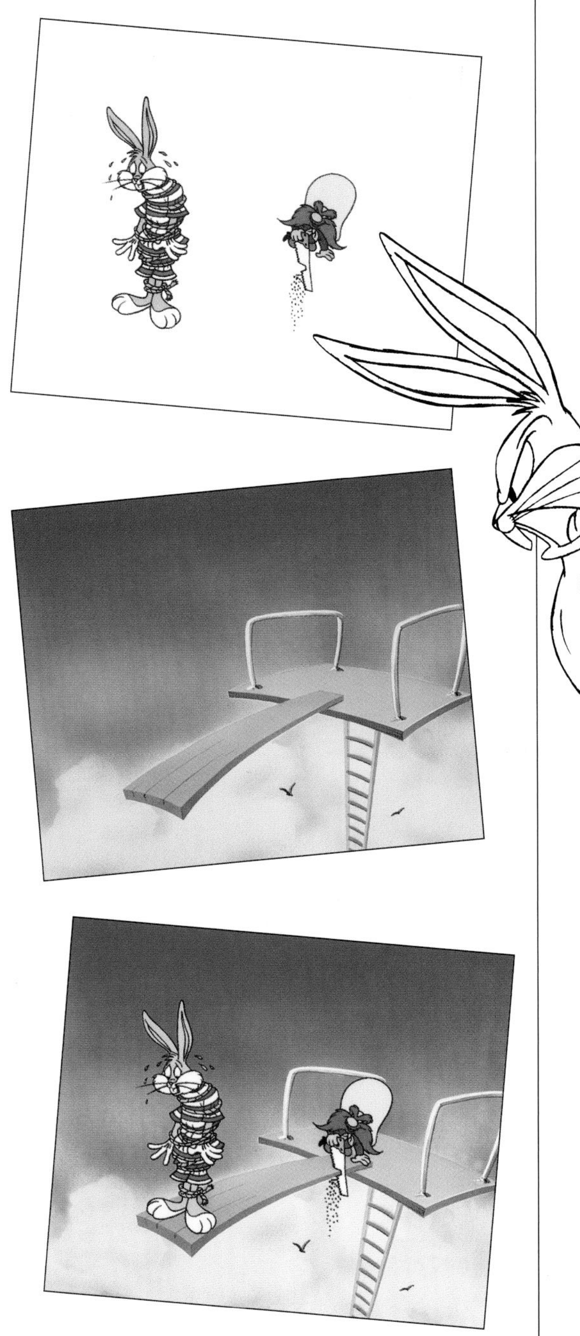

Bugs and Yosemite Sam appear on a cel by Friz Freleng (top). Animators would ink each moment of action onto a sheet of celluloid, lay it over a painted background (center), and capture the combination (bottom) on film. This scene is from High Diving Hare—in which Sam's half of the diving platform falls, while Bugs remains suspended in air. This violates the law of gravity, "but," Bugs says, "I never studied law."

The Next Generation of Animation

As technology evolved, so did animation. In 1988's *Who Framed Roger Rabbit*—starring Bob Hoskins as a 1940s detective, and cartoon character Roger Rabbit as a murder suspect *(right)*—Disney and Steven Spielberg's Amblin Entertainment blended the animated and real worlds seamlessly. "If Roger comes into a room and sits down on a big chair, you should see the cushion go down and a puff of dust," Spielberg said.

After live-action sequences were filmed, animators crafted drawings to fit precisely into the footage. Cartoon characters had to hold real objects in a believable way. To match each movement of the camera, drawings needed to shift perspective subtly. Layers of highlight and shadow made the animated figures seem three-dimensional or created other effects, such as the shimmer of a sequined gown worn by sultry Jessica Rabbit.

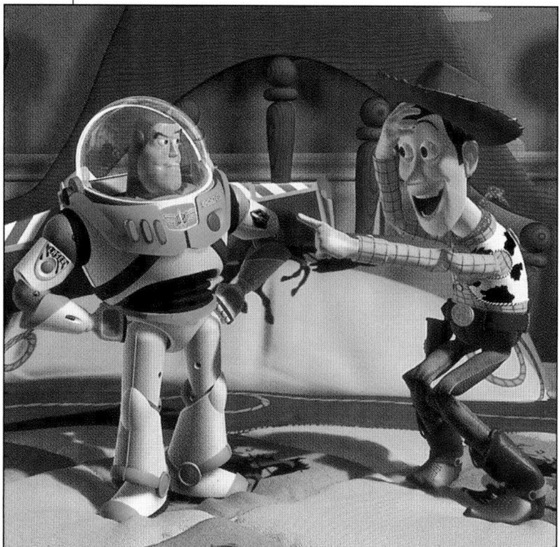

An even bigger breakthrough was 1995's *Toy Story,* the first feature film animated entirely by computer. The story of Woody *(inset, right)* and Buzz *(inset, left),* toys who compete for their owner's affection, required four years of work from Disney and computer-graphics studio Pixar. Programmers and animators created computer models for every character, setting, and object. Then they designed surface "textures" for each model to make this virtual world convincingly tactile.

In *Snow White,* Walt Disney created animation's first realistic human characters; *Toy Story* did the same in the realm of computer animation. The two lead toy characters received a high level of realism as well, with carefully nuanced facial expressions. "For the audience to believe in them, Woody and Buzz have to look like they're thinking," Pixar's John Lasseter said. *Toy Story* had a happy ending, winning both a special Academy Award and box-office success.

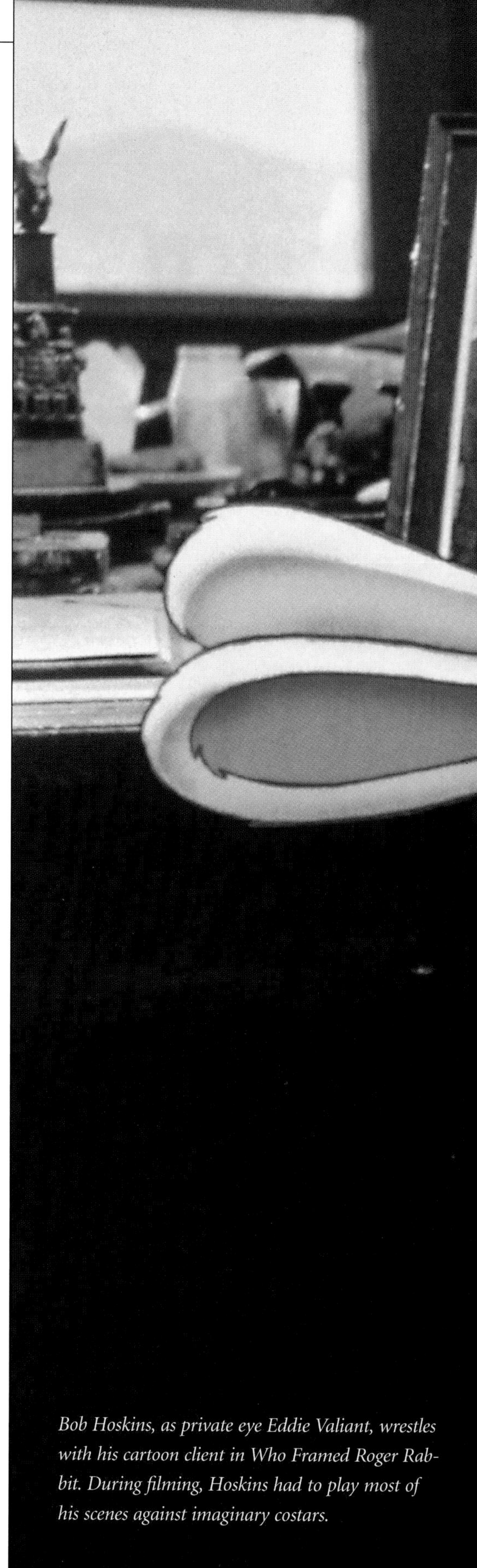

Bob Hoskins, as private eye Eddie Valiant, wrestles with his cartoon client in Who Framed Roger Rabbit. During filming, Hoskins had to play most of his scenes against imaginary costars.

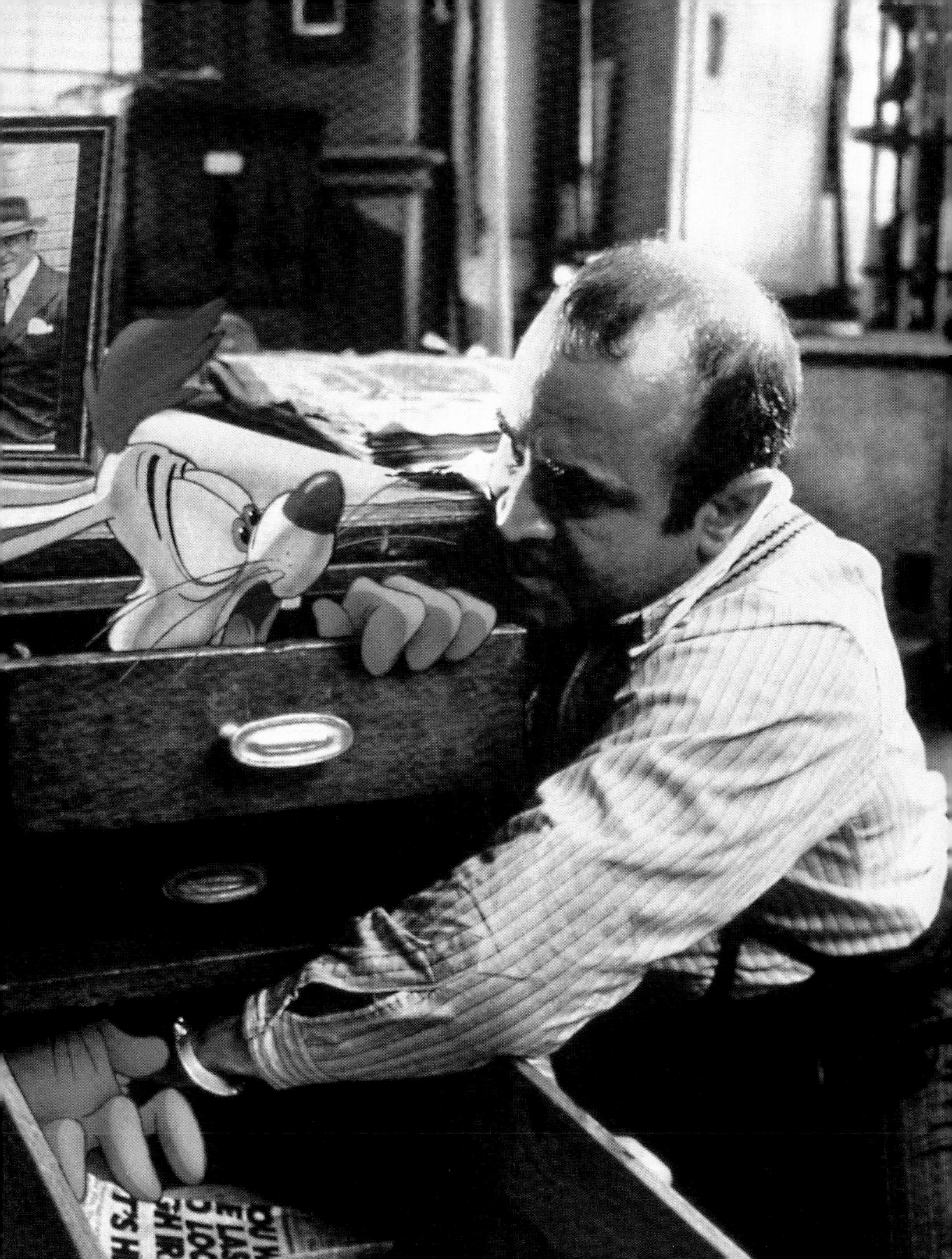

Kids and Animals

HARD ACTS TO FOLLOW

Never work with kids and animals," warned W. C. Fields. "They'll steal your best scene with their behind to the camera." The grumpy comedian knew what he was talking about. Movie audiences found it difficult to resist a noble dog like Lassie or a lovable pig *(inset)*. But if Hollywood's critters often upstaged their grown-up human costars, children were even bigger scene stealers.

At first producers were slow to catch on to this phenomenon, and youngsters in film served largely as props. By the 1930s, however, child stars shone so brightly in the movieland firmament that ambitious mothers were besieging the studios, dragging along a kid who was sure to be the next little person to make it big.

The one who made it biggest of all had a dimpled smile and precisely 56 corkscrew curls. For four years in a row, beginning in 1935 when she was seven years old, Shirley Temple *(right)* outdrew every other Hollywood star at the box office. Her sunny on-screen optimism was infectious, buoying the spirits of a nation mired in the Great Depression. She could sing. She could dance. She was impossibly cute. And she was such a quick study that she always remembered her lines—and didn't shy away from prompting her adult fellow actors if they forgot theirs.

Two babes who made the grade in Tinseltown: Above, a talking pig had the title role in Babe (1995). At right, sipping milk, Shirley Temple was America's image of wholesome goodness during the mid-1930s.

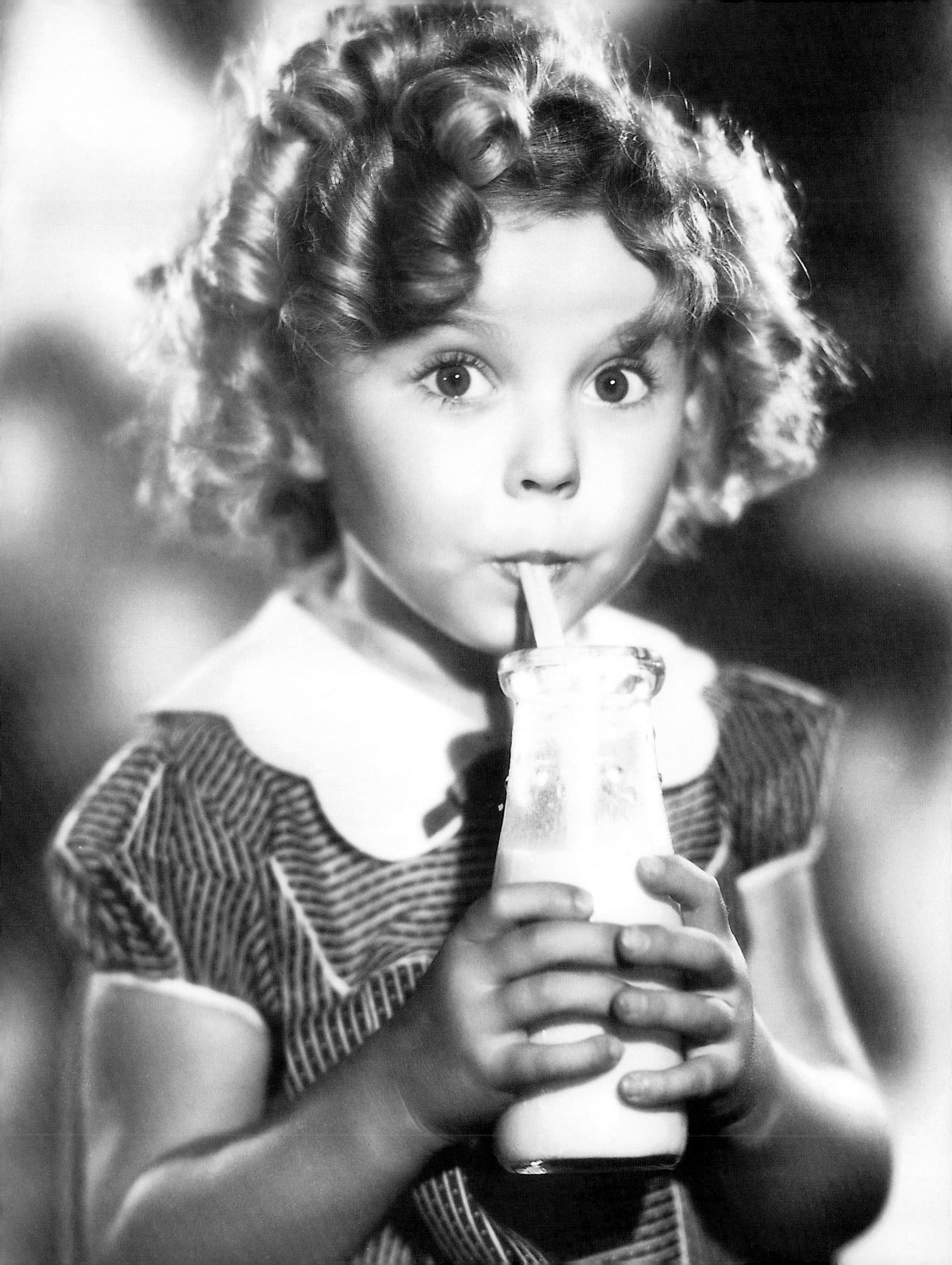

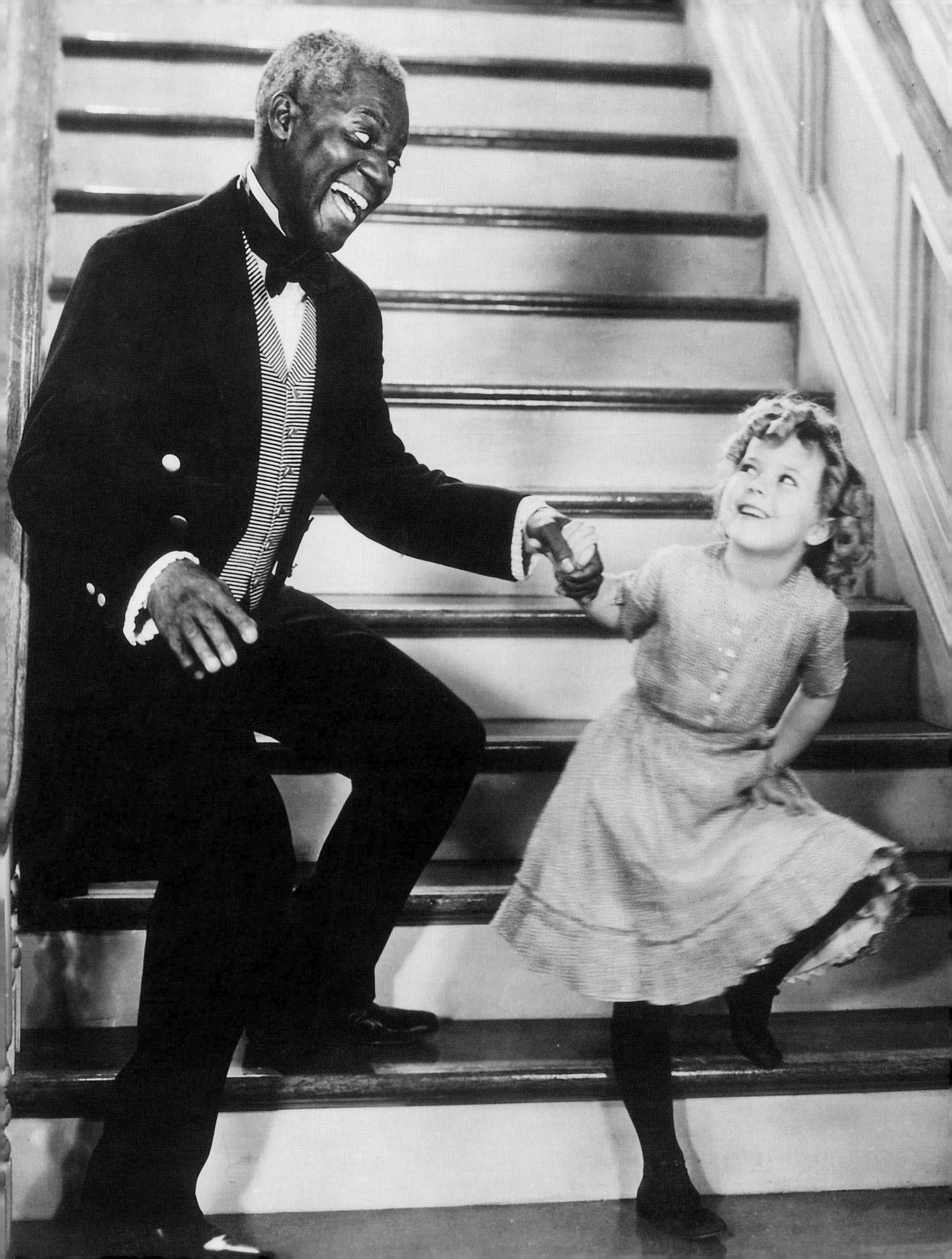

Temple was a natural. At age two she was keeping time with her feet to music on the radio. At three she was enrolled in dancing school, where a talent scout discovered her. Before she was four she had her first film contract, making one-reelers. In 1934, when she turned six, she made no fewer than eight feature films and was awarded a special miniature Oscar for bringing "more happiness to millions of children and millions of grownups than any child of her years in the history of the world."

Such was her popularity that Temple's studio, 20th Century-Fox, maintained a staff of 19 writers to develop scripts for her. These screenplays typically featured treacly plots, but if the films were forgettable, Temple never was. "Sparkle, Shirley, sparkle!" her mother would remind her. And for 15 cents at their neighborhood theaters Americans could watch that sparkle and momentarily forget their woes. It was no wonder that she was photographed more than anyone in the world, including her adoring fan President Franklin D. Roosevelt.

By the time she reached puberty, Temple had earned three million dollars and saved the studio from bankruptcy. Only then did she learn that she was actually 13, not 12; her parents and the studio had shaved a year off her age to make her seem even more precocious. By then her best days on the screen were behind her.

In a reversal of the usual filmland scenario, Temple was succeeded as Hollywood's most popular child star by someone who was actually older than she—a teenager with the stage name Mickey Rooney *(right).* Born Joe Yule Jr. into a vaudeville family in Brooklyn, Rooney made his stage debut, playing a dwarf, when he was scarcely out of diapers. In 1926, at age six, he appeared in his first movie, and his freckled face soon became familiar in such films as *Boys' Town* and *Captains Courageous.* He made the first of 15 Andy Hardy films in 1937, playing an all-American adolescent with such verve that he was number one at the box office three years running.

Unlike Temple, Rooney stayed in show business. In an up-and-down career spanning three-quarters of a cen-

"Don't ask me how she does it. You've heard of chess champions at eight and violin virtuosos at 10? Well, she's Ethel Barrymore at six."

Costar Adolphe Menjou on Shirley Temple

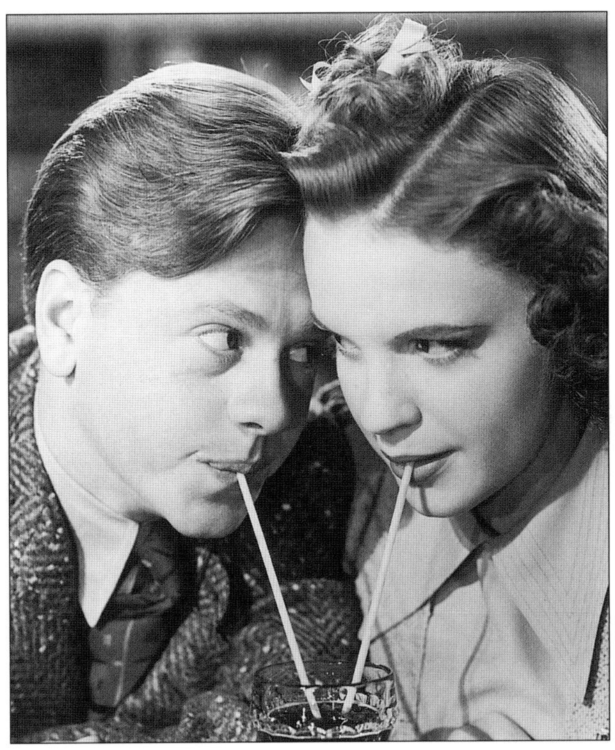

In the famous malt-shop scene from Love Finds Andy Hardy, Mickey Rooney as Andy and Judy Garland as the girl next door share one soda with two straws. Between 1937 and 1943 Rooney and Garland made a total of nine films together—five of them musicals.

Opposite: Shirley Temple and favorite dance partner Bill "Bojangles" Robinson tap a classic sequence in The Little Colonel. Robinson said, "God made her just all by herself—no series, just one."

tury, he had roles in 189 films. "I've been coming back like a rubber ball for years," he said. "I couldn't live without acting."

Rooney's frequent costar, Judy Garland *(page 151)*, was also the offspring of vaudevillians. Born Frances Gumm in Minnesota, she sang with her two older sisters in the unsuccessful "Gumm Sisters Kiddie Act." But when she was 13 her emotive voice so impressed Louis B. Mayer of MGM that he signed her to a contract—the first person in the studio's history to be signed without a screen test or sound test. Twice she was cast opposite Rooney in teenage pictures before she found her unforgettable role as Dorothy in *The Wizard of Oz (right).*

Garland was MGM's second choice for the role of the Kansas girl flung by a tornado into the Land of Oz. The studio wanted Temple but could not work out a deal with 20th Century-Fox. Garland was 16 when filming started in 1938. To mask her maturing figure and make her fit the role of 11-year-old Dorothy, the studio strapped her into a corset and bound her breasts. Later, the effort of maintaining the slender look demanded by Hollywood bedeviled Garland throughout a brilliant and troubled adult career that included such classics as *Meet Me in St. Louis* and *A Star Is Born.* Amphetamines she took to lose weight paved the way for alcohol abuse and, finally, death at age 47 from an unintentional overdose of sleeping pills.

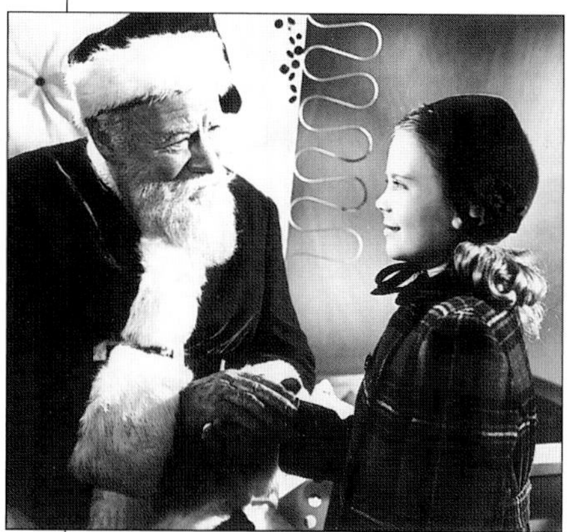

Natalie Wood meets Santa

Playing Garland's young sister in *Meet Me in St. Louis* was Margaret O'Brien, who became the major child star of the 1940s. Even at seven, Margaret knew how to turn on the emotional spigot. But just to make sure he got copious tears during a key scene, director Vincente Minnelli once took the youngster aside before shooting and told her that her dog had been killed by a car. It worked. O'Brien's roles belonged to the long Hollywood tradition of childhood innocence exemplified by Shirley Temple. Nine-year-old Natalie Wood, as Susan Walker *(inset, above)*, worked the same vein in *Miracle on 34th Street.* In that classic, released in 1947 and shown practically every Christmas since then, little Susan's

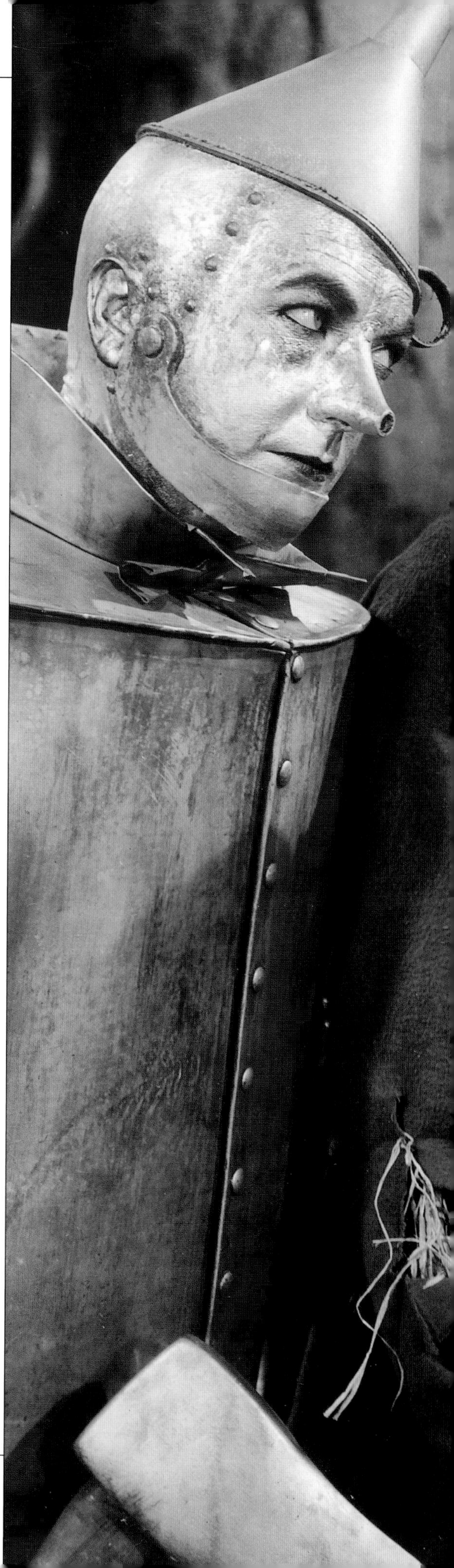

In The Wizard of Oz, Dorothy (Judy Garland) ministers to the Cowardly Lion (Bert Lahr) as the Tin Man (Jack Haley) and the Scarecrow (Ray Bolger) watch.

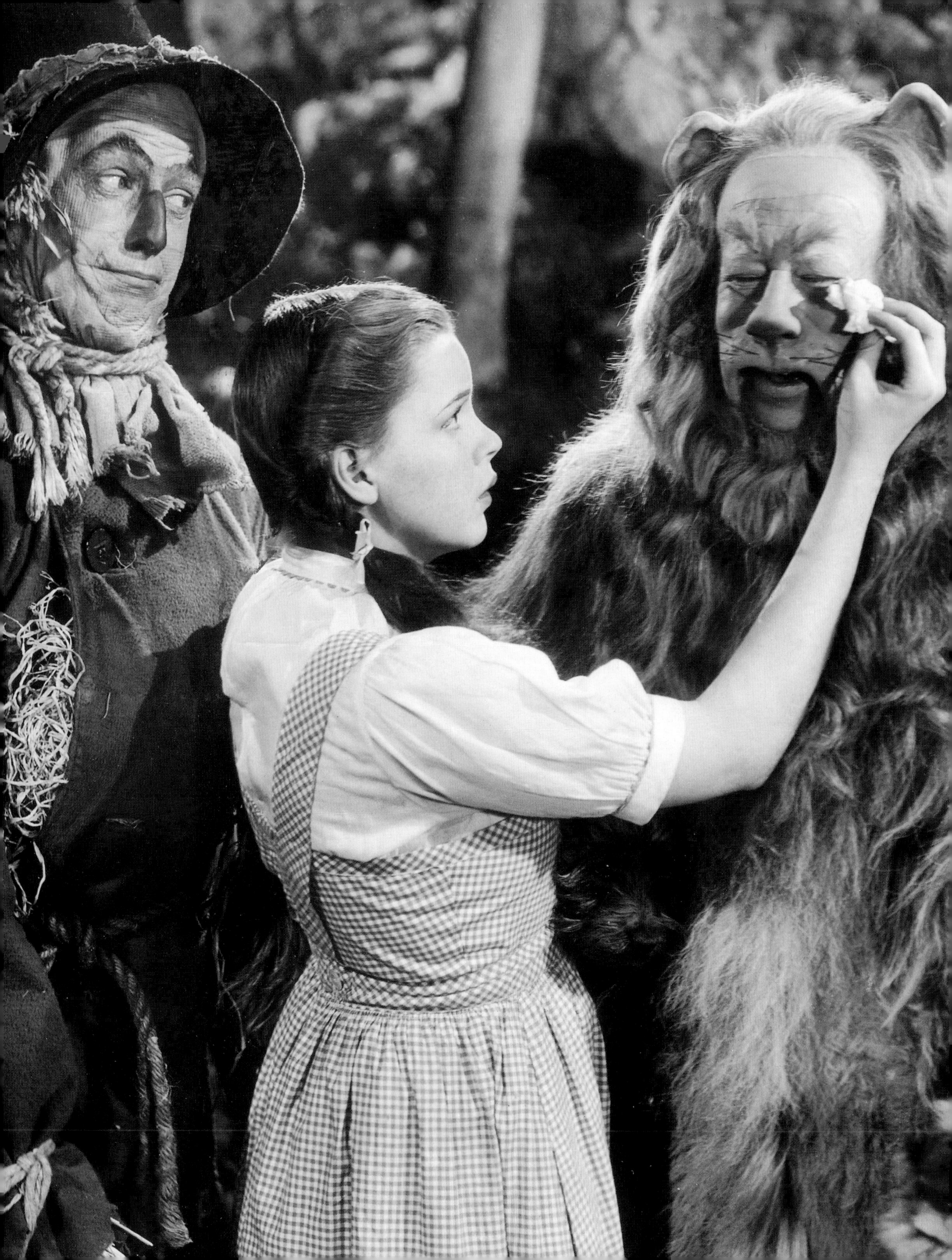

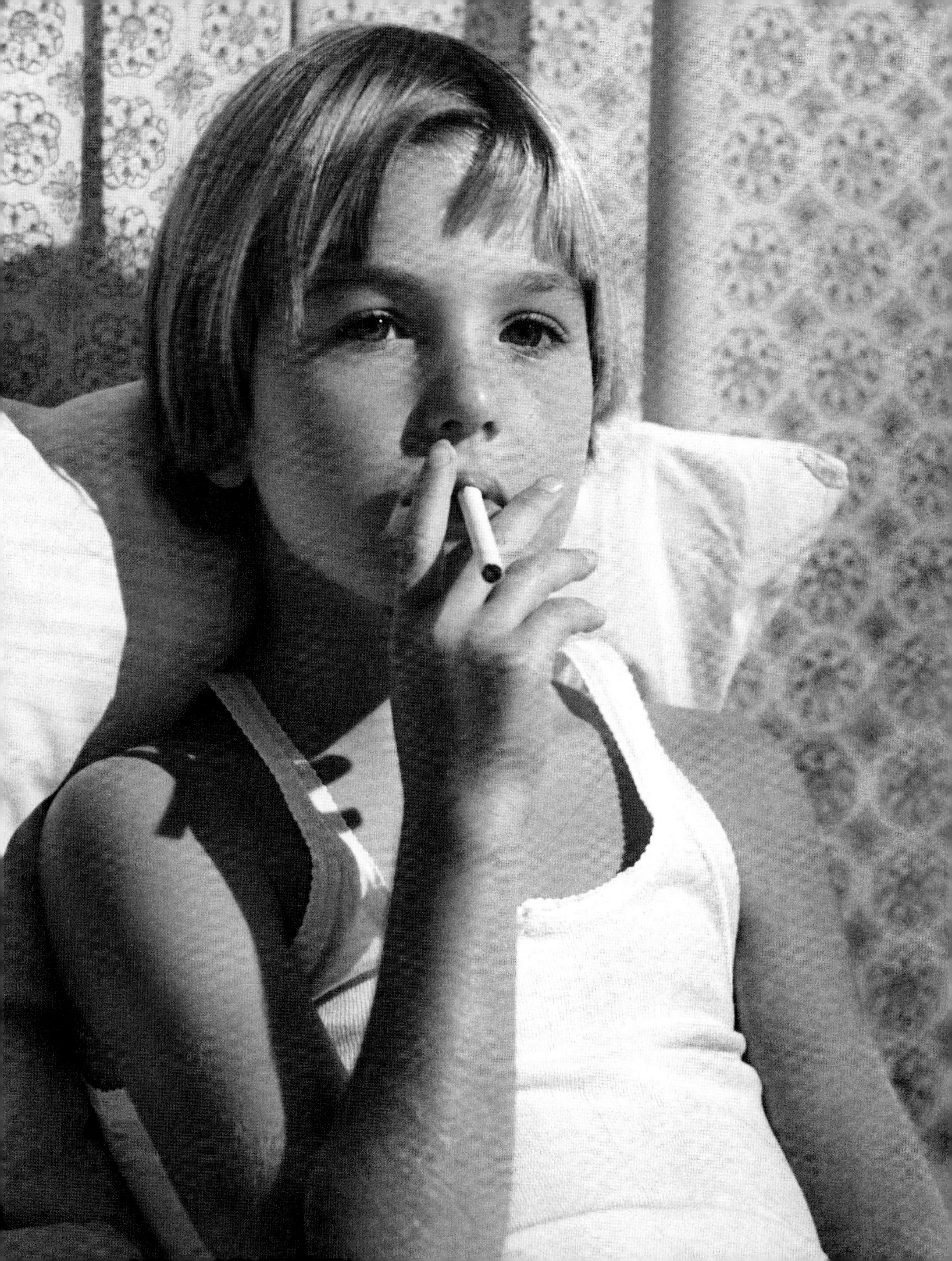

skepticism about the existence of Santa Claus is transformed into fervent belief.

After World War II, screen roles for children began evolving with the rapidly changing times. The new screenplays reflected a more realistic view of childhood, stripped of some of the contrived if endearing charm of little Shirley tap-dancing or Judy in the Land of Oz. In *The Parent Trap,* 15-year-old Hayley Mills—daughter of British actor John Mills—showed a shrewder aspect of adolescence, portraying twins *(below, right)* who trick their separated parents into reconciling.

In *Paper Moon* (1973), a natural con artist who smoked, cursed, and bilked lonely widows out of their money was nine-year-old Tatum O'Neal *(left).* Teamed up with a traveling swindler, played by her real-life father, Ryan O'Neal, she demonstrated that more than the old innocence was gone. Unlike Temple, who remembered everyone's lines, O'Neal had to be bribed to learn hers. But she delivered them so persuasively that she won an Oscar for Best Supporting Actress. One of the other nominees that year was 14-year-old Linda Blair, for her chilling performance in *The Exorcist.*

As roles available to child actors changed, so did the youngsters' treatment in the media. Intimate matters that once would have been hushed up, such as Garland's pill problems, became the everyday stuff of TV and tabloids. Perhaps the first child star to endure such exposure was Patty Duke. At 16 her performance in *The Miracle Worker* (1962) as the young Helen Keller *(above, right)*—blind, deaf, and mute—won the Academy Award for Best Supporting Actress. But along with the accolades came reports that she threw temper tantrums on the set—and her life off it proved no less troubled. Her father, who left home when she was six, was an alcoholic. Her mother had to be hospitalized repeatedly for mental illness. As a teenager, Duke herself drank heavily, suffered from manic-

Tatum O'Neal puffs away in Paper Moon. The actress admitted she had already been smoking secretly for three years.

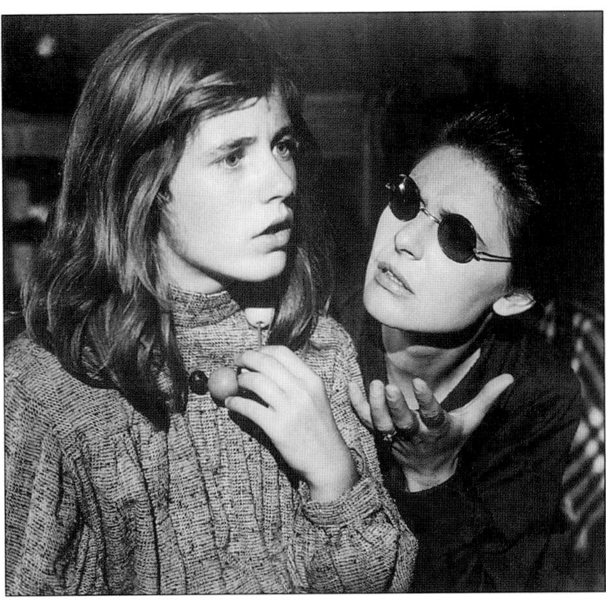

Helen Keller (Patty Duke) takes a lesson from her teacher, Annie Sullivan (Anne Bancroft), in The Miracle Worker. Duke and Bancroft were reprising roles that had won them acclaim on Broadway.

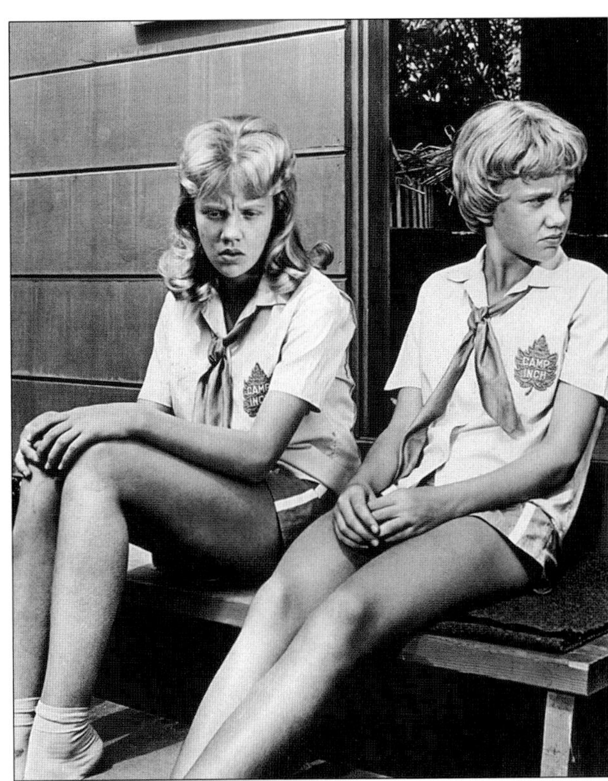

With the help of cinematic sleight of hand, Hayley Mills portrays twin sisters Susan and Sharon in the 1961 classic The Parent Trap.

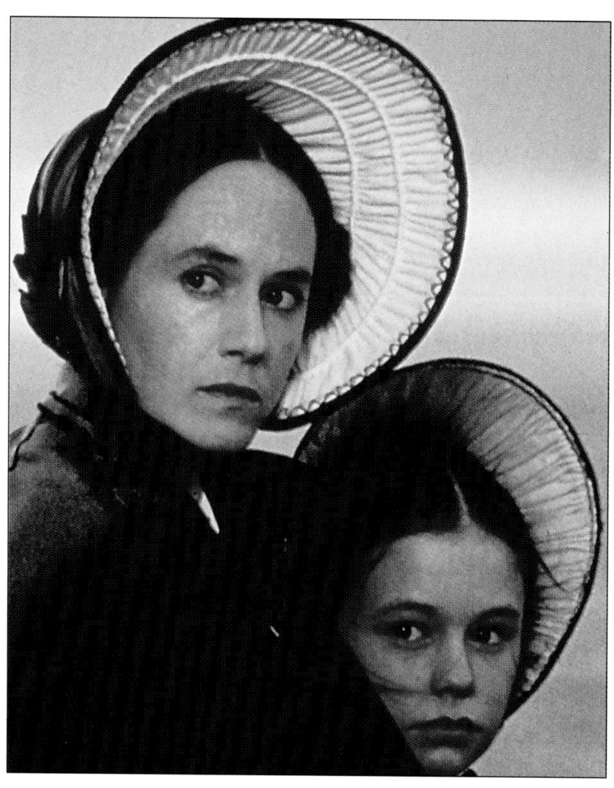

Anna Paquin and Holly Hunter won Oscars for their roles in The Piano. Hunter was Best Actress; Paquin became, next to Tatum O'Neal, the youngest winner of the Best Supporting Actress award.

Ten-year-old Macaulay Culkin is adept at demonstrating fear—and cunning—when confronted with burglars in Home Alone (1990).

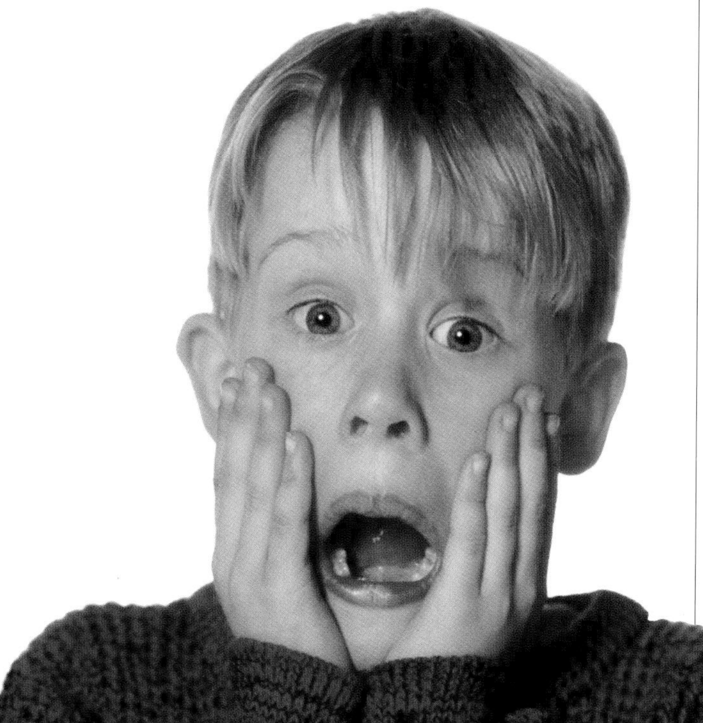

depressive illness, and was, she later charged, sexually abused by her managers.

The media also went to town on 10-year-old Macaulay Culkin. The hilarious difficulties he encountered in the hit *Home Alone (below, left)* paled alongside the highly publicized feuding that followed in his real-life family. Culkin, who earned an estimated $50 million in his first five years as a child star, retreated from the movies while his parents waged a bitter fight over custody of him and his six siblings; he then married at the age of 17.

In kids' roles, too, the kid gloves were off. Increasingly, children were being cast in R-rated films that, by law, they were not even allowed to view in theaters. Many of these roles demanded a new range of acting abilities. In 1994, 11-year-old Anna Paquin of New Zealand took the Oscar for Best Supporting Actress for her performance in the passionate 19th-century drama *The Piano (left).* Paquin had to develop a Scottish accent and learn to interpret the gestures through which her mute screen mother communicated. Yet her only previous acting experience had been the role of a skunk in a school play.

Unprecedented roles as child prostitutes were played by Brooke Shields and Jodie Foster. Both began their professional careers precociously—Shields as a baby model, Foster as the bare-bottomed three-year-old in a suntan-lotion commercial. Both played 12-year-old prostitutes—Shields in *Pretty Baby* (1978), Foster in *Taxi Driver* (1976) *(right).* Both actresses later went to Ivy League universities—Shields to Princeton, Foster to Yale. Shields later starred in her own TV series, *Suddenly Susan.* Foster went on to win two Best Actress Oscars and to direct her own films. Appropriately, when she appeared in front of the camera as well as behind it in her directorial debut, *Little Man Tate* (1991), she played the mother of a child prodigy.

Jodie Foster, 13, plays a child prostitute in Taxi Driver. In her next films she was a gangster's moll and a murderer.

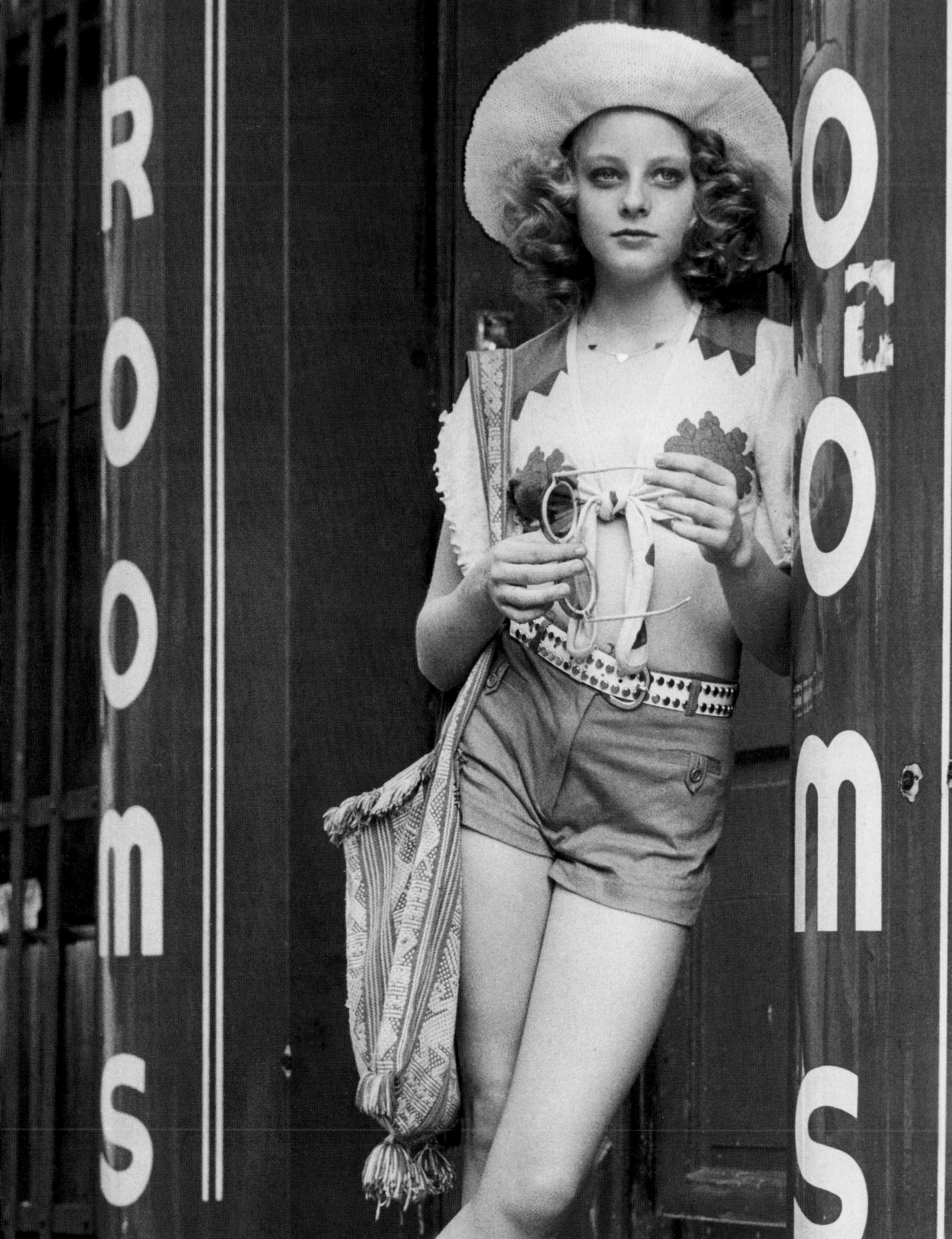
ROOMS

A Menagerie of Matinee Idols

Hollywood's first animal superstar was a refugee German shepherd *(opposite, top)*, saved from a bombed-out building in France during World War I. His rescuer, Lee Duncan, an American pilot, named him Rin Tin Tin after a character in a popular French story and taught him hundreds of tricks. Audiences flocked to his debut in the silent adventure film *Where the North Begins* (1923). His 21 subsequent movies were so popular that "Rinty" single-pawedly brought Warner Bros. back from near bankruptcy. Two of his descendants would follow him into the character in films, and a successor appeared in TV's *The Adventures of Rin Tin Tin*. But none could top the original. At the height of his nine-year career, Rinty lived in a mansion across the street from Jean Harlow and received more than a million pieces of fan mail annually.

Pete the Pup *(below)* was the featured canine of Our Gang, the series of short comedies produced between 1922 and 1944. Pete, a gentle pit bull terrier, first joined the gang of mischief-loving kids in 1927. He had a distinctive ring around his right eye that had been applied with liquid dye for another movie and would not come off. Over the next decade, as many as a dozen different terriers played Pete, and all of them wore the trademark eye-encircling paint. Audiences scarcely noticed that on all dogs but the first, the circle shifted back and forth between eyes—sometimes in the same film. "We just painted the ring around whichever eye would show it off the best," producer Hal Roach said. Whenever trouble loomed for his young comrades, each Pete would perform his primary trick: As if to say "Oh no, not again!" he would lie down, put his paws over his head, and close his eyes.

The best-known animal performer of all, Lassie *(right)*, was actually a female impersonator. The script for *Lassie Come Home* had called for a female collie, and a pedigreed female was cast in the role. But when the starring canine refused to go near the water in a critical scene, the director summoned her stand-in, Pal, a male with a somewhat questionable résumé. Pal's first owner had hired trainer Rudd Weatherwax to break the dog of chasing motorcycles and chewing up furniture, then let Weatherwax have him in lieu of payment. But when opportunity knocked, Pal came through. He swam the swollen stream,

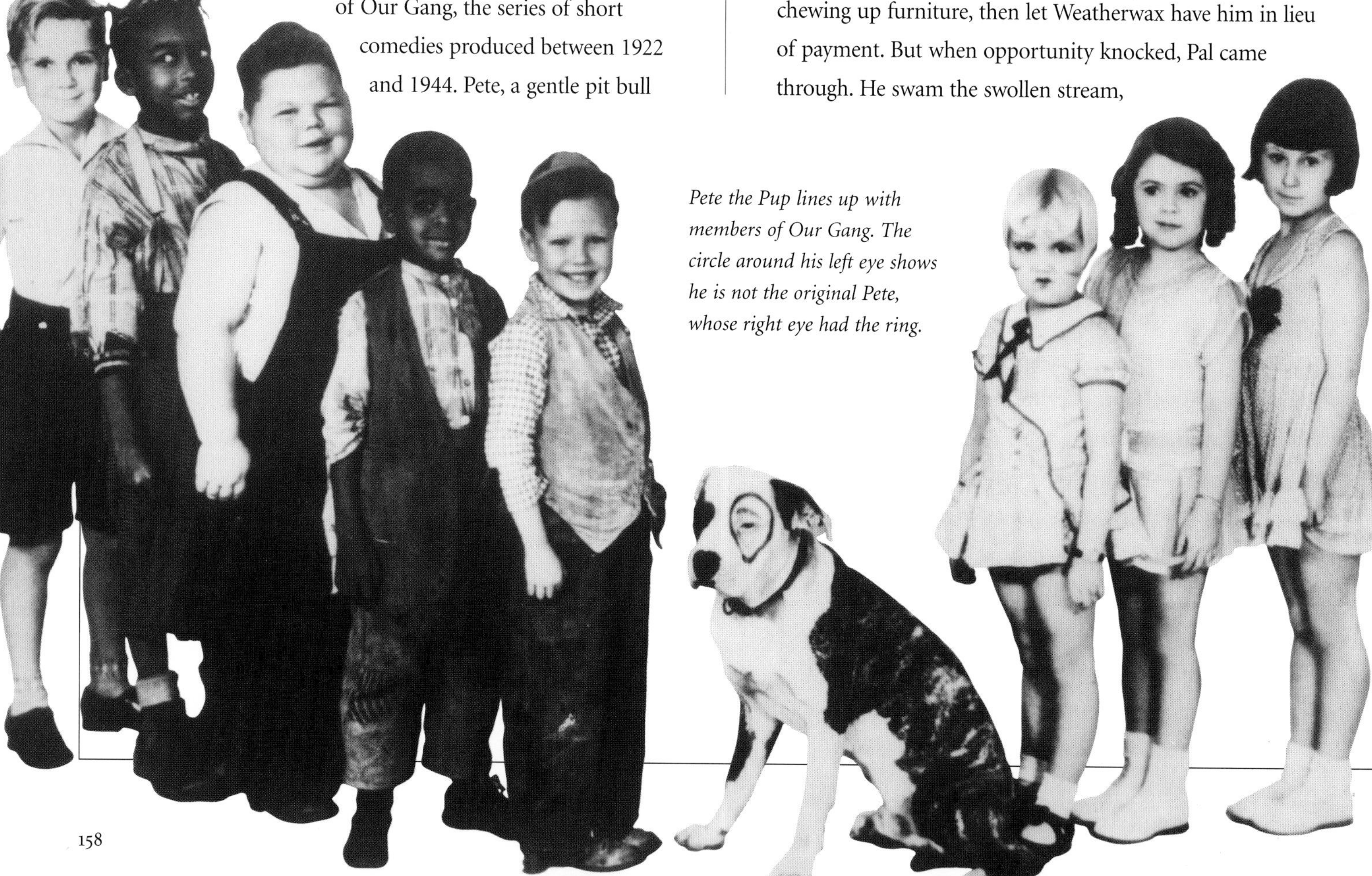

Pete the Pup lines up with members of Our Gang. The circle around his left eye shows he is not the original Pete, whose right eye had the ring.

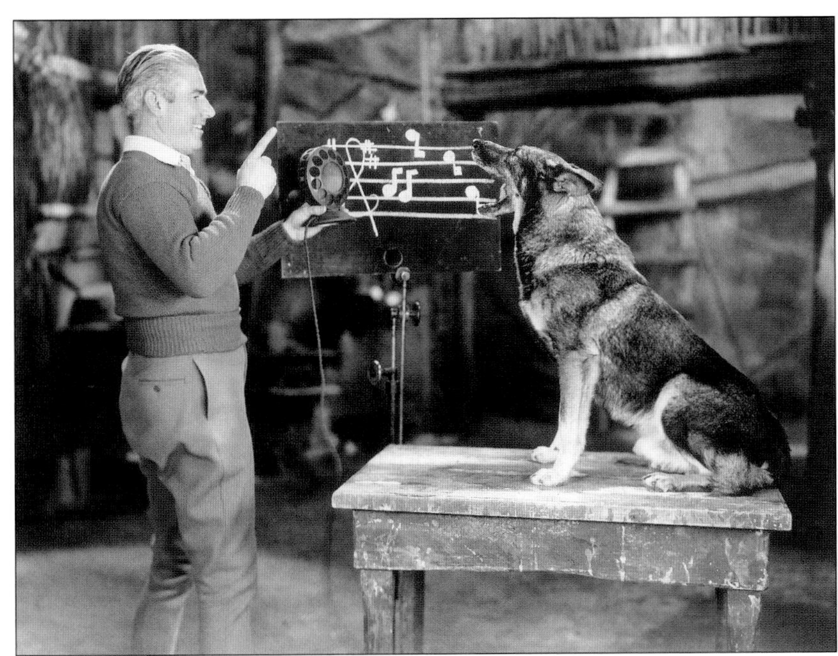

Taking a sound test in 1929, Rin Tin Tin shows he is ready for the talkies. Many of his fellow silent-screen stars could not make the switch.

"We can't even house-break him. Do you think you can train him?"

First owner of Pal (Lassie) to Rudd Weatherwax

The original Lassie was paid more for his work in the 1943 classic Lassie Come Home than his 11-year-old costar, Elizabeth Taylor.

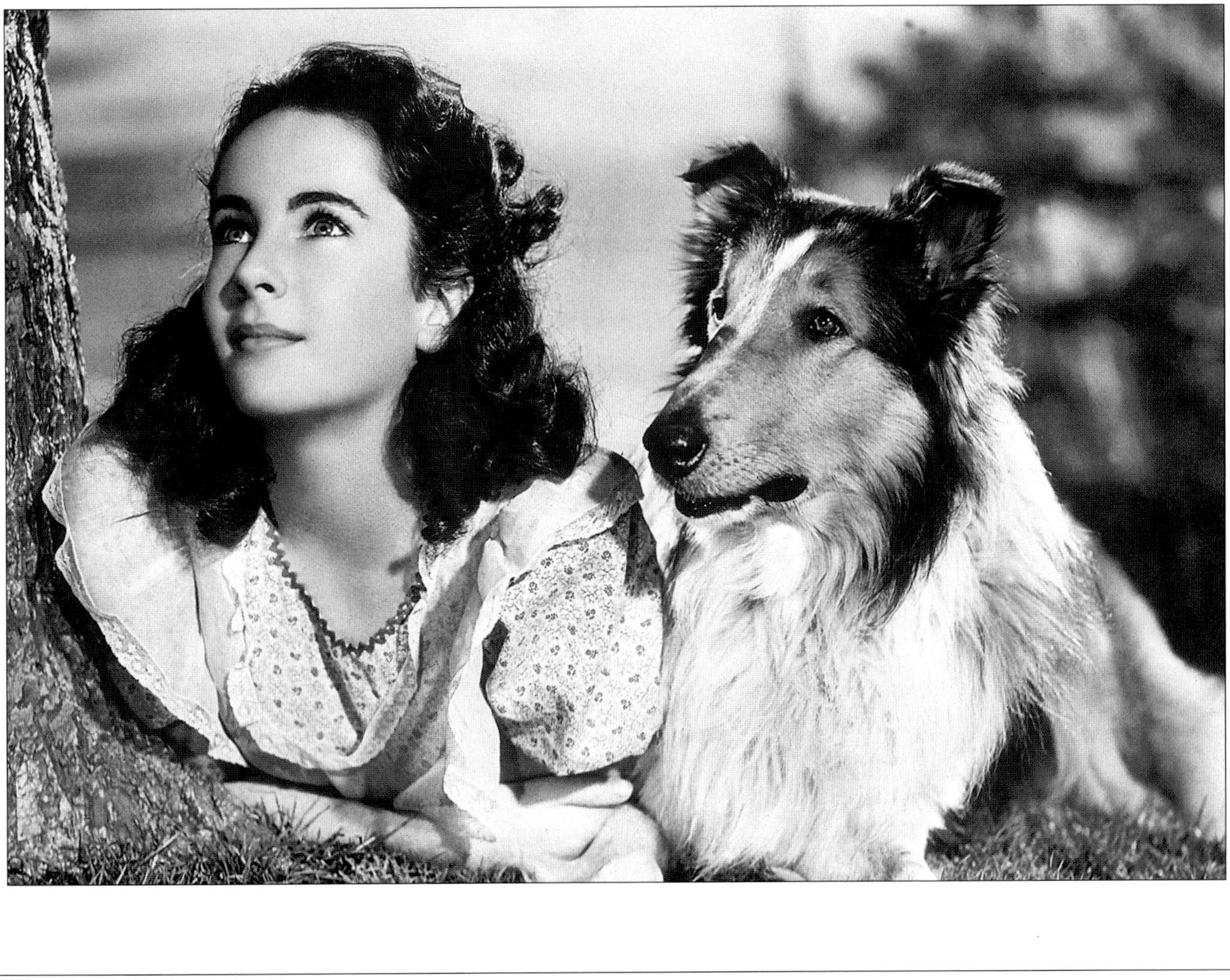

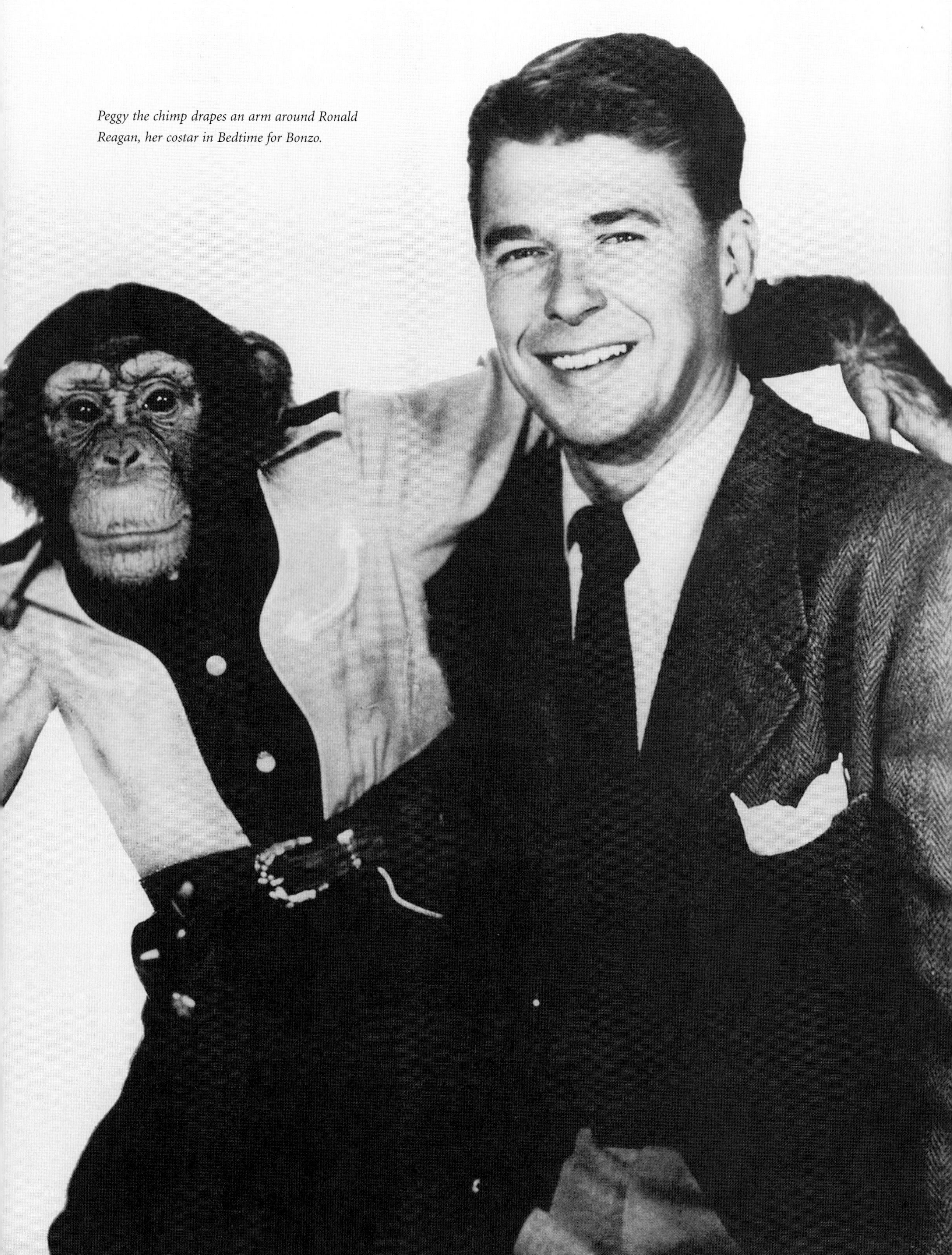

Peggy the chimp drapes an arm around Ronald Reagan, her costar in Bedtime for Bonzo.

emerged from the water, and, instead of shaking himself as any normal, red-blooded dog would, slumped down exhausted on cue. He got the role and shared the screen with two other promising newcomers—Roddy McDowall and Elizabeth Taylor. Pal starred in seven Lassie films. Later, five generations of his descendants—all male—played Lassie in movies or on TV.

Other animal stars have made their mark in comic roles. In *Bedtime for Bonzo* (1951), a chimpanzee named Peggy *(left)* became the only animal ever to share top billing with a future president. Ronald Reagan played a psychologist who raises a chimp to prove that environment rather than genes shapes behavior. Reagan found Peggy "adorable to work with" but unpredictable: She once grabbed his necktie and nearly strangled him.

Francis the Talking Mule *(right, top)* dispensed advice to Donald O'Connor and other human costars in seven films during the 1950s. His voice came from the veteran character actor Chill Wills, an old mule skinner who knew the critters so well he sometimes ignored the script and adlibbed Francis's dialogue. The mule's lips moved because the trainer manipulated them with thread or by pressing the muscles on the side of the head. After her first film, Francis—in reality a female named Molly—let stardom go to her head. She put on the feedbag with such gusto that for her next movie she had to lose 200 pounds by jogging the Hollywood hills and sweating in a custom-made steam cabinet. Molly could climb stairs, wink on cue, and execute almost all of the other necessary tricks. But she had her standards; she stubbornly refused to sit down, and that feat had to be performed by a stand-in.

The title role in *Babe* (1995) belonged to no fewer than 48 different white Yorkshire pigs. Because Yorkshires grow so quickly, four-week-old shoats were trained in groups of six so they could begin filming about 12 weeks later. Each wore a toupee to simulate the tuft of dark hair on Babe's forehead *(right)*. Animatronic clones and computer graphics created facial expressions and the

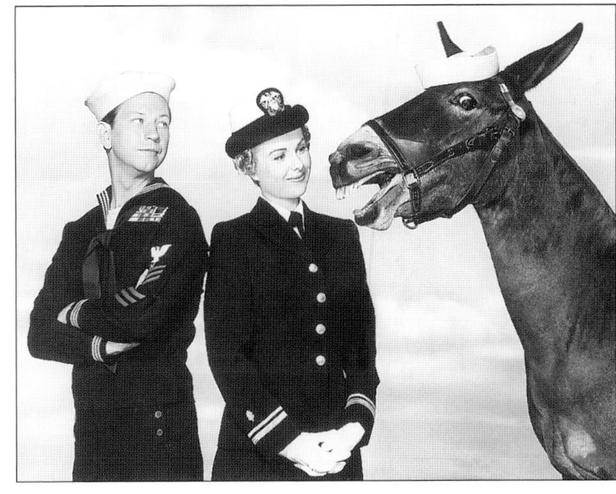

Francis the Talking Mule (Molly) advises fellow sailors Donald O'Connor and Martha Hyer in Francis in the Navy (1955).

"What trick is there to talking? Any fool can do it."

Francis the Talking Mule, in *Francis Joins the Wacs* (1954)

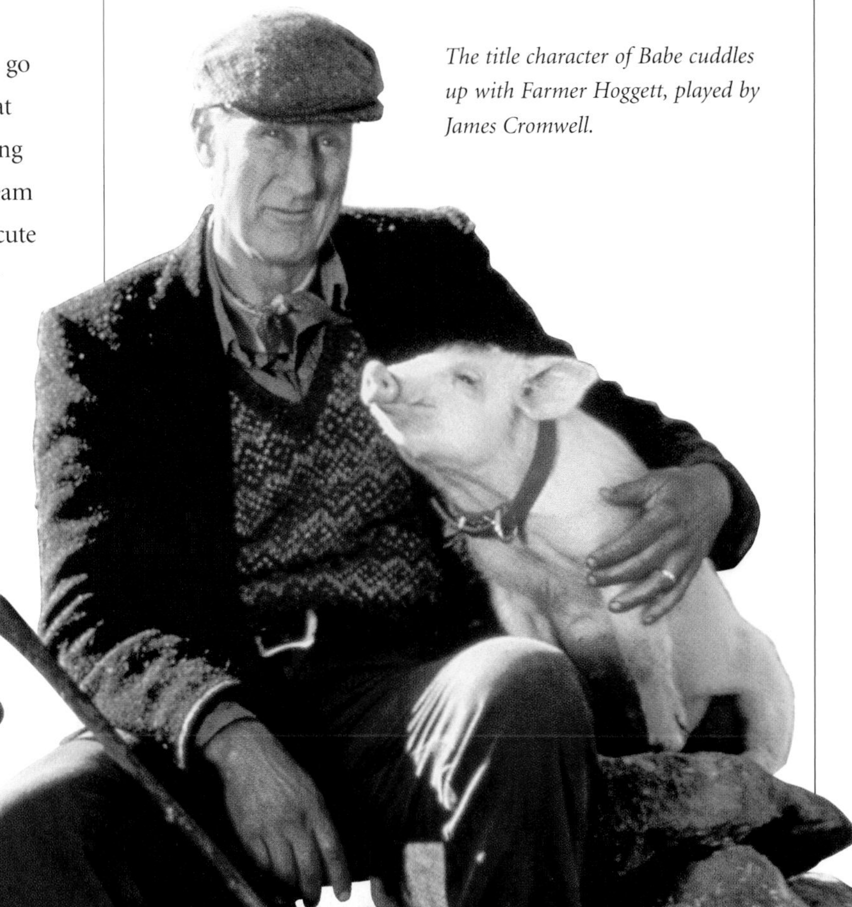

The title character of Babe cuddles up with Farmer Hoggett, played by James Cromwell.

appearance of speech for Babe and the 800 other animals cast in this charming fable.

During the 1990s, animal films tended to reflect environmental concerns. *Fly Away Home* (1996) grew out of the experiences of Canadian artist Bill Lishman, who taught a domesticated flock of geese how to migrate by leading them south to winter quarters in an ultralight plane. In the film, Anna Paquin, Academy Award winner for *The Piano (page 156),* finds an abandoned nest of goose eggs and becomes surrogate mother to the goslings. When it is time to migrate, they don't know where to go, but Anna shows them the way in a little goose-shaped aircraft *(below).*

Life imitated art in the saga of Keiko the killer whale—star of *Free Willy* (1993). In the film, Keiko plays Willy, a captive in an amusement park with an unscrupulous owner. A 12-year-old boy helps the whale gain his freedom *(right).* In real life, it turned out, after the film was shot Keiko was returned to a seaquarium in Mexico City, where he lived in a cramped, filthy pool, lost weight, and developed a severe skin disease. An exposé in *Life* magazine touched off a worldwide campaign to rescue Keiko. Millions of dollars in contributions poured in, and the Free Willy-Keiko Foundation was formed to return the whale to the North Atlantic near Iceland, where he had been captured in 1979. Keiko was airlifted in 1996 to a rehabilitation facility in Oregon, where he recovered, gained weight, and learned to hunt. Two years later he was flown to Iceland to move into a new temporary home in a huge floating pen. Nylon mesh sides enabled him to acclimate to the ocean around him as he underwent preparation for release into his native waters.

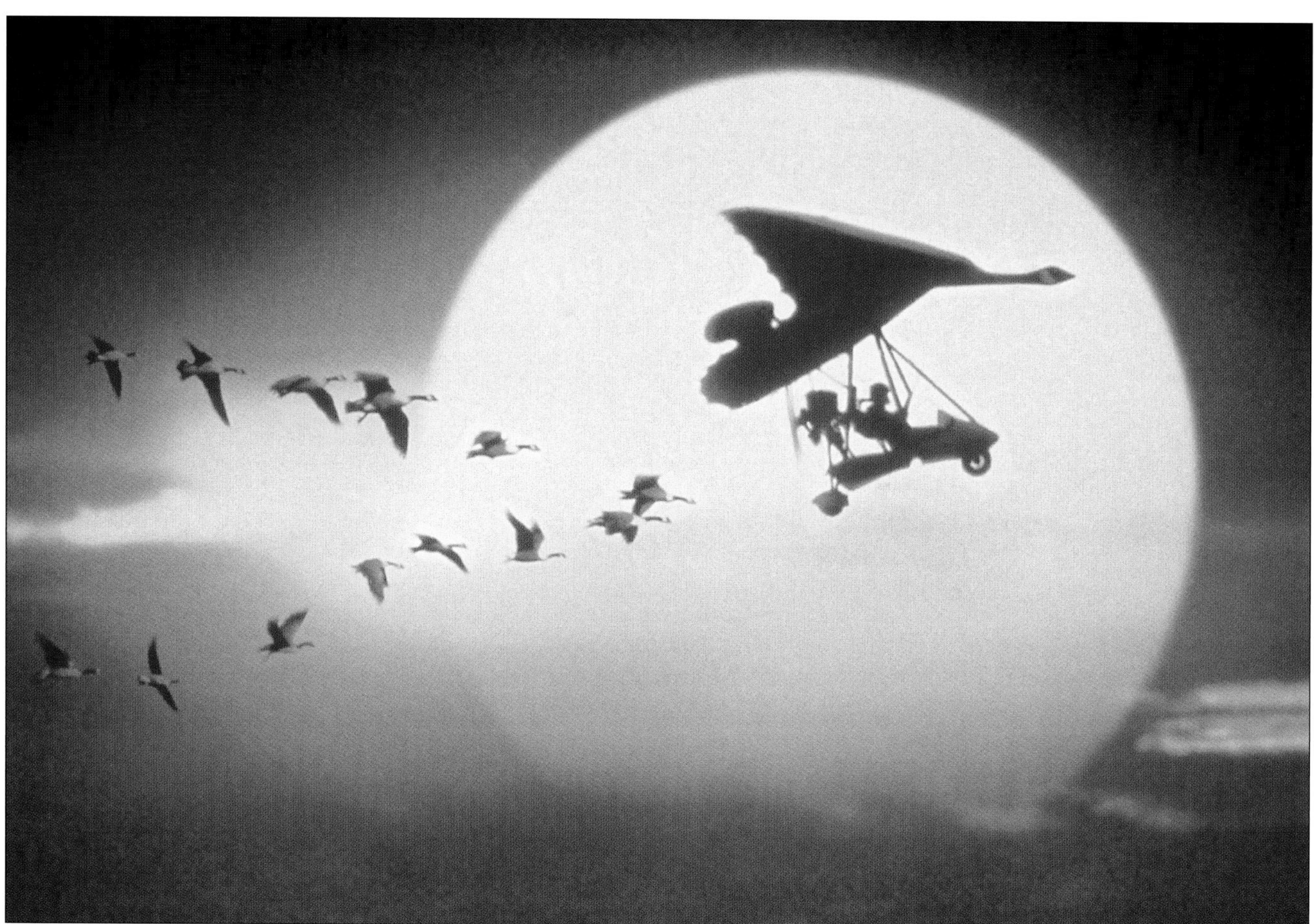

Piloting a goose-shaped ultralight aircraft, Anna Paquin leads a flock of Canada geese on their first migration south in Fly Away Home.

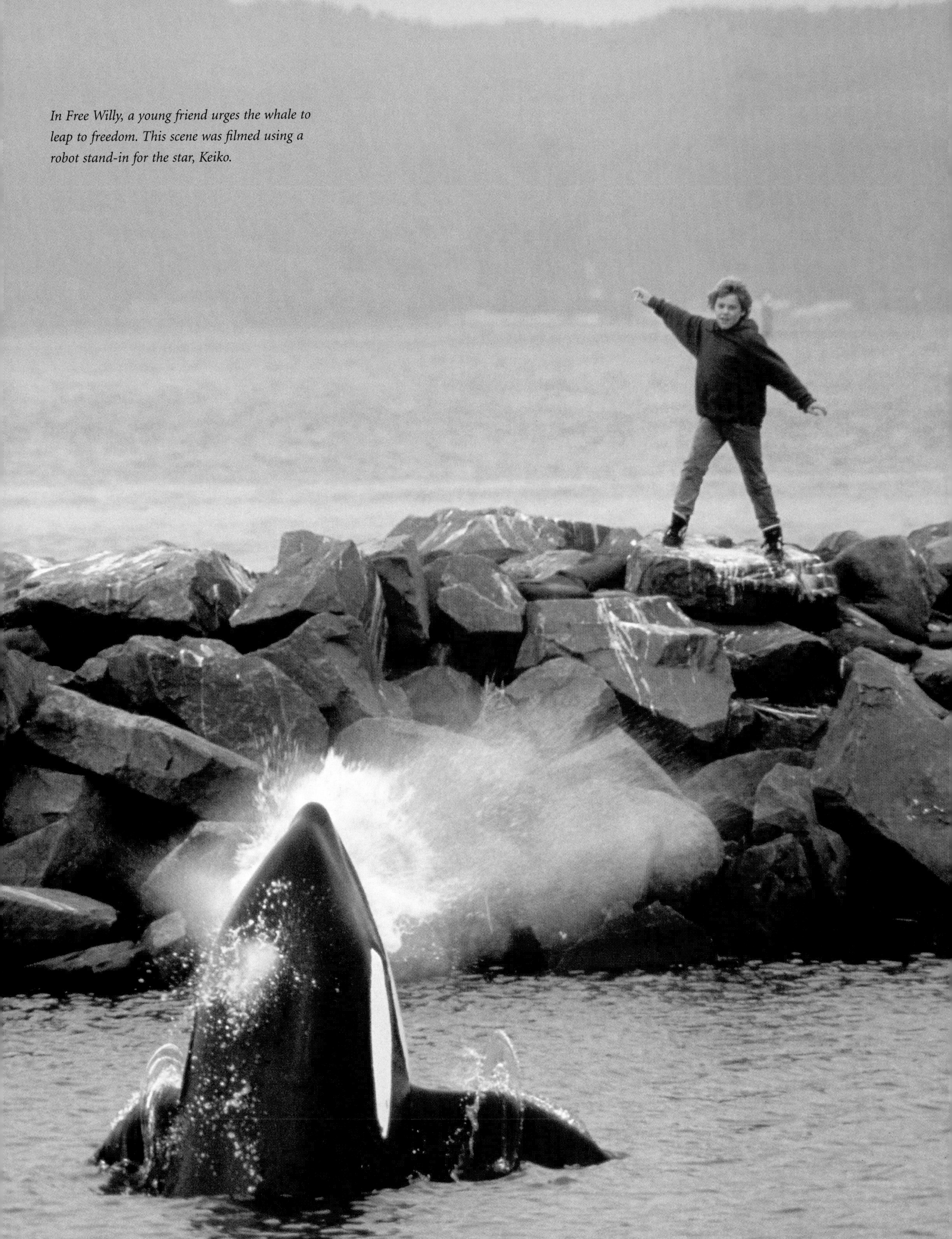

In Free Willy, a young friend urges the whale to leap to freedom. This scene was filmed using a robot stand-in for the star, Keiko.

The Lights in Hollywood's Sky

★

CELEBRATING THE STARS

The headline in the November 21, 1913, issue of the showbiz newspaper *Variety* reported a new phenomenon—an outrageous one, in the minds of the studio bosses of the day: "Picture Actors Are Asking for Names on the Screen." Farsighted in many ways, the pioneer movie moguls nonetheless did not yet perceive that their business would ride to riches primarily on star power.

Although those early actors had not asked for much, the process of celebrating them—once it began—did not stop at mere recognition. Smiling or sneering into the camera, they were a new kind of popular hero. After their names became as well known as their faces, Americans were willing—indeed, eager—to pay not only to watch their work but also to see pictures of them at play and to read and hear about their lives and loves and frailties and follies. The actors were now called stars, an apt celestial metaphor, for as they stood before the camera they were literally suffused with light and seemed to sparkle. Hollywood's galaxy became as familiar as the night sky and equally out of reach. And like the heavens in perpetual movement, they were in a constant process of change—in one film beggar, in another prince.

With their fame the stars reaped almost unimaginable wealth, adulation, and, for some of the serious actors among them, a token of recognition almost equally valued—an Oscar *(inset)*.

The very essence of that elusive something called star quality, 26-year-old Elizabeth Taylor exudes a smoldering sexuality as Maggie in the 1958 film version of Tennessee Williams's Cat on a Hot Tin Roof.

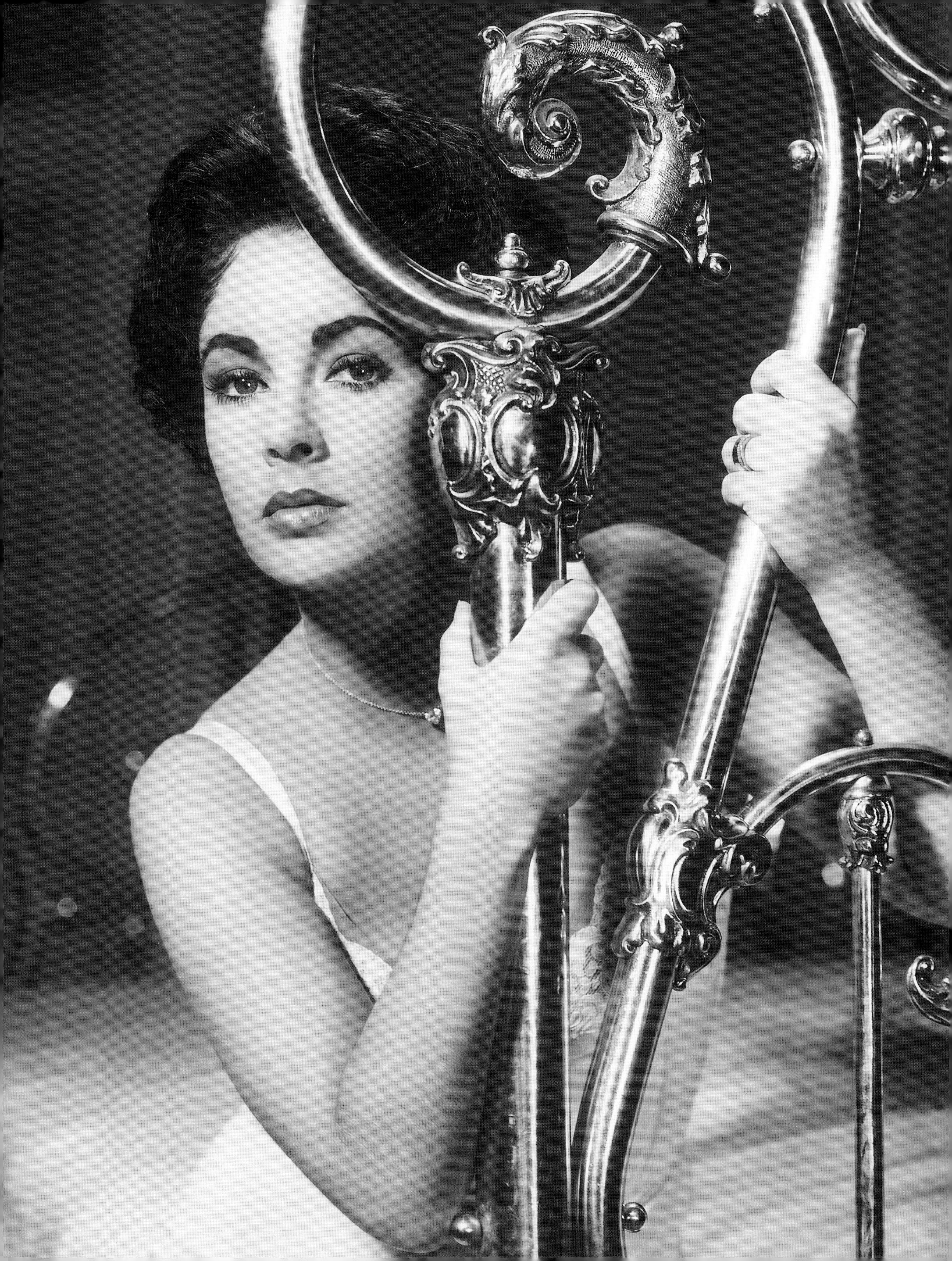

The Making of a Movie Star

Almost from the beginning, the possibility of film stardom exerted a gravitational pull on American youth. Although some of the biggest Hollywood names—James Stewart and Katharine Hepburn, for example—came from the stage, for thousands of hometown prom queens and handsome quarterbacks, the promise of a life in the movies was irresistible. They dreamed of being "discovered." Few ever were, but just one story like Lana Turner's was enough to keep the dream alive. She was spotted at 15, cutting school, sipping a Coke—although not in Schwab's Drugstore, as legend would have it—by Billy Wilkerson, publisher of the *Hollywood Reporter.* Asked if she'd like to be in pictures, she replied simply, "I'll have to ask my mother."

The fortunate few who survived the compulsory screen test—and sometimes the notorious casting couch—were taken in hand by the strong arm of the studio. There they were made, and made over, into images. Restyled, renamed, buffed to dental perfection, and tutored in makeup, voice, and comportment, an Iowa farm girl might come off the assembly line a glamorous temptress in a skintight gown.

Thus reconfigured, new stars went into the studio inventory and were protected from mishap with great care. "You can't imagine how the studios cosseted us in those days," said Robert Taylor, born Spangler Arlington Brugh in Filley, Nebraska. "They had to. If we weren't looked after and guarded, the fans would tear us to pieces."

The fans were ravenous indeed, and to gratify their insatiable curiosity, the publicity function expanded beyond

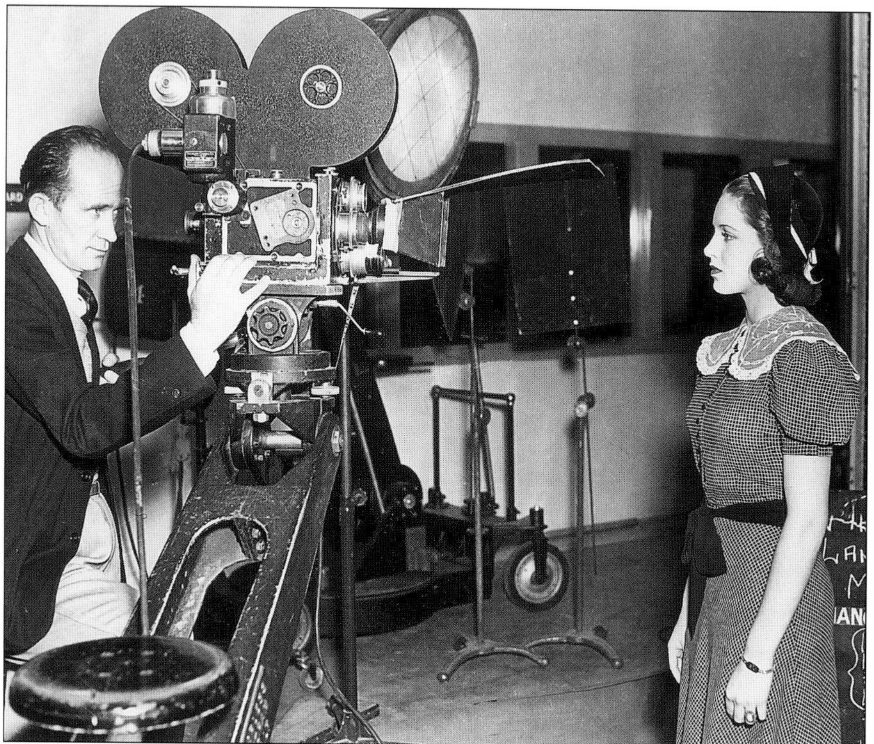

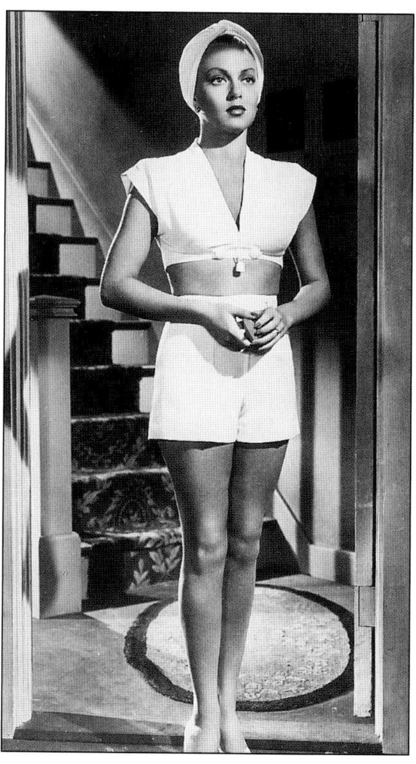

A sunbonnet set amid her auburn curls, Julia Jean Turner, 16, stands before the camera for her 1937 screen test (left). By the time she starred as the seductive but cold-blooded wife in 1946's The Postman Always Rings Twice (right), Lana Turner had made the real-life journey from virgin to vixen.

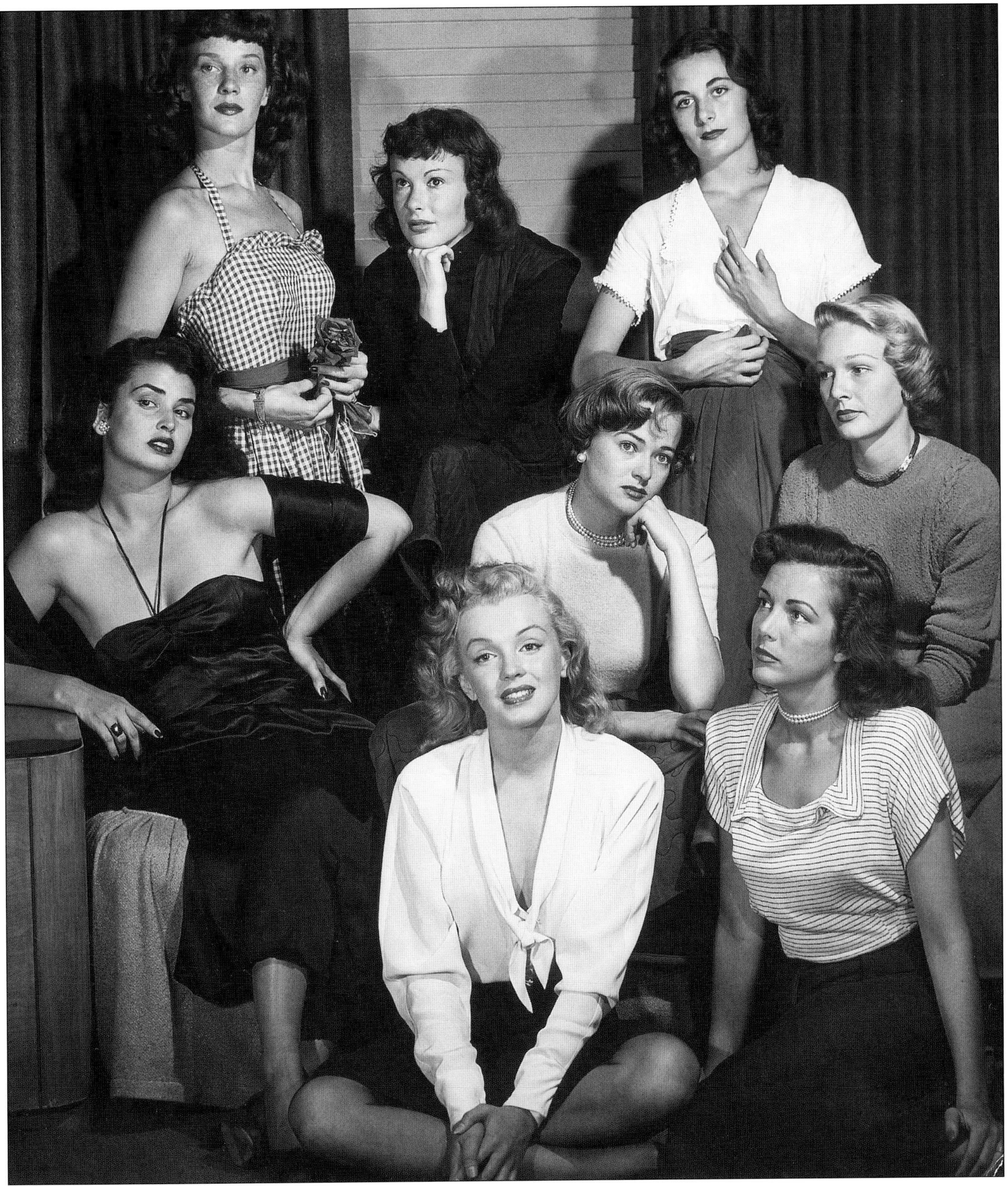

The Hollywood publicity machine would manage to crank out only one prize graduate from this 1949 class of starlets—but what a one: With her wistful vulnerability, Marilyn Monroe seems to project the most affecting—and genuine—expression.

the control of the studios into a journalistic genre of its own. No one better represented the power of the celebrity press than the newspaper columnists: Walter Winchell, Hedda Hopper *(inset)*, and Louella Parsons. Hopper and Parsons—rival scoopsters, gargoyles of gossip—became Tinseltown celebrities in their own right; Winchell was an American institution.

Because Parsons and Hopper together had a daily readership of 75 million people—more than half the U.S. population in the 1940s—they had tremendous power. A favorable mention by either was an incalculable boost to an actor's career; a slight could end it. Hopper candidly referred to her Beverly Hills mansion as "the house that fear built." Winchell wielded vast influence in political as well as entertainment circles. Once, accosted by an angry film fan, he cried, "You can't talk to me that way! I'm God!"

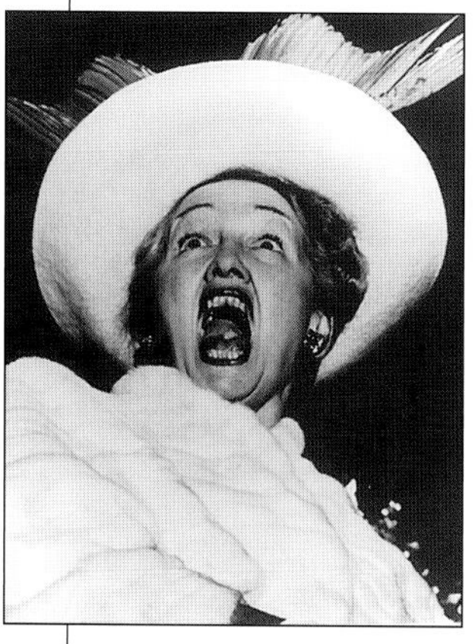

Hedda Hopper

After *Life* magazine was launched in 1936, it soon came to seem that the magazine and Hollywood were made for each other. Many would-be stars found that publicity shots taken by *Life*'s staff photographers could help them win that all-important first part. And many of the magazine's most popular covers *(right)* featured the screen's best-known faces.

The end of World War II brought changes to Hollywood. The studio system began a period of decline from which it would never recover. New actors came on the scene, many trained by top acting coaches in New York. Independent, schooled in theory, and less obsessed with the tinsel than their predecessors, stars such as Marlon Brando, James Dean, Paul Newman, Dustin Hoffman, and Joanne Woodward eschewed the usual contrivances of mainstream publicity. Gone were the fantasies concocted by studio press agents. The new breed insulated themselves with entourages of assistants, pressed for creative control of their

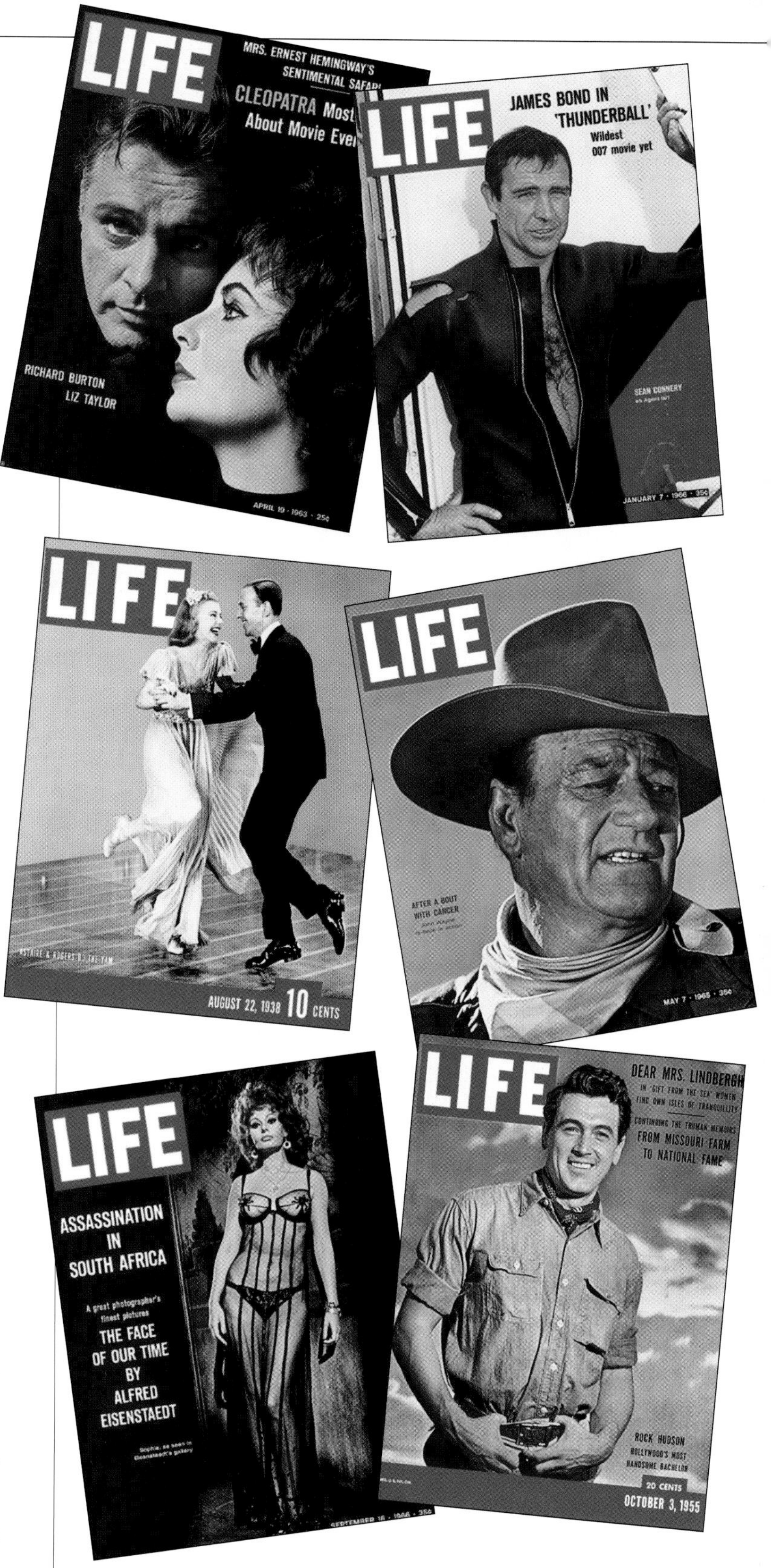

Whether featuring a supernova or an ingenue, Life always found a fond place for the movie star portrait. During its 36 years as a weekly, the magazine devoted 290 covers to Hollywood royalty.

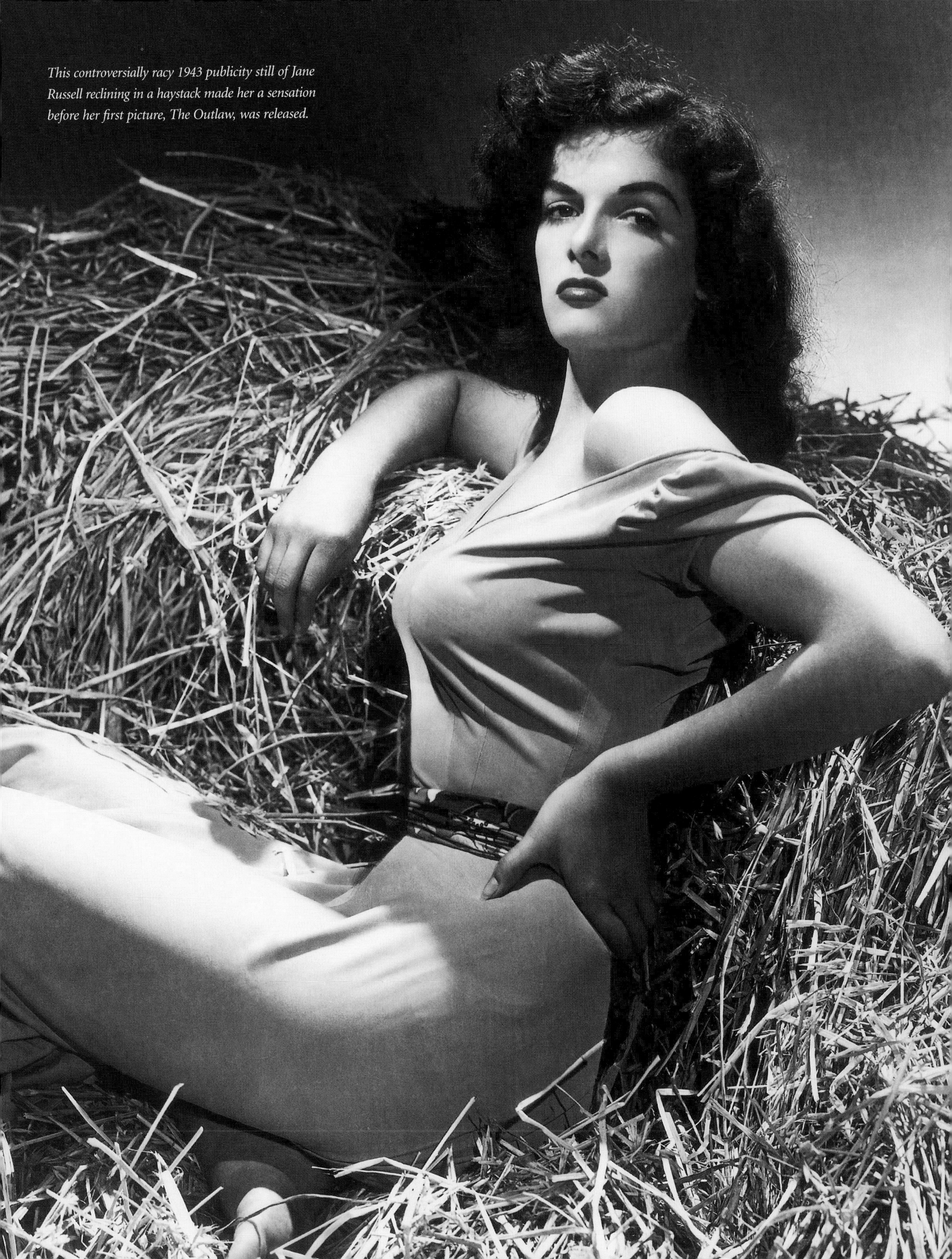

This controversially racy 1943 publicity still of Jane Russell reclining in a haystack made her a sensation before her first picture, The Outlaw, was released.

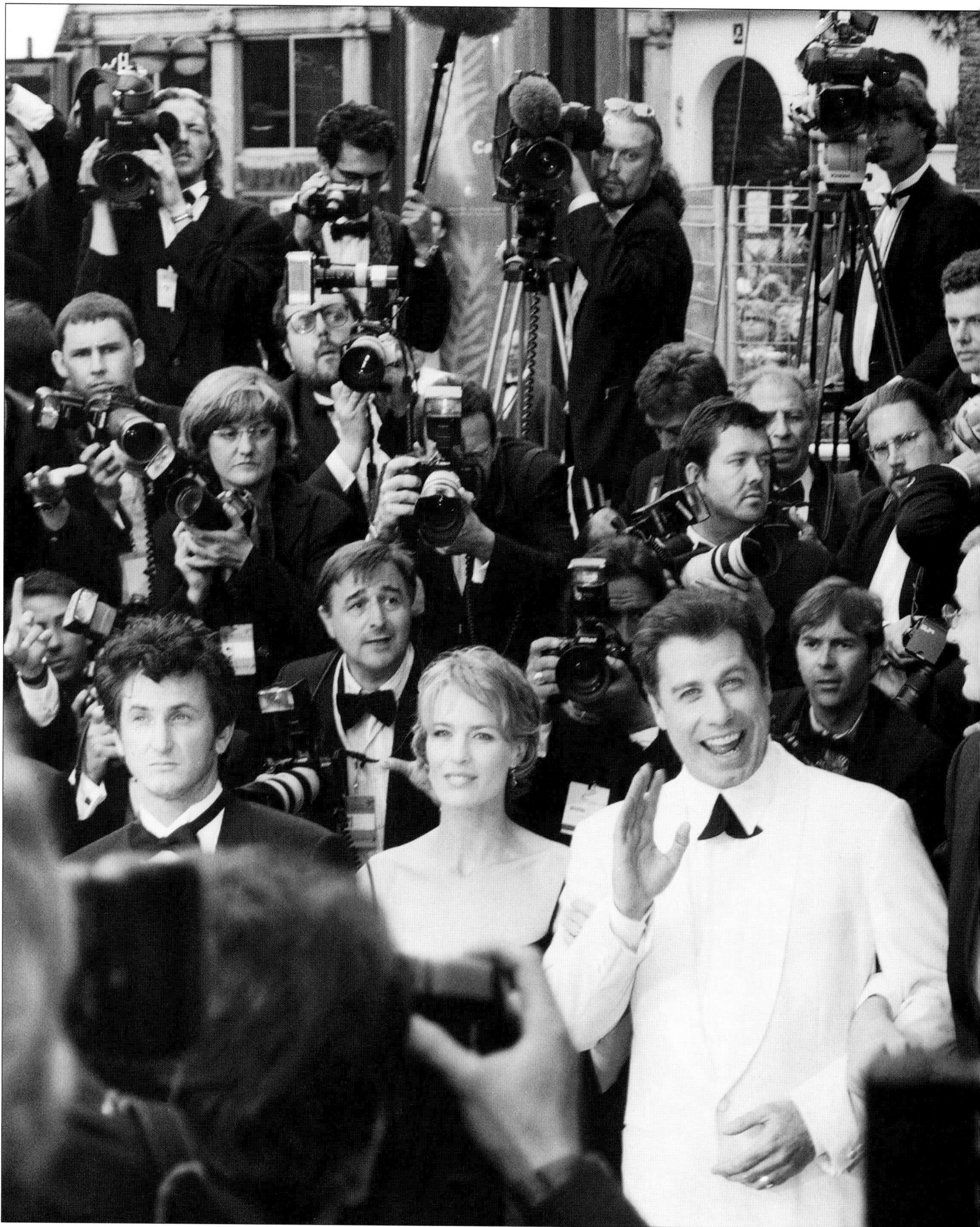

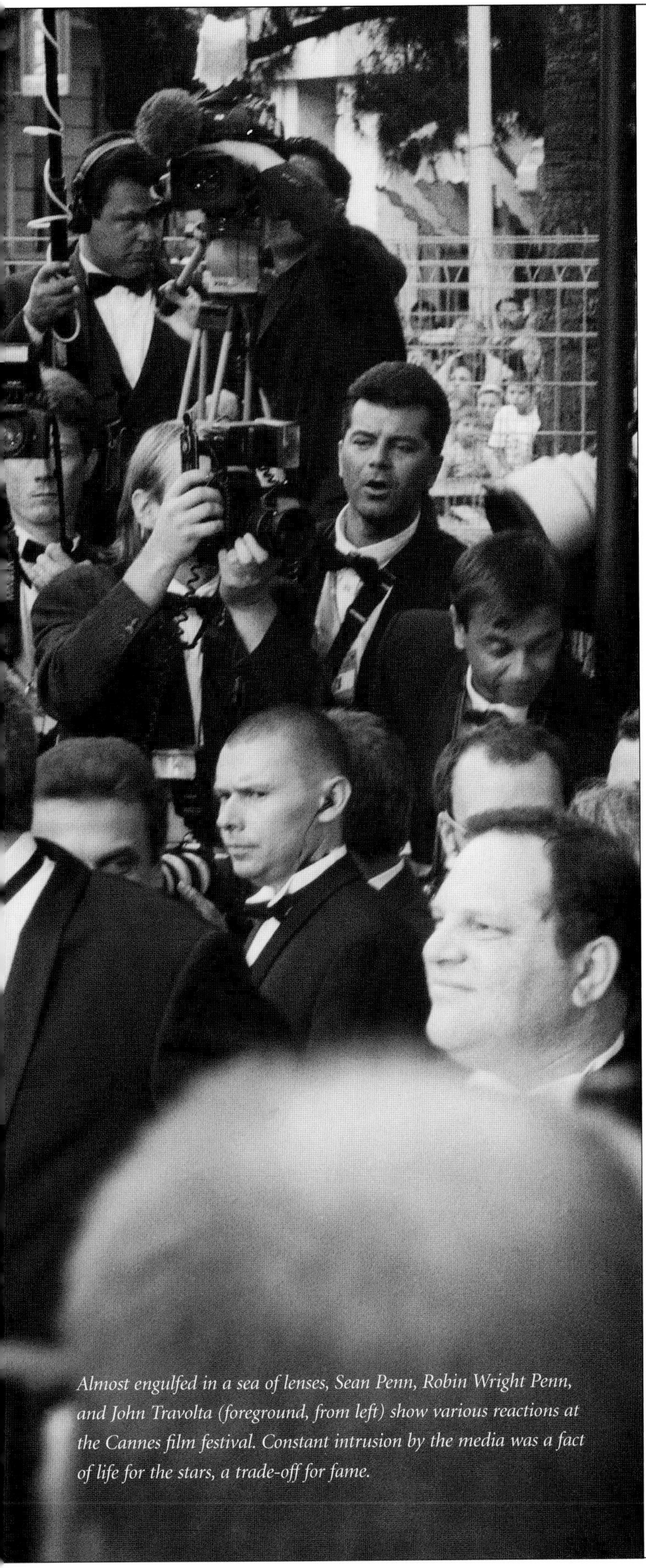

projects, and frequently produced and directed their own films instead of acting under the direction of others.

But Americans still wanted to see behind the dark glasses. The public's interest in the stars' private lives became, if anything, a greater obsession than ever. And, in the relatively forthright spirit of the times, many stars were surprisingly candid in their self-revelations. For a long time the job of conveying the stories to the public remained the province of the magazines. *Life* ended its weekly run in 1972, but two years later *People* arrived to fill the gap.

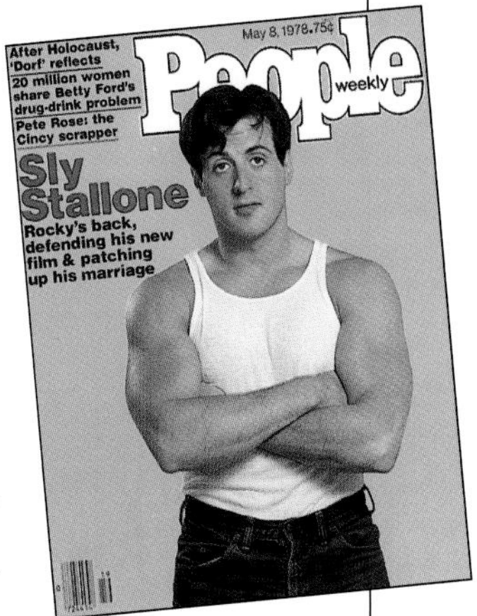

Later, magazines like *Vanity Fair* and *Entertainment Weekly* added impetus to the trend, elevating celebrity to a fetish. With a seemingly inexhaustible supply of uninhibited and insanely rich young stars eager to tell—and show—all, the magazines published fresh and often audacious interviews and cutting-edge pictures by photographers who were famous in their own right. Coverage of film stars began to be given equal weight with articles about world leaders, captains of industry, and aristocrats.

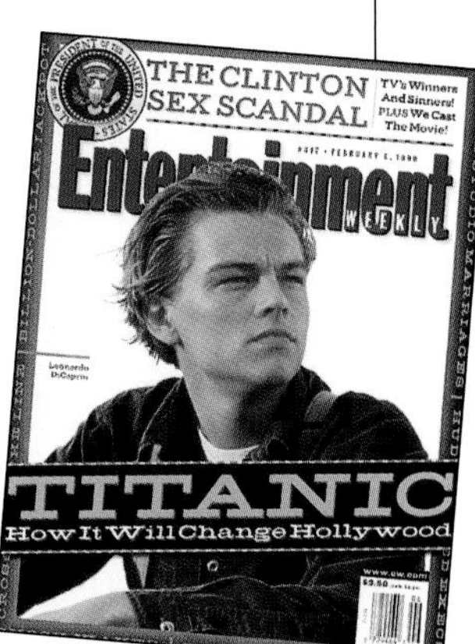

With seemingly no end in sight to the public's craving for the lowdown on the stars, television got into the act with nightly entertainment-news programs, followed soon after by countless sites on the World Wide Web. Internet users could get the purported inside dope on their favorite stars—everything from latest love affair to choice of shampoo.

Whether they were the studio-controlled glamour pusses of Hollywood's golden age or the independent-minded actors of a latter day, the stars' appeal remained the same. With their wealth, their pure visual impact, and their fame, movie stars gave their fans vicarious access to dreams, a high-flying slice of life to titillate an earthbound audience.

Almost engulfed in a sea of lenses, Sean Penn, Robin Wright Penn, and John Travolta (foreground, from left) show various reactions at the Cannes film festival. Constant intrusion by the media was a fact of life for the stars, a trade-off for fame.

Laurence Olivier
Hamlet, 1948

"More Stars Than in the Heavens"

In the days when each studio had its roster of actors under contract, MGM used the headline above as a slogan. Those days are long gone, but the stars still shine. Some of the best known adorn these and the following pages.

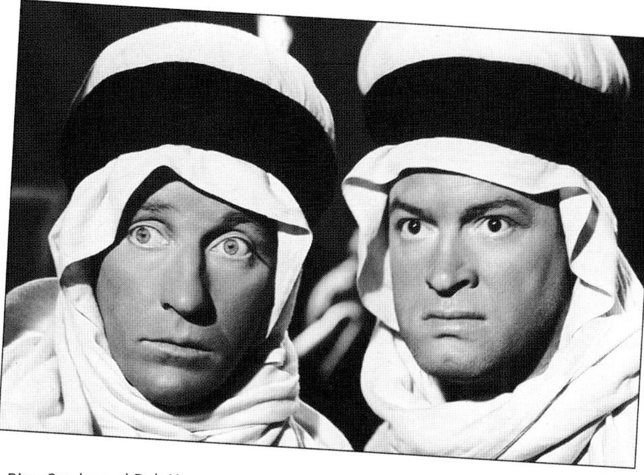

Bing Crosby and Bob Hope
The Road to Morocco, 1942

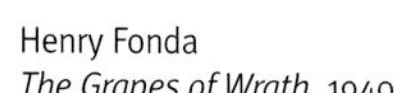

Henry Fonda
The Grapes of Wrath, 1940

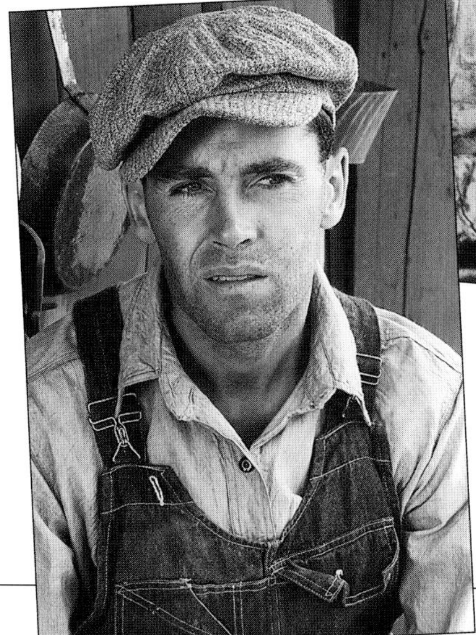

Spencer Tracy
The Old Man and the Sea, 1958

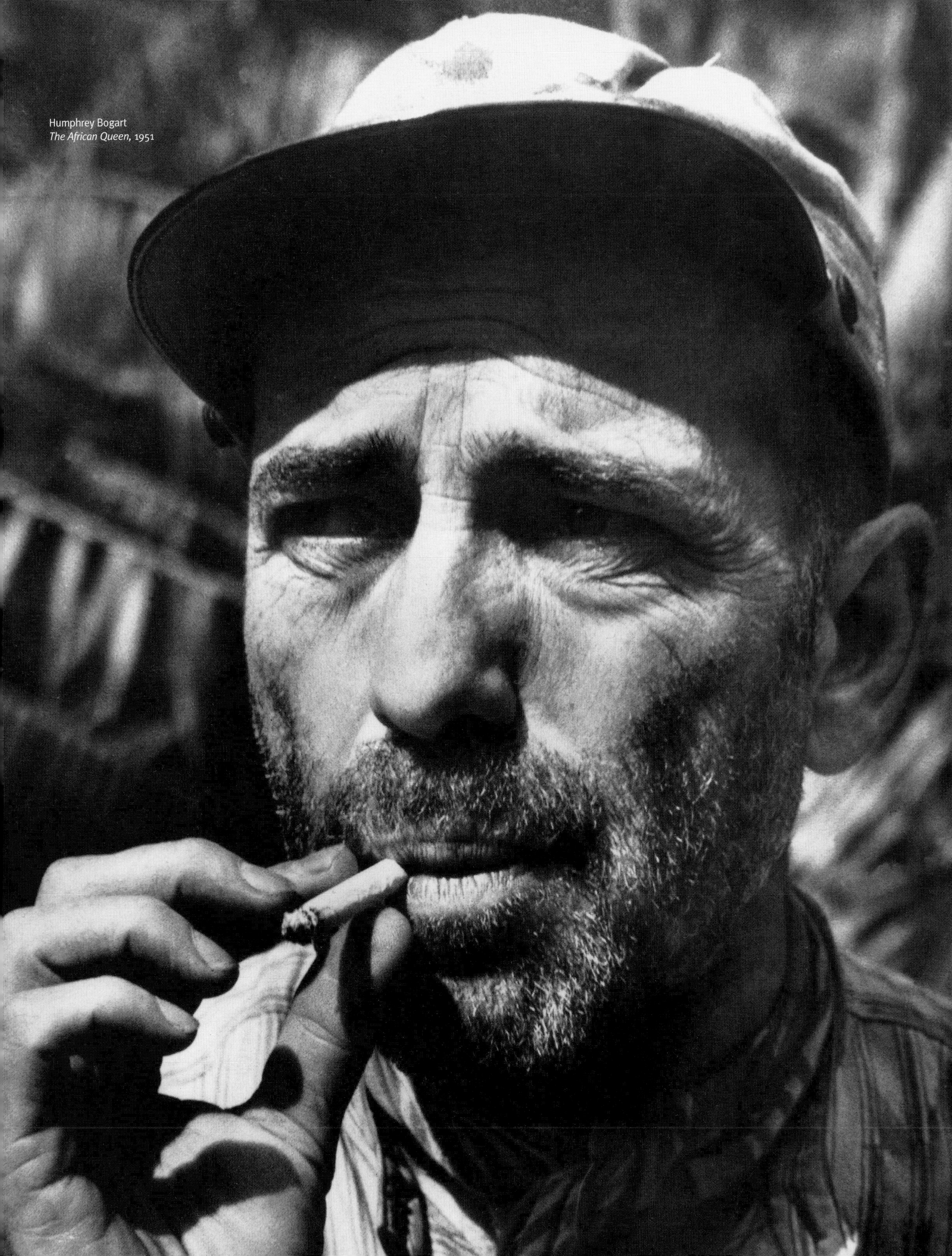

Humphrey Bogart
The African Queen, 1951

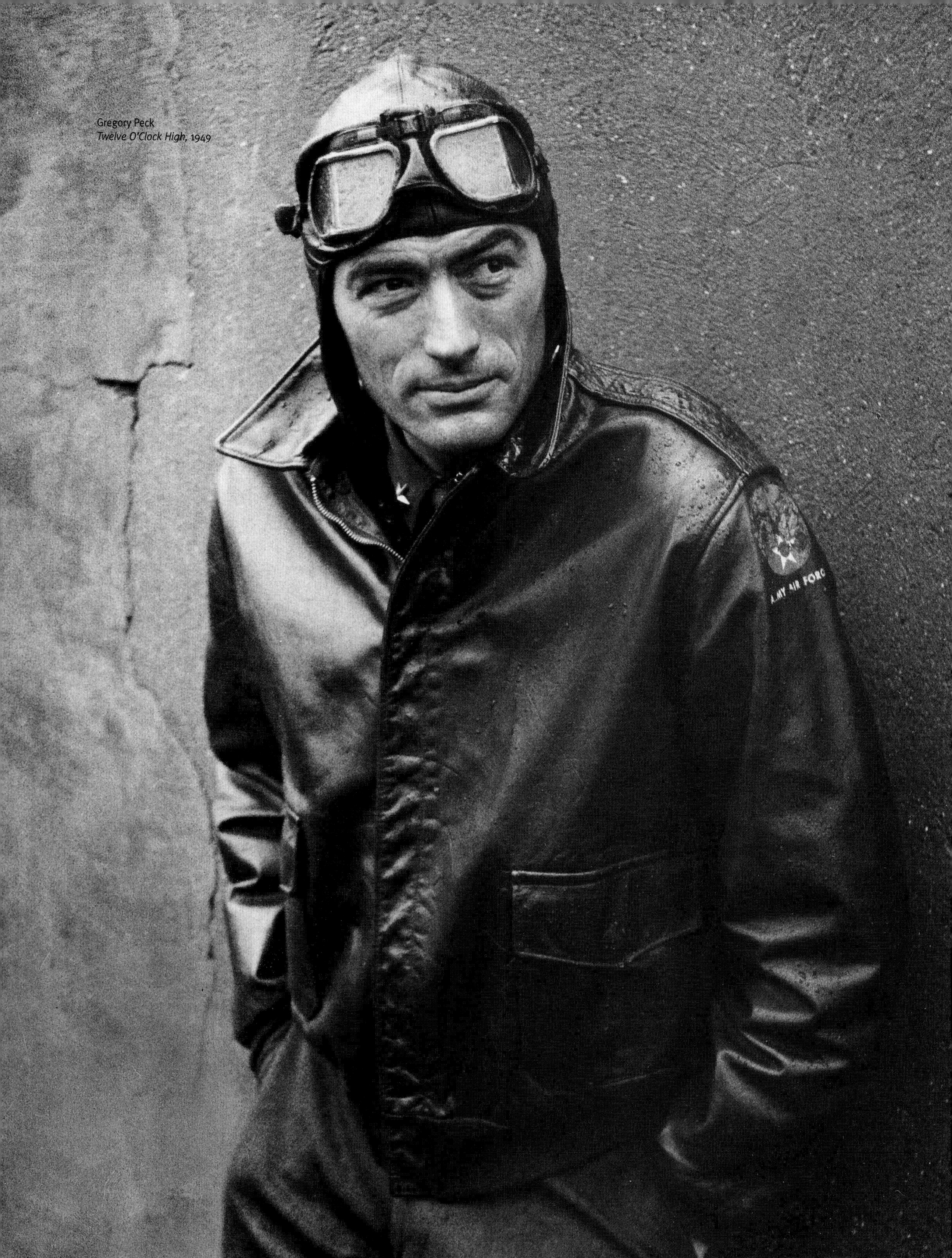

Gregory Peck
Twelve O'Clock High, 1949

Jack Lemmon
The Odd Couple, 1968

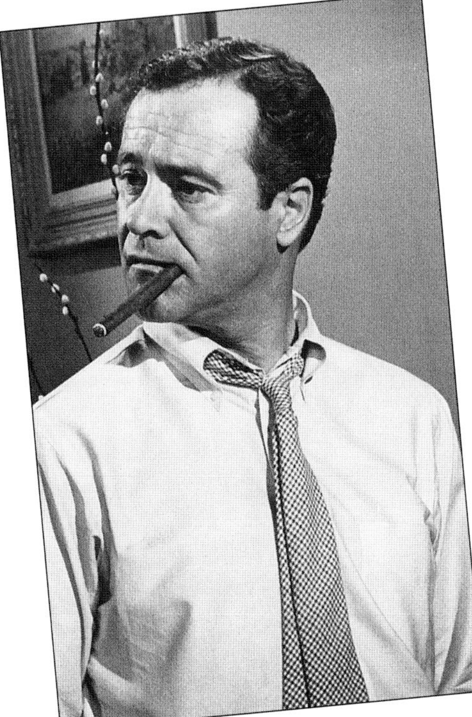

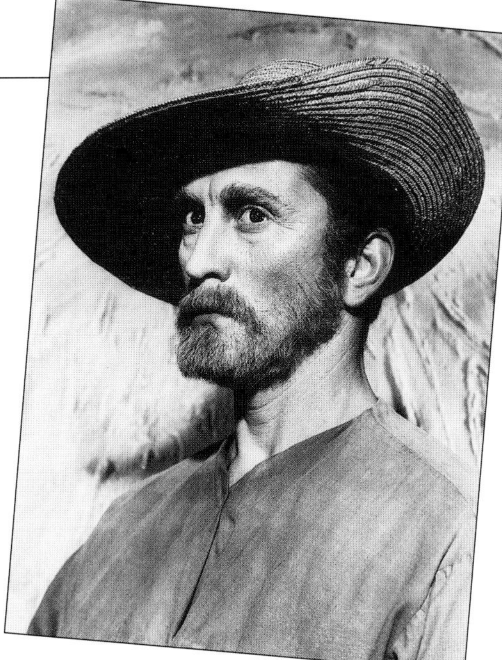

Kirk Douglas
Lust for Life, 1956

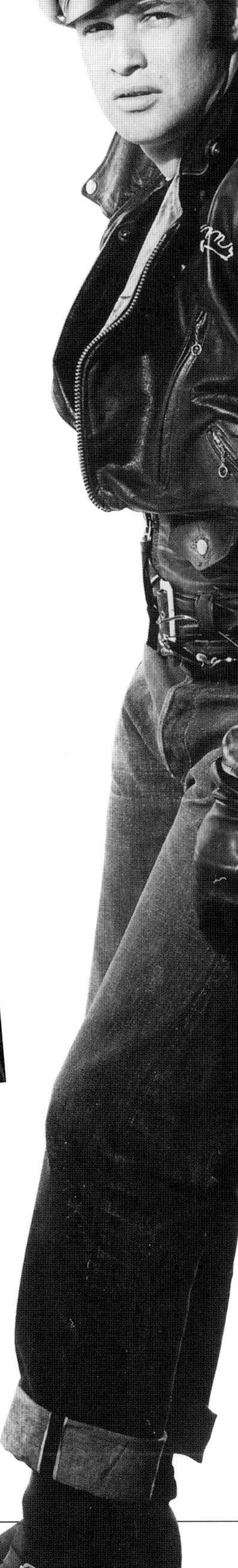

James Dean
Giant, 1956

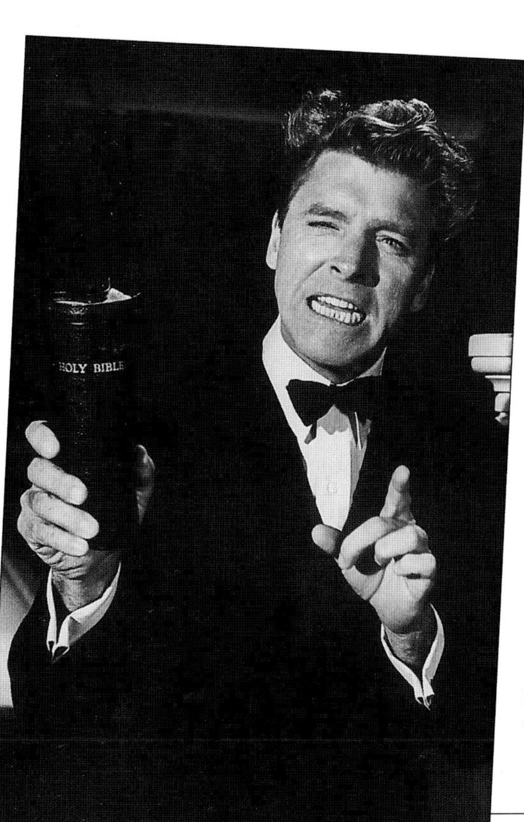

Marlon Brando
The Wild One, 1953

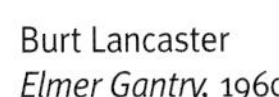

Burt Lancaster
Elmer Gantry, 1960

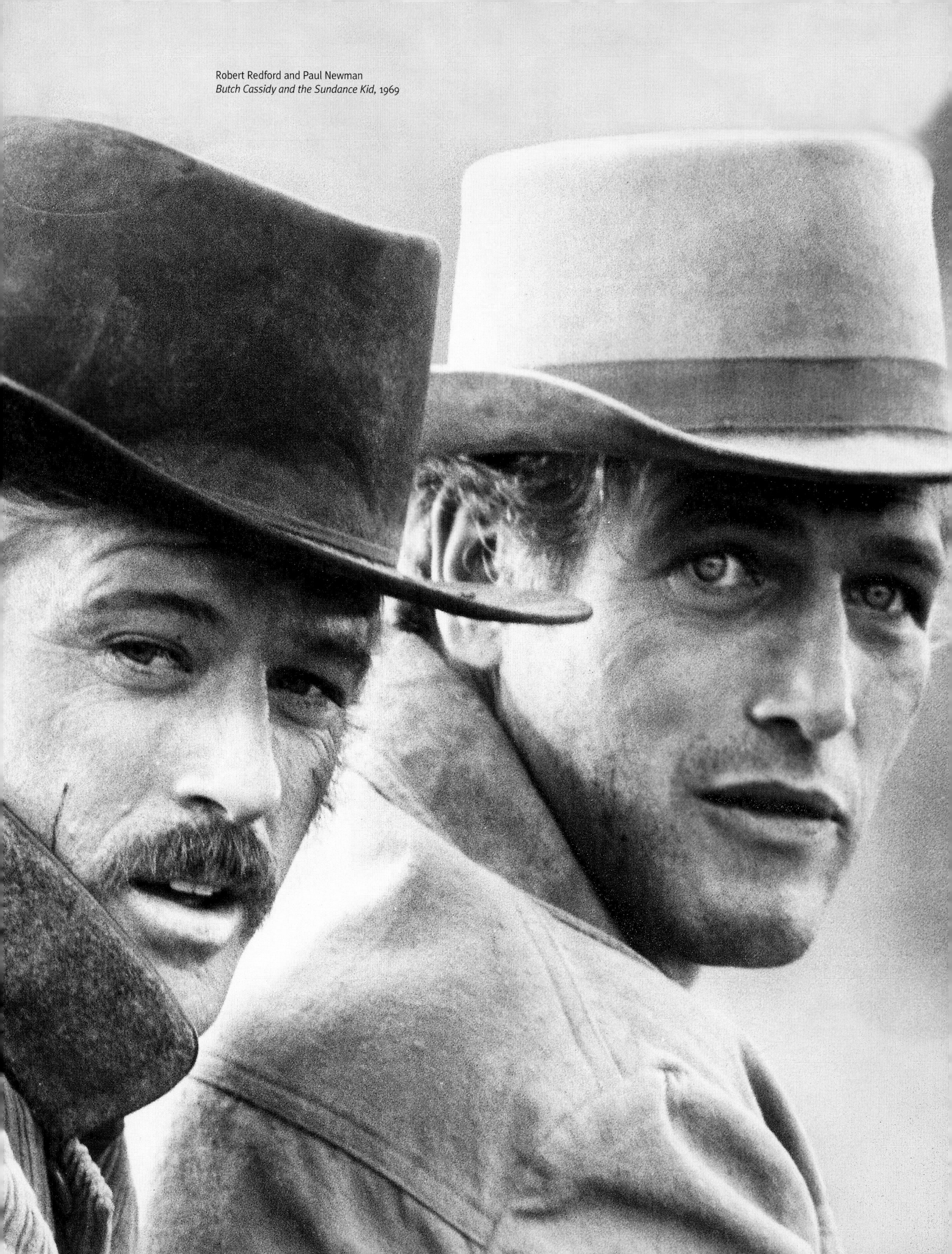

Robert Redford and Paul Newman
Butch Cassidy and the Sundance Kid, 1969

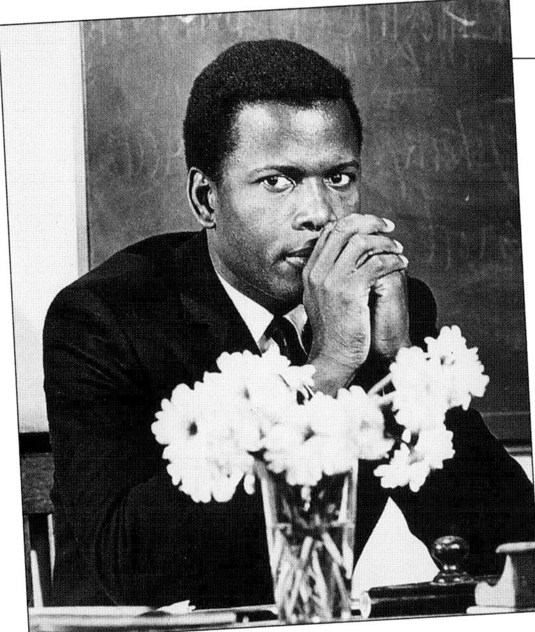

Sidney Poitier
To Sir, With Love, 1967

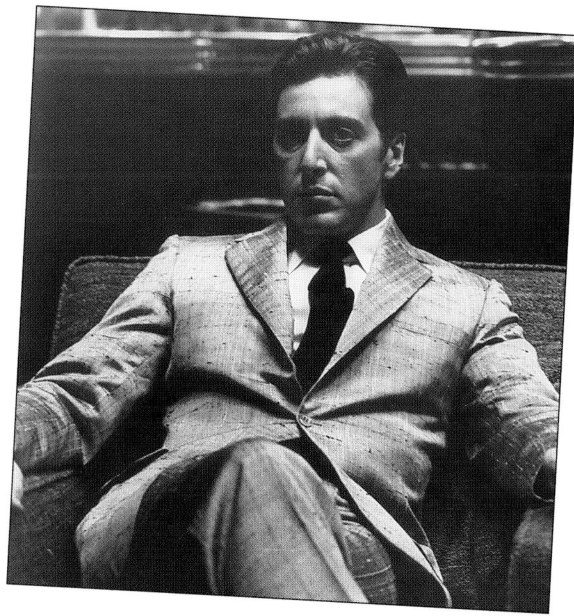

Al Pacino
The Godfather Part II, 1974

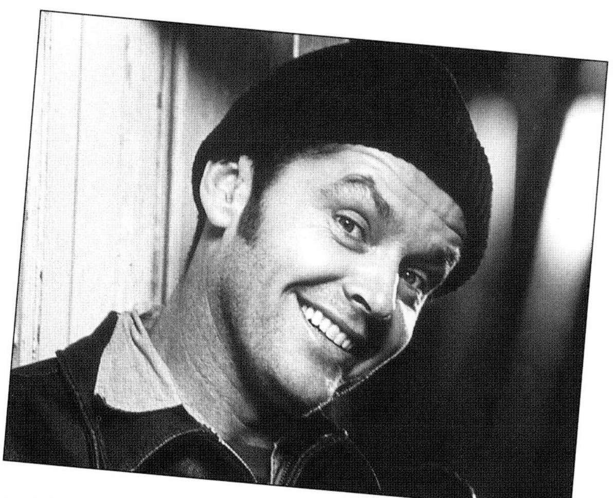

Jack Nicholson
One Flew Over the Cuckoo's Nest, 1975

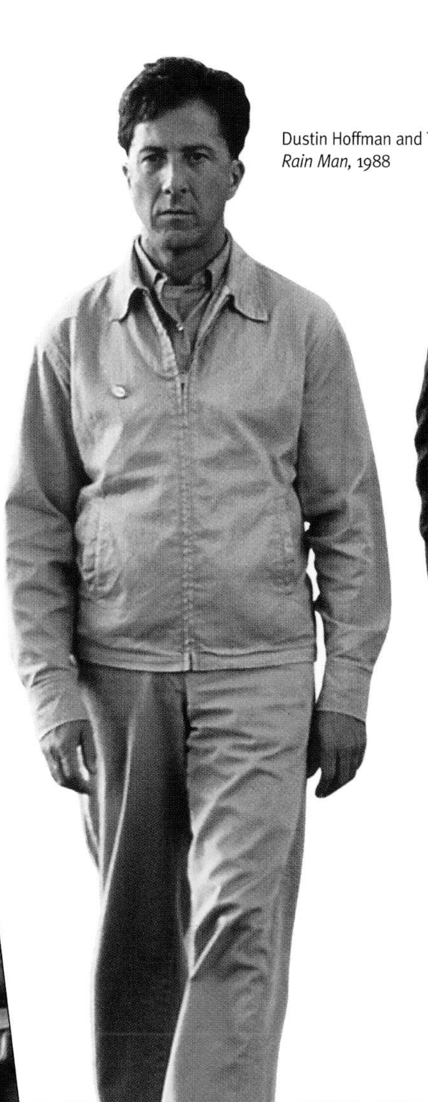

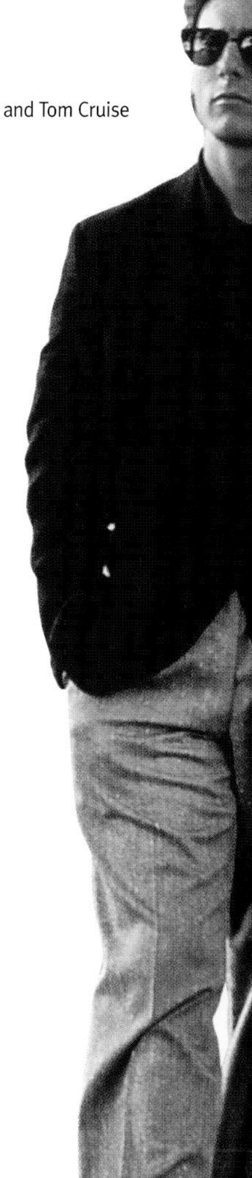

Dustin Hoffman and Tom Cruise
Rain Man, 1988

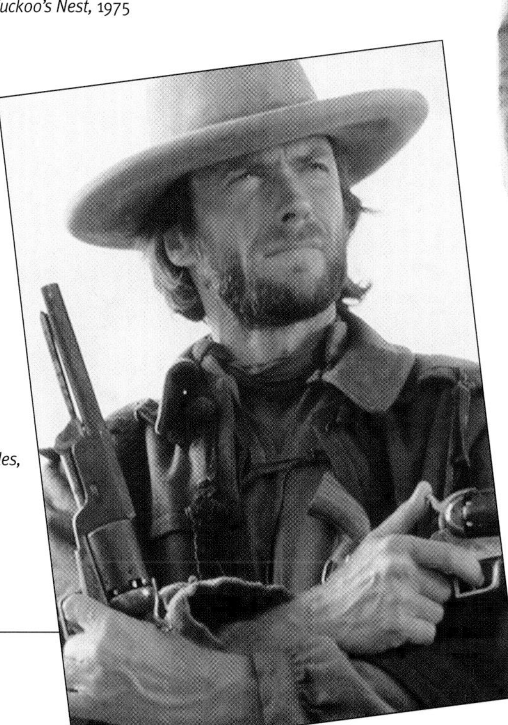

Clint Eastwood
The Outlaw Josey Wales,
1976

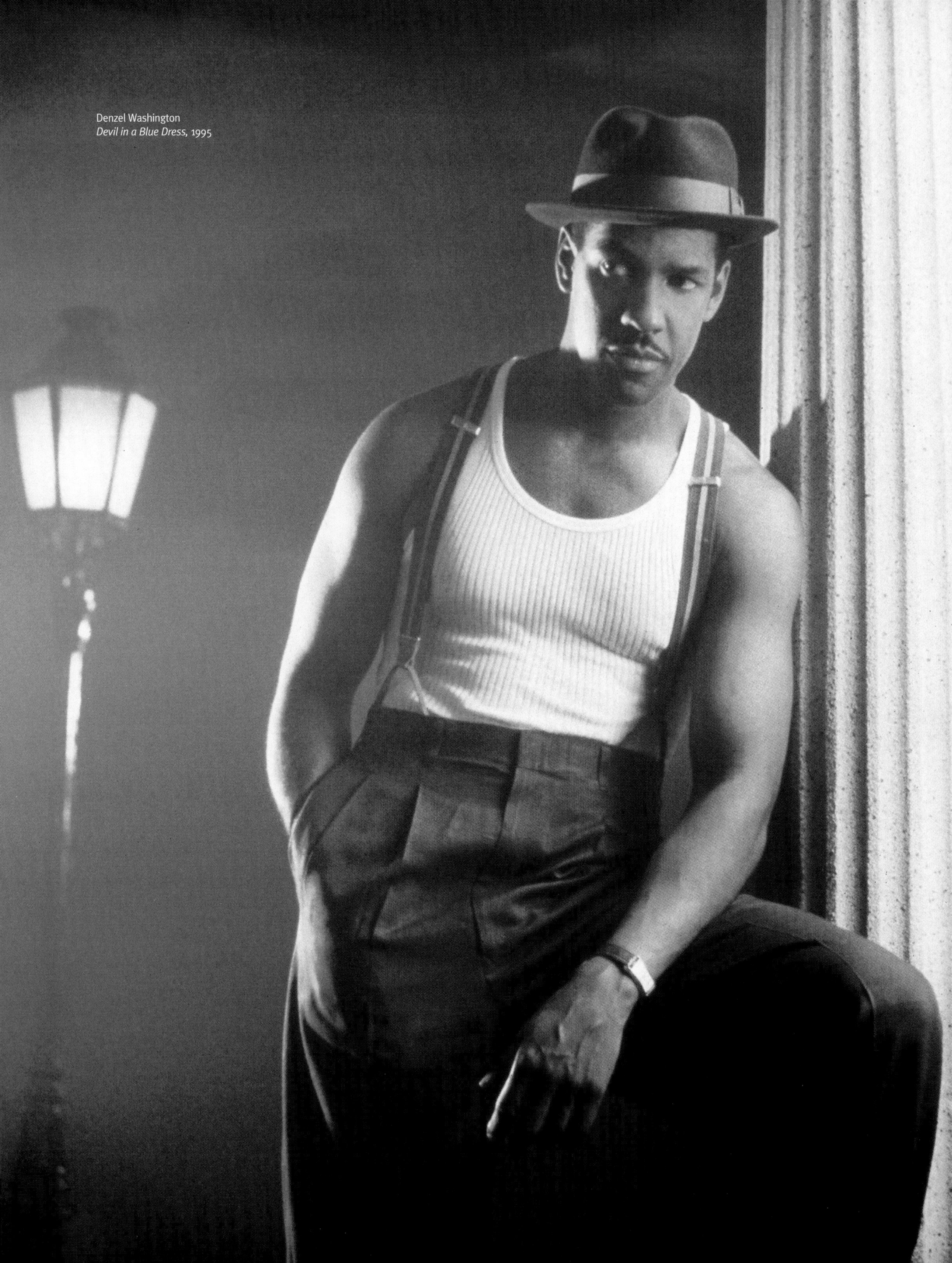

Denzel Washington
Devil in a Blue Dress, 1995

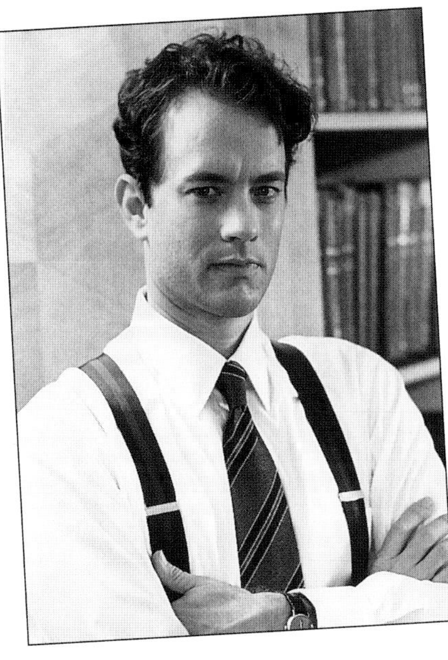

Tom Hanks
Philadelphia, 1993

Mel Gibson
Braveheart, 1995

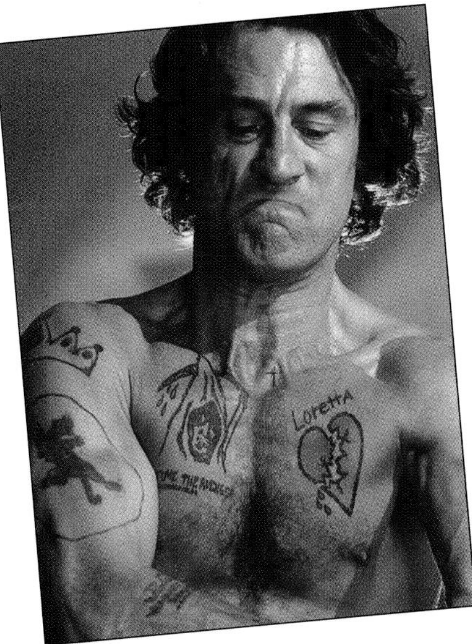

Robert De Niro
Cape Fear, 1991

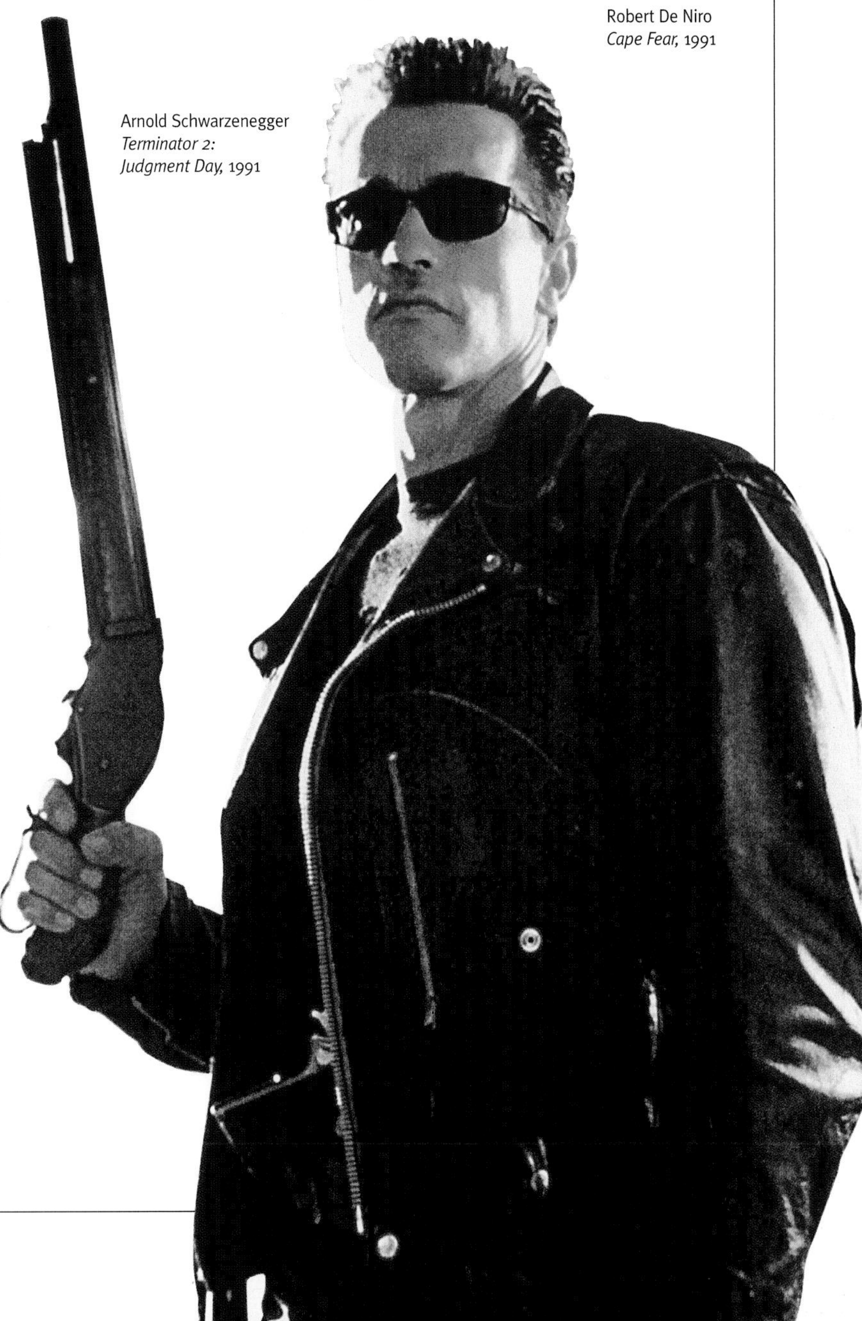

Arnold Schwarzenegger
Terminator 2: Judgment Day, 1991

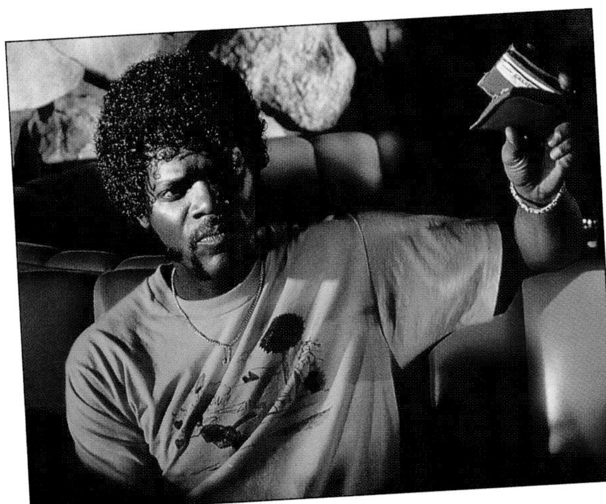

Samuel L. Jackson
Pulp Fiction, 1994

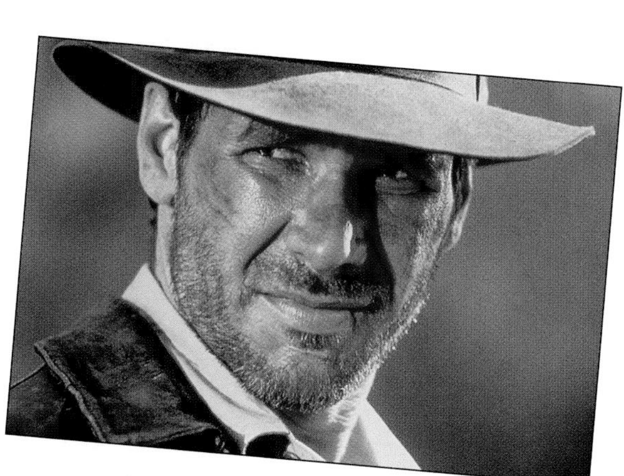

Harrison Ford
Raiders of the Lost Ark, 1981

Rita Hayworth
Gilda, 1946

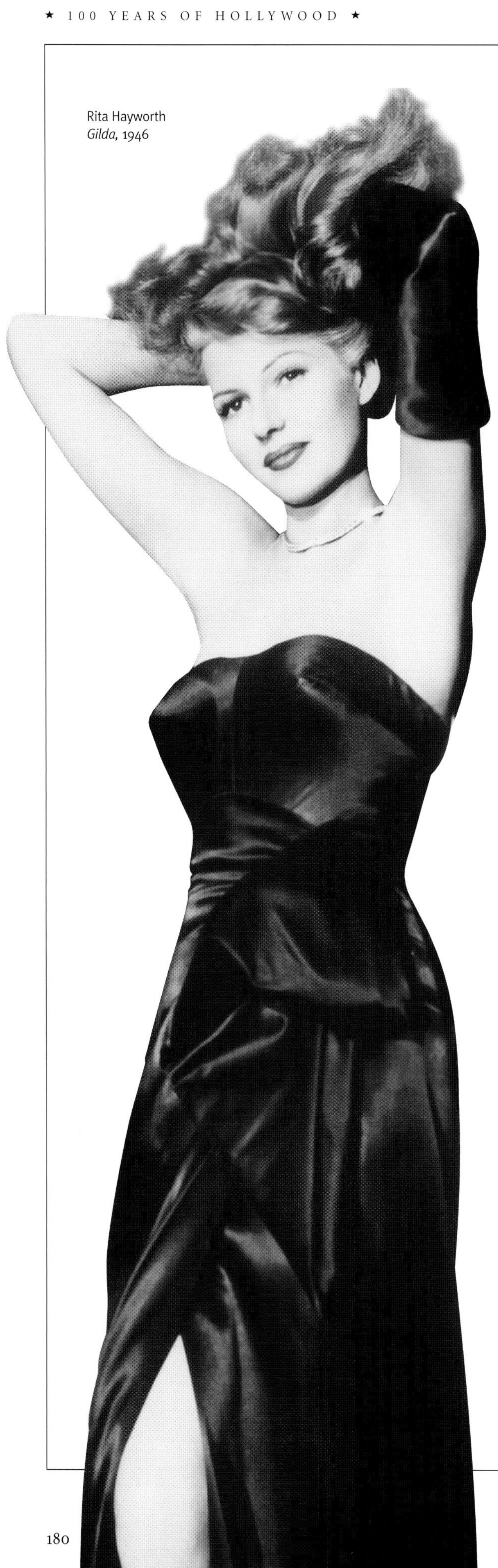

Bette Davis
All About Eve, 1950

Mae West
She Done Him Wrong, 1933

Joan Crawford
Sudden Fear, 1952

Katharine Hepburn
Woman of the Year, 1942

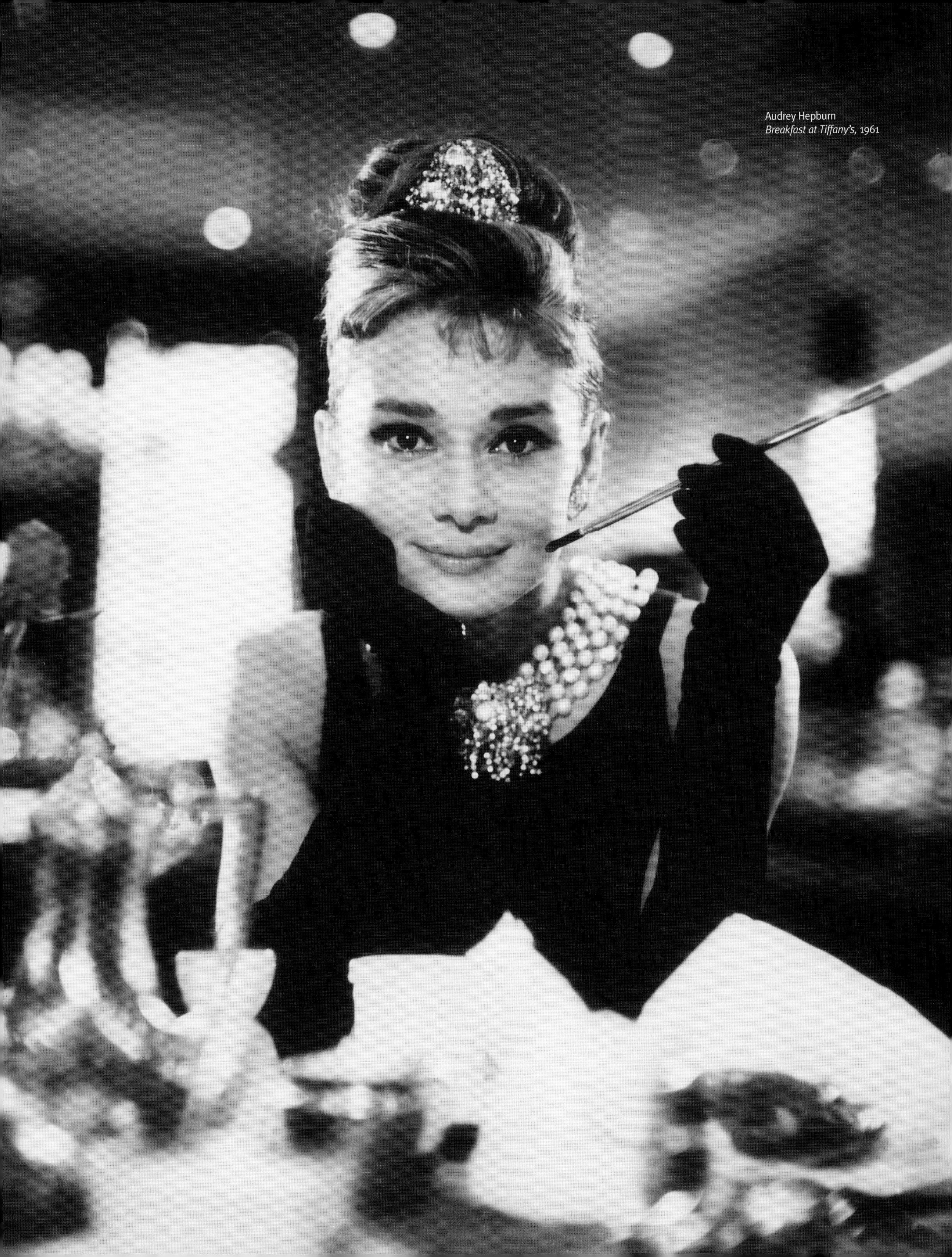

Audrey Hepburn
Breakfast at Tiffany's, 1961

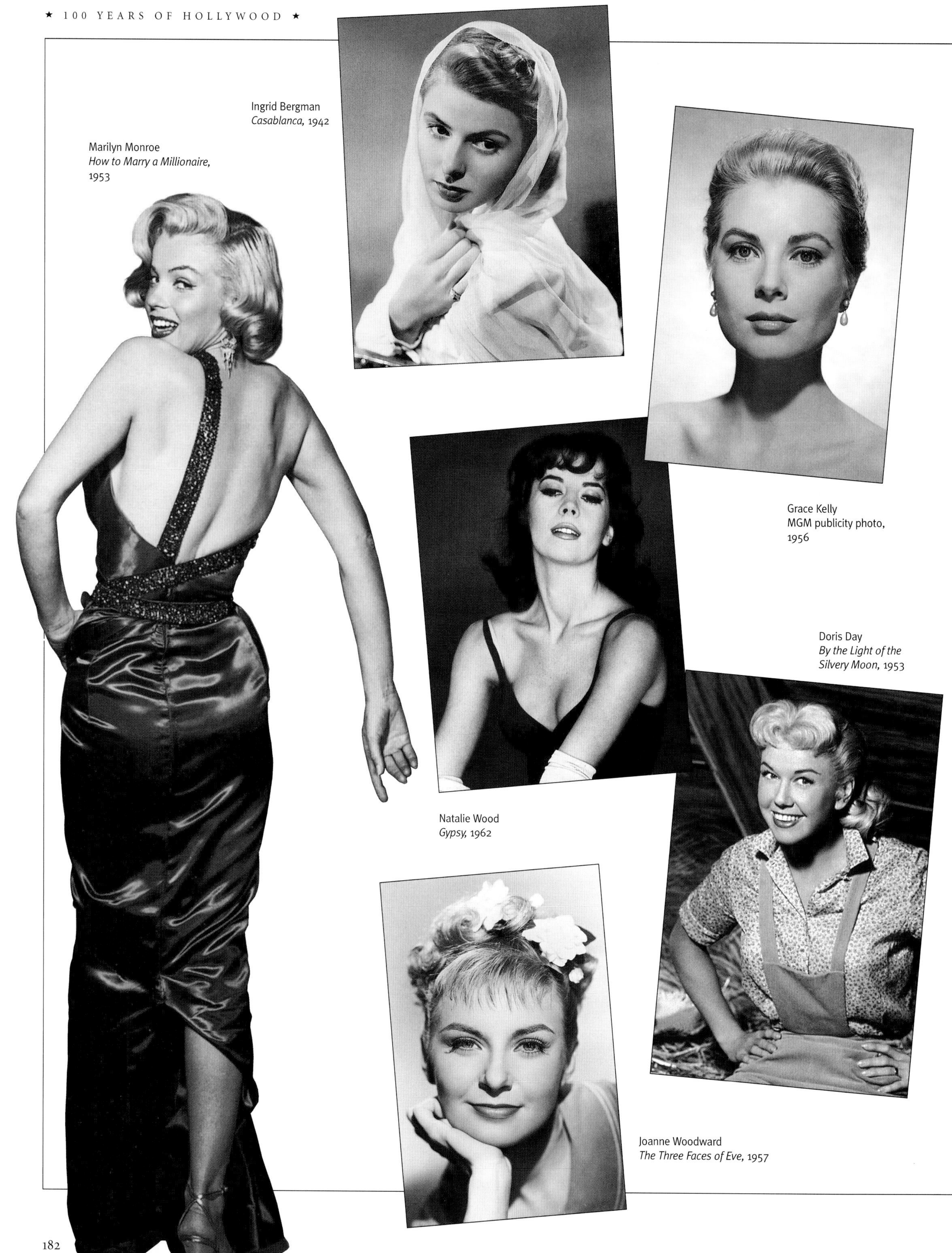

Ingrid Bergman
Casablanca, 1942

Marilyn Monroe
How to Marry a Millionaire, 1953

Grace Kelly
MGM publicity photo, 1956

Doris Day
By the Light of the Silvery Moon, 1953

Natalie Wood
Gypsy, 1962

Joanne Woodward
The Three Faces of Eve, 1957

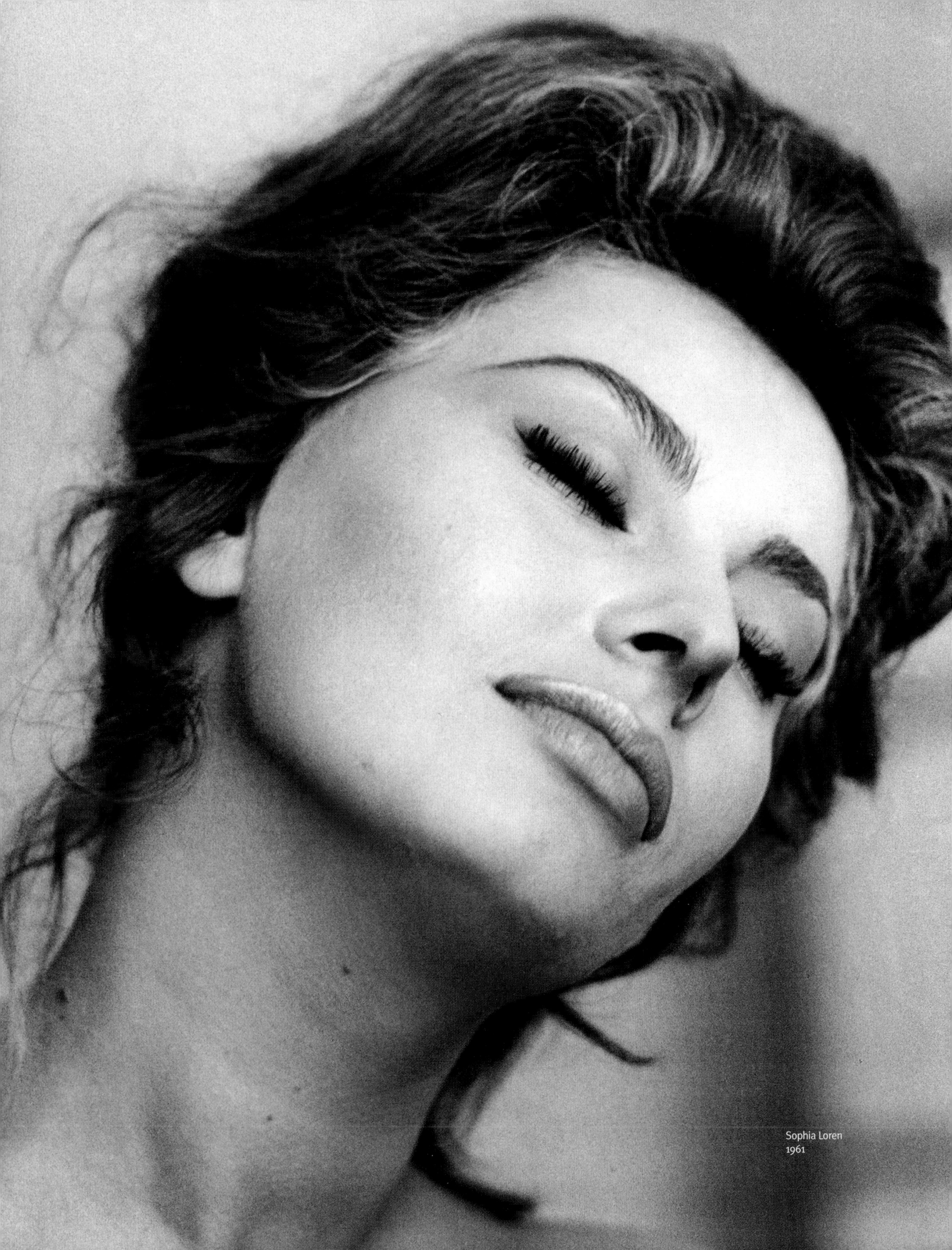

Sophia Loren
1961

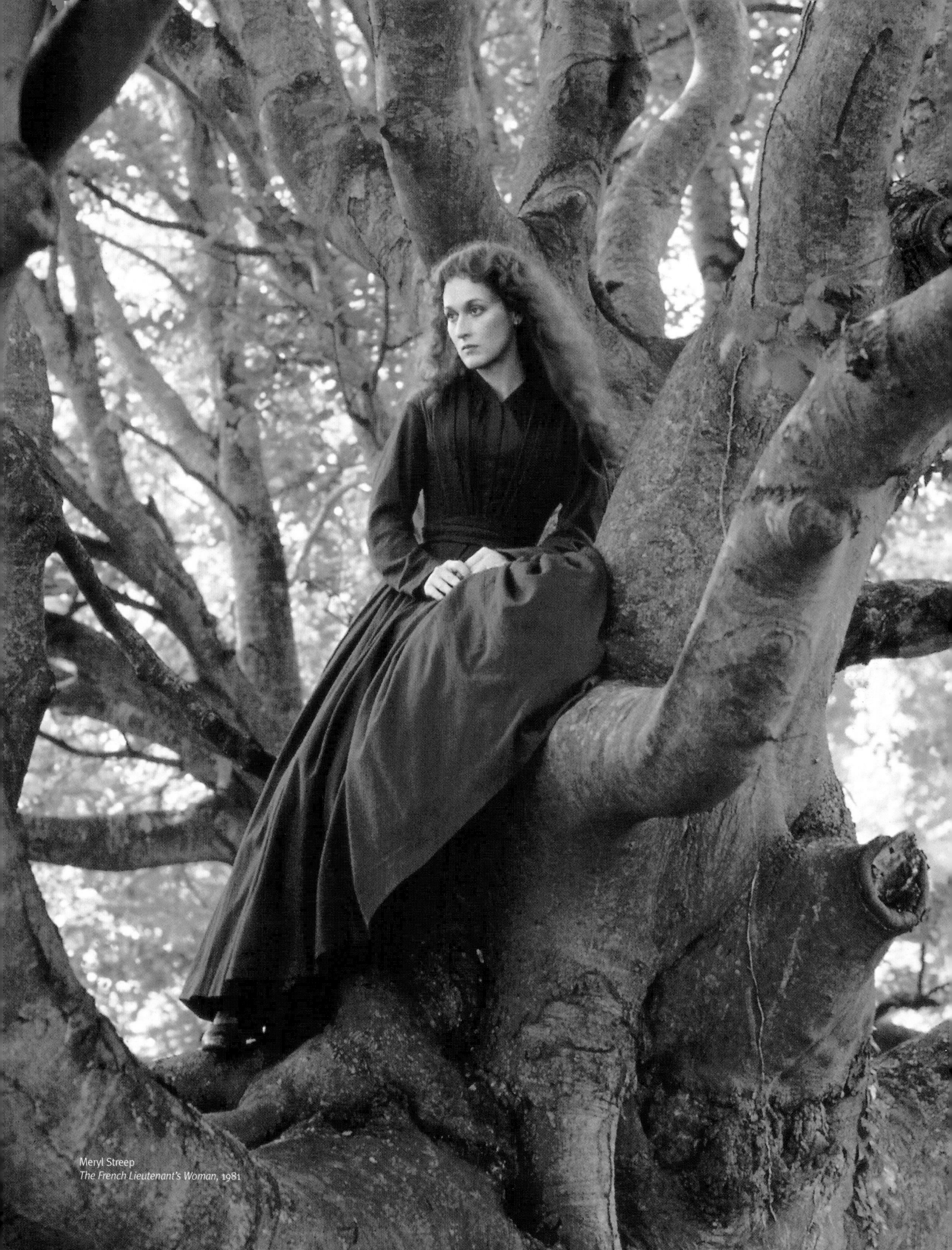

Meryl Streep
The French Lieutenant's Woman, 1981

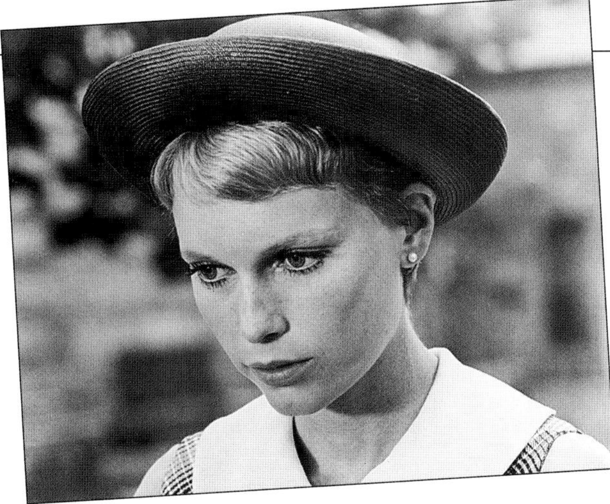

Mia Farrow
Rosemary's Baby, 1968

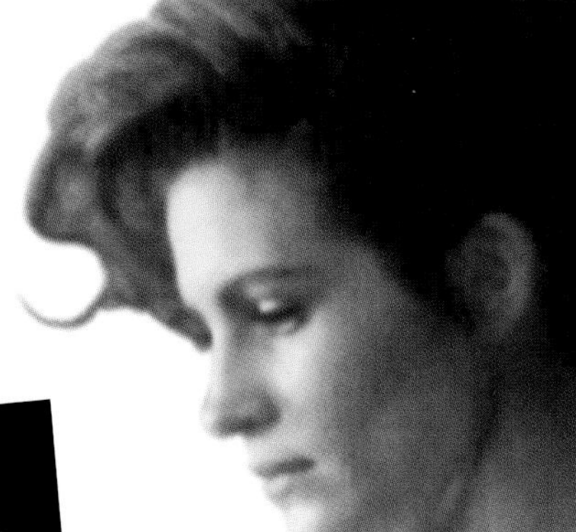

Julia Roberts
Pretty Woman, 1990

Goldie Hawn
Private Benjamin, 1980

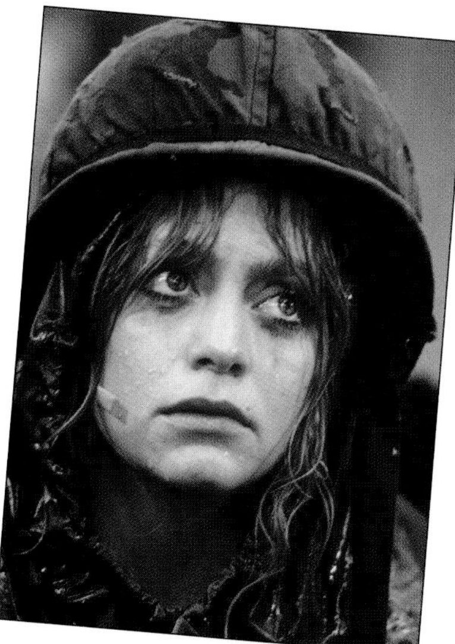

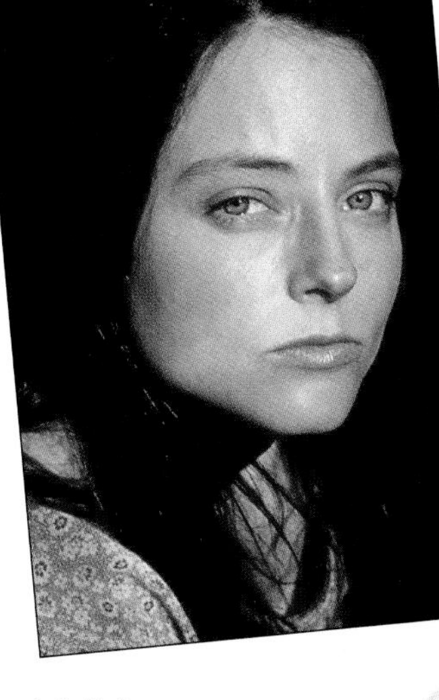

Jodie Foster
Nell, 1994

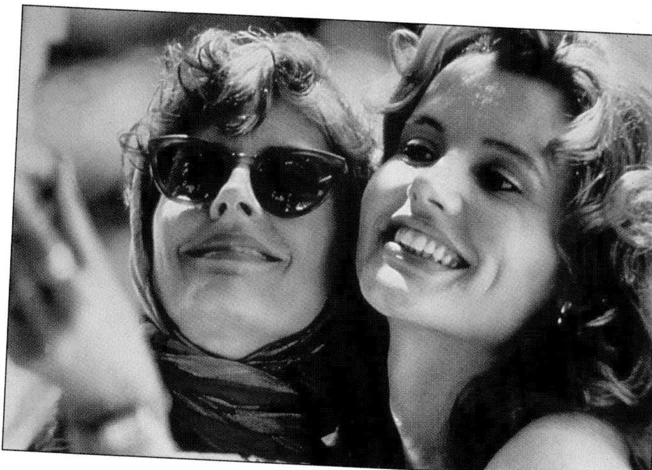

Susan Sarandon and Geena Davis
Thelma & Louise, 1991

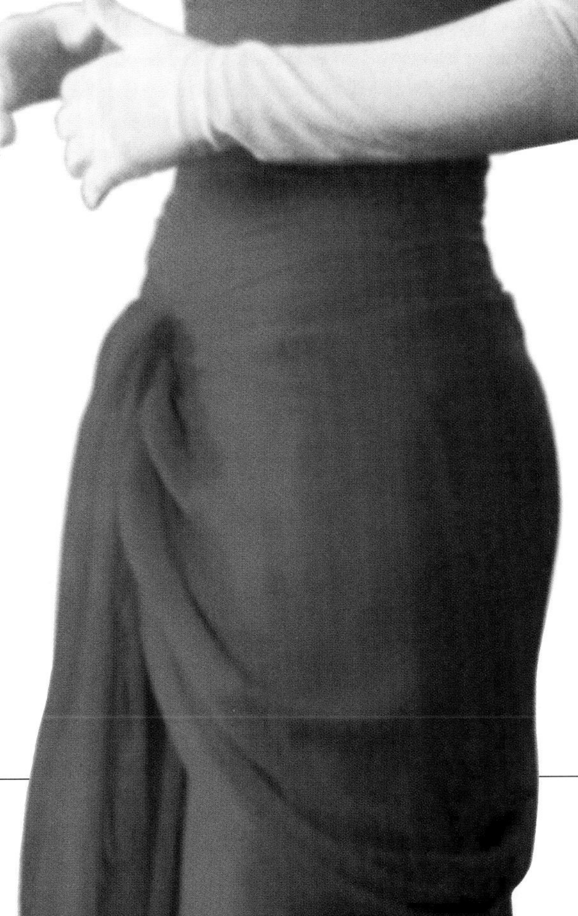

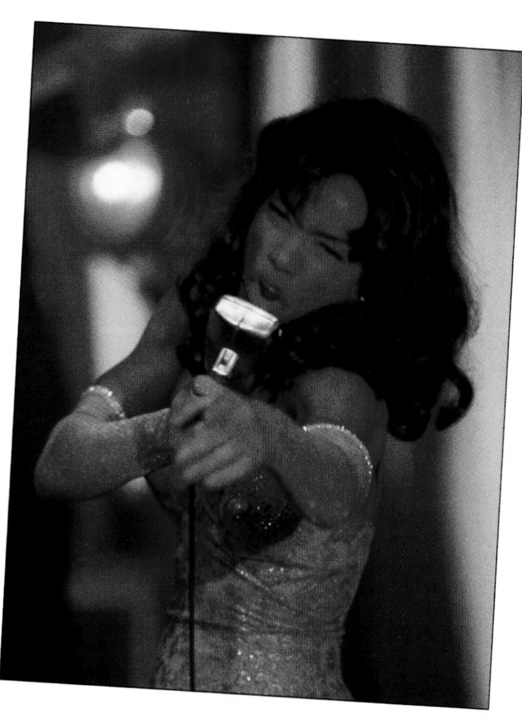

Angela Bassett
What's Love Got to Do With It, 1993

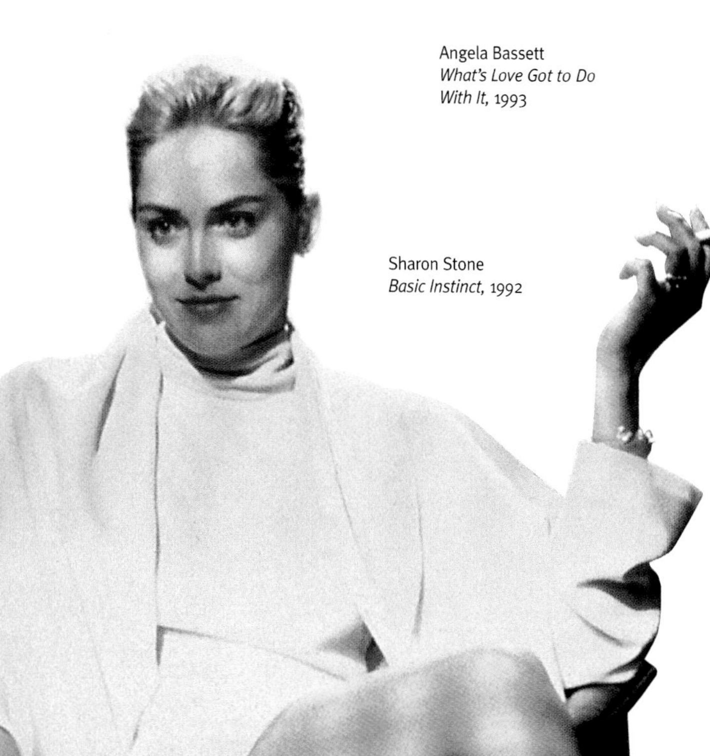

Sharon Stone
Basic Instinct, 1992

Gwyneth Paltrow
Shakespeare in Love, 1998

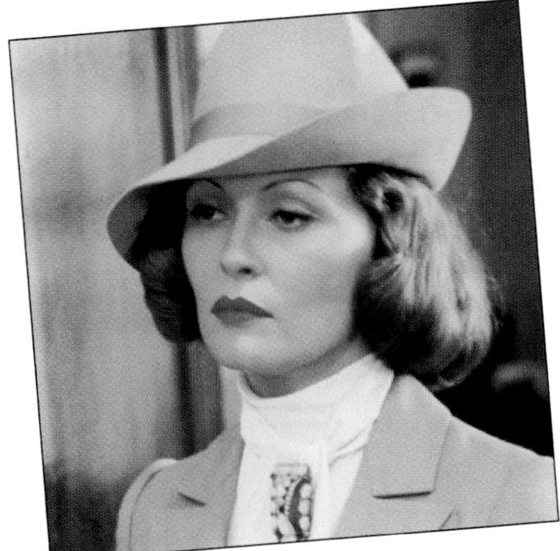

Faye Dunaway
Chinatown, 1974

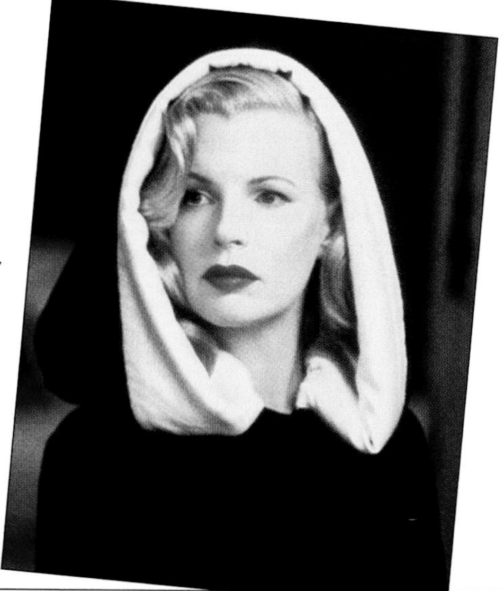

Kim Basinger
L.A. Confidential, 1997

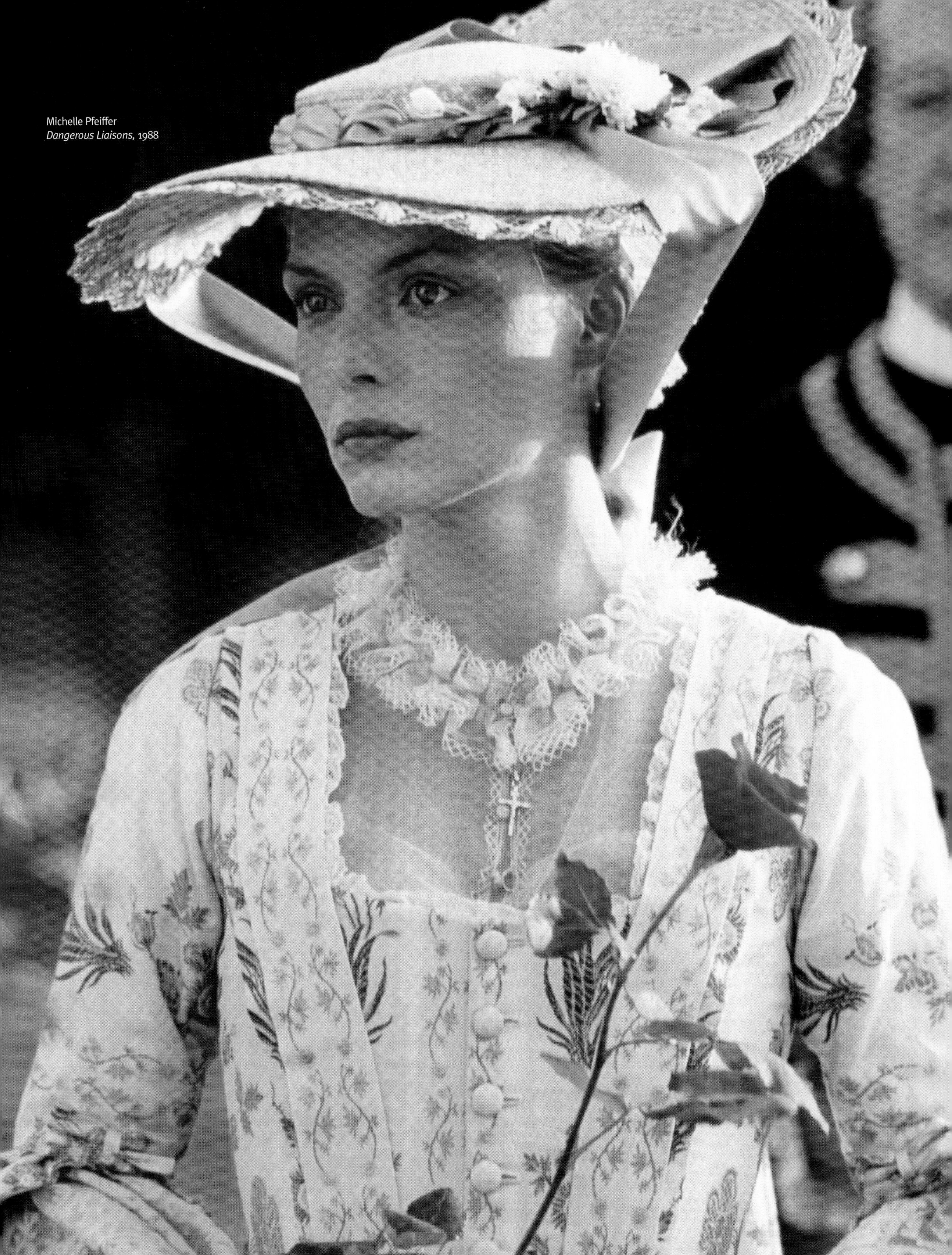

Michelle Pfeiffer
Dangerous Liaisons, 1988

ACKNOWLEDGMENTS

The editors wish to thank the following individuals and institutions for their valuable assistance in the preparation of this volume:
Margaret Adamic, Disney Publishing Group, Burbank, Calif.; Richard Allen, Lynden, Wash.; Jeanne Cole, Lucasfilm, Nicasio, Calif.; Tom Conroy, Movie Still Archives, Harrison, Nebr.; Mary Corliss, Museum of Modern Art, New York; Marlene Eastman, Warner Bros., Burbank, Calif.; Bruce Hershenson, West Plains, Mo.; Christopher Holm, Lucasfilm, Nicasio, Calif.; Mary Ison and Staff, Library of Congress, Washington, D.C.; Michael Key, *Make-up Artist* Magazine, Sunland, Calif.; Kristine Krueger, Academy of Motion Picture Arts and Sciences, Beverly Hills, Calif.; Janice Madhu, George Eastman House, Rochester, N.Y.; Diane Masuda, Warner Bros. Animation, Burbank, Calif.; Madeline Matz, Library of Congress, Washington, D.C.; Ellen Pasternak, Lucas Digital, San Rafael, Calif.; Judith Singer, Warner Bros., Burbank, Calif.; Paul C. Spehr, Fairfield, Pa.; Suzy Starke, Lucas Digital, San Rafael, Calif.; Marc Wanamaker, Bison Archives, Hollywood, Calif.

PICTURE CREDITS

The sources for the illustrations in this book appear below. Credits from left to right are separated by semicolons, from top to bottom by dashes.

Cover: The Kobal Collection, New York (Kobal Collection); Movie Still Archives, Harrison, Nebr.; Kobal Collection; Photofest, New York; Kobal Collection; Movie Still Archives, Harrison, Nebr; courtesy Globe Photos, New York—CORBIS/ Bettmann.
3: Photofest, New York. **6-9:** Kobal Collection. **10:** Photofest, New York. **11-18:** Kobal Collection. **19:** Photofest, New York. **20, 21:** Marc Wanamaker/Bison Archives, Hollywood, Calif. (Bison Archives); The Joel Finler Collection, London. **22, 23:** U.S. Department of the Interior, National Park Service, Edison National Historic Site. **24:** Museum of Modern Art (MOMA) Film Stills Archive, New York. **25:** Brown Brothers, Sterling, Pa.—MOMA Film Stills Archive, New York. **26:** MOMA Film Stills Archive, New York—U.S. Department of the Interior, National Park Service, Edison National Historic Site (2). **27:** The Joel Finler Collection, London; David Francis—Richard Koszarski Collection. **28:** MOMA Film Stills Archive, New York—courtesy the Academy of Motion Picture Arts and Sciences, Beverly Hills, Calif. (2). **29:** Bison Archives—courtesy the Academy of Motion Picture Arts and Sciences, Beverly Hills, Calif. **30:** MOMA Film Stills Archive, New York—Movie Still Archives, Harrison, Nebr. **31, 32:** Bison Archives. **33:** Brown Brothers, Sterling, Pa.—Bison Archives. **34:** Bison Archives. **35:** Warner Bros./Archive Photos, New York—The Joel Finler Collection, London. **36:** CORBIS/Bettmann—Bison Archives. **37:** Movie Still Archives, Harrison, Nebr.; courtesy George Eastman House. **38:** Culver Pictures, New York—The Granger Collection, New York; Movie Still Archives, Harrison, Nebr. **39:** Movie Still Archives, Harrison, Nebr.—Culver Pictures, New York (2); MOMA Film Stills Archive, New York. **40:** Kobal Collection. **41:** MOMA Film Stills Archive, New York—courtesy the Academy of Motion Picture Arts and Sciences, Beverly Hills, Calif. **42:** Hershenson-Allen Archive, West Plains, Mo.; Bison Archives. **43:** Movie Still Archives, Harrison, Nebr. **44, 45:** Culver Pictures, New York; Movie Still Archives, Harrison, Nebr.—J. W. Sandison Collection, Whatcom Museum of History and Art, Bellingham, Wash.; MOMA Film Stills Archive, New York. **46, 47:** MOMA Film Stills Archive, New York; Brown Brothers, Sterling, Pa. **48:** MGM, courtesy Kobal Collection—Kobal Collection (3). **49:** © Dick Busher, courtesy 5th Avenue Theatre, Seattle, Wash.—courtesy Eddie Brandt's Saturday Matinee, North Hollywood, Calif.; photograph © Ben Martin from *Hollywood at Your Feet.* Pomegranate Press, Ltd. **50, 51:** Famous Players/Paramount, courtesy Kobal Collection. **52:** Kobal Collection. **53:** Paramount, courtesy Kobal Collection—Bison Archives; Photofest, New York. **54, 55:** Studio Still of Ramon Navarro, John Gilbert, and Roy D'Arcy © 1926 Turner Entertainment Co. All rights reserved. Photo courtesy Kobal Collection—DR. JEYKLL AND MR. HYDE © 1920 Turner Entertainment Co. All rights reserved. Photo courtesy Movie Still Archives, Harrison, Nebr.; HE WHO GETS SLAPPED © 1924 Turner Entertainment Co. All rights reserved. Photo courtesy the Academy of Motion Picture Arts and Sciences, Beverly Hills, Calif. **56, 57:** Photofest, New York. **58:** W. Eugene Smith, *Life* Magazine. **59:** Bison Archives—Warner Bros., courtesy Kobal Collection. **60:** Movie Still Archives, Harrison, Nebr.—© Estate of Garry Winogrand, courtesy Fraenkel Gallery, San Francisco. **61:** Universal, courtesy Kobal Collection—courtesy Globe Photos, New York. **62:** Movie Still Archives, Harrison, Nebr. **63:** Movie Still Archives, Harrison, Nebr.—LAWRENCE OF ARABIA 1962 © Columbia Pictures Industries, Inc. All rights reserved. Courtesy Columbia Pictures. **64:** Culver Pictures, New York. **65:** RKO, courtesy Kobal Collection—MOMA Film Stills Archive, New York—MGM, courtesy Kobal Collection. **66:** United Artists, courtesy Kobal Collection. **67, 68:** Movie Still Archives, Harrison, Nebr. **69:** The Joel Finler Collection, London—Susan Gray ©, New York. **70:** Warner Bros., courtesy Kobal Collection. **71:** Hershenson-Allen Archive, West Plains, Mo.—Movie Still Archives, Harrison, Nebr. **72, 73:** Movie Still Archives, Harrison, Nebr.—Photofest, New York; Movie Still Archives, Harrison, Nebr. (2). **74:** Rex Hardy Jr., *Life* Magazine © Time Inc. **75:** RKO, courtesy Kobal Collection—Columbia Pictures, Inc., courtesy Kobal Collection. **76:** Photofest, New York. **77:** Movie Still Archives, Harrison, Nebr.—Hershenson-Allen Archive, West Plains, Mo.—BLOOD ALLEY © 1955 Batjac Productions, Inc. **78, 79:** BONNIE AND CLYDE © 1967 Warner Bros.-Seven Arts and Tatira-Hiller Productions. All rights reserved; Movie Still Archives, Harrison, Nebr. **80:** Movie Still Archives, Harrison, Nebr.; Hershenson-Allen Archive, West Plains, Mo. (3)—20th Century Fox Studios, courtesy Kobal Collection. **81, 82:** Movie Still Archives, Harrison, Nebr. **83:** Movie Still Archives, Harrison, Nebr. (2); © 1954 Elliott Erwitt/Magnum Photos, New York. **84:** Photofest, New York. **85:** Susan Gray ©, New York—Movie Still Archives, Harrison, Nebr. **86:** United Artists, courtesy Kobal Collection—Movie Still Archives, Harrison, Nebr. **87:** Paramount, courtesy Kobal Collection. **88:** Columbia Pictures, courtesy Kobal Collection—Movie Still Archives, Harrison, Nebr. **89:** Courtesy Globe Photos, New York—Hershenson-Allen Archive, West Plains, Mo. **90:** MGM, courtesy Kobal Collection—Hershenson-Allen Archive, West Plains, Mo.—SINGIN' IN THE RAIN © 1952 Turner Entertainment Co. A Time Warner Company. All rights reserved. **91:** MGM Inc., courtesy Kobal Collection. **92:** Movie Still Archives, Harrison, Nebr.—Everett Collection, New York. **93:** ABC Pictures, courtesy Kobal Collection; CABARET © 1972 ABC Pictures Corp. and Allied Artists Corp.—photography by Harry Benson. **94, 95:** Hershenson-Allen Archive, West Plains, Mo. (5); Movie Still Archives, Harrison, Nebr. (2). **96, 97:** Hershenson-Allen Archive, West Plains, Mo.; Movie Still Archives, Harrison, Nebr. (4). **98:** Photofest, New York; Movie Still Archives, Harrison, Nebr. **99:** Hershenson-Allen Archive, West Plains, Mo. (4)—Photofest, New York. **100:** Hershenson-Allen Archive, West Plains, Mo. (5)—Philippe Halsman © Halsman Estate. **101:** Photofest, New York. **102:** Michael Abramson/Onyx, Los Angeles—Warner Bros., courtesy Kobal Collection. **103:** Warner Bros., courtesy Kobal Collection—© Roland Neveu/Liaison Agency, New York. **104:** Movie Still Archives, Harrison, Nebr. **105:** Jerry Ohlinger's Movie Material Store, New York. **106:** Louis Goldman. **107:** Movie Still Archives, Harrison, Nebr.—Miramax, courtesy Kobal Collection—United Artists, courtesy Kobal Collection. **108, 109:** Gregory Heisler/CORBIS Outline. **110, 111:** Courtesy Always Superior Books, Marietta, Ga.; David O. Selznick Collection, Harry Ransom Humanities Research Center, University of Texas at Austin—GONE WITH THE WIND © 1939 Turner Entertainment Co. A Time Warner Company. All rights reserved. **112, 113:** NORTH BY NORTHWEST © 1959 Turner Entertainment Co. A Time Warner Company. All rights reserved. Photo courtesy the Academy of Motion Picture Arts and Sciences, Beverly Hills, Calif., except right center © Michael Webb, Los Angeles. **114, 115:** THE WIZARD OF OZ © 1939 Turner Entertainment Co. A Time Warner Company. All rights reserved. Photo p. 115 courtesy Kobal Collection. **116:** Allan Grant, *Life* Magazine © Time Inc. **117:** Sketch © Estate of Edith Head, courtesy Bibliothèque du Film, Paris—Paramount, courtesy Kobal Collection. **118:** Sketch by Cecil Beaton, by courtesy of the National Portrait Gallery, London/photo from BFI, London; MY FAIR LADY © CBS Broadcasting Inc., courtesy Kobal Collection. **119:** George Zeno, New York; design and drawing by Theadora Van Runkle, photo © 1999 Christopher Casler; INDIANA JONES AND THE TEMPLE OF DOOM © 1984 by Paramount Pictures and © Lucasfilm Ltd. & TM. All rights reserved. Used under authorization. Courtesy Paramount Pictures and Lucasfilm Ltd.—Sketch © Estate of William Travilla, photo © 1999 Christopher Casler; BONNIE AND CLYDE © 1967 Warner Bros.-Seven Arts and Tatira-Hiller Productions. All rights reserved. Photo courtesy Movie Still Archives, Harrison, Nebr.; INDIANA JONES AND THE TEMPLE OF DOOM © Lucasfilm Ltd. & TM. All rights reserved. Used under authorization. Courtesy Lucasfilm Ltd. **120, 121:** Photofest, New York; Dick Smith, Branford, Conn. (3). **122:** Express Newspapers/Archive Photos, New York—courtesy Globe Photos, New York; Universal, courtesy Kobal Collection (3).

123: Photos by Bob Romero reprinted from *Make-up Artist* Magazine. **124, 125:** Photos by David James for the motion picture *Saving Private Ryan* © 1998 Dream Works, reprinted with permission of Dream Works L.L.C. **126, 127:** Bison Archives; BOYZ N' THE HOOD 1991 © Columbia Pictures Industries, Inc. All rights reserved. Courtesy Columbia Pictures (2). **128:** Movie Still Archives, Harrison, Nebr. **129:** Louis Goldman—Dick Smith, Branford, Conn.; Movie Still Archives, Harrison, Nebr. (2). **130:** LETHAL WEAPON 4 © 1998 Warner Bros. A division of Time Warner Entertainment Company, L.P. All rights reserved. **131:** LAST ACTION HERO 1993 © Columbia Pictures Industries, Inc. All rights reserved. Courtesy Columbia Pictures; 20th Century Fox Studios courtesy Lucas Digital Ltd. (2). **132-135:** *Star Wars, The Empire Strikes Back,* and *Return of the Jedi* © Lucasfilm Ltd. & TM. All rights reserved. Used under authorization. **136:** 20th Century Fox Studios, courtesy Lucas Digital Ltd. **137:** Still from *Terminator 2: Judgment Day* appears courtesy Canal Plus Distribution, courtesy Lucas Digital Ltd., LLC. Used with permission of Robert Patrick; stills from *Terminator 2: Judgment Day* appear courtesy Canal Plus Distribution, courtesy Lucas Digital Ltd., LLC. (2). **138, 139:** Copyright © 1999 by Universal City Studios, Inc. Courtesy Universal Studios Publishing Rights. All rights reserved. Photo courtesy Lucas Digital Ltd. **140, 141:** New Line Cinema, courtesy Lucas Digital Ltd. **142:** © Disney Enterprises, Inc. **143:** © Disney Enterprises, Inc., photo courtesy Kobal Collection—© Disney Enterprises, Inc.; © Disney Enterprises, Inc.—© Disney Enterprises, Inc., photos courtesy Photofest, New York (2). **144:** PORKY PIG in Looney Tunes Bull's Eye, LOONEY TUNES, characters, names, and all related indicia are trademarks of Warner Bros. © 1999; BUGS BUNNY Model Sheet © 1992 Warner Bros. All rights reserved—courtesy Blanc Communications. Bugs Bunny's likeness in photo of Mel Blanc with carrot used with permission of Warner Bros. Photo courtesy Movie Still Archives, Harrison, Nebr.—BUGS BUNNY Model Sheet © 1992 Warner Bros. All rights reserved. **145:** BUGS BUNNY Model Sheet © 1992 Warner Bros. All rights reserved—courtesy Sybil Freleng Bergman and Hope Freleng Shan. SYLVESTER & TWEETY "HE DID IT" Limited Edition Cel by Friz Freleng TM & © 1990 Warner Bros. Inc. All rights reserved; courtesy Sybil Freleng Bergman and Hope Freleng Shan. BUGS BUNNY & YOSEMITE SAM "HIGH DIVING HARE" Limited Edition Cel by Friz Freleng © 1993 Warner Bros. Inc. All rights reserved (3); BUGS BUNNY Model Sheet © 1992 Warner Bros. All rights reserved. **146, 147:** © Disney Enterprises, Inc.; © Disney Enterprises, Inc. and Amblin Entertainment, Inc. **148, 149:** Hershenson-Allen Archive, West Plains, Mo.; Photofest, New York. **150-151:** Movie Still Archives, Harrison, Nebr. **152, 153:** Movie Still Archives, Harrison, Nebr.; THE WIZARD OF OZ © 1939 Turner Entertainment Co. A Time Warner Company. All rights reserved. Photo courtesy Movie Still Archives, Harrison, Nebr. **154:** Steve Schapiro/Black Star, New York. **155:** Movie Still Archives, Harrison, Nebr.—© Disney Enterprises, Inc., photo courtesy Photofest, New York. **156:** Courtesy Globe Photos, New York—Timothy White/CORBIS Outline. **157:** Columbia Pictures, courtesy Kobal Collection. **158:** Archive Photos, New York. **159:** Photofest, New York—MGM/Archive Photos, New York. **160:** Copyright © 1999 by Universal City Studios, Inc. Courtesy Universal Studios Publishing Rights. All rights reserved. **161:** Movie Still Archives, Harrison, Nebr.—Carolyn Jones/Fotos International/Archive Photos, New York. **162:** Archive Photos, New York. **163:** Jason James Richter/Kobal Collection. **164, 165:** Bill Eppridge, *Life* Magazine © Time Inc.; Movie Still Archives, Harrison, Nebr. **166:** Courtesy Lou Valentino Collection; MGM, courtesy Kobal Collection. **167:** Philippe Halsman © Halsman Estate. **168:** Weegee/ICP/Liaison Agency, New York; Bert Stern, New York, *Life* Magazine © Time Inc.; Loomis Dean, *Life* Magazine © Time Inc.—Rex Hardy Jr., *Life* Magazine © Time Inc; John R. Hamilton/Globe Photos, New York, *Life* Magazine © Time Inc.—Alfred Eisenstaedt, *Life* Magazine © Time Inc.; Sanford H. Roth/ Photo Researchers, New York, *Life* Magazine © Time Inc. **169:** RKO, courtesy Kobal Collection. **170, 171:** © 1997 Peter Mikelbank, Paris; *PEOPLE* Weekly is a registered trademark of Time Inc., used with permission—Merie W. Wallace/AP/Wide World Photos, *ENTERTAINMENT* Weekly © Time Inc. **172:** Rank, courtesy Kobal Collection; Paramount, courtesy Kobal Collection—THE OLD MAN AND THE SEA © 1958 Leland Hayward Prod., Inc.—Movie Still Archives, Harrison, Nebr. **173:** Eliot Elisofon, *Life* Magazine © Time Inc. **174:** W. Eugene Smith, *Life* Magazine © Time Inc. **175:** Movie Still Archives, Harrison, Nebr. (3)—Liaison Agency, New York; Photofest, New York. **176:** Movie Still Archives, Harrison, Nebr. **177:** Columbia Pictures/Archive Photos, New York; Movie Still Archives, Harrison, Nebr.—Peter Sorel/CORBIS Sygma, New York—Warner Bros., courtesy Kobal Collection; United Artists, courtesy Kobal Collection. **178:** Courtesy Globe Photos, New York. **179:** Courtesy Globe Photos, New York; Paramount Pictures, courtesy Kobal Collection; Photofest, New York—Photofest, New York (2); courtesy Globe Photos, New York. **180, 181:** Columbia Pictures/Archive Photos, New York; Movie Still Archives, Harrison, Nebr. (5). **182:** Mirror Syndication International, London; CASABLANCA © 1943 Turner Entertainment Co. A Time Warner Company. All rights reserved; MGM, courtesy Kobal Collection—Don Ornitz, courtesy Globe Photos, New York; Culver Pictures, New York—Movie Still Archives, Harrison, Nebr. **183:** Alfred Eisenstaedt, *Life* Magazine © Time Inc. **184:** Snowdon/Camera Press, London. **185:** Movie Still Archives, Harrison, Nebr.—Photofest, New York (2)—BIS/Camera Press/courtesy Globe Photos, New York; PRETTY WOMAN © 1990 Touchstone Pictures. **186:** Touchstone, courtesy Kobal Collection; Miramax, courtesy Kobal Collection—Photofest, New York—Columbia TriStar/Archive Photos, New York; courtesy Globe Photos, New York. **187:** George/CORBIS Sygma, New York.

BIBLIOGRAPHY

BOOKS

Adamson, Joe. *Bugs Bunny: Fifty Years and Only One Grey Hare.* New York: Henry Holt, 1990.

Aylesworth, Thomas G. *Hollywood Kids.* New York: E. P. Dutton, 1987.

Barson, Michael. *The Illustrated Who's Who of Hollywood Directors, Vol. 1: The Sound Era.* New York: Noonday Press, 1995.

Bartel, Pauline. *Amazing Animal Actors.* Dallas: Taylor, 1997.

Basinger, Jeanine. *American Cinema: One Hundred Years of Filmmaking.* New York: Rizzoli, 1994.

Bayer, William. *The Great Movies.* New York: Grosset & Dunlap, 1973.

Beck, Jerry, and Will Friedwald:

Looney Tunes and Merrie Melodies. New York: Henry Holt, 1989.

Warner Bros. Animation Art. [N.p]: Hugh Lauter Levin, 1997.

Berg, A. Scott. *Goldwyn: A Biography.* New York: Riverhead Books, 1989.

Bergan, Ronald. *The United Artists Story.* New York: Crown Publishers, 1986.

Bowser, Eileen. *The Transformation of Cinema: 1907-1915,* Vol. 2 of *History of the American Cinema.* New York: Charles Scribner's Sons, 1990.

Brady, John. *The Craft of the Screenwriter.* New York: Simon and Schuster, 1981.

Brownlow, Kevin:

Hollywood: The Pioneers. London: Collins, 1979.

The War, the West, and the Wilderness. New York: Alfred A. Knopf, 1979.

Cahn, William. *A Pictorial History of the Great Comedians.* New York: Grosset & Dunlap, 1970.

Chierichetti, David. *Hollywood Costume Design.* London: Cassell & Collier Macmillan, 1976.

Chronicle of the Cinema. London: Dorling Kindersley, 1995.

Collins, Ace. *Lassie: A Dog's Life.* New York: Penguin Books, 1993.

Draigh, David. *Behind the Screen: Who Does What in Motion Pictures and Television.* New York: Abbeville Press, 1988.

Eames, John Douglas. *The Paramount Story.* New York: Crown, 1985.

Edelson, Edward. *Great Kids of the Movies.* Garden City, N.Y.: Doubleday, 1979.

Everson, William K. *The American Movie.* New York: Atheneum, 1963.

Fahey, David, and Linda Rich. *Masters of Starlight.* New York: Ballantine Books, 1987.

Finch, Christopher:

The Art of Walt Disney. New York: Abrams, 1999.

Special Effects: Creating Movie Magic. New York: Abbeville Press, 1984.

Gabler, Neal. *An Empire of Their Own: How the Jews Invented Hollywood.* New York: Doubleday, 1988.

Goldman, Louis. *Lights, Camera, Action!* New York: Harry N. Abrams, 1986.

Griffith, Richard, Arthur Mayer, and Eileen Bowser. *The Movies.* New York: Simon and Schuster, 1981.

Guttmacher, Peter:

Legendary Horror Films. New York: MetroBooks, 1995.

Legendary War Movies. New York: MetroBooks, 1996.

Hall, Ben M. *The Golden Age of the Movie Palace.* New York: Clarkson N. Potter, 1961.

Harmetz, Aljean. *The Making of the Wizard of Oz.* New York: Delta, 1977.
Hay, Peter. *MGM: When the Lion Roars.* Atlanta: Turner, 1991.
Head, Edith, and Jane Kesner Ardmore. *The Dress Doctor.* Boston: Little, Brown, 1959.
Heisner, Beverly. *Hollywood Art: Art Direction in the Days of the Great Studios.* Jefferson, N.C.: McFarland, 1990.
Henderson, Amy, and Dwight Blocker Bowers. *Red, Hot & Blue: A Smithsonian Salute to the American Musical.* Washington, D.C.: Smithsonian Institution Press, 1996.
Hirschhorn, Clive:
The Hollywood Musical. New York: Crown, 1981.
The Warner Bros. Story. New York: Crown, 1979.
Hollywood: Legend and Reality. Boston: Little, Brown, 1986.
Javna, John. *Animal Superstars.* Milwaukee: Hal Leonard Books, 1986.
Kerr, Walter. *The Silent Clowns.* New York: Alfred A. Knopf, 1975.
Koszarski, Richard. *An Evening's Entertainment: The Age of the Silent Feature Picture, 1915-1928,* Vol. 3 of *History of the American Cinema.* New York: Charles Scribner's Sons, 1990.
Lambert, Gavin. *GWTW: The Making of Gone With the Wind.* Boston: Little, Brown, 1973.
Lasseter, John, and Steve Daly. *The Art and Making of the Animated Film.* New York: Hyperion, 1995.
LaVine, W. Robert. *In a Glamorous Fashion.* New York: Charles Scribner's Sons, 1980.
Maltin, Leonard, ed. *Leonard Maltin's Movie & Video Guide.* New York: Plume, 1996.
Maltin, Leonard, and Richard W. Bann. *The Little Rascals: The Life and Times of Our Gang.* New York: Crown Trade, 1992.
Musser, Charles. *The Emergence of Cinema: The American Screen to 1907,* Vol. 1 of *History of the American Cinema.* New York: Charles Scribner's Sons, 1990.
Naughton, John, and Adam Smith. *Movies: A Crash Course.* New York: Watson-Guptill, 1998.
O'Conner, Jane, and Katy Hall. *Magic in the Movies: The Story of Special Effects.* Garden City, N.Y.: Doubleday, 1980.
Oxford History of World Cinema. Ed. by Geoffrey Nowell-Smith. Oxford: Oxford University Press, 1996.
Powers, Tom. *Special Effects in the Movies.* San Diego, Calif.: Lucent, 1989.
Ramsaye, Terry. *A Million and One Nights.* New York: Simon and Schuster, 1954.
Robinson, David. *From Peep Show to Palace: The Birth of American Film.* New York: Columbia University Press, 1996.
The St. James Film Directors Encyclopedia. Ed. by Andrew Sarris. Detroit: Visible Ink, 1998.
Scorsese, Martin, and Michael Henry Wilson. *A Personal Journey with Martin Scorsese through American Movies.* New York: Hyperion, 1997.
Sennett, Robert S. *Setting the Scene: The Great Hollywood Art Directors.* New York: Harry N. Abrams, 1994.
Sennett, Ted:
Great Movie Directors. New York: Harry N. Abrams, 1986.
Hollywood Musicals. New York: Harry N. Abrams, 1981.
Sklar, Robert. *Film: An International History of the Medium.* New York: Harry N. Abrams, 1993.
Smith, Thomas G. *Industrial Light & Magic.* New York: Ballantine Books, 1986.
Spehr, Paul C. *The Movies Begin: Making Movies in New Jersey, 1887-1920.* Newark, N.J.: Newark Museum, 1977.
Taub, Eric. *Gaffers, Grips, and Best Boys.* New York: St. Martin's Press, 1994.
Thomas, Bob. *Disney's Art of Animation: From Mickey Mouse to Hercules.* New York: Hyperion, 1992.
Vaz, Mark Cotta. *Industrial Light & Magic: Into the Digital Realm.* New York: Ballantine Books, 1996.
Vieira, Mark A. *Hurrell's Hollywood Portraits: The Chapman Collection.* New York: Harry N. Abrams, 1997.
Windeler, Robert. *The Films of Shirley Temple.* New York: Citadel Press, 1995.

PERIODICALS

Collins, Amy Fine. "Anything for an Oscar." *Vanity Fair,* March 1998.
Make-up Artist, August-September 1996.
Probst, Christopher. "The Last Great War." *American Cinematographer,* August 1998.
Spiller, Roger J. "War in the Dark." *American Heritage,* February-March 1999.

OTHER SOURCES

Internet Movie Database. Available: http://imdb.com August 24, 1999.

INDEX

Numerals in italics indicate an illustration of the subject mentioned.

A

B

C

D

E

F

G

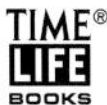

Time-Life Books is a division of Time Life Inc.

TIME LIFE INC.
PRESIDENT and CEO: George Artandi

TIME-LIFE BOOKS
PUBLISHER/MANAGING EDITOR: Neil Kagan
SENIOR VICE PRESIDENT, MARKETING: Joseph A. Kuna
VICE PRESIDENT, NEW PRODUCT DEVELOPMENT: Amy Golden

OUR AMERICAN CENTURY

EDITORS: Loretta Britten, Paul Mathless
DIRECTOR, NEW PRODUCT DEVELOPMENT: Elizabeth D. Ward
DIRECTOR OF MARKETING: Pamela R. Farrell

100 Years of Hollywood
Deputy Editor: Roxie France-Nuriddin
Text Editor: Elizabeth Hedstrom
Associate Editor/Research and Writing: Kerry Hamilton
Associate Marketing Manager: Terri Miller
Picture Associate: Anne Whittle
Senior Copyeditor: Judith Klein
Technical Art Specialist: John Drummond
Photo Coordinator: Betty H. Weatherley
Editorial Assistant: Christine Higgins

Design for **Our American Century** by Antonio Alcalá, Studio A, Alexandria, Virginia.

Special Contributors: George Constable (writing and editing); Ronald H. Bailey, Mimi Harrison, James Michael Lynch, Ellen Phillips, Robert Speziale, Henry Wiencek (writing); Jane Coughran, Corinna Luyken, Norma Shaw (research); Marti Davila, Richard Friend (design); Susan Nedrow (index).

Correspondents: Christine Hinze (London), Christina Lieberman (New York), Maria Vincenza Aloisi (Paris). Valuable assistance was also provided by Valerie Bassett (Hollywood).

Director of Finance: Christopher Hearing
Directors of Book Production: Marjann Caldwell, Patricia Pascale
Director of Publishing Technology: Betsi McGrath
Director of Photography and Research: John Conrad Weiser
Director of Editorial Administration: Barbara Levitt
Manager, Technical Services: Anne Topp
Senior Production Manager: Ken Sabol
Production Manager: Virginia Reardon
Quality Assurance Manager: James King
Chief Librarian: Louise D. Forstall

Separations by the Time-Life Imaging Department

First printing. Printed in U.S.A.
School and library distribution by Time-Life Education, P.O. Box 85026, Richmond, Virginia 23285-5026

EDITORIAL CONSULTANT
Richard B. Stolley is currently senior editorial adviser at Time Inc. After 19 years at *Life* magazine as a reporter, bureau chief, and assistant managing editor, he became the first managing editor of *People* magazine, a position he held with great success for eight years. He then returned to *Life* magazine as managing editor and later served as editorial director for all Time Inc. magazines. In 1997 Stolley received the Henry Johnson Fisher Award for Lifetime Achievement, the magazine industry's highest honor.

Library of Congress Cataloging-in-Publication Data
100 years of Hollywood / by the editors of Time-Life Books.
p. cm. — (Our American century)
Includes bibliographical references and index.
ISBN 0-7835-5515-6
1. Motion pictures—United States—History. I. Title: One hundred years of Hollywood. II. Series. III. Time-Life Books.
PN1993.5.U6A17 1999
791.43'0973—dc21 99-38437
CIP

Other History Publications:

World War II
The American Story
The American Indians
Lost Civilizations
Mysteries of the Unknown
What Life Was Like
Voices of the Civil War
Time Frame
The Civil War
Cultural Atlas

For information on and a full description of any of the Time-Life Books series listed above, please call 1-800-621-7026 or write: Reader Information, Time-Life Customer Service, P.O. Box C-32068, Richmond, Virginia 23261-2068

On the cover:
Reprising on film his blockbuster Broadway performance in Tennessee Williams's A Streetcar Named Desire, Marlon Brando smolders as Stanley Kowalski, whose thin sheen of civilization barely covered a powerfully coarse, brutish nature. Nominated for a 1951 Best Actor Oscar, Brando lost to Humphrey Bogart in The African Queen. Did he care? He represented a new breed of movie star, his attitude perhaps conveyed by one of his lines in Streetcar—that he was not taken in "by this Hollywood glamour stuff." Pictured across the top of the cover are other film greats: Rudolph Valentino, Lauren Bacall, Alfred Hitchcock, Grace Kelly, Sophia Loren, and Denzel Washington. Humphrey Bogart is shown on the spine.